MW00997491

WEST ACADEMIC PUBLISHING'S
LAW SCHOOL ADVISORY BOARD

JESSE H. CHOPER
Professor of Law and Dean Emeritus
University of California, Berkeley

JOSHUA DRESSLER
Distinguished University Professor Emeritus, Frank R. Strong Chair in Law
Michael E. Moritz College of Law, The Ohio State University

YALE KAMISAR
Professor of Law Emeritus, University of San Diego
Professor of Law Emeritus, University of Michigan

MARY KAY KANE
Professor of Law, Chancellor and Dean Emeritus
University of California, Hastings College of the Law

LARRY D. KRAMER
President, William and Flora Hewlett Foundation

JONATHAN R. MACEY
Professor of Law, Yale Law School

ARTHUR R. MILLER
University Professor, New York University
Formerly Bruce Bromley Professor of Law, Harvard University

GRANT S. NELSON
Professor of Law Emeritus, Pepperdine University
Professor of Law Emeritus, University of California, Los Angeles

A. BENJAMIN SPENCER
Justice Thurgood Marshall Distinguished Professor of Law
University of Virginia School of Law

JAMES J. WHITE
Robert A. Sullivan Professor of Law Emeritus
University of Michigan

INTERACTIVE CASEBOOK SERIES^{SM}

DOMESTIC RELATIONSHIPS

A Contemporary Approach

SECOND EDITION

———————

Ann Laquer Estin
ALIBER FAMILY CHAIR IN LAW
UNIVERSITY OF IOWA COLLEGE OF LAW

———————

WEST
ACADEMIC
PUBLISHING

The publisher is not engaged in rendering legal or other professional advice and this publication is not a substitute for the advice of an attorney. If you require legal or other expert advice, you should seek the services of a competent attorney or other professional.

Interactive Casebook Series is a servicemark registered in the U.S. Patent and Trademark Office.

© 2013 LEG, Inc. d/b/a West Academic Publishing
© 2019 LEG, Inc. d/b/a West Academic
    444 Cedar Street, Suite 700
    St. Paul, MN 55101
    1-877-888-1330

West, West Academic Publishing, and West Academic are trademarks of West Publishing Corporation, used under license.

Printed in the United States of America

ISBN: 978-1-64242-530-7

Preface

Domestic Relationships: A Contemporary Approach follows a trail marked by Homer H. Clark, Jr., whose long and distinguished academic career included writing the leading Domestic Relations treatise of the era and five editions of an important casebook.

Family law has changed in many dramatic ways since Homer's first book appeared in 1965, and this book addresses a much wider range of contemporary family forms and issues. As part of the Interactive Casebook series, it also includes new features designed to help students engage more deeply with the materials and the subject.

I owe thanks to many people for their help with this project. Melanie Stutzman has provided enormous assistance with this and all the projects I undertake. My students at the University of Iowa have offered useful feedback over many years. Two student research assistants, Jordan Davis and Paden Hanson, helped with checking and updating citations for this edition. This book is dedicated to the memory of Homer Clark, with my affection and gratitude for his scholarship as well as his support and friendship along the way.

Table of Contents

Chapter 3: *Adoption and Assisted Reproduction* 305

Table of Cases

The principal cases are in **bold** type. Cases cited or discussed in the text are in roman type. References are to pages. Cases cited in principal cases and within other quoted materials are not included.

Introduction

Students may enroll in Family Law because of a particular interest in the subject, based on their prior experiences working with families or children, or because the subject is commonly tested on the bar exam. Often, students discover that the field does match their preconceptions. Family lawyers must be pragmatic problem-solvers, helping their clients navigate a wide range of legal, financial, and personal problems, using many different types of lawyering skills. At the same time, family law includes broad and important social, political, and constitutional questions.

Go Online

The outline of family law topics tested on the Multistate Essay Examination is available from the web site of the National Conference of Bar Examiners.

Families in the United States are increasingly diverse, with demographers telling us that fewer than half of all households in the United States today are headed by a husband-wife married couple. Nuclear families formed by marriage remain at the center of family law, but the subject also reaches the large numbers of adults and children who live in households headed by a single adult, households formed by cohabiting couples, and extended family or multi-generational households. Policy-makers have responded slowly to these demographic changes, but lawyers and judges see many kinds of domestic relationships in the cases they handle every day.

One goal of this book is to address the full range of family types, and to prompt discussion of how and why the law treats these families differently. For example, cases addressing the financial rights of cohabiting partners are included in Chapter 1, Chapter 4, and Chapter 6. Parent-child relationships formed outside of marriage are discussed in Chapter 2, Chapter 3, and Chapter 7. Relationships between adult family members, and various extended family forms, are considered in Chapter 4.

Because family law is primarily a state law subject, and families tend to be mobile, the field has always raised a wealth of jurisdictional and conflict of laws problems. In the modern era, national constitutional and statutory law have significantly shaped state family law rules and practices. Increasingly, family law also operates on a transnational level, and its global dimensions are regularly noted in these pages.

Family law has a rich history, marked by compelling and contentious public policy questions. Today's students have watched as the controversy over same-sex marriage made its way through legislatures and the state and federal courts. In past generations, divorce laws were the subject of an equally difficult national debate. During the century from the Civil War to the civil rights movement, laws punishing marriage and family relationships across the color line were a flashpoint for regional and national politics. This history is deeply important to understanding the complex intersection of public and private interests in the family, and how we arrived at our current approach to regulating family life.

Further Reading: Historical Perspectives

- Nelson Blake, The Road to Reno (1962).

- Nancy F. Cott, Public Vows: A History of Marriage and the Nation (2001).

- Peggy Cooper Davis, Neglected Stories: The Constitution and Family Values (1997).

- J. Herbie Di Fonzo, Beneath the Fault Line: The Popular and Legal Culture of Divorce in Twentieth Century America (1997).

- Mary Ann Glendon, The Transformation of Family Law: State, Law and Family in the United States and Western Europe (1989).

- Michael Grossberg, Governing the Hearth: Law and the Family in Nineteenth-Century America (1985).

- Hendrik Hartog, Man and Wife in America: A History (2000).

- Herbert Jacob, Silent Revolution: The Transformation of Divorce Law in the United States (1988).

Family Law is deeply interdisciplinary, both in terms of the fields of law that it covers—evidence, procedure, criminal law, tax, bankruptcy, international law—and also in a wider sense. Fields such as sociology, economics, and psychology offer useful perspectives on larger questions of family policy, and experts in these fields may consult or serve as expert witnesses in the litigation of particular cases.

Further Reading: Social Science Perspectives

- Paul R. Amato, et al., Alone Together: How Marriage in America is Changing (2007).
- Gary S. Becker, A Treatise on the Family (Enlarged ed. 1991).
- Andrew J. Cherlin, Marriage, Divorce, Remarriage (Rev. & Enlarged ed. 1992).
- Kathryn Edin & Maria Kefalas, Promises I Can Keep: Why Poor Women Put Motherhood Before Marriage (2005).
- Joseph Goldstein, Anna Freud & Albert J. Solnit, Beyond the Best Interests of the Child (1973).
- Christopher Lasch, Haven in a Heartless World: The Family Besieged (1977).
- Susan Moller Okin, Justice, Gender and the Family (1989).
- Judith S. Wallerstein et al., The Unexpected Legacy of Divorce: A 25-Year Landmark Study (2000).

Features of this Casebook

This book is part of West's Interactive Casebook Series, which offers students a parallel electronic version of the text. The e-book provides an easy means to search and highlight the materials. Citations to cases, statutes and articles have been underlined to indicate embedded hyperlinks to *Westlaw* and other online resources. This feature makes it easy to check the full version of an edited opinion, the facts recited in a previous ruling, or the case on which a study problem was based.

Throughout the book, text boxes associated with the reading provide opportunities for students to reflect on the material or extend their learning with supplemental sources and information. In the electronic version, many of these boxes provide links to important resources including government agency information and reports, recordings of the oral arguments in Supreme Court cases, tables and summaries of state statutes, professional conduct rules, and the web sites of organizations such as the American Bar Association, the American Academy of Matrimonial Lawyers, the Uniform Law Commission and the Hague Conference on Private International Law.

Practice Pointer
These boxes address legal practice questions and challenges raised by the material covered in the text.

Ethical Issue
These boxes point out potential ethics problems, and identify sources that can help address those issues.

Global View
These boxes offer comparative and international law perspectives.

What's That?
These boxes explain the meaning of legal terms that appear in the main text. *Black's Law Dictionary* definitions may be accessed by clicking on the terms that appear in blue type.

For More Information
These boxes suggest additional resources on particular subjects.

Go Online!
These boxes direct you to relevant online resources.

Think About It
These boxes present critical reading questions directing you to important issues raised directly or indirectly by the text.

Take Note
These boxes call attention to a particular aspect of a case or a point that deserves further thought or attention.

Make the Connection
These boxes highlight concepts and information that are relevant to other law school courses or point to material covered elsewhere in this course.

FYI
These boxes provide additional information, including subsequent history of a case, summaries of any omitted sections or additional opinions, or further background information.

Please note that in preparing this book, we have edited cases, sometimes extensively. Places where material has been deleted from cases or statutes are marked with an ellipsis (* * *) or a text box summarizing the omitted section. Many citations and footnotes have been removed without those omissions being indicated, and original footnote numbers have been preserved for all footnotes that appear in the text. All statutory citations included in the text and notes were checked on Westlaw in 2018, and this date is given in parentheses as part of the citation.

CHAPTER 1

Marriage and Its Alternatives

In addition to its personal and private meanings, and its importance in religious communities, marriage is a legal institution, shaped and defined by state and federal laws that define the many rights and obligations that flow from marital status, and determine when and how individuals may enter into or exit from a marriage. Although all governments seek to shape marriage and family life, contemporary discourse frames the right to marry as a fundamental human right, protected by the United States Constitution and the Universal Declaration of Human Rights.

Go Online

According to a 1997 report by the U.S. General Accounting Office (GAO), there are more than 1000 federal statutory provisions in which benefits, rights and privileges are contingent on marital status, or in which marital status is a factor. The GAO issued an updated report in 2004.

This chapter begins with an exploration of the constitutional framework for marriage and private life, and then considers the role of private ordering of marriage relationships through contracts. It continues with coverage of the process for entering into marriage, including requirements for licensing and solemnization, and restrictions on who may marry. Because state law controls these questions in the United States, and there are significant variations among the state laws, marriage regulation generates significant conflict of laws problems. This chapter also considers civil union and domestic partnerships, and how the law responds to unmarried cohabitation relationships.

A. Marriage and Privacy Rights

Early decisions of the Supreme Court affirmed the broad plenary power of the state and federal governments to regulate marriage. In *Reynolds v. United States*, 98 U.S. 145 (1878), the Court rejected the argument that the First Amendment limited legislation criminalizing the practice of polygamy, concluding that it was "impossible to believe that the constitutional guaranty of religious freedom was intended to prohibit legislation in respect to this most important feature of social life." Similarly, in <u>*Maynard v. Hill*, 125 U.S. 190 (1888)</u>, the Court upheld a legislative divorce issued to a husband with no notice to his wife, writing: "Marriage, as creating the most important relation in life, as having more to do with the morals and civilization of a people than any other institution, has always been subject to the control of the legislature."

During the 1960s, however, the Supreme Court began to fix limits on state power over marriage. The Court looked to several earlier cases that had extended protection under the Due Process Clause of the Fourteenth Amendment to aspects of private and family life. These earlier cases included several that protected parents' rights to determine how their children would be educated, and the decision in <u>*Skinner v. Oklahoma*, 316 U.S. 535 (1942)</u> which described marriage and procreation as among the "basic civil rights of man" and "fundamental to the very existence and survival of the race."

Fourteenth Amendment, U.S. Constitution, Section 1

All persons born or naturalized in the United States and subject to the jurisdiction thereof, are citizens of the United States and of the State wherein they reside. No State shall make or enforce any law which shall abridge the privileges or immunities of citizens of the United States; nor shall any State deprive any person of life, liberty, or property, without due process of law; nor deny to any person within its jurisdiction the equal protection of the laws.

Griswold v. Connecticut

<u>381 U.S. 479 (1965)</u>

MR. JUSTICE DOUGLAS delivered the opinion of the Court.

Appellant Griswold is Executive Director of the Planned Parenthood League of Connecticut. Appellant Buxton is a licensed physician and a professor at the Yale Medical School who served as Medical Director for the

Go Online

Listen to the <u>oral arguments</u> in *Griswold* on the Oyez Project website.

League at its Center in New Haven—a center open and operating from November 1 to November 10, 1961, when appellants were arrested.

They gave information, instruction, and medical advice to *married persons* as to the means of preventing conception. They examined the wife and prescribed the best contraceptive device or material for her use. Fees were usually charged, although some couples were serviced free.

The statutes whose constitutionality is involved in this appeal are §§ 53–32 and 54–196 of the General Statutes of Connecticut (1958 rev.). The former provides:

> "Any person who uses any drug, medicinal article or instrument for the purpose of preventing conception shall be fined not less than fifty dollars or imprisoned not less than sixty days nor more than one year or be both fined and imprisoned."

Section 54–196 provides:

> "Any person who assists, abets, counsels, causes, hires or commands another to commit any offense may be prosecuted and punished as if he were the principal offender."

The appellants were found guilty as accessories and fined $100 each, against the claim that the accessory statute as so applied violated the Fourteenth Amendment.

* * *

Coming to the merits, we are met with a wide range of questions that implicate the Due Process Clause of the Fourteenth Amendment. Overtones of some arguments suggest that <u>Lochner v. New York, 198 U.S. 45 (1905)</u>, should be our guide. But we decline that invitation. * * * We do not sit as a super-legislature to determine the wisdom, need, and propriety of laws that touch economic problems, business affairs, or social conditions. This law, however, operates directly on an intimate relation of husband and wife and their physician's role in one aspect of that relation.

The association of people is not mentioned in the Constitution nor in the Bill of Rights. The right to educate a child in a school of the parents' choice—whether public or private or parochial—is also not mentioned.

Take Note

Justice Douglas distinguishes the Court's analysis here from its famous opinion in *Lochner*, which held that protective labor legislation in New York violated the liberty of contract protected by the Due Process Clause.

Nor is the right to study any particular subject or any foreign language. Yet the First Amendment has been construed to include certain of those rights.

By *Pierce v. Society of the Sisters of the Holy Names of Jesus and Mary*, [268 U.S. 510 (1925)] the right to educate one's children as one chooses is made applicable to the States by the force of the First and Fourteenth Amendments. By *Meyer v. Nebraska*, [262 U.S. 390 (1923)] the same dignity is given the right to study the German language in a private school. In other words, the State may not, consistently with the spirit of the First Amendment, contract the spectrum of available knowledge. The right of freedom of speech and press includes not only the right to utter or to print, but the right to distribute, the right to receive, the right to read and freedom of inquiry, freedom of thought, and freedom to teach—indeed the freedom of the entire university community. Without those peripheral rights the specific rights would be less secure. And so we reaffirm the principle of the *Pierce* and the *Meyer* cases.

In *NAACP v. Alabama*, 357 U.S. 449, 462 (1958), we protected the "freedom to associate and privacy in one's associations," noting that freedom of association was a peripheral First Amendment right. Disclosure of membership lists of a constitutionally valid association, we held, was invalid "as entailing the likelihood of a substantial restraint upon the exercise by petitioner's members of their right to freedom of association." In other words, the First Amendment has a penumbra where privacy is protected from governmental intrusion. In like context, we have protected forms of "association" that are not political in the customary sense but pertain to the social, legal, and economic benefit of the members. *NAACP v. Button*, 371 U.S. 415, 430–431 (1963). * * *

Those cases involved more than the "right of assembly"—a right that extends to all irrespective of their race or ideology. The right of "association," like the right of belief, is more than the right to attend a meeting; it includes the right to express one's attitudes or philosophies by membership in a group or by affiliation with it or by other lawful means. Association in that context is a form of expression of opinion; and while it is not expressly included in the First Amendment its existence is necessary in making the express guarantees fully meaningful.

The foregoing cases suggest that specific guarantees in the Bill of Rights have penumbras, formed by emanations from those guarantees that help give them life and substance. See *Poe v. Ullman*, 367 U.S. 497 (1961) (dissenting opinion). Various guarantees create zones of privacy. The right of association contained in the penumbra of the First Amendment is one, as we have seen. The Third Amendment in its prohibition against the quartering of soldiers "in any house" in time of peace without the consent of the owner is another facet of that privacy. The Fourth Amendment explicitly affirms the "right of the people to be secure in their persons, houses, papers, and effects, against unreasonable searches and seizures." The Fifth Amendment in its Self-Incrimination Clause enables the citizen to create a zone of privacy which government may not force him to surrender to his detriment. The Ninth Amendment provides: "The enumeration in the Constitution, of certain rights, shall not be construed to deny or disparage others retained by the people."

* * *

We have had many controversies over these penumbral rights of "privacy and repose." * * * These cases bear witness that the right of privacy which presses for recognition here is a legitimate one.

The present case, then, concerns a relationship lying within the zone of privacy created by several fundamental constitutional guarantees. And it concerns a law which, in forbidding the use of contraceptives rather than regulating their manufacture or sale, seeks to achieve its goals by means having a maximum destructive impact upon that relationship. Such a law cannot stand in light of the familiar principle, so often applied by this Court, that a "governmental purpose to control or prevent activities constitutionally subject to state regulation may not be achieved by means which sweep unnecessarily broadly and thereby invade the area of protected freedoms." <u>NAACP v. Alabama, 377 U.S. 288, 307 (1964)</u>. Would we allow the police to search the sacred precincts of marital bedrooms for telltale signs of the use of contraceptives? The very idea is repulsive to the notions of privacy surrounding the marriage relationship.

Think About It

Justice Douglas concludes here that the Connecticut statute sweeps too broadly. Would a more narrowly tailored statute be constitutional?

We deal with a right of privacy older than the Bill of Rights—older than our political parties, older than our school system. Marriage is a coming together for better or for worse, hopefully enduring, and intimate to the degree of being sacred. It is an association that promotes a way of life, not causes; a harmony in living, not political faiths; a bilateral loyalty, not commercial or social projects. Yet it is an association for as noble a purpose as any involved in our prior decisions.

Reversed.

MR. JUSTICE GOLDBERG, whom THE CHIEF JUSTICE and MR. JUSTICE BRENNAN join, concurring.

I agree with the Court that Connecticut's birth-control law unconstitutionally intrudes upon the right of marital privacy, and I join in its opinion and judgment. Although I have not accepted the view that "due process" as used in the Fourteenth

Amendment incorporates all of the first eight Amendments * * *, I do agree that the concept of liberty protects those personal rights that are fundamental, and is not confined to the specific terms of the Bill of Rights. * * *

* * *

This Court, in a series of decisions, has held that the Fourteenth Amendment absorbs and applies to the States those specifics of the first eight amendments which express fundamental personal rights. The language and history of the Ninth Amendment reveal that the Framers of the Constitution believed that there are additional fundamental rights, protected from governmental infringement, which exist alongside those fundamental rights specifically mentioned in the first eight constitutional amendments.

Take Note

At the time the Supreme Court decided *Griswold*, it was deeply engaged in debating the question referred to here: to what extent does the Fourteenth Amendment require the states to respect the rights included in the Bill of Rights?

The Ninth Amendment reads, "The enumeration in the Constitution, of certain rights, shall not be construed to deny or disparage others retained by the people." The Amendment is almost entirely the work of James Madison. It was introduced in Congress by him and passed the House and Senate with little or no debate and virtually no change in language. It was proffered to quiet expressed fears that a bill of specifically enumerated rights could not be sufficiently broad to cover all essential rights and that the specific mention of certain rights would be interpreted as a denial that others were protected.

* * * [T]he Framers did not intend that the first eight amendments be construed to exhaust the basic and fundamental rights which the Constitution guaranteed to the people.

While this Court has had little occasion to interpret the Ninth Amendment, "[i]t cannot be presumed that any clause in the constitution is intended to be without effect." *Marbury v. Madison, 1 Cranch 137, 174 (1803)*. In interpreting the Constitution, "real effect should be given to all the words it uses." *Myers v. United States, 272 U.S. 52, 151 (1926)*. The Ninth Amendment to the Constitution may be regarded by some as a recent discovery and may be forgotten by others, but since 1791 it has been a basic part of the Constitution which we are sworn to uphold. To hold that a right so basic and fundamental and so deep-rooted in our society as the right of privacy in marriage may be infringed because that right is not guaranteed in so many words by the first eight amendments to the

Constitution is to ignore the Ninth Amendment and to give it no effect whatsoever. Moreover, a judicial construction that this fundamental right is not protected
by the Constitution because it is not mentioned in explicit terms by one of the
first eight amendments or elsewhere in the Constitution would violate the Ninth
Amendment, which specifically states that "[t]he enumeration in the Constitution,
of certain rights, shall not be construed to deny or disparage others retained by
the people." (Emphasis added.)

* * *

In determining which rights are fundamental, judges are not left at large to
decide cases in light of their personal and private notions. Rather, they must look
to the "traditions and [collective] conscience of our people" to determine whether
a principle is "so rooted [there] * * * as to be ranked as fundamental." *Snyder v.
Massachusetts, 291 U.S. 97, 105 (1934)*. The inquiry is whether a right involved
"is of such a character that it cannot be denied without violating those 'fundamental principles of liberty and justice which lie at the base of all our civil and political
institutions' * * *." *Powell v. Alabama, 287 U.S. 45, 67 (1932)*. "Liberty" also
"gains content from the emanations of * * * specific [constitutional] guarantees"
and "from experience with the requirements of a free society." *Poe v. Ullman, 367
U.S. 497, 517 (1961)* (dissenting opinion of Mr. Justice Douglas).

I agree fully with the Court that, applying these tests, the right of privacy is
a fundamental personal right, emanating "from the totality of the constitutional
scheme under which we live."* * *

The Connecticut statutes here involved deal with a particularly important
and sensitive area of privacy—that of the marital relation and the marital home.
* * *

The entire fabric of the Constitution and the purposes that clearly underlie
its specific guarantees demonstrate that the rights to marital privacy and to marry
and raise a family are of similar order and magnitude as the fundamental rights
specifically protected.

Although the Constitution does not speak in so many words of the right of
privacy in marriage, I cannot believe that it offers these fundamental rights no
protection. The fact that no particular provision of the Constitution explicitly
forbids the State from disrupting the traditional relation of the family—a relation
as old and as fundamental as our entire civilization—surely does not show that
the Government was meant to have the power to do so. Rather, as the Ninth
Amendment expressly recognizes, there are fundamental personal rights such as

this one, which are protected from abridgment by the Government though not specifically mentioned in the Constitution.

* * *

The logic of the dissents would sanction federal or state legislation that seems to me even more plainly unconstitutional than the statute before us. Surely the Government, absent a showing of a compelling subordinating state interest, could not decree that all husbands and wives must be sterilized after two children have been born to them. Yet by their reasoning such an invasion of marital privacy would not be subject to constitutional challenge because, while it might be "silly," no provision of the Constitution specifically prevents the Government from curtailing the marital right to bear children and raise a

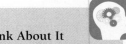

Think About It

Is Justice Goldberg's analogy to mandatory sterilization persuasive? How could a mandatory sterilization law be distinguished from a law prohibiting access to contraception?

family. While it may shock some of my Brethren that the Court today holds that the Constitution protects the right of marital privacy, in my view it is far more shocking to believe that the personal liberty guaranteed by the Constitution does not include protection against such totalitarian limitation of family size, which is at complete variance with our constitutional concepts. Yet, if upon a showing of a slender basis of rationality, a law outlawing voluntary birth control by married persons is valid, then, by the same reasoning, a law requiring compulsory birth control also would seem to be valid. In my view, however, both types of law would unjustifiably intrude upon rights of marital privacy which are constitutionally protected.

In a long series of cases this Court has held that where fundamental personal liberties are involved, they may not be abridged by the States simply on a showing that a regulatory statute has some rational relationship to the effectuation of a proper state purpose. "Where there is a significant encroachment upon personal liberty, the State may prevail only upon showing a subordinating interest which is compelling," <u>Bates v. Little Rock, 361 U.S. 516, 524 (1960)</u>. The law must be shown "necessary, and not merely rationally related, to the accomplishment of a permissible state policy." <u>McLaughlin v. Florida, 379 U.S. 184, 196 (1964)</u>.

Although the Connecticut birth-control law obviously encroaches upon a fundamental personal liberty, the State does not show that the law serves any "subordinating [state] interest which is compelling" or that it is "necessary * * * to the accomplishment of a permissible state policy." The State, at most, argues that there is some rational relation between this statute and what is admittedly a legitimate subject of state concern—the discouraging of extra-marital relations. It says that preventing the use of birth-control devices by married persons helps prevent the indulgence by some in such extra-marital relations. The rationality of this justification is dubious, particularly in light of the admitted widespread availability to all persons in the State of Connecticut, unmarried as well as married, of birth-control devices for the prevention of disease, as distinguished from the prevention of conception, see *Tileston v. Ullman,* 129 Conn. 84, 26 A.2d 582 (1942). But, in any event, it is clear that the state interest in safeguarding marital fidelity can be served by a more discriminately tailored statute, which does not like the present one, sweep unnecessarily broadly, reaching far beyond the evil sought to be dealt with and intruding upon the privacy of all married couples. * * * The State of Connecticut does have statutes, the constitutionality of which is beyond doubt, which prohibit adultery and fornication. See Conn.Gen.Stat.

Justice Harlan concurred in the judgment, concluding that the Connecticut statute violated basic values implicit in the concept of ordered liberty. Justice White concurred, concluding that the statute interfered with a fundamental right— the right to participate in family life— without sufficient justification.

Justice Black and Justice Stewart dissented. Calling the Connecticut statute "an uncommonly silly law," they nevertheless concluded that the Due Process Clause does not restrict state powers beyond the limitations imposed by the Bill of Rights, and found that none of those provisions applied to this case.

For more of the story behind this case, see Catherine E. Roraback, *Griswold v. Connecticut: A Brief Case History,* 16 Ohio N.U. L. Rev. 395 (1989).

§§ 53–218, 53–219 et seq. These statutes demonstrate that means for achieving the same basic purpose of protecting marital fidelity are available to Connecticut without the need to "invade the area of protected freedoms." * * *

Finally, it should be said of the Court's holding today that it in no way interferes with a State's proper regulation of sexual promiscuity or misconduct. * * *

In sum, I believe that the right of privacy in the marital relation is fundamental and basic—a personal right "retained by the people" within the meaning of the Ninth Amendment. Connecticut cannot constitutionally abridge this fundamental right, which is protected by the Fourteenth Amendment from infringement by the States. I agree with the Court that petitioners' convictions must therefore be reversed.

Points for Discussion

a. Constitutional Balancing

Griswold raises significant questions of constitutional law. What is the liberty interest protected by the Court in this case? What is Connecticut's interest in regulating contraception? Why is that interest not sufficient for the state to prevail in this case? After *Griswold*, when and how can a state regulate contraceptives?

How far can *Griswold* be extended? Does the decision in *Griswold* suggest that other laws regulating marriage or contraceptive use are invalid? See Kenneth L. Karst, *The Freedom of Intimate Association*, 89 Yale L.J. 624 (1980).

b. Role of History

Marriage has been heavily regulated by the state throughout our history, but the opinions of Justices Douglas and Goldberg do not discuss this fact. The Court acknowledged this pervasive state regulation in *Boddie v. Connecticut*, 401 U.S. 371, 376, 389 (1971), when it held that a state may not deny access to divorce to those who cannot pay court fees. State and federal legislation restricting access to contraception was extremely widespread from the late nineteenth century to the mid-twentieth century. How might the history be relevant to the constitutional arguments in *Griswold*?

Before *Griswold*, the courts relied on the concept of marital privacy in refusing to address domestic violence or resolve disputes between husbands and wives. See Chapter 4. Is this different from the marital privacy norm invoked in *Griswold*?

c. Rights of Married Couples

Do married people have other rights protected by the Constitution? The suit in *Kerry v. Din*, 576 U.S. ___, 135 S.Ct. 2128 (2015), was brought by a U.S.-citizen wife seeking an explanation of the reasons why her non-citizen husband was denied a visa to enter the United States. A plurality of three justices decided that Din had not been deprived of any right that entitled her to due process protection. Two justices concurred, finding that even if Din had a protected liberty interest, the government procedures were adequate on the facts of her case. Four members of the Court dissented, concluding that given the central importance of marriage in the law, Din's "freedom to live together with her husband in the United States" merited greater procedural protection than she received. *Din* is not unique; on the broader problems faced by married couples with mixed citizenship or immigration status, see Beth Caldwell, *Deported by Marriage: Americans Forced to Choose Between Love and Country*, 82 Brook. L. Rev. 1 (2016).

Loving v. Commonwealth of Virginia

388 U.S. 1 (1967)

Mr. CHIEF JUSTICE WARREN delivered the opinion of the Court.

This case presents a constitutional question never addressed by this Court: whether a statutory scheme adopted by the State of Virginia to prevent marriages between persons solely on the basis of racial classifications violates the Equal Protection and Due Process Clauses of the Fourteenth Amendment. For reasons which seem to us to reflect the central meaning of those constitutional commands, we conclude that these statutes cannot stand consistently with the Fourteenth Amendment.

Go Online

Listen to the oral arguments in *Loving* on the Oyez Project web site.

In June 1958, two residents of Virginia, Mildred Jeter, a Negro woman, and Richard Loving, a white man, were married in the District of Columbia pursuant to its laws. Shortly after their marriage, the Lovings returned to Virginia and established their marital abode in Caroline County. At the October Term, 1958, of the Circuit Court of Caroline County, a grand jury issued an indictment charging the Lovings with violating Virginia's ban on interracial marriages. On January 6, 1959, the Lovings pleaded guilty to the charge and were sentenced to one year in jail; however, the trial judge suspended the sentence for a period of 25 years on the condition that the Lovings leave the State and not return to Virginia together for 25 years. He stated in an opinion that:

> 'Almighty God created the races white, black, yellow, malay and red, and he placed them on separate continents. And but for the interference with his arrangement there would be no cause for such marriages. The fact that he separated the races shows that he did not intend for the races to mix.'

After their convictions, the Lovings took up residence in the District of Columbia. On November 6, 1963, they filed a motion in the state trial court to vacate the judgment and set aside the sentence on the ground that the statutes which they had violated were repugnant to the Fourteenth Amendment. The motion not having been decided by October 28, 1964, the Lovings instituted a class action in the United States District Court for the Eastern District of Virginia requesting that a three-judge court be convened to declare the Virginia antimiscegenation statutes unconstitutional and to enjoin state officials from enforcing their convictions. On January 22, 1965, the state trial judge denied the motion to vacate the sentences, and the Lovings perfected an appeal to the Supreme Court of Appeals of Virginia.

On February 11, 1965, the three-judge District Court continued the case to allow the Lovings to present their constitutional claims to the highest state court.

The Supreme Court of Appeals upheld the constitutionality of the antimiscegenation statutes and, after modifying the sentence, affirmed the convictions. [206 Va. 924, 147 S.E.2d 78 (1966).] The Lovings appealed this decision, and we noted probable jurisdiction on December 12, 1966.

The two statutes under which appellants were convicted and sentenced are part of a comprehensive statutory scheme aimed at prohibiting and punishing interracial marriages. The Lovings were convicted of violating § 20–58 of the Virginia Code:

> 'Leaving State to evade law.—If any white person and colored person shall go out of this State, for the purpose of being married, and with the intention of returning, and be married out of it, and afterwards return to and reside in it, cohabiting as man and wife, they shall be punished as provided in § 20–59, and the marriage shall be governed by the same law as if it had been solemnized in this State. The fact of their cohabitation here as man and wife shall be evidence of their marriage.'

Section 20–59, which defines the penalty for miscegenation, provides:

> 'Punishment for marriage.—If any white person intermarry with a colored person, or any colored person intermarry with a white person, he shall be guilty of a felony and shall be punished by confinement in the penitentiary for not less than one nor more than five years.'

Take Note!

The sections of the Virginia Code cited here state that the term white person: "shall apply only to such person as has no trace whatever of any blood other than Caucasian; but persons who have one-sixteenth or less of the blood of the American Indian and have no other non-Caucasic blood shall be deemed to be white persons." For a history of this statute, see Walter Wadlington, *The Loving Case; Virginia's Anti-Miscegenation Statute in Historical Perspective*, 52 Va. L. Rev. 1189 (1966).

Other central provisions in the Virginia statutory scheme are § 20–57, which automatically voids all marriages between 'a white person and a colored person' without any judicial proceeding, and §§ 20–54 and 1–14 which, respectively, define 'white persons' and 'colored persons and Indians' for purposes of the statutory prohibitions. The Lovings have never disputed in the course of this litigation that Mrs. Loving is a 'colored person' or that Mr. Loving is a 'white person' within the meanings given those terms by the Virginia statutes.

Virginia is now one of 16 States which prohibit and punish marriages on the basis of racial classifications.[5] Penalties for miscegenation arose as an incident to slavery and have been common in Virginia since the colonial period. The present statutory scheme dates from the adoption of the Racial Integrity Act of 1924, passed during the period of extreme nativism which followed the end of the First World War. The central features of this Act, and current Virginia law, are the absolute prohibition of a 'white person' marrying other than another 'white person,' a prohibition against issuing marriage licenses until the issuing official is satisfied that the applicants' statements as to their race are correct, certificates of 'racial composition' to be kept by both local and state registrars, and the carrying forward of earlier prohibitions against racial intermarriage.

I.

In upholding the constitutionality of these provisions in the decision below, the Supreme Court of Appeals of Virginia referred to its 1955 decision in *Naim v. Naim*, 197 Va. 80, 87 S.E.2d 749, as stating the reasons supporting the validity of these laws. In *Naim*, the state court concluded that the State's legitimate purposes were 'to preserve the racial integrity of its citizens,' and to prevent 'the corruption of blood,' 'a mongrel breed of citizens,' and 'the obliteration of racial pride,' obviously an endorsement of the doctrine of White Supremacy. The court also reasoned that marriage has traditionally been subject to state regulation without federal intervention, and, consequently, the regulation of marriage should be left to exclusive state control by the Tenth Amendment.

While the state court is no doubt correct in asserting that marriage is a social relation subject to the State's police power, *Maynard v. Hill*, 125 U.S. 190 (1888), the State does not contend in its argument before this Court that its powers to regulate marriage are unlimited notwithstanding the commands of the Fourteenth Amendment. Nor could it do so in light of *Meyer v. State of Nebraska*, 262 U.S. 390 (1923), and *Skinner v. State of Oklahoma*, 316 U.S. 535 (1942). Instead, the State argues that the meaning of the Equal Protection Clause, as illuminated by the statements of the Framers, is only that state penal laws containing an interracial element as part of the definition of the offense must apply equally to whites and Negroes in the sense that members of each race are punished to the same degree. Thus, the State contends that, because its miscegenation statutes punish equally

[handwritten: state argument]

---

[5]   After the initiation of this litigation, Maryland repealed its prohibitions against interracial marriage, leaving Virginia and 15 other States with statutes outlawing interracial marriage: Alabama, Arkansas, Delaware, Florida, Georgia, Kentucky, Louisiana, Mississippi, Missouri, North Carolina, Oklahoma, South Carolina, Tennessee, Texas, West Virginia.

Over the past 15 years, 14 States have repealed laws outlawing interracial marriages: Arizona, California, Colorado, Idaho, Indiana, Maryland, Montana, Nebraska, Nevada, North Dakota, Oregon, South Dakota, Utah, and Wyoming. The first state court to recognize that miscegenation statutes violate the Equal Protection Clause was the Supreme Court of California. *Perez v. Sharp*, 32 Cal.2d 711, 198 P.2d 17 (1948).

both the white and the Negro participants in an interracial marriage, these statutes, despite their reliance on racial classifications do not constitute an invidious discrimination based upon race. The second argument advanced by the State assumes the validity of its equal application theory. The argument is that, if the Equal Protection Clause does not outlaw miscegenation statutes because of their reliance on racial classifications, the question of constitutionality would thus become whether there was any rational basis for a State to treat interracial marriages differently from other marriages. On this question, the State argues, the scientific evidence is substantially in doubt and, consequently, this Court should defer to the wisdom of the state legislature in adopting its policy of discouraging interracial marriages.

Because we reject the notion that the mere 'equal application' of a statute containing racial classifications is enough to remove the classifications from the Fourteenth Amendment's proscription of all invidious racial discriminations, we do not accept the State's contention that these statutes should be upheld if there is any pos-

Think About It

What are Virginia's arguments in defense of this statute? What does the Court conclude regarding the purposes of the law?

sible basis for concluding that they serve a rational purpose. The mere fact of equal application does not mean that our analysis of these statutes should follow the approach we have taken in cases involving no racial discrimination where the Equal Protection Clause has been arrayed against a statute discriminating between the kinds of advertising which may be displayed on trucks in New York City, or an exemption in Ohio's ad valorem tax for merchandise owned by a non-resident in a storage warehouse. In these cases, involving distinctions not drawn according to race, the Court has merely asked whether there is any rational foundation for the discriminations, and has deferred to the wisdom of the state legislatures. In the case at bar, however, we deal with statutes containing racial classifications, and the fact of equal application does not immunize the statute from the very heavy burden of justification which the Fourteenth Amendment has traditionally required of state statutes drawn according to race.

* * *

There can be no question but that Virginia's miscegenation statutes rest solely upon distinctions drawn according to race. The statutes proscribe generally accepted conduct if engaged in by members of different races. Over the years, this Court has consistently repudiated '(d)istinctions between citizens solely because of their ancestry' as being 'odious to a free people whose institutions are founded upon the doctrine of equality.' *Hirabayashi v. United States, 320 U.S. 81 (1943).*

At the very least, the Equal Protection Clause demands that racial classifications, especially suspect in criminal statutes, be subjected to the 'most rigid scrutiny,' _Korematsu v. United States, 323 U.S. 214, 216 (1944)_, and, if they are ever to be upheld, they must be shown to be necessary to the accomplishment of some permissible state objective, independent of the racial discrimination which it was the object of the Fourteenth Amendment to eliminate. Indeed, two members of this Court have already stated that they 'cannot conceive of a valid legislative purpose * * * which makes the color of a person's skin the test of whether his conduct is a criminal offense.' _McLaughlin v. Florida, supra, 379 U.S. at 198_ (Stewart, J., joined by Douglas, J., concurring).

There is patently no legitimate overriding purpose independent of invidious racial discrimination which justifies this classification. The fact that Virginia prohibits only interracial marriages involving white persons demonstrates that the racial classifications must stand on their own justification, as measures designed to maintain White Supremacy. We have consistently denied the constitutionality of measures which restrict the rights of citizens on account of race. There can be no doubt that restricting the freedom to marry solely because of racial classifications violates the central meaning of the Equal Protection Clause.

II.

These statutes also deprive the Lovings of liberty without due process of law in violation of the Due Process Clause of the Fourteenth Amendment. The freedom to marry has long been recognized as one of the vital personal rights essential to the orderly pursuit of happiness by free men.

Marriage is one of the 'basic civil rights of man,' fundamental to our very existence and survival. _Skinner v. State of Oklahoma, 316 U.S. 535, 541 (1942)_. See also _Maynard v. Hill, 125 U.S. 190 (1888)_. To deny this fundamental freedom on so unsupportable a basis as the racial classifications embodied in these statutes, classifications so directly subversive of the principle of equality at the heart of the Fourteenth Amendment, is surely to deprive all the State's citizens of liberty without due process of law. The Fourteenth Amendment requires that the freedom of choice to marry not be restricted by invidious racial discriminations. Under our Constitution, the freedom to marry or not marry, a person of another race resides with the individual and cannot be infringed by the State.

These convictions must be reversed. It is so ordered.

Reversed.

Mr. JUSTICE STEWART, concurring.

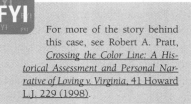

For more of the story behind this case, see Robert A. Pratt, *Crossing the Color Line: A Historical Assessment and Personal Narrative of Loving v. Virginia*, 41 Howard L.J. 229 (1998).

I have previously expressed the belief that 'it is simply not possible for a state law to be valid under our Constitution which makes the criminality of an act depend upon the race of the actor.' *McLaughlin v. State of Florida*, 379 U.S. 184, 198 (concurring opinion). Because I adhere to that belief, I concur in the judgment of the Court.

Points for Discussion

a. Equal Protection and Due Process

The decision in *Loving* concluded that the Virginia law enacted a racial classification that violated the Equal Protection Clause, and that it infringed the Lovings' fundamental freedom to marry in violation of the Due Process Clause. Are each of these grounds independently sufficient to support the Court's ruling?

b. Race and Families

The 2010 U.S. census found that almost seven percent of married couple households consisted of spouses of different races, while 14% of unmarried partner households had partners of different races. The rates were highest in the western states, and lowest in the midwest. See Daphne Lofquist et al., Households and Families: 2010 (Census Briefs, 2012). For a study exploring the experiences of contemporary multiracial couples, see Angela Onwuachi-Willig, According to *Our Hearts: Rhinelander v. Rhinelander and the Law of the Multiracial Family* (2013).

Issues of race are important across many aspects of family law. See, for example, the material on transracial adoption in Chapter 3, on race and the child welfare system in Chapter 5, and the decision in Palmore v. Sidoti, 466 U.S. 429 (1984), reprinted in Chapter 7.

Zablocki v. Redhail

434 U.S. 374 (1978)

Mr. JUSTICE MARSHALL delivered the opinion of the Court.

At issue in this case is the constitutionality of a Wisconsin statute, <u>Wis.
Stat. §§ 245.10(1), (4), (5) (1973)</u>,
which provides that members of a certain class of Wisconsin residents may

Go Online

Listen to the <u>oral arguments</u> in
Zablocki on the Oyez Project website.

not marry, within the State or elsewhere, without first obtaining a court order
granting permission to marry. The class is defined by the statute to include any
"Wisconsin resident having minor issue not in his custody and which he is under
obligation to support by any court order or judgment." The statute specifies that
court permission cannot be granted unless the marriage applicant submits proof
of compliance with the support obligation and, in addition, demonstrates that the
children covered by the support order "are not then and are not likely thereafter to
become public charges." No marriage license may lawfully be issued in Wisconsin
to a person covered by the statute, except upon court order; any marriage entered
into without compliance with § 245.10 is declared void; and persons acquiring
marriage licenses in violation of the section are subject to criminal penalties.

After being denied a marriage license because of his failure to comply with
§ 245.10, appellee brought this class action under <u>42 U.S.C. § 1983</u>, challenging
the statute as violative of the Equal Protection and Due Process Clauses of the
Fourteenth Amendment and seeking declaratory and injunctive relief. * * *

I

Appellee Redhail is a Wisconsin resident who, under the terms of <u>§ 245.10</u>,
is unable to enter into a lawful marriage in Wisconsin or elsewhere so long as he
maintains his Wisconsin residency. The facts, according to the stipulation filed by
the parties in the District Court, are as follows. In January 1972, when appellee
was a minor and a high school student, a paternity action was instituted against
him in Milwaukee County Court, alleging that he was the father of a baby girl
born out of wedlock on July 5, 1971. After he appeared and admitted that he was
the child's father, the court entered an order on May 12, 1972, adjudging appellee
the father and ordering him to pay $109 per month as support for the child until
she reached 18 years of age. From May 1972 until August 1974, appellee was
unemployed and indigent, and consequently was unable to make any support
payments.

On September 27, 1974, appellee filed an application for a marriage license with appellant Zablocki, the County Clerk of Milwaukee County, and a few days later the application was denied on the sole ground that appellee had not obtained a court order granting him permission to marry, as required by § 245.10. Although appellee did not petition a state court thereafter, it is stipulated that he would not have been able to satisfy either of the statutory prerequisites for an order granting permission to marry. First, he had not satisfied his support obligations to his illegitimate child, and as of December 1974 there was an arrearage in excess of $3,700. Second, the child had been a public charge since her birth, receiving benefits under the Aid to Families with Dependent Children program. It is stipulated that the child's benefit payments were such that she would have been a public charge even if appellee had been current in his support payments.

On December 24, 1974, appellee filed his complaint in the District Court, on behalf of himself and the class of all Wisconsin residents who had been refused a marriage license pursuant to § 245.10(1) by one of the county clerks in Wisconsin. * * * The complaint alleged, among other things, that appellee and the woman he desired to marry were expecting a child in March 1975 and wished to be lawfully married before that time. The statute was attacked on the grounds that it deprived appellee, and the class he sought to represent of equal protection and due process rights secured by the First, Fifth, Ninth, and Fourteenth Amendments to the United States Constitution.

* * *

II

In evaluating §§ 245.10(1), (4), (5) under the Equal Protection Clause, "we must first determine what burden of justification the classification created thereby must meet, by looking to the nature of the classification and the individual interests affected." *Memorial Hospital v. Maricopa County,* 415 U.S. 250, 253 (1974). Since our past decisions make clear that the right to marry is of fundamental importance, and since the classification at issue here significantly interferes with the exercise of that right, we believe that "critical examination" of the state interests advanced in support of the classification is required.

The leading decision of this Court on the right to marry is *Loving v. Virginia,* 388 U.S. 1 (1967). In that case, an interracial couple who had been convicted of violating Virginia's miscegenation laws challenged the statutory scheme on both equal protection and due process grounds. The Court's opinion could have rested solely on the ground that the statutes discriminated on the basis of race in violation of the Equal Protection Clause. *Id., at 11–12.* But the Court went on to hold that the laws arbitrarily deprived the couple of a fundamental liberty protected by the Due Process Clause, the freedom to marry. * * *

Although *Loving* arose in the context of racial discrimination, prior and subsequent decisions of this Court confirm that the right to marry is of fundamental importance for all individuals. Long ago, in *Maynard v. Hill*, 125 U.S. 190 (1888), the Court characterized marriage as "the most important relation in life," *id., at 205*, and as "the foundation of the family and of society, without which there would be neither civilization nor progress," *id., at 211*. In *Meyer v. Nebraska*, 262 U.S. 390 (1923), the Court recognized that the right "to marry, establish a home and bring up children" is a central part of the liberty protected by the Due Process Clause, *id., at 399*, and in *Skinner v. Oklahoma ex rel. Williamson*, *supra*, marriage was described as "fundamental to the very existence and survival of the race," 316 U.S., at 541.

More recent decisions have established that the right to marry is part of the fundamental "right of privacy" implicit in the Fourteenth Amendment's Due Process Clause. In *Griswold v. Connecticut*, 381 U.S. 479 (1965), the Court observed:

> "We deal with a right of privacy older than the Bill of Rights—older than our political parties, older than our school system. Marriage is a coming together for better or for worse, hopefully enduring, and intimate to the degree of being sacred. It is an association that promotes a way of life, not causes; a harmony in living, not political faiths; a bilateral loyalty, not commercial or social projects. Yet it is an association for as noble a purpose as any involved in our prior decisions." *Id., at 486*.

Cases subsequent to *Griswold* and *Loving* have routinely categorized the decision to marry as among the personal decisions protected by the right of privacy. * * *

It is not surprising that the decision to marry has been placed on the same level of importance as decisions relating to procreation, childbirth, child rearing, and family relationships. As the facts of this case illustrate, it would make little sense to recognize a right of privacy with respect to other matters of family life and not with respect to the decision to enter the relationship that is the foundation of the family in our society. The woman whom appellee desired to marry had a fundamental right to seek an abortion of their expected child, see *Roe v. Wade*, *supra*, or to bring the child into life to suffer the myriad social, if not economic, disabilities that the status of illegitimacy brings, see *Trimble v. Gordon*, 430 U.S. 762, 768–770, and n. 13 (1977); *Weber v. Aetna Casualty & Surety Co.*, 406 U.S. 164, 175–176 (1972). Surely, a decision to marry and raise the child in a traditional family setting must receive equivalent protection. And, if appellee's right to procreate means anything at all, it must imply some right to enter the only relationship in which the State of Wisconsin allows sexual relations legally to take place.[11]

---

[11] Wisconsin punishes fornication as a criminal offense:

"Whoever has sexual intercourse with a person not his spouse may be fined not more than $200 or imprisoned not more than 6 months or both." Wis.Stat. § 944.15 (1973).

By reaffirming the fundamental character of the right to marry, we do not mean to suggest that every state regulation which relates in any way to the incidents of or prerequisites for marriage must be subjected to rigorous scrutiny. To the contrary, reasonable regulations that do not significantly interfere with decisions to enter into the marital relationship may legitimately be imposed. See *Califano v. Jobst,* 434 U.S. 47, n. 12, *infra.* The statutory classification at issue here, however, clearly does interfere directly and substantially with the right to marry.

Under the challenged statute, no Wisconsin resident in the affected class may marry in Wisconsin or elsewhere without a court order, and marriages contracted in violation of the statute are both void and punishable as criminal offenses. Some of those in the affected class, like appellee, will never be able to obtain the necessary court order, because they either lack the financial means to meet their support obligations or cannot prove that their children will not become public charges. These persons are absolutely prevented from getting married. Many others, able in theory to satisfy the statute's requirements, will be sufficiently burdened by having to do so that they will in effect be coerced into forgoing their right to marry. And even those who can be persuaded to meet the statute's requirements suffer a serious intrusion into their freedom of choice in an area in which we have held such freedom to be fundamental.

III

When a statutory classification significantly interferes with the exercise of a fundamental right, it cannot be upheld unless it is supported by sufficiently important state interests and is closely tailored to effectuate only those interests. Appellant asserts that two interests are served by the challenged statute: the permission-to-marry proceeding furnishes an opportunity to counsel the applicant as to the necessity of fulfilling his prior support obligations; and the welfare of the out-of-custody children is protected. We may accept for present purposes that these are legitimate and substantial interests, but, since the means selected by the State for achieving these interests unnecessarily impinge on the right to marry, the statute cannot be sustained.

There is evidence that the challenged statute, as originally introduced in the Wisconsin Legislature, was intended merely to establish a mechanism whereby persons with support obligations to children from prior marriages could be counseled before they entered into new marital relationships and incurred further support obligations. Court permission to marry was to be required, but apparently permission was automatically to be granted after counseling was completed. The statute actually enacted, however, does not expressly require or provide for any counseling whatsoever, nor for any automatic granting of permission to marry by the court, and thus it can hardly be justified as a means for ensuring counseling of the persons within its coverage. Even assuming that counseling does take place—a fact as to which there is no evidence in the record—this interest obviously cannot support the withholding of court permission to marry once counseling is completed.

With regard to safeguarding the welfare of the out-of-custody children, appellant's brief does not make clear the connection between the State's interest and the statute's requirements. At argument, appellant's counsel suggested that, since permission to marry cannot be granted unless the applicant shows that he has satisfied his court-determined support obligations to the prior children and that those children will not become public charges, the statute provides incentive for the applicant to make support payments to his children. Tr. of Oral Arg. 17–20. This "collection device" rationale cannot justify the statute's broad infringement on the right to marry.

First, with respect to individuals who are unable to meet the statutory requirements, the statute merely prevents the applicant from getting married, without delivering any money at all into the hands of the applicant's prior children. More importantly, regardless of the applicant's ability or willingness to meet the statutory requirements, the State already has numerous other means for exacting compliance with support obligations, means that are at least as effective as the instant statute's and yet do not impinge upon the right to marry. * * *

There is also some suggestion that § 245.10 protects the ability of marriage applicants to meet support obligations to prior children by preventing the applicants from incurring new support obligations. But the challenged provisions of § 245.10 are grossly underinclusive with respect to this purpose, since they do not limit in any way new financial commitments by the applicant other than those arising out of the contemplated marriage. The statutory classification is substantially overinclusive as well: Given the possibility that the new spouse will actually better the applicant's financial situation, by contributing income from a job or otherwise, the statute in many cases may prevent affected individuals from improving their ability to satisfy their prior support obligations. And, although it is true that the applicant will incur support obligations to any children born during the contemplated marriage, preventing the marriage may only result in the children being born out of wedlock, as in fact occurred in appellee's case. Since the support obligation is the same whether the child is born in or out of wedlock, the net result of preventing the marriage is simply more illegitimate children.

The statutory classification created by §§ 245.10(1), (4), (5) thus cannot be justified by the interests advanced in support of it. The judgment of the District Court is, accordingly,

Affirmed.

Mr. JUSTICE STEWART, concurring in the judgment.

Four members of the Court joined Justice Marshall's majority opinion in *Zablocki*. Justices Stewart, Powell and Stevens filed opinions concurring in the result, and Justice Rehnquist dissented. Excerpts from these opinions are included here.

I cannot join the opinion of the Court. To hold, as the Court does, that the Wisconsin statute violates the Equal Protection Clause seems to me to misconceive the meaning of that constitutional guarantee. The Equal Protection Clause deals not with substantive rights or freedoms but with invidiously discriminatory classifications. * * * The paradigm of its violation is, of course, classification by race. <u>McLaughlin v. Florida, 379 U.S. 184</u>; <u>Loving v. Virginia, 388 U.S. 1, 13</u> (concurring opinion).

Like almost any law, the Wisconsin statute now before us affects some people and does not affect others. But to say that it thereby creates "classifications" in the equal protection sense strikes me as little short of fantasy. The problem in this case is not one of discriminatory classifications, but of unwarranted encroachment upon a constitutionally protected freedom. I think that the Wisconsin statute is unconstitutional because it exceeds the bounds of permissible state regulation of marriage, and invades the sphere of liberty protected by the Due Process Clause of the Fourteenth Amendment.

* * *

The Wisconsin law makes no allowance for the truly indigent. The State flatly denies a marriage license to anyone who cannot afford to fulfill his support obligations and keep his children from becoming wards of the State. We may assume that the State has legitimate interests in collecting delinquent support payments and in reducing its welfare load. We may also assume that, as applied to those who can afford to meet the statute's financial requirements but choose not to do so, the law advances the State's objectives in ways superior to other means available to the State. The fact remains that some people simply cannot afford to meet the statute's financial requirements. To deny these people permission to marry penalizes them for failing to do that which they cannot do. Insofar as it applies to indigents, the state law is an irrational means of achieving these objectives of the State.

* * *

Mr. Justice Powell, concurring in the judgment.

I concur in the judgment of the Court that Wisconsin's restrictions on the exclusive means of creating the marital bond * * * cannot meet applicable constitutional standards. I write separately because the majority's rationale sweeps too broadly in an area which traditionally has been subject to pervasive state regulation. The Court apparently would subject all state regulation which "directly and substantially" interferes with the decision to marry in a traditional family setting to "critical examination" or "compelling state interest" analysis. Presumably, "reasonable regulations that do not significantly interfere with decisions to enter into the marital relationship may legitimately be imposed." The Court does not present, however, any principled means for distinguishing between the two types of regulations. Since state regulation in this area typically takes the form of a prerequisite or barrier to marriage or divorce, the degree of "direct" interference with the decision to marry or to divorce is unlikely to provide either guidance for state legislatures or a basis for judicial oversight.

* * *

In my view, analysis must start from the recognition of domestic relations as "an area that has long been regarded as a virtually exclusive province of the States." Sosna v. Iowa, 419 U.S. 393, 404 (1975). The marriage relation traditionally has been subject to regulation, initially by the ecclesiastical authorities, and later by the secular state. As early as Pennoyer v. Neff, 95 U.S. 714, 734–735 (1878), this Court noted that a State "has absolute right to prescribe the conditions upon which the marriage relation between its own citizens shall be created, and the causes for which it may be dissolved." The State, representing the collective expression of moral aspirations, has an undeniable interest in ensuring that its rules of domestic relations reflect the widely held values of its people.

State regulation has included bans on incest, bigamy, and homosexuality, as well as various preconditions to marriage, such as blood tests. Likewise, a showing of fault on the part of one of the partners traditionally has been a prerequisite to the dissolution of an unsuccessful union. A "compelling state purpose" inquiry would cast doubt on the network of restrictions that the States have fashioned to govern marriage and divorce.

State power over domestic relations is not without constitutional limits. The Due Process Clause requires a showing of justification "when the government intrudes on choices concerning family living arrangements" in a manner which is contrary to deeply rooted traditions. * * * Due process constraints also limit the extent to which the State may monopolize the process of ordering certain human relationships while excluding the truly indigent from that process. Boddie v. Connecticut, 401 U.S. 371 (1971). Furthermore, under the Equal Protection Clause the means chosen by the State in this case must bear " 'a fair and substantial relation' " to the object of the legislation.

* * *

The marriage applicant is required by the Wisconsin statute not only to submit proof of compliance with his support obligation, but also to demonstrate—in some unspecified way—that his children "are not then and are not likely thereafter to become public charges." This statute * * * tells the truly indigent, whether they have met their support obligations or not, that they may not marry so long as their children are public charges or there is a danger that their children might go on public assistance in the future. Apparently, no other jurisdiction has embraced this approach as a method of reducing the number of children on public assistance. Because the State has not established a justification for this unprecedented foreclosure of marriage to many of its citizens solely because of their indigency, I concur in the judgment of the Court.

Mr. JUSTICE STEVENS, concurring in the judgment.

* * *

A classification based on marital status is fundamentally different from a classification which determines who may lawfully enter into the marriage relationship. The individual's interest in making the marriage decision independently is sufficiently important to merit special constitutional protection. It is not, however, an interest which is constitutionally immune from evenhanded regulation. Thus, laws prohibiting marriage to a child, a close relative, or a person afflicted with venereal disease, are unchallenged even though they "interfere directly and substantially with the right to marry." This Wisconsin statute has a different character.

Under this statute, a person's economic status may determine his eligibility to enter into a lawful marriage. A noncustodial parent whose children are "public charges" may not marry even if he has met his court-ordered obligations. Thus, within the class of parents who have fulfilled their court-ordered obligations, the rich may marry and the poor may not. This type of statutory discrimination is, I believe, totally unprecedented, as well as inconsistent with our tradition of administering justice equally to the rich and to the poor.

* * *

Mr. JUSTICE REHNQUIST, dissenting.

I substantially agree with my Brother Powell's reasons for rejecting the Court's conclusion that marriage is the sort of "fundamental right" which must invariably trigger the strictest judicial scrutiny. I disagree with his imposition of an "intermediate" standard of review, which leads him to conclude that the statute, though generally valid as an "additional collection mechanism" offends the Constitution by its "failure to make provision for those without the means to comply with child-support obligations." For similar reasons, I disagree with my Brother Stewart's conclusion that the statute is invalid for its failure to exempt those persons who "simply cannot afford to meet the statute's financial requirements." I would view this legislative judgment in the light of the traditional presumption of validity. I think that under the Equal Protection Clause the statute need pass only the "rational basis test," and that under the Due Process Clause it need only be shown that it bears a rational relation to a constitutionally permissible objective. The statute so viewed is a permissible exercise of the State's power to regulate family life and to assure the support of minor children, despite its possible imprecision in the extreme cases envisioned in the concurring opinions.

* * *

Two of the opinions concurring in the judgment seem to agree that the statute is sufficiently rational except as applied to the truly indigent. Under this view, the statute could, I suppose, be constitutionally applied to forbid the marriages of those applicants who had willfully failed to contribute so much as was in their means to the support of their dependent children. Even were I to agree that a statute based upon generally valid assumptions could be struck down on the basis of "selected, atypical examples," I could not concur in the judgment of the Court, because there has been no showing that this appellee is so truly indigent that the State could not refuse to sanction his marriage.

Points for Discussion

a. Right to Marry

Under *Zablocki*, what kinds of marriage regulations can states enact? Does the opinion also limit statutory classifications that are based on marriage? For example, under the federal income tax laws, two spouses sometimes pay more in income tax when they are married than they would if they were single and filed separately. Given the constitutional stature of the right to marry considered in *Loving* and *Zablocki*, are these provisions of the Internal Revenue Code unconstitutional? See <u>*Druker v. Commissioner*, 697 F.2d 46 (2d Cir.1982)</u>.

After *Zablocki*, how far can a state go in establishing rules that may restrict access to marriage? The Supreme Court considered the right to marry again in <u>Turner v. Safley, 482 U.S. 78 (1987)</u>, which considered Missouri prison regulations requiring that inmates have the prison superintendent's permission to marry, which permission was available only in limited circumstances. Recognizing that the right to marry was "subject to substantial restrictions as a result of incarceration," the majority nevertheless concluded that the right recognized in *Loving* and *Zablocki* also extended to prisoners. The Court held that the Missouri regulations were too broad to be sustained by the state's legitimate security and rehabilitation concerns.

b. Families, Poverty, and the Law

The Justices disagreed about whether *Zablocki* was an Equal Protection or Due Process case, and what type of scrutiny should be applied. The opinions also reflect different views as to how courts should consider the impact of marriage laws on "the truly indigent."

The Court has not generally been willing to apply heightened scrutiny to laws that have a more serious impact on poor people, but it has held, because of the important rights at stake in family cases, that states may not deny access to the courts in divorce or termination of parental rights cases when individuals cannot afford to pay court fees. See <u>Boddie v. Connecticut, 401 U.S. 371 (1971)</u>; <u>M.L.B. v. S.L.J., 519 U.S. 102 (1996)</u>.

Global View: Marriage and the Family in
International Human Rights Law

According to Article 16 of the <u>Universal Declaration of Human Rights</u> (1948):

> 1. Men and women of full age, without any limitation due to race, nationality or religion, have the right to marry and found a family. They are entitled to equal rights as to marriage, during marriage, and at its dissolution.
> 2. Marriage shall be entered into only with the free and full consent of the intending spouses.
> 3. The family is the natural and fundamental group until of society and is entitled to protection by society and the State.

These provisions are implemented in other human rights instruments, including the United Nations <u>International Covenant on Civil and Political Rights</u>, ratified by the United States in 1992.

Problem 1-1

Heather is a U.S. citizen who lives with her partner Jose and their son in the United States. Jose is a Mexican citizen who entered the United States without authorization. When Heather and Jose apply for a marriage license, the local registrar refuses to grant the license unless Jose can present a U.S. Permanent Resident Card (also known as a "Green Card") along with other valid identification documents. Can Heather and Jose challenge this policy? (See <u>Buck v. Stankovic, 485 F.Supp.2d 576 (M.D. Pa. 2007)</u>.

Eisenstadt v. Baird

<u>405 U.S. 438 (1972)</u>

Go Online

Listen to the <u>oral arguments</u> in *Eisenstadt* on the Oyez Project web site.

Mr. Justice Brennan delivered the opinion of the Court.

Appellee William Baird was convicted at a bench trial in the Massachusetts Superior Court under <u>Massachusetts General Laws Ann., c. 272, § 21</u>, first, for exhibiting contraceptive articles in the course of delivering a lecture on contraception to a group of students at Boston University and, second, for giving a young woman a package of Emko vaginal foam at the close of his address. The Massachusetts Supreme Judicial Court unanimously set aside the conviction for exhibiting contraceptives on the ground that it violated Baird's First Amendment rights, but by a four-to-three vote sustained the conviction for giving away the foam. <u>Commonwealth v. Baird, 355 Mass. 746, 247 N.E.2d 574 (1969)</u>. * * *

<u>Massachusetts General Laws Ann., c. 272, § 21</u>, under which Baird was convicted, provides a maximum five-year term of imprisonment for "whoever. . .gives away. . .any drug, medicine, instrument or article whatever for the prevention of conception," except as authorized in § 21A. Under § 21A, "(a) registered physician may administer to or prescribe for any married person drugs or articles intended for the prevention of pregnancy or conception. (And a) registered pharmacist actually engaged in the business of pharmacy may furnish such drugs or articles to any married person presenting a prescription from a registered physician." As interpreted by the State Supreme Judicial Court, these provisions make it a felony for anyone, other than a registered physician or pharmacist acting in accordance with the terms of § 21A, to dispense any article with the intention that it be used

for the prevention of conception. The statutory scheme distinguishes among three distinct classes of distributees—*first*, married persons may obtain contraceptives to prevent pregnancy, but only from doctors or druggists on prescription; *second*, single persons may not obtain contraceptives from anyone to prevent pregnancy; and, *third*, married or single persons may obtain contraceptives from anyone to prevent, not pregnancy, but the spread of disease. This construction of state law is, of course, binding on us. * * *

The legislative purposes that the statute is meant to serve are not altogether clear. In *Commonwealth v. Baird, supra*, the Supreme Judicial Court noted only the State's interest in protecting the health of its citizens: "(T)he prohibition in § 21," the court declared, "is directly related to" the State's goal of "preventing the distribution of articles designed to prevent conception which may have undesirable, if not dangerous, physical consequences," In a subsequent decision, *Sturgis v. Attorney General, 358 Mass. 37, 260 N.E.2d 687, 690 (1970)*, the court, however, found "a second and more compelling ground for upholding the statute"—namely, to protect morals through "regulating the private sexual lives of single persons."[3] The Court of Appeals, for reasons that will appear, did not consider the promotion of health or the protection of morals through the deterrence of fornication to be the legislative aim. Instead, the court concluded that the statutory goal was to limit contraception in and of itself—a purpose that the court held conflicted "with fundamental human rights" under *Griswold v. Connecticut, 381 U.S. 479 (1965)*, where this Court struck down Connecticut's prohibition against the use of contraceptives as an unconstitutional infringement of the right of marital privacy.

We agree that the goals of deterring premarital sex and regulating the distribution of potentially harmful articles cannot reasonably be regarded as legislative aims of §§ 21 and 21A. And we hold that the statute, viewed as a prohibition on contraception *per se*, violates the rights of single persons under the Equal Protection Clause of the Fourteenth Amendment.

Think About It

Why does the Court reject Massachusetts's argument regarding the purpose of the statute?

* * *

---

[3]   Appellant suggests that the purpose of the Massachusetts statute is to promote marital fidelity as well as to discourage premarital sex. Under § 21A, however, contraceptives may be made available to married persons without regard to whether they are living with their spouses or the uses to which the contraceptives are to be put. Plainly the legislation has no deterrent effect on extramarital sexual relations.

II

The basic principles governing application of the Equal Protection Clause of the Fourteenth Amendment are familiar. * * *

The question for our determination in this case is whether there is some ground of difference that rationally explains the different treatment accorded married and unmarried persons under Massachusetts General Laws Ann., c. 272, §§ 21 and 21A. For the reasons that follow, we conclude that no such ground exists.

First. Section 21 stems from Mass. Stat.1879, c. 159, § 1, which prohibited without exception, distribution of articles intended to be used as contraceptives. In *Commonwealth v. Allison*, 227 Mass. 57, 62, 116 N.E. 265, 266 (1917), the Massachusetts Supreme Judicial Court explained that the law's "plain purpose is to protect purity, to preserve chastity, to encourage continence and self restraint, to defend the sanctity of the home, and thus to engender in the State and nation a virile and virtuous race of men and women." Although the State clearly abandoned that purpose with the enactment of § 21A, at least insofar as the illicit sexual activities of married persons are concerned, see n. 3, *supra*, the court reiterated in *Sturgis v. Attorney General, supra*, that the object of the legislation is to discourage premarital sexual intercourse. Conceding that the State could, consistently with the Equal Protection Clause, regard the problems of extramarital and premarital sexual relations as "(e)vils. . .of different dimensions and proportions, requiring different remedies," *Williamson v. Lee Optical Co.*, 348 U.S. 483, 489 (1955), we cannot agree that the deterrence of premarital sex may reasonably be regarded as the purpose of the Massachusetts law.

It would be plainly unreasonable to assume that Massachusetts has prescribed pregnancy and the birth of an unwanted child as punishment for fornication, which is a misdemeanor under Massachusetts General Laws Ann., c. 272, § 18. Aside from the scheme of values that assumption would attribute to the State, it is abundantly clear that the effect of the ban on distribution of contraceptives to unmarried persons has at best a marginal relation to the proffered objective. What Mr. Justice Goldberg said in *Griswold v. Connecticut, supra*, 381 U.S., at 498 (concurring opinion), concerning the effect of Connecticut's prohibition on the use of contraceptives in discouraging extramarital sexual relations, is equally applicable here. "The rationality of this justification is dubious, particularly in light of the admitted widespread availability to all persons in the State of Connecticut, unmarried as well as married, of birth-control devices for the prevention of disease, as distinguished from the prevention of conception." See also *id., at 505–507* (White, J., concurring in judgment). Like Connecticut's laws, §§ 21 and 21A do not at all regulate the distribution of contraceptives when they are to be used to prevent, not pregnancy, but the spread of disease. Nor, in making contraceptives available to married persons without regard to their intended use, does Massachusetts attempt to deter married persons from engaging in illicit sexual relations with unmarried persons. Even on the assumption that the fear of pregnancy operates as a deterrent to fornication, the Massachusetts statute is thus so riddled with exceptions that deterrence of premarital sex cannot reasonably be regarded as its aim.

Moreover, §§ 21 and 21A on their face have a dubious relation to the State's criminal prohibition on fornication. As the Court of Appeals explained, "Fornication is a misdemeanor (in Massachusetts), entailing a thirty dollar fine, or three months in jail. Massachusetts General Laws Ann. c. 272, § 18. Violation of the present statute is a felony, punishable by five years in prison. We find it hard to believe that the legislature adopted a statute carrying a five-year penalty for its possible, obviously by no means fully effective, deterrence of the commission of a ninety-day misdemeanor." Even conceding the legislature a full measure of discretion in fashioning means to prevent fornication, and recognizing that the State may seek to deter prohibited conduct by punishing more severely those who facilitate than those who actually engage in its commission, we, like the Court of Appeals, cannot believe that in this instance Massachusetts has chosen to expose the aider and abetter who simply *gives away* a contraceptive to *20* times the *90-day* sentence of the offender himself. The very terms of the State's criminal statutes, coupled with the *de minimis* effect of §§ 21 and 21A in deterring fornication, thus compel the conclusion that such deterrence cannot reasonably be taken as the purpose of the ban on distribution of contraceptives to unmarried persons.

Second. Section 21A was added to the Massachusetts General Laws by Stat. 1966, c. 265, § 1. The Supreme Judicial Court in *Commonwealth v. Baird, supra*, held that the purpose of the amendment was to serve the health needs of the community by regulating the distribution of potentially harmful articles. It is plain that Massachusetts had no such purpose in mind before the enactment of § 21A. As the Court of Appeals remarked, "Consistent with the fact that the statute was contained in a chapter dealing with 'Crimes Against Chastity, Morality, Decency and Good Order,' it was cast only in terms of morals. A physician was forbidden to prescribe contraceptives even when needed for the protection of health. *Commonwealth v. Gardner, 1938, 300 Mass. 372, 15 N.E.2d 222*." Nor did the Court of Appeals "believe that the legislature (in enacting § 21A) suddenly reversed its field and developed an interest in health. Rather, it merely made what it thought to be the precise accommodation necessary to escape the *Griswold* ruling." *Ibid.*

Again, we must agree with the Court of Appeals. If health were the rationale of § 21A, the statute would be both discriminatory and overbroad. Dissenting in *Commonwealth v. Baird, 355 Mass., at 758, 247 N.E.2d, at 581*, Justices Whittemore and Cutter stated that they saw "in § 21 and § 21A, read together, no public health purpose. If there is need to have a physician prescribe (and a pharmacist dispense) contraceptives, that need is as great for unmarried persons as for married persons." The Court of Appeals added: "If the prohibition (on distribution to unmarried persons). . .is to be taken to mean that the same physician who can prescribe for married patients does not have sufficient skill to protect the health of patients who lack a marriage certificate, or who may be currently divorced, it is illogical to the point of irrationality."[8] Furthermore, we must join the Court of Appeals in noting that not all contraceptives are potentially dangerous.[9] * * *

But if further proof that the Massachusetts statute is not a health measure is necessary, the argument of Justice Spiegel, who also dissented in *Commonwealth v. Baird*, 355 Mass. at 759, 247 N.E.2d, at 582, is conclusive: "It is at best a strained conception to say that the Legislature intended to prevent the distribution of articles 'which may have undesirable, if not dangerous, physical consequences.' If that was the Legislature's goal, § 21 is not required" in view of the federal and state laws *already* regulating the distribution of harmful drugs. See Federal Food, Drug, and Cosmetic Act, § 503, 52 Stat. 1051, as amended, 21 U.S.C. § 353; Mass.Gen. Laws Ann., c. 94, § 187A, as amended. We conclude, accordingly, that, despite the statute's superficial earmarks as a health measure, health, on the face of the statute, may no more reasonably be regarded as its purpose than the deterrence of premarital sexual relations.

Third. If the Massachusetts statute cannot be upheld as a deterrent to fornication or as a health measure, may it, nevertheless, be sustained simply as a prohibition on contraception? The Court of Appeals analysis "led inevitably to the conclusion that, so far as morals are concerned, it is contraceptives per se that are considered immoral—to the extent that *Griswold* will permit such a declaration." The Court of Appeals went on to hold:

"To say that contraceptives are immoral as such, and are to be forbidden to unmarried persons who will nevertheless persist in having inter-

---

[8] Appellant insists that the unmarried have no right to engage in sexual intercourse and hence no health interest in contraception that needs to be served. The short answer to this contention is that the same devices the distribution of which the State purports to regulate when their asserted purpose is to forestall pregnancy are available without any controls whatsoever so long as their asserted purpose is to prevent the spread of disease. It is inconceivable that the need for health controls varies with the purpose for which the contraceptive is to be used when the physical act in all cases is one and the same.

[9] The Court of Appeals stated, 429 F.2d, at 1401:

"[W]e must take notice that not all contraceptive devices risk 'undesirable. . .(or) dangerous physical consequences.' It is 200 years since Casanova recorded the ubiquitous article which, perhaps because of the birthplace of its inventor, he termed a 'redingote anglais.' The reputed nationality of the condom has now changed, but we have never heard criticism of it on the side of health. We cannot think that the legislature was unaware of it, or could have thought that it needed a medical prescription. We believe the same could be said of certain other products."

course, means that such persons must risk for themselves an unwanted pregnancy, for the child, illegitimacy, and for society, a possible obligation of support. Such a view of morality is not only the very mirror image of sensible legislation; we consider that it conflicts with fundamental human rights. In the absence of demonstrated harm, we hold it is beyond the competency of the state."

We need not and do not, however, decide that important question in this case because, whatever the rights of the individual to access to contraceptives may be, the rights must be the same for the unmarried and the married alike.

If under *Griswold* the distribution of contraceptives to married persons cannot be prohibited, a ban on distribution to unmarried persons would be equally impermissible. It is true that in *Griswold* the right of privacy in question inhered in the marital relationship. Yet the marital couple is not an independent entity with a mind and heart of its own, but an association of two individuals each with a separate intellectual and emotional makeup. If the right of privacy means anything, it is the right of the individual, married or single, to be free from unwarranted governmental intrusion into matters so fundamentally affecting a person as the decision whether to bear or beget a child. See <u>Stanley v. Georgia, 394 U.S. 557 (1969)</u>. See also <u>Skinner v. Oklahoma, 316 U.S. 535 (1942)</u>; <u>Jacobson v. Massachusetts, 197 U.S. 11, 29 (1905)</u>.

On the other hand, if *Griswold* is no bar to a prohibition on the distribution of contraceptives, the State could not, consistently with the Equal Protection Clause, outlaw distribution to unmarried but not to married persons. In each case the evil, as perceived by the State, would be identical, and the underinclusion would be invidious. * * * We hold that by providing dissimilar treatment for married and unmarried persons who are similarly situated, <u>Massachusetts General Laws Ann., c. 272, §§ 21 and 21A</u>, violate the Equal Protection Clause. The judgment of the Court of Appeals is

Affirmed.

Justice Powell and Justice Rehnquist took no part in this case. Justice Douglas filed a concurring opinion, arguing that Baird's conviction violated the First Amendment. Justice White, joined by Justice Blackmun, also concurred in the result. Noting that contraceptive foam was widely available without prescription, and that there was no evidence of hazards from use of the foam, Justice White concluded that the record did not support the state's claim that restrictions on distribution of vaginal foam were essential to achieving an important public health purpose. Justice Burger dissented.

Points for Discussion

a. Rights of Unmarried Adults

Eisenstadt was widely understood as extending to unmarried adults the same sexual privacy rights that *Griswold* recognized for married couples. See Kenneth Karst, *The Freedom of Intimate Association,* 89 Yale. L.J. 624 (1980). A more narrow reading of the case holds that it concerns only the right of access to contraceptives. See Bruce Hafen, *The Constitutional Status of Marriage, Kinship and Sexual Privacy-Balancing the Individual and Social Interests,* 81 Mich. L. Rev. 463 (1983). Justice Brennan's opinion in *Eisenstadt* concludes that "whatever the rights of the individual to access to contraceptives may be, the rights must be the same for the married and the unmarried alike." Why is this? Does this suggest a constitutional problem with other rights that are extended only to married people?

b. Families or Individuals?

Professor Janet Dolgin has argued that *Eisenstadt* is "singularly important" as evidence of an important ideological shift, which she describes as "the transformation of the American family into an association of separate individuals." Janet Dolgin, *The Family in Transition: From* Griswold *to* Eisenstadt *and Beyond,* 82 Geo. L. J. 1519 (1994). Would you agree? Can you identify other indications of this transformation?

Make the Connection

Does the Constitution protect family relationships beyond those of marital couples or parents and children? These issues are considered in Chapter 4.

Lawrence v. Texas

539 U.S. 558 (2003)

JUSTICE KENNEDY delivered the opinion of the Court.

Liberty protects the person from unwarranted government intrusions into a dwelling or other private places. In our tradition the State is not omnipresent in the home. And there are other spheres of our lives and existence, outside the home, where the State should not be a dominant presence. Freedom extends beyond spatial bounds. Liberty presumes an autonomy of self that includes freedom of thought, belief, expression, and certain intimate

Go Online

Listen to the oral arguments in *Lawrence* on the Oyez Project web site.

conduct. The instant case involves liberty of the person both in its spatial and more transcendent dimensions.

I

The question before the Court is the validity of a Texas statute making it a crime for two persons of the same sex to engage in certain intimate sexual conduct.

In Houston, Texas, officers of the Harris County Police Department were dispatched to a private residence in response to a reported weapons disturbance. They entered an apartment where one of the petitioners, John Geddes Lawrence, resided. The right of the police to enter does not seem to have been questioned. The officers observed Lawrence and another man, Tyron Garner, engaging in a sexual act. The two petitioners were arrested, held in custody over night, and charged and convicted before a Justice of the Peace.

The complaints described their crime as "deviate sexual intercourse, namely anal sex, with a member of the same sex (man)." The applicable state law is Tex. Penal Code Ann. § 21.06(a) (2003). It provides: "A person commits an offense if he engages in deviate sexual intercourse with another individual of the same sex." The statute defines "[d]eviate sexual intercourse" as follows:

> "(A) any contact between any part of the genitals of one person and the mouth or anus of another person; or
> "(B) the penetration of the genitals or the anus of another person with an object." § 21.01(1).

The petitioners * * * challenged the statute as a violation of the Equal Protection Clause of the Fourteenth Amendment and of a like provision of the Texas Constitution. Tex. Const., Art. 1, § 3a. Those contentions were rejected. The petitioners, having entered a plea of *nolo contendere,* were each fined $200 and assessed court costs of $141.25.

* * *

We granted certiorari to consider three questions:

> 1. Whether Petitioners' criminal convictions under the Texas 'Homosexual Conduct' law—which criminalizes sexual intimacy by same-sex couples, but not identical behavior by different-sex couples—violate the Fourteenth Amendment guarantee of equal protection of laws?
> 2. Whether Petitioners' criminal convictions for adult consensual sexual intimacy in the home violate their vital interests in liberty and privacy protected by the Due Process Clause of the Fourteenth Amendment?
> 3. Whether *Bowers v. Hardwick,* 478 U.S. 186 (1986), should be overruled?".

The petitioners were adults at the time of the alleged offense. Their conduct was in private and consensual.

II

We conclude the case should be resolved by determining whether the petitioners were free as adults to engage in the private conduct in the exercise of their liberty under the Due Process Clause of the Fourteenth Amendment to the Constitution. For this inquiry we deem it necessary to reconsider the Court's holding in *Bowers*.

There are broad statements of the substantive reach of liberty under the Due Process Clause in earlier cases, including <u>*Pierce v. Society of the Sisters of the Holy Names of Jesus and Mary,* 268 U.S. 510 (1925)</u>, and <u>*Meyer v. Nebraska,* 262 U.S. 390 (1923)</u>; but the most pertinent beginning point is our decision in <u>*Griswold v. Connecticut,* 381 U.S. 479 (1965)</u>.

In *Griswold* the Court invalidated a state law prohibiting the use of drugs or devices of contraception and counseling or aiding and abetting the use of contraceptives. The Court described the protected interest as a right to privacy and placed emphasis on the marriage relation and the protected space of the marital bedroom.

After *Griswold* it was established that the right to make certain decisions regarding sexual conduct extends beyond the marital relationship. In <u>*Eisenstadt v. Baird,* 405 U.S. 438 (1972)</u>, the Court invalidated a law prohibiting the distribution of contraceptives to unmarried persons. The case was decided under the Equal Protection Clause, but with respect to unmarried persons, the Court went on to state the fundamental proposition that the law impaired the exercise of their personal rights. It quoted from the statement of the Court of Appeals finding the law to be in conflict with fundamental human rights, and it followed with this statement of its own:

> "It is true that in *Griswold* the right of privacy in question inhered in the marital relationship. . . . If the right of privacy means anything, it is the right of the *individual,* married or single, to be free from unwarranted governmental intrusion into matters so fundamentally affecting a person as the decision whether to bear or beget a child."

The opinions in *Griswold* and *Eisenstadt* were part of the background for the decision in <u>*Roe v. Wade,* 410 U.S. 113 (1973)</u>. As is well known, the case involved a challenge to the Texas law prohibiting abortions, but the laws of other States were affected as well. Although the Court held the woman's rights were not absolute, her right to elect an abortion did have real and substantial protection as an exercise of her liberty under the Due Process Clause. * * *

In *Carey v. Population Services Int'l*, 431 U.S. 678 (1977), the Court confronted a New York law forbidding sale or distribution of contraceptive devices to persons under 16 years of age. Although there was no single opinion for the Court, the law was invalidated. Both *Eisenstadt* and *Carey*, as well as the holding and rationale in *Roe*, confirmed that the reasoning of *Griswold* could not be confined to the protection of rights of married adults. This was the state of the law with respect to some of the most relevant cases when the Court considered *Bowers v. Hardwick*.

* * *

The Court began its substantive discussion in *Bowers* as follows: "The issue presented is whether the Federal Constitution confers a fundamental right upon homosexuals to engage in sodomy and hence invalidates the laws of the many States that still make such conduct illegal and have done so for a very long time." That statement, we now conclude, discloses the Court's own failure to appreciate the extent of the liberty at stake. To say that the issue in *Bowers* was simply the right to engage in certain sexual conduct demeans the claim the individual put forward, just as it would demean a married couple were it to be said marriage is simply about the right to have sexual intercourse. The laws involved in *Bowers* and here are, to be sure, statutes that purport to do no more than prohibit a particular sexual act. Their penalties and purposes, though, have more far-reaching consequences, touching upon the most private human conduct, sexual behavior, and in the most private of places, the home. The statutes do seek to control a personal relationship that, whether or not entitled to formal recognition in the law, is within the liberty of persons to choose without being punished as criminals.

This, as a general rule, should counsel against attempts by the State, or a court, to define the meaning of the relationship or to set its boundaries absent injury to a person or abuse of an institution the law protects. It suffices for us to acknowledge that adults may choose to enter upon this relationship in the confines of their homes and their own private lives and still retain their dignity as free persons. When sexuality finds overt expression in intimate conduct with another person, the conduct can be but one element in a personal bond that is more enduring. The liberty protected by the Constitution allows homosexual persons the right to make this choice.

Think About It

What is the constitutional liberty interest the Court identifies in this case?

Having misapprehended the claim of liberty there presented to it, and thus stating the claim to be whether there is a fundamental right to engage in consensual sodomy, the *Bowers* Court said: "Proscriptions against that conduct have ancient roots." In academic writings, and in many of the scholarly *amicus* briefs filed to assist the Court in this case, there are fundamental criticisms of the historical premises relied upon by the majority and concurring opinions in *Bowers*. Brief for Cato Institute as *Amicus Curiae* 16–17; Brief for American Civil Liberties Union et al. as *Amici Curiae* 15–21; Brief for Professors of History et al. as *Amici Curiae* 3–10. We need not enter this debate in the attempt to reach a definitive historical judgment, but the following considerations counsel against adopting the definitive conclusions upon which *Bowers* placed such reliance.

* * *

FYI

The Court discusses the history of prohibitions on sodomy, writing that early laws "were not directed at homosexuals as such but instead sought to prohibit non-procreative sexual activity more generally." The Court notes that these laws "do not seem to have been enforced against consenting adults acting in private." Laws targeted at homosexual conduct did not emerge until the 1970s, and of the nine states that singled out same sex relations for criminal prosecution at one time, five have since moved toward abolishing these prohibitions.

In summary, the historical grounds relied upon in *Bowers* are more complex than the majority opinion and the concurring opinion by Chief Justice Burger indicate. Their historical premises are not without doubt and, at the very least, are overstated.

It must be acknowledged, of course, that the Court in *Bowers* was making the broader point that for centuries there have been powerful voices to condemn homosexual conduct as immoral. The condemnation has been shaped by religious beliefs, conceptions of right and acceptable behavior, and respect for the traditional family. For many persons these are not trivial concerns but profound and deep convictions accepted as ethical and moral principles to which they aspire and which thus determine the course of their lives. These considerations do not answer the question before us, however. The issue is whether the majority may use the power of the State to enforce these views on the whole society through operation of the criminal law. "Our obligation is to define the liberty of all, not to mandate our own moral code." *Planned Parenthood of Southeastern Pa. v. Casey*, 505 U.S. 833 (1992).

Chief Justice Burger joined the opinion for the Court in *Bowers* and further explained his views as follows: "Decisions of individuals relating to homosexual conduct have been subject to state intervention throughout the history of Western civilization. Condemnation of those practices is firmly rooted in Judeao-Christian moral and ethical standards." 478 U.S., at 196. As with Justice White's assumptions about history, scholarship casts some doubt on the sweeping nature of the statement by Chief Justice Burger as it pertains to private homosexual conduct between consenting adults. See, *e.g.,* Eskridge, Hardwick and Historiography, 1999 U. Ill. L.Rev. 631, 656. In all events we think that our laws and traditions in the past half century are of most relevance here. These references show an emerging awareness that liberty gives substantial protection to adult persons in deciding how to conduct their private lives in matters pertaining to sex. "[H]istory and tradition are the starting point but not in all cases the ending point of the substantive due process inquiry." *County of Sacramento v. Lewis*, 523 U.S. 833, 857 (1998) (Kennedy, J., concurring).

* * *

In our own constitutional system the deficiencies in *Bowers* became even more apparent in the years following its announcement. The 25 States with laws prohibiting the relevant conduct referenced in the *Bowers* decision are reduced now to 13, of which 4 enforce their laws only against homosexual conduct. In those States where sodomy is still proscribed, whether for same-sex or heterosexual conduct, there is a pattern of nonenforcement with respect to consenting adults acting in private. The State of Texas admitted in 1994 that as of that date it had not prosecuted anyone under those circumstances. *State v. Morales*, 869 S.W.2d 941, 943.

FYI

The Court describes the decision to omit criminal penalties for private consensual sexual relations from the Model Penal Code in 1955 and the widespread abandonment of these statutes by the states beginning in 1961. The Court also notes a decision by the European Court of Human Rights in 1981 finding that laws prohibiting consensual homosexual conduct were invalid under the European Convention on Human Rights.

Two principal cases decided after *Bowers* cast its holding into even more doubt. In *Planned Parenthood of Southeastern Pa. v. Casey*, 505 U.S. 833 (1992), the Court reaffirmed the substantive force of the liberty protected by the Due Process Clause. The *Casey* decision again confirmed that our laws and tradition afford constitutional protection to personal decisions relating to marriage, procreation, contraception, family relationships, child rearing, and education. * * *

The second post-*Bowers* case of principal relevance is *Romer v. Evans*, 517 U.S. 620 (1996). There the Court struck down class-based legislation directed at homosexuals as a violation of the Equal Protection Clause. *Romer* invalidated an amendment to Colorado's constitution which named as a solitary class persons who were homosexuals, lesbians, or bisexual either by "orientation, conduct, practices or relationships," and deprived them of protection under state antidiscrimination laws. We concluded that the provision was "born of animosity toward the class of persons affected" and further that it had no rational relation to a legitimate governmental purpose.

As an alternative argument in this case, counsel for the petitioners and some *amici* contend that *Romer* provides the basis for declaring the Texas statute invalid under the Equal Protection Clause. That is a tenable argument, but we conclude the instant case requires us to address whether *Bowers* itself has continuing validity. Were we to hold the statute invalid under the Equal Protection Clause some might question whether a prohibition would be valid if drawn differently, say, to prohibit the conduct both between same-sex and different-sex participants.

Equality of treatment and the due process right to demand respect for conduct protected by the substantive guarantee of liberty are linked in important respects, and a decision on the latter point advances both interests. If protected conduct is made criminal and the law which does so remains unexamined for its substantive validity, its stigma might remain even if it were not enforceable as drawn for equal protection reasons. When homosexual conduct is made criminal by the law of the State, that declaration in and of itself is an invitation to subject homosexual persons to discrimination both in the public and in the private spheres. The central holding of *Bowers* has been brought in question by this case, and it should be addressed. Its continuance as precedent demeans the lives of homosexual persons.

* * *

The foundations of *Bowers* have sustained serious erosion from our recent decisions in *Casey* and *Romer.* When our precedent has been thus weakened, criticism from other sources is of greater significance. In the United States criticism of *Bowers* has been substantial and continuing, disapproving of its reasoning in all respects, not just as to its historical assumptions. The courts of five different States have declined to follow it in interpreting provisions in their own state constitutions parallel to the Due Process Clause of the Fourteenth Amendment, see *Jegley v. Picado,* 349 Ark. 600, 80 S.W.3d 332 (2002); *Powell v. State,* 270 Ga. 327, 510 S.E.2d 18, 24 (1998); *Gryczan v. State,* 283 Mont. 433, 942 P.2d 112 (1997); *Campbell v. Sundquist,* 926 S.W.2d 250 (Tenn.App.1996); *Commonwealth v. Wasson,* 842 S.W.2d 487 (Ky.1992).

To the extent *Bowers* relied on values we share with a wider civilization, it should be noted that the reasoning and holding in *Bowers* have been rejected elsewhere. The European Court of Human Rights has followed not *Bowers* but its own decision in *Dudgeon v. United Kingdom.* See *P.G. & J.H. v. United Kingdom,* App. No.

Think About It

The majority's references to European human rights law in this opinion drew sharp criticism from the dissenters. Why was this controversial?

00044787/98, & ¶ 56 (Eur.Ct.H. R., Sept. 25, 2001); *Modinos v. Cyprus,* 259 Eur. Ct. H.R. (1993); *Norris v. Ireland,* 142 Eur. Ct. H.R. (1988). Other nations, too, have taken action consistent with an affirmation of the protected right of homosexual adults to engage in intimate, consensual conduct. See Brief for Mary Robinson et al. as *Amici Curiae* 11–12. The right the petitioners seek in this case has been accepted as an integral part of human freedom in many other countries. There has been no showing that in this country the governmental interest in circumscribing personal choice is somehow more legitimate or urgent.

* * *

The rationale of *Bowers* does not withstand careful analysis. In his dissenting opinion in *Bowers* Justice Stevens came to these conclusions:

> "Our prior cases make two propositions abundantly clear. First, the fact that the governing majority in a State has traditionally viewed a particular practice as immoral is not a sufficient reason for upholding a law prohibiting the practice; neither history nor tradition could save a law prohibiting miscegenation from constitutional attack. Second, individual decisions by married persons, concerning the intimacies of their physical relationship, even when not intended to produce offspring, are a form of 'liberty' protected by the Due Process Clause of the Fourteenth Amendment. Moreover, this protection extends to intimate choices by unmarried as well as married persons."

Justice Stevens' analysis, in our view, should have been controlling in *Bowers* and should control here.

Bowers was not correct when it was decided, and it is not correct today. It ought not to remain binding precedent. <u>Bowers v. Hardwick</u> should be and now is overruled.

The present case does not involve minors. It does not involve persons who might be injured or coerced or who are situated in relationships where consent might not easily be refused. It does not involve public conduct or prostitution. It does not involve whether the government must give formal recognition to any relationship that homosexual persons seek to enter. The case does involve two adults who, with full and mutual consent from each other, engaged in sexual practices common to a homosexual lifestyle. The petitioners are entitled to respect for their private lives. The State cannot demean their existence or control their destiny by making their private sexual conduct a crime. Their right to liberty under the Due Process Clause gives them the full right to engage in their conduct without intervention of the government. "It is a promise of the Constitution that there is a realm of personal liberty which the government may not enter." The Texas statute furthers no legitimate state interest which can justify its intrusion into the personal and private life of the individual.

Had those who drew and ratified the Due Process Clauses of the Fifth Amendment or the Fourteenth Amendment known the components of liberty in its manifold possibilities, they might have been more specific. They did not presume to have this insight. They knew times can blind us to certain truths and later generations can see that laws once thought necessary and proper in fact serve only to oppress. As the Constitution endures, persons in every generation can invoke its principles in their own search for greater freedom.

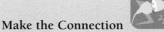

> Justice O'Connor wrote a concurring opinion in which she refused to join the Court in overturning *Bowers*, and expressed her view that the Texas statute violated the Equal Protection Clause by banning homosexual sodomy and not heterosexual sodomy. Justice Scalia wrote a dissenting opinion, joined by Justice Thomas and Chief Justice Rehnquist, arguing that *Bowers* was correctly decided and concluding that the majority opinion in *Lawrence* "effectively decrees the end of all morals legislation." Justice Thomas also issued a separate dissenting opinion.

The judgment of the Court of Appeals for the Texas Fourteenth District is reversed, and the case is remanded for further proceedings not inconsistent with this opinion.

It is so ordered.

Points for Discussion

a. Constitutional Liberty and Privacy

Consider the line of cases beginning with *Griswold* and *Loving* and running through *Eisenstadt* to *Lawrence*. Are there common themes uniting these cases? How has the Court's analysis changed over the period covered by these decisions?

b. Morals Legislation

Does the reasoning in *Lawrence* invalidate other state laws prohibiting private, consensual sexual conduct? After *Lawrence*, can states continue to prohibit **adultery** or **fornication**? *Marcum v. McWhorter*, 308 F.3d 635

Make the Connection

In *Griswold*, *Eisenstadt*, *Loving* and *Baird*, the Supreme Court struck down state statutes that criminalized various types of behavior: contraceptive use, interracial marriage, and homosexual sex. Why did states enact these types of criminal laws? How significant was the fact that these cases involved criminal convictions to the result in each case?

On the broader question of whether the criminal law is an appropriate vehicle to regulate the intimate activities of mature persons, see Jennifer M. Collins, Ethan J. Leib and Dan Markel, *Punishing Family Status*, 88 B.U. L. Rev. 1327, 1390-1416 (2008).

(6th Cir. 2002), upheld the termination of a sheriff's department employee for an extramarital cohabitation relationship. Does *Lawrence* cast doubt on the validity of this ruling?

Does *Lawrence* go far enough? What about privacy rights for sexual conduct that does not promote emotional intimacy? See Laura A. Rosenbury & Jennifer E. Rothman, *Sex In and Out of Intimacy*, 59 Emory L.J. 810 (2010).

c. Heterosexual Couples

Prior to the decision in *Lawrence*, courts considered whether state statutes criminalizing sodomy or "lewd and lascivious acts" by married or unmarried heterosexual couples violated the privacy rights recognized in *Griswold* and *Eisenstadt*. Has *Lawrence* changed the analysis applicable to these cases?

Obergefell v. Hodges

576 U.S.   , 135 S. Ct. 2584 (2015)

JUSTICE KENNEDY delivered the opinion of the Court.

Go Online

Listen to the oral arguments in *Obergefell* on the Oyez Project website.

The Constitution promises liberty to all within its reach, a liberty that includes certain specific rights that allow persons, within a lawful realm, to define and express their identity. The petitioners in these cases seek to find that liberty by marrying someone of the same sex and having their marriages deemed lawful on the same terms and conditions as marriages between persons of the opposite sex.

I

These cases come from Michigan, Kentucky, Ohio, and Tennessee, States that define marriage as a union between one man and one woman. See, *e.g.*, Mich. Const., Art. I, § 25; Ky. Const. § 233A; Ohio Rev. Code Ann. § 3101.01 (Lexis 2008); Tenn. Const., Art. XI, § 18. The petitioners are 14 same-sex couples and two men whose same-sex partners are deceased. The respondents are state officials responsible for enforcing the laws in question. The petitioners claim the respondents violate the Fourteenth Amendment by denying them the right to marry or to have their marriages, lawfully performed in another State, given full recognition.

Petitioners filed these suits in United States District Courts in their home States. Each District Court ruled in their favor. * * * [T]he United States Court of Appeals for the Sixth Circuit * * * consolidated the cases and reversed the judgments of the District Courts. * * *

The petitioners sought certiorari. This Court granted review, limited to two questions. The first, presented by the cases from Michigan and Kentucky, is whether the Fourteenth Amendment requires a State to license a marriage between two people of the same sex. The second, presented by the cases from Ohio, Tennessee, and, again, Kentucky, is whether the Fourteenth Amendment requires a State to recognize a same-sex marriage licensed and performed in a State which does grant that right.

II

Before addressing the principles and precedents that govern these cases, it is appropriate to note the history of the subject now before the Court.

A

From their beginning to their most recent page, the annals of human history reveal the transcendent importance of marriage. The lifelong union of a man and a woman always has promised nobility and dignity to all persons, without regard to their station in life. Marriage is sacred to those who live by their religions and offers unique fulfillment to those who find meaning in the secular realm. Its dynamic allows two people to find a life that could not be found alone, for a marriage becomes greater than just the two persons. Rising from the most basic human needs, marriage is essential to our most profound hopes and aspirations.

* * *

Recounting the circumstances of three of these cases illustrates the urgency of the petitioners' cause from their perspective. Petitioner James Obergefell, a plaintiff in the Ohio case, met John Arthur over two decades ago. They fell in love and started a life together, establishing a lasting, committed relation. In 2011, however, Arthur was diagnosed with amyotrophic lateral sclerosis, or ALS. This debilitating disease is progressive, with no known cure. Two years ago, Obergefell and Arthur decided to commit to one another, resolving to marry before Arthur died. To fulfill their mutual promise, they traveled from Ohio to Maryland, where same-sex marriage was legal. It was difficult for Arthur to move, and so the couple were wed inside a medical transport plane as it remained on the tarmac in Baltimore. Three months later, Arthur died. Ohio law does not permit Obergefell to be listed as the surviving spouse on Arthur's death certificate. By statute, they must remain strangers even in death, a state-imposed separation Obergefell deems "hurtful for the rest of time." He brought suit to be shown as the surviving spouse on Arthur's death certificate.

* * *

The cases now before the Court involve other petitioners as well, each with their own experiences. Their stories reveal that they seek not to denigrate marriage but rather to live their lives, or honor their spouses' memory, joined by its bond.

B

The ancient origins of marriage confirm its centrality, but it has not stood in isolation from developments in law and society. The history of marriage is one of both continuity and change. That institution—even as confined to opposite-sex relations—has evolved over time.

For example, marriage was once viewed as an arrangement by the couple's parents based on political, religious, and financial concerns; but by the time of the Nation's founding it was understood to be a voluntary contract between a man and a woman. See N. Cott, Public Vows: A History of Marriage and the Nation 9–17 (2000); S. Coontz, Marriage, A History 15–16 (2005). As the role and status of women changed, the institution further evolved. Under the centuries-old doctrine of coverture, a married man and woman were treated by the State as a single, male-dominated legal entity. See 1 W. Blackstone, Commentaries on the Laws of England 430 (1765). As women gained legal, political, and property rights, and as society began to understand that women have their own equal dignity, the law of coverture was abandoned. See Brief for Historians of Marriage et al. as Amici Curiae 16–19. These and other developments in the institution of marriage over the past centuries were not mere superficial changes. * * *

These new insights have strengthened, not weakened, the institution of marriage. Indeed, changed understandings of marriage are characteristic of a Nation where new dimensions of freedom become apparent to new generations, often through perspectives that begin in pleas or protests and then are considered in the political sphere and the judicial process.

* * *

This Court first gave detailed consideration to the legal status of homosexuals in *Bowers v. Hardwick*, 478 U.S. 186 (1986). There it upheld the constitutionality of a Georgia law deemed to criminalize certain homosexual acts. Ten years later, in *Romer v. Evans*, 517 U.S. 620 (1996), the Court invalidated an amendment to Colorado's Constitution that sought to foreclose any branch or political subdivision of the State from protecting persons against discrimination based on sexual orientation. Then, in 2003, the Court overruled Bowers, holding that laws making same-sex intimacy a crime "demea[n] the lives of homosexual persons." *Lawrence v. Texas*, 539 U.S. 558, 575.

Against this background, the legal question of same-sex marriage arose. In 1993, the Hawaii Supreme Court held Hawaii's law restricting marriage to opposite-sex couples constituted a classification on the basis of sex and was therefore subject to strict scrutiny under the Hawaii Constitution. *Baehr v. Lewin*, 74 Haw. 530, 852 P.2d 44. Although this decision did not mandate that same-sex marriage be allowed, some States were concerned by its implications and reaffirmed in their laws that marriage is defined as a union between opposite-sex partners. So too in 1996, Congress passed the Defense of Marriage Act (DOMA), 110 Stat. 2419, defining marriage for all federal-law purposes as "only a legal union between one man and one woman as husband and wife." 1 U.S.C. § 7.

The new and widespread discussion of the subject led other States to a different conclusion. In 2003, the Supreme Judicial Court of Massachusetts held the State's Constitution guaranteed same-sex couples the right to marry. See *Goodridge v. Department of Public Health*, 798 N.E.2d 941 (Mass. 2003). After that ruling, some additional States granted marriage rights to same-sex couples, either through judicial or legislative processes. * * * Two Terms ago, in *United States v. Windsor*, 570 U.S. 744 (2013), this Court invalidated DOMA to the extent it barred the Federal Government from treating same-sex marriages as valid even when they were lawful in the State where they were licensed. DOMA, the Court held, impermissibly disparaged those same-sex couples "who wanted to affirm their commitment to one another before their children, their family, their friends, and their community."

* * *

III

Under the Due Process Clause of the Fourteenth Amendment, no State shall "deprive any person of life, liberty, or property, without due process of law." The fundamental liberties protected by this Clause include most of the rights enumerated in the Bill of Rights. See *Duncan v. Louisiana*, 391 U.S. 145, 147–149 (1968). In addition these liberties extend to certain personal choices central to individual dignity and autonomy, including intimate choices that define personal identity and beliefs. See, *e.g.*, *Eisenstadt v. Baird*, 405 U.S. 438, 453 (1972); *Griswold v. Connecticut*, 381 U.S. 479, 484–486 (1965).

The identification and protection of fundamental rights is an enduring part of the judicial duty to interpret the Constitution. That responsibility, however, "has not been reduced to any formula." *Poe v. Ullman*, 367 U.S. 497, 542 (1961)

(Harlan, J., dissenting). Rather, it requires courts to exercise reasoned judgment in identifying interests of the person so fundamental that the State must accord them its respect. See *ibid.* That process is guided by many of the same considerations relevant to analysis of other constitutional provisions that set forth broad principles rather than specific requirements. History and tradition guide and discipline this inquiry but do not set its outer boundaries. See Lawrence, supra, at 572. That method respects our history and learns from it without allowing the past alone to rule the present.

The nature of injustice is that we may not always see it in our own times. The generations that wrote and ratified the Bill of Rights and the Fourteenth Amendment did not presume to know the extent of freedom in all of its dimensions, and so they entrusted to future generations a charter protecting the right of all persons to enjoy liberty as we learn its meaning. When new insight reveals discord between the Constitution's central protections and a received legal stricture, a claim to liberty must be addressed.

Applying these established tenets, the Court has long held the right to marry is protected by the Constitution. In *Loving v. Virginia*, 388 U.S. 1, 12 (1967), which invalidated bans on interracial unions, a unanimous Court held marriage is "one of the vital personal rights essential to the orderly pursuit of happiness by free men." The Court reaffirmed that holding in *Zablocki v. Redhail*, 434 U.S. 374, 384 (1978), which held the right to marry was burdened by a law prohibiting fathers who were behind on child support from marrying. The Court again applied this principle in *Turner v. Safley*, 482 U.S. 78, 95 (1987), which held the right to marry was abridged by regulations limiting the privilege of prison inmates to marry. Over time and in other contexts, the Court has reiterated that the right to marry is fundamental under the Due Process Clause. * * *

It cannot be denied that this Court's cases describing the right to marry presumed a relationship involving opposite-sex partners. The Court, like many institutions, has made assumptions defined by the world and time of which it is a part. This was evident in *Baker v. Nelson*, 409 U.S. 810, a one-line summary decision issued in 1972, holding the exclusion of same-sex couples from marriage did not present a substantial federal question.

Still, there are other, more instructive precedents. This Court's cases have expressed constitutional principles of broader reach. In defining the right to marry these cases have identified essential attributes of that right based in history, tradition, and other constitutional liberties inherent in this intimate bond. See, *e.g.*, *Lawrence*, 539 U.S., at 574; *Turner, supra*, at 95; *Zablocki, supra*, at 384; *Loving, supra*, at 12; *Griswold, supra*, at 486. And in assessing whether the force and rationale of its cases apply to same-sex couples, the Court must respect the basic reasons why the right to marry has been long protected. See, *e.g., Eisenstadt, supra*, at 453–454; *Poe, supra*, at 542–553 (Harlan, J., dissenting).

This analysis compels the conclusion that same-sex couples may exercise the right to marry. The four principles and traditions to be discussed demonstrate that the reasons marriage is fundamental under the Constitution apply with equal force to same-sex couples.

A first premise of the Court's relevant precedents is that the right to personal choice regarding marriage is inherent in the concept of individual autonomy. This abiding connection between marriage and liberty is why *Loving* invalidated inter-racial marriage bans under the Due Process Clause. See 388 U.S., at 12; see also *Zablocki, supra*, at 384 (observing Loving held "the right to marry is of funda-mental importance for all individuals"). Like choices concerning contraception, family relationships, procreation, and childrearing, all of which are protected by the Constitution, decisions concerning marriage are among the most intimate that an individual can make. See *Lawrence, supra*, at 574. Indeed, the Court has noted it would be contradictory "to recognize a right of privacy with respect to other matters of family life and not with respect to the decision to enter the relationship that is the foundation of the family in our society." *Zablocki, supra*, at 386.

Choices about marriage shape an individual's destiny. As the Supreme Judicial Court of Massachusetts has explained, because "it fulfils yearnings for security, safe haven, and connection that express our common humanity, civil marriage is an esteemed institution, and the decision whether and whom to marry is among life's momentous acts of self-definition." *Goodridge, 798 N.E.2d, at 955*.

The nature of marriage is that, through its enduring bond, two persons together can find other freedoms, such as expression, intimacy, and spirituality. This is true for all persons, whatever their sexual orientation. See *Windsor*, 570 U.S., at ___ (slip op., at 22–23). There is dignity in the bond between two men or two women who seek to marry and in their autonomy to make such profound choices. Cf. *Loving, supra*, at 12 ("[T]he freedom to marry, or not marry, a person of another race resides with the individual and cannot be infringed by the State").

A second principle in this Court's jurisprudence is that the right to marry is fundamental because it supports a two-person union unlike any other in its importance to the committed individuals. This point was central to *Griswold v. Connecticut*, which held the Constitution protects the right of married couples to use contraception. 381 U.S., at 485. Suggesting that marriage is a right "older than the Bill of Rights." * * *

And in *Turner*, the Court again acknowledged the intimate association pro-tected by this right, holding prisoners could not be denied the right to marry because their committed relationships satisfied the basic reasons why marriage is a fundamental right. See 482 U.S., at 95–96. The right to marry thus dignifies couples who "wish to define themselves by their commitment to each other." *Windsor, supra,* at ___ (slip op., at 14). Marriage responds to the universal fear that a lonely person might call out only to find no one there. It offers the hope of companionship and understanding and assurance that while both still live there will be someone to care for the other.

As this Court held in *Lawrence,* same-sex couples have the same right as opposite-sex couples to enjoy intimate association. Lawrence invalidated laws that made same-sex intimacy a criminal act. And it acknowledged that "[w]hen sexuality finds overt expression in intimate conduct with another person, the conduct can be but one element in a personal bond that is more enduring." 539 U.S., at 567. But while *Lawrence* confirmed a dimension of freedom that allows individuals to engage in intimate association without criminal liability, it does not follow that freedom stops there. Outlaw to outcast may be a step forward, but it does not achieve the full promise of liberty.

A third basis for protecting the right to marry is that it safeguards children and families and thus draws meaning from related rights of childrearing, procreation, and education. See *Pierce v. Society of Sisters,* 268 U.S. 510 (1925); *Meyer,* 262 U.S., at 399. The Court has recognized these connections by describing the varied rights as a unified whole: "[T]he right to 'marry, establish a home and bring up children' is a central part of the liberty protected by the Due Process Clause." *Zablocki,* 434 U.S., at 384 (quoting *Meyer, supra,* at 399). Under the laws of the several States, some of marriage's protections for children and families are material. But marriage also confers more profound benefits. By giving recognition and legal structure to their parents' relationship, marriage allows children "to understand the integrity and closeness of their own family and its concord with other families in their community and in their daily lives." *Windsor, supra,* at ___ (slip op., at 23). Marriage also affords the permanency and stability important to children's best interests. See Brief for Scholars of the Constitutional Rights of Children as *Amici Curiae* 22–27.

As all parties agree, many same-sex couples provide loving and nurturing homes to their children, whether biological or adopted. And hundreds of thousands of children are presently being raised by such couples. See Brief for Gary J. Gates as *Amicus Curiae* 4. Most States have allowed gays and lesbians to adopt, either as individuals or as couples, and many adopted and foster children have same-sex parents, see *id.,* at 5. This provides powerful confirmation from the law itself that gays and lesbians can create loving, supportive families.

Excluding same-sex couples from marriage thus conflicts with a central premise of the right to marry. Without the recognition, stability, and predictability marriage offers, their children suffer the stigma of knowing their families are somehow lesser. They also suffer the significant material costs of being raised by unmarried parents, relegated through no fault of their own to a more difficult and uncertain family life. The marriage laws at issue here thus harm and humiliate the children of same-sex couples. See *Windsor, supra*, at ___ (slip op., at 23).

That is not to say the right to marry is less meaningful for those who do not or cannot have children. An ability, desire, or promise to procreate is not and has not been a prerequisite for a valid marriage in any State. In light of precedent protecting the right of a married couple not to procreate, it cannot be said the Court or the States have conditioned the right to marry on the capacity or commitment to procreate. The constitutional marriage right has many aspects, of which childbearing is only one.

Fourth and finally, this Court's cases and the Nation's traditions make clear that marriage is a keystone of our social order. Alexis de Tocqueville recognized this truth on his travels through the United States almost two centuries ago. * * * In *Maynard v. Hill*, 125 U.S. 190, 211 (1888), the Court echoed de Tocqueville, explaining that marriage is "the foundation of the family and of society, without which there would be neither civilization nor progress." Marriage, the *Maynard* Court said, has long been " 'a great public institution, giving character to our whole civil polity.' " *Id.*, at 213. This idea has been reiterated even as the institution has evolved in substantial ways over time, superseding rules related to parental consent, gender, and race once thought by many to be essential. See generally N. Cott, Public Vows. Marriage remains a building block of our national community.

For that reason, just as a couple vows to support each other, so does society pledge to support the couple, offering symbolic recognition and material benefits to protect and nourish the union. Indeed, while the States are in general free to vary the benefits they confer on all married couples, they have throughout our history made marriage the basis for an expanding list of governmental rights, benefits, and responsibilities. These aspects of marital status include: taxation; inheritance and property rights; rules of intestate succession; spousal privilege in the law of evidence; hospital access; medical decisionmaking authority; adoption rights; the rights and benefits of survivors; birth and death certificates; professional ethics rules; campaign finance restrictions; workers' compensation benefits; health insurance; and child custody, support, and visitation rules. See Brief for United States as *Amicus Curiae* 6–9; Brief for American Bar Association as *Amicus Curiae* 8–29. Valid marriage under state law is also a significant status for over a thousand provisions of federal law. See *Windsor*, 570 U.S., at ___ – ___ (slip op., at 15–16). The States have contributed to the fundamental character of the marriage right by placing that institution at the center of so many facets of the legal and social order.

There is no difference between same- and opposite-sex couples with respect to this principle. Yet by virtue of their exclusion from that institution, same-sex couples are denied the constellation of benefits that the States have linked to marriage. This harm results in more than just material burdens. Same-sex couples are consigned to an instability many opposite-sex couples would deem intolerable in their own lives. As the State itself makes marriage all the more precious by the significance it attaches to it, exclusion from that status has the effect of teaching that gays and lesbians are unequal in important respects. It demeans gays and lesbians for the State to lock them out of a central institution of the Nation's society. Same-sex couples, too, may aspire to the transcendent purposes of marriage and seek fulfillment in its highest meaning.

The limitation of marriage to opposite-sex couples may long have seemed natural and just, but its inconsistency with the central meaning of the fundamental right to marry is now manifest. With that knowledge must come the recognition that laws excluding same-sex couples from the marriage right impose stigma and injury of the kind prohibited by our basic charter.

* * *

The right to marry is fundamental as a matter of history and tradition, but rights come not from ancient sources alone. They rise, too, from a better informed understanding of how constitutional imperatives define a liberty that remains urgent in our own era. Many who deem same-sex marriage to be wrong reach that conclusion based on decent and honorable religious or philosophical premises, and neither they nor their beliefs are disparaged here. But when that sincere, personal opposition becomes enacted law and public policy, the necessary consequence is to put the imprimatur of the State itself on an exclusion that soon demeans or stigmatizes those whose own liberty is then denied. Under the Constitution, same-sex couples seek in marriage the same legal treatment as opposite-sex couples, and it would disparage their choices and diminish their personhood to deny them this right.

The right of same-sex couples to marry that is part of the liberty promised by the Fourteenth Amendment is derived, too, from that Amendment's guarantee of the equal protection of the laws. The Due Process Clause and the Equal Protection Clause are connected in a profound way, though they set forth independent principles. Rights implicit in liberty and rights secured by equal protection may rest on different precepts and are not always co-extensive, yet in some instances each may be instructive as to the meaning and reach of the other. In any particular case one Clause may be thought to capture the essence of the right in a more accurate and comprehensive way, even as the two Clauses may converge in the identification and definition of the right. This interrelation of the two principles furthers our understanding of what freedom is and must become.

The Court's cases touching upon the right to marry reflect this dynamic. In *Loving* the Court invalidated a prohibition on interracial marriage under both the Equal Protection Clause and the Due Process Clause. The Court first declared the prohibition invalid because of its unequal treatment of interracial couples. It stated: "There can be no doubt that restricting the freedom to marry solely because of racial classifications violates the central meaning of the Equal Protection Clause." 388 U.S., at 12. With this link to equal protection the Court proceeded to hold the prohibition offended central precepts of liberty: "To deny this fundamental freedom on so unsupportable a basis as the racial classifications embodied in these statutes, classifications so directly subversive of the principle of equality at the heart of the Fourteenth Amendment, is surely to deprive all the State's citizens of liberty without due process of law." *Ibid.* The reasons why marriage is a fundamental right became more clear and compelling from a full awareness and understanding of the hurt that resulted from laws barring interracial unions.

The synergy between the two protections is illustrated further in *Zablocki*. There the Court invoked the Equal Protection Clause as its basis for invalidating the challenged law, which, as already noted, barred fathers who were behind on child-support payments from marrying without judicial approval. The equal protection analysis depended in central part on the Court's holding that the law burdened a right "of fundamental importance." It was the essential nature of the marriage right, discussed at length in *Zablocki*, that made apparent the law's incompatibility with requirements of equality. Each concept—liberty and equal protection—leads to a stronger understanding of the other.

Indeed, in interpreting the Equal Protection Clause, the Court has recognized that new insights and societal understandings can reveal unjustified inequality within our most fundamental institutions that once passed unnoticed and unchallenged. To take but one period, this occurred with respect to marriage in the 1970's and 1980's. Notwithstanding the gradual erosion of the doctrine of coverture, invidious sex-based classifications in marriage remained common through the mid-20th century. These classifications denied the equal dignity of men and women. One State's law, for example, provided in 1971 that "the husband is the head of the family and the wife is subject to him; her legal civil existence is merged in the husband, except so far as the law recognizes her separately, either for her own protection, or for her benefit." Ga.Code Ann. § 53–501 (1935). Responding to a new awareness, the Court invoked equal protection principles to invalidate laws imposing sex-based inequality on marriage. * * * Like *Loving* and *Zablocki*, these precedents show the Equal Protection Clause can help to identify and correct inequalities in the institution of marriage, vindicating precepts of liberty and equality under the Constitution.

* * *

In *Lawrence* the Court acknowledged the interlocking nature of these constitutional safeguards in the context of the legal treatment of gays and lesbians. See 539 U.S., at 575. Although *Lawrence* elaborated its holding under the Due Process Clause, it acknowledged, and sought to remedy, the continuing inequality that resulted from laws making intimacy in the lives of gays and lesbians a crime against the State. *Lawrence* therefore drew upon principles of liberty and equality to define and protect the rights of gays and lesbians, holding the State "cannot demean their existence or control their destiny by making their private sexual conduct a crime.

This dynamic also applies to same-sex marriage. It is now clear that the challenged laws burden the liberty of same-sex couples, and it must be further acknowledged that they abridge central precepts of equality. Here the marriage laws enforced by the respondents are in essence unequal: same-sex couples are denied all the benefits afforded to opposite-sex couples and are barred from exercising a fundamental right. Especially against a long history of disapproval of their relationships, this denial to same-sex couples of the right to marry works a grave and continuing harm. The imposition of this disability on gays and lesbians serves to disrespect and subordinate them. And the Equal Protection Clause, like the Due Process Clause, prohibits this unjustified infringement of the fundamental right to marry. See, *e.g.*, *Zablocki, supra*, at 383–388; *Skinner, 316 U.S., at 541*.

These considerations lead to the conclusion that the right to marry is a fundamental right inherent in the liberty of the person, and under the Due Process and Equal Protection Clauses of the Fourteenth Amendment couples of the same-sex may not be deprived of that right and that liberty. The Court now holds that same-sex couples may exercise the fundamental right to marry. No longer may this liberty be denied to them. *Baker v. Nelson* must be and now is overruled, and the State laws challenged by Petitioners in these cases are now held invalid to the extent they exclude same-sex couples from civil marriage on the same terms and conditions as opposite-sex couples.

* * *

V

These cases also present the question whether the Constitution requires States to recognize same-sex marriages validly performed out of State. As made clear by the case of Obergefell and Arthur, * * * the recognition bans inflict substantial and continuing harm on same-sex couples.

Being married in one State but having that valid marriage denied in another is one of "the most perplexing and distressing complication[s]" in the law of domestic relations. *Williams v. North Carolina*, 317 U.S. 287, 299 (1942) (internal quotation marks omitted). Leaving the current state of affairs in place would maintain and promote instability and uncertainty. For some couples, even an ordinary drive into a neighboring State to visit family or friends risks causing severe hardship in the event of a spouse's hospitalization while across state lines. In light of the fact that many States already allow same-sex marriage—and hundreds of thousands of these marriages already have occurred—the disruption caused by the recognition bans is significant and ever-growing.

As counsel for the respondents acknowledged at argument, if States are required by the Constitution to issue marriage licenses to same-sex couples, the justifications for refusing to recognize those marriages performed elsewhere are undermined. See Tr. of Oral Arg. on Question 2, p. 44. The Court, in this decision, holds same-sex couples may exercise the fundamental right to marry in all States. It follows that the Court also must hold—and it now does hold—that there is no lawful basis for a State to refuse to recognize a lawful same-sex marriage performed in another State on the ground of its same-sex character.

* * *

No union is more profound than marriage, for it embodies the highest ideals of love, fidelity, devotion, sacrifice, and family. In forming a marital union, two people become something greater than once they were. As some of the petitioners in these cases demonstrate, marriage embodies a love that may endure even past death. It would misunderstand these men and women to say they disrespect the idea of marriage. Their plea is that they do respect it, respect it so deeply that they seek to find its fulfillment for themselves. Their hope is not to be condemned to live in loneliness, excluded from one of civilization's oldest institutions. They ask for equal dignity in the eyes of the law. The Constitution grants them that right.

The judgment of the Court of Appeals for the Sixth Circuit is reversed.

It is so ordered.

CHIEF JUSTICE ROBERTS, with whom JUSTICE SCALIA and JUSTICE THOMAS join, dissenting.

Petitioners make strong arguments rooted in social policy and considerations of fairness. They contend that same-sex couples should be allowed to affirm their love and commitment through marriage, just like opposite-sex couples. That position has undeniable appeal; over the past six years, voters and legislators in eleven States and the District of Columbia have revised their laws to allow marriage between two people of the same sex.

But this Court is not a legislature. Whether same-sex marriage is a good idea should be of no concern to us. Under the Constitution, judges have power to say what the law is, not what it should be. The people who ratified the Constitution authorized courts to exercise "neither force nor will but merely judgment." The Federalist No. 78, p. 465 (C. Rossiter ed. 1961) (A.Hamilton) (capitalization altered).

Although the policy arguments for extending marriage to same-sex couples may be compelling, the legal arguments for requiring such an extension are not. The fundamental right to marry does not include a right to make a State change its definition of marriage. And a State's decision to maintain the meaning of marriage that has persisted in every culture throughout human history can hardly be called irrational. In short, our Constitution does not enact any one theory of marriage. The people of a State are free to expand marriage to include same-sex couples, or to retain the historic definition.

Today, however, the Court takes the extraordinary step of ordering every State to license and recognize same-sex marriage. Many people will rejoice at this decision, and I begrudge none their celebration. But for those who believe in a government of laws, not of men, the majority's approach is deeply disheartening. Supporters of same-sex marriage have achieved considerable success persuading their fellow citizens—through the democratic process—to adopt their view. That ends today. Five lawyers have closed the debate and enacted their own vision of marriage as a matter of constitutional law. Stealing this issue from the people will for many cast a cloud over same-sex marriage, making a dramatic social change that much more difficult to accept.

* * *

The Court's accumulation of power does not occur in a vacuum. It comes at the expense of the people. And they know it. Here and abroad, people are in the midst of a serious and thoughtful public debate on the issue of same-sex marriage. They see voters carefully considering same-sex marriage, casting ballots in favor or opposed, and sometimes changing their minds. They see political leaders similarly reexamining their positions, and either reversing course or explaining adherence to old convictions confirmed anew. They see governments and businesses modifying policies and practices with respect to same-sex couples, and participating actively in the civic discourse. They see countries overseas democratically accepting profound social change, or declining to do so. This deliberative process is making people take seriously questions that they may not have even regarded as questions before.

When decisions are reached through democratic means, some people will inevitably be disappointed with the results. But those whose views do not prevail at least know that they have had their say, and accordingly are—in the tradition of our political culture—reconciled to the result of a fair and honest debate. In addition, they can gear up to raise the issue later, hoping to persuade enough on the winning side to think again. "That is exactly how our system of government is supposed to work." *Post*, at 2–3 (SCALIA, J., dissenting).

But today the Court puts a stop to all that. By deciding this question under the Constitution, the Court removes it from the realm of democratic decision. There will be consequences to shutting down the political process on an issue of such profound public significance. Closing debate tends to close minds. People denied a voice are less likely to accept the ruling of a court on an issue that does not seem to be the sort of thing courts usually decide. As a thoughtful commentator observed about another issue, "The political process was moving. . ., not swiftly enough for advocates of quick, complete change, but majoritarian institutions were listening and acting. Heavy-handed judicial intervention was difficult to justify and appears to have provoked, not resolved, conflict." Ginsburg, Some Thoughts on Autonomy and Equality in Relation to *Roe v. Wade*, 63 N.C.L.Rev. 375, 385–386 (1985) (footnote omitted). Indeed, however heartened the proponents of same-sex marriage might be on this day, it is worth acknowledging what they have lost, and lost forever: the opportunity to win the true acceptance that comes from persuading their fellow citizens of the justice of their cause. And they lose this just when the winds of change were freshening at their backs.

Federal courts are blunt instruments when it comes to creating rights. They have constitutional power only to resolve concrete cases or controversies; they do not have the flexibility of legislatures to address concerns of parties not before the court or to anticipate problems that may arise from the exercise of a new right. Today's decision, for example, creates serious questions about religious liberty. Many good and decent people oppose same-sex marriage as a tenet of faith, and their freedom to exercise religion is—unlike the right imagined by the majority—actually spelled out in the Constitution. Amdt. 1.

Respect for sincere religious conviction has led voters and legislators in every State that has adopted same-sex marriage democratically to include accommodations for religious practice. The majority's decision imposing same-sex marriage cannot, of course, create any such accommodations. The majority graciously suggests that religious believers may continue to "advocate" and "teach" their views of marriage. *Ante*, at 27. The First Amendment guarantees, however, the freedom to "*exercise*" religion. Ominously, that is not a word the majority uses.

Hard questions arise when people of faith exercise religion in ways that may be seen to conflict with the new right to same-sex marriage—when, for example, a religious college provides married student housing only to opposite-sex married couples, or a religious adoption agency declines to place children with same-sex married couples. Indeed, the Solicitor General candidly acknowledged that the tax exemptions of some religious institutions would be in question if they opposed same-sex marriage. There is little doubt that these and similar questions will soon be before this Court. Unfortunately, people of faith can take no comfort in the treatment they receive from the majority today.

* * *

In the face of all this, a much different view of the Court's role is possible. That view is more modest and restrained. It is more skeptical that the legal abilities of judges also reflect insight into moral and philosophical issues. It is more sensitive to the fact that judges are unelected and unaccountable, and that the legitimacy of their power depends on confining it to the exercise of legal judgment. It is more attuned to the lessons of history, and what it has meant for the country and Court when Justices have exceeded their proper bounds. And it is less pretentious than to suppose that while people around the world have viewed an institution in a particular way for thousands of years, the present generation and the present Court are the ones chosen to burst the bonds of that history and tradition.

* * *

If you are among the many Americans—of whatever sexual orientation—who favor expanding same-sex marriage, by all means celebrate today's decision. Celebrate the achievement of a desired goal. Celebrate the opportunity for a new expression of commitment to a partner. Celebrate the availability of new benefits. But do not celebrate the Constitution. It had nothing to do with it.

I respectfully dissent.

Points for Discussion

a. Due Process and Equal Protection

In reaching the conclusion that same-sex couples may not be deprived of the fundamental right to marry, the Court's opinion in *Obergefell* does not reference the different levels of scrutiny traditionally invoked in due process and equal protection cases. How does the majority opinion reach its conclusion? How does the Court understand the interaction of these two guarantees?

b. Dissenting Opinions

Justices Ginsburg, Breyer, Sotomayor and Kagan joined Justice Kennedy's majority opinion, reprinted here. Justices Scalia and Thomas joined Chief Justice Roberts's dissenting opinion, excerpted above. In addition, Justice Alito wrote a dissent, which was joined by Justices Scalia and Thomas, and Justice Scalia and Justice Thomas wrote their own dissents.

Justice Alito concluded that the Constitution leaves the question of same-sex marriage to be decided by the people of each state, arguing that the traditional understanding of marriage was "inextricably linked" to procreation and that states should be free to adhere to that understanding. Justice Scalia's dissent emphasized that when the Fourteenth Amendment was ratified in 1868, "every State limited marriage to one man and one woman, and no one doubted the constitutionality of doing so." He criticized the majority for its "hubris" in discovering a fundamental right "overlooked by every person alive at the time of ratification, and almost everyone else in the time since." Justice Thomas extended this argument, emphasizing his view that the Due Process Clause should not be seen "as a font of substantive rights." Justice Thomas pointed out that the Court's previous decisions regarding the right to marry, such as *Loving v. Virginia* and *Zablocki v. Redhail*, rejected state-imposed criminal sanctions on private behavior, and he distinguished this understanding of liberty from the claim in *Obergefell* for state recognition and benefits. How does the majority opinion respond to these arguments?

During his thirty years on the Supreme Court, Justice Kennedy wrote the Court's majority opinions—and typically cast the deciding vote—in all of its cases involving same-sex marriage and the rights of gays and lesbians. With his retirement in 2018, many observers have asked whether the Court's future opinions may bear a closer resemblance to these dissenting opinions in *Obergefell*.

c. Marriage Recognition and the Defense of Marriage Act (DOMA)

By the time *Obergefell* was decided, same-sex couples had obtained the right to marry under state law, as a result of judicial decisions or legislation, in California, Connecticut, Delaware, Hawaii, Illinois, Iowa, Maine, Maryland, Massachusetts, New Hampshire, New Jersey, New York, Rhode Island, Vermont, Washington, and the District of Columbia. A number of other states had established an alternative legal status, such as civil union or domestic partnership, extending some or all of the rights and obligations of marriage under state law to same-sex couples.

The differences among the states generated significant conflict of laws questions. Congress had attempted to limit recognition for same-sex marriage with the Defense of Marriage Act (DOMA) in 1996. DOMA provided that states would not be required to recognize same-sex marriages from other states, see 28 U.S.C. § 1738C, and defined marriage for purposes of federal law to include only opposite-sex marriages, see 1 U.S.C. § 7. Many states enacted similar rules by statute or constitutional amendment.

Two years before *Obergefell*, the Supreme Court struck down the provision in DOMA that excluded same-sex couples with marriages that were valid under state law from the rights and obligations of marriage under federal law. Justice Kennedy's majority opinion for the Court in United States v. Windsor, 570 U.S. 744 (2013), emphasized federalism arguments, concluding that this aspect of DOMA interfered with "state sovereign choices about who may be married" and had the purpose and effect of interfering with the equal dignity of those in same-sex marriages recognized as valid under state law. In *Obergefell*, when the Court concluded that all states must recognize same-sex marriages that are valid in another state, it effectively overruled the rest of DOMA.

d. Religious Objections to Same-Sex Marriage

The dissenting opinions in *Obergefell* raised the question of how the decision might affect people who oppose same-sex marriage on religious grounds. Three years later, in Masterpiece Cakeshop Ltd., v. Colorado Civil Rights Commission, 584 U.S.   , 138 S.Ct. 1719 (2017), the Court considered the claim of a baker who had refused on religious grounds to make a wedding cake a same-sex couple. After the couple complained to the state's Civil Rights Commission, which ruled in their favor under the state's anti-discrimination law, the baker challenged this finding as a violation of his First Amendment rights to free speech and free exercise of religion. Writing for a majority of six justices, Justice Kennedy did not reach the broader constitutional questions, however, concluding that in this case the Colorado Civil Rights Commission had not acted "with the religious neutrality that the Constitution requires."

Same-Sex Marriage Litigation

Same-sex couples began to challenge marriage license laws in the early 1970s. but achieved the first significant legal victory in Baehr v. Lewin, 852 P.2d 44 (Haw. 1993), which held that that state laws limiting marriage to opposite-sex couples imposed a classification based on sex that was presumptively invalid under the Hawaii Constitution. The court remanded the case, allowing the state an opportunity to establish that its marriage statutes furthered compelling state interests and were narrowly drawn to prevent unnecessary infringements of constitutional rights. The state's voters subsequently approved an amendment to Hawaii's Constitution, giving the state legislature the authority to reserve marriage to opposite sex couples, and the litigation was dismissed as moot in 1999.

After the decision in *Baehr*, in light of the prospect that same-sex marriage would become legal in Hawaii, the question arose whether same-sex couples living in other states would be able to come to Hawaii to marry and return home with the expectation that their marriages would be recognized. Many states responded by enacting legislation or constitutional amendments to prohibit both contracting of same-sex marriage within the state, and recognition of same-sex marriages celebrated elsewhere.

Advocates of same-sex marriage achieved a significant victory with <u>Baker v. State, 744 A.2d 864 (Vt. 1999)</u>, which held that the state could not exclude same-sex couples from the legal benefits and protections that it provided to married opposite-sex couples. *Baker* left the question of a remedy to the state's legislature, which implemented the court's ruling by enacting a civil union statute. Same-sex couples had the opportunity to enter into civil unions in Vermont from 2000 until 2009, when new legislation extended full marriage rights to same-sex couples.

The first state to extend full marriage rights to same-sex couples was Massachusetts, following the ruling in <u>Goodridge v. Department of Public Health, 798 N.E.2d 941 (Mass. 2001)</u>. The court held that the state could not deny the "protections, benefits, and obligations conferred by civil marriage to two individuals of the same sex who wish to marry," and reaffirmed in a subsequent opinion that providing for civil union would not be a sufficient remedy, because it would create "a second-class citizen status for same-sex couples by excluding them from the institution of civil marriage." <u>Opinions of the Justices to the Senate, 802 N.E.2d 565, 571 (Mass. 2004)</u>. See Edward Stein, *The Story of* Goodridge v. Department of Public Health: *The Bumpy Road to Marriage for Same-Sex Couples, in Family Law Stories* 27 (Carol Sanger, ed. 2008).

B. Marital Agreements

Marriage is often described as a contract, but marriage relationships have been also subject to extensive regulation by the state. In this sense, marriage is a legal status, giving rise to many rights and obligations as a matter of law. Despite the important financial and legal consequences of marriage for individuals and their families, many of these consequences may not be readily negotiated by the parties to the marriage.

During the past generation, laws and customs have shifted to allow individuals greater freedom to determine the terms of their private lives. Courts have begun to permit and enforce marital and premarital agreements, and agreements to divorce. Couples are more likely to live together without marriage, and most states enforce agreements between unmarried cohabitants concerning their property and support rights. The legal rules applied to these contracts are distinct from the rules that govern business or commercial contracts, however. Even as the law

Think About It

Status refers to a condition imposed by law on certain classes of persons, traditionally including husbands and wives, minors, persons born out of wedlock, and slaves.

has opened more room for private ordering of relationships, the state interest in regulating family life still plays a noticeable role. See generally Jana Singer, _The Privatization of Family Law_, 1992 Wis. L. Rev. 1443.

Premarital agreements, also referred to as prenuptial or antenuptial agreements, have long been used in the United States by older persons planning to marry who wish to adjust spousal inheritance rights, typically in order to provide for children of former marriages or other obligations. Until 1970, however, state courts nearly unanimously held that prenuptial agreements regarding the financial and property aspects of divorce could not be enforced. The court in Fricke v. Fricke, 42 N.W.2d 500 (Wis. 1950), explained the policy in these terms: "At least a majority, if not all of the courts which have considered the matter have held that any antenuptial contract which provides for, or facilitates, or tends to induce a separation or divorce of the parties after marriage, is contrary to public policy and is therefore void. Quite generally the courts have said that the contract itself invites dispute, encourages separation and incites divorce proceedings."

Think About It

As you read this material, consider whether, and in what ways, marriage is still a status relationship.

Starting with the Florida Supreme Court decision in Posner v. Posner, 233 So.2d 381 (Fla.1970), the law began to shift direction. Courts in the United States now conclude that premarital agreements determining alimony and property rights on divorce do not violate public policy, and many states have enacted legislation to define the circumstances in which premarital agreements will be enforced. Twenty-two states and the District of Columbia have enacted some version of the Uniform Premarital Agreement Act (UPAA), 9C U.L.A. 48 (2001), discussed below.

In general, a premarital agreement will be enforced against an individual who entered into it freely, without fraud, duress, coercion or overreaching, and if that individual had either full disclosure or knowledge of the other spouse's property before entering into the agreement. The test of validity is framed differently in different states, however, with some states much more likely to scrutinize the reasonableness of the agreement when it was entered into or its effects at the time the marriage ends in death or divorce. States also take notably different positions on whether married couples may enter into postmarital agreements regarding their property and support rights.

Simeone v. Simeone

581 A.2d 162 (Pa. 1990)

FLAHERTY, JUSTICE.

At issue in this appeal is the validity of a prenuptial agreement executed between the appellant, Catherine E. Walsh Simeone, and the appellee, Frederick A. Simeone. At the time of their marriage, in 1975, appellant was a twenty-three year old nurse and appellee was a thirty-nine year old neurosurgeon. Appellee had an income of approximately $90,000 per year, and appellant was unemployed. Appellee also had assets worth approximately $300,000. On the eve of the parties' wedding, appellee's attorney presented appellant with a prenuptial agreement to be signed. Appellant, without the benefit of counsel, signed the agreement. Appellee's attorney had not advised appellant regarding any legal rights that the agreement surrendered. The parties are in disagreement as to whether appellant knew in advance of that date that such an agreement would be presented for signature. Appellant denies having had such knowledge and claims to have signed under adverse circumstances, which, she contends, provide a basis for declaring it void.

The agreement limited appellant to support payments of $200 per week in the event of separation or divorce, subject to a maximum total payment of $25,000. The parties separated in 1982, and, in 1984, divorce proceedings were commenced. Between 1982 and 1984 appellee made payments which satisfied the $25,000 limit. In 1985, appellant filed a claim for alimony *pendente lite*. A master's report upheld the validity of the prenuptial agreement and denied this claim. Exceptions to the master's report were dismissed by the Court of Common Pleas of Philadelphia County. The Superior Court affirmed. *Simeone v. Simeone*, 380 Pa.Super. 37, 551 A.2d 219 (1988).

What's That?

Alimony pendente lite, also referred to as "temporary alimony," may be ordered to support a spouse while litigation is pending.

We granted allowance of appeal because uncertainty was expressed by the Superior Court regarding the meaning of our plurality decision in *Estate of Geyer,* 516 Pa. 492, 533 A.2d 423 (1987). The Superior Court viewed *Geyer* as permitting a prenuptial agreement to be upheld if it *either* made a reasonable provision for the spouse *or* was entered after a full and fair disclosure of the general financial positions of the parties and the statutory rights being relinquished. Appellant contends that this interpretation of *Geyer* is in error insofar as it requires disclosure of statutory rights *only* in cases where there has not been made a reasonable provision for the spouse. Inasmuch as the courts below held that the provision made for appellant was a reasonable one, appellant's efforts to overturn the agreement have focused upon an assertion that there was an inadequate disclosure of statutory rights. Appellant continues to assert, however, that the payments provided in the agreement were less than reasonable.

* * *

While the decision of the Superior Court reflects, perhaps, a reasonable interpretation of *Geyer,* we do not view this case as a vehicle to affirm that interpretation. Rather, there is need for a reexamination of the foundations upon which *Geyer* and earlier decisions rested, and a need for clarification of the standards by which the validity of prenuptial agreements will be judged.

There is no longer validity in the implicit presumption that supplied the basis for *Geyer* and similar earlier decisions. Such decisions rested upon a belief that spouses are of unequal status and that women are not knowledgeable enough to understand the nature of contracts that they enter. Society has advanced, however, to the point where women are no longer regarded as the "weaker" party in marriage, or in society generally. Indeed, the stereotype that women serve as homemakers while men work as breadwinners is no longer viable. Quite often today both spouses are income earners. Nor is there viability in the presumption that women are uninformed, uneducated, and readily subjected to unfair advantage in marital agreements. Indeed, women nowadays quite often have substantial education, financial awareness, income, and assets.

Accordingly, the law has advanced to recognize the equal status of men and women in our society. See, e.g., Pa.Const. art. 1, § 28 (constitutional prohibition of sex discrimination in laws of the Commonwealth). Paternalistic presumptions and protections that arose to shelter women from the inferiorities and incapacities which they were perceived as having in earlier times have, appropriately, been discarded. It would be inconsistent, therefore, to perpetuate the standards governing prenuptial agreements that were described in *Geyer* and similar decisions, as these reflected a paternalistic approach that is now insupportable.

Further, *Geyer* and its predecessors embodied substantial departures from traditional rules of contract law, to the extent that they allowed consideration of the knowledge of the contracting parties and reasonableness of their bargain as factors governing whether to uphold an agreement. Traditional principles of contract law provide perfectly adequate remedies where contracts are procured through fraud, misrepresentation, or duress. Consideration of other factors, such as the knowledge of the parties and the reasonableness of their bargain, is inappropriate. Prenuptial agreements are contracts, and, as such, should be evaluated under the same criteria as are applicable to other types of contracts. Absent fraud, misrepresentation, or duress, spouses should be bound by the terms of their agreements.

Contracting parties are normally bound by their agreements, without regard to whether the terms thereof were read and fully understood and irrespective of whether the agreements embodied reasonable or good bargains. Based upon these principles, the terms of the present prenuptial agreement must be regarded as binding, without regard to whether the terms were fully understood by appellant. *Ignorantia non excusat.*

Accordingly, we find no merit in a contention raised by appellant that the agreement should be declared void on the ground that she did not consult with independent legal counsel. To impose a *per se* requirement that parties entering a prenuptial agreement must obtain independent legal counsel

What's That?

This maxim is sometimes framed as ***ignorantia juris non excusat***, or "ignorance of the law is no excuse."

would be contrary to traditional principles of contract law, and would constitute a paternalistic and unwarranted interference with the parties' freedom to enter contracts.

Further, the reasonableness of a prenuptial bargain is not a proper subject for judicial review. *Geyer* and earlier decisions required that, at least where there had been an inadequate disclosure made by the parties, the bargain must have been reasonable at its inception. Some have even suggested that prenuptial agreements should be examined with regard to whether their terms remain reasonable at the time of dissolution of the parties' marriage.

By invoking inquiries into reasonableness, however, the functioning and reliability of prenuptial agreements is severely undermined. Parties would not have entered such agreements, and, indeed, might not have entered their marriages, if they did not expect their agreements to be strictly enforced. If parties viewed an agreement as reasonable at the time of its inception, as evidenced by their having signed the agreement, they should be foreclosed from later trying to evade its terms by asserting that it was not in fact reasonable. Pertinently, the present agreement contained a clause reciting that "each of the parties considers this agreement fair, just and reasonable. * * * "

Further, everyone who enters a long-term agreement knows that circumstances can change during its term, so that what initially appeared desirable might prove to be an unfavorable bargain. Such are the risks that contracting parties routinely assume. Certainly, the possibilities of illness, birth of children, reliance upon a spouse, career change, financial gain or loss, and numerous other events that can occur in the course of a marriage cannot be regarded as unforeseeable. If parties choose not to address such matters in their prenuptial agreements, they must be regarded as having contracted to bear the risk of events that alter the value of their bargains.

We are reluctant to interfere with the power of persons contemplating marriage to agree upon, and to act in reliance upon, what *they* regard as an acceptable distribution scheme for their property. A court should not ignore the parties' expressed intent by proceeding to determine whether a prenuptial agreement was, in the court's view, reasonable at the time of its inception or the time of divorce. These are exactly the sorts of judicial determinations that such agreements are designed to avoid. Rare indeed is the agreement that is beyond possible challenge when reasonableness is placed at issue. Parties can routinely assert some lack of fairness relating to the inception of the agreement, thereby placing the validity of the agreement at risk. And if reasonableness at the time of divorce were to be taken into account an additional problem would arise. Virtually nonexistent is the marriage in which there has been absolutely no change in the circumstances of either spouse during the course of the marriage. Every change in circumstance, foreseeable or not, and substantial or not, might be asserted as a basis for finding that an agreement is no longer reasonable.

In discarding the approach of *Geyer* that permitted examination of the reasonableness of prenuptial agreements and allowed inquiries into whether parties had attained informed understandings of the rights they were surrendering, we do not depart from the longstanding principle that a full and fair disclosure of the financial positions of the parties is required. Absent this disclosure, a material misrepresentation in the inducement for entering a prenuptial agreement may be asserted. Parties to these agreements do not quite deal at arm's length, but rather at the time the contract is entered into stand in a relation of mutual confidence and trust that calls for disclosure of their financial resources. It is well settled that this disclosure need not be exact, so long as it is "full and fair." In essence therefore, the duty of disclosure under these circumstances is consistent with traditional principles of contract law.

If an agreement provides that full disclosure has been made, a presumption of full disclosure arises. If a spouse attempts to rebut this presumption through an assertion of fraud or misrepresentation then this presumption can be rebutted if it is proven by clear and convincing evidence.

Think About It

What does it mean to say that the parties "stand in a relation of mutual confidence and trust"? How does this affect the legal test for validity of prenuptial agreement?.

The present agreement recited that full disclosure had been made, and included a list of appellee's assets totalling approximately $300,000. Appellant contends that this list understated by roughly $183,000 the value of a classic car collection which appellee had included at a value of $200,000. The master, reviewing the parties' conflicting testimony regarding the value of the car collection, found that appellant failed to prove by clear and convincing evidence that the value of the collection had been understated. The courts below affirmed that finding. We have examined the record and find ample basis for concluding that the value of the car collection was fully disclosed. Appellee offered expert witnesses who testified to a value of approximately $200,000. Further, appellee's disclosure included numerous cars that appellee did not even own but which he merely hoped to inherit from his mother at some time in the future. Appellant's contention is plainly without merit.

Appellant's final contention is that the agreement was executed under conditions of duress in that it was presented to her at 5 p.m. on the eve of her wedding, a time when she could not seek counsel without the trauma, expense, and embarrassment of postponing the wedding. The master found this claim not credible. The courts below affirmed that finding, upon an ample evidentiary basis.

Although appellant testified that she did not discover until the eve of her wedding that there was going to be a prenuptial agreement, testimony from a number of other witnesses was to the contrary. Appellee testified that, although the final version of the agreement was indeed presented to appellant on the eve of the wedding, he had engaged in several discussions with appellant regarding the contents of the agreement during the six month period preceding that date. Another witness testified that appellant mentioned, approximately two or three weeks before the wedding, that she was going to enter a prenuptial agreement. Yet another witness confirmed that, during the months preceding the wedding, appellant participated in several discussions of prenuptial agreements. And the legal counsel who prepared the agreement for appellee testified that, prior to the eve of the wedding, changes were made in the agreement to increase the sums payable to appellant in the event of separation or divorce. He also stated that he was present when the agreement was signed and that appellant expressed absolutely no reluctance about signing. It should be noted, too, that during the months when the agreement was being discussed appellant had more than sufficient time to consult with independent legal counsel if she had so desired. Under these circumstances, there was plainly no error in finding that appellant failed to prove duress.

Hence, the courts below properly held that the present agreement is valid and enforceable. Appellant is barred, therefore, from receiving alimony *pendente lite*.

Order affirmed.

PAPADAKOS, JUSTICE, concurring.

Although I continue to adhere to the principles enunciated in <u>Estate of Geyer, 516 Pa. 492, 533 A.2d 423 (1987)</u>, I concur in the result because the facts fully support the existence of a valid and enforceable agreement between the parties and any suggestion of duress is totally negated by the facts. The full and fair disclosure, as well as the lack of unfairness and inequity, standards reiterated in *Geyer* are supported by the facts in this case so that I can concur in the result.

However, I cannot join the opinion authored by Mr. Justice Flaherty, because, it must be clear to all readers, it contains a number of unnecessary and unwarranted declarations regarding the "equality" of women. Mr. Justice Flaherty believes that, with the hard-fought victory of the Equal Rights Amendment in Pennsylvania, all vestiges of inequality between the sexes have been erased and women are now treated equally under the law. I fear my colleague does not live in the real world. If I did not know him better I would think that his statements smack of male chauvinism, an attitude that "you women asked for it, now live with it." If you want to know about equality of women, just ask them about comparable wages for comparable work. Just ask them about sexual harassment in the workplace. Just ask them about the sexual discrimination in the Executive Suites of big business. And the list of discrimination based on sex goes on and on.

I view prenuptial agreements as being in the nature of contracts of adhesion with one party generally having greater authority than the other who deals in a subservient role. I believe the law protects the subservient party, regardless of that party's sex, to insure equal protection and treatment under the law.

The present case does not involve the broader issues to which the gratuitous declarations in question are addressed, and it is injudicious to offer declarations in a case which does not involve those issues. Especially when those declarations are inconsistent with reality.

McDermott, Justice, dissenting.

I dissent. I would reverse and remand to the trial court for further consideration of the validity of the prenuptial agreement executed by the appellee, Dr. Frederick Simeone, and Catherine Simeone, on the eve of their wedding.

Let me begin by setting forth a common ground between my position in this matter and that of the majority. There can be no question that, in the law and in society, men and women must be accorded equal status. * * *

* * *

In my view, one seeking to avoid the operation of an executed pre-nuptial agreement must first establish, by clear and convincing evidence, that a full and fair disclosure of the worth of the intended spouse was not made at the time of the execution of the agreement. This Court has recognized that full and fair disclosure is needed because, at the time of the execution of a pre-nuptial agreement, the parties do not stand in the usual arm's length posture attendant to most other types of contractual undertakings, but "stand in a relation of mutual confidence and trust that calls for the highest degree of good faith. . . . " *See Gelb Estate, 425 Pa. 117, 123, 228 A.2d 367, 369 (1967)*. In addition to a full and fair disclosure of the general financial pictures of the parties, I would find a pre-nuptial agreement voidable where it is established that the parties were not aware, at the time of contracting, of existing statutory rights which they were relinquishing upon the signing of the agreement. * * *

At the time of dissolution of the marriage, a spouse should be able to avoid the operation of a pre-nuptial agreement upon clear and convincing proof that, despite the existence of full and fair disclosure at the time of the execution of the agreement, the agreement is nevertheless so inequitable and unfair that it should not be enforced in a court of this state. * * *

Thus, I believe that the door should remain open for a spouse to avoid the application of a pre-nuptial agreement where clear and convincing proof establishes that the result will be inequity and unfairness under the circumstances of the particular case and the public policy of this state. Some pre-nuptial agreements will be unfair and inequitable from their beginning. * * *

I would emphasize that there are circumstances at the inception of marriage that render a pre-nuptial agreement not only fair and equitable, but a knowing and acceptable reservation of ownership. Such are usually the circumstances surrounding a second marriage. * * *

It is also apparent that, although a pre-nuptial agreement is quite valid when drafted, the passage of time accompanied by the intervening events of a marriage, may render the terms of the agreement completely unfair and inequitable. While parties to a pre-nuptial agreement may indeed foresee, generally, the events which may come to pass during their marriage, one spouse should not be made to suffer for failing to foresee all of the surrounding circumstances which may attend the dissolution of the marriage. Although it should not be the role of the courts to void pre-nuptial agreements merely because one spouse may receive a better result in an action under the Divorce Code to recover alimony or equitable distribution, it should be the role of the courts to guard against the enforcement of pre-nuptial agreements where such enforcement will bring about only inequity and hardship. * * *

* * *

I can likewise conceive of a situation where, after a long marriage, the value of property may have increased through the direct efforts of the spouse who agreed not to claim it upon divorce or death. In such a situation, the court should be able to decide whether it is against the public policy of the state, and thus inequitable and unfair, for a spouse to be precluded from receiving that increase in the value of property which he or she had, at least in part, directly induced. I marvel at the majority's apparent willingness to enforce a pre-nuptial agreement in the interest of freedom to contract at any cost, even where unforeseen and untoward illness has rendered one spouse unable, despite his own best efforts, to provide reasonable support for himself. I would further recognize that a spouse should be given the opportunity to prove, through clear and convincing evidence, that the amount of time and energy necessary for that spouse to shelter and care for the children of the marriage has rendered the terms of a pre-nuptial agreement inequitable, and unjust and thus, avoidable.

* * *

I would remand this matter to provide the appellant with an opportunity to challenge the validity of the pre-nuptial agreement on two grounds. Although alimony *pendente lite* was mentioned in the pre-nuptial agreement,[6] appellant should have an opportunity to establish that the mere recitation of this legal term did not advise her of the general nature of the statutory right she was relinquishing with the signing of the agreement.[7] Appellant must establish this lack of full

---

[6]   The agreement stated in relevant part: "Frederick's obligation to make payments to Catherine for her support and maintenance or as alimony (including, without limitation, alimony pendente lite) shall be limited to and shall not exceed the $200 per week as above provided, and Catherine does hereby acknowledge that the foregoing provision for the payment of $200 per week is fair, just and reasonable."

[7]   This would not apply to any claim for alimony, as the statutory right to alimony did not arise until the enactment of the Divorce Code of 1980.

and fair disclosure of her statutory rights with clear and convincing evidence. Further, I would allow appellant the opportunity, with the same standard of proof, to challenge the validity of the pre-nuptial agreement's support provisions, relating to alimony *pendente lite* and alimony, for undue unfairness and inequity. I would express no opinion, however, on the appropriate final resolution of these issues. An appellate court should defer to the trial court in these determinations, and the trial court order should not be reversed absent an error of law or an abuse of discretion.

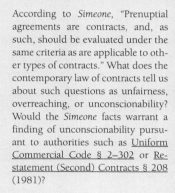

Make the Connection

According to *Simeone,* "Prenuptial agreements are contracts, and, as such, should be evaluated under the same criteria as are applicable to other types of contracts." What does the contemporary law of contracts tell us about such questions as unfairness, overreaching, or unconscionability? Would the *Simeone* facts warrant a finding of unconscionability pursuant to authorities such as Uniform Commercial Code § 2–302 or Restatement (Second) Contracts § 208 (1981)?

Points for Discussion

a. Confidential Relationships

Simeone holds that the parties to prenuptial agreements are in relationships of "mutual confidence and trust that calls for a disclosure of their financial resources." The disclosure need not be exact so long as it is "full and fair." Does this mean that it would be sufficient if the prospective wife knew in general that her fiancé was quite wealthy and had a large annual income?

The position of *Simeone,* that there is a confidential relationship between the parties to a prenuptial agreement, is generally but not universally shared by other courts. After marriage, the husband and wife relationship is treated like other relationships the law characterizes as confidential, such as trustee and beneficiary, guardian and ward, lawyer and client, or principal and agent. What factors justify extending the concept of the confidential relationship to prospective spouses prior to marriage?

b. Agreements Concerning Inheritance Rights

Before 1970, the case law on premarital agreements focused primarily on their consequences for inheritance rights. Premarital and marital agreements still routinely include provisions concerning spouses' rights in the event the marriage ends with the death of one partner. Disclosure requirements usually apply in this context; see, e.g., Uniform Probate Code § 2–213, but see Stregack v. Moldofsky, 474 So.2d 206 (Fla.1985) (disclosure not required under Florida law for waiver of elective share). Should the test for validity of a premarital agreement be different depending whether a waiver of divorce or inheritance rights is at issue?

A premarital agreement must clearly address inheritance rights in order to be effective as a waiver of these rights. See, e.g. Pysell v. Pysell, 559 S.E.2d 677 (Va. 2002); Matter of Estate of Zimmerman, 579 N.W.2d 591 (N.D.1998). In this context, the parties to the agreement should have sufficient understanding of their inheritance rights to make a knowing and enforceable waiver of those rights. In most cases, clients should also be advised to write or revise wills soon after their marriage. In many cases, more extensive estate planning will be required.

c. Postnuptial Agreements

Laws in many states permit married couples to enter contracts concerning their property and financial rights in the event of divorce. In these states, the test for enforceability of postnuptial agreements is similar to that applied to prenuptial agreements. See, e.g., Marriage of Traster, 339 P.3d 778 (Kan. 2014). In some states, postnuptial agreements are not enforceable, or they are subject to more stringent fairness review. See, e.g., Bedrick v. Bedrick, 17 A.3d 17 (Conn. 2011); Ansin v. Craven-Ansin, 929 N.E.2d 955 (Mass. 2010); Marriage of Grossman, 106 P.3d 618 (Or. 2005). Some states allow postnuptial agreements with respect to rights of inheritance, but not divorce or separation. See, *e.g.*, Devney v. Devney, 886 N.W.2d 61 (Neb. 2016). What considerations might justify taking a stricter approach to postnuptial agreements? How might the court in *Simeone* respond to this question?

The Uniform Premarital and Marital Agreements Act (UPMAA), adopted in 2012 by the Uniform Law Commission, addresses agreements entered into by spouses during their marriage that modify or waive rights that would otherwise arise at the time of separation, divorce or the death of one of the spouses. The threshold requirements for enforcement are higher under the UPMAA than under the 1983 Uniform Premarital Agreement Act, discussed in the following case.

d. Statutes of Frauds

Prenuptial agreements are subject to the Statute of Frauds, which requires promises made in contemplation of marriage, other than promises to marry, to be in writing and signed by the party to be charged. New York requires that pre- and postnuptial agreements be signed and acknowledged; see Matisoff v. Dobi, 681 N.E.2d 376 (N.Y. 1997). A couple's oral prenuptial agreement to keep their finances separate, fully performed during the marriage, was enforced under the part-performance exception to the statute of frauds in Dewberry v. George, 62 P.3d 525 (Wash Ct. App. 2003).

Should one party's premarital promise to "take care of" the other forever be legally enforceable? Dane v. Dane, 368 P.3d 914 (Wyo. 2016), held that a contract or promissory estoppel claim in this situation was barred by the statute of frauds and also the state's heart balm statute. The court concluded that evidence of such promises could be taken into account by the court in dividing the marital estate, however.

Practice Pointer: Pension Benefits

In some situations, the disposition of an older person's pension benefits upon death may be the primary issue that a prenuptial agreement seeks to address. Specifically, the agreement may be intended to preserve some portion of these benefits for the spouse or children from a previous marriage.

The rights of a surviving spouse to benefits from a private pension plan are governed by the federal Employees Retirement Income Security Act (ERISA), discussed in Chapter 6. If, as part of a prenuptial agreement, a soon-to-be spouse agrees to waive rights to the surviving spouse's benefits in a private pension plan, the waiver must comply with ERISA. On the malpractice risks for lawyers in attempting to navigate these complex rules, see <u>Merchant v. Kelly, Haglund, Garnsey and Kahn, 874 F.Supp. 300 (D.Colo.1995)</u> (malpractice claim against law firm for drafting postnuptial agreement dividing pension benefits in violation of federal tax law.)

Marriage of Porter

<u>381 P.3d 873 (Or. Ct. App. 2016)</u>

DUNCAN, P.J.

Husband appeals from a dissolution judgment that includes an award of spousal support and a division of property, asserting, among other contentions, that the trial court erred in concluding that the parties' "prenuptial agreement" was unenforceable because wife signed it involuntarily and because it was unconscionable. * * * [We] conclude that the trial court correctly ruled that the agreement is not enforceable, because wife did not enter into it voluntarily, as required by <u>ORS 108.725</u> and our case law interpreting that statute. * * *

The facts relevant to our determination are largely undisputed. The parties were married for 10 years and have four minor children, ages four to nine. At the time of trial, wife was 42 and husband was 57. Husband is well to do, and the parties lived comfortably during the marriage. Wife grew up in Germany but she is fluent in English. She spent one year of high school in the United States as an exchange student, and has advanced degrees in English and linguistics, which she earned from German universities before moving to the United States in July 2001 to do research and to teach at Portland State University.

The parties met in May 2002 and started dating that summer. Wife knew that husband had been married twice before. She was also aware that he did not have a financial need to work full time. The parties' versions of the facts differ slightly with respect to the circumstances surrounding the execution of the agreement. The trial court made an explicit finding that wife's version is credible. Wife testified that, in early December 2002, although the parties had not yet discussed marriage, husband mentioned that he was going to have his attorney prepare a prenuptial agreement, in the event that they should decide to get married. Wife testified that she told husband that she had never heard of a prenuptial agreement and that husband explained to her that it is something people sign when they want to get married, and

> "he just wanted to make sure that I wasn't in this relationship for his money. And I responded, 'If that's what it is about, I can sign it.'"

Wife testified that the parties had no further conversation about marriage until the afternoon of December 24, 2002. They were running errands together when husband suddenly pulled up to a bank and said, "We are going to the bank to sign the prenuptial agreement." At the bank, husband requested a notary and presented wife with three copies of a document to sign. Wife testified that that was the first time she had seen the prenuptial agreement or the list of husband's assets attached to it as an exhibit. She testified that she did not read every word of the document because she did not understand most of it, especially the legal terminology, but that she did not remember asking husband to explain any of the terms. In addition, wife testified that she trusted husband and believed that the document was "rather insignificant," because only a notary (and not a lawyer) was present. Wife testified that she thought that, just as husband had told her, the agreement was only to reassure him that, if the parties ever married, she was not marrying him for his money. Wife testified that husband pointed to the places in the agreement where she needed to sign the agreement, but that she did not feel forced. The parties spent about five minutes at the bank.

Wife testified that she did not understand that the agreement provided that, in the event of divorce, she would not be entitled to spousal support or to any portion of husband's property. Wife testified that, had she understood the agreement, she would not have signed it and would have consulted a lawyer. Earlier that day, at husband's suggestion, wife had made an appointment to see a lawyer with regard to another matter, but it did not occur to wife to have that lawyer review the agreement, either before or after she signed it.

After the parties signed the agreement, they went to husband's house, where he placed two original copies of the agreement in a file folder in his office. He mailed the third copy to his attorney. The parties became engaged that night. Wife moved into husband's home in early March 2003, and the parties were married on April 19, 2003.

Wife filed the petition for dissolution in November 2011. She simultaneously sought a declaration that the agreement was unenforceable. The agreement is a 12-page single-spaced document that was prepared by husband's attorney. It includes a list of each party's assets, as well as recitals that each party has been fully informed of the nature of the agreement and has knowingly entered into the agreement. Substantively, the agreement provides that all of the property and income of each party owned at the time of the marriage and acquired in the sole name of either party "shall remain the separate property of each of them." It further provides that, upon divorce or death, each party released and relinquished "all claims to and rights in the Separate Property" of the other, and that "[n]either party shall make any claim for alimony or spousal support from the other party." The agreement states that

> "[t]he parties acknowledge they have had ample opportunity to consult with independent legal counsel regarding the effects of this Agreement, the rights and privileges waived hereunder, the rights and privileges granted hereunder, the binding effect of the present and future consequences hereof, and all other matters pertaining to this Agreement. The parties hereby acknowledge their complete understanding of such legal effects of this Agreement."

After a hearing, the trial court ruled that the agreement was unenforceable, both because it had not been entered into voluntarily and because it was unconscionable. The court then tried the dissolution matter without regard to the agreement and awarded wife spousal support as well as personal property and an equalizing award of $ 612,047.

* * *

The parties' agreement was subject to the provisions of the Uniform Premarital Agreement Act (UPAA), ORS 108.700 to 108.740. Under ORS 108.710, parties may enter into a premarital agreement with respect to most matters to be resolved at dissolution, including the division of property and the award of spousal support. A premarital agreement becomes effective upon marriage. ORS 108.715. When a party challenges the enforceability of a premarital agreement, the court is required to evaluate it under ORS 108.725, which provides, in relevant part:

> "(1) A premarital agreement is not enforceable if the party against whom enforcement is sought proves that:
> "(a) That party did not execute the agreement voluntarily; or

"(b) The agreement was unconscionable when it was executed and, before execution of the agreement, that party:

"(A) Was not provided a fair and reasonable disclosure of the property or financial obligations of the other party;

"(B) Did not voluntarily and expressly waive, in writing, any right to disclosure of the property or financial obligations of the other party beyond the disclosure provided; and

"(C) Did not have, or reasonably could not have had, an adequate knowledge of the property or financial obligations of the other party."

The trial court's conclusion that the parties' agreement is unenforceable was based primarily on the court's findings concerning the circumstances of its execution, which led the court to conclude that wife had not signed the agreement voluntarily and that it was unconscionable. The court further found that the parties had not had a "meeting of the minds."

In support of its conclusions, the trial court found that the parties had not discussed the terms of the agreement in advance; that wife had not seen a copy of the agreement before husband asked her to sign it and had not had an opportunity to review its terms or the list of husband's assets in advance; that wife did not have a chance to negotiate the terms of the agreement; that wife did not have time to fully read or understand the agreement; and that, despite the recitals of the agreement, wife had not been informed of and did not fully understand the nature of the agreement or the rights that were being determined. The court was particularly troubled that husband, who had had experience with premarital agreements, had not recommended that wife have an attorney review the agreement. The court found that husband had made an intentional effort to create circumstances in which wife would sign the agreement without sufficient time to review it or to have it reviewed by an attorney.

On appeal, husband assigns error to the trial court's ruling that the agreement is not enforceable, contending that the court erroneously concluded that wife did not sign it voluntarily and that it was unconscionable. Wife responds that the trial court's findings in support of its conclusions are supported by the evidence. Because we agree with wife that the evidence supports the trial court's conclusion that wife did not execute the agreement "voluntarily," as that term is used in ORS 108.725, we agree with the trial court's conclusion that the agreement was unenforceable.

As husband correctly contends, under ORS 108.725, the party seeking a determination that a premarital agreement is not enforceable bears the burden of proving either that the party did not execute the agreement voluntarily or that the agreement was unconscionable when it was executed. ORS 108.725 ("premarital agreement is not enforceable if the party against whom enforcement is sought proves" involuntariness or unconscionability).

In *Rudder and Rudder*, 217 P.3d 183, *rev. den.*, 222 P.3d 1091 (Or. 2009), we addressed the meaning of "voluntarily," as used in ORS 108.725(1)(a). In the absence of a statutory definition for the term, we referred to dictionary definitions, concluding that the term "voluntarily" suggests "independent action, free from coercion and intimidation; an element of 'choice' is evident." We then cited a discussion by the California Supreme Court in its opinion in *In re Marriage of Bonds*, 5 P.3d 815 (Cal. 2000). That opinion is cited frequently for its discussion of the meaning of the term "voluntarily," as used in the UPAA. We quoted with approval the California Supreme Court's explanation that the Uniform Law Commission's official comments

> "demonstrate the commissioners' belief that a number of factors are relevant to the issue of voluntariness. In considering defenses proffered against enforcement of a premarital agreement, the court should consider whether the evidence indicates coercion or lack of knowledge * * *. Specifically, the cases cited in the comment * * * direct consideration of the impact upon the parties of such factors as the coercion that may arise from the proximity of execution of the agreement to the wedding, or from surprise in the presentation of the agreement; the presence or absence of independent counsel; inequality of bargaining power—in some cases indicated by the relative age and sophistication of the parties; whether there was full disclosure of assets; the parties' understanding of the rights being waived under the agreement or at least their awareness of the intent of the agreement."

217 P.3d 183 (quoting *Marriage of Bonds*, 5 P.3d 815). The significance of that discussion for purposes of this case is that it suggests that involuntariness does not relate only to the immediate circumstances of the signing and whether they were coercive. In *Rudder*, we agreed with the California Supreme Court that the factors relevant to determining the element of voluntariness in the execution of a premarital agreement include the proximity of the document's presentation to the time of the wedding; any surprise in its presentation; the presence or absence of legal counsel; an inequality of bargaining power; disclosure of assets; an understanding of rights waived under the agreement; and, an awareness of the intent of the document. We also noted and agreed with the California court's observation that "[t]he commissioners also clearly anticipated that ordinary contract defenses, 'such as lack of capacity, fraud, duress, and undue influence,' would apply in assessing the voluntariness of an agreement."

In *Rudder*, we explicitly rejected an interpretation by the Iowa Supreme Court in *In re Marriage of Shanks*, 758 N.W.2d 506, 517–18 (Iowa 2008), that involuntariness requires proof of duress or undue influence, as those terms are understood in contract law. Rather, we concluded that the uniform law's comment showed that "the drafters of the UPAA intended a broader meaning of voluntariness to apply."

We further said in *Rudder* that the California Supreme Court's reading of the UPAA was consistent with the view expressed in the legislative history of Oregon's enactment that the uniform law represented, essentially, a codification of common law. Our analysis of Oregon's case law led to our conclusion in *Rudder* that, in determining the validity of a premarital agreement,

> "courts primarily considered the sophistication of the party against whom the agreement was being enforced, whether the party had a reasonable opportunity to review the agreement and to seek independent counsel, whether the party was aware of the purpose of the agreement, and, finally whether the party was aware of or should have been aware of the nature and extent of the property that would be affected. * * * It thus follows that the Oregon legislature, like California's, understood the term 'voluntarily' as used in ORS 108.725(1)(a) to imply a lack of coercion, intimidation, or undue pressure, as well as some modicum of knowledge of the terms of the agreement and the property affected. The timing of the agreement in relation to the wedding, and an adequate opportunity to consult with independent counsel, the relative sophistication of the parties, and a sufficient disclosure of assets are among the factors bearing on that question."

Id. at 455, 217 P.3d 183 (citations and footnotes omitted).

In concluding in *Rudder* that the wife had met her burden to show that she had not entered into the premarital agreement voluntarily, we cited the trial court's findings that the parties had first discussed the agreement in general terms a few weeks before their wedding; that the wife first saw the agreement on the day before the parties were scheduled to travel to Las Vegas for their wedding; that, although the wife had expressly requested the presence of her attorney at the signing, he was not present; that the husband urged the wife to sign the agreement because the wedding plans were made; and that the entire meeting lasted no more than 30 minutes. In further support for our conclusion that the signing was involuntary, we cited evidence that the wife lacked sufficient knowledge of the extent of the property affected by the agreement; that the list of the husband's assets attached to the agreement was incomplete and did not include values; that the wife had limited knowledge of the husband's financial holdings; that the wife's experience in business affairs was limited; and that she was relatively unsophisticated in financial matters. We concluded on *de novo* review that "those circumstances created a sufficiently coercive environment so as to render wife's agreement involuntary."

Here, based on our application of the _Rudder_ factors to the facts found by the trial court, we conclude that the record supports the trial court's conclusion that wife did not sign "voluntarily." It is true, as husband contends, that unlike in _Rudder_, husband presented the agreement to wife several months, rather than days, before the wedding (and indeed before the parties were even engaged), and wife testified that she did not feel pressured to sign it. But there are other factors that the trial court cited and that support its conclusion. Wife, although highly educated, was considerably less sophisticated than husband in matters of this nature, because English is not her first language and because of her lack of personal experience with legal matters relating to dissolution in the United States. The court found that wife was credible and accepted her testimony that, although the parties had spoken briefly and in general terms about husband's reason for wanting a prenuptial agreement, they never discussed the specific terms of the agreement. The court found, further, that wife did not understand the agreement's legal significance or its practical effect and did not have sufficient time at the signing to do so. The trial court's findings support its conclusion that wife did not sign the agreement voluntarily as required by ORS 108.725(1)(a), and as that term has been interpreted in _Rudder_. Wife was considerably disadvantaged by her lack of familiarity with divorce in the United States and with English legal terminology; husband took advantage of that circumstance by implying that the document was relatively inconsequential and by presenting it to her suddenly, without sufficient time to review it or to have it reviewed by a lawyer.

It certainly is true, as husband points out, that a party has an independent obligation to protect his or her own interests and to read documents before signing them. Husband cites our opinion in _Knoll and Knoll, 671 P.2d 718 (Or. 1983)_, as setting forth a rule that a party's failure to read an agreement before signing it does not excuse a party's failure to understand the agreement. But _Knoll_ is distinguishable. In that case, the wife, who had been presented with a premarital agreement nine months before the wedding, knew the purpose of the agreement, knew a great deal about the husband's financial affairs, and was repeatedly advised to seek independent counsel, yet failed even to read the agreement. Here, wife attempted to read the agreement but could not understand it; further, she testified that she signed the agreement without asking for an explanation because she trusted husband's implicit representations that the agreement was not significant and was only to reassure him that she would not marry him for his money. The trial court believed wife. The trial court did not err in concluding that the premarital agreement was not enforceable because wife did not sign it voluntarily, as required by the UPAA, because of her failure to understand its purpose and consequences.

Affirmed on appeal and on cross-appeal.

Points for Discussion

a. Voluntariness

As discussed in *Porter*, an agreement under may be challenged the Uniform Premarital Agreement Act (UPAA) if it was not executed voluntarily, or if it was unconscionable when it was executed. How does *Porter* interpret the term "voluntary" in the UPAA? What made the wife's execution involuntary?

b. Uniform (and Non-Uniform) Premarital Agreement Act

The Uniform Premarital Agreement Act (UPAA) has been adopted, with some modifications, by twenty-six states and the District of Columbia. Current information on the UPAA is available from the web site of the Uniform Law Commission. Would the *Simeone* case have been decided differently if the Act had been in force? Would the adoption of the UPAA affect the outcome of the cases stated in the problems below?

After the California decision in In re the Marriage of Bonds, 5 P.3d 815 (Cal. 2000), cited in *Porter,* California's legislature amended its version of the UPAA to provide greater safeguards. As amended, the California UPAA now requires "fair, reasonable and full disclosure" instead of "fair and reasonable disclosure." The California statute also includes a new subsection providing that a premarital agreement shall not be deemed to have been executed voluntarily unless two requirements are met. The court must find that the party against whom enforcement was sought had seven days between the time the agreement was first presented and the time it was signed, and must also find that the party against whom enforcement is sought was represented by independent legal counsel or expressly waived representation and was fully informed in writing of the terms and basic effect of the agreement and the rights being released. Cal. Fam. Code § 1615 (c) (2018). If applicable, would this statute have changed the outcome of either *Simeone* or *Rudder*?

As noted by the Court in *Porter*, Iowa's courts have taken a different approach to the voluntariness question. Under Iowa's version of the UPAA, a premarital agreement is not enforceable if a party proves any one of three things: that he or she did not execute the agreement voluntarily, that it was unconscionable when executed, or that the party did not receive fair and reasonable disclosure or have an adequate knowledge of the other party's assets. See Iowa Code § 596.8 (2018). In addition, the Iowa version of the UPAA states that "The right of a spouse or child to support shall not be adversely affected by a premarital agreement." Iowa Code § 596.5. How does this approach compare with the provision in UPAA §6(b), reprinted below?

The 2012 <u>Uniform Premarital and Marital Agreements Act</u> (UPMAA) applies both to premarital agreements and agreements entered into during a marriage, and includes somewhat more stringent requirements for enforceability than the earlier uniform act, including a requirement that the party have access to independent legal representation or, in the alternative, that the agreement includes a notice of waiver of rights or "an explanation in plain language of the marital rights or obligations being modified or waived by the agreement." UPMAA § 9. Two states have enacted the UPMAA.

Uniform Premarital Agreement Act § 6

(a) A premarital agreement is not enforceable if the party against whom enforcement is sought proves that:

    (1) that party did not execute the agreement voluntarily; or

    (2) the agreement was unconscionable when it was executed and, before execution of the agreement, that party:

        (i) was not provided a fair and reasonable disclosure of the property or financial obligations of the other party;

        (ii) did not voluntarily and expressly waive, in writing, any right to disclosure of the property or financial obligations of the other party beyond the disclosure provided; and

        (iii) did not have, or reasonably could not have had, an adequate knowledge of the property or financial obligations of the other party.

(b) If a provision of a premarital agreement modifies or eliminates spousal support and that modification or elimination causes one party to the agreement to be eligible for support under a program of public assistance at the time of separation or marital dissolution, a court, notwithstanding the terms of the agreement, may require the other party to provide support necessary to avoid that eligibility.

(c) An issue of unconscionability of a premarital agreement shall be decided by the court as a matter of law.

<u>Uniform Premarital Agreement Act § 6</u> (UPAA), 9C U.L.A. 48 (2001).

---

c. Disclosure Obligations

In *Porter*, a list of the husband's assets was attached to the agreement the wife signed. If the court had considered the agreement to be unconscionable, would this be sufficient to satisfy the requirements of § 6(a)(2)? If this had not been attached, would that fact be sufficient standing alone as a basis to set aside a premarital agreement under the Oregon statute? Under the California statute? See generally <u>Friezo v. Friezo, 914 A.2d 533 (Conn. 2007)</u> (discussing what is "fair and reasonable" disclosure). See also UPMAA § 9(d).

d. Changes in Circumstances and Spousal Support

Courts in some jurisdictions consider whether enforcement of a premarital agreement would be unconscionable based upon circumstances existing at the time of a divorce. These courts are particularly concerned with changes that would leave a spouse "without sufficient property, maintenance, or appropriate employment to support herself." <u>DeMatteo v. DeMatteo, 762 N.E.2d 797, 811–13 (Mass. 2002)</u>. California's version of the UPAA, as amended after the decision in <u>Pendleton v. Fireman, 5 P.3d 839 (Cal. 2000)</u>, states that premarital agreements concerning spousal support are not enforceable if the party against whom enforcement is sought was not represented by independent counsel at the time the agreement was signed or if the provision is unconscionable at the time of enforcement. <u>Cal. Fam. Code § 1612(c) (2018)</u>. What are the arguments for treating support rights differently from property rights in this context? What does the court in *Simeone* have to say on this question?

If a couple's standard of living improved significantly after the time they executed a premarital or marital agreement, due to a large increase in one spouse's earnings, so that the effect of the agreement would be to reduce the other spouse's standard of living dramatically in the event of a divorce, should that be a sufficient change of circumstances to justify a court in refusing to enforce the agreement? Compare <u>Gross v. Gross, 464 N.E.2d 500 (Ohio 1984)</u> (finding maintenance provided by agreement to be unconscionable in view of husband's greatly increased earnings and property), with <u>In re Marriage of Drag, 762 N.E.2d 1111 (Ill. 2002)</u> (change in parties' economic fortunes during marriage is not sufficient basis to modify prenuptial agreement).

Represented and Unrepresented Parties

If the couple in *Porter* had come to the office of the husband's attorney to sign the agreement, would his attorney have any obligations to the wife? Is it enough for the attorney to tell the wife he is representing only the husband? See American Bar Association <u>Model Rules of Professional Conduct Rule 4.3</u>; American Academy of Matrimonial Lawyers, <u>Bounds of Advocacy</u> 3.2 (requiring that a lawyer tell the client's spouse that the lawyer cannot also advise the spouse and recommend that he or she consult another attorney).

Could a lawyer, when approached by both prospective spouses with a request to draft an prenuptial agreement for them, represent both parties? See ABA Model Rules of Professional Conduct, Rule 1.7; American Academy of Matrimonial Lawyers, Bounds of Advocacy 3.1. For a decision concluding that a premarital agreement was invalid where one lawyer attempted to advise both parties, see Ware v. Ware, 687 S.E.2d 382 (W.Va. 2009).

If the agreement were held invalid in this situation, should the attorney who drafted it be held liable for malpractice? If so, to whom? Note that in many jurisdictions, lawyers do not have malpractice liability to third parties unless the client intended that the third party be the beneficiary of the legal services. See, e.g., Pelham v. Griesheimer, 440 N.E.2d 96 (Ill. 1982) (children have no cause of action for malpractice against mother's divorce lawyer).

e. Choice of Law

In light of the different legal standards applied to premarital and postmarital agreements in different states, how should courts treat cases in which spouses enter into an agreement in one state and subsequently divorce in another? See Lewis v. Lewis, 748 P.2d 1362 (Haw. 1988) (applying Hawaii law to a New York premarital agreement because Hawaii had the most significant contacts with the parties at the time of divorce); Estate of Davis, 184 S.W.3d 231 (Tenn. Ct. App. 2004) (applying Tennessee law to Florida prenuptial agreement where Florida law, which does not require disclosure of assets in the estate context, violated Tennessee's public policy).

To assure that the law of a particular state will govern the agreement, the drafter can include a choice of law provision, which will usually be given effect. Restatement (Second) of Conflict of Laws §§ 187, 188 (1971). E.g. DeLorean v. DeLorean, 511 A.2d 1257 (N.J. Super. Ct. Ch. Div. 1986); Gamache v. Smurro, 904 A.2d 91 (Vt. 2006). See also Fernandez v. Fernandez, 15 Cal.Rptr. 374 (Ct. App. 1961) (upholding validity of Mexican premarital agreement in California divorce). However, absolute assurance on the choice of law question at the time of execution does not appear possible under the Restatement approach. See Gustafson v. Jensen, 515 So.2d 1298 (Fla.1987).

f. Scope of Marital Agreements

Even as courts began to allow parties autonomy in regulating their support and property obligations on divorce or death, they still hesitated to enforce agreements dealing with support or other conduct during the marriage. In Osborne v. Osborne, 428 N.E.2d 810 (Mass. 1981), the court was careful to say that "We express no opinion on the validity of antenuptial contracts that purport to limit the duty of each spouse to support the other during the marriage." This reflects a longstanding practice of courts declining to adjudicate marital disputes; see Kilgrow v. Kilgrow, 107 So.2d 885 (Ala. 1958) (dispute over child's school enrollment); McGuire v. McGuire, 59 N.W.2d 336 (Neb. 1953) (dispute over marital finances).

Section 3(a) of the Uniform Premarital Agreement Act lists a variety of subjects that parties may address in a premarital agreement including "any other matter, including their personal rights and obligations, not in violation of public policy or a statute imposing a criminal penalty." (Under § 3(b), however, "The right of a child to support may not be adversely affected by a premarital agreement." See also UPMAA § 10(b)(1)). The UPAA Commissioner's Comment states that "[A]n agreement may provide for such matters as the choice of abode, the freedom to pursue career opportunities, the upbringing of children, and so on." The UPAA does not address the question of what remedies might be available for the breach of such provisions, and its section on enforcement makes no distinctions between the different kinds of provisions that may be included in premarital agreements.

How should a court in a jurisdiction in which the UPAA is in force approach a marital contract dispute concerning an agreement as to where the couple will reside, the number and spacing of children, or the sharing of financial obligations and household chores? Should courts lend their assistance to spouses who wish to structure their married life by means of contract? How should a court evaluate a marital agreement articulating an obligation of "emotional and sexual fidelity" between the parties, and providing for payment of liquidated damages in the event of a breach of this provision? See Diosdado v. Diosdado, 118 Cal.Rptr.2d 494 (Cal. Ct. App. 2002). What about a contract that specifies that neither party will be allowed to obtain a no-fault divorce? See Coggins v. Coggins, 601 So.2d 109 (Ala.Civ.App.1992), cert. denied.

UPMAA § 10 treats a number of these potential terms as unenforceable, including provisions that would limit or restrict a remedy available to a victim of domestic violence, modify the grounds on which a separation or divorce may be obtained, or penalize a party for initiating divorce or separation proceedings.

Agreements regarding custodial rights are always subject to review by a court with appropriate jurisdiction in order to protect the best interests of any minor children. See, e.g., <u>In re Marriage of Littlefield, 940 P.2d 1362 (Wash. 1997)</u>. This limitation is made clear in UPMAA §10(c), which provides that: "A term in a premarital agreement or marital agreement which defines the rights or duties of the parties regarding custodial responsibility is not binding on the court."

Global View: Religious Marital Agreements

Courts in many states have considered enforcement of premarital agreements entered into by Muslim or Jewish couples, either in the United States or in another country where marriage and divorce issues are governed by religious law. In those religious and legal traditions, husbands have broad rights to divorce their wives, and wives have relatively few property or support rights. Agreements signed at the time of a marriage provide some financial security to a wife in the event of her husband's death or the dissolution of their marriage. Depending on the circumstances, a traditional marital agreement might provide a wife with more or less than what she would be entitled to receive under the law that would apply in the state where the divorce takes place. Compare <u>In re Marriage of Noghrey, 215 Cal.Rptr. 153 (Ct. App. 1985)</u> with <u>In re Marriage of Shaban, 105 Cal.Rptr.2d 863 (Ct. App. 2001)</u>. How should a state court determine whether to enforce these agreements? How do the Establishment and Free Exercise Clauses of the First Amendment affect this question?

Premarital agreements signed by some Jewish couples include provisions concerning a religious dissolution of the marriage, in the event of a civil divorce, or provisions placing jurisdiction over marital disputes with a rabbinic tribunal known as a *bet din*. Courts have been divided on whether such promises are enforceable in the civil courts. Compare <u>In re Marriage of Goldman, 554 N.E.2d 1016 (Ill. 1990)</u> (ordering specific performance of promise to appear before bet din) with <u>Aflalo v. Aflalo, 685 A.2d 523 (N.J. Super. Ct. Ch. Div. 1996)</u>, and <u>In re Marriage of Victor, 866 P.2d 899 (Ariz. Ct. App.1993)</u> (refusing to order performance of promise to deliver religious divorce document). In <u>Avitzur v. Avitzur, 446 N.E.2d 136 (N.Y. 1983)</u>, the court interpreted a provision placing jurisdiction over marital disputes with the rabbinic court as an arbitration clause, and held that it was enforceable under neutral principles of contract law. See generally Ann Laquer Estin, <u>*Embracing Tradition: Pluralism in American Family Law*, 63 Md. L. Rev. 540 (2004)</u>.

Client Counseling: Premarital Agreement

Imagine that you have been consulted by a new client who intends to be married next month and would like you to prepare a premarital agreement. Based on *Simeone*, *Rudder*, and the other materials in this section, prepare a checklist of the issues you would want to be certain to address in that agreement and the steps you would take to assure that the agreement will stand up if it is ever challenged in court. What questions would you have for your client before beginning to draft the agreement?

Problem 1-2

Robert and Christie decided to get married when Christie became pregnant. She was eighteen and a recent graduate from high school. She had no property, but Robert had property worth $151,000. Several days before the wedding Robert had his lawyer draft a prenuptial agreement and told Christie that if she did not sign it there would be no wedding. She signed in the lawyer's office, although she was suffering from morning sickness. The agreement released all claims to Robert's property that Christie might have as a result of their marriage and contained a list of his property, with its value, stating that this was a full and complete disclosure of all his property. The lawyer did not advise Christie about the effect of the agreement, but Robert told her that it would protect her from his debts if the marriage ended. Eleven months later Robert drowned, dying intestate. Robert's father filed an application to be appointed administrator of his estate, opposed by Christie, who sought a decree that the agreement was invalid. Was Christie coerced? Does your answer change if Robert did not know Christie was pregnant? (See Rowland v. Rowland, 599 N.E.2d 315 (Ohio Ct. App. 1991).)

Problem 1-3

While they were engaged, A.J. told Sara his financial advisors had said that he needed a prenuptial agreement to protect his construction business. In fact, A.J.'s statement was false. When Sara refused to sign any prenuptial agreement. A.J. dropped the matter, and they set a wedding date. Without telling Sara, A.J. had his lawyer draft an agreement in which they both agreed that any property acquired by either during the marriage would belong to the party acquiring it, and that in the event of divorce neither would receive any support. Five days before the wedding, A.J. sent the agreement to Sara, telling her to consult a lawyer and offering to pay her lawyer's fee. Sara was upset, but did consult a lawyer, who advised her that under the agreement she would get nothing if the couple divorced. The day before the wedding, A.J. and Sara met together with their lawyers. After a heated discussion, Sara asked A.J. if he wanted her to sign. He said yes, and she signed. During the parties' six-year marriage, A.J.'s net worth increased from $2.4 million to $6.5 million. When Sara sued for divorce, she requested support and a share in A.J.'s increased property. What should be the result? (See In re the Marriage of Spiegel, 553 N.W.2d 309 (Iowa 1996).)

Problem 1-4

James, age forty-five, and Peggy, age twenty-two, began living together when Peggy worked as a bookkeeper in one of James' companies. James was worth about $1.2 million. Peggy's net worth was $8,200. They lived together for three years, during which time James was physically violent with Peggy on three occasions. After each episode, he apologized profusely. Peggy continued to work in James' businesses before and during their later marriage. After three years they decided to marry. James had the lawyer for his businesses draft a prenuptial agreement precluding the accumulation of marital property and containing Peggy's waiver of any claim to alimony. Peggy knew this lawyer and respected him, but he told her plainly in writing that he was acting for James and that she should employ her own lawyer. The agreement was presented to Peggy two days before the wedding and she signed it a day later, although she had known for two weeks that it was being prepared. Nine years later Peggy sued for divorce and contended that the agreement should be disregarded. During the marriage James also inflicted serious physical and emotional abuse on Peggy, leaving her in need of treatment for post-traumatic stress disorder. Under *Simeone*, should the agreement be enforced? What about the UPAA? (See Matter of Marriage of Foran, 834 P.2d 1081 (Wash. Ct. App. 1992); see also Sogg v. Nevada State Bank, 832 P.2d 781 (Nev. 1992).)

Problem 1-5

Warren and Carol signed a valid prenuptial agreement several days before their marriage which included a waiver of claims for support. Eight years later, Carol was very seriously injured in a traffic accident. Two years after the accident, her medical bills totaled more than a million dollars and she was still mentally and physically devastated by her injuries. Warren, who has substantial separate property, has filed for divorce, and asked the court to enforce Carol's support waiver. Should the court enforce the agreement? If the court denies enforcement, how should it determine an appropriate amount of support? (See Marriage of Rosendale, 15 Cal.Rptr.3d 137 (Cal.Ct.App. 2004)).

Problem 1-6

Robert and Laurie signed a premarital agreement three days before their wedding that included this language: "This Agreement shall become null and void and of no further force and effect upon the seventh (7th) anniversary of the parties' marriage." Robert filed an action for divorce three months before their seventh wedding anniversary. At the divorce hearing, several months after their anniversary, Laurie asked the court not to enforce the agreement, arguing that it had expired and also that an agreement with a "sunset" provision violated public policy by encouraging Robert to file for divorce. How should the court rule? (See Peterson v. Sykes-Peterson, 37 A.3d 173 (Conn. Ct. App. 2012); see also Sides v. Sides, 717 S.E.2d 472 (Ga. 2011).)

Problem 1-7

Two years after Cynthia and Michael were married, Cynthia demanded that Michael sign an agreement promising that if he were ever guilty of statutory grounds for divorce, Cynthia could divorce him and he would be required to pay her half of his assets and half of all his future income. When they signed the agreement, Michael was in medical school. When Cynthia filed for divorce on grounds of adultery fifteen years later, he was an orthopedic surgeon earning $500,000 a year. Cynthia had a part time career in real estate. Should this agreement be enforceable? Should the answer to this question depend on whether the claim is brought in a fault-based or no-fault divorce jurisdiction? (See Bratton v. Bratton, 136 S.W.3d 595 (Tenn.2004); see also Mehren v. Dargan, 13 Cal.Rptr.3d 522 (Cal. Ct. App. 2004).)

Further Reading: Marital Agreements

- American Law Institute, Principles of the Law of Family Dissolution §§ 7.01–7.08 (2002).

- Homer H. Clark, Jr., Domestic Relations § 1.1 (Student 2d ed. 1988).

- Linda J. Ravdin, Premarital Agreements: Drafting and Negotiation (2d ed. 2017).

- Brett R. Turner and Laura W. Morgan, Attacking and Defending Marital Agreements (2d ed. 2013)

C. Getting Married

Marriage patterns have changed dramatically around the world over the past fifty years. Although the majority of all adults over age 30 in the United States have married, the percentages of men and women who marry have been declining and the median age at first marriage has been increasing. As marriage rates have decreased, other trends have also emerged: divorce rates have leveled off, cohabitation has become more common, and marriage is now more common among those who are better off socioeconomically and have more education. Between twenty and twenty-five percent of all currently married couples have at least one partner who had been married previously.

Rates of marriage across different racial, ethnic and religious groups are also increasing. Government data indicate that one in every ten women under age 45 who are currently in their first marriage is married to an individual of a different racial or ethnic group. (In these surveys, the groups identified are non-Hispanic White, non-Hispanic Black, non-Hispanic Asian, non-Hispanic other, and Hispanic.)

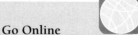

Go Online

The U.S. National Center for Health Statistics, based in the Centers for Disease Control and Prevention (CDC), collects marriage and divorce statistics from state authorities and makes them available through the National Vital Statistics System. Survey data on marriage and divorce are available from the U.S. Census Bureau. See Rose M. Kreider and Renee Ellis, Number, Timing, and Duration of Marriages and Divorces: 2009 (Current Population Reports, May 2011), and Diana B. Elliott and Tavia Simmons, Marital Events of Americans: 2009 (American Community Survey Reports, 2011).

1. Licensing and Solemnization

In all of the American states, there are statutes regulating entry into marriage. Much of this legislation governs procedures for licensing and solemnization of ceremonial marriages. In all states, individuals who wish to be married must obtain a license, usually from some public official such as the county clerk or a clerk of court. Where common law marriage or some other form of informal marriage is recognized, these statutory requirements may be by-passed. Statutes in some states impose a waiting period, to run between the application for the license and its issuance or between the issuance of the license and the marriage.

Most statutes authorize marriages to be solemnized by such religious leaders as priests, rabbis and ministers and by various civil officers, including judges, justices of the peace, county clerks and others. Some statutes explicitly allow solemnization in accordance with the rules of any denomination, e.g., Ill. Ann.

Stat. 750 ILCS 5/209 (2018); Mass. Ann. L. ch. 207, § 38 (2018), or in accordance with the customs of an Indian Nation, Tribe or Native Group, see Uniform Marriage and Divorce Act § 206, 9A U.L.A. (Part 1) 182 (1998). See also Center for Inquiry, Inc. v. Marion Circuit Court Clerk, 758 F.3d 869 (7th Cir. 2014), which held state marriage statutes that accommodate the practices of some religions may not exclude other religions or secular groups such as humanist societies. A Colorado statute provides that a marriage may be solemnized by the parties to the marriage. Colo. Rev. Stat. Ann. § 14–2–109 (2018). Statutes typically require two witnesses, whose names or signatures appear on the marriage certificate. The certificate usually must be filled out by the person solemnizing the marriage and sent to the place of recording. Marriage certificates are then kept as public records.

Think About It

What is the purpose of these solemnization rules?

In addition to formal, ceremonial marriage under these statutes, many jurisdictions in the United States recognized the validity of informal, or "common law" marriages, discussed further below. This institution traces its roots to the English ecclesiastical courts, which recognized until 1753 a form of marriage called ***sponsalia per verba de praesenti*** entered into without a ceremony. Such a marriage was held valid to the extent of prevailing over a subsequent ceremonial marriage meeting all the formal requirements, although the common law courts would not recognize it for purposes of awarding dower to a woman who was married in this fashion. Once relatively widespread, common law marriage has been on the decline in the United States, with only nine states and the District of Columbia allowing common law marriages.

Accounts Management, Inc. v. Litchfield

576 N.W.2d 233 (S.D. 1998)

KONENKAMP, JUSTICE.

Today we must decide whether failure to record a marriage license invalidates a marriage. A widow denies responsibility for her deceased husband's medical bills contending her marriage was void for lack of recording with the register of deeds. Because we construe our licensing statutes to favor validation of marriages even when a statutory formality was overlooked, we declare the marriage valid and conclude our statutes make her financially responsible for his medical care. Her debt is affirmed.

Facts

Fredrick Klusman and Claudia Caswell submitted an application for a marriage license to the Pennington County Register of Deeds on December 20, 1984. They were married four days later by an ordained Presbyterian minister in the company of a few friends and relatives. On October 14, 1986, Fredrick was in Mitchell, South Dakota on a business trip when he suffered a severe heart attack. Emergency personnel transported him to St. Joseph Hospital. Claudia signed, as his wife, an "Admission Consent Form" and an "Authorization for Medical and/or Surgical Treatment." Fredrick was in the intensive care unit for seven days. As a result of his heart attack, Fredrick's brain was deprived of oxygen for eight to ten minutes resulting in severe and irreversible brain damage. Claudia obtained guardianship of his person and assumed responsibility for all his affairs until his death from cancer in 1989.

The medical bill at St. Joseph totaled $14,170. Claudia made consistent, monthly payments for nearly eight years. Distressed the balance was not decreasing as quickly as she anticipated, she stopped paying in August 1994. Accounts Management, Inc. (AMI), the successor in interest to the balance owed St. Joseph, brought suit for the remaining amount. Following a hearing, the circuit court granted AMI's motion for summary judgment. Claudia appeals believing genuine issues of fact persist on whether she has any obligation to pay Fredrick's medical bills because an unrecorded marriage is invalid, there is no official proof she was ever legally married to him, and his medical expenses were not "necessaries."

* * *

Analysis and Decision

1. Failure to Record Marriage License

After their marriage ceremony, Claudia evidently believed she was married to Fredrick. Now she feels the marriage should be deemed void as the license was never recorded. Our law makes recording mandatory. "After performing the ceremony, the person solemnizing the marriage shall deliver the marriage certificate to the persons married and return, within ten days, the license and record of marriage to the county register of deeds." SDCL 25–1–35. Then, the "register of deeds shall maintain. . . records of marriages solemnized in that register's county." SDCL 25–1–37. With the use of the word "shall" in SDCL 25–1–35 and–37, was it the Legislature's intent to require recording before a marriage is legitimized?

We aspire to preserve the sanctity of marriage and family, so when the validity of a marital union is challenged, we examine the pertinent legislative enactments with respectful care * * * These statutes should be construed to favor validation even when full compliance with statutory formalities may be deficient. * * * Only two states, Alaska and Oklahoma, have statutes which appear to provide that noncompliance with licensing requirements will render a marriage invalid. *See* Lynn D. Wardle et al., *Contemporary Family Law*, § 3.09, at 47 (1988).

Our law defines marriage as "consent" followed by "solemnization." SDCL 25–1–1. Although SDCL 25–1–29 provides that a "marriage must be solemnized, authenticated, and recorded as provided in this chapter," no statute makes recordation essential to legalize a marriage. Rather than the newlyweds, SDCL 25–1–35 commands "the person solemnizing the marriage" to deliver the license to the register of deeds and SDCL 25–1–37 specifically directs the register of deeds to "maintain. . .records of marriages solemnized in that register's county." Neither of these statutes require action or compliance by the parties to the marriage. With this in mind, we cannot imagine our legislators intended that the mere act of recording would be necessary to "perfect" the marital relationship as if akin to a UCC filing. If so, what would be the status of the parties during the interim between the ceremony and the recording?

The real question here is whether there was any genuine issue of fact about the parties' relationship. Competent evidence of a marriage may be proven by direct or circumstantial evidence. AMI submitted an affidavit from the secretary of the Big Bend Presbyterian Church, confirming Claudia and Fredrick were married by an ordained minister in the church. No record of the marriage can be found with the register of deeds in accord with SDCL 25–1–37, but Claudia and Fredrick did take out a valid license, exchanged vows in a marriage ceremony, and lived together as a married couple. Claudia signed the hospital admission and consent papers as "Claudia Klusman, wife," and later signed a petition swearing under oath she was married to Fredrick. No genuine issue of fact exists. Fredrick and Claudia were husband and wife.

2. Deceased Spouse's Medical Bills

Claudia believes the Legislature intended spouses to be liable for nothing more than food, clothing, and fuel. SDCL 25–2–11 provides:

> Every husband and wife shall be jointly and severally liable for the purchase price, if such price be stated or agreed upon at the time of purchase, and if not so stated or agreed upon, for the reasonable value of *all the necessaries of life*, consisting of food, clothing, and fuel purchased by either husband or wife for their family while they are living together as husband and wife.

(emphasis added). Her argument has facial merit if we apply the maxim of *expressio unius est exclusio alterius*, the enumeration of particular things excludes those things not mentioned. Yet, statutory rules of construction, applied senselessly, yield absurd results. Will a wife be responsible for her husband's fuel, but not his life saving medical treatment? If we accept this interpretation, then we cannot reconcile SDCL 25–7–4, which makes it a felony for able persons to neglect to provide medical care to their spouses.

> Every person with sufficient ability to provide for his or her spouse's support, or who is able to earn the means of the spouse's support, who intentionally abandons and leaves his or her spouse in a destitute condition, or who refuses or neglects to provide such spouse with necessary food, clothing, shelter or medical attendance, unless, by the spouse's misconduct, he or she is justified in abandoning the spouse or failing to so provide is guilty of a Class 6 felony.

In determining legislative intent, we must give words "a reasonable, natural, and practical meaning." Husbands and wives must stand accountable for each other's bills when third-party creditors provide necessaries to their respective spouses. That was the obvious intent behind these statutes—marriage as a partnership, with a duty to care for each other, hence the broad modifier "all" to the words "necessaries of life." * * * Other statutes also enforce a spouse's obligation to pay medical bills as Chief Justice Dunn recognized when he wrote for a unanimous Court in *Faulk County Mem'l Hosp. v. Neilan*, 269 N.W.2d 121, 123 (S.D.1978): "[W]e hold that under SDCL 25–7–1, 25–7–2 and 25–7–4 the general duty of a husband to support his wife is applicable and, therefore, Bernard is responsible for Blanche's hospital bills." Considering this overall statutory scheme, which applies to husbands and wives equally, a spouse's duty to pay for necessaries inescapably includes medical care and treatment.

* * *

Affirmed.

<hr>

Points for Discussion

a. Marriage Validation

The question sometimes arises whether a marriage that is solemnized without a license, or pursuant to a defective license, is valid. Many cases uphold the validity of such marriages. E.g. Carabetta v. Carabetta, 438 A.2d 109 (Conn. 1980); Levick v. MacDougall, 805 S.E.2d 775 (Va. 2017); State v. Denton, 983 P.2d 693 (Wash. Ct. App. 1999). See also N.Y. Dom. Rel. L. § 25 (2018). But see Moran v. Moran, 933 P.2d 1207 (Ariz. Ct.App.1996) (holding marriage invalid where ceremony was conducted without license); Becker v. Judd, 646 F.Supp.2d 923 (M.D. Tenn. 2009) (religious ceremony did not give rise to valid marriage where couple made deliberate choice not to obtain marriage license). The fact that a marriage is solemnized by a person not authorized to do so may not invalidate the marriage if either or both parties are not aware of the disqualification. E.g. Helfond v. Helfond, 280 N.Y.S.2d 990 (Sup. Ct. 1967).

b. Estoppel

The parties in this case acted in all respects as if married for five years. Should an estoppel doctrine be applied to bar Claudia from attacking the validity of her marriage? Would your answer be different if she had been challenging the validity of their marriage in a divorce or inheritance case? Estoppel and validation principles are discussed following the next case.

c. Spousal Necessaries

In *Accounts Management*, the validity of the marriage was asserted by a creditor seeking to collect a debt. Under the common law, a husband was required to pay debts incurred by his wife or children for "necessaries." Since the late 1960s, in many states, these obligations have been extended by statute to both husband and wife, in order to avoid discrimination based on sex. In what other legal contexts might someone other than a husband or wife seek to challenge or uphold the validity of a marriage?

Farah v. Farah

429 S.E.2d 626 (Va. Ct. App. 1993)

COLEMAN, JUDGE.

In this appeal from a declaratory judgment and divorce decree, we hold that a proxy marriage celebrated in England will not be recognized as a valid marriage in Virginia. Accordingly, we hold that the trial judge erred by declaring the Farahs' marriage to be valid in Virginia based on the trial judge's finding that the marriage was valid under Islamic or Pakistani law. Thus, because no valid marriage existed under Virginia law, the trial judge erred by granting the parties a divorce and by equitably distributing their property pursuant to Code § 20–107.3. We remand the case to the trial court to vacate the declaratory judgment and divorce decree and for such further proceedings as may be necessary.

Ahmed Farah is a citizen of Algeria. Naima Mansur is a citizen of Pakistan. They have resided in Virginia for several years. They belong to different Muslim sects. They signed a proxy marriage form (the "Nikah") that is used to solemnize marriages by members of the Ahmadiyya Muslim community. The "Nikah" or marriage contract also provided that Ahmed Farah would receive a deferred payment of $20,000 as the wife's dower. On July 31, 1988, Ahmed Farah and Naima Mansur purported to enter into a Muslim marriage through their proxies in London, England. Neither Ahmed Farah nor Naima Mansur was present in England during the ceremony. No marriage certificate was issued by any court or governmental authority in England. According to testimony at trial, under Islamic law and Pakistani law, which generally recognizes Islamic religious law, the parties to the "Nikah" are legally married once the proxy ceremony is complete. During the ceremony, a member of the Muslim community solemnizes the marriage in the presence of the parties' proxy representatives and their witnesses.

What's That?

A **proxy marriage** is a marriage contracted or celebrated through agents who represent one or both parties. Only a few states in the United States allow proxy marriages. See, e.g., <u>Mont. Code § 40-1-301 (4)</u> (allowing proxy marriage if one party is either a resident of Montana or a member of the U.S. armed forces on active duty).

Approximately one month after the "Nikah" was solemnized in London, the parties went to Pakistan for three days, where Naima Mansur's father held a reception (the "Rukhsati") in their honor. Under the tradition of the wife's Islamic sect, the "Rukhsati" symbolizes the sending away of the bride with her husband. The parties returned to Virginia in September of 1988 and purchased a house that was jointly titled in both names. They had intended to have a civil marriage ceremony when they returned to the United States, but they never did so. They lived together in Virginia as husband and wife for about one year when, on June 29, 1989, they separated, and Ahmed Farah filed a bill to have the marriage declared void and Naima Mansur filed for divorce and equitable distribution.

At trial, Ahmed Farah introduced testimony from a solicitor of the Supreme Court of England and Wales that a marriage performed in England is void *ab initio* unless all statutory formalities of the Marriage Act are satisfied. The Marriage Act of England requires issuance of a marriage license, fifteen-day residence in England by one of the parties before the marriage, and the issuance of a certificate of marriage by a duly authorized registrar of marriages. Ahmed Farah and Naima Mansur, in their proxy marriage, did not obtain a special license nor did they comply with any of the formalities required by the Marriage Act of England.

Naima Mansur contends that, even though they did not comply with the requirements of the Marriage Act of England, her marriage to Ahmed Farah is valid and must be recognized in Virginia. She asserts that the English law governing her marriage is not applicable because the marriage ceremony was completed in Pakistan by conducting the "Rukhsati," and, furthermore, that the proxy marriage conducted in London was valid under Pakistani law, which recognizes a valid Islamic marriage.

A marriage that is valid under the law of the state or country where it is celebrated is valid in Virginia, unless it is repugnant to public policy. *Kleinfield v. Veruki*, 7 Va.App. 183, 186, 372 S.E.2d 407, 409 (1988). A marriage that is void where it was celebrated is void everywhere. *Spradlin v. State Compensation Commissioner*, 113 S.E.2d 832, 834 (W.Va.1960). Although the trial judge found that the marriage was celebrated in England, he ruled, however, that

> the marriage of the parties took place in London under Moslem law which was applicable to the parties, that the marriage by proxy is sanctioned under Moslem law and that the law of the state of Pakistan sanctions marriages performed under the personal law of the parties which in this case was Moslem law * * *. The Commonwealth of Virginia recognizes the marriage as consistent with Islamic law and therefore as valid by a state, viz., Pakistan, to which the comity of recognition is due.

The trial court granted the parties a divorce based upon a separation of more than one year and ordered equitable distribution of their jointly owned marital residence by evenly dividing the equity of approximately $62,000. The fact that Pakistan may recognize the parties' marriage as valid because it was valid according to Islamic religious law does not control the issue of the validity of the marriage under Virginia law. In Virginia, whether a marriage is valid is controlled by the law of the place where the marriage was celebrated. *Kleinfield*, 7 Va.App. at 186, 372 S.E.2d at 409. Thus, the question is whether aspects of the marriage were performed in Pakistan, as the wife contends, so that it was a marriage celebrated in Pakistan, or whether it was a valid marriage celebrated in England.

Take Note!

The court gives the traditional rule for determining the validity of a marriage: a marriage valid in the place of celebration is valid everywhere.

The only aspect of the Muslim ceremony that occurred in Pakistan was the "Rukhsati," or reception, which the evidence showed is merely a custom that has no legal significance and is not a formality required for a legal marriage in Pakistan. Furthermore, at trial, evidence was presented that even Pakistan would not recognize the proxy marriage in England as valid because, contrary to Islamic law, the parties had not signed the "Nikah" at the same time and also because the wife was a member of a controversial Muslim sect that the Pakistani government did not recognize. No evidence established that a marriage ceremony, or any part of it, occurred in Pakistan or that it was celebrated in any jurisdiction other than England.

Because the marriage was contracted and celebrated in England, the validity of the marriage is determined according to English law. *Id.* at 186, 372 S.E.2d at 409. The Marriage Act of England requires that a marriage be contracted in strict compliance with its statutory formalities. None of those formalities were complied with in the proxy marriage. Therefore, the marriage was void *ab initio* in England and is void in Virginia.

Furthermore, Ahmed Farah and Naima Mansur did not enter into a common-law marriage that Virginia recognizes. Virginia does not recognize common-law marriages where the relationship is created in Virginia. *Offield v. Davis,* 100 Va. 250, 253, 40 S.E. 910, 914 (1902). Virginia does recognize a common-law marriage that is valid under the laws of the jurisdiction where the common-law relationship was created. *Kleinfield,* 7 Va.App. at 186, 372 S.E.2d at 409; *Metropolitan Life Ins. Co. v. Holding,* 293 F.Supp. 854, 857 (E.D.Va.1968). There is no evidence, however, that Ahmed Farah and Naima Mansur created a common-law marriage by entering into a relationship as husband and wife in any jurisdiction that recognizes common-law marriages.

For these reasons, we hold that Ahmed Farah and Naima Mansur never entered into a marriage that is recognized as valid in Virginia. Accordingly, no marriage existed from which the trial judge could grant a divorce according to Virginia law. Therefore, we reverse the trial judge's declaratory judgment finding that the parties entered into a valid marriage, and we remand the matter for the circuit court to vacate the divorce decree and order of equitable distribution. We leave the parties to seek such other remedies as are appropriate to determine and resolve their property rights.

Reversed and remanded.

Points for Discussion

a. Choice of Law Principles

Farah recites the traditional choice of law rule of **lex loci celebrationis**, sometimes referred to as **lex loci contractus**: the validity of a marriage is determined based on the law of the place where it is celebrated or contracted. Statutes in a number of states incorporate this principle. See also Uniform Marriage and Divorce Act § 210, 9A U.L.A. (Part 1) 194 (1998).

A different rule is included in Restatement (Second) of Conflict of Laws § 283 (1971), which states that the "validity of a marriage is to be determined by the local law of the state which, with respect to the particular issue, has the most significant relationship to the spouses and the marriage." Restatement §6 lists these factors as bearing on the question of significant relationship: (a) the needs of the interstate and international systems; (b) the relevant policies of the forum; (c) the relevant policies of other interested states and the relative interests of those states in the determination of the particular issue; (d) the protection of justified expectations; (e) the basic policies underlying the particular field of law; (f) certainty, predictability and uniformity of result; (g) ease in the determination and application of the law to be applied. See, e.g., Donlann v. Macgurn, 55 P.3d 74 (Ariz. Ct.App.2002) (applying § 283 to uphold validity in Arizona of marriage that was invalid under the law of Mexico, where it was celebrated). The results in *Farah* could be found either to support or reject the Restatement approach, since the Restatement does not indicate which factors should be given the greatest weight. Which of the listed factors are most important in this case? When the Restatement speaks of protecting expectations, to whose expectations is it referring?

b. Marriage Validation

A number of English cases have held that in some circumstances, English common law marriage principles could serve to validate foreign marriages contracted without the proper formalities. In Taczanowska (Orse. Roth) v. Taczanowski, [1957] P. 301, 2 All E.R. 563, the court refused to annul a marriage performed in Italy at the end of World War II by a Roman Catholic priest serving as a Polish army chaplain. The bride and groom were both Polish nationals, the bride a civilian refugee and the groom an officer in the Polish army serving in Italy. The couple did not observe the marriage formalities of either Poland or Italy. They became domiciled in England a year later, and had one child in that year. The Court of Appeal upheld the marriage as a common law marriage under English law, notwithstanding the foreign nationality and domicile of the parties at the date of the ceremony. Other English cases have reached similar results. Cf. Lazarewicz v. Lazarewicz, [1962] P. 171, 2 All E.R. 5 (marriage invalid where parties clearly chose to submit to Italian law). A number of U.S. cases reach the same conclusion, upholding the validity of marriages solemnized in a traditional or religious ceremony in another country, despite a failure to comply with the formalities required in the place of celebration. See, e.g., Xiong ex rel. Edmondson v. Xiong, 648 N.W.2d 900 (Wis. Ct. App. 2002); Amsellem v. Amsellem, 730 N.Y.S.2d 212 (Sup. Ct. 2001).

Professor Alfred Ehrenzweig defended the result in *Taczanowska* on a principle of validation: if some reasonable argument can be made in favor of recognizing a marriage, that should be done, rather than frustrating the parties' expectations by applying technical rules which are not based on important policies. Alfred Ehrenzweig, Conflict of Laws, 378–379 (1962). Could the Virginia Court of Appeals have upheld the marriage in *Farah* on this basis?

c. Estoppel

There are strong public policy reasons for upholding marriages despite defects in solemnization, particularly when one of the parties raises the challenge. In <u>Yun v. Yun, 908 S.W.2d 787 (Mo. Ct. App. 1995)</u> the court rejected husband's argument that there was no valid marriage where a license was not properly obtained prior to the ceremony. Among other grounds for its decision, the court concluded that he should be equitably estopped from denying the validity of the marriage. "Mr. Yun engaged in a marriage ceremony, cohabitation, and other conduct consistent with the existence of a marriage relationship. He obtained the benefits of marriage to Mrs. Yun, and lived the life of a married man. He participated in bringing children into the marriage and did not disavow the existence of a marriage. . . . Mr. Yun never, until after Mrs. Yun decided to seek dissolution, informed Mrs. Yun that he would take the position there was no marriage. He now seeks to avoid the marriage only to deprive Mrs. Yun of the relief which the law would provide her." Should this estoppel principle have been invoked in *Farah*?

Engagement

Under the English common law, a broken engagement might be followed by a lawsuit for **breach of promise to marry**. During the sixteenth century, when marriages among the wealthy were often extensively negotiated property transactions, the remedies in such an action were similar to those for breach of a commercial contract. In later years, the action came to look more like a tort action, in which damages might be given for injury to the plaintiff's feelings, health, and reputation and for expenses such as costs incurred in preparing for a wedding.

Widespread criticism of the suit for breach of promise to marry (as well as related tort actions including **seduction** and **alienation of affections**) led to the passage of **heartbalm statutes** abolishing these claims in many jurisdictions in the United States beginning in the 1930s. See <u>Gilbert v. Barkes, 987 S.W.2d 772 (Ky.1999)</u> (listing 28 other jurisdictions in which the action has been abolished.) The action is still recognized in some jurisdictions; see, e.g., <u>Finch v. Dasgupta, 555 S.E.2d 22 (Ga. Ct. App. 2001)</u>. See also 1 Homer H. Clark, Jr., Domestic Relations, 1–31 (2d ed. 1987), and Rebecca Tushnet, Note, <u>*Rules of Engagement,* 107 Yale L.J. 2583 (1998)</u>.

Another type of controversy that may follow a broken engagement concerns ownership of gifts such as engagement rings. Gifts made in contemplation of marriage are usually understood to be conditional upon the marriage taking place and may be recovered if it does not. In some jurisdictions, a donor who breaks an engagement without justification is not permitted to recover a gift such as a ring; e.g. Albinger v. Harris, 48 P.3d 711 (Mont.2002). Other courts have adopted a "no fault" approach, requiring return of engagement gifts without regard to which party terminated the engagement. E.g. Cooper v. Smith, 800 N.E.2d 372 (Ohio Ct. App. 2003) (treating engagement ring as conditional gift that must be returned to donor, but other engagement gifts as irrevocable). For an empirical analysis, linking the growth of the custom of diamond engagement rings with abolition of the action for breach of promise to marry, see Margaret F. Brinig, *Rings and Promises*, 6 J. L. Econ. & Org. 203 (1990).

2. Common Law and Putative Marriage

The doctrines of common law marriage and putative marriage are expressions of the marriage validation principle, which seeks to uphold marriages whenever possible. These doctrines serve an important remedial purpose, allowing courts to extend the legal rights and obligations of marriage to couples who behaved as if they were married. In this respect, the doctrines are similar to other rules and presumptions in favor of marriage considered in this chapter. In addition, common law marriage served to legitimate the children of couples who had not complied with marriage licensing requirements. The Supreme Court considered these arguments in Meister v. Moore, 96 U.S. 76 (1877).

Cohabitation alone, even for an extended period of time, does not give rise to a common law marriage in any state. The couple must have an agreement to be married, expressed in words of the present tense. This is often proved indirectly by circumstantial evidence of cohabitation and repute: that the couple lived together and that they held themselves out in the community as husband and wife.

Although once widely recognized, fewer than a dozen jurisdictions in the United States still permit common-law marriage. In states that have abolished common law marriage relatively recently, these issues still arise with respect to marriages entered into before the date when common law marriage was abolished. In addition, states that never permitted common law marriage or abolished it many years ago often recognize common-law marriages from other states under the *lex loci contractus* rule.

Lewis v. Anderson

173 S.W.3d 556 (Tex. App. 2005)

Opinion by JUSTICE MOSELEY.

In this case, we must determine whether the evidence supports the jury's finding that a common law or informal marriage existed between Mindy Jane Anderson and Harold Ray Lewis. In three issues, Lewis claims the evidence is legally and factually insufficient to support that finding and that the trial court improperly commented on the weight of the evidence in its instructions to the jury. We affirm the trial court's judgment.

BACKGROUND

In 1998, Anderson left Lewis and filed for divorce. After Lewis denied the existence of a marriage, the trial court conducted a separate trial on the existence of an informal marriage. A jury found that Anderson and Lewis were informally married and the trial court entered a judgment declaring the existence of an informal marriage. This judgment was later severed from the divorce action. After the trial court denied his motion for judgment notwithstanding the verdict and for new trial, Lewis perfected this appeal.

The record indicates that Anderson, a nurse, and Lewis, a medical doctor, were married in a formal ceremony in December 1974. They bought a house in 1976. Lewis testified that in 1976 or 1977, it became clear to him that a divorce was necessary. One of his reasons was that Anderson was reluctant to sign documents about financial matters. Anderson resisted the divorce, saying she was committed to the marriage. Lewis determined that divorce was absolutely necessary because he would not allow his "financial situation to be jeopardized by her emotional state." Lewis prepared the divorce papers himself without a lawyer and Anderson signed the waiver of service and divorce decree. Lewis presented the documents to the court and the divorce decree was signed on May 26, 1977.

Following the signing of the divorce decree, Anderson conveyed her interest in the residence to Lewis in August 1977. However, except for a few weeks in 1978 when Lewis (according to Anderson) locked her out of the house, Anderson and Lewis lived together for the next twenty years, until 1998. During this time, they joined a church as "Hal and Mindy Lewis" and adopted two children. Documents in both adoption proceedings referred to Anderson and Lewis as husband and wife, "Dr. and Mrs. Lewis," or "Harold and Mindy Lewis."

The couple attended Lewis family functions together and celebrated wedding anniversaries. Lewis wore a wedding ring until the couple separated in 1998. The record contains one tax return filed by the couple in 1997 as married filing jointly. Lewis could not remember whether earlier tax returns were filed jointly or singly, but said the 1997 return was a mistake and he had notified the IRS of the mistake.

Anderson testified she did not remember the 1977 divorce decree until sometime after this suit was filed in 1998. However, she wrote to Lewis sometime in 1978 about the termination of their marriage the previous year. She did not dispute the divorce or her signature on the waiver and divorce decree. The jury found the parties were informally married as of September 21, 1982, the date they filed the petition to adopt their first child.

DISCUSSION

Lewis's first and second issues challenge the legal and factual sufficiency of the evidence to support the finding of an informal marriage. Specifically, he challenges the sufficiency of the evidence of an agreement to be married.

1. Legal Sufficiency of the Evidence

* * *

A common law, or informal, marriage may be proved by evidence that: (1) the parties agreed to be married and after the agreement; (2) they lived together in Texas as husband and wife; and (3) there represented to others that they were married. TEX. FAM. CODE ANN. § 2.401(a)(2) (Vernon 1998). The proponent of a common law marriage may prove an agreement to be married by circumstantial as well as direct evidence. *Russell v. Russell,* 865 S.W.2d 929, 933 (Tex.1993). The legislature has not excluded the finding of a tacit agreement to be married, but circumstantial evidence must be "more convincing" than before the 1989 amendments to the statute. Direct evidence of an agreement to be married is not required. Evidence of cohabitation and representations that the couple is married may constitute circumstantial evidence of an agreement to be married, but "the circumstances of each case must be determined based upon its own facts."

Lewis makes three arguments in support of his first issue: (a) the evidence conclusively negates an agreement to be married; (b) there is no evidence of the holding out of a new marriage; and (c) there is no evidence of the date of the marriage found by the jury.

(a) Evidence of Agreement to be Married

The record contains evidence that after the 1977 divorce, Lewis and Anderson lived together as husband and wife in Texas and represented to others that they were presently married. In 1978, Anderson wrote Lewis a note expressing regret over their situation and acknowledging "the termination of our marriage and the resulting property settlement." She also stated, "I continue to be committed to a marriage with you and our future." After a few weeks of separation in 1978, the couple resumed living together and continued to live together for the next twenty years. They joined a church together in 1979 as "Hal and Mindy Lewis" and Anderson heard Lewis tell the pastor that they were married. The pastor testified the couple represented themselves as "Hal and Mindy Lewis" and he knew both of them by the name Lewis.

In 1982, the couple hired an attorney to adopt their first child in a private adoption. Correspondence from the adoption attorney referred to them as "Dr. and Mrs. Lewis." Anderson testified that Lewis told the attorney they were married. Lewis admitted he reviewed the lawyer's correspondence and never told the lawyer they were not married or were divorced. The petitions for termination of the parental rights of the birth mother and for adoption of the child signed by their attorney identified Anderson and Lewis as husband and wife. Correspondence arranging the social study for the adoption was addressed to "Dr. & Mrs. Harold Ray Lewis." Anderson heard Lewis tell the social worker they were married. She also heard Lewis testify in court at the adoption hearing that they were married. The decree of adoption signed by the judge on February 11, 1983 recites that "On this day Petitioners, Harold Ray Lewis and wife, Malinda Jane Lewis, appeared in person and by attorney and announced ready for trial." Lewis testified that he did not tell his attorney, the social worker, or the adoption court that he and Anderson were not married and were divorced because he did not feel it was important or relevant.

In 1985, the couple adopted another child through Hope Cottage. They signed a custody agreement with Hope Cottage as "Harold Ray Lewis and Malinda J. Anderson Lewis, husband and wife respectively." The document obligated them to reimburse Hope Cottage for expenses of the child and mother in the amount of $5000. Anderson heard Lewis tell Hope Cottage and testify in court that they were married. The adoption decree identified the parties as "Harold and Mindy Lewis." Anderson also heard Lewis tell their children that they were married, but never heard him tell the children they were divorced. Anderson testified that she and Lewis represented themselves as married to the children's schools.

Lewis argues there is no evidence of an agreement to be married after the divorce and that the evidence conclusively shows the opposite—that the couple did not agree to be married. Lewis points to some of Anderson's testimony that after the divorce, she and Lewis did not have discussions that they were "common law married" and that the only date she asserted they were married was the date of their 1974 ceremonial marriage. He also relies on Anderson's testimony that she felt her agreement to be married to Lewis began in 1974 and never ended. Lewis testified that there was no agreement to be married after the divorce.

Anderson also testified, however, that during the period after the divorce, she felt they were husband and wife. She said, "we had an agreement that we were married every year. We celebrated our anniversary every year." During cross-examination, she testified:

> Q I'm sorry. You had discussions between 1977 and 1998 that you were informally married?
> A We agreed that we were.
> Q Is that what you just testified to?
> A We had—we agreed that we were married. We didn't have a discussion as to whether it was formal or informal.
> Q I apologize, I'm a little lost. Just a moment ago you testified, we had discussions that we were informally and formally married. Is that accurate?
> A That's not accurate.
> Q Okay. Thank you.
> A We had discussions—
> Q Did you—
> A —that we were married.

While Anderson agreed that she and Lewis had not discussed being "common law married," she testified that they did agree they were married and had an agreement they were married every year. After the 1977 divorce, she did not believe there was any reason to talk about a common law marriage with or remarrying Lewis, "[b]ecause he told me we were married."

The issue here of course is not whether Anderson agreed to be married—she testified that she agreed to be married to Lewis from 1974 until she filed this action. The issue is whether there is some evidence that after the divorce, Lewis also agreed to be married to Anderson. Anderson's testimony that in the years after the divorce, she and Lewis agreed they were married and that Lewis told her they were married is at least some evidence that Lewis did agree to be married to Anderson after the divorce. That Anderson did not remember the divorce later, does not negate an agreement to be married after the divorce. *See Dalworth Trucking Co. v. Bulen*, 924 S.W.2d 728, 737 (Tex.App.-Texarkana 1996, no writ) ("She may have been mistaken about the effectiveness of the divorce decree, but so long as she and Ricky met the requirements of a common law marriage sometime after the divorce and before he died, they were capable of entering into a new marriage after the acknowledged divorce."). It is undisputed that Lewis knew about the divorce; yet there is evidence that afterwards he told Anderson and others they were married. Anderson wanted to be married to Lewis and there is evidence that Lewis agreed with her after the divorce.

In addition to Anderson's direct testimony of an agreement to be married, the evidence of cohabitation and representations to others is circumstantial evidence of an agreement to be married. *See Russell*, 865 S.W.2d at 933 (stating agreement to be married may be shown by direct or circumstantial evidence or both). The jury could reasonably infer that Lewis and Anderson agreed to be married after their divorce.

* * *

Lewis relies primarily on *Gary v. Gary*, 490 S.W.2d 929 (Tex.Civ.App.-Tyler 1973, writ ref'd n.r.e.), a case decided some twenty years before *Russell*. However, each case must be decided on its own facts, *Russell*, 865 S.W.2d at 933, and we conclude *Gary* is distinguishable. * * *

The evidence of an express agreement, the lack of doubt about the validity of the divorce, the long cohabitation and adoption of children, the representations of a present marriage for an extended time, and Lewis's willingness to sign or accept without question legal documents referring to an existing marriage with Anderson distinguish this case from *Gary*. We also distinguish *Gary* because the evidence of holding out in this case is more convincing than in *Gary*. *See Russell*, 865 S.W.2d at 932 ("evidence of holding-out must be more convincing than before the 1989 [amendment]") (quoting Joseph W. McKnight, *Family Law: Husband and Wife*, 44 SW.L.J. 1, 2–3 (1990)).

(b) Holding out of a New Marriage

Lewis argues that the fact that he and Anderson did not tell anyone they were divorced, negates a holding out of a subsequent informal marriage. He argues the evidence they represented they were married following the divorce, was a holding out of the earlier ceremonial marriage (that was dissolved by the 1977 divorce). We disagree. While the parties did not discuss the divorce,[2] the divorce decree was a matter of public record and its validity was never disputed. As a matter of law, the 1974 ceremonial marriage was terminated. Thus, when the parties later represented that they were presently married, the representation was of a new, current marriage rather than the old, previously terminated ceremonial marriage.

---

[2]   There is evidence in the record that Lewis told his brother at some point that he and Anderson were divorced, and Lewis testified that Anderson told the staff of Hope Cottage during the second adoption that she and Lewis were divorced.

* * * Lewis argues it would be reasonable to infer from the evidence that the parties represented they remained married under the 1974 ceremonial marriage after the divorce. We disagree. There is evidence that after the divorce, both Lewis and Anderson represented to others that they were presently married. Some of this evidence was disputed; however, a reasonable jury could disbelieve the disputed evidence and resolve the disputes in favor of the finding of an agreement and holding out. Although there was evidence that the parties submitted the 1974 marriage certificate to the social worker in one or both of the adoptions, the undisputed facts remain that the ceremonial marriage was terminated by the 1977 divorce and that they represented they were presently married at the time of the adoptions.

Because the earlier ceremonial marriage had been terminated by the divorce, it is not reasonable to infer that the later representations of a present marriage were representations of the terminated marriage instead of a new agreement to be married. Certainly Lewis was aware of the divorce and the termination of the ceremonial marriage. The evidence that he later represented to others that he was presently married to Anderson leads to only one logical inference—the representation was of a new post-divorce marriage. Any inference that the parties could unilaterally nullify the divorce decree by holding out that they remained married under the 1974 ceremonial marriage would not reasonable.

(c) Date of the Marriage

Lewis argues there is no evidence to support the jury's finding that they were informally married on September 21, 1982, the date the first adoption petition was filed. This date is significant because the petition was a representation by the couple through their attorney that they were husband and wife. The couple had been living together since 1978. Anderson testified that she and Lewis had an agreement they were married every year. There is evidence that Lewis told the attorney who prepared the petition that he and Anderson were married. Evidence that the parties continued to represent that they were married when they later adopted a second child tends to corroborate that they were married by the time of the first adoption. Thus, there is evidence that by the time the first adoption petition was filed, all of the elements of an informal marriage existed. *See Winfield v. Renfro,* 821 S.W.2d 640, 646 (Tex.App.-Houston [1st Dist.] 1991, writ denied) (elements may occur at different times, but until all three exist there is no common law marriage).

(d) Conclusion

Viewing the evidence in the light most favorable to the jury's finding, we conclude the evidence is such that reasonable minds could differ in their conclusions about whether Lewis and Anderson had an informal marriage. Crediting all favorable evidence that reasonable jurors could believe and disregarding all contrary evidence except that which they could not ignore, we conclude the evidence is legally sufficient to support the jury's verdict. We resolve Lewis's first issue against him.

2. Factual Sufficiency of the Evidence

Lewis also argues the evidence is factually insufficient. * * *

Lewis argues there is no direct evidence of an agreement to be married nor of a holding out of a post-divorce informal marriage. We have already concluded there is legally sufficient evidence of an agreement to be married after the divorce and that the representations that the couple was married in the years following the divorce was a representation of a current marriage post-dating the termination of the ceremonial marriage. We do not repeat that discussion.

In support of the factual insufficiency issue, Lewis points to his testimony that he and Anderson never agreed to be married following their divorce and never discussed whether they were married or were going to be married. He also testified that in 1994, he made arrangements to remarry Anderson, but she refused, saying she would not consent to being married to him. He denied ever representing to anyone (their pastor, lawyer, the social workers, or the adoption courts) that he was married to Anderson after the divorce. He testified that Anderson told the representatives of Hope Cottage that she and Lewis were divorced. He said the 1997 joint tax return was a mistake and he had contacted the IRS about the mistake.

There is also evidence that Lewis and Anderson kept separate banking arrangements and that Anderson continued to use her maiden name. For example, in 1980, Anderson purchased a house individually as "Mindy Anderson, a single woman." However, when Anderson sold the house in 1985, the deed referred to her as "Mindy Anderson Lewis," but was signed on her behalf by her agent.

The record indicates much of the testimony was conflicting. The jury is the sole judge of the credibility of the witnesses and the weight to be given their testimony. While not always clear and consistent, Anderson did testify to an agreement and holding out. It was up to the jury "to resolve conflicts and inconsistencies in the testimony of any one witness as well as in the testimony of different witnesses." *Ford v. Panhandle & Santa Fe Ry. Co.*, 151 Tex. 538, 542, 252 S.W.2d 561, 563 (1952). After reviewing all the evidence, we cannot say the evidence is so weak that the jury finding of an informal marriage on September 21, 1982 is clearly wrong and unjust. Thus the evidence is factually sufficient to support the verdict. We resolve Lewis's second issue against him.

* * *

We affirm the trial court's judgment.

Points for Discussion

a. *Lewis*

What evidence served to support the finding of common law marriage in this case? What evidence tended to negate it? What evidence do you think was most persuasive to the jury? In your view, does the fact that the couple divorced in 1977 make this case easier or more difficult to decide? Would an estoppel theory have been preferable here?

b. Proof of Common Law Marriage

Under the leading English authority on common law marriage, Dalrymple v. Dalrymple, 2 Hagg.Cons. 53, 161 Eng.Rep. 665 (1811) the only requirement is proof of " * * * the consent of two parties expressed in words of present mutual acceptance * * * ." Courts in the United States sometimes find a common law marriage based on evidence that the parties were thought by their friends and relatives to be married, and that they referred to each other as husband and wife in official documents or otherwise, even though there was little or no evidence of an explicit agreement to be married. See, e.g., In re Marriage of Winegard, 257 N.W.2d 609 (Iowa 1977); In re Estate of Benjamin, 311 N.E.2d 495 (N.Y. 1974). This has been true even under the Texas statute applied in *Lewis* and reprinted below. How did the court in *Lewis* explain the elements required under the Texas statute?

In cases in which there is clear evidence of a present agreement to be husband and wife, but the parties either never told people they were married, or they told some people they were married and told others they were not married, results are mixed, with some cases finding that a common law marriage existed. See, e.g., Ridley v. Grandison, 389 S.E.2d 746 (Ga. 1990). The Utah statute adopted in 1987 sets forth requirements to establish an "unsolemnized marriage" including cohabitation, the mutual assumption of marital rights, duties and obligations, and a general reputation as husband and wife. The statute, which was enacted for the purpose of preventing welfare fraud, does not require evidence of a present agreement to be married. See Clark v. Clark, 27 P.3d 538 (Utah), cert. den., 534 U.S. 1066 (2001).

An Islamic religious ceremony followed by representation in the community that the parties were married was held to constitute a valid common law marriage by <u>State v. Phelps, 652 N.E.2d 1032 (Ohio Ct. App. 1995)</u>, so that the wife was incompetent to testify against the husband in a criminal case. If Virginia had recognized common law marriage, would the parties in the *Farah* case have had a valid common law marriage?

Texas Family Code § 2.401 (2018): Proof of Informal Marriage

(a) In a judicial, administrative, or other proceeding, the marriage of a man and woman may be proved by evidence that:

(1) a declaration of their marriage has been signed as provided by this subchapter; or

(2) the man and woman agreed to be married and after the agreement they lived together in this state as husband and wife and there represented to others that they were married.

(b) If a proceeding in which a marriage is to be proved as provided by Subsection (a)(2) is not commenced before the second anniversary of the date on which the parties separated and ceased living together, it is rebuttably presumed that the parties did not enter into an agreement to be married.

(c) A person under 18 years of age may not:

(1) be a party to an informal marriage; or

(2) execute a declaration of informal marriage under Section 2.402.

(d) A person may not be a party to an informal marriage or execute a declaration of an informal marriage if the person is presently married to a person who is not the other party to the informal marriage or declaration of an informal marriage, as applicable.

---

c. Common Law Marriage Jurisdictions

Common law marriages can still be contracted in the jurisdictions shown in the chart below. Although New York no longer recognizes common law marriage, it does recognize a marriage contracted by a written, signed, witnessed and acknowledged document. <u>N.Y.Dom.Rel.L. § 11(4) (2018)</u>. In New Hampshire, a statute provides that: "Persons cohabiting and acknowledging each other as husband and wife, and generally reputed to be such, for the period of 3 years, and until the decease of one of them, shall thereafter be deemed to have been legally married." N.H. Rev. Stat. § 457:39 (2018).

Common Law Marriage Jurisdictions	
Colorado	**Oklahoma** But see Okla. Stat. Ann. tit. 43, § 1 (2018)
District of Columbia	**Rhode Island**
Iowa See Iowa Code Ann. § 595.11 (2018)	**South Carolina**
Kansas But see Kan. Stat. Ann. § 23–2502 (2018)	**Texas** See Texas Family Code § 2.401 (2018)
Montana See Mont. Code Ann. §§ 26–1–602(30), 40–1–403 (2018).	**Utah** See Utah Code Ann. § 30–1–4.5(2) (2018)

In recent years, common law marriage has been abolished by statute in Alabama (as of Jan. 1, 2017), and Pennsylvania (as of Jan. 1, 2005). These states continue to recognize common law marriages that commenced before the dates when the laws took effect. What are the policy arguments against recognizing common law marriages? Does common law marriage encourage fraud and perjury, or debase conventional marriage? What policy arguments support continuing or restoring recognition for common law marriage? See Cynthia Grant Bowman, *A Feminist Proposal to Bring Back Common Law Marriage*, 75 Or. L. Rev. 709 (1996); Note, *Common Law Marriage and Unmarried Cohabitation: An Old Solution to a New Problem*, 39 U. Pitt. L. Rev. 579 (1978).

d. Common Law Marriage and Same-Sex Couples

Under *Obergefell*, states must extend same-sex couples access to marriage on the same terms as opposite-sex couples. This includes common law marriage, where that is recognized. See Ranolls v. Dewling, 223 F. Supp. 3d 613 (E.D. Tex. 2016), which read the Texas informal marriage statute reprinted above to include same-sex couples. *Ranolls* and other cases also ruled that *Obergefell* should be applied retroactively to common law marriage claims. See id. at 622–24; see also Estate of Carter, 159 A.3d 970 (Pa. Super. Ct. 2017).

Problem 1-8

Two young graduate students, Hank and Winnie, begin living together in a state that recognizes common law marriage. Although they believe that marriage is an immoral restraint on individual freedom, they begin to represent themselves as married in order to make it possible to live together in the university's family housing and to make Winnie eligible for the lower resident tuition rate. Hank and Winnie also tell their parents that they have gotten married. After living in this way for three years, Hank is killed in an automobile accident. May Winnie recover as a surviving spouse under the wrongful death statute in the state? May Winnie take Hank's property against his will? If Winnie or Hank had consulted you after they began living together in this way, what would you have advised them about their legal rights? (Cf. Schrader v. Schrader, 484 P.2d 1007 (Kan. 1971).)

Problem 1-9

Assume that Hank and Winnie move in together in the circumstances described above, but that before they do so they execute a notarized "Affidavit of Common Law Marriage" prepared by the university housing office. If they live together for three years and then separate, are they required to get a divorce before marrying again? If Winnie has significant assets, can Hank seek a division of property? (See Bell v. Ferraro, 849 A.2d 1233 (Pa. Super. Ct. 2004).)

Renshaw v. Heckler

787 F.2d 50 (2nd Cir. 1986)

GEORGE C. PRATT, CIRCUIT JUDGE:

This appeal presents a single question: did the Secretary of Health and Human Services and the district court err in determining that, under Pennsylvania law, plaintiff Edith L. Renshaw was not the common-law wife of the decedent Albert Renshaw, and therefore not entitled to widow's insurance benefits under Title II of the Social Security Act. Finding that Edith and Albert Renshaw had entered into a valid common-law marriage under the laws of the Commonwealth of Pennsylvania, we reverse the decision of the district court and remand to the Secretary for action consistent with this opinion.

BACKGROUND

After a brief courtship following their respective divorces from other individuals, Albert and Edith Renshaw began living together on July 5, 1958 in Baltimore, Maryland. Although the couple did not have a formal ceremonial marriage, Mrs. Renshaw testified that when she and Mr. Renshaw began living together they agreed to live "just as though [they] were married" and that they considered themselves "husband and wife". The evidence supports her assertion.

Edith immediately adopted the last name Renshaw and a short time later, changed the name on her social security card—the only identification she had at that time—to reflect her new status. The couple told friends and relatives that they had been married, and introduced each other to relatives, friends, and acquaintances as husband and wife.

Mr. Renshaw gave Mrs. Renshaw a wedding band shortly after they began to live together, and throughout the 21 years they lived together they celebrated July 5 as their marriage anniversary. The couple never separated or broke up, and Mrs. Renshaw testified that neither ever had relationships with others during this time. Moreover, the couple filed joint tax returns as husband and wife, and Mr. Renshaw listed Mrs. Renshaw as his wife and beneficiary on his life insurance policy.

Immediately after their marriage the Renshaws lived in Maryland for several months. After that, they moved to Buffalo, New York, where they lived for the next twenty years. During this time, the couple had one child, Lorna Gail Renshaw.

On approximately eight occasions between 1968 and 1975, the Renshaws drove to Virginia and North Carolina to visit relatives. Since the visits required a lengthy drive each way, the Renshaws always spent the night at the Port Motel in Port Treverton, Pennsylvania, a state that recognizes common-law marriage. Their daughter always accompanied them on these trips; on occasions when Mr. Renshaw's mother was in Buffalo, she also traveled with them.

It is unknown whether the couple signed the register as husband and wife since the motel records were unavailable and since Mrs. Renshaw never accompanied her husband to the motel office when he signed the guest register. However, she did recall hearing him make reservations by phone and specifying the date and the fact that he would be there with himself, his wife, and his daughter.

While at the motel in Pennsylvania, the Renshaws would check into their room, eat dinner at the restaurant, walk around the motel grounds, retire for the evening, and continue their journey the next morning. With the exception of a coincidental meeting with her brother, who believed that she and Mr. Renshaw were legally married, the couple never met anyone they knew while in Pennsylvania.

DISCUSSION

Section 202(e) of the Social Security Act, 42 U.S.C. § 402(e), provides that a widow of an individual who died while fully insured is entitled to widow's insurance benefits, if she meets certain other conditions not in issue on this appeal. Section 216(h)(1)(A) of the Social Security Act, 42 U.S.C. § 416(h)(1)(A), provides that an applicant is the widow of an insured individual if the courts of the state in which the insured individual was domiciled at the time of his death would find that the applicant and insured individual were validly married at the time of his death. Since Mr. and Mrs. Renshaw were domiciled in New York at the time of his death, New York law governs her status as a widow.

Think About It

Federal statutes such as the Social Security Act typically rely on state law to determine who qualifies as a "spouse" or "child" for purposes of the federal law. Consider how this case would have been decided if the Renshaws had spent their entire lives living in Baltimore, and how it would have turned out if they had lived from the outset of their relationship in Pennsylvania. Does this influence the court's decision? Should it?

Although New York does not itself recognize common-law marriages, a common-law marriage contracted in another state will be recognized as valid in New York if it is valid where contracted. *Mott v. Duncan Petroleum Trans.*, 51 N.Y.2d 289, 292, 434 N.Y.S.2d 155, 157, 414 N.E.2d 657, 659 (1980). The law to be applied in determining the validity of such a marriage is the law of the state in which the marriage occurred. Since plaintiff claims that she contracted a common-law marriage with her husband in Pennsylvania during their travels through the state, the appropriate law to apply is the law of Pennsylvania.

The Commonwealth of Pennsylvania recognizes the institution of common-law marriage. In re *Estate of Stauffer*, 504 Pa. 626, 476 A.2d 354, 356 (1984). Believing that common-law marriage is a fruitful source of perjury and fraud, however, the Pennsylvania courts have imposed a heavy burden on one who grounds his or her claim on an allegation of common-law marriage.

Generally, a common-law marriage may be created by uttering words in the present tense with the intent to establish a marital relationship, *Commonwealth v. Sullivan*, 484 Pa. 130, 398 A.2d 978, 980 (1979); but where no such utterance is proved, Pennsylvania law also permits a finding of marriage based on reputation and cohabitation when established by satisfactory proof. In re *Estate of Wagner*, 398 Pa. 531, 159 A.2d 495, 498 (1960).

In reaching his determination that the Renshaws had not entered into a valid common-law marriage under Pennsylvania law, the magistrate—to whom the case was referred on consent of the parties—noted that "if the facts had shown that the Renshaws lived their lives primarily in Pennsylvania, and conducted themselves there as the evidence indicates they conducted their lives in New York, their marriage would be declared a valid common-law marriage by a Pennsylvania court."

"Under this hypothetical", he continued, "the facts would show the plaintiff clearly was entitled to the presumption of marriage by her showing of the continuous relationship and the holding of themselves out as husband and wife." Magistrate's Decision and Order, at 9. The magistrate declined to make such a finding, however, since "at best only 16 days out of Mr. Renshaw's lifetime were spent in Pennsylvania [and] the overwhelming bulk of the supporting evidence rests on actions taken outside of Pennsylvania in non-common law states." Relying on *Peart v. T.D. Bross Line Construction Co.*, 45 A.D.2d 801, 357 N.Y.S.2d 53 (3d Dep't 1974), the magistrate concluded that absent proof of some present intent to marry while in Pennsylvania, the parties had not contracted a valid common-law marriage under Pennsylvania law.

> **FYI**
>
> Note that the Pennsylvania legislature abolished common law marriage in 2004 for any marriage contracted after January 1, 2005. 23 Pa.Cons.Stat. § 1103 (2018).

The facts admittedly present a unique situation. Although we have found no Pennsylvania cases directly on point, New York courts have recognized valid common-law marriages under similar factual situations. *McCullon v. McCullon*, 96 Misc.2d 962, 410 N.Y.S.2d 226 (Erie County 1978) (valid common-law marriage where New York residents vacationed in Pennsylvania for two to four weeks at a time over a 30-year period); *Skinner v. Skinner*, 4 Misc.2d 1013, 150 N.Y.S.2d 739 (New York County 1956) (valid common-law marriage found on the basis of a three week visit to Pennsylvania). *But see Peart v. T.D. Bross Line Construction Co.*, 45 A.D.2d 801, 357 N.Y.S.2d 53 (3d Dep't 1974) (three or four days' stay as a cohabiting couple in Pennsylvania did not establish the existence of a common-law marriage). We think that a New York court would find that the Renshaws had contracted a valid common-law marriage in Pennsylvania.

Although Mrs. Renshaw furnished no proof of words in the present tense establishing a marriage contract while in Pennsylvania, she did present proof of cohabitation and reputation. The Renshaws' stays in Pennsylvania were admittedly short; but they cohabitated during the entire time that they were there. While the evidence of reputation is not extensive, they held themselves out as husband and wife to every individual they knew that they saw in Pennsylvania—his mother, her brother, and their daughter. Moreover, Mrs. Renshaw testified that when Mr. Renshaw made reservations over the phone, he indicated on at least one occasion that the reservations were for himself, his wife, and their daughter.

In different circumstances, such facts alone might not prove sufficient. But the uncontroverted evidence as to their 21 year relationship, their intent to live as husband and wife during that time, and the fact that until these proceedings began all of their relatives, friends, and acquaintances assumed that they were married, negates the possibility that Mrs. Renshaw is attempting to engage in perjury or fraud and provides the additional assurance that Pennsylvania courts seem to have required before giving judicial approval to such a relationship. *Cf. Chlieb v. Heckler,* 777 F.2d 842 (2d Cir.1985) (absent other evidence of marriage relationship and in light of contrary intent, couple's two nights in Pennsylvania and one night in Ohio failed to establish common-law marriage).

In reaching our conclusion, we recognize that there is no evidence of some present tense intent to create the marriage while in Pennsylvania. The magistrate found this absence fatal to Mrs. Renshaw's claim, reasoning that "some conscious recognition by the parties that they intended to establish or at least consciously reaffirm their marriage" while in Pennsylvania was required. We disagree.

In *Sullivan v. American Bridge Company,* 115 Pa.Super. 536, 176 A. 24 (1935), a couple had exchanged marriage vows in a state that did not recognize common-law marriages while under the impression that in using the words they did use they were entering into a valid marriage. Subsequently, the couple moved to Pennsylvania. When the husband died, the widow sought benefits under the workman's compensation act. In objecting to her claim that she was the legal widow of her husband, her husband's employer relied

> on the general rule that a marriage, if valid in the state where it is contracted, is valid everywhere; and its corollary, which is not so well established, that, if the marriage is invalid in the state where it is contracted, it is invalid everywhere, and * * * that, as the attempted marriage in Maryland was invalid under the laws of that state, and there was no proof of any subsequent contract of marriage, in *verba de praesenti,* entered into between the parties, * * * in * * * Pennsylvania * * * there never was a valid marriage between them, and claimant never became his lawful wife.

The Pennsylvania court reasoned that the corollary to the general rule—that if the marriage is invalid in the state where it is contracted it is invalid everywhere—had been held subject to exceptions by the Supreme Courts of both Pennsylvania and the United States. *See Phillips v. Gregg,* 10 Watts 158, 168 (1840); *Travers v. Reinhardt,* 205 U.S. 423, 27 S.Ct. 563, 51 L.Ed. 865 (1907). The court held that, even in the absence of a "new contract in *verba de praesenti* "in Pennsylvania, "the subsequent conduct of the parties was equivalent to a declaration by each that they did, and during their joint lives were to, occupy the relation of husband and wife." *Sullivan,* 176 A. at 25. We think that the Renshaws' conduct while in Pennsylvania and elsewhere is similarly sufficient to support finding such a declaration here, and conclude that the Renshaws entered into a valid common-law marriage under Pennsylvania law.

If the Secretary's findings as to any fact are supported by substantial evidence in the record, they should not be disturbed by a court on review. 42 U.S.C. § 405(g). Under Pennsylvania law, however, the question as to whether a person has been legally married to another is a mixed question of law and fact for the purpose of review, In re *Cummings Estate,* 330 Pa.Super. 255, 479 A.2d 537, 541 (1984), and since the underlying facts are undisputed, we are not bound by the substantial evidence standard of review on this issue. Accordingly, we hold that the Secretary erred in finding that the Renshaws had not entered into a valid common-law marriage.

CONCLUSION

The judgment of the district court is reversed and the case is remanded to the Secretary for the purpose of determining: (1) whether Edith Renshaw, as the legal widow of Albert Renshaw, is eligible for widow's insurance benefits, and (2) the amount of benefits due.

Points for Discussion

a. Proof of a New Agreement

The Magistrate who initially decided the case ruled against Mrs. Renshaw because she had not proved that they had made a new agreement to be married while they were in Pennsylvania. How does the appellate court resolve this question? Compare Marriage of Swanner-Renner, 209 P.3d 238 (Mont. 2009) with Callen v. Callen, 620 S.E.2d 59 (S.C. 2005).

In Travers v. Reinhardt, 205 U.S. 423 (1907), the parties lived together in various states that did not recognize common law marriage before moving to New Jersey, which did recognize common law marriage. The Supreme Court held that they contracted a common law marriage in New Jersey, although there was no evidence of any new agreement to be husband and wife made after moving to that state, and although they only lived there for a short time before the husband died. In his dissent, Justice Holmes remarked: "To live in New Jersey and think you are married does not constitute a marriage by the law of that state."

b. Choice of Law and Common Law Marriage

Should the choice of law principle applicable to recognition and validity of ceremonial marriages also be applied to test the validity of common law marriages? This is the New York conflicts principle, applied by the court in *Renshaw*, but other states take different approaches.

In states with strong public policies against common law marriage, courts do not recognize common law marriages contracted in other states if the parties maintained their domicile in a non-common law marriage state at the time they were alleged to have contracted a common law marriage. See for example, Lynch v. Bowen, 681 F.Supp. 506 (N.D.Ill.1988) which held, on the basis of Illinois law, that four visits to states which recognized common law marriage, during which about twenty four days were spent in those states, did not produce a common law marriage. As a result, despite the fact that the parties lived together thirty-eight years and had three children, the woman was denied social security widow's benefits on the man's death.

Courts in another group of states recognize out-of-state common law marriages by their domiciliaries so long as the parties have an established place of abode in the common law marriage state. For example, In re Estate of Bivians, 652 P.2d 744 (N.M. 1982) held that a man and woman domiciled in New Mexico did not succeed in contracting a common law marriage during several business and pleasure trips to Texas and Colorado, concluding: "Where the couple was not domiciled in a common law marriage state, evidence of substantial contacts with the common law state must be presented."

In states that take the New York approach, and recognize common law marriages contracted in a state where the parties have no domicile or substantial connections, how much of a stay in the common law marriage state should be necessary to produce a valid marriage? An overnight visit? A drive through the state without stopping overnight? A two-week summer or winter vacation? Should the result be different if the parties were domiciled in a state which did not recognize common law marriage, but visited a common law marriage state for the purpose of contracting a marriage there?

The answers to these doctrinal questions are influenced by different views of the wisdom of common law marriage as an institution, and often seem to be affected by the factual context of the particular case. To what extent should the law individualize results in this context? Are there better solutions to the problems that common law marriage seeks to solve?

Global View: Cohabitation vs. Common Law Marriage

Individuals sometimes argue that cohabitation relationships that are accorded legal effects in other countries, such as *concubinage* in Mexico, should be recognized as common law marriages in the United States. Courts have consistently refused to do this unless the legal status under foreign law confers all of the rights and benefits of marriage. E.g. In re Estate of Duval, 777 N.W.2d 380 (S.D. 2010); Rosales v. Battle, 7 Cal.Rptr.3d 13 (Ct. App. 2004).

c. Federal and State Law

As the court notes, the Social Security Act provisions under which Edith Renshaw sought widow's insurance benefits rely on state law to define marital status and other family relationships. This is also true in many other contexts, such as federal income tax and immigration laws. Would it be preferable for these programs to have uniform nationwide application? The broader issue is debated in Kahn v. Immigration and Naturalization Service 36 F.3d 1412 (9th Cir.1994) (considering common law type relationship as factor in granting waiver of deportation).

Make the Connection

For those states that have abolished common law marriage, what effect should this determination have on the legal treatment of cohabiting couples who make claims such as those in *Marvin v. Marvin*, discussed later in this chapter?

Putative Marriage

Putative marriage was adopted from the Napoleonic Code in states with a civil law tradition, such as California, Louisiana and Texas. The purpose of the doctrine is to protect parties to invalid marriages. Putative marriage occurs when a marriage is contracted at a time when an existing impediment makes the purported marriage either void or voidable and when one or both of the parties are ignorant of the impediment. Under these circumstances a party who entered the marriage in the good faith belief that it was valid is entitled to assert financial or property claims based upon the marriage, such as the claim to share in community property, the right to inherit from the putative spouse, the right to sue for wrongful death, or the right to social security benefits. If the impediment is later removed, the putative marriage becomes fully valid.

The putative spouse doctrine is now widely recognized in many states, either by statute or judicial decision. The Uniform Marriage and Divorce Act § 209, 9A U.L.A. (Part 1) 192 (1998), defines a putative spouse as "any person who has cohabited with another to whom he is not legally married in the good faith belief that he was married to that person."

Problem 1-10

Dave, a professional baseball player, learned that his girlfriend, Sandra, was pregnant. During a three-day stay together at the honeymoon suite of a hotel in Texas, they agreed to be "informally married." The hotel suite was booked for them as "Mr. and Mrs. David Winfield." Dave refused to have a ceremonial marriage, because he was concerned that his career and his image in the media would suffer if it were known that he had fathered a child before marriage. He bought a condominium in Texas for Sandra to live in, and spent about 100 days there with her during the off-seasons over the next two years. Sandra told her mother that they were married, but neither Dave nor Sandra wore a wedding ring, and Dave continued to see other women. Sandra's tax returns, bank and pay records, and insurance forms all identified her as single. Can Sandra obtain a divorce and property division under the Texas statute? (See Winfield v. Renfro, 821 S.W.2d 640 (Tex. App. 1991).)

Problem 1-11

After Robert filed for divorce from his first wife, he began living with Feather. When they learned that the judge would sign Robert's stipulated divorce judgment on April 5, he and Feather made plans to be married that weekend in Acapulco, Mexico. On April 4, Robert and Feather went to a government office in Acapulco, filled out some forms, signed a document before witnesses, and at the end of the proceedings were told by an official that they were married. The next day, April 5, they found an English-speaking minister who performed a religious marriage ceremony for them, telling them that by Mexican law it was not a valid marriage unless there had been an earlier valid civil ceremony. Robert and Feather returned home to Nebraska, and lived together as husband and wife. Feather sued Robert for divorce more than twenty years later, and he defended on the ground that they were not validly married. Should the Court find that Feather was never married to Robert, and therefore that she has no financial or other claims upon him? (See Randall v. Randall, 345 N.W.2d 319 (Neb. 1984).)

Problem 1-12

Yang and Xiong, both refugees from Laos, met in Minnesota and two weeks later had a Hmong cultural marriage ceremony. At the time, Yang was 16, and too young to marry under state law. Five years later, the couple went to the court-house, signed some papers, and obtained a marriage license, and continued living together as a married couple. Years later, Yang objected when Xiong brought home a second wife. When Yang went to speak to a lawyer about getting a divorce, she learned that a marriage license was not the same thing as a marriage certificate. Minnesota does not recognize common-law marriage. Can Yang seek property division and support from Xiong? (See In re Marriage of Xiong, 800 N.W.2d 187 (Minn. Ct. App. 2011).

Problem 1-13

Sonemaly and Stella are two women who began living together in Texas in 2004, and celebrated their marriage with a commitment ceremony there in 2008. Although Texas did not permit or recognize same-sex marriages until after Stella died in 2014, Sonemaly would like to be recognized as her spouse for inheritance and other purposes. What arguments should she make? (Cf. Ranolls v. Dewling, 223 F. Supp. 3d 613 (E.D. Tex. 2016). See Lauren McGaughy, *In a first, Texas court recognizes same-sex common law marriage*, Houston Chronicle (Sept. 16, 2015).)

---

3. Marital Capacity and Consent

A marriage in which one party was below a minimum age, or where a party lacked capacity to consent to or consummate the marriage, or where consent was induced by fraud or duress or as a jest or dare, is traditionally treated as voidable. These marriages are fully valid, however, unless one of the parties (or a parent or guardian) brings an action for annulment or declaration of invalidity of the marriage. Standing to seek annulment of a marriage, and the time periods within which such an action may be brought, depend upon the specific grounds for annulment. See, e.g., Uniform Marriage and Divorce Act § 208, 9A U.L.A. (Part 1) 186–87 (1998).

Most states today set the age of consent for marriage at eighteen, although many states allow children below the statutory age to marry with the consent of their parents or approval of a court. Failure to obtain a parent's consent does not invalidate the marriage, however, so long as the parties are above the minimum marriageable age. Most states set a minimum age for marriage at sixteen, but in a few states the minimum age follows the common law rule, which allowed marriage at age fourteen for boys and at age twelve for girls. Many states have begun to raise their minimum age for marriage, and in 2018 Delaware and New Jersey became the first states to completely prohibit child marriage. See Del. Code Ann. tit. 13, § 123 (2018); N.J. Stat. Ann. § 37:1–6 (2018).

The authorities agree that "Marriage being a contract is of course consensual * * * for it is of the essence of all contracts to be constituted by the consent of parties." Dalrymple v. Dalrymple, 2 Hagg.Cons. 54, 161 Eng.Rep. 665, 668 (1811). This implies that the consent must be freely and voluntarily given. Religious teachings have also emphasized that the marriage contract requires a free consent. When consent has been induced by fraud, duress, or undue influence, the marriage can be annulled. See, e.g., Clark v. Foust-Graham, 615 S.E.2d 398 (N.C. Ct. App. 2005); Estate of Laubenheimer, 833 N.W.2d 735 (Wis. 2013).

Global View: Forced Marriage

International human rights laws take a strong position against child marriage and forced marriage, reflected in Article 16(2) of the Universal Declaration of Human Rights and Article 23 of the International Covenant on Civil and Political Rights. Women and men, children and adults may be subject to marriage coercion, both domestically and in international settings. The U.S. State Department provides information and assistance with forced marriage prevention for U.S. citizens who may be facing marriage coercion in another country.

Janda v. Janda

984 So.2d 434 (Ala. Civ. App. 2007)

MOORE, JUDGE.

Jiri Janda appeals from a judgment of the Baldwin Circuit Court annulling his marriage to Antoinette Walters Janda. We affirm.

Background

On February 14, 2007, Antoinette filed a petition for an annulment of her marriage to Jiri. In support of her petition, Antoinette asserted that Jiri, a native of the Czech Republic, had fraudulently induced her to marry him; that, at the time of the marriage, Jiri had no intention of honoring his marital obligations; and that Jiri had married her only so that he could obtain a "green card," which would permit him to remain in the United States. Jiri answered the complaint, denying those allegations; he counterclaimed for a divorce.

The Baldwin Circuit Court conducted a hearing on May 8, 2007, at which both parties appeared pro se and presented ore tenus evidence. At that hearing, Antoinette testified that she and Jiri were married on June 5, 2005, after a courtship of only a few months. She also testified that she and Jiri had "honeymooned" by camping in the Smokey Mountains; that, throughout their honeymoon, they had had no sexual relations; and that they had slept in separate tents the entire time. She further testified that, when they returned to live in her home in Baldwin County, Jiri would not share a bedroom with her.

Antoinette testified that throughout their marriage she and Jiri had never had a sexual relationship of any kind. Antoinette initially believed that their differing expectations regarding a sexual relationship resulted from cultural differences. Antoinette testified that she eventually asked Jiri about the lack of a sexual relationship between them, and, according to Antoinette, Jiri had reported that he was unhappy with Antoinette's weight. Antoinette then lost 65 pounds, but, she testified, Jiri still showed no romantic interest in her. Antoinette testified that, after 20 months of marriage, she realized that Jiri had married her never intending to engage in marital intercourse with her.

According to Jiri's testimony, he is a native of the Czech Republic. He came to the United States in October 2001.[1] Jiri claimed that he became a permanent resident of the United States as a result of his marriage to Antoinette. Jiri acknowledged that if his marriage to Antoinette was annulled, he would be deported back to the Czech Republic. Jiri testified that if his marriage was terminated by divorce, rather than by annulment, whether he could remain in the United States was "between him and the immigration service."

Jiri denied that he had proposed to Antoinette; he claimed that Antoinette had proposed to him in March 2005. He agreed that they had married in June 2005 and that he and Antoinette had purchased a grill and a television together after they were married. Jiri acknowledged that he had voluntarily quit work-

---

[1]   It appears that Jiri was in the United States on a temporary green card, valid for two years, before or at the time of his marriage to Antoinette. Jiri testified that he had visited the United States on two other occasions, once in 1996 and again in 1997. On those occasions, he had obtained "B2" tourist visas; Jiri also testified that, at one point, he had applied for a temporary work permit.

ing at some of his jobs. Jiri also admitted that he was unhappy with Antoinette's weight, with the difficulties Antoinette experienced with her 19-year-old son, and with changes that had occurred in Antoinette's personality and behavior following a hysterectomy. Jiri testified that he had maintained his own bedroom because Antoinette was "messy" while he was tidy. Jiri also complained that Antoinette at times would mistakenly call him by her son's name.

The trial court entered an order annulling the marriage on May 8, 2007, specifically finding that the parties had not consummated the marriage and had not acted as a married couple, but had acted more as roommates, during their marriage. Jiri appeals, asserting that the trial court should have entered a judgment of divorce rather than an annulment.

Analysis

In this appeal, we must determine whether the trial court properly annulled the marriage of Jiri and Antoinette. Under long-standing Alabama caselaw, a court may annul a marriage because of fraudulent inducement going to "the essence of the marriage relation." *Williams v. Williams*, 268 Ala. 223, 226, 105 So.2d 676, 678 (1958); *Hyslop v. Hyslop*, 241 Ala. 223, 226, 2 So.2d 443, 445 (1941); and *Raia v. Raia*, 214 Ala. 391, 392, 108 So. 11, 12 (1926). The existence of fraud is a question for the trier of fact—in this case, the trial court—to determine. This court may not predicate error on a finding of fact based on oral testimony unless that finding is plainly and palpably wrong, without supporting evidence, or manifestly unjust.

* * *

We note that in both *Williams, supra*, and *Hyslop, supra*, the Alabama Supreme Court cited with approval the case of *Millar v. Millar*, 175 Cal. 797, 167 P. 394 (1917). We find *Millar* to be directly on point. In that case, the California court annulled the parties' marriage, after eight months of cohabitation, because the wife had refused to engage in a sexual relationship with her husband since the date of their marriage ceremony. The California court concluded that, despite the parties' cohabitation, the wife's secret intent to refuse to matrimonial intercourse provided a proper basis for an annulment. * * *

Despite the age of these cited cases, we find no reason, and none has been urged in this case, to depart from their long-standing recognition of the nature of the marital relationship, the public policy attendant to that relationship, and the impact of a fraudulent intent, held at the time of the marriage, upon that relationship. We agree with *Millar* that a fraud perpetrated at the time of the marriage and going to the essence of the marital relationship renders the marriage voidable by the injured party. *See Williams, supra*, and *Hyslop, supra* (both citing *Millar* with approval). Also, as recognized in *Millar, supra*, we agree that traditionally a sexual relationship is implicit in marriage vows and that an unstated intent, held at the time of the marriage ceremony, to utterly refuse to engage in a sexual relationship with the other party is a fraud that alters the very essence of the marriage. Finally, the continued viability of the principles stated above is evidenced by their application in more recent cases from other jurisdictions.[4]

In this case, the trial court heard testimony indicating that, immediately after the marriage ceremony, Jiri refused to share a bed with Antoinette and refused to engage in sexual relations with her. Antoinette testified that she had remained in the marriage because she originally believed Jiri's reluctance to engage in marital intercourse with her resulted from cultural differences between them. Jiri subsequently told Antoinette that he would not engage in marital intercourse with her because of her weight. However, after Antoinette lost 65 pounds, Jiri persisted in his refusal to engage in marital intercourse with her. Antoinette testified that, after some 20 months of marriage, she realized that Jiri had married her never intending to engage in marital intercourse with her. Upon that realization, she petitioned the court for an annulment. As recognized in *Millar, supra*, these circumstances gave rise to a marriage that was voidable by Antoinette. By filing her petition, Antoinette sought to void her marriage to Jiri.

We acknowledge that, because of the length of time the parties cohabitated together, this is a close case and could have been resolved either way. However, the trial court resolved the evidence in favor of an annulment. Because the ore tenus rule applies and because the record contains substantial evidence to support the trial court's judgment, we will not disturb that judgment. We, therefore, affirm the trial court's judgment.

---

[4]   *See, e.g., In re the Marriage of Meagher,* 131 Cal.App.4th 1, 7, 31 Cal.Rptr.3d 663, 667 (2005) (recognizing that annulments on the basis of fraud are generally granted only in cases in which the fraud related in some way to the sexual or procreative aspects of marriage); *In re Marriage of Liu,* 197 Cal.App.3d 143, 155–56, 242 Cal.Rptr. 649, 656–57 (1987) (annulling marriage because wife had fraudulently induced husband into marriage so that the wife could obtain a "green card"); *Stojcevska v. Anic* (No. 210144, Jan. 11, 2000) (Mich.Ct.App.2000) (not reported in Mich.App. or N.W.2d) (annulling marriage, upon wife's request, because evidence indicated that wife's parents had arranged her marriage to her cousin so that he could obtain a visa to United States); *V.J.S. v. M.J.B.,* 249 N.J.Super. 318, 320, 592 A.2d 328, 329 (Chan.Div.1991) ("Where the marriage has been consummated, the fraud of defendant will entitle plaintiff to an annulment only when the fraud is of an extreme nature, going to one of the essentials of marriage."); *Bishop v. Bishop,* 62 Misc.2d 436, 308 N.Y.S.2d 998 (N.Y.Sup.Ct.1970) (denying husband's petition for annulment based on fraudulent inducement; court found no fraud in wife's attempt to obtain a divorce and in her refusal to consummate the marital relationship because husband himself testified that he and wife had agreed they would marry and then immediately divorce; such an agreement did not contemplate marital intercourse).

Points for Discussion

a. Essentials of the Marriage

At a time when divorces were difficult to obtain, courts defined "the essentials of marriage" very narrowly, including only misrepresentations concerning the ability and willingness to have sexual relations and to bear children. The leading early authority for that view is <u>Reynolds v. Reynolds, 85 Mass. 605, 3 Allen (85 Mass.) 605 (1862)</u>. In that case the wife concealed from her husband her pregnancy by another man. The parties had not had pre-marital sexual relations. In granting a decree annulling the marriage the court explained its reasoning in these terms:

> "The great object of marriage in a civilized and Christian community is to secure the existence and permanence of the family relation, and to insure the legitimacy of offspring. It would tend to defeat this object, if error or disappointment in personal qualities or character was allowed to be the basis of proceedings on which to found a dissolution of the marriage tie. The law therefore wisely requires that persons who act on representations or belief in regard to such matters should bear the consequences which flow from contracts into which they have voluntarily entered, after they have been executed, and affords no relief for the results of a 'blind credulity, however it may have been produced' ".

> * * *

> "But a very different question arises where, as in the case at bar, a marriage is contracted and consummated on the faith of a representation that the woman is chaste and virtuous, and it is afterwards ascertained not only that this statement was false, but that she was at the time of making it and when she entered into the marriage relation pregnant with child by a man other than her husband. * * * In such a case, the concealment and false statement go directly to the essentials of the marriage contract, and operate as a fraud of the gravest character on him with whom she enters into that relation. * * * "

<u>85 Mass. 605, 3 Allen (85 Mass.) 605, 607, 609</u>.

b. Fraud

Over time, there has been an expansion of the kinds of fraud that courts recognize as an appropriate basis for granting an annulment. *Janda* repeats the rule that the fraud must relate to the essentials of the marriage in order to justify an annulment. Does the court define essentials? If Jiri had been willing to "honor his marital obligations" to Antoinette, could she have had the marriage annulled by proving that he married her only to obtain immigration benefits?

c. Sham Marriage

Courts hearing annulment actions have disagreed as to whether a marriage contracted for some ulterior reason should be treated as valid. For example, a Connecticut court refused to annul a marriage contracted for the sole purpose of "giving a child a name," without any intention that the parties would live together as husband and wife. Schibi v. Schibi, 69 A.2d 831 (Conn. 1949). The court in Faustin v. Lewis, 427 A.2d 1105 (N.J. 1981) granted an annulment of a marriage the plaintiff had entered into for the purpose of becoming eligible for permanent residence in the United States.

Global View: Marriage and Immigration Law

Marriages that are valid in the place of celebration are generally recognized for purposes of federal immigration law, with specific restrictions applicable to proxy marriages and polygamous marriages. See generally Ann Laquer Estin, International Family Law Desk Book 38-39 (2d ed. 2016).

Under the 1986 Immigration Marriage Fraud Amendments, codified at 8 U.S.C.A. § 1186a (2018) an immigrant spouse in a marriage that has lasted less than two years is limited to a two-year conditional permanent residence status, and the spouses must usually petition jointly to have the condition removed at the end of two years. The procedures are included at 8 CFR § 216 (2018) and described on the U.S. Citizenship and Immigration Services web site.

Haacke v. Glenn

814 P.2d 1157 (Utah Ct. App. 1991)

GARFF, JUDGE:

Appellant LeslieAnn Haacke appeals a final order denying her a decree of annulment and granting her a decree of divorce. Appellant asserts that the court erred because the findings supported a decree of annulment. We reverse and remand.

Facts

Appellant, LeslieAnn Haacke and appellee, Mark Mitchell Glenn participated in a marriage ceremony on December 16, 1989 in Bountiful, Utah. At the time of the ceremony, Haacke was employed as an attorney for the Inspector General's Division of the Utah Department of Corrections. As part of her job she had unlimited access to criminal files and records. Thus, a marriage with a convicted felon would create a severe conflict of interest and would place Haacke in violation of state policy and procedure, and state statute.

Prior to and during the parties' marriage, Glenn deliberately and intentionally concealed from Haacke the fact that he had been convicted of a second degree felony, theft of property, in Alabama. In fact, Glenn told Haacke that the purpose for his frequent travels to Alabama was to take care of prior child support obligations, when in fact he was using the parties' joint funds for payment of fines and restitution attendant to his felony conviction. Haacke did not become aware of Glenn's criminal record until she was informed by her employer. Subsequently, Gary W. DeLand, Executive Director of the Utah Department of Corrections, in a letter dated September 4, 1990, told Haacke that because of her marriage to a convicted felon, the Attorney General had determined there was a conflict of interest and, therefore, her employment with the department would terminate effective September 14, 1990. DeLand told her that she would be considered for reemployment in the event "the current circumstances were to change, eliminating the conflict of interest." In a later letter, Haacke was informed that, even if she were to dissolve her marriage through divorce, the department would investigate whether or not she had been aware of Glenn's criminal record prior to the marriage.

In response to discovering Glenn's deception, Haacke filed a complaint for divorce. She later amended her complaint to request an annulment. The parties entered into a stipulation in which they consented to the entry of a decree of annulment. However, when the court heard the matter on September 14, 1990, it refused to grant the annulment, and instead granted a divorce. The court based the grounds for divorce on the following finding:

> Plaintiff should be awarded a Decree of Divorce in this matter in that prior to the marriage, Defendant did make fraudulent misrepresentations concerning his honesty, trustworthiness and lack of criminal involvement. Defendant failed to inform Plaintiff that he had been convicted of a felony in the state of his previous residence, Alabama; he informed Plaintiff that he was traveling to Alabama to take care of prior child support obligations and problems when in reality he was utilizing the funds of these parties for payment of fines and restitution, and he failed to inform Plaintiff of his prior criminal activity, much to Plaintiff's detriment in the form of loss of her employment with the State of Utah, Department of Corrections.

Haacke does not challenge the court's findings, but appeals the court's conclusion that she is not entitled to an annulment.

Annulment

Utah Code Ann. § 30–1–17.1(1) specifies two general categories of grounds for annulment. The first is for marriages that do not conform to Utah Code Ann. § 30–1–1. The second category allows for annulment "upon grounds existing at common law." Utah Code Ann. § 30–1–17.1(2). Haacke claims that the lower court erred in failing to grant her an annulment on the common law ground of fraud.

Under common law, a marriage could be annulled for a fraud going to the essence of the marriage. The fraud must be such that directly affects the marriage relationship rather than "merely such fraud as would be sufficient to rescind an ordinary civil contract." The misrepresentation must go to present and not future facts. Further, the fraud must be material to such a degree that, had the deceived party known of the fraud, he or she would not have consented to the marriage. "The test in all cases is whether the false representations or concealment were such as to defeat the essential purpose of the injured spouse inherent in the contracting of a marriage."

As to the form the fraud takes, it may "consist of an affirmative false representation or the withholding of the truth when it should be disclosed."

In determining fraud, courts have adopted a subjective standard and have considered the facts of the particular marriage. *Wolfe*, 19 Ill.Dec. at 311, 378 N.E.2d at 1186 (where husband concealed his prior marital history from Roman Catholic wife); *Costello*, 282 A.2d 432 (where husband omitted to tell wife of his heroin addiction); *Lamberti v. Lamberti*, 77 Cal.Rptr. 430, 432, 272 Cal.App.2d 482 (1969) (where husband's secret intent in marrying was to acquire an advantageous alien status and where he falsely promised to go through a subsequent religious ceremony); *Parks v. Parks*, 418 S.W.2d 726 (Ky.1967) (where wife falsely represented at time of marriage that she was pregnant); *Kober v. Kober*, 16 N.Y.2d 191, 211 N.E.2d 817, 264 N.Y.S.2d 364 (1965) (where husband failed to disclose his extreme anti-Semitism to wife); *Handley v. Handley*, 179 Cal.App.2d 742, 3 Cal.Rptr. 910 (1960) (where wife secretly intended not to live with husband and not to adopt his name); *Osborne v. Osborne*, 134 A.2d 438 (D.C.1957) (where husband secretly intended not to live with his wife); *Rathburn v. Rathburn*, 138 Cal.App.2d 568, 292 P.2d 274, 277 (1956) (where wife secretly intended not to consummate the marriage); *Vileta v. Vileta*, 53 Cal.App.2d 794, 128 P.2d 376, 377 (1942) (where wife did not disclose her infertility); *Rubman v. Rubman*, 140 Misc. 658, 251 N.Y.S. 474 (1931) (where husband falsely told wife he loved her and did not disclose that real reason for marriage was to avoid deportation). *See also*

Leventhal v. Liberman, 262 N.Y. 209, 186 N.E. 675 (1933) (where husband did not disclose he had tuberculosis and was a narcotics addict).

Courts have recognized that justice may demand that an annulment be granted even though there is no case with the same set of specific facts. This includes cases where the grounds pleaded for annulment could also constitute grounds for divorce, such as here.

As to the factual pattern of this case, courts have granted annulments where one spouse has concealed from the other a criminal background. *Lockwood v. Lockwood*, 29 Misc.2d 114, 220 N.Y.S.2d 718 (1961) (where husband did not disclose his former drug addiction and prior criminal record); *Douglass*, 307 P.2d at 676 ("the fraud of the defendant in concealing his criminal record and true character was deceit so gross and cruel as to prove him to plaintiff to be a man unworthy of trust, either with respect to his truthfulness, his moral character or a disposition to be a law-abiding citizen.").

The court's findings in the instant case present a strong case for annulment on the common law ground of fraud. Glenn's fraud went to the fact, present at the time of the marriage, that he had a felony criminal record. He affirmatively represented to Haacke that he traveled to Alabama to take care of child support arrearages. He falsely represented that joint funds were being used for child support when, in reality, the real purpose was to pay fines and restitution. Not only did Glenn's fraudulent misrepresentation affect Haacke's career, but, more importantly, it defeated "the essential purpose of the injured spouse inherent in the contracting of a marriage." *Douglass*, 307 P.2d at 675. We think the same considerations given by the *Douglass* court have validity here. "There was no reason whatever to doubt that in consenting to marry defendant her purposes were . . .namely, to have a home, a husband of honorable character whom she could respect and trust, one whom she would be proud to have as a companion and to introduce to her friends, and who would be a suitable [father] for her children." *Douglass*, 307 P.2d at 676.

Considering the relevant case law, and applying a subjective analysis to the particular marriage, we conclude that the original false representations and concealments by Glenn so violated the essential purpose of the marriage, that Haacke is entitled to an annulment. We therefore reverse the decree of divorce and remand for the court to enter a decree of annulment.

Reversed and remanded.

BENCH and BILLINGS, JJ., concur.

Points for Discussion

a. Materiality

The *Haacke* case seems to have adopted a materiality principle to determine when fraud will justify an annulment. Is this the same as or different from the principle applied in *Reynolds* and *Janda*? How does the materiality test compare to rules governing the disaffirmance of commercial contracts for fraud? See, e.g., Restatement (Second) Contracts § 162 (1981); 12 Williston, Contracts, § 1490 (3d ed. Jaeger 1970). Can you devise a reasonably clear statutory provision which would assist the courts in determining what types of misrepresentation or non-disclosure justify an annulment for fraud?

b. Annulment vs. Divorce

Why did Ms. Haacke seek an annulment rather than a divorce? With divorce now readily available in every state on no-fault grounds, actions for annulment are very rare. What purposes does the law of annulment serve today? When might you advise a client to pursue an annulment rather than a divorce?

Annulment and Declaration of Invalidity

An annulment, also known as a declaration of invalidity, is available for a marriage that is voidable based on a lack of capacity or consent. An action for annulment may also be brought by either party to a void marriage, such as one that is bigamous or that falls within the prohibited degrees of family relationship. In some circumstances, a parent or guardian may have standing to bring an action for annulment. See generally Uniform Marriage and Divorce Act (UMDA) § 208, 9A U.L.A. (Part 1) 186–87 (1998).

Actions for annulment lay within the jurisdiction of the ecclesiastical courts in England, and served an important function in the time before absolute divorce was permitted. An action for annulment usually resulted in a declaration that no marriage ever existed between the parties, either because the marriage was void *ab initio* or because the court's decree nullified the marriage retroactively. Under the common law, this had the result of bastardizing any children born of the marriage, and denying the spouse any possibility of alimony. With the emergence of statutes governing annulment and divorce in the United States, the distinction between the two was that a divorce terminated a valid existing marriage for the future, while an annulment declared that no valid marriage had ever occurred.

Today there may be important legal consequences from void or voidable marriages. Contemporary statutes protect the legitimacy of children born in void or voidable marriages, and grant courts authority to order financial remedies including spousal support or equitable division of property in an action for annulment or declaration of invalidity. See, e.g., UMDA § 208(d) and (e). See also Fontana v. Callahan, 999 F.Supp. 304 (E.D.N.Y.1998) (allowing social security benefits to wife whose 27-year marriage ended in annulment rather than divorce).

Because of the rule that an annulment terminates a marriage retroactively, it has some consequences that are different from the consequences of divorce. For example, couples who filed joint income tax returns prior to having their marriage annulled are obligated to re-file separate returns. A spouse who had been receiving alimony from a prior marriage, subject to termination on his or her remarriage, may request that the initial alimony obligation be revived if the later marriage is annulled. See, e.g., Joye v. Yon, 586 S.E.2d 131 (S.C. 2003); Amundson v. Amundson, 645 N.W.2d 837 (S.D.2002).

D. Restrictions on Marriage

In addition to regulations governing licensing and solemnization of marriages, and laws defining the requirements of marital capacity and consent, state laws include substantive restrictions on the entry into marriage. Marriage is not permitted in any state if either party was previously married, and that marriage has not been terminated by death or divorce. Marriage is also not permitted if the parties are related by blood or marriage within certain degrees. Bigamous or incestuous marriages are treated as prohibited and void. See, e.g., Uniform Marriage and Divorce Act § 207. Bigamy and incest may also be punishable under state criminal laws.

Before the Supreme Court's ruling in *Loving v. Virginia*, reprinted above, many states also prohibited interracial marriages and subjected the parties to the threat of criminal prosecution. These boundaries were enforced for many years with laws that also criminalized nonmarital cohabitation or sexual relationships across the color line. One such law was upheld by the Court in Pace v. Alabama, 106 U.S. 583 (1883), and *Pace* remained good law until it was overruled in McLaughlin v. Florida, 379 U.S. 184 (1964). Because states took different approaches to interracial marriages, many courts considered whether an interracial marriage that was valid in the state of celebration must be recognized in other states.

Similarly, same-sex couples could not marry in any state before 2004, and states took different approaches to recognition of same-sex marriage until the Supreme Court ruling in *Obergefell v. Hodges*.

1. Successive Marriages: Bigamy?

Monogamy is the controlling principle of Anglo-American marriage law: a person may have only one spouse at a time. This rule is expressed in civil statutes that treat a subsequent marriage as void if one partner has a living spouse from whom he or she has not been divorced, and also in criminal statutes that impose penalties for bigamy, for attempting to contract a marriage when a prior marriage remains undissolved, or for bigamous cohabitation, the crime of living with a person of the opposite sex as a spouse when there is an earlier marriage still in existence. See, e.g., Cal. Penal Code §§ 281, 282, 283, 284 (2018); Colo. Rev. Stat.Ann. § 18–6–201 (2018); Tenn. Code Ann. § 39–15–301 (2018); Model Penal Code § 230.1 (Official Draft 1985). See also Marjorie A. Shields, Annotation, *Validity of Bigamy and Polygamy Statutes and Constitutional Provisions*, 22 A.L.R.6th 1 (2007).

Despite this strong principle, rules against bigamy are not enforced very often. Criminal prosecutions are rare, although one famous case, Williams v. North Carolina, 317 U.S. 287 (1942) and 325 U.S. 226 (1945), did involve a bigamy prosecution, and there are several more recent examples involving fundamentalist Mormon communities. See, e.g., State v. Green, 99 P.3d 820 (Utah 2004). On the civil side, various doctrines dilute the force of the monogamy principle. One such doctrine is the presumption of the validity of the later marriage, addressed in the cases that follow. In many of the cases applying this presumption, there was no divorce ending the earlier marriage, yet the courts presumed that a divorce had occurred without great concern that one or both of the parties might be bigamists.

In the wake of decisions extending recognition to same-sex marriages, scholars have begun to reconsider the reasons behind the ban on polygamy. See Martha Bailey and Amy J. Kaufman, Polygamy in the Monogamous World: Multicultural Challenges for Western Law and Policy (2010).

Chandler v. Central Oil Corporation, Inc.

853 P.2d 649 (Kan. 1993)

LOCKETT, JUSTICE:

Claimant, Mary Glin Chandler, appeals a judgment of the district court which affirmed the decisions of an Administrative Law Judge (ALJ) and the Director of Workers Compensation which awarded benefits to another claimant, Eliza Davis Chandler, as the surviving widow of Fred R. Chandler, Sr., deceased. Mary Chandler appealed, claiming that the district court erred in failing to require the claimed common-law wife to overcome the presumption of validity of the subsequent ceremonial marriage between claimant Mary and the deceased. In an unpublished opinion filed August 28, 1992, the Court of Appeals reversed and remanded for further proceedings. 839 P.2d 82. Eliza Chandler's petition for review was granted by this court.

Fred R. Chandler, Sr., was shot during a robbery in the course of his employment as a gas station attendant for Central Oil Corporation, Inc., respondent. Fred died on July 18, 1988, as a result of his injury.

Fred fathered three children with three different women. Fred had a son named Ruben Holmes who was born on March 6, 1955, to Dorothy R. Johnson. Fred and Dorothy were never married. Ruben was 33 years old when Fred was killed. Ruben never appeared in this action.

After his relationship with Dorothy, Fred married three women and fathered two other children. He first married Noletta J. Carter on June 20, 1964. Fred and Noletta were divorced on June 1, 1973. There were no children born of this marriage.

The second wife, Eliza, began living with Fred in 1969. Rosalin Chandler, the daughter of Fred and Eliza, was born August 27, 1971. She turned 18 on August 27, 1989, after Fred's death, while this case was pending. Eliza and Fred were married in Arkansas on July 7, 1972. Eliza did not know that Fred was still married to Noletta at the time. Eliza and Fred continued to live together after Fred's divorce from Noletta became final.

Mary, the third wife, and Fred began living together in April 1982. They were married on July 10, 1985, in Kansas City, Kansas. Fred R. Chandler, Jr., the son of Fred and Mary, was born July 14, 1983. Mary also had six children who were not Fred's natural children. Fred and Mary lived together until his death on July 18, 1988.

After Fred's death, both Eliza and Mary claimed to be the surviving spouse. In determining whether Eliza or Mary was entitled to Fred's workers compensation death benefits, the ALJ concluded that, because Eliza and Fred continued to live together and hold themselves out as husband and wife after Fred's divorce from Noletta became final, a common-law marriage existed between Eliza and Fred. Under these facts, Fred lacked capacity to enter into the subsequent marriage with Mary because his prior common-law marriage to Eliza had not been dissolved. The ALJ found that

Think About It

Draw a timeline showing the chronology of Fred's relationships with Dorothy, Noletta, Eliza and Mary. What is the basis for the ALJ's ruling that Eliza and Fred had a valid marriage? When did it become valid?

because Eliza was the common-law wife of Fred at the time of his death, Eliza and her children were entitled to receive benefits in various amounts and at various periods of time. The ALJ denied benefits to Mary and her children, except for Fred, Jr.'s, own benefits. Mary appealed to the Director of Workers Compensation. The Director upheld the ALJ. Mary appealed to the district court.

The district court observed the only issue on review was who was the surviving spouse of Fred R. Chandler, Sr. After reviewing the testimony, the exhibits, the submission letters of the parties, and oral arguments, the district court affirmed the ALJ and the Director's determination that Eliza Chandler was the surviving spouse and, as a result, entitled to the benefits.

The district court noted that well-settled law in Kansas recognizes a common-law marriage if three elements are present: (1) the requisite capacities of the parties to marry; (2) a present marriage agreement between the parties; and (3) a holding out of each other as husband and wife to the public. * * * The district court pointed out that both the award of the ALJ and the order of the Director recognized the prerequisites for a common-law marriage and set forth in detail the factual basis for concluding that such a relationship existed between Fred and Eliza at the time Fred died. The district court concluded the three elements required for a common-law marriage existed between Fred and Eliza. Because the subsequent marriage of Fred to Mary Chandler was void and of no legal effect, Eliza, as the surviving spouse of Fred Chandler, Sr., was entitled to all benefits allowed under the Workers Compensation Act to the surviving widow. The district court affirmed the award of the ALJ and the Director. Mary appealed to the Court of Appeals.

In an unpublished opinion, the Court of Appeals noted that in proceedings under the Workers Compensation Act, the burden of proof is on the claimant to establish the claimant's right to an award of compensation and to prove the various conditions on which the claimant's right depends. In determining whether the claimant has satisfied this burden of proof, the trier of fact considers the whole record. K.S.A.1991 Supp. 44–501(a). It observed that K.S.A.1991 Supp. 44–508(g) defines burden of proof under workers compensation as "the burden of a party to persuade the trier of facts by a preponderance of the credible evidence that such party's position on an issue is more probably true than not true on the basis of the whole record." It observed that under these statutes, both Mary and Eliza had the burden to prove by a preponderance of the evidence they were entitled to benefits as Fred's surviving spouse. The Court of Appeals noted that Mary claims she is entitled to a presumption that her subsequent marriage to Fred was valid under *Harper v. Dupree*, 185 Kan. 483, Syl. ¶ 2, 345 P.2d 644 (1959).

In *Harper*, a husband sought to have his marriage annulled because his alleged wife had a surviving spouse from a previous marriage. * * *

The *Harper* court noted that *the majority view is that a second or subsequent marriage of a person is presumed to be valid;* that such presumption is stronger than and overcomes or rebuts the presumption of the continuance of the previous marriage, and that the burden of proving the continuance of the previous marriage, and the invalidity of the second marriage, is upon the party attacking the validity of the subsequent marriage. To overcome the presumption of validity, and to sustain the burden of proving the invalidity of a marriage, every reasonable possibility of validity must be negatived, and the evidence to overcome the presumption of validity of the subsequent marriage must be clear, strong, and satisfactory and so persuasive as to leave no room for reasonable doubt. In other words, the burden of proving that a divorce has not been granted to either party to a former marriage is substantial and is not met by proof of facts from which mere inferences may be drawn. 185 Kan. at 487, 345 P.2d 644.

* * *

Eliza argues that this presumption applies only when a party to the marriage seeks to annul the marriage; because she is not a party to the marriage, the presumption does not apply. The Court of Appeals pointed out that Eliza's argument is inconsistent with *Hawkins v. Weinberger*, 368 F.Supp. 896 (D.Kan.1973), in which the United States District Court for the District of Kansas applied the presumption of validity of the second marriage against the alleged spouse of a prior common-law marriage who was attempting to obtain social security benefits as the decedent's surviving widow. * * * The Court of Appeals found that this case is controlled by *Harper* and that the *Hawkins* rationale applies because here, as in *Hawkins*, the prior common-law spouse sought to invalidate the decedent's subsequent ceremonial marriage in order to receive dependent benefits.

Think About It

There are two presumptions in conflict here: the presumption that Fred's marriage to Eliza is continuing, and the presumption that his second or subsequent marriage to Mary is valid. How does the court resolve the conflict between these two presumptions?

* * *

The Court of Appeals reversed and remanded the cause with directions to the district court to (1) apply the presumption of validity to the marriage of Fred and Mary and then permit Eliza the opportunity to rebut such presumption; and (2) after deciding which of the claimants was the wife of the worker at the time of his death, determine how the benefits for dependent children/stepchildren should be divided. The Court of Appeals held that if the district court after remand concludes that Mary was the surviving spouse of Fred, the court must also consider whether Mary's children from a previous marriage were entitled to dependent benefits as stepchildren pursuant to K.S.A.1991 Supp. 44–508(c)(3)(B) and (C).

* * *

We agree with the Court of Appeals' statement that, because of the peculiar nature of the relationship of marriage and the grave consequences attendant upon its subversion, the law raises a presumption of validity of a subsequent marriage, and such presumption is " 'one of the strongest known to the law.' " *Harper v. Dupree*, 185 Kan. at 488 (quoting *Shepard v. Carter*, 86 Kan. 125, 130, 119 P. 533 [1911]). Where an attempt is made to annul a marriage on the ground of a prior subsisting marriage of the other party, the presumption of validity of the subsequent marriage is stronger than and overcomes the presumption of the continuance of the previous marriage, and one who seeks to impeach the subsequent marriage assumes the burden of proving by evidence " 'so cogent as to compel conviction' " that the previous marriage has not been dissolved. *Harper v. Dupree*, 185 Kan. at 488, 345 P.2d 644.

On remand, to overcome the presumption of validity and to sustain the burden of proving the invalidity of the marriage of Mary and Fred, every reasonable possibility of validity of that marriage must be negatived, and Eliza's evidence of a continuing common-law marriage to overcome the presumption of validity of the subsequent marriage must be clear, strong, and satisfactory and so persuasive as to leave no room for reasonable doubt. Clear and convincing evidence is evidence that is certain, unambiguous, and plain to the understanding and so reasonable and persuasive as to cause the trier of fact to believe it. Clear and convincing evidence is not a quantum of proof, but rather a quality of proof; thus, a party establishes a claim by a preponderance of the evidence, but this evidence must be clear and convincing in nature.

> **FYI**
>
> *Chandler* was modified by In re B.D.-Y., 187 P.3d 594 (Kan. 2008), which described the "clear and convincing" standard as falling between proof by a preponderance of evidence and proof beyond a reasonable doubt. The court said that clear and convincing evidence is "that which is sufficient to establish that the truth of the facts asserted is 'highly probable.' " Id. at 601.

Judgment of the district court is reversed and the case is remanded. Judgment of the Court of Appeals is affirmed as modified.

Points for Discussion

a. Presumption of Validity

What is the basis for the presumption of the validity of the later marriage? Is it that the probabilities of the situation favor the validity of that marriage? Or is it some consideration of social policy?

To rebut the presumption in this case, Eliza must prove that her marriage to Fred was not terminated in some fashion prior to his death. How could their marriage have been terminated without Eliza being aware of that fact? The possibility of **ex parte divorce** is addressed in Chapter 6. As a practical matter, what evidence would Eliza have to present to "negative every reasonable possibility" that Fred's marriage to Mary is valid?

b. Removal of Impediments

As described in *Chandler*, Fred Chandler married his second wife, Eliza, in 1972, while he was still married to his first wife. The trial court concluded that Fred and Eliza's continued cohabitation after the termination of Fred's first marriage gave rise to a common law marriage under Kansas law. Most cases take the position that if a married couple begin living together when there is an impediment to their marriage, usually a prior existing marriage, and they continue to live together after the impediment is removed, as by divorce or death, a common law marriage results if either or both parties had begun living together in bona fide ignorance of the impediment. In states that do not recognize common law marriage, the same result may be reached through statutes or judicial decisions. See, e.g., Mass. Ann. L. ch. 207, § 6 (2018); Wis. Stat. Ann. § 765.24 (2018).

c. Presumptions in Favor of Marriage

Once a marriage has been proved, various presumptions flow from this fact. These include the presumption that the marriage was contracted in good faith, that it was performed by a person having authority, and that the parties had the capacity to marry. In other words, the marriage is presumed valid, and the party attacking it has the burden of proving it invalid. As in *Chandler*, a conflict may arise between the presumption that a marriage once contracted is valid and continues, and the presumption that the later of two marriages is valid. The latter presumption is often said to be the stronger. Stewart v. Hampton, 506 So.2d 70 (Fla.Ct.App.1987). The presumption of validity of the later marriage, without proof, was held not sufficient to support a bigamy conviction in State v. Rivera, 977 P.2d 1247 (Wash. Ct. App. 1999). For further discussion of these presumptions and the presumption of the validity of the later marriage, see Homer H. Clark, Jr., Domestic Relations § 2.7 (Student 2d ed. 1988).

Gomez v. Windows on the World

804 N.Y.S.2d 849 (App. Div. 2005)

CARDONA, P.J.

Appeal from a decision of the Workers' Compensation Board, filed July 6, 2004, which ruled that claimant is the legal widow of decedent and awarded her workers' compensation death benefits.

Wilder Gomez (hereinafter decedent) died on September 11, 2001 in the terrorist attacks upon the World Trade Center in New York City. When claimant applied for a workers' compensation death benefit as decedent's surviving spouse, Elisa Gomez Escalante objected and likewise sought a death benefit as decedent's surviving spouse. It appears that decedent married Escalante in his native Colombia in 1984 and, following his solitary emigration to the United States in 1991, decedent married claimant in New York in 1992.

After decedent's work-related death was established, a Workers' Compensation Law Judge (hereinafter WCLJ) concluded that claimant was decedent's surviving spouse and awarded benefits. Upon Escalante's application for further review, the Workers' Compensation Board affirmed, prompting this appeal.

Initially, we agree with Escalante that the Board should have formally considered certain evidence which had not been presented to the WCLJ but which was submitted as part of her application for Board review. Escalante indicated to the WCLJ that she had been married to one Guillermo Rojas in 1981 but divorced him before her marriage to decedent. In support of this claim, Escalante submitted her Colombian "civil registry record of birth" which noted, among other facts, that she had obtained a "separación de cuerpos" from Rojas and thereafter "contracted civil matrimony" with decedent. Based upon the Spanish-to-English translation provided and representations made by Escalante's counsel, the WCLJ apparently concluded that Escalante and Rojas had merely been legally separated (see generally Domestic Relations Law art. 11) and that, as a result, her subsequent marriage to decedent was "questionable." Therefore, according to the WCLJ, that proof failed to overcome the presumptive validity of decedent's marriage to claimant (see Matter of Seidel v. Crown Indus., 132 A.D.2d 729, 730, 517 N.Y.S.2d 310 [1987]).

In her application for Board review, however, Escalante submitted a copy of the actual order of separación de cuerpos and an affidavit of an experienced Colombian attorney, Sulamita Kaim Torres. Kaim Torres attested that the "birth registry" submitted by Escalante is a statutorily-derived, "unique and definitive" catalogue of facts relating to a person's legal capacity and status. Moreover, Kaim

Torres indicated that, under then-existing Colombian law, a separacion de cuerpos was used to civilly dissolve a canonic or religious marriage—such as purportedly existed between Escalante and Rojas—and that the device served as the functional equivalent to a divorce in that context.

Assuming the Board's unfamiliarity with the laws of Colombia, which are pertinent to the resolution of the instant dispute, and inasmuch as Escalante proffered a credible excuse for failing to present the evidence in question to the WCLJ, we conclude that the Board should have formally considered this additional proof. However, in light of the fact that the Board stated that the new evidence, even if considered, would not change its determination, we decline to remit the matter for additional factfinding, and will instead review the record before us to ascertain whether the Board's determination in favor of claimant is supported by substantial evidence (see generally 111 NY Jur.2d, Workers Compensation § § 772, 773).

It has long been the rule that, where a marriage has been proven by the facts adduced, there exists a presumption that such marriage is valid. However, where, as here, two competing putative spouses have come forth with adequate proof establishing the existence of their respective matrimonies, the law further presumes that it is the second marriage which is valid and that the first marriage was dissolved by death, divorce or annulment. Thus, it was Escalante's burden to prove that the more recent marriage of decedent to claimant was invalid due to the continued existence of her own marriage to decedent. Regardless of whether Escalante's burden of persuasion is set at a clear and convincing standard or something less stringent, it is our view that Escalante has sufficiently established the vitality of her marriage to decedent and thus rebutted the presumptive validity of claimant's marriage to decedent.

As discussed above, Escalante produced documentary proof that a Columbian court issued a judgment of separación de cuerpos dissolving her marriage to Rojas, a fact further evidenced by a consistent notation on her Colombian civil registry form. This evidence, in conjunction with Colombian documentation of her subsequent marriage to decedent, sufficiently resolves any question concerning Escalante's capacity to marry decedent. Moreover, Escalante affirmatively testified that she and decedent never divorced and that decedent continued to provide for her and their three children following his emigration. Escalante's assertion is further buttressed by the fact that decedent disavowed any prior marriages on the marriage certificate associated with his marriage to claimant. Significantly, the notarized Colombian marriage registration documenting the union between Escalante and decedent, as well as Escalante's civil registry, both of which were generated by Colombian authorities after decedent's death, make no mention of any dissolution of the marriage. Again, Kaim Torres explained the significance of the absence of such notation on Escalante's registry form and, further, there is record evidence indicating that no divorce action involving decedent or Escalante has been commenced anywhere within New York City. Accordingly, inasmuch as we find the presumptive validity of decedent's marriage to claimant to be sufficiently rebutted by Escalante's proof, and insofar as claimant has failed to adduce affirmative proof of the invalidity of Escalante's marriage to decedent, we find the decision unsupported by substantial evidence.

holding [

ORDERED that the decision is reversed, without costs, and matter remitted to the Workers' Compensation Board for further proceedings not inconsistent with this Court's decision.

Points for Discussion

a. *Gomez*

Is the standard the New York court applied in *Gomez* different from the one articulated by the Kansas court in *Chandler*? If not, what explains the different outcome?

b. Proof of Personal Status

There is no U.S. equivalent to the Colombian birth registry described in *Gomez*, which is also found in other civil law countries. In the United States, birth, death, and marriage certificates are public records maintained by local or state authorities in the place where the birth, death or marriage occurred. For a single individual, these records may be scattered in different jurisdictions. In most states, the only official record of a divorce is the court decree issued in a divorce proceeding, available from the clerk of the local court. Because there is no central registry of divorce proceedings or decrees, it can be difficult to know where to search. What evidence other than her "birth registry" was Escalante's lawyer able to present in this case? Would that have been sufficient to establish her right to the workers' compensation benefits?

Problem 1-14

John and Barbara were married in 1996 in Texas. They lived together for about three years in Texas and in Maryland, except for a time while John was in prison and later when he was in the army. They had two children. John left the family in September 1999 while they were living in Texas. He telephoned Barbara three months later to tell her he would not return. In 2003, Barbara telephoned John to ask for his cooperation in obtaining a divorce. John said she should have a lawyer draw the papers, send them to him, and he would sign and return them with half the money for the lawyer's fee. Barbara did so, but John never returned either the papers or the fee.

In 2007, after John was killed in an auto accident, Barbara applied for social security benefits. The Social Security Administration investigated, found no divorce decree, and awarded survivor benefits to Barbara as John's widow and to their children. Barbara later learned that John had married a woman named Nancy in North Carolina in December 1999. John and Nancy lived together for eight years in Maryland and Virginia, and had three children. After John's death, Nancy brought a wrongful death action. She obtained a settlement of $400,000, and Barbara was notified of the settlement. Can Barbara claim the $400,000? What does she need to prove to be entitled to the money? (See Hewitt v. Firestone Tire & Rubber Co., 490 F.Supp. 1358 (E.D.Va.1980).)

Polygamous Marriages

Polygamy, or more specifically polygyny, is a form of marriage in which a man marries and lives at one time with several wives and their children. Polygamous marriages are legally permitted in many countries around the world, particularly in Africa and in Muslim countries. Polygamy is practiced in a few places in the United States, but the practice was harshly suppressed in the nineteenth century in federal legislation. The argument that polygamy based on religious belief came within the protection of the First Amendment was rejected in Reynolds v. United States, 98 U.S. 145 (1878). See generally Nancy F. Cott, Public Vows: A History of Marriage and the Nation 105-131 (2000).

Criminal prosecutions of polygamists in the western United States have continued in more recent years. A Utah man with multiple wives and more than 25 children was convicted for failure to provide child support, multiple counts of bigamy, and other crimes related to marrying and fathering a child with a 13-year-old girl. State v. Green, 99 P.3d 820 (Utah 2004). Some individuals attempt to avoid violation of the criminal law by entering into a legal marriage with only one of their several "wives;" see, e.g., Barlow v. Blackburn, 798 P.2d 1360 (Ariz. Ct.App.1990); State v. Holm, 137 P.3d 726 (Utah 2006). In the *Green* and *Holm* cases the court sustained Utah's statute criminalizing bigamous cohabitation. The statute was challenged directly in Brown v. Buhman, 947 F. Supp. 2d 1170 (D. Utah 2013), by members of a polygamous family known for their appearance in a reality television series. After the action was filed, the local county attorney's office adopted a policy limiting prosecution under the statute to cases involving misrepresentation, fraud, or abuse. The trial court ruled that the prohibition of polygamous cohabitation was facially unconstitutional under the First Amendment, but the judgment was later vacated on mootness grounds. <u>Brown v. Buhman, 822 F.3d 1151 (10th Cir. 2016)</u>.

Despite the universal rule in the United States that polygamous marriages are not valid, courts have been willing to grant non-matrimonial relief based on a polygamous foreign marriage that was valid in the place where it was contracted. See In <u>re Dalip Singh Bir's Estate, 188 P.2d 499 (Cal.Ct.App. 1948)</u> (recognizing valid polygamous marriage for purposes of intestate succession). Immigration laws expressly exclude polygamists from entry into the United States, and polygamous marriages are not recognized in this context. See <u>8 U.S.C. § 1182(a)(10)(A) (2012)</u>; Kerry Abrams, <u>*Immigration Law and the Regulation of Marriage,* 91 Minn. L. Rev. 1625 (2007)</u>.

Problem 1-15

When G applies for a license to marry J, the local official refuses to issue a license because G is already married to D. G and J challenge the state statutory and constitutional provisions that prohibit their marriage as a violation of their rights under the First Amendment, <u>Lawrence v. Texas, 539 U.S. 558 (2003)</u>, and <u>Obergefell v. Hodges, 576 U.S.   , 135 S.Ct. 2584 (2015)</u>. All three individuals subscribe to the religious doctrine of plural marriage. How should the court evaluate this claim? (Cf. <u>Bronson v. Swensen, 394 F.Supp.2d 1329 (D. Utah 2005)</u>; <u>Bronson v. Swensen, 500 F.3d 1099 (10th Cir. 2007)</u>.)

---

2. Marriages Within Families: Incest?

All states have statutes prohibiting marriages within various degrees of kinship, and most of these provide that such marriages are void. All states prohibit marriages between ancestors and descendants, and between brothers and sisters of the half-blood as well as the whole blood, illegitimate as well as legitimate. Nearly all states prohibit the marriages of uncle and niece and aunt and nephew, and a large number prohibit the marriages of first cousins. Many states forbid marriages between stepparents and stepchildren, and a few prohibit marriages in which there is some other family relationship by marriage.

Incest prohibitions are also enforced through criminal laws that punish sexual relations or marriage between certain family members. See, e.g., Model Penal Code § 230.2, 10A U.L.A. 601 (2001); Colo. Rev. Stat. § 18–6–301 (2018). In addition, the issue sometimes arises in child protection proceedings. See In re Zachary B., 662 N.W.2d 360 (Wis. Ct. App. 2003) (considering statute permitting involuntary termination of parental rights on basis of incestuous parenthood).

Nguyen v. Holder

21 N.E.3d 1023 (N.Y. 2014)

MEMORANDUM

Following certification of a question by the United States Court of Appeals for the Second Circuit and acceptance of the question by this Court, and after hearing argument by counsel for the parties and consideration of the briefs and the record submitted, certified question answered in the negative. A marriage where a husband is the half brother of the wife's mother is not void as incestuous under Domestic Relations Law § 5(3).

Smith, J. (concurring).

The United States Court of Appeals for the Second Circuit has asked us whether a marriage between a half uncle and half niece is void as incestuous under Domestic Relations Law § 5(3). I agree, for the following reasons, that we should answer that it is not.

I

Petitioner is a citizen of Vietnam. In January of 2000, at the age of 19, she was married in Rochester, New York to Vu Truong, who was 24 and a naturalized American citizen. Later that year, petitioner was granted the status of a conditional permanent resident in the United States on the basis of her marriage.

According to the factual findings of the United States Board of Immigration Appeals, which the Second Circuit accepted as supported by substantial evidence, petitioner's mother was born in 1950 to a woman named Nguyen Thi Ba. Twenty-five years later, Nguyen Thi Ba gave birth to Vu Truong. Petitioner's mother and Vu Truong had different fathers. Thus petitioner's mother was Vu Truong's half sister, and petitioner is his half niece.

An immigration judge ordered petitioner removed from the country on the ground that her purported marriage to an American citizen was void, and the Board of Immigration Appeals affirmed. Petitioner sought review of that ruling in the Second Circuit, and the Second Circuit certified the following question to us:

> "Does section 5(3) of New York's Domestic Relations Law void as incestuous a marriage between an uncle and niece 'of the half blood' (that is, where the husband is the half-brother of the wife's mother)?"(743 F.3d 311, 317 [2014].)

II

Section 5 of the Domestic Relations Law reads in full:

> "A marriage is incestuous and void whether the relatives are legitimate or illegitimate between either:

> "1. An ancestor and a descendant;
> "2. A brother and sister of either the whole or the half blood;
> "3. An uncle and niece or an aunt and nephew.

> "If a marriage prohibited by the foregoing provisions of this section be solemnized it shall be void, and the parties thereto shall each be fined not less than fifty nor more than one hundred dollars and may, in the discretion of the court in addition to said fine, be imprisoned for a term not exceeding six months. Any person who shall knowingly and wilfully solemnize such marriage, or procure or aid in the solemnization of the same, shall be deemed guilty of a misdemeanor and shall be fined or imprisoned in like manner."

We must decide whether subdivision (3) of this statute should be read to include a half uncle and half niece (or half aunt and half nephew). There is something to be said on both sides of this question.

In common speech, the half brother of one's mother or father would usually be referred to as an uncle, and the daughter of one's half sister or half brother would usually be referred to as a niece; the terms "half uncle" and "half niece" are not in common use. Thus it is perfectly plausible to read subdivision (3) as including half blood relatives. On the other hand, the authors of Domestic Relations Law § 5(2), when prohibiting brother-sister marriages, went to the trouble of adding the words "of either the whole or the half blood." No similar words appear in section 5(3), arguably implying that the legislature did not intend the uncle-niece prohibition to reach so far. The statute is ambiguous. Perhaps the likeliest inference is that the authors of section 5(3) gave no particular thought to the half uncle/half niece question, since if they had they could easily have clarified it either way.

Nor does New York case law point to any clear conclusion. In _Audley v. Audley,_ 187 N.Y.S. 652 (1st Dept.1921), the Appellate Division held a marriage between a half uncle and a half niece to be void under section 5(3). But in _Matter of Simms,_ 257 N.E.2d 627 (N.Y. 1970) we, without deciding the question, expressed doubt about _Audley's_ conclusion:

> "If the Legislature had intended that its interdiction on this type of marriage should extend down to the rather more remote relationship of half blood between uncle and niece, it could have made suitable provision. Its failure to do so in the light of its explicit language relating to brothers and sisters suggests it may not have intended to carry the interdiction this far."

Thus there is a holding from the Appellate Division pointing in one direction, and dictum from this Court pointing in the other. Neither is binding on us. I would resolve the issue by considering the nature and the purpose of the statute we interpret.

Domestic Relations Law § 5 is in part a criminal statute: it says that the participants in a prohibited marriage may be fined, and may be imprisoned for up to six months. Penal Law § 255.25, using language very similar to that of Domestic Relations Law § 5 ("ancestor, descendant, brother or sister of either the whole or the half blood, uncle, aunt, nephew or niece"), makes entry into a prohibited marriage a class E felony. Where a criminal statute is ambiguous, courts will normally prefer the more lenient interpretation, and the courts of several other states have followed that rule in interpreting their criminal laws not to prohibit relationships between uncles and nieces, or aunts and nephews, of the half blood. The government says that these cases are distinguishable because they were criminal cases; but we are here interpreting a statute that applies in both civil and criminal cases, and it would be strange at best to hold that the same words in the same statute mean different things in different kinds of litigation.

I also conclude that the apparent purpose of section 5(3) supports a reading that excludes half uncle/half niece marriages from its scope. Section 5 as a whole may be thought of as serving two purposes: it reflects long-held and deeply-rooted values, and it is also concerned with preventing genetic diseases and defects. Section 5(1) and (2), prohibiting primarily parent-child and brother-sister marriages, are grounded in the almost universal horror with which such marriages are viewed—a horror perhaps attributable to the destructive effect on normal family life that would follow if people viewed their parents, children, brothers and sisters as potential sexual partners. As the Appellate Division explained in _Matter of May,_ 117 N.Y.S.2d 345 (3d Dept.1952), _aff'd._ 114 N.E.2d 4 (N.Y. 1953), these relationships are "so incestuous in degree as to have been regarded with abhorrence since time immemorial."

There is no comparably strong objection to uncle-niece marriages. Indeed, until 1893 marriages between uncle and niece or aunt and nephew, of the whole or half blood, were lawful in New York. And 60 years after the prohibition was enacted we affirmed, in *May,* a judgment recognizing as valid a marriage between a half uncle and half niece that was entered into in Rhode Island and permitted by Rhode Island law. It seems from the Appellate Division's reasoning in *May* that the result would have been the same even if a full uncle and full niece had been involved. Thus Domestic Relations Law § 5(3) has not been viewed as expressing strong condemnation of uncle-niece and aunt-nephew relationships.

The second purpose of section 5's prohibition of incest is to prevent the increased risk of genetic disorders generally believed to result from "inbreeding." (It may be no coincidence that the broadening of the incest statute in 1893 was roughly contemporaneous with the development of the modern science of genetics in the late nineteenth century.) We are not geneticists, and the record and the briefs in this case do not contain any scientific analysis; but neither party disputes the intuitively correct-seeming conclusion that the genetic risk in a half uncle, half niece relationship is half what it would be if the parties were related by the full blood. Indeed, both parties acknowledged at oral argument that the risk in a half uncle/half niece marriage is comparable to the risk in a marriage of first cousins. First cousins are allowed to marry in New York, and I conclude that it was not the legislature's purpose to avert the similar, relatively small, genetic risk inherent in relationships like this one.

GRAFFEO, J. (concurring).

Under our long-standing principles of statutory construction, I conclude that a marriage between a half uncle and half niece, or a half aunt and half nephew, is permissible in New York based on the structure of Domestic Relations Law § 5. As this Court observed in *Matter of Simms,* 257 N.E.2d 627 (N.Y. 1970), the legislature included language in subdivision (2) of this statute that prohibits a marriage between a brother and sister of "the half blood," but there is no comparable clause in subdivision (3) voiding marriages between uncles and nieces or aunts and nephews. When the legislature includes a condition in one provision but excludes it from another within the same statute, there arises an "irrefutable inference" that the omission was intentional. Hence, the contrast in the plain language of Domestic Relations Law § 5(2) and (3) compels the conclusion that marriages between half siblings are outlawed but marriages involving half uncles and half nieces or half aunts and half nephews are permissible.

Nevertheless, I write separately to emphasize that the legislature may see fit to revisit this provision. The record before us does not address the question of genetic ramifications for the children of these unions. Some of my colleagues assert that marriages between half uncles and half nieces, or half aunts and half nephews, are no different than marriages between first cousins. Perhaps there is no genetic basis for precluding such unions, but this Court was not presented with any scientific evidence upon which to draw an informed conclusion on this point.

From a public policy perspective, there may be other important concerns. Such relationships could implicate one of the purposes underlying incest laws, i.e., "maintaining the stability of the family hierarchy by protecting young family members from exploitation by older family members in positions of authority, and by reducing competition and jealous friction among family members." Similar intrafamilial concerns may arise regardless of whether the uncle or aunt in the marriage is of whole or half blood in relation to the niece or nephew. The issue of unequal stature in a family or cultural structure may not be implicated in this case but certainly could exist in other contexts, and a number of states have retained statutory prohibitions involving such marriages. These considerations are more appropriately evaluated in the legislative process.

Points for Discussion

a. Marriage Restrictions

Statutes prohibiting the marriage of close family members trace to the ecclesiastical law and to marriage prohibitions in the Bible (Leviticus 18: 6–18). There is a large literature in the social sciences on the origins of incest taboos, which are believed to exist in every human society. Geneticists have explored the harmful consequences resulting from inbreeding, which is often cited as a basis for these statutes. See A.H. Bittles and M.L. Black, *Consanguineous Marriage and Human Evolution*, 39 Ann. Rev. of Anthropology 193 (2010); Bernadette Modell and Aamra Darr, *Genetic Counselling and Customary Consanguineous Marriage*, 3 Nature Reviews 225 (2003).

In re May's Estate, 114 N.E.2d 4 (N.Y. 1953), an earlier case discussed in *Nguyen*, involved a half-uncle and niece who went from New York to Rhode Island to be married, because the statute in Rhode Island permitted Jewish people to marry "within the degrees of affinity or consanguinity allowed by their religion." See R.I. Gen. L. § 15–1–4 (2018). The Uniform Marriage and Divorce Act § 207, 9A U.L.A. (Part 1) 183–84 (1998), forbids uncle-niece and aunt-nephew marriages, "except * * * marriages permitted by the established customs of aboriginal cultures." These statutes are unusual in their acknowledgment of religious and cultural differences concerning the rules for marriage. See generally Ann Laquer

Estin, *Embracing Tradition: Pluralism in American Family Law*, 63 Md. L. Rev. 540 (2004).

b. Scope of Incest Prohibitions

Beyond the central prohibitions on marriage between siblings and marriage between parents or grandparents and their descendants, incest prohibitions in state marriage statutes are different in many respects. For example, many but not all states prohibit marriage between cousins. See Mason v. Mason, 775 N.E.2d 706 (Ind. Ct. App. 2002) (recognizing validity of Tennessee marriage between first cousins as a matter of comity). This variation is even more pronounced when the question is considered in a broader cross-cultural perspective. Other societies accept and even encourage marriages between cousins. See generally Martin Ottenheimer, Forbidden Relatives: The American Myth of Cousin Marriage (1996), which argues that prohibitions on cousin marriage serve a cultural rather than biological purpose.

Note also that statutes in some states forbid marriages between certain persons related by marriage, who have no genetic relationship at all. See, e.g., Mass. Gen. L. Ann. c. 207, §§ 1, 2 (2018); Miss. Code Ann. § 93–1–1 (2018). Although Uniform Marriage and Divorce Act § 207 prohibits marriages of adoptive siblings, Israel v. Allen, 577 P.2d 762 (Colo. 1978), found that a state statute based this provision was unconstitutional, as a violation of equal protection. The court concluded that because there was no blood relationship between the parties the statute failed to satisfy a "minimum rationality" test. On this reasoning, would a prohibition on the marriage of a father and adopted daughter also be unconstitutional?

These questions are not purely hypothetical. See, e.g., In re Adoption of M, 722 A.2d 615 (N.J. Super. Ch. Div. 1998) (vacating adoption so pregnant adoptive daughter could marry her recently-divorced adoptive father). According to the Commissioners' Note to UMDA § 207, "Marriages of brothers and sisters by adoption are prohibited because of the social interest in discouraging romantic attachments between such persons even if there is no genetic risk."

Similar issues arise in interpretation and application of criminal incest statutes. See State v. Rogers, 133 S.E.2d 1 (N.C. 1963) (holding no criminal violation occurred when a father had sexual relations with his adopted daughter), but see State v. George B., 785 A.2d 573 (Conn. 2001) (concluding that lack of a biological relationship was not a defense in grandfather's prosecution for sexual assault). How should this policy be implemented in the criminal law? Should statutes distinguish between consensual and nonconsensual incest? How do cases such as *Lawrence v. Texas* affect this question? See Brett H. McDonnell, *Is Incest Next?* 10 Cardozo Women's L.J. 337 (2004); Note, *Inbred Obscurity: Improving Incest Laws in the Shadow of the "Sexual Family,"* 119 Harv. L. Rev. 2464 (2006).

c. Conflict of Laws and Marriage Evasion

The uncle-niece couple in *May's Estate*, noted above, went from New York to Rhode Island to be married, and then returned to live together in New York for more than thirty years. The opinion in *May* began with the traditional conflict of laws rule, under which courts recognize a marriage if it is valid under the law of the place of celebration, unless it is contrary to a strong public policy in the forum state. See generally Peter Hay, et al., Conflict of Laws § 13.5 (6th ed. 2018). The problem in *May*, and many other cases, was how widely to define the public policy exception to the rule. The Court in *May* decided that the Rhode Island marriage did not violate its strong public policy, even if it would not have been permitted it New York. But some states refuse to recognize marriages of people domiciled in the state who travel somewhere else to enter into a marriage that is not permitted at home. For example, statutes based on the Uniform Marriage Evasion Act bar recognition of a marriage like the one in *May*. The Illinois version of the Act, 750 Ill.Comp.Stat.Ann. § 5/216 (2018), reads as follows:

> "§ 216 Prohibited marriages void if contracted in another state. That if any person residing and intending to continue to reside in this state and who is * * * prohibited from contracting marriage under the laws of this state, shall go into another state or country and there contract a marriage prohibited and declared void by the law of this state, such marriage shall be null and void for all purposes in this state with the same effect as though such prohibited marriage had been entered into in this state."

See also Iowa Code § 595.20 (2018), which treats a marriage solemnized in another jurisdiction as valid in Iowa if it was valid in that jurisdiction and if the parties meet the requirements for a valid marriage under Iowa law. Both Illinois and Iowa prohibit uncle-niece marriages. Conversely, Uniform Marriage and Divorce Act §210 includes a broad marriage recognition principle, validating all marriages "that were valid at the time of the contract or subsequently validated by the laws of the place in which they were contracted or by the domicil of the parties."

Under Restatement (Second) Conflict of Laws § 283(1) (1971), marriage validity is determined by "the local law of the state which, with respect to the particular issue, has the most significant relationship to the spouses and the marriage." Comments to this section suggest that the state where a marriage was celebrated will primarily be concerned with marriage formalities, such as the requirement of a license or ceremony. In cases of conflict as to more substantive aspects of marriage regulation, other states, such as the state where one or both spouses are domiciled at the time of the marriage or immediately afterward, may have a stronger interest. Section 283(2) states that a marriage that meets the requirements of the place of celebration "will everywhere be recognized as valid unless it violates the strong public policy of another state which had the most significant relationship to the spouses and the marriage at the time of the marriage."

What would be the result in a case such as *May* under these approaches? What if the marriage had been invalid in Rhode Island, but valid in New York? See also Catalano v. Catalano, 170 A.2d 726 (Conn. 1961); Leszinske v. Poole, 798 P.2d 1049 (N.M. App. 1990), cert. denied 797 P.2d 983 (N.M.1990).

Note that similar questions arose during the time when same-sex marriages were recognized in some but not all states. See, e.g., Port v. Cowan, 44 A.3d 970 (Md. 2012); Godfrey v. Spano, 920 N.E.2d 328 (N.Y. 2009). See generally Andrew Koppelman, *Interstate Recognition of Same-Sex Marriages and Civil Unions: A Handbook for Judges*, 153 U. Pa. L. Rev. 2143 (2005).

Problem 1-16

Tahereh married her first first cousin, Hamid, in Iran in 1976 and gave birth to their son a year later. She remained behind when Hamid went to the United States on a student visa. Hamid eventually became a U.S. citizen and sponsored the admission of his son to the United States in 1995. In 2005, the son sponsored his mother's immigration. After arriving in the United States, Tahereh filed an action for divorce against Hamid. First cousins are not permitted to marry in the state where Tahereh and Hamid both live now. What issues will the court need to consider to determine whether Tahereh and Hamid have a valid marriage? (See Ghassemi v. Ghassemi, 998 So.2d 731 (La. Ct. App. 2008).)

E. Unmarried Partners

Many couples in the United States live together without marriage. These individuals and their families live with significant legal uncertainty, in terms of their financial and other rights and responsibilities to each other and to third parties. To the extent that unmarried couples have children together, the rules described in the chapters that follow have largely taken marriage out of the equation as a determinant of parental rights and responsibilities. Marriage is still relevant in many parentage determinations, however.

Formal substitutes for marriage such as civil union and registered partnership address these issues at the state level, conferring all or many of the rights and responsibilities of marriage on couples who fulfill the statutory requirements. Where these alternatives are not available, or for couples who choose not to marry, form a civil union or register their partnership, the law provides a much more limited set of rights and remedies.

1. Marriage Alternatives: Civil Union and Registered Partnership

Civil unions were instituted in Vermont in 2000 following the decision in Baker v. State of Vermont, 744 A.2d 864 (Vt. 1999). The Vermont legislation allowed same-sex couples to apply for a license from a town clerk and receive a certificate of civil union. Parties to a civil union have the same legal rights and obligations under state law as married individuals; if their relationship ends, the union must be dissolved through a divorce in a family court. See 1999 Vermont House Bill No. 847, codified at Vt. Stat. Ann. Tit. 15 §§ 1201–1207 and tit. 18 §§ 5160–5169 (2018). When Vermont legalized same-sex marriage in 2009, it allowed couples with civil unions the option of converting to marriage or retaining civil union status.

Like Vermont, New Jersey instituted civil union as an alternative to marriage for same-sex couples in the wake of a court decision. See Lewis v. Harris, 908 A.2d 196 (N.J. 2006). New Jersey had already enacted a statewide domestic partnership registration program which made more a limited set of health care, property and inheritance rights available to same-sex couples and to opposite-sex couples age 62 or older. Civil union laws conferring substantially the same rights and obligations as marriage under state law were also enacted in Connecticut (2005), Delaware (2011), Hawaii (2011), Illinois (2011), New Hampshire (2007), and Rhode Island (2011). Changes came frequently in this area, with several states moving to allow same-sex marriages within a few years after enacting a civil union law.

Another group of states established registered partnership laws for same-sex couples, with a range of legal consequences. In California, Nevada, and Oregon, the rights and obligations of registered partners are substantially the same as those of married couples, while in Colorado, Maine, Maryland and Wisconsin registered couples receive a narrower range of protections.

In states that provide for domestic partnership or civil union, state statutes also provide for dissolution of these partnerships or unions. In states where this status is equivalent to marriage, dissolution follows the same rules applied to divorce. See, e.g. In re Domestic Partnership of Ellis, 76 Cal.Rptr.3d 401 (Ct. App. 2008) (applying putative spouse doctrine to registered partner).

Some state registration laws are also open to opposite-sex couples, or two individuals without a **conjugal** partner relationship, such as siblings. Registration in the District of Columbia is available to any two persons who are at least 18 and competent to contract who are not married or in another domestic partnership.

D.C. Code § 32–702(i) (2018). See also Colo. Rev. Stat. §§ 15–22–101 to –112 (2018). Hawaii allows any two individuals who are legally prohibited from marrying under state law to declare a "reciprocal beneficiary" relationship, including siblings and other pairs of relatives, such as "a widowed mother and her unmarried son." Haw. Rev. Stat. § 572C–1 et seq. (2018).

When same-sex couples gained full access to marriage after *Obergefell*, some states converted civil unions to marriages and phased out the alternative status. Other states continued to allow couples to enter a civil union or register as partners, including California, Colorado, Hawaii, Illinois, Maine, Nevada, New Jersey, Oregon, Washington, and the District of Columbia.

The frequent changes in these laws have generated numerous complications. For example, Estate of Wilson, 150 Cal.Rptr.3d 699 (Ct. App. 2012), addressed the property rights of same-sex spouses who signed a "Pre-Registration Domestic Partnership Agreement" several years before they were able to marry under California law, and concluded that their agreement should be given effect under the state's Uniform Premarital Agreement Act in subsequent inheritance proceedings.

Cross-Border Recognition of Civil Union and Registered Partnership

Marriage alternatives recognized in different states have no effect at the federal level. Moreover, because the definitions and incidents of civil union or registered partnership are slightly different in each state, it can be difficult for these couples to predict what consequences their relationship will have in other states. Some states with civil union or registered partnership laws have statutes addressing this question. See, e.g., Cal. Fam. Code §299.2 (2018); N.J. Stat. Ann. §§ 26:8A–6(c); 37:1–34 (2018). Courts in some states without these laws have recognized an out-of-state civil union or registered partnership as equivalent to marriage based on comity, for the limited purpose of dissolving it. See, e.g., Hunter v. Rose, 975 N.E.2d 857 (Mass. 2012); Neyman v. Buckley, 153 A.3d 1010 (Pa. Super. Ct. 2016).

Make the Connection

Chapter 6 addresses dissolution of civil unions and domestic partnerships.

By contrast, a number of states moved to prevent any recognition of civil unions or other marriage alternatives. See, e.g., Ga. Code Ann. § 19–3–3.1 (2018); Va. Code § 20–45.3 (2018). Note, however, that recognition of adoption, parentage or custody orders involving same-sex couple families is governed by the Full Faith and Credit Clause and the federal Parental Kidnapping Prevention Act (PKPA), 28 U.S.C. § 1738A (2018), discussed in Chapter 7. See, e.g.,

Miller-Jenkins v. Miller-Jenkins, 912 A.2d 951 (Vt. 2006) and Miller-Jenkins v. Miller-Jenkins, 637 S.E.2d 330 (Va. Ct. App. 2006).

How should a state, which does not recognize civil union or registered partnership, handle a case in which an individual seeking to marry in the state has a prior undissolved union or partnership from another state? See Elia-Warnken v. Elia, 972 N.E.2d 17 (Mass. 2012), which treated a same-sex marriage in Massachusetts as bigamous and invalid when one of the partners had entered into a previous civil union in Vermont that had not been properly terminated.

Problem 1-17

Neil and John had lived together for many years when they traveled to a nearby state to have a civil union ceremony. Several years later, back in their home state, Neil was injured in a car accident and died following surgery at a local hospital. John wants to bring an action against the hospital. The applicable statute provides that the personal representative of a decedent "who is survived by distributees" may maintain an action to recover damages for wrongful death. "Distributees" are defined in the statute to include a spouse, children, parents, parents' children, grandparents, grandparents' children, and grandparents' grandchildren, in that order. Will John be permitted to bring the action? If Neil died without a will, can John inherit as his spouse? (See Langan v. St. Vincent's Hospital, 802 N.Y.S.2d 476 (App. Div. 2005).)

Global View: Civil Union and Registered Partnership

Same-sex couple relationships were first extended legal recognition at the national level in the Scandinavian countries, beginning with Denmark's Registered Partnership Act in 1989. Over time, many other countries also moved to create new institutions such as civil union or registered partnership. Some types of alternative status have significant differences from marriage, such as the PACS (*pacte civil de solidarité*) in France. For a sense of the complexity that these differences generated within Europe, see Ian Curry-Sumner, *Interstate Recognition of Same-Sex Relationships in Europe*, 13 J. Gender Race & Just. 59 (2009) (listing 17 European countries with different registration schemes).

The European Court of Human Rights ruled in Oliari v. Italy, [2015] ECtHR 716, that countries must provide access to legal recognition for same-sex couples, and in numerous countries this has taken the form of civil union or registered partnership.

2. Cohabitation Relationships

One of the most dramatic changes in family life over the past generation has been a steep increase in the number of cohabiting couples, which has taken place as marriage rates have dropped and the age of first marriages has increased. A majority of couples who marry live together first, but most cohabiting couples do not go on to marry. Cohabitation relationships are generally shorter in duration than marriages, and marital relationships that are preceded by cohabitation seem to be less stable in the aggregate, although it is not clear whether there is a causal link between premarital cohabitation and marital instability. Patterns of marriage and cohabitation are significantly different based on factors such as race, ethnicity, education and economic status. See Pamela J. Smock and Wendy D. Manning, _Living Together Unmarried in the United States: Demographic Perspectives and Implications for Family Policy_, 26 Law & Pol'y 87 (2004), Cynthia Grant Bowman, _Social Science and Legal Policy: The Case of Heterosexual Cohabitation_, 9 J. L & Fam. Stud. 1 (2007).

Demographers have concluded that at least half of all cohabiting couples live with children, and a substantial portion of nonmarital children are born to cohabiting parents. Data collected in 2012 showed that although the majority of first births occur in marital relationships, there has been a notable decline over time. For women age 15 to 50 whose first child was born before 1992, almost 70% had been married and about 14% were cohabiting with a partner at the time of the child's birth. For those whose first child was born in 2007 or later, 52% were married and 25% cohabiting. See Lindsay M. Monte and Renee R. Ellis, Fertility of Women in the United States: June 2012 (Current Population Reports, 2014).

Go Online

According to the 2010 Census, there were 116.7 million households in the United States, including 56.5 million husband-wife married couple households and 7.7 million unmarried partner households. See Daphne Lofquist et al., Households and Families: 2010 (Census Briefs, 2012).

Despite these broad changes, the law of cohabitation has not changed significantly in most states in the past forty years. As a result, cohabiting couples may have particular need of legal advice to address problems that are not governed by statutes or other sources of law. Legal scholars have focused attention on these trends, describing the rise of "nonmarriage," or "postmarital" family life, and pointing out the need for new thinking and new legal rules. As you read the materials in this section, consider how well the principles described here address the range of legal issues for cohabiting couples.

Marvin v. Marvin

557 P.2d 106 (Cal.1976)

TOBRINER, JUSTICE.

During the past 15 years, there has been a substantial increase in the number of couples living together without marrying.[1] Such nonmarital relationships lead to legal controversy when one partner dies or the couple separates. Courts of Appeal, faced with the task of determining property rights in such cases, have arrived at conflicting positions: two cases (*In re Marriage of Cary* (1973) 34 Cal. App.3d 345, 109 Cal.Rptr. 862; *Estate of Atherley* (1975) 44 Cal.App.3d 758, 119 Cal.Rptr. 41) have held that the Family Law Act (Civ.Code, § 4000 et seq.) requires division of the property according to community property principles, and one decision (*Beckman v. Mayhew* (1974) 49 Cal.App.3d 529, 122 Cal.Rptr. 604) has rejected that holding. We take this opportunity to resolve that controversy and to declare the principles which should govern distribution of property acquired in a nonmarital relationship.

We conclude: (1) The provisions of the Family Law Act do not govern the distribution of property acquired during a nonmarital relationship; such a relationship remains subject solely to judicial decision. (2) The courts should enforce express contracts between nonmarital partners except to the extent that the contract is explicitly founded on the consideration of **meretricious** sexual services. (3) In the absence of an express contract, the courts should inquire into the conduct of the parties to determine whether that conduct demonstrates an implied contract, agreement of partnership or joint venture, or some other tacit understanding between the parties. The courts may also employ the doctrine of quantum meruit, or equitable remedies such as constructive or resulting trusts, when warranted by the facts of the case.

Take Note!

In 1970, the U.S. census recorded 523,000 unmarried partner households in the United States. What is the relevance of this data for Justice Tobriner?

In the instant case plaintiff and defendant lived together for seven years without marrying; all property acquired during this period was taken in defendant's name. When plaintiff sued to enforce a contract under which she was entitled to half the property and to support payments, the trial court granted judgment on the pleadings for defendant, thus leaving him with all property accumulated by

---

[1]   "The 1970 census figures indicate that today perhaps eight times as many couples are living together without being married as cohabited ten years ago." (Comment, *In re Cary: A Judicial Recognition of Illicit Cohabitation* (1974) 25 Hastings L.J. 1226.)

the couple during their relationship. Since the trial court denied plaintiff a trial on the merits of her claim, its decision conflicts with the principles stated above, and must be reversed.

1. The factual setting of this appeal

Since the trial court rendered judgment for defendant on the pleadings, we must accept the allegations of plaintiff's complaint as true, determining whether such allegations state, or can be amended to state, a cause of action. We turn therefore to the specific allegations of the complaint.

Plaintiff avers that in October of 1964 she and defendant "entered into an oral agreement" that while "the parties lived together they would combine their efforts and earnings and would share equally any and all property accumulated as a result of their efforts whether individual or combined." Furthermore, they agreed to "hold themselves out to the general public as husband and wife" and that "plaintiff would further render her services as a companion, homemaker, housekeeper and cook to * * * defendant."

Shortly thereafter plaintiff agreed to "give up her lucrative career as an entertainer [and] singer" in order to "devote her full time to defendant * * * as a companion, homemaker, housekeeper and cook;" in return defendant agreed to "provide for all of plaintiff's financial support and needs for the rest of her life."

Plaintiff alleges that she lived with defendant from October of 1964 through May of 1970 and fulfilled her obligations under the agreement. During this period the parties as a result of their efforts and earnings acquired in defendant's name substantial real and personal property, including motion picture rights worth over $1 million. In May of 1970, however, defendant compelled plaintiff to leave his household. He continued to support plaintiff until November of 1971, but thereafter refused to provide further support.

On the basis of these allegations plaintiff asserts two causes of action. The first, for declaratory relief, asks the court to determine her contract and property rights; the second seeks to impose a constructive trust upon one half of the property acquired during the course of the relationship.

* * *

2. Plaintiff's complaint states a cause of action for breach of an express contract

In _Trutalli v. Meraviglia (1932) 215 Cal. 698, 12 P.2d 430_, we established the principle that nonmarital partners may lawfully contract concerning the ownership of property acquired during the relationship. We reaffirmed this principle in

<u>*Vallera v. Vallera* (1943) 21 Cal.2d 681, 685, 134 P.2d 761, 763</u>, stating that "If a man and woman [who are not married] live together as husband and wife under an agreement to pool their earnings and share equally in their joint accumulations, equity will protect the interests of each in such property."

In the case before us plaintiff, basing her cause of action in contract upon these precedents, maintains that the trial court erred in denying her a trial on the merits of her contention. Although that court did not specify the ground for its conclusion that plaintiff's contractual allegations stated no cause of action, defendant offers some four theories to sustain the ruling; we proceed to examine them.

Defendant first and principally relies on the contention that the alleged contract is so closely related to the supposed "immoral" character of the relationship between plaintiff and himself that the enforcement of the contract would violate public policy. He points to cases asserting that a contract between nonmarital partners is unenforceable if it is "involved in" an illicit relationship, or made in "contemplation" of such a relationship. A review of the numerous California decisions concerning contracts between nonmarital partners, however, reveals that the courts have not employed such broad and uncertain standards to strike down contracts. The decisions instead disclose a narrower and more precise standard: a contract between nonmarital partners is unenforceable only *to the extent* that it *explicitly* rests upon the immoral and illicit consideration of meretricious sexual services.

* * *

Although the past decisions hover over the issue in the somewhat wispy form of the figures of a Chagall painting, we can abstract from those decisions a clear and simple rule. The fact that a man and woman live together without marriage, and engage in a sexual relationship, does not in itself invalidate agreements between them relating to their earnings, property, or expenses. Neither is such an agreement invalid merely because the parties may have contemplated the creation or continuation of a nonmarital relationship when they entered into it. Agreements between nonmarital partners fail only to the extent that they rest upon a consideration of meretricious sexual services. Thus the rule asserted by defendant, that a contract fails if it is "involved in" or made "in contemplation" of a nonmarital relationship, cannot be reconciled with the decisions.

What's That?

The word "**meretricious**" refers here to **prostitution**, or the exchange of money for sex.

The three cases cited by defendant which have *declined* to enforce contracts between nonmarital partners involved consideration that *was* expressly founded upon an illicit sexual services. In <u>Hill v. Estate of Westbrook, supra</u>, the woman promised to keep house for the man, to live with him as man and wife, and to bear his children; the man promised to provide for her in his will, but died without doing so. Reversing a judgment for the woman based on the reasonable value of her services, the Court of Appeal stated that "the action is predicated upon a claim which seeks, among other things, the reasonable value of living with decedent in meretricious relationship and bearing him two children * * *. The law does not award compensation for living with a man as a concubine and bearing him children. * * * As the judgment is, at least in part, for the value of the claimed services for which recovery cannot be had, it must be reversed." Upon retrial, the trial court found that it could not sever the contract and place an independent value upon the legitimate services performed by claimant. We therefore affirmed a judgment for the estate.

In the only other cited decision refusing to enforce a contract, <u>Updeck v. Samuel (1954), 123 Cal.App.2d 264, 266 P.2d 822</u>, the contract "was based on the consideration that the parties live together as husband and wife." Viewing the contract as calling for adultery, the court held it illegal.

The decisions in the *Hill* and *Updeck* cases thus demonstrate that a contract between nonmarital partners, even if expressly made in contemplation of a common living arrangement, is invalid only if sexual acts form an inseparable part of the consideration for the agreement. In sum, a court will not enforce a contract for the pooling of property and earnings if it is explicitly and inseparably based upon services as a paramour. The Court of Appeal opinion in *Hill,* however, indicates that even if sexual services are part of the contractual consideration, any *severable* portion of the contract supported by independent consideration will still be enforced.

* * *

Defendant secondly relies upon the ground suggested by the trial court: that the 1964 contract violated public policy because it impaired the community property rights of Betty Marvin, defendant's lawful wife. * * * But whether or not defendant's contract with plaintiff exceeded his authority as manager of the community property (see former Civ.Code, § 172), defendant's argument fails for the reason that an improper transfer of community property is not void *ab initio,* but merely voidable at the instance of the aggrieved spouse.

In the present case Betty Marvin, the aggrieved spouse, had the opportunity to assert her community property rights in the divorce action. The interlocutory and final decrees in that action fix and limit her interest. Enforcement of the contract between plaintiff and defendant against property awarded to defendant by the divorce decree will not impair any right of Betty's, and thus is not on that account violative of public policy.

Defendant's third contention is noteworthy for the lack of authority advanced in its support. He contends that enforcement of the oral agreement between plaintiff and himself is barred by Civil Code section 5134, which provides that "All contracts for marriage settlements must be in writing * * *." A marriage settlement, however, is an agreement in contemplation of marriage in which each party agrees to release or modify the property rights which would otherwise arise from the marriage. (See *Corker v. Corker* (1891) 87 Cal. 643, 648, 25 P. 922.) The contract at issue here does not conceivably fall within that definition, and thus is beyond the compass of section 5134.[9]

* * *

In summary, we base our opinion on the principle that adults who voluntarily live together and engage in sexual relations are nonetheless as competent as any other persons to contract respecting their earnings and property rights. Of course, they cannot lawfully contract to pay for the performance of sexual services, for such a contract is, in essence, an agreement for prostitution and unlawful for that reason. But they may agree to pool their earnings and to hold all property acquired during the relationship in accord with the law governing community property; conversely they may agree that each partner's earnings and the property acquired from those earnings remains the separate property of the earning partner. So long as the agreement does not rest upon illicit meretricious consideration, the parties may order their economic affairs as they choose, and no policy precludes the courts from enforcing such agreements.

In the present instance, plaintiff alleges that the parties agreed to pool their earnings, that they contracted to share equally in all property acquired, and that defendant agreed to support plaintiff. The terms of the contract as alleged do not rest upon any unlawful consideration. We therefore conclude that the complaint furnishes a suitable basis upon which the trial court can render declaratory relief. The trial court consequently erred in granting defendant's motion for judgment on the pleadings.

3. Plaintiff's complaint can be amended to state a cause of action founded upon theories of implied contract or equitable relief

As we have noted, both causes of action in plaintiff's complaint allege an express contract; neither assert any basis for relief independent from the contract.

---

[9]   Our review of the many cases enforcing agreements between nonmarital partners reveals that the majority of such agreements were oral. In two cases (*Ferguson v. Schuenemann, supra,* 167 Cal.App.2d 413, 334 P.2d 668; *Cline v. Festersen, supra,* 128 Cal.App.2d 380, 275 P.2d 149), the court expressly rejected defenses grounded upon the statute of frauds.

In *In re Marriage of Cary, supra*, 34 Cal.App.3d 345, 109 Cal.Rptr. 862, however, the Court of Appeal held that, in view of the policy of the Family Law Act, property accumulated by nonmarital partners in an actual family relationship should be divided equally. Upon examining the *Cary* opinion, the parties to the present case realized that plaintiff's alleged relationship with defendant might arguably support a cause of action independent of any express contract between the parties. The parties have therefore briefed and discussed the issue of the property rights of a nonmarital partner in the absence of an express contract. Although our conclusion that plaintiff's complaint states a cause of action based on an express contract alone compels us to reverse the judgment for defendant, resolution of the *Cary* issue will serve both to guide the parties upon retrial and to resolve a conflict presently manifest in published Court of Appeal decisions.

Both plaintiff and defendant stand in broad agreement that the law should be fashioned to carry out the reasonable expectations of the parties. Plaintiff, however, presents the following contentions: that the decisions prior to *Cary* rest upon implicit and erroneous notions of punishing a party for his or her guilt in entering into a nonmarital relationship, that such decisions result in an inequitable distribution of property accumulated during the relationship, and that *Cary* correctly held that the enactment of the Family Law Act in 1970 overturned those prior decisions. Defendant in response maintains that the prior decisions merely applied common law principles of contract and property to persons who have deliberately elected to remain outside the bounds of the community property system.[11] *Cary,* defendant contends, erred in holding that the Family Law Act vitiated the force of the prior precedents.

* * *

Janet and Paul Cary had lived together, unmarried, for more than eight years. They held themselves out to friends and family as husband and wife, reared four children, purchased a home and other property, obtained credit, filed joint income tax returns, and otherwise conducted themselves as though they were married. Paul worked outside the home, and Janet generally cared for the house and children.

---

[11]   We note that a deliberate decision to avoid the strictures of the community property system is not the only reason that couples live together without marriage. Some couples may wish to avoid the permanent commitment that marriage implies, yet be willing to share equally any property acquired during the relationship; others may fear the loss of pension, welfare, or tax benefits resulting from marriage (see *Beckman v. Mayhew, supra*, 49 Cal.App.3d 529, 122 Cal.Rptr. 604). Others may engage in the relationship as a possible prelude to marriage. In lower socioeconomic groups the difficulty and expense of dissolving a former marriage often leads couples to choose a nonmarital relationship; many unmarried couples may also incorrectly believe that the doctrine of common law marriage prevails in California, and thus that they are in fact married. Consequently we conclude that the mere fact that a couple have not participated in a valid marriage ceremony cannot serve as a basis for a court's inference that the couple intend to keep their earnings and property separate and independent; the parties' intention can only be ascertained by a more searching inquiry into the nature of their relationship.

In 1971 Paul petitioned for "nullity of the marriage." Following a hearing on that petition, the trial court awarded Janet half the property acquired during the relationship, although all such property was traceable to Paul's earnings. The Court of Appeal affirmed the award.

Reviewing the prior decisions which had denied relief to the homemaking partner, the Court of Appeal reasoned that those decisions rested upon a policy of punishing persons guilty of cohabitation without marriage. The Family Law Act, the court observed, aimed to eliminate fault or guilt as a basis for dividing marital property. But once fault or guilt is excluded, the court reasoned, nothing distinguishes the property rights of a nonmarital "spouse" from those of a putative spouse. Since the latter is entitled to half the "quasi marital property" (Civ.Code, § 4452), the Court of Appeal concluded that, giving effect to the policy of the Family Law Act, a nonmarital cohabitator should also be entitled to half the property accumulated during an "actual family relationship."

* * *

If *Cary* is interpreted as holding that the Family Law Act requires an equal division of property accumulated in nonmarital "actual family relationships," then we agree with <u>Beckman v. Mayhew</u> that *Cary* distends the act. No language in the Family Law Act addresses the property rights of nonmarital partners, and nothing in the legislative history of the act suggests that the Legislature considered that subject. The delineation of the rights of nonmarital partners before 1970 had been fixed entirely by judicial decision; we see no reason to believe that the Legislature, by enacting the Family Law Act, intended to change that state of affairs.

But although we reject the reasoning of *Cary* and *Atherley*, we share the perception of the *Cary* and *Atherley* courts that the application of former precedent in the factual setting of those cases would work an unfair distribution of the property accumulated by the couple. * * *

The principal reason why the pre-*Cary* decisions result in an unfair distribution of property inheres in the court's refusal to permit a nonmarital partner to assert rights based upon accepted principles of implied contract or equity. We have examined the reasons advanced to justify this denial of relief, and find that none have merit.

First, we note that the cases denying relief do not rest their refusal upon any theory of "punishing" a "guilty" partner. Indeed, to the extent that denial of relief "punishes" one partner, it necessarily rewards the other by permitting him to retain a disproportionate amount of the property. Concepts of "guilt" thus cannot justify an unequal division of property between two equally "guilty" persons.

Other reasons advanced in the decisions fare no better. The principal argument seems to be that "[e]quitable considerations arising from the reasonable expectation of * * * benefits attending the status of marriage * * * are not present [in a nonmarital relationship]." (*Vallera v. Vallera, supra,* 21 Cal.2d at p. 685, 134 P.2d 761, 763.) But, although parties to a nonmarital relationship obviously cannot have based any expectations upon the belief that they were married, other expectations and equitable considerations remain. The parties may well expect that property will be divided in accord with the parties' own tacit understanding and that in the absence of such understanding the courts will fairly apportion property accumulated through mutual effort. We need not treat nonmarital partners as putatively married persons in order to apply principles of implied contract, or extend equitable remedies; we need to treat them only as we do any other unmarried persons.[22]

The remaining arguments advanced from time to time to deny remedies to the nonmarital partners are of less moment. There is no more reason to presume that services are contributed as a gift than to presume that funds are contributed as a gift; in any event the better approach is to presume, as Justice Peters suggested, "that the parties intend to deal fairly with each other." (*Keene v. Keene, supra,* 57 Cal.2d 657, 674, 21 Cal.Rptr. 593, 603, 371 P.2d 329, 339 (dissenting opn.)).

The argument that granting remedies to the nonmarital partners would discourage marriage must fail; as *Cary* pointed out, "with equal or greater force the point might be made that the pre-1970 rule was calculated to cause the income producing partner to avoid marriage and thus retain the benefit of all of his or her accumulated earnings." Although we recognize the well-established public policy to foster and promote the institution of marriage, perpetuation of judicial rules which result in an inequitable distribution of property accumulated during a nonmarital relationship is neither a just nor an effective way of carrying out that policy.

In summary, we believe that the prevalence of nonmarital relationships in modern society and the social acceptance of them, marks this as a time when our courts should by no means apply the doctrine of the unlawfulness of the so-called meretricious relationship to the instant case. As we have explained, the nonenforceability of agreements expressly providing for meretricious conduct rested upon the fact that such conduct, as the word suggests, pertained to and encompassed prostitution. To equate the nonmarital relationship of today to such a subject matter is to do violence to an accepted and wholly different practice.

---

[22]   In some instances a confidential relationship may arise between nonmarital partners, and economic transactions between them should be governed by the principles applicable to such relationships.

We are aware that many young couples live together without the solemnization of marriage, in order to make sure that they can successfully later undertake marriage. This trial period, preliminary to marriage, serves as some assurance that the marriage will not subsequently end in dissolution to the harm of both parties. We are aware, as we have stated, of the pervasiveness of nonmarital relationships in other situations.

The mores of the society have indeed changed so radically in regard to cohabitation that we cannot impose a standard based on alleged moral considerations that have apparently been so widely abandoned by so many. Lest we be misunderstood, however, we take this occasion to point out that the structure of society itself largely depends upon the institution of marriage, and nothing we have said in this opinion should be taken to derogate from that institution. The joining of the man and woman in marriage is at once the most socially productive and individually fulfilling relationship that one can enjoy in the course of a lifetime.

We conclude that the judicial barriers that may stand in the way of a policy based upon the fulfillment of the reasonable expectations of the parties to a nonmarital relationship should be removed. As we have explained, the courts now hold that express agreements will be enforced unless they rest on an unlawful meretricious consideration. We add that in the absence of an express agreement, the courts may look to a variety of other remedies in order to protect the parties' lawful expectations.[24]

The courts may inquire into the conduct of the parties to determine whether that conduct demonstrates an implied contract or implied agreement of partnership or joint venture, or some other tacit understanding between the parties. The courts may, when appropriate, employ principles of constructive trust or resulting trust. Finally, a nonmarital partner may recover in quantum meruit for the reasonable value of household services rendered less the reasonable value of support received if he can show that he rendered services with the expectation of monetary reward.[25]

---

[15]   We do not seek to resurrect the doctrine of common law marriage, which was abolished in California by statute in 1895. Thus we do not hold that plaintiff and defendant were "married," nor do we extend to plaintiff the rights which the Family Law Act grants valid or putative spouses; we hold only that she has the same rights to enforce contracts and to assert her equitable interest in property acquired through her effort as does any other unmarried person.

[16]   Our opinion does not preclude the evolution of additional equitable remedies to protect the expectations of the parties to a nonmarital relationship in cases in which existing remedies prove inadequate; the suitability of such remedies may be determined in later cases in light of the factual setting in which they arise.

Since we have determined that plaintiff's complaint states a cause of action for breach of an express contract, and, as we have explained, can be amended to state a cause of action independent of allegations of express contract,[26] we must conclude that the trial court erred in granting defendant a judgment on the pleadings.

The judgment is reversed and the cause remanded for further proceedings consistent with the views expressed herein.

Take Note!

Justice Clark dissented from the second part of the *Marvin* opinion. He agreed that a contract between the parties should be enforced, but he did not think that in the absence of a contract an award should be made in reliance upon "general equitable principles."

* * *

FYI

After the case was remanded to the trial court, Judge Arthur K. Marshall rejected Ms. Marvin's claim to half of the property, but awarded her $104,000, or the equivalent of $1,000 per week for two years, "for rehabilitation purposes." The complete text of Judge Marshall's opinion is reproduced in 5 Fam. L. Rep. 3077 (1979); see also Henry H. Foster, Jr. & Doris Jonas Freed, Marvin v. Marvin: *New Wine in Old Bottles*, 5 Fam. L. Rep. 4001 (1979). Judge Marshall found that there was no express contract between the parties, and no basis for a constructive trust or a resulting trust. He based his award on footnote 25 of the *Marvin* decision, noting her recent resort to unemployment insurance benefits, the fact that her return to a career as a singer was doubtful, and the fact that the market value of Lee Marvin's property at time of separation exceeded $1,000,000. On appeal, the $104,000 award was reversed. The California Court of Appeals held that the rehabilitative support awarded by the trial court was not within the issues framed by the pleadings and that, as the plaintiff had benefited economically and socially from her association with the defendant, the defendant had no equitable obligation to provide support for her. Marvin v. Marvin, 176 Cal.Rptr. 555 (Ct.App.1981).

For more on what followed the case, see Ann Laquer Estin, *Ordinary Cohabitation*, 76 Notre Dame L. Rev. 1381 (2001).

---

[17]   We do not pass upon the question whether, in the absence of an express or implied contractual obligation, a party to a nonmarital relationship is entitled to support payments from the other party after the relationship terminates.

Points for Discussion

a. Express Contracts

The first part of <u>Marvin</u> holds that unmarried cohabitants may make enforceable contracts concerning their financial and property affairs. This principle is widely accepted by courts around the country, which routinely enforce express contracts made by cohabitants; see. e.g., <u>Wilcox v. Trautz, 693 N.E.2d 141 (Mass. 1998)</u>; <u>Boland v. Catalano, 521 A.2d 142 (Conn. 1987)</u>. Courts in a few jurisdictions refuse to enforce cohabitation contracts, however. See <u>Hewitt v. Hewitt, 394 N.E.2d 1204 (Ill. 1979)</u>; <u>Rehak v. Mathis, 238 S.E.2d 81 (Ga. 1977)</u>; and <u>Schwegmann v. Schwegmann, 441 So.2d 316 (La. App. 1983)</u>, cert. denied <u>467 U.S. 1206 (1984)</u>.

Should cohabitation agreements be tested for disclosure and fair dealing? <u>Wilcox v. Trautz, *supra*</u>, concluded that a cohabitation agreement is enforceable "so long as it conforms to the ordinary rules of contract law." What defenses might be asserted in a case seeking enforcement of a cohabitation contract? How does the law governing cohabitation contracts compare with the rules for premarital and marital agreements?

b. Implied Contracts and Equitable Relief

The second branch of *Marvin* holds that even in the absence of any contract, relief may be granted based on an "implied contract" theory or on equitable grounds, such as implied partnership, **constructive trust**, **resulting trust**, or **quantum meruit**. The use of these equitable remedies to compensate unmarried cohabitants at the end of their relationship is discussed in the next case and the notes that follow it.

Courts in other states disagree on whether to enforce implied agreements between cohabitants. In <u>Morone v. Morone, 413 N.E.2d 1154 (N.Y. 1980)</u>, the court refused to follow this aspect of *Marvin*, finding "an implied contract such as was recognized in [*Marvin*] to be conceptually so amorphous as practically to defy enforcement, and inconsistent with the legislative policy enunciated in 1933 when common law marriages were abolished in New York. . . ." In contrast, <u>Watts v. Watts, 405 N.W.2d 303 (Wis. 1987)</u>, followed *Marvin*. See also <u>Goode v. Goode, 396 S.E.2d 430 (W. Va. 1990)</u>. In some of these cases it is unclear whether the court is finding an **implied-in-fact contract** or an **implied-in-law contract**. What kind of evidence would be sufficient to prove that an unmarried couple had an unspoken agreement regarding their financial rights and responsibilities to each other? See, e.g., <u>Cook v. Cook, 691 P.2d 664 (Ariz. 1984)</u> (finding agreement from parties' course of conduct).

Courts in a few jurisdictions may enter property distribution orders in long term cohabitation cases based on "general equitable principles," without looking for evidence of an agreement or grounds for a restitution claim. See, e.g., Eaton v. Johnston, 681 P.2d 606 (Kan. 1984); Williams v. Mason, 556 So.2d 1045 (Miss.1990); Beal v. Beal, 577 P.2d 507 (Or. 1978). In Washington, courts have taken the step that the court refused to take in *Marvin*, applying the state's community property laws to unmarried cohabitants in settled, long-term relationships "by analogy." See Connell v. Francisco, 898 P.2d 831 (Wash. 1995); Matter of Marriage of Lindsey, 678 P.2d 328 (Wash. 1984). See also Tomal v. Anderson, 426 P.3d 915 (Alaska 2018); Western States Const. Inc. v. Michoff, 840 P.2d 1220 (Nev. 1992).

Claims for "palimony"—ongoing support payments after the termination of a cohabitation relationship—have been recognized in California based on *Marvin*, but the overwhelming weight of authority around the country rejects this kind of claim. See Devaney v. L'Esperance, 949 A.2d 743 (N.J. 2008). Although New Jersey did allow palimony claims, as described in *Devaney*, these cases were superseded by statute in 2010, and "palimony" contracts are no longer enforceable in New Jersey unless the terms are in writing and both parties were represented by counsel.

c. Common Law Marriage

How does the court in *Marvin* deal with the fact that California had abolished common law marriage? Is there any distinction between common law marriage and the relationship of the parties in *Marvin*? How does the remedy granted in *Marvin* differ from the rights available to a common-law spouse?

Other courts have felt constrained by state laws abolishing common law marriage in deciding how far to allow claims by unmarried couples at the end of their cohabitation. See *Morone*, cited above, in which the parties lived together twelve years in a "marriage-like" relationship, had two children, and described themselves as husband and wife in various documents such as income tax returns and deeds to property. See also *Hewitt*, which concluded that enforcement of express cohabitation contracts would contravene the public policies reflected in the statutes governing marriage and divorce, particularly the law abolishing common law marriage in 1905. Why did most states abolish common law marriage? Are those reasons relevant to these cohabitation cases?

d. Consideration

What was the consideration alleged by Michelle Marvin in support of her contract claims? After *Marvin*, what would be considered an illicit or meretricious basis for a contract? See, e.g., Della Zoppa v. Della Zoppa, 103 Cal.Rptr.2d 901 (Ct. App. 2001).

Could one cohabitant enforce the other's promise to make a gift of property? See, e.g., <u>Williams v. Ormsby, 966 N.E.2d 255 (Ohio 2012)</u>.

e. Statutes of Frauds

Legislatures in several states have enacted statutes of frauds to require that cohabitation contracts must be signed and in writing. See <u>Tex. Bus. & Com. Code §§ 26.01(b)(3)(2018)</u>, applied in <u>Zaremba v. Cliburn, 949 S.W.2d 822 (Tex. Ct. App. 1997)</u>, and <u>Minn. Stat. Ann. §§ 513.075, 513.076 (2018)</u>, applied in <u>In re Estate of Eriksen, 337 N.W.2d 671 (Minn.1983)</u>. These statutes may not bar restitution claims, however; see <u>In re Estate of Palmen, 588 N.W.2d 493 (Minn.1999)</u>, reversing <u>574 N.W.2d 743 (Minn. Ct. App. 1998)</u> (allowing unjust enrichment claim despite lack of written contract). See also <u>N.J. Stat. Ann. § 25:1–5(h) (2018)</u>, which requires that support contracts made by cohabitants must be in writing and made with independent advice of counsel on both sides.

f. Same-Sex Couples and Cohabitation Agreements

Courts have provided the same range of remedies to same-sex cohabiting couples that are available to opposite-sex couples. See, e.g., <u>Posik v. Layton, 695 So.2d 759 (Fla. Ct. App. 1997)</u>; <u>Weekes v. Gay, 256 S.E.2d 901 (Ga. 1979)</u>; <u>Seward v. Mentrup, 622 N.E.2d 756 (Ohio Ct. App. 1993)</u>; <u>Ireland v. Flanagan, 627 P.2d 496 (Or. Ct. App. 1981)</u>; <u>Gormley v. Robertson, 83 P.3d 1042 (Wash. Ct. App. 2004)</u>. As with other cohabitant agreements, the question of meretricious consideration may be an issue these cases. See <u>Whorton v. Dillingham, 248 Cal. Rptr. 405 (Cal. Ct. App. 1988)</u>, which found that the sexual component of the consideration recited in the parties' agreement was severable from the rest of the contract.

g. Property Law Remedies

If an unmarried couple has jointly-owned property, such as a bank account or real estate, a partition action allows the court to divide that asset. See, for example, <u>Hofstad v. Christie, 240 P.3d 816 (Wyo. 2010)</u>, reprinted in Chapter 6. See also <u>Blumenthal v. Brewer, 69 N.E.3d 834 (Ill. 2016)</u>, which approved partition of a couple's jointly-owned home but rejected counterclaims for equitable division of other property.

Client Counseling: Cohabitation

If you had a wealthy client who was contemplating a *Marvin* relationship, what legal advice would you offer? Would you recommend some sort of contract, and if so, what should it provide?

Problem 1-18

After dating Russell for six years, based on his representation that he was getting a divorce from his wife, Gail quit her job as an elementary school teacher and moved into his apartment. Russell and Gail entertained and traveled extensively and maintained a lavish lifestyle, paid for by Russell, for eighteen years. When Russell broke up with Gail, he had still never gotten a divorce. Gail brought an action for promissory estoppel, fraud, breach of promise to marry, and intentional infliction of emotional distress. She alleges that if not for Russell's repeated promises to divorce his wife, marry her, and support her for the rest of her life, she would ended the relationship years earlier. Should the court allow Gail's claims to proceed? (See Norton v. McOsker, 407 F.3d 501 (1st Cir. 2005).)

Problem 1-19

Laura and Dena lived together in a committed relationship for 20 years without marrying. Each of them gave birth to a child, and each adopted the other's child. After their first child was born, the couple agreed that Laura would give up her full time employment to work part time and take primary responsibility for the couple's children. They have recently separated, and Laura seeks an equal share of all assets acquired by either partner during their years together. What legal theories can she use, and what does she need to plead and prove in order to recover? (See Dee v. Rakower, 976 N.Y.S.2d 470 (App. Div. 2013).)

Porter v. Zuromski

6 A.3d 372 (Md. Ct. Spec. App. 2010)

ZARNOCH, J.

Is this, as appellant contends, "nothing more than a palimony case," or is it, as appellee argues, unjust enrichment of one partner in an unmarried relationship at the expense of the other, justifying the imposition of an implied trust? After a February 2009 bench trial, Anne Arundel County Circuit Judge Michele Jaklitsch sided with appellee/plaintiff Donna Zuromski, and against appellant/defendant, Sean Porter. This appeal of the circuit court's decision calls upon us to address, for the first time, property rights issues oft-litigated in other jurisdictions. *See* Annot., *Property Rights Arising From Relationship of Couple Cohabiting Without Marriage, 69 A.L.R.5th 219 (1999, 2010 Supp.)* (*"Cohabitation-Property Rights"*). For reasons set forth below, we affirm the judgment of the circuit court.

FACTS AND PROCEEDINGS

This is a dispute over real property located on Washington Avenue in Shady Side, Maryland. In her March 31, 2007 Memorandum Opinion, the trial judge summarized the relevant facts in this case:

The parties were romantically involved from 1993 through June 2007. They became engaged to be married in 1995, but postponed their wedding after Plaintiff's brother was injured in an accident in 1996. The parties lived with Plaintiff's mother in Fort Washington, Maryland, for approximately three years, during which time Defendant assisted around the house and in caring for Plaintiff's brother, and Plaintiff paid the rent of $600 each month to allow Defendant to save money for the parties. Defendant deposited his savings into a joint checking account held in both parties' names.

In 1997, the parties decided to purchase a home together. Defendant found a house, and in February 1998, the parties applied for a mortgage loan together at Severn Savings Bank to finance the purchase. Because of Plaintiff's credit score and impending bankruptcy filing (filed in May 1999), the parties were unable to qualify for a loan jointly. The parties then agreed that Defendant would apply for a mortgage loan again, this time in his name only. Defendant paid a down payment of $4500 from the parties' joint checking account, and Plaintiff paid Defendant $3700 for her contribution toward the down payment. The parties agreed that although Plaintiff could not qualify for a mortgage, the parties would act as joint owners of the property and Plaintiff would pay Defendant one half the mortgage expenses, and one half of all other property expenses each month.[1] The parties never had an agreement that Plaintiff would be a tenant; rather, they agreed that she was to be a joint owner. The parties agreed that Defendant's name would appear on the deed, but he would hold the property for both parties.[2] Defendant promised Plaintiff that in the future he would put Plaintiff's name on the deed and that the property would be held in joint tenancy.

The parties made significant improvements to the house, with each of them working extensively to the best of their capabilities, and with the help of friends of both parties. Plaintiff's mother's friend, Allen Keller, installed the HVAC system with the understanding that the house was to be jointly owned by both Plaintiff and Defendant. Defendant's friends installed drywall and other improvements.

Plaintiff paid one half of all mortgage, construction loan, utility, and other expense payments on the property until the parties' relationship deteriorated in mid-2007. In January 2007, the parties ended their engagement, but the parties stayed together as a couple and Plaintiff con-

---

[1]   This agreement was never reduced to writing.
[2]   Zuromski testified that in 2003 Porter again said he would put her name on the deed.

tinued making mortgage and home expense payments to Defendant. In May 2007, Defendant moved out of the parties' shared bedroom in the house. In July 2007, on the termination of their romantic relationship, Defendant ordered Plaintiff to vacate the property. Defendant refused the Plaintiff's request to divide the equity in the home, and he instituted a refinancing on the property which stripped a substantial portion of the equity out of the property.

On October 18, 2007, Zuromski filed a six-count complaint in the circuit court, asserting that Porter's actions: 1) warranted imposition of a constructive trust; 2) required the establishment of a resulting trust; 3) unjustly enriched Porter; 4) constituted a promissory estoppel; 5) required entry of a declaratory judgment declaring that Zuromski was entitled to one-half ownership of the property; and 6) mandated injunctive relief. Porter answered and denied liability.

In February 2009, a two-day trial was held. The following month, the trial judge issued a memorandum opinion and order. The court found that Zuromski had "established the existence of a constructive trust as an equitable remedy for unjust enrichment." It emphasized that in cases where only one party holds title, a constructive trust should be imposed, not only where fraud or misrepresentation exists, but also "when the circumstances render it inequitable for the party holding the title to retain it." The court said that this standard was satisfied in this case.

The circuit court also found an additional basis for imposing a constructive trust. Porter, as holder of legal title to the property, was the dominant party in a confidential relationship.[7]

Finally, the court said that, even absent a confidential relationship between the parties, it would find a constructive trust on the basis of unjust enrichment. As a result, the court declared that the parties each had an "undivided one half interest in the subject property as tenants in common." It denied any specific monetary award, an injunction, and other claimed relief, but did not expressly address the resulting trust claim.[8] The court declared that each party had an undivided interest in the property and appointed a trustee to transfer title and to cause a new deed to be prepared reflecting joint ownership. This appeal followed.

---

[7]   Specifically, the court found:

The parties' testimony indicates that Plaintiff and Defendant were engaged in an intimate romantic relationship and were planning marriage. Defendant purported to act in Plaintiff's best interests when he discussed placing her name on the deed in the future. The parties' sexual relationship was not the sole consideration for this agreement. Plaintiff had no reason to believe that Defendant may be motivated by anything other than his feelings for her and interest in a financially secure future together. Under the circumstances, Plaintiff was "justified in assuming" that Defendant would act in her best interest and that a written agreement establishing the joint tenancy was not required. . . . As such, this Court finds that a confidential relationship did exist between Defendant and Plaintiff.

[8]   Of course, the court was under no obligation to address the issue in light of the fact that the constructive trust count sought the identical relief pursued under the resulting trust theory.

QUESTIONS PRESENTED

Porter has raised a single issue in this appeal:

On the facts of this case, did the trial judge commit reversible error by imposing a constructive trust on real property owned by Appellant and appointing a Trustee to transfer title to the same?

Zuromski has raised an alternative ground for upholding the judgment in the circuit court, which we have phrased as the following question:

Was there sufficient evidence before the trial court to support the imposition of a resulting trust?[10]

DISCUSSION

1. Constructive Trust

A constructive trust is a remedy that converts the holder of legal title to property into a trustee for one who in good conscience should reap the benefits of the property. _Wimmer v. Wimmer_, 287 Md. 663, 668, 414 A.2d 1254 (1980). Its purpose is to prevent the unjust enrichment of the holder of the property. This remedy applies "where a property has been acquired by fraud, misrepresentation, or other improper method, or where the circumstances render it inequitable for the party holding the title to retain it." Ordinarily, such factors must be shown by clear and convincing evidence. However, this rule changes, " [o]nce a confidential relationship is shown.[12] Then, a presumption arises that confidence was placed in the dominant party and that the transaction complained of resulted from fraud or undue influence and superiority or abuse of the confidential relationship by which the dominant party profited." This presumption shifts the burden to the defendant to show the fairness and reasonableness of the transaction. Of course, our review of whether the trial judge's findings of fact on these points are supported in the record is governed by the clearly erroneous rule. _See_ Md. Rule 8–131(c) (Appellate court "will not set aside the judgment of the trial court on the evidence unless clearly erroneous, and will give due regard to the opportunity of the trial court to judge the credibility of the witnesses.").

A. Fraud

At the outset, Porter challenges some of these principles that guided the circuit court's decision. He particularly takes aim at the trial court's reliance on _Hartsock v. Strong, supra_, 21 Md.App. at 116, 318 A.2d 237, for the proposition

---

[10]   A constructive trust and a resulting trust are both implied trusts. _Jahnigen v. Smith_, 143 Md.App. 547, 557–58, 795 A.2d 234 (2002).

[12]   A confidential relationship exists "where one party is under the domination of another or where, under the circumstances, such party is justified in assuming that the other will not act in a manner inconsistent with his or her welfare." _Bass v. Smith_, 189 Md. 461, 469, 56 A.2d 800 (1948).

that a constructive trust may arise from some equitable principle independent of fraud. He suggests that *Hartsock* may have been weakened by our decision in *Jahnigen v. Smith*, 143 Md.App. 547, 795 A.2d 234 (2002), where, at one point in our opinion, we noted: "[T]he facts as presented do not support an action for constructive trust because there has been no allegation of misrepresentation, fraud, or other improper methods of obtaining title." However, *Jahnigen* flatly states that, in addition to fraud and these other grounds, a constructive trust may be found "where the circumstances render it inequitable for the party holding title to retain it." Moreover, just six months after *Jahnigen* was decided, we once again restated the principles governing imposition of a constructive trust, noting that the remedy could be invoked for inequitable circumstances independent of fraud. *Turner v. Turner*, 147 Md.App. 350, 421–22, 809 A.2d 18 (2002).

Porter also contends that *Wimmer* undercuts the circuit court decision here. In *Wimmer*, the Court of Appeals overturned the imposition of a constructive trust upon a one-half interest in a marital home purchased with the husband's funds and titled in his name. In rejecting the wife's claim, the Court emphasized that the wife parted with no money or labor with respect to the property and thus, the title holder was not unjustly enriched. The very facts found missing in *Wimmer* are present here. To be sure, the *Wimmer* court also noted that the husband made no misrepresentations as to the title to the property. But *Wimmer* is clearly not a case of absence-of-fraud equals no-claim. It is one "where the circumstances [did not] render it inequitable for the party holding the title to retain it," because he was not unjustly enriched at the expense of the plaintiff. Thus, nothing in *Wimmer* suggests that Zuromski would have to make a showing of fraud in order to prevail here.

B. Palimony

Porter denigrates Zuromski's constructive trust claim as a palimony action not recognized in this State. This argument is misplaced here. The appellee was not seeking "alimony from or for a pal." *See Attorney Grievance Commission v. Ficker*, 319 Md. 305, 320, 572 A.2d 501 (1990).[14] Nor was her lawsuit an action for support. *See* Annot. *"Palimony" Actions for Support Following Termination of Nonmarital Relationships*, 21 A.L.R.6th 351 (2005, 2010 Supp.). It was not "based on" promises or commitments to marriage, *see Miller v. Ratner*, 114 Md.App. 18, 50, 688 A.2d 976 (1997), or predicated upon meretricious sexual services. *Ficker*, 319 Md. at 319, 572 A.2d 501; *Baxter v. Wilburn*, 172 Md. 160, 162–63, 190 A. 773 (1937). Rather, Zuromski's claim arises from her financial contributions to the property and the unjust enrichment that would consequently occur if Porter retained sole title to the house.

---

[14] *Ficker* discusses the many permutations of the term "palimony." 319 Md. at 318–22, 572 A.2d 501.

C. Joint Banking Account

Porter contends that "[a] key element of Appellee's case and the trial court's decision was that the parties established a joint bank account into which Appellant deposited virtually all of the funds while Appellee used her money to pay rent to her mother, in whose house the parties were living." He goes on to argue that "[t]he law is that no gift of Appellant's funds to the Appellee was complete until she withdrew them from that joint account, which she did not do, and that, to the extent Appellant may have withdrawn any funds she had deposited into that account, a gift from her to him was completed at that time."

A fair reading of the trial court's opinion does not support the contention that the joint banking account for the house was a "key element" of the decision to impose a constructive trust. What was critical was that Zuromski made substantial financial contributions toward the purchase of the house and paid half of the mortgage charges and other home expenses.

This is not a case where one party to a joint banking account claims an interest in property purchased with funds withdrawn solely by the other account holder, exclusively for his own purposes. *See Hamilton v. Caplan*, 69 Md.App. 566, 586, 518 A.2d 1087 (1987). Nor does Zuromski assert that Porter's withdrawal of funds from the account were improper. *See Kornmann v. Safe Deposit & Trust Co.*, 180 Md. 270, 23 A.2d 692 (1942). Rather, when the Shady Side property was purchased in 1999, both parties drew checks on the account to pay the down payment: Porter's was payable to the lender and Zuromski's was payable to Porter, apparently to be endorsed and paid over to the mortgage holder. This record belies the contention that these withdrawals and others by Zuromski were gifts to Porter. On the contrary, she withdrew funds in accordance with the couple's plan to save money for a home, and their agreement to pay for it jointly—a factor that supports a finding of a constructive trust. *See* 76 Am.Jur.2d *Trusts, supra* at § 132 ("[A] constructive trust is independent of any agreement between the parties—although the existence of some agreement may serve as a factor in determining whether to impose a constructive trust. . .").

D. Appellant's Other Legal Objections

A volley of additional legal arguments from Porter's scattershot attack on the circuit court decision all miss their target. He contends that the trial court should not have ignored his testimony that he never intended that Zuromski have title to the property. However, a constructive trust is independent of any agreement between the parties. Restatement of the Law, *Restitution* at § 160 Comment b. ("A constructive trust is imposed not because of the intention of the parties but because the person holding the title to the property would profit by a wrong or would be unjustly enriched if he were permitted to keep the property."); 76

Am.Jur.2d *Trusts* § 132 (2005) ("A constructive trust is independent of any agreement between the parties. . ."). Even if the circuit court found Porter's testimony credible, it would have not called into question the trial judge's conclusion that, by operation of law, a constructive trust was required to be imposed.

* * *

E. Sufficiency of Evidence

Porter's question presented asks whether "[o]n the facts of this case" the trial court erred by imposing a constructive trust. In our view, the answer to this question is a resounding "no."

The evidence in this case clearly supports the imposition of a constructive trust. Porter testified that he told Zuromski he would put her on the title to the property, but privately he never really intended to do so. Such conduct smacks of misrepresentation if not fraud. But fraud need not be found here to uphold the circuit court's judgment. Zuromski's monetary and non-monetary investments in the property demonstrated that she clearly relied on Porter's representation that she would become co-owner of the house. In our view, these circumstances would render it inequitable for Porter to retain exclusive title and would justify imposition of a constructive trust.

On this record, the same result is reached if Porter's conduct is examined as an abuse of a confidential relationship. We think there is no doubt that a confidential relationship existed between the parties. This Court recently noted that, in the context of prenuptial agreements, while there is no presumption that spouses are in a confidential relationship, an engaged couple could occupy a confidential relationship. *Lasater v. Guttmann*, 194 Md.App. 431, 459 n. 19, 5 A.3d 79, 95 (2010). Out of state cases, more directly on point, also recognize that couples cohabitating or planning to marry can be parties to a confidential relationship, the breach of which can lead to imposition of a constructive trust on property. *See Hatton v. Meade*, 23 Mass.App.Ct. 356, 502 N.E.2d 552, 557 (1987); *Hudson v. DeLonjay*, 732 S.W.2d 922, 929 (Mo.App.1987); *Rhue v. Rhue*, 189 N.C.App. 299, 658 S.E.2d 52, 59 (2008). *See generally Cohabitation-Property Rights, supra*, 69 A.L.R.5th at § 3.

Other factors support the finding of a confidential relationship here. Porter's sole name on the title made him a dominant party in the relationship and, by his representation that he would put Zuromski on the title, she was justified in assuming that Porter would not act inconsistent with her welfare. Porter's attempt to profit from the relationship by solely retaining title to the property abused the confidential relationship, shifting the burden to him to show the fairness and reasonableness of his action. On this record, he has failed to meet this burden and a constructive trust was justified.

2. Resulting Trust

In the alternative, Zuromski contends that the record before the trial court also supported the finding of a resulting trust. In *Jahnigen, supra, 143 Md.App. at 558, 795 A.2d 234*, we noted that "[w]here a transfer of property is made to one person, and only a part of the purchase price is paid by another, a resulting trust arises in favor of the person by whom said payment is made. . . ." A resulting trust has also been described in the following fashion:

> Under compelling circumstances, courts may impose a resulting trust. A resulting trust is not a trust at all, but rather it is an equitable remedy designed to prevent unjust enrichment and to ensure that legal formalities do not frustrate the original intent of the transacting parties. Such a trust is implied by law from the acts and conduct of the parties and the facts and circumstances which at the time exist and surround the transaction out of which it arises. Broadly speaking, a resulting trust arises from the nature or circumstances of consideration involved in a transaction whereby one person becomes invested with a legal title but is obligated in equity to hold his or her legal title for the benefit of another, and there ordinarily being no fraud or constructive fraud involved.

76 Am.Jur.2d *Trusts* § 135.

One legal observer, seemingly predicting the scenario of this case, has said:

> Resulting trusts, also known as purchase money resulting trusts, arise when one partner, intending the property bought to be for his or her benefit and not that of another, pays all or part of the purchase price but title is taken in the name of another.

Mary L. Bonauto, *Advising Non-Traditional Families,* 40 Boston Bar Journ. 10, 11 (Sept.–Oct. 1996). In a resulting trust, the intent of the parties that a trust relationship result is important. 76 Am.Jur.2d, *Trusts, supra* at § 132.

Some of the facts of this case raise the possibility of a resulting trust and courts in other jurisdictions—where circumstances required—have found a resulting trust where unmarried cohabitants were involved. *See Cohabitation-Property Rights, supra, 69 A.L.R.5th at § 3.* However, this is an issue the circuit court did not decide, and we need not decide it here. For all of the reasons set forth above, we affirm the circuit court's imposition of a constructive trust, its declaration that each party has an undivided interest in the property, and the appointment of a trustee to transfer title.

JUDGMENT OF THE CIRCUIT COURT FOR ANNE ARUNDEL COUNTY AFFIRMED. COSTS TO BE PAID BY APPELLANT.

Points for Discussion

a. Constructive and Resulting Trusts

What relief does the court award Ms. Zuromski in this case? Based on the discussion in *Porter*, what is the distinction between a constructive trust and a resulting trust? Why do you think the trial court based its ruling on the constructive trust theory? Resulting trusts are described in the <u>Restatement (Third) of Trusts § 7 (2003)</u>; constructive trusts are discussed in the <u>Restatement (Third) of Restitution and Unjust Enrichment § 55 (2011)</u>.

b. Restitution-Based Remedies

In many cohabitation cases, courts have required compensation for one party's financial investment in the other's property or business. See, e.g., <u>Salzman v. Bachrach, 996 P.2d 1263, 1266 (Colo. 2000)</u>; <u>Bass v. Bass, 814 S.W.2d 38 (Tenn. 1991)</u>; <u>Weekes v. Gay, 256 S.E.2d 901, 904 (Ga. 1979)</u>. Courts also routinely order recovery in quantum meruit for services such as work for a partner's business or on home construction and renovation. See, e.g., <u>Suggs v. Norris, 364 S.E.2d 159 (N.C. Ct. App.)</u>, cert. denied <u>370 S.E.2d 236 (N.C. 1988)</u>; <u>Harman v. Rogers, 510 A.2d 161, 165 (Vt. 1986)</u>.

Courts have generally refused to order compensation for such contributions as household services, paying household expenses, raising or supporting children or stepchildren, or assisting with a partner's career. E.g. <u>Maria v. Freitas, 832 P.2d 259 (Haw. 1992)</u>. See also Ann Laquer Estin, <u>*Ordinary Cohabitation*, 76 Notre Dame L. Rev. 1381 (2001)</u>.

Make the Connection

Chapter 6 includes further discussion of financial remedies for unmarried cohabitants.

On restitution-based claims of cohabitants, see generally <u>Restatement (Third) of Restitution and Unjust Enrichment § 28 (2011)</u>.

Problem 1-20

For the first four years of their relationship, Sandra and Dennis lived together in Sandra's apartment, where she paid the rent as well as all household expenses. Dennis saved his earnings for the down payment on a house. When Dennis had accumulated $11,000, he used it to purchase a house, which was titled in his name alone. Sandra and Dennis moved into the house and lived together there for eight years. Although they were engaged throughout this time, they never married. Dennis made all mortgage and tax payments; Sandra paid for groceries and the utility bills. She did the cooking, cleaning and laundry, and he did maintenance work. At the time their relationship ended, Dennis had $90,000 in equity in the house. Does Sandra have a claim against Dennis? (See <u>Ward v. Jahnke, 583 N.W.2d 656 (Wis. Ct. App. 1998)</u>.)

Problem 1-21

Kurt and Stephanie, both college students, lived together for 16 months. After they broke up, Kurt filed in small claims court, seeking reimbursement of $2500 worth of expenses he incurred on Stephanie's behalf during their relationship. These expenses included $800 for her share of the rent during the last four months they lived together, $640 toward her car payments, $300 for a plane ticket, and the rest for books, magazines, movie rentals and groceries. Can Kurt recover under either an implied contract or restitution theory? (See <u>Soderholm v. Kosty, 676 N.Y.S.2d 850 (Justice Ct. 1998)</u>.)

Global View: Cohabitation Law

Judicial rulings and legislation in many Canadian provinces extend certain rights and protections to cohabitants in marriage-like or "common law" relationships at the federal and provincial level. See Julien D. Payne & Marilyn A. Payne, Canadian Family Law 38-57 (6th ed. 2015). Civil law countries including France extend some legal rights to a cohabiting partner, referred to as a *concubine,* and many Latin American countries recognize the de facto union or *unión marital de hecho.* Informal statuses that are not fully equivalent to marriage are not given any effect in legal proceedings in the United States. See, <u>e.g., Bandsa v. Wheeler, 995 A.2d 189 (D.C. 2010)</u>; <u>American Airlines v. Mejia, 766 So.2d 305 (Fla. Ct. App. 2000)</u>.

New Zealand has extended property rights automatically to couples who have lived together for three years or more, including inheritance rights and a right to division of relationship property at the end of their "de facto relationship." Couples may enter into an agreement to opt out of the statutory scheme. See generally Bill Atkin, <u>*The Challenge of Unmarried Cohabitation—The New Zealand Response,* 37 Fam. L.Q. 303 (2003)</u>. What are the benefits and disadvantages of this approach? Would you favor enacting it into law in your jurisdiction?

Legal Effects of Unmarried Cohabitation

Cases such as *Marvin* and *Porter* address the financial claims and remedies that may be available between cohabitants at the end of their relationship, but do not address the question of whether and when cohabitation relationships should have broader legal consequences. Here are some of the other questions courts have considered.

(a) Should an unmarried cohabitant, on separation, be granted a share of the other partner's pension rights? See Wilbur v. DeLapp, 850 P.2d 1151 (Or. Ct. App. 1993) (awarding share of pension rights); Boulds v. Nielsen, 323 P.3d 58 (Alaska 2014).

(b) Should the surviving member of a cohabiting couple have the same inheritance rights as a spouse? See Olver v. Fowler, 168 P.3d 348 (Wash. 2007) (allowing distribution of jointly acquired property, but not partner's separate property, under the "meretricious relationship" doctrine), and Northrup v. Brigham, 826 N.E.2d 239 (Mass. Ct. App. 2005) (allowing cohabitant to bring quantum meruit claim against partner's estate).

(c) Courts in some states treat a husband as the "equitable parent" of a child born to his wife during the marriage, even if that child is not his biological child, provided that he has treated the child as his own. Should the doctrine be extended to a cohabiting partner who lived with the child's mother, supporting and caring for the child? See Van v. Zahorik, 597 N.W.2d 15 (Mich.1999).

(d) Should cohabiting couples come within the scope of civil and criminal laws addressing domestic violence? See Petrowsky v. Krause, 588 N.W.2d 318 (Wis. Ct. App. 1998). Cf. Peterman v. Meeker, 855 So.2d 690 (Fla. Ct. App. 2003).

(e) Can unmarried cohabitants claim marital evidentiary privileges? See People v. Delph, 156 Cal.Rptr. 422 (Ct. App. 1979).

(f) Should an automobile insurance policy that includes coverage for a policyholder's "spouse" be construed to include a cohabiting partner? See Cole v. State Farm Insurance Company, 128 P.3d 171 (Alaska 2006).

(g) Should one partner be permitted to sue in tort if the other is negligently and seriously injured by a third party, in circumstances in which a spouse would have a claim for loss of consortium? *Compare* Lozoya v. Sanchez, 66 P.3d 948 (N.M. 2003) (allowing consortium claim) with Elden v. Sheldon, 758 P.2d 582

(Cal. 1988) and Medley v. Strong, 558 N.E.2d 244 (Ill. App. Ct. 1990) (no consortium claim). See also Dunphy v. Gregor, 642 A.2d 372 (N.J. 1994) (cohabitant may have claim as bystander for negligent infliction of emotional distress).

(h) If the wage-earning member of a couple were killed in an industrial accident, should the other partner be entitled to recover workers' compensation benefits? Should the partner recover for wrongful death if the decedent died as a result of another's negligence? See Sykes v. Propane Power Corp., 541 A.2d 271 (N.J. Super. Ct. App. Div. 1988) (denying recovery). Cf. Or. Rev. Stat. § 656.226 (2018), which provides that where two unmarried individuals have cohabited as spouses for more than a year in Oregon and have children, the surviving cohabitant and children are entitled to worker's compensation as if there had been a legal marriage.

(i) Should a landlord's refusal to rent an apartment to a cohabiting couple violate an ordinance or statute prohibiting discrimination based on marital status? Compare Donahue v. Fair Employment and Housing Commission, 2 Cal. Rptr.2d 32 (Ct. App. 1991), petition for review granted 825 P.2d 766 (Cal. 1992) review dismissed and cause remanded 859 P.2d 671 (Cal. 1993) (refusal to rent to unmarried couple violated city ordinance) with County of Dane v. Norman, 497 N.W.2d 714 (Wis. 1993) (refusal did not violate ordinance).

Given the limited range of protections for cohabitants in the law, unmarried couples should consider not only cohabitation agreements but also how they title assets and other measures such as writing wills, making beneficiary designations, and preparing durable powers of attorney and heath care advance directives. One popular guide on these questions is Frederick Hertz and Lina Guillen, Living Together: A Legal Guide for Unmarried Couples (16th ed. 2017).

Ending Marriage?

The decline in marriage rates and rise in unmarried cohabitation, the advent of same-sex marriage and the invention of civil union and registered partnership laws prompted writers from different political perspectives to call for abolishing state-sanctioned civil marriage, and replacing it with some other form of contract-based family regulation. See, for example, Nancy D. Polikoff, *Ending Marriage as We Know It*, 32 Hofstra L. Rev. 201 (2003), which argues against laws that confer special privileges on marital relationships. See also *Symposium on Abolishing Civil Marriage*, 27 Cardozo L. Rev. 1155 (2006), and Elizabeth S. Scott, *A World Without Marriage*, 41 Fam. L.Q. 537 (2007).

Further Reading: Cohabitation

- Albertina Antognini, <u>The Law of Nonmarriage, 58 B.C. L. Rev. 1 (2017)</u>.

- Cynthia Grant Bowman, *Unmarried Couples, Law, and Public Policy* (2010).

- June Carbone and Naomi Cahn, *Nonmarriage*, 76 Md L. Rev. 55 (2016)

- Marsha Garrison, <u>*Is Consent Necessary? An Evaluation of the Emerging Law of Cohabitant Obligation*, 52 UCLA L. Rev. 815 (2005)</u>.

- Clare Huntington, <u>*Postmarital Family Law: A Legal Structure for Non-marital Families*, 67 Stan. L. Rev. 167 (2015)</u>.

CHAPTER 2

———

Having Children

———

Parent-child relationships are created by law and biology, and by the lived experiences of family members. Until recent scientific advances made it possible to determine a child's genetic parentage, the law constructed parent-child relationships almost exclusively on the basis of marriage, and children born outside of marriage bore the stigma of illegitimacy. Law has also regulated reproduction, shaping access to contraception and abortion and defining rights during pregnancy and on the birth of a child. This chapter begins with reproductive rights and regulations, and then turns to the definition of parent-child relationships for children born within and outside of marriage. Chapter 3 considers the laws that shape and respond to adoption and assisted reproduction as additional means of creating families.

A. Reproductive Rights and Regulations

Although some methods of preventing and terminating pregnancy are ancient, laws regulating pregnancy, contraception, and abortion emerged in the United States during the nineteenth century. Congress passed legislation known as the Comstock Law in 1873, which defined contraceptives as obscene and forbid both importing into the United States and sending through the mails any article designed for the prevention of conception as well as writings describing such articles. The Comstock Law remained in the United States Code until 1971, and many states adopted similar laws. Historians have explored the relationship between these laws and changing patterns of economic and family life during this period, as well as the campaign led by Margaret Sanger to challenge restrictions on birth control in the early twentieth century. See, e.g., Linda Gordon, Woman's Body, Woman's Right: Birth Control in America (rev. ed. 1990).

Even as many states restricted access to contraception by the early twentieth century, a substantial number of states also enacted statutes authorizing involuntary sterilization of some individuals on eugenic grounds. In 1927, Buck v. Bell, 274 U.S. 200 (1927) upheld a statute permitting Virginia to sterilize an 18-year-old resident of a state institution. Accepting the evidence that Carrie Buck and her mother were "feeble-minded," and the lower court's conclusion that she was "the probably potential parent of socially inadequate offspring," Justice Holmes's opinion for the Supreme Court observed that "Three generations of imbeciles are enough." Id. at 207. The real story of Carrie Buck, however, was significantly different from the version presented to the Court. See Paul A. Lombardo, Three Generations, No Imbeciles: Eugenics, the Supreme Court and Buck v. Bell (2008).

An important turning point came in 1941, when the Supreme Court found that an Oklahoma statute that provided for sterilization of "habitual criminals" was unconstitutional. Skinner v. Oklahoma, 316 U.S. 535 (1942). The statute applied to persons convicted three times of felonies involving "moral turpitude," a category that included stealing chickens but did not include some felony offenses such as embezzlement. Writing for the Court, in the first opinion to employ "strict scrutiny" under the Equal Protection Clause, Justice Douglas wrote:

> We are dealing here with legislation which involves one of the basic civil rights of man. Marriage and procreation are fundamental to the very existence and survival of the race. The power to sterilize, if exercised, may have subtle, far reaching and devastating effects. In evil or reckless hands it can cause races or types which are inimical to the dominant group to wither and disappear. There is no redemption for the individual whom the law touches. Any experiment which the State conducts is to his irreparable injury. He is forever deprived of a basic liberty. We mention these matters not to reexamine the scope of the police power of the States. We advert to them merely in emphasis of our view that strict scrutiny of the classification which a State makes in a sterilization law is essential, lest unwittingly or otherwise invidious discriminations are made against groups or types of individuals in violation of the constitutional guaranty of just and equal laws.

316 U.S. at 541. With this language, *Skinner* set the stage for the Court's later decisions treating the rights to marriage and procreation as fundamental.

1. Contraception, Pregnancy, and Childbirth

In spite of criminal prosecutions under federal and state statutes during the nineteenth and early twentieth centuries, birth control was practiced in this country and there was substantial use of the contraceptive devices that became available. The application of the federal Comstock Law to contraceptives was effectively overruled by the decision in United States v. One Package, 13 F.Supp. 334 (S.D. N.Y. 1936), *aff'd* 86 F.2d 737 (2d Cir. 1936), leaving the subject to regulation by state laws. In this period, condoms, the diaphragm and spermicides were the primary forms of contraception available, with birth control pills first marketed in 1960.

The Supreme Court entered the debate over contraception with its 1965 decision in *Griswold v. Connecticut*, holding that Connecticut's law prohibiting the use of contraceptives by married couples violated their privacy rights under the Constitution. The Court went further in 1972 in *Eisenstadt v. Baird*, holding as a matter of equal protection that unmarried persons have the same rights to use contraceptives as married couples.

Make the Connection

Griswold and *Eisenstadt* are reprinted in Chapter 1.

The scope of constitutional privacy rights surrounding contraception came before the Supreme Court again in Carey v. Population Services International, 431 U.S. 678 (1977), which considered a New York statute that imposed various restrictions on advertising and sale of nonprescription contraceptives, including a prohibition on distribution to individuals under age 16. Citing *Griswold* and *Eisenstadt*, as well as its recent decisions in several abortion cases, the Court concluded that "the right to privacy in connection with decisions affecting procreation extends to minors as well as to adults." Accordingly, state restrictions on the privacy rights of minors must serve a "significant state interest. . .that is not present in the case of an adult." The Court rejected the state's argument that free availability of contraceptives would lead to increased sexual activity among the young, noting that the state had offered no evidence to support this claim.

Teenage pregnancy and minors' access to sex education and contraception have remained controversial. In 1981, Congress passed the Adolescent Family Life Demonstration Projects Act, 42 U.S.C.A. §§ 300z et seq. (2018), intended to reduce the "severe adverse health, social and economic consequences" of pregnancy and

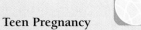

Teen Pregnancy

Statistics and other information on teen pregnancy is available from the web site of the U.S. Centers for Disease Control and Prevention (CDC).

childbirth among unmarried adolescents. In order to do this, the Act authorized federal grants to public and nonprofit private organizations, including religious organizations, for research and services respecting adolescent sexual activity and pregnancy. The Supreme Court upheld the constitutionality of this Act under the Establishment Clause of the First Amendment in Bowen v. Kendrick, 487 U.S. 589 (1988).

Regulations issued by the Department of Health and Human Services, requiring all family planning clinics receiving grant funds from the United States pursuant to 42 U.S.C.A. § 300 et seq. (2018) (The Public Health Service Act) to

(1) notify parents or guardians within ten days of prescribing contraceptives to unemancipated minors and (2) comply with any state laws requiring parental notice of or consent to the provision of family planning services to minors, were held not to be within the agency's statutory authority in Planned Parenthood Fed. of America v. Heckler, 712 F.2d 650 (D.C.Cir.1983); State of N.Y. v. Heckler, 719 F.2d 1191 (2d Cir.1983). If the regulations were within the statutory authority, would they be constitutional under *Carey*? See Note, *Parental Consent Requirements and Privacy Rights of Minors: The Contraceptive Controversy*, 88 Harv. L. Rev. 1001 (1975).

Sterilization

In the past, there was some doubt whether voluntary sterilization could be lawfully performed on a consenting adult as a birth control measure. See Glanville Williams, The Sanctity of Life and the Criminal Law 74–76 (1957). Sterilization for contraceptive purposes is now legal in all states. Jessin v. Shasta County, 79 Cal.Rptr. 359 (Ct. App. 1969); Kent Greenawalt, *Criminal Law and Population Control*, 24 Vand. L. Rev. 465 (1971). As noted above, involuntary sterilization on eugenic grounds was approved in Buck v. Bell, 274 U.S. 200 (1927), and many states still have statutes authorizing the involuntary sterilization of limited classes of persons, usually the mentally incompetent. See, e.g., Ark. Code Ann. §§ 20–49–201 et seq. (2018); Colo. Rev. Stat. Ann. § 25.5–10–233 (2018); Conn. Gen. Stat. §§ 45a–690 to 45a–700 (2018); Del. Code Ann. tit. 16, §§ 5701 to 5708 (2018); Ga. Code Ann. §§ 31–20–1 to 31–20–4 (2018); Idaho Code §§ 39–3901 to 39–3910 (2018); Me. Rev. Stat. Ann. tit. 34–B, §§ 7001 to 7017 (2018); Ore. Rev. Stat. Ann. §§ 436.205 to 436.335 (2018); Vt. Stat. Ann. tit. 18, §§ 8705 to 8716 (2018); and Va. Code §§ 54.1–2974 to 54.1–2980 (2018). In light of the Supreme Court's opinion in Skinner v. Oklahoma, 316 U.S. 535 (1942), concluding that a compulsory sterilization law violated the Equal Protection Clause, these statutes may no longer be valid. See, e.g., McKinney v. McKinney, 805 S.W.2d 66 (Ark. 1991) (holding section of statute authorizing sterilization without a judicial proceeding to be unconstitutional).

Falling somewhere between voluntary and involuntary sterilization are cases in which family members of an individual with a serious mental disability decide that a tubal ligation or vasectomy would be in the individual's best interests and seek authorization to consent to this procedure. See, for example, In re Grady, 426 A.2d 467 (N.J. 1981), in which the court concluded:

> The right to choose among procreation, sterilization and other methods of contraception is an important privacy right of all individuals. Our courts must preserve that right. Where an incompetent person lacks the mental capacity to make that choice, a court should ensure the exercise of that right on behalf of the incompetent in a manner that reflects his or her best interests.
>
> Id. at 475. See also Elisabeth S. Scott, *Sterilization of Mentally Retarded Persons: Reproductive Rights and Family Privacy*, 1986 Duke L.J. 806.

Problem 2-1

A superintendent of public schools, with authorization from the school board, publishes a memorandum allowing school nurses to issue free condoms to students in the junior high and high schools, and allowing condom vending machines to be placed in the boys' and girls' restrooms in the schools. The parents of four junior high and four high school students, and their children, sue to enjoin the institution of this program. What should be the result of their suit? (See Curtis v. School Committee of Falmouth, 652 N.E.2d 580 (Mass. 1995).)

Problem 2-2

David entered a "no contest" plea to three felony counts of intentional failure to support the nine children he had fathered with four different women. Finding that David's defaults were "obvious, consistent, and inexcusable," the trial judge sentenced him to a three-year prison term to be followed by five years of probation. As a condition of his probation, the judge ordered that David could not have any more children unless he could demonstrate that he had the ability to support them and that he was supporting the children he already had. David challenges this sentence, arguing that it violated his fundamental right to procreate. How should the appellate court decide his appeal? (See State v. Oakley, 629 N.W.2d 200 (Wis. 2001), cert. denied, 537 U.S. 813 (2002); State v. Talty, 814 N.E.2d 1201 (Ohio 2004).)

Problem 2-3

If you were a member of a state legislature, would you vote for a bill that offers an additional $200 per month of public assistance to women who agree to have Norplant implanted? Would this legislation raise constitutional concerns under the cases discussed above? (See Susan Frelich Appleton, *Standards for Con-*

stitutional Review of Privacy-Invading Welfare Reforms: Distinguishing the Abortion Funding Cases and Redeeming the Undue-Burden Test, 49 Vand. L. Rev. 1 (1996); Linda C. McClain, *"Irresponsible" Reproduction*, 47 Hastings L. J. 339 (1996).)

Pregnancy

Although privacy norms stand at the center of the case law on contraception and abortion, laws regulating pregnancy have been analyzed primarily as a matter of gender equality. The Supreme Court has sometimes struck pregnancy regulations as a violation of Due Process rights under the Fourteenth Amendment, see Cleveland Board of Education v. LaFleur, 414 U.S. 632 (1974), or under the 1964 Civil Rights Act, see Nashville Gas Co. v. Satty, 434 U.S. 136 (1977). At the same time, the Court has permitted private discrimination based on pregnancy, on the theory that it was not gender-based; see General Electric Co. v. Gilbert, 429 U.S. 125 (1976) rehearing denied 429 U.S. 1079 (1977); Geduldig v. Aiello, 417 U.S. 484 (1974).

Congress responded to the Court's decisions in cases such as *Gilbert* by passing the Pregnancy Discrimination Act of 1978, amending the Civil Rights Act to specify that sex discrimination includes discrimination on the basis of pregnancy. Subsequent decisions considered the requirements of this act, including California Federal Sav. & Loan Ass'n v. Guerra, 479 U.S. 272 (1987), and International Union, United Automobile Workers of America v. Johnson Controls, Inc., 499 U.S. 187 (1991). See generally Joanna L. Grossman, *Pregnancy, Work and the Promise of Equal Citizenship*, 98 Geo. L.J. 567 (2010).

In 1993, Congress passed the Family and Medical Leave Act (FMLA), 29 U.S.C.A. § 2601 et seq. (2018). Employees covered by the FMLA, whether they are male or female, must be permitted to take up to 12 weeks unpaid leave per year within the first year after birth of a baby, adoption of a child, or placement of a foster child, or in case of the employee's own serious health condition or the need to care for a spouse, parent or child with a serious health condition. More recently, the FMLA was expanded to include certain military family leave entitlements. See U.S. Department of Labor, The Employee's Guide to the Family and Medical Leave Act (2012).

Nevada Department of Human Resources v. Hibbs

538 U.S. 721 (2003)

CHIEF JUSTICE REHNQUIST delivered the opinion of the Court.

The Family and Medical Leave Act of 1993 (FMLA or Act) entitles eligible employees to take up to 12 work weeks of unpaid leave annually for any of several reasons, including the onset of a "serious health condition" in an employee's spouse, child, or parent.

Go Online

Listen to the oral arguments in *Hibbs* at the Oyez Project web site.

107 Stat. 9, 29 U.S.C. § 2612(a)(1)(C). The Act creates a private right of action to seek both equitable relief and money damages "against any employer (including a public agency) in any Federal or State court of competent jurisdiction,"§ 2617(a)(2), should that employer "interfere with, restrain, or deny the exercise of" FMLA rights, § 2615(a)(1). We hold that employees of the State of Nevada may recover money damages in the event of the State's failure to comply with the family-care provision of the Act.

Petitioners include the Nevada Department of Human Resources (Department) and two of its officers. Respondent William Hibbs (hereinafter respondent) worked for the Department's Welfare Division. In April and May 1997, he sought leave under the FMLA to care for his ailing wife, who was recovering from a car accident and neck surgery. The Department granted his request for the full 12 weeks of FMLA leave and authorized him to use the leave intermittently as needed between May and December 1997. Respondent did so until August 5, 1997, after which he did not return to work. In October 1997, the Department informed respondent that he had exhausted his FMLA leave, that no further leave would be granted, and that he must report to work by November 12, 1997. Respondent failed to do so and was terminated.

Respondent sued petitioners in the United States District Court seeking damages and injunctive and declaratory relief for, *inter alia,* violations of 29 U.S.C. § 2612(a)(1)(C). The District Court awarded petitioners summary judgment on the grounds that the FMLA claim was barred by the Eleventh Amendment and that respondent's Fourteenth Amendment rights had not been violated. Respondent

Take Note!

Mr. Hibbs's claim was that the Department should not have treated his leave under the FMLA as running concurrently with catastrophic leave that he was also entitled to take.

appealed, and the United States intervened under 28 U.S.C. § 2403 to defend the validity of the FMLA's application to the States. The Ninth Circuit reversed. 273 F.3d 844 (2001).

We granted certiorari, to resolve a split among the Courts of Appeals on the question whether an individual may sue a State for money damages in federal court for violation of § 2612(a)(1)(C).

For over a century now, we have made clear that the Constitution does not provide for federal jurisdiction over suits against nonconsenting States. *Board of Trustees of Univ. of Ala. v. Garrett,* 531 U.S. 356, 363 (2001); *Kimel v. Florida Bd. of Regents,* 528 U.S. 62, 72–73 (2000); * * *.

Congress may, however, abrogate such immunity in federal court if it makes its intention to abrogate unmistakably clear in the language of the statute and acts pursuant to a valid exercise of its power under § 5 of the Fourteenth Amendment. The clarity of Congress' intent here is not fairly debatable. The Act enables employees to seek damages "against any employer (including a public agency) in any Federal or State court of competent jurisdiction," 29 U.S.C. § 2617(a)(2), and Congress has defined "public agency" to include both "the government of a State or political subdivision thereof" and "any agency of . . .a State, or a political subdivision of a State,"§§ 203(x), 2611(4)(A)(iii). We held in *Kimel* that, by using identical language in the Age Discrimination in Employment Act of 1967 (ADEA), Congress satisfied the clear statement rule * * *. This case turns, then, on whether Congress acted within its constitutional authority when it sought to abrogate the States' immunity for purposes of the FMLA's family-leave provision.

> **FYI**
>
> The Court discusses the scope of Congress's authority under § 5 of the Fourteenth Amendment, concluding that it extends to enacting prophylactic legislation designed to remedy and to deter conduct that the Court has not found to be unconstitutional. Under its previous cases, particularly City of Boerne v. Flores, 521 U.S. 507 (1997), the Court reserves to itself the "ultimate interpretation and determination of the Fourteenth Amendment's substantive meaning." This means that Congress may not undertake a "substantive redefinition of the Fourteenth Amendment right at issue," and therefore its § 5 legislation must exhibit "congruence and proportionality between the injury to be prevented or remedied and the means adopted to that end."

* * *

The FMLA aims to protect the right to be free from gender-based discrimination in the workplace.[2] We have held that statutory classifications that distinguish between males and females are subject to heightened scrutiny. See, *e.g., Craig v. Boren, 429 U.S. 190 (1976)*. For a gender-based classification to withstand such scrutiny, it must "serv[e] important governmental objectives," and "the discriminatory means employed [must be] substantially related to the achievement of those objectives." *United States v. Virginia, 518 U.S. 515, 533 (1996)* (citations and internal quotation marks omitted). The State's justification for such a classification "must not rely on overbroad generalizations about the different talents, capacities, or preferences of males and females." We now inquire whether Congress had evidence of a pattern of constitutional violations on the part of the States in this area.

The history of the many state laws limiting women's employment opportunities is chronicled in—and, until relatively recently, was sanctioned by—this Court's own opinions. For example, in *Bradwell v. State, 16 Wall. 130, (1873)* (Illinois), and *Goesaert v. Cleary, 335 U.S. 464, 466 (1948)* (Michigan), the Court upheld state laws prohibiting women from practicing law and tending bar, respectively. State laws frequently subjected women to distinctive restrictions, terms, conditions, and benefits for those jobs they could take. In *Muller v. Oregon, 208 U.S. 412, 419, n. 1 (1908)*, for example, this Court approved a state law limiting the hours that women could work for wages, and observed that 19 States had such laws at the time. Such laws were based on the related beliefs that (1) a woman is, and should remain, "the center of home and family life," *Hoyt v. Florida, 368 U.S. 57, 62 (1961)*, and (2) "a proper discharge of [a woman's] maternal functions—having in view not merely her own health, but the well-being of the race—justif[ies] legislation to protect her from the greed as well as the passion of man," *Muller, supra, at 422*. Until our decision in *Reed v. Reed, 404 U.S. 71 (1971)*, "it remained the prevailing doctrine that government, both federal and state, could withhold from women opportunities accorded men so long as any 'basis in reason' "—such as the above beliefs—"could be conceived for the discrimination." *Virginia, supra, at 531* (quoting *Goesaert, supra, at 467*).

Take Note

The Court notes here that its opinions in *Bradwell, Goesart, Muller,* and *Hoyt* approved gender-based legislation principally on the basis of women's maternal roles.

---

[2]   The text of the Act makes this clear. Congress found that, "due to the nature of the roles of men and women in our society, the primary responsibility for family caretaking often falls on women, and such responsibility affects the working lives of women more than it affects the working lives of men." 29 U.S.C. § 2601(a)(5). In response to this finding, Congress sought "to accomplish the [Act's other] purposes. . .in a manner that. . .minimizes the potential for employment discrimination **on the basis of sex** by ensuring generally that leave is available. . .on a gender-neutral basis[,] and to promote the goal of equal employment opportunity for women and men (4)27" §§ 2601(b)(4) and (5) (emphasis added).

Congress responded to this history of discrimination by abrogating States' sovereign immunity in Title VII of the Civil Rights Act of 1964, 78 Stat. 255, 42 U.S.C. § 2000e–2(a), and we sustained this abrogation in *Fitzpatrick [v. Bitzer,* 427 U.S. 445 (1976)]. But state gender discrimination did not cease. "[I]t can hardly be doubted that. . .women still face pervasive, although at times more subtle, discrimination. . .in the job market." *Frontiero v. Richardson,* 411 U.S. 677, 686 (1973). According to evidence that was before Congress when it enacted the FMLA, States continue to rely on invalid gender stereotypes in the employment context, specifically in the administration of leave benefits. Reliance on such stereotypes cannot justify the States' gender discrimination in this area. *Virginia, supra,* at 533. The long and extensive history of sex discrimination prompted us to hold that measures that differentiate on the basis of gender warrant heightened scrutiny; here, as in *Fitzpatrick,* the persistence of such unconstitutional discrimination by the States justifies Congress' passage of prophylactic § 5 legislation.

As the FMLA's legislative record reflects, a 1990 Bureau of Labor Statistics (BLS) survey stated that 37 percent of surveyed private-sector employees were covered by maternity leave policies, while only 18 percent were covered by paternity leave policies. S.Rep. No. 103–3, pp. 14–15 (1993), U.S.Code Cong. & Admin.News 1993, p. 3. The corresponding numbers from a similar BLS survey the previous year were 33 percent and 16 percent, respectively. While these data show an increase in the percentage of employees eligible for such leave, they also show a widening of the gender gap during the same period. Thus, stereotype-based beliefs about the allocation of family duties remained firmly rooted, and employers' reliance on them in establishing discriminatory leave policies remained widespread.

Congress also heard testimony that "[p]arental leave for fathers. . .is rare. Even. . .[w]here child-care leave policies do exist, men, *both in the public and private sectors,* receive notoriously discriminatory treatment in their requests for such leave." Joint Hearing 147 (Washington Council of Lawyers) (emphasis added). Many States offered women extended "maternity" leave that far exceeded the typical 4- to 8-week period of physical disability due to pregnancy and childbirth, but very few States granted men a parallel benefit: Fifteen States provided women up to one year of extended maternity leave, while only four provided men with the same. M. Lord & M. King, The State Reference Guide to Work-Family Programs for State Employees 30 (1991). This and other differential leave policies were not attributable to any differential physical needs of men and women, but rather to the pervasive sex-role stereotype that caring for family members is women's work.

Finally, Congress had evidence that, even where state laws and policies were not facially discriminatory, they were applied in discriminatory ways. It was aware of the "serious problems with the discretionary nature of family leave," because when "the authority to grant leave and to arrange the length of that leave rests with individual supervisors," it leaves "employees open to discretionary and possibly unequal treatment." H.R.Rep. No. 103–8, pt. 2, pp. 10–11 (1993). Testimony supported that conclusion, explaining that "[t]he lack of uniform parental and medical leave policies in the work place has created an environment where [sex] discrimination is rampant." 1987 Senate Labor Hearings, pt. 2, at 170 (testimony of Peggy Montes, Mayor's Commission on Women's Affairs, City of Chicago).

* * *

Furthermore, the dissent's statement that some States "had adopted some form of family-care leave" before the FMLA's enactment, glosses over important shortcomings of some state policies. First, seven States had childcare leave provisions that applied to women only. Indeed, Massachusetts required that notice of its leave provisions be posted only in "establishment [s] in which females are employed." These laws reinforced the very stereotypes that Congress sought to remedy through the FMLA. Second, 12 States provided their employees no family leave, beyond an initial childbirth or adoption, to care for a seriously ill child or family member. Third, many States provided no statutorily guaranteed right to family leave, offering instead only voluntary or discretionary leave programs. Three States left the amount of leave time primarily in employers' hands. Congress could reasonably conclude that such discretionary family-leave programs would do little to combat the stereotypes about the roles of male and female employees that Congress sought to eliminate. Finally, four States provided leave only through administrative regulations or personnel policies, which Congress could reasonably conclude offered significantly less firm protection than a federal law. Against the above backdrop of limited state leave policies, no matter how generous petitioners' own may have been, see *post,* at 1992 (dissent), Congress was justified in enacting the FMLA as remedial legislation.

In sum, the States' record of unconstitutional participation in, and fostering of, gender-based discrimination in the administration of leave benefits is weighty enough to justify the enactment of prophylactic § 5 legislation.

* * *

Here, however, Congress directed its attention to state gender discrimination, which triggers a heightened level of scrutiny. Because the standard for demonstrating the constitutionality of a gender-based classification is more difficult to meet than our rational-basis test—it must "serv[e] important governmental objectives" and be "substantially related to the achievement of those objectives," *Virginia*, 518 U.S., at 533, it was easier for Congress to show a pattern of state constitutional violations. Congress was similarly successful in *South Carolina v. Katzenbach*, 383 U.S. 301 (1966), where we upheld the Voting Rights Act of 1965: Because racial classifications are presumptively invalid, most of the States' acts of race discrimination violated the Fourteenth Amendment.

The impact of the discrimination targeted by the FMLA is significant. Congress determined:

> "Historically, denial or curtailment of women's employment opportunities has been traceable directly to the pervasive presumption that women are mothers first, and workers second. This prevailing ideology about women's roles has in turn justified discrimination against women when they are mothers or mothers-to-be." Joint Hearing 100.

Stereotypes about women's domestic roles are reinforced by parallel stereotypes presuming a lack of domestic responsibilities for men. Because employers continued to regard the family as the woman's domain, they often denied men similar accommodations or discouraged them from taking leave. These mutually reinforcing stereotypes created a self-fulfilling cycle of discrimination that forced women to continue to assume the role of primary family caregiver, and fostered employers' stereotypical views about women's commitment to work and their value as employees. Those perceptions, in turn, Congress reasoned, lead to subtle discrimination that may be difficult to detect on a case-by-case basis.

We believe that Congress' chosen remedy, the family-care leave provision of the FMLA, is "congruent and proportional to the targeted violation," *Garrett, supra,* at 374. Congress had already tried unsuccessfully to address this problem through Title VII and the amendment of Title VII by the Pregnancy Discrimination Act, 42 U.S.C. § 2000e(k). Here, as in *Katzenbach, supra,* Congress again confronted a "difficult and intractable proble[m]," *Kimel, supra,* at 88, where previous legislative attempts had failed. See *Katzenbach, supra,* at 313 (upholding the Voting Rights Act). Such problems may justify added prophylactic measures in response. *Kimel, supra,* at 88.

Justices Souter, Ginsburg, Breyer, and Stevens concurred. Justices Scalia, Kennedy and Thomas dissented.

After the case was remanded, Hibbs was ultimately unable to establish a violation of the FMLA. See Hibbs v. Nevada Department of Human Resources, 2004 WL 5267600 (D. Nev. 2004).

By creating an across-the-board, routine employment benefit for all eligible employees, Congress sought to ensure that family-care leave would no longer be stigmatized as an inordinate drain on the workplace caused by female employees, and that employers could not evade leave obligations simply by hiring men. By setting a minimum standard of family leave for *all* eligible employees, irrespective of gender, the FMLA attacks the formerly state-sanctioned stereotype that only women are responsible for family caregiving, thereby reducing employers' incentives to engage in discrimination by basing hiring and promotion decisions on stereotypes.

* * *

For the above reasons, we conclude that § 2612(a)(1)(C) is congruent and proportional to its remedial object, and can "be understood as responsive to, or designed to prevent, unconstitutional behavior."

The judgment of the Court of Appeals is therefore

Affirmed.

Points for Discussion

a. Family Care and Gender Discrimination

Is Mr. Hibbs alleging that there was gender-based discrimination in his case? The Court had to decide in *Hibbs* whether Congress was justified in enacting the FMLA as a response to a pattern of discrimination in state child care leave provisions. To make this determination, the Court referred to its case law on gender-based discrimination. See Reva B. Siegel, *You've Come a Long Way, Baby: Rehnquist's New Approach to Pregnancy Discrimination in* Hibbs, 58 Stan. L. Rev. 1871 (2006). Once the Court determined that the FMLA fell within Congress's power under § 5 of the Fourteenth Amendment, however, the question that remained was whether Nevada had complied with the requirements of the statute when it terminated Mr. Hibbs.

b. *Hibbs* and the Maternal Wall

Joan Williams places *Hibbs* in the context of "maternal wall" cases, which consider employment discrimination against women based on gender stereotypes associated with mothering and child care responsibilities. See Joan C. Williams, Hibbs *as a Federalism Case,* Hibbs *as a Maternal Wall Case*, 73 U. Cin. L. Rev. 365 (2004). What language in the opinion supports this reading? How might *Hibbs* be useful in such cases? See, e.g., Back v. Hastings on Hudson, 365 F.3d 107 (2d Cir. 2004).

c. FMLA

Studies suggest that the Family and Medical Leave Act has been utilized mostly in medical leave situations, with the family leave provisions used much less frequently. See Michael Selmi, *Is Something Better Than Nothing? Critical Reflec-*

tions on Ten Years of the FMLA, 15 Wash. U. J.L. & Pol'y 65 (2004). Women also remain far more likely to take family leaves than men. See Joanna L. Grossman, *Job Security Without Equality: The Family and Medical Leave Act of 1993*, 15 Wash. U. J.L. & Pol'y 17 (2004). Consider the description of the FMLA at the start of the Court's opinion in *Hibbs*. What might explain the fact that the FMLA is not used widely for family leave?

---

2. Abortion

Laws criminalizing abortion, enacted in the nineteenth century, had become the subject of significant debate by the middle of the twentieth century. Illegal abortions were common, presenting serious health risks and a significant death rate, particularly for poor women. In 1962, the American Law Institute's Model Penal Code § 230.3 proposed that abortion by a licensed physician should be legal if the physician believed that continuing the pregnancy would endanger the woman's physical or mental health, if the child would be born with a severe defect, or if the pregnancy resulted from rape or incest. Over the next ten years, more than a dozen states enacted new laws based on this model, providing for what was known as therapeutic abortion. By 1973, New York, Washington, Alaska and Hawaii had substantially repealed their antiabortion statutes. On the politics of the era, see Linda Greenhouse and Reva B. Siegel, *Before (and After) Roe v. Wade: New Questions About Backlash*, 120 Yale L.J. 2028 (2011).

Roe v. Wade

410 U.S. 113 (1973)

Mr. Justice Blackmun delivered the opinion of the Court.

Go Online

Listen to the oral arguments in *Roe* on the Oyez Project web site.

This Texas federal appeal and its Georgia companion, *Doe v. Bolton*, present constitutional challenges to state criminal abortion legislation. The Texas statutes under attack here are typical of those that have been in effect in many States for approximately a century. The Georgia statutes, in contrast, have a modern cast and are a legislative product that, to an extent at least, obviously reflects the influences of recent attitudinal change, of advancing medical knowledge and techniques, and of new thinking about an old issue.

FYI At this point, the Court described the plaintiffs, including "Jane Roe," an unmarried pregnant woman who wanted a safe, physician-performed abortion in Texas. The Court concluded that Jane Roe had standing to sue, that her case presented a case or controversy, and that it was not moot, even though it was obvious that her pregnancy, which had existed in 1970 when the suit was brought, must have long since ended. The other plaintiffs' claims were dismissed on various grounds.

* * *

I

The Texas statutes that concern us here are Arts. 1191–1194 and 1196 of the State's Penal Code[1]. These make it a crime to "procure an abortion," as therein defined, or to attempt one, except with respect to "an abortion procured or attempted by medical advice for the purpose of saving the life of the mother." Similar statutes are in existence in a majority of the States.

* * *

V

The principal thrust of appellant's attack on the Texas statutes is that they improperly invade a right, said to be possessed by the pregnant woman, to choose to terminate her pregnancy. Appellant would discover this right in the concept of

---

[1] "Article 1191. Abortion

"If any person shall designedly administer to a pregnant woman or knowingly procure to be administered with her consent any drug or medicine, or shall use towards her any violence or means whatever externally or internally applied, and thereby procure an abortion, he shall be confined in the penitentiary not less than two nor more than five years; if it be done without her consent, the punishment shall be doubled. By 'abortion' is meant that the life of the fetus or embryo shall be destroyed in the woman's womb or that a premature birth thereof be caused.

"Art. 1192. Furnishing the means

"Whoever furnishes the means for procuring an abortion knowing the purpose intended is guilty as an accomplice.

"Art. 1193. Attempt at abortion

"If the means used shall fail to produce an abortion, the offender is nevertheless guilty of an attempt to produce abortion, provided it be shown that such means were calculated to produce that result, and shall be fined not less than one hundred nor more than one thousand dollars.

"Art. 1194. Murder in producing abortion

"If the death of the mother is occasioned by an abortion so produced or by an attempt to effect the same it is murder."

"Art. 1196. By medical advice

"Nothing in this chapter applies to an abortion procured or attempted by medical advice for the purpose of saving the life of the mother."

The foregoing Articles, together with Art. 1195, compose Chapter 9 of Title 15 of the Penal Code. Article 1195, not attacked here, reads:

"Art. 1195. Destroying unborn child

"Whoever shall during parturition of the mother destroy the vitality or life in a child in a state of being born and before actual birth, which child would otherwise have been born alive, shall be confined in the penitentiary for life or for not less than five years."

personal "liberty" embodied in the Fourteenth Amendment's Due Process Clause; or in personal, marital, familial, and sexual privacy said to be protected by the Bill of Rights or its penumbras, see <u>Griswold v. Connecticut, 381 U.S. 479 (1965)</u>; <u>Eisenstadt v. Baird, 405 U.S. 438 (1972)</u>; <u>Id., at 460</u> (White, J., concurring in result); or among those rights reserved to the people by the Ninth Amendment, <u>Griswold v. Connecticut, 381 U.S., at 486</u> (Goldberg, J., concurring). * * *

* * *

VII

Three reasons have been advanced to explain historically the enactment of criminal abortion laws in the 19th century and to justify their continued existence.

The Court's opinion provides a long historical account of attitudes toward abortion and of the development of the common law and statutory law on the subject.

Take Note!

How does Texas justify its abortion law? What does the Court say about these purposes?

It has been argued occasionally that these laws were the product of a Victorian social concern to discourage illicit sexual conduct. Texas, however, does not advance this justification in the present case, and it appears that no court or commentator has taken the argument seriously. The appellants and *amici* contend, moreover, that this is not a proper state purpose at all and suggest that, if it were, the Texas statutes are overbroad in protecting it since the law fails to distinguish between married and unwed mothers.

A second reason is concerned with abortion as a medical procedure. When most criminal abortion laws were first enacted the procedure was a hazardous one for the woman. This was particularly true prior to the development of antisepsis. Antiseptic techniques, of course, were based on discoveries by Lister, Pasteur, and others first announced in 1867, but were not generally accepted and employed until about the turn of the century. Abortion mortality was high. Even after 1900, and perhaps until as late as the development of antibiotics in the 1940's, standard modern techniques such as dilation and curettage were not nearly so safe as they are today. Thus, it has been argued that a State's real concern in enacting a criminal abortion law was to protect the pregnant woman, that is, to restrain her from submitting to a procedure that placed her life in serious jeopardy.

Modern medical techniques have altered this situation. Appellants and various *amici* refer to medical data indicating that abortion in early pregnancy, that is, prior to the end of the first trimester, although not without its risk, is now relatively safe. Mortality rates for women undergoing early abortions, where the procedure is legal, appear to be as low as or lower than the rates for normal child-birth. Consequently, any interest of the State in protecting the woman from an inherently hazardous procedure, except when it would be equally dangerous for her to forgo it, has largely disappeared. Of course, important state interests in the areas of health and medical standards do remain. The State has a legitimate inter-est in seeing to it that abortion, like any other medical procedure, is performed under circumstances that insure maximum safety for the patient. This interest obviously extends at least to the performing physician and his staff, to the facilities involved, to the availability of after-care, and to adequate provision for any com-plication or emergency that might arise. The prevalence of high mortality rates at illegal "abortion mills" strengthens, rather than weakens, the State's interest in regulating the conditions under which abortions are performed. Moreover, the risk to the woman increases as her pregnancy continues. Thus, the State retains a definite interest in protecting the woman's own health and safety when an abor-tion is proposed at a late stage of pregnancy.

The third reason is the State's interest—some phrase it in terms of duty—in protecting prenatal life. Some of the argument for this justification rests on the theory that a new human life is present from the moment of conception. The State's interest and general obligation to protect life then extends, it is argued, to prenatal life. Only when the life of the pregnant mother herself is at stake, bal-anced against the life she carries within her, should the interest of the embryo or fetus not prevail. Logically, of course, a legitimate state interest in this area need not stand or fall on acceptance of the belief that life begins at conception or at some other point prior to live birth. In assessing the State's interest, recognition may be given to the less rigid claim that as long as at least *potential* life is involved, the State may assert interests beyond the protection of the pregnant woman alone.

Parties challenging state abortion laws have sharply disputed in some courts the contention that a purpose of these laws, when enacted, was to protect prenatal life. Pointing to the absence of legislative history to support the contention, they claim that most state laws were designed solely to protect the woman. Because medical advances have lessened this concern, at least with respect to abortion in early pregnancy, they argue that with respect to such abortions the laws can no longer be justified by any state interest. There is some scholarly support for this view of original purpose. The few state courts called upon to interpret their laws in the late 19th and early 20th centuries did focus on the State's interest in protecting the woman's health rather than in preserving the embryo and fetus. Proponents of this view point out that in many States, including Texas, by statute or judicial interpretation, the pregnant woman herself could not be prosecuted for self-abortion or for cooperating in an abortion performed upon her by another. They claim that adoption of the "quickening" distinction through received common law and state statutes tacitly recognizes the greater health hazards inherent in late abortion and impliedly repudiates the theory that life begins at conception.

It is with these interests, and the weight to be attached to them, that this case is concerned.

VIII

The Constitution does not explicitly mention any right of privacy. In a line of decisions, however, going back perhaps as far as <u>Union Pacific R. Co. v. Botsford, 141 U.S. 250, 251 (1891)</u>, the Court has recognized that a right of personal privacy, or a guarantee of certain areas or zones of privacy, does exist under the Constitution. In varying contexts, the Court or individual Justices have, indeed, found at least the roots of that right in the First Amendment, * * * in the Fourth and Fifth Amendments, * * *; in the penumbras of the Bill of Rights, <u>Griswold v. Connecticut, 381 U.S., at 484–485</u>; in the Ninth Amendment, <u>id., at 486</u> (Goldberg, J., concurring); or in the concept of liberty guaranteed by the first section of the Fourteenth Amendment, * * * These decisions make it clear that only personal rights that can be deemed "fundamental" or "implicit in the concept of ordered liberty," <u>Palko v. Connecticut, 302 U.S. 319, 325 (1937)</u>, are included in this guarantee of personal privacy. They also make it clear that the right has some extension to activities relating to marriage, <u>Loving v. Virginia, 388 U.S. 1, 12 (1967)</u>; procreation, <u>Skinner v. Oklahoma, 316 U.S. 535, 541–542 (1942)</u>; contraception, <u>Eisenstadt v. Baird, 405 U.S., at 453–454</u>; <u>id., at 460, 463–465</u> (White, J., concurring in result); family relationships, <u>Prince v. Massachusetts, 321 U.S. 158, 166 (1944)</u>; and child rearing and education, <u>Pierce v. Society of the Sisters of the Holy Names of Jesus and Mary, 268 U.S. 510, 535 (1925)</u>, Meyer v. Nebraska, *supra*.

This right of privacy, whether it be founded in the Fourteenth Amendment's concept of personal liberty and restrictions upon state action, as we feel it is, or, as the District Court determined, in the Ninth Amendment's reservation of rights to the people, is broad enough to encompass a woman's decision whether or not to terminate her pregnancy. The detriment that the

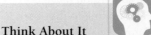

Think About It

How does the Court define the individual right it considers in this case? What is the basis in the Constitution for this right?

State would impose upon the pregnant woman by denying this choice altogether is apparent. Specific and direct harm medically diagnosable even in early pregnancy may be involved. Maternity, or additional offspring, may force upon the woman a distressful life and future. Psychological harm may be imminent. Mental and physical health may be taxed by child care. There is also the distress, for all concerned, associated with the unwanted child, and there is the problem of bringing a child into a family already unable, psychologically and otherwise, to care for it. In other cases, as in this one, the additional difficulties and continuing stigma of unwed motherhood may be involved. All these are factors the woman and her responsible physician necessarily will consider in consultation.

On the basis of elements such as these, appellant and some *amici* argue that the woman's right is absolute and that she is entitled to terminate her pregnancy at whatever time, in whatever way, and for whatever reason she alone chooses. With this we do not agree. Appellant's arguments that Texas either has no valid interest at all in regulating the abortion decision, or no interest strong enough to support any limitation upon the woman's sole determination, are unpersuasive. The Court's decisions recognizing a right of privacy also acknowledge that some state regulation in areas protected by that right is appropriate. As noted above, a State may properly assert important interests in safeguarding health, in maintaining medical standards, and in protecting potential life. At some point in pregnancy, these respective interests become sufficiently compelling to sustain regulation of the factors that govern the abortion decision. The privacy right involved, therefore, cannot be said to be absolute. In fact, it is not clear to us that the claim asserted by some *amici* that one has an unlimited right to do with one's body as one pleases bears a close relationship to the right of privacy previously articulated in the Court's decisions. The Court has refused to recognize an unlimited right of this kind in the past. * * *

We, therefore, conclude that the right of personal privacy includes the abortion decision, but that this right is not unqualified and must be considered against important state interests in regulation.

* * *

Although the results are divided, most of these courts have agreed that the right of privacy, however based, is broad enough to cover the abortion decision; that the right, nonetheless, is not absolute and is subject to some limitations; and that at some point the state interests as to protection of health, medical standards, and prenatal life, become dominant. We agree with this approach.

Where certain "fundamental rights" are involved, the Court has held that regulation limiting these rights may be justified only by a "compelling state interest," Kramer v. Union Free School District, 395 U.S. 621, 627 (1969); Shapiro v. Thompson, 394 U.S. 618, 634 (1969); Sherbert v. Verner, 374 U.S. 398, 406 (1963), and that legislative enactments must be narrowly drawn to express only the legitimate state interests at stake. * * * see Eisenstadt v. Baird, 405 U.S., at 460, 463–464 (White, J., concurring in result).

* * *

IX

* * *

A. The appellee and certain *amici* argue that the fetus is a "person" within the language and meaning of the Fourteenth Amendment. In support of this, they outline at length and in detail the well-known facts of fetal development. If this suggestion of personhood is established, the appellant's case, of course, collapses, for the fetus' right to life would then be guaranteed specifically by the Amendment. The appellant conceded as much on reargument. On the other hand, the appellee conceded on reargument that no case could be cited that holds that a fetus is a person within the meaning of the Fourteenth Amendment.

The Constitution does not define "person" in so many words. Section 1 of the Fourteenth Amendment contains three references to "person." The first, in defining "citizens," speaks of "persons born or naturalized in the United States." The word also appears both in the Due Process Clause and in the Equal Protection Clause. "Person" is used in other places in the Constitution: in the listing of qualifications for Representatives and Senators, Art. I, § 2, cl. 2, and § 3, cl. 3; in the Apportionment Clause, Art. I, § 2, cl. 3;[53] in the Migration and Importation provision, Art. I, § 9, cl. 1; in the Emolument Clause, Art. I, § 9, cl. 8; in the Electors provisions, Art. II, § 1, cl. 2, and the superseded cl. 3; in the provision outlining qualifications for the office of President, Art. II, § 1, cl. 5; in the Extradition provisions, Art. IV, § 2, cl. 2, and the superseded Fugitive Slave Clause 3; and in the Fifth, Twelfth, and Twenty-second Amendments, as well as in §§ 2 and 3 of the Fourteenth Amendment. But in nearly all these instances, the use of the word is such that it has application only postnatally. None indicates, with any assurance, that it has any possible pre-natal application.[54]

---

[53] We are not aware that in the taking of any census under this clause, a fetus has ever been counted.

[54] When Texas urges that a fetus is entitled to Fourteenth Amendment protection as a person, it faces a dilemma. Neither in Texas nor in any other State are all abortions prohibited. Despite broad proscription, an exception always exists. The exception contained in Art. 1196, for an abortion procured or attempted by medical advice for the purpose of saving the life of the mother, is typical. But if the fetus is a person who is not to be deprived of life without due process of law, and if the mother's condition is the sole determinant, does not the Texas exception appear to be out of line with the Amendment's command?

There are other inconsistencies between Fourteenth Amendment status and the typical abortion statute. It has already been pointed out, that in Texas the woman is not a principal or an accomplice with respect to an abortion upon her. If the fetus is a person, why is the woman not a principal or an accomplice? Further, the penalty for criminal abortion specified by Art. 1195 is significantly less than the maximum penalty for murder prescribed by Art. 1257 of the Texas Penal Code. If the fetus is a person, may the penalties be different?

All this, together with our observation, *supra*, that throughout the major portion of the 19th century prevailing legal abortion practices were far freer than they are today, persuades us that the word "person," as used in the Fourteenth Amendment, does not include the unborn. This is in accord with the results reached in those few cases where the issue has been squarely presented. * * * Indeed, our decision in United States v. Vuitch, 402 U.S. 62 (1971), inferentially is to the same effect, for we there would not have indulged in statutory interpretation favorable to abortion in specified circumstances if the necessary consequence was the termination of life entitled to Fourteenth Amendment protection.

This conclusion, however, does not of itself fully answer the contentions raised by Texas, and we pass on to other considerations.

B. The pregnant woman cannot be isolated in her privacy. She carries an embryo and, later, a fetus, if one accepts the medical definitions of the developing young in the human uterus. See Dorland's Illustrated Medical Dictionary 478–479, 547 (24th ed. 1965). The situation therefore is inherently different from marital intimacy, or bedroom possession of obscene material, or marriage, or procreation, or education, with which *Eisenstadt* and *Griswold, Stanley, Loving, Skinner* and *Pierce* and *Meyer* were respectively concerned. As we have intimated above, it is reasonable and appropriate for a State to decide that at some point in time another interest, that of health of the mother or that of potential human life, becomes significantly involved. The woman's privacy is no longer sole and any right of privacy she possesses must be measured accordingly.

Texas urges that, apart from the Fourteenth Amendment, life begins at conception and is present throughout pregnancy, and that therefore, the State has a compelling interest in protecting that life from and after conception. We need not resolve the difficult question of when life begins. When those trained in the respective disciplines of medicine, philosophy, and theology are unable to arrive at any consensus, the judiciary, at this point in the development of man's knowledge, is not in a position to speculate as to the answer.

* * *

In areas other than criminal abortion, the law has been reluctant to endorse any theory that life, as we recognize it, begins before live birth or to accord legal rights to the unborn except in narrowly defined situations and except when the rights are contingent upon live birth. For example, the traditional rule of tort law denied recovery for prenatal injuries even though the child was born alive. That rule has been changed in almost every jurisdiction. In most States, recovery is said to be permitted only if the fetus was viable, or at least quick, when the injuries were sustained, though few courts have squarely so held. In a recent development, generally opposed by the commentators, some States permit the parents of a still-born child to maintain an action for wrongful death because of prenatal injuries. Such an action, however, would appear to be one to vindicate the parents' interest and is thus consistent with the view that the fetus, at most, represents only the potentiality of life. Similarly, unborn children have been recognized as acquiring rights or interests by way of inheritance or other devolution of property, and have been represented by guardians *ad litem*. Perfection of the interests involved, again, has generally been contingent upon live birth. In short, the unborn have never been recognized in the law as persons in the whole sense.

X

In view of all this, we do not agree that, by adopting one theory of life, Texas may override the rights of the pregnant woman that are at stake. We repeat, however, that the State does have an important and legitimate interest in preserving and protecting the health of the pregnant woman, whether she be a resident of the State or a nonresident who seeks medical consultation and treatment there, and that it has still *another* important and legitimate interest in protecting the potentiality of human life. These interests are separate and distinct. Each grows in substantiality as the woman approaches term and, at a point during pregnancy, each becomes "compelling."

With respect to the State's important and legitimate interest in the health of the mother, the "compelling" point, in the light of present medical knowledge, is at approximately the end of the first trimester. This is so because of the now-established medical fact, * * * that until the end of the

> **Think About It**
>
> The Court concludes here that the appropriate constitutional analysis changes with different stages of a woman's pregnancy. What defines these different phases?

first trimester mortality in abortion may be less than mortality in normal childbirth. It follows that, from and after this point, a State may regulate the abortion procedure to the extent that the regulation reasonably relates to the preservation and protection of maternal health. Examples of permissible state regulation in this area are requirements as to the qualifications of the person who is to perform the abortion; as to the licensure of that person; as to the facility in which the procedure is to be performed, that is, whether it must be a hospital or may be a clinic or some other place of less-than-hospital status; as to the licensing of the facility; and the like.

This means, on the other hand, that, for the period of pregnancy prior to this "compelling" point, the attending physician, in consultation with his patient, is free to determine, without regulation by the State, that, in his medical judgment, the patient's pregnancy should be terminated. If that decision is reached, the judgment may be effectuated by an abortion free of interference by the State.

With respect to the State's important and legitimate interest in potential life, the "compelling" point is at viability. This is so because the fetus then presumably has the capability of meaningful life outside the mother's womb. State regulation protective of fetal life after viability thus has both logical and biological justifications. If the State is interested in protecting fetal life after viability, it may go so far as to proscribe abortion during that period, except when it is necessary to preserve the life or health of the mother.

Measured against these standards, Art. 1196 of the Texas Penal Code, in restricting legal abortions to those "procured or attempted by medical advice for the purpose of saving the life of the mother," sweeps too broadly. The statute makes no distinction between abortions performed early in pregnancy and those performed later, and it limits to a single reason, "saving" the mother's life, the legal justification for the procedure. The statute, therefore, cannot survive the constitutional attack made upon it here.

This conclusion makes it unnecessary for us to consider the additional challenge to the Texas statute asserted on grounds of vagueness.

XI

To summarize and to repeat:

1. A state criminal abortion statute of the current Texas type, that excepts from criminality only a *life-saving* procedure on behalf of the mother, without regard to pregnancy stage and without recognition of the other interests involved, is violative of the Due Process Clause of the Fourteenth Amendment.

(a) For the stage prior to approximately the end of the first trimester, the abortion decision and its effectuation must be left to the medical judgment of the pregnant woman's attending physician.

(b) For the stage subsequent to approximately the end of the first trimester, the State, in promoting its interest in the health of the mother, may, if it chooses, regulate the abortion procedure in ways that are reasonably related to maternal health.

(c) For the stage subsequent to viability, the State in promoting its interest in the potentiality of human life may, if it chooses, regulate, and even proscribe, abortion except where it is necessary, in appropriate medical judgment, for the preservation of the life or health of the mother.

2. The State may define the term "physician," as it has been employed in the preceding numbered paragraphs of this Part XI of this opinion, to mean only a physician currently licensed by the State, and may proscribe any abortion by a person who is not a physician as so defined.

In *Doe v. Bolton*, post, procedural requirements contained in one of the modern abortion statutes are considered. That opinion and this one, of course, are to be read together.

This holding, we feel, is consistent with the relative weights of the respective interests involved, with the lessons and examples of medical and legal history, with the lenity of the common law, and with the demands of the profound problems of the present day. The decision leaves the State free to place increasing restrictions on abortion as the period of pregnancy lengthens, so long as those restrictions are tailored to the recognized state interests. The decision vindicates the right of the physician to administer medical treatment according to his professional judgment up to the points where important state interests provide compelling justifications for intervention. Up to those points, the abortion decision in all its aspects is inherently, and primarily, a medical decision, and basic responsibility for it must rest with the physician. If an individual practitioner abuses the privilege of exercising proper medical judgment, the usual remedies, judicial and intra-professional, are available.

XII

Our conclusion that Art. 1196 is unconstitutional means, of course, that the Texas abortion statutes, as a unit, must fall. * * *

* * *

Mr. Justice Rehnquist, dissenting.

The Court's opinion brings to the discussion of this troubling question both extensive historical fact and a wealth of legal scholarship. While the opinion thus commands my respect, I find myself nonetheless in fundamental disagreement with those parts of it that invalidate the Texas statute in question, and therefore dissent.

* * *

* * * I have difficulty in concluding, as the Court does, that the right of "privacy" is involved in this case. Texas, by the statute here challenged, bars the performance of a medical abortion by a licensed physician on a plaintiff such as Roe. A transaction resulting in an operation such as this is not "private" in the ordinary usage of that word. Nor is the "privacy" that the Court finds here even a distant relative of the freedom from searches and seizures protected by the Fourth Amendment to the Constitution, which the Court has referred to as embodying a right to privacy. <u>Katz v. United States, 389 U.S. 347 (1967)</u>.

If the Court means by the term "privacy" no more than that the claim of a person to be free from unwanted state regulation of consensual transactions may be a form of "liberty" protected by the Fourteenth Amendment, there is no doubt that similar claims have been upheld in our earlier decisions on the basis of that liberty. I agree with the statement of Mr. Justice Stewart in his concurring opinion that the "liberty," against deprivation of which without due process the Fourteenth Amendment protects, embraces more than the rights found in the Bill of Rights. But that liberty is not guaranteed absolutely against deprivation, only against deprivation without due process of law. The test traditionally applied in the area of social and economic legislation is whether or not a law such as that challenged has a ratio-

In the companion case, <u>Doe v. Bolton, 410 U.S. 179 (1973)</u>, the Court struck down Georgia's abortion statute, enacted in 1968 based on the Model Penal Code, which permitted a licensed physician to perform an abortion only if continuation of the pregnancy would endanger a woman's life or health, if the fetus would likely be born with a serious mental or physical defect, or if the pregnancy had resulted from forcible or statutory rape.

In <u>Doe</u>, the Court also held unconstitutional provisions of that act which required that abortions be performed only in accredited hospitals, required that a hospital abortion committee and two licensed physicians (in addition to the pregnant woman's physician) agree with the decision to perform an abortion; and which limited the availability of abortions to Georgia residents. Justices White and Rehnquist dissented in both *Roe* and *Doe*. Chief Justice Burger and Justices Stewart and Douglas filed separate concurrences in both cases, Justice Douglas relying on his own opinion in <u>Griswold v. Connecticut</u>.

The story of the young lawyer who argued and won the *Roe* case is recounted in her memoir: Sarah Weddington, A Question of Choice (1993). The plaintiff told her story in Norma McCorvey & Andy Meisler, I am Roe: My Life, Roe v. Wade, and Freedom of Choice (1994).

nal relation to a valid state objective. <u>Williamson v. Lee Optical Co., 348 U.S. 483, 491 (1955)</u>. The Due Process Clause of the Fourteenth Amendment undoubtedly does place a limit, albeit a broad one, on legislative power to enact laws such as this. If the Texas statute were to prohibit an abortion even where a mother's life is in jeopardy, I have little doubt that such a statute would lack a rational relation to a valid state objective under the test stated in <u>Williamson, supra.</u> But the Court's sweeping invalidation of any restrictions on abortion during the first trimester is impossible to justify under that standard, and the conscious weighing of competing factors that the Court's opinion apparently substitutes for the established test is far more appropriate to a legislative judgment than a judicial one.

* * *

Points for Discussion

a. Constitutional Basis for Abortion Rights

What is the constitutional basis for the holding in *Roe*? Could you draft a better reasoned opinion supporting the result?

A number of writers, including now-Justice Ruth Bader Ginsburg, have suggested that it would have been preferable for the Supreme Court to base the ruling in *Roe* on gender equality grounds under the Equal Protection Clause of the Fourteenth Amendment, and the Due Process Clause of the Fifth Amendment. Ruth Bader Ginsburg, <u>Some Thoughts on Autonomy and Equality in Relation to</u> Roe v. Wade, 63 N.C. L. Rev. 375 (1985). See also Sylvia A. Law, <u>Rethinking Sex and the Constitution, 132 U. Pa. L. Rev. 955, 1008, 1013–1028 (1984)</u>; Catharine A. MacKinnon, <u>Reflections on Sex Equality Under Law, 100 Yale L.J. 1281, 1311–1324 (1991)</u>; Reva Siegel, <u>Reasoning From the Body: A Historical Perspective on Abortion Regulation and Questions of Equal Protection, 44 Stan. L. Rev. 261, 347–381 (1992)</u>.

A number of prominent scholars have proposed alternative opinions that the Supreme Court might have written using materials available as of the date when *Roe v. Wade* was handed down. See What Roe v. Wade Should Have Said: The Nation's Top Legal Experts Rewrite America's Most Controversial Opinion (Jack M. Balkin, ed., 2005).

b. Criticism of Roe v. Wade

The *Roe* decision was subjected to criticism, with respect to both its reasoning and its social policy. For an early critique, see John Hart Ely, <u>The Wages of Crying Wolf: A Comment on</u> Roe v. Wade, 82 Yale L.J. 920 (1973), which argued that the *Griswold* case was based on the state's choice of a means of preventing conception that required the invasion of people's homes for the acquisition of evidence, a factor not present in *Roe*. With respect to the tragic conflict between the harms that an unwanted pregnancy inflicts on the mother, and the destruction of the fetus caused by the abortion, Ely concluded that the privacy right announced by *Roe* cannot be inferred from the Constitution. See also Archibald Cox, *The Supreme Court and Abortion*, 2 Hum. Life Rev. 15, 18 (1976) ("My criticism of *Roe v. Wade* is that the Court failed to establish the legitimacy of the decision by not articulating a precept of sufficient abstractness to lift the ruling above the level of a political judgment based upon the evidence currently available from the medical, physical and social sciences.")

Mary Ann Glendon, in Abortion and Divorce in Western Law 58–62 (1989) suggested that *Roe* prevents the law from sending the humane message that the fetus is entitled to some protection, and thereby from providing a beneficial influence on public behavior and opinions. Leaving the abortion issue to the legislatures, in her view, would have enabled them to work out a better balance between the interests of the mother and those of the fetus, one which most Americans would favor.

The majority in *Roe* concluded that the word "person" as used in the Fourteenth Amendment did not include the unborn. This aspect of the holding has been strenuously disputed. See, for example, John T. Noonan, Jr., A Private Choice: Abortion in America in the Seventies (1979). In Webster v. Reproductive Health Services, 492 U.S. 490 (1989), the Court considered Missouri abortion legislation that included a preamble finding that "[t]he life of each human being begins at conception," and that "unborn children have protectable interests in life, health, and well-being." The Court decided that it did not need to pass on the constitutionality of this preamble in order to sustain the substantive provisions of the Missouri statute.

c. Abortion Clinic Violence

As the abortion debate became more intense and polarized after *Roe*, some abortion opponents resorted to violence. One organization, Operation Rescue, blockaded clinics, trespassed on clinic property, prevented both patients and doctors from entering clinics and in general engaged in unlawful conduct designed to interrupt the operation of abortion clinics. Clinics brought lawsuits seeking injunctive relief in response to this conduct under the Ku Klux Klan Act of 1871, now 42 U.S.C.A. § 1985(3) (2018). These suits were not ultimately successful, but in 1994, Congress enacted the Freedom of Access to Clinic Entrances Act (FACE), codified at 18 U.S.C.A. § 248 (2018), which makes it a federal crime to use force or threat of force to injure, intimidate, or interfere with persons attempting to obtain or provide reproductive health services. In Hill v. Colorado, 530 U.S. 703 (2000), the Court sustained a "bubble law" enacted in Colorado which required that individuals passing out literature or engaged in "oral protest, education, or counseling" must remain at least eight feet away from people entering or leaving any health care facility. In McCullen v. Coakley, 573 U.S.   , 134 S.Ct.

2518 (2014), however, the Justices ruled that a Massachusetts statute establishing a 35-foot buffer zone around non-hospital facilities where abortions were performed violated the First Amendment, because it was not sufficiently narrowly tailored to the government's interests in protecting safety and access.

d. Abortion Litigation After *Roe*

After its decision in *Roe*, the Supreme Court decided many other cases defining the scope of abortion rights and how far the state and federal governments may go to try to discourage or prevent abortions. These cases considered various procedural restrictions on abortion, including record-keeping requirements and informed consent procedures, prohibitions on public funding or use of public facilities to provide abortions, and prohibitions of particular procedures such as what has been called a "partial birth abortion" during the later stages of pregnancy. The Court upheld many of these restrictions.

In <u>Planned Parenthood of Central Missouri v. Danforth, 428 U.S. 52 (1976)</u> and <u>Planned Parenthood of Southeastern Pennsylvania v. Casey, 505 U.S. 833 (1992)</u>, the Supreme Court rejected laws that required a married woman to notify or secure consent from her husband prior to an abortion. This section of the Casey opinion is reprinted below. In a series of decisions considering parental notice and consent requirements for a minor seeking an abortion, the Court has consistently required that such laws include access to a judicial "bypass proceeding" to allow a mature minor to demonstrate that she should be permitted an abortion without her parents being informed or being required to consent. This was addressed in <u>Hodgson v. Minnesota, 497 U.S. 417 (1990)</u>, discussed below.

e. What's Left of *Roe*?

The Supreme Court's abortion decisions have cut back on the principles announced in *Roe* without expressly overruling the case. For example, the majority opinion in <u>Webster v. Reproductive Health Services, 492 U.S. 490 (1989)</u>, written by Chief Justice Rehnquist (one of the original dissenters in *Roe*) sustained many aspects of a restrictive Missouri abortion statute, but did so without overruling *Roe*.

In 1992, in its decision in <u>Planned Parenthood of Southeastern Pennsylvania v. Casey, 505 U.S. 833 (1992)</u>, the Court reaffirmed what it called the "essential holding" of *Roe* while abandoning its "rigid trimester framework" and changing the standard to be used in testing the validity of abortion legislation. Chief Justice Rehnquist and Justices White, Scalia and Thomas dissented in *Casey*, arguing that *Roe* should be overruled. The "joint opinion" issued by Justices O'Connor,

Kennedy and Souter concluded that the abortion right protected in *Roe* is within the liberty protected by the Due Process Clause of the Fourteenth Amendment. The Court emphasized that the states have a legitimate interest in protecting the potential life of the fetus, and went on to hold that only where the state regulation imposed an undue burden on the woman's decision to have an abortion would the regulation be unconstitutional. "Undue burden" was later defined as a short way of saying that the "state regulation has the purpose or effect of placing a substantial obstacle in the path of a woman seeking an abortion of a nonviable fetus." Although the Court rejected the trimester framework of *Roe*, it retained the distinction between nonviable and viable fetuses, holding that a woman should be free to terminate her pregnancy before viability.

In Gonzales v. Carhart, 550 U.S. 124 (2007), five members of the Supreme Court voted to uphold the federal Partial Birth Abortion Act, 18 U.S.C. § 1531, which barred a particular abortion procedure without providing an exception to allow use of the procedure when necessary to preserve the health of the mother. In an opinion written by Justice Kennedy that did not decide whether *Casey* was still good law, the majority rejected a facial challenge to the statute, concluding that it did not impose an undue burden under *Casey*. Four dissenters joined an opinion written by Justice Ginsburg that included this language:

> "Today's decision is alarming. It refuses to take *Casey* and *Stenberg* seriously. It tolerates, indeed applauds, federal intervention to ban nationwide a procedure found necessary and proper in certain cases by the American College of Obstetricians and Gynecologists (ACOG). It blurs the line, firmly drawn in *Casey*, between previability and postviability abortions. And, for the first time since *Roe*, the Court blesses a prohibition with no exception safeguarding a woman's health."

In 2016, the Court held in Whole Woman's Health v. Hellerstedt, 579 U.S. ___, 136 S.Ct. 2292 (2016), that Texas laws requiring that physicians performing abortions have admitting privileges at a local hospital, and that any "abortion facility" must meet the state standards for ambulatory surgical centers, placed substantial obstacles in the path of women seeking a previability abortion, and were therefore unconstitutional under *Casey*. In the same term, the Court declined to review Edwards v. Beck, 786 F.3d 1113 (8th Cir. 2015), which held that a state may not prohibit all second trimester abortions after a fetal heartbeat is detected.

———————————

Planned Parenthood of Southeastern Pennsylvania v. Casey

505 U.S. 833 (1992)

This excerpt is Part V(C) of the "joint opinion" issued by Justices O'Connor, Kennedy and Souter, considering the constitutionality of the Pennsylvania's requirement that married women must notify their spouses of their intent to obtain an abortion.

C

Section 3209 of Pennsylvania's abortion law provides, except in cases of medical emergency, that no physician shall perform an abortion on a married woman without receiving a signed statement from the woman that she has notified her spouse that she is about to undergo an abortion. The woman has the option of providing an alternative signed statement certifying that her husband is not the man who impregnated her; that her husband could not be located; that the pregnancy is the result of spousal sexual assault which she has reported; or that the woman believes that notifying her husband will cause him or someone else to inflict bodily injury upon her. A physician who performs an abortion on a married woman without receiving the appropriate signed statement will have his or her license revoked, and is liable to the husband for damages.

Go Online

Listen to the <u>oral arguments</u> in *Casey* on the Oyez Project web site.

The District Court heard the testimony of numerous expert witnesses, and made detailed findings of fact regarding the effect of this statute. These included:

> "273. The vast majority of women consult their husbands prior to deciding to terminate their pregnancy. * * *

> * * *

> "281. Studies reveal that family violence occurs in two million families in the United States. This figure, however, is a conservative one that substantially understates (because battering is usually not reported until it reaches life-threatening proportions) the actual number of families affected by domestic violence. In fact, researchers estimate that one of every two women will be battered at some time in their life. * * *

> "282. A wife may not elect to notify her husband of her intention to have an abortion for a variety of reasons, including the husband's illness, concern about her own health, the imminent failure of the marriage, or the husband's absolute opposition to the abortion. * * *

"283. The required filing of the spousal consent form would require plaintiff-clinics to change their counseling procedures and force women to reveal their most intimate decision-making on pain of criminal sanctions. The confidentiality of these revelations could not be guaranteed, since the woman's records are not immune from subpoena. * * *

* * *

"289. Mere notification of pregnancy is frequently a flashpoint for battering and violence within the family. The number of battering incidents is high during the pregnancy and often the worst abuse can be associated with pregnancy. * * * The battering husband may deny parentage and use the pregnancy as an excuse for abuse. * * *

"290. Secrecy typically shrouds abusive families. Family members are instructed not to tell anyone, especially police or doctors, about the abuse and violence. Battering husbands often threaten their wives or her children with further abuse if she tells an outsider of the violence and tells her that nobody will believe her. A battered woman, therefore, is highly unlikely to disclose the violence against her for fear of retaliation by the abuser. * * *

* * *

"294. A woman in a shelter or a safe house unknown to her husband is not 'reasonably likely' to have bodily harm inflicted upon her by her batterer, however her attempt to notify her husband pursuant to section 3209 could accidentally disclose her whereabouts to her husband. Her fear of future ramifications would be realistic under the circumstances.

"295. Marital rape is rarely discussed with others or reported to law enforcement authorities, and of those reported only few are prosecuted. * * *

"296. It is common for battered women to have sexual intercourse with their husbands to avoid being battered. While this type of coercive sexual activity would be spousal sexual assault as defined by the Act, many women may not consider it to be so and others would fear disbelief. * * *"

* * *

These findings are supported by studies of domestic violence. The American Medical Association (AMA) has published a summary of the recent research in this field, which indicates that in an average 12-month period in this country, approximately two million women are the victims of severe assaults by their male partners. In a 1985 survey, women reported that nearly one of every eight husbands had assaulted their wives during the past year. The AMA views these figures as "marked underestimates," because the nature of these incidents discourages women from reporting them, and because surveys typically exclude the very poor, those who do not speak English well, and women who are homeless or in institutions or hospitals when the survey is conducted. According to the AMA, "[r]esearchers on family violence agree that the true incidence of partner violence is probably *double* the above estimates; or four million severely assaulted women per year. Studies on prevalence suggest that from one-fifth to one-third of all women will be physically assaulted by a partner or ex-partner during their lifetime." AMA Council on Scientific Affairs, Violence Against Women 7 (1991) (emphasis in original). * * *

* * *

The limited research that has been conducted with respect to notifying one's husband about an abortion, although involving samples too small to be representative, also supports the District Court's findings of fact. The vast majority of women notify their male partners of their decision to obtain an abortion. In many cases in which married women do not notify their husbands, the pregnancy is the result of an extramarital affair. Where the husband is the father, the primary reason women do not notify their husbands is that the husband and wife are experiencing marital difficulties, often accompanied by incidents of violence. Ryan & Plutzer, When Married Women Have Abortions: Spousal Notification and Marital Interaction, 51 J. Marriage & the Family 41, 44 (1989).

This information and the District Court's findings reinforce what common sense would suggest. In well-functioning marriages, spouses discuss important intimate decisions such as whether to bear a child. But there are millions of women in this country who are the victims of regular physical and psychological abuse at the hands of their husbands. Should these women become pregnant, they may have very good reasons for not wishing to inform their husbands of their decision to obtain an abortion. Many may have justifiable fears of physical abuse, but may be no less fearful of the consequences of reporting prior abuse to the Commonwealth of Pennsylvania. Many may have a reasonable fear that notifying their husbands will provoke further instances of child abuse; these women are not exempt from § 3209's notification requirement. Many may fear devastating forms of psychological abuse from their husbands, including verbal harassment, threats of future violence, the destruction of possessions, physical confinement to the home, the withdrawal of financial support, or the disclosure of the abortion to family and friends. These methods of psychological abuse may act as even more of a deterrent to notification than the possibility of physical violence, but women who are the victims of the abuse are not exempt from § 3209's notification requirement. And many women who are pregnant as a result of sexual assaults by their husbands will be unable to avail themselves of the exception for spousal sexual assault, § 3209(b)(3), because the exception requires that the woman have notified law enforcement authorities within 90 days of the assault, and her husband will be notified of her report once an investigation begins. § 3128(c). If anything in this field is certain, it is that victims of spousal sexual assault are extremely reluctant to report the abuse to the government; hence, a great many spousal rape victims will not be exempt from the notification requirement imposed by § 3209.

The spousal notification requirement is thus likely to prevent a significant number of women from obtaining an abortion. It does not merely make abortions a little more difficult or expensive to obtain; for many women, it will impose a substantial obstacle. We must not blind ourselves to the fact that the significant number of women who fear for their safety and the safety of their children are likely to be deterred from procuring an abortion as surely as if the Commonwealth had outlawed abortion in all cases.

Respondents attempt to avoid the conclusion that § 3209 is invalid by pointing out that it imposes almost no burden at all for the vast majority of women seeking abortions. They begin by noting that only about 20 percent of the women who obtain abortions are married. They then note that of these women about 95 percent notify their husbands of their own volition. Thus, respondents argue, the effects of § 3209 are felt by only one percent of the women who obtain abortions. Respondents argue that since some of these women will be able to notify their husbands without adverse consequences or will qualify for one of the exceptions, the statute affects fewer than one percent of women seeking abortions. For this reason, it is asserted, the statute cannot be invalid on its face. We disagree with respondents' basic method of analysis.

The analysis does not end with the one percent of women upon whom the statute operates; it begins there. Legislation is measured for consistency with the Constitution by its impact on those whose conduct it affects. For example, we would not say that a law which requires a newspaper to print a candidate's reply to an unfavorable editorial is valid on its face because most newspapers would adopt the policy even absent the law. See *Miami Herald Publishing Co. v. Tornillo, 418 U.S. 241 (1974)*. The proper focus of constitutional inquiry is the group for whom the law is a restriction, not the group for whom the law is irrelevant.

Respondents' argument itself gives implicit recognition to this principle, at one of its critical points. Respondents speak of the one percent of women seeking abortions who are married and would choose not to notify their husbands of their plans. By selecting as the controlling class women who wish to obtain abortions, rather than all women or all pregnant women, respondents in effect concede that § 3209 must be judged by reference to those for whom it is an actual rather than irrelevant restriction. Of course, as we have said, § 3209's real target is narrower even than the class of women seeking abortions identified by the State: it is married women seeking abortions who do not wish to notify their husbands of their intentions and who do not qualify for one of the statutory exceptions to the notice requirement. The unfortunate yet persisting conditions we document above will mean that in a large fraction of the cases in which § 3209 is relevant, it will operate as a substantial obstacle to a woman's choice to undergo an abortion. It is an undue burden, and therefore invalid.

* * *

We recognize that a husband has a "deep and proper concern and interest * * * in his wife's pregnancy and in the growth and development of the fetus she is carrying." _Danforth, supra, at 69_. With regard to the children he has fathered and raised, the Court has recognized his "cognizable and substantial" interest in their custody. _Stanley v. Illinois, 405 U.S. 645, 651–652 (1972)_; see also _Quilloin v. Walcott, 434 U.S. 246 (1978)_; _Caban v. Mohammed, 441 U.S. 380 (1979)_; _Lehr v. Robertson, 463 U.S. 248 (1983)_. If these cases concerned a State's ability to require the mother to notify the father before taking some action with respect to a living child raised by both, therefore, it would be reasonable to conclude as a general matter that the father's interest in the welfare of the child and the mother's interest are equal.

Before birth, however, the issue takes on a very different cast. It is an inescapable biological fact that state regulation with respect to the child a woman is carrying will have a far greater impact on the mother's liberty than on the father's. The effect of state regulation on a woman's protected liberty is doubly deserving of scrutiny in such a case, as the State has touched not only upon the private sphere of the family but upon the very bodily integrity of the pregnant woman. The Court has held that "when the wife and the husband disagree on this decision, the view of only one of the two marriage partners can prevail. Inasmuch as it is the woman who physically bears the child and who is the more directly and immediately affected by the pregnancy, as between the two, the balance weighs in her favor." _Danforth, supra, 428 U.S., at 71_. This conclusion rests upon the basic nature of marriage and the nature of our Constitution: "[T]he marital couple is not an independent entity with a mind and heart of its own, but an association of two individuals each with a separate intellectual and emotional makeup. If the right of privacy means anything, it is the right of the _individual,_ married or single, to be free from unwarranted governmental intrusion into matters so fundamentally affecting a person as the decision whether to bear or beget a child." _Eisenstadt v. Baird, 405 U.S., at 453_ (emphasis in original). The Constitution protects individuals, men and women alike, from unjustified state interference, even when that interference is enacted into law for the benefit of their spouses.

There was a time, not so long ago, when a different understanding of the family and of the Constitution prevailed. In _Bradwell v. State, 16 Wall. 130, 21_

L.Ed. 442 (1872), three Members of this Court reaffirmed the common-law principle that "a woman had no legal existence separate from her husband, who was regarded as her head and representative in the social state; and, notwithstanding some recent modifications of this civil status, many of the special rules of law flowing from and dependent upon this cardinal principle still exist in full force in most States." Id., at 141 (Bradley, J., joined by Swayne and Field, JJ., concurring in judgment). Only one generation has passed since this Court observed that "woman is still regarded as the center of home and family life," with attendant "special responsibilities" that precluded full and independent legal status under the Constitution. Hoyt v. Florida, 368 U.S. 57, 62 (1961). These views, of course, are no longer consistent with our understanding of the family, the individual, or the Constitution.

In keeping with our rejection of the common-law understanding of a woman's role within the family, the Court held in *Danforth* that the Constitution does not permit a State to require a married woman to obtain her husband's consent before undergoing an abortion. The principles that guided the Court in *Danforth* should be our guides today. For the great many women who are victims of abuse inflicted by their husbands, or whose children are the victims of such abuse, a spousal notice requirement enables the husband to wield an effective veto over his wife's decision. Whether the prospect of notification itself deters such women from seeking abortions, or whether the husband, through physical force or psychological pressure or economic coercion, prevents his wife from obtaining an abortion until it is too late, the notice requirement will often be tantamount to the veto found unconstitutional in *Danforth*. The women most affected by this law—those who most reasonably fear the consequences of notifying their husbands that they are pregnant—are in the gravest danger.

The husband's interest in the life of the child his wife is carrying does not permit the State to empower him with this troubling degree of authority over his wife. The contrary view leads to consequences reminiscent of the common law. A husband has no enforceable right to require a wife to advise him before she exercises her personal choices. If a husband's interest in the potential life of the child outweighs a wife's liberty, the State could require a married woman to notify her husband before she uses a postfertilization contraceptive. Perhaps next in line would be a statute requiring pregnant married women to notify their husbands before engaging in conduct causing risks to the fetus. After all, if the husband's interest in the fetus' safety is a sufficient predicate for state regulation, the State could reasonably conclude that pregnant wives should notify their husbands before drinking alcohol or smoking. Perhaps married women should notify their husbands before using contraceptives or before undergoing any type of surgery that may have complications affecting the husband's interest in his wife's reproductive organs. And if a husband's interest justifies notice in any of these cases, one might reasonably argue that it justifies exactly what the *Danforth* Court held it did not justify—a requirement of the husband's consent as well. A State may not give to a man the kind of dominion over his wife that parents exercise over their children.

Chief Justice Rehnquist's dissent, joined by Justices White, Scalia and Thomas, concluded that the spousal notification provision advanced legitimate state interests: the husband's interest in procreation within marriage, and the state's interest in promoting the integrity of the marital relationship by improving truthful communication between spouses and by encouraging collaborative decision-making. The dissent also asserted that spousal notification is less intrusive than consent, and that the provision could not be said to be irrational.

Section 3209 embodies a view of marriage consonant with the common-law status of married women but repugnant to our present understanding of marriage and of the nature of the rights secured by the Constitution. Women do not lose their constitutionally protected liberty when they marry. The Constitution protects all individuals, male or female, married or unmarried, from the abuse of governmental power, even where that power is employed for the supposed benefit of a member of the individual's family. These considerations confirm our conclusion that § 3209 is invalid.

* * *

Points for Discussion

a. Unwed Fathers

In <u>Coe v. County of Cook, 162 F.3d 491 (7th Cir.1998)</u> the court relied on *Danforth* and *Casey* in ruling that Cook County Hospital had no obligation to notify a non-marital father before the mother could obtain an abortion. Rights of non-marital fathers are discussed in more detail in Chapter 3. What might the dissenters in *Casey* have to say about this situation? Are the constitutional questions different where married and unmarried fathers are concerned?

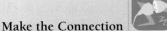

Make the Connection

Domestic violence issues, central to the joint opinion in *Casey*, are discussed in Chapter 4.

b. Minors and Abortion

Beginning shortly after *Roe*, the Court heard a series of cases challenging parental notice and consent requirements for minors seeking abortions. These cases involve a difficult conflict between respect for parents' rights and responsibility for raising their children, the state's interest in protecting the welfare of minors, and the liberty and privacy interests of young pregnant women. Although the Court sustained many of these regulations, it has required exceptions for cases involving medical emergencies and a "judicial bypass" procedure in cases involving mature minors or situations in which parental notification would not be in the minor's best interests. The process of judicial bypass proceedings was described in Patricia Donovan, *Judging Teenagers: How Minors Fare When They Seek Court-Authorized Abortions*, 15 Fam. Plan. Persp. 259 (1983).

More recent litigation has focused on when exceptions or a judicial bypass procedure must be available. In <u>Ayotte v. Planned Parenthood of Northern New England, 546 U.S. 320 (2006)</u>, the Court considered a parental notification statute with no exception for medical emergencies, but it addressed only the remedial problem, concluding that a more narrowly tailored injunctive remedy might be more appropriate than an injunction invalidating the law in its entirety.

Make the Connection

The court in *Casey* upheld a parental consent requirement, writing that a state "may not give to a man the kind of dominion over his wife that parents exercise over their children." What does this mean? To the extent that the Court is rejecting the common law of marital status, discussed in Chapter 4, does *Casey* have wider implications?

B. Marital and Nonmarital Families

Traditionally, children born to a married couple were deemed to be legitimate, and this status gave them all of the rights, benefits and protections that flow from the parent-child relationship, including rights of support and inheritance; the right to receive public benefits such as Social Security and worker's compensation payments if a parent was injured, disabled or killed; and the right to sue for a parent's wrongful death. Conversely, parents who were married when their children were born are treated by law as entitled to the full range of parental rights with respect to those children. For children born to unmarried parents, the picture was much more complex. The law traditionally labeled such children as illegitimate, and a large number of legal and social disabilities flowed from their status as illegitimate children. These disabilities have been greatly reduced over the past fifty years, due in significant part to a series of constitutional rulings from the United States Supreme Court.

Over the same time period, there has been a sharp increase in the percentage of nonmarital births in the United States and in other countries. These demographic trends have increased the importance of procedures for establishing parentage. Sophisticated genetic testing has made this process much easier than it once was. Federal laws have required the states to implement simplified legal procedures for paternity establishment, in order to help secure more extensive financial support for nonmarital children from their biological parents.

Go Online

Data compiled for 2012 showed that 62% of the 4.1 million women who gave birth that year were married, and 12% were living with a cohabiting partner. See Lindsay M. Monte and Renee R. Ellis, U.S. Census Bureau, *Fertility of Women in the United States: 2012* (July 2014).

Parents of nonmarital children also seek to establish parentage in order to enjoy the legal benefits and rights of parenthood. Here as well, there has been a substantial shift in the law, marked in a series of Supreme Court decisions addressing the constitutional rights of unwed fathers.

1. Protections for Nonmarital Children

Anglo-American law traditionally defined the legitimate child as one whose parents were married at the time of the child's conception or before the child's birth, or one who was "born in lawful wedlock or within a competent time afterwards." 1 Blackstone, Commentaries on the Law of England, 446, 447 (Cooley 4th ed. 1899). All other children were treated as illegitimate. Thus, a child conceived before the parents' marriage but born after it was legitimate. A child born after his or her parents' divorce was legitimate if the birth was near enough to the divorce so that the child would have been conceived during the marriage. If a child was born before the parents married, however, the child remained illegitimate even if they married later.

At common law, the illegitimate child was considered to be "**filius nullius**," that is, the child of no one. As a result of this status, an illegitimate child could not inherit from either parent. Although it is often asserted that illegitimate children had no right to support from their fathers, there were ecclesiastical remedies by which fathers could be ordered to support their illegitimate children, and the

Elizabethan Poor Law gave illegitimate children the right to be supported by their fathers. See generally Homer H. Clark, Jr., Domestic Relations § 4.3–4.5 (Student 2d ed. 1988), and Harry D. Krause, Illegitimacy: Law and Social Policy (1971).

Contemporary statutes have gradually improved the circumstances of nonmarital children. For example, in many states, the child of an invalid marriage was deemed to be legitimate, and statutes in all states allowed parents to legitimate their nonmarital children either by marrying each other after the child's birth, by marriage followed by acknowledgment of the child, by acknowledgment alone, or by other acts indicating an assumption of parentage. Statutes in all states impose a duty of support upon both parents of the nonmarital child, and permit nonmarital children to inherit from their fathers under certain circumstances.

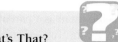

What's That?

The term "natural" is used to describe biological family relationships. A **birth mother** may be described as the child's **natural mother**, a **biological father** as the **natural father**, and a child who has a biological or genetic tie to the parent as a **natural child**.

The most comprehensive attempt to protect the legal position of nonmarital children and to deal with the complexities of parentage determinations was the Uniform Parentage Act, 9B U.L.A. 377 (2001) (UPA 1973), promulgated in 1973 and adopted by eighteen states. A revised version of the UPA, passed in 2000 and amended in 2002, was enacted in eleven jurisdictions. See Uniform Parentage Act, 9B U.L.A. 295 (2001 & Supp. 2018) (UPA 2002). The current version of the UPA was approved in 2017, following the Supreme Court's rulings in Obergefell v. Hodges, 576 U.S. ___, 135 S.Ct. 2584 (2015) and Pavan v. Smith, 582 U.S. ___, 137 S.Ct. 2075 (2017). See Uniform Parentage Act (2017), 9B U.L.A. (Supp. 2018). Information on these acts is available from the Uniform Law Commission, and selected provisions of the UPA 2017 are reprinted in the Appendix.

Levy v. Louisiana

391 U.S. 68 (1968)

MR. JUSTICE DOUGLAS delivered the opinion of the Court.

Appellant sued on behalf of five illegitimate children to recover, under

Go Online

Listen to the oral arguments in *Levy* on the Oyez Project web site.

a Louisiana statute[1] (La.Civ.Code Ann. Art. 2315 (Supp.1967)) for two kinds of damages as a result of the wrongful death of their mother: (1) the damages to them for the loss of their mother; and (2) those based on the survival of a cause of action which the mother had at the time of her death for pain and suffering. Appellees are the doctor who treated her and the insurance company.

We assume in the present state of the pleadings that the mother, Louise Levy, gave birth to these five illegitimate children and that they lived with her; that she treated them as a parent would treat any other child; that she worked as a domestic servant to support them, taking them to church every Sunday and enrolling them, at her own expense, in a parochial school. The Louisiana District Court dismissed the suit. The Court of Appeal affirmed, holding that "child" in Article 2315 means "legitimate child," the denial to illegitimate children of "the right to recover" being "based on morals and general welfare because it discourages bringing children into the world out of wedlock." 192 So.2d 193, 195. The Supreme Court of Louisiana denied certiorari. 250 La. 25, 193 So.2d 530.

The case is here on appeal; and we noted probable jurisdiction, the statute as construed having been sustained against challenge under both the Due Process and Equal Protection Clauses of the Fourteenth Amendment.

Think About It

What language in the Louisiana statute prevents the Levy children from bringing suit? Why does the Louisiana court construe that language as it does?

We start from the premise that illegitimate children are not "non-persons." They are humans, live, and have their being. They are clearly "persons" within the meaning of the Equal Protection Clause of the Fourteenth Amendment.[4]

---

[1]   "Every act whatever of man that causes damage to another obliges him by whose fault it happened to repair it.

"The right to recover damages to property caused by an offense or quasi offense is a property right which, on the death of the obligee, is inherited by his legal, instituted, or irregular heirs, subject to the community rights of the surviving spouse.

"The right to recover all other damages caused by an offense or quasi offense, if the injured person dies, shall survive for a period of one year from the death of the deceased in favor of: (1) the surviving spouse and child or children of the deceased, or either such spouse or such child or children; (2) the surviving father and mother of the deceased, or either of them, if he left no spouse or child surviving; and (3) the surviving brothers and sisters of the deceased, or any of them, if he left no spouse, child, or parent surviving. The survivors in whose favor this right of action survives may also recover the damages which they sustained through the wrongful death of the deceased. A right to recover damages under the provisions of this paragraph is a property right which, on the death of the survivor in whose favor the right of action survived, is inherited by his legal, instituted, or irregular heirs, whether suit has been instituted thereon by the survivor or not.

"As used in this article, the words 'child,' 'brother,' 'sister,' 'father,' and 'mother' include a child, brother, sister, father, and mother, by adoption, respectively."

[4]   No State shall "deny to any person within its jurisdiction the equal protection of the laws."

While a State has broad power when it comes to making classifications it may not draw a line which constitutes an invidious discrimination against a particular class. See *Skinner v. State of Oklahoma, 316 U.S. 535, 541–542 (1942)*. Though the test has been variously stated, the end result is whether the line drawn is a rational one.

In applying the Equal Protection Clause to social and economic legislation, we give great latitude to the legislature in making classifications. Even so, would a corporation, which is a "person," for certain purposes, within the meaning of the Equal Protection Clause be required to forgo recovery for wrongs done its interest because its incorporators were all bastards? However that might be, we have been extremely sensitive when it comes to basic civil rights and have not hesitated to strike down an invidious classification even though it had history and tradition on its side. The rights asserted here involve the intimate, familial relationship between a child and his own mother. When the child's claim of damage for loss of his mother is in issue, why, in terms of "equal protection," should the tortfeasors go free merely because the child is illegitimate? Why should the illegitimate child be denied rights merely because of his birth out of wedlock? He certainly is subject to all the responsibilities of a citizen, including the payment of taxes and conscription under the Selective Service Act. How under our constitutional regime can he be denied correlative rights which other citizens enjoy?

Legitimacy or illegitimacy of birth has no relation to the nature of the wrong allegedly inflicted on the mother. These children, though illegitimate, were dependent on her; she cared for them and nurtured them; they were indeed hers in the biological and in the spiritual sense; in her death they suffered wrong in the sense that any dependent would.

We conclude that it is invidious to discriminate against them when no action, conduct, or demeanor of theirs is possibly relevant to the harm that was done the mother.

Reversed.

MR. JUSTICE HARLAN, whom MR. JUSTICE BLACK and MR. JUSTICE STEWART join, dissenting.

These decisions can only be classed as constitutional curiosities.

At common law, no person had a legally cognizable interest in the wrongful death of another person,

> **FYI**
>
> The Court decided *Levy* with a companion case, Glona v. American Guarantee & Liability Insurance Co., 391 U.S. 73 (1968), which held that the mother of an illegitimate child must be allowed to bring an action for the child's wrongful death after an automobile accident in Louisiana. Three Justices dissented to both *Levy* and *Glona*, filing this opinion.

and no person could inherit the personal right of another to recover for tortious injuries to his body. By statute, Louisiana has created both rights in favor of certain classes of persons. The question in these cases is whether the way in which Louisiana has defined the classes of persons who may recover is constitutionally permissible. The Court has reached a negative answer to this question by a process that can only be described as brute force.

One important reason why recovery for wrongful death had everywhere to await statutory delineation is that the interest one person has in the life of another is inherently intractable. Rather than hear offers of proof of love and affection and economic dependence from every person who might think or claim that the bell had tolled for him, the courts stayed their hands pending legislative action. Legislatures, responding to the same diffuseness of interests, generally defined classes of proper plaintiffs by highly arbitrary lines based on family relationships, excluding issues concerning the actual effect of the death on the plaintiff.

Louisiana has followed the traditional pattern. There the actions lie in favor of the surviving spouse and children of the deceased, if any; if none, then in favor of the surviving parents of the deceased, if any; if none, then in favor of the deceased's brothers and sisters, if any; if none, then no action lies. According to this scheme, a grown man may sue for the wrongful death of parents he did not love, even if the death relieves him of a great economic burden or entitles him to a large inheritance. But an employee who loses a job because of the death of his employer has no cause of action, and a minor child cared for by neighbors or relatives "as if he were their own son" does not therefore have a right to sue for their death. Perhaps most dramatic, a surviving parent, for example, of a Louisiana deceased may sue if and only if there is no surviving spouse or child: it does not matter who loved or depended on whom, or what the economic situation of any survivor may be, or even whether the spouse or child elects to sue. In short, the whole scheme of the Louisiana wrongful death statute, which is similar in this respect to that of most other States, makes everything the Court says about affection and nurture and dependence altogether irrelevant. The only question in any case is whether the plaintiff falls within the classes of persons to whom the State has accorded a right of action for the death of another.

Louisiana has chosen, as have most other States in one respect or another, to define these classes of proper plaintiffs in terms of their legal rather than their biological relation to the deceased. A man may recover for the death of his wife, whether he loved her or not, but may not recover for the death of his paramour. A child may recover for the death of his adopted parents. An illegitimate may recover for the wrongful death of a parent who has taken a few hours to acknowledge him formally, but not for the death of a person who he claims is his parent but who has not acknowledged him. A parent may recover for the death of an illegitimate child he has acknowledged, but not for the death of an illegitimate child whom he did not bother to acknowledge until the possibility of tort recovery arose.

The Court today, for some reason which I am at a loss to understand, rules that the State must base its arbitrary definition of the plaintiff class on biological rather than legal relationships. Exactly how this makes the Louisiana scheme even marginally more "rational" is not clear, for neither a biological relationship nor legal acknowledgment is indicative of the love or economic dependence that may exist between two persons. * * * The rights at issue here stem from the existence of a family relationship, and the State has decided only that it will not recognize the family relationship unless the formalities of marriage, or of the acknowledgment of children by the parent in question, have been complied with.

Think About It

Did the majority hold that the state must define the class of potential plaintiffs based on "biological rather than legal relationships"?

There is obvious justification for this decision. If it be conceded, as I assume it is, that the State has power to provide that people who choose to live together should go through the formalities of marriage and, in default, that people who bear children should acknowledge them, it is logical to enforce these requirements by declaring that the general class of rights that are dependent upon family relationships shall be accorded only when the formalities as well as the biology of those relationships are present. Moreover, and for many of the same reasons why a State is empowered to require formalities in the first place, a State may choose to simplify a particular proceeding by reliance on formal papers rather than a contest of proof. That suits for wrongful death, actions to determine the heirs of intestates, and the like, must as a constitutional matter deal with every claim of biological paternity or maternity on its merits is an exceedingly odd proposition.

The Equal Protection Clause states a complex and difficult principle. Certain classifications are "inherently suspect," which I take to mean that any reliance upon them in differentiating legal rights requires very strong affirmative justification. The difference between a child who has been formally acknowledged and one who has not is

FYI

The underlying medical malpractice claim in *Levy* alleged that when Louise Levy came to the Charity Hospital in New Orleans on March 12 with symptoms of tiredness, dizziness, chest pain and slowness of breath, the doctor on duty did not take her blood pressure or conduct any other tests, either at that time or when she returned a week later with more severe symptoms. On March 22 she was brought back to the hospital in a comatose condition, and she died on March 29 of hypertension uremia.

hardly one of these. Other classifications are impermissible because they bear no intelligible proper relation to the consequences that are made to flow from them. This does not mean that any classification this Court thinks could be better drawn is unconstitutional. But even if the power of this Court to improve on the lines that Congress and the States have drawn were very much broader than I consider it to be, I could not understand why a State which bases the right to recover for wrongful death strictly on family relationships could not demand that those relationships be formalized.

I would affirm the decisions of the state court and the Court of Appeals for the Fifth Circuit.

Points for Discussion

a. *Levy*

The Court in *Levy* seems to lay down the general proposition that legislative classifications violate the Equal Protection Clause if they are "invidious," but do not if they are "rational." What was invidious about the Louisiana statute? Is it that the illegitimate children were dependent upon and loved by their mother, as much so as legitimate children could be? Is it that illegitimate children bear the same biological relationship to their mother as legitimate children, and all distinctions between persons having the same biological relationships constitute **invidious discrimination**?

The appellants' brief in *Levy* (available at 1967 WL 113865) framed the challenge to the Louisiana statute as a matter of civil rights, arguing that classifications based on legitimacy of birth were like classifications based on race or ancestry and should be constitutionally suspect, noting that "statutes directed against illegitimates tend to fall most heavily on Negroes, as in this case, and in some instances may have been designed to achieve this end." In addition, the brief argued that there was no reasonable relationship between the classification made in the statute and its purpose. Did the Court accept these arguments? See John C. Gray, Jr. and David Rudovsky, *The Court Acknowledges the Illegitimate:* Levy v. Louisiana *and* Glona v. American Guarantee & Liability Insurance Co., 118 U. Pa. L. Rev. 1, 5 (1969).

b. *Glona*

In the companion case, Glona v. American Guarantee & Liability Insurance Co., 391 U.S. 73 (1968), the mother of an illegitimate child sought to recover for the child's wrongful death in an automobile accident. Do the same policy arguments apply in this context? The majority in *Glona* had this to say:

[W]e see no possible rational basis for assuming that if the natural mother is allowed recovery for the wrongful death of her illegitimate child, the cause of illegitimacy will be served. It would, indeed, be farfetched to assume that women have illegitimate children so that they can be compensated in damages for their death. A law which creates an open season on illegitimates in the area of automobile accidents gives a windfall to tortfeasors. But it hardly has a causal connection with the "sin," which is, we are told, the historic reason for the creation of the disability. To say that the test of equal protection should be the "legal" rather than the biological relationship is to avoid the issue. For the Equal Protection Clause necessarily limits the authority of a State to draw such "legal" lines as it chooses.

c. Mothers and Fathers

At the time *Levy* was decided, Louisiana appeared to be the only state that applied the strict version of **filius nullius**, under which illegitimate children had no legal relationship to their mothers. A much larger number of states continued to treat nonmarital children as having no legal relationship to their biological fathers. Is the *Levy* decision authority for the principle that a statute would be unconstitutional if it did not permit illegitimate children to recover for the wrongful death of their *father?* Most cases since *Levy* have reached this conclusion. See Brookbank v. Gray, 658 N.E.2d 724 (Ohio 1996).

Should unwed fathers have the same rights that *Glona* recognized for unwed mothers? Parham v. Hughes, 441 U.S. 347 (1979), upheld a Georgia statute permitting the mother but not the father of an illegitimate child to sue for the child's wrongful death. The Court concluded that the statute did not improperly discriminate between men and women because mothers and fathers of nonmarital children were not similarly situated and that the statute was a rational means of dealing with problems of proof of paternity.

Supreme Court Developments After *Levy*

Labine v. Vincent

During the decade after deciding *Levy* and *Glona*, the Supreme Court considered many more cases challenging the constitutionality of statutes drawing distinctions based on legitimacy of birth. The first of these, *Labine v. Vincent*, 401 U.S. 532 (1971), rehearing denied 402 U.S. 990 (1971), upheld various Louisiana rules governing the disabilities of illegitimate children in taking property from their fathers by intestacy or by will. The Court said, "*Levy* did not say and cannot fairly be read to say that a State can never treat an illegitimate child differently from legitimate offspring." 401 U.S. at 536. The opinion distinguished *Levy* by stating that in *Levy* the state had created an "insurmountable barrier" to the illegitimate child, while in *Labine* no such barrier was created. In addition, *Labine* seemed to hold that rules about the devolution of property on death did not violate either the Equal Protection Clause or the Due Process Clause, because the state was attempting to protect the traditional family, and that in doing so it had plenary power over inheritance.

Weber v. Aetna Casualty

A year after *Labine*, <u>Weber v. Aetna Casualty & Surety Co., 406 U.S. 164 (1972)</u> held that the Louisiana workers' compensation statute violated the Equal Protection Clause of the Fourteenth Amendment when it provided that illegitimate children could recover benefits for the death of their father on the same terms with legitimate children only if their father had formally acknowledged them. The Court held that *Weber* was controlled by *Levy*, and distinguished *Labine* as based on the state's traditional authority to regulate the disposition of property on death, and because the deceased father in *Labine* could easily have ameliorated the illegitimate child's disfavored position. The Court found that the statute did not serve the state's interest in protecting legitimate family relationships, because it required proof of dependency as a condition on recovery by any offspring, legitimate or illegitimate, thereby ensuring that the relationships would reflect "familial care and affection."

Trimble v. Gordon

The only basis for the different outcomes in *Levy*, *Labine* and *Weber* seemed to be the difference between statutes governing inheritance, which might constitutionally classify on the basis of legitimacy, and statutes addressing wrongful death or worker's compensation claims which can not make this classification. In <u>Trimble v. Gordon, 430 U.S. 762 (1977)</u>, however, the Court struck an Illinois statute barring illegitimate children from intestate succession through their fathers. The decedent was a homicide victim who had been adjudicated to be the father of the claimant and ordered to contribute to her support in a state court paternity action prior to his death. She was not entitled to inherit his estate, consisting of a new 1974 Plymouth worth $2500, because the Illinois statute permitted illegitimate children to inherit only if they had been legitimated based on their parents' subsequent marriage.

Writing for the Court, Justice Powell's opinion in *Trimble* held that statutory classifications based on legitimacy would be subject to an intermediate level of scrutiny, somewhere between strict scrutiny, which is applied in equal protection cases involving either a suspect classification or a fundamental right, and the scrutiny applied in other cases which requires only a rational relationship between the statutory purpose and the classification made. The Court stated that this intermediate scrutiny would not be "toothless," and rejected the state's claim that its interest in promoting legitimate family relationships was a sufficient basis for the classification. The Court also found that the state's interest in assuring accuracy and efficiency in the disposition of property at death could be met without such a broad exclusion of illegitimate children.

Lalli v. Lalli

Although *Trimble* represented the twelfth time the Court had considered the constitutionality of classifications based on legitimacy, the Justices returned to the issue a year later in <u>Lalli v. Lalli, 439 U.S. 259 (1978)</u>, and shifted course once again. *Lalli* presented a challenge to the New York inheritance laws, which allowed nonmarital children to inherit from their fathers by intestate succession only if the father's paternity had been declared in a judicial proceeding prior to the father's death. Robert and Maureen Lalli presented proof that their father, Mario Lalli, had provided for their financial support and openly acknowledged them as his children.

The distinction between the Illinois statute that the Court struck in *Trimble* and the New York statute it sustained in *Lalli* was that the Illinois statute swept more broadly, excluding nonmarital children from inheritance rights unless the children had been legitimated by the marriage of their parents. While the Illinois law had been defended as a means of encouraging legitimate family relationships, the New York law was enacted after an assessment of the practical problems of estate administration in order to "provide for the just and orderly disposition of property after death."

Although *Lalli* and *Trimble* can be reconciled, only Justice Powell agreed with the outcome in both cases, and the Justices disagreed as to the effect of *Lalli* on the *Trimble* decision. Several years later, the Court relied on *Trimble* to strike down a Texas statute foreclosing inheritance by an illegitimate child, without making any attempt to distinguish *Lalli*. See <u>Reed v. Campbell, 476 U.S. 852 (1986)</u>. *Levy* and the cases that followed it are discussed in Homer H. Clark, Jr., Domestic Relations § 4.2 (Student 2d ed. 1988).

Points for Discussion

a. Proof of Paternity

The Court held in *Lalli* that New York may discriminate against illegitimate children in order to avoid difficult problems of proving paternity. These problems are not unique to intestacy cases, and may arise in any case in which the alleged father or the child has died before the proceeding is begun. Does *Lalli* mean that a state statute may bar a wrongful death suit by any child whose paternity has not been legally established?

Why has the Court been so reluctant to hold that nonmarital children must have the same inheritance rights as children born to married parents? In view of the advances that have been made in establishing parentage, what social policy is served by laws that require a particular form of proof of paternity during the father's lifetime?

b. Uniform Parentage Acts

The 1973 Uniform Parentage Act (UPA 1973), 9B U.L.A. 377 (2001), defined the parent-child relationship for all purposes, including a nonmarital child's claims for inheritance, workers' compensation benefits, wrongful death or child support, and provided procedures for proof of paternity. Under UPA 1973 § 2, "The parent and child relationship extends equally to every child and to every parent, regardless of the marital status of the parents." Section 4 of the UPA created a series of presumptions of paternity based on marriage or on the fact that an individual "receives the child into his home and openly holds out the child as his natural child." The most recent version of the Uniform Parentage Act (UPA 2017), 9B U.L.A. (Supp. 2018) has a similar series of parentage presumptions in § 204. These provisions are discussed later in this chapter, and reprinted in the Appendix.

c. Disposition of Property at Death

The Court in *Lalli* upholds the New York statute because it accomplishes the "just and orderly disposition of property at death," a state interest of "considerable magnitude." Should it matter that New York could have drafted a statute that achieves a just and orderly disposition of decedents' estates and also permits illegitimate children to inherit from their fathers? For example, the original Uniform Probate Code, drafted in 1969, addressed this question by providing that "for purposes of intestate succession by, through, or from a person, an individual is the child of his or her natural parents, regardless of their marital status." Uniform Probate Code (UPC) § 2–114(a), 8 U.L.A. (Part I) 1 (2013). Other provisions of the UPC deal with notice, res judicata and limitation on claims.

d. Child Support

In 1973, the Supreme Court held in <u>Gomez v. Perez, 409 U.S. 535 (1973)</u>, that a Texas statute was unconstitutional because it permitted legitimate children to enforce a right to support against their fathers while denying that right to illegitimate children. In subsequent cases, the Court struggled to determine what limitations periods states may place on paternity actions. The Court has held that the period of limitations must be long enough to give the child or his representative a reasonable opportunity to assert the claim, and that the period of limitation must be substantially related to the state's interest in preventing the assertion of stale or fraudulent claims. See <u>Mills v. Habluetzel, 456 U.S. 91 (1982)</u> (statute barring claims brought after the child is one year old held invalid); <u>Pickett v. Brown, 462 U.S. 1 (1983)</u> (two-year statute unconstitutional); <u>Clark v. Jeter, 486 U.S. 456 (1988)</u> (six-year statute unconstitutional). Federal statutes now require that all states have procedures that permit the establishment of paternity at any time before the child reaches age 18. See <u>42 U.S.C. § 666(a)(5)(A) (2018)</u>.

Problem 2-4

Delores and Herman were living together when Delores discovered she was pregnant. Herman told his friends about the child, and said that he and Delores planned to get married before the baby was born. However, before they were married, when Delores was seven months pregnant, Herman was killed in an auto accident, leaving a substantial amount of property. After the child was born, Delores filed claims for support and inheritance on his behalf. The state statute provided that an illegitimate child could inherit from his father only where paternity had been adjudicated by a court during the lifetime of the father, or where the child was acknowledged by the father. Neither of these had occurred in this case. If a legitimate child would recover in these circumstances, must an illegitimate child also be permitted to recover? (See <u>Estate of Blumreich, 267 N.W.2d 870 (Wis. 1978)</u>, dismissed for want of a substantial federal question, <u>Caldwell v. Kaquatosh, 439 U.S. 1061 (1979)</u>.) Should the result be different if the posthumously born child sought to bring a wrongful death action? (See <u>Le Fevre v. Schrieber, 482 N.W.2d 904 (Wis. 1992)</u>.)

Problem 2-5

Edith and Pat lived together as an unmarried couple for several years and had a son, Pat Jr. Edith and Pat Jr. were both killed in an auto accident when Pat Jr. was eight months old. Pat filed a petition to be appointed administrator of his son's estate and for an advance distribution from the estate, pursuant to the local practice. The petition was opposed by Pat Jr.'s half-sister. The applicable statute provided that any person claiming to be the father of a child born out of wedlock might file a claim of paternity during the life of the child in a specified court, or could acknowledge paternity if agreed to by the mother of the child, or could legitimate the child by marrying the mother. Pat had taken none of these actions. Is the statute unconstitutional? (See <u>Ganim v. Roberts, 529 A.2d 194 (Conn. 1987)</u>; see also <u>Rainey v. Chever, 510 S.E.2d 823 (Ga. 1999)</u>.)

Global View: Immigration and Citizenship Rights of Nonmarital Children

Distinctions based on legitimacy of birth have affected important immigration and citizenship rights. In <u>Fiallo v. Bell, 430 U.S. 787 (1977)</u>, the Supreme Court upheld a federal statute that denied to those nonmarital children whose fathers were U.S. citizens or lawful permanent residents eligibility for the special preference immigration status normally accorded to children of U.S. citizens and lawful permanent residents. Following the Court's decision in *Fiallo*, Congress amended the statute to grant preference status to nonmarital children of U.S. citizen or permanent resident fathers "if the father has or had a bona fide parent-child relationship" with the child. <u>8 U.S.C. § 1101(b) (1)(D) (2018)</u>.

Several subsequent decisions from the Supreme Court considered the federal statute that defines eligibility for United States citizenship. The statute requires that a nonmarital child born outside of the United States to a non-citizen mother and a U.S.-citizen father be legitimated before age 18 in order to acquire U.S. citizenship by birth. By contrast, a nonmarital child born outside the United States to a citizen mother and a non-citizen father is a U.S. citizen from birth. <u>8 U.S.C. § 1409 (2018)</u>. The requirement that unwed citizen fathers—but not mothers—must formally acknowledge their foreign-born children to transmit their U.S. citizenship was held not to violate equal protection in <u>Miller v. Albright, 523 U.S. 420 (1998)</u>, and <u>Nguyen v. I.N.S., 533 U.S. 53 (2001)</u>. *Miller* and *Nguyen* are critiqued in Martha F. Davis, <u>*Male Coverture: Law and the Illegitimate Family*, 56 Rutgers L. Rev. 73 (2003)</u>, and Kristin Collins, <u>*When Father's Rights Become Mother's Duties: The Failure of Equal Protection in* Miller v. Albright, 109 Yale L.J. 1669 (2000)</u>.

A different section of the statute requires that U.S.-citizen parents have a minimum period of physical presence in the United States before their child is born in order to transmit their citizenship to a child born abroad. For married parents and unmarried fathers, the residence requirement is five years, while for unmarried mothers the statute requires only one year. In <u>Sessions v. Morales-Santana, 582 U.S. ___, 137 S.Ct. 1678 (2017)</u>, the Court held that the different requirements for physical presence based on gender were "stunningly anachronistic" and could not be sustained.

2. Marriage and Parenthood

Until the Supreme Court's 1972 decision in *Stanley v. Illinois*, unwed biological fathers had few legally enforceable rights with respect to their nonmarital children. Fathers were sometimes awarded custody or visitation, but both the responsibilities of parenthood and the right to make decisions concerning nonmarital children fell almost entirely to their mothers. Statutes generally provided that if the child's birth mother wished to place the child for adoption, her consent was sufficient to free the child for adoption. Nonmarital children were also made available for adoption if the mother's parental rights were terminated involuntarily. These statutes facilitated the adoption of nonmarital children, and served to help protect the privacy of mothers who had given birth to them, but cut fathers out of the picture almost entirely.

Stanley v. Illinois

<u>405 U.S. 645 (1972)</u>

MR. JUSTICE WHITE delivered the opinion of the Court.

Joan Stanley lived with Peter Stanley intermittently for 18 years, during which time they had three children. When Joan Stanley died, Peter Stanley

Go Online

Listen to the <u>oral arguments</u> in *Stanley* on the Oyez Project web site.

lost not only her but also his children. Under Illinois law, the children of unwed fathers become wards of the State upon the death of the mother. Accordingly, upon Joan Stanley's death, in a dependency proceeding instituted by the State of

Illinois, Stanley's children were declared wards of the State and placed with court-appointed guardians. Stanley appealed, claiming that he had never been shown to be an unfit parent and that since married fathers and unwed mothers could not be deprived of their children without such a showing, he had been deprived of the equal protection of the laws guaranteed him by the Fourteenth Amendment. The Illinois Supreme Court accepted the fact that Stanley's own unfitness had not been established but rejected the equal protection claim, holding that Stanley could properly be separated from his children upon proof of the single fact that he and the dead mother had not been married. Stanley's actual fitness as a father was irrelevant. *In re Stanley*, 45 Ill.2d 132, 256 N.E.2d 814 (1970).

Stanley presses his equal protection claim here. The State continues to respond that unwed fathers are presumed unfit to raise their children and that it is unnecessary to hold individualized hearings to determine whether particular fathers are in fact unfit parents before they are separated from their children. We granted certiorari, to determine whether this method of procedure by presumption could be allowed to stand in light of the fact that Illinois allows married fathers—whether divorced, widowed, or separated—and mothers—even if unwed—the benefit of the presumption that they are fit to raise their children.

I

* * *

We must therefore examine the question that Illinois would have us avoid: Is a presumption that distinguishes and burdens all unwed fathers constitutionally repugnant? We conclude that, as a matter of due process of law, Stanley was entitled to a hearing on his fitness as a parent before his children were taken from him and that, by denying him a hearing and extending it to all other parents whose custody of their children is challenged, the State denied Stanley the equal protection of the laws guaranteed by the Fourteenth Amendment.

II

Illinois has two principal methods of removing non-delinquent children from the homes of their parents. In a dependency proceeding it may demonstrate that the children are wards of the State because they have no surviving parent or guardian. Ill.Rev.Stat., c. 37, §§ 702–1, 702–5. In a neglect proceeding it may show that children should be wards of the State because the present parent(s) or guardian does not provide suitable care. Ill.Rev.Stat., c. 37, §§ 702–1, 702–4.

The State's right—indeed, duty—to protect minor children through a judicial determination of their interests in a neglect proceeding is not challenged here. Rather, we are faced with a dependency statute that empowers state officials to circumvent neglect proceedings on the theory that an unwed father is not a "parent" whose existing relationship with his children must be considered. "Parents," says the State, "means the father and mother of a legitimate child, or the survivor of them, or the natural mother of an illegitimate child, and includes any adoptive parent," Ill.Rev.Stat., c. 37, § 701–14, but the term does not include unwed fathers.

Under Illinois law, therefore, while the children of all parents can be taken from them in neglect proceedings, that is only after notice, hearing, and proof of such unfitness as a parent as amounts to neglect, an unwed father is uniquely subject to the more simplistic dependency proceeding. By use of this proceeding, the State, on showing that the father was not married to the mother, need not prove unfitness in fact, because it is presumed at law. Thus, the unwed father's claim of parental qualification is avoided as "irrelevant."

In considering this procedure under the Due Process Clause, we recognize, as we have in other cases, that due process of law does not require a hearing "in every conceivable case of government impairment of private interest." *Cafeteria Workers v. McElroy, 367 U.S. 886, 894 (1961)*. That case explained that "[t]he very nature of due process negates any concept of inflexible procedures universally applicable to every imaginable situation" and firmly established that "what procedures due process may require under any given set of circumstances must begin with a determination of the precise nature of the government function involved as well as of the private interest that has been affected by governmental action."

The private interest here, that of a man in the children he has sired and raised, undeniably warrants deference and, absent a powerful countervailing interest, protection. It is plain that the interest of a parent in the companionship, care, custody, and management of his or her children "come[s] to this Court with a momentum for respect lacking when appeal is made to liberties which derive merely from shifting economic arrangements." *Kovacs v. Cooper, 336 U.S. 77, 95 (1949)* (Frankfurter, J., concurring).

The Court has frequently emphasized the importance of the family. The rights to conceive and to raise one's children have been deemed "essential," *Meyer v. Nebraska, 262 U.S. 390, 399 (1923)*, "basic civil rights of man," *Skinner v. Oklahoma, 316 U.S. 535, 541 (1942)*, and "[r]ights far more precious * * * than property rights," *May v. Anderson, 345 U.S. 528, 533 (1953)*. "It is cardinal with us that the custody, care and nurture of the child reside first in the parents, whose primary function and freedom include preparation for obligations the state can neither supply nor hinder." *Prince v. Massachusetts, 321 U.S. 158, 166 (1944)*. The integrity of the family unit has found protection in the Due Process Clause of the Fourteenth Amendment, *Meyer v. Nebraska, supra, 262 U.S., at 399*, the Equal Protection Clause of the Fourteenth Amendment, *Skinner v. Oklahoma, supra, 316*

U.S., at 541 and the Ninth Amendment, _Griswold v. Connecticut, 381 U.S. 479, 496 (1965)_ (Goldberg, J., concurring).

Nor has the law refused to recognize those family relationships unlegitimized by a marriage ceremony. The Court has declared unconstitutional a state statute denying natural, but illegitimate, children a wrongful-death action for the death of their mother, emphasizing that such children cannot be denied the right of other children because familial bonds in such cases were often as warm, enduring, and important as those arising within a more formally organized family unit. _Levy v. Louisiana, 391 U.S. 68, 71–72 (1968)._ "To say that the test of equal protection should be the 'legal' rather than the biological relationship is to avoid the issue. For the Equal Protection Clause necessarily limits the authority of a State to draw such 'legal' lines as it chooses." _Glona v. American Guarantee Co., 391 U.S. 73, 75–76 (1968)._

These authorities make it clear that, at the least, Stanley's interest in retaining custody of his children is cognizable and substantial.

For its part, the State has made its interest quite plain: Illinois has declared that the aim of the Juvenile Court Act is to protect "the moral, emotional, mental, and physical welfare of the minor and the best interests of the community" and to "strengthen the minor's family ties whenever possible, removing him from the custody of his parents only when his welfare or safety or the protection of the public cannot be adequately safeguarded without removal * * *." Ill.Rev.Stat., c. 37, § 701–2. These are legitimate interests, well within the power of the State to implement. We do not question the assertion that neglectful parents may be separated from their children.

But we are here not asked to evaluate the legitimacy of the state ends, rather, to determine whether the means used to achieve these ends are constitutionally defensible. What is the state interest in separating children from fathers without a hearing designed to determine whether the father is unfit in a particular disputed case? We observe that the State registers no gain towards its declared goals when it separates children from the custody of fit parents. Indeed, if Stanley is a fit father, the State spites its own articulated goals when it needlessly separates him from his family.

* * *

[I]t may be argued that unmarried fathers are so seldom fit that Illinois need not undergo the administrative inconvenience of inquiry in any case, including Stanley's. The establishment of prompt efficacious procedures to achieve legitimate state ends is a proper state interest worthy of cognizance in constitutional adjudication. But the Constitution recognizes higher values than speed and efficiency. Indeed, one might fairly say of the Bill of Rights in general, and the Due Process Clause in particular, that they were designed to protect the fragile values of a vulnerable citizenry from the overbearing concern for efficiency and efficacy that may characterize praiseworthy government officials no less, and perhaps more, than mediocre ones.

Procedure by presumption is always cheaper and easier than individualized determination. But when, as here, the procedure forecloses the determinative issues of competence and care, when it explicitly disdains present realities in deference to past formalities, it needlessly risks running roughshod over the important interests of both parent and child. It therefore cannot stand.

<u>Bell v. Burson</u> [402 U.S. 535 (1971)] held that the State could not, while purporting to be concerned with fault in suspending a driver's license, deprive a citizen of his license without a hearing that would assess fault. Absent fault, the State's declared interest was so attenuated that administrative convenience was insufficient to excuse a hearing where evidence of fault could be considered. That drivers involved in accidents, as a statistical matter, might be very likely to have been wholly or partially at fault did not foreclose hearing and proof in specific cases before licenses were suspended.

We think the Due Process Clause mandates a similar result here. The State's interest in caring for Stanley's children is *de minimis* if Stanley is shown to be a fit father. It insists on presuming rather than proving Stanley's unfitness solely because it is more convenient to presume than to prove. Under the Due Process Clause that advantage is insufficient to justify refusing a father a hearing when the issue at stake is the dismemberment of his family.

Chief Justice Burger and Justice Blackmun dissented in *Stanley,* taking the position that the Equal Protection Clause was not violated by Illinois' refusal to recognize the father-child relationship when it did not arise "in the context of family units bound together by legal obligations arising from marriage or from adoption proceedings." <u>405 U.S. at 663</u>. The dissenters found the purpose of the Illinois rule to be the protection of the welfare of illegitimate children. Stanley's own position in relation to the children they found to be somewhat unclear, since he had turned the children over to the care of a Mr. and Mrs. Ness, did not seek custody or offer to become legally responsible for them and was concerned with the loss of welfare payments if others were appointed guardians for the children.

On September 13, 1973, Mr. Stanley was declared to be an "unfit" parent by a Juvenile Court in Chicago and deprived of custody of his two children, who were placed in the permanent custody of the Illinois Department of Children and Family Services. Chi. Daily News, Sept. 14, 1973, at 6.

III

The State of Illinois assumes custody of the children of married parents, divorced parents, and unmarried mothers only after a hearing and proof of neglect. The children of unmarried fathers, however, are declared dependent children without a hearing on parental fitness and without proof of neglect. Stanley's claim in the state courts and here is that failure to afford him a hearing on his parental qualifications while extending it to other parents denied him equal protection of the laws. We have concluded that all Illinois parents are constitutionally entitled to a hearing on their fitness before their children are removed from their custody. It follows that denying such a hearing to Stanley and those like him while granting it to other Illinois parents is inescapably contrary to the Equal Protection Clause.

The judgment of the Supreme Court of Illinois is reversed and the case is remanded to that court for proceedings not inconsistent with this opinion.

Points for Discussion

a. Notice Requirements

According to *Stanley*, what rights must the states extend to parents in dependency and neglect proceedings? Does the opinion have implications for nonmarital fathers whose children are placed for adoption? How does *Stanley* apply if the whereabouts or identity of the father is unknown?

Many states passed legislation in response to *Stanley* addressing the question of what notice is due to unmarried fathers in adoption proceedings. Under these statutes, notice may be made by publication when the father's identity or location is unknown. This presents other difficulties, however: what information should be included in a published notice? Wisconsin's statute authorizes the court to order publication of the mother's name only where she has consented. Wis.Stat.Ann. § 48.42(4)(b)5 (2018). Is this provision consistent with the holding in *Stanley*?

b. Custody and Visitation Claims

Since the decision in *Stanley v. Illinois,* the claims of nonmarital parents for custody and visitation rights have been decided largely on the same basis as other parents, once parentage has been established. The primary consideration is the welfare or best interests of the child, and courts may refer to the factors set forth in divorce statutes. See, e.g., Custody of Kali, 792 N.E.2d 635 (Mass. 2003); Rosero v. Blake, 581 S.E.2d 41 (N.C. 2003); Heffernan v. Harbeson, 861 A.2d 1149 (Vt. 2004). See also Druckman v. Ruscitti, 327 P.3d 511 (Nev. 2014) (unmarried parents have equal custody rights absent judicial order to the contrary).

c. Stepparent Adoption

Following *Stanley v. Illinois,* the Supreme Court decided two cases concerning the rights of nonmarital fathers to consent or withhold consent to a proposed stepparent adoption that would have the effect of terminating their parental rights. In Quilloin v. Walcott, 434 U.S. 246 (1978), rehearing denied 435 U.S. 918 (1978), the Court allowed the stepparent adoption to go forward, concluding that neither the Due Process Clause nor the Equal Protection Clause protected the father's parental rights. In Caban v. Mohammed, 441 U.S. 380 (1979), however, the Court concluded that an adoption statute requiring the consent of an unwed mother but not the consent of an unwed father violated the Equal Protection Clause.

Quilloin v. Walcott

The child in *Quilloin* had lived with his mother and her husband for about eight years and wanted to be adopted by his stepfather. The child's father was given notice of the adoption petition, appeared in that action, and sought to block the adoption, seeking also to legitimate the child and to obtain visitation rights. Although the father had visited his child on many occasions, he had furnished support only on an irregular basis. In ruling against the biological father, the Court relied on the fact that the "result of the adoption in this case is to give full recognition to a family unit already in existence" and said the state need only establish that the adoption was in the child's best interests. The Court concluded that the father's interests were "readily distinguishable from those of a separated or divorced father," and accordingly the state was warranted in giving him less of a veto power than would be given to a married father. The Court in *Quilloin* made no real attempt to distinguish *Stanley,* other than to say that in *Quilloin* the countervailing interests were more substantial than in *Stanley.*

Caban v. Mohammed

Caban involved an unmarried couple who lived together for five years, during which time they had two children. After they separated, each of the parents married, and both parents petitioned with their new spouses for stepparent adoption. Applying a statute requiring the consent of the mother but not the father for adoption of a nonmarital child, the New York courts granted the petition of the mother and her husband to adopt the children. The Supreme Court concluded that the New York statute violated the Equal Protection Clause. The Court recognized the importance of the state interests in promoting adoption and providing for the well-being of illegitimate children, but found that the gender-based distinction in the statute did not bear a substantial relation to this purpose. The Court noted: "Even if unwed mothers as a class were closer than unwed fathers to their newborn infants, this generalization concerning parent-child relations would become less acceptable as a basis for legislative distinctions as the age of the child increased."

In this case, the Court found that the father's relationship with the children was fully comparable with that of the mother.

Justice Stevens dissented in *Caban,* arguing that the constitutional principles should reflect the different functions of men and women in pregnancy and the early life of children. His view was that the state has an interest in the welfare of the child that is often furthered by facilitating the child's adoption, and requirements for obtaining an unwed father's consent can frustrate this purpose. Justice Stevens characterized the holding in *Caban* as being limited to cases involving the adoption of older children whose fathers have admitted paternity and have participated in the rearing of their children. Four years later, this view was reflected in his opinion for the Court in Lehr v. Robertson, 463 U.S. 248 (1983).

Lehr v. Robertson

463 U.S. 248 (1983)

JUSTICE STEVENS delivered the opinion of the Court.

Go Online

Listen to the oral arguments in *Lehr* on the Oyez Project web site.

The question presented is whether New York has sufficiently protected an unmarried father's inchoate relationship with a child whom he has never supported and rarely seen in the two years since her birth. The appellant, Jonathan Lehr, claims that the Due Process and Equal Protection Clauses of the Fourteenth Amendment, as interpreted in Stanley v. Illinois, 405 U.S. 645 (1972), and Caban v. Mohammed, 441 U.S. 380 (1979), give him an absolute right to notice and an opportunity to be heard before the child may be adopted. We disagree.

Jessica M. was born out of wedlock on November 9, 1976. Her mother, Lorraine Robertson, married Richard Robertson eight months after Jessica's birth. On December 21, 1978, when Jessica was over two years old, the Robertsons filed an adoption petition in the Family Court of Ulster County, New York. The court heard their testimony and received a favorable report from the Ulster County Department of Social Services. On March 7, 1979, the court entered an order of adoption. In this proceeding, appellant contends that the adoption order is invalid because he, Jessica's putative father, was not given advance notice of the adoption proceeding.

The State of New York maintains a "putative father registry." A man who files with that registry demonstrates his intent to claim paternity of a child born out of wedlock and is therefore entitled to receive notice of any proceeding to adopt that child. Before entering Jessica's adoption order, the Ulster County Family Court had the putative father registry examined. Although appellant claims to be Jessica's natural father, he had not entered his name in the registry.

In addition to the persons whose names are listed on the putative father registry, New York law requires that notice of an adoption proceeding be given to several other classes of possible fathers of children born out of wedlock—those who have been adjudicated to be the father, those who have been identified as the father on the child's birth certificate, those who live openly with the child and the child's mother and who hold themselves out to be the father, those who have been identified as the father by the mother in a sworn written statement, and those who were married to the child's mother before the child was six months old. Appellant admittedly was not a member of any of those classes. He had lived with appellee prior to Jessica's birth and visited her in the hospital when Jessica was born, but his name does not appear on Jessica's birth certificate. He did not live with appellee or Jessica after Jessica's birth, he has never provided them with any financial support, and he has never offered to marry appellee. Nevertheless, he contends that the following special circumstances gave him a constitutional right to notice and a hearing before Jessica was adopted.

On January 30, 1979, one month after the adoption proceeding was commenced in Ulster County, appellant filed a "visitation and paternity petition" in the Westchester County Family Court. In that petition, he asked for a determination of paternity, an order of support, and reasonable visitation privileges with Jessica. Notice of that proceeding was served on appellee on February 22, 1979. Four days later appellee's attorney informed the Ulster County Court that appellant had commenced a paternity proceeding in Westchester County; the Ulster County judge then entered an order staying appellant's paternity proceeding until he could rule on a motion to change the venue of that proceeding to Ulster County. On March 3, 1979, appellant received notice of the change of venue motion and, for the first time, learned that an adoption proceeding was pending in Ulster County.

On March 7, 1979, appellant's attorney telephoned the Ulster County judge to inform him that he planned to seek a stay of the adoption proceeding pending the determination of the paternity petition. In that telephone conversation, the judge advised the lawyer that he had already signed the adoption order earlier that day. According to appellant's attorney, the judge stated that he was aware of the pending paternity petition but did not believe he was required to give notice to appellant prior to the entry of the order of adoption.

Thereafter, the Family Court in Westchester County granted appellee's motion to dismiss the paternity petition, holding that the putative father's right to seek paternity "must be deemed severed so long as an order of adoption exists." Appellant did not appeal from that dismissal. On June 22, 1979, appellant filed a petition to vacate the order of adoption on the ground that it was obtained by fraud and in violation of his constitutional rights. The Ulster County Family Court received written and oral argument on the question whether it had "dropped the ball" by approving the adoption without giving appellant advance notice. After deliberating for several months, it denied the petition, explaining its decision in a thorough written opinion. *In re Adoption of Martz*, 102 Misc.2d 102, 423 N.Y.S.2d 378 (1979).

* * *

The New York Court of Appeals also affirmed by a divided vote. *In re Adoption of Jessica "XX,"* 54 N.Y.2d 417, 430 N.E.2d 896 (1981). * * *

Appellant has now invoked our appellate jurisdiction. He offers two alternative grounds for holding the New York statutory scheme unconstitutional. First, he contends that a putative father's actual or potential relationship with a child born out of wedlock is an interest in liberty which may not be destroyed without due process of law; he argues therefore that he had a constitutional right to prior notice and an opportunity to be heard before he was deprived of that interest. Second, he contends that the gender-based classification in the statute, which both denied him the right to consent to Jessica's adoption and accorded him fewer procedural rights than her mother, violated the Equal Protection Clause.

The Due Process Claim

The Fourteenth Amendment provides that no State shall deprive any person of life, liberty, or property without due process of law. When that Clause is invoked in a novel context, it is our practice to begin the inquiry with a determination of the precise nature of the private interest that is threatened by the State. Only after that interest has been identified, can we properly evaluate the adequacy of the State's process. We therefore first consider the nature of the interest in liberty for which appellant claims constitutional protection and then turn to a discussion of the adequacy of the procedure that New York has provided for its protection.

I

The intangible fibers that connect parent and child have infinite variety. They are woven throughout the fabric of our society, providing it with strength, beauty, and flexibility. It is self-evident that they are sufficiently vital to merit constitutional protection in appropriate cases. In deciding whether this is such a case, however, we must consider the broad framework that has traditionally been used to resolve the legal problems arising from the parent-child relationship.

In the vast majority of cases, state law determines the final outcome. Rules governing the inheritance of property, adoption, and child custody are generally specified in statutory enactments that vary from State to State. Moreover, equally varied state laws governing marriage and divorce affect a multitude of parent-child relationships. The institution of marriage has played a critical role both in defining the legal entitlements of family members and in developing the decentralized structure of our democratic society. In recognition of that role, and as part of their general overarching concern for serving the best interests of children, state laws almost universally express an appropriate preference for the formal family.

In some cases, however, this Court has held that the Federal Constitution supersedes state law and provides even greater protection for certain formal family relationships. In those cases, as in the state cases, the Court has emphasized the paramount interest in the welfare of children and has noted that the rights of the parents are a counterpart of the responsibilities they have assumed. Thus, the "liberty" of parents to control the education of their children that was vindicated in _Meyer v. Nebraska,_ 262 U.S. 390 (1923), and _Pierce v. Society of the Sisters of the Holy Names of Jesus and Mary,_ 268 U.S. 510 (1925), was described as a "right, coupled with the high duty, to recognize and prepare [the child] for additional obligations." _Id., at 535._ The linkage between parental duty and parental right was stressed again in _Prince v. Massachusetts,_ 321 U.S. 158, 166 (1944), when the Court declared it a cardinal principle "that the custody, care and nurture of the child reside first in the parents, whose primary function and freedom include preparation for obligations the state can neither supply nor hinder." _Ibid._ In these cases the Court has found that the relationship of love and duty in a recognized family unit is an interest in liberty entitled to constitutional protection.

There are also a few cases in which this Court has considered the extent to which the Constitution affords protection to the relationship between natural parents and children born out of wedlock. In some we have been concerned with the rights of the children, see, _e.g., Trimble v. Gordon,_ 430 U.S. 762 (1977); _Jimenez v. Weinberger,_ 417 U.S. 628 (1974); _Weber v. Aetna Casualty & Surety Co.,_ 406 U.S. 164 (1972). In this case, however, it is a parent who claims that the State has improperly deprived him of a protected interest in liberty. This Court has examined the extent to which a natural father's biological relationship with his child receives protection under the Due Process Clause in precisely three cases: _Stanley v. Illinois,_ 405 U.S. 645 (1972), _Quilloin v. Walcott,_ 434 U.S. 246 (1978), and _Caban v. Mohammed,_ 441 U.S. 380 (1979).

* * *

The difference between the developed parent-child relationship that was implicated in *Stanley* and *Caban,* and the potential relationship involved in *Quilloin* and this case, is both clear and significant. When an unwed father demonstrates a full commitment to the responsibilities of parenthood by "com[ing] forward to participate in the rearing of his child," *Caban, 441 U.S., at 392,* his interest in personal contact with his child acquires substantial protection under the Due Process Clause. At that point it may be said that he "act[s] as a father toward his children." *Id., at 389,* n. 7. But the mere existence of a biological link does not merit equivalent constitutional protection. The actions of judges neither create nor sever genetic bonds. * * *

The significance of the biological connection is that it offers the natural father an opportunity that no other male possesses to develop a relationship with his offspring. If he grasps that opportunity and accepts some measure of responsibility for the child's future, he may enjoy the blessings of the parent-child relationship and make uniquely valuable contributions to the child's development. If he fails to do so, the Federal Constitution will not automatically compel a State to listen to his opinion of where the child's best interests lie.

In this case, we are not assessing the constitutional adequacy of New York's procedures for terminating a developed relationship. Appellant has never had any significant custodial, personal, or financial relationship with Jessica, and he did not seek to establish a legal tie until after she was two years old. We are concerned only with whether New York has adequately protected his opportunity to form such a relationship.

II

The most effective protection of the putative father's opportunity to develop a relationship with his child is provided by the laws that authorize formal marriage and govern its consequences. But the availability of that protection is, of course, dependent on the will of both parents of the child. Thus, New York has adopted a special statutory scheme to protect the unmarried father's interest in assuming a responsible role in the future of his child.

> **Think About It**
>
> The dissent describes consistent efforts made by Lehr after the birth of his child to provide support and develop a relationship with the child. These efforts were thwarted by the mother, who apparently had no desire to have him involved in the child's life. Assuming these facts to be true, in what ways did the New York statutory scheme protect Mr. Lehr's "opportunity interest"?

After this Court's decision in *Stanley,* the New York Legislature appointed a special commission to recommend legislation that would accommodate both the interests of biological fathers in their children and the children's interest in prompt and certain adoption procedures. The commission recommended, and the legislature enacted, a statutory adoption scheme that automatically provides notice to seven categories of putative fathers who are likely to have assumed some responsibility for the care of their natural children. If this scheme were likely to omit many responsible fathers, and if qualification for notice were beyond the control of an interested putative father, it might be thought procedurally inadequate. Yet, as all of the New York courts that reviewed this matter observed, the right to receive notice was completely within appellant's control. By mailing a postcard to the putative father registry, he could have guaranteed that he would receive notice of any proceedings to adopt Jessica. The possibility that he may have failed to do so because of his ignorance of the law cannot be a sufficient reason for criticizing the law itself. The New York Legislature concluded that a more open-ended notice requirement would merely complicate the adoption process, threaten the privacy interests of unwed mothers, create the risk of unnecessary controversy, and impair the desired finality of adoption decrees. Regardless of whether we would have done likewise if we were legislators instead of judges, we surely cannot characterize the State's conclusion as arbitrary.

Appellant argues, however, that even if the putative father's opportunity to establish a relationship with an illegitimate child is adequately protected by the New York statutory scheme in the normal case, he was nevertheless entitled to special notice because the court and the mother knew that he had filed an affiliation proceeding in another court. This argument amounts to nothing more than an indirect attack on the notice provisions of the New York statute. The legitimate state interests in facilitating the adoption of young children and having the adoption proceeding completed expeditiously that underlie the entire statutory scheme also justify a trial judge's determination to require all interested parties to adhere precisely to the procedural requirements of the statute. The Constitution does not require either a trial judge or a litigant to give special notice to nonparties who are presumptively capable of asserting and protecting their own rights. Since the New York statutes adequately protected appellant's inchoate interest in establishing a relationship with Jessica, we find no merit in the claim that his constitutional rights were offended because the Family Court strictly complied with the notice provisions of the statute.

The Equal Protection Claim

* * *

The legislation at issue in this case, N.Y.Dom.Rel.Law §§ 111 and 111–a (McKinney 1977 and Supp.1982–1983), is intended to establish procedures for adoptions. Those procedures are designed to promote the best interests of the child, to protect the rights of interested third parties, and to ensure promptness and finality. To serve those ends, the legislation guarantees to certain people the right to veto an adoption and the right to prior notice of any adoption proceeding. The mother of an illegitimate child is always within that favored class, but only certain putative fathers are included. Appellant contends that the gender-based distinction is invidious.

As we have already explained, the existence or nonexistence of a substantial relationship between parent and child is a relevant criterion in evaluating both the rights of the parent and the best interests of the child. In *Quilloin v. Walcott,* we noted that the putative father, like appellant, "ha[d] never shouldered any significant responsibility with respect to the daily supervision, education, protection, or care of the child. Appellant does not complain of his exemption from these responsibilities. . . . " 434 U.S., at 256. We therefore found that a Georgia statute that always required a mother's consent to the adoption of a child born out of wedlock, but required the father's consent only if he had legitimated the child, did not violate the Equal Protection Clause. Because appellant, like the father in *Quilloin,* has never established a substantial relationship with his daughter, see supra, at 262, the New York statutes at issue in this case did not operate to deny appellant equal protection.

We have held that these statutes may not constitutionally be applied in that class of cases where the mother and father are in fact similarly situated with regard to their relationship with the child. In *Caban v. Mohammed,* 441 U.S. 380 (1979), the Court held that it violated the Equal Protection Clause to grant the mother a veto over the adoption of a 4-year-old girl and a 6-year-old boy, but not to grant a veto to their father, who had admitted paternity and had participated in the rearing of the children. The Court made it clear, however, that if the father had not "come forward to participate in the rearing of his child, nothing in the Equal Protection Clause [would] preclud[e] the State from withholding from him the privilege of vetoing the adoption of that child." *Id.,* at 392.

> Justice White dissented in *Lehr* with Justices Marshall and Blackmun, arguing that the "biological connection" itself creates a constitutionally-protected interest, and concluding that procedures developed by the State must represent a reasonable effort to determine the identity of the putative father and to give him adequate notice.

Jessica's parents are not like the parents involved in *Caban*. Whereas appellee had a continuous custodial responsibility for Jessica, appellant never established any custodial, personal, or financial relationship with her. If one parent has an established custodial relationship with the child and the other parent has either abandoned or never established a relationship, the Equal Protection Clause does not prevent a State from according the two parents different legal rights.

The judgment of the New York Court of Appeals is

Affirmed.

Points for Discussion

a. *Lehr*

As described above, the Supreme Court in *Quilloin* upheld the termination of Mr. Quilloin's parental rights. Quilloin had notice and an opportunity for a hearing, but was denied the right to insist that his consent to the adoption was necessary absent proof of his unfitness. The Court upheld the trial court's refusal to hear any evidence at all from Mr. Lehr concerning the child's best interests, since under New York law Lehr was not entitled to notice or an opportunity to be heard. What state purposes are furthered by restricting fathers such as Lehr from participating in proceedings to terminate their parental rights?

b. Notice Requirements

What is left of the holding in *Stanley* after the Court's decision in *Lehr*? Why wasn't it a violation of the Due Process or Equal Protection Clauses to refuse to give notice and a hearing to a father whose whereabouts were known both by the trial court and the mother? In light of *Lehr*, how should a state court proceed in determining who should be notified of a proposed adoption? Should the court hold a hearing to determine the extent to which a child's biological father has developed a relationship with his child, in order to determine whether he has a right to receive notice and an opportunity to be heard at a proceeding to terminate his parental rights? What evidence is relevant to this determination?

c. Adoption Laws

The line of cases from *Stanley* to *Lehr* left state courts and legislatures with very little guidance on the constitutional parameters for state adoption laws, and the Court has not returned to these questions in the decades since *Lehr* was decided. State statutes

Go Online

Find state laws on the rights of unmarried fathers through the Child Welfare Information Gateway web site.

have attempted to enable nonmarital fathers to protect their parental rights in accordance with *Lehr* and at the same time provide workable rules for placement agencies and adoptive parents. These issues are discussed further in Chapter 3.

d. Unmarried Fathers and ICWA

Although the Court has not said more on the general subject of rights for nonmarital fathers since its ruling in *Lehr*, the issue came up indirectly in Adoptive Couple v. Baby Girl, 570 U.S. 637 (2013), a case decided under the unique provisions of the Indian Child Welfare Act. The Court held that an unmarried Cherokee father of a child placed for adoption (by her non-Indian mother) who was not entitled to notice of the adoption under South Carolina law was not a "parent" within the meaning of ICWA. Justice Breyer, whose vote was necessary for the majority to prevail, wrote a concurring opinion suggesting that an unmarried biological father without formal custody rights might be entitled to these protections in different circumstances. Four justices dissented, noting that the Court had regularly recognized the principle that the biological bond between parent and child is meaningful, and pointed out that many states extend greater protection to unwed biological fathers than South Carolina does. ICWA is discussed in more detail in Chapter 3 and Chapter 5.

Problem 2-6

Ann, a girl of fourteen, was impregnated by Rob, a man of twenty-one. Rob pleaded guilty to sexual assault in the second degree. Ann released her parental rights and the child was placed for adoption without notice to Rob. The state statute provides that notice is not required to one "who may be the father of a child conceived as the result of a sexual assault, if a physician attests to his or her belief that a sexual assault has occurred". Does this procedure meet the constitutional requirements of *Stanley* or *Lehr*? Does *Lehr* mean that if the father knows of the existence of the baby and makes some effort to maintain financial, personal or custodial contact with the child, he would have a right to prevent the adoption? (See Matter of SueAnn A.M., 500 N.W.2d 649 (Wis. 1993).)

(Not entitled to Notice

Michael H. v. Gerald D.

<u>491 U.S. 110 (1989)</u>

JUSTICE SCALIA announced the judgment of the Court and delivered an opinion, in which THE CHIEF JUSTICE joins, and in all but note 6 of which JUSTICE O'CONNOR and JUSTICE KENNEDY join.

Under California law, a child born to a married woman living with her husband is presumed to be a child of the marriage. <u>Cal.Evid.Code Ann. § 621 (West Supp.1989)</u>. The presumption of legitimacy may be rebutted only by the husband or wife, and then only in limited circumstances.

Go Online

Listen to the <u>oral arguments</u> in *Michael H.* on the Oyez Project web site.

The instant appeal presents the claim that this presumption infringes upon the due process rights of a man who wishes to establish his paternity of a child born to the wife of another man, and the claim that it infringes upon the constitutional right of the child to maintain a relationship with her natural father.

I

The facts of this case are, we must hope, extraordinary. On May 9, 1976, in Las Vegas, Nevada, Carole D., an international model, and Gerald D., a top executive in a French oil company, were married. The couple established a home in Playa del Rey, California in which they resided as husband and wife when one or the other was not out of the country on business. In the summer of 1978, Carole became involved in an adulterous affair with a neighbor, Michael H. In September 1980, she conceived a child, Victoria D., who was born on May 11, 1981. Gerald was listed as father on the birth certificate and has always held Victoria out to the world as his daughter. Soon after delivery of the child, however, Carole informed Michael that she believed he might be the father.

In the first three years of her life, Victoria remained always with Carole, but found herself within a variety of quasi-family units. In October 1981, Gerald moved to New York City to pursue his business interests, but Carole chose to remain in California. The end of that month, Carole and Michael had blood tests of themselves and Victoria, which showed a 98.07% probability that Michael was Victoria's father. In January 1982, Carole visited Michael in St. Thomas, where his primary business interests were based. There Michael held Victoria out as his child. In March, however, Carole left Michael and returned to California, where she took up residence with yet another man, Scott K. Later that spring, and again in the summer, Carole and Victoria spent time with Gerald in New York City, as well as on vacation in Europe. In the fall, they returned to Scott in California.

In November 1982, rebuffed in his attempts to visit Victoria, Michael filed a filiation action in California Superior Court to establish his paternity and right to visitation. In March 1983, the court appointed an attorney and guardian ad litem to represent Victoria's interests. Victoria then filed a cross-complaint asserting that if she had more than one psychological or *de facto* father, she was entitled to maintain her filial relationship, with all of the attendant rights, duties, and obligations, with both. In May 1983, Carole filed a motion for summary judgment. During this period, from March through July of 1983, Carole was again living with Gerald in New York. In August, however, she returned to California, became involved once again with Michael, and instructed her attorneys to remove the summary judgment motion from the calendar.

For the ensuing eight months, when Michael was not in St. Thomas he lived with Carole and Victoria in Carole's apartment in Los Angeles, and held Victoria out as his daughter. In April 1984, Carole and Michael signed a stipulation that Michael was Victoria's natural father. Carole left Michael the next month, however, and instructed her attorneys not to file the stipulation. In June 1984, Carole reconciled with Gerald and joined him in New York, where they now live with Victoria and two other children since born into the marriage.

In May 1984, Michael and Victoria, through her guardian ad litem, sought visitation rights for Michael *pendente lite*. To assist in determining whether visitation would be in Victoria's best interests, the Superior Court appointed a psychologist to evaluate Victoria, Gerald, Michael, and Carole. The psychologist recommended that Carole retain sole custody, but that Michael be allowed continued contact with Victoria pursuant to a restricted visitation schedule. The court concurred and ordered that Michael be provided with limited visitation privileges *pendente lite*.

On October 19, 1984, Gerald, who had intervened in the action, moved for summary judgment on the ground that under Cal.Evid.Code § 621 there were no triable issues of fact as to Victoria's paternity. This law provides that "the issue of a wife cohabiting with her husband, who is not impotent or sterile, is conclusively presumed to be a child of the marriage." Cal.Evid.Code Ann. § 621(a) (West Supp.1989). The presumption may be rebutted by blood tests, but only if a motion for such tests is made, within two years from the date of the child's birth, either by the husband or, if the natural father has filed an affidavit acknowledging paternity, by the wife. §§ 621(c) and (d).

On January 28, 1985, having found that affidavits submitted by Carole and Gerald sufficed to demonstrate that the two were cohabiting at conception and birth and that Gerald was neither sterile nor impotent, the Superior Court granted Gerald's motion for summary judgment, rejecting Michael's and Victoria's challenges to the constitutionality of § 621. The court also denied their motions for continued visitation pending the appeal under Cal.Civ.Code § 4601, which provides that a court may, in its discretion, grant "reasonable visitation rights * * * to any * * * person having an interest in the welfare of the child." Cal.Civ.Code Ann. § 4601 (West Supp.1989). It found that allowing such visitation would "violat[e] the intention of the Legislature by impugning the integrity of the family unit."

* * *

II

The California statute that is the subject of this litigation is, in substance, more than a century old. * * * In their present form, the substantive provisions of the statute are as follows:

"§ 621. Child of the marriage; notice of motion for blood tests
"(a) Except as provided in subdivision (b), the issue of a wife cohabiting with her husband, who is not impotent or sterile, is conclusively presumed to be a child of the marriage.
"(b) Notwithstanding the provisions of subdivision (a), if the court finds that the conclusions of all the experts, as disclosed by the evidence based upon blood tests performed pursuant to Chapter 2 (commencing with Section 890) of Division 7 are that the husband is not the father of the child, the question of paternity of the husband shall be resolved accordingly.
"(c) The notice of motion for blood tests under subdivision (b) may be raised by the husband not later than two years from the child's date of birth.
"(d) The notice of motion for blood tests under subdivision (b) may be raised by the mother of the child not later than two years from the child's date of birth if the child's biological father has filed an affidavit with the court acknowledging paternity of the child.
"(e) The provisions of subdivision (b) shall not apply to any case coming within the provisions of Section 7005 of the Civil Code [dealing with artificial insemination] or to any case in which the wife, with the consent of the husband, conceived by means of a surgical procedure."

III

We address first the claims of Michael. At the outset, it is necessary to clarify what he sought and what he was denied. California law, like nature itself, makes no provision for dual fatherhood. Michael was seeking to be declared *the* father of Victoria. The immediate benefit he evidently sought to obtain from that status was visitation rights. See Cal.Civ.Code Ann. § 4601 (West 1983) (parent has statutory right to visitation "unless it is shown that such visitation would be detrimental to the best interests of the child"). But if Michael were successful in being declared the father, other rights would follow—most importantly, the right to be considered as the parent who should have custody, Cal.Civ.Code Ann. § 4600 (West 1983), a status which "embrace[s] the sum of parental rights with respect to the rearing of a child, including the child's care; the right to the child's services and earnings; the right to direct the child's activities; the right to make decisions regarding the control, education, and health of the child; and the right, as well as the duty, to prepare the child for additional obligations, which includes the teaching of moral standards, religious beliefs, and elements of good citizenship." 4 California Family Law § 60.02[1][b] (C. Markey ed. 1987) (footnotes omitted). All parental rights, including visitation, were automatically denied by denying Michael status as the father. While Cal.Civ.Code Ann. § 4601 places it within the discretionary power of a court to award visitation rights to a nonparent, the Superior Court here, affirmed by the Court of Appeal, held that California law denies visitation, against the wishes of the mother, to a putative father who has been prevented by § 621 from establishing his paternity. See 191 Cal.App.3d, at 1013, 236 Cal.Rptr., at 821, citing *Vincent B. v. Joan R.*, 126 Cal.App.3d, at 627–628 179 Cal.Rptr., at 13.

Michael raises two related challenges to the constitutionality of § 621. First, he asserts that requirements of procedural due process prevent the State from terminating his liberty interest in his relationship with his child without affording him an opportunity to demonstrate his paternity in an evidentiary hearing. We believe this claim derives from a fundamental misconception of the nature of the California statute. While § 621 is phrased in terms of a presumption, that rule of evidence is the implementation of a substantive rule of law. California declares it to be, except in limited circumstances, *irrelevant* for paternity purposes whether a child conceived during and born into an existing marriage was begotten by someone other than the husband and had a prior relationship with him. * * *

This Court has struck down as illegitimate certain "irrebuttable presumptions." See, *e.g.*, *Stanley v. Illinois*, 405 U.S. 645 (1972); *Vlandis v. Kline*, 412 U.S. 441 (1973); *Cleveland Board of Education v. LaFleur*, 414 U.S. 632 (1974). Those holdings did not, however, rest upon *procedural* due process. A conclusive presumption does, of course, foreclose the person against whom it is invoked from demonstrating, in a particularized proceeding, that applying the presumption to him will in fact not further the lawful governmental policy the presumption is designed to effectuate. But the same can be said of any legal rule that establishes general classifications, whether framed in terms of a presumption or not. In this respect there is no difference between a rule which says that the marital husband shall be irrebuttably presumed to be the father, and a rule which says that the adulterous natural father shall not be recognized as the legal father. *Both* rules deny someone in Michael's situation a hearing on whether, in the particular circumstances of his case, California's policies would best be served by giving him parental rights. Thus, as many commentators have observed, our "irrebuttable presumption" cases must ultimately be analyzed as calling into question not the adequacy of procedures but—like our cases involving classifications framed in other terms, the adequacy of the "fit" between the classification and the policy that the classification serves. We therefore reject Michael's procedural due process challenge and proceed to his substantive claim.

Michael contends as a matter of substantive due process that because he has established a parental relationship with Victoria, protection of Gerald's and Carole's marital union is an insufficient state interest to support termination of that relationship. This argument is, of course, predicated on the assertion that Michael has a constitutionally protected liberty interest in his relationship with Victoria.

It is an established part of our constitutional jurisprudence that the term "liberty" in the Due Process Clause extends beyond freedom from physical restraint. See, *e.g.*, *Pierce v. Society of the Sisters of the Holy Names of Jesus and Mary,* 268 U.S. 510 (1925); *Meyer v. Nebraska,* 262 U.S. 390 (1923). Without that core textual meaning as a limitation, defining the scope of the Due Process Clause "has at times been a treacherous field for this Court," giving "reason for concern lest the only limits to. . .judicial intervention become the predilections of those who happen at the time to be Members of this Court." *Moore v. East Cleveland,* 431 U.S. 494 (1977). * * *

In an attempt to limit and guide interpretation of the Clause, we have insisted not merely that the interest denominated as a "liberty" be "fundamental" (a concept that, in isolation, is hard to objectify), but also that it be an interest traditionally protected by our society. As we have put it, the Due Process Clause affords only those protections "so rooted in the traditions and conscience of our people as to be ranked as fundamental." *Snyder v. Massachusetts,* 291 U.S. 97, 105 (1934) (Cardozo, J.). * * *

This insistence that the asserted liberty interest be rooted in history and tradition is evident, as elsewhere, in our cases according constitutional protection to certain parental rights. Michael reads the landmark case of *Stanley v. Illinois,* 405 U.S. 645 (1972), and the subsequent cases of *Quilloin v. Walcott,* 434 U.S. 246 (1978), *Caban v. Mohammed,* 441 U.S. 380 (1979) and *Lehr v. Robertson,* 463 U.S. 248 (1983), as establishing that a liberty interest is created by biological fatherhood plus an established parental relationship—factors that exist in the present case as well. We think that distorts the rationale of those cases. As we view them, they rest not upon such isolated factors but upon the historic respect—indeed, sanctity would not be too strong a term—traditionally accorded to the relationships that develop within the unitary family. In *Stanley,* for example, we forbade the destruction of such a family when, upon the death of the mother, the state had sought to remove children from the custody of a father who had lived with and supported them and their mother for 18 years. As Justice Powell stated for the plurality in _Moore v. East Cleveland, supra,_ 431 U.S., at 503: "Our decisions establish that the Constitution protects the sanctity of the family precisely because the institution of the family is deeply rooted in this Nation's history and tradition."

Thus, the legal issue in the present case reduces to whether the relationship between persons in the situation of Michael and Victoria has been treated as a protected family unit under the historic practices of our society, or whether on any other basis it has been accorded special protection. We think it impossible to find that it has. In fact, quite to the contrary, our traditions have protected the marital family (Gerald, Carole, and the child they acknowledge to be theirs) against the sort of claim Michael asserts.

The presumption of legitimacy was a fundamental principle of the common law. H. Nicholas, Adulturine Bastardy 1 (1836). Traditionally, that presumption could be rebutted only by proof that a husband was incapable of procreation or had had no access to his wife during the relevant period. As explained by Blackstone, nonaccess could only be proved "if the husband be out of the king-dom of England (or, as the law somewhat loosely phrases it, _extra quatuor maria_ [beyond the four seas]) for above nine months. . . . " 1 Blackstone's Commentaries 456 (Chitty ed. 1826). And, under the common law both in England and here, "neither husband nor wife [could] be a witness to prove access or nonaccess." J. Schouler, Law of the Domestic Relations § 225, p. 306 (3d ed. 1882); R. Graveson & F. Crane, A Century of Family Law: 1857–1957, p. 158 (1957). The primary policy rationale underlying the common law's severe restrictions on rebuttal of the presumption appears to have been an aversion to declaring children illegiti-mate, thereby depriving them of rights of inheritance and succession, and likely making them wards of the state. A secondary policy concern was the interest in promoting the "peace and tranquility of States and families," a goal that is obvi-ously impaired by facilitating suits against husband and wife asserting that their children are illegitimate. Even though, as bastardy laws became less harsh, "[j]udges in both [England and the United States] gradually widened the acceptable range of evidence that could be offered by spouses, and placed restraints on the 'four seas rule'. . .[,] the law retained a strong bias against ruling the children of married women illegitimate."

We have found nothing in the older sources, nor in the older cases, address-ing specifically the power of the natural father to assert parental rights over a child born into a woman's existing marriage with another man. Since it is Michael's burden to establish that such a power (at least where the natural father has estab-lished a relationship with the child) is so deeply embedded within our traditions as to be a fundamental right, the lack of evidence alone might defeat his case. But the evidence shows that even in modern times—when, as we have noted, the rigid protection of the marital family has in other respects been relaxed—the ability of a person in Michael's position to claim paternity has not been generally acknowledged. * * *

Moreover, even if it were clear that one in Michael's position generally possesses, and has generally always possessed, standing to challenge the marital child's legitimacy, that would still not establish Michael's case. As noted earlier, what is at issue here is not entitlement to a state pronouncement that Victoria was begotten by Michael. It is no conceivable denial of constitutional right for a State to decline to declare facts unless some legal consequence hinges upon the requested declaration. What Michael asserts here is a right to have himself declared the natural father *and thereby to obtain parental prerogatives.* What he must establish, therefore, is not that our society has traditionally allowed a natural father in his circumstances to establish paternity, but that it has traditionally accorded such a father parental rights, or at least has not traditionally denied them. Even if the law in all States had always been that the entire world could challenge the marital presumption and obtain a declaration as to who was the natural father, that would not advance Michael's claim. Thus, it is ultimately irrelevant, even for purposes of determining *current* social attitudes towards the alleged substantive right Michael asserts, that the present law in a number of States appears to allow the natural father—including the natural father who has not established a relationship with the child—the theoretical power to rebut the marital presumption, see Note, Rebutting the Marital Presumption: A Developed Relationship Test, 88 Col.L.Rev. 369, 373 (1988). What counts is whether the States in fact award substantive parental rights to the natural father of a child conceived within, and born into, an extant marital union that wishes to embrace the child. We are not aware of a single case, old or new, that has done so. This is not the stuff of which fundamental rights qualifying as liberty interests are made.

FYI

Footnote 6 of Justice Scalia's plurality opinion, joined by only one other member of the Court, defends his approach of "using historical traditions specifically relating to the rights of an adulterous natural father, rather than inquiring more generally 'whether parenthood is an interest that historically has received our attention and protection.'" As a general comment on his methodology, Justice Scalia writes: "We refer to the most specific level at which a relevant tradition protecting, or denying protection to, the asserted right can be identified. If, for example, there were no societal tradition, either way, regarding the rights of the natural father of a child adulterously conceived, we would have to consult, and (if possible) reason from, the traditions regarding natural fathers in general. But there is such a more specific tradition, and it unqualifiedly denies protection to such a parent."

In *Lehr v. Robertson*, a case involving a natural father's attempt to block his child's adoption by the unwed mother's new husband, we observed that "[t]he significance of the biological connection is that it offers the natural father an opportunity that no other male possesses to develop a relationship with his offspring," and we assumed that the Constitution might require some protection of that opportunity. Where, however, the child is born into an extant marital family, the natural father's unique opportunity conflicts with the similarly unique opportunity of the husband of the marriage; and it is not unconstitutional for the State to give categorical preference to the latter. In *Lehr* we quoted approvingly from Justice Stewart's dissent in *Caban v. Mohammed*, to the effect that although " '[i]n some circumstances the actual relationship between father and child may suffice to create in the unwed father parental interests comparable to those of the married father,' " " 'the absence of a legal tie with the mother may in such circumstances appropriately place a limit on whatever substantive constitutional claims might otherwise exist.' " In accord with our traditions, a limit is also imposed by the circumstance that the mother is, at the time of the child's conception and birth, married to, and cohabiting with, another man, both of whom wish to raise the child as the offspring of their union. It is a question of legislative policy and not constitutional law whether California will allow the presumed parenthood of a couple desiring to retain a child conceived within and born into their marriage to be rebutted.

We do not accept Justice Brennan's criticism that this result "squashes" the liberty that consists of "the freedom not to conform." It seems to us that reflects the erroneous view that there is only one side to this controversy—that one disposition can expand a "liberty" of sorts without contracting an equivalent "liberty" on the other side. Such a happy choice is rarely available. Here, to *provide* protection to an adulterous natural father is to *deny* protection to a marital father, and vice versa. If Michael has a "freedom not to conform" (whatever that means), Gerald must equivalently have a "freedom to conform." One of them will pay a price for asserting that "freedom"—Michael by being unable to act as father of the child he has adulterously begotten, or Gerald by being unable to preserve the integrity of the traditional family unit he and Victoria have established. Our disposition does not choose between these two "freedoms," but leaves that to the people of California. Justice Brennan's approach chooses one of them as the constitutional imperative, on no apparent basis except that the unconventional is to be preferred.

IV

We have never had occasion to decide whether a child has a liberty interest, symmetrical with that of her parent, in maintaining her filial relationship. We need not do so here because, even assuming that such a right exists, Victoria's claim must fail. Victoria's due process challenge is, if anything, weaker than Michael's. Her basic claim is not that California has erred in preventing her from establishing that Michael, not Gerald, should stand as her legal father. Rather, she claims a due process right to maintain filial relationships with both Michael and Gerald. This assertion merits little discussion, for, whatever the merits of the guardian ad litem's belief that such an arrangement can be of great psychological benefit to a child, the claim that a State must recognize multiple fatherhood has no support in the history or traditions of this country. Moreover, even if we were to construe Victoria's argument as forwarding the lesser proposition that, whatever her status vis-à-vis Gerald, she has a liberty interest in maintaining a filial relationship with her natural father, Michael, we find that, at best, her claim is the obverse of Michael's and fails for the same reasons.

Victoria claims in addition that her equal protection rights have been violated because, unlike her mother and presumed father, she had no opportunity to rebut the presumption of her legitimacy. We find this argument wholly without merit. We reject, at the outset, Victoria's suggestion that her equal protection challenge must be assessed under a standard of strict scrutiny because, in denying her the right to maintain a filial relationship with Michael, the State is discriminating against her on the basis of her illegitimacy. See *Gomez v. Perez*, 409 U.S. 535, 538 (1973). Illegitimacy is a legal construct, not a natural trait. Under California law, Victoria is not illegitimate, and she is treated in the same manner as all other legitimate children: she is entitled to maintain a filial relationship with her legal parents.

We apply, therefore, the ordinary "rational relationship" test to Victoria's equal protection challenge. The primary rationale underlying § 621's limitation on those who may rebut the presumption of legitimacy is a concern that allowing persons other than the husband or wife to do so may undermine the integrity of the marital union. When the husband or wife contests the legitimacy of their child, the stability of the marriage has already been shaken. In contrast, allowing a claim of illegitimacy to be pressed by the child—or, more accurately, by a court-appointed guardian ad litem—may well disrupt an otherwise peaceful union. Since it pursues a legitimate end by rational means, California's decision to treat Victoria differently from her parents is not a denial of equal protection.

The judgment of the California Court of Appeal is

Affirmed.

Justice Brennan, with whom Justice Marshall and Justice Blackmun join, dissenting.

In a case that has yielded so many opinions as has this one, it is fruitful to begin by emphasizing the common ground shared by a majority of this Court. Five Members of the Court refuse to foreclose "the possibility that a natural father might ever have a constitutionally protected interest in his relationship with a child whose mother was married to and cohabiting with another man at the time of the child's conception and birth." (Stevens, J., concurring in judgment). Five Justices agree that the flaw inhering in a conclusive presumption that terminates a constitutionally protected interest without any hearing whatsoever is a *procedural* one. (Stevens, J., concurring in judgment). Four Members of the Court agree that Michael H. has a liberty interest in his relationship with Victoria (White, J., dissenting), and one assumes for purposes of this case that he does. (Stevens, J., concurring in judgment).

In contrast, only two Members of the Court fully endorse Justice Scalia's view of the proper method of analyzing questions arising under the Due Process Clause. (O'Connor, J., concurring in part). Nevertheless, because the plurality opinion's exclusively historical analysis portends a significant and unfortunate departure from our prior cases and from sound constitutional decisionmaking, I devote a substantial portion of my discussion to it.

I

Once we recognized that the "liberty" protected by the Due Process Clause of the Fourteenth Amendment encompasses more than freedom from bodily restraint, today's plurality opinion emphasizes, the concept was cut loose from one natural limitation on its meaning. This innovation paved the way, so the plurality hints, for judges to substitute their own preferences for those of elected officials. Dissatisfied with this supposedly unbridled and uncertain state of affairs, the plurality casts about for another limitation on the concept of liberty.

It finds this limitation in "tradition." * * * Because reasonable people can disagree about the content of particular traditions, and because they can disagree even about which traditions are relevant to the definition of "liberty," the plurality has not found the objective boundary that it seeks.

* * *

It is ironic that an approach so utterly dependent on tradition is so indifferent to our precedents. * * *

It is not that tradition has been irrelevant to our prior decisions. Throughout our decisionmaking in this important area runs the theme that certain interests and practices—freedom from physical restraint, marriage, childbearing, childrearing, and others—form the core of our definition of "liberty." * * *

Today's plurality, however, does not ask whether parenthood is an interest that historically has received our attention and protection; the answer to that question is too clear for dispute. Instead, the plurality asks whether the specific variety of parenthood under consideration—a natural father's relationship with a child whose mother is married to another man—has enjoyed such protection.

If we had looked to tradition with such specificity in past cases, many a decision would have reached a different result. * * * If we had asked, therefore, * * * whether the specific interest under consideration had been traditionally protected, the answer would have been a resounding "no." That we did not ask this question in those cases highlights the novelty of the interpretive method that the plurality opinion employs today.

* * *

The document that the plurality construes today is unfamiliar to me. It is not the living charter that I have taken to be our Constitution; it is instead a stagnant, archaic, hidebound document steeped in the prejudices and superstitions of a time long past. *This* Constitution does not recognize that times change, does not see that sometimes a practice or rule outlives its foundations. I cannot accept an interpretive method that does such violence to the charter that I am bound by oath to uphold.

II

The plurality's reworking of our interpretive approach is all the more troubling because it is unnecessary. * * *

* * * The better approach—indeed the one commanded by our prior cases and by common sense—is to ask whether the specific parent-child relationship under consideration is close enough to the interests that we already have protected to be deemed an aspect of "liberty" as well. On the facts before us, therefore, the question is not what "level of generality" should be used to describe the relationship between Michael and Victoria, but whether the relationship under consideration is sufficiently substantial to qualify as a liberty interest under our prior cases.

On four prior occasions, we have considered whether unwed fathers have a constitutionally protected interest in their relationships with their children. See *Stanley v. Illinois, supra; Quilloin v. Walcott, 434 U.S. 246 (1978); Caban v. Mohammed, 441 U.S. 380 (1979)*; and *Lehr v. Robertson, 463 U.S. 248 (1983)*. Though different in factual and legal circumstances, these cases have produced a unifying theme: although an unwed father's biological link to his child does not, in and of itself, guarantee him a constitutional stake in his relationship with that child, such a link combined with a substantial parent-child relationship will do so. * * * Michael H. is almost certainly Victoria D.'s natural father, has lived with her as her father, has contributed to her support, and has from the beginning sought to strengthen and maintain his relationship with her.

* * *

The evidence is undisputed that Michael, Victoria, and Carole did live together as a family; that is, they shared the same household, Victoria called Michael "Daddy," Michael contributed to Victoria's support, and he is eager to continue his relationship with her. Yet they are not, in the plurality's view, a "unitary family," whereas Gerald, Carole, and Victoria do compose such a family. The only difference between these two sets of relationships, however, is the fact of marriage. The plurality, indeed, expressly recognizes that marriage is the critical fact in denying Michael a constitutionally protected stake in his relationship with Victoria: no fewer than six times, the plurality refers to Michael as the "*adulterous* natural father." * * * However, the very premise of *Stanley* and the cases following it is that marriage is not decisive in answering the question whether the Constitution protects the parental relationship under consideration. These cases are, after all, important precisely because they involve the rights of *unwed* fathers. It is important to remember, moreover, that in *Quilloin, Caban* and *Lehr,* the putative father's demands would have disrupted a "unitary family" as the plurality defines it; in each case, the husband of the child's mother sought to adopt the child over the objections of the natural father. Significantly, our decisions in those cases in no way relied on the need to protect the marital family. Hence the plurality's claim that *Stanley, Quilloin, Caban,* and *Lehr* were about the "unitary family," as that family is defined by today's plurality, is surprising indeed.

* * *

The plurality's premature consideration of California's interests is evident from its careful limitation of its holding to those cases in which "the mother is, at the time of the child's conception and birth, married to and cohabitating with another man, *both of whom wish to raise the child as the offspring of their union.*" (emphasis added). See also <u>ante,</u> (describing Michael's liberty interest as the "substantive parental rights [of] the natural father of a child conceived within and born into an *extant marital union that wishes to embrace the child*"). The highlighted language suggests that if Carole or Gerald alone wished to raise Victoria, or if both were dead and the State wished to raise her, Michael and Victoria might be found to have a liberty interest in their relationship with each other. But that would be to say that whether Michael and Victoria have a liberty interest varies with the State's interest in recognizing that interest, for it is the State's interest in protecting the marital family—and not Michael and Victoria's interest in their relationship with each other—that varies with the status of Carole and Gerald's relationship. It is a bad day for due process when the State's interest in terminating a parent-child relationship is reason to conclude that that relationship is not part of the "liberty" protected by the Fourteenth Amendment.

* * *

III

Because the plurality decides that Michael and Victoria have no liberty interest in their relationship with each other, it need consider neither the effect of § 621 on their relationship nor the State's interest in bringing about that effect. It is obvious, however, that the effect of § 621 is to terminate the relationship between Michael and Victoria before affording any hearing whatsoever on the issue whether Michael is Victoria's father. This refusal to hold a hearing is properly analyzed under our procedural due process cases, which instruct us to consider the State's interest in curtailing the procedures accompanying the termination of a constitutionally protected interest. * * *

A

We must first understand the nature of the challenged statute: it is a law that stubbornly insists that Gerald is Victoria's father, in the face of evidence showing a 98 percent probability that her father is Michael. * * * By depriving him of this opportunity, California prevents Michael from taking advantage of the best-interest standard embodied in § 4601 of California's Civil Code, which directs that *parents* be given visitation rights unless "the visitation would be detrimental to the best interests of the child." Cal.Civ.Code Ann. § 4601 (West Supp.1989).

As interpreted by the California courts, however, § 621 not only deprives Michael of the benefits of the best-interest standard; it also deprives him of any chance of maintaining his relationship with the child he claims to be his own. When, as a result of § 621, a putative father may not establish his paternity, neither may he obtain discretionary visitation rights as a "nonparent" under § 4601. * * *

* * *

B

The question before us, therefore, is whether California has an interest so powerful that it justifies granting Michael *no* hearing before terminating his parental rights.

* * *

The purported state interests here, however, stem primarily from the State's antagonism to Michael and Victoria's constitutionally protected interest in their relationship with each other and not from any desire to streamline procedures. Gerald D. explains that § 621 promotes marriage, maintains the relationship between the child and presumed father, and protects the integrity and privacy of the matrimonial family. It is not, however, § 621, but the best-interest principle, that protects a stable marital relationship and maintains the relationship between the child and presumed father. These interests are implicated by the determination of who gets parental rights, *not* by the determination of who is the father; in the hearing that Michael seeks, parental rights are not the issue. Of the objectives that Gerald stresses, therefore, only the preservation of family privacy is promoted by the refusal to hold a hearing itself. Yet § 621 furthers even this objective only partially.

> FYI
>
> In addition to Justice Scalia's plurality opinion for four members of the Court, Justice Stevens wrote an opinion concurring in the result. Justice Stevens agreed with the outcome because the California statutes permitted Michael to seek visitation with Victoria, but he noted that he would not foreclose the possibility of a constitutionally-protected relationship in a case such as this. In addition to Justice Brennan's dissent, Justice White wrote a dissent, joined by Justice Brennan, arguing that Michael H. had met the conditions for asserting paternity outlined in *Lehr v. Robertson*, and that Michael therefore had a constitutionally protected interest in asserting his paternity of Victoria.

* * *

Make no mistake: to say that the State must provide Michael with a hearing to prove his paternity is not to express any opinion of the ultimate state of affairs between Michael and Victoria and Carole and Gerald. In order to change the current situation among these people, Michael first must convince a court that he is Victoria's father, and even if he is able to do this, he will be denied visitation rights if that would be in Victoria's best interests. See Cal.Civ.Code Ann. § 4601 (West Supp.1989). It is elementary that a determination that a State must afford procedures before it terminates a given right is not a prediction about the end result of those procedures.

IV

The atmosphere surrounding today's decision is one of make-believe. Beginning with the suggestion that the situation confronting us here does not repeat itself every day in every corner of the country, moving on to the claim that it is tradition alone that supplies the details of the liberty that the Constitution protects, and passing finally to the notion that the Court always has recognized a cramped vision of "the family," today's decision lets stand California's pronouncement that Michael—whom blood tests show to a 98 percent probability to be Victoria's father—is not Victoria's father. When and if the Court awakes to reality, it will find a world very different from the one it expects.

Points for Discussion

a. *Michael H.*

Can *Michael H.* be reconciled with the Court's decisions in *Stanley* through *Lehr*? How does the plurality opinion in *Michael H.* distinguish these cases? What about the principles announced in the line of cases from *Levy* to *Lalli*? See Melissa Murray, *What's So New About the New Illegitimacy?*, 20 Am. U. J. Gender, Soc. Pol'y & L. 387, 409, (2012), for a useful reading of the line of cases from *Levy* through *Michael H.*

b. Presumption of Legitimacy

The provision of the California Evidence Code at issue in *Michael H.* was amended in 1992 to permit a presumed father who is not the child's mother's husband to move for blood testing to establish paternity within two years of a child's birth. See Cal. Family Code §§ 7540 and 7541 (2018). Other states continue to apply a rebuttable presumption that a child born to a married woman is legitimate. The effect of this is to place the burden of persuasion on a person asserting that the child is illegitimate. It is generally a strong presumption that may be rebutted only by clear and convincing or even more persuasive evidence. Cases discussing the presumption include Strauser v. Stahr, 726 A.2d 1052 (Pa. 1999); David V.R. v. Wanda J.D., 907 P.2d 1025 (Okla.1995); Atkinson v. Hall, 556 A.2d 651 (Me.1989); In Interest of S.C.V., 750 S.W.2d 762 (Tex.1988). Cf. Brinkley v. King, 701 A.2d 176 (Pa. 1997) (presumption not applicable where husband and wife have separated or divorced).

An influential Massachusetts case abolished the traditional presumption that the child of a married woman is the legitimate child of her husband, reasoning that this was no longer needed to protect the child, "[i]n view of the gradual betterment of the illegitimate's legal position * * * coupled with the corresponding recognition of the interests of unwed putative fathers * * *." A putative father may pursue his claim of paternity if he can prove by clear and substantial evidence that he is the child's father and also that he has a "substantial parent-child relationship" with the child, notwithstanding that the child's mother was married when the child was conceived. C.C. v. A.B., 550 N.E.2d 365 (Mass. 1990). See also

Weidenbacher v. Duclos, 661 A.2d 988 (Conn. 1995); Callender v. Skiles, 591 N.W.2d 182 (Iowa 1999).

c. Parentage Presumptions

State laws based on the original Uniform Parentage Act (UPA) include a presumption of maternity based on a woman's giving birth to the child, see UPA 1973 § 3(1); and presumptions of paternity based on a man's marriage or attempted marriage to the child's birth mother, see UPA 1973 § 4(a)(1)–(3); or his living with and openly acknowledging the child as his own, see UPA 1973 § 4(a)(4). The presumption based on living as a family helped to address cases such as *Stanley v. Illinois* involving children with unmarried parents. In a case with facts like the ones in *Michael H.*, however, there might be two different men who are both presumed fathers under the UPA.

Under UPA 1973 § 4(b), a presumption of paternity can be rebutted only by clear and convincing evidence, and when two or more presumptions arise which conflict with each other, "the presumption which on the facts is founded on the weightier considerations of policy and logic controls." Many cases have considered how to apply this language in a case like *Michael H.*, when one man is a presumed father based on marriage, and the other based on holding out as a parent. State laws must also include a presumption of paternity based on genetic testing results, discussed later in this chapter. What considerations of policy and logic should be weighed in balancing these different presumptions?

d. Multiple Fatherhood

According to Justice Stevens' concurring opinion, the trial court in *Michael H.* denied visitation because the existence of two fathers as male authority figures would confuse Victoria and not be in her best interests. How would this differ from the situation when a child lives with a mother who has divorced and remarried, so that the child lives with a stepfather but also spends time with his or her father?

A statute enacted in California, effective January 1, 2014, allows for recognition of more than two parents, "if the court finds that recognizing only two parents would be detrimental to the child." See Cal. Fam. Code § 7612(c) and (d) (2018). The statute is applied in In re Donovan L. Jr., 198 Cal.Rptr. 3d 550 (Cal. Ct. App. 2016), reprinted later in this chapter.

e. Estoppel and Equitable Parenthood

Justice Scalia's opinion suggests that the facts of the *Michael H.* case must be "extraordinary," but published case reports indicate otherwise. State courts have demonstrated substantial creativity in wrestling with different variations of the problem in *Michael H.*, developing a number of doctrines that do some of the work of the traditional presumption of legitimacy. These include **parentage by estoppel**, under which a husband who is not the biological father of a child born to his wife during the marriage may be estopped from later denying paternity if he has acted as a father with knowledge that the child may not be his. See, e.g., Pietros v. Pietros, 638 A.2d 545 (R.I.1994); D.L.B. v. D.J.B. (In re Paternity of J.R.W.), 814 P.2d 1256 (Wyo.1991); but see B.E.B v. R.L.B., 979 P.2d 514 (Alaska 1999); Adams v. Arnold, 701 N.E.2d 1131 (Ill. App. Ct. 1998). Similarly, some courts hold that a wife is estopped from challenging her husband's paternity in divorce proceedings or subsequent to a divorce. See, e.g. Ex parte Presse, 554 So.2d 406 (Ala.1989); Adoption of Young, 364 A.2d 1307 (Pa. 1976); Pettinato v. Pettinato, 582 A.2d 909 (R.I.1990).

Under an **equitable parent** approach, a husband who reasonably believes that he is the father of a child born to his wife during their marriage may be treated as the child's father regardless of biological paternity. See, e.g., In re the Marriage of Gallagher, 539 N.W.2d 479 (Iowa 1995); Atkinson v. Atkinson, 408 N.W.2d 516 (Mich.Ct.App.1987); In re Paternity of D.L.H., 419 N.W.2d 283 (Wis. Ct.App.1987); Alan Stephens, Annotation, *Parental Rights of Man Who Is Not Biological or Adoptive Father of Child But Was Husband or Cohabitant of Mother When Child Was Conceived or Born*, 84 A.L.R.4th 655 (1991).

Courts have generally not been willing to apply these principles where the mother's nonmarital partner was led to believe that he was the father of her child. See, e.g., Van v. Zahorik, 597 N.W.2d 15 (Mich. 1999); Simmons v. Comer, 438 S.E.2d 530 (W.Va. 1993). Why would courts treat this situation differently? See W. v. W., 728 A.2d 1076 (Conn. 1999) (mother's cohabitant equitably estopped from denying paternity).

f. Tort Claims

State courts are divided on the question whether a husband who learns that he is not the biological father of a child born during his marriage may sue for tort damages. Koestler v. Pollard, 471 N.W.2d 7 (Wis. 1991), approved the dismissal of a man's action for intentional infliction of emotional distress brought against the biological father of a child born to his wife during their marriage. See also Day v. Heller, 653 N.W.2d 475 (Neb. 2002) (refusing to allow husband's suit against wife on theories of fraud and emotional distress); but see Bailey v. Searles-Bailey, 746 N.E.2d 1159 (Ohio Ct. App. 2000) (holding that claim for intentional infliction of emotional distress states cause of action but claim was not established on facts of this case). Denzik v. Denzik, 197 S.W.3d 108 (Ky. 2006), upheld a jury verdict for more than $50,000 in a paternity fraud action brought by a husband against his former wife concerning a 13-year-old child born during their marriage. After a man married his pregnant girlfriend based on her assurance that he was the biological father of her child, and then discovered that he was not when the child was 15 years old, <u>Hodge v. Craig, 382 S.W. 3d 325 (Tenn. 2012)</u> allowed his claim for damages based on her intentional misrepresentation.

On the facts of *Michael H.*, should Gerald be allowed to sue in tort?

Problem 2-7

Catherine and Gregory were married in 1989. Later that year Catherine met Leslie, who was also married, and they had a sexual relationship for several months. In 1990 Catherine found she was pregnant, and sued Gregory for divorce. Her daughter Jennifer was born in January, 1991, and the divorce decree was entered in May of that year. No father was named on Jennifer's birth certificate, and the divorce petition stated that there were no children of the marriage. Later in 1991 Catherine sued Leslie, alleging paternity and asking the court to order support for Jennifer. Blood tests established that Gregory was not Jennifer's father. Leslie relied on the statutory conclusive presumption that a child of a married woman cohabiting with her husband is a child of the marriage, with limited exceptions not relevant here, like the California statute in *Michael H.* What should be the result in this case? (See <u>County of Orange v. Leslie B., 17 Cal.Rptr.2d 797 (Cal. Ct. App. 1993)</u>.)

Pavan v. Smith

582 U.S. ___ , 137 S.Ct. 2075 (2017)

PER CURIAM.

As this Court explained in <u>Obergefell v. Hodges, 576 U.S. ___ , 135 S.Ct. 2584 (2015)</u>, the Constitution entitles same-sex couples to civil marriage "on the same terms and conditions as opposite-sex couples." <u>Id., at ___ , 135 S.Ct., at 2605</u>. In the decision below, the Arkansas Supreme

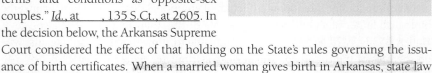

Go Online

Information about *Pavan* is available on the <u>Oyez Project</u> web site.

Court considered the effect of that holding on the State's rules governing the issuance of birth certificates. When a married woman gives birth in Arkansas, state law generally requires the name of the mother's male spouse to appear on the child's birth certificate—regardless of his biological relationship to the child. According to the court below, however, Arkansas need not extend that rule to similarly situated same-sex couples: The State need not, in other words, issue birth certificates including the female spouses of women who give birth in the State. Because that differential treatment infringes *Obergefell's* commitment to provide same-sex couples "the constellation of benefits that the States have linked to marriage," *id., at   , 135 S.Ct., at 2601*, we reverse the state court's judgment.

The petitioners here are two married same-sex couples who conceived children through anonymous sperm donation. Leigh and Jana Jacobs were married in Iowa in 2010, and Terrah and Marisa Pavan were married in New Hampshire in 2011. Leigh and Terrah each gave birth to a child in Arkansas in 2015. When it came time to secure birth certificates for the newborns, each couple filled out paperwork listing both spouses as parents—Leigh and Jana in one case, Terrah and Marisa in the other. Both times, however, the Arkansas Department of Health issued certificates bearing only the birth mother's name.

The department's decision rested on a provision of Arkansas law, Ark.Code § 20–18–401 (2014), that specifies which individuals will appear as parents on a child's state-issued birth certificate. "For the purposes of birth registration," that statute says, "the mother is deemed to be the woman who gives birth to the child." § 20–18–401(e). And "[i]f the mother was married at the time of either conception or birth," the statute instructs that "the name of [her] husband shall be entered on the certificate as the father of the child." § 20–18–401(f)(1). There are some limited exceptions to the latter rule—for example, another man may appear on the birth certificate if the "mother" and "husband" and "putative father" all file affidavits vouching for the putative father's paternity. *Ibid.* But as all parties agree, the requirement that a married woman's husband appear on her child's birth certificate applies in cases where the couple conceived by means of artificial insemination with the help of an anonymous sperm donor. See Pet. for Cert. 4; Brief in Opposition 3–4; see also Ark.Code § 9–10–201(a) (2015) ("Any child born to a married woman by means of artificial insemination shall be deemed the legitimate natural child of the woman and the woman's husband if the husband consents in writing to the artificial insemination").

The Jacobses and Pavans brought this suit in Arkansas state court against the director of the Arkansas Department of Health—seeking, among other things, a declaration that the State's birth-certificate law violates the Constitution. The trial court agreed, holding that the relevant portions of § 20–18–401 are inconsistent with *Obergefell* because they "categorically prohibi[t] every same-sex married couple. . .from enjoying the same spousal benefits which are available to every opposite-sex married couple." App. to Pet. for Cert. 59a. But a divided Arkansas Supreme Court reversed that judgment, concluding that the statute "pass[es] constitutional muster." 2016 Ark. 437, 505 S.W.3d 169, 177. In that court's view, "the statute centers on the relationship of the biological mother and the biological father to the child, not on the marital relationship of husband and wife," and so it "does not run afoul of *Obergefell*." *Id., at 178*. Two justices dissented from that view, maintaining that under *Obergefell* "a same-sex married couple is entitled to a birth certificate on the same basis as an opposite-sex married couple." 505 S.W.3d, at 184 (Brill, C.J., concurring in part and dissenting in part); accord, *id.*, at 190 (Danielson, J., dissenting).

The Arkansas Supreme Court's decision, we conclude, denied married same-sex couples access to the "constellation of benefits that the Stat [e] ha[s] linked to marriage." *Obergefell*, 576 U.S., at ___, 135 S.Ct., at 2601. As already explained, when a married woman in Arkansas conceives a child by means of artificial insemination, the State will—indeed, *must*—list the name of her male spouse on the child's birth certificate. See § 20–18–401(f)(1); see also § 9–10–201; *supra*, at 2077. And yet state law, as interpreted by the court below, allows Arkansas officials in those very same circumstances to omit a married woman's female spouse from her child's birth certificate. See 505 S.W.3d, at 177–178. As a result, same-sex parents in Arkansas lack the same right as opposite-sex parents to be listed on a child's birth certificate, a document often used for important transactions like making medical decisions for a child or enrolling a child in school. See Pet. for Cert. 5–7 (listing situations in which a parent might be required to present a child's birth certificate).

Obergefell proscribes such disparate treatment. As we explained there, a State may not "exclude same-sex couples from civil marriage on the same terms and conditions as opposite-sex couples." 576 U.S., at ___, 135 S.Ct., at 2605. Indeed, in listing those terms and conditions—the "rights, benefits, and responsibilities" to which same-sex couples, no less than opposite-sex couples, must have access— we expressly identified "birth and death certificates." *Id.*, at ___, 135 S.Ct., at 2601. That was no accident: Several of the plaintiffs in *Obergefell* challenged a State's refusal to recognize their same-sex spouses on their children's birth certificates. See *DeBoer v. Snyder*, 772 F.3d 388, 398–399 (C.A.6 2014). In considering those challenges, we held the relevant state laws unconstitutional to the extent they treated same-sex couples differently from opposite-sex couples. See 576 U.S., at ___, 135 S.Ct., at 2605. That holding applies with equal force to § 20–18–401.

Echoing the court below, the State defends its birth-certificate law on the ground that being named on a child's birth certificate is not a benefit that attends marriage. Instead, the State insists, a birth certificate is simply a device for recording biological parentage—regardless of whether the child's parents are married. But Arkansas law makes birth certificates about more than just genetics. As already discussed, when an opposite-sex couple conceives a child by way of anonymous sperm donation—just as the petitioners did here—state law requires the placement of the birth mother's husband on the child's birth certificate. See *supra*, at 2077. And that is so even though (as the State concedes) the husband "is definitively not the biological father" in those circumstances. Brief in Opposition 4.* Arkansas has thus chosen to make its birth certificates more than a mere marker of biological relationships: The State uses those certificates to give married parents a form of legal recognition that is not available to unmarried parents. Having made that choice, Arkansas may not, consistent with *Obergefell*, deny married same-sex couples that recognition.

Justices Gorsuch, Thomas and Alito dissented, arguing that summary reversal was not appropriate, because "nothing in *Obergefell* indicates that a birth registration regime based on biology, no doubt with many analogues across the country and throughout history, offends the Constitution. To the contrary, to the extent they speak to the question at all, this Court's precedents suggest just the opposite conclusion." (citing *Michael H.* and *Ngyen v. I.N.S.*, 533 U.S. 53 (2001)).

The petition for a writ of certiorari and the pending motions for leave to file briefs as *amici curiae* are granted. The judgment of the Arkansas Supreme Court is reversed, and the case is remanded for further proceedings not inconsistent with this opinion.

It is so ordered.

Points for Discussion

a. Same-Sex Couple Families

In a birth certificate case decided before *Obergefell*, <u>Gartner v. Department of Public Health, 830 N.W.2d 335 (Iowa 2013)</u>, held that the state's refusal to list a married woman's non-birthing female spouse as a parent on her child's birth certificate violated the equal protection guarantee of the state constitution. Other cases have also held that presumptions of parentage that arise from marriage must be extended equally to same-sex couples. See, e.g., <u>McLaughlin v. Jones, 401 P.3d 492 (Ariz. 2017)</u>; <u>Wendy G-M v. Erin G-M, 985 N.Y.S.2d 845 (N.Y. Sup. Ct. 2014)</u>. Similarly, courts have required a gender-neutral application of state parentage statutes in cases involving same sex couples with a registered partnership or civil union, see, e.g., <u>Miller-Jenkins v. Miller-Jenkins, 912 A.2d 951, 965–971 (Vt. 2006)</u>. Before states extended legal recognition to same-sex relationships, couples made use of other strategies to share parental rights and obligations, including

---

* As the petitioners point out, other factual scenarios (beyond those present in this case) similarly show that the State's birth certificates are about more than genetic parentage. For example, when an Arkansas child is adopted, the State places the child's original birth certificate under seal and issues a new birth certificate—unidentifiable as an amended version—listing the child's (nonbiological) adoptive parents. See Ark.Code §§ 20–18–406(a)(1), (b) (2014); <u>Ark. Admin. Code 007.12.1–5.5(a) (Apr. 2016)</u>.

second-parent or co-adoption, discussed in Chapter 3, and claims of de facto parentage, discussed in Chapter 7.

b. Gender and Parentage

State statutes based on the 1973 and 2002 versions of the Uniform Parentage Act include gender-specific presumptions of maternity and paternity, with the added proviso in UPA (2002) § 106 that: "Provisions of this Act relating to determination of paternity apply to determinations of maternity." Courts in a number of states have sought to apply these statutes in a gender-neutral manner. For example, Elisa B. v. Superior Court, 117 P.3d 660 (Cal. 2005), concluded that a woman may be a presumed parent if she "receives the child into [her] home and openly holds out the child as [her] natural child." See also Partanen v. Gallagher, 59 N.E.3d 1133 (Mass. 2016); Guardianship of Madelyn B., 98 A.3d 494 (N.H. 2014); and Chatterjee v. King, 280 P.3d 283 (N.M. 2012).

For a thoughtful exploration of these challenges, see Susan Frelich Appleton, *Presuming Women: Revisiting the Presumption of Legitimacy in the Same-Sex Couples Era,* 86 B.U. L. Rev. 227 (2006).

C. Establishing Parentage

For many generations, the primary purpose of paternity determination was to help provide for the financial support of nonmarital children. This is still an important purpose, but contemporary parentage laws also provide the basis on which a biological parent or a person acting as a parent may claim parental rights and responsibilities. Because there are now large numbers of children born outside of marriage every year, these rules define parentage for millions of children. The project of determining parentage was further complicated by the shift toward recognition of same-sex couple relationships and the new possibility that a child could have two legal mothers or fathers.

After the decisions in cases such as *Levy v. Louisiana* and *Stanley v. Illinois*, states needed to develop new approaches to establishing parentage that did not rely exclusively on marriage. The National Conference of Commissioners on Uniform State Laws, now known as the Uniform Law Commission, adopted the Uniform Parentage Act (UPA) in 1973, 9B U.L.A. 377 (2001), and a revised UPA in 2000 and 2002. See Uniform Parentage Act (UPA 2002), 9B U.L.A. 295 (2001 & Supp. 2018). In 2017, the Uniform Law Commission approved a new revision of the UPA, designed to ensure equal treatment of children born to same-sex couples. Uniform Parentage Act (UPA 2017), 9B U.L.A. (Supp. 2018). About 20 states have some version of the UPA; selected provisions from the UPA 2017 are included in the Appendix.

State parentage laws have also been shaped by federal law under Title IV-D of the Social Security Act. All states must have plans in place for paternity determination and establishment and enforcement of child support in order to receive federal funding for the Temporary Assistance for Needy Families (TANF) program. Federal law requires states to have expedited administrative and judicial procedures for determining paternity, 42 U.S.C.A. § 666(a)(2)(2018); procedures permitting the establishment of paternity until a child reaches the age of 18, § 666(a)(5)(A); and simplified procedures for voluntary paternity acknowledgment, including hospital-based programs that allow fathers to acknowledge paternity at the time of the child's birth, § 666(a)(5)(C). State laws must provide for genetic testing, § 666(a)(5)(B), and establish thresholds at which genetic testing results are given presumptive effect, §666(a)(5)(G). Under the Social Security Act, substantial pressure is brought to bear on unmarried mothers who seek TANF benefits: states must reduce or terminate support to an individual who does not cooperate in establishing paternity or obtaining child support without good cause to do so. See 42 U.S.C.A. § 608 (a)(2) (2018).

> **Make the Connection**
>
> Child support enforcement and the federal IV-D program are discussed in Chapter 7.

In 2017, the Uniform Parentage Act was revised to ensure compliance with all federal requirements and equal treatment for children of same-sex couples. The statute allows a parent-child relationship to be established in a variety of ways, including:

- Giving birth to the child
- Based on an acknowledgment of parentage
- Based on a presumption of parentage
- Based on an adjudication of parentage

See UPA 2017 § 201. Parent-child relationships may also be established by adoption, consent to assisted reproduction, or surrogacy arrangements, discussed in Chapter 3.

1. Acknowledging Parentage

Prompted by federal law, all states have simplified procedures for acknowledgment of parentage, with a particular focus on encouraging in-hospital voluntary paternity establishment at the time a child is born. Hospitals provide unmarried parents with educational materials and an opportunity to sign an acknowledgment form. These programs are also intended to help connect unmarried fathers with their children and encourage them to remain involved in the child's life. See Ronald Mincy, et al., *In-Hospital Paternity Establishment and Father Involvement in Fragile Families*, 67 J. Marriage & Fam. 611 (2005).

Cesar C. v. Alicia L.

800 N.W.2d 249 (Neb. 2011)

MILLER-LERMAN, J.

NATURE OF CASE

The district court for Dawson County awarded Alicia L. custody of Jaime C. based on its application of the parental preference doctrine. Cesar C. appeals and assigns various errors, and Alicia cross-appeals. We conclude that the district court erred when it failed to give proper legal effect to a notarized acknowledgment of paternity signed by Cesar and Alicia at the time of Jaime's birth. In the absence of a successful challenge directed at the acknowledgment, the acknowledgment had the effect of establishing that Cesar was the legal father of Jaime and matters of custody and child support should have been considered within this legal framework. We therefore reverse the decision of the district court and remand the cause for further proceedings.

STATEMENT OF FACTS

Cesar and Alicia lived together and had an intimate relationship between 2004 and 2006. During that time, Alicia became pregnant. Cesar and Alicia are not married.

Alicia gave birth to Jaime in 2006, and Cesar was present at the birth. On the day after Jaime's birth, Cesar and Alicia both signed a form provided by the Nebraska Department of Health and Human Services titled "Acknowledgement of Paternity," in which both Cesar and Alicia acknowledged that Cesar was Jaime's biological father. Their signatures were notarized. Cesar was named as the father on the birth certificate.

When Alicia and Jaime left the hospital, they returned to a home Cesar and Alicia had rented in Lexington, Nebraska. Shortly thereafter, Alicia learned that there was an outstanding federal warrant for her arrest for conspiracy to deliver methamphetamine. Without notifying Cesar, Alicia fled Lexington and left Jaime with Cesar. Alicia was arrested in Colorado on October 5, 2006, and was later convicted and sentenced to imprisonment in a federal facility in Texas. She was in federal custody until August 2008, when she was released to a halfway house in Omaha, Nebraska, where she lived until she moved into a house in February 2009. After arriving in Omaha, Alicia resumed contact with Cesar and Jaime, who for the last 2 years had been living together in Lexington. The relationship between Cesar and Alicia did not resume.

On June 8, 2009, Cesar filed a complaint in the district court for Dawson County to establish paternity, custody, and child support with respect to Jaime. Cesar asserted that at all times, Jaime had been in his physical care, custody, and control and that they had lived in Lexington Jaime's entire life. Cesar sought an order declaring him to be Jaime's father, granting him custody of Jaime, and ordering Alicia to pay child support. Cesar also filed a motion for temporary custody; in an affidavit in support of the motion, he asserted that on June 7, Alicia had taken Jaime to Omaha without Cesar's knowledge or consent. The court granted Cesar's motion for temporary custody of Jaime.

Although on June 9, 2009, Alicia filed a separate action in the district court for Douglas County in which she asserted that Cesar was Jaime's father, she answered Cesar's complaint in this case with a counter-complaint for custody and child support in which she asserted that Cesar was "potentially" Jaime's father. In a separate motion, Alicia asserted that it was possible that Cesar was not Jaime's biological father and she requested that the court order Cesar to submit to genetic testing to determine paternity. The court granted the request. After the genetic testing excluded Cesar as being Jaime's biological father, Alicia filed a motion for summary judgment and motions to, inter alia, grant her temporary custody of Jaime and vacate the order directing her to pay child support.

Cesar filed a motion for leave to file an amended complaint which alleged that immediately after Jaime's birth, he asked Alicia whether he was Jaime's father; that Alicia told Cesar that he was Jaime's father; and that at no time since, until the present action, had Alicia indicated to Cesar that he was not Jaime's father. Cesar also alleged that Alicia was unfit to have custody of Jaime for various reasons including, inter alia, her involvement with drugs, her conviction "for one or more federal felonies," and her abandonment of Jaime. Cesar further alleged that he was an " 'equitable parent' " to Jaime, that Alicia should be equitably estopped from denying his paternity, and that he had acted in loco parentis to Jaime.

The district court granted Cesar leave to file the amended complaint. The court overruled Alicia's motion for summary judgment and other motions after it determined that there were genuine issues of material fact relating to the claims raised by Cesar in his amended complaint and that there was legal authority to support Cesar's claims that he had the rights of a parent. Alicia answered Cesar's amended complaint by alleging, inter alia, that Cesar was unfit to have custody of Jaime.

At a final hearing on all pending matters in this case, Cesar offered into evidence the notarized acknowledgment of paternity signed by Cesar and Alicia at Jaime's birth. Without objection by Alicia, the court received the acknowledgment into evidence. Following the hearing, the court entered an order on August 19, 2010, ruling on both parties' various claims. The court first determined that Cesar had proved by clear and convincing evidence each of the elements of equitable estoppel. In making such determination, the court found as an incidental matter that the acknowledgment of paternity had been signed; however, the court did not consider the legal effect of the acknowledgment. The court concluded that Cesar could use the doctrine of equitable estoppel to prevent Alicia from terminating the relationship between Cesar and Jaime.

In its order, the court noted that genetic testing excluded Cesar as being Jaime's biological father. The court therefore applied the parental preference doctrine and concluded that Alicia, as the biological parent of Jaime, had the superior right to custody unless such custody would be detrimental to Jaime's welfare. The court found that Cesar failed to establish that Alicia was unfit to parent Jaime or that she had forfeited her parental rights by substantial, continuous, and repeated neglect of Jaime. The court awarded custody of Jaime to Alicia.

Despite its conclusion that Cesar had not rebutted the presumption of custody in Alicia, the court found that Cesar had established that his relationship with Jaime was protected by the in loco parentis doctrine and that therefore, Cesar was entitled to parenting time with Jaime. The court found that Cesar should have "extensive and liberal parenting time" with Jaime and set forth a parenting plan to provide such time. Finally, the court determined that because Cesar stood in loco parentis to Jaime, he had an obligation to support Jaime; the court therefore ordered Cesar to pay monthly child support.

Cesar filed a motion for a new trial or to reconsider or modify the August 19, 2010, order. The court granted a new trial limited to a specific evidentiary issue. Cesar noted that at the prior hearing, the court did not explicitly rule on Alicia's offering into evidence the results of the genetic testing that excluded Cesar as Jaime's biological father. When Alicia again offered the evidence at the new trial, Cesar objected. Cesar argued that based on equitable estoppel, Alicia should not be allowed to present evidence that he was not Jaime's biological father. The court overruled Cesar's objection, stating that equitable estoppel did not prevent admission of the evidence. In an order entered September 16, the court concluded that admission of the evidence did not change the findings and conclusions it had reached in its August 19 order.

Cesar appeals the August 19 and September 16, 2010, orders. Alicia cross-appeals.

ASSIGNMENTS OF ERROR

In his appeal, Cesar claims that the district court erred when it (1) found that Alicia was not equitably estopped from offering the results of genetic testing to establish that Cesar was not Jaime's biological father, (2) found that Alicia was not unfit to have custody of Jaime, and (3) did not order Alicia to pay child support.

In her cross-appeal, Alicia claims that the district court erred when it concluded that Cesar had established the elements of equitable estoppel by clear and convincing evidence.

* * *

ANALYSIS

Before considering the assigned errors, we note plain error which requires reversal: to wit, the district court failed to give proper legal effect to the signed and notarized acknowledgment of paternity. Because such error resolves the appeal, we need not consider the errors assigned by Cesar or those assigned by Alicia in her cross-appeal. Instead, we reverse the August 19 and September 16, 2010, orders of the district court which encompassed the court's rulings on custody and the admission of genetic testing, and remand the cause for further proceedings consistent with this opinion.

Although an appellate court ordinarily considers only those errors assigned and discussed in the briefs, the appellate court may, at its option, notice plain error. Plain error is error plainly evident from the record and of such a nature that to leave it uncorrected would result in damage to the integrity, reputation, or fairness of the judicial process. We note plain error in the district court's failure to give proper legal effect to the notarized acknowledgment of paternity signed by Cesar and Alicia at Jaime's birth, and we determine that to leave the error uncorrected would result in damage to the integrity, reputation, or fairness of the judicial process, because the error affected Cesar's legal relationship to Jaime and beyond doubt affected the court's decisions with respect to evidentiary matters and custody.

At Jaime's birth, Cesar and Alicia executed a notarized acknowledgment of paternity in which they asserted that Cesar was Jaime's biological father. Cesar offered the notarized acknowledgment into evidence at the hearing in this case, and the court received the evidence without objection by Alicia. The court noted in its August 19, 2010, order that the acknowledgment was signed. However, the court failed to give proper legal effect to the signed, unchallenged acknowledgment. As explained below, the proper legal effect of a signed, unchallenged acknowledgment of paternity is a finding that the individual who signed as the father is in fact the legal father.

With regard to the legal effect of a notarized acknowledgment of paternity, Neb.Rev.Stat. § 43–1409 (Reissue 2008) provides as follows:

> The signing of a notarized acknowledgment, whether under section 43–1408.01 or otherwise, by the alleged father shall create a rebuttable presumption of paternity as against the alleged father. The signed, notarized acknowledgment is subject to the right of any signatory to rescind the acknowledgment within the earlier of (1) sixty days or (2) the date of an administrative or judicial proceeding relating to the child, including a proceeding to establish a support order in which the signatory is a party. *After the rescission period a signed, notarized acknowledgment is considered a legal finding* which may be challenged only on the basis of fraud, duress, or material mistake of fact with the burden of proof upon the challenger, and the legal responsibilities, including the child support obligation, of any signatory arising from the acknowledgment shall not be suspended during the challenge, except for good cause shown. Such a signed and notarized acknowledgment or a certified copy or certified reproduction thereof shall be admissible in evidence in any proceeding to establish support.

(Emphasis supplied.)

We also note that Neb.Rev.Stat. § 43–1402 (Reissue 2008), regarding the liability of parents to support a child, refers to the "father of a child whose paternity is established either by judicial proceeding or by acknowledgment as hereinafter provided." Section 43–1402 therefore contemplates that paternity may be established by acknowledgment and that establishment of paternity by acknowledgment is the equivalent of establishment of paternity by a judicial proceeding. Reading these statutes together, we interpret the provision in § 43–1409 that the acknowledgment is a "legal finding" to mean that it legally establishes paternity in the person named in the acknowledgment as the father.

* * *

Finally, we note that under § 43–1409, any signatory has a right to rescind the acknowledgment within the earlier of 60 days or the date of a legal proceeding related to the child. There is no indication in this case that either party rescinded the acknowledgment within the statutory rescission period, and no proceeding relating to the child was noted during the rescission period. Thus, the acknowl-edgment remained in full force and effect.

* * *

In the present case, at the time Cesar initiated the current proceedings, the notarized acknowledgment signed by Cesar and Alicia legally established Cesar's paternity as to Jaime. A judicial proceeding was not needed to establish Cesar's paternity. The legal finding of paternity that is implicit in the acknowledgment is made explicit by the terms of §§ 43–1402 and 43–1409. Upon finding that the notarized acknowledgment of paternity had been signed, the court should have treated Cesar's paternity as having been legally established and treated this action as one solely to determine issues of custody and support as between two legal parents, and not one to establish paternity.

In her answer, Alicia questioned Cesar's status as Jaime's father by alleg-ing that another man might be the bio-logical father and requested the court to order Cesar to submit to genetic testing. However, under the statutory scheme, before Alicia could challenge paternity and subject Cesar to genetic testing, she needed to overcome the acknowledgment that she and Cesar had both signed which established that Cesar was Jaime's legal father.

Think About It

How would the court's analysis be different in an action to determine custody between two legal parents?

Section 43–1409 provides that an acknowledgment that has become a legal finding of paternity "may be challenged only on the basis of fraud, duress, or material mistake of fact with the burden of proof upon the challenger." Under § 43–1409, Alicia had the burden to prove fraud, duress, or material mistake of fact with regard to the execution of the acknowledgment. Alicia made no allega-tion of fraud, duress, or material mistake and therefore did not properly challenge the acknowledgment under § 43–1409. The acknowledgment remained a legal finding, and Cesar had the legal status as father. Because such legal status had been established and the acknowledgment was unchallenged, the results of genet-ic testing were not relevant to any issue properly raised in the case and the district court should not have ordered or considered genetic testing. See § 43–1412.01.

Courts in other states have similarly found that an acknowledgment has the effect of a judgment and can only be challenged on the bases stated in the statutes. * * *

* * *

We agree with these authorities that not only do the applicable statutes require that an unchallenged acknowledgment have the effect of making the acknowledged father the legal father but that the best interests of the child are ordinarily served by certain parentage determinations and continuity in the child's life.

The court in this case committed plain error when it failed to give proper legal effect to the acknowledgment. Such failure resulted in the court's ordering Cesar to submit to genetic testing, which led to a determination that Cesar was not Jaime's biological father, which in turn led the court to apply the parental preference doctrine and conclude that Alicia had a superior right to custody of Jaime. If the court had given proper legal effect to the acknowledgment, the court would have viewed both Cesar and Alicia as legal parents to Jaime, and the issues in this case would have, and should have, been considered within this legal framework. The orders of August 19 and September 16, 2010, are reversed. Because our finding of plain error resolves this appeal, we need not consider the assignments of error raised by the parties.

CONCLUSION

We conclude that the district court erred when it failed to give proper legal effect to the acknowledgment of paternity that was signed by Cesar and Alicia and notarized at the time of Jaime's birth, named Cesar as Jaime's father, and was not challenged by Alicia. The acknowledgment established Cesar as Jaime's legal father. See § 43–1409. We reverse the August 19 and September 16, 2010, orders regarding custody and other issues, and remand the cause to the district court for further proceedings. In the absence of a challenge to the acknowledgment, the court should consider the issues raised in this proceeding regarding custody and support within the framework that under the applicable statutes, Cesar is legally Jaime's father.

REVERSED AND REMANDED FOR FURTHER PROCEEDINGS.

Points for Discussion

a. *Cesar C.*

What if Cesar and Alicia had not signed the "Acknowledgment of Paternity" form, but all of the other facts in this case had been the same? Could Cesar have obtained parental rights on another basis?

b. Parentage Acknowledgment

Under Article 3 of the UPA 2017, a woman who gives birth to a child and an alleged genetic father, an intended parent (in cases of assisted reproduction), or a presumed parent may sign an acknowledgment to establish parentage for the child. A presumed parent or alleged genetic parent may sign a denial of parentage in some circumstances, provided that another individual has filed an acknowledgment. An acknowledgment or denial of parentage may be rescinded within 60 days after its effective date or until the date of the first hearing adjudicating an issue concerning the child, whichever is earlier, and after this time may be challenged only on the basis of fraud, duress, or material mistake of fact and only within two years of the effective date.

c. Birth Certificates

If a child is born to unmarried parents, federal law provides that the father's name may be included on a birth certificate only if there has been a voluntary paternity acknowledgment or an adjudication of paternity. See 42 U.S.C. § 666(a)(5)(D) (2018). Why would Congress have included this requirement in the law?

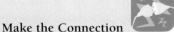

Make the Connection

Custody, visitation, and child support claims of parents and third parties are considered in Chapter 7.

2. Adjudicating Parentage

State laws such as the Uniform Parentage Act provide a framework for adjudicating parentage disputes, whether they involve a presumed parent (or parents) or an alleged genetic parent. In the UPA 2017, Article 5 governs genetic testing, and Article 6 addresses proceedings to adjudicate parentage, defining who has standing to initiate a parentage action, who must participate in such a proceeding, and within what time periods the action must be brought.

Interest of C.L.S., a Child

313 P.3d 662 (Colo. Ct. App. 2011)

Opinion by Judge Bernard.

When two men seek to be declared the father of a child, Colorado's paternity statutes establish a process to resolve their claims and to declare which man will be the child's father under the law. The statutes accomplish this end by creating presumptions of paternity. These presumptions may be rebutted by clear and convincing evidence. If two men each establish a presumption that is not rebutted, the statutes prescribe a method for resolving the conflict between them: the trial court determines which presumption should control based on the weightier considerations of policy and logic. Our supreme court addressed this method in *N.A.H. v. S.L.S.*, 9 P.3d 354, 359–65 (Colo.2000), concluding that it must include consideration of the child's best interests.

In this case, two men each established presumptions of paternity that were not rebutted. To resolve these competing presumptions, the magistrate applied the statutory method and, as a result, named one of them the child's legal father. In doing so, the magistrate did not articulate the burden of proof he used to resolve the conflict.

On review, the district court held that the burden of proof used to resolve competing presumptions is the preponderance standard. On appeal, we are asked to reverse this legal conclusion because, one party asserts, the correct burden of proof is the clear and convincing standard. We disagree with that assertion, and, as a result, we affirm.

I. Background

A. The Parties

S.V. (mother) and T.V. (husband) had been married a short time when a son, C.L.S., was conceived in early 2006. Mother also had a short, intimate relationship with T.R.S. (boyfriend) at the same time.

Mother filed for dissolution of marriage later in 2006, before the son was born. Mother and husband executed a separation agreement a few days before the son's birth, which did not refer to any children or a pregnancy. The dissolution decree, issued in February 2007 after the son was born at the end of 2006, also does not refer to any children.

At the time of the son's birth, his birth certificate did not list a father.

Mother and boyfriend began dating again in the spring of 2007, about three months after the son was born. Genetic testing was performed a short time later. It excluded boyfriend as the son's biological father. However, although he was aware of these results, boyfriend acted as the son's father, signed an acknowledgement of paternity, and added his name to the son's birth certificate as the son's father.

Mother did not notify husband that boyfriend had been listed on the birth certificate as the son's father. Husband did not know that boyfriend had formally acknowledged being the son's father.

Boyfriend, mother, and the son then began to live together. Mother and boyfriend had another child. They ended their relationship in the summer of 2008.

Boyfriend then asked a court to grant him parental responsibilities for the son. The court awarded him some parenting time. He paid mother child support, and maintained health insurance on both children.

B. The Proceedings

In the course of applying for governmental benefits, mother worked with the local child support enforcement unit. Based on information that mother provided, the enforcement unit sought an order establishing husband as the son's legal father and requiring him to pay mother a regular amount to support the son. In October 2008, genetic testing established a 99.99% probability that husband was the son's biological father.

Once the enforcement unit learned that boyfriend had signed an acknowledgement that he was the son's father and that boyfriend's name had been placed on the son's birth certificate, the unit filed this case to determine the son's legal father, naming both husband and boyfriend. Husband then sought an allocation of parental responsibilities for the son.

After a hearing, the magistrate entered a series of findings. First, he found that there were competing statutory presumptions of paternity. On the one hand, husband was presumed to be the son's legal father because he was married to mother when the child was conceived and born, and genetic testing indicated that he was the son's biological father. On the other hand, boyfriend was presumed to be the son's legal father because he voluntarily acknowledged that he was the son's father, and he held the son out as his child.

Second, the magistrate made findings about husband's and boyfriend's conduct. Husband knew mother was pregnant when they separated and before their marriage was dissolved; however he did not take any action to claim the son as his child. Boyfriend knew that he was not the son's biological father, but he decided to have his name entered on the son's birth certificate as the son's father, and he cared for the son as his own child while he lived with mother.

Third, the magistrate resolved the competing presumptions of paternity by finding that it was in the child's best interests to declare boyfriend to be the son's legal father.

Husband asked the district court to review the magistrate's order. He asserted that the facts did not establish the statutory presumption that boyfriend voluntarily acknowledged that he was the son's father. Then, he argued that the magistrate did not articulate the burden of proof that he used to resolve the competing presumptions of paternity, and that the clear and convincing standard should apply.

The district court concluded that the magistrate's finding that boyfriend satisfied the statutory presumption that he voluntarily acknowledged paternity "appear[ed] to be error." This statutory presumption requires that any other man presumed to be the father must consent in writing to the acknowledgement. That did not happen here. However, the district court concluded that this error was "ultimately harmless" because boyfriend had also established a second presumption of paternity.

The district court then held that the proper burden of proof to be employed when resolving competing presumptions of paternity is the preponderance standard. The court reasoned that (1) the statute establishing the method for resolving competing paternity presumptions is ambiguous; (2) applying the clear and convincing evidence standard would lead to absurd results; (3) the language describing the resolution method uses language "impl[ying]" that the preponderance standard should apply; and (4) because the resolution method requires that the presumptions be balanced against each other and with the child's best interests, "a preponderance standard seems to be the only rational standard to apply." Reviewing the magistrate's order based on the preponderance standard, the district court upheld the magistrate's decision.

On appeal, husband contends that the district court committed reversible error by rejecting the clear and convincing standard in favor of the preponderance standard. We disagree.

II. Analysis

* * *

B. General Principles

* * *

Because the paternity statutes at issue here are part of the Colorado Children's Code, we must liberally construe them "to serve the welfare of children and the best interests of society." § 19–1–102(2), C.R.S.2011; *People in Interest of S.X.M., 271 P.3d 1124, 1130 (Colo.App.2011)*. We must "avoid any technical reading. . .that would disregard the best interests of the child." *C.S., 83 P.3d at 635*.

Colorado's paternity statutes are based on the Uniform Parentage Act (UPA). *N.A.H., 9 P.3d at 360*. Because our statutes are based on a model code, we may look to authority from other states interpreting their versions of the code for persuasive authority. *See Swan v. American Family Mut. Ins. Co., 8 P.3d 546, 548 (Colo. App.2000)*; *see also* § 19–4–126, C.R.S.2011 (paternity statutes to be construed "to effectuate its general purpose to make uniform the law. . .among states enacting it").

C. Colorado's Paternity Statutes and *N.A.H.*

Our paternity statutes establish a mechanism for establishing a father-child relationship. § 19–4–104, C.R.S.2011. The first step in this process is determining whether a man is presumed to be a child's father. § 19–4–105(1), C.R.S.2011. There are six statutory presumptions. § 19–4–105(1)(a)–(f), C.R.S.2011.

The magistrate found that four of these presumptions existed here. Two applied to husband:

- § 19–4–105(1)(a) (the man and the child's mother were married and the child was born during the marriage) (also known as the presumption of legitimacy); and
- § 19–4–105(1)(f) (genetic tests establish that the probability of a man's parentage of the child is 97% or higher) (also known as the presumption of biology).

Two applied to boyfriend:

- § 19–4–105(1)(d) (the man received the child into his home and openly held the child out as his natural child); and
- § 19–4–105(1)(e) (the man acknowledges his paternity in writing, but, if another man is also presumed to be the father, the other man has given written consent to the acknowledgement).

Once presumptions are established, they may be rebutted by clear and convincing evidence. § 19–4–105(2)(a), C.R.S.2011. That did not occur here. However, on review, the district court determined that the evidence did not support one of the presumptions applying to boyfriend because husband did not provide written consent for boyfriend to acknowledge the son as his child. Thus, the district court concluded, this presumption was rebutted, in effect, because one of the factors necessary to establish it was not met. See *Courtney v. Roggy*, 302 S.W.3d 141, 146 (Mo.Ct.App.2009) (under Missouri's version of the UPA, the first step in the process is to determine whether a presumption of paternity is rebutted by clear and convincing evidence).

The second step in the process occurs after the presumptions are established and have not been rebutted. "If two or more presumptions arise which conflict with each other, the presumption which on the facts is founded on the weightier considerations of policy and logic controls." § 19–4–105(2)(a). This language establishes the method to resolve competing presumptions of paternity that is the focus of this appeal. *N.A.H.*, 9 P.3d at 360; *see also Courtney*, 302 S.W.3d at 146 (the second step of the process is to weigh any remaining competing unrebutted presumptions to determine the one which is, on the facts, based on the weightier considerations of policy and logic).

N.A.H. reached two conclusions that guide our analysis. First, none of the statutory presumptions of paternity is conclusive. 9 P.3d at 361. That means, as relevant here, that neither the presumption of biology, nor the presumption of legitimacy, is conclusive, and neither presumption "automatically eliminates other presumptions of fatherhood." *Id.* at 361–62.

Second, assuming that competing presumptions have not been disproved by clear and convincing evidence, the trial court must then decide, under section 19–4–105(2)(a), which man should be declared the child's legal father based on the "weightier considerations of policy and logic." This is a "fact-intensive" inquiry; "all the facts considered. . .should bear directly on the child's best interests"; and the trial court resolves the competing presumptions by focusing on "the best interests of the child and mak[ing] determinations of paternity with that standard at the forefront." *N.A.H.,* 9 P.3d at 362, 365.

The requirement that the child's best interests be the focus stems from the observation that "despite the numerous burdens and benefits of being a father . . .it is the child who has the most at stake in a paternity proceeding." *Id.* at 364 (quoting *McDaniels v. Carlson,* 108 Wash.2d 299, 311, 738 P.2d 254, 262 (1987)). Indeed, our supreme court observed that, "[in] some cases, the child's best interests may not match the best interests of any of the adults involved." *N.A.H.,* 9 P.3d at 365.

These two holdings—that none of the statutory presumptions is conclusive and that the child's best interests are a necessary consideration in weighing competing presumptions—lead us to a third. When there are competing unrebutted presumptions of paternity, the main object of Colorado's paternity statutes is not necessarily to "identify as the father the man most likely to have been the biological father of the child." *See* David D. Meyer, *Parenthood in a Time of Transition: Tensions Between Legal, Biological, and Social Conceptions of Parenthood,* 54 Am. J. Comp. L. 125, 130 (Fall 2006) (stating that the main object of the UPA is to determine who is the biological father).

The result of a final determination of paternity is to render one presumptive father the child's parent. The other presumptive father becomes a nonparent who does not have rights to visit a child or to make any decisions about the child's education, health, or upbringing. *In re Marriage of Ohr,* 97 P.3d 354, 357 (Colo.App.2004). This is because a child can have only one legal father. *N.A.H.,* 9 P.3d at 360.

When *N.A.H.* was decided, the legislature had not "define[d] the best interests of the child in the context of a paternity proceeding." *Id.* at 364. There was no reference in section 19–4–105(2)(a) to what factors the trial court should consider as part of its evaluation of the "weightier considerations of policy and logic."

We note that this changed in 2003. Then, the legislature amended section 19–4–105(2)(a) by adding eight factors that the judge or magistrate "shall consider" when evaluating the "weightier considerations of policy and logic." § 19–4–105(2)(a)(I)–(VIII), C.R.S.2011. At least five of the eight factors focus on the child, such as "[t]he length of time during which the presumed father has assumed the role of father of the child," section 19–4–105(2)(a)(II); "[t]he nature of the father-child relationship," section 19–4–105(2)(a)(IV); "[t]he age of the child," section 19–4–105(2)(a)(V); "[t]he relationship of the child to any presumed father or fathers," section 19–4–105(2)(a)(VI); and "[a]ny other factors that may affect the equities arising from the disruption of the father-child relationship between the child and the presumed father or fathers or the chance of other harm to the child," section 19–4–105(2)(a)(VIII).

These factors were taken almost verbatim from the 2000 version of the UPA. They are found in section 608(b) of that act, which requires courts to evaluate the "best interest" of the child, "including the following factors," when deciding whether to deny a motion requesting genetic testing. UPA § 608(b), 9B U.L.A. 343 (2000).

We also note that, in 2003, the legislature amended the statute that addresses genetic tests to determine parentage, section 13–25–126, C.R.S.2011, in ways that are pertinent here. First, the legislature softened the effect of biological testing on the presumption of legitimacy. It changed the language "the presumption of legitimacy. . .is overcome" by genetic tests "show[ing] that the husband. . .is not the parent" to "the presumption of legitimacy. . .may be overcome" by such tests. *Compare* ch. 42, sec. 1, § 13–25–126(1)(e)(IV), 1991 Colo. Sess. Laws 248, *with* ch. 163, sec. 1, § 13–25–126(1)(i), 2003 Colo. Sess. Laws 1240 (emphasis added).

Second, before the 2003 amendments, the statute prescribed different effects on the presumption of paternity for genetic tests resulting in a probability of parentage less than 97% and a probability of parentage of 97% or greater. Now, the statute only creates a presumption when genetic tests indicate a probability of parentage of 97% or greater. *Compare* ch. 42, sec. 1, § 13–25–126(1)(e)(II)–(III), 1991 Colo. Sess. Laws 248, *with* ch. 163, sec. 1, § 13–25–126(1)(g), 2003 Colo. Sess. Laws 1240.

Third, the amendments specified the type of evidence that a man can use to rebut the presumption that he is the father based on genetic testing. Before 2003, the statute read that "[o]ther expert testimony can be offered to rebut the presumption, but cannot prohibit the presumption from attaching." Now, this presumption may only be rebutted by a genetic test that either excludes a man as the child's father or identifies another man as the father. Compare ch. 42, sec. 1, § 13–25–126(1)(e)(III), 1991 Colo. Sess. Laws 248, with ch. 163, sec. 1, § 13–25–126(1)(h), 2003 Colo. Sess. Laws 1240.

The parties do not contend that these legislative changes have any effect on the analysis of the appropriate burden of proof. However, as described below, we conclude that the changes have some effect.

D. The Proper Burden of Proof for Resolving Competing Presumptions

Several Colorado appellate decisions, including *N.A.H.*, recognize that evidence must be clear and convincing to rebut any established presumptions of paternity. However, the parties do not cite, and our research has not found, any decisions that discuss what burden of proof should be applied to resolve competing presumptions based on the weightier considerations of policy and logic.

* * *

We conclude that a trial court should determine the weightier considerations of policy and logic by employing the preponderance standard for the following reasons.

1. The legislature has stated generally that the preponderance standard is the burden of proof in civil cases, section 13–25–127(1), and paternity cases are civil cases, *S.E.G.*, 934 P.2d at 922.

2. By using the word "weightier," the plain language of section 19–4–105(2)(a) indicates that the preponderance standard applies.

3. Our supreme court and two divisions of this court have stated that the preponderance standard applies to paternity cases. See *People v. Smith*, 183 P.3d 726, 729 (Colo.App.2008) (Colorado Court of Appeals is bound by decisions of Colorado Supreme Court).

4. The use of the preponderance standard most effectively furthers our supreme court's direction in *N.A.H.* that a trial court must consider the best interests of the child when determining the weightier considerations of policy and logic. *See also* § 19–1–102(2); *L.L.*, 10 P.3d at 1277–78; *C.S.*, 83 P.3d at 635. Applying this authority, we conclude that employing the clear and convincing standard at this point of the decision-making process would make it harder to promote the child's best interests and reduce the prospect of a viable solution because this elevated standard of proof would (a) put greater weight on the rights of the presumed fathers than those of the child, when "it is the child who has the most at stake in a paternity proceeding," *N.A.H.*, 9 P.3d at 364; (b) change the focus of the analysis to the interests of the presumed fathers, even though "[in] some cases, the child's best interests may not match the best interests of

any of the adults involved," id. at 365; and (c) make it more difficult to determine which presumed father should become the legal one, lessening the prospect of a workable result.

5. The cases cited above, such as *A.M.D.*, which require the clear and convincing standard, recognize the fundamentally important legal rights of *parents*. In paternity cases, the goal of the proceeding is to determine *whether* a man is a child's legal parent. Until that issue has been resolved, presumptive fathers are not yet parents. See N.A.H., 9 P.3d at 360; Ohr, 97 P.3d at 357. Thus, they are not entitled to the same due process protections that are given to parents by use of the clear and convincing standard. This reasoning is consistent with our supreme court's decisions in cases such as *B.J.*, *Reese*, and *C.A.*, in which *nonparents* were required to provide clear and convincing evidence to overcome the rights of *parents*. Cf. H.S. v. N.S., 173 Cal.App.4th 1131, 1140–41, 93 Cal.Rptr.3d 470, 476–77 (2009) (when resolving custody dispute between natural parent and nonparent-de facto parent, removing child from de facto parent's "long-standing stable home where the child's physical and emotional needs are met" creates a clear and convincing rebuttable presumption of harm to a child, which a natural parent can rebut by a preponderance of the evidence; this statutory arrangement of a presumption based on clear and convincing evidence to overcome the natural parent's rights, and allowing the natural parent to rebut the presumption in favor of the nonparent by a preponderance of the evidence, satisfies due process).

6. Presumptions of paternity can only be rebutted by clear and convincing evidence. The use of this standard provides the rights of presumed fathers with sufficient protection, see, e.g., R.H.N., 710 P.2d at 488 n. 5. Because, as we recognize above, presumed fathers are not parents, it is unnecessary to repeat this standard when deciding which presumptions are weightier.

7. We recognize that the presumption of legitimacy has historically been given significant weight. See W.C. in Interest of A.M.K., 907 P.2d 719, 722 (Colo.App.1995)("The public policy of Colorado favors legitimacy."). However, N.A.H. made clear that the legislature had not established any presumptions as conclusive, and that, based on the facts of the case, (a) any of them, including the presumptions of legitimacy and biology, may be rebutted; and (b) none of them automatically controls the analysis of which presumption is weightier. N.A.H., 9 P.3d at 361; see also id. at 357 ("a question of paternity is not automatically resolved by biological testing").

8. The legislature's 2003 amendment to section 19–4–105(2)(a) demonstrates its intent to reinforce the holding of *N.A.H.* It does so by focusing the analysis of the weightier considerations of policy and logic on specific factors that involve the child's best interests. Of the eight specific

factors, at least five of them emphasize considerations directly applicable to the child. § 19–4–105(2)(a)(II), (IV)–(VI), (VIII). These same factors are found in section 608(b) of the 2000 UPA, which directs courts to evaluate the "best interest" of the child when deciding whether to deny a motion requesting genetic testing. This amendment therefore makes clear that the legislature intended that the process of weighing considerations of policy and logic must emphasize the child's best interests over the interests of the presumptive fathers, which are inherent in the presumptions of paternity.

9. The legislature's 2003 amendments to section 13–25–126 also demonstrate its intent to reinforce *N.A.H.*'s holding. Those changes (a) moderated the effect of the results of genetic tests on the presumption of legitimacy; (b) established clearer parameters for the presumption of biology based on genetic testing; and (c) limited the kinds of evidence that can be used to rebut the presumption of biology based on such tests. We do not interpret these modifications as evidence of the legislature's intent to elevate the presumption of biology to conclusive status. Rather, these alterations support our view that the process of rebutting presumptions focuses upon the presumption itself: for example, can a man presumed to be the biological father overcome the presumption of paternity by providing a genetic test that excludes him, or that identifies another man, as the father? However, once that presumption is established and is not subsequently rebutted, the issue turns to whether there are competing presumptions and how that competition should be resolved. *See N.A.H., 9 P.3d at 362* ("[I]t is evident from the statutory scheme as a whole that presumptions of fatherhood can be the starting point for an adjudication of paternity, not the end of the inquiry.").
10. Finally, the combination of the previous nine reasons leads us to reject husband's argument that employing the preponderance standard would render section 19–4–105(2) unconstitutional.

We recognize that our reasoning is somewhat different from the district court's. For example, we respectfully disagree with the district court's conclusion that section 19–4–105(2)(a) is ambiguous because we conclude that the plain language of the statute is clear. *See W. Fire Truck, Inc., 134 P.3d at 573*. Nonetheless, we may affirm on grounds different from those employed by the district court. *See Negron v. Golder, 111 P.3d 538, 542 (Colo.App.2004)*.

III. Conclusion

In his brief, husband "emphasizes that he is not asking for any ruling beyond an establishment of the proper standard of proof [and]. . .seeks only a retrial under the proper evidentiary standard." We have now, after conducting our de novo review, resolved the narrow issue that husband has asked us to decide.

Therefore, the judgment is affirmed.

Points for Discussion

a. Conflicting Presumptions

The Colorado legislation applied in *C.L.S.* was an amended version of the original Uniform Parentage Act (1973), under which there were different presumptions in favor of the mother's husband and her boyfriend respectively. The court determines that none of the statutory presumptions is conclusive, and that the child's best interests are a necessary consideration in weighing the competing presumptions. Why does the court decide that a preponderance standard (rather than clear and convincing evidence) is correct in this situation? Why did the magistrate decide that it was in the child's best interests to declare the boyfriend to be the child's legal father? Note that one judge on the panel dissented from this ruling, as discussed below.

Other cases dealing with conflicting presumptions of parentage include Minnesota v. Thomas, 584 N.W.2d 421 (Minn.Ct.App. 1998); A.J.S. v. M.T.H. (In re the Paternity of B.J.H.), 573 N.W.2d 99 (Minn.Ct.App. 1998); L.C. v. T.L., 870 P.2d 374 (Wyo. 1994).

b. Competing Parentage Claims Under the UPA

Using the presumptions of parentage set forth in UPA 2017 § 204, would both of these individuals entitled to presumptions of parentage? The husband would be a presumed father under § 204(a)(1)(A), but on the facts described it does not appear that the boyfriend would qualify for the presumption under § 204(a)(2), which includes a durational element: "the individual resided in the same household with the child for the first two years of the life of the child, including any period of temporary absence, and openly held out the child as the individual's child." See also UPA 2017 § 608, which describes the process for adjudicating parentage of a child with a presumed parent. Is there a way on these facts in which the boyfriend's claim could prevail under the UPA 2017? How would the analysis be different if testing had indicated that the boyfriend was the child's genetic parent? See UPA 2017 §§ 607(c), 608(c) and 613.

c. Best Interests Principle

Courts in some states may require that a determination of the child's best interests be made before the court orders or considers genetic testing to establish the biological paternity of a child born to a married woman. See, e.g., UPA (2002) § 608; Evans v. Wilson, 856 A.2d 679 (Md. 2004). With the UPA 2017, the child's best interests factor into the evaluation of competing claims of parentage under § 613, and may be a basis for denying a motion for genetic testing under § 503. Applying these rules, there are numerous cases in which a child has a genetic parent who is not determined to be the child's legal parent. See, e.g., Department of Health and Rehabilitative Services v. Privette, 617 So.2d 305 (Fla.1993); In re Ross, 783 P.2d 331 (Kan. 1989); In the Matter of the Paternity of Adam, 903 P.2d 207 (Mont. 1995); In re Paternity of C.A.S., 468 N.W.2d 719 (Wis. 1991); Mak-M v. SM, 854 P.2d 64 (Wyo.1993); cf. Tedford v. Gregory, 959 P.2d 540 (N.M.Ct.App.1998).

d. Role of Genetic Evidence

One judge dissented from the ruling in *C.L.S.*, based in part on his view that under the Colorado statute "there are no equitable considerations which countervail the paternity of a biological father." He wrote:

> I reject the notion that the presumptions set forth in section 19–4–105 are merely factors to be considered in determining who would be the better father. Indeed, the purpose of the statute in my view is to determine the identity of the true father. The magistrate here should have conducted a fact-finding examination that considered not only the best interests of the child but the legitimacy of T.V.'s claim to paternity based upon his DNA testing and T.R.S.'s genetic exclusion.

C.L.S., 313 P.3d at 674 (Graham, J., dissenting). As compared to a presumption "based upon mere declaration," he argued that "the presumption afforded by a 99.99% test should be conclusive and unrebuttable." Id. at n. 2.

The federal laws governing paternity determination, discussed above, require states to implement genetic testing in some circumstances, see 42 U.S.C. § 666(a)(5)(B) (2018), and to enact rules defining conditions for admissibility of the results of genetic testing, § 666(a)(5)(F). The laws also provide for these results to be given presumptive effect at certain threshold levels, see § 666(a)(5)(G). See generally Alan Z. Litovsky and Kirsten Schultz, *Scientific Evidence of Paternity: A Survey of State Statutes*, 39 Jurimetrics 79 (Fall 1998). The federal law does not state that genetic testing results should be determinative, or indicate when a presumption should be rebuttable.

If a legislature enacted a statute making genetic test results "conclusive and unrebuttable," would this be a wise public policy? What arguments would you make for or against this approach?

Genetic Testing and Parentage Disputes

Genetic testing produces a "probability of parentage," a statistic that measures the likelihood that the particular combination of traits inherited by the child would occur in a randomly selected individual of the ethnic or racial group to which the tested individual belongs. See UPA 2017 § 501(4). A probability of parentage of 99.5 percent means that only five individuals out of 1000 within the relevant population have the right combination of genetic traits to be the child's parent. This figure is based on an evaluation of genetic information in the context of a "prior probability of parentage" estimate reflecting other facts, such as the relationship between an alleged genetic father and the child's mother.

For a careful analysis of this problem in a paternity proceeding, see Plemel v. Walter, 735 P.2d 1209 (Or. 1987). See generally Christopher B. Mueller and Laird C. Kirkpatrick, Evidence § 7.19 (6th ed. 2018); David L. Faigman, David H. Kaye, Michael J. Saks, & Joseph Sanders, Modern Scientific Evidence: The Law and Science of Expert Testimony § 26–1.5 (2002).

e. Jurisdiction and Procedure

Standing to maintain a parentage proceeding is defined in UPA 2017 § 602, and extends to the child, the woman who gave birth to the child, an individual who is a parent under the act or whose parentage is to be adjudicated, a child-support agency, an adoption agency, or a representative authorized to act for one of these individuals who is deceased, incapacitated, or a minor. A court must have personal jurisdiction over an individual to adjudicate that person's parentage of a child. See UPA 2017 § 604(a); see also e.g., In re S.M., 874 So.2d 720 (Fla. Dist. Ct. App. 2004); In re Paternity of Carlin L.S., 593 N.W.2d 486 (Wis. Ct. App. 1999). This jurisdiction may be exercised over a nonresident as prescribed in the Uniform Interstate Family Support Act, 9 U.L.A. Part 1B 159 (2005) (UIFSA).

Under UIFSA § 201, any person who has sexual intercourse within a state submits to the jurisdiction of its courts with respect to a child who may have been conceived by that act. UIFSA provides that, if it is not possible to obtain long-arm jurisdiction over a respondent in a paternity action, the petition for determination of parentage may be forwarded to another state in which it is possible to obtain jurisdiction. In a case contrasting the jurisdictional requirements for parentage adjudication with child custody proceedings under the UCCJEA, which do not require personal jurisdiction, a New York court ruled in Rajic v. George, 994 N.Y.S.2d 292 (N.Y. Sup. Ct. 2014), that it did not have jurisdiction over the putative father, a professional basketball player whose only contacts with the state involved trips a few times each year to play the New York Knicks or the Brooklyn Nets.

Paternity may be established based upon a preponderance of the evidence; see Rivera v. Minnich, 483 U.S. 574 (1987). Although paternity claims were once tried to juries rather than judges, jury trial in paternity actions have been eliminated under the federal guidelines. See 42 U.S.C.A. § 666(a)(5)(I) (2018). These guidelines also require that states must allow for the establishment of the paternity of a child at any time until the child reaches age 18, see 42 U.S.C.A. § 666(a)(5)(A)(i) (2018).

Under UPA 2017 §§ 610 and 611, challenges to the parentage of a child with an acknowledged or adjudicated parent are limited to a period of two years after the effective date of the acknowledgment or adjudication. In addition, the court must find that permitting the proceeding is in the best interest of the child. Proceedings to overcome a presumption of parentage must be commenced within two years of a child's birth, unless the court also finds that the presumed parent is not a genetic parent, never resided with the child, and never held out the child as the presumed parent's child, or if the child has more than one presumed parent.

In Bryan M. v. Anne B., 874 N.W.2d 824 (Neb. 2016), the court rejected a biological father's constitutional challenge to the four-year statute of limitations governing his paternity claim under Nebraska law. What policy arguments support the limitations periods defined in these statutes?

f. Disestablishing Parentage

When should a presumed or acknowledged parent be permitted to disestablish parentage? As with other types of judgments, a challenge to a parentage judgment is generally limited by res judicata, with very narrow grounds for reopening that judgment. See, e.g., Paternity of Cheryl, 746 N.E.2d 488 (Mass. 2001) (no basis to reopen stipulated judgment based upon father's voluntary paternity acknowledgment after he learned he was not the child's genetic parent). In divorce cases, language included in the court's orders that identifies a child as a "child of the marriage" also constitutes an adjudication of parentage, which can ordinarily be challenged only under rules permitting reopening of a judgment. See, e.g., UPA 2017 § 623(c). Note that a child's birth mother may also be barred by res judicata from seeking to disestablish the parentage of her child's other parent; see Doe v. Doe, 52 P.3d 255 (Haw. 2002).

Several states, however, have removed obstacles to the disestablishment of paternity when a legal father offers genetic evidence of nonpaternity, even if many years have passed since paternity was adjudicated. These laws are discussed and applied in Langston v. Riffe, 754 A.2d 389 (Md. 2000); In re Kates, 761 N.E.2d 153 (Ill. 2001).

Courts generally hold that an order disestablishing parentage terminates any ongoing obligation to pay child support, but state laws are divided on whether such an order discharges the obligation to pay support arrearages. Compare Ferguson v. State, Department of Revenue, 977 P.2d 95 (Alaska 1999) (prospective relief only) with Bouchard v. Frost, 840 A.2d 109 (Me. 2004); Walter v. Gunter, 788 A.2d 609 (Md. 2002) (relief both prospectively and from arrearages). Cases and statutes have not permitted the disestablished parent to recoup support payments already made. See generally Paula Roberts, *Truth and Consequences: Part III. Who Pays When Paternity is Disestablished?* 37 Fam. L. Q. 69 (2003). Courts set aside orders more readily when child support enforcement agencies seek to enforce obligations against individuals who were mistakenly identified as fathers, particularly when a paternity judgment was entered by default without genetic evidence. See, e.g., County of Los Angeles v. Navarro, 14 Cal.Rptr.3d 905 (Cal. Ct. App. 2004), applying California's Child Support Enforcement Fairness Act of 2000.

Problem 2-8

While Mary is married to James, she has an extra-marital affair with Ben and gives birth to a child several months later. Ben believes that the baby is his biological child, but Mary rejects his attempts to acknowledge paternity and to visit with the child. Ben would like to secure an order for genetic testing and obtain custody and visitation rights. Can Ben pursue this claim under the UPA 2017? (Cf. Witso v. Overby, 627 N.W.2d 63 (Minn. 2001).)

[handwritten margin note: Mary is married to someone else ↓ rebut. presump]

Problem 2-9

During their marriage, Leslie and Tim had a daughter, Tory. Tim was killed in an accident, and Leslie brought a wrongful death action on Tory's behalf. The defendant, alleging that Tim was not Tory's biological father, requests that the court enter orders for genetic testing. Does the defendant have standing to challenge Tory's parentage under the UPA 2017? Would the answer be different if the challenge was brought by the executor of Tim's estate? (See Johnson Controls, Inc. v. Forrester, 704 N.E.2d 1082 (Ind.Ct.App.1999); cf. Estate of Jagdowski, 83 N.E.3d 656 (Ill. App. Ct. 2017).)

Problem 2-10

Many years after his divorce from Bonnie, Roy discovers that one of their three children, Darren, who was then almost 30 years old, had most likely been fathered by another man, named Patrick. A year later, Roy filed an action seeking a determination that Patrick was Darren's biological father and requesting reimbursement of the costs of supporting Darren to adulthood as well as compensatory and punitive damages. Voluntary DNA testing has confirmed that Roy is not Darren's father. How should the court proceed in this case? (See R.A.C. v. P.J.S. Jr., 927 A.2d 97 (N.J. 2007).)

Problem 2-11

When Randy filed for a divorce from his wife of ten years, Norma, she filed a counterclaim seeking to disestablish Randy's paternity of their young daughter. Norma claims that she had an affair with another man, Brendan, during the period when the child was conceived, and seeks to have Brendan declared to be the legal father. Randy has been the girl's primary caregiver for the past year, and would like to continue in that role. As Randy's lawyer, what advice would you give him? Should he oppose genetic testing? (Cf. Randy A.J. v. Norma I.J., 677 N.W.2d 630 (Wis. 2004).)

Problem 2-12

Megan was dating Frank when she learned that she was pregnant. Based on the timing, she assumed that her former boyfriend, Russ, was the child's father, and she stopped seeing Frank and moved in with Russ. They did not marry, but Russ they signed and filed a parentage acknowledgment after the baby was born.

Megan and Russ split up when the child was a year old, and the court designated Russ as her primary residential parent. Megan has gotten back together with Frank, and they have recently obtained genetic testing that established Frank as the child's biological father. In this situation, can Frank be adjudicated to be the child's legal father? (See Parentage and Custody of M.J.M., 294 P.3d 746 (Wash. Ct. App. 2013).

In re Donovan L., Jr.

198 Cal.Rptr.3d 550 (Cal. Ct. App. 2016)

IRION, J.

Shannon L., the biological mother of minor Donovan L., Jr. (DJ), and her husband Donovan L., Sr. (Donovan) appeal from the juvenile court's June 2015 disposition order. The juvenile court ruled that although Donovan was DJ's conclusively presumed father under Family Code section 7540, David S. was DJ's presumed father under section 7611, subdivision (d), and DJ had three parents under recently enacted section 7612, subdivision (c). Section 7612, subdivision (c) provides that in an appropriate action, "if the court finds that recognizing only two parents would be detrimental to the child," a court may find a child has more than two parents. We conclude the juvenile court erred in applying section 7612, subdivision (c) in this case, given its determination that David and DJ lacked an existing parent-child relationship. Accordingly, we reverse the disposition order insofar as it determines David is DJ's presumed father under Family Code section 7612, subdivision (c) and orders services and visitation for David.

I.

FACTUAL AND PROCEDURAL BACKGROUND

In March 2015, the San Diego County Health and Human Services Agency (Agency) filed a juvenile dependency petition under Welfare and Institutions Code, section 300, subdivision (b), alleging risk of harm to DJ due to Shannon's substance abuse. The 2015 case is the third dependency proceeding involving four-year-old DJ; as described below, the Agency previously filed petitions in 2012 and 2014.

Shannon was married to Donovan at the time of DJ's conception in 2010 and birth in 2011. In 2010, Shannon had an affair with David and informed him she was pregnant. David did not seek involvement in Shannon's pregnancy or DJ's rearing until he saw Shannon and one-year-old DJ at a shopping center parking lot in July 2012. Seeing a resemblance, David took a paternity test on his own initiative and determined he was DJ's biological father. He told friends and family he was DJ's father and asked Shannon for visits with DJ. She facilitated a few visits between DJ and David, unbeknown to Donovan.

Shannon and DJ stayed at David's apartment for two weeks in August 2012, when she and Donovan were having marital problems. During that time, Shannon called the police because David locked her out after they fought over child custody. When officers arrived, they found David and DJ "passed out" on the bed with approximately 50 marijuana plants growing in the apartment. Following this incident, the Agency filed the 2012 dependency petition under Welfare and Institutions Code, section 300, subdivision (b).

At the detention hearing in the 2012 case, the juvenile court found Donovan to be DJ's conclusively presumed father under section 7540 and authorized the Agency to release DJ to Donovan.[2] David initially sought presumed father status, but he later withdrew that request and asked to be named DJ's biological father. In October 2012, the court conferred biological father status to David, "[b]ased on the agreement of all parties and the LabCorp paternity test results." In November 2012, the court terminated jurisdiction in the 2012 case, after the parties voluntarily agreed to facilitate visitation between David and DJ.

In 2014, Shannon tested positive for methadone when giving birth to her second child. Shannon and Donovan agreed to a voluntary case and services to address Shannon's addiction issues.

The Agency became involved with DJ for a third time in March 2015, after Shannon tested positive for hydromorphone when giving birth to her third child. The 2015 dependency petition underlies the present appeal. At the detention hearing on March 24, 2015, the juvenile court noted Donovan was DJ's conclusively presumed father under section 7540 and allowed DJ to live with him, provided that Shannon move out of their home.

In April 2015, David appeared at the disposition hearing and requested presumed father status under section 7611, subdivision (d).[3] The court noted that Donovan had already been named a conclusively presumed father and continued the disposition hearing to May 2015. At the continued hearing, the court made a true finding on the Agency's petition and ordered supervised visitation for David. The court deferred the paternity issue, explaining:

> "First of all, there's a question of fact whether or not [David] is presumed. That's going to require an evidentiary hearing. Secondly, if he is found to be a presumed father, he is not entitled to a weighing process because a *[section] 7540* father [Donovan] is a conclusively presumed father. Thirdly, there's a question of fact whether or not the court, under [section

---

[2]   Section 7540 provides: "Except as provided in *Section 7541*, the child of a wife cohabiting with her husband, who is not impotent or sterile, is conclusively presumed to be a child of the marriage." *Section 7541* provides an exception to the conclusive presumption based on blood tests performed before the child's second birthday. (§ 7541, subd. (b); *Craig L. v. Sandy S. (2004) 125 Cal.App.4th 36, 46[22 Cal.Rptr.3d 606]*.)

[3]   Pursuant to *section 7611, subdivision (d)*, a person is a presumed parent if he or she "receives the child into his or her home and openly holds out the child as his or her natural child."

7612, subdivision (c),[4] the new statute, should recognize him as a father and give [DJ] two fathers."

At the contested disposition hearing on June 12, 2015, the court heard testimony from the social worker, David, David's mother, Shannon, Donovan, and Donovan's father. DJ's position, expressed during closing arguments, was that David did not qualify as a third parent under section 7612, subdivision (c). The court took judicial notice of orders from the 2012 dependency case and received into evidence the Agency's reports and the parties' paternity questionnaires. On the basis of this evidence, the court declared David to be DJ's presumed father under section 7611, subdivision (d), and applying section 7612, subdivision (c), held DJ would suffer detriment were the court to rule he had only two parents.

In pronouncing its ruling, the court expressed "no doubt" that Donovan had been "a great father" and a "superlative dad," stating it could make that finding "beyond a reasonable doubt, conclusively." The court believed Shannon sought out David in 2012 because she wanted options while facing marital problems with Donovan. The court did not rule David was a *Kelsey S.*[5] father, but suggested that to the extent Shannon initially sought out David and later changed her mind, the case supported a *Kelsey S.* argument to some degree. The court believed Donovan and Shannon would likely prevent DJ from learning David was his biological father and that Donovan sought to move the family to Arizona to "get as far away as possible" from David.

The court credited David's testimony that although he did not get involved with DJ initially, he decided to seek visitation and parental status after seeing DJ in 2012. Although David withdrew his request for presumed father status in the 2012 case, the court concluded he did so because of an agreement between the parties that "made the whole case go away." The court relied on the social worker's testimony and photographs to conclude that DJ had "nice visits" with David and "seem[ed] pretty happy at these various events." The court rejected "very similar

---

[4] Section 7612, subdivision (c) provides: "In an appropriate action, a court may find that more than two persons with a claim to parentage under this division are parents if the court finds that recognizing only two parents would be detrimental to the child. In determining detriment to the child, the court shall consider all relevant factors, including, but not limited to, the harm of removing the child from a stable placement with a parent who has fulfilled the child's physical needs and the child's psychological needs for care and affection, and who has assumed that role for a substantial period of time. A finding of detriment to the child does not require a finding of unfitness of any of the parents or persons with a claim to parentage."

[5] In *Adoption of Kelsey S. (1992)* 1 Cal.4th 816, 849 [4 Cal.Rptr.2d 615, 823 P.2d 1216] (*Kelsey S.*), the Supreme Court recognized a "child's well-being is presumptively best served by continuation of the [biological] father's parental relationship" where "an unwed [biological] father promptly comes forward and demonstrates a full commitment to his parental responsibilities—emotional, financial, and otherwise—" but is precluded from establishing a meaningful relationship with the child as a result of actions unilaterally taken by a third party.

and consistent" testimony from Shannon, Donovan, and Donovan's father that DJ referred to David as a "mean man" and exhibited behavioral problems after supervised visits began in May 2015, instead attributing those behavioral problems to Shannon's departure from the home.

Finding David to be a presumed parent under section 7611, the court turned to section 7612, subdivision (c) and determined DJ would suffer detriment if the court found he had only two parents. In reaching this decision, the juvenile court relied heavily on David's biological ties to DJ:

"With regard to 7612(c), I would find that it would be detrimental for this child to only have two parents.

"Now, I want to be clear. [The statute] says 'in determining detriment to the child, the court shall consider all rel[evant] factors.' And that's what I'm considering. In particular, I am considering the fact that this child has a cultural heritage; that this child has DNA running through his veins; that this child has another family that was introduced to him at a younger [stage of his] life who seemed to want to be involved with him; that this child will, in fact, have to do those family trees; that this child will, if he finds out at age 21 that he had a different bio father that was hidden from him, will have an effect on him. It will affect him—because I've been doing this a long time and I've seen those type of effects. It's just one of those things. It's not fair to lie to these kids about this type of situation, it just isn't.

"Under certain circumstances they may not [find] out. But under this circumstance, lying is not going to do any good. And I don't believe for a second that either [Donovan or Shannon] have any real intention of introducing [David], this father, in the near future. Because I don't know when the good time would be. . . . They want their own family together. If this marriage falls apart, and [Donovan] for some reason gets custody, he's not going to warm up to [David], considering [David] slept with his wife. Those are all the types of problems that can arise in this very complex situation, which is all fueled by drugs. So I will make that detriment finding, because I think that the evidence supports it.

"Now, I understand that it says that I have to consider the harm of removing the child from a stable placement with a parent who has fulfilled the child's physical needs. [Donovan] defines that exactly. I'm not removing the child from [Donovan]. I don't know if it will ever happen. But the fact of the matter is, I envision more visitation happening, that [DJ] learns about this 'mean man,' [David], and that he warms up to him and that he will learn to have two fathers like a lot of kids learn. Like kids learn that they have two moms. There is a book out there, *Heather Has Two Mommies*. This is 2015. This is the 21st century. I didn't create all this stuff, but it's out there. And I have an obligation to view these statutes and apply the facts to the statutes."

Significantly, in finding detriment under section 7612, subdivision (c), the court found no existing bond between David and DJ, stating: "I'm going to note that [David] *does not have a strong relationship with this child.* " (Italics added.) The court granted visitation to David, finding he had "done everything [he was] supposed to do," but ordered DJ's initial visits with David to be supervised while DJ and David developed a relationship: "At least maybe the first two, you want to see how the exchange goes. . . . I'm not concerned that he's a danger to the child but *because he has to develop a relationship*, and there is some testimony about the child's reactions, I wanted to just cover that." (Italics added.) The court granted the Agency discretion to allow unsupervised and overnight visits with 48 hours' notice to counsel, "as the child warms up and feels comfortable."

Turning to the dispositional findings, the court found there was clear and convincing evidence of a substantial risk to DJ's "physical health, safety, protection or physical or emotional well being" if he were returned to Shannon's custody. The court placed DJ with Donovan and ordered services and visitation for Donovan, Shannon, and David. Shannon and Donovan each filed a timely notice of appeal.

II.

DISCUSSION

* * *

As we will explain, David is not barred under equitable principles from seeking presumed father status. However, this is not "an appropriate action" to recognize three parents under section 7612, subdivision (c). Because the juvenile court determined DJ did not have an existing relationship with David, there is no substantial evidence to support a finding that "recognizing only two parents would be detrimental to the child" within the meaning of section 7612, subdivision (c).

* * *

B. *Section 7611, Subdivision (d)*

Shannon and Donovan argue the juvenile court erred in finding David to be DJ's presumed father under section 7611, subdivision (d). Under section 7611, subdivision (d), a person is presumed a parent if he or she "receives the child into his or her home and openly holds out the child as his or her natural child." The court heard testimony that DJ lived with David for two weeks in August 2012 and that, beginning in 2012, David told friends and family that DJ was his son.[8] We will assume, without deciding, that there is substantial evidence to support the juvenile court's ruling that David qualifies as a presumed parent under section 7611, subdivision (d).

C. Parentage Presumptions

Donovan argues that, as a conclusively presumed father under section 7540, his parentage claim defeats any claim to parentage that David may assert under section 7611, subdivision (d). Because DJ is more than two years old, Donovan's conclusive marital presumption may no longer be rebutted. The Agency does not dispute that Donovan is DJ's conclusively presumed father, but it contends parentage law changed in 2014 so as to allow David to assert a parallel parentage claim under section 7612.[10]

As a general rule, " 'there can be only one presumed father.' " (*In re Jesusa V.* (2004) 32 Cal.4th 588, 603[10 Cal.Rptr.3d 205, 85 P.3d 2].) *Unless section 7612, subdivision (c) applies*, which we address below, Donovan's conclusive marital presumption under section 7540 defeats any parentage claim in David.

D. Section 7612, Subdivision (c)

Central to this appeal is the application of section 7612, subdivision (c). In 2013, the Legislature enacted section 7612, subdivision (c) to allow courts to 7 recognize that a child has more than two parents in certain limited contexts:

> "*In an appropriate action*, a court may find that more than two persons with a claim to parentage under this division are parents *if the court finds that recognizing only two parents would be detrimental to the child.* In determining detriment to the child, the court shall consider all relevant factors, including, but not limited to, the harm of removing the child from a stable placement with a parent who has fulfilled the child's physical needs and the child's psychological needs for care and affection, and who has assumed that role for a substantial period of time. A finding of detriment to the child does not require a finding of unfitness of any of the parents or persons with a claim to parentage."

(§ 7612, subd. (c), italics, added by Stats. 2013, ch. 564, § 6.5.) The statute went into effect on January 1, 2014. The parties agree that section 7612, subdivision (c)

---

[8]   The court also heard testimony that DJ had weekly visits with David from August to November 2012 and periodic visits thereafter; spent two Easters and one Christmas Eve with David and his family; received Christmas and birthday gifts from David; received diapers, toys, and clothing from David; and had a birthday party scheduled with David's family (that did not ultimately occur).

allows a court to recognize three parents only in "rare cases" where a child truly has more than two parents, but they disagree as to whether this is such a case.

The juvenile court determined DJ would face detriment under section 7612, subdivision (c) if the court were to find he had only two parents and therefore ruled David was to be DJ's third parent under the statute. Shannon and Donovan contest this ruling. Specifically, Shannon and Donovan challenge the court's finding of detriment under the statute, arguing there is no evidence DJ was missing anything from his life that David could provide. DJ joins in their arguments, contending there is no evidence he ever formed any real emotional attachment with David to support a finding of detriment under section 7612, subdivision (c). In response, the Agency suggests David and DJ shared a close bond between July 2012 and December 2014, such that "DJ would suffer great harm if his relationship with David ended." The Agency nevertheless concedes "David is not the poster boy for application of the statute."

As we explain, this is not "an appropriate action" for application of section 7612, subdivision (c). Because the juvenile court determined David and DJ lacked an existing parent-child relationship, there is no substantial evidence to support a finding that "recognizing only two parents would be detrimental to the child" within the meaning of the statute. (§ 7612, subd. (c).)

1. Legal Principles

* * *

We will interpret the statute de novo, as we must. (*In re J.P.* (2014) 229 Cal. App.4th 108, 122[176 Cal.Rptr.3d 792]; *In re Alanna A.* (2005) 135 Cal.App.4th 555, 563[37 Cal.Rptr.3d 579].) Then, in applying the statute to this case, we will determine whether the juvenile court's findings under section 7612, subdivision (c) are supported by substantial evidence. This analysis is the same under either the substantial evidence or abuse of discretion standard of review. Because we will conclude substantial evidence is lacking to support a finding of detriment within the meaning of section 7612, subdivision (c), we need not decide the standard of review for all rulings in which the juvenile court finds that a child has more than two parents under section 7612, subdivision (c).

As with any statute, " '[w]e begin with the fundamental rule that our primary task is to determine the lawmakers' intent.' " (*In re B.A.* (2006) 141 Cal.App.4th 1411, 1418[47 Cal.Rptr.3d 115].) "Where the language of the statute is clear and unambiguous, we follow the plain meaning of the statute and need not examine other indicia of legislative intent." (*In re J.P., supra,* 229 Cal.App.4th at p. 123, 176 Cal.Rptr.3d 792.) Section 7612, subdivision (c) is ambiguous as to what constitutes "an appropriate action" so as to allow a court to find a child has more than two parents. Therefore, on our own motion, we take judicial notice of the legislative history of Senate Bill No. 274 (2013–2014 Reg. Sess.) to resolve the ambiguity. (Evid. Code, §§ 452, 459; *In re J.W.* (2002) 29 Cal.4th 200, 210[126 Cal.Rptr.2d 897, 57 P.3d 363].)

2. *Legislative History*

Section 7612, subdivision (c) directs that a court "may find that more than two persons with a claim to parentage under this division are parents if the court finds that recognizing only two parents would be detrimental to the child." In determining detriment in this context, courts must "consider all relevant factors, including, but not limited to, the harm of removing the child from a stable placement with a parent who has fulfilled the child's physical needs and the child's psychological needs for care and affection, and who has assumed that role for a substantial period of time." (§ 7612, subd. (c).)[12]

The Legislature borrowed the "detriment to the child" standard from section 3041, which governs custody awards to a nonparent over the objection of a parent.[13] (See Sen. Com. on Judiciary, Rep. on Sen. Bill No. 274 (2013–2014 Reg. Sess.) as amended Apr. 1, 2013, p. 6.) Detriment under section 3041 considers "the prospect that a *successful, established* custodial arrangement would be disrupted") or the harm in "removing a child from what has been a *stable, continuous,* and *successful placement* is detrimental to the child". Although courts have concluded detriment under section 3041 may include the loss of an *existing* relationship with a nonparent, the parties have not pointed us to, nor have we found, any case applying section 3041 to protect a parental relationship that has not yet developed.

Indeed, legislative reports indicate that *section 7612, subdivision (c)* seeks to "protect[ ] children from harm by *preserving the bonds* between children and their parents" (Sen. Rules Com., Off. of Sen. Floor Analyses, 3d reading analysis

---

[12]   An earlier version of the bill, which the Governor vetoed, was based on the "best interest of the child" standard. (Sen. Bill No. 1476 (2011–2012 Reg. Sess.) § 5 ["In an appropriate action, a court may find that a child has more than two natural or adoptive parents if required to serve the best interest of the child."]; Governor's veto message to Sen. on Sen. Bill No. 1476 (Sept. 30, 2012) (2011–2012 Reg. Sess.).) Redrafting the legislation in 2013, the Legislature incorporated the "detriment to the child" standard.

[13]   *Section 3041, subdivision (c)* provides that " 'detriment to the child' includes the harm of removal from a stable placement of a child with a person who has assumed, on a day-to-day basis, the role of his or her parent, fulfilling both the child's physical needs and the child's psychological needs for care and affection, and who has assumed that role for a substantial period of time. A finding of detriment does not require any finding of unfitness of the parents."

of Sen. Bill No. "274 (2013–2014 Reg. Sess.) as amended May 14, 2013, p. 7, italics added) and avoid the "disastrous emotional, psychological, and financial consequences for a child, who may be separated from one or both of the parents *he or she has always known.*" (Assem. Com. on Judiciary, analysis of Sen. Bill No. 274 (2013–2014 Reg. Sess.) as amended May 14, 2013, pp. 4–5, italics added.) These authorities suggest that "an appropriate action" for application of *section 7612, subdivision (c)* is one in which a court finds an *existing*, rather than potential, relationship between a child and a putative third parent, such that "recognizing only two parents would be detrimental to the child." (*§ 7612, subd. (c)*.)[14]

* * *

3. Harmonizing Section 7612 With the Uniform Parentage Act

As our Supreme Court has explained, " 'every statute should be construed with reference to the whole system of law of which it is a part so that all may be harmonized and have effect.' " (*Briggs v. Eden Council for Hope & Opportunity (1999) 19 Cal.4th 1106, 1118–1119[81 Cal.Rptr.2d 471, 969 P.2d 564]*; see *People v. Verduzco (2012) 210 Cal.App.4th 1406, 1414[149 Cal.Rptr.3d 200]* [courts must "consider the consequences that will flow from a particular statutory interpretation"].) Our interpretation of what constitutes "an appropriate action" under *section 7612, subdivision (c)* harmonizes the statute with the broader statutory framework under the Uniform Parentage Act (UPA); § 7600 et seq.).

In making parentage determinations under the UPA, courts seek to protect *existing* relationships rather than foster *potential* relationships. (See *Rodney F. v. Karen M., supra, 61 Cal.App.4th at p. 239, 71 Cal.Rptr.2d 399* ["There is. . .an obvious distinction between a biological father who has actually established a parent and child relationship, and a man who has not established such a relationship but would like to do so."]; *In re D.M. (2012) 210 Cal.App.4th 541, 555[148 Cal.Rptr.3d 349]* [juvenile court erred in focusing on the "possibility that [the mother's boyfriend] would develop a parental relationship with the child, not that the relationship already existed"]; *In re A.A. (2003) 114 Cal.App.4th 771, 788[7 Cal.Rptr.3d 755]* ["[T]he state's interest in these matters includes preserving developed parent-child relationships whether or not the father figure has biological ties to the child."].)

Over the past three decades, courts increasingly have looked to the *nature* of the parent-child relationship to resolve paternity disputes. (*Brian C. v. Ginger K. (2000) 77 Cal.App.4th 1198, 1210–1216[92 Cal.Rptr.2d 294]* [collecting cases].) "The courts have repeatedly held, in applying paternity presumptions, that the extant father-child relationship is to be preserved at the cost of biological ties." (*In re Nicholas H. (2002) 28 Cal.4th 56, 65[120 Cal.Rptr.2d 146, 46 P.3d 932]*.) The

" ' "social relationship" ' " between a putative father and child " ' "is much more important, to the child at least, than a biological relationship of actual paternity." ' " (In re Marriage of Freeman (1996) 45 Cal.App.4th 1437, 1445[53 Cal.Rptr.2d 439].) Thus, although our Supreme Court has rejected the notion that an unwed biological father has a protected liberty interest in *establishing* a relationship with his child, the court has recognized a biological father's liberty interest "in *maintaining and preserving an existing* parent-child relationship." (*Dawn D. v. Superior Court* (1998) 17 Cal.4th 932, 942, [72 Cal.Rptr.2d 871, 952 P.2d 1139], italics added; see *Lisa I. v. Superior Court* (2005) 133 Cal.App.4th 605, 616[34 Cal. Rptr.3d 927] [a biological father does not have a liberty interest "in the *opportunity* to develop a relationship with" the child].)[16] Biological paternity may be afforded greater weight when the child is an infant; however, as the child gets older, courts seek to preserve the stronger social bond over biological ties. (*In re Kiana A.* (2001) 93 Cal.App.4th 1109, 1120[113 Cal.Rptr.2d 669].)

Together, these authorities support our statutory interpretation as applied here to four-year-old DJ: "an appropriate action" for application of *section 7612, subdivision (c)* requires a court to find an existing, rather than potential, relationship between a putative third parent and the child, such that "recognizing only two parents would be detrimental to the child." (*§ 7612, subd. (c).*) This interpretation harmonizes *section 7612, subdivision (c)* with the broader statutory framework under the UPA.

4. *Application*

The juvenile court found that David "does not have a strong relationship" with DJ and ordered visits to be supervised "because [David] has to develop a relationship." Despite these findings, the court applied *section 7612, subdivision (c)*, relying on David's biological ties to DJ and the potential harm to DJ from possibly not finding out about his roots until later in his life. This was error.

There is no indication the Legislature intended *section 7612, subdivision (c)* to apply to a person like David, who, at the time of the contested disposition hearing on parentage, lacked an existing relationship with the child. A person who lacks an existing parent-child relationship is not a child's "parent in every way." (Sen. Bill No. 274 (2013–2014 Reg. Sess.) § 1, subd. (a).) Nor would separation from such a person cause "devastating psychological and emotional impact on the

---

[16] An exception to this general principle can be found in *Kelsey S., supra,* 1 Cal.4th at pages 848–849, 4 Cal.Rptr.2d 615, 823 P.2d 1216, which recognized a liberty interest where a biological father is *precluded* from establishing a relationship with his child. Here, however, the juvenile court did not make a ruling under *Kelsey S.*, and the issue of whether David might qualify as a *Kelsey S.* father is not before us on appeal. The policy motivations underlying *Kelsey S.* therefore do not apply.

child." (*Ibid.*) The court's speculation as to potential harm from DJ discovering his biological father later in life is not substantial evidence supporting a finding of detriment within the meaning of <u>section 7612, subdivision (c)</u>.

Application of <u>section 7612, subdivision (c)</u> to the facts presented here would open the floodgates to virtually all biological fathers who may qualify as a presumed parent under section 7611 and seek to form a relationship with the child. Such an interpretation would apply far beyond the "rare case" envisioned by the Legislature. Indeed, application of the statute here would call into question the continued viability of <u>section 7612, subdivision (b)</u>. If the possible loss of a potential relationship were sufficient to find detriment and recognize three parents under <u>section 7612, subdivision (c)</u>, we question when, if ever, a court would weigh competing parentage presumptions under <u>section 7612, subdivision (b)</u>. Such a result would be untenable, given the express legislative intent to leave <u>section 7612, subdivision (b)</u>'s weighing test intact:

> "[E]xisting law anticipates the situation where two or more presumptions of paternity conflict under the Family Code, and provides the following guidance: the presumption which on the facts is founded on the weightier considerations of policy and logic controls. Courts therefore, under current law, apply a critical analysis to situations where more than two presumptions exist. *This bill does not limit that analysis.*"

(Assem. Com. on Judiciary, com. on Sen. Bill No. 274 (2013–2014 Reg. Sess.) as amended May 14, 2013, p. 7, italics added; see *id.* at p. 5 [explaining the legislation gives courts "flexibility": where there are more than two presumed parents, a "court *can, but is not required to,* recognize more than two people as legal parents of the child if it would otherwise be detrimental to the child" (italics added)].)

For these reasons, we conclude "an appropriate action" for application of <u>section 7612, subdivision (c)</u> is one in which there is an existing parent-child relationship between the child and the putative third parent, such that "recognizing only two parents would be detrimental to the child." Because the juvenile court determined David did not have an existing parent-child relationship with DJ, there is no substantial evidence to support a finding of detriment under the statute. This is not the "rare case" in which <u>section 7612, subdivision (c)</u> allows a court to find that a child has more than two parents. Consequently, <u>section 7612, subdivision (c)</u> does not apply, and Donovan's conclusive marital presumption under <u>section 7540</u> defeats David's parentage claim under section 7611, subdivision (d).

* * *

DISPOSITION

The juvenile court's June 12, 2015 disposition order is reversed insofar as it determines David is DJ's presumed father under *Family Code section 7612, subdivision (c)* and orders services (including the preparation of a case plan) and visitation for David. In all other respects, the disposition order is affirmed.

————————————

Points for Discussion

a. Recognition of More than Two Legal Parents

Along with California, statutes in a number of other states permit a court to recognize more than two people as the child's legal parents in some circumstances. See, e.g., Me. Rev. Stat. tit. 19–a, § 1853(2) (2018). In the most recent revision of the Uniform Parentage Act, the drafters provided two alternative versions of § 613(c), one of which allows a court adjudicating competing claims of parentage to adjudicate a child to have more than two parents, "if the court finds that failure to recognize more than two parents would be detrimental to the child." How does this test compare with the statute considered in *Donovan L.*?

b. DeFacto Parentage

When a child's legal parent allows or encourages a person to develop a strong parent-like relationship with a child, that person may be accorded standing to seek parental rights and responsibilities under various legal theories, including that the individual stands in loco parentis to the child, or is the child's psychological parent. The individual may be a stepparent, or a family member who cares for a child when the parents cannot. This status is distinct from the presumption of parentage that may arise from living with and acknowledging the child as one's own under statutes such as the Uniform Parentage Act. Cases considering third-party custody and visitation claims are discussed in Chapter 7.

Statutes in several states authorize courts to recognize individuals in this situation as legal parents. See, e.g., Del Code Ann., tit. 13, §8–201 (2018); Me. Rev. Stat. tit. 19–a, § 1891 (2018). Under the UPA 2017, § 609 adopts this approach, allowing an individual who claims to be a de facto parent of a child to commence a proceeding before the child reaches age 18 to establish parentage. The individual must establish a series of key facts by clear and convincing evidence.

c. Child Support Obligations

When should de facto parents have support obligations? Compare T.F. v. B.L., 813 N.E.2d 1244 (Mass. 2004) (rejecting argument that a child support obligation may be premised on an implied parenthood contract) with <u>H.M. v. E.T., 930 N.E.2d 206 (N.Y. 2010)</u> (finding that court had subject matter jurisdiction to adjudicate parentage and impose support obligation on parent's former same-sex partner); <u>L.S.K. v. H.A.N., 813 A.2d 872 (Pa. Super. Ct. 2002)</u> (affirming child support obligation imposed on mother's former same-sex partner).

d. Recognition of Parentage Orders

As a constitutional matter, every state must give Full Faith and Credit to parentage and adoption decrees entered by a court with competent jurisdiction in another state. See <u>V.L. v. E.L., 577 U.S. ___, 136 S.Ct. 1017 (2016) (per curiam)</u>. Before the Supreme Court rulings in *Obergefell* and *Pavan*, parental rights that resulted from a legally valid same-sex marriage or partnership were often not recognized by the federal government or in states that did not recognize these unions. For this reason, it was important for same-sex couples to obtain an adoption decree or parentage order confirming the parental rights of both parents. See <u>Adoption of Sebastian, 879 N.Y.S.2d 677 (Surr. Ct. 2009)</u> ("[A]lthough it is also true that an adoption should be unnecessary because Sebastian was born to parents whose marriage is legally recognized in this state, the best interests of this child require a judgment that will ensure recognition of both Ingrid and Mona as his legal parents throughout the entire United States.")

Problem 2-13

James and Andrea began living together when James was twenty-five and Andrea seventeen. About six months after they began living together, Andrea gave birth to a son, Andrew. James paid Andrea's prenatal and hospital expenses, and paid $50 per week for child support after Andrew was born. He shared half of the caretaking duties for Andrew as long as he and Andrea lived together. When Andrew was 18 months old, Andrea moved out, and two years later she married someone else. James continued to pay child support, although he knew he was not Andrew's father. James visited Andrew, often cared for him on weekends, and behaved in all ways as a parent. When Andrew was almost five, Andrea notified James that he could no longer visit or have contact with Andrew, telling him in a letter that he should get on with his life and have a family and children of his own. James immediately brought suit for a declaration of paternity, asking for visitation and that the court approve his payments of $50 per week. A blood test excluded James as Andrew's father. What should be the result of this suit? (See <u>Petition of Ash, 507 N.W.2d 400 (Iowa 1993)</u>.)

Problem 2-14

Kiana's mother was living with Kevin when she became pregnant, but they separated before Kiana was born. The mother began living with another man, Mario, whose name is listed as Kiana's father on her birth certificate. Mario and Kiana's mother were married two years after Kiana was born. They remained married for seven years, but Mario was incarcerated for most of that time. Over the years, Kevin has given Kiana's mother money to buy food and clothing for Kiana, and Kiana has stayed at Kevin's home for periods of time up to three months. Kiana's mother was arrested when Kiana was 12, and Kiana called Kevin and asked him to pick her up. In neglect proceedings brought against Kiana's mother in the juvenile court, Kevin has petitioned to be determined as Kiana's father. Kiana calls Kevin "Daddy," and wants to live with him. Can Kevin be declared to be Kiana's legal father? (Cf. In re Kiana A., 113 Cal.Rptr.2d 669 (Cal. Ct. App. 2001); see also In re Nicholas H., 46 P.3d 932 (Cal. 2002).)

Problem 2-15

Alicia and Jose, a married couple from Guatemala, agreed that their child should be raised by a woman named Leticia. When the child was born, Alicia checked into the hospital using Leticia's name, and that was the name given on the child's birth certificate. Leticia has raised the child, Karen, who is now twelve. Karen has never had any contact with her biological parents, who returned to Guatemala shortly after her birth. When these facts come to the attention of the state authorities, Leticia files a petition seeking to be recognized as Karen's legal mother. Should the court grant this relief? (See In re Karen C., 124 Cal.Rptr.2d 677 (Cal. Ct. App. 2002); see also In re Salvador M., 4 Cal.Rptr.3d 705 (Cal. Ct. App. 2003).)

CHAPTER 3

Adoption and Assisted Reproduction

Adoption creates new family relationships when the legal rights and responsibilities of one or both of the child's natural parents are terminated and the law substitutes new rights and responsibilities of adoptive parents. State statutes govern both steps, the termination of one set of rights and the creation of the other, which may occur in the course of one legal proceeding or two separate proceedings.

This chapter begins with the termination of the rights and obligations of natural parents, which may be accomplished voluntarily or involuntarily. Voluntary termination occurs when a natural parent initiates a proceeding for the relinquishment of his or her child, or when the parent completes a valid consent to adoption. In some circumstances, state statutes allow the authorities to proceed without obtaining the natural parent's consent. Involuntary termination is usually accomplished in a statutory proceeding initiated by a state agency. The involuntary termination process raises fundamental questions about parental rights and child welfare that are addressed in Chapter 5.

Go Online

Approximately 119,500 children were adopted in 2012 in the United States, with about 44 percent of these adoptions occurring through public child welfare agencies, 7 percent as intercountry adoptions, and the remaining 49 percent from other sources, including private agency, independent and stepparent adoptions. See U.S. Department of Health and Human Services, *Child Welfare Information Gateway, Trends in U.S. Adoptions: 2008–2012 (2016)*.

After the rights of the natural parents have been terminated, adoption laws define how adoptive parents may establish legal parental ties with a child. Placement of children for adoption may be decided by a public or private adoption agency, or by the natural parents themselves, sometimes with the assistance of an intermediary. In all states, a court must approve the placement and determine whether adoption is in the child's best interests.

State statutes also regulate different methods of assisted reproduction, including artificial insemination, in vitro fertilization and embryo transfer, and surrogacy. In these cases, there may be many adults with conflicting parentage claims, and adoption is sometimes necessary to formalize the legal relationship between the intended parents and the child. Legal regulation has not kept up with medical advances in this area, raising particularly difficult legal and ethical problems.

Some of the most contentious issues in the law of adoption and assisted reproduction center on families that form across racial, ethnic, or international borders. In recent years, there were also significant disputes in some states regarding the rights of gay and lesbian individuals and same-sex couples to these modes of family formation. In addition, wide differences among the laws in different states generate problematic jurisdictional and conflict of laws questions.

A. Parental Consent to Adoption

Consent to adoption describes a procedure through which a child's legal parents or guardian relinquish all of their rights and responsibilities concerning that child. The process is governed by state statutes, and these procedures vary significantly in different states. Consent must generally be obtained from the child's birth mother, and from the birth father if his paternity has been established or if he is a "presumed father" or otherwise entitled to notice and consent under state law. Older children must also give consent to their own adoption. Some states require counseling for birth parents prior to relinquishment, and many states have a waiting period after the child's birth before an

Go Online

Information on state laws governing consent to adoption is available online from the Child Welfare Information Gateway.

effective consent to adoption can be made. The specifics of these rules may be different for birth mothers and birth fathers. State laws also vary on whether—and in what circumstances—a consent to adoption may subsequently be revoked.

Petition of Steve B.D.

723 P.2d 829 (Idaho 1986)

SHEPARD, Justice. This is an appeal from an order of the district court which affirmed an order of the magistrate court, which denied a petition to revoke consent to the adoption of a child. We *affirm.*

Appellant Mary Ann DeBernardi gave birth to a child on March 5, 1984. On March 7, 1984, before a magistrate, DeBernardi executed a consent to the adoption of that newborn child by Mr. and Mrs. D. Mr. and Mrs. D. filed a petition for adoption of the child on March 9, 1984. DeBernardi filed a written revocation of her consent to the adoption of the child on March 20, 1984. A hearing was held on the attempted revocation of consent in May of 1984 before a magistrate who denied the attempted revocation. That order of the magistrate was appealed to the district court which affirmed the order of the magistrate in March of 1985. The appeal before this Court was heard in January 1986. In the interim there have been no further adoption proceedings and no decree of adoption. The child has lived with Mr. and Mrs. D. since March 7, 1984.

In 1982 DeBernardi, a 36-year-old woman who had four children, was recently divorced after a long marriage, and had minimal financial resources. She responded to a newspaper advertisement which sought surrogate mothers. She consulted with attorney Bert Osborn who had placed the advertisement. He informed her that prospective adoptive parents were willing to pay her $7,000.00 plus her medical and legal expenses to be a surrogate mother. Negotiations for such surrogate parenthood were never completed.

Sometime later DeBernardi met and sporadically began living with one Chet Swan during 1982 and 1983. In July 1983 DeBernardi learned she was pregnant, allegedly by Swan. Swan left DeBernardi in September 1983. Thereupon DeBernardi recontacted Osborn to inform him of her pregnancy and of her desire to have the child placed for adoption. Osborn advised DeBernardi to hire another attorney, and she then sought advice from McDonald, an attorney who had previously handled her divorce.

On September 15, 1983 a written contract was executed between DeBernardi and Mr. and Mrs. D. in which DeBernardi agreed to give up her as yet unborn child for adoption, and Mr. and Mrs. D. agreed to adopt the child when born. The contract provided for the payment of DeBernardi's legal and medical costs, but did not provide for any payment to be made to DeBernardi herself. * * *

Prior to, and again after the execution of the contract, DeBernardi met with and discussed the proposed adoption with Davenport, a counselor with the Department of Health and Welfare. In December 1983 attorney Osborn withdrew from the proceedings and referred the prospective adoptive parents to attorney McDonald who in turn referred them to attorney Fouser.

DeBernardi gave birth to a child at 2:00 a.m., March 5, 1984. During the time that she was in the hospital she twice consulted with Bev Putnam, director of social services for the hospital. Putnam testified that she spent over an hour reviewing the question of adoption, and the alternatives thereto, with DeBernardi.

The child was delivered to Mr. and Mrs. D. who took the child home on March 7, 1984.

1st hearing

On March 7, 1984 DeBernardi appeared before Magistrate Birnbaum to execute a consent to the adoption of the newborn child by Mr. and Mrs. D. and to terminate her parental rights. At that time she testified under oath that she did not know the identity of the child's father, and that she had contemplated the adoption for nine months. She testified that no one had threatened or coerced her into giving her consent. DeBernardi then executed the consent document before the magistrate.

On March 17, 1984, the current counsel for DeBernardi notified Mr. and Mrs. D. that DeBernardi had revoked her consent, and on March 20, 1984 DeBernardi filed with the court a written revocation of consent. A hearing on DeBernardi's petition to revoke her consent and dismiss the adoption petition of Mr. and Mrs. D. was held on May 11, 1984, before Magistrate Drescher. * * *

At the conclusion of the hearing, Magistrate Drescher denied DeBernardi's attempted revocation and her petition to dismiss the adoption petition. * * *

Magistrate Drescher rendered his decision denying DeBernardi's attempted revocation of her consent and denying her petition to dismiss the adoption proceedings on the basis of what he perceived to be the standards of *Matter of Andersen*, 99 Idaho 805, 589 P.2d 957 (1978). Magistrate Drescher therefore held that DeBernardi was estopped from revoking her consent to the adoption.

In *Andersen*, a young unwed mother decided to privately place her child for adoption, and she chose the Crapos as the adoptive parents. As she went into labor she changed her mind and informed the Crapos that the baby would not be adopted. Shortly after the birth of the child the mother married the father of the child. A month later she called the Crapos to inform them that they could adopt the child. The Crapos and the Andersens met, and the baby was delivered to the Crapos. The parties signed an adoption form and had their signatures notarized at a bank. The Andersens went to California and twice called the Crapos requesting the return of the child. During a third telephone call the Andersens apologized for the demands for the return of the child, and indicated they would not attempt to regain custody. An adoption proceeding was initiated by the Crapos and a decree of adoption was issued. Approximately two months later the Andersens again demanded the return of the child, and when met with a refusal filed a petition for writ of habeas corpus. After a hearing before the district court the adoption decree was set aside and the child ordered returned to the Andersens.

The adopting parents appealed to this Court, and the district court order was affirmed. A majority of this Court held that a natural parent should be permitted to revoke a valid consent to adoption unless estopped from doing so. The Andersens were held not to be estopped from revoking their otherwise valid consent. The Court held that the following factors were to be considered in determining whether or not natural parents should be estopped to revoke their otherwise valid consent to adoption:

> "the circumstances under which the consent was given; the length of time elapsing, and the conduct of the parties, between the giving of consent and the attempted withdrawal; whether or not the withdrawal was made before or after the institution of adoption proceedings; the nature of the natural parent's conduct with respect to the child both before and after consenting to its adoption; and the 'vested rights' of the proposed adoptive parents with respect to the child."

* * *

Think About It

How was the relinquishment handled in *Andersen*? How does that compare with the facts of this case?

At the hearing before Magistrate Drescher, DeBernardi testified that she had received no counseling prior to the birth of the baby, and that at the time she entered the hospital she had decided not to go through with the adoption. She indicated that she had purchased various furniture and clothes in anticipation of bringing the baby home. She further testified that attorney McDonald had told her to state at the hearing before Magistrate Birnbaum that she did not know who the father was. She also testified that in February she decided to make her consent to adoption conditional upon agreement that the child would be raised out-of-state, that it would be reared in the Catholic faith, and that the adoptive parents would be childless. She further testified that attorney McDonald had exerted influence upon her to give the child up for adoption.

On the other hand, McDonald testified at the hearing that he had reviewed the consent form with DeBernardi and discussed its legal ramifications, and denied that DeBernardi ever attached any conditions to the adoption. He testified that DeBernardi had never expressed any desire to take her child home with her from the hospital, and that one of the continuing concerns of DeBernardi was the fact that she worked a night shift. McDonald denied that he had ever coached DeBernardi to testify that the father was unknown at the hearing before Magistrate Birnbaum, and testified that DeBernardi gave conflicting versions of the paternity of the child.

Although DeBernardi testified that while she was in the hospital she told the director of social services that she was being pressured to consent to the adoption,

Putnam, the director of social services at the hospital, testified that she counseled with DeBernardi at least twice, and that DeBernardi appeared to be firm in her decision to consent to adoption and give up the child.

Mr. and Mrs. D. both testified at the hearing. Both testified that they have had uninterrupted custody of the child since March 7, 1984, and that they love the child and consider him a part of the family. Mrs. D. testified that adoption had been contemplated since July 1983, and that she and her husband had paid DeBernardi's legal fees in the amount of $2,000.00 to McDonald, and $2,500.00 for DeBernardi's medical expenses.

* * *

Magistrate Drescher reviewed the five factors set out in *Andersen* to be considered by a court in passing upon a revocation of consent to adoption. Magistrate Drescher contrasted the mature woman in the instant case, and the distress of a young woman without any advice, as in *Andersen*. He indicated that DeBernardi was a mature woman who "had the benefit of counsel throughout the period of pregnancy and for a material period of time before; she had reviewed the matter on a number of occasions with her attorney and also discussed and reviewed the pros and cons of the adoption versus other alternatives. She also had the benefit of consultation with a social worker during the term of her pregnancy. * * * " Magistrate Drescher contrasted DeBernardi's situation with that of the natural mother in *Andersen* who attempted to care for the child for some considerable period of time in the home of her parents. In the instant case DeBernardi had very brief contact with the child at the hospital. The magistrate indicated that Mr. and Mrs. D. had uninterrupted custody of the child since March 1984, that they have renamed the child, that they had expended considerable sums in regard to medical attention as well as legal fees. The magistrate found that the above factors, together with the emotional attachment to the child, required a holding that DeBernardi was estopped from revoking her consent. Additionally, the magistrate court noted that there was "not the slightest bit of evidence that the consent was induced by fraud or duress" and that in contrast to the Andersen proceeding DeBernardi had a full judicial proceeding in the securing of her execution of consent and "Mrs. DeBernardi in fact executed the consent freely, voluntarily, intelligently, knowingly and with full knowledge of its consequence."

We hold, therefore, that under the standards enunciated in *Andersen,* that the magistrate court as affirmed by the district court, was correct in its holding that DeBernardi was estopped to revoke her consent to the adoption, and in denying DeBernardi's petition to dismiss the adoption proceedings brought by Mr. and Mrs. D. Although we have held that the trial court was correct in its decision that the facts in the instant case satisfied the estoppel requirements as set forth in <u>*Andersen, supra,*</u> we today overrule *Andersen* and its "estoppel" approach to an attempted revocation of a consent to adoption.

The central issue in *Andersen,* as in the case at bar, is whether in the absence of fraud, duress or undue influence a natural parent who has executed a consent to adoption has the right for an indeterminate period to simply change his or her mind and revoke consent as in *Andersen,* even after an adoption procedure has been completed. We now hold that in the absence of fraud, duress, or undue influence, consents to adoption become final and irrevocable upon execution of the consent to adoption by the natural parents, and delivery and surrender of the child to the adoptive parents. We so hold in the view of thus promoting the child's welfare and subordinate to that welfare the protection of the interests of the natural and the adoptive parents.

It was well stated that the estoppel approach of *Andersen* inevitably will breed litigation and uncertainty with the future of potentially adoptive children remaining in a state of limbo for years.

"Uncertainty, as this case verifies, breeds litigation which, regardless of how the issues are ultimately decided by the courts, often results in tragedy for the child. . . . Much of this could be avoided by a clear, decisive and easily ascertainable standard for determining, short of prolonged litigation, when and if a consent is revocable. In this respect the majority opinion fails egregiously. The standard adopted by the majority, estoppel, does not provide the public with any clear guidelines. It is a standard only the courts can apply. Under that standard, questions concerning revocation cannot be resolved with any certainty without litigation." <u>*Andersen,* 99 Idaho at 818–819, 589 P.2d at 970–971</u> (Bakes, J., dissenting).

We perceive the majority opinion in *Andersen* as focusing unduly on the rights of and consideration for the interests of the natural parents to the exclusion of the welfare of the child. Although this Court has long recognized the right of natural parents to the care and custody of their own children, case law pre-*Andersen* does not establish any rule primarily favoring the rights of natural parents in a case such as presented here. As well pointed out by the dissenting opinion of Bakes, J., in <u>*Andersen,*</u> where the child has been delivered to and has been for some period of time in the custody of the prospective adoptive parents, emotional ties and bonds are established between the child and the adoptive parents, the severance of which will be as traumatic, if not more so, than the severance of the ties between the child and the natural parents.

As stated in the dissenting opinion of Bakes, J., in *Andersen:*

"However, the natural parents actually have the least interest in the specific point at which a consent becomes irrevocable, though they certainly have a strong interest in knowing when it is. Unlike the child and the adoptive parents, the natural parents have complete control over when the consent is given. There is no deadline for the natural parents. They can surrender the child and consent to the adoption at any time which best fits their needs and interests. That most natural parents choose to give the child for adoption at birth recognizes the sociological fact that the longer the decision for adoption is delayed the more difficult it is to sever the emotional bonds between the mother and the child. But the decision is solely the natural parents' to make, and in the absence of fraud, coercion, or undue influence they should be bound by it, because after the consent is given and the child placed with the adoptive parents, the same emotional bonds are forged with the new parents. By changing her mind the natural mother is not merely exercising what the majority apparently finds to be the natural right of an 'extremely distraught, concerned and upset' woman, but is destroying the emotional bonds which the child has forged with its new parents and, in most cases, the only parents and family it has ever known.

* * *

"Nevertheless, I do believe the fact that the natural mother, subsequent to consenting to the adoption, has had a change of heart and now is desirous and willing to care for the child may be significant in the adoption proceedings. I.C. § 16–1507 requires that before entering a final order of adoption the judge must be 'satisfied that the interests of the child will be promoted by the adoption.' Certainly the natural parents' desire to regain custody of the child and their present willingness to assume the parental responsibility for the child are relevant to the judge's determination whether the proposed adoption is in the child's best interests. If convinced that the best interests of the child would be promoted by returning the child to the natural parents, the judge, in my view, would be entitled under I.C. § 16–1507 to deny the adoption petition and order the child returned to the natural parents. However, such decision must be based upon careful findings that such action would in fact serve the child's best interests and not merely upon the fact that the natural parents have changed their minds. * * * * "

We hold that while natural parental ties are one factor to be considered in determining the best interests of the child, such ties are not to be treated as a presumption in favor of the natural parents. When, in the absence of fraud, duress, or undue influence a consent to adoption has been executed and the child has been delivered to the potential adopting parents, the general rule favoring natural parents is inoperative and rather a judicial inquiry is triggered into the best interest of the child. The best interest of the child test is much more than a mere comparison of the social status and economic means of the competing sets of parents, and our courts are well equipped to make inquiry into the child's best interest, going well beyond a balance sheet financial comparison. As indicated in S.O. v. W.S., 643 P.2d 997 (Alaska 1982), the best interest of the child standard is not a mere comparison of the economic and social benefits which competing sets of parents can provide. * * *

* * *

Finally, we examine DeBernardi's assertion that her attorney-client relationship with attorney McDonald was tainted because McDonald's fees were paid by Mr. and Mrs. D. Our Disciplinary Rule 5–107 provides:

"A. *Except with the consent of his client after full disclosure,* a lawyer shall not:
1. Accept compensation for his legal services from one other than his client.
2. Accept from one other than his client anything of value related to his representation of or his employment by his client.
"B. A lawyer shall not permit a person who recommends, employs, or pays him to render legal services for another to direct or regulate his professional judgment in rendering such legal services." (Emphasis added.)

> **FYI**
>
> The order entered by Magistrate Drescher and a transcript of the consent proceeding were published as attachments to the court's opinion. See Petition of Steve B.D., 723 P.2d 829, 839–847 (Idaho 1986).

In the instant case the record clearly indicates that DeBernardi, in the written agreement, not only consented to the payment of her legal fees by Mr. and Mrs. D., but undoubtedly insisted upon it, since at that time she was in severe financial straits. While such an arrangement is less than ideal, under such circumstances and absent an offer of *pro bono* assistance, there appears no other practical method by which DeBernardi, nor most natural mothers giving up a child for adoption, could obtain legal advice. Further, there is no evidence in the record, and we see no inference, that McDonald allowed Mr. and Mrs. D. to regulate his professional judgment in rendering services to Mrs. DeBernardi.

* * *

All parties to the instant action have endured a lengthy and undoubtedly painful litigation which has perhaps best demonstrated the unworkability and unfairness of the "estoppel" rule enunciated by the majority in *Andersen,* and lends even greater credence to the Bakes, J. dissent in *Andersen.* * * *

* * *

Points for Discussion

a. Consent Proceedings

Several states require that an adoption consent be executed under judicial supervision. E.g., Colo.Rev.Stat. § 19–5–103 (2018); 23 Pa.Cons.Stat. § 2503 (2018). In New York, a consent to a private placement adoption which is executed before a judge is irrevocable, whereas an extrajudicial consent remains revocable for forty-five days after execution. N.Y.Dom.Rel.Law § 115–b(3) (a) (McKinney 2018). What is the purpose of requiring judicial supervision? Whose interests are being protected? What is the proper role for lawyers in a consent proceeding? Should the parents be appointed an attorney if they cannot afford one? Should counseling be required? In the *Andersen* case, discussed in *Steve B.D.*, the birth parents gave their consent to adoption on a form they had notarized at a bank. How should the legal rules concerning the consent process influence the rules regarding revocation of consent? See also Brown v. Baby Girl Harper, 766 S.E.2d 375 (S.C. 2014), holding that a consent to adoption was invalid where there was not strict compliance with the statutory formalities.

b. Whose Consent Is Required?

Practice Pointer

Review the transcript of the consent proceeding in *Steve B.D.* that is appended to the opinion. Did that proceeding assure that Ms. DeBernardi's consent was knowing and voluntary? Should she have been asked different or additional questions?

Chester Swan, the biological father of the child in *Steve B.D.*, appeared at the revocation of consent hearing on May 11 and "testified as to his paternity, his wish to reunite the child 'with his mother and his brothers and sisters,' and his desire to help raise the child." Steve B.D. v. Swan, 730 P.2d 942 (Idaho 1986). Swan presented uncontroverted evidence that Mary Anne did not inform him she had placed the child for adoption and that she consistently misled him, promising that he would see the child soon. The Supreme Court of Idaho found that Chet's consent was not required since he had not developed a substantial relationship with the child sufficient to create a constitutionally protected interest under *Lehr*, *Caban* and *Stanley*. Should a father in Chet's position have a right to notice and consent?

c. Revocation of Consent

The questions of whether and under what circumstances a consent to an adoption may be revoked have been the subject of extensive litigation and differing legislative treatment. Some statutes permit revocation only on the grounds of fraud or duress. E.g., 750 Ill.Comp.Stat.Ann. § 50/11 (2018). Others authorize revocation within a short time after the consent was executed. E.g. Ark.Code Ann. § 9–9–209(b) (1) (2018) (10 calendar days); Minn.Stat.Ann. § 259.24(6a) (2018) (10 working days). Other statutes provide that the consent when executed may not be withdrawn unless that is shown to be in the child's best interests as found by a court, Haw.Rev.Stat. § 578–2(f)(2018). In the absence of statute, there has been a shift in the case law away from the rights of the natural parent in favor of protecting the interests of the child. See generally Homer H. Clark, Jr., Domestic Relations 883–887 (Student 2d ed. 1988). How does the court in *Steve B.D.* justify its abandonment of the parental preference doctrine?

d. Uniform Adoption Act

The 1994 Uniform Adoption Act, 9 U.L.A. (Part 1A) 11 (1999) (enacted only in Vermont) specifies what must be included in a written consent or relinquishment in § 2–406. Although the consent may be executed before a judge, the Act also provides for an adoption agency, lawyer, or other public official to take the consent, see § 2–405. The consent may not be executed before the child is born, and may be revoked for any reason within 192 hours (8 days) after the child's birth. § 2–404. If executed more than 192 hours after the child's birth, a parent's consent is revocable only on proof by clear and convincing evidence, before a decree of adoption has been issued, that the consent was obtained by fraud or duress. §§ 2–408, 2–409. Before executing a consent or relinquishment, a parent must have been informed of the meaning and consequences of adoption and the availability of personal and legal counseling, as well as procedures for releasing health and other information to the adoptee or the adoptive parents. § 2–404. Would these procedures have been preferable to the ones applied in *Steve B.D.*?

e. Fraud and Duress

How would you define the level of duress that would be a sufficient basis for setting aside a consent? Courts have frequently held that "duress of circumstances" is not an adequate ground for revocation of a consent to adopt. See, e.g., D.S. v. United Catholic Social Services of Archdiocese of Omaha, Inc., 419 N.W.2d 531 (Neb. 1988); Matter of Adoption of Doe, 543 So.2d 741 (Fla.1989). Should a minor relinquishing a child for adoption have legal counsel? See Adoption of A.L.O., 132 P.3d 543 (Mont. 2006).

Fraud claims have been sustained in circumstances in which a birth parent is somehow misled about the proceeding or precluded from participation; see Adoption of E.L., 733 N.E.2d 846 (Ill. App. Ct. 2000) (stepparent adoption set aside based on fraud committed upon the court and on father in procurement of judgment); Wunderlich v. Alexander, 92 S.W.3d 715 (Ark. Ct. App. 2002) ("pretend" adoption by maternal grandparents set aside). Courts have also considered claims of fraud in cases in which birth parents signed relinquishments without understanding what they were signing as a result of language barriers. See, e.g.,

F.E. v. G.F.M., 547 S.E.2d 531 (Va. Ct. App. 2001) (setting aside consent form signed by father who thought it was a medical consent form); cf. In the Interest of L.M.I., 119 S.W.3d 707 (Tex. 2003) (relinquishment affidavits not translated into Spanish, but father's claim was not properly preserved for appeal; dissent concludes that termination of parental rights violated father's due process rights).

Ethics and Adoption Lawyers

What obligations do attorneys owe to their clients and to other parties in the adoption context? Sanctions were applied against the lawyer for a birth mother where there were defects in her consent, where the child's father refused to consent, and the attorney failed to make reasonable inquiries as to whether the father's rights could be terminated. Matter of Adoption of R.N.L., 913 P.2d 761 (Utah Ct.App.1996). In Kessel v. Leavitt, 511 S.E.2d 720 (W. Va. 1998), the biological father of a child placed for adoption in Canada (to avoid the need for his consent) obtained a substantial award of damages and punitive damages against an adoption attorney.

Can a lawyer represent both the adoptive and biological parents in a private adoption proceeding? Although some jurisdictions have permitted this, provided that the clients are fully informed as to potential conflicts of interest, the ABA has taken the position that a lawyer may not ethically undertake joint representation in this context on the ground that there are inherent conflicts of interest that cannot be reconciled. ABA Committee on Professional Ethics and Professional Responsibility, Informal Opinion 87–1523 (1987). See generally ABA Model Rules of Professional Conduct Rule 1.7. Cases illustrating the problems that arise from conflicts in adoption cases include Matter of Petrie, 742 P.2d 796 (Ariz. 1987); Matter of Swihart, 517 N.E.2d 792 (Ind.1988).

The court in *Steve B.D.* rejected the mother's claim that the payment of her attorney's fees by the adoptive parents tainted her attorney-client relationship, citing Disciplinary Rule 5–107 from the Model Code of Professional Responsibility. For the more current version of this rule, see Model Rules of Professional Conduct Rule 1.8(f). Based on the evidence from this opinion, and the transcript of the consent proceeding, do you think Mr. McDonald was compromised in his representation of Ms. DeBernardi?

f. Open Adoption

Birth parents have sometimes attempted to condition their consent or relinquishment on maintaining the right to see and visit the child. Courts have frequently found these consents to be invalid; see K.W.E. v. People, 500 P.2d 167 (Colo. Ct. App. 1972); McLaughlin v. Strickland, 309 S.E.2d 787 (S.C. Ct.App.1983). Some courts have permitted adoptions to go forward based on this type of consent, however, allowing enforcement of the visitation provision if it is in the child's best interests. See In re Adoption of a Minor, 291 N.E.2d 729 (Mass. 1973). The question of "open adoption" is discussed further in the next part of this chapter.

g. Indian Child Welfare Act

Any adoption involving a child who may fall within the coverage of the Indian Child Welfare Act (ICWA), 25 U.S.C.A. § 1901 et seq. (2018), is subject to special jurisdictional, procedural and substantive rules that override the provisions of state adoption laws. The statute applies to any "Indian child", defined as a child who is either a member of an Indian tribe, or eligible for membership and the biological child of a member of an Indian tribe. 25 U.S.C.A. § 1903. ICWA is generally more protective of parental rights than state adoption laws.

In an adoption subject to ICWA, " * * * the consent of the parent may be withdrawn for *any* reason at *any* time prior to the entry of a final decree of termination or adoption, * * * and the child *shall* be returned to the parent". 25 U.S.C.A. § 1913(c) (emphasis added). A number of cases have found this provision to be mandatory, despite the passage of a considerable period of time during which the child had lived with the prospective adoptive parents. See, e.g., A.B.M. v. M.H., 651 P.2d 1170 (Alaska 1982), cert. denied 461 U.S. 914 (1983); Matter of Appeal in Pima County, 635 P.2d 187 (Ariz. Ct. App.1981), cert. denied 455 U.S. 1007 (1982). The application of ICWA to unmarried fathers has been complicated by the decision in Adoptive Couple v. Baby Girl, 570 U.S. 637 (2013), discussed in more detail in the notes following Mississippi Band of Choctaw Indians v. Holyfield, 490 U.S. 30 (1989), later in this Chapter.

Problem 3-1

Claire gives birth to a child in New York and signs a consent form which reads as follows:

> I hereby irrevocably consent to the private placement adoption of my son. I understand that since this consent has not been executed before a judge it shall be irrevocable thirty days after the commencement of the adoption proceeding unless written notice of revocation thereof shall be received by this Court within said thirty days.

Claire files a notice to withdraw her consent with the court within the thirty day period, believing that she will be entitled to the return of her child. However, the law in New York is that if the adoptive parents oppose the revocation, the child may be returned to the natural mother only if it would be in the child's best interests. N.Y.Dom.Rel.Law § 115–b(4) (a) (iv) (McKinney 2012). Further, the law explicitly rejects any presumption in favor of the natural parent in making this determination. N.Y.Dom.Rel.Law § 115–b(6) (d) (v) (McKinney 2012). What arguments would you make on Claire's behalf to invalidate the consent? (See Matter of Adoption of Daniel C., 473 N.E.2d 31 (N.Y. 1984).)

Problem 3-2

Four months after placing her newborn child for adoption, a birth mother seeks to revoke her consent on the ground that it was given involuntarily and as a result of coercion and duress. She alleges that she became pregnant as a junior in college; the child's father was a married man with children who wanted her to have an abortion or give the child up for adoption. When her parents learned of her pregnancy, they would not allow her to return home and threatened to stop assisting with her educational expenses. She spoke with her priest, a counselor and her physician, who all told her she should give the child up for adoption. Five days after the child was born, the mother signed the adoption consent forms but felt very uneasy about it. In a state which follows the approach of *Steve B.D.*, how should the court rule? Should the result be different if the mother sought to revoke her consent within a few days of signing it? Should it matter if the father was unmarried, and came forward immediately after the relinquishment to marry the mother and acknowledge paternity? (See D.S. v. United Catholic Social Services of Archdiocese of Omaha, Inc., 419 N.W.2d 531 (Neb. 1988); Matter of Adoption of Doe, 543 So.2d 741 (Fla.1989).)

Problem 3-3

Donna and Brian were divorced when their daughter, Brianna, was two. Donna remarried several years later, and her new husband filed a petition to adopt Brianna. At the same time, Brian was facing felony charges for failing to pay child support. As a result of negotiations, Brian was allowed to plead guilty to a misdemeanor charge in exchange for relinquishing his parental rights. Brian challenged the relinquishment the next day, arguing that his consent was coerced. Should Brian's consent be set aside? (See In re Adoption of Gatley, 742 N.E.2d 728 (Ohio Ct. App. 2000).)

Heidbreder v. Carton

645 N.W.2d 355 (Minn. 2002)

Russell A. Anderson, Justice.

Appellant Dale "J.R." Heidbreder, an Iowa resident, registered with the Minnesota Fathers' Adoption Registry 31 days after his former girlfriend Katie Carton gave birth to a girl, K.M.C. After registering, Heidbreder commenced a paternity action in Stearns County District Court in an attempt to block the pending adoption of K.M.C. in Minnesota. The prospective adoptive parents, respondents M.J.P. and M.B.P., intervened and moved to dismiss the paternity action under Minn. R. Civ. P. 12.03 on the grounds that Heidbreder's suit was barred under Minn. Stat. § 259.52, subd. 8 (2000), because Heidbreder was not entitled to notice of the adoption petition under Minn.Stat. § 259.49 (2000) and he failed to register with the Fathers' Adoption Registry within 30 days of K.M.C.'s birth. The district court treated the motion as a motion for summary judgment under Minn. R. Civ. P. 56. The district court granted respondents summary judgment and the court of appeals affirmed. We also affirm.

In November 1999, Carton, Heidbreder's girlfriend at the time, informed him that she was pregnant and due in August 2000. At the time, both lived in Fort Madison, Iowa. Carton was 18 years old and had graduated from high school in the spring of 1999. Heidbreder was a year older. According to Heidbreder, he and Carton had one discussion about adoption early in Carton's pregnancy. Carton expressed some interest in exploring adoption but Heidbreder told her he was "absolutely against" adoption and that he believed adoption was "not right." Heidbreder testified in his deposition that Carton told him she would "never ever" put his child up for adoption. While respondents dispute whether Carton made an affirmative promise to Heidbreder not to put the child up for adoption, we view the facts in the light most favorable to Heidbreder as the nonmoving party at the summary judgment stage and assume, for purposes of our decision, that Carton did in fact make such a promise to Heidbreder during their discussion of adoption.

In the spring of 2000, Carton moved out of her mother's house and went to Carthage, Illinois, for approximately 2 weeks. She then moved back to her mother's house. In June 2000, Carton and Heidbreder rented an apartment together in Fort Madison. Carton paid the security deposit and the rent for the month of June. Heidbreder occasionally paid for meals for Carton, but he never provided financial support to Carton for pregnancy-related expenses.

While Carton and Heidbreder were living together, Carton learned that her mother was moving to Minnesota. Carton's relationship with her mother was strained because of the pregnancy and because Carton's mother believed Heidbreder did not treat Carton well. Carton told Heidbreder she would not move to Minnesota with her mother. However, Heidbreder knew Carton had other relatives living in Minnesota.

Carton and Heidbreder argued during the time they lived together. In mid-June, Carton decided to leave Heidbreder. Carton testified in her deposition that she left Heidbreder because they were not getting along. Heidbreder testified that he did not know why Carton left but that at the time she left, Carton was "scared and confused."

Carton moved to St. Cloud, Minnesota, and lived with her grandparents for a few days. She then moved to New Beginnings, a home for pregnant teenage girls in St. Cloud. Carton's mother moved to Minnesota in late June or early July.

While Carton maintained contact with Heidbreder through e-mail, she did not tell him where she was and she instructed her family and friends not to give Heidbreder any information about her location. Although Heidbreder asked for information, Carton's family and friends refused to tell him where Carton was. Heidbreder testified in his deposition that he believed Carton had returned to Illinois and he never considered the possibility that Carton was in Minnesota because of Carton's poor relationship with her mother.

According to Heidbreder, after Carton left he met with an attorney in Iowa to discuss visitation and child support. Heidbreder testified he did not discuss his rights in the event Carton put the child up for adoption because he did not believe Carton would do that. However, he also testified that the attorney told him that his child could not be adopted in Iowa without his consent. The attorney and Heidbreder considered hiring a private detective to find Carton, but never did so, and other than talking to Carton's family and friends, Heidbreder did not take any steps to locate Carton. Nor did Heidbreder take any steps to commence a paternity action, to register with the Iowa Declaration of Paternity Registry under Iowa Code § 144.12A (2001), or to learn whether the laws of Illinois—where Heidbreder believed Carton was—required him to do anything to preserve his parental rights.[1] Heidbreder explained in his deposition that he did not take any action after talking to the attorney because he and the attorney "figured [Carton] would * * * send [Heidbreder] papers."

---

[1] Minnesota law regarding when putative fathers are entitled to notice of a pending adoption and when they are required to register with the state's adoption registry is almost identical to the law of Illinois. See 750 Ill. Comp. Stat. Ann. 50/7 (notice), 50/8 (consent), 50/12.1 (Illinois Putative Father Registry) (West 1999). As in Minnesota, a putative father not entitled to notice of an adoption petition has no right to make a claim to a child who is the subject of a petition for adoption in Illinois unless he registered with the Illinois Putative Father Registry before the child is more than 30 days old. See id.

While living at New Beginnings, Carton decided to give her child up for adoption. Through the Children's Home Society (CHS), Carton selected the couple she wanted to adopt K.M.C., respondents M.J.P. and M.B.P. During a meeting with a representative from CHS, Carton expressed concern that Heidbreder would stop the adoption. The representative explained to Carton that under Minnesota law, she was not required to name Heidbreder on the birth certificate and that if he was not named on the birth certificate, Heidbreder could not prevent the adoption unless he registered with the Minnesota Fathers' Adoption Registry no later than 30 days after the birth of the child.

Think About It

As you read this case, consider what Heidbreder's attorney could have done differently to help protect Heidbreder's interests.

Carton gave birth to a girl, K.M.C., on August 12, 2000. Carton did not identify a father on K.M.C.'s birth certificate and the space for identifying K.M.C.'s father was left blank. K.M.C. left the hospital with respondents on August 14, 2000, and respondents filed a petition to adopt K.M.C. in Washington County District Court.

On September 12, 2000, 31 days after K.M.C.'s birth, Heidbreder learned from a third party that Carton was in Minnesota, had given birth to a girl and had put her up for adoption. Heidbreder contacted Carton by e-mail. That night, Carton told Heidbreder over the telephone that she had given birth and had put the child up for adoption. She also told him it was too late for him to stop the adoption. The same day, Heidbreder found a website with information on the Minnesota Fathers' Adoption Registry and completed and mailed the necessary forms. The forms were postmarked September 12, 2000, 31 days after K.M.C.'s birth.

Heidbreder then commenced a paternity action in Stearns County District Court seeking a paternity adjudication and custody of K.M.C. Carton counterclaimed for custody in the event Heidbreder's attempt to block the adoption of K.M.C. was successful. Pursuant to a stipulation between Heidbreder, Carton, and respondents, the district court allowed respondents to intervene. Action on respondents' adoption petition was stayed pending resolution of Heidbreder's paternity action. K.M.C. has remained in respondents' care throughout these proceedings.

Respondents moved to dismiss Heidbreder's paternity action on the grounds that Minn.Stat. § 259.52, subd. 8, barred Heidbreder from asserting parental rights to K.M.C. because he failed to register with the Minnesota Fathers' Adoption Registry before K.M.C. was more than 30 days old and he was not otherwise entitled to notice of an adoption petition under Minn.Stat. § 259.49, subd. 1(b) (2000). Heidbreder argued that his failure to timely file should be excused because Carton engaged in fraud by failing to disclose her location. He also challenged the constitutionality of Minn.Stat. §§ 259.49 and 259.52.

The district court treated respondents' motion to dismiss as a motion for summary judgment under Minn. R. Civ. P. 56. *See* Minn. R. Civ. P. 12.03 (allowing district court to treat motion to dismiss as motion for summary judgment if matters outside the pleadings are presented). The district court granted respondents summary judgment.

* * *

Heidbreder appealed and the court of appeals affirmed. We granted review to address Heidbreder's claims that (1) his failure to comply with the requirements of Minn.Stat. §§ 259.49 and 259.52 is excused due to fraud by Carton; (2) he should be permitted to pursue his paternity action because he substantially complied with Minn.Stat. § 259.52; (3) the deadline for registration with the Minnesota Fathers' Adoption Registry is a statute of limitations that is tolled by Carton's fraudulent concealment of her location; (4) equitable estoppel bars respondents and Carton from challenging the timeliness of his registration; and (5) Minn.Stat. §§ 259.49 and 259.52 as applied to Heidbreder violate due process and equal protection.

* * *

II.

Historically, most states, including Minnesota, did not recognize a putative father's[2] parental rights to a child and did not require that the putative father be given notice of the filing of a petition for adoption or that he consent to an adoption. * * *

In 1972, the United States Supreme Court recognized that a putative father with an established relationship with his children has a liberty interest in the "companionship, care, custody, and management of his * * * children" and that this interest warrants protection absent a "powerful countervailing interest." *Stanley v. Illinois,* 405 U.S. 645, 651, 92 S.Ct. 1208, 31 L.Ed.2d 551 (1972). The court invalidated an Illinois statute that had the effect of presuming all putative fathers unfit to parent and rejected Illinois' assertion that because "most unmarried fathers are unsuitable and neglectful parents," it could deem *all* putative fathers

[2]   A "putative father" is a man who may be the child's father but who was not married to the birth mother on or before the date of birth and has not established paternity in a court proceeding. Minn. Stat. § 259.21, subd. 12 (2000).

unfit. The court held that Illinois' interest in convenience did not justify denying a putative father a hearing on his fitness.

Following *Stanley*, the Minnesota Legislature amended the adoption laws to recognize the rights of a putative father. * * *

The court describes legislation enacted in 1974, and notes that while the new laws protected putative fathers' rights, they also had adverse effects on the permanence and stability of adoptions. In response to these difficulties, the legislature amended the statutes in 1997 to limit a putative father's rights regarding a child who is the subject of a pending adoption petition.

The legislature continued to require that the putative father's consent to the adoption be obtained if the putative father is entitled to notice of the adoption. Minn.Stat. § 259.24, subd. 1 (2000). It also continued to require that notice of the adoption be given to any putative father who is named on the birth certificate, has substantially supported the child, has married the birth mother, is openly living with the child or the person designated as the natural mother on the child's birth certificate, or has been adjudicated a parent of the child. Minn.Stat. § 259.49, subd. 1(b) (2000). However, the legislature limited a putative father's right to thwart a pending adoption by commencing a paternity action. The legislature provided that a putative father who commences a paternity action is entitled to notice, and therefore may block the adoption by withholding consent, if he commences his paternity action "within 30 days after the child's birth and the action is still pending" at the time the adoption petition is filed. Minn.Stat. § 259.49, subd. 1(b)(6). The statute does not require that the putative father commence his paternity action in Minnesota. The legislature also eliminated the 90/60-day rule and replaced it with a provision that entitles a putative father to notice if he registers with the newly created Minnesota Fathers' Adoption Registry under Minn.Stat. § 259.52. Minn.Stat. § 259.49, subd. 1(b)(8).

Minnesota Statutes § 259.52 provides that *any* putative father may register with the Minnesota Fathers' Adoption Registry but requires that the putative father register no later than 30 days after the birth of the child in order to retain any interest in a child who is the subject of a pending adoption petition. Minn. Stat. § 259.52, subds. 6, 7 (2000).[4] If a putative father is not entitled to notice of a petition for adoption under Minn.Stat. § 259.49, subd. 1, and does not register with the Minnesota Fathers' Adoption Registry before the child is more than 30 days old, the putative father:

---

[4]   While this change gives a putative father less time after the birth of the child to protect his parental rights than the 90/60-day rule, a putative father may register upon knowledge of the possibility of conception, i.e. upon the occurrence of sexual intercourse. Thus, the putative father has up to 10 months (9 months of pregnancy plus 30 days) to register.

(1) is barred thereafter from bringing or maintaining an action to assert any interest in the child during the pending adoption proceeding concerning the child;

(2) is considered to have waived and surrendered any right to notice of any hearing in any judicial proceeding for adoption of the child, and consent of that person to the adoption of the child is not required; and

(3) is considered to have abandoned the child.

Minn.Stat. § 259.52, subd. 8.

The legislature limited the circumstances under which a court can excuse a putative father's failure to timely register. A putative father's failure to timely register is excused if he proves by clear and convincing evidence that:

(i) it was not possible for him to register within the period of time specified in subdivision 7;

(ii) his failure to register was through no fault of his own; and

(iii) he registered within 10 days after it became possible for him to file.

The legislature further limited a putative father's right to be excused from the registration requirement by providing that "lack of knowledge of the pregnancy or birth is not an acceptable reason for failure to register."

III.

The issue in this case is whether Heidbreder's paternity action must be dismissed due to his failure to register with the Minnesota Fathers' Adoption Registry before K.M.C. was more than 30 days old. Heidbreder is barred under Minn. Stat. § 259.52, subd. 8, from maintaining his paternity action unless (1) he was entitled to notice of the adoption under Minn.Stat. § 259.49, subd. 1, (2) he timely registered with the Minnesota Fathers' Adoption Registry, or (3) his failure to timely register is excused under Minn.Stat. § 259.52, subd. 8.

Heidbreder admits he does not meet any of the criteria for notice of the adoption under Minn.Stat. § 259.49, subd. 1(b). He argues, however, that he should be "deemed" entitled to notice because he would have been named on the birth certificate but for "fraudulent collusion" by Carton and CHS and because he would have timely commenced a paternity action had Carton revealed her location. This argument is without merit. There is no basis in the language of Minn. Stat. § 259.49, subd. 1(b), for expanding the categories of putative fathers entitled to notice beyond those specifically listed.

Heidbreder concedes that his registration, filed one day late, was untimely. He argues that his failure to timely register should be excused because it was "not possible" for him to timely register and that his failure to timely register was "through no fault of his own" under Minn.Stat. § 259.52, subd. 8(i)–(iii). He asserts that it was "not possible" for him to register in Minnesota because Carton concealed her location and he did not know she was in Minnesota.

The legislature specifically provided that lack of knowledge of pregnancy or birth would not excuse a putative father's failure to timely register. Minn.Stat. § 259.52, subd. 8. It is apparent from this statutory language that the legislature intended not to excuse an untimely registration based on concealment of the fact of pregnancy or birth by the birth mother even if the concealment made it "not possible" for the putative father to timely register and his failure to timely register was "through no fault of his own." It follows that concealment by the birth mother of facts related to the pregnancy or birth, such as her location during pregnancy or at the time of birth, would also not excuse a putative father's failure to timely register even if he otherwise met the requirements of Minn.Stat. § 259.52, subd. 8(i)–(iii). Therefore, the fact that Carton concealed her location from Heidbreder does not excuse his failure to timely register with the Minnesota Fathers' Adoption Registry.

Heidbreder characterizes Carton's concealment as "fraud" and asserts that this excuses his failure to timely register because Carton's "fraud" made it "not possible" for him to timely register and made his failure to register "no fault of his own" under Minn.Stat. § 259.52, subd. 8.

We need not resolve the question of whether fraud by the birth mother excuses a putative father's failure to timely register under Minn.Stat. § 259.52 because Heidbreder cannot, as a matter of law, establish that Carton engaged in fraud.

To establish fraud, a plaintiff must demonstrate:

[T]hat [the] defendant (1) made a representation (2) that was false (3) having to do with a past or present fact (4) that is material (5) and susceptible of knowledge (6) that the representor knows to be false or is asserted without knowing whether the fact is true or false (7) with the intent to induce the other person to act (8) and the person in fact is induced to act (9) in reliance on the representation [and] (10) that the plaintiff suffered damages (11) attributable to the misrepresentation.

M.H. v. Caritas Family Servs., 488 N.W.2d 282, 289 (Minn.1992). A misrepresentation may be made by an affirmative statement that is itself false or by concealing or not disclosing certain facts that render facts disclosed misleading.

Carton's statements that she would "never ever" choose adoption and would not move to Minnesota with her mother fail to satisfy at least three elements of fraud. First, the statements concern future facts—adoption and moving to Minnesota—not past or present facts. Second, there is no evidence that at the time Carton made these statements she knew they were false. Heidbreder has presented no evidence that Carton intended to put the child up for adoption or that Carton intended to move to Minnesota when she told him she would not do either of these things. Carton testified that she moved to Minnesota on the "spur of the moment" and that she decided to put the child up for adoption after moving to Minnesota. The record does not support the conclusion that Carton knew her statements were untrue at the time she made them. Finally, there is no evidence that Carton made these statements intending to prevent Heidbreder from exercising his rights as the putative father or to induce him not to protect himself in the event she placed the child up for adoption. Thus, Heidbreder's claim that Carton committed fraud fails as a matter of law.

Heidbreder's claim that Carton engaged in fraudulent nondisclosure also fails as a matter of law. Nondisclosure does not give rise to a fraud claim unless there is "a legal or equitable obligation" to communicate facts to a particular person and that person is entitled to the information. *L & H Airco, Inc. v. Rapistan Corp., 446 N.W.2d 372, 380 (Minn.1989)*. A duty to disclose facts may exist when a fiduciary relationship exists between the parties or when disclosure would be necessary to clarify information already disclosed.

Heidbreder does not assert that Carton had a duty to clarify her prior statements that she would not put the child up for adoption and would not move to Minnesota. Rather, he asks the court to hold that Carton, as the mother of his unborn child, owed him a fiduciary duty to disclose her location because her nondisclosure prevented him from protecting his interest in K.M.C. as a putative father. At oral argument, Heidbreder's attorney clarified when the fiduciary duty on the birth mother to disclose her location should attach. He stated that the fiduciary duty should not attach based solely on the occurrence of sexual intercourse and a resulting pregnancy. Rather, he asked us to hold that a fiduciary duty attaches at the time of birth and that upon giving birth, the birth mother is required to disclose her location to a putative father whom she knows is attempting to locate her.

We decline to impose a fiduciary duty on an unmarried birth mother to disclose her location to the putative father even if she knows he wants to know her location or establish a relationship with his child. We are not aware of any court that has imposed such a fiduciary duty on an unmarried birth mother to the putative father. There are numerous situations in which an unmarried birth mother would be justified in keeping information from a putative father, including situations where the woman has fled an abusive relationship, where the pregnancy was the result of nonconsensual intercourse, or where the putative father poses a danger to the child.

Furthermore, there is no need to impose such a duty on the birth mother in the interest of protecting a putative father's interests because the legislature has provided a means for the putative father to assert his interest in his child independent of the birth mother through registration with the Minnesota Fathers' Adoption Registry. Because a putative father is able to protect his interest in his child without any assistance or information from the birth mother, the birth mother is not in a position superior to the putative father such that she should be required to provide him with information regarding her location.

Because we decline to impose a fiduciary duty on a birth mother to notify a putative father of her location at the time of birth, Carton had no duty to disclose her location to Heidbreder, and thus Heidbreder's claim of fraudulent nondisclosure fails as a matter of law.

In the absence of evidence to support a finding of fraud or fraudulent nondisclosure, there is no reason to address whether either would make it "not possible" for a putative father to register or make the putative father's failure to register "no fault of his own" under Minn.Stat. § 259.52, subd. 8(i)–(ii).

Because the legislature has provided that lack of knowledge of pregnancy or birth does not excuse a putative father's failure to timely register, it is clear that the legislature intended to foreclose the argument that the birth mother's concealment of any information relating to the pregnancy or birth, including her location during pregnancy or at the time of birth, excuses a putative father's failure to register, regardless of whether the concealment made it "not possible" for the putative father to timely register and his failure to timely register "no fault of his own." Therefore, Heidbreder's failure to timely register cannot be excused under Minn. Stat. § 259.52, subd. 8, based on Carton's concealment of her location. Because Carton did not engage in fraud, there is no need to address whether fraud by the birth mother could excuse a putative father's failure to timely register with the Minnesota Fathers' Adoption Registry.

IV.

Heidbreder argues that his registration with the Minnesota Fathers' Adoption Registry should be deemed timely because he substantially complied with the statute.

* * *

We decline to carve out a substantial compliance exception to the statutory requirement that a putative father not otherwise entitled to notice of petition for adoption under Minn.Stat. § 259.49, subd. 1, must register with the Minnesota Fathers' Adoption Registry no later than 30 days after the birth of the child in order to assert an interest in a child who is the subject of a petition for adoption. The legislature created the Minnesota Fathers' Adoption Registry after the court of appeals' decision in *A.M.P.* but did not include a substantial compliance exception. The legislature's decision to excuse a putative father's failure to timely register only if he can establish by "clear and convincing evidence" that it was "not possible" for him to have timely registered and that his failure to register was "through no fault of his own," indicates that the legislature did not want untimely registration to be excused based on the putative father's substantial compliance with the registration deadline.

We agree with Heidbreder that the purpose of the Minnesota Fathers' Adoption Registry is to provide a mechanism for identifying putative fathers and giving them notice of adoption proceedings. *See* Minn.Stat. § 259.52, subd. 1. However, adoption registries are also intended to balance the putative father's interests with those of the child, the birth mother, and adoptive parents. *See In re* Petition of K.J.R., 293 Ill.App.3d 49, 227 Ill.Dec. 190, 687 N.E.2d 113, 117 (1997). Adoption registries serve the interests of the child and adoptive parents by establishing a clear cut-off date after which there is little risk that a putative father who has failed to timely register and who is not otherwise entitled to notice can disrupt the adoptive placement. While recognizing a substantial compliance exception would benefit putative fathers who fail to timely register, such an exception would also weaken the permanence and stability adoption registries give adopted children.

In enacting Minn.Stat. § 259.52, the legislature has decided that a putative father must act promptly to assert his interest in a child. We recognize that Heidbreder's registration was only one day late. However, under the statute, Heidbreder's registration cannot be treated any differently than a registration that is one week, one month, one year, or one decade late. The state cannot give a putative father an infinite amount of time to claim an interest in the child. At some point, the putative father's interest in knowing and raising his child gives way to the child's interest in having a permanent and stable home. While the deadline here may seem unjustly short to the putative father who misses the deadline, the period is justified by the need for early permanent and stable placement. No matter how much time the legislature provides for registration, the possibility that a putative father will miss the deadline by one day can never be eliminated. We will not undermine the legislature's determination that a putative father not otherwise entitled to notice of an adoption proceeding under Minn.Stat. § 259.49, subd. 1, must register within 30 days of the child's birth to protect his interests by recognizing a substantial compliance exception for a putative father who misses the statutory deadline but claims his registration should nonetheless be recognized because he acted promptly upon learning of the need to register.

* * *

Because creating a substantial compliance exception would defeat one of the purposes of the Minnesota Fathers' Adoption Registry—permanent and stable adoptive placements—we hold that substantial compliance with the registration requirements does not excuse a putative father's failure to timely register.

V.

We also reject Heidbreder's claim that the registration deadline of 30 days after birth in Minn.Stat. § 259.52, subd. 7, is a statute of limitations that can be tolled by fraudulent concealment. Generally, a statute of limitations affects a party's remedy not his right. *See State ex rel. Moser v. Kaml,* 181 Minn. 523, 527, 233 N.W. 802, 804 (1930). Here, Minn.Stat. § 259.52 does not provide any remedy to a putative father but rather terminates a putative father's substantive rights to a child who is the subject of an adoption petition if he fails to timely register. Minn.Stat. § 259.52, subd. 8. Therefore, the registration deadline is not a statute of limitations.

Even if we were to treat the registration deadline as a statute of limitations that could be tolled by fraudulent concealment, Heidbreder would not be entitled to relief because Carton had no duty to inform Heidbreder of her location or otherwise assist him in protecting his rights. *See Lehr,* 463 U.S. at 265 n. 23, 103 S.Ct. 2985 (noting that "[i]t is a generally accepted feature of our adversary system that a potential defendant who knows that the statute of limitations is about to run has no duty to give the plaintiff advice").

VI.

Heidbreder also argues that promissory estoppel bars respondents and Carton from seeking dismissal of his paternity action because Carton promised him she would "never ever" put his child up for adoption. He also contends that respondents and Carton are barred from opposing equitable relief because Carton has "unclean hands."

A party seeking to invoke the doctrine of equitable or promissory estoppel has the burden of proving (1) that promises or inducements were made; (2) that he reasonably relied upon the promises; and (3) that he will be harmed if estoppel is not applied. We assume, as we must in reviewing summary judgment, that Carton promised Heidbreder she would never put the child up for adoption. Nonetheless, Heidbreder's promissory estoppel claim fails because we conclude that, as a matter of law, it was unreasonable for Heidbreder to rely on Carton's promise after she left him.

Carton effectively ended her romantic relationship with Heidbreder when she moved to Minnesota and refused to tell him where she was. Once that relationship ended, Heidbreder could not reasonably expect that Carton, who as far as he knew would be raising the child alone, would not reconsider her promise not to put the child up for adoption. Heidbreder was aware that Carton had suggested the possibility of adoption and that her promise not to put the child up for adoption was made after he told her he was "absolutely against" adoption because it is "not right." Heidbreder also believed Carton was "scared and confused" when she left him. Under these circumstances, Heidbreder could not reasonably believe that a "scared and confused" Carton would not reconsider adoption after she ended their relationship, moved away, and refused to reveal her location. Indeed, such actions by a birth mother, if anything, are consistent with a birth mother's decision to put her child up for adoption without interference from the putative father and would put a putative father on notice of the need to protect his rights.

Heidbreder argues that respondents and Carton cannot oppose equitable relief because Carton acted with "unclean hands." The doctrine of "unclean hands" bars a party who acted inequitably from obtaining equitable relief. It does not bar a party with "unclean hands" from opposing a request for equitable relief by the other side. Here, it is Heidbreder, not respondents, seeking equitable relief and it is irrelevant whether anyone other than Heidbreder acted with "unclean hands." Therefore, we do not need to address whether Carton, while not engaging in any fraud, acted with "unclean hands" such that respondents would not be entitled to equitable relief if they were seeking such relief.

VII.

We now turn to Heidbreder's constitutional arguments that <u>Minn.Stat. §§ 259.49 and 259.52</u> violate due process and equal protection as applied to him because they deprived him of his parental rights and gave Carton greater rights in the adoption proceeding than him.

The constitutionality of a statute is question of law that is reviewed de novo on appeal. <u>*Associated Builders & Contractors v. Ventura,* 610 N.W.2d 293, 298 (Minn.2000)</u>. Statutes are presumed to be constitutional and the party challenging the constitutionality of a statute "must meet the very heavy burden of demonstrating beyond a reasonable doubt that the statute is unconstitutional."

A. Procedural Due Process

A person may not allege a procedural due process violation unless the person has a protected property or liberty interest at stake. Heidbreder argues that he has a protected liberty interest in having a relationship with K.M.C. because he is her biological father. However, the mere existence of a biological connection between a child and a putative father does not confer due process protection on the putative father's parental interests. <u>*Lehr,* 463 U.S. at 260–61, 103 S.Ct. 2985</u> (citing <u>*Caban v. Mohammed,* 441 U.S. 380, 397, 99 S.Ct. 1760, 60 L.Ed.2d 297 (1979)</u> (Stewart, J., dissenting)). A putative father's interest in knowing his child is entitled to due process protection only when the father "demonstrates a full commitment to the responsibilities of parenthood by 'com[ing] forward to participate in the rearing of his child.' " *Lehr,* 463 U.S. at 261, 103 S.Ct. 2985 (quoting *Caban,* 441 U.S. at 392, 99 S.Ct. 1760). While the Court has never addressed the degree of involvement a putative father must have to demonstrate "a full commitment" to the responsibilities of parenthood, it has recognized that a putative father could demonstrate the required commitment if he has a "significant custodial, personal, or financial relationship" with the child. *Lehr,* 463 U.S. at 262, 103 S.Ct. 2985.

Here, Heidbreder is not entitled to due process protection of his interest in K.M.C. because he does not have a custodial, personal or financial relationship with K.M.C. Heidbreder never had a custodial right to K.M.C. *See* Minn.Stat. § 257.541, subd. 1 (2000) (providing that birth mother who is not married to child's father at time of conception or birth has sole custody of child until paternity is established in a judicial proceeding). In addition, there is no evidence in the record that would support a conclusion that Heidbreder had a personal relationship with K.M.C. The record is also void of any evidence that Heidbreder provided, or attempted to provide, financial support to Carton during her pregnancy or to K.M.C. following her birth. Therefore, due process does not require recognition of Heidbreder's interest in K.M.C. as a putative father.

> **FYI**
>
> The court discusses and quotes from the Supreme Court opinion in *Lehr,* noting the Court's observations that under the New York statutes considered in that case the right to receive notice was completely within the putative father's control, and that "a more open-ended notice requirement would merely complicate the adoption process, threaten the privacy interests of unwed mothers, create the risk of unnecessary controversy, and impair the desired finality of adoption decrees."

Because Heidbreder did not have an established relationship with K.M.C., the only due process issue is whether the state "has adequately protected his opportunity to form such a relationship." *Lehr,* 463 U.S. at 262–63, 103 S.Ct. 2985.

* * *

Heidbreder argues that the requirement that he register with the Minnesota Fathers' Adoption Registry before K.M.C. was more than 30 days old to protect his interests as a putative father is inadequate because he did not know Carton was in Minnesota, he did not know Minnesota law required him to register, and he was not required to do anything under Iowa law to receive notice of termination of his parental rights and pending adoption of his child in Iowa. However, the issue here is not whether one part of the statutory scheme—the Minnesota Fathers' Adoption Registry—adequately protected Heidbreder's interests, but whether the entire scheme adopted by the legislature adequately protected Heidbreder's opportunity to form a relationship with K.M.C. We conclude that the statutes, as applied to Heidbreder, adequately protected his opportunity to establish a relationship with K.M.C.

The statutory scheme here is almost identical to the statutory scheme upheld in *Lehr*. The only material factual distinction between the two cases is that here the putative father is not a resident of the state in which he was required to register. However, the fact that Heidbreder is not a Minnesota resident does not make the statutory scheme unconstitutional as applied to him because the scheme is not "likely to omit many responsible fathers" who live outside of Minnesota and "qualification for notice [is] not beyond the control of an interest putative father" living outside the state, *Lehr*, 463 U.S. at 264, 103 S.Ct. 2985.

In addition to registering with the Minnesota Fathers' Adoption Registry, a non-resident putative father can ensure that his parental rights are not terminated under Minn.Stat. § 259.52, subd. 8, by commencing a paternity action. *See* Minn.Stat. § 259.49, subd. 1(b)(6) (2000). There is no requirement in Minn.Stat. § 259.49, subd. 1(b)(6), that the paternity action be commenced in Minnesota. Therefore, a putative father may protect his interest in a child by commencing a paternity action in his own state before the child is more than 30 days old.

Furthermore, even though Heidbreder is an Iowa resident, Minnesota law did not foreclose his opportunity to establish the required relationship with K.M.C. Heidbreder knew or had sufficient reason to believe that Carton was not in Iowa. Therefore, it was not reasonable for him to assume he could rely exclusively on the provisions of Iowa law to protect his interests. Under the circumstances, Heidbreder could have done more than simply assume Carton "would * * * send [him] papers." Heidbreder had opportunities under Iowa law to establish a sufficient commitment. He could have registered with the Iowa Declaration of Paternity Registry or commenced a paternity action in Iowa.[14] In addition, while Heidbreder did not know with certainty where Carton was, he had sufficient information to put him on notice that it was possible she was in Illinois or Minnesota. Both Illinois and Minnesota provided Heidbreder with the opportunity to establish a commitment. Heidbreder could have commenced a paternity action in either state or registered with the adoption registries provided by both states. Any of the above options would have put Heidbreder in a position to argue he established a sufficient commitment to warrant due process protection.[16] Therefore, as applied

---

[14]   A putative father may commence a paternity action in Iowa according to the same procedure applicable to a paternity action brought by the birth mother. See Iowa Code § 600B.7 (2001). A birth mother may commence a paternity action during the pregnancy. Iowa Code § 600B.9 (2001).

[16]   We note that registration with another state's registry does not entitle a putative father to notice under Minn.Stat. §§ 259.49 or 259.52. If registration with an adoption registry in any state is, by itself, sufficient to demonstrate a substantial commitment to the child, then arguably a putative father is entitled to due process protection regardless of whether state law recognizes such registration. We need not address the issue here because we are not presented with a situation in which a putative father registered with another state's registry.

to the circumstances of this case, Minn.Stat. §§ 259.49 and 259.52 adequately protected Heidbreder's opportunity to establish the required commitment necessary for due process protection to arise.

That the statutes could provide more time or greater opportunity for the putative father to establish the required relationship is a policy decision that is left to the legislature. The Court recognized in *Lehr* that the legislature may require strict adherence to statutory procedures as long as the statute satisfies due process constraints. 463 U.S. at 265, 103 S.Ct. 2985. The Minnesota Legislature has made policy choices similar to those made by the New York Legislature at issue in *Lehr.* Because the statutes provide adequate notice and opportunity to be heard to someone who has established a sufficient relationship to create a protected liberty interest and also adequately protected Heidbreder's opportunity to create such a relationship, the statutes satisfy due process requirements.

B. Equal Protection

Heidbreder claims that Minn.Stat. §§ 259.49 and 259.52 violate equal protection as applied to him because Carton receives more favorable treatment under the statutes than he in the proceeding for the adoption of K.M.C. This argument is without merit. It is well established that the state can treat unmarried parents differently with respect to their rights in an adoption proceeding based on each parent's relationship to the child. *Lehr,* 463 U.S. at 267–68, 103 S.Ct. 2985. Equal protection does not prohibit the state from treating a birth mother with an established custodial relationship with the child more favorably than a putative father who does not have an established relationship. *Id.* As the birth mother, Carton had an established custodial relationship with K.M.C. under Minnesota law. *See* Minn.Stat. § 257.541, subd. 1. In contrast, Heidbreder did not have an established relationship with K.M.C., nor did he avail himself of the opportunities provided to him to establish such a relationship. Under these circumstances, Carton and Heidbreder were not similarly situated with respect to their relationship to K.M.C., and equal protection does not require the legislature to give Heidbreder the same opportunity as Carton to voice an opinion about K.M.C.'s best interests or to block the adoption by withholding consent.

VIII.

The dissent asserts that in our "arrogance" we have foreclosed the possibility that the best interests of the child can be met by having a permanent and stable relationship with the child's biological father. The legislature has concluded, however, that a child's best interests will be served in an adoption proceeding if the rights of any putative father not entitled to notice of her adoption under Minn.

Stat. § 259.49 are terminated unless the putative father registered with the Minnesota Fathers' Adoption Registry before the child is more than 30 days old or the putative father's failure to register is excused under Minn.Stat. § 259.52, subd. 8(i)–(iii). Our decision today is not made in arrogance, but rather in deference to the legislature's determination of when a child's interest in permanence and stability in an adoptive placement takes priority over any interest a putative father has in establishing a relationship with the child. The legislature has carefully balanced the different interests of the child and putative father, and its decision, as applied to Heidbreder, does not violate the constitution. Under these circumstances, nothing would be more arrogant than for us to disregard the legislature's decision concerning the best interests of a child out of a desire to give a putative father time beyond that prescribed by the legislature to assert an interest in a child.

> **FYI**
>
> Three justices dissented, concluding that Heidbreder's failure to file with the Registry within thirty days of the child's birth should have been excused under the statute: "As a practical matter, it was 'not possible' for Heidbreder to register in any state, given that he did not know and had no way of knowing where Carton was living after she left Iowa." The dissenters also concluded that Heidbreder had "grasped the opportunity and demonstrated a full commitment to the responsibilities of parenthood by coming forward to participate in the rearing of his child" and therefore that denying him a remedy was a violation of his constitutional rights under *Lehr*. Heidbreder's petition for certiorari was denied. Heidbreder v. Carton, 537 U.S. 1046 (2002).

Affirmed.

Points for Discussion

a. Nonmarital Father's Constitutional Rights

After *Lehr v. Robertson*, state courts and legislatures confronted the question of when unmarried biological fathers had the right to receive notice and give consent before their parental rights were terminated in an adoption. With respect to older children, *Lehr's* focus on whether the father had filed in the state paternity registry and developed a relationship with the child—an approach sometimes described as "biology

> **Make the Connection**
>
> *Lehr v. Robertson* is reprinted in Chapter 2.

plus"—presented a fairly clear standard for when biological fathers had the right to participate in adoption proceedings. The ruling encouraged states to utilize putative father registries like the one the Supreme Court approved in *Lehr*.

In cases involving very young children, however, and fathers who have had little or no opportunity to step forward after their child was born, *Lehr* is less helpful. This is not surprising: Justice Stevens, author of the majority opinion in *Lehr*, had previously filed a dissent in <u>*Caban v. Mohammed*</u>, arguing that men and women are differently situated in the context of pregnancy and childbirth, and that mothers should have the exclusive right to consent to adoption of a newborn nonmarital child. On the other side, three justices dissented in *Lehr*, arguing that a unmarried father's biological connection should be sufficient standing alone to trigger some level of constitutional protection. Since *Lehr*, the Supreme Court has repeatedly declined to consider whether the Due Process or Equal Protection Clauses protect an unwed father's opportunity to develop a relationship with his biological child, leaving the problem to be resolved by state courts and legislatures.

See generally Deborah L. Forman, <u>*Unwed Fathers and Adoption: A Theoretical Analysis in Context*, 72 Tex. L. Rev. 967 (1994)</u>; Mary L. Shanley, <u>*Unwed Fathers' Rights, Adoption, and Sex Equality: Gender-Neutrality and the Perpetuation of Patriarchy*, 95 Colum. L. Rev. 60 (1995)</u>.

Go Online

Find state laws on the <u>rights of unmarried fathers</u> through the <u>Child Welfare Information Gateway</u> web site.

b. Statutory Protections for Putative Fathers

All states have provisions for voluntary acknowledgement of parentage of a nonmarital child as discussed in Chapter 2. Many states have putative father registries, and others allow for filing an affidavit or acknowledgment with a court. See also Laura Oren, <u>*Thwarted Fathers or Pop-Up Pops?: How to Determine When Putative Fathers Can Block the Adoption of Their Newborn Children*, 40 Fam. L.Q. 153, 170–75 (2006)</u>. Would the result in *Heidbreder* have been different if he had registered with the Iowa putative fathers registry before the child's birth? Cf. <u>In re Mary G., 59 Cal.Rptr.3d 703 (Cal. Ct. App. 2007)</u>; <u>Adoption of K.C.J., 184 P.3d 1239 (Utah Ct. App. 2008)</u>.

Under the Minnesota statute applied in *Heidbreder*, what if the father had registered with the putative father registry in Iowa or Illinois before the child's birth? <u>Nevares v. M.L.S., 345 P.3d 719 (Utah 2015)</u>, applied a Utah statute requiring notice to an unmarried biological father who has fully complied with any requirements to preserve the right to notice under the law of the state where the child was conceived, or the last state where he knew or should have known that the mother had resided before executing her consent to adoption of the child. In that case, the child was conceived in Colorado, where the law preserves the parental rights of an unwed father and requires that courts inquire into his identity and provide notice of proceedings.

c. Parentage Laws and Adoption

By defining who is a "parent," state parentage laws define who is entitled to parental rights, including the right to notice and to consent to an adoption. For example, UPA 1973 § 24 required that notice of adoption proceedings be provided to any presumed father, and § 25 provided that when a mother proposed to relinquish a child with no presumed or adjudicated father, the court must "cause inquiry to be made of the mother" in order to identify the natural father. Any person identified as a possible natural father was entitled to receive notice of the proceeding. If the court was unable to identify the natural father, it was required to determine whether notice by publication or public posting would be likely to lead to identification of the unknown father. If no father was determined, the court could enter an order terminating the unknown father's parental rights, which became final after a period of six months.

Under the UPA 2017, § 402 requires that a man file with the paternity registry before the child's birth or not later than 30 days after the child's birth in order to be notified of adoption or termination of parental rights proceedings regarding his genetic child, but provides that he is not required to register if his parent-child relationship has been legally established or if he commences a proceeding to adjudicate parentage before a court terminates his parental rights. For a child under one year of age, § 405 states that notice to a man who may be a genetic father is not required if the man did not register and is not exempt from registration under § 402. For a child who has attained one year of age, § 405 states that notice of a proceeding for adoption or termination of parental rights must be given "to each alleged genetic father of the child, whether or not he has registered. . .unless his parental rights have already been terminated." Would this statute have protected Mr. Heidbreder's claim to notice and an opportunity for a hearing? What policies explain this distinction between younger and older children?

d. Thwarted Fathers

As judges and legislators have confronted the problem considered in *Heidbreder*, two different approaches have emerged. A number of states take the approach described in *Heidbreder,* requiring nonmarital fathers to take specific steps in order to participate in adoption proceedings, often within a very short time after the child's birth. In Nebraska, for example, the time limit may be as short as five days. See Neb. Rev. Stat. §43–104.02 (2012). As in *Heidbreder*, courts in these states generally refused to grant equitable relief from these deadlines. E.g. Paternity of M.G.S., 756 N.E.2d 990 (Ind.Ct.App. 2001) (refusing to excuse delay based on mother's representations); Adoption of Baby Girl H., 635 N.W.2d 256 (Neb. 2001) (denying relief where father's petition was filed in county rather than district court). But see Jeremiah J. v. Dakota D., 826 N.W.2d 242 (Neb. 2013), holding that a birth mother might be equitably estopped from invoking the five-day limit in the Nebraska statute when the father had filed two days after the baby's due date and the mother had taken steps to hide the fact of the child's birth from him.

In another group of states, including New York and California, courts hold that a nonmarital father has a constitutional right under *Lehr* to prevent termination of his parental rights for a third-party adoption if he can show that he has demonstrated a substantial commitment to becoming a parent. Courts in these states inquire into the father's conduct both before and after the child's birth, considering such matters as the father's willingness to assume custody of the child and his contribution toward pregnancy and birth expenses. Because of the focus on pre-birth conduct, fathers who do not act until after the child is born may be not be able to veto an adoption. See Adoption of Kelsey S., 823 P.2d 1216 (Cal. 1992); and In re Raquel Marie X., 559 N.E.2d 418 (N.Y. 1990), cert. denied sub nom. Robert C. v. Miguel T., 498 U.S. 984 (1990).

Under either approach, the most difficult cases are ones involving perjured testimony or coordinated efforts to exclude an unmarried biological father from the adoption consent process. In *Heidbreder*, what should the result have been under the Minnesota statute if the birth mother had told the agency representative the name of the child's birth father, and the agency had concealed that information from the court? Fathers thwarted by this kind of misconduct may have greater success in having an adoption set aside. See, e.g., In re Baby Boy W., 988 P.2d 1270 (Okla. 1999). See generally Laura Oren, *Thwarted Fathers or Pop-Up Pops?: How to Determine When Putative Fathers Can Block the Adoption of Their Newborn Children*, 40 Fam. L.Q. 153 (2006); see also Ardis L. Campbell, Annotation, *Rights of Unwed Father to Obstruct Adoption of His Child by Withholding Consent*, 61 A.L.R.5th 151(1998).

Baby Jessica and Baby Richard

Several "thwarted father" cases drew wide attention in the 1990s, particularly when courts ordered that young children must be returned to their biological fathers after living for several years with adoptive families. One was the "Baby Jessica" case, litigated in Iowa and Michigan, which was highlighted on the cover of Time magazine and in Lucinda Franks, *The War for Baby Clausen*, The New Yorker, Mar. 22, 1993, at 56. See In Interest of B.G.C., 496 N.W.2d 239 (Iowa 1992), and In re Clausen, 502 N.W.2d 649 (Mich. 1993). Several years later, the "Baby Richard" decision in Illinois drew similar criticism; see In re Doe, 638 N.E.2d 181 (Ill. 1994), cert. denied sub nom Baby Richard v. Kirchner, 513 U.S. 994 (1994), and In re Kirchner, 649 N.E.2d 324 (Ill. 1995), cert. denied sub nom. Doe v. Kirchner, 515 U.S. 1152 (1995) overruled on other grounds in In re R.L.S., 844 N.E.2d 22 (Ill. 2006).

In cases such as these, how should the courts consider the effects on the child of changing custody after a long period in the care of the prospective adoptive parents? If an adoption consent is held to be invalid, should the court go on to consider whether or not returning custody to the natural parents is in the child's best interests? Could a different remedy be ordered? Should the child or the adoptive parents be understood to have any constitutionally-protected rights to continue their relationship?

Problem 3-4

When Stephanie, age 16, learned that she was pregnant, she and her boyfriend, Mark, agreed that the child should be placed for adoption with John and Margaret. Mark wanted to marry Stephanie, but she declined to marry him until she finished high school and he quit drinking and using drugs. Mark was arrested after a violent outburst, and he spent the final months of Stephanie's pregnancy in a rehabilitation program, where he resolved to get his life together and decided that he did not want to give up his child for adoption. Mark found an attorney, who called John and Margaret and learned that the baby had been born a week earlier. Mark immediately filed an action seeking determination of his parental rights and custody. He purchased supplies to care for the baby and sent out birth announcements. John and Margaret filed a petition to terminate Mark's parental rights and adopt the child. Under the applicable statute, Mark was not a presumed father and was therefore not entitled to notice or a right to veto the proposed adoption. How should the court evaluate Mark's claim? Has he "promptly come forward and demonstrated a full commitment to his parental responsibilities"? Should it make a difference if the sexual relationship between Mark and Stephanie was illegal in the state based on the difference in their ages? (See Adoption of Michael H., 898 P.2d 891 (Cal. 1995); In re Kyle F., 5 Cal.Rptr.3d 190 (Ct. App. 2003).)

Problem 3-5

Mary was involved in a sexual relationship with Frank that resulted in Mary giving birth to a daughter. Mary never told Frank that she was pregnant and ended the relationship before the child was born. She placed the child for adoption immediately after her birth, and refused to disclose the name of Frank to the court. She told the court that Frank was extremely aggressive and that if he found out about the child he would harass her and her family. Furthermore, she felt that Frank would neither be able to care for the child, nor would he want to. The court determined that under these facts, Frank was not entitled to notice of the adoption proceedings and terminated both parents' parental rights. Is this procedure constitutional? (See In re Karen A.B., 513 A.2d 770 (Del.1986).)

Problem 3-6

Melanie, an unmarried girl of fourteen, became pregnant. After talking it over with her parents and with a social worker, she decides she would like to place the baby for adoption. She took the appropriate steps under local law to relinquish the child as soon as it is born, telling the social worker that she does not know who the father of the child is. She says she got drunk at a party and had sexual relations with three boys, none of whose names she knew. She has never seen any of the boys again. If you represent the adoption agency, and want to ensure that the baby's adoption is not vulnerable to a legal challenge, how would you draft a notice for publication that satisfies the Due Process Clause and does not violate the privacy rights of the mother or the child? Should the mother's name be included in the notice? (Cf. G.P. v. State, 842 So.2d 1059 (Fla. Dist. Ct. App. 2003); Jones v. South Carolina Department of Social Services, 534 S.E.2d 713 (S.C. Ct. App.2000).)

Problem 3-7

Natalie, an unwed teenage mother, secretly placed her newborn child for adoption out of state with the help of her parents. Joey, Natalie's boyfriend, had made several attempts to assert his parental rights and gain custody of the child, both before and after the child's birth. Under the applicable state statute, fathers in Joey's situation are not entitled to notice of an adoption proceeding, and their assent to the child's adoption is not required. Joey has sued Natalie and her parents for intentional infliction of emotional distress. Should he be entitled to pursue this claim? (See Smith v. Malouf, 722 So.2d 490 (Miss.1998); Kessel v. Leavitt, 511 S.E.2d 720 (W.Va. 1998).)

Newborn "Safe Haven" Laws

Legislatures in virtually every state and Puerto Rico have responded to news stories about newborn children who are found abandoned by enacting laws that allow relinquishment of very young children anonymously or with an assurance of confidentiality and with no risk of criminal prosecution unless there is evidence of abuse of neglect. In some states, the child must not be more than 72 hours old, in others the child may be up to one month old, and most other states have limits of less than a month, although a few allow relinquishment of children up to a year of age. See, e.g., Tex. Fam. Code Ann. §262.301 et seq. (Vernon 2018) (up to 60 days). A summary and links to safe haven laws are available through from the Child Welfare Information Gateway.

Although several states require a search of the putative father registry for a child who has been abandoned in this manner, it is obviously difficult to provide notice when there is no information available about the child's history. How should state legislatures weigh the interests and constitutional rights of unknown fathers in this context? See Laura Oren, *Thwarted Fathers or Pop-Up Pops?: How to Determine When Putative Fathers Can Block the Adoption of Their Newborn Children*, 40 Fam. L.Q. 153 (2006).

In the Matter of J.J.J., A Minor

718 P.2d 948 (Alaska 1986)

OPINION

MOORE, JUSTICE.

This is an expedited appeal from an adoption decree whereby a 7-year-old boy was adopted by his stepfather over the objections of the boy's biological father. Because of the biological father's history of nonsupport, his consent was deemed unnecessary.

The primary issue in this case is whether the master erred in finding that for at least a 12-month period, the biological father failed significantly without justifiable cause to provide support required by judicial decree. This finding was sustained by the superior court. A second issue is whether the superior court erred in reversing the master's determination that it was not in the best interests of the child for the adoption to be granted. Lastly, at issue is whether the superior court erred in ruling that the biological father could, upon a proper showing be granted enforceable post-adoption visitation rights.

We conclude that the superior court correctly affirmed the master's finding with respect to support and correctly reversed her best interests determination. However, the superior court erred in allowing for post-adoption visitation rights.[2]

I. BACKGROUND SUMMARY

On May 25, 1982 the boy's biological parents were divorced. B.J., the biological mother, was awarded custody of the boy and J.B., the biological father, was ordered to pay $200 per month as child support. J.B. made no payments until August 1982, when he made a single $200 payment after being contacted by the Child Support Enforcement Agency (C.S.E.A.).

Thereafter, from September 1982 through March 1983, J.B. made no payments toward the support of the boy. In April and May of 1983 the C.S.E.A. garnished a total of $1,000 of J.B.'s wages to apply toward his child support arrearages. Thereafter, from May through October 1983, J.B. continued to pay nothing toward the boy's support.[3]

---

[2] This precise issue was recently decided in *In the Matter of W.E.G. and J.R.G.*, 710 P.2d 410 (Alaska 1985). We held that AS 25.23.130 precludes granting post-adoption visitation to biological relatives of an adopted child.

[3] J.B.'s earnings in 1982 appear to have been $22,518; his earnings during three quarters of 1983 appear to have been $18,750.

In August 1983 the boy's mother and his stepfather, S.J., decided that S.J. should seek to adopt the boy and so advised J.B. In November 1983, shortly before the filing of the adoption petition, J.B. and his new wife paid $1,800 against part of his child support arrearages, after again being contacted by the C.S.E.A.

From December 1981 until the filing of the adoption petition, on December 19, 1983, J.B. had almost no contact with the boy. Twice during the last six months of this period J.B. reportedly informed the boy's mother, B.J., that he now wanted to visit the boy. However, B.J. resisted J.B.'s request for unsupervised visitation with the boy, stating that she believed that J.B. should slowly develop a relationship with the boy after having had no contact with him for such a long period. It does appear that, beginning well before the divorce, J.B. virtually ignored the boy.

During the period since his marriage to B.J., the boy's stepfather evidently established a close parental relationship with the boy.

In December 1983 the boy's stepfather, S.J., filed the petition to adopt him. The biological father, J.B., refused to consent to the adoption. The stepfather contended that J.B.'s consent was unnecessary pursuant to AS 25.23.050(a) (2) (B), because J.B. had "failed significantly, without justifiable cause. . .to provide for the care and support of the child as required by law or judicial decree."

The probate master found that J.B. had, for at least a year, significantly and unjustifiably failed to provide court-ordered support and had lost his right to withhold consent to the adoption. However, the master also found that the adoption decree would not be in the boy's best interests because he was curious about his biological father and seemed interested in knowing him (notwithstanding the boy's attachment to his stepfather). By law an adoption decree would terminate J.B.'s parental rights regarding the boy.

The superior court sustained the master's finding on consent, but overturned the "best interest" finding as clearly erroneous. The court also concluded that the adoption should be granted and that "upon a proper showing, the biological father can be afforded visitation rights." This expedited appeal followed.

II. DISCUSSION

A. STEPPARENT ADOPTION IN ALASKA

As commentators have noted, the very problem now before us is an increasingly common occurrence, given the increase in divorce and remarriage in our society. Nevertheless, despite voluntarily assumed obligations and the existence of a strong bond between stepparent and stepchild, such a relationship lacks legal protection in the event of the desertion or death of the stepparent's spouse (the custodial "natural" parent). In such an event the noncustodial "natural" parent, even a parent who has rarely paid child support or merely made an occasional gesture of communication, may automatically assert primary rights to take legal custody of the child, despite the child's need for a stable and continuous family relationship. Stepparent adoption assures that the child may remain with his existing family. However, adoption has seemed a harsh remedy when the biological parent refuses consent. In Alaska, as in most states, an adoption decree has the effect of terminating an adopted child's legal relationship with all of his blood relatives.

Well-known commentators have proposed "incomplete adoption" as a middle approach that would better accommodate the interests of both the stepparent and the noncustodial natural parent by giving equal custody rights to each. However, the Alaska legislature apparently has not yet considered this modern approach that would allow the courts a more reasonable choice in deciding stepfamily cases. Unfortunately, the present law's all-or-nothing approach is unrealistic and often compels an unfair result for a child, for a stepfamily, or for a noncustodial "natural" parent. We are therefore left with the harsh choices inherent in deciding between adoption or no adoption at all.

Alaska has adopted a modified version of the <u>Uniform Adoption Act</u>.[12] The Uniform Adoption Act sets forth the circumstances under which an adoption should be granted without a natural parent's consent, including a provision indicating that the court must consider the best interests of the child in determining whether to grant an adoption.[13] Alaska's version of the Act focuses on a noncustodial parent's failure to meaningfully communicate with a child, significant failure to pay child support, and other acts of abandonment.

In this court's prior decisions in this area we have declined to dispense with a noncustodial parent's right to withhold consent to a stepparent adoption as long as the noncustodial parent had made a few perfunctory communications or an occasional gesture of support. In <u>*Matter of Adoption of K.M.M.*, 611 P.2d</u>

---

[12] * * *

Alaska is not among those states whose approach to allowing stepparent adoptions without the noncustodial natural parent's consent emphasizes the best interests of the child. Indeed, this court has repeatedly ruled that a child's best interest is not relevant to a determination of whether a noncustodial natural parent's consent is unnecessary. <u>D.L.J. v. W.D.R., 635 P.2d 834 (Alaska 1981)</u>; <u>*Adoption of L.A.H.*, 597 P.2d 513 (Alaska 1979)</u>; <u>*Adoption of K.S.*, 543 P.2d 1191 (Alaska 1975)</u>. Many other states, however, have taken a different position and favor considering the child's best interests. *See, e.g.,* <u>Ariz. Rev.Stat.Ann. § 8–106</u> (West Supp.1980–81); <u>Conn.Gen.Stat.Ann. § 45–61F(d)</u> (West Supp.1980); <u>D.C.Code Ann. § 16–304 (1973)</u>; <u>Idaho Code §§ 16–1504, 16–2005 (1979)</u>; Md.Ann.Code art. 16, § 74 (1981); and <u>Mass.Gen.Laws Ann. ch. 210, § 3</u> (West Supp.1981). *See also* Comment, *A Survey Of State Law Authorizing Stepparent Adoptions Without The Non-Custodial Parent's Consent,* 15 Akron L.Rev. 567, 577–79 (1982).

[13] Uniform Adoption Code § 6, 9 U.L.A. 26 (Amended 1971).

84 (Alaska 1980), we found that the biological father's unwillingness to visit his children for over one year was justified by "the mere fact that it was emotionally traumatic for the natural father to see his children and former wife living with a man who had been the father's closest friend." R.N.T. v. J.R.G., 666 P.2d 1036, 1039 (Alaska 1983), discussing *Matter of Adoption of K.M.M.* In R.N.T. v. J.R.G. this court reversed a superior court's decision to allow a stepfather to adopt the children of R.N.T. because R.N.T. had not maintained meaningful communication with his young children during the 14-month period that he was in prison. We emphasized that parental conduct that causes the loss of a parent's right to consent must be *willful,* noting that the commentary to the Uniform Adoption Act makes it clear that the willfulness requirement was intended to be continued in the Uniform Adoption Act. * * * Upon reflection, however, we now find that the *R.N.T.* dissent actually presented the better approach:

* * *

> It is true * * * that the adoption statutes must be strictly construed in favor of the natural parent. We did not, however, judicially abrogate the provision by which the consent of a parent is not required if the parent has failed significantly without justifiable cause to communicate meaningfully with the children. This court concludes that anytime a parent is precluded from communicating with his or her children, whether or not the constraints are a result of the parent's own conduct, "the failure to communicate is properly considered non-willful and thus justifiable cause." * * * Such a result can frequently reward the guilty and punish the innocent. This is certainly not mandated by Alaska's statutes.

R.N.T. v. J.R.G., 666 P.2d at 1041–42 (Compton, J., dissenting).

We take this opportunity to clarify that, in order for a noncustodial parent to block a stepparent adoption, he or she must have maintained *meaningful* contact with a child, and must have provided regular payments of child support, unless prevented from doing so by circumstances beyond the noncustodial parent's control. Circumstances resulting from the noncustodial parent's own conduct cannot excuse such a parent's significant failure to provide support or maintain meaningful communication. Moreover, failure to support or to maintain contact with a child should not be excused by the emotional antagonism or awkwardness that may exist between former spouses. * * *

B. J.B.'S SIGNIFICANT FAILURE TO SUPPORT

AS 25.23.050(a) specifies: "Persons as to whom consent and notice not required" in adoption cases. This provision provides that consent is not required of

(1) . . .a parent who has abandoned a child for not less than six months,

(2) a parent of a child in the custody of another, if the parent for a period of at least one year has failed significantly without justifiable cause, including but not limited to indigency,

(A) to communicate meaningfully with the child, or

(B) to provide for the care and support of the child as required by law or judicial decree. . . .

J.B. contends that the "period of at least one year" of significant nonsupport must immediately precede the adoption petition. We disagree, as do other courts. J.B. also suggests that his occasional payment should suffice to preserve his right to withhold consent to any adoption of J.J.J.

The statute does *not* say that the period of "at least one year" must immediately precede the filing of an adoption petition. One year is the minimum period which may be considered. Thus the superior court correctly considered the entire 17-month period during which J.B. made only one voluntary payment of $200 on his court-ordered obligation to contribute to J.J.J.'s support.

Sporadic partial payments do not preclude a finding of significant failure to provide child support. Child support payments should be substantial or "regular" and constitute a "material factor" in the support of a child. * * *

The dissent insists that "no rule of law or principle of logic" requires that child support must be "uncompelled". However, the purpose of the waiver-of-consent statute was to provide an *objective measure* (at least one year) of when a parent has, in the *practical* sense, forsaken a child. It would make no sense at all to infer parental concern from payments that a government agency has to garnish from the income of a parent who has refused to provide support. Nevertheless, the dissent suggests that payments garnished from a recalcitrant parent's income should signify the same parental concern that voluntary support payments signify, because all court-ordered child support is "compelled" and "there is no certainty what the terms 'compulsion' or 'voluntary' mean" in this context. Actually, at common law all parents have a *duty* (not a "voluntary" option) to support their children. Court orders for child support set forth the amount of the parent's obligation. Most parents *choose* to *abide* by what the courts determine to be the child's financial needs. Garnishment occurs only as a last resort, when a parent has *refused* to meet this important obligation. Common sense tells us that a person who chooses to meet his obligations shows more responsibility than a person who forces the C.S.E.A. to garnish his income or attach his assets. The existence of an *obligation* does not mean that an individual's choices have no significance. We decline to dwell any further on this aspect of the "free will" debate.

As for J.B.'s 11th-hour (or 19th-month) payment to partially pay off his arrearages a few weeks before the adoption petition was filed, it would be absurd to believe that the legislature meant for a last-minute balloon payment to cancel out the import of a substantial period of nonsupport and noninvolvement.

* * *

We hold that courts shall consider a parent's *entire history* of support or nonsupport to determine whether that parent has waived his or her right to block a child's adoption by a stepparent.[21]

* * *

J.B. also argues that his significant failure to support the boy was the excusable result of his ex-wife's resistance to his belated interest in having the boy visit him, in August 1983, after more than a year of no communication at all with him. This, however, is no justification at all. Many decisions have held, and we agree, that a parent's duty to provide child support is not excused by the conduct of others unless that conduct actually prevents performance of the child-support obligation. *See, e.g., Pender v. McKee,* 582 S.W.2d at 935–36; *Adoption of Infants Reynard,* 252 Ind. 632, 251 N.E.2d 413, 417 (1969).

C. THE CHILD'S BEST INTERESTS

The probate master found that although J.B.'s consent to the boy's adoption was unnecessary because of his significant failure to provide support, the adoption should nonetheless be denied because the boy might benefit from renewed contact with J.B. We conclude that the superior court correctly overruled the probate master on this issue. The master's finding that the boy's adoption would not be in his best interest was clearly erroneous.

In AS 25.24.150(c) the legislature has set forth statutory standards to guide the trial courts in the difficult determination of a child's best interests in custody disputes. The statute directs the courts to consider:

(1) the physical, emotional, mental, religious, and social needs of the child;
(2) the capability and desire of each parent to meet these needs;
(3) the child's preference if the child is of sufficient age and capacity to form a preference;
(4) the love and affection existing between the child and each parent;

---

[21] If, for instance, four years ago a parent significantly failed to support a child for a year, but thereafter (for the next three years) fully supported the child until the filing of an adoption petition, a court should find that that parent had *not* waived his or her right to withhold consent to the child's adoption. Although the dissent labels our position "harsh," this opinion actually considers the broader picture of the problems posed and recognizes that a child *needs* regular support (and meaningful communication) in the here-and-now. A young child's needs cannot be put on hold for years until a parent *might* have a "change of heart."

(5) the length of time the child has lived in a stable, satisfactory environment and the desirability of maintaining continuity;

(6) the desire and ability of each parent to allow an open and loving frequent relationship between the child and the other parent.

Although the probate master correctly considered the boy's curiosity about his long-absent biological father, this single factor is far outweighed by other significant factors and thus does not justify the master's finding that the adoption would not be in the boy's best interests. * * * Most of the factors listed above greatly favor the strong relationship between the boy and his stepfather. The evidence demonstrated that J.B. was a virtual stranger to the boy. In contrast to J.B.'s extended period of noninvolvement with the boy, the record shows that the stepfather has been an exceptionally involved and devoted parent.

* * *

* * * Even though we have liberally construed the controlling statute in the noncustodial parent's favor, we are not compelled to render it so meaningless that courts can never dispense with a noncustodial parent's consent to an adoption.

* * *

THEREFORE, except for the superior court's order as to the possibility of granting post-adoption visitation to J.B., the superior court's decree of adoption is AFFIRMED.

> **FYI**
>
> There was a dissent in *J.J.J.*, arguing that the one-year period in the statute should be construed to refer to the year immediately preceding the filing of the petition, and also taking the position that all of the father's payments should count.

Points for Discussion

a. Stepparent Adoption

Although the United States does not maintain comprehensive adoption statistics, it appears that a substantial majority of adoptions are by persons already related to the child, particularly stepparents. As illustrated by *Matter of J.J.J.,* stepparent adoptions are generally favored under the law.

J.B.'s parental rights could not have been involuntarily terminated in a dependency and neglect action without considerably greater procedural and substantive protection than he was afforded in this case. Moreover, in involuntary termination proceedings parents are often given an opportunity to rehabilitate themselves in order to avoid termination of their parental rights. These laws are addressed in Chapter 5. In both situations, however, the result is a complete severance of the natural parent's rights. What justifies the different standard for termination in a stepparent adoption proceeding? Should a court consider as a factor in a stepparent adoption whether the natural parent has demonstrated that despite his past failure to pay support, he is willing and able to pay his arrears and provide consistent support in the future? See E.R.S. v. O.D.A., 779 P.2d 844 (Colo.1989) (court must consider whether there is any likelihood that the natural parent will provide child support); see also Del.Code.Ann. tit. 13 § 1103 (2018). If B.J. and J.B. had been granted joint legal custody, could J.B.'s parental rights have been terminated under the statute applied in *J.J.J.*? See In re AJR, 834 N.W.2d 904 (Mich. Ct. App. 2013).

Practice Pointer

Given the high rate of remarriage after divorce, the availability and grounds for stepparent adoption should be discussed with all parties as part of their representation in a divorce.

b. Failure to Support

The one-year nonsupport requirement is common to many stepparent adoption statutes, although as noted by the court in *J.J.J.*, states differ in their interpretation of this rule. Some statutes explicitly define the twelve month period as that immediately preceding the filing of the adoption petition. E.g., Ohio Rev.Code § 3107.07(A) (2018); Oregon Rev.Stat. § 109.324 (2018); Wyo. Stat. § 1–22–110(a)(iv) (2018). In a later case, the Alaska Supreme Court concluded that the one-year rule should be strictly construed in favor of the biological parent, holding that a father had only failed to support his child for 11 months when he made support payments on August 15, 1995 and August 16, 1996. In re Adoption of A.F.M., 960 P.2d 602 (Alaska 1998).

In *Matter of J.J.J.*, nineteen months had passed between the divorce and the petition for stepparent adoption. At the time the petition was filed, the father was only three months in arrears on his support; however, his payments were not timely and the payments he made were paid either in a lump sum after the payments were overdue or were garnished from his wages. The Alaska court dismissed the significance of support paid as a result of collection efforts, finding that such payments did not adequately reflect a recognition on the father's part of his duty of support. Is the statutory test failure to pay support for twelve months, or failure to willingly and voluntarily pay for twelve months? What does the court's interpretation of this provision suggest about its view of stepparent adoptions?

c. Meaningful Contact

The dissent in *J.J.J.* points out that the trial court refused to find that the father had unjustifiably failed to significantly communicate with his son, based on testimony that the mother interfered with visitation between father and son, suggested that the father write letters and then did not read them to the son, and did not permit visitation until after the adoption petition had been filed. In addition, several months before stepfather filed his adoption petition, the father filed a motion to enforce his visitation rights. When the court ordered specific visitation in November 1983, the mother refused to comply with the order. Matter of J.J.J., 718 P.2d 948, 955 (Alaska 1986). Regardless of whose fault it was, the court relied on the fact that the father did not maintain meaningful contact with his son in deciding that the adoption would be in the child's best interests.

If the father in *J.J.J.,* although failing in his support obligation had succeeded better in maintaining a meaningful relationship with his son, would the adoption be in the child's best interests? Would termination of the father's parental rights be consistent with the holdings of *Stanley, Quilloin, Caban* and *Lehr?*

d. Best Interests

Should the court in a stepparent adoption case focus on the conduct of the natural parent, the best interests of the child, or both? In footnote 12, the court states that the best interest of the child is not relevant to a determination of whether a noncustodial natural parent's consent is unnecessary. The best interests of the child are evaluated only after the consent is determined to be unnecessary. The facts of *J.J.J.* offer a clear example of a situation in which a parent's rights seem to conflict with the child's best interests.

Statutes in some jurisdictions permit courts to allow adoptions to go forward without consent of the parent whose rights will be terminated, when there is clear and convincing evidence that a parent's consent is being withheld contrary to the child's best interests. See, e.g., In re J.G.Jr., 831 A.2d 992 (D.C.2003) (child had been placed with great aunt for four years following serious abuse by parent; mother not able to provide a home); R.F. v. S.S. and J.S., 928 P.2d 1194 (Alaska 1996) (child lived with grandparents; father in prison following conviction for second degree murder of the child's mother in the child's presence).

e. Incomplete Adoption

The Court refers to a middle approach, "incomplete adoption," whereby the stepparent would be awarded custody, but parental rights would not be terminated and the natural parent would retain visitation rights. What are the advantages and disadvantages of this approach? Should the father in *J.J.J.* have been granted post-adoption visitation rights? What difficulties, if any, would you foresee?

f. Termination Without Adoption?

Should courts permit a custodial parent to petition for termination of the noncustodial parent's rights where no stepparent adoption is being sought? What if both parents agree? For example, in Ex parte Brooks, 513 So.2d 614 (Ala.1987), overruled on other grounds by Ex parte Beasley, 564 S.2d 950 (Ala.1990), the divorced parents of a child jointly petitioned the court to terminate the father's parental rights. The parties were divorced before the child was born, the father had never paid child support and testified that he had no desire to visit with or know his child. The child's guardian *ad litem* argued that termination of the father's parental rights would not be in child's best interests since it would allow the father to avoid his obligation to provide support with no corresponding benefit to the child. The court denied the petition, stating that termination of parental rights should not be used for the convenience of parents.

Problem 3-8

After Mother and Father were divorced, Father paid support for several years. He stopped paying support for a year after his ex-wife remarried a wealthy man and moved to another state with the child, in part because he felt that the sole purpose of the move was to prevent his continued visitation with the child. Father had a new family of his own and knew that the child was being well provided for; he also remained in contact with the child by phone and mail although he was unable to afford the cost of visitation. Immediately after the year of nonsupport had passed, Mother's new husband filed a petition for stepparent adoption. What arguments would you make on Father's behalf? Should it make a difference if Father had offered to pay, and Mother had refused his payments? (See Matter of Adoption of D.J.V., 796 P.2d 1076 (Mont. 1990).)

Problem 3-9

When Stacy was two years old, her biological father was convicted for armed robbery and sentenced to three years in prison. After he had served two of the three years, Stacy's mother and her husband filed a petition for stepparent adoption. Although Stacy's father has not paid any child support, he has sent her letters once a month and opposes any termination of his parental rights. Under the statute applied in *J.J.J.*, does he have the right to prevent the adoption? (See Application to Adopt H.B.S.C., 12 P.3d 916 (Kan. Ct. App. 2000); see also Adoption of C.D.M., 39 P.3d 802 (Okla.2001).)

Second-Parent Adoption

Many state courts have considered whether state adoption statutes permit stepparent adoption by an adult who is cohabiting with but not legally married to the child's custodial parent. Many of these cases involved same-sex couples who were not able to marry. Second-parent adoptions were approved by courts in a number of jurisdictions. See, e.g., Sharon S. v. Superior Court, 73 P.3d 554 (Cal. 2003); In re M.M.D., 662 A.2d 837 (D.C.1995); Adoption of Tammy, 619 N.E.2d 315 (Mass. 1993); Matter of the Adoption of a Child by J.M.G., 632 A.2d 550 (N.J. Super. Ct. 1993); and Matter of Jacob, 660 N.E.2d 397 (N.Y. 1995); Adoptions of B.L.V.B and E.L.V.B., 628 A.2d 1271 (Vt. 1993). See also In re Adoption No. 90072022/CAD, 590 A.2d 1094 (Md. Ct. Spec. App. 1991), and Adoption of R.B.F., 803 A.2d 1195 (Pa. 2002). For statutes addressing second parent adoption, see 15A Vt. Stat. Ann. § 1–102(b) (2018).

Courts in another group of states concluded that state adoption statutes did not allow second parent adoptions by unmarried partners. See Matter of Adoption of T.K.J., 931 P.2d 488 (Colo.Ct.App.1996); Adoption of Luke, 640 N.W.2d 374 (Neb.2002); and In Interest of Angel Lace M., 516 N.W.2d 678 (Wis. 1994). A statute in Mississippi, which expressly prohibited co-adoption by same-sex couples, was found to be unconstitutional in Campaign for Southern Equality v. Mississippi Department of Human Services, 175 F.Supp.3d 691 (S.D. Miss. 2016).

B. Adoption Proceedings

A public or private adoption agency may place a child for adoption after the child becomes eligible for adoption based on a relinquishment proceeding or an involuntary termination of parental rights. Some states also permit independent or private placements, in which a child's birth parents place their child directly with prospective adoptive parents, sometimes with the assistance of an intermediary. Although most states do not prohibit independent adoptions, statutes vary widely and many states require that a licensed agency be involved in the process at some point. The differences among state laws lead to forum shopping in some cases and difficult problems of jurisdiction and conflict of laws.

Adoptive placements made by agencies begin with an investigation of the prospective adoptive parents, but private placements may not include this step. Agencies typically have detailed placement criteria, and may have long waiting lists of parents seeking to adopt. For adoptive parents, one advantage of an independent adoption is that they may avoid agency procedures and waiting lists. In an independent adoption, prospective adoptive parents often pay the birth mother's medical and legal expenses. Beyond certain permitted expenses, however, payment in connection with adoption is unlawful in all or nearly all states. E.g., State v. Runkles, 605 A.2d 111 (Md. 1992); State v. Verde, 770 P.2d 116 (Utah 1989).

In all states, a court must ultimately approve any adoptive placement when the adoptive parents petition for a decree of adoption. Most adoption statutes provide that an adoption terminates the rights of the natural parents and establishes new parental rights and obligations in the adoptive parent or parents.

There has been a dramatic shift away from the secrecy and confidentiality that once characterized the adoption process. Some states permit open adoption, in which the adopted child will continue to have some form of contact with members of his or her biological family. State laws are divided

Go Online

Summaries of state laws on domestic adoption are available online at the Child Welfare Information Gateway.

on whether agreements for this type of post-adoption visitation can be incorporated into an adoption decree and specifically enforced.

Adoption History

Various forms of adoption and foster care have been practiced for centuries, but Massachusetts enacted the first comprehensive adoption statute in the United States in 1851. The early history is discussed in Stephen B. Presser, *The Historical Background of the American Law of Adoption*, 11 J. Fam. L. 443 (1972). There is now a significant literature on these issues. The Adoption History Project at the University of Oregon maintains a useful web page with an extensive bibliography. See also Ellen Herman, Kinship by Design: A History of Adoption in the Modern United States (2008).

1. Who May Adopt

State laws define who may adopt a child, typically setting a minimum age for adoptive parents and sometimes imposing residency requirements. All states require some type of criminal background investigation for prospective foster and adoptive parents, and most require checks of child abuse and neglect registries. See 42 U.S.C. § 671(a)(20) (2018); see generally Child Welfare Information Gateway, *Background Checks for Prospective Foster, Adoptive, and Kinship Caregivers* (2016).

State statutes frequently give some preference to relatives in placing a child for foster care or adoption. This is consistent with the federal foster care and adoption assistance program under Title IV-E of the Social Security Act. See 42 U.S.C. § 671(a)(19) (2018). Many states streamline the adoption process when a child is placed with relatives, and sometimes require agencies to make reasonable efforts to identify and notify relatives when a child is removed from the care of his or her parents. Courts have rejected the claim, however, that family members have constitutional rights to placement or adoption of children with whom they share a genetic link; see Mullins v. Oregon, 57 F.3d 789 (9th Cir. 1995) (dismissing grandparents' action under 42 U.S.C. § 1983). See Child Welfare Information Gateway, *Placement of Children with Relatives* (2018).

Adoption of M.A

930 A.2d 1088 (Me. 2007)

LEVY, J.

[¶ 1] A.C. and M.K. appeal from the judgment of the Cumberland County Probate Court (*Mazziotti, J.*) dismissing their joint petitions for adoption and name change as to their foster children, M.A. and R.A. A.C. and M.K. contend that the court erred in concluding that it lacks jurisdiction, pursuant to 18–A M.R.S. § 9–301 (2006), to consider joint petitions for adoption filed by two unmarried individuals. Because we conclude that the court has jurisdiction and the petitions are not otherwise barred by section 9–301, we vacate the court's judgment and remand for further proceedings.

I. BACKGROUND

[¶ 2] The petitions allege the following facts, which are presumed to be true for the purposes of the pending appeals. In early 2001, A.C. and M.K., an unmarried, same-sex couple, became foster parents to the minor children and biological siblings, M.A. and R.A. At the time, M.A. was one week shy of her fourth birthday and R.A. was four months old. The Department of Health and Human Services received the custody of the children as a result of a jeopardy order entered in a child protection proceeding in the District Court (Biddeford, *Foster, J.*). The parental rights of the children's birth parents were subsequently terminated by the court with their consent. Both children have been diagnosed with post-traumatic stress disorder, reactive attachment disorder, and attention deficit and hyperactivity disorder.

[¶ 3] Nearly two years after the children came into the Department's custody, A.C. and M.K. applied to the Department to adopt the children. An independent home study was completed in early 2006 as required by 18–A M.R.S. § 9–304(a–1) (2006). The home study report recommended that A.C. and M.K. be approved to jointly adopt the children, concluding that:

> [A.C. and M.K.] are able to parent children with moderate to severe special needs that include attachment disorders, mental illness, ADHD/ADD, learning disabilities and delays. They are able to parent children who require a wide range of services and may not live independently as. . .adult[s].

[¶ 4] The children's court-appointed guardian ad litem recommended in favor of the adoption, concluding that "[h]aving two legal parents forever will clearly be in the children's best interests." The Department's adoption worker and adoption supervisor responsible for the children also issued reports strongly supporting the adoptions, recommending that the adoptions "be legalized as soon as possible to provide [each child] with the security that only permanence can provide." In April 2006, the Department, acting through its Commissioner, consented to the joint adoption of both children by A.C. and M.K.

[¶ 5] A.C. and M.K. filed two petitions for adoption in the Cumberland County Probate Court in May 2006: one to jointly adopt M.A., and the other to jointly adopt R.A. The court ordered the two petitions consolidated pursuant to M.R. Prob. P. 42(a). The following month, the court denied the petitions in a written order that simply stated that each was "denied for lack of jurisdiction pursuant to 18–A M.R.S.A. [§] 9–301," without addressing the merits of the petitions. Section 9–301 provides: "A husband and wife jointly or an unmarried person, resident or nonresident of the State, may petition the Probate Court to adopt a person, regardless of age, and to change that person's name." 18–A M.R.S. § 9–301 (2006). These appeals followed. The Attorney General, as well as several organizations and associations, submitted briefs as amici curiae pursuant to M.R.App. P. 9(e)(1).

II. DISCUSSION

[¶ 6] The Probate Court concluded that it lacked jurisdiction to consider A.C. and M.K.'s joint petitions to adopt M.A. and R.A. based on the language of section 9–301. We review the Probate Court's rulings on questions of law de novo. * * *

[¶ 7] In the present case, the Probate Court has personal jurisdiction over the petitioners and the children they seek to adopt. A.C., M.K., and the children have resided continuously in Maine since R.A.›s birth in 2000. The Probate Court also has exclusive subject-matter jurisdiction over adoption petitions. *See* 4 M.R.S. § 251 (2006) (providing that a judge of probate has jurisdiction "to grant leave to adopt children"); 18–A M.R.S. § 9–103(a)(1) (2006) (granting exclusive jurisdiction over adoption petitions). Regardless of whether the adoption petitions filed in this case may be filed individually or jointly, that procedural issue does not affect the Probate Court's subject-matter jurisdiction.

[¶ 8] Because the Probate Court has personal jurisdiction over the parties and the children, and subject-matter jurisdiction to act on petitions for adoption, the Probate Court erred in dismissing the petitions for lack of jurisdiction. However, to the extent the Probate Court inferred that a joint petition by unmarried persons is prohibited by section 9–301, we must still determine whether a joint petition for adoption filed by two unmarried persons is procedurally barred because the statute addresses joint petitions only in connection with a husband and wife, but not in connection with two unmarried persons. *Cf. Mason v. City of Augusta,* 2007 ME 101, ¶ 15, 927 A.2d 1146, 1150 (addressing whether a complaint stated a claim upon which relief can be granted after concluding that the trial court improperly dismissed the complaint for lack of jurisdiction).

A. The Plain Meaning of Section 9–301

[¶ 9] In construing a statute, we look first to its plain meaning. In addition, we do not read exceptions, limitations, or conditions into an otherwise clear and unambiguous statute.

[¶ 10] The petitioners and the Attorney General both assert that section 9–301 is clear and unambiguous. They observe that the statute does not expressly prohibit two unmarried persons from jointly petitioning to adopt a child. The petitioners urge us to treat the statute's language permitting a petition to adopt by a "husband and wife jointly" as functioning solely as a restriction on petitions brought by married persons. They note that other jurisdictions have construed similar statutes on this basis and have recognized that the purpose of requiring a married person to join his or her spouse to an adoption petition is "specific to the marital relationship and its attendant legal obligations." *In re Infant Girl W.,* 845 N.E.2d 229, 242–43 (Ind.Ct.App.2006), *transfer denied sub nom. In re Adoption of M.W.,* 851 N.E.2d 961 (Ind.2006); *see also In re M.M.D.,* 662 A.2d 837, 848 (D.C.1995); *Adoption of Tammy,* 416 Mass. 205, 619 N.E.2d 315, 318 n. 3 (1993); *In re Jacob,* 86 N.Y.2d 651, 636 N.Y.S.2d 716, 660 N.E.2d 397, 400 (1995).

* * *

[¶ 14] * * * The statute is silent as to whether an unmarried person may or may not be a party to a joint petition. As a general principle of statutory construction, if a statute does not contain "a limiting adverb such as 'solely,' we refuse to imply such a restriction." *Eagle Rental, Inc. v. City of Waterville*, 632 A.2d 130, 131 (Me.1993). One cannot conclude that the statute prohibits two unmarried persons from proceeding by way of a joint petition without reaching beyond the actual language of the statute so as to interpret it to state: "[a] husband and wife jointly or an unmarried person, resident or nonresident of the State, [individually, but not jointly,] may petition the Probate Court to adopt a person." 18–A M.R.S. § 9–301.

[¶ 15] A plain reading of the statute is not only saddled by the need to engage in an inference that introduces the restriction "individually, but not jointly," into the text, but also leads to possibly absurd or illogical results. The adoption statute expressly permits unmarried persons to adopt children and does not expressly prohibit a child from being adopted by two unmarried persons. Therefore, unless one reads section 9–301 as also implicitly establishing a bar that prohibits more than one unmarried person from adopting a particular child, A.C. and M.K. could achieve a joint adoption of the children by filing separate individual petitions for adoption, and then moving to consolidate the petitions into a single adoption proceeding in accordance with M.R. Prob. P. 42(a). In addition, A.C. and M.K. could also proceed by having one file an individual petition to adopt the children and, if successful, that person consenting to a second adoption petition filed by the other, resulting in the adoption of the children by both. In short, if we infer that section 9–301 prohibits joint petitions by unmarried persons, but does not prohibit joint adoption by two unmarried persons, unmarried persons can still accomplish a joint adoption through successive or consolidated individual petitions. With this in mind, construing section 9–301 as prohibiting a joint petition by unmarried persons elevates form over substance to an illogical degree.

[¶ 16] Accordingly, we do not accept the petitioners' contention that the plain language of section 9–301 is free from ambiguity and requires no further inquiry beyond the application of the rule of construction stated in 1 M.R.S. § 71(9). Because the statute is reasonably susceptible of different constructions, it is ambiguous, and we turn to consider its history and purpose for further guidance.

B. Legislative History and Purpose

1. History

[¶ 17] The legal adoption of another person's child was unknown at common law and was first introduced to American jurisprudence through statutory enactments in the mid-nineteenth century. *See Estate of Skolfield*, 121 Me. 97, 101,

115 A. 765, 767 (Me.1922). Maine's current adoption law can be traced back to its first statutory enactment in 1855. *See* P.L. 1855, ch. 189. The original statute contained the following provisions regarding who may petition to adopt:

> SECT. 1. Any inhabitant of this state may petition the judge of probate in the county wherein he or she may reside, for leave to adopt a child not his or her own by birth.

Sections 2 and 3 of the Act addressed who must give consent for an adoption. Section 4 established a restriction on petitions brought by married persons:

> SECT. 4. No petition by a person having a lawful wife, shall be allowed, unless such wife shall join therein; and no petition by a person having a lawful husband shall be allowed, unless such husband shall join therein.

Accordingly, at its genesis, Maine's adoption statute imposed a joinder requirement on married persons, but did not impose any restrictions on petitions filed by unmarried inhabitants of the State.

[¶ 18] In 1855 the Legislature also adopted a "Resolves providing for a revision of the public laws of this state." The resolve authorized commissioners to "faithfully. . .revise, collate and arrange all the public laws of this State." The resolve resulted in the Maine Revised Statutes, enacted in 1857. As it pertains to adoptions, the 1857 revision abridged the first four sections of the 1855 Act into a single section * * *. There is no evidence in the legislative record that this consolidation and simplification of the first four sections of the 1855 Act into a single section in the 1857 revision was intended to cause a substantive change.

[¶ 19] As is apparent, the language in the 1857 Act—"Any inhabitant of this state not married, or any husband and wife jointly, may petition"—is the direct antecedent of the current language in section 9–301—"A husband and wife jointly or an unmarried person, resident or nonresident of the State, may petition." The legislative history that documents the intervening enactments that have refined the language of the 1857 Act to the current language of section 9–301 does not indicate that the refinements were intended to cause a substantive change in the law as to who may be a party to an adoption petition.

[¶ 20] The legislative history establishes that the provision regarding joint petitions by husbands and wives began with the 1855 Act and was intended to restrict petitions brought by married persons. There is nothing in the legislative history associated with the 1857 revision, or any of the subsequent legislative refinements resulting in the language that appears today in section 9–301, to suggest that the statute, in its current form, should impose a restriction on petitions by unmarried persons.

[¶ 21] It is nearly certain that in the mid-nineteenth century the Legislature could not have contemplated the possibility of an adoption arising from a foster care placement of children with an unmarried couple as the result of a child protection proceeding. The specific question, however, is not whether the Legislature entertained this possibility, but rather, whether the Legislature intended by its enactment to define "all possible categories of persons leading to adoptions in the best interests of children." *Adoption of Tammy*, 619 N.E.2d at 319; *see also In re Jacob*, 636 N.Y.S.2d 716, 660 N.E.2d at 405; *Adoption of B.L.V.B.*, 160 Vt. 368, 628 A.2d 1271, 1274 (1993). Our answer to this question must adhere to the principle that "[s]tatutes framed in general terms apply to new cases that arise and to new subjects that are created, from time to time, and which come within their general scope and policy." *Appeal of Cummings*, 126 Me. 111, 114, 136 A. 662, 664 (1927) (citation omitted); *see also* 2B SUTHERLAND STATUTORY CONSTRUCTION § 49.02 (6th ed.2000) (collecting cases).

[¶ 22] Although the historical record is not definitive, it does not establish that section 9–301 is intended to impose a restriction that would bar a joint petition by unmarried persons.

C. Purpose of Adoption Law

[¶ 23] When we find a statute ambiguous, we may also look to the statute's underlying purpose to ascertain legislative intent. As a prelude to construing the purpose of section 9–301, we first address the role that purpose should play in our construction of the statute.

[¶ 24] Although statutes adopted in derogation of the common law are to be strictly construed, we have previously recognized that "[w]e construe our adoption statutes to protect the rights and privileges of the child being adopted." *Dept of Human Servs. v. Sabattus*, 683 A.2d 170, 172 (Me.1996). This is consistent with the central role the best interests of the children play in the statutory factors the court is required to consider in evaluating an adoption petition. *See* 18–A M.R.S. § 9–308(a)(5), (b)(1)–(3) (2006). Accordingly, it is established in our jurisprudence that:

> Adoption statutes, as well as matters of procedure leading up to adoption, should be liberally construed to carry out the beneficent purposes of the adoption institution and to protect the adopted child in the rights and privileges coming to it as a result of the adoption.

In re Estate of Goodwin, 147 Me. 237, 244, 86 A.2d 88, 91 (1952) (quotation marks omitted).

[¶ 25] This construction also comports with the Probate Code's general rule of statutory construction: "This Code shall be liberally construed and applied to promote its underlying purposes and policies." 18–A M.R.S. § 1–102(a) (2006). The first stated purpose of the Probate Code is "to simplify and clarify the law concerning the affairs of decedents, missing persons, protected persons, *minors* and incapacitated persons." *Id.* § 1–102(b)(1) (2006) (emphasis added). We applied the Code's liberal rule of construction in *Guardianship of Zachary Z.* so as to interpret the term "residence" broadly to include, as residents of Maine, children who formerly, but no longer, lived in Maine. 677 A.2d 550, 552–53 (Me.1996). We reasoned that "[s]uch liberal construction allows the Probate Court to protect children who are removed from their Maine homes for the duration of guardianship proceedings by persons seeking to avoid a Maine forum." We also observed that a liberal construction of the statute better comports "with the purposes of the Probate Code, which subscribe generally to judicial efficiency and simplification of process."

[¶ 26] The construction of section 9–301 that will most promote the rights and privileges of children such as M.A., R.A., and other similarly situated children, and will simplify and clarify the law of adoption, is one that does not infer a procedural bar that would disqualify the joint petitions filed by A.C. and M.K. In contrast to a narrow reading of section 9–301 that infers a restriction not expressed in the statute, a broader construction is more in keeping with the statute's overriding objective of protecting the welfare of children. A joint adoption assures that in the event of either adoptive parent's death, the children's continued relationship with the surviving adoptive parent is fixed and certain. A joint adoption also enables the children to be eligible for a variety of public and private benefits, including Social Security, worker's compensation, and intestate succession, as well as employment benefits such as health insurance and family leave, on account of not one, but two legally recognized parents. Most importantly, a joint adoption affords the adopted children the love, nurturing, and support of not one, but two parents.

[¶ 27] In addition, a construction of section 9–301 that allows a joint petition will enable the Probate Court to conduct a single proceeding in which it can evaluate the statutory best interest criteria as applied to M.A. and R.A. relative to their relationships to both A.C. and M.K. A joint petition will permit the court to evaluate, among other things, "[t]he love, affection and other emotional ties existing between the adoptee and the adopting. . .persons," 18–A M.R.S. § 9–308(b) (1), from the perspective of the established family unit that has emerged since the children went into the Department's custody in 2001. A single joint petition makes it unnecessary for the parties to proceed by way of separate, consolidated or consecutive adoption petitions, with the added costs and delay that arise from a more convoluted process. A single joint petition best comports "with the purposes of the Probate Code, which subscribe generally to judicial efficiency and simplification of process." *Guardianship of Zachary Z., 677 A.2d at 553.*

[¶ 28] There is also a broader, systemic reason for opting in favor of a construction of section 9–301 that permits the joint petitions filed in this case. The

Probate Code requires the court to evaluate the best interest factors in order "to give the adoptee a *permanent home* at the earliest possible date." 18–A M.R.S. § 9–308(b) (emphasis added). As we recognized in *In re Thomas H.,* "[p]ermanency planning was embraced by Congress in the Adoption and Safe Families Act of 1997 (ASFA) in direct response to the documented inability of state child welfare systems to bring about stable and final outcomes for children within a timeframe reasonably designed to meet their needs." 2005 ME 123, ¶ 23, 889 A.2d 297, 304 (citation omitted). We described permanency as "a central tenet of ASFA and the corresponding amendments to Maine['s] child protective laws," noting that our Legislature had declared "instability and impermanency [as] contrary to the welfare of children." We concluded that because of "the strong public policy favoring permanency for children [that] must inform the trial court's exercise of judicial discretion associated with determining a child's best interest," a disposition that will result in a child remaining in long-term foster care can only be sustained if there is a compelling reason for it.

[¶ 29] This adoption proceeding is the final phase of a continuum of a legal process that began in 2001 when M.A. and R.A. first came into the Department's custody and were placed in the joint care of A.C. and M.K. The construction of section 9–301 that permits the Probate Court to consider a single joint petition to adopt advances the strong public policy favoring permanency at the earliest possible date as applied to children, such as M.A. and R.A., who have been in a long-term, pre-adoptive foster care placement for most of their lives.

[¶ 30] The question of statutory construction presented by this case does not arise in a vacuum. We cannot be oblivious to the fact that if the statute is construed to permit the Probate Court to consider a joint adoption petition by unmarried persons, there will be a greater incentive for other unmarried persons to undertake the profound and difficult responsibility of serving as pre-adoptive foster parents for young children with significant special needs. Absent the incentive that the possibility of joint adoption provides, there will be fewer homes for such children.

Take Note!

The court suggests an important public policy argument here: encouraging adults to serve as foster and adoptive parents for children with special needs.

[¶ 31] Viewing the petitions and the supporting reports and documents in the light most favorable to the petitioners, it is clear that a construction of section 9–301 that imposes a procedural bar that would further complicate and delay, or even prohibit, the court from considering a joint adoption petition is inimical to the children's interests and bears no connection to the child welfare goals of our adoption and child protection statutes. When faced with competing constructions of a statute, we choose the construction "that avoids a result adverse to the public interest." *See South Portland Civil Serv. Comm'n v. City of S. Portland, 667 A.2d 599, 601 (Me.1995)*. We conclude that section 9–301 does not prohibit a joint adoption petition by two unmarried persons.

The entry is:

Judgment vacated and remanded to the Probate Court for further proceedings consistent with this opinion.

Points for Discussion

a. Adoption from Foster Care

Most children adopted from foster care are adopted by their relatives or their foster parents. Laws in many states seek to facilitate adoptions by foster parents. E.g., In re Adoption of A.K.S.R., 71 S.W.3d 715 (Tenn.Ct.App.2001) (applying statute giving preference to foster parents). See generally Child Welfare Information Gateway, Foster Parents Considering Adoption (2012).

Many children spend significant time in the public foster care system before they are freed for adoption, and the court in *M.A.* notes the "profound and difficult responsibility of serving as pre-adoptive foster parents for young children with significant special needs." These adoptions raise complex issues, as many children in foster care have experienced separation and loss, multiple placements, abuse, neglect, or other trauma. Older children, sibling groups, children of color and children with disabilities are also more difficult to place for adoption. Since the federal Adoption Assistance and Child Welfare Act of 1980, state programs offering financial assistance to families who adopt these children have been subsidized by the federal government under Title IV-E of the Social Security Act. See 42 U.S.C. §§ 673–74 (2018).

b. Joint Adoption by Unmarried Adults

Courts have approved requests for joint adoption by unmarried same-sex and opposite-sex couples, see Adoption of Emilio R., 742 N.Y.S.2d 22 (App. Div.2002), and joint adoption by a parent and grandparent, see In re Abby D., 839 A.2d 1222 (R.I.2004). But see e.g. Adoption of K.M.W., 718 A.2d 332 (Pa. Super. Ct.1998) (declining grandmother's petition to adopt child without termination of mother's parental rights). Utah amended its adoption statutes in 2000 to provide that a child may be adopted by "adults who are legally married to each other in accordance with the laws of this state," or by any single adult, unless that person "is cohabiting in a relationship that is not a legally valid and binding marriage under the laws of this state." Utah Code § 78B–6–117 (2018). Moving in the other direction, New York amended its statutes after the *Emilio* decision to allow joint adoption by "any two unmarried adult intimate partners." N.Y. Dom. Rel. L. § 110 (2018). See, e.g., Adoption of G., 978 N.Y.S.2d 622 (Sur. Ct. 2013) (approving adoption by two close personal friends).

Why should state laws restrict adoption to couples who are married or living together in a conjugal relationship? Why not allow adult siblings to become joint parents to a child? Angela Mae Kupenda has argued that adoption alternatives for African-American children would be improved if the law permitted joint adoption by a pair of single parents. Angela Mae Kupenda, *Two Parents are Better Than None: Whether Two Single, African-American Adults Who Are not in a Traditional Marriage or a Romantic or Sexual Relationship with Each Other Should Be Allowed to Jointly Adopt and Co-Parent African-American Children*, 35 J. Fam. L. 703 (1997).

c. Sexual Orientation and Adoption

A number of states have attempted to restrict adoption by gay or lesbian individuals. A Florida statute prohibiting adoption by homosexuals was sustained by the federal courts, see Lofton v. Secretary of the Department of Children and Family Services, 358 F.3d 804 (11th Cir. 2004), but later held to be unconstitutional under the Florida Constitution in Florida Dept. of Children and Families v. Adoption of X.X.G., 45 So.3d 79 (Fla. Dist. Ct. App. 2010). See generally Ann K. Wooster, Annotation, *Adoption of Child by Same-Sex Partners*, 61 A.L.R.6th 1 (2011). States that prohibited joint adoption by unmarried couples had the effect of preventing joint adoption by same-sex couples until the ruling in *Obergefell*.

Differences between state laws led to conflict of laws disputes in this area. For example, Oklahoma's 2004 "Adoption Invalidation Law" provided that state agencies and courts "shall not recognize an adoption by more than one individual of the same sex from any other state or foreign jurisdiction." 10 Okla. Stat. § 7502–1.4(A) (2012). Finstuen v. Crutcher, 496 F.3d 1139 (10th Cir. 2007), held that this nonrecognition provision was unconstitutional on full faith and credit grounds. In a short per curiam opinion, the Supreme Court ruled in V.L. v. E.L., 577 U.S. ___, 136 S.Ct. 1017 (2016) (per curiam), that state courts must recognize and give effect to adoption judgments entered in other states.

———————

Race and Adoption

In the past, adoption agencies tried to match children with prospective parents of similar traits and background, so that the new family would appear to be biologically related. This practice, as well as the secrecy with which relinquishment and adoption proceedings were handled, reflected a wider set of norms in which nonmarital childbirth and infertility carried a significant social stigma. Matching policies went beyond the child's physical traits, extending to ethnicity and religion. Courts have upheld religious matching practices in adoptive against constitutional challenges under the First and Fourteenth Amendments. For example, Dickens v. Ernesto, 281 N.E.2d 153 (N.Y. 1972), sustained provisions of the state constitution and statutes requiring placement of a child "when practicable" with adoptive parents of the same religious background as the child's birth parents.

During the 1950s, some adoptive parents became more willing to adopt across racial or international borders. Transracial adoption practices developed slowly, and became controversial in 1972 when the National Association of Black Social Workers (NABSW) registered its opposition to the practice. In a statement, the NABSW asserted that "Black children belong physically, psychologically and culturally in Black families in order that they receive the total sense of themselves and develop a sound projection of their future. Human beings are products of their environment and develop their sense of values, attitudes and self concept within their family structures. Black children in white homes are cut off from the healthy development of themselves as Black people". (Quoted in Margaret Howard, *Transracial Adoption: Analysis of the Best Interests Standard,* 59 Notre Dame L. Rev. 503, 517 (1984).) In response, many agencies and organizations revised their policies to encourage same-race placements.

In 1978, Congress enacted the Indian Child Welfare Act (ICWA), codified at 25 U.S.C. §§ 1901–1963 (2018), which significantly restructured child welfare and adoption practices in order to protect the ties between Indian children and their tribes. ICWA is addressed in Mississippi Band of Choctaw Indians v. Holyfield, 490 U.S. 30 (1989), reprinted below, and the notes that follow. In other contexts, race-matching policies were challenged repeatedly under the federal civil rights laws. For example, Drummond v. Fulton County Department of Family and Children's Services, 563 F.2d 1200 (5th Cir.1977), cert. denied 437 U.S. 910 (1978), held that consideration of race as a "relevant factor" in the child placement process was constitutional, so long as it was not used "in an automatic fashion." Other courts held that using race as the sole factor in denying adoption or in placing children in foster homes was a violation of the Equal Protection Clause. See, e.g., Compos v. McKeithen, 341 F.Supp. 264 (E.D.La.1972); and In re Adoption of Gomez, 424 S.W.2d 656 (Tex.Civ.App.1967).

The Supreme Court has never addressed transracial adoption, but the Court found a constitutional violation in Palmore v. Sidoti, 466 U.S. 429 (1984), when a white child was removed from the custody of her mother, who had married a black man, and placed in the custody of her father. The Court held that the risk that the child would be subjected to pressures and stresses resulting from private biases against multi-racial families when living with a stepparent of a different race could not be allowed to affect the custody decision under the Fourteenth Amendment.

State and federal courts struggled to determine how *Palmore* should be applied to racial matching policies in the adoption setting. For example, Reisman v. Tennessee Department of Human Services, 843 F. Supp. 356 (W.D. Tenn. 1993) struck down poli-

Make the Connection

Palmore v. Sidoti is reproduced in Chapter 7.

cies that treated white and black families differently with respect to placement of mixed-race children, but concluded that biracial children should be placed with biracial families if possible. DeWees v. Stevenson, 779 F. Supp. 25 (E.D.Pa.1991), held that an agency's refusal to let white foster parents adopt a biracial child was not unconstitutional when the agency decision was based not on race but on the foster parents' attitudes about race. Congress weighed in on this controversy with the Multiethnic Placement Act of 1994 (MEPA), which it amended in 1996, codified at 42 U.S.C. §1996b (2018).

MEPA is discussed in Joan Heifetz Hollinger, A Guide to the Multiethnic Placement Act of 1994 as Amended by the Interethnic Adoption Provisions of 1996 (1998). Government data suggest that MEPA has been accompanied by a small increase in the rate of transracial adoptions of black children from foster care, but black children are still disproportionately represented on the foster care system and have lower adoption rates than children of other ethnicities. U.S. Government Accountability Office, *African American Children in Foster Care: Additional HHS Assistance Needed to Help States Reduce the Proportion in Care* (2007). One report surveying these data and other research has concluded that "transracial adoption brings additional challenges to adoptive children and their families— challenges that need to be addressed in matching children with families and in preparing families to meet their children's needs." See Evan B. Donaldson Adoption Institute, *Finding Families for African American Children: The Role of Race & Law in Adoption from Foster Care* (2008). See also the resources on Transracial/Transcultural Adoption available on the Child Welfare Information Gateway.

Multiethnic Placement Act

42 U.S.C. §1996b. Interethnic Adoption

(1) Prohibited conduct.

A person or government that is involved in adoption or foster care placements may not—

(A) deny to any individual the opportunity to become an adoptive or a foster parent, on the basis of the race, color, or national origin of the individual, or of the child, involved; or

(B) delay or deny the placement of a child for adoption or into foster care, on the basis of the race, color, or national origin of the adoptive or foster parent, or the child, involved.

(2) Enforcement.

Noncompliance with paragraph (1) is deemed a violation of title VI of the Civil Rights Act of 1964 [42 U.S.C.A. § 2000d et seq.].

(3) No effect on the Indian Child Welfare Act of 1978.

This subsection shall not be construed to affect the application of the Indian Child Welfare Act of 1978 [25 U.S.C.A. §§ 1901 et seq.]

Problem 3-10

Mr. and Mrs. H were white foster parents of a black infant and sought to adopt the child after she had been in their care for several months. The evidence was undisputed that they provided excellent care for the child. They had four other children, one of whom was a black child they had adopted some years before. They testified at length about their awareness of the need to instill a sense of black identity in their adopted children. The child's black grandparents intervened in the adoption proceeding and filed a petition to adopt the child. They too appeared to be fit parents, able to care for the child. In evaluating these petitions, may the court consider the grandparents' ability to provide a good home in a same race household? (See Petition of R.M.G., 454 A.2d 776 (D.C.1982).)

Problem 3-11

Mr. and Mrs. D. became foster parents for Dante, a two-month old biracial child, and he had lived with them for two years when his parents' parental rights were terminated. Although the Ds sought to adopt Dante, the adoption director of the county child welfare agency refused their request. While recognizing that there was a strong bond between Dante and the Ds, the director concluded that they lacked sensitivity to racial issues and lacked the inter-racial network of community resources needed to raise the child properly. Do Mr. and Mrs. D. have any basis to challenge the director's decision? (See DeWees v. Stevenson, 779 F. Supp. 25 (E.D.Pa.1991).)

Further Reading: Transracial Adoption

- Richard Banks, *The Color of Desire: Fulfilling Adoptive Parents Racial Preferences through Discriminatory State Action*, 107 Yale L. J. 875 (1998).

- Elizabeth Bartholet, *Where to Black Children Belong? The Politics of Race Matching in Adoption*, 139 U. Pa. L. Rev. 1163 (1991).

- Randall Kennedy, Interracial Intimacies: Sex, Marriage, Identity and Adoption 402–79 (2003).

- Twila L. Perry, *The Transracial Adoption Controversy: An Analysis of Discourse and Subordination*, 21 N.Y.U. Rev. L. & Soc. Change 33 (1994).

- Dorothy Roberts, Shattered Bonds: The Color of Child Welfare 149–72 (2002).

Mississippi Band of Choctaw Indians v. Holyfield

490 U.S. 30 (1989)

JUSTICE BRENNAN delivered the opinion of the Court.

This appeal requires us to construe the provisions of the Indian Child Welfare Act that establish exclusive tribal jurisdiction over child custody proceedings involving Indian children domiciled on the tribe's reservation.

Go Online

Listen to the oral arguments in *Holyfield* on the Oyez Project web site.

I

A

The Indian Child Welfare Act of 1978 (ICWA), 92 Stat. 3069, <u>25 U.S.C. §§ 1901–1963</u>, was the product of rising concern in the mid-1970's over the consequences to Indian children, Indian families, and Indian tribes of abusive child welfare practices that resulted in the separation of large numbers of Indian children from their families and tribes through adoption or foster care placement, usually in non-Indian homes. Senate oversight hearings in 1974 yielded numerous examples, statistical data, and expert testimony documenting what one witness called "the wholesale removal of Indian children from their homes, * * * the most tragic aspect of Indian life today." Indian Child Welfare Program, Hearings before the Subcommittee on Indian Affairs of the Senate Committee on Interior and Insular Affairs, 93d Cong., 2d Sess., 3 (hereinafter 1974 Hearings) (statement of William Byler). Studies undertaken by the Association on American Indian Affairs in 1969 and 1974, and presented in the Senate hearings, showed that 25 to 35% of all Indian children had been separated from their families and placed in adoptive families, foster care, or institutions. *Id.*, at 15; see also <u>H.R.Rep. No. 95–1386, p. 9</u> (1978) (hereinafter House Report), U.S.Code Cong. & Admin.News 1978, pp. 7530, 7531. Adoptive placements counted significantly in this total: in the State of Minnesota, for example, one in eight Indian children under the age of 18 was in an adoptive home, and during the year 1971–1972 nearly one in every four infants under one year of age was placed for adoption. The adoption rate of Indian children was eight times that of non-Indian children. Approximately 90% of the Indian placements were in non-Indian homes. A number of witnesses also testified to the serious adjustment problems encountered by such children during adolescence, as well as the impact of the adoptions on Indian parents and the tribes themselves.

Further hearings, covering much the same ground, were held during 1977 and 1978 on the bill that became the ICWA. While much of the testimony again focused on the harm to Indian parents and their children who were involuntarily separated by decisions of local welfare authorities, there was also considerable emphasis on the impact on the tribes themselves of the massive removal of their children. For example, Mr. Calvin Isaac, Tribal Chief of the Mississippi Band of Choctaw Indians and representative of the National Tribal Chairmen's Association, testified as follows:

> "Culturally, the chances of Indian survival are significantly reduced if our children, the only real means for the transmission of the tribal heritage, are to be raised in non-Indian homes and denied exposure to the ways of their People. Furthermore, these practices seriously undercut the tribes' ability to continue as self-governing communities. Probably in no area is

it more important that tribal sovereignty be respected than in an area as socially and culturally determinative as family relationships."

Chief Isaac also summarized succinctly what numerous witnesses saw as the principal reason for the high rates of removal of Indian children:

"One of the most serious failings of the present system is that Indian children are removed from the custody of their natural parents by nontribal government authorities who have no basis for intelligently evaluating the cultural and social premises underlying Indian home life and childrearing. Many of the individuals who decide the fate of our children are at best ignorant of our cultural values, and at worst contemptful of the Indian way and convinced that removal, usually to a non-Indian household or institution, can only benefit an Indian child."

The congressional findings that were incorporated into the ICWA reflect these sentiments. The Congress found:

"(3) that there is no resource that is more vital to the continued existence and integrity of Indian tribes than their children * * *;

"(4) that an alarmingly high percentage of Indian families are broken up by the removal, often unwarranted, of their children from them by nontribal public and private agencies and that an alarmingly high percentage of such children are placed in non-Indian foster and adoptive homes and institutions; and

"(5) that the States, exercising their recognized jurisdiction over Indian child custody proceedings through administrative and judicial bodies, have often failed to recognize the essential tribal relations of Indian people and the cultural and social standards prevailing in Indian communities and families." 25 U.S.C. § 1901.

At the heart of the ICWA are its provisions concerning jurisdiction over Indian child custody proceedings. Section 1911 lays out a dual jurisdictional scheme. Section 1911(a) establishes exclusive jurisdiction in the tribal courts for proceedings concerning an Indian child "who resides or is domiciled within the reservation of such tribe," as well as for wards of tribal courts regardless of domicile. Section 1911(b), on the other hand, creates concurrent but presumptively tribal jurisdiction in the case of children not domiciled on the reservation: on petition of either parent or the tribe, state-court proceedings for foster care placement or termination of parental rights are to be transferred to the tribal court, except in cases of "good cause," objection by either parent, or declination of jurisdiction by the tribal court.

Various other provisions of ICWA Title I set procedural and substantive standards for those child custody proceedings that do take place in state court. The procedural safeguards include requirements concerning notice and appointment of counsel; parental and tribal rights of intervention and petition for invalidation of illegal proceedings; procedures governing voluntary consent to termination of parental rights; and a full faith and credit obligation in respect to tribal court decisions. See §§ 1901–1914. The most important substantive requirement imposed on state courts is that of § 1915(a), which, absent "good cause" to the contrary, mandates that adoptive placements be made preferentially with (1) members of the child's extended family, (2) other members of the same tribe, or (3) other Indian families.

The ICWA thus, in the words of the House Report accompanying it, "seeks to protect the rights of the Indian child as an Indian and the rights of the Indian community and tribe in retaining its children in its society." House Report, at 23, U.S.Code Cong. & Admin.News 1978, at 7546. It does so by establishing "a Federal policy that, where possible, an Indian child should remain in the Indian community," and by making sure that Indian child welfare determinations are not based on "a white, middle-class standard which, in many cases, forecloses placement with [an] Indian family."

B

This case involves the status of twin babies, known for our purposes as B.B. and G.B., who were born out of wedlock on December 29, 1985. Their mother, J.B., and father, W.J., were both enrolled members of appellant Mississippi Band of Choctaw Indians (Tribe), and were residents and domiciliaries of the Choctaw Reservation in Neshoba County, Mississippi. J.B. gave birth to the twins in Gulfport, Harrison County, Mississippi, some 200 miles from the reservation. On January 10, 1986, J.B. executed a consent-to-adoption form before the Chancery Court of Harrison County. W.J. signed a similar form. On January 16, appellees Orrey and Vivian Holyfield filed a petition for adoption in the same court, and the chancellor issued a Final Decree of Adoption on January 28. Despite the court's apparent awareness of the ICWA, the adoption decree contained no reference to it, nor to the infants' Indian background.

Two months later the Tribe moved in the Chancery Court to vacate the adoption decree on the ground that under the ICWA exclusive jurisdiction was vested in the tribal court. On July 14, 1986, the court overruled the motion, holding that the Tribe "never obtained exclusive jurisdiction over the children involved herein. * * * " The court's one-page opinion relied on two facts in reaching that conclusion. The court noted first that the twins' mother "went to some efforts to see that they were born outside the confines of the Choctaw Indian Reservation" and that the parents had promptly arranged for the adoption by the Holyfields. Second, the court stated: "At no time from the birth of these children to the present date have either of them resided on or physically been on the Choctaw Indian Reservation."

The Supreme Court of Mississippi affirmed. <u>511 So.2d 918 (1987)</u>. It rejected the Tribe's arguments that the state court lacked jurisdiction and that it, in any event, had not applied the standards laid out in the ICWA. The court recognized that the jurisdictional question turned on whether the twins were domiciled on the Choctaw Reservation. It answered that question as follows:

> "At no point in time can it be said the twins resided on or were domiciled within the territory set aside for the reservation. Appellant's argument that living within the womb of their mother qualifies the children's residency on the reservation may be lauded for its creativity; however, apparently it is unsupported by any law within this state, and will not be addressed at this time due to the far-reaching legal ramifications that would occur were we to follow such a complicated tangential course."

The court distinguished Mississippi cases that appeared to establish the principle that "the domicile of minor children follows that of the parents," It noted that "the Indian twins * * * were voluntarily surrendered and legally abandoned by the natural parents to the adoptive parents, and it is undisputed that the parents went to some efforts to prevent the children from being placed on the reservation as the mother arranged for their birth and adoption in Gulfport Memorial Hospital, Harrison County, Mississippi." Therefore, the court said, the twins' domicile was in Harrison County and the state court properly exercised jurisdiction over the adoption proceedings. Indeed, the court appears to have concluded that, for this reason, *none* of the provisions of the ICWA was applicable. ("these proceedings * * * actually escape applicable federal law on Indian Child Welfare"). In any case, it rejected the Tribe's contention that the requirements of the ICWA applicable in state courts had not been followed: "[T]he judge did conform and strictly adhere to the minimum federal standards governing adoption of Indian children with respect to parental consent, notice, service of process, etc."[13]

Because of the centrality of the exclusive tribal jurisdiction provision to the overall scheme of the ICWA, as well as the conflict between this decision of the Mississippi Supreme Court and those of several other state courts, we granted plenary review. We now reverse.

Think About It

The Court notes that the lower court ignored ICWA's placement preferences in <u>§1915(a)</u>. How should the Mississippi courts have applied that section of the statute?

---

[13]   The lower court may well have fulfilled the applicable ICWA procedural requirements. It clearly did not, however, comply with or even take cognizance of the substantive mandate of <u>§ 1915(a)</u>: "In any adoptive placement of an Indian child *under State law*, a preference shall be given, in the absence of good cause to the contrary, to a placement with (1) a member of the child's extended family; (2) other members of the Indian child's tribe; or (3) other Indian families" [emphasis added]. <u>Section 1915(e)</u>, moreover, requires the court to maintain records "evidencing the efforts to comply with the order of preference specified in this section." Notwithstanding the Tribe's argument below that <u>§ 1915</u> had been violated, the Mississippi Supreme Court made no reference to it, merely stating in conclusory fashion that the "minimum federal standards" had been met.

II

Tribal jurisdiction over Indian child custody proceedings is not a novelty of the ICWA. Indeed, some of the ICWA's jurisdictional provisions have a strong basis in pre-ICWA case law in the federal and state courts. * * * In enacting the ICWA Congress confirmed that, in child custody proceedings involving Indian children domiciled on the reservation, tribal jurisdiction was exclusive as to the States.

The state-court proceeding at issue here was a "child custody proceeding." That term is defined to include any " 'adoptive placement' which shall mean the permanent placement of an Indian child for adoption, including any action resulting in a final decree of adoption." 25 U.S.C. § 1903(1) (iv). Moreover, the twins were "Indian children." See 25 U.S.C. § 1903(4). The sole issue in this case is, as the Supreme Court of Mississippi recognized, whether the twins were "domiciled" on the reservation.

A

The meaning of "domicile" in the ICWA is, of course, a matter of Congress' intent. The ICWA itself does not define it. The initial question we must confront is whether there is any reason to believe that Congress intended the ICWA definition of "domicile" to be a matter of state law. * * *

Take Note!

ICWA defines "Indian child" as "any unmarried person who is under age eighteen and is either (a) a member of an Indian tribe or (b) is eligible for membership in an Indian tribe and is the biological child of a member of an Indian tribe." 25 U.S.C. §1903(4) (2012).

* * *

First, and most fundamentally, the purpose of the ICWA gives no reason to believe that Congress intended to rely on state law for the definition of a critical term; quite the contrary. It is clear from the very text of the ICWA, not to mention its legislative history and the hearings that led to its enactment, that Congress was concerned with the rights of Indian families and Indian communities vis-à-vis state authorities. More specifically, its purpose was, in part, to make clear that in certain situations the state courts did *not* have jurisdiction over child custody proceedings. * * * Under these circumstances it is most improbable that Congress would have intended to leave the scope of the statute's key jurisdictional provision subject to definition by state courts as a matter of state law.

Second, Congress could hardly have intended the lack of nationwide uniformity that would result from state-law definitions of domicile. An example will illustrate. In a case quite similar to this one, the New Mexico state courts found exclusive jurisdiction in the tribal court pursuant to § 1911(a), because the illegitimate child took the reservation domicile of its mother at birth—notwithstanding that the child was placed in the custody of adoptive parents two days after its off-reservation birth and the mother executed a consent to adoption ten days later. *In re Adoption of Baby Child,* 102 N.M. 735, 737–738, 700 P.2d 198, 200–201 (App. 1985). Had that mother traveled to Mississippi to give birth, rather than to Albuquerque, a different result would have obtained if state-law definitions of domicile applied. The same, presumably, would be true if the child had been transported to Mississippi for adoption after her off-reservation birth in New Mexico. While the child's custody proceeding would have been subject to exclusive tribal jurisdiction in her home State, her mother, prospective adoptive parents, or an adoption intermediary could have obtained an adoption decree in state court merely by transporting her across state lines. Even if we could conceive of a federal statute under which the rules of domicile (and thus of jurisdiction) applied differently to different Indian children, a statute under which different rules apply from time to time to the same child, simply as a result of her transport from one State to another, cannot be what Congress had in mind.

We therefore think it beyond dispute that Congress intended a uniform federal law of domicile for the ICWA.

B

It remains to give content to the term "domicile" in the circumstances of the present case. The holding of the Supreme Court of Mississippi that the twin babies were not domiciled on the Choctaw Reservation appears to have rested on two findings of fact by the trial court: (1) that they had never been physically present there, and (2) that they were "voluntarily surrendered" by their parents. The question before us, therefore, is whether under the ICWA definition of "domicile" such facts suffice to render the twins nondomiciliaries of the reservation.

We have often stated that in the absence of a statutory definition we "start with the assumption that the legislative purpose is expressed by the ordinary meaning of the words used." * * * We therefore look both to the generally accepted meaning of the term "domicile" and to the purpose of the statute.

* * *

"Domicile" is, of course, a concept widely used in both federal and state courts for jurisdiction and conflict-of-laws purposes, and its meaning is generally uncontroverted. * * * For adults, domicile is established by physical presence in a place in connection with a certain state of mind concerning one's intent to remain there. * * * Since most minors are legally incapable of forming the requisite intent to establish a domicile, their domicile is determined by that of their parents. In the case of an illegitimate child, that has traditionally meant the domicile of its mother. Under these principles, it is entirely logical that "[o]n occasion, a child's domicile of origin will be in a place where the child has never been." Restatement [(Second) of Conflicts of Laws (1971)] § 14, Comment *b.*

It is undisputed in this case that the domicile of the mother (as well as the father) has been, at all relevant times, on the Choctaw Reservation. Thus, it is clear that at their birth the twin babies were also domiciled on the reservation, even though they themselves had never been there. The statement of the Supreme Court of Mississippi that "[a]t no point in time can it be said the twins * * * were domiciled within the territory set aside for the reservation," may be a correct statement of that State's law of domicile, but it is inconsistent with generally accepted doctrine in this country and cannot be what Congress had in mind when it used the term in the ICWA.

Nor can the result be any different simply because the twins were "voluntarily surrendered" by their mother. Tribal jurisdiction under § 1911(a) was not meant to be defeated by the actions of individual members of the tribe, for Congress was concerned not solely about the interests of Indian children and families, but also about the impact on the tribes themselves of the large numbers of Indian children adopted by non-Indians. See 25 U.S.C. §§ 1901(3) ("[T]here is no resource that is more vital to the continued existence and integrity of Indian tribes than their children"), 1902 ("promote the stability and security of Indian tribes"). The numerous prerogatives accorded the tribes through the ICWA's substantive provisions, * * * must, accordingly, be seen as a means of protecting not only the interests of individual Indian children and families, but also of the tribes themselves.

In addition, it is clear that Congress' concern over the placement of Indian children in non-Indian homes was based in part on evidence of the detrimental impact on the children themselves of such placements outside their culture. Congress determined to subject such placements to the ICWA's jurisdictional and other provisions, even in cases where the parents consented to an adoption, because of concerns going beyond the wishes of individual parents. * * *

These congressional objectives make clear that a rule of domicile that would permit individual Indian parents to defeat the ICWA's jurisdictional scheme is inconsistent with what Congress intended. The appellees in this case argue strenuously that the twins' mother went to great lengths to give birth off the reservation so that her children could be adopted by the Holyfields. But that was precisely part of Congress' concern. Permitting individual members of the tribe to avoid tribal exclusive jurisdiction by the simple expedient of giving birth off the reservation would, to a large extent, nullify the purpose the ICWA was intended to accomplish. The Supreme Court of Utah expressed this well in its scholarly and sensitive opinion in what has become a leading case on the ICWA:

> "To the extent that [state] abandonment law operates to permit [the child's] mother to change [the child's] domicile as part of a scheme to facilitate his adoption by non-Indians while she remains a domiciliary of the reservation, it conflicts with and undermines the operative scheme established by subsections [1911(a)] and [1913(a)] to deal with children of domiciliaries of the reservation and weakens considerably the tribe's ability to assert its interest in its children. The protection of this tribal interest is at the core of the ICWA, which recognizes that the tribe has an interest in the child which is distinct from but on a parity with the interest of the parents. This relationship between Indian tribes and Indian children domiciled on the reservation finds no parallel in other ethnic cultures found in the United States. It is a relationship that many non-Indians find difficult to understand and that non-Indian courts are slow to recognize. It is precisely in recognition of this relationship, however, that the ICWA designates the tribal court as the exclusive forum for the determination of custody and adoption matters for reservation-domiciled Indian children, and the preferred forum for nondomiciliary Indian children. [State] abandonment law cannot be used to frustrate the federal legislative judgment expressed in the ICWA that the interests of the tribe in custodial decisions made with respect to Indian children are as entitled to respect as the interests of the parents." *In re Adoption of Halloway*, 732 P.2d 962, 969–970 (1986).

Think About It

Is there any way that parents like J.B. and W.J. could prevent the application of ICWA in a future case?

We agree with the Supreme Court of Utah that the law of domicile Congress used in the ICWA cannot be one that permits individual reservation-domiciled tribal members to defeat the tribe's exclusive jurisdiction by the simple expedient of giving birth and placing the child for adoption off the reservation. Since, for purposes of the ICWA, the twin babies in this case were domiciled on the reservation when adoption proceedings were begun, the Choctaw tribal court possessed exclusive jurisdiction pursuant to 25 U.S.C. § 1911(a). The Chancery Court of Harrison County was, accordingly, without jurisdiction to enter a decree of adoption; under ICWA § 104, 25 U.S.C. § 1914, its decree of January 28, 1986, must be vacated.

III

We are not unaware that over three years have passed since the twin babies were born and placed in the Holyfield home, and that a court deciding their fate today is not writing on a blank slate in the same way it would have in January

1986. Three years' development of family ties cannot be undone, and a separation at this point would doubtless cause considerable pain.

Whatever feelings we might have as to where the twins should live, however, it is not for us to decide that question. We have been asked to decide the legal question of *who* should make the custody determination concerning these children—not what the outcome of that determination should be. The law places that decision in the hands of the Choctaw tribal court. Had the mandate of the ICWA been followed in 1986, of course, much potential anguish might have been avoided, and in any case the law cannot be applied so automatically to "reward those who obtain custody, whether lawfully or otherwise, and maintain it during any ensuing (and protracted) litigation." *Halloway, 732 P.2d, at 972*. It is not ours to say whether the trauma that might result from removing these children from their adoptive family should outweigh the interest of the Tribe—and perhaps the children themselves—in having them raised as part of the Choctaw community. Rather, "we must defer to the experience, wisdom, and compassion of the [Choctaw] tribal courts to fashion an appropriate remedy." *Ibid*.

> **FYI**
>
> Justices Stevens and Kennedy and Chief Justice Rehnquist dissented, disagreeing with the meaning the Court gives to "domicile" in the statute. The dissenters argued that Indian parents should be able to invoke state court jurisdiction over an adoption without establishing a new domicile.
>
> For more of the story behind the *Holyfield* case, and a discussion of what happened after the Supreme Court's decision, see Solangel Maldonado, The Story of the Holyfield Twins: *Mississippi Band of Choctaw Indians v. Holyfield, in* Family Law Stories 113 (Carol Sanger, ed. 2008).

The judgment of the Supreme Court of Mississippi is reversed and the case remanded for further proceedings not inconsistent with this opinion.

It is so ordered.

Points for Discussion

a. Scope of ICWA

State courts must follow the requirements of the Indian Child Welfare Act in any child custody proceeding involving an Indian child. ICWA's definition of "child custody proceeding," includes foster care placement, termination of parental rights, and preadoptive and adoptive placements, but it does not include placements "based on an act which, if committed by an adult, would be deemed a crime" or to the award of custody in divorce proceedings. 25 U.S.C. § 1903(1)

(2018). Under the statute, an Indian child is any child who is either a member of an Indian tribe or eligible for membership and the biological child of a member of an Indian tribe. 25 U.S.C.A. § 1903(4). See, e.g., Welfare of S.N.R., 617 N.W.2d 77 (Minn.Ct.App.2000); In re Arianna R.G., 259 Wis.2d 563, 657 N.W.2d 363 (2003). An adoption decree entered in violation of the provisions of the Act can be invalidated by the tribe or custodian at any time after the decree is entered. 25 U.S.C. § 1913(1).

b. Jurisdiction Under ICWA

Holyfield discusses the jurisdictional rule in § 1911(a), which applies in child custody proceedings concerning Indian children who are domiciled on their tribe's reservation. Under § 1911(b), proceedings concerning Indian children who are not domiciled on the reservation are subject to trans-

> **Make the Connection**
>
> ICWA's application to cases in which children are removed from their parents' care are discussed in Chapter 5.

fer to tribal court at the request of either the child's parent or the tribe, unless the tribal court declines jurisdiction, the parent objects to the transfer, or the court concludes there is "good cause" to retain jurisdiction. The Bureau of Indian Affairs (BIA) has issued guidelines for determining whether good cause exists; see Guidelines for State Courts and Agencies in Indian Child Custody Proceedings, 80 Fed. Reg. 10146 (2015), applied in Interest of Tavian B., 874 N.W.2d 456 (Neb. 2016).

c. ICWA Placement Rules

ICWA mandates that adoptive placement of a child, absent good cause to the contrary, be made with a member of the child's family or tribe or other Indian families. 25 U.S.C. § 1915(a). A court may deviate from the placement preferences of ICWA if there is good cause to deviate, and the BIA Guidelines suggest that there may be good cause based on the request of the biological parents or the child (if the child is of sufficient age), the extraordinary physical or emotional needs of the child as established by a qualified expert witness, or the unavailability of suitable families for placement after a diligent search has been completed for families meeting the preference criteria. How would these criteria apply to a case like *Holyfield*, if it were appropriately within the state court's jurisdiction?

How can the placement preferences in ICWA be reconciled with the Multiethnic Placement Act (MEPA), discussed above? Should it be considered a violation of the Equal Protection Clause to restrict Indian children and parents from placement options that are available to non-Indians? Under Morton v. Mancari, 417 U.S. 535 (1974), legislation enacted by Congress containing classifications based on membership in a federally-recognized Indian tribe will be upheld "as long as the special treatment can be tied rationally to the fulfillment of Congress' unique obligation toward the Indians." Note also that Congress expressly exempted cases under ICWA when it enacted MEPA, reprinted above.

The Supreme Court has not addressed the constitutionality of ICWA, and state courts have reached different conclusions. Matter of Guardianship of D.L.L. & C.L.L., 291 N.W.2d 278 (S.D.1980), held that ICWA was not unconstitutional as racial discrimination because it was based not on race but on political status and the quasi-sovereign nature of Indian tribes, and that it did not violate the Tenth Amendment in light of Congress's plenary power to legislate concerning Indians under Article I, section 8 of the Constitution. In re Santos Y., 112 Cal. Rptr.2d 692, 716–17 (Ct. App. 2001) reached the opposite conclusion.

d. "Existing Indian Family" Exception?

Some state courts have avoided implementation of ICWA by holding that it applies only when the state is seeking to break up an "existing Indian family". The initial decision taking this approach was In re Adoption of Baby Boy L., 643 P.2d 168 (Kan. 1982), but the same court later abandoned it in Matter of A.J.S., 204 P.3d 543 (Kan. 2009). This approach has been criticized as contrary to the congressional intent behind the act; see Joan Heifetz

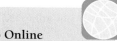

Go Online

Information on the Indian Child Welfare Act is available from the Child Welfare Information Gateway, and the Practical Guide to the Indian Child Welfare Act available on the web site of the Native American Rights Foundation.

Hollinger, *Beyond the Best Interests of the Tribe: The Indian Child Welfare Act and the Adoption of Indian Children*, 66 U. Det. Mercy L. Rev. 451, 477 (1989).

In California, some of the state's appellate courts have embraced the "existing Indian family" rule, see In re Santos Y., 112 Cal.Rptr.2d 692, 716–17 (Cal. Ct. App. 2001), and others have rejected it, see In re Vincent M., 59 Cal.Rptr.3d 321 (Cal. Ct. App. 2007). The court in *Santos Y.* concluded that recognition of the existing Indian family doctrine was necessary to the constitutionality of ICWA, finding that the

Further Reading: ICWA

B.J. Jones, et al., The Indian Child Welfare Act: A Legal Guide to the Custody and Adoption of Native American Children (2d ed. 2010).

statute would be unconstitutional as a matter of substantive due process and equal protection law if applied to an Indian child based solely on the child's genetic heritage, without "substantial social, cultural, or political affiliations between the child's family and a tribal community." The court in *Vincent M.* held that the exception contradicted "an unambiguous federal statute and an unambiguous state statute," and rejected the assertion that application of ICWA would otherwise be unconstitutional. In re Alexandria P., 176 Cal.Rptr.3d 468 (Ct. App. 2014), also rejected the "existing Indian family" exception and remanded for consideration of whether foster parents seeking to adopt an Indian child had demonstrated good cause to depart from ICWA's placement preferences by clear and convincing evidence.

e. *Adoptive Couple v. Baby Girl*

In addition to its *Mississippi Band* decision, the Supreme Court considered ICWA in Adoptive Couple v. Baby Girl, 570 U.S. 637 (2013). In a 5–4 ruling, the Court narrowed the scope of ICWA by limiting the application of two sections of the statute imposing heightened requirements for the termination of parental rights of an Indian parent. (This aspect of ICWA is addressed in Chapter 5.) The Court did not address the broader question presented: whether ICWA's definition of "parent" in 25 U.S.C. § 1903(9) should be read to include an nonmarital father who had not complied with rules under state law for attaining legal status as a parent. For a critique of the decision, see Bethany R. Berger, *In the Name of the Child: Race, Gender, and Economics in Adoptive Couple v. Baby Girl*, 67 Fla. L. Rev. 295 (2015).

Problem 3-12

B, an Indian, is married to S, a non-Indian. They have been unable to have a child and enter into a surrogacy agreement with S's sister whereby she is artificially inseminated with B's sperm and agrees to relinquish her parental rights to the child. When the child is born, the sister surrenders custody to B and S and signs a consent to adopt. B and S obtain an adoption decree, but sixteen months later S's sister seeks to have it set aside for non-compliance with a provision of ICWA requiring that consent be executed before a judge. B and S argue that since the adoption proceeding terminated the rights of the non-Indian parent and did not affect the rights of B, who is the Indian parent, ICWA should not apply. Does ICWA govern this case? (See Matter of Adoption of T.N.F., 781 P.2d 973 (Alaska 1989).)

Problem 3-13

Based on a history of abuse and neglect, the state removed Julian B. from his mother's care and terminated her parental rights. Julian's tribe has requested that he be placed for adoption with S, his mother's uncle, age 71, and D, S's companion, age 48. The state social services agency opposes placement with S because S is not married to D, based on S's age, and his prior history of alcohol abuse and a criminal conviction for driving under the influence and vehicular manslaughter. The tribe argues that S is active and in good health, that S and D have lived together for almost thirty years and consider themselves married based on their traditions, and that S's conviction was twenty years ago and he has been sober for more than fifteen years. In addition, S speaks the tribal language and participates in tribal and community activities. The agency has proposed an alternative placement with a "young, active" couple consisting of a wife and a husband who is part Cherokee. The couple is willing to help Julian remain connected to his own tribe. How should the court make the placement determination? (See In re Jullian B., 99 Cal.Rptr.2d 241 (Cal. Ct. App. 2000).)

2. Adoption Procedures

Jurisdiction over adoption has become an extremely complex question, often treated as a specialized case of the larger problem of child custody jurisdiction addressed in Chapter 7. Numerous cases have concluded that adoption jurisdiction is governed by statutes such as the Uniform Child Custody Jurisdiction Act, 9 U.L.A. (pt. IA) 261 (1999) (or its successor, the Uniform Child Custody Jurisdiction and Enforcement Act (UCCJEA), 9 U.L.A. (pt. IA) 649 (1999)), and the federal Parental Kidnapping Prevention Act, 28 U.S.C. § 1738A (2018). See, e.g., Matter of B.B.R., 566 A.2d 1032 (D.C. 1989); In re Baby Girl Clausen, 502 N.W.2d 649 (Mich. 1993).

Another school of thought holds that the use of these statutes in adoption cases is a mistake and should be replaced by use of the jurisdiction provisions of the 1994 Uniform Adoption Act (UAA). See Herma Hill Kay, *Adoption in the Conflict of Laws: The UAA, Not the UCCJA, Is the Answer*, 84 Cal. L. Rev. 703 (1996). The UAA was only enacted in Vermont, however and has been withdrawn. The problem is further complicated by the fact that the UCCJEA, which is in force in every state except Massachusetts, was designed to work with the UAA, and expressly excludes adoption proceedings from its scope. Many proceedings related to an adoption, however, such as an action to terminate parental rights, fall within the scope of the UCCJEA. See In the Interest of A.J.C., 88 P.3d 599 (Colo.2004) (discussing interaction of the UAA, the UCCJA, the PKPA and the UCCJEA in failed adoption cases); and State ex rel. Garrett v. Costine, 100 N.E.3d 368 (Ohio 2018) (holding that Ohio court could not order adoption when West Virginia had continuing jurisdiction under the UCCJEA and PKPA)

An interstate adoptive placement must also comply with the Interstate Compact on the Placement of Children (ICPC) which has been enacted in every state as well as the District of Columbia and the U.S. Virgin Islands. See Bernadette W. Hartfield, *The Role of the Interstate Compact on the Placement of Children in Interstate Adoption*, 68 Neb. L. Rev. 292 (1989). Unfortunately, there has been considerable noncompliance with the compact caused by a lack of awareness of its existence, a lack of uniformity in court decisions applying the compact and a lack of adequate remedies for violations. Some courts have been reluctant to deny an adoption for noncompliance, but other courts have dismissed adoption petitions where there has been a violation of the ICPC, particularly when a natural parent has objected to the adoption. See, e.g., In re Adoption of A.M.M., 949 P.2d 1155 (Kan. Ct. App. 1997).

Once it is final, a state court adoption decree is entitled to recognition in every state under the Full Faith and Credit Clause of the U.S. Constitution, provided that it was entered in accordance with the requirements of due process. These principles were reaffirmed in V.L. v. E.L., 577 U.S. ___, 136 S.Ct. 1017 (2016), and Finstuen v. Crutcher, 496 F.3d 1139 (10th Cir. 2007).

State courts have sometimes refused to extend recognition on the basis of comity to adoption decrees entered by foreign courts on procedural or other grounds, but as international adoption has become increasingly common many states have enacted statutes addressing recognition of foreign adoption decrees. E.g. Fla. Stat. § 63.192 (2018); Tex. Fam. Code § 162.023(a) (2018).

Global View: International Adoption

As the availability of healthy infants for adoption in the United States diminished, prospective adoptive parents turned to international adoptions. Adoptive parents must obtain a U.S. visa in order to bring a child they have adopted in another country into the United States, and federal immigration laws have been the primary point of regulation for international adoption. Similar procedures apply when U.S. citizen parents obtain placement of a child abroad with the expectation that their adoption of the child will be finalized in state court after the child enters the United States. In 1992, the United States issued an annual total of 6,472 "orphan visas" in incoming adoption cases, and this number peaked in 2004 with visas issued for 22,884 children.

Various factors have contributed to a reduction in the numbers of international adoptions since 2004; in the 2017 fiscal year the annual total had dropped to 4,714. The numbers of children made available for international adoption in countries such as China, Russia and South Korea declined significantly during this period. At the same time, concerns regarding a lack of appropriate safeguards for children and parents led U.S. authorities to suspend approval for further visas in intercountry adoption cases from several other countries including Guatemala. In 2017, 83 children were adopted from the United States to foreign countries including Canada, the Netherlands, and Ireland.

The United States participates in the Hague Convention on Intercountry Adoption, 32 I.L.M. 1134–1146 (1993). The Adoption Convention was implemented with the Intercountry Adoption Act of 2000, 42 U.S.C. § 14901 et seq.(2018), and came into force in the United States in 2008. The Convention establishes a system for international cooperation to ensure that intercountry adoptions take place in the best interests of the child. Authorities in the child's state of origin must determine that the child is adoptable, that intercountry adoption is in the child's best interests, and that appropriate consents have been given. Authorities in the receiving state are responsible for determining that the prospective adoptive parents are eligible and suited to adopt, that they have been counseled, and that the child will be authorized to enter the new country and reside there permanently. Each country that ratifies or accedes to the Adoption Convention must designate a Central Authority to handle these cases. In the United States, the Central Authority is located in the Bureau of Consular Affairs in the State Department.

Implementing regulations in the United States include rules for accreditation and approval of agencies and persons to provide adoption services. See 22 C.F.R. § 96 (2018). The Convention also applies to outgoing cases, in which a child who is habitually resident in the United States will be adopted and taken to live in another Convention country. See 22 C.F.R. § 97 (2018) (issuance of Hague adoption certificates); 22 C.F.R. § 98 (2018) (preservation of adoption records) and 22 C.F.R. § 99 (2018) (reporting requirement in outgoing cases). Detailed information on intercountry adoption is available on the U.S. State Department web site. Resources and information about the Hague Adoption Convention are available on the Hague Conference on Private International Law web site.

In re Adoption of M.S.

103 Cal.Rptr.3d 715 (Ct. App. 2010)

SIMS, J.

This is a tragic case in which there can be no good ending for anyone.

Appellants Eleanor P. and Martin S. appeal from an order denying their petition to set aside their Ukrainian adoption of a Ukrainian girl, M.S. The petition was opposed by the California Department of Social Services (the Department or DSS). Appellants contend the trial court erred in construing Family Code section 9100,[1] which authorizes the court to vacate adoptions, as inapplicable to an "intercountry adoption" completed in Ukraine.[2]

This is a case with equities on both sides. However, when we apply the governing statutes enacted by the Legislature, we conclude the trial court was correct. We shall affirm the judgment.

FACTUAL AND PROCEDURAL BACKGROUND

In early 2003, appellants began the process to adopt a foreign-born child. Appellants engaged a California lawyer and a private California adoption agency, Heartsent Adoptions, Inc. (Heartsent), which was licensed by the Department to provide noncustodial intercountry adoption services.

In late 2003, appellants spent several weeks in Ukraine for the adoption. On December 15, 2003, by decree of a Ukrainian court, appellants adopted M.S., a three-year-old Ukrainian girl. The Ukrainian court decree stated in part: "It was found out from the case documents that the child's [biological] mother is mentally sick. She left the child at the hospital and never visited her. The place of father's residence was not identified. Since February 2002 the child has been made the

---

[1]   Undesignated statutory references are to the Family Code.

Section 9100 provides:

"(a) If a child adopted pursuant to the law of this state shows evidence of a developmental disability or mental illness as a result of conditions existing before the adoption to an extent that the child cannot be relinquished to an adoption agency on the grounds that the child is considered unadoptable, and of which conditions the adoptive parent or parents had no knowledge or notice before the entry of the order of adoption, a petition setting forth those facts may be filed by the adoptive parents or parent with the court that granted the adoption petition. If these facts are proved to the satisfaction of the court, it may make an order setting aside the order of adoption. [¶] (b) The petition shall be filed within five years after the entry of the order of adoption. [¶] (c) The court clerk shall immediately notify the department at Sacramento of the petition. Within 60 days after the notice, the department shall file a full report with the court and shall appear before the court for the purpose of representing the adopted child."

[2]   An "intercountry adoption" is "the adoption of a foreign-born child for whom federal law makes a special immigration visa available. Intercountry adoption includes completion of the adoption in the child's native country or completion of the adoption in this state." (§ 8527.)

ward of the government. The medical history of the girl says that she is almost healthy though psychologically delayed." A hospital record says the mother has epilepsy.

Appellants' declarations assert they believed M.S. was healthy, were not aware of this medical background information until after the adoption was finalized, and the documents were not translated for them until after the adoption was completed.

Appellants brought M.S. to live in their Davis home. They did not "readopt" M.S. in California, as authorized by <u>section 8919</u>.

In California, various evaluations were performed due to M.S.'s low level of functioning. Healthcare professionals diagnosed her with spastic cerebral palsy, reactive attachment disorder, oppositional defiance disorder, moderate mental retardation, global development delay, ataxia, fetal alcohol syndrome or effect, microcephaly, and post-traumatic stress disorder. Appellants assert M.S. cannot live in a normal home environment, is unadoptable, and has been living in intensive foster care placement in Arizona since 2005.

On May 20, 2008, appellants filed in Yolo County Superior Court a "MOTION TO SET ASIDE ORDER OF ADOPTION UNDER FAMILY CODE SECTION 9100" (the petition). This petition was served on the Department, which filed an opposition. The opposition argued section 9100 is inapplicable to intercountry adoptions; the statutory remedy is not appropriate because the child could not be returned to Ukraine; the records gave notice of potential problems; and the Department did not have access to underlying investigative reports or documentation it would need to fulfill its obligation to make a full report to the court.

On October 31, 2008, after hearing oral argument, the superior court issued an "ORDER DENYING PETITION TO SET ASIDE INTERCOUNTRY ADOPTION PURSUANT TO FAMILY CODE SECTION 9100." The order denied the petition on the ground the court lacked jurisdiction to make a ruling on the matter.

DISCUSSION

I. *Standard of Review*

"Where, as here, the issue presented is one of statutory construction, our fundamental task is 'to ascertain the intent of the lawmakers so as to effectuate the purpose of the statute.' [Citations.] We begin by examining the statutory language because it generally is the most reliable indicator of legislative intent. [Citation.] We give the language its usual and ordinary meaning, and '[i]f there is no ambiguity, then we presume the lawmakers meant what they said, and the plain meaning of the language governs.' [Citation.]"

II. *Section 9100*

Appellants cite no legal authority for un-doing the Ukraine adoption except section 9100.

Section 9100 authorizes the superior court to vacate an adoption of a child "adopted pursuant to the law of this state."

Appellants contend the superior court erred in construing section 9100's language "pursuant to the law of this state" to mean that an adoption must have occurred within California's borders in order to be afforded section 9100 relief to vacate the adoption.

However, the language of section 9100 itself, plus the language of a companion statute—section 9101—clearly show that section 9100 is limited to un-doing adoptions that were granted by California state courts.[7]

Thus, section 9100 says a petition under that section "may be filed with the court that granted the adoption petition." " 'It is a conceded principle that the laws of a state have no force, *proprio vigor* beyond its territorial limits. . . .' " (*Estate of Lund* (1945) 26 Cal.2d 472, 489, 159 P.2d 643, quoting *Hoyt v. Thompson*, 5 N.Y. 320, 340.) With this in mind, the California Legislature surely did not intend to legislate court filings in a Ukrainian court. We therefore infer "the court that granted the adoption petition" in section 9100 must be a California state court. Moreover, when two statutes touch upon a common subject, they are to be construed in reference to each other. In the event an adoption is vacated under section 9100, section 9101 places responsibility for the support of the now unadopted child on "[t]he county in which the proceeding for adoption was had." In this case, there is no such county in California, and the California Legislature obviously has no power to order a Ukrainian county (if such even exists) to support the child. Where section 9100 requires the petition to be filed "with the court that granted the adoption petition," the reference is to a court within the state of California. In this case, the petition was not filed "with the court that granted the adoption petition." Accordingly, the Yolo County Superior Court correctly ruled that it had no authority to adjudicate the petition.

Appellants offer two main arguments against our conclusion.

First, they say that where section 9100 provides that a petition "may be filed. . .with the court that granted the adoption petition," the word "may" is permissive, not mandatory. Section 12 provides, " '[s]hall' is mandatory and 'may'

---

[7] We have no occasion in this case to determine whether section 9100 may be used to set aside a readoption pursuant to section 8919 because the child, M.S., was not readopted in California.

is permissive." In other words, appellants argue section 9100 does not require a petition to be filed "with the court that granted the adoption petition."

For reasons that follow, we do not agree.

The sentence in which the word "may" occurs is as follows: "(a) If a child adopted pursuant to the law of this state shows evidence of a developmental disability or mental illness as a result of conditions existing before the adoption to an extent that the child cannot be relinquished to an adoption agency on the grounds that the child is considered unadoptable, and of which conditions the adoptive parent or parents had no knowledge or notice before the entry of the order of adoption, a petition setting forth those facts may be filed by the adoptive parents or parent with the court that granted the adoption petition." (§ 9100.)

In this sentence, the word "may" is used in the permissive sense of giving a parent or parents discretion whether to file a petition under section 9100. This is in stark contrast to section 8919, which *requires* a readoption of a child adopted in a foreign country "if it is required by the Department of Homeland Security."

So, by its use of "may," section 9100 makes clear that the parent or parents have discretion whether to file a petition under that statute.

However, once the decision is made to file a petition, the petition must be filed "with the court that granted the adoption petition." This is the only construction that makes sense. No other court is designated as the proper place for the filing of a petition. If the petition could be filed in *any* court, then reference to "the court that granted the adoption petition" would be unnecessary. Moreover, since the petition seeks to unadopt a child, it is only reasonable to require the petition to be filed in the court that has the records of the original adoption. Thus, if a petition under section 9100 is filed, it *must* be filed "with the court that granted the adoption petition."

Appellants next argue that section 9100 should receive a liberal construction.

However, the doctrine of "liberal construction" has its limits. "As a rule, a command that a constitutional provision or a statute be liberally construed 'does not license either enlargement or restriction of its evident meaning.' (*People v. Cruz* (1974) 12 Cal.3d 562, 566[, 116 Cal.Rptr. 242, 526 P.2d 250].)" (*Apartment Assn. of Los Angeles County, Inc. v. City of Los Angeles* (2001) 24 Cal.4th 830, 844, 102 Cal.Rptr.2d 719, 14 P.3d 930.) Whatever may be thought of the wisdom, expediency, or policy of a statute, we have no power to rewrite the statute to make it conform to a presumed intention that is not expressed. In our view, appellants are asking us to re-write the statutory scheme. This we will not do.

For these reasons, then, we conclude that section 9100 applies only to adoptions granted by a California state court. This is the law that must be applied in this difficult case. The trial court correctly found that section 9100 could not be used to undo the Ukrainian adoption.

III. *Withdrawal of Contention re Readoption*

In their opening brief, appellants argued in the alternative that they should be allowed to amend the pleading to readopt the child in California under section 8919 (with the intent that they would then petition to set aside the adoption under section 9100). In their reply brief, appellants withdraw this argument, and we therefore need not address it.

DISPOSITION

The judgment (order) is affirmed. The parties shall bear their own costs on appeal. (Cal. Rules of Court, rule 8.278(a)(5).)

Points for Discussion

a. Annulment of Adoption

In a domestic case, could the adoptive parents have prevailed in a suit to annul the adoption decree on the basis of fraud or non-disclosure? Courts have not readily agreed to set aside adoption decrees, see Matter of Adoption of T.B., 622 N.E.2d 921 (Ind.1993); Allen v. Allen, 330 P.2d 151 (Or. 1958); Wimber v. Timpe, 818 P.2d 954 (Or. Ct. App. 1991). For a case applying the California statute cited in *M.S.*, see Adoption of Kay C., 278 Cal.Rptr. 907 (Ct. App. 1991). Most states have short statutes of limitations governing adoption challenges, reflecting the strong public policy favoring family stability. See, e.g., Colo. Rev. Stat. Ann. § 19–5–214 (2018), which includes the proviso that the court shall sustain the decree unless there is clear and convincing evidence that the decree is not in the best interests of the child.

b. Disclosure Rules

Many modern statutes require adoption agencies to provide adoptive parents with detailed health and genetic information about the child and its natural parents. E.g., Ariz. Rev. Stat. Ann. § 8–129 (2018); N.Y. Soc. Serv. L. § 373–a (2018). The New York law requires disclosure of drugs and medications taken during pregnancy. If an unmarried mother relinquishes her baby to an agency, and refuses to discuss her family history or that of the baby's father, how should the agency proceed?

c. Tort Actions Following Adoption

Mohr v. Commonwealth, 653 N.E.2d 1104 (Mass. 1995), and Mallette v. Children's Friend and Service, 661 A.2d 67 (R.I.1995), both held that an adoption agency could be liable for negligent or intentional misrepresentations concerning the adopted child's medical, genetic or social background. Gibbs v. Ernst, 647 A.2d 882 (Pa. 1994), held that although the agency had no duty to investigate the child's background, it must make a good faith effort to discover the child's medical history. Here the agency was liable for not disclosing that the child had a long history of physical and sexual abuse, which they knew before the adoption placement. Jackson v. State, 956 P.2d 35 (Mont. 1998), held that adoptive parents could bring an action for negligent misrepresentation, negligent nondisclosure, negligence based on a lack of informed consent and negligent supervision against the state adoption agency. Wolford v. Children's Home Society of West Virginia, 17 F. Supp. 2d 577 (S.D.W.Va.1998) allowed a suit for misrepresentation of facts concerning a birth mother's alcohol abuse during her pregnancy. See also Dresser v. Cradle of Hope Adoption Center, 358 F. Supp. 2d 620 (E.D. Mich. 2005), which allowed a negligence action to proceed against the agencies that arranged a foreign adoption and failed to deliver the child's medical records to his adoptive parents within a reasonable time.

d. Unregulated Custody Transfers

News stories have reported on a practice referred to as "rehoming," in which parents who have adopted children from foster care or through intercountry adoption transfer custody informally when they find they are not able to meet the challenges of parenting children with complex needs. This practice presents enormous risks to children, and has been explicitly criminalized in a number of states. See, e.g., La. Rev. Stat. § 14:46.4 (2018). See generally Child Welfare Information Gateway, *Unregulated Custody Transfers of Adopted Children* (2018).

Problem 3-14

Mary and Robert applied to become adoptive parents with their local state adoption service, and were investigated and accepted. They told the service they did not want a handicapped or special needs child or one who had prenatal drug exposure. The agency placed an infant, Alex, with them. Although Alex was in generally good health for the first few months of his life, his development began to slow. Mary and Robert were referred to specialists who tentatively diagnosed Alex as having cerebral palsy. Although Mary and Robert tried to get more information about Alex, they were not successful. The adoption decree was entered when Alex was nine months old, and shortly thereafter a definite diagnosis of "global neuro-developmental dysfunction" was made. This condition meant that Alex would not live a normal life, and that he would require expensive medical care and round-the-clock supervision. Should Mary and Robert recover damages from the agency on the ground that they were not told (i) that public subsidies for the care of special needs children were available, and (ii) that they should postpone finalizing the adoption until the child's health difficulties were fully diagnosed? (See MacMath v. Maine Adoption Placement Services, 635 A.2d 359 (Me.1993).)

Consequences of an Adoption Decree

State statutes define the consequences of adoption, generally providing that adoption terminates the rights of the natural parents and creates new rights and obligations of the adoptive parents. The adopted child inherits from his or her adoptive parents, and the descendants of a deceased adopted child also usually inherit from the adoptive parents. See, e.g., N.Y. Dom. Rel. § 117(c) (2018). In some states, however, an adopted child is not included in class gifts made by will or inter vivos transfer, where the gift is to "heirs", "issue", "children" etc. of the adoptive parent. Under Uniform Probate Code § 2–705, 8 U.L.A. (Part I) 1 (2013), adopted persons are included in class gift terminology in accordance with the rules for determining relationships for purposes of intestate succession.

Courts have had some trouble with the issue raised when the adopted child attempts to take by intestacy from his natural parents. Modern statutes often contain express provisions that the child does not inherit from or through his genetic parents after he is adopted. See Uniform Probate Code § 2–119, 8 U.L.A. 1 (2013). Since this is essentially a statutory subject, and the statutes are frequently changing, the inheritance rights of an adopted child in any specific jurisdiction can only be determined by a detailed investigation of the local law.

Many courts have recognized equitable adoption, based either on the rationale that there was a contract to adopt the child, or that a party is estopped from denying that adoption had occurred. In either event some or all of the consequences of adoption may follow even if the parties did not comply with the adoption statute. Claims of equitable adoption often arise in intestacy proceedings after the "adoptive" parents have died, and courts may require proof by clear and convincing evidence. See, e.g., Estate of Ford, 82 P.3d 747 (Cal.2004). Courts have concluded that child support obligations may be imposed on the basis of equitable adoption; see, e.g., Johnson v. Johnson, 617 N.W.2d 97 (N.D.2000). See also D'Accardi v. Chater, 96 F.3d 97 (4th Cir.1996), holding that New Jersey law recognized an oral contract to adopt, entitling the child to social security benefits under the doctrine of equitable adoption; and Weidner v. American Family Mutual Ins. Co., 928 S.W.2d 401(Mo.Ct.App.1996), holding that stepdaughter did not provide sufficient evidence of equitable adoption to acquire standing to pursue a wrongful death action following stepfather's death.

Adult Adoption

Most states permit adoption of an adult, which is usually contemplated for inheritance purposes. An adult adoption may serve to formalize an informal parent-child relationship that began when the child was a minor, when adoption was not possible for some reason. Alternatively, adoption may be intended primarily to secure some legal or financial benefit that depends upon a family relationship. Same-sex couples who could not marry sometimes relied on adoption as a substitute, but this was not permitted in every state. See Matter of Adoption of Robert Paul P., 471 N.E.2d 424 (N.Y. 1984). Some states have age restrictions, or rules that prohibit adoption of a spouse. Many of the decided cases involve adoptions that were intended to confer inheritance rights through the adoptive parent under the terms of a will or trust. For example, in Goodman v. Goodman, 126 So.3d 310 (Fla. Dist. Ct. App. 2013), a man's adult adoption of his girlfriend in Florida, carried out without notice to other family members, was set aside when it would have diminished his children's interest in a trust established for them as part of his divorce from their mother. See generally Sarah Ratliff, Comment, *Adult Adoption: Intestate Succession and Class Gifts Under the Uniform Probate Code*, 105 Nw. U. L. Rev. 1777 (2011); see also 2 Homer H. Clark, Jr., Domestic Relations § 21.10 (2d ed. 1987).

In the Matter of the Adoption of Anthony

448 N.Y.S.2d 377 (Fam. Ct. 1982)

GERTRUD MAINZER, JUDGE:

In this adoption proceeding filed on July 8, 1980 by Dennis and Dorothy P. the Court signed an Order of Adoption which included a provision that the adoptive child have continued contact and visitation with his biological siblings (hereinafter the "birth siblings"). Recognizing that some decisions have held it to be beyond the authority of the Court to provide for visitation with members of the biological family (hereinafter the "birth family") after adoption, this Court felt compelled to set forth its reasoning in a written decision. * * *

The pertinent facts are as follows:

Anthony, the adoptive child, was born on April 9, 1969. He was the fourth child of Barbara B. and William R., his putative father. The records of the Children's Aid Society, the agency having custody and guardianship of Anthony, indicate that William R. died on December 22, 1969. The cause of death stated in his death certificate was fatty liver attributed to chronic alcoholism. Subsequent to the death of William R., Anthony's mother married Robert K.

Anthony was first placed in a shelter boarding home on September 12, 1969. At that time, his mother, who was alleged to be emotionally unstable was unable to care for him. On November 25, 1970, when Anthony was 18 months old, he was placed with his present family, with whom he has continuously resided. On September 3, 1975 the parental rights of both Anthony's mother and Robert K. were terminated under Section 384 of the Social Services Law.

Anthony's three older birth siblings had been previously freed for adoption. All three were placed with and adopted by the same foster family. At the time Anthony came into placement, the foster family who adopted his birth siblings was unable to accommodate another child and, consequently Anthony was placed in his present adoptive home.

Despite the separation from his birth siblings, Anthony has maintained an ongoing relationship with them. He has visited them and been in phone contact with them up to the time this proceeding was filed. Anthony knows their adoptive names and address. The Children's Aid Society, following sound agency policy, as well as Anthony's adoptive parents have encouraged and supported Anthony's relationship with his birth siblings.

After finding that all formal requirements for Anthony's adoption had been met and after examining the background of Anthony's adoptive and birth families, this Court discussed Anthony's contact with his birth siblings with all parties. Both the Agency and the adoptive parents agreed that Anthony's relationship with his birth siblings was most important to Anthony's well being and should be continued. However, the Agency maintained that such contact be continued on an informal basis or, alternatively, that a letter of consent by the adoptive parents be attached to the adoption order. After considering both proposals, this Court found that neither arrangement would adequately safeguard Anthony's interests. While the adoptive parents may presently feel that Anthony's contact with his birth siblings is essential, Anthony's interests would not be protected should his adoptive parents change their minds in the future. Therefore, this Court determined that the only way to ensure Anthony's interests after his adoption was to include a direction in the Order of Adoption that Anthony have continued contact including visitation with his birth siblings.

This Court is well aware of the legal consequences of adoption as defined in Section 117 of the Domestic Relations Law providing for the termination of parental rights and obligations of the birth parents and the creation of such rights and obligations in the adoptive parents. Section 114 of the Domestic Relations Law further provides that an adoption order shall be approved only if the judge or surrogate is satisfied that the *best interests* of the child will be promoted by the adoption. Though the adoption procedure is primarily intended to promote the welfare of children, the statute nowhere specifically defines the interests to be considered by the Court, nor are there any provisions to ensure that such interests will be protected after the child's adoption. In this regard, it has been increasingly recognized that the concept of an "open adoption", one in which contact, including visitation, is permitted between the adopted child and members of his birth family may serve to promote the best interests of the child in certain cases and should be available as an alternative form of adoption.

In the past, the typical adoption involved an infant, usually illegitimate, who was taken into the adoptive home with no previous relationship or contact with his birth family. In such cases, adoption was conceptualized as a complete substitution of one family by another and secrecy in the adoption was primarily intended to protect the child against the stigma of illegitimacy and to guarantee an undisturbed family environment.

Significant social changes have occurred, however, which have undermined many of the traditional assumptions upon which adoption practices are based. In the last decade the number of infants surrendered for adoption at birth has been steadily decreasing. The greater use of birth control, the legalization of abortion and changing social attitudes have all contributed to this decline. The social stigma attached to illegitimacy has lessened and many unwed mothers now keep their babies.

While the number of infants being adopted at birth has been decreasing, there has been an increase in the number of older children now being adopted. The high rates of divorce and remarriage has been accompanied by an increase in step-parent adoptions of older children. In addition, there has been an increase in the number of foster children now being adopted by their foster parents. Many of these children have lived in foster care for extended periods, are older and have physical or mental handicaps. In these adoptions, secrecy is not only frequently impossible, but often inadvisable since these children remember their past and have emotional ties to their birth families.

Research by psychiatrists and psychologists has also revealed the importance of a child's links to known ancestral, religious, ethnic and cultural backgrounds. Recent studies indicate that shrouding a child's background in an air of mystery, even for a child adopted at birth, can cause psychological harm, retarding emotional development and self-identity. Moreover, in a longitudinal investigation of foster care,[11] Professors David Fanshel of Columbia University and Eugene B. Shinn of Hunter College found that the intellectual, psychological and physical development of children in long term foster care was enhanced by visitation and contact, however minimal, with the biological family. Although no studies are available for adopted children, it seems likely that visitation with members of a child's birth family after adoption would be similarly beneficial. Furthermore, the need to know family medical history for the diagnosis, prevention and treatment of congenital diseases[12] as well as for family planning is now widely recognized. Many genetic illnesses are not apparent at birth. Others do not occur until adult life. In such instances continued contact with the birth family and knowledge of their medical history may be essential.

In view of these developments the need for and the advantages of an open adoption are clear. This concept offers an enlightened alternative for dealing with those situations in which the traditional adoption would be inappropriate. Accordingly, where adoption cannot be a total replacement of the birth family, but rather a legal means of assuring the adoptive parents and the child that their relationship is permanent, an open adoption may guarantee this permanency without unnecessarily severing important relationships with known members of the child's birth family existing prior to the adoption.[13]

Although open adoptions are not specifically authorized by statute, there is legal precedent supporting the proposition that the court has the necessary authority to provide for visitation between the adopted child and members of his birth family where such visitation is in the best interests of the adopted child and does not unduly interfere with the adoptive relationship. That the Court has such power was recognized as early as 1917 in *Matter of McDevitt, 176 A.D. 418, 162 N.Y.S. 1032 (2d Dept.1917)*, where a mother was granted visitation rights with her child following adoption. There the Court held that ample power exists at law and in equity to promote the welfare of the child, notwithstanding a legal adoption.

---

[11] Fanshel, D., Shinn, E.B., Children in Foster Care, Columbia University Press, 1978.

[12] There are approximately 2,000 genetic diseases. Examples of the more common diseases are sickle cell anemia, thalassemia, Huntington disease, hemophilia and Wilson's disease.

[13] The most recent amendments to the New Jersey adoption statute incorporates the requirement that due regard be given to the rights of all persons affected by an adoption and provides for the termination of all rights between the adopted child and his parents, as well as the rights of any person which are derived from that parent-child relationship except such rights which have vested prior to the entry of the order of adoption. N.J.S. 9:3–37 and 9:3–50. These provisions have been applied to permit continuing contact between the adopted child and members of his birth family where such relationships were established prior to the child's adoption and are beneficial to the child.

More recently it was held that a Surrogate has equitable jurisdiction to make orders of visitation incident to an adoption proceeding. *Matter of Raana Beth N., 78 Misc.2d 105, 355 N.Y.S.2d 956 (Surr.Ct.N.Y.Co.1974)*. In that case, a 51/2 year old child who was adopted by her stepfather was permitted to visit her birth father. The Court found that although it was preferable for the child to become a full member of her mother's and stepfather's family through adoption, visitation with the birth father would be beneficial to the child and should be continued. See also: *Matter of Widrick, 25 Misc.2d 1078, 212 N.Y.S.2d 350 (Surr.Ct.Lawrence Co.1960)* (an adoption of children by their stepfather would not divest the natural father of his visitation rights).

In *Matter of Patricia A.W., 89 Misc.2d 368, 392 N.Y.S.2d 180 (Fam.Ct.Kings Co.1977)* the Court addressed the issue of visitation between siblings. There a petition was brought to terminate the parental rights of a father who had two girls, ages 7 and 9, who were in foster care and an older boy, age 11, who lived with a grandparent. The boy expressed a strong desire to maintain his relationship with his sisters, despite their separation. The Court ordered parental rights terminated but preserved visitation rights between the boy and his sisters.

Finally and most recently in *People ex rel. Sibley v. Sheppard, 54 N.Y.2d 320, 445 N.Y.S.2d 420, 429 N.E.2d 1049, 1981*, the Court of Appeals affirmed an order of the Supreme Court permitting a grandparent visitation with her grandchild despite the child's adoption and the objections of the adoptive parents.[14] In doing so, the Court of Appeals recognized that an adoption does not automatically sever all contacts between the adoptive child and members of the birth family and that the Court has the authority to preserve such contacts when necessary to protect the best interests of the child even when opposed by the adoptive parents.

Think About It

Does the reasoning in *Adoption of Anthony* apply equally to continued contact with the natural parent, or is it limited to sibling contact?

Before this Court is a twelve year old child who knows the facts surrounding his adoption, who has visited and maintained a relationship with his siblings over the years and who strongly desires to continue his relationship with his siblings. The adoptive parents and the child's birth siblings know each other. Thus, there are no privacy concerns here, nor are there any claims that visitation between the child and his birth siblings will hinder the adoptive family unit. Indeed, the adoptive parents admit that it is in the child's

---

[14]   While Section 72 of the Domestic Relations Law specifically provides a grandparent with a right to seek visitation with a grandchild where either or both parents of the child are deceased, the principles enunciated by the Court of Appeals are applicable to other family members even where no such statutory provision exists.

best interests to continue to visit his birth siblings. In light of these facts this Court finds that contact and visitation with his birth siblings is necessary to promote Anthony's best interests and furthermore finds that this Court has the necessary power to order this adoption with the direction that Anthony have continued contact including visitation with his birth siblings.

Points for Discussion

a. Open Adoption

In an open adoption, the parties agree that the adopted child will continue to have some form of contact with members of his or her biological family. Proponents of open adoption assert that adoptions that would be in the child's best interest do not take place in some cases due to the extreme consequence of complete severance of ties to the biological family, and that continued contact with the biological family after adoption would best meet the needs of all parties. See Carol Amadio and Stuart L. Deutsch, *Open Adoption: Allowing Adopted Children to "Stay in Touch" With Blood Relatives*, 22 J. Fam. L. 59 (1983–84). In the case of an older child who has an established relationship with the natural parent, or where the grounds for involuntary termination do not exist but the child would be better off living with an adoptive family, open adoption may provide a useful alternative to full termination of parental rights.

Open adoption may be particularly important in communities with a pattern of strong extended families. See Gilbert A. Holmes, *The Extended Family System in the Black Community: A Child Centered Model for Adoption Policy*, 68 Temple L. Rev. 1649 (1995), which criticizes adoption policies that are based on a simple nuclear family model for ignoring the complex family structures of adopted children, and argues that "law should facilitate adopted children's connection with both their adoptive kin and birth kin." Open adoption has also been suggested as a means to resolve disputes under the Indian Child Welfare Act in which a adoption decree may be set aside long after the child has been integrated into a non-Indian family. See Adoption of Halloway, 732 P.2d 962 (Utah 1986); Joan Heifetz Hollinger, *Beyond the Best Interests of the Tribe: The Indian Child Welfare Act and the Adoption of Indian Children*, 66 U. Det. Mercy L. Rev. 451, 497–498 (1989).

b. Post-Adoption Visitation Agreements

State laws are divided on whether agreements for post-adoption visitation can be incorporated into an adoption decree and specifically enforced. In many states, provisions for continued contact after an adoption are inconsistent with the requirements for termination of parental rights. See In re M.M., 619 N.E.2d 702

(Ill. 1993); Birth Mother v. Adoptive Parents, 59 P.3d 1233 (Nev. 2002). In other states, statutes allow enforcement of these agreements. See, e.g., Cal. Fam. Code § 8616.5 (2018), Mass. Ann. Laws ch. 210 § 6C (2018), Minn. Stat. Ann. § 259.58 (2018); Or. Rev. Stat. § 109.305(2) (2018). See generally Margaret M. Mahoney, *Open Adoption in Context: The Wisdom and Enforceability of Visitation Orders for Former Parents under Uniform Adoption Act § 4–113*, 51 Fla. L. Rev. 89 (1999). What is the source of the New York court's authority to order continued contact with the siblings in *Adoption of Anthony*?

c. Adoption Secrecy

Adoption laws and practices were structured in the past to maintain a complete separation between the child's biological and adoptive families. This was achieved by the termination of all legal and social ties between the child and his or her natural parents and by strict secrecy surrounding adoption proceedings and records. More recent thinking challenged these traditions, with some studies supporting the view that the secrecy that has surrounded adoption proceedings has had a profoundly detrimental effect on both the child and the relinquishing parent in many instances. See, e.g., Arthur D. Sorosky, et. al., The Adoption Triangle: The Effects of the Sealed Record on Adoptees, Birth Parents, and Adoptive Parents 219–229 (1978).

Today, birth parents often select adoptive parents from detailed dossiers of information about the candidates, a significant shift away from the secrecy that was fundamental to adoption in the past. See Annette Ruth Appell, *Blending Families Through Adoption: Implications for Collaborative Adoption Law and Practice*, 75 B.U. L. Rev. 997 (1995), which discusses changes in adoption practice, the continuing need of adopted children to know about their birth parents and the flexible concept of open adoption, and the need for the law to change correspondingly.

d. Adoption Records

Adoption records have traditionally been sealed in order to protect the privacy of the parties and the integrity of the adoption process. With the movement towards open adoption has come a legislative trend toward opening of adoption records. Some states now allow an adult adoptee to obtain his or her original birth certificate in some circumstances. E.g., Kan. Stat. Ann. § 65–2423(a) (2018). More states have established a voluntary registry which will release information if both the adoptee and the birth parent register their consent. E.g., Cal. Fam. Code §§ 9203–9206 (2018). In a few states, statutes provide that the state agency will affirmatively search for the birth parent, inform him or her of the request for access to the records and ask for consent to release the information. E.g., Ky. Rev. Stat. Ann. § 199.572 (2018); Neb. Rev. Stat. § 43–140 (2018).

Adoptees in search of information about their natural parents and siblings have also sought to obtain greater access to their adoption records through judicial challenges based on the First Amendment, the Equal Protection and Due Process Clauses of the Fourteenth Amendment and the right to privacy. These have consistently failed.; see Alma Soc. Inc. v. Mellon, 601 F.2d 1225 (2d Cir.1979), cert. denied 444 U.S. 995 (1979); In re Roger B., 418 N.E.2d 751 (Ill. 1981); Adoption of S.J.D., 641 N.W.2d 794 (Iowa 2002); Application of Maples, 563 S.W.2d 760 (Mo.1978).

Efforts to obtain legislative change have been more successful, and some state statutes authorize a court to open adoption records based on a finding of "good cause." See, e.g., N.J. Stat. Ann. § 9:3–52(a) (2018). Courts seem reluctant to define clearly what constitutes good cause, and the burden of proof is usually placed on the person seeking to open the records. See Linda F.M. v. Department of Health, 418 N.E.2d 1302 (N.Y. 1981). Natural parents have also been denied relief when they sought to locate children they gave up for adoption; see In re Adoption of Baby S., 705 A.2d 822 (N.J. Super. 1997); In re Christine, 397 A.2d 511 (R.I. 1979).

Go Online

For a survey of state laws, see Child Welfare Information Gateway, Access to Adoption Records (2016).

With the opening of adoption records, legal challenges have also come from the opposite direction, arguing that opening such records violates rights of familial and reproductive privacy under the United States Constitution. See Does v. Oregon, 993 P.2d 822 (Or. Ct. App.1999) (sustaining measure passed as a ballot initiative opening birth records to adoptees over age 21); Doe v. Sundquist, 2 S.W.3d 919 (Tenn.1999) (holding that statute did not unconstitutionally impair any vested rights); Doe v. Sundquist, 106 F.3d 702 (6th Cir.1997) (upholding the 1996 Tennessee adoption records statute against various federal constitutional attacks).

Problem 3-15

Before her baby was born, M decided to place the child for adoption and met with Mr. and Mrs. A., a couple recommended to M by her doctor. Mrs. A described their previous experience with an open adoption and the contacts they maintained with the birth family of their adopted son. M met with Mrs. A on several occasions, and Mrs. A was present when M's baby was born. M signed consent forms for the adoption twelve hours after the child was born. The next day, M called Mrs. A to ask when she could visit with the baby. Mrs. A refused to let her visit, and a week later M sought to revoke her consent to the adoption on the basis of fraud and mistake. How should the court evaluate her claim? (See <u>Adoption of Baby Girl T., 21 P.3d 581 (Kan.Ct.App.2001)</u>.)

Problem 3-16

Vito tested positive for cocaine at his birth, and has been placed with a foster family for eight years. Vito's biological mother is no longer using drugs, and has visited Vito once a month for several years. Vito acknowledges her as his "other mother," but he has a very strong attachment to his foster parents, who would like to adopt him. In proceedings to terminate the parental rights of Vito's biological mother, the court concluded that she was unfit, but denied the adoption plan, ruling that it should provide for some post-adoption contact between Vito and his biological family. In particular, the judge noted her concern that a connection to his birth family and culture would be crucial for Vito's racial and cultural development and adjustment as he grew older. The foster parents and the state social services agency have appealed. Is post-adoption visitation improper in these circumstances? (See <u>Adoption of Vito, 728 N.E.2d 292 (Mass. 2000)</u>.)

C. Assisted Reproduction

Adoption provides an important path to parenthood for adults who are not able to have children through a traditional pregnancy. Beyond adoption, new techniques for assisting with conception and pregnancy have allowed many individuals and couples to become parents of children with whom they also share a genetic relationship. Often, the birth of these children is only possible through the use of donor sperm or egg cells, or the assistance of a woman who carries the child and gives birth as a surrogate mother. In contrast to adoption, which is governed by detailed adoption laws, many aspects of assisted or alternative reproduction are not regulated in the United States.

1. Artificial Insemination

For two centuries, people have turned to artificial insemination in response to infertility, with the practice becoming more widespread and sophisticated in the years after World War II. Also known as intrauterine

Go Online

For information on <u>fertility, reproductive health and assisted reproductive technologies,</u> see the web page of the U.S. Centers for Disease Control and Prevention (CDC).

insertion (IUI), this technique utilizes sperm from a woman's husband (AIH) or sperm from a known or unknown donor (AID). All states have laws regulating these practices to some extent, but many complex and unresolved questions remain. For example, state laws differ on questions such as whether private insemination agreements are enforceable, and whether a child conceived posthumously may establish a legal parent-child relationship with his or her deceased genetic father for purposes of inheritance or federal Social Security benefits.

Most statutes addressing artificial insemination provide that when a married woman in inseminated with donor sperm with her husband's consent, the husband is the legal father of the child and the donor has no parental rights or obligations. E.g., N.Y. Dom. Rel. Law § 73 (2018). Many fewer address the parental rights of a sperm donor when an unmarried woman conceives a child by artificial insemination. See, e.g., Cal. Fam. Code § 7613(b) (2018); Or. Rev. Stat. § 109.239 (2018).

E.E. v. O.M.G.R.

20 A.3d 1171 (N.J. Super Ct. 2011)

Opinion

Sandson, J.S.C.

The question presented to the court is whether two parties can enter into a private contract regarding a self-administered "artificial insemination" procedure whereby one party may contract with another to terminate their parental rights. This is a case of first impression under New Jersey law. This court has determined, first, that parties cannot by contract terminate their parental rights under common law. Rather, the termination of parental rights is controlled by statute. Second, the Legislature did not intend for this type of procedure to lead to the termination of parental rights under the New Jersey Artificial Insemination statute N.J.S.A. 9:17–44, and therefore the parental rights of the donor in this matter will not be terminated.

The facts of this case are unusual. Plaintiff is a single woman without a partner who wished to have a child. She did not wish to assume the expense of purchasing sperm through a sperm bank or use a licensed physician in order to effect the insemination. Rather she secured her friend, O.M.G.R., to donate his sperm, which she transported to its intended location with a kitchen turkey baster. Shortly following the child's conception, the parties entered into an agreement dated April 12, 2010, whereby defendant contracted to surrender and terminate all future rights and responsibilities to the child and plaintiff assumed all financial responsibility for the child. The Agreement contained the following provisions:

Voluntary Relinquishment/Termination of Parental Rights

This is a voluntary relinquishment of any and all parental rights and obligations such as child support, visitation and custody in relationship to the donation of the sperm either through in-vitro fertilization, artificial insemination/intrauterine insemination or sexual relations from [defendant] to [plaintiff].

If a child is conceived or born through the sperm donations given by [defendant] through in-vitro fertilization, artificial insemination/intrauterine insemination or sexual relations to [plaintiff] this document serves as a voluntary relinquishment of any and all parental rights and obligations such as child support, visitation & custody in relation to the born child or children in the event of multiple birth.

This relinquishment & termination of all legal parental rights to the sperm, fetus, or born child is completely voluntary and without force, gift, monetary exchange or promises.

[Plaintiff] shall be the sole parent and provider for the child and relinquishes any rights to seek financial or emotional support from [defendant] at any time.

Both parties signed and dated the document in the presence of a notary on April 19, 2010.

On December 17, 2010, the child, G.J.E., was born. No name was listed on the birth certificate as the child's father. Following the child's birth, the parties again signed a consent order, indicating again that defendant had surrendered all rights and responsibilities relating to the child and plaintiff had assumed full responsibility for the child's health and well-being. The consent order was submitted to this court.

Under New Jersey law, a child has the right to the security of two parents at the time of birth. The Supreme Court of New Jersey noted that parental rights can be legally terminated under New Jersey law only when a parent has been declared unfit, an adoption has taken place, or if [the Division of Youth and Family Services] has removed a child from a parent. Accordingly, the parental rights of one parent may not be terminated by consent except when it is accompanied by the adoption of the child by another party. *See, e.g., R.H. v. M.K.*, 254 N.J.Super. 480, 484, 603 A.2d 995 (Ch.Div.1991). A detailed consent agreement designed to terminate a biological father's parental rights and spell out the mother's ability to fully care for the child was definitively struck down by the court in *R.H., supra*. The parties in *R.H.*, with the help of counsel, entered into a comprehensive agreement, whereby the biological father fully and unequivocally gave up his rights to the child that the parties had conceived. The parties argued, under the adoption procedure then in effect, that a natural parent may consent to an adoption of a child conceived per N.J.S.A. 9:3–48.

By analogy, the parties argued, since they both consented to the termination of plaintiff's parental rights, their agreement should be upheld by the court. The court did not find the analogy persuasive and held the agreement invalid. The court reasoned, first, the adoption statute provides for an approved agency investigation, a preliminary hearing and a finding of fitness. Secondly, the court reasoned that an adoptive parent is a second parent to the child noting "[t]he adopted child will be raised (presumably) by two individuals with different (perhaps complementary) strengths and weaknesses."

The guiding principle necessary to resolve the case at hand is that a permanent contractual surrender of parental rights is not provided for under New Jersey law. *In re Baby M*, [537 A.2d 1227 (N.J. 1988]. The Court has unequivocally stated that a child's relationship with his or her parents is so significant that all doubts are to be resolved against the destruction of that relationship. Rather, the case law demonstrates that the termination of parental rights is strictly governed by statute. *In re Baby M, supra*. In this case, there is no second party to adopt the child. Therefore, the termination of defendant's rights cannot be accomplished by the parties' contract.

The parental rights of the biological father are presumptively established by the father's genetic relationship to the child under N.J.S.A. 9:17–41(b).[2] However, the New Jersey Legislature has recognized that biology is not always controlling in the area of parentage and has created statutory exceptions to the presumption that the biological father has parental rights in the area of artificial insemination. The issue presented by this case is whether a party may avail themselves of the

---

[2]   N.J.S.A. 9:17–41(b) reads as follows:

[The parent and child relationship between a child and] [t]he natural father, may be established by proof that his paternity has been adjudicated under prior law; under the laws governing probate; by giving full faith and credit to a determination of paternity made by any other state or jurisdiction, whether established through voluntary acknowledgment or through judicial or administrative processes; by a Certificate of Parentage. . .that is executed by the father, including an unemancipated minor, prior to or after the birth of a child, and filed with the appropriate State agency; by a default judgment or order of the court; or by an order of the court based on a blood test or genetic test that meets or exceeds the specific threshold probability. . .creating a rebuttable presumption of paternity.

The statute seems to indicate that a biological relationship, although not necessary, leads to the presumption of paternity. An interesting question raised by this case is whether the biological father's rights existed prior to the filing of this action. Implicit in the motion to terminate parental rights is an acknowledgement of the paternity of the child as the biological issue of plaintiff and defendant. This recognition triggers the existence of parental rights. As noted previously, defendant does not appear on the birth certificate, he did not sign a Certificate of Parentage, and he does not have a legal relationship with plaintiff that would lead to the presumption of parenthood.

protection set forth by <u>N.J.S.A. 9:17–44(b)</u> when they have not strictly complied with a provision within the statute.

The statute deals directly with artificial insemination and states in pertinent part that

> Unless the donor of semen and the woman have entered into a written contract to the contrary, the donor of semen provided to a licensed physician for use in artificial insemination of a woman other than the donor's wife is treated in law as if he were not the father of a child thereby conceived and shall have no rights or duties stemming from the conception of a child.

In this case, there was no physician involved in the insemination process. Rather, plaintiff procured sperm from defendant and inseminated herself.

There has been no case in New Jersey that carries a similar factual scenario to this case since the enactment of the statute. However, since the statute itself is a variation of the Uniform Parentage Act ("UPA"), similar provisions have been enacted in other areas of the country. It is therefore appropriate to turn to our sister states for guidance on this issue. In a California case, <u>*Jhordan C. v. Mary K., Victoria T.,* 179 Cal.App.3d 386, 224 Cal.Rptr. 530, 531–32 (1986)</u>, a known sperm donor petitioned for parental rights relating to a child that had been conceived at home with sperm he provided. The court held that the issue was controlled by the artificial insemination statute in California, which stated in pertinent part that "a 'donor of semen provided to a licensed physician for use in artificial insemination of a woman other than the donor's wife is treated in law as if he were not the natural father of a child thereby conceived.' " (quoting <u>Cal. Civ.Code, § 7005(b)</u>). The court concluded that where impregnation takes place by artificial insemination, and the parties have failed to take advantage of this statutory basis for preclusion of paternity (i.e. the use of a licensed physician in the process), the donor of semen can be determined to be the father of the child in a paternity action.

* * * The court believed there were significant, logical reasons for the statutory requirement of a physician. These included health considerations, including medical histories relating to both parties, which might impact the resulting child. In addition, the court believed the presence of a professional third party created a formal, documented structure for the donor-recipient relationship. Although the court acknowledged that artificial insemination could easily be carried out without a physician's involvement, and even that there are some privacy considerations against requiring a physician, the court concluded that Mary K. could have taken advantage of the statute through the minimal use of a licensed physician, either to procure the sperm or to effectuate the insemination.[5]

Similarly, the Kansas Supreme Court most recently held in the case *In re the Paternity of K.C.H. and K.M.H., 285 Kan. 53, 169 P.3d 1025, 1042 (2007)* that the physician did not need to be directly involved in the procurement of the sperm as long as he was involved in the insemination. Rather, the court analyzed the language of the statute and did not discuss the Kansas Legislature's process in crafting the statute at issue. The fact that the mother supplied the donor's sperm to the physician did not prevent application of the statute because the court held that the use of a physician was sufficient to trigger the statute. Rather, the court applied the statute as written and refused to read in additional requirements than the ones laid out.

Our Supreme Court has consistently held that the best indicators of legislative intent are the plain words of the statute. In reviewing the statutory language, courts should "ascribe to the statutory words their ordinary meaning and significance, and read them in context with related provisions so as to give sense to the legislation as a whole." The Court has cautioned against " 'rewrit[ing] a plainly-written enactment of the Legislature or presum[ing] that the Legislature intended something other than that expressed by way of the plain language.' " This court is not interested in debating the merits of the purpose behind the "licensed physician" provision within our statute. The court notes that the New Jersey Legislature, in enacting the UPA, could have removed the requirement of a licensed physician, as other states have done.[7]

---

[5] The court in *Jhordan* wrote,
We wish to stress that our opinion in this case is not intended to express any judicial preference toward traditional notions of family structure or toward providing a father where a single woman has chosen to bear a child. Public policy in these areas is best determined by the legislative branch of government, not the judicial. Our Legislature has already spoken and has afforded to unmarried women a statutory right to bear children by artificial insemination (as well as a right of men to donate semen) without fear of a paternity claim, through provision of the semen to a licensed physician. *Jhordan, supra, 224 Cal.Rptr. at 537*.
This court agrees.

[7] See *McIntyre v. Crouch, 98 Or.App. 462, 780 P.2d 239 (1989)*, cert. denied *495 U.S. 905, 110 S.Ct. 1924, 109 L.Ed.2d 288 (1990)*. In this case, an unmarried woman artificially inseminated herself with a known donor's semen. The donor sought recognition of his paternity, and both he and the woman sought summary judgment. The Oregon artificial insemination statute read:
If the donor of semen used in artificial insemination is not the mother's husband: (1) Such donor shall have no right, obligation or interest with respect to a child born as a result of the artificial insemination; and (2) A child born as a result of the artificial insemination shall have no right, obligation or interest with respect to the donor. *Ore.Rev.Stat. § 109.239 (1977)*.
On appeal, the court held that summary judgment was inappropriate because the court still had to consider whether the parties had verbally agreed to allow the donor to have a relationship with the child. This court notes that the artificial insemination contemplated in the Oregon statute does not mention the presence of a physician.

Although this court can see by the parties' original agreement that the intent was to have defendant's role limited to supplying biological material and for defendant to be absolved from further liability, the parties failed to abide by the statute in failing to use a physician. In no case did the self-designation of a party as a "sperm donor" excuse this statutory deviation. Accordingly, this court is bound to follow the language of the statute and may not ignore a portion of the statute because of the parties' intent.

The court notes that the case law favors the application of the statute to limit the rights of the donor when the donor seeks to exercise his parental rights by virtue of his biological relationship. The existence of parental rights and the exercise of those rights are different. Defendant, who was present for this hearing via phone but chose not to participate, has made the choice not to exercise his parental rights and, should that continue by agreement between the parties, the court sees no reason to impose a different result. In accordance with the testimony presented by plaintiff, this court grants sole custody of G.J.E. to plaintiff. Defendant has been granted no parenting time with G.J.E. Plaintiff has made the choice not to seek child support. The court believes this order is currently in the best interest of G.J.E. because plaintiff has testified to her ability to fully provide for the child both financially and emotionally, and defendant has expressed, through the consent order, his desire not to have any relationship with the child. The court expresses no opinion as to the appropriateness of the termination of defendant's parental rights at a later date. However, this court feels under the case law and the instant statute, defendant's rights cannot be terminated in the manner proposed and are not encompassed under the artificial insemination statute.

Accordingly, plaintiff's motion to terminate defendant father's parental relationship is denied. Plaintiff's motion for sole custody and no parenting time for defendant is granted.

Points for Discussion

a. *E.E.*

Why did the Court in *E.E.* conclude that it could not enforce the agreement the parties signed? What would the result be under the New Jersey statute if the donor had changed his mind after signing, and wanted to claim parental rights? Given the holding in this case, what advice would you give a woman who wants to avoid the risk that a sperm donor will seek to establish his paternity of her child? See also Bruce v. Boardwine, 770 S.E.2d 774 (Va. Ct. App. 2015) (concluding that man who donated sperm to woman for her self-insemination process was genetic and legal father entitled to seek custody and visitation).

b. Medical Supervision

Artificial insemination is a relatively simple procedure which can be performed without the assistance of a physician. One case discussed by the court in *E.E.*, Jhordan C. v. Mary K., 224 Cal.Rptr. 530 (Cal. Ct. App.1986), involved insemination with no medical supervision. California's statute also provides that a donor who provides semen to a licensed physician for use in artificial insemination is "treated in law as if he were not the natural father of a child thereby conceived". Cal. Fam. Code § 7613(b) (2018). Mary argued that the California statute, by requiring involvement of a physician in order to protect her against a donor's claim of paternity, violated her rights to procreative choice and family autonomy. How would you analyze these claims?

The court in *Jhordan C.* also discussed many of the pros and cons of physician involvement, conceding that "nothing inherent in artificial insemination requires the involvement of a physician." Why do the majority of the statutes governing artificial insemination cover only situations where there is physician involvement? See Sheila M. O'Rourke, *Family Law in a Brave New World: Private Ordering of Parental Rights and Responsibilities for Donor Insemination*, 1 Berkeley Women's L.J. 140 (2004). At least two states specifically prohibit self-insemination and provide criminal penalties for insemination performed by anyone other than a physician. See Ga. Code Ann. § 43–34–37 (2018); Or. Rev. Stat. §§ 677.360, 677.990 (2018). Are these statutes constitutional? Are they good policy?

Article 7 of the UPA 2017, 9B U.L.A. (Supp. 2018) defines the parentage of children conceived with assisted reproduction technologies. Section 702 states: "A donor is not a parent of a child conceived by means of assisted reproduction", and § 703 states: "An individual who consents under § 704 to assisted reproduction by a woman with the intent to be a parent of a child conceived by the assisted reproduction is a parent of the child." Is this a preferable approach? Why or why not?

c. Insemination Agreements

Courts have enforced visitation provisions included in insemination agreements; see Matter of Tripp v. Hinckley, 736 N.Y.S.2d 506 (App.Div.2002); Matter of LaChapelle v. Mitten, 607 N.W.2d 151 (Minn.Ct.App.2000). In McIntyre v. Crouch, 780 P.2d 239 (Or. Ct. App. 1989), discussed in *E.E.*, the court concluded that the state statute precluded the donor from asserting his parental rights, even though he was known to the mother and no physician was involved. The court did state, however, that it would violate the donor's due process rights to deprive him of his parental rights if he had donated his semen in reliance on an agreement with the mother that he would have parental rights and obligations. The court concluded that "[t]he Due Process clause can afford no different protection to petitioner as the biological father because the child was conceived by artificial insemination rather than by sexual intercourse." Kansas requires that insemination agreements addressing the parental rights of a known donor must be in writing. See Kan. Stat. Ann. § 38–1114(f)(2018), applied in Interest of K.M.H., 169 P.3d 1025 (Kan. 2007).

d. Known and Unknown Donors

When a physician utilizes sperm donated to a sperm bank by an anonymous donor, there is little risk that the donor will later seek to assert parental rights. However, there are several reasons why a woman may prefer a known donor rather than using a sperm bank. A known donor allows the mother to make a more informed choice about the type of father she would like for her child. In addition, she can obtain detailed family and medical history and has more choices about providing the child with information about the child's father's background. Denise S. Kaiser, Note, *Artificial Insemination: Donor Rights In Situations Involving Unmarried Recipients*, 26 J. Fam. L. 793 (1987–1988).

Should doctors be required to screen donors prior to utilizing their semen for artificial insemination? See Idaho Code § 39–5408 (2018); Ohio Rev. Code Ann. § 3111.91 (2018). If it was discovered after the fact that a donor had been carrying, for example, the AIDS virus, should the physician or clinic performing the insemination be liable for malpractice for failure to screen the donor? See Johnson v. Superior Court, 124 Cal.Rptr.2d 650 (Ct.App.2002) (action for fraud and malpractice against sperm bank that

> **Make the Connection**
>
> As discussed above, there has been a movement in adoption cases toward disclosure of information about natural parents. Does the same reasoning support a child's right to know the identity of an egg or sperm donor? See Joan Heifetz Hollinger, *From Coitus to Commerce: Legal and Social Consequences of Noncoital Reproduction*, 18 U. Mich. J. L. Reform 865, 922–924 (1985).

did not identify risks associated with anonymous donor's family history of hereditary kidney disease). Should legislatures enact statutes requiring comprehensive genetic testing for all persons contributing sperm or eggs for use in assisted reproduction?

e. Children's Identity Rights

A number of different jurisdictions around the globe prohibit anonymous donation of sperm or eggs, in order to assure that donor-conceived children will have access to information about their genetic origins. This is sometimes based on Article 8 of the United Nations Convention on the Rights of the Child, which recognizes a child's right "to preserve his or her identity, including nationality, name and family relations as recognized by law." Should "identity" in this context include genetic identity? See generally Petra Nordqvsit and Carol Smart, Relative Strangers: Family Life, Genes, and Donor Conception (2014).

Posthumous Conception

Sperm banks accept sperm from anonymous donors, and also from men who wish to store sperm for their own future use, particularly before undergoing treatment for cancer or other terminal illnesses. The possibility of posthumous reproduction raises a number of legal questions, such as whether a child conceived in this manner qualifies as a legal heir of the decedent. See, e.g. Woodward v. Commissioner of Social Security, 760 N.E.2d 257 (Mass. 2002) (holding that twin girls conceived by posthumous artificial insemination would be entitled to inherit under state law if they could establish a genetic tie and in addition that their deceased parent had consented "clearly and unequivocally. . .not only to posthumous reproduction but also to the support of any resulting child.") A posthumously conceived child may qualify for federal Social Security benefits as the child of a deceased individual under 42 U.S.C. § 416(h)(2)(A) (2018), but only if the child could inherit from his or her deceased biological father under the intestate inheritance laws of the state where the father was domiciled at the time of his death. See Astrue v. Capato, 566 U.S. 541 (2012).

In Hecht v. Superior Court, 20 Cal.Rptr.2d 275 (Cal. Ct. App. 1993), the court considered a will in which decedent had bequeathed his frozen sperm to his girlfriend. The man's grown children from a former marriage challenged the will, arguing that the court should adopt a policy against posthumous conception. The probate court entered an order requiring that the sperm be destroyed, but that order was stayed and then reversed as an abuse of discretion by the California Court of Appeals. Should the girlfriend be permitted to use the sperm to conceive a child? If so, should any child conceived with the sperm be entitled to inherit from the decedent's estate? See Anne Reichman Schiff, Arising from the Dead: Challenges of Posthumous Procreation, 75 N. C. L. Rev. 901 (1997); see also UPA 2017 § 708, which addresses the parental status of an individual who dies before the transfer of his or her gametes or embryos for assisted reproduction, or during the period between a transfer and the birth of the child.

Problem 3-17

Sandra and Robin, a lesbian couple living in New York, each have a child conceived by artificial insemination. Thomas, who is the biological father of Robin's daughter, is a gay man who lives in California. Robin and Thomas agreed, informally, that Sandra and Robin would raise the child, and that Thomas would have no parental rights or obligations. When the daughter was five years old, the children became curious about "the men who helped make them." Sandra and Robin arranged for the children to meet Thomas. He visited with them several times a year for the next five years, and eventually brought a proceeding to establish paternity. Can Sandra and Robin have his parental rights terminated? (See Thomas S. v. Robin Y., 618 N.Y.S.2d 356 (App. Div. 1994), appeal dismissed 655 N.E.2d 708 (N.Y. 1995).)

Problem 3-18

After several years of trying to become pregnant, Alexis and her boyfriend, Raymond, learned that he was infertile. Raymond encouraged her to pursue artificial insemination, helped Alexis select an anonymous donor who resembled Raymond, and provided financial assistance for the procedure. After Alexis gave birth to twin boys, Raymond treated the children as his own, providing various forms of financial support and taking vacations with Alexis and the twins. When the boys were three years old, Alexis learned that Raymond had hidden from her his true name and the fact that he was married rather than divorced. Alexis has ended their relationship, but she would like to have Raymond declared to be the boys' father and have child support orders entered. What arguments should she make? (See Parentage of M.J., 787 N.E.2d 144 (Ill. 2003).) What if Raymond wanted to claim parental rights, and Alexis was opposed to this? (See Dunkin v. Boskey, 98 Cal. Rptr.2d 44 (Ct. App. 2000).)

2. Assisted Reproductive Technology (ART)

Fertility treatments that involve manipulation of both eggs and sperm are known as Assisted Reproductive Technology (ART). In 1978, Louise Brown was the first child born as a result of in vitro fertilization (IVF), and these techniques now account for more than 60,000 children born each year in the United States. ART created the possibility that eggs could be collected and donated as well as sperm, and the possibility that a surrogate mother might carry a child with whom she had no genetic relationship. With the advent of ART a child could be born with many more potential "parents" whose claims might come into conflict, including the egg and sperm donors, the gestational mother and the intending or commissioning parent or parents.

Egg donation is analogous in many respects to sperm donation, but there are relatively few statutes that attempt to define the parties' parental rights in these cases. Clinics around the country obtain eggs both from women who are undergoing in vitro fertilization procedures and from women who are recruited and paid a fee for serving as egg donors. The Uniform Parentage Act 2017 addresses both egg and sperm donation in § 702, which states that: "A donor is not a parent of a child conceived by means of assisted reproduction." Is there any policy reason to treat egg donation differently from sperm donation?

Although ART raises an enormous range of scientific, legal and moral challenges, the fertility industry in the United States is largely unregulated. Groups such as the American Society for Reproductive Medicine (ASRM) and the Society for Assisted Reproductive Technology (SART) have worked with the U.S. Centers for Disease Control and Prevention (CDC) to collect data and monitor ART usage and outcomes. For a thoughtful exploration of these issues, see Naomi R. Cahn, Test Tube Families: Why the Fertility Market Needs Legal Regulation (2009).

The ability to freeze and store fertilized preembryos for later implantation has also generated legal dilemmas regarding the status of embryos created in ART procedures. Embryo donation is possible as another means of assisted reproduction, and may be treated under the same principles as egg and sperm donation. See UPA 2017 § 102(4)(c). Some states treat embryo donation differently from donation of eggs or sperm, however. Louisiana defines an in vitro fertilized human ovum as a juridical person, and provides that if IVF patients renounce their parental rights their embryos will be available for "adoptive" implantation." See La. Rev. Stat. Ann. §9:121–133 (2018). State laws also vary on the treatment accorded to unused frozen embryos, particularly if the intending parents disagree on how to dispose of them. Some states require clinics to provide information to their patients and ask them to enter a written agreement as to the disposition of unused eggs, sperm and embryos in the event of death, divorce, or other unforeseen circumstances. See, e.g., Fla. Stat. Ann. § 742.17 (2018).

Go Online

Data and information on ART are available from the U.S. Centers for Disease Control and Prevention (CDC) web page.

Judges have confronted these questions in cases such as Kass v. Kass, 696 N.E.2d 174 (N.Y. 1998) which enforced a term in an informed consent document providing that, if the parties did not agree on a different disposition, their embryos would be retained by program for approved research purposes. In contrast to *Kass*, A.Z. v. B.Z., 725 N.E.2d 1051 (Mass. 2000), enjoined a wife from having embryos implanted over her former husband's objections after their divorce, holding that their prior written agreement was ambiguous and should not be enforced when one party had reconsidered.

Davis v. Davis

Davis v. Davis, 842 S.W.2d 588 (Tenn.1992), addressed the status of seven frozen embryos a married couple had created together, which had not been implanted at the time of their divorce. The wife sought an order that would allow her to have them implanted, but the husband opposed this, arguing that the implantation would subject him to parenthood against his wishes. The trial court judge awarded custody of the pre-embryos to the wife after concluding that "human life begins at the moment of conception," and that the "best interest of the children, in vitro," would be to make them available to the wife for implantation.

The Tennessee Supreme Court reversed this order, holding that the preembryos were neither persons nor property, and ruling that they "occupy an interim category that entitles them to special respect because of their potential for human life." 842 S.W.2d at 597. The court concluded that the relative interests of the parties in using or not using the preembryos must be weighed, addingt: "Ordinarily, the party wishing to avoid procreation should prevail, assuming that the other party has a reasonable possibility of achieving parenthood by means other than use of the preembryos in question." 842 S.W.2d at 604. *Davis* suggested that if the parties had agreed at the outset about the disposition of the preembryos in the event of contingencies such as death or divorce, that agreement would be presumed valid and enforced.

For additional discussion of the *Davis* case, see Margaret Margaret F. Brinig, *The Story of Mary Sue and Junior Davis*, in Family Law Stories 195 (Carol Sanger, ed. 2008).

3. Surrogacy

Surrogate parenting agreements fall in one of two categories: "traditional" or "genetic" surrogacy, in which a woman agrees to be inseminated on behalf of a commissioning parent, or "gestational" surrogacy, in which IVF techniques and gametes from other individuals are utilized to create an embryo that is implanted into the uterus of a woman who agrees to carry the child for the intending parent or parents. In traditional surrogacy, the woman who gives birth to the child is also its genetic mother, while in gestational surrogacy the woman who gives birth has no genetic tie to the child. As with other areas of alternative reproduction, state laws vary widely regarding surrogacy and the respective rights of sperm and egg donors, gestational mothers, and intending parents. Beyond the question whether and to what extent surrogacy agreements may be enforceable, there are many other issues, such as who will be named as the parents on the child's birth certificate, how the child's parentage will ultimately be determined, and who may bring a claim for custody or adoption of the child.

R.R. v. M.H.

689 N.E.2d 790 (Mass. 1998)

WILKINS, CHIEF JUSTICE.

On a report by a judge in the Probate and Family Court, we are concerned with the validity of a surrogacy parenting agreement between the plaintiff (father) and the defendant (mother). Both the mother and the father are married but not to each other. A child was conceived through artificial insemination of the mother with the father's sperm, after the mother and father had executed the surrogate parenting agreement. The agreement provided that the father would have custody of the child. During the sixth month of her pregnancy and after she had received funds from the father pursuant to the surrogacy agreement, the mother changed her mind and decided that she wanted to keep the child.

The father thereupon brought this action and obtained a preliminary order awarding him temporary custody of the child. * * * The question of the enforceability of the surrogacy agreement is before us and, although we could defer any ruling until there is a final judgment entered, the issue is one on which we elect to comment because it is fully briefed and is of importance to more than the parties. This court has not previously dealt with the enforceability of a surrogacy agreement.

The Facts

The baby girl who is the subject of this action was born on August 15, 1997, in Leominster. The defendant mother and the plaintiff father are her biological parents. The father and his wife, who live in Rhode Island, were married in June, 1989. The wife is infertile. Sometime in 1994, she and the father learned of an egg donor program but did not pursue it because the procedure was not covered by insurance and had a relatively low success rate. Because of their ages (they were both in their forties), they concluded that pursuing adoption was not feasible. In April, 1996, responding to a newspaper advertisement for surrogacy services, they consulted a Rhode Island attorney who had drafted surrogacy contracts for both surrogates and couples seeking surrogacy services. On the attorney's advice, the father and his wife consulted the New England Surrogate Parenting Advisors (NESPA), a for-profit corporation that helps infertile couples find women willing to act as surrogate mothers. They entered into a contract with NESPA in September, 1996, and paid a fee of $6,000.

Meanwhile, in the spring of 1996, the mother, who was married and had two children, responded to a NESPA advertisement. She reported to NESPA that her family was complete and that she desired to allow others less fortunate than herself to have children. The mother submitted a surrogacy application to NESPA. The judge found that the mother was motivated to apply to NESPA by a desire to be pregnant, in order to earn money, and to help an infertile couple.

In October, Dr. Angela Figueroa of NESPA brought the mother together with the father and his wife. They had a seemingly informative exchange of information and views. The mother was advised to seek an attorney's advice concerning the surrogacy agreement. Shortly thereafter, the mother, the father, and his wife met again to discuss the surrogacy and other matters. The mother also met with a clinical psychologist as part of NESPA's evaluation of her suitability to act as a surrogate. The psychologist, who also evaluated the father and his wife, advised the mother to consult legal counsel, to give her husband a chance to air his concerns, to discuss arrangements for contact with the child, to consider and discuss her expectations concerning termination of the pregnancy, and to arrange a meeting between her husband and the father and his wife.[2] The psychologist concluded that the mother was solid, thoughtful, and well grounded, that she would have no problem giving the child to the father, and that she was happy to act as a surrogate. The mother told the psychologist that she was not motivated by money, although she did plan to use the funds received for her children's education. The mother's husband told the psychologist by telephone that he supported his wife's decision.

The mother signed the surrogate parenting agreement and her signature was notarized on November 1. The father signed on November 18. The agreement stated that the parties intended that the "Surrogate shall be inseminated with

---

[2]   Her husband had had a vasectomy in 1994 and did not have sexual relations with the mother after October, 1996.

the semen of Natural Father" and "that, on the birth of the child or children so conceived, Natural Father, as the Natural Father, will have the full legal parental rights of a father, and surrogate will permit Natural Father to take the child or children home from the hospital to live with he [sic] and his wife." The agreement acknowledged that the mother's parental rights would not terminate if she permitted the father to take the child home and have custody, that the mother could at any time seek to enforce her parental rights by court order, but that, if she attempted to obtain custody or visitation rights, she would forfeit her rights under the agreement and would be obligated to reimburse the father for all fees and expenses paid to her under it. The agreement provided that its interpretation would be governed by Rhode Island law.

The agreement provided for compensation to the mother in the amount of $10,000 "for services rendered in conceiving, carrying and giving birth to the Child." Payment of the $10,000 was to be made as follows: $500 on verification of the pregnancy; $2,500 at the end of the third month; $3,500 at the end of the sixth month; and $3,500 at the time of birth "and when delivery of child occurs." The agreement stated that no payment was made in connection with adoption of the child, the termination of parental rights, or consent to surrender the child for adoption. The father acknowledged the mother's right to determine whether to carry the pregnancy to term, but the mother agreed to refund all payments if, without the father's consent, she had an abortion that was not necessary for her physical health. The father assumed various expenses of the pregnancy, including tests, and had the right to name the child. The mother would be obliged, however, to repay all expenses and fees for services if tests showed that the father was not the biological father of the child, or if the mother refused to permit the father to take the child home from the hospital. The agreement also provided that the mother would maintain some contact with the child after the birth.

The judge found that the mother entered into the agreement on her own volition after consulting legal counsel. There was no evidence of undue influence, coercion, or duress. The mother fully understood that she was contracting to give custody of the baby to the father. She sought to inseminate herself on November 30 and December 1, 1996. The attempt at conception was successful.

The lawyer for the father sent the mother a check for $500 in December, 1996, and another for $2,500 in February. In May, the father's lawyer sent the mother a check for $3,500. She told the lawyer that she had changed her mind and wanted to keep the child. She returned the check uncashed in the middle of June. The mother has made no attempt to refund the amounts that the father paid her, including $550 that he paid for pregnancy-related expenses.

Procedure

Approximately two weeks after the mother changed her mind and returned the check for $3,500, and before the child was born, the father commenced this action against the mother seeking to establish his paternity, alleging breach of contract, and requesting a declaration of his rights under the surrogacy agreement. Subsequently, the wife's husband was added as a defendant. The judge appointed a guardian ad litem to represent the interests of the unborn child. Proceedings were held on aspects of the preliminary injunction request (now resolved) and on the mother's motion to determine whether surrogacy contracts are enforceable in Massachusetts.

On August 4, 1997, the judge entered an order directing the mother to give the child to the father when it was discharged from the hospital and granting the father temporary physical custody of the child. She did so based on her determination that the father's custody claim was likely to prevail on the merits of the contract claim, and, if not on that claim, then on the basis of the best interests of the child. The mother was granted the right to frequent visits.

* * *

Other Jurisdictions

A significant minority of States have legislation addressing surrogacy agreements. Some simply deny enforcement of all such agreements. See Ariz.Rev. Stat. Ann. § 25–218(A) (West 1991); D.C.Code Ann. § 16–402(a) (1997); Ind. Code Ann. §§ 31–20–1–1, 31–20–1–2 (Michie 1997); Mich. Comp. Laws Ann. § 722.855 (West 1993); N.Y. Dom. Rel. Law § 122 (McKinney Supp.1997);[4] N.D. Cent.Code § 14–18–05 (1991); Utah Code Ann. § 76–7–204 (1995). Others expressly deny enforcement only if the surrogate is to be compensated. See Ky. Rev. Stat. Ann§ 199.590(4) (Michie 1995);[5] La. Rev. Stat. Ann. § 9:2713 (West 1991); Neb. Rev. Stat. § 25–21,200 (1995); Wash. Rev. Code §§ 26.26.230, 26.26.240 (1996). Some States have simply exempted surrogacy agreements from provisions making it a crime to sell babies. See Ala. Code § 26–10A–34 (1992); Iowa Code § 710.11 (1997). A few States have explicitly made unpaid surrogacy agreements lawful. See Fla. Stat. ch. 742.15 (1995); Nev. Rev. Stat. § 126.045 (1995); N.H. Rev. Stat. Ann. § 168–B:16 (1994 & Supp.1996); Va. Code Ann. §§ 20–159,

---

[4] This statute changed the law established in *Adoption of Baby Girl L.J.*, 132 Misc.2d 972, 505 N.Y.S.2d 813 (N.Y.Sur.Ct.1986), in which the court approved the terms of a surrogate parenting agreement which required the payment of compensation to the surrogate and delivery of the child to the natural father and his wife for adoption. See *Adoption of Paul*, 146 Misc.2d 379, 385, 550 N.Y.S.2d 815 (N.Y.Fam.Ct.1990), voiding a surrogacy agreement and approving adoption of the child only if the surrogate agreed not to accept compensation from the intended parents.

[5] This statute in effect overruled *Surrogate Parenting Assocs., Inc. v. Commonwealth ex rel. Armstrong*, 704 S.W.2d 209 (Ky.1986), in which the Supreme Court of Kentucky held that a compensated surrogate parenting procedure did not violate a statute prohibiting the buying and selling of babies. *Id. at 211*.

20–160(B) (4) (Michie 1995). Florida, New Hampshire, and Virginia require that the intended mother be infertile. See Fla. Stat. ch. 742.15(2) (a); N.H. Rev. Stat. Ann. § 168–B:17(II) (1994); Va. Code Ann. § 20–160(B) (8). New Hampshire and Virginia place restrictions on who may act as a surrogate and require advance judicial approval of the agreement. See N.H. Rev. tat. Ann. §§ 168–B:16(I) (b), 168–B:17; Va. Code Ann. §§ 20–159(B), 20–160(B) (6).[6] Last, Arkansas raises a presumption that a child born to a surrogate mother is the child of the intended parents and not the surrogate. Ark. Code Ann. § 9–10–201(b), (c) (Michie 1993).

There are few appellate court opinions on the enforceability of traditional surrogacy agreements. The Kentucky Legislature, as indicated in note 5 above, has provided that a compensated surrogacy agreement is unenforceable (Ky.Rev.Stat. Ann. § 199.590[4]), thus changing the rule that the Supreme Court of Kentucky announced in *Surrogate Parenting Assocs., Inc. v. Commonwealth ex rel. Armstrong*, 704 S.W.2d 209 (Ky.1986). In In re Marriage of Moschetta, 25 Cal.App.4th 1218, 30 Cal.Rptr.2d 893 (1994), the court declined to enforce a traditional surrogacy agreement because it was incompatible with California parentage and adoption statutes. The surrogate, who was to be paid $10,000, had agreed that (a) the father could obtain sole custody of any resulting child, (b) she would agree to terminate her parental rights, and (c) she would aid the father's wife in adopting the child. The court sent the case back to the trial court for a determination whether the father should be awarded primary physical custody.

The best known opinion is that of the Supreme Court of New Jersey in *Matter of Baby M.*, 109 N.J. 396, 537 A.2d 1227 (1988), where the court invalidated a compensated surrogacy contract because it conflicted with the law and public policy of the State. The Baby M surrogacy agreement involved broader concessions from the mother than the agreement before us because it provided that the mother would surrender her parental rights and would allow the father's wife to adopt the child. The agreement, therefore, directly conflicted with a statute prohibiting the payment of money to obtain an adoption and a statute barring enforcement of an agreement to adoption made prior to the birth of the child. The court acknowledged that an award of custody to the father was in the best interests of the child, but struck down orders terminating the mother's parental rights and authorizing the adoption of the child by the husband's wife. The court added that it found no "legal prohibition against surrogacy when the surrogate mother volunteers, without any payment, to act as a surrogate and is given the right to change her mind and to assert her parental rights."

---

[6]   New Hampshire permits the surrogate to opt out of the agreement to surrender custody at any time up to seventy-two hours after birth. N.H.Rev.Stat. Ann. § 168–B:25(IV) (1994). Virginia allows a surrogate who is the child's genetic mother to terminate the agreement within 180 days of the last assisted conception. Va.Code Ann. § 20–161(B) (Michie 1995).

Discussion

1. *The Governing Law.* The agreement before us provided that "Rhode Island Law shall govern the interpretation of this agreement." No party has argued that Rhode Island law has any application to the issues before us.[7] We are, in any event, not concerned with "the interpretation of this agreement," but rather with the legal significance, if any, of its provisions. The child was conceived and born in Massachusetts, and the mother is a Massachusetts resident, all as contemplated in the surrogacy arrangement. The significance, if any, of the surrogacy agreement on the relationship of the parties and on the child is appropriately determined by Massachusetts law.

2. *General Laws c. 46, § 4B.* The case before us concerns traditional surrogacy, in which the fertile member of an infertile couple is one of the child's biological parents. Surrogate fatherhood, the insemination of the fertile wife with sperm of a donor, often an anonymous donor, is a recognized and accepted procedure. If the mother's husband consents to the procedure, the resulting child is considered the legitimate child of the mother and her husband. G.L. c. 46, § 4B.[9] Section 4B does not comment on the rights and obligations, if any, of the biological father, although inferentially he has none. In the case before us, the infertile spouse is the wife. No statute decrees the consequences of the artificial insemination of a surrogate with the sperm of a fertile husband. This situation presents different considerations from surrogate fatherhood because surrogate motherhood is never anonymous and her commitment and contribution is unavoidably much greater than that of a sperm donor.[10]

We must face the possible application of G.L. c. 46, § 4B, to this case. Section 4B tells us that a husband who consents to the artificial insemination of his wife with the sperm of another is considered to be the father of any resulting child. In the case before us, the birth mother was married at the time of her artificial insemination. Despite what he told the psychologist, her husband was not supportive of her desire to become a surrogate parent but acknowledged that

---

[7] It appears that Rhode Island does not have statutes similar to those in Massachusetts (G.L. c. 210, §§ 2, 11A) which, as will be seen, provide us guidance.

[9] General Laws c. 46, § 4B, states: "Any child born to a married woman as a result of artificial insemination with the consent of her husband, shall be considered the legitimate child of the mother and such husband."

[10] A situation which involves considerations different from those in the case before us arises when the birth mother has had transferred to her uterus an embryo formed through in vitro fertilization of the intended parents' sperm and egg. This latter process in which the birth mother is not genetically related to the child (except coincidentally if an intended parent is a relative) has been called gestational surrogacy. In *Johnson v. Calvert,* 5 Cal.4th 84, 96, 19 Cal.Rptr.2d 494, 851 P.2d 776, cert. denied, 510 U.S. 874, 114 S.Ct. 206, 126 L.Ed.2d 163, and cert. dismissed sub nom. *Baby Boy J. v. Johnson,* 510 U.S. 938, 114 S.Ct. 374, 126 L.Ed.2d 324 (1993), the Supreme Court of California gave effect to a contract that provided that the mother of a child born as a result of a gestational surrogacy would be the egg donor and not the surrogate.

it was her decision and her body. The husband, who filed a complaint for divorce on August 8, 1997, may have simply been indifferent because he knew that the marriage was falling apart. The judge found that he was not the biological father of the child. His interest might have been vastly greater if he had been informed that § 4B literally says that any child produced by the artificial insemination of his wife with his consent would be his legitimate child whom he would have a duty to support. It is doubtful, however, that the Legislature intended § 4B to apply to the child of a married surrogate mother. Section 4B seems to concern the status of a child born to a fertile mother whose husband, presumably infertile, consented to her artificial insemination with the sperm of another man so that the couple could have a child biologically related to the mother.

3. *Adoption Statutes.* Policies underlying our adoption legislation suggest that a surrogate parenting agreement should be given no effect if the mother's agreement was obtained prior to a reasonable time after the child's birth or if her agreement was induced by the payment of money. Adoption legislation is, of course, not applicable to child custody, but it does provide us with some guidance. Although the agreement makes no reference to adoption and does not concern the termination of parental rights or the adoption of the child by the father's wife, the normal expectation in the case of a surrogacy agreement seems to be that the father's wife will adopt the child with the consent of the mother (and the father). Under G.L. c. 210, § 2, adoption requires the written consent of the father and the mother but, in these circumstances, not the mother's husband. Any such consent, written, witnessed, and notarized, is not to be executed "sooner than the fourth calendar day after the date of birth of the child to be adopted." *Id.* That statutory standard should be interpreted as providing that no mother may effectively agree to surrender her child for adoption earlier than the fourth day after its birth, by which time she better knows the strength of her bond with her child. Although a consent to surrender custody has less permanency than a consent to adoption, the legislative judgment that a mother should have time after a child's birth to reflect on her wishes concerning the child weighs heavily in our consideration whether to give effect to a prenatal custody agreement. No private agreement concerning adoption or custody can be conclusive in any event because a judge, passing on custody of a child, must decide what is in the best interests of the child.[11]

Think About It

In what important ways is traditional surrogacy similar to or different from adoption?

---

[11] In the case of a divorce, a judge may approve an agreement between parents concerning child custody unless the judge makes specific findings that the agreement would not be in the best interests of the child. G.L. c. 208, § 31.

Adoptive parents may pay expenses of a birth parent but may make no direct payment to her. See G.L. c. 210, § 11A; 102 Code Mass. Regs. § 5.09 (1997). Even though the agreement seeks to attribute that payment of $10,000, not to custody or adoption, but solely to the mother's services in carrying the child, the father ostensibly was promised more than those services because, as a practical matter, the mother agreed to surrender custody of the child. She could assert custody rights, according to the agreement, only if she repaid the father all amounts that she had received and also reimbursed him for all expenses he had incurred. The statutory prohibition of payment for receiving a child through adoption suggests that, as a matter of policy, a mother's agreement to surrender custody in exchange for money (beyond pregnancy-related expenses) should be given no effect in deciding the custody of the child.

4. *Conclusion.* The mother's purported consent to custody in the agreement is ineffective because no such consent should be recognized unless given on or after the fourth day following the child's birth. In reaching this conclusion, we apply to consent to custody the same principle which underlies the statutory restriction on when a mother's consent to adoption may be effectively given. Moreover, the payment of money to influence the mother's custody decision makes the agreement as to custody void. Eliminating any financial reward to a surrogate mother is the only way to assure that no economic pressure will cause a woman, who may well be a member of an economically vulnerable class, to act as a surrogate. It is true that a surrogate enters into the agreement before she becomes pregnant and thus is not presented with the desperation that a poor unwed pregnant woman may confront. However, compensated surrogacy arrangements raise the concern that, under financial pressure, a woman will permit her body to be used and her child to be given away.

There is no doubt that compensation was a factor in inducing the mother to enter into the surrogacy agreement and to cede custody to the father. If the payment of $10,000 was really only compensation for the mother's services in carrying the child and giving birth and was unrelated to custody of the child, the agreement would not have provided that the mother must refund all compensation paid (and expenses paid) if she should challenge the father's right to custody. Nor would the agreement have provided that final payment be made only when the child is delivered to the father. We simply decline, on public policy grounds, to apply to a surrogacy agreement of the type involved here the general principle that an

Think About It

How should policy-makers address the risk that economic pressure might cause a woman to agree to be a surrogate?

agreement between informed, mature adults should be enforced absent proof of duress, fraud, or undue influence.

We recognize that there is nothing inherently unlawful in an arrangement by which an informed woman agrees to attempt to conceive artificially and give birth to a child whose father would be the husband of an infertile wife. We suspect that many such arrangements are made and carried out without disagreement.

If no compensation is paid beyond pregnancy-related expenses and if the mother is not bound by her consent to the father's custody of the child unless she consents after a suitable period has passed following the child's birth, the objections we have identified in this opinion to the enforceability of a surrogate's consent to custody would be overcome. Other conditions might be important in deciding the enforceability of a surrogacy agreement, such as a requirement that (a) the mother's husband give his informed consent to the agreement in advance; (b) the mother be an adult and have had at least one successful pregnancy; (c) the mother, her husband, and the intended parents have been evaluated for the soundness of their judgment and for their capacity to carry out the agreement; (d) the father's wife be incapable of bearing a child without endangering her health; (e) the intended parents be suitable persons to assume custody of the child; and (f) all parties have the advice of counsel. The mother and father may not, however, make a binding best-interests-of-the-child determination by private agreement. Any custody agreement is subject to a judicial determination of custody based on the best interests of the child.

The conditions that we describe are not likely to be satisfactory to an intended father because, following the birth of the child, the mother can refuse to consent to the father's custody even though the father has incurred substantial pregnancy-related expenses. A surrogacy agreement judicially approved before conception may be a better procedure, as is permitted by statutes in Virginia and New Hampshire. A Massachusetts statute concerning surrogacy agreements, pro or con, would provide guidance to judges, lawyers, infertile couples interested in surrogate parenthood, and prospective surrogate mothers.

We do not reach but comment briefly on the mother's argument that the agreement was unconscionable. She actively sought to become a surrogate and entered into the surrogacy agreement voluntarily, advised by counsel, not under duress, and fully informed. Unconscionability is not apparent on this record.

A declaration shall be entered that the surrogacy agreement is not enforceable. Such further orders as may be appropriate, consistent with this opinion, may be entered in the Probate and Family Court.

So ordered.

Baby M.

The court in *R.R.* discusses the most widely known surrogacy case, Matter of Baby M., 537 A.2d 1227 (N.J. 1988), which invalidated a traditional surrogacy contract. Mary Beth Whitehead and William Stern agreed that Mary Beth would become pregnant by artificial insemination using William's sperm, would have the child, deliver it to him and do whatever was necessary to terminate her own parental rights so that William's wife could adopt the child. The contract provided for a payment of $10,000. After the child's birth, the parties carried on a high-profile struggle over her custody, eventually leading to an order granting custody to William and visitation to Mary Beth. The New Jersey Supreme Court concluded that the contract violated statutes prohibiting the use of money in connection with adoption, laws requiring proof of unfitness or abandonment before parental rights can be terminated, and laws that make surrender of custody and consent to adoption revocable in private placement adoptions. Because the contract was not enforceable and there was no basis to terminate Whitehead's parental rights, Mrs. Stern was not permitted to adopt the child. After reviewing extensive evidence offered at the trial of the case, the court granted custody of *Baby M.* to Mr. Stern and remanded the issue of visitation to the trial court.

For additional discussion of the Baby M. case, see Carol Sanger, *Developing Markets in Baby-Making*: In the Matter of Baby M., 30 Harv. J. L. & Gender 67 (2007).

Points for Discussion

a. Gestational Surrogacy

In the early surrogacy cases, including *R.R.* and *Baby M.*, the child was conceived by a surrogate who had been artificially inseminated with the contracting father's sperm. With the development of IVF techniques, it is now far more common for a gestational mother to carry a child that was implanted in her womb as an embryo, with which she has no genetic tie. In Johnson v. Calvert, 851 P.2d 776 (Cal. 1993), a married couple, Mark and Crispina Calvert, contracted with a woman named Anna to serve as a gestational surrogate. Crispina had had a hysterectomy, but her ovaries were still capable of producing eggs. One of her eggs was fertilized with Mark's sperm and the zygote implanted in Anna. During the pregnancy, the relationship between Anna and the Calverts deteriorated, and the parties filed lawsuits before the child was born. After the baby was born, blood tests confirmed that Mark and Crispina were the child's genetic parents.

The court in *Johnson* began by considering whether Crispina or Anna was the child's mother, and concluded that when two women present proof of maternity, the one who affirmatively intended "to bring about the birth of a child that she intended to raise as her own" will be the child's natural mother under California law. The court rejected Anna's argument that gestational surrogacy agreements violate the state's adoption laws, concluding that gestational surrogacy "differs in crucial respects from adoption."

Three years after its decision in *R.R.*, the same court decided <u>Culliton v. Beth Israel Deaconess Medical Center, 756 N.E.2d 1133 (Mass. 2001)</u>, approving a request of the genetic parents in a gestational surrogacy case for a declaration of parentage and a pre-birth order that their names be entered on the birth certificates of twins being carried by the gestational mother. Distinguishing gestational surrogacy issues from those addressed in *R.R.*, the court relied on the facts that the plaintiffs were the "sole genetic sources" of the twins, that the gestational carrier agreed with the relief sought, and that no one had contested the petition. The court also noted the importance of establishing the rights and responsibilities of parents as soon as practically possible.

b. Surrogacy Statutes

Early debates about surrogacy contracts focused on two concerns: that surrogacy amounted to baby-selling, and that it risked demeaning and exploiting women. A number of state legislatures passed statutes regulating or prohibiting surrogacy; the opinion in *R.R.* lists many of these. The Michigan statute, denying enforcement of all surrogacy agreements, was held to be constitutional in <u>Doe v. Attorney General, 487 N.W.2d 484 (Mich. Ct. App. 1992)</u>, while the Utah statute was found unconstitutional in <u>J.R. v. Utah, 261 F.Supp.2d 1268 (D.Utah 2002)</u>.

More recent legislation has taken a more permissive approach, focused primarily on gestational surrogacy. Article 8 of the UPA 2017, 9B U.L.A. (Supp. 2018), reprinted in the Appendix, addresses "Gestational Agreements," with commentary pointing to the fact that "thousands of children are born each year pursuant to gestational agreements" and arguing that "a child born under these circumstances is entitled to have its status clarified." Article 8 authorizes gestational agreements, provides a mechanism for judicial review and makes agreements enforceable if they have been approved by a court. State statutes permitting and regulating gestational surrogacy include <u>750 Ill. Comp. Stat. 47/25 (2018)</u> and <u>N.H. Rev.</u>

Stat. ch. 168–B (2018). On the shifting politics behind these two waves of legislation, see Elizabeth S. Scott, *Surrogacy and the Politics of Commodification*, 72 L. & Contemp. Probs. 109 (2009).

c. Recognition of Parentage Judgments

Given the differences among state surrogacy laws, intending parents may decide to travel to another state where the law is more favorable to enter into a surrogacy agreement. A court order declaring parentage of the intending parents, entered in the state where the child is born, will be entitled to full faith and credit in other states. See, e.g., Berwick v. Wagner, 509 S.W.3d 411 (Tex. App. 2014).

d. Altruism and Commodification

Popular and academic discussion of surrogacy has shifted between a debate over the risks of commodification of children and women and a more altruistic conception of surrogacy. The courts in both *R.R.* and *Baby M* concluded that surrogacy contracts were not illegal if no fee is paid and the mother retains the right to change her mind. Is it the payment of a large fee that makes the arrangement objectionable? See generally Margaret Jane Radin, *Market-Inalienability*, 100 Harv. L. Rev. 1849, 1928–1936 (1987); Martha Field, Surrogate Motherhood 17–32 (1988); but see also Richard A. Posner, *The Ethics and Economics of Enforcing Contracts of Surrogate Motherhood*, 5 J. Contemp. Health L. & Pol'y 21 (1989).

To the extent that gestational surrogacy seems less problematic, what is it about the separation of the genetic and gestational aspects of surrogacy that has made these arrangements more widely acceptable? See Scott, *supra* at 139–42. How are the policy concerns for lawmakers different when surrogacy is framed as an altruistic practice?

Note that even if surrogates or birth parents receive no compensation from the intending parents, adoption and assisted reproduction can be extremely expensive. Many other participants in the process profit significantly, including "a wide array of fertility specialists, agents, brokers, facilitators and other intermediaries." Kimberly A. Krawiec, *Altruism and Intermediation in the Market for Babies*, 66 Wash. & Lee L. Rev. 203, 207 (2009). Krawiec suggests that these intermediaries benefit from the altruistic model and from baby-selling restrictions that allow them to capture the full profits of the implicit market in babies.

e. Determining Maternity

With IVF techniques, there are now two different sources of biological motherhood. A woman who conceives a child using IVF and donated eggs will give birth to a child with whom she has no genetic connection. Courts have divided on the question whether it is possible for a child to have two biological mothers. *Johnson* concluded that the intended mother should be recognized as the child's natural mother under the Uniform Parentage Act. <u>Andres A. v. Judith N., 591 N.Y.S.2d 946 (Fam.Ct.1992)</u> held that the genetic mother of children born to a surrogate was not entitled to declaration of maternity, but that she might seek to adopt the children. In <u>K.M. v. E.G., 117 P.3d 673 (Cal. 2005)</u>, the court concluded that both lesbian partners were legal parents of children born after one partner donated her eggs so that the other could bear a child through in vitro fertilization, despite the fact that the donor had signed a consent form that relinquished any claim to legal parentage.

If a gestational surrogacy agreement is held to be unenforceable, should the contracting genetic parents have a right to seek recognition of their parental relationship with the child? Several courts have identified constitutional rights in this situation; see <u>J.R. v. Utah, 261 F.Supp.2d 1268 (D.Utah 2002)</u> (finding that surrogacy statute precluding genetic/biological parents from establishing parentage was unconstitutional as applied); <u>Soos v. Superior Court, 897 P.2d 1356 (Ariz. App.1994) rev. denied (1995)</u> (finding surrogacy statute unconstitutional in the case of gestational surrogacy).

In a number of states, laws permit intending parents to obtain a birth certificate for the child that lists their names and not the surrogate's. For example, <u>In re Roberto d.B., 923 A.2d 115 (Md. 2007)</u>, granted the father's request to omit from his children's birth certificate the name of the gestational carrier who bore the children, who were conceived from his sperm and donor eggs. See also <u>Culliton v. Beth Israel Deaconess Medical Center, 756 N.E.2d 1133 (Mass. 2001)</u>, noted above, and <u>Raftopol v. Ramey, 12 A.3d 783 (Conn. 2011)</u>.

f. Unmarried Couples and Assisted Reproduction

Courts have experienced some difficult in sorting out the parental rights of unmarried couples who use various forms of assisted reproduction. Compare <u>Steven S. v. Deborah D., 25 Cal. Rptr.3d 482 (Cal. Ct. App. 2005)</u>, which held that a sperm donor had no parental rights despite his intimate relationship with the mother when conception occurred as a result of artificial insemination rather than sexual intercourse, with <u>In re Parentage of J.M.K., 119 P.3d 840 (Wash. 2005)</u>, which held that the statute terminating the parental rights and obligations of a sperm donor was not applicable to a man who donated sperm to his lover for IVF. See also <u>In re C.K.G., 173 S.W.3d 714 (Tenn. 2005)</u>, holding that a woman who conceived children by IVF using donor eggs and her partner's sperm was entitled to parental rights after the couple ended their relationship.

g. Surrogacy Torts

What responsibilities do the intermediaries arranging surrogacy contracts have to the other participants and to children who may be born? Several courts have recognized the possibility of tort liability in these cases. In <u>Stiver v. Parker,</u>

975 F.2d 261 (6th Cir.1992), a woman agreed to be inseminated by Malahoff and to deliver the baby to him on its birth. Malahoff changed his mind and abandoned the baby, who was born with an infection that the surrogate believed was caused by the insemination which caused the baby serious mental and physical disorders. The court allowed the mother's suit to proceed against the "broker," a lawyer, and four doctors who participated in the surrogacy program.

In Huddleston v. Infertility Center of America, Inc., 700 A.2d 453 (Pa.Super. Ct.1997), a surrogate's action against Infertility Center of America (ICA) was allowed to proceed on claims for negligence, breach of fiduciary duty, wrongful death, negligent infliction of emotional distress and fraud. Patricia had agreed to be impregnated by James' sperm and act as a surrogate mother, with the child to be turned over to James, in response to an advertisement by the ICA. James paid a fee to ICA for its services and agreed to pay Patricia $13,000 as a surrogate fee. She gave birth to a boy, Jonathan, and physical custody was given to James. Six weeks later, Jonathan died as a result of serious physical abuse by James.

Global View: International ART

Internationally, countries take different approaches to surrogacy, ranging from complete prohibition in France, Germany, and Italy to a largely permissive approach in Nepal, Russia, the Ukraine, and a number of U.S. states. As a result, there has been a dramatic expansion in global surrogacy, leading to serious conflict of laws problems that leave some children with uncertain legal parentage or citizenship. See generally Hague Conference on Private International Law, *A Preliminary Report on the Issues Arising from International Surrogacy Arrangements*, Prel. Doc. No. 10 (March 2012).

U.S. citizens who use surrogacy or other forms of ART in another country may face difficulties when they seek to return to the United States with their children. A child born outside the United States may not be eligible for U.S. citizenship unless the child has a genetic or gestational relationship with a U.S.-citizen parent. Unless the intending parents—and clinics—are extremely careful to assure that either the egg or sperm comes from a known U.S. citizen, the child may be left stateless. Information on Assisted Reproductive Technology (ART) and Surrogacy Abroad is available on the U.S. State Department web page.

Problem 3-19

Luanne and John arranged to have a surrogate bear a child for them, using IVF with donor and egg and sperm. Shortly before the child's birth, John filed for a divorce, disclaiming any responsibility for the child. Luanne would like to raise the child, and asks the court to declare John to be the child's father. What arguments would you make for and against her petition? (See In re Marriage of Buzzanca, 72 Cal.Rptr.2d 280 (Ct. App.) rev. denied (1998).)

Problem 3-20

Robert and Denise contracted with an anonymous donor for eggs to be fertilized with Robert's sperm and implanted into Denise. From this process, thirteen embryos were created. Several of these were implanted, and Denise gave birth to a son. After their child was born, Robert and Denise learned that three of the embryos produced for them were mistakenly implanted into another woman, Susan, who had come to the clinic seeking an embryo created from anonymous donors. Robert has filed an action seeking to be declared the father of the child Susan delivered, and Robert and Denise seek custody or visitation rights with the child. Should their request be granted? (Robert B. v. Susan B., 135 Cal.Rptr.2d 785 (Ct. App. 2003).)

Further Reading: Assisted Reproduction

- Naomi R. Cahn, Test Tube Families: Why the Fertility Market Needs Legal Regulation (2009).

- Charles P. Kindregan and Maureen McBrien, Assisted Reproductive Technology: A Lawyer's Guide to Emerging Law and Science (2d ed. 2010)

- John A. Robertson, Children of Choice: Freedom and the New Reproductive Technologies (1996).

CHAPTER 4

Family Rights and Responsibilities

Law shapes families both with rules for forming and dissolving family relationships, and with rules that govern the rights and obligations of family members. The common law of domestic relations constructed the status relationships of husband and wife and parent and child in strongly gendered and hierarchical terms. This heritage still influences our approach to family relationships, but several centuries of legislation established a more egalitarian basis for marriage and gradually expanded the protections available for dependent family members. This chapter explores spousal and parent-child relationships, and contrasts this with the legal treatment of unmarried partners, elderly or disabled adult family members, and extended families. The large subject of child abuse and neglect is considered in Chapter 5.

A. Husbands, Wives and Partners

Marital status defined a large number of rights and obligations under the English common law, including significant legal disabilities for married women. As described in William Blackstone's Commentaries on the Laws of England, first published in 1765–1769, at Book 1, Chapter 15:

> By marriage, the husband and wife are one person in law, that is, the legal existence of the woman is suspended during marriage, or at least is incorporated into that of her husband, under whose protection and cover, she does everything, and is therefor called by French law, a *feme covert*, or under the protection of the husband, her baron and lord, and her condition during marriage is one of coverture.

Based on the system of **coverture**, a husband was entitled to control virtually all of his wife's property. A married woman had no legal capacity to make contracts or to sue and be sued in her own name. Her husband was held responsible for her crimes or torts. These aspects of coverture were gradually eliminated by **Married Women's Property Acts** that were enacted in all states, beginning in the 1830s, and gave married women the right to own and control their own property, to make contracts, to sue and be sued, and made them responsible for their own crimes and torts. The Married Women's Property Acts did not address many other aspects of coverture, however, which continued well into the twentieth century. See generally Homer H. Clark, Jr. Domestic Relations §§ 7.1–7.2 (Student 2d ed. 1988).

Building on the idea that a wife's legal existence had merged into her husband's, the common law held that a married couple could not contract with each other, could not enter into a criminal conspiracy with each other, and could not commit torts against each other. A wife could not establish her own legal domicile. A husband had the right of **consortium**, encompassing her services, society, companionship and sexual relations. Although a wife had a right of financial support, which could be enforced by the state or by creditors who provided her with necessaries, she could enforce this right only in an action for separate maintenance, and only if she was living apart from her husband.

Over time, courts began to characterize the tradition of noninterference in family life in terms of respect for marital privacy or preserving marital harmony rather than on the basis of coverture or **spousal unity**. Reva Siegel has described how this type of transformation effectively preserved the substance of the older rules. See Reva B. Siegel, *Home as Work: The First Woman's Rights Claims Concerning Wives' Household Labor, 1850–1880*, 103 Yale L.J. 1073 (1994), and Reva B. Siegel, "The Rule of Love": Wife Beating as Prerogative and Privacy, 105 Yale L.J. 2117 (1996). A significant body of contemporary case law wrestles with the legacies of coverture in many areas of the law.

Spousal Contracts. Since 1970, states have begun to allow a wider range of premarital and separation agreements, as discussed in Chapter 1 and Chapter 6. Courts remain reluctant to enforce agreements between spouses with respect to their ongoing marital obligations, however. See, e.g., Graham v. Graham, 33 F.Supp. 936 (E.D. Mich. 1940) In Romeo v. Romeo, 418 A.2d 258 (N.J. 1980), a case involving a husband who had been employed at his wife's tavern, the court concluded that a husband and wife may enter into a valid employment contract, but it was surprisingly careful to limit its ruling to the context of workers' compensation claims.

Spousal Support Obligations. In 1979, Orr v. Orr, 440 U.S. 268 (1979), invalidated a state statute authorizing alimony awards for wives only on equal protection grounds. Contemporary statutes and case law assign the support duty equally to husbands and wives, to be shared in proportion to their financial means. See, e.g., Colo. Rev. Stat. Ann. § 14–6–110 (2018); Conn. Gen. Stat. § 46b–37(b) (2018); Wash. Rev. Code § 26.16.205 (2018); Yale University School of Medicine v. Collier, 536 A.2d 588 (Conn. 1988).

Courts will not take jurisdiction over support claims while the couple lives together, however. The well-known case of McGuire v. McGuire, 59 N.W.2d 336

(Neb. 1953), reversed a lower court ruling that had ordered a husband "with a reputation for more than ordinary frugality" to make repairs and improvements to the family home (including installing indoor plumbing), buy a car with a working heater, and pay his wife a personal allowance of $50 a month. Noting that the couple had been married 33 years and were still living together, the court concluded that: "The living standards of a family are a matter of concern to the household, and not for the courts to determine, even though the husband's attitude toward his wife, according to his wealth and circumstances, leaves little to be said in his behalf." See Hendrik Hartog, *The Scene of a Marriage*: McGuire v. McGuire, *in* Family Law Stories 219 (Carol Sanger, ed. 2008).

Spousal Necessaries. Creditors continue to rely on the **family expense statutes** and the **necessaries** doctrine in order to hold one spouse responsible for the

Make the Connection

The spousal necessaries rule was applied in Accounts Management, Inc. v. Litchfield, 576 N.W.2d 233 (S.D. 1998), reprinted in Chapter 1.

other's debts. Often, these are debts for medical care incurred at the end of life. Faced with the requirement of gender equality, most state courts and legislatures have expanded the doctrine to impose obligations on both spouses. See, e.g., Landmark Medical Center v. Gauthier, 635 A.2d 1145 (R.I.1994). Cf. Connor v. Southwest Florida Regional Medical Center Inc., 668 So.2d 175 (Fla.1995) rehearing den. (1996) (abrogating the common law doctrine of necessaries, and leaving the question for the state legislature); North Ottawa Community Hospital v. Kieft, 457 Mich. 394, 578 N.W.2d 267 (1998) (holding necessaries doctrine to be unconstitutional).

Spousal Tort Immunities. The traditional rule of **interspousal tort immunity** was often justified with the argument that such suits might disturb the harmony of the marriage, even in cases of serious domestic violence, see Thompson v. Thompson, 218 U.S. 611 (1910). Another frequent argument was that allowing such suits might lead to fraud and collusion between spouses, see Lyons v. Lyons, 208 N.E.2d 533 (Ohio 1965). A large majority of the states eventually abolished or limited the traditional immunity; see generally Carl Tobias, *Interspousal Tort Immunity in America*, 23 Ga. L. Rev. 359 (1989). Marital torts are considered further in the materials below.

Spousal Evidentiary Privileges. The common law gave husband and wife the right to prevent adverse testimony from the other spouse. Under federal law, this **marital privilege** was modified to give the witness-spouse the choice whether or not to testify adversely. See Trammel v. United States, 445 U.S. 40 (1980). In addition, evidence law recognizes a privilege for confidential communications between husband and wife, which may be asserted by the spouse by whom a communication was made. There are exceptions to these privileges; see, e.g., United States v. Martinez, 44 F.Supp.2d 835 (W.D. Texas 1999) (holding that spousal communications privilege does not apply where parent is charged with child abuse). See generally Christopher B. Mueller, Laird C. Kirkpatrick, & Liesa L. Richter, Evidence §§ 5.31–5.32 (6th ed. 2018).

Spousal Violence. The most egregious aspects of the common law of coverture were rules that condoned spousal abuse. According to Blackstone, the "old law" allowed a husband to "correct" or "chastise" his wife by inflicting corporal punishment or restraining her of her liberty. In addition, courts concluded that a husband could not be guilty of raping his wife, on the basis that by consenting to marry the wife had consented to sexual intercourse with her husband. These rules remained largely intact until challenged during women's movement of the 1970s.

───────

Despite the changes to the common law tradition over the past two centuries, marriage still has significant legal consequences for husbands and wives, both in relation to each other and to the state and third parties. Marital property law is an important and complex field, with implications for how couples manage their assets during marriage as well as how property is distributed when the marriage ends by death or divorce. Marriage has important consequences in tort law and in criminal law, in the law of evidence, and in the law of debtors and creditors. Married individuals have the right to make certain medical decisions for an incompetent spouse. Under federal law, marriage plays a significant role in matters such as income and inheritance taxes, bankruptcy law, eligibility for social security and other public benefits, and family immigration rights.

Go Online

For the original GAO list, see U.S. General Accounting Office, *Defense of Marriage Act,* GAO/OGC–97–16 (January 31, 1997).
For the updated report, see U.S. General Accounting Office, *Defense of Marriage Act,* GAO 04–1353R (January 23, 2004)

According to a 1997 report by the U.S. General Accounting Office (GAO), there were 1049 federal laws in which benefits, rights or privileges were dependent on marital status or in which marital status is a factor. An updated report prepared in 2004 placed the number at 1138. Marital status is equally or more important under state law. See, for example, the discussion of the protections, benefits and obligations conferred by marriage in the same-sex marriage cases, including Goodridge v. Department of Public Health, 798 N.E.2d 941, 955–56 (Mass. 2003), and Varnum v. Brien, 763 N.W.2d

862, 902 n.28 (Iowa 2009), as well as Obergefell v. Hodges, 576 U.S. ___, 135 S.Ct. 2584 (2015), reprinted in Chapter 1.

Schlueter v. Schlueter

975 S.W.2d 584 (Tex. 1998)

GONZALEZ, JUSTICE, delivered the opinion of the Court, in which ENOCH, OWEN, BAKER, ABBOTT and HANKINSON, JUSTICES, joined.

This divorce case answers the question of what remedies are available to a spouse alleging fraud on the community committed by the other spouse. The husband transferred various community assets to his father shortly before he filed for divorce. The wife counterclaimed for divorce and brought independent tort claims against her husband and father-in-law, seeking damages for fraud, breach of fiduciary duty, and conspiracy. Based on favorable jury findings, the trial court ordered a disproportionate division of the community estate favoring the wife, and rendered judgment for the wife against the husband and his father for actual and exemplary damages. Holding that a tort cause of action for fraud on the community exists independent of a divorce proceeding, the court of appeals affirmed. 929 S.W.2d 94. We granted writ to resolve a conflict among courts of appeals. Because a wronged spouse has an adequate remedy for fraud on the community through the "just and right" property division upon divorce, we hold that there is no independent tort cause of action between spouses for damages to the community estate. Accordingly, we reverse the judgment against the husband and remand for a new division of the marital estate. We affirm the remainder of the court of appeals' judgment.

I

Richard and Karen Schlueter married in 1969. In December 1992, Mr. Schlueter began investing in emus. He contributed $3250 of community funds toward two pairs of the birds, but eventually sold his interest to his father, Hudson Schlueter, for $1,000. The emu business was worth at least $10,000 when the sale occurred. Mrs. Schlueter did not know the details of the business and did not find out that her husband had sold his interest to her father-in-law until after Mr. Schlueter filed for divorce.

Shortly before he filed for divorce, Mr. Schlueter accepted a $30,360.41 check from his employer as an incentive for early retirement. Mr. Schlueter turned the check over to his father for deposit in his father's account. His father then wrote himself a check for $12,565, allegedly to reimburse past loans to Mr. Schlueter. About a week later, Mr. Schlueter filed for divorce.

Mrs. Schlueter counterclaimed for divorce and added independent tort claims against her husband and father-in-law for fraud, breach of fiduciary duty, and conspiracy. All of Mrs. Schlueter's claims against her husband and father-in-law involve their depriving the Schlueters' community estate of assets. Mrs. Schlueter makes no claim that she was deprived of her separate property.

The jury heard the fraud and conspiracy claims in a bifurcated trial. The jury found that Mr. Schlueter committed actual and constructive fraud in dealing with the community assets, that he and his father had fraudulently transferred assets between them, and that they had engaged in a civil conspiracy to injure Mrs. Schlueter. The jury found that $12,850 would compensate the community for Mr. Schlueter's and his father's actions. It found that $35,000 would compensate the community for damage caused by the conspiracy. Finally, the jury found that Mr. Schlueter should pay $50,000 and his father $15,000 in exemplary damages.

At a later date, the trial court heard the divorce action without a jury, divided the marital assets, and rendered judgment on the jury verdict against Mr. Schlueter and his father jointly and severally for $12,850. In its Findings of Fact, the trial court determined that the joint and several judgment was part of the community estate. The court also awarded Mrs. Schlueter $30,000 in exemplary damages against her husband and $15,000 in exemplary damages against her father-in-law, and awarded Mrs. Schlueter $18,500 from her husband for attorney's fees on appeal.

The court of appeals affirmed. The court held that a spouse may bring an independent tort claim against the other spouse for fraud for which exemplary damages may be awarded, even when the fraud resulted only in a depletion of community assets and not the wronged spouse's separate estate. 929 S.W.2d at 99–100. The court of appeals based its holding on this Court's abrogation of the doctrine of interspousal immunity in the *Bounds*, *Price*, and *Twyman* decisions, and concluded that a person may bring any cause of action against his or her spouse. 929 S.W.2d at 99–100 (construing *Twyman v. Twyman*, 855 S.W.2d 619, 624 (Tex.1993); *Price v. Price*, 732 S.W.2d 316, 319 (Tex.1987); and *Bounds v. Caudle*, 560 S.W.2d 925, 927 (Tex.1977)). The court of appeals also affirmed the judgment against the father-in-law, holding that the trial court had not abused its discretion in admitting into evidence a copy of a divorce decree involving Mr. Schlueter's brother.

Relying on *Belz v. Belz*, 667 S.W.2d 240, 247 (Tex.App.-Dallas 1984, writ ref'd n.r.e.), and *In re Marriage of Moore*, 890 S.W.2d 821, 829 (Tex.App.-Amarillo 1994, no writ), Mr. Schlueter alleges that the court of appeals committed reversible error in recognizing a separate cause of action for fraud on the community. Mr. Schlueter and his father, in the father's only point of error, also assert that the court of appeals erred in holding that the trial court did not abuse its discretion in admitting into evidence a copy of the decree from Mr. Schlueter's brother's divorce.

II

The court of appeals reads the *Twyman*, *Price*, and *Bounds* decisions too broadly; these decisions do not control this case. In *Bounds*, we dealt with whether the interspousal immunity doctrine prevented a deceased woman's children from suing their stepfather for their mother's wrongful death. The stepfather had allegedly shot and killed his wife. We concluded that interspousal immunity should be abolished for willful or intentional torts. From a policy perspective, we stated that suits for willful and intentional torts such as the physical attack in that case would not disrupt domestic tranquility in "a home which has already been strained to the point where an intentional physical attack could take place."

We re-examined the doctrine in *Price v. Price*, 732 S.W.2d 316 (Tex.1987). A wife sued her husband for negligence in causing her injuries in a motorcycle accident. Again this Court considered and rejected the argument that "peace and harmony" in the home would be damaged by suits between spouses, commenting that "[i]t is difficult to fathom how denying a forum for the redress of any wrong could be said to encourage domestic tranquility." We followed up on our holding in *Bounds* by stating, "We now abolish [the interspousal immunity doctrine] completely as to any cause of action. We do not limit our holding to suits involving vehicular accidents only."

Finally, in *Twyman*, we expressly adopted the tort of intentional infliction of emotional distress, and a plurality held that such a claim could be brought in a divorce proceeding. The plurality noted that under *Bounds* and *Price*, there was no legal impediment to bringing a tort claim in a divorce action "based on either negligence or an intentional act such as assault or battery." Of course, by its facts, *Twyman* expanded that statement by allowing an intentional tort claim for emotional distress, which does not necessarily involve the physical aspects of assault or battery.

The salient characteristic distinguishing *Bounds*, *Price*, and *Twyman* from the case before us is that all three involved personal injury tort claims. *Twyman, 855 S.W.2d at 621* (intentional infliction of emotional distress); *Price, 732 S.W.2d at 316* (negligence claim for personal injuries); *Bounds, 560 S.W.2d at 926* (wrongful death). Cf. *Cleaver v. George Staton Co., Inc., 908 S.W.2d 468, 471* n. 2 (Tex. App.-Tyler 1995, writ denied) (distinguishing *Twyman*, which involved outrageous spousal conduct, and noting that the trial court could sort out the husband's claims against wife for breach of fiduciary duty and fraud on community estate in the property division, not by a separate cause of action). In discussing the potential for double recovery in _Twyman_, the Court pointed out that recovery for personal injuries of a spouse, including pain and suffering, is the separate property of the injured spouse, and therefore does not add to the marital estate. _Twyman_, 855 S.W.2d at 625 n. 20 (citing (Tex. Fam.Code) § 5.01(a)(3) (Act of May 31, 1969, 61st Leg., R.S., ch. 888, 1969 Tex. Gen. Laws 2707, 2726, _repealed by_ Act of April 3, 1997, 75th Leg., R.S., ch. 7, § 3, 1997 Tex. Gen. Laws 8, 43)) (current version at Tex. Fam. Code Ann. § 3.001(3)).

Likewise, in response to the concern that interspousal suits would result in fraud and collusion between the participants, the _Price_ court stated, "we are unable to distinguish interspousal suits from other actions for personal injury." Therefore, despite its broad language stating that the Court was abolishing the interspousal immunity doctrine "completely as to any cause of action," the action in _Price_ was one for personal injury, for which any recovery would be separate property of the injured spouse.

Moreover, a factor in _Price_ that weighed heavily toward abolishing interspousal immunity "as to any cause of action" was the need to remedy the problem of denying a litigant a forum for the redress of a wrong. The Court summed up the holding by saying that the result in the case was "compelled by the fundamental proposition of public policy that the courts should afford [such] redress." However, redress is available in the present case without the creation of a separate tort cause of action between spouses.

Mrs. Schlueter sued her husband for improperly depleting community assets. This state's community property system provides that upon divorce, the trial court must enter a division of a married couple's estate "in a manner that the court deems just and right," considering the rights of the parties and any children of the marriage. Tex. Fam. Code Ann. § 7.001. Such a standard may at times lead to a disproportionate division of assets and liabilities of the parties, depending on the circumstances that courts may consider in refusing to divide the marital estate equally.

As this Court stated in _Cameron v. Cameron_, 641 S.W.2d 210, 223 (Tex.1982), "Community property owes its existence to the legal fact of marriage, and when the parties to that compact determine their relationship should end, property acquired during marriage is and should be divided among them in a just and right manner." This is distinguishable from recovery of separate property through an independent tort, which we allowed in _Twyman_, because "separate property. . .owes its existence to wholly extramarital factors, things unrelated to the marriage. In relation to that property, the parties are, in essence, strangers; they are separate." With these differences in mind, we hold that the well-developed "just and right" standard should continue to be the sole method used to account for and divide community property upon divorce.

Of course, there are also aspects of this state's community property system that provide additional remedies against a spouse for improper conduct involving the community estate. Texas recognizes the concept of fraud on the community, which is a wrong by one spouse that the court may consider in its division of the estate of the parties and that may justify an unequal division of the property. *See Belz v. Belz*, 667 S.W.2d 240, 247 (Tex.App.-Dallas 1984, writ ref'd n.r.e.). As the court in *Belz* aptly described it:

> [A] claim of fraud on the community is a means to an end, either to re-cover specific property wrongfully conveyed, . . . or . . .to obtain a greater share of the community estate upon divorce, in order to compensate the wronged spouse for his or her lost interest in the community estate.

Just as in the present case, *Belz* involved alleged intentional deprivation of the wife's share of community assets. Nevertheless, despite the intentional nature of the claim, because the fraud was perpetrated on the community, the court correctly distinguished it from cases involving personal injuries for which recovery belongs to the separate estate.

Additionally, it is well settled that a trial court may award a money judgment to one spouse against the other in order to achieve an equitable division of the community estate. *See Murff v. Murff*, 615 S.W.2d 696, 699 (Tex.1981) (allowing money judgment against husband in division of community property where he had substantial sums in savings before separation that had disappeared by the time of trial). Of course, the money judgment can only be used as a means for the wronged spouse to recoup the value of his or her share of the community estate lost through the wrongdoer spouse's actions. *See Mazique v. Mazique*, 742 S.W.2d 805, 808 (Tex.App.-Houston [1st Dist.] 1987, no writ). Because the amount of the judgment is directly referable to a specific value of lost community property, it will never exceed the total value of the community estate. Still, a sound policy in favor of the wronged spouse is advanced: he or she should not suffer just because when it is time to divide the community, the other spouse has depleted the estate such that there is not enough money or property left to effect a just and right division.

* * *

Trial courts also have wide discretion and are allowed to take many factors into consideration in making a just and right division, *see Murff*, 615 S.W.2d at 698–99, including wasting of community assets. *See* Barbara Anne Kazen, *Division of Property at the Time of Divorce*, 49 Baylor L. Rev. 417, 424–28 (1997) (discussing factors that may be considered by a trial court in effecting a just and right property division). This too allows injured spouses like Mrs. Schlueter to recover her appropriate share of not only that property existing in the community at the time of divorce, but also that which was improperly depleted from the community estate. Waste of community assets is similar to the allegations against the husband here: that without the wife's knowledge or consent, he wrongfully depleted the community of assets of which Mrs. Schlueter was entitled a share. Such behavior is properly considered when dividing a community estate.

Mrs. Schlueter argues that allowing a separate tort cause of action for actual fraud is necessary so that exemplary damages may be awarded for the intentional acts of the wrongdoer spouse. However, heightened culpability does not change the essential character of the wrong: a deprivation of community assets as opposed to a tort committed against a person or his or her separate property. As discussed, the "just and right" standard with accompanying consideration of a wrongdoer spouse's fraud on community assets provides wronged spouses such as Mrs. Schlueter with redress. Moreover, as we have previously held, "recovery of punitive damages requires a finding of an independent tort with accompanying actual damages." *Twin City Fire Ins. Co. v. Davis*, 904 S.W.2d 663, 665 (Tex.1995); *Federal Express Corp. v. Dutschmann*, 846 S.W.2d 282, 284 (Tex.1993); *cf. Amoco Prod. Co. v. Alexander*, 622 S.W.2d 563, 571 (Tex.1981) (explaining in breach of contract action that even if breach is malicious, intentional, or capricious, punitive damages not recoverable without a tort). Because of our holding in the present case that there is no independent tort cause of action for wrongful disposition by a spouse of community assets, the wronged spouse may not recover punitive damages from the other spouse.

However, despite the inappropriateness of punitive damages, it is a logical extension of a standard that calls for a "just and right" division to allow the court to consider that a spouse not only deprived the community of assets to the detriment of the other spouse, but may have done so with dishonesty of purpose or intent to deceive. *See Land v. Marshall*, 426 S.W.2d 841, 846 n. 3 (Tex.1968). This is the culpability needed for actual fraud on the community, which is one of the allegations by Mrs. Schlueter against Mr. Schlueter. Therefore, while we hold that a separate and independent tort action for actual fraud and accompanying exemplary damages against one's spouse do not exist in the context of a deprivation of community assets, if the wronged spouse can prove the heightened culpability of actual fraud, the trial court may consider it in the property division.[1]

III

With regard to the causes of action against Mr. Schlueter's father, he has not argued that these separate and independent tort claims against him as a third-

---

[1]   For a thorough discussion of issues relevant to this case, *see* Bradley L. Adams, *The Doctrine of Fraud on the Community*, 49 Baylor L. Rev. 445, 450–64 (1997).

party defendant should also be abolished. Therefore, we do not reach that issue. We note that the trial court's $12,850 judgment of actual damages against Mrs. Schlueter's father-in-law was awarded to the community estate. That judgment represents an asset returned to the community estate, making it monetarily whole. Therefore, the trial court, in its just and right division, may not effect a disproportionate property division solely to make up for that formerly lost asset. However, as we have already discussed, the trial court may take into account Mr. Schlueter's conduct that resulted in a defrauding of the community estate.

* * *

For all the foregoing reasons, we reverse the court of appeals' judgment against Richard Schlueter for actual and exemplary damages, and attorney's fees on appeal, and remand this cause to the trial court for a new property division. We affirm the remainder of the court of appeals' judgment.

> **FYI**
>
> One dissenting opinion in *Schlueter* rejected the conclusion that a spousal fraud claim should be actionable only in divorce proceedings and not in an independent tort action. Another dissent argued that a plaintiff spouse should be entitled to recover punitive damages from the defendant spouse's separate estate.

Points for Discussion

a. *Schlueter*

Why does the court distinguish between financial torts and personal injury tort claims? What practical differences are there for a spouse between the remedies available in tort and those available in a division of community or marital property? Should Mrs. Schlueter be entitled to punitive damages in this case?

b. Property Division

The court holds in *Schlueter* that the husband's fraud may be taken into account in the division of property in the couple's divorce. Rules governing the division of marital and community property in divorce are discussed in Chapter 6. With the passage of "no-fault" divorce laws, many states also enacted laws that prohibit courts from considering marital misconduct in division of marital property. Despite this rule, courts in these states have sometimes approved awards taking financial misconduct into account. See, e.g., Sands v. Sands, 497 N.W.2d 493 (Mich. 1993). Another case concluding that a claim for depletion of marital assets must be resolved under the divorce law rather than as a tort claim for fraud is Beers v. Beers, 724 So.2d 109 (Fla.Ct.App.1998).

c. Marital Torts

With the demise of interspousal immunities, courts have had to decide what behavior should be treated as tortious between married individuals. Claims for assault and battery are commonly recognized, and may permit financial recovery for a spouse who has been the victim of domestic violence. E.g. Waite v. Waite, 618 So.2d 1360 (Fla.1993) (husband attacked wife with a machete); Heacock v. Heacock, 520 N.E.2d 151 (Mass. 1988) (husband repeatedly struck his wife's head against a door frame, causing dizzy spells, blackouts and traumatic epilepsy); Aubert v. Aubert, 529 A.2d 909 (N.H. 1987) (woman deliberately shot her husband in the face at point-blank range.) Spouses have also sued after being infected by a partner with a sexually transmitted disease; see, e.g., McPherson v. McPherson, 712 A.2d 1043 (Me.1998) (human papillomavirus), M.M.D. v. B.L.G., 467 N.W.2d 645 (Minn.App.1991) (genital herpes); Endres v. Endres, 912 A.2d 975 (Vt. 2006) (HPV infection).

In cases raising claims of outrageous conduct, or negligent or intentional infliction of emotional distress, courts have struggled to determine what level of outrageousness is necessary to state a claim for relief. Twyman v. Twyman, 855 S.W.2d 619 (Tex.1993), cited by the court in *Schlueter,* recognized a claim for intentional infliction of emotional distress when a wife who had been raped prior to the marriage was traumatized by her husband's attempts to force her to engage in sexual bondage. Other courts have not been willing to recognize emotional distress claims, in part due to a concern that some emotional distress is part of the normal process of marital life and marital breakdown. E.g. Hakkila v. Hakkila, 812 P.2d 1320 (N.M. Ct.App.1991) (alleging that husband insulted wife in front of guests, locked her out of the house during winter, refused to have sex with her or used too much force during sex, slammed trunk lid on her hands). See generally Leonard Karp & Cheryl L. Karp, Domestic Torts: Family Violence, Conflict and Sexual Abuse (rev. ed. 2005). Marital tort claims for domestic violence are considered further below.

How should marital tort claims be treated in states that permit consideration of fault in a divorce action? Professors Ira Ellman and Stephen Sugarman have argued against permitting emotional distress claims for conduct such as bullying or infidelity, on the basis that these are really claims for breach of the marital relationship. The argue that recognition of emotional abuse torts undermines the policy goals of no-fault divorce laws, and urge that tort recoveries should be limited to those based on conduct that is also criminal. Ira Mark Ellman & Stephen D. Sugarman, *Spousal Emotional Abuse as a Tort?* 55 Md. L. Rev. 1268 (1996); cf. Harry D. Krause, *On the Danger of Allowing Marital Fault to Re-Emerge in the Guise of Torts,* 73 Notre Dame L. Rev. 1355 (1998).

d. Community and Common-Law Property

Texas is one of eight states with **community property** laws; the others are Arizona, California, Idaho, Louisiana, Nevada, New Mexico and Washington. In these states, property acquired by either partner during the marriage belongs to both spouses, with the exception of property acquired by gift, devise or inheritance. Generalizations about community property laws are difficult, however, as there are many variations among the laws in these eight states. See Homer H. Clark, Jr., Domestic Relations 296–98 (Student 2d ed. 1988).

Community property principles have had significant influence on states with a common law property tradition, most of which now classify the spouses' property as either separate or marital at the time of divorce, and require equitable division of the marital property. Common law states also give one spouse an interest in the other spouse's property owned at the time of death. The central difference between the two property systems today is that, in a common law state, one spouse's interest in property held by the other does not vest until a divorce proceeding is filed.

Wisconsin has enacted the Uniform Marital Property Act (UMPA), 9A U.L.A. (Part I) 103 (1998), which provides that each spouse has an undivided one-half interest in all marital property during the marriage. The UMPA gives both spouses powers of management and control of marital property, creating in effect, a community property regime. Wis. Stat. Ann. § 766.001 et seq. (2018).

Tort Claims and the Marital Relationship

In the common law, a husband could bring an action for loss of **consortium** if his wife was injured through the defendant's negligence. The first case that permitted a married woman to bring a similar suit was Hitaffer v. Argonne Co., 183 F.2d 811 (D.C.Cir.1950), cert. denied 340 U.S. 852 (1950), but almost every state now permits either spouse to bring this type of action. Cf. Boucher v. Dixie Medical Center, a Div. of IHC Hospitals, Inc., 850 P.2d 1179 (Utah 1992) (neither husband nor wife have claim for loss of consortium). Damages are intended to compensate for impairment of the spouse's interest in society, companionship and sexual relations with the other spouse. See generally 1 Homer H. Clark, Jr., Domestic Relations § 12.5 (2d ed.1987); Homer H. Clark, Jr., Domestic Relations § 11.3 (Student 2d ed.1988).

Courts generally refuse to extend consortium claims to couples living together who are not married; see, e.g., Elden v. Sheldon, 758 P.2d 582 (Cal. 1988); Laws v. Griep, 332 N.W.2d 339 (Iowa 1983); Feliciano v. Rosemar Silver Co., 514 N.E.2d

1095 (Mass. 1987); but see <u>Lozoya v. Sanchez, 66 P.3d 948 (N.M. 2003)</u>. Several courts have permitted cohabitants to bring a bystander action for negligent infliction of emotional distress after witnessing fatal injuries inflicted on their partners. See <u>Graves v. Estabrook, 818 A.2d 1255 (N.H. 2003)</u>; <u>Dunphy v. Gregor, 642 A.2d 372 (N.J. 1994)</u>.

In cases of intentional interference with a marital relationship, the common law permitted actions for **alienation of affections**, based on proof that there was some wrongful conduct by defendant with the plaintiff's spouse, and that there was a loss of affection or consortium as a result. These cases are sometimes brought against family members or even counselors who break up a marriage by giving advice, but the cases hold that if the advice is given honestly, reasonably and in good faith, the defendant is not liable. Although it may be joined with an action for alienation of affections, the common law action for **criminal conversation** allowed a husband to recover if his wife committed adultery, based on proof that the defendant had intercourse with the plaintiff's wife. See generally 1 Homer H. Clark, Jr., Domestic Relations § 12.2 and 12.3 (2d ed. 1987). In some cases, the claim for alienation of affection may overlap with other tort claims, such as fraud or intentional infliction of emotional distress. See, e.g., <u>Coulson v. Steiner, 390 P.3d 1139 (Alaska 2017)</u>.

Heartbalm legislation in many states has abolished, in whole or in part, suits for alienation of affections and criminal conversation. Several other states have abolished these actions by judicial decision. See, e.g., <u>Hoye v. Hoye, 824 S.W.2d 422 (Ky.1992)</u>; <u>Bearbower v. Merry, 266 N.W.2d 128 (Iowa 1978)</u>. Courts have had some difficulty in determining precisely what kinds of suits the legislation abolishes, since plaintiffs' counsel are often astute enough to frame their claims in ways which may not ostensibly resemble alienation of affections or criminal conversation. See, e.g., <u>Destefano v. Grabrian, 763 P.2d 275 (Colo.1988)</u>; <u>Schieffer v. Catholic Archdiocese of Omaha, 508 N.W.2d 907 (Neb. 1993)</u>. The Heart Balm statute was held not to bar a suit by a husband for emotional distress after he learned that defendant was the biological father of his children, <u>C.M. v. J.M., 726 A.2d 998 (N.J. Super. Ct. 1999)</u>. In Illinois, the damages that may be awarded in heart balm actions are limited by statute; see <u>Murphy v. Colson, 999 N.E.2d 372 (Ill. App. Ct. 2013)</u> (upholding constitutionality of limitations).

In <u>Veeder v. Kennedy, 589 N.W.2d 610 (S.D. 1999)</u>, the court sustained a jury verdict for $265,000 in compensatory and punitive damages, rejecting defendant's request to abrogate the claim for alienation of affections, which has a statutory basis in South Dakota. The court noted, however, that the tort remained a legitimate cause of action in only nine states (Illinois, Hawaii, Missouri, Mississippi, New Hampshire, New Mexico, North Carolina, South Dakota and Utah.) <u>Knight v. Woodfield, 50 So.3d 995 (Miss. 2011)</u>, found that the court had long-arm jurisdiction over a non-resident defendant in an alienation of affections case based on emails, text messages, and phone calls he sent to plaintiff's wife in Mississippi. A contemporary case sustaining a jury verdict in a criminal conversation case is Horner v. Byrnett, 511 S.E.2d 342 (N.C. Ct. App. 1999) (awarding $1.00 in compensatory damages and $85,000 in punitive damages.)

Problem 4-1

When John and Jane had been married for almost seven years, John discovered that Jane had been having an affair with her employer for some period of time. Blood tests revealed that John was the biological father of only one of the couple's three children. John filed for divorce on the ground of adultery, and sought damages from Jane for fraud and intentional infliction of emotional distress. John, who has had a close relationship with the children, has also requested custody of all three. Should the court permit his tort action to proceed against Jane? (See Doe v. Doe, 747 A.2d 617 (Md. 2000).) Should John be permitted to sue Jane's employer, and if so on what basis?

In re the Guardianship of Atkins

868 N.E.2d 878 (Ind. Ct. App. 2007)

BAKER, CHIEF JUDGE.

Appellant-petitioner Brett Conrad[1] appeals from the trial court's order that, among other things, appointed appellees-cross-petitioners Thomas and Jeanne Atkins (collectively, the Atkinses) as co-guardians of Patrick Atkins and Patrick's estate. Specifically, Brett raises the following arguments: (1) Brett should have been appointed as Patrick's guardian or, at a minimum, should have visitation rights; (2) the trial court erred by declining to require Patrick's physical attendance at trial and refusing to interview or meet with Patrick; (3) Patrick's Charles Schwab account should not have been entirely set off to the guardianship estate; and (4) a portion of Brett's attorney fees and expenses should have been paid from the guardianship estate.

We find, among other things, that although the trial court did not abuse its discretion by naming the Atkinses to be Patrick's co-guardians, there is over-

---

[1] On June 9, 2006, Brett filed a motion to permit identification of the parties by their initials. The motions panel directed the parties to use full names in their pleadings and reserved the ruling on Brett's motion for the writing panel. Brett has offered no citation to authority or rule in support of his request to identify the parties herein by their initials and we see no compelling reason to grant this request. Consequently, the motion is denied.

whelming evidence in the record establishing that it is in Patrick's best interest to continue to have contact with Brett, his life partner of twenty-five years. We also find that the trial court erroneously refused Brett's request to have a portion of his attorney fees and costs paid by the guardianship estate. Thus, we affirm in part, reverse in part, and remand with instructions to grant Brett the visitation and contact with Patrick that he requested and to calculate the amount of Brett's attorney fees and costs to be paid by the guardianship estate.

FACTS

Patrick and Brett met and became romantically involved beginning in 1978 when they attended Wabash College together. Since that time—for twenty-five years—the men have lived together and have been in a committed and loving relationship.

Patrick's family vehemently disapproves of his relationship with Brett. Patrick, however, was able to reconcile his religious faith with his homosexuality and in 2000, Patrick wrote a letter to his family, begging them to accept him and welcome Brett:

> I want you all to know that Brett is my best friend in the whole world and I love him more than life itself. I beg all of you to reach out to him with the same love you have for me, he is extremely special and once you know him you will understand why I love him so much. Trust me, God loves us all so very much, and I know he approves of the love that Brett and I have shared for over 20 years.

Patrick's family, however, has steadfastly refused to accept their son's lifestyle. Jeanne believes that homosexuality is a grievous sin and that Brett and his relatives are "sinners" and are "evil" for accepting Brett and Patrick's relationship. She testified that no amount of evidence could convince her that Patrick and Brett were happy together or that they had a positive and beneficial relationship.

Neither Patrick nor Brett earned a degree from Wabash College. In 1982, Patrick began working for the family business, Atkins, Inc. d/b/a Atkins Elegant Desserts and Atkins Cheesecake, and he ultimately became the CEO of that business. Patrick's annual income prior to his incapacitation was approximately $130,000. Brett is a waiter, has been working for Puccini's restaurants for the past ten years, and has an annual income of approximately $31,800. Patrick and Brett pooled their earnings, depositing them into a checking account that was titled solely in Patrick's name but was used as a joint account for payment of living expenses. They used some of their accumulated savings to make extra mortgage payments and periodically transferred the remaining savings into a Charles Schwab account that was titled solely in Patrick's name.

Between 1980 and 1992, Brett and Patrick lived together in various apartments. In 1992, they bought a house together in Fishers as joint tenants, and the home is still titled jointly.

On March 11, 2005, Patrick was on a business trip in Atlanta when he collapsed and was admitted to a hospital. Doctors determined that he had suffered a ruptured aneurysm and an acute subarachnoid hemorrhage. Patrick remained in the Intensive Care Unit (ICU) of the Atlanta hospital for six weeks. At some point during his stay in the ICU, Patrick suffered a stroke.

Brett traveled to the Atlanta hospital to be with Patrick; Patrick's family did as well. Patrick's brother testified that Brett's mere presence in the hospital was "hurting" Jeanne and offending her religious beliefs. Jeanne told Brett that if Patrick was going to return to his life with Brett after recovering from the stroke, she would prefer that he not recover at all.

Shortly after Brett's first visit with Patrick in the ICU, Patrick's family restricted the times and duration of Brett's visits. Subsequently, Brett was allowed to see Patrick for only fifteen minutes at a time after the close of regular visiting hours so that Patrick's family would not have to see Brett at all. Eventually, a sign was placed in Patrick's ICU space reading "immediate family and clergy only," purporting to exclude Brett altogether. Nevertheless, hospital staff defied the family's instructions and allowed Brett to continue to visit with Patrick early in the morning and in the evenings, outside of regular visiting hours.

On April 27, 2005, Patrick was moved from the Atlanta hospital to Manor-Care at Summer Trace (Summer Trace), a nursing facility in Carmel. In May and June 2005, Brett visited Patrick daily at Summer Trace, with his visits usually taking place after regular visiting hours so that Patrick's relatives would not see him. Brett was well-received by the Summer Trace staff, who observed that his visits had a positive impact on Patrick's recovery.

On June 20, 2005, Brett filed a guardianship petition, requesting that he be appointed guardian of Patrick's person and property. The Atkinses filed an answer to the petition, a motion to intervene, and a cross-petition requesting that they be appointed co-guardians of Patrick's person and property. Brett eventually voluntarily withdrew his request to be appointed guardian of Patrick's property, seeking only to be named as guardian of Patrick's person.

In mid-August 2005, Patrick was admitted to Zionsville Meadows, another nursing facility, for physical rehabilitation and speech therapy. Brett continued to visit Patrick after regular visiting hours at Zionsville Meadows. Notwithstanding the conclusions of the court-appointed guardian ad litem (GAL) and a neuropsychologist that it would be beneficial to Patrick and his recovery process for Brett to continue to have contact with Patrick, in early November 2005, the Atkinses moved Patrick into their home and have refused to allow Brett to visit with Patrick since that time. The Atkinses have refused phone calls from Brett and requests from Brett and his family members to visit Patrick.[2]

At the time of trial, Patrick was able to walk, dress, bathe, and feed himself with some supervision or prompting, to read printed matter aloud with good accuracy but only 25% comprehension, to engage in simple conversations, to communicate his basic wants and needs, and to answer questions with some prompting. He still required close and constant supervision and had significant problems with short-term memory, attention span, problem-solving, multi-step commands, reacting in urgent situations, and decision-making. The Atkinses took turns supervising or caring for Patrick in their Carmel home and were assisted by a certified home health aide who worked with Patrick daily from 8:30 a.m. until 5:00 p.m.

A trial was held beginning on November 23, 2005. On that same day, Brett filed a motion seeking the payment of a portion of his attorney fees and costs from the guardianship estate.

On January 11, 2006, Brett filed a petition for an order requiring the Atkinses to allow him to visit and have contact with Patrick. At trial, the Atkinses acknowledged that it was "probably true" that if the trial court did not order them to allow visitation between Patrick and Brett, they would not allow any contact between the life partners.

On May 10, 2006, the trial court entered two orders, making very limited findings of fact and disposing of the case by:

- Appointing the Atkinses as co-guardians of Patrick's person and estate;
- Denying Brett's visitation petition and ordering that "it is and shall be the ultimate and sole responsibility of [the Atkinses] to determine and control visitation with and access of visitors to Patrick Atkins in his best interest";
- Denying Brett's attorney fee petition;
- Determining that the home owned by Patrick and Brett should be split equally between Brett and the guardianship estate after reimbursing the estate for mortgage payments, taxes, insurance, utilities, and maintenance expenses incurred after March 10, 2005, and permitting the Atkinses to maintain the real estate, to sever and sell it, or to bring an action for partition;

---

[2]   Brett's relatives accepted Brett and Patrick's relationship and consider Patrick to be a member of their family. Therefore, they have also suffered a loss stemming from Patrick's incapacitation and the Atkinses' refusal to allow Brett or any members of his family from talking with or visiting Patrick.

• Ordering that $16,469.73—approximately one-third of the balance in Patrick's checking account—be disbursed to Brett as the portion attributable to his earnings and contributions, with the rest to be set off to the guardianship estate;

• Ordering that the funds in the Charles Schwab account be set off to the guardianship estate;

• Ordering that the household goods and other tangible property be split equally between Brett and the guardianship estate; and

• Ordering Patrick's interest as a shareholder in the family business to be set off to the family estate.

Brett now appeals.

DISCUSSION AND DECISION

As we consider Brett's challenges to the trial court's judgment, we observe that the trial court is vested with discretion in making determinations as to the guardianship of an incapacitated person. See Ind. Code § 29–3–2–4. This discretion extends to both its findings and its order. Id. Thus, we apply the abuse of discretion standard to review the trial court's findings and order. *In re Guardianship of V.S.D.*, 660 N.E.2d 1064, 1066 (Ind.Ct.App.1996). An abuse of discretion occurs when the trial court's decision is clearly against the logic and effect of the facts and circumstances presented. *J.M. v. N.M.*, 844 N.E.2d 590, 602 (Ind.Ct.App.2006), *trans. denied.*

I. Guardianship

Brett first argues that the trial court erroneously appointed the Atkinses as Patrick's guardian. A guardianship action is initiated by filing a petition seeking appointment to serve as guardian of an incapacitated person. *See* Ind.Code § 29–3–5–1. The guardianship statutes provide that the following

> are entitled to consideration for appointment as a guardian. . .in the order listed:
>
> (1) a person designated in a durable power of attorney;
> (2) the spouse of an incapacitated person;
> (3) an adult child of an incapacitated person;
> (4) a parent of an incapacitated person, or a person nominated by will of a deceased parent of an incapacitated person. . .;
> (5) any person related to an incapacitated person by blood or marriage with whom the incapacitated person has resided for more than six (6) months before the filing of the petition;
> (6) a person nominated by the incapacitated person who is caring for or paying for the care of the incapacitated person.

I.C. § 29–3–5–5(a). With respect to persons having equal priority, however, "the court shall select the person it considers best qualified to serve as guardian." *Id.* at

§ –5(b). Additionally, the trial court is authorized to "pass over a person having priority and appoint a person having a lower priority or no priority" if the trial court believes that action to be in the incapacitated person's best interest. The trial court's paramount consideration in making its determination of the person to be appointed guardian is "the best interest of the incapacitated person."

Patrick did not designate Brett for guardianship consideration in a durable power of attorney. Therefore, only if the trial court concluded that it was in Patrick's best interest that Brett be appointed his guardian would his appointment have been proper. Brett makes a sincere and compelling argument that, based on his long-term relationship with Patrick and his heartfelt desire to take care of his life partner, "Patrick's best interest will be served by appointing Brett as guardian over Patrick's person." Under these circumstances, however, our standard of review does not permit us to conduct a de novo analysis of what is in Patrick's best interest. Instead, we must assess whether the trial court abused its discretion when it found that it was in Patrick's best interest that the Atkinses be appointed co-guardians of his person and estate.

Think About It

Consider how this statute would have applied if Patrick and Brett had been married to each other. How else could Brett have been eligible to become Patrick's guardian?

The evidence presented established that the Atkinses' home was appropriate for Patrick's care. The Atkinses were actively involved in Patrick's care from the time of his hospitalization in Atlanta until his release to their care, and they have adequately cared for Patrick in their home since November 2005. Other family members are willing and able to assist with Patrick's care as might be necessary in the future. The Atkinses were committed to providing Patrick with the best possible care by applying their own personal efforts, employing outside assistance, and pursing potentially helpful therapies.

We conclude that there is sufficient evidence in the record supporting a conclusion that the Atkinses and Brett are equally well-equipped to care for Patrick's physical needs. Given the Atkinses' lack of support of their son's personal life through the years and given his mother's astonishing statement that she would rather that he *never recover* than see him return to his relationship with Brett, we are extraordinarily skeptical that the Atkinses are able to take care of Patrick's emotional needs. But we cannot conclude that the record shows that the trial court abused its discretion in denying Brett's guardianship petition. Under these circumstances, therefore, the trial court had two passable options from which to choose, neither of which was presumptively incorrect. Based upon the evidence presented, the trial court did not abuse its discretion when it found that it was in Patrick's best interest to appoint the Atkinses as co-guardians of his person.

II. Visitation

Brett next argues that the trial court erroneously denied his request for visitation and telephonic contact with Patrick. Turning to the record herein, we note that after observing interactions between Brett and Patrick and between Patrick and his family, the GAL concluded, among other things, as follows:

> . . .It also seems evident that Patrick loves Brett very much and it is evident that Brett loves Patrick.
> The challenge in this case seems to be how to provide for all parties to coexist in the best interest of Patrick. It appears that the involvement of *all parties* is paramount to Patrick's continued improvement. . . .

> * * *

> . . .[T]his Guardian Ad Litem strongly believes that an order should be implemented ensuring that *all parties* have regular access to Patrick regardless of who is appointed guardian. All parties to this litigation appear to be truly committed to Patrick's best interest and have no ulterior motives that this Guardian Ad Litem can determine.

Appellant's App. p. 58–60 (emphases added). The GAL later testified that "cutting back on one of those sources of stimulation or one of those sources of familiarity would just seem to me not to be in Patrick's best interest."

An impartial neuropsychologist who evaluated Patrick testified that people in his profession treating someone with memory problems, such as Patrick, strive to have as many "familiar cues" as possible for the patient "to help try to trigger access to long-term memory as well as to facilitate or try and promote his learning or recognition of new information." The neuropsychologist went on to testify as follows:

> A. [A]ssuming that there was a long relationship [between Brett and Patrick] and assuming that. . .that relationship was a significant relationship emotionally and in time it would ordinarily be our objective to reintegrate the patient into that environment so that they can participate in activities and situations with which they're familiar.
> Q. Based on your examination and evaluation of Patrick do you have a professional opinion as a neuropsychologist within a reasonable certainty about whether it is appropriate in terms of Patrick's long-term care and rehabilitation and recovery for Patrick's parents to have him continue to live in their home and to prohibit visits from or with Brett?
> A. Well, my experience in interacting with the patient and his family were that it seemed that [the Atkinses] were indeed generally interested in his care and were very invested in it. I think, however, that if this relationship [between Brett and Patrick] has persisted as long as you describe that *including Brett in that situation would be at least from a clinical standpoint something that we would recommend.*

* * *

Q. Based on what you know and your, of Patrick's background, his family situation, his history, and also on your examination and evaluations of Patrick, do you believe as his neuropsychologist within a reasonable certainty that it would be detrimental to Patrick's health or recovery if he were to see Brett or spend time with Brett outside Patrick's parents' home?

A. I have no reason to believe that it would be detrimental. *I suspect it would be helpful.*

Id. at 236–39 (emphases added).

Although the Atkinses argue that there was evidence that "visitation with Brett poses a risk of diminishing Patrick's chance for normalcy of life and possibly causing irreparable psychological harm," they provide no citation in support of this assertion and, indeed, the overwhelming evidence in the record supports a contrary conclusion. The only evidentiary support to which the Atkinses direct our attention in support of their position that Brett should be barred from visiting Patrick is testimony from their expert witness, psychologist Dr. Jonathon Mangold. Dr. Mangold met with Patrick only once for one hour, performed no psychological testing on Patrick, never spoke with Brett, and never observed Patrick and Brett together. On January 10, 2006, Dr. Mangold testified that he did not have enough factual background to form an opinion as to whether visitation with Brett would be harmful to Patrick. Three weeks later, at trial, Dr. Mangold suddenly testified that he *could* give an opinion regarding visitation, opining that visitation with Brett may not be positive for Patrick from a psychological standpoint. He reached this new conclusion based solely upon second-hand information that he obtained in interviews with Patrick's family members.

Thus, the *sole* support of the trial court's conclusion that Brett should be barred from visiting Patrick consists of the changed opinion of the Atkinses' expert witness who based his opinion *not* on testing of Patrick, an interview of Brett, or observations of the two men interacting, but on secondhand information gleaned from Patrick's family members. Indeed, the overwhelming wealth of evidence in the record, as well as common sense, establishes that it is in Patrick's best interest that he continue to have contact with Brett, his life partner of over twenty-five years. We cannot conclude, therefore, that the evidence in the record supports the trial court's order denying Brett's request for visitation.

The trial court was required to enter orders to "encourage development of the incapacitated person's self-improvement, self-reliance, and independence" and to "contribute to the incapacitated person's living as normal a life as that person's condition and circumstances permit without psychological or physical harm to the incapacitated person." I.C. § 29–3–5–3(b). The trial court was also required to order appropriate relief if it found that the Atkinses were not acting in Patrick's best interest. Ind. Code § 16–36–1–8(d). Given that the evidence overwhelmingly establishes that it is in Patrick's best interest to spend time with Brett and that the Atkinses have made it crystal clear that, absent a court order requiring to do so, they will not permit Brett to see their son, it was incumbent upon the trial court to order visitation as requested by Brett. Consequently, we reverse the judgment of the trial court on this basis and direct it to amend its order to grant Brett visitation and contact with Patrick as Brett requested.

* * *

IV. Charles Schwab Account

Brett next argues that the trial court erred when it set off the entire $85,000 Charles Schwab account in Patrick's name to the guardianship estate. The trial court determined that Brett was entitled to approximately one-third of the balance in the checking account that was solely in Patrick's name, having found the one-third "portion. . .attributable to Brett's earnings and contributions" to the checking account. Brett emphasizes that the evidence indicated that the Charles Schwab account was funded by checks written from Patrick's checking account. Therefore, Brett insists that one-third of the Charles Schwab account should also be found to be attributable to his earnings and contributions.

According to the evidence presented, at the time of his aneurysm, Patrick's annual salary was approximately $130,000. Brett's 2004 tax return showed that Brett earned about $31,800 annually. Patrick's earnings, therefore, were more than four times greater than Brett's. Brett testified that he had deposited most of his earnings into the checking account. But Brett also testified that all of Patrick's earnings had been deposited into that account as well. Thus, by awarding Brett one-third of the checking account, the trial court gave Brett a greater portion of the account than would be attributable to him had he deposited all of his earnings into it. We also observe that the checking account and Charles Schwab account were titled solely in Patrick's name.[4] Under these circumstances, we cannot conclude that the trial court abused its discretion by ordering that Patrick's Charles Schwab account be set aside to the guardianship estate.

* * *

---

[4]   The Atkinses urge us to consider the fact that Brett received half of the equity in the parties' jointly-owned home as we analyze the proper recipient of the Charles Schwab account. But Brett and Patrick do, in fact, own the home as joint tenants. Consequently, Brett is entitled to half of that equity regardless of his contribution to mortgage payments and it would have been erroneous for the trial court to have awarded less than half of the home's value to Brett. *See Cunningham v. Hastings, 556 N.E.2d 12, 13–14 (Ind.Ct.App.1990)* (holding that "[r]egardless of who provided the money to purchase the land, the creation of a joint tenancy relationship entitles each party to an equal share of the proceeds of the sale upon partition" and an equal right to share in the enjoyment of the real estate while both joint tenants are alive).

VI. CONCLUSION

We are confronted here with the heartbreaking fracture of a family. Brett and Patrick have spent twenty-five years together as life partners—longer than Patrick lived at home with his parents—and their future life together has been destroyed by Patrick's tragic medical condition and by the Atkinses' unwillingness to accept their son's lifestyle.

Although we are compelled to affirm the trial court's order that the Atkinses be appointed Patrick's co-guardians under our standard of review, we reverse the trial court with respect to Brett's request for visitation, inasmuch as all credible evidence in the record establishes that it is in Patrick's best interest to continue to have contact with his life partner. We also find that the trial court should have required Patrick's presence at the hearing but that Patrick's GAL waived that right by failing to enforce it. Additionally, we conclude that the trial court properly set off the entirety of the Charles Schwab account to the guardianship estate. Finally, we find that the trial court erroneously refused Brett's request that the guardianship estate pay a portion of his attorney fees and costs and remand for a calculation of the amount to be paid therefrom.

The judgment of the trial court is affirmed in part, reversed in part, and remanded with instructions to grant Brett visitation and contact with Patrick and to calculate the amount of Brett's attorney fees and costs to be paid by the guardianship estate.

> **FYI**
>
> Under federal regulations in effect since 2011, a hospital patient has the right to receive the visitors whom he or she designates, "including, but not limited to, a spouse, domestic partner (including a same-sex domestic partner), another family member, or a friend." 42 C.F.R. § 482.13(h) (2018).

Points for Discussion

a. Guardianship and Powers of Attorney

Atkins illustrates several important distinctions between marital and non-marital partner relationships, and suggests the importance of financial and other planning devices for committed unmarried couples, including durable powers of attorney. Another case raising similar issues is In re Guardianship of Kowalski, 478 N.W.2d 790 (Minn. Ct. App. 1991).

> **Make the Connection**
>
> The role of guardians for children is considered later in this chapter and in Chapters 5 and 7.

A guardian is a person appointed to protect various interests of another person, called the ward, who may be a child or a person under a disability. The guardian may be appointed as guardian of the person or the property of the ward or both. Under the Indiana statute applied in *Atkins*, the guardian is responsible for the incapacitated person's care and custody and preservation of the incapacitated person's property. See Ind. Code § 29–3–8–1(b) (2018).

In *Atkins*, the court also appointed a guardian ad litem (GAL) to represent Patrick's interests in the legal proceeding. How did the GAL contribute to the resolution of the case?

b. Property Rights of Unmarried Couples

What was the basis for the court's orders in *Atkins* regarding the division of the home Patrick and Brett owned and their other assets? Chapter 6 covers the use of a partition action to divide property of an unmarried couple at the end of their cohabitation relationship. What would be the result in a case like *Atkins* if Patrick had died as a result of his aneurysm? See, e.g., Olver v. Fowler, 168 P.3d 348 (Wash. 2007) (distributing jointly acquired property after the death of one partner) and Northrup v. Brigham, 826 N.E.2d 239 (Mass. Ct. App. 2005).

Medical Decisions for Adult Family Members

Every state has laws that allow individuals to execute an advance directive regarding medical treatment or appoint a health care surrogate or proxy decision maker who may or may not be a family member. If a patient is not able to make a decision, and has not signed an advance directive or appointed a proxy, many states permit courts to make a "substituted judgment" decision for the patient regarding whether or not to continue life-prolonging procedures. The widely discussed case of Karen Ann Quinlan in the 1970s set standards that were influential in other states; see Matter of Quinlan, 355 A.2d 647 (N.J. 1976).

Most states have laws that define a hierarchy of individuals to make health care decisions in such situations. See, e.g., Fla. Stat. Ann. § 765.401(1)(b) (2018). After a variety of different relatives, the list includes "a close friend of the patient." Another highly public case began with a disagreement in Florida between the husband and the parents of Terry Schiavo about withdrawing hydration and nutrition after she had been in a persistent vegetative state for years. The case became extraordinarily political, highlighting the ambiguities of the substituted judgment approach. See Bush v. Schiavo, 885 So.2d 321 (Fla. 2004); Schiavo ex rel Schindler v. Schiavo, 403 F.3d 1289 (11th Cir.), cert. den. 125 S.Ct. 1692 (2005); see generally John A. Robertson, Schiavo *and its (In)significance*, 35 Stetson L. Rev. 101 (2005).

Standards of evidence required in a substituted judgment proceeding are higher in some states. In Cruzan v. Director, Missouri Department of Health, 497 U.S. 261 (1990), Nancy Cruzan's parents sought to end hydration and nutrition procedures, offering evidence that Nancy had made statements at about age 25 that if she were sick or injured, she would not wish to continue her life unless she could function "halfway normally." The Missouri courts concluded that Cruzan's parents' consent was not effective under state law because it was not based either on compliance with the state's living will statute, or on clear and convincing evidence of Nancy's intentions. The U.S. Supreme Court held that the Due Process Clause of the Fourteenth Amendment includes a liberty interest in refusing medical treatment, but concluded that Missouri's insistence that an incompetent person's wishes must be proved by clear and convincing evidence served legitimate state interests.

Friendship and the Law

Should friendship be a basis for any kind of legal consequences? A number of family law scholars have pointed out that close relationships that may not be based on sexual intimacy provide significant caregiving, but do not receive the kinds of social, legal and financial support accorded to relationships based on marriage or parent-child ties. See, e.g., David L. Chambers, *For the Best of Friends and for Lovers of All Sorts, A Status Other Than Marriage,* 76 Notre Dame L. Rev. 1347 (2001). Some states have partnership registration laws that allow any two people who are not already married or in a registered partnership to register for a set of reciprocal legal rights. See, e.g., D.C. Code §§ 32–701 to 32–710 (2018), which creates a family relationship and grants registered partners rights to family leave, to hospital visitation, and to purchase health insurance benefits. See also Colo. Rev. Stat. §§ 15–22–101 to 15–22–112 (2018) (Designated Beneficiary Agreement Act); Haw. Rev. Stat. §§ 572C–1 to 572C–7 (2018) (Reciprocal Beneficiaries Act).

Apart from a formal registration scheme, should law recognize and encourage friendship? See Ethan J. Leib, *Friendship and the Law,* 54 UCLA L. Rev. 631 (2007), which considers circumstances in which courts have imposed duties based on friendship, such as a duty to rescue in tort, duties of disclosure and fair dealing in business dealings, or duties of confidentiality. See also Laura A. Rosenbury, *Friends with Benefits?* 106 Mich. L. Rev. 189 (2007), which suggests that friendship should not be treated as a functional equivalent to marriage, but as a fluid and nonexclusive alternative that might exist along with marriage, arguing that this would help promote gender equality.

Global View: Beyond Conjugality

In 2001, the Law Commission of Canada produced a report called *Beyond Conjugality: Recognizing and Supporting Close Personal Adult Relationships*, which argued for looking beyond "the nuclear family centered on the conjugal couple" and extending legal recognition and support to "the full range of close personal relationship among adults." The report pointed to "adult siblings sharing a home, widows and widowers forming blended families, and multigenerational families," as well as households with adult children who have returned home to live with their parents, and persons with disabilities and their caregivers. The report recommended a comprehensive reconsideration of existing and proposed laws that depend on personal relationships to achieve values including personal security, privacy, autonomy, religious freedom, equality among different types of relationships, and equality within relationships. See Law Commission of Canada, Beyond Conjugality: Recognizing and Supporting Close Personal Adult Relationships (2001.)

B. Family Violence

Domestic violence is an intractable social problem in the United States. According to the U.S. Department of Justice, intimate partner violence has declined since 1993, but despite this decline there were about 907,000 intimate partner victimizations in 2010. See <u>U.S. Department of Justice, Bureau of Justice Statistics, Intimate Partner Violence, 1993–2010 (November 2012)</u>. Women were victims in almost 80% percent of these incidents, but men have also benefitted from the campaign to address family violence. From 1993 to 2004, the number of women murdered by intimates declined by 26 percent, while the number of men murdered by intimates declined by 45 percent. See U.S. Department of Justice, Bureau of Justice Statistics, <u>Intimate Partner Violence in the U.S.</u> (December 2006). In this analysis, "intimate partner" is defined to include a current or former spouse, boyfriend, girlfriend or same-sex partner. Violence and other forms of abuse may also occur between family members who are not intimate partners. Abuse of elderly and other dependent adult family members is considered later in this chapter. Child abuse, addressed in Chapter 5, often occurs in combination with adult abuse.

As noted earlier in this chapter, some authorities suggest that the common law gave a husband the right to "correct" or "chastise" his wife, so that only extremely serious assaults would be punished by the criminal law. See, e.g., Bradley v. State, 1 Miss. (Walker) 156 (1824); State v. Rhodes, 61 N.C. 453 (1868); but cf. State v. Oliver, 70 N.C. 60 (1874). Because the common

Go Online

Information on intimate partner violence, including data from the 2015 National Intimate Partner and Sexual Violence Survey, is available from the U.S. Centers for Disease Control and Prevention (CDC).

law prevented spouses from suing each other, a wife could not recover in tort for injuries suffered at the hands of her husband. See Thompson v. Thompson, 218 U.S. 611 (1910). Under the common law, a husband could not be convicted for rape if he forced his wife to have sexual relations, and this rule was later codified in criminal statutes in many states. In 1984, People v. Liberta, 474 N.E.2d 567 (N.Y. 1984) noted that 40 states still retained some form of marital exemption for rape.

Beginning in the 1970s, women's advocates began to press states to enact legislation to prevent, control and respond to domestic violence. Initially, states provided for civil remedies for victims including ex parte temporary injunctions against an abusive partner, permanent injunctions and other protective orders, and enforcement of these orders by contempt sanctions. See, e.g., Cal. Family Code §§ 6200 to 6409 (2018); Fla. Stat. Ann. §§ 39.901 to 39.908 (2018) and 741.30 (2018); 750 Ill. Comp. Stat. 60/101 to 60/305 (2018); N.J. Stat. Ann. §§ 30:14–1 to 30:14–14 (2018); N.Y. Fam. Ct. Act §§ 812 to 847 (2018); Wash. Rev. Code Ann. §§ 10.99.010 to 10.99.900 and 26.50.010 to 26.50.903 (2018).

Protection order statutes include different definitions of who is eligible for protection. Some laws apply to any "family or household member," including a spouse, parent, child, sibling or cohabitant. Compare State v. Williams, 683 N.E.2d 1126 (Ohio 1997) (upholding domestic abuse conviction based on cohabitation relationship) with Petrowsky v. Krause, 588 N.W.2d 318 (Wis. Ct.App.1998) (concluding that unmarried couple not residing together on a continuous basis were not "household members" for purposes of the state's domestic abuse statute). See also Patole v. Marksberry, 329 P.3d 50 (Utah Ct. App. 2014), which held that a son-in-law was "related by marriage" to his father-in-law and entitled to seek a protective order under the state's Cohabitant Abuse Act. Laws that include cohabitation relationships within the definition of domestic violence are applicable to same-sex as well as opposite-sex couples; see, e.g., Peterman v.

Meeker, 855 So.2d 690 (Fla. Ct. App. 2003); Ireland v. Davis, 957 S.W.2d 310 (Ky. Ct. App.1997). See David Frazee et al., eds., Violence Against Women: Law and Litigation §§ 16:4–16:11 (1997). In some states, domestic abuse laws may apply to dating relationships. See Mass. Gen. Laws ch. 209A § 3 (2018), applied in C.O. v. M.M., 815 N.E.2d 582 (Mass. 2004); and N.J. Stat. § 2C:25–19 (2018), discussed in Andrews v. Rutherford, 832 A.2d 379 (N.J. Super. Ct. 2003).

One important early result of the movement against domestic violence was that communities began to establish shelters for victims, and provide new opportunities for counseling and police training. Subsequent efforts focused on the criminal justice system, with new mandatory arrest laws and "no-drop" prosecution policies, which have since become controversial. See Leigh Goodmark, *Autonomy Feminism: An Anti-Essentialist Critique of Mandatory Interventions in Domestic Violence Cases*, 37 Fla. St. U. L. Rev. 1 (2009). In some states, new domestic abuse laws provided enhanced penalties for general crimes such as assault committed against family or household members. States have also gradually modified or eliminated the marital rape exemption, but most states retain some form of the traditional rule. See Jill Elaine Hasday, *Contest and Consent: A Legal History of Marital Rape*, 88 Cal. L. Rev. 1373, 1484–90 (2000).

Violence Against Women Act (VAWA)

At the national level, Congress enacted the Violence Against Women Act (VAWA) in 1994. VAWA includes a variety of civil and criminal provisions intended to address problems of gender-based violence, including funding for prevention, training, and research programs and provisions establishing new civil and criminal claims under federal law. The new law established the Office on Violence Against Women in the Department of Justice, which administers grant programs and works to implement the mandates of the legislation.

VAWA established two new federal domestic violence crimes. The first made it a crime to travel across state lines with the intention to commit domestic violence and then to commit such a crime. 18 U.S.C. § 2261 (2018). See, e.g., United States v. Al-Zubaidy, 283 F.3d 804 (6th Cir. 2002). The second made it a crime to cross state lines with the intention to violate a protective order and then to do so. 18 U.S.C. § 2262 (2018). See, e.g., United States v. Von Foelkel, 136 F.3d 339 (2d Cir.1998). VAWA also enacted the Protective Order Gun Ban, 18 U.S.C. § 922(g)(8) (2018), criminalizing the possession of a firearm by anyone subject to a domestic violence restraining order, and a ban on possession of firearms by anyone who has been convicted of a misdemeanor crime of domestic violence, 18 U.S.C. § 922(g)(9) (2018). These provisions have been repeatedly sustained by the federal courts against constitutional challenges. See also Voisine v. United

States, 579 U.S. ___, 136 S.Ct. 2272 (2016) and <u>United States v. Castleman, 572 U.S. ___, 134 S.Ct. 1405 (2014)</u> (construing § 922(g)(9)).

In addition, VAWA mandated that all states give full faith and credit to protective orders issued in other states. <u>18 U.S.C. § 2265 (2018)</u>. See generally Catherine F. Klein, <u>*Full Faith and Credit: Interstate Enforcement of Protection Orders Under the Violence Against Women Act of 1994,* 29</u> Fam. L.Q. 253 (1995). With VAWA, Congress sought to improve the circumstances of domestic violence victims within immigrant communities, enacting amendments to the Immigration and Nationality Act to permit victims of domestic violence to leave their partners and sponsor their own applications for permanent residence, <u>8 U.S.C. § 1154(a)(1) (2018)</u>, and to permit cancellation of removal (formerly known as suspension of deportation) for a battered spouse or child in cases of extreme hardship, <u>8 U.S.C. § 1229(b)(2) (2018)</u>. See also <u>Hernandez v. Ashcroft, 345 F.3d 824 (9th Cir.2003)</u> (construing "extreme cruelty" requirement in federal statute that allows suspension of deportation for some domestic violence victims).

The most controversial aspect of VAWA was its establishment of a federal civil rights remedy, initially codified in <u>42 U.S.C. § 13981(c)</u>, that would permit the victim of a "crime of violence motivated by gender" to recover compensatory and punitive damages and injunctive relief. See generally Reva B. Siegel, <u>*"The Rule of Love": Wife Beating as Prerogative and Privacy,* 105</u> Yale L.J. 2117 (1996). Despite extensive congressional findings on the economic effects of gender-motivated violence, the Supreme Court held in <u>United States v. Morrison, 529 U.S. 598 (2000)</u>, that the Commerce Power does not allow Congress "to regulate non-economic, violent criminal conduct based solely on that conduct's aggregate effect on interstate commerce." In addition, the Court rejected the argument that the legislation could be upheld as an exercise of Congress's remedial power under § 5 of the Fourteenth Amendment, holding that this power does not permit Congress to enact laws directed at "purely private conduct" and rejecting the argument that the legislation was enacted to remedy gender-based disparate treatment by state authorities. Justices Souter, Stevens, Ginsburg and Breyer dissented.

Felton v. Felton

<u>679 N.E.2d 672 (Ohio 1997)</u>

ALICE ROBIE RESNICK, JUSTICE.

This case presents two issues. The first is whether a court may issue a domestic protection order pursuant to <u>R.C. 3113.31</u> when, as part of the dissolution decree, the parties have agreed to a provision prohibiting harassment of each other. The second issue is what is the correct burden of proof that a court must use when issuing a protection order pursuant to R.C. 3113.31.

I

The court of appeals held that because the parties' dissolution decree contained a no-harassment provision, a domestic violence protection order would be unnecessary and superfluous. We disagree.

Initially we note that R.C. 3113.31(G) states, "The remedies and procedures provided in this section are *in addition to, and not in lieu of,* any other available civil or criminal remedies." (Emphasis added.) Thus, nothing in the statutes precludes the court from issuing a protection order even though the no-harassment provision of the dissolution decree continues to govern the parties' actions towards each other.

The court of appeals further held that the "provision in the final judgment entry [of the dissolution decree] is of much more force and effect than one which [the court] might issue in the domestic violence action for only a period of one year." This is patently incorrect.

The General Assembly enacted the domestic violence statutes specifically to criminalize those activities commonly known as domestic violence and to authorize a court to issue protection orders designed to ensure the safety and protection of a complainant in a domestic violence case. Ohio Legislative Service Commission, Summary of 1978 Enactments, June–December (1979), at 9–14; Legislative Service Commission Analysis of Sub. H.B. No. 835 as reported by Senate Judiciary Committee (1978), at 2 and 7 (Comment A); Legislative Service Commission Analysis of Am. Sub. H.B. No. 835 as enacted (1978), at 1 and 2.[1] Accordingly, R.C. 3113.31 authorizes a court in an ex parte hearing to issue a temporary protection order when the court finds there to be an "[i]mmediate and present danger of domestic violence to the family or household member." R.C. 3113.31(D). Subsequent to this, the court proceeds as in a normal civil action and grants a full hearing. R.C. 3113.31(D). After such hearing, the court may issue a protection order that may direct the respondent to refrain from abusing the family or household members, grant possession of the household to the petitioner to the exclusion of the respondent, temporarily allocate parental rights and responsibilities and visitation rights, require the respondent to maintain support, require all

---

[1]   A pending bill proposing amendments to the various statutory provisions that are concerned with domestic violence, 1997 Sub.S.B. No. 1, would continue to emphasize the prevention of domestic violence. In its analysis of S.B. No. 1, the Legislative Service Commission notes that a "court may grant *any* civil protection order or approve any consent agreement * * * to bring about a cessation of domestic violence against the family or household members." Bill Analysis, Sub.S.B. No. 1 (as passed by the Senate, 1997).

parties to seek counseling, require the respondent to refrain from entering the residence, school, business, or place of employment of the petitioner, and grant any other relief that the court considers equitable and fair. R.C. 3113.31(E)(1).

The no-harassment provision, by contrast, contains only a general prohibition. As read by the trial court judge, the dissolution agreement states: " 'Each party shall hereafter continue to live separate and apart from the other and each shall go his or her own way without direction, control, or molestation from the other the same as though unmarried[.]' * * * 'Further, each shall not annoy, harass, or interfere with the other in any manner whatsoever.' "

The statute gives the trial court extensive authority to tailor the domestic violence protection order to the exact situation before it at the time, while the no-harassment provision in the dissolution decree is general in nature and application and does not take into account any changes in custody, housing, transportation, and any other household needs that may have arisen since the dissolution.

Additionally, with a protection order come several features not available with a dissolution or divorce decree. First, the results of violating the R.C. 3113.31 protection order are much more immediate and consequential than the results of violating a provision of a divorce or dissolution decree. A person who violates a protection order is subject to criminal prosecution for a violation of R.C. 2919.27, and punishment for contempt of court. R.C. 3113.31(L)(1). Punishment for contempt of court does not preclude subsequent criminal prosecution under R.C. 2919.27. R.C. 3113.31(L)(2). Anyone who recklessly violates any terms of a protection order issued pursuant to R.C. 2919.26 or 3113.31 is guilty of violating a protection order, which is a misdemeanor of the first degree. R.C. 2919.27(B)(1)(a).[2] The penalty for a misdemeanor of the first degree is imprisonment for not more than six months and/or a fine of not more than one thousand dollars. R.C. 2929.21. If the violator has previously been convicted or pleaded guilty to two or more violations of R.C. 2919.27, 2903.211 (menacing by stalking), or 2911.211 (aggravated trespass), the violation is a felony of the fifth degree. R.C. 2919.27(B)(1)(b). The penalty for a felony of the fifth degree is imprisonment for six to twelve months or a community control sanction (which may be made up of a combination of residential [*e.g.*, jail and halfway house] and nonresidential [day reporting, house arrest, community service, *inter alia*] sanctions) and/or a fine of not more than $2,500. R.C. 2929.13 through 2929.18.

In contrast, a violation of a dissolution or divorce decree is subject to contempt of court for violating a court's final judgment entry. R.C. 2705.02(A). Anyone who is found guilty of contempt of court may be subject to a fine of not more

2   The General Assembly has amended R.C. 2919.27 since appellant filed her petition pursuant to R.C. 3113.31. However, the current version of the statute would apply to any *violation* that occurred now.

than $250 and/or imprisonment of not more than thirty days in jail (first offense), a fine of not more than $500 and/or imprisonment of not more than sixty days in jail (second offense), or a fine of not more than $1,000 and/or imprisonment of not more than ninety days in jail (third or greater offense). R.C. 2705.05(A). It is quite apparent that the penalties for violating a protection order are considerably more substantial and punitive and thus more deterring than those for violating a court's judgment entry.

Second, the statutes provide for the preferred arrest of a violator of a protection order. No such policy applies to violators of a court order or judgment entry. The preferred-arrest policy states that if a peace officer has reasonable grounds to believe that a violation of a protection order has been committed and reasonable cause to believe that a particular person is guilty of committing the offense, "it is the preferred course of action in this state that the officer arrest and detain that person * * * until a warrant can be obtained." R.C. 2935.03(B)(3)(b). If the officer does not make an arrest when it is the preferred course of action in this state, "the officer shall articulate in the written report of the incident * * * a clear statement of the officer's reasons for not arresting and detaining that person until a warrant can be obtained." R.C. 2935.03(B)(3)(c). A finding of contempt of court does not carry with it any of the foregoing rights and powers. Nor are those proceedings generally on a fast track.

Third, R.C. 3113.31(F)(1) requires that a copy of the protection order be issued to all law enforcement agencies that have jurisdiction to enforce the order or agreement, R.C. 3113.31(F)(1), and that all law enforcement agencies establish and maintain an index of the protection orders sent to them. R.C. 3113.31(F)(2). In addition, any law enforcement officer shall enforce a protection order issued by any court in this state regardless of whether the petitioner has registered the order in the county of the law enforcement officer's jurisdiction. R.C. 3113.31(F)(3). With this statewide enforcement, communication, indexing, and authority, enforcement of the protection order is much more apt to occur than a contempt order.

And, fourth, a protection order is easier for a petitioner to enforce than a "no-harassment" provision in a dissolution or divorce decree. As described above, R.C. 3113.31(B) provides for enforcement of a protection order by the police. Upon threat of a violation of a civil protection order, a petitioner need only call the police, who are available at all times of the day or night. By contrast, in order to enforce a provision in a dissolution or divorce decree, the petitioner must move the court to find the violator in contempt. The court is available only during normal business hours and often a motion for contempt is so complicated as to require the services of an attorney. Moreover, because of the congested dockets of most domestic relations courts, the process can take an extremely lengthy time to get a hearing scheduled. The police, by enforcing a protection order, are thus in a much better position than is the court, through a contempt action, to prevent further domestic violence.

Finally, the court of appeals appears to have been swayed by the temporary nature of a protection order. Pursuant to R.C. 3113.31(E)(3)(a), any protection order issued pursuant to that statute is valid for a maximum period of two years. The court of appeals stated that, because the dissolution decree has no termination date, it is more powerful. However, a protection order issued pursuant to R.C. 3113.31 is fully renewable in the same manner as the original order was issued. R.C. 3113.31(E)(3)(c). Thus, the overwhelming benefits to the victim of domestic violence that the protection order offers far outweigh any concerns about the temporary nature of the protection order, which can be renewed at the end of the effective period.

Last, we note that there are strong policy reasons for allowing a court to issue a protection order after a divorce or dissolution has become final. Violence against a former spouse does not stop with the separation:

"Women who are divorced or separated are at higher risk of assault than married women.[3] The risk of assault is greatest when a woman leaves or threatens to leave an abusive relationship.[4] Nonfatal violence often escalates once a battered woman attempts to end the relationship.[5] Furthermore, studies in Philadelphia and Chicago revealed that twenty-five percent of women murdered by their male partners were separated or divorced from their assailants.[6] Another twenty-nine percent of women were murdered during the separation or divorce process.[7] State statutes need to protect women and children during and after the break-up of relationships because of their continuing, and often heightened,

---

[3]   "Stark & Flitcraft [Violence Among Intimates: An Epidemiological View, in Handbook of Family Violence (Van Hassett et al. Ed.1987) 293, 301], at 307–08."

[4]   "*See* Ganley [Domestic Violence: The What, Why and Who, as Relevant to Civil Court Cases, in Domestic Violence in Civil Court Cases: A National Model for Judicial Education (Jacqueline A. Agtuca et al. Ed.1992)], at 24. Separated or divorced women are six times more likely to be victims of violent crime than widows and four and one half times more likely than married women. Harlow [U.S. Dept. of Justice, Female Victims of Violent Crime (1991)], at 5; *see also* Elis Desmond, *Post-Separation Woman Abuse: The Contribution of Lawyers as 'Barracudas,' 'Advocates,' and 'Counselors,'* 10 Int'l J.L. & Psych. 403, 408 (1987)."

[5]   "David Adams, *Identifying the Assaultive Husband in Court: You Be the Judge*, 13 Response to the Victimization Women & Children 13 (1990). Perpetrators of domestic violence view the abused party's attempts to leave the relationship as the ultimate act of resistance and consequently increase their violence in response to attempts by the victim to leave."

[6]   "Ganley, *supra* note [4], at 24."

[7]   "Noel A. Casanave & Margaret A. Zahn, Women, Murder, and Male Domination: Police Reports of Domestic Homicide in Chicago and Philadelphia, Paper Presented at the American Society of Criminology Annual Meeting (Oct.1986). This paper additionally found that husbands were commonly motivated to kill their wives because they felt abandoned or feared they were losing control over them. In one study of spousal homicide, over one-half of the male defendants were separated from their victims. Franklin E. Zimring et al., *Intimate Violence: A Study of Intersexual Homicide, 50 U. Chi. L.Rev. 910, 916 (1983)*."

vulnerability to violence." (Footnotes renumbered.) Klein and Orloff, <u>Providing Legal Protection for Battered Women: An Analysis of State Statutes and Case Law (1993), 21 Hofstra L.Rev. 801, 816</u>.

In Ohio, the domestic violence statutes grant police and courts great authority to enforce protection orders, and violations of those protection orders incur harsh penalties. Therefore, protection orders issued pursuant to R.C. 3113.31 are the more appropriate and efficacious method to prevent future domestic violence and thus accomplish the goals of the legislation. Accordingly, a court is not precluded by statute or public policy reasons from issuing a protection order pursuant to Ohio's civil domestic violence statute, R.C. 3113.31, where the parties' dissolution or divorce decree already prohibits the parties from harassing each other.

II

We will now address the issue of the burden of proof to be used when issuing a protection order. The trial court requested arguments from the parties as to which standard of proof to apply and then decided upon the preponderance of the evidence.

<u>R.C. 3113.31</u> is silent as to the appropriate burden of proof required to issue a protection order. The Ohio courts of appeals are divided over whether to apply the clear-and-convincing standard or the lesser standard of preponderance of the evidence. The courts applying the clear-and-convincing standard reason that a protective order issued pursuant to <u>R.C. 3113.31</u> is analogous to an injunction and, as an action for equitable relief, as opposed to monetary damages, the issuance of a protection order is subject to the clear-and-convincing standard. <u>O'Hara v. Dials (Feb. 2, 1996), Erie App. No. E–95–044, unreported, at 4–7, 1996 WL 38810</u>. See, also, <u>Moman v. Smith (Oct. 14, 1996), Clermont App. No. CA96–05–047, unreported, 1996 WL 586771</u>; <u>Tischler v. Vahcic (Nov. 16, 1995), Cuyahoga App. No. 68053, unreported, 1995 WL 680928</u>; <u>Coughlin v. Lancione (Feb. 25, 1992), Franklin App. No. 91AP–950, unreported, 1992 WL 40557</u> (requiring clear and unequivocal evidence).

Courts applying a lesser standard of proof appear to base that standard upon the statutory language. <u>Thomas v. Thomas (1988), 44 Ohio App.3d 6, 8, 540 N.E.2d 745, 746</u> ("The statutory criterion * * * is the existence or threatened existence of domestic violence."). See, also, <u>Deacon v. Landers (1990), 68 Ohio App.3d 26, 587 N.E.2d 395</u>; <u>Snyder v. Snyder (Aug. 15, 1995), Ross App. No. 94 CA 2068, unreported, at 10, 1995 WL 493998</u> (The court reviewed trial court record for "sufficient competent, credible evidence to support a finding that appellant committed domestic violence against appellee.").

R.C. 3113.31 directs only that the court "proceed as in a normal civil action." R.C. 3113.31(D). In *Walden v. State* (1989), 47 Ohio St.3d 47, 53, 547 N.E.2d 962, this court observed:

"The General Assembly, had it wanted to do so, knew how to specify a 'clear and convincing' standard. A review of the Revised Code reveals at least nineteen sections in which the General Assembly has specified a 'clear and convincing' standard by using the words 'clear and convincing.' See, *e.g.*, R.C. 709.07(D) (petition to enjoin annexation); 1533.92 (appeal from denial of fishing tournament permit); 1701.59 (breach of fiduciary duty by corporate directors); 2307.80 (punitive damages in products liability actions); 3111.03 (rebuttal of presumption of paternity); 4731.22 (summary suspension of license to practice medicine); 5122.15 (civil commitment of mentally ill person). Accordingly, it is clear that the General Assembly intended to apply the usual preponderance of the evidence standard to civil proceedings under R.C. 2305.02."

The same reasoning applies to R.C. 3113.31. Had the General Assembly intended that the clear-and-convincing standard apply, it certainly knew how to specify that standard. Thus, we hold that when granting a protection order, the trial court must find that petitioner has shown by a preponderance of the evidence that petitioner or petitioner's family or household members are in danger of domestic violence. R.C. 3113.31(D).

In the case *sub judice*, the trial court determined that after presenting her evidence, appellant had shown a prima facie case supporting a protection order. Subsequently, however, the court held in its final judgment that appellee's answer to appellant's petition for a protection order was evidence enough to controvert appellant's evidence, and the court dismissed the petition.[8]

* * *

Specifically, our review of the record shows sufficient, credible evidence to support a finding that appellant was in danger of domestic violence R.C. 3113.31(D). Domestic violence is defined in part as:

---

[8]   The court's final judgment entry states in full:

"This matter came on for a merits hearing this date upon the petitioner's complaint in civil domestic violence, filed September 8, 1994, pursuant to R.C. 3113.31. Present were both parties and their respective counsel. In his September 20, 1994 answer, the respondent had entered a general denial to the petitioner's substantive allegations.

"At the conclusion of the evidence and upon consideration, the court finds that petitioner has failed to prove her case by a preponderance of the evidence (see record).

"Accordingly, it is hereby ordered that this action is dismissed for lack of evidence, without prejudice.

"Court costs are taxed to the parties equally."

" * * * the occurrence of one or more of the following acts against a family or household member:

"(a) Attempting to cause or recklessly causing bodily injury;

"(b) Placing another person by the threat of force in fear of imminent serious physical harm * * *." <u>R.C. 3113.31(A)(1)</u>.

Appellant testified that appellee's assaults upon her increased during her marriage, and continued after the divorce, culminating in a violent episode occurring on July 26, 1994 in which appellee attempted to strangle her. Moreover, she stated that appellee would harass her on the phone. She also testified that she was afraid that if she did anything to anger appellee, he would actually try to kill her. Paul Long testified that approximately one to one and a half years prior to the hearing, at around the time of the Feltons' dissolution, appellant told him that appellee had hit her two or three times and that Long had seen a bruised mark on appellant's shoulder. Without controverting evidence, this testimony presents sufficient, credible evidence to prove by a preponderance of the evidence that appellee had engaged in acts of domestic violence. <u>R.C. 3113.31(A)(1)</u>. The trial judge in effect held that this evidence did not meet the preponderance-of-the-evidence standard. Rather, the trial judge would require corroborating eyewitness testimony or medical evidence to establish domestic violence by a preponderance of the evidence. It appears from the comments of the trial judge that a victim's testimony, standing alone, would never be sufficient to establish proof by a preponderance of the evidence. Domestic violence is seldom committed in the presence of eyewitnesses. Moreover, in many cases medical evidence is absent. Often the only evidence of domestic violence is the testimony of the victim. Generally, the victim will not photograph bruises or share these episodes of abuse with others. In the case sub judice, after thoroughly considering the record, we find that the evidence presented by the appellant was sufficient to meet the preponderance-of-the-evidence standard. The trial court thus erred by not granting appellant's petition for a protection order.[9]

---

[9]   In order to grant appellant's petition for a protection order, the trial court erroneously required appellant to present some evidence which would corroborate her testimony. Upon reaching the final decision to dismiss the petition, the court stated:

"[Respondent and his attorney] have the burden of proving nothing. [Petitioner] carries the burden of proving that these incidents took place by a preponderance of the evidence. We have no police reports. We have no physician or hospital reports. We have no eyewitnesses. We have no admission by the, other than her [sic]. We have no admission from the defendant and I thought surely you would have called the son to testify because he is the one that uh, according to your client's testimony, was the one who pulled the father off and stopped the strangulation, at least for the purpose of corroborating that the incident took place.
" * * *

"Well, how as a matter of law does this rise to a preponderance of the evidence? I'm not disputing that what your client said isn't true, but I'm saying from a purely legal standpoint when he has entered a denial by virtue of his answer and has to prove nothing how, how on earth can I find that by a preponderance of the evidence your client has established a case. She says it happened. He says it didn't. Does [that] not make the evidence equally balanced?"

However, R.C. 3113.31 does not set forth the type of evidence to be considered by the court, other than to state that the proceeding should be handled as any other civil action, nor does it require any corroboration of the petitioner's own testimony. R.C. 3113.31(D).

In conclusion, we note that because the domestic violence statutes give the courts decision-making authority, the courts have an obligation to carry out the legislative goals to protect the victims of domestic violence. In his article entitled "The Domestic Violence Civil Protection Order and the Role of the Court," Judge Michael J. Voris of the Clermont County Domestic Relations Court, cogently expressed this obligation:

"Advanced societies take intra-family violence seriously. Only in the last twelve years has this problem become a focus of attention and national concern. The Ohio Legislature has passed one of the most comprehensive set of statutes authorizing Civil Protection Orders to combat domestic violence. Because the language of the statutes is broad, the response of the Court has a profound impact in protecting victims of domestic violence. Judges have the power and authority to implement the legislation. It is critical that Judges and Referees be aware of the severity of the domestic violence problem and make efforts to remain informed about the recent domestic violence legislation. Continuing education as to the realities of all forms of domestic violence will help to remove the shroud of secrecy and break the cycle of violence. Judges and Referees can play a leadership role in enlightening and educating attorneys, parties and the community in general about the severity of the domestic violence issues and the civil legal remedies that exist for victims of domestic violence. The Attorney General's Task Force on Family Violence urges Judges not to underestimate their ability to influence the respondent's behavior. Judges can communicate a powerful message about the justice system's view of domestic violence within their own courtrooms.

"The Ohio Legislature has made a laudatory beginning in responding to the problems of domestic violence. The legislation that provides for Civil Protection Orders is responsive to the immediate needs of the victims and provides a necessary alternative and supplement to criminal legal remedies. However, the legislation cannot achieve its full potential without the careful and responsible utilization by Judges and Referees." (Footnotes omitted.) Voris, The Domestic Violence Civil Protection Order and the Role of the Court (1990), 24 Akron L.Rev. 423, 432. See, also, Recommendations to the Supreme Court of Ohio, Goal 4, Report of the Supreme Court of Ohio Domestic Violence Task Force (1996), at 18.

The consequences of domestic violence are serious and severe. Protection orders can be an effective tool when used in conjunction with provisions in divorce and dissolution decrees and other separation agreements. Ohio's courts must make themselves aware of the authority they have been granted by the legislation to implement all of these protection orders.

Accordingly, we reverse the judgment of the court of appeals and remand the cause to the trial court for an order granting appellant's petition for a protection order and for the trial court to fashion that protection order pursuant to its authority as granted in R.C. 3113.31.

Judgment reversed and cause remanded.

Points for Discussion

a. Separation Violence

As *Felton* notes, the risk of lethal violence is particularly serious at the time a battered partner leaves or attempts to leave an abusive relationship. Screening for domestic violence is an important skill for lawyers in many areas of practice, but it is especially critical in family law and criminal law. Where there is a history of violence, lawyers should also assist clients with making plans for their own safety. See American Bar Association Commission on Domestic Violence, The Impact of Domestic Violence on Your Legal Practice: A Lawyer's Handbook, (Deborah M. Goelman et al., eds 1996).

b. Interstate Protection Orders

In addition to provisions of VAWA mandating interstate recognition of protection orders, the Uniform Interstate Enforcement of Domestic-Violence Protection Orders Act, 9 U.L.A. (Part 1B) (Supp. 2018), establishes procedures for enforcing out-of-state protection orders. Implementing these laws has proved to be difficult, however. See Emily J. Sack, *Domestic Violence Across State Lines: The Full Faith and Credit Clause, Congressional Power, and Interstate Enforcement of Protection Orders,* 98 Nw. U. L. Rev. 827 (2004). See also the Uniform Recognition and Enforcement of Canadian Domestic-Violence Protection Orders Act, 9 U.L.A. (Part 1B) (Supp. 2018).

If there is not already an order in place, an individual who is attempting to escape family violence may seek a protection order after moving to a new state. In McNair v. McNair, 856 A.2d 5 (N.H. 2004), a New Hampshire court found that it had long arm jurisdiction over a woman's nonresident husband for purposes of entering domestic abuse protection orders. The husband had previously obtained a default divorce in Texas after his wife had left for New Hampshire. Based on a series of harassing and threatening telephone calls to the wife—as many as forty a day— the court concluded there were sufficient minimum contacts with the state to support issuance of protective orders. See also <u>Hemenway v. Hemenway, 992 A.2d 575 (N.H. 2010)</u> and <u>Shah v. Shah, 875 A.2d 931 (N.J. 2005)</u>, which held that courts could grant protection orders on an ex parte basis, but could not order any type of affirmative relief without personal jurisdiction over the restrained spouse. Case law from a number of states is reviewed in <u>Fox v. Fox, 106 A.3d 919 (Vt. 2014)</u>.

c. Protection Orders Permitting Ongoing Contact

What if a person with an abusive partner or family member does not want to end the relationship? For an argument that protection orders should be customized to express the victim's preferences for how much and what kind of contact should be allowed, see Sally F. Goldfarb, *Reconceiving Civil Protection Orders for Domestic Violence: Can Law Help End the Abuse Without Ending the Relationship?* 29 Cardozo L. Rev. 1487 (2008).

Battered Woman Syndrome Evidence

Domestic violence presents a complex problem in the criminal law when a woman kills her partner after significant spousal or partner abuse. Numerous cases have concluded that an abused woman who shot and killed her husband while he slept should not be acquitted by reason of self-defense because the evidence did not show that she reasonably believed that she was confronted by a threat of imminent death or great bodily harm. See, e.g., <u>State v. Stewart, 763 P.2d 572 (Kan. 1988)</u>, <u>State v. Norman, 378 S.E.2d 8 (N.C. 1989)</u>. In some cases, women have offered testimony based on the "battered woman syndrome," elaborated by psychologist Lenore E. Walker in The Battered Woman (1979). <u>State v. Kelly, 478 A.2d 364 (N.J. 1984)</u>, reversed the manslaughter conviction of a battered wife when a defense witness was not permitted to testify concerning battered woman syndrome. Although courts frequently admit this evidence in criminal prosecutions, they have also held regularly that the existence of battered woman syndrome is not, in and of itself, a defense to murder charges. See generally Kit Kinports, *Defending Battered Women's Self-Defense Claims, 67 Or. L. Rev. 393 (1988)*; Richard A. Rosen, *On Self-Defense, Imminence, and Women Who Kill Their Batterers, 71 N.C. L. Rev. 371 (1993)*. Although the syndrome is now widely accepted by courts, it has also come under criticism. See generally Myrna S. Raeder, *The Double-Edged Sword: Admissibility of Battered Woman Syndrome By and Against Batterers in Cases Implicating Domestic Violence, 67 U. Colo. L. Rev. 789 (1996)*. One criticism is that the syndrome contributes to stigmatization of battered women as passive and helpless; see

Anne M. Coughlin, *Excusing Women*, 82 Cal. L. Rev. 1 (1994); Martha R. Mahoney, *Legal Images of Battered Women: Redefining the Issue of Separation*, 90 Mich. L. Rev. 1 (1991). Another criticism is that the experiences of battered women are too diverse to fit a single profile; see Mary Ann Dutton, *Understanding Women's Responses to Domestic Violence: A Redefinition of Battered Woman Syndrome*, 21 Hofstra L. Rev. 1191 (1993).

Problem 4-2

Betty had a restraining order issued against her ex-husband Joseph in October. Six months later, she invited Joseph into her home for a birthday celebration for one of their children. During the course of the evening, Betty and Joseph drank together, began arguing, and eventually came to blows. Joseph sustained a broken and dislocated elbow and head injuries, and Betty suffered a bruised nose. Joseph was charged with violation of the protection order, and Betty was charged with domestic violence and with aiding and abetting Joseph's violation of the protective order. Should both of these charges be allowed to proceed? Would the answer be different if Betty had not gotten the better of Joseph in their altercation? (State v. Lucas, 795 N.E.2d 642 (Ohio 2003).)

Town of Castle Rock v. Gonzales

545 U.S. 748 (2005)

JUSTICE SCALIA delivered the opinion of the Court.

We decide in this case whether an individual who has obtained a state-law restraining order has a constitutionally protected property interest in having the police enforce the restraining order when they have probable cause to believe it has been violated.

Go Online

Listen to the oral arguments in *Gonzales* at the Oyez Project web site.

I

The horrible facts of this case are contained in the complaint that respondent Jessica Gonzales filed in Federal District Court. (Because the case comes to us on appeal from a dismissal of the complaint, we assume its allegations are true.) Respondent alleges that petitioner, the town of Castle Rock, Colorado, violated the Due Process Clause of the Fourteenth Amendment to the United States Constitution when its police officers, acting pursuant to official policy or custom, failed to respond properly to her repeated reports that her estranged husband was violating the terms of a restraining order.

The restraining order had been issued by a state trial court several weeks earlier in conjunction with respondent's divorce proceedings. The original form order, issued on May 21, 1999, and served on respondent's husband on June 4, 1999, commanded him not to "molest or disturb the peace of [respondent] or of any child," and to remain at least 100 yards from the family home at all times. The bottom of the preprinted form noted that the reverse side contained "IMPORTANT NOTICES FOR RESTRAINED PARTIES AND LAW ENFORCEMENT OFFICIALS." (emphasis deleted). The preprinted text on the back of the form included the following **"WARNING"**:

> "**A KNOWING VIOLATION OF A RESTRAINING ORDER IS A CRIME**. . . . A VIOLATION WILL ALSO CONSTITUTE CONTEMPT OF COURT. **YOU MAY BE ARRESTED** WITHOUT NOTICE IF A LAW ENFORCEMENT OFFICER HAS PROBABLE CAUSE TO BELIEVE THAT YOU HAVE KNOWINGLY VIOLATED THIS ORDER." <u>Id., at</u> <u>1144</u> (emphasis in original).

The preprinted text on the back of the form also included a **"NOTICE TO LAW ENFORCEMENT OFFICIALS,"** which read in part:

> "YOU SHALL USE EVERY REASONABLE MEANS TO ENFORCE THIS RESTRAINING ORDER. YOU SHALL ARREST, OR, IF AN ARREST WOULD BE IMPRACTICAL UNDER THE CIRCUMSTANCES, SEEK A WARRANT FOR THE ARREST OF THE RESTRAINED PERSON WHEN YOU HAVE INFORMATION AMOUNTING TO PROBABLE CAUSE THAT THE RESTRAINED PERSON HAS VIOLATED OR ATTEMPTED TO VIOLATE ANY PROVISION OF THIS ORDER AND THE RESTRAINED PERSON HAS BEEN PROPERLY SERVED WITH A COPY OF THIS ORDER OR HAS RECEIVED ACTUAL NOTICE OF THE EXISTENCE OF THIS ORDER."

On June 4, 1999, the state trial court modified the terms of the restraining order and made it permanent. The modified order gave respondent's husband the right to spend time with his three daughters (ages 10, 9, and 7) on alternate weekends, for two weeks during the summer, and, " 'upon reasonable notice,' " for a midweek dinner visit " 'arranged by the parties' "; the modified order also allowed him to visit the home to collect the children for such "parenting time."

According to the complaint, at about 5 or 5:30 p.m. on Tuesday, June 22, 1999, respondent's husband took the three daughters while they were playing outside the family home. No advance arrangements had been made for him to see the daughters that evening. When respondent noticed the children were missing, she suspected her husband had taken them. At about 7:30 p.m., she called the Castle Rock Police Department, which dispatched two officers. The complaint continues: "When [the officers] arrived. . ., she showed them a copy of the TRO and requested that it be enforced and the three children be returned to her immediately. [The officers] stated that there was nothing they could do about the TRO and suggested that [respondent] call the Police Department again if the three children did not return home by 10:00 p.m."

At approximately 8:30 p.m., respondent talked to her husband on his cellular telephone. He told her "he had the three children [at an] amusement park in Denver." She called the police again and asked them to "have someone check for" her husband or his vehicle at the amusement park and "put out an [all points bulletin]" for her husband, but the officer with whom she spoke "refused to do so," again telling her to "wait until 10:00 p.m. and see if" her husband returned the girls.

At approximately 10:10 p.m., respondent called the police and said her children were still missing, but she was now told to wait until midnight. She called at midnight and told the dispatcher her children were still missing. She went to her husband's apartment and, finding nobody there, called the police at 12:10 a.m.; she was told to wait for an officer to arrive. When none came, she went to the police station at 12:50 a.m. and submitted an incident report. The officer who took the report "made no reasonable effort to enforce the TRO or locate the three children. Instead, he went to dinner."

At approximately 3:20 a.m., respondent's husband arrived at the police station and opened fire with a semiautomatic handgun he had purchased earlier that evening. Police shot back, killing him. Inside the cab of his pickup truck, they found the bodies of all three daughters, whom he had already murdered.

On the basis of the foregoing factual allegations, respondent brought an action under Rev. Stat. § 1979, <u>42 U.S.C. § 1983</u>, claiming that the town violated the Due Process Clause because its police department had "an official policy or custom of failing to respond properly to complaints of restraining order violations" and "tolerate[d] the non-enforcement of restraining orders by its police officers." The complaint also alleged that the town's actions "were taken either willfully, recklessly or with such gross negligence as to indicate wanton disregard and deliberate indifference to" respondent's civil rights.

Before answering the complaint, the defendants filed a motion to dismiss under <u>Federal Rule of Civil Procedure 12(b)(6)</u>. The District Court granted the motion, concluding that, whether construed as making a substantive due process or procedural due process claim, respondent's complaint failed to state a claim upon which relief could be granted.

* * *

II

The Fourteenth Amendment to the United States Constitution provides that a State shall not "deprive any person of life, liberty, or property, without due process of law." Amdt. 14, § 1. In <u>42 U.S.C. § 1983</u>, Congress has created a federal cause of action for "the deprivation of any rights, privileges, or immunities secured by the Constitution and laws." Respondent claims the benefit of this provision on the ground that she had a property interest in police enforcement of the restraining order against her husband; and that the town deprived her of this property without due process by having a policy that tolerated nonenforcement of restraining orders.

As the Court of Appeals recognized, we left a similar question unanswered in <u>DeShaney v. Winnebago County Dept. of Social Servs., 489 U.S. 189 (1989)</u>, another case with "undeniably tragic" facts: Local child-protection officials had failed to protect a young boy from beatings by his father that left him severely brain damaged. We held that the so-called "substantive" component of the Due Process Clause does not "requir[e] the State to protect the life, liberty, and property of its citizens against invasion by private actors." We noted, however, that the petitioner had not properly preserved the argument that—and we thus "decline[d] to consider" whether-state "child protection statutes gave [him] an 'entitlement' to receive protective services in accordance with the terms of the statute, an entitlement which would enjoy due process protection."

Make the Connection

<u>DeShaney v. Winnebago County</u> is reprinted in Chapter 5.

The procedural component of the Due Process Clause does not protect everything that might be described as a "benefit": "To have a property interest in a benefit, a person clearly must have more than an abstract need or desire" and "more than a unilateral expectation of it. He must, instead, have a legitimate claim of entitlement to it." <u>Board of Regents of State Colleges v. Roth, 408 U.S. 564, 577 (1972)</u>. Such entitlements are, " 'of course,. . .not created by the Constitution. Rather, they are created and their dimensions are defined by existing rules or understandings that stem from an independent source such as state law.' " <u>Paul v. Davis, 424 U.S. 693, 709 (1976)</u> (quoting <u>Roth, supra, at 577</u>).

* * *

B

The critical language in the restraining order came not from any part of the order itself (which was signed by the state-court trial judge and directed to the restrained party, respondent's husband), but from the preprinted notice to law-enforcement personnel that appeared on the back of the order. That notice effectively restated the statutory provision describing "peace officers' duties" related to the crime of violation of a restraining order. At the time of the conduct at issue in this case, that provision read as follows:

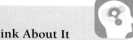

Think About It

Why does the Court ask whether Gonzales had a "property interest" in the restraining order?

"(a) Whenever a restraining order is issued, the protected person shall be provided with a copy of such order. *A peace officer shall use every reasonable means to enforce a restraining order.*

"(b) *A peace officer shall arrest, or, if an arrest would be impractical under the circumstances, seek a warrant for the arrest of a restrained person* when the peace officer has information amounting to probable cause that:

"(I) The restrained person has violated or attempted to violate any provision of a restraining order; and

"(II) The restrained person has been properly served with a copy of the restraining order or the restrained person has received actual notice of the existence and substance of such order.

"(c) In making the probable cause determination described in paragraph (b) of this subsection (3), a peace officer shall assume that the information received from the registry is accurate. *A peace officer shall enforce a valid restraining order whether or not there is a record of the restraining order in the registry.*" <u>Colo.Rev.Stat. § 18–6–803.5(3) (Lexis 1999)</u> (emphases added).

The Court of Appeals concluded that this statutory provision—especially taken in conjunction with a statement from its legislative history,[6] and with another statute restricting criminal and civil liability for officers making arrests[7]—established the Colorado Legislature's clear intent "to alter the fact that the police were not enforcing domestic abuse restraining orders," and thus its intent "that the recipient of a domestic abuse restraining order have an entitlement to its enforcement." Any other result, it said, "would render domestic abuse restraining orders utterly valueless."

This last statement is sheer hyperbole. Whether or not respondent had a right to enforce the restraining order, it rendered certain otherwise lawful conduct by her husband both criminal and in contempt of court. See §§ 18–6–803.5(2)(a), (7). The creation of grounds on which he could be arrested, criminally prosecuted, and held in contempt was hardly "valueless"—even if the prospect of those sanctions ultimately failed to prevent him from committing three murders and a suicide.

We do not believe that these provisions of Colorado law truly made enforcement of restraining orders *mandatory*. A well established tradition of police discretion has long coexisted with apparently mandatory arrest statutes.

> "In each and every state there are long-standing statutes that, by their terms, seem to preclude nonenforcement by the police. . . . However, for a number of reasons, including their legislative history, insufficient resources, and sheer physical impossibility, it has been recognized that such statutes cannot be interpreted literally. . . . [T]hey clearly do not mean that a police officer may not lawfully decline to . . . make an arrest. As to third parties in these states, the full-enforcement statutes simply have no effect, and their significance is further diminished." 1 ABA Standards for Criminal Justice 1–4.5, commentary, pp. 1–124 to 1–125 (2d ed.1980) (footnotes omitted).

The deep-rooted nature of law-enforcement discretion, even in the presence of seemingly mandatory legislative commands, is illustrated by _Chicago v. Morales, 527 U.S. 41 (1999)_, which involved an ordinance that said a police officer " 'shall order' " persons to disperse in certain circumstances. This Court rejected out of

---

6   The Court of Appeals quoted one lawmaker's description of how the bill " 'would really attack the domestic violence problems' ":

> " '[T]he entire criminal justice system must act in a consistent manner, which does not now occur. The police must make probable cause arrests. The prosecutors must prosecute every case. Judges must apply appropriate sentences, and probation officers must monitor their probationers closely. And the offender needs to be sentenced to offender-specific therapy.

> " '[T]he entire system must send the same message. . .[that] violence is criminal. And so we hope that House Bill 1253 starts us down this road.' " 366 F.3d, at 1107 (quoting Tr. of Colorado House Judiciary Hearings on House Bill 1253, Feb. 15, 1994; emphasis deleted).

7   Under Colo.Rev.Stat. § 18–6–803.5(5) (Lexis 1999), "[a] peace officer arresting a person for violating a restraining order or otherwise enforcing a restraining order" was not to be held civilly or criminally liable unless he acted "in bad faith and with malice" or violated "rules adopted by the Colorado supreme court."

hand the possibility that "the mandatory language of the ordinance. . .afford[ed] the police *no* discretion." It is, the Court proclaimed, simply "common sense that *all* police officers must use some discretion in deciding when and where to enforce city ordinances." (emphasis added).

Against that backdrop, a true mandate of police action would require some stronger indication from the Colorado Legislature than "shall use every reasonable means to enforce a restraining order" (or even "shall arrest. . . or . . .seek a warrant"), §§ 18–6–803.5(3)(a), (b). That language is not perceptibly more mandatory than the Colorado statute which has long told municipal chiefs of police that they "shall pursue and arrest any person fleeing from justice in any part of the state" and that they "shall apprehend any person in the act of committing any offense. . .and, forthwith and without any warrant, bring such person before a. . .competent authority for examination and trial." Colo.Rev.Stat. § 31–4–112 (Lexis 2004). It is hard to imagine that a Colorado peace officer would not have some discretion to determine that—despite probable cause to believe a restraining order has been violated—the circumstances of the violation or the competing duties of that officer or his agency counsel decisively against enforcement in a particular instance. The practical necessity for discretion is particularly apparent in a case such as this one, where the suspected violator is not actually present and his whereabouts are unknown.

* * *

Even if the statute could be said to have made enforcement of restraining orders "mandatory" because of the domestic-violence context of the underlying statute, that would not necessarily mean that state law gave *respondent* an entitlement to *enforcement* of the mandate. Making the actions of government employees obligatory can serve various legitimate ends other than the conferral of a benefit on a specific class of people. The serving of public rather than private ends is the normal course of the criminal law because criminal acts, "besides the injury [they do] to individuals,. . .strike at the very being of society; which cannot possibly subsist, where actions of this sort are suffered to escape with impunity." 4 W. Blackstone, Commentaries on the Laws of England 5 (1769); see also *Huntington v. Attrill,* 146 U.S. 657, 668 (1892). This principle underlies, for example, a Colorado district attorney's discretion to prosecute a domestic assault, even though the victim withdraws her charge.

Respondent's alleged interest stems only from a State's *statutory* scheme— from a restraining order that was authorized by and tracked precisely the statute on which the Court of Appeals relied. She does not assert that she has any common-law or contractual entitlement to enforcement. If she was given a statutory entitlement, we would expect to see some indication of that in the statute itself. Although Colorado's statute spoke of "protected person[s]" such as respondent, it did so in connection with matters other than a right to enforcement. It said that a "protected person shall be provided with a copy of [a restraining] order" when it is issued, § 18–6–803.5(3)(a); that a law enforcement agency "shall make all reasonable efforts to contact the protected party upon the arrest of the restrained person," § 18–6–803.5(3)(d); and that the agency "shall give [to the protected person] a copy" of the report it submits to the court that issued the order, § 18–6–803.5(3)(e). Perhaps most importantly, the statute spoke directly to the protected person's power to "initiate contempt proceedings against the restrained person if the order [was] issued in a civil action or request the prosecuting attorney to initiate contempt proceedings if the order [was] issued in a criminal action." § 18–6–803.5(7). The protected person's express power to "initiate" civil contempt proceedings contrasts tellingly with the mere ability to "request" initiation of criminal contempt proceedings—and even more dramatically with the complete silence about any power to "request" (much less demand) that an arrest be made.

The creation of a personal entitlement to something as vague and novel as enforcement of restraining orders cannot "simply g[o] without saying." We conclude that Colorado has not created such an entitlement.

C

Even if we were to think otherwise concerning the creation of an entitlement by Colorado, it is by no means clear that an individual entitlement to enforcement of a restraining order could constitute a "property" interest for purposes of the Due Process Clause. Such a right would not, of course, resemble any traditional conception of property. Although that alone does not disqualify it from due process protection, as *Roth* and its progeny show, the right to have a restraining order enforced does not "have some ascertainable monetary value," as even our "*Roth*-type property-as-entitlement" cases have implicitly required. Merrill, The Landscape of Constitutional Property, 86 Va. L.Rev. 885, 964 (2000). Perhaps most radically, the alleged property interest here arises *incidentally,* not out of some new species of government benefit or service, but out of a function that government actors have always performed—to wit, arresting people who they have probable cause to believe have committed a criminal offense.

* * *

III

We conclude, therefore, that respondent did not, for purposes of the Due Process Clause, have a property interest in police enforcement of the restraining order against her husband. It is accordingly unnecessary to address the Court of

Appeals' determination that the town's custom or policy prevented the police from giving her due process when they deprived her of that alleged interest.

In light of today's decision and that in *DeShaney*, the benefit that a third party may receive from having someone else arrested for a crime generally does not trigger protections under the Due Process Clause, neither in its procedural nor in its "substantive" manifestations. This result reflects our continuing reluctance to treat the Fourteenth Amendment as " 'a font of tort law,' " *Parratt v. Taylor,* 451 U.S. 527 (1981) (quoting *Paul v. Davis,* 424 U.S., at 701), but it does

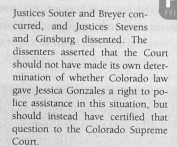

Justices Souter and Breyer concurred, and Justices Stevens and Ginsburg dissented. The dissenters asserted that the Court should not have made its own determination of whether Colorado law gave Jessica Gonzales a right to police assistance in this situation, but should instead have certified that question to the Colorado Supreme Court.

not mean States are powerless to provide victims with personally enforceable remedies. Although the framers of the Fourteenth Amendment and the Civil Rights Act of 1871, 17 Stat. 13 (the original source of § 1983), did not create a system by which police departments are generally held financially accountable for crimes that better policing might have prevented, the people of Colorado are free to craft such a system under state law.[15]

The judgment of the Court of Appeals is

Reversed.

Points for Discussion

a. Mandatory Enforcement

The Court in *Gonzales* concluded that the Colorado statute did not create a personal entitlement to enforcement of the restraining order the plaintiff had obtained, and that this would be necessary in order to have an interest protected by the Due Process Clause. What language could the state legislature have used to make enforcement mandatory and give someone like Jessica Gonzales a basis for

---

[15] In Colorado, the general statutory immunity for government employees does not apply when "the act or omission causing. . .injury was willful and wanton." Colo.Rev.Stat. § 24–10–118(2)(a) (Lexis 1999). Respondent's complaint does allege that the police officers' actions "were taken either willfully, recklessly or with such gross negligence as to indicate wanton disregard and deliberate indifference to" her civil rights.

recovery in similar circumstances? What are the policy arguments for and against this approach?

See also <u>Burella v. City of Philadelphia, 501 F.3d 134 (3d Cir. 2007)</u>, decided after *Gonzales*, which concluded that a plaintiff who was shot by her estranged husband did not have procedural or substantive due process rights to police protection based on the restraining orders she had obtained under the Pennsylvania Protection from Abuse Act.

b. Public and Private Actors

Gonzales reaffirms the Court's conclusion in <u>DeShaney v. Winnebago County Dept. of Social Services, 489 U.S. 189 (1989)</u>, reprinted in Chapter 5, that a state is not constitutionally required to "to protect the life, liberty, and property of its citizens against invasions by private actors." *DeShaney* was a child protection case, in which the state agency became involved after receiving reports that the child was being abused by his father. The Court rejected the argument that the child had been unconstitutionally deprived of his liberty when the caseworkers failed to protect him from his father's violence. In reading these cases, it is important to understand that the U.S. Constitution applies to state action, and not to discriminatory or wrongful conduct by private individuals.

The distinction between the actions of state officials and actions by private actors was also an issue in <u>United States v. Morrison, 529 U.S. 598 (2000)</u>, in which the Court concluded that Congress's powers to remedy civil rights violations under § 5 of the Fourteenth Amendment did not extend to enacting legislation to remedy private violence motivated by gender. Two members of the Court disagreed with this aspect of the ruling.

c. Positive and Negative Rights

The constitutional tradition in the United States, as described in *DeShaney* and *Gonzales*, imposes limits on the power of governments to act that are sometimes described as creating negative rights or liberties. Our tradition has not been understood to protect positive rights, such as a right to police protection or health care or education, which would impose affirmative obligations on governments. Contemporary international human rights instruments recognize both negative and positive rights, however, which are addressed in two separate treaties that comprise the United Nations Bill of Rights. The United States has ratified the <u>International Covenant on Civil and Political Rights (ICCPR)</u>, which has parallels to the rights protected by the U.S. Constitution and Bill of Rights. The United States has not ratified the <u>International Covenant on Economic, Social and Cultural Rights (ICESCR)</u>, which focuses on positive rights.

Global View: Domestic Violence and Human Rights

After losing in the U.S. Supreme Court, Jessica Lenahan (formerly Gonzales) filed a petition with the <u>Inter-American Commission on Human Rights</u>, arguing that the failure of the Castle Rock police to protect her and her children, and the failure of the U.S. courts to provide her with a remedy, violated various provisions of the American Declaration of the Rights and Duties of Man. The <u>Commission's report</u> concluded that members of the Organization of American States, including the United States, have a duty to prevent and respond to acts of domestic violence by private actors, and that the failure to meet this duty with due diligence violated the rights of Jessica and her children.

Feltmeier v. Feltmeier

<u>777 N.E.2d 1032 (Ill. App. Ct. 2002)</u>; aff'd <u>798 N.E.2d 75 (Ill. 2003)</u>

JUSTICE KUEHN delivered the opinion of the court:

It took the law a long time to recognize domestic violence for what it is.[1] In 1986, our legislature awoke to the reality that "the legal system has ineffectively dealt with family violence in the past, allowing abusers to escape effective prosecution or financial liability." <u>750 ILCS 60/102(3) (West 2000)</u>.

The Illinois Domestic Violence Act of 1986 (the Act) (<u>750 ILCS 60/101</u> *et seq.* (West 2000)) created the crime of domestic battery and provides serious penalties for those who committed it. While the Act provides a number of remedies in an effort to protect abused spouses and family members, it did not create a civil cause of action to remedy the damages done. This case addresses the question of whether a victim of domestic violence can maintain a civil action to recover monetary damages for a pattern of marital abuse, inflicted over a number of years and resulting in severe emotional distress.

The plaintiff wants to recover damages from her former husband for the way he treated her during the course of their 11 year failed marriage. The complaint

---

[1] Battered wives were not always looked upon as crime victims. An angry husband could whip his wife, provided that he employed the use of a rod no larger than the diameter of his thumb. Called the "Rule of Thumb," this English common law acknowledged, condoned, and perpetuated the physical abuse of women. See W. Blackstone, 1 Commentaries on the Law of England, at 445–46 (1765).

alleges a pattern of physical and mental abuse, along with the allegation that it inflicted severe and lasting emotional distress. We are asked to decide whether a former wife can maintain such an action against her erstwhile husband and, if so, whether an alleged pattern of domestic abuse constitutes one continuous tort, so that the statute of limitations begins to run only after the final abusive act has occurred.

As a rule of thumb, we rarely review questions that arise during litigation's course. However, if an interlocutory appeal can resolve novel legal questions and thereby facilitate judicial economy, we sometimes accept the review of questions certified for our consideration prior to a final adjudication in the trial court. 155 Ill.2d R. 308(a). In this case, we have accepted three issues certified for review by the trial judge. Their resolution leads us to conclude that this plaintiff can maintain an action at law to recover monetary damages proximately caused by her ex-husband's pattern of abusive treatment during the course of their ill-fated marriage.

Lynn Feltmeier and Robert Feltmeier entered the bonds of matrimony on October 11, 1986. The ensuing marriage failed to measure up to the sacred vows under which it was entered. Lynn was awarded a divorce from Robert on December 16, 1997. She prevailed on grounds of mental cruelty. The judgment incorporated the terms of a December 10, 1997, marital settlement agreement, which contained a provision that called for the mutual release of all future claims that either party might have against the other.

On August 25, 1999, Lynn sued Robert for the intentional infliction of emotional distress. According to the allegations contained in the complaint, Robert engaged in a pattern of domestic abuse—both physical and mental in nature—that began shortly after the exchange of the marital vows, continued throughout the marriage, and did not cease even after the marriage ended. Lynn's complaint was very specific about the details and time frames of the alleged physical and emotional abuse. Lynn alleged that she was physically beaten at least 11 times. She claimed that many of the beatings were administered while her children were at hand to witness them. Lynn further alleged that she was physically restrained against her will on more than one occasion. In addition to the physical abuse, Lynn repeatedly found herself on the receiving end of verbal attacks and flying objects hurled in her direction. She alleged that her husband systematically isolated her from family and friends. Finally, she alleged that when she took action to rid herself of the abuse, Robert stalked her. The complaint specifically alleged more than 45 episodes of abusive behavior.

On October 20, 1999, Robert filed a motion to dismiss the lawsuit. Robert maintained that the complaint failed to allege facts that give rise to an action for the intentional infliction of emotional distress. He argued that the conduct alleged was neither extreme nor outrageous in nature. He also argued that even if the conduct alleged was actionable, the claim was still not viable because the statute of limitations had run on most of the alleged misconduct.

On February 14, 2000, the trial judge denied Robert's motion. Immediately thereafter, Robert filed an amended motion to dismiss that raised the marital settlement agreement as a release from the various claims presented by Lynn's lawsuit. The trial judge denied that motion on June 23, 2000.

On April 10, 2001, using the language of Supreme Court Rule 308(a) (155 Ill.2d R. 308(a)) the trial judge found that the interlocutory orders denying Robert's motions to dismiss involved questions of law "as to which there is substantial ground for difference of opinion" and that an immediate appeal from the orders "may materially advance the ultimate termination of the litigation."

The issues certified for review are as follows:

1. Whether the plaintiff's complaint states a cause of action for the intentional infliction of emotional distress.
2. Whether the plaintiff's claims for the intentional infliction of emotional distress based on conduct prior to August 25, 1997, are barred by the applicable statute of limitations.
3. Whether the plaintiff's claim against the defendant for the intentional infliction of emotional distress has been released by the language of the marital settlement agreement.

We will address each issue in the order presented. * * *

Stating a Cause of Action

When a trial judge is presented with a motion to dismiss a case for the failure to state a cause of action pursuant to section 2–615 of the Code of Civil Procedure (735 ILCS 5/2–615 (West 1998)), he or she must determine whether the complaint sets forth sufficient facts that, if established, could entitle the plaintiff to relief. The judge must accept all well-pleaded facts in the complaint as true and draw reasonable inferences from those facts that are favorable to the plaintiff. Because the judge is not being called upon to weigh any witness's credibility or weigh facts, on appeal we review the matter *de novo*. The same standard of review applies when determining the propriety of an order denying a motion to dismiss pursuant to section 2–619 of the Code of Civil Procedure (735 ILCS 5/2–619 (West 1998)).

To state a valid cause of action for the intentional infliction of emotional distress, the plaintiff must plead certain facts. To maintain her action, Lynn had to initially allege that Robert engaged in conduct that was truly extreme and outrageous. She had to further allege that Robert intended to inflict severe emotional distress or knew that there was a high probability that his actions would cause severe emotional distress. Finally, Lynn had to allege that as a result of Robert's conduct, she actually suffered severe emotional distress. *McGrath v. Fahey*, 126 Ill.2d 78, 86, 127 Ill.Dec. 724, 533 N.E.2d 806, 809 (1988). These elements are taken from section 46 of the Restatement (Second) of Torts. *McGrath*, 126 Ill.2d at 86, 127 Ill.Dec. 724, 533 N.E.2d at 809; Restatement (Second) of Torts § 46 (1965). The court system only intervenes in such matters when " 'the distress inflicted is so severe that no reasonable [person] could be expected to endure it.' " *McGrath*, 126 Ill.2d at 86, 127 Ill.Dec. 724, 533 N.E.2d at 809 (quoting Restatement (Second) of Torts § 46, Comment j, at 77 (1965)).

Robert asks us to evaluate Lynn's claim in light of the marital context in which it arose. He draws upon several cases from other jurisdictions that have rejected efforts to maintain actions for the intentional infliction of emotional distress based upon marital misconduct. See *Pickering v. Pickering*, 434 N.W.2d 758, 761 (S.D.1989) (The husband could not maintain an action for the intentional infliction of emotional distress based upon his wife's extramarital affair. Such an action does not lie, as a matter of public policy, when it is predicated upon conduct that leads to a divorce.); see also *Hakkila v. Hakkila*, 112 N.M. 172, 812 P.2d 1320 (App.1991). We recognize that the family relationship is an important consideration in analyzing intrafamily torts.

In order to fully appreciate the importance of the marital context to a cause of action for the intentional infliction of emotional distress, we must generally review some of the policy considerations that underlie restrictions of the tort's scope. Liability does not flow from every act that intends to cause, and does cause, emotional distress. It is reserved for those who engage in "extreme and outrageous" conduct intended to cause such distress.

There are several simple reasons to support this limitation on the cause of action. The law simply cannot impose a degree of civility beyond human capacity. Courts cannot police every intentional infliction of emotional distress in a society where, like it or not, incivility is quite pervasive. Nor should they. As one noted scholar has observed, "[I]t would be unfortunate if the law closed all the safety valves through which irascible tempers might legally blow off steam." C. Magruder, *Mental and Emotional Disturbance in the Law of Torts*, 49 Harv. L.Rev. 1033, 1053 (1936). Most everyone needs some leeway to vent emotions in order to preserve proper mental health.

Making another person unhappy or upset may actually serve a useful purpose, other than simply maintaining a degree of mental health. Hence, witnesses at a trial have to suffer the anguish of harsh, and sometimes humiliating, cross-examination, just like young soldiers must suffer the distress that flows from a drill sergeant's wrath during basic training.

Basic liberty interests serve to justify the limitation of the tort's scope. "There is still, in this country, such a thing as liberty to express an unflattering opinion of another, however wounding it may be to his feelings * * *." W. Prosser, *Insult and Outrage*, 44 Cal. L.Rev. 40, 44 (1956). Similarly, an interest in personal autonomy has led courts to reject lawsuits where a person intentionally causes emotional distress by engaging in an extramarital affair. <u>Pickering, 434 N.W.2d at 761</u>.

Finally, the restriction of this tort to extreme and outrageous behavior provides protection against unfounded and frivolous lawsuits, offering reliable confirmation of injury and causation, the other two elements of the tort. When conduct is truly extreme and outrageous, it is more likely that severe emotional distress suffered by the victim was actually caused by that conduct.

These considerations, limiting the liability for the intentional infliction of emotional distress to only outrageous behavior, caution a very limited scope for the tort in the marital context.

* * *

Mindful that this kind of tort deserves circumscription in the marital setting, we nonetheless find that Lynn's complaint states a proper cause of action for the intentional infliction of emotional distress. We reject the contention that the complaint fails to meet the law's desire for careful detail in alleging this kind of tort. The complaint sets forth the alleged pattern of marital misconduct in great detail. We also disagree with the contention that the complaint falls short of adequately alleging the existence of severe emotional distress. Lynn specifically alleges that she suffered severe emotional distress, including a loss of self-esteem. She translates that distress into ongoing symptoms through numerous allegations about its effects on her mental state. She alleges that she has been diagnosed as suffering from posttraumatic stress disorder, manifested by depression and fear of other men and her inability to form relationships with them. She alleges that her mental distress has resulted in medical and psychological expenses, which she will continue to incur into the unforeseeable future.

Given the alleged pattern of abuse, it is reasonable to infer that Robert knew or should have known that his conduct would have long-lasting ramifications. Robert does not argue a contrary position. However, he does take issue with the allegation that his conduct amounted to extreme and outrageous behavior.

Robert argues that any objectively reasonable woman could have endured the abuse that he is alleged to have administered, without suffering severe emotional distress. He maintains that his alleged misconduct, having taken place in the context of an 11 year marriage, was neither extreme nor outrageous. At oral argument, in an effort to minimize the abusive conduct that Lynn alleged and in order to demonstrate that it was not extreme, Robert's attorney looked at the number of alleged acts and argued that the abuse claimed occurred only three or four times per year over the course of the marriage. The argument suggested that one beating a year, coupled with an act of physical restraint or an annual pelting from flying missiles, when spread out over an 11 year span, constituted marital conduct that any reasonable wife should be able to endure without suffering emotional distress.

We cannot accept this position. As previously noted, we understand that married couples will get into arguments and that, on occasion, those arguments will become heated. Spouses will most assuredly bruise each other's feelings. And, from time to time, a husband will touch his wife with an angry hand. However, the marital conduct alleged in this particular case is different. It cannot be trivialized below the threshold of outrageousness that is actionable, by calculating the annual number of abusive events and arguing that there were not enough of them per year to matter.

The allegations of Lynn's complaint typify the kind of abusive relationship that spawns a series of posttraumatic stress symptoms coined the "battered wife syndrome." This syndrome results from domestic violence and abuse that recurs but is not necessarily constant or all that frequent. It routinely occurs between relatively long periods of normal and routine family life. This accounts, in part, for why its victims tend to hold steadfast to the hope that the most immediate abusive episode will be the last of its kind. They cling to the love and affection the abuser is eager to provide after his attacks, and they resist the need for any assistance as the abusive pattern develops. Most cries for help are heard only after the psychological, and in some cases physical, damage is irreversible. Even though the abusive events may only occur a handful of times over the course of a year, the repeated pattern of abuse inflicts daily psychic torment. Its victims live in a constant state of silent fear, generated by the knowledge that their spouse, the very person with whom they sleep every night, harbors the capacity to hurt them. While the abusive episodes may not significantly increase in number, they do tend to increase in terms of the harm inflicted. The victims begin to realize that the abuse is certain to come again, but they are unable to predict its appointed hour. They also begin to fear the intensity of the next episode.

Domestic violence and domestic abuse can take many forms. The kind alleged here is extreme enough to be actionable. It combines more than a decade of verbal insults and humiliations with episodes where freedom of movement was deprived and where physical injury was often inflicted. The alleged pattern of abuse, combined with its duration, worked a humiliation and loss of self-esteem. Regardless of the form in which it arrived, violence was certain to erupt, and when seasons of spousal abuse turn to years that span the course of a decade, we are unwilling to dismiss it on grounds that it is unworthy of outrage.

We find that the complaint clearly articulates a pattern of conduct that satisfies the standard necessary to state a cause of action for the intentional infliction of emotional distress. We have not been directed to, nor could we independently find, any Illinois case holding that marital domestic abuse can be sufficiently outrageous to sustain a tortious cause of action. * * *

Illinois has determined that domestic violence presents sufficient problems to warrant its own legislative act to deal with the violence. By enacting these statutes, our legislature is saying that such behavior is unacceptable, and from that finding it can be inferred that violent behavior in the domestic setting is outrageous. Our supreme court has found that the duration of the behavior at issue is one factor to consider in determining whether that behavior is outrageous. <u>McGrath, 126 Ill.2d at 86, 127 Ill.Dec. 724, 533 N.E.2d at 809</u>. A pattern, course, and accumulation of acts can make an individual's conduct "sufficiently extreme to be actionable, whereas one instance of such behavior might not be." <u>Pavlik v. Kornhaber, 326 Ill. App.3d 731, 746, 260 Ill.Dec. 331, 761 N.E.2d 175, 187 (2001)</u>. This duration factor is not new law. Its foundation lies in section 46 of the Restatement (Second) of Torts. See <u>Restatement (Second) of Torts § 46, Comment j, at 77–78 (1965)</u>. The duration of Robert's alleged abusive behavior helps to support the outrageous nature of the conduct alleged in the complaint. We conclude that Lynn has alleged facts which, if proven, could entitle her to relief. The trial court's order to that effect was correct.

Statute of Limitations

Robert contends that each separate act of abuse triggered a new statute of limitations so that all acts of abuse which occurred more than two years prior to the date on which Lynn filed her complaint would be barred.

Given the type of psychological damage Lynn experienced, she asks this court to adopt the continuing-tort theory in the context of domestic violence and abuse. The applicable statute of limitations for a cause of action alleging the intentional infliction of emotional distress is two years, because the tort is a form of personal injury. <u>735 ILCS 5/13–202 (West 1998)</u>. The purpose of the statute of limitations is to discourage old claims. <u>Pavlik, 326 Ill.App.3d at 744–45, 260 Ill.Dec. 331, 761 N.E.2d at 186</u>. The continuing-tort theory advanced by Lynn looks at the behavior of the defendant as a continuous whole. If the theory is applied, the statute of limitations would not start until either the continuing behavior at issue stopped or the last such act occurred.

* * *

We agree with the decision of the First District Appellate Court in *Pavlik* in applying the continuing-tort theory to claims for the intentional infliction of emotional distress.

We are also in agreement with other states that have recognized the continuing-tort theory in the context of domestic abuse cases. See, *e.g., Curtis v. Firth*, 123 Idaho 598, 850 P.2d 749 (1993); *Cusseaux v. Pickett*, 279 N.J.Super. 335, 652 A.2d 789, 794 (App.1994).

The alleged domestic violence and abuse endured by Lynn in this case spanned the entire 11-year marriage. No one disputes that the allegations set forth the existence of ongoing abusive behavior. Lynn's psychologist, Dr. Michael E. Althoff, found that Lynn suffered from the "battered wife syndrome." He described the psychological process as one that unfolds over time. The process by which a spouse exerts coercive control is based upon "a systematic, repetitive infliction of psychological trauma" designed to "instill terror and helplessness." Dr. Althoff indicated that the posttraumatic stress disorder from which Lynn suffered was the result of the entire series of abusive acts, not just the result of one specific incident.

"The mate who is responsible for creating the condition suffered by the battered victim must be made to account for his actions—*all* his actions. Failure to allow affirmative recovery under these circumstances would be tantamount to the courts condoning the continued abusive treatment of women in the domestic sphere." (Emphasis in original.) *Cusseaux*, 652 A.2d at 794. We find that the statute of limitations did not begin to run until the date of the last injury Lynn suffered or when Robert's tortious acts ceased to occur. The complaint includes allegations relative to Robert's behavior through August 1999. Accordingly, Lynn's complaint was timely filed, and the trial court's orders denying Robert's motions to dismiss were correct.

Release of Claims by Marital Settlement Agreement

Robert contends that there are two clauses in the marital settlement agreement, executed by the parties on December 11, 1997, that operate to release the claim brought by Lynn in this suit. Before addressing the merits of this argument, we look to the specific language at issue. Paragraph 8(a) of the agreement is as follows:

"To the fullest extent by law permitted to do so, and except as herein otherwise provided, each of the parties does hereby forever relinquish, release, waive, and forever quitclaim and grant to the other, his or her heirs, personal representatives[,] and assignees[ ] all rights of dower, inheritance, descent, distribution, community interest, marital property, and all other right, title, claim, tort claims, interest, and estate as husband and wife, widow or widower, or otherwise, by reason of the marital relations existing between the parties hereto, under any present or future law, or which he or she otherwise has or might have or be entitled to claim in, to, or against the property and assets of the other, real, personal, or mixed, or his or her estate, whether now owned or hereafter in any manner acquired by the other party, or whether in possession or in expectancy, whether vested or contingent, and each party further covenants and agrees for himself or herself, his or her heirs, personal representatives[,] and assignees[ ] that neither of them will at any time hereafter sue the other or his or her heirs, personal representatives, grantees, devisees[,] or assignees, for the purpose of enforcing any of the rights specified in and relinquished under this paragraph 8(a), and further agrees that in the event any suit shall be commenced, this release, when pleaded, shall be and constitute a complete defense to any claim or suit so instituted by either party hereto, and [each party] further agrees to execute, acknowledge[,] and deliver at the request of the other party[ ] or his or her heirs, personal representatives, grantees, devisees[,] or assignees [ ] any or all such deeds, releases[,] or other instruments[ ] and further assurances as may be required or reasonably requested to effect or evidence such release, waiver, relinquishment[,] or extinguishment of such rights; provided, however, that nothing herein contained shall operate or be construed as a waiver or release by either party to the other party of any obligation imposed upon or undertaken by a party under this Agreement."

Paragraph 8(d) provides as follows:

"Save and except as herein otherwise provided, and to the fullest extent that they may lawfully do so, all the rights, claims, and demands of every kind, nature[,] and description[ ] which each party has, or may hereafter have, or claim to have against the other[ ] shall be and the same hereby are forever discharged, extinguished, released, and ended, and all matters and charges whatsoever, and any and all manner of actions or causes of actions, suits, debts, dues, accounts, bonds, covenants, contracts, agreements, judgments, claims, and demands whatsoever, in law or in equity, which each party ever had [or] now has[ ] or which he or she, his or her heirs, executors, administrators, or assignees, or any of them[ ] hereafter can, shall, or may have against the other (as the case may be) for or by reason of any cause, matter[,] or thing whatsoever, from the beginning of the world to the effective date hereof, shall be and the same are[ ] extinguished; provided, however, that nothing herein contained shall release or limit the obligation of either of the parties hereto to comply with the other provisions of this Agreement or with any Order of Protection or Restraining Order that may exist in favor of one party against the other."

Robert asks us to conclude that these two provisions release him from liability for the abusive behavior he inflicted upon Lynn during and after their marriage.

Initially, we note that the question can be simply answered in the negative in light of our holding on the continuing-tort theory. Lynn's cause of action did not arise until, at the earliest, mid-1999. This agreement was signed a little less than two years before.

A release with very general boilerplate language, such as the two provisions at issue, cannot be construed to release future causes of action between the parties. Such language would be contrary to public policy. General release language simply cannot operate to release unknown claims. Neither Lynn nor Robert was aware of Lynn's claim when they signed the agreement. Consequently, this release can only release the specific claims listed.

The language of paragraph 8(a) involves claims derived from the marital relationship itself. Domestic abuse is not one such claim. The provision is meant to deal with traditional common law marital issues, such as dower.

Turning to the language of paragraph 8(d), we note that it contains catch-all release language. No type of claim is specifically released. As already stated, general boilerplate language is simply ineffective to release specific types of claims.

Consequently, the marital settlement agreement does not bar Lynn's suit against Robert for the intentional infliction of emotional distress that arose after the agreement's execution. Additionally, the general language of the relevant release provisions is insufficient to bar Lynn's suit.

* * *

Conclusion

Accordingly, we answer the first certified question in the affirmative and the second and third certified questions in the negative. We also respond in the negative to the additional immunity issue brought forth by Robert in this appeal. We remand this cause for further proceedings.

Certified questions answered; cause remanded.

GOLDENHERSH, J., concurs.

JUSTICE WELCH, concurring in part and dissenting in part:

I concur with the majority that Lynn's complaint satisfies the standard necessary to state a cause of action for the intentional infliction of emotional distress, but I respectfully dissent from the remainder of the majority's opinion.

First, regarding the statute of limitations, Robert contends that each separate act of abuse triggered a new statute of limitations so that all acts of abuse which occurred more than two years prior to the date on which Lynn filed her complaint are barred. I agree. Although I am sympathetic to Lynn's alleged plight and I understand that the majority is well-intentioned in applying the continuing-tort theory in the context of domestic violence and abuse, I believe that the law dictates otherwise.

* * *

Here, I simply believe that each alleged act of abuse by Robert resulted in a separate cause of action for the intentional infliction of emotional distress. Applying the statutory language, I would hold that Lynn's causes of action accrued at the time of the alleged abuse. Moreover, I cannot discern any unjust result, because Lynn has alleged actionable, noncumulative, tortious conduct within the limitations period. Therefore, I believe that the circuit court erred by denying Robert's motion to dismiss the allegations of conduct outside the limitations period.

Second, I agree with Robert's contention that paragraph 8(d) of the marital settlement agreement, executed by the parties on December 11, 1997, released the claim brought by Lynn in this suit. Paragraph 8(d) provides in pertinent part as follows:

> "[A]ll the rights, claims, and demands of every kind, nature[,] and description[ ] which each party has, or may hereafter have, or claim to have against the other[ ] shall be and the same hereby are forever discharged, extinguished, released, and ended, and * * * any and all manner of actions or causes of actions, suits, * * * claims, and demands whatsoever, in law or in equity, which each party ever had * * * or may have against the other (as the case may be) for or by reason of any cause, matter[,] or thing whatsoever, from the beginning of the world to the effective date hereof, shall be and the same are[ ] extinguished[.]"

A question of contract construction is reviewed *de novo*. Absent ambiguity, the meaning and intent of a contract must be ascertained by the language utilized in the contract. A contractual release relinquishes a claim, but not future claims or uncontemplated claims.

Here, the language of the settlement agreement extinguishes all current and future causes of action between the parties. Although the waiver of future claims is prohibited as a matter of law as mentioned above, we are not dealing here with a future claim. Here, Lynn either knew or should have reasonably known of her current claim for emotional distress at the time she executed the marital settlement agreement. Thus, she elected to release it under the terms of the settlement agreement.

The ruling was affirmed unanimously in <u>Feltmeier v. Feltmeier, 798 N.E.2d 75 (Ill. 2003)</u>, which accepted the continuing tort approach, concluding that because Lynne's cause of action did not accrue until the last tortious act in August 1999, her claim could not have been released in the December 1997 settlement agreement.

* * * Here, the majority fails to point to any specific language in the agreement that overcomes the general. Nevertheless, Lynn argues that the specific provisions in paragraph 8(a) limit the general provisions of paragraph 8(d). I would give this argument weight if paragraph 8 of the settlement agreement was cohesive. It is not. I need only point out that paragraph 8(f) involves social security law and paragraph 8(g) involves applicable governing law.

Therefore, I believe that the marital settlement agreement bars Lynn's suit against Robert for the intentional infliction of emotional distress for incidents arising prior to the agreement's execution.

* * *

For the foregoing reasons, I concur in part and dissent in part.

Points for Discussion

a. Statutes of Limitations

The *Feltmeier* continuing tort doctrine was adopted in <u>Pugliese v. Los Angeles County Superior Court, 53 Cal.Rptr.3d 681 (Cal. Ct. App. 2007)</u>. In New Jersey, <u>Cusseaux v. Pickett, 652 A.2d 789 (N.J. Super. Ct. 1994)</u>, embraced the continuing tort theory, but a subsequent ruling held that that when there is expert testimony to establish that a spouse was suffering from battered woman syndrome, causing "an inability to take any action to improve or alter the circumstances in her marriage unilaterally," the statute of limitations could be tolled during the period in which the condition existed. <u>Giovine v. Giovine, 663 A.2d 109 (N.J. Super. Ct. App.Div.1995)</u>. Would Lynne Feltmeier have been able to bring her claim under this approach?

b. Joinder

Marital tort claims pose significant questions for courts and litigants, including whether such claims should be joined with a divorce claim, whether a plaintiff in a tort suit that is joined with a divorce proceedings is entitled to a jury trial, and to what extent res judicata and collateral estoppel apply to a marital tort suit tried after a divorce proceeding. See, e.g., Xiao Yang Chen v. Fischer, 843 N.E.2d 723 (N.Y. 2005); Stuart v. Stuart, 421 N.W.2d 505 (Wis. 1988). See also Steven J. Gaynor, Annotation, *Joinder of Tort Actions Between Spouses with Proceeding for Dissolution of Marriage,* 4 A.L.R.5th 972 (1992).

c. Settlement Agreements

As suggested in *Feltmeier*, agreements settling claims in a divorce case may preclude the parties from filing suit after the divorce for marital torts; see e.g. Cerniglia v. Cerniglia, 679 So.2d 1160 (Fla.1996). If the abuse described in *Feltmeier* had not continued after the parties' divorce, would Lynn Feltmeier's claim have been barred?

Problem 4-3

During the three years they lived together, Sam committed frequent acts of physical and emotional abuse against Sarah. A year before leaving Sam, Sarah sought treatment from a therapist who diagnosed her as suffering from post-traumatic stress disorder, anxiety disorder, depression and insomnia as a result of the abuse. Two years after leaving Sam, Sarah comes to you to discuss the possibility of bringing an action for damages against Sam. What issues would you want to explore or research to decide whether Sarah may be able to recover? (See Graham v. Brown, 26 A.3d 823 (Me. 2011).)

Elder and Adult Abuse

Elderly or incapacitated individuals are at risk of mistreatment from family members or other caregivers in or out of the home. This may include physical and emotional abuse, sexual abuse, neglect or abandonment by caregivers, or financial exploitation. Every state has laws to address elder abuse and systems for reporting suspected abuse or neglect. In most states, Adult Protective Services will investigate these reports and offer services.

> **Go Online**
>
> Information and resources on elder abuse is available from the National Institute on Aging in the National Institutes of Health, and the National Center on Elder Abuse in the U.S. Department of Health and Human Services.

See, e.g., Fla. Stat. Ann. §§ 415.101—415.113 (2018). In addition, state laws may create separate criminal offenses or provide for enhanced sentences in cases of elder abuse. See James L. Buchwalter, Annotation, <u>Validity, Construction, and Application of State Civil and Criminal Elder Abuse Laws, 113 A.L.R.5th 431 (2003 & Supp.)</u>

Boyce v. Fernandes

<u>77 F.3d 946 (7th Cir. 1996)</u>

POSNER, CHIEF JUDGE.

Claudine Boyce appeals from the dismissal, on summary judgment, of a damages suit for false arrest that she brought against Vera Fernandes, a Peoria police officer, and the City of Peoria. The suit against Fernandes is based exclusively on <u>42 U.S.C. § 1983</u> and was dismissed on the ground of public officers' immunity. A supplemental state law claim naming both Fernandes and the City as defendants was also dismissed.

Take Note

Defendants in a civil rights action under § 1983 are entitled to a qualified immunity from liability when they carry out discretionary public functions, provided that they do not violate clearly established statutory or constitutional rights.

Where the only issue bearing on immunity is whether the defendant had probable cause to make the search or arrest that is challenged, merits and immunity merge; the dispositive question is simply whether the defendant did have probable cause. * * * It is apparent that Fernandes had probable cause to make the arrest, and this makes the issue of immunity academic.

Elder abuse is a growing problem in this country because of the growing number of elderly people. Like child abuse, elder abuse is a difficult crime to detect and prosecute. In both types of case the victim is often an unreliable witness because of limited mental capacity—undeveloped in the case of the child, impaired by old age in the case of the elder. Claudine Boyce was employed by a woman of 75 named Auda Tunis who was afflicted by senile dementia caused either by alcoholism or by Parkinson's disease. Detective Fernandes began her investigation of Boyce at the instance of Tunis's granddaughter, who told the detective that she thought Boyce might be stealing from her grandmother. The granddaughter had discovered that all the furniture had been removed from Tunis's home and that she had been placed in a nursing home. The granddaughter had visited her grandmother in the nursing home and found that she seemed confused at first but later recognized the granddaughter and the granddaughter's husband. Tunis told them she did not know why she was there, that Boyce had badgered her into signing what she thought was a document that said merely that she would think about signing a power of attorney, and that she was ashamed of the situation she was in and had not wanted to complain to the granddaughter.

The nursing home had told the granddaughter that Tunis had granted Boyce (who had signed Tunis into the nursing home) both a general power of attorney and a health-care power of attorney. Detective Fernandes therefore called the lawyer who had prepared the powers of attorney. He expressed surprise that Tunis had a granddaughter—he had thought she had no living relatives. Fernandes interviewed employees of the nursing home. They told her that Tunis had been in a shocking condition when admitted to the home, with multiple bruises and lacerations, and that the jewelry Tunis had worn on her previous admission to the nursing home was gone. Fernandes reported that the staff had told her that "Tunis seemed to be in a state of shock and her condition was completely opposite of the first time she had been admitted to the home several weeks prior. She now appeared confused and withdrawn and her clothing was unkempt and old appearing." The staff suspected elder abuse and decided to institute proceedings to obtain a new power of attorney, in which the nursing home would be the power holder.

Fernandes then spoke to Tunis herself, who in this interview and a subsequent one on December 26 told Fernandes that Boyce had threatened, slapped, and shoved her, had plied her with liquor, and might have (subsequent investigation revealed that she had) deposited her social security checks, without her authorization, in a joint checking account in Boyce's and her name; and that Boyce had taken Tunis's furniture and other personal property without her authorization and Tunis did not know what she had done with it. Two days later, December 28, Fernandes learned that Tunis's Cadillac was parked in Boyce's driveway and that the car, formerly registered to Tunis's deceased husband, was now registered to Boyce. A few days later Fernandes arrested Boyce, without a warrant, for the theft of the Cadillac, a felony. Boyce was held in the county jail for 42 hours before being released on bond. Subsequent investigation brought to light that Boyce had in all likelihood forged a bill of sale of the Cadillac to herself for $100. Nevertheless, she has not been prosecuted.

Accusations by demented persons must always be viewed with a certain skepticism, especially since paranoid suspicions are a common incident of dementia. It would have been imprudent for the detective to have reposed automatic, unquestioning credence in Tunis's accusations against Boyce. She did not. Tunis's accusations were corroborated by the granddaughter, by the staff of the nursing home, and by the lawyer, who was upset to learn that Tunis had granted a power of attorney to her housekeeper when (as Boyce well knew) she had an adult granddaughter. Further corroboration came from the fact that Boyce, though knowing of Tunis's granddaughter, had never informed her that Boyce had a power of attorney, that she was managing Tunis's affairs, and that she was preparing Tunis's property for sale. There thus were grounds for suspicion that Boyce was trying to conceal what she was doing from Tunis's only relative.

Tunis's accusations themselves, moreover, had a degree of particularity that reduced the likelihood that they were merely senile fantasies. It is a common mistake to exaggerate the degree to which senile dementia renders an individual mentally incompetent. There are different types and severities of dementia. The most serious—senile dementia of the Alzheimer's type—is progressive. Some persons afflicted with it exhibit only short-term memory loss and occasional disorientation, while others are so far demented as to have forgotten their own name, to have lost the power of speech, and to be unable to recognize their spouse or their children. See generally Fred Plum, "Dementia," in 1 *Encyclopedia of Neuroscience* 309 (George Adelman ed. 1987). A further complication is that, until the terminal stage that we have just described is reached, the severity of the dementia varies from day to day, even from hour to hour. Mrs. Tunis apparently had good days and bad days. The second interview with Fernandes evidently took place on a good day, because she spoke coherently and precisely, exhibiting a good memory, and nothing she said was bizarre or seemed delusional. Contract law, property law, and criminal law alike have rejected a per se rule that demented persons are legally incompetent. We do not think there should be a different rule for witnesses.

To all this Boyce replies that she had a power of attorney and thus was authorized to take and sell Tunis's personal property. She says that she had stored the furniture in her own garage in preparation for sale, and that if she sold the Cadillac to herself at its market value and gave the proceeds to Tunis she was doing nothing more than transforming Tunis's property into a more convenient form. She adds that if the power of attorney was invalid because Tunis was incompetent at the time she signed it, or even if it was abused, these things would not in themselves convict the power holder of theft in exercising it. And this of course is true. But this is just to say that Fernandes did not have conclusive proof of the theft of the Cadillac. She had a strong, reasonably grounded suspicion and that is all that is required for probable cause. The intimation that a power of attorney immunizes the power holder from a charge of conversion is nonsense. The power creates a fiduciary relation, *In re Estate of Rybolt*, 258 Ill.App.3d 886, 197 Ill.Dec. 570, 573, 631 N.E.2d 792, 795 (1994), and thus an opportunity for abuse by the power holder that is at best tortious and at worst criminal. We were disturbed by the insistence by Boyce's lawyer at argument that the power holder is authorized to convert to her own use any of the grantor's property that has no market value. Although market value is relevant to the gravity of a theft and therefore the length of the thief's sentence, the theft of an item that has no market value is still theft, *Hessel v. O'Hearn*, 977 F.2d 299, 303 (7th Cir.1992), and neither explicitly nor implicitly does a power of attorney authorize the power holder to steal from his grantor. *In re Estate of Rybolt, supra,* 197 Ill.Dec. at 573, 631 N.E.2d at 795. Indeed, the breach of a fiduciary obligation to an elderly person is explicitly a crime in Illinois. 720 ILCS 5/16–1.3(a), (c). No doubt this sort of thing is common, which may be why the legislature decided to single it out for specific prohibition, but crime does not become legal by being widespread.

The lawyer also disparaged the evidence of physical abuse on the ground that his client had not been arrested for such abuse. But the evidence of abuse, like the evidence of the unexplained disappearance of the jewelry and Boyce's failure to disclose to the lawyer that Mrs. Tunis had an adult granddaughter, cast light on Boyce's probable intentions in registering the Cadillac in her own name. The facts turned up in the investigation that preceded her arrest, when they are taken as a whole, would have indicated to a reasonable police officer that Boyce was trying to despoil a vulnerable old woman. The protection of the vulnerable is a noble duty of government. Fernandes is rather to be commended for the speed and thoroughness of her investigation than condemned for having acted before she had assembled conclusive proof of criminal misconduct. The fact that in the end Boyce was not prosecuted does not establish the absence of probable cause, and not only because the legal standard and the evidentiary requirements for probable cause are more stringent at the preliminary hearing than at the arrest stage, the point emphasized in *Williams v. Kobel,* 789 F.2d 463, 469 (7th Cir.1986). The majority of lawfully arrested persons are not prosecuted. Prosecutors' time and other resources are severely limited in relation to the amount of crime in this country, and prosecution may be declined merely because the evidence of guilt is not overwhelming. The State's Attorney may have believed this to be such a case or may have thought that Boyce's arrest would suffice to deter her and perhaps other caretakers of the elderly from abusing their positions. Boyce is herself an elderly woman and prosecuting her for elder abuse might strike a jury as an uncomfortable irony.

It is unfortunate that Boyce, herself a woman of 63 when arrested, was kept in jail for 42 hours. Fernandes cannot be criticized for this sequel to the arrest, however, for she was required to hand Boyce over to the sheriff, and he administers the county jail. Given the overcrowding of American jails, we venture to suggest that a practice of automatic incarceration of all arrested persons, regardless of circumstances, is as wasteful as it is uncivilized. Which is not to say that it entitles the plaintiff to any relief—and certainly not against Detective Fernandes.

* * *

Points for Discussion

a. Adult Neglect

The most common form of elder abuse is neglect, often by a family member or other caregiver who may be overwhelmed with the burdens of providing care. Typically, state statutes provide a basis for charging a paid caregiver with neglect. See, e.g., 18 Pa. Cons. Stat. Ann. § 2713 (2018). Individuals who are not caretakers within the statutory definition, however, may not have a legal duty to act to protect an adult family member from abuse or neglect. If Boyce had been an unpaid family member living with Ms. Tunis, would she have been liable for neglect on these facts? See, e.g., People v. Heitzman, 886 P.2d 1229 (Cal. 1994). See generally Lara Queen Plaisance, *Will You Still . . . When I'm Sixty-Four: Adult Children's Obligation to Aging Parents,* 21 J. Am. Acad. Matrim. Law. 245 (2008).

b. Financial Exploitation

State statutes punish exploitation of an elderly person or disabled adult, typically applying to any individual who has a business relationship with or is in a position of trust and confidence with respect to the victim. See, e.g., Fla. Stat. Ann. § 825.103 (2018). In addition to a caregiver or family member, these statutes may reach various types of mail fraud, telemarketing fraud and other schemes designed to separate the elderly from their money. See generally Shelby A.D. Moore, Jeanettte Schaefer, *Remembering the Forgotten Ones: Protecting the Elderly from Financial Abuse,* 41 San Diego L. Rev. 505 (2004).

c. Protection Orders

State laws often provide a basis for a civil protection orders for elderly or dependent adults. See, e.g., Cal. Wel. & Inst. Code § 15657.03 (2018), applied in Gdowski v. Gdowski, 95 Cal.Rptr.3d 799 (Ct. App. 2009) and Bookout v. Nielsen, 67 Cal.Rptr.3d 2 (Cal. Ct. App. 2007). For a useful survey of issues for practicing lawyers that explores the range of remedies available in one state, see Denis Culley & Hanna Sanders, *Exploitation and Abuse of the Elderly During the Great Recession: A Maine Practitioner's Perspective,* 62 Me. L. Rev. 429 (2010).

────────

C. Parents and Children

Cases decided by the Supreme Court beginning in the 1920s concluded that parents have a liberty interest, protected by the Due Process Clause of the U.S. Constitution, in determining the education and upbringing of their children. Meyer v. Nebraska, 262 U.S. 390 (1923), struck down a state law prohibiting the teaching of foreign languages in public and private schools, and Pierce v. Society of the Sisters of the Holy Names of Jesus and Mary, 268 U.S. 510 (1925), struck a law requiring parents to send their children to public schools. These decisions were deeply conservative, based on the tradition that accorded parents extensive authority and control over their children and reflecting the judicial philosophy of the *Lochner* era. See generally Barbara Bennett Woodhouse, "Who Owns the Child?": Meyer *and* Pierce *and the Child as Property*, 33 Wm. & Mary L. Rev. 995 (1992). The Court reaffirmed the broad principle of *Meyer* and *Pierce* in later cases, however, including Wisconsin v. Yoder, 406 U.S. 205 (1972), which found protection in the First Amendment for parents' decision on religious grounds to keep their children out of school after the eighth grade.

Along with the strong legal protections for parental rights, there are important limits on these rights. The state, acting as **parens patriae** on behalf of its youngest citizens, has a compelling interest in protecting children, reflected in laws requiring parental support and prohibiting child neglect and abuse. In cases of serious harm, the state may remove children from their parents' custody and ultimately terminate parental rights. These issues are covered in Chapter 5. Moreover, contemporary cases have determined that children have some rights of constitutional dimension that may limit their parents' control over decisions such as whether they may use contraception or have an abortion, as addressed in Chapter 3.

Troxel v. Granville

530 U.S. 57 (2000)

Go Online

Listen to the oral arguments in *Troxel* at the Oyez Project web site.

JUSTICE O'CONNOR announced the judgment of the Court and delivered an opinion, in which THE CHIEF JUSTICE, JUSTICE GINSBURG, and JUSTICE BREYER join.

Section 26.10.160(3) of the Revised Code of Washington permits "[a]ny person" to petition a superior court for visitation rights "at any time," and authorizes that court to grant such visitation rights whenever "visitation may serve the best interest of the child." Petitioners Jenifer and Gary Troxel petitioned a

Washington Superior Court for the right to visit their grandchildren, Isabelle and Natalie Troxel. Respondent Tommie Granville, the mother of Isabelle and Natalie, opposed the petition. The case ultimately reached the Washington Supreme Court, which held that § 26.10.160(3) unconstitutionally interferes with the fundamental right of parents to rear their children.

I

Tommie Granville and Brad Troxel shared a relationship that ended in June 1991. The two never married, but they had two daughters, Isabelle and Natalie. Jenifer and Gary Troxel are Brad's parents, and thus the paternal grandparents of Isabelle and Natalie. After Tommie and Brad separated in 1991, Brad lived with his parents and regularly brought his daughters to his parents' home for weekend visitation. Brad committed suicide in May 1993. Although the Troxels at first continued to see Isabelle and Natalie on a regular basis after their son's death, Tommie Granville informed the Troxels in October 1993 that she wished to limit their visitation with her daughters to one short visit per month.

In December 1993, the Troxels commenced the present action by filing, in the Washington Superior Court for Skagit County, a petition to obtain visitation rights with Isabelle and Natalie. The Troxels filed their petition under two Washington statutes, Wash. Rev.Code §§ 26.09.240 and 26.10.160(3) (1994). Only the latter statute is at issue in this case. Section 26.10.160(3) provides: "Any person may petition the court for visitation rights at any time including, but not limited to, custody proceedings. The court may order visitation rights for any person when visitation may serve the best interest of the child whether or not there has been any change of circumstances." At trial, the Troxels requested two weekends of overnight visitation per month and two weeks of visitation each summer. Granville did not oppose visitation altogether, but instead asked the court to order one day of visitation per month with no overnight stay. In 1995, the Superior Court issued an oral ruling and entered a visitation decree ordering visitation one weekend per month, one week during the summer, and four hours on both of the petitioning grandparents' birthdays.

Granville appealed, during which time she married Kelly Wynn. Before addressing the merits of Granville's appeal, the Washington Court of Appeals remanded the case to the Superior Court for entry of written findings of fact and conclusions of law. On remand, the Superior Court found that visitation was in Isabelle and Natalie's best interests:

> "The Petitioners [the Troxels] are part of a large, central, loving family, all located in this area, and the Petitioners can provide opportunities for the children in the areas of cousins and music.

". . .The court took into consideration all factors regarding the best interest of the children and considered all the testimony before it. The children would be benefitted from spending quality time with the Petitioners, provided that that time is balanced with time with the childrens' [sic] nuclear family. The court finds that the childrens' [sic] best interests are served by spending time with their mother and stepfather's other six children."

Approximately nine months after the Superior Court entered its order on remand, Granville's husband formally adopted Isabelle and Natalie.

FYI

The Court explains that the Washington Supreme Court reversed the visitation order, holding that § 26.10.160(3) unconstitutionally infringed on the fundamental right of parents to rear their children. That court found the statute unconstitutional because it required no threshold showing of harm before the state interfered with parents' decisions, and because the statute allowed "any person" to petition for visitation at "any time" with the only requirement being that the visitation serve the best interest of the child.

* * *

We granted certiorari, and now affirm the judgment.

II

The demographic changes of the past century make it difficult to speak of an average American family. The composition of families varies greatly from household to household. While many children may have two married parents and grandparents who visit regularly, many other children are raised in single-parent households. In 1996, children living with only one parent accounted for 28 percent of all children under age 18 in the United States. U.S. Dept. of Commerce, Bureau of Census, Current Population Reports, 1997 Population Profile of the United States 27 (1998). Understandably, in these single-parent households, persons outside the nuclear family are called upon with increasing frequency to assist in the everyday tasks of child rearing. In many cases, grandparents play an important role. For example, in 1998, approximately 4 million children—or 5.6 percent of all children under age 18—lived in the household of their grandparents. U.S. Dept. of Commerce, Bureau of Census, Current Population Reports, Marital Status and Living Arrangements: March 1998 (Update), p. i (1998).

The nationwide enactment of nonparental visitation statutes is assuredly due, in some part, to the States' recognition of these changing realities of the American family. Because grandparents and other relatives undertake duties of a parental nature in many households, States have sought to ensure the welfare of the children therein by protecting the relationships those children form with such third parties. The States' nonparental visitation statutes are further supported by a recognition, which varies from State to State, that children should have the opportunity to benefit from relationships with statutorily specified persons—for example, their grandparents. The extension of statutory rights in this area to persons other than a child's parents, however, comes with an obvious cost. For example, the State's recognition of an independent third-party interest in a child can place a substantial burden on the traditional parent-child relationship. Contrary to Justice STEVENS' accusation, our description of state nonparental visitation statutes in these terms, of course, is not meant to suggest that "children are so much chattel." Rather, our terminology is intended to highlight the fact that these statutes can present questions of constitutional import. In this case, we are presented with just such a question. Specifically, we are asked to decide whether § 26.10.160(3), as applied to Tommie Granville and her family, violates the Federal Constitution.

The Fourteenth Amendment provides that no State shall "deprive any person of life, liberty, or property, without due process of law." We have long recognized that the Amendment's Due Process Clause, like its Fifth Amendment counterpart, "guarantees more than fair process." Washington v. Glucksberg, 521 U.S. 702 (1997). The Clause also includes a substantive component that "provides heightened protection against government interference with certain fundamental rights and liberty interests." Id., at 720; see also Reno v. Flores, 507 U.S. 292, 301–302 (1993).

Think About It

How does the Court define the constitutional right it recognizes in this case?

The liberty interest at issue in this case—the interest of parents in the care, custody, and control of their children—is perhaps the oldest of the fundamental liberty interests recognized by this Court. More than 75 years ago, in Meyer v. Nebraska, 262 U.S. 390, 399, 401 (1923), we held that the "liberty" protected by the Due Process Clause includes the right of parents to "establish a home and bring up children" and "to control the education of their own." Two years later, in Pierce v. Society of the Sisters of the Holy Names of Jesus and Mary, 268 U.S. 510, 534–535 (1925), we again held that the "liberty of parents and guardians" includes the right "to direct the upbringing and education of children under their control." We explained in Pierce that "[t]he child is not the mere creature of the State; those who nurture him and direct his destiny have the right, coupled with the high duty, to recognize and prepare him for additional obligations." Id., at 535. We returned to the subject in Prince v. Massachusetts, 321 U.S. 158 (1944), and again confirmed that there is a constitutional dimension to the right of parents to direct the upbringing of their children. "It is cardinal with us that the custody, care and nurture of the child reside first in the parents, whose primary function and freedom include preparation for obligations the state can neither supply nor hinder."

In subsequent cases also, we have recognized the fundamental right of parents to make decisions concerning the care, custody, and control of their children. See, e.g., Stanley v. Illinois, 405 U.S. 645, 651 (1972) ("It is plain that the interest of a parent in the companionship, care, custody, and management of his or her children 'come[s] to this Court with a momentum for respect lacking when appeal is made to liberties which derive merely from shifting economic arrangements' "(citation omitted)); Wisconsin v. Yoder, 406 U.S. 205, 232 (1972) ("The history and culture of Western civilization reflect a strong tradition of parental concern for the nurture and upbringing of their children. This primary role of the parents in the upbringing of their children is now established beyond debate as an enduring American tradition"); Quilloin v. Walcott, 434 U.S. 246, 255 (1978) ("We have recognized on numerous occasions that the relationship between parent and child is constitutionally protected"); Parham v. J. R., 442 U.S. 584, 602 (1979) ("Our jurisprudence historically has reflected Western civilization concepts of the family as a unit with broad parental authority over minor children. Our cases have consistently followed that course"); Santosky v. Kramer, 455 U.S. 745, 753 (1982) (discussing "[t]he fundamental liberty interest of natural parents in the care, custody, and management of their child"); Glucksberg, supra, at 720 ("In a long line of cases, we have held that, in addition to the specific freedoms protected by the Bill of Rights, the 'liberty' specially protected by the Due Process Clause includes the righ[t]. . .to direct the education and upbringing of one's children" (citing Meyer and Pierce)). In light of this extensive precedent, it cannot now be doubted that the Due Process Clause of the Fourteenth Amendment protects the fundamental right of parents to make decisions concerning the care, custody, and control of their children.

Section 26.10.160(3), as applied to Granville and her family in this case, unconstitutionally infringes on that fundamental parental right. The Washington nonparental visitation statute is breathtakingly broad. According to the statute's text, "[a]ny person may petition the court for visitation rights at any time," and the court may grant such visitation rights whenever "visitation may serve the best interest of the child." § 26.10.160(3) (emphases added). That language effectively permits any third party seeking visitation to subject any

Think About It

The plurality concludes that the Washington statute is unconstitutional as applied in this case. How or when could the statute be applied in a manner that these four justices would find to be constitutional?

decision by a parent concerning visitation of the parent's children to state-court review. Once the visitation petition has been filed in court and the matter is placed before a judge, a parent's decision that visitation would not be in the child's best interest is accorded no deference. Section 26.10.160(3) contains no requirement that a court accord the parent's decision any presumption of validity or any weight whatsoever. Instead, the Washington statute places the best-interest determination solely in the hands of the judge. Should the judge disagree with the parent's estimation of the child's best interests, the judge's view necessarily prevails. Thus, in practical effect, in the State of Washington a court can disregard and overturn any decision by a fit custodial parent concerning visitation whenever a third party affected by the decision files a visitation petition, based solely on the judge's determination of the child's best interests. The Washington Supreme Court had the opportunity to give § 26.10.160(3) a narrower reading, but it declined to do so.

Turning to the facts of this case, the record reveals that the Superior Court's order was based on precisely the type of mere disagreement we have just described and nothing more. The Superior Court's order was not founded on any special factors that might justify the State's interference with Granville's fundamental right to make decisions concerning the rearing of her two daughters. To be sure, this case involves a visitation petition filed by grandparents soon after the death of their son—the father of Isabelle and Natalie—but the combination of several factors here compels our conclusion that § 26.10.160(3), as applied, exceeded the bounds of the Due Process Clause.

First, the Troxels did not allege, and no court has found, that Granville was an unfit parent. That aspect of the case is important, for there is a presumption that fit parents act in the best interests of their children. As this Court explained in *Parham*:

> "[O]ur constitutional system long ago rejected any notion that a child is the mere creature of the State and, on the contrary, asserted that parents generally have the right, coupled with the high duty, to recognize and prepare [their children] for additional obligations. . . .The law's concept of the family rests on a presumption that parents possess what a child lacks in maturity, experience, and capacity for judgment required for making life's difficult decisions. More important, historically it has recognized that natural bonds of affection lead parents to act in the best interests of their children." 442 U.S., at 602, 99 S.Ct. 2493 (alteration in original) (internal quotation marks and citations omitted).

Accordingly, so long as a parent adequately cares for his or her children (i.e., is fit), there will normally be no reason for the State to inject itself into the private realm of the family to further question the ability of that parent to make the best decisions concerning the rearing of that parent's children.

The problem here is not that the Washington Superior Court intervened, but that when it did so, it gave no special weight at all to Granville's determination of her daughters' best interests. More importantly, it appears that the Superior Court applied exactly the opposite presumption. In reciting its oral ruling after the conclusion of closing arguments, the Superior Court judge explained:

> "The burden is to show that it is in the best interest of the children to have some visitation and some quality time with their grandparents. I think in most situations a commonsensical approach [is that] it is normally in the best interest of the children to spend quality time with the grandparent, unless the grandparent, [sic] there are some issues or problems involved wherein the grandparents, their lifestyles are going to impact adversely upon the children. That certainly isn't the case here from what I can tell."

The judge's comments suggest that he presumed the grandparents' request should be granted unless the children would be "impact[ed] adversely." In effect, the judge placed on Granville, the fit custodial parent, the burden of disproving that visitation would be in the best interest of her daughters. The judge reiterated moments later: "I think [visitation with the Troxels] would be in the best interest of the children and I haven't been shown it is not in [the] best interest of the children."

The decisional framework employed by the Superior Court directly contravened the traditional presumption that a fit parent will act in the best interest of his or her child. See Parham, supra, at 602. In that respect, the court's presumption failed to provide any protection for Granville's fundamental constitutional right to make decisions concerning the rearing of her own daughters. Cf., e.g., Cal. Fam.Code Ann. § 3104(e) (West 1994) (rebuttable presumption that grandparent visitation is not in child's best interest if parents agree that visitation rights should not be granted); Me.Rev.Stat. Ann., Tit. 19A, § 1803(3) (1998) (court may award grandparent visitation if in best interest of child and "would not significantly interfere with any parent-child relationship or with the parent's rightful authority over the child"); Minn.Stat. § 257.022(2)(a)(2) (1998) (court may award grandparent visitation if in best interest of child and "such visitation would not interfere with the parent-child relationship"); Neb.Rev.Stat. § 43–1802(2) (1998) (court must find "by clear and convincing evidence" that grandparent visitation "will not adversely interfere with the parent-child relationship"); R.I. Gen. Laws § 15–5–24.3(a)(2)(v) (Supp.1999) (grandparent must rebut, by clear and convincing evidence, presumption that parent's decision to refuse grandparent visitation was reasonable); Utah Code Ann. § 30–5–2(2)(e) (1998) (same); Hoff v. Berg, 595 N.W.2d 285, 291–292 (N.D.1999) (holding North Dakota grandparent visitation statute unconstitutional because State has no "compelling interest in presuming visitation rights of grandparents to an unmarried minor are in the child's best interests and forcing parents to accede to court-ordered grandparental visitation unless the parents are first able to prove such visitation is not in the best interests of their minor child"). In an ideal world, parents might always seek to cultivate the bonds between grandparents and their grandchildren. Needless to say, however, our world is far from perfect, and in it the decision whether such an intergenerational relationship would be beneficial in any specific case is for the parent to make in the first instance. And, if a fit parent's decision of the kind at issue here becomes subject to judicial review, the court must accord at least some special weight to the parent's own determination.

Finally, we note that there is no allegation that Granville ever sought to cut off visitation entirely. Rather, the present dispute originated when Granville informed the Troxels that she would prefer to restrict their visitation with Isabelle and Natalie to one short visit per month and special holidays. In the Superior Court proceedings Granville did not oppose visitation but instead asked that the duration of any visitation order be shorter than that requested by the Troxels. While the Troxels requested two weekends per month and two full weeks in the summer, Granville asked the Superior Court to order only one day of visitation per month (with no overnight stay) and participation in the Granville family's holiday celebrations. The Superior Court gave no weight to Granville's having assented to visitation even before the filing of any visitation petition or subsequent court intervention. The court instead rejected Granville's proposal and settled on a middle ground, ordering one weekend of visitation per month, one week in the summer, and time on both of the petitioning grandparents' birthdays. Significantly, many other States expressly provide by statute that courts may not award visitation unless a parent has denied (or unreasonably denied) visitation to the concerned third party. See, e.g., Miss.Code Ann. § 93–16–3(2)(a) (1994) (court must find that "the parent or custodian of the child unreasonably denied the grandparent visitation rights with the child"); Ore.Rev.Stat. § 109.121(1)(a)(B) (1997) (court may award visitation if the "custodian of the child has denied the grandparent reasonable opportunity to visit the child"); R.I. Gen. Laws § 15–5–24.3(a)(2)(iii)–(iv) (Supp.1999) (court must find that parents prevented grandparent from visiting grandchild and that "there is no other way the petitioner is able to visit his or her grandchild without court intervention").

Considered together with the Superior Court's reasons for awarding visitation to the Troxels, the combination of these factors demonstrates that the visitation order in this case was an unconstitutional infringement on Granville's fundamental right to make decisions concerning the care, custody, and control of her two daughters. The Washington Superior Court failed to accord the determination of Granville, a fit custodial parent, any material weight. In fact, the Superior Court made only two formal findings in support of its visitation order. First, the Troxels "are part of a large, central, loving family, all located in this area, and the [Troxels] can provide opportunities for the children in the areas of cousins and music." Second, "[t]he children would be benefitted from spending quality time with the [Troxels], provided that that time is balanced with time with the childrens' [sic] nuclear family." These slender findings, in combination with the court's announced presumption in favor of grandparent visitation and its failure to accord significant weight to Granville's already having offered meaningful visitation to the Troxels, show that this case involves nothing more than a simple disagreement between the Washington Superior Court and Granville concerning her children's best interests. The Superior Court's announced reason for ordering one week of visitation in the summer demonstrates our conclusion well: "I look back on some personal experiences. . . . We always spen[t] as kids a week with one set of grandparents and another set of grandparents, [and] it happened to work out in our family that [it] turned out to be an enjoyable experience. Maybe that can, in this family, if that is how it works out." As we have explained, the Due Process Clause does not permit a State to infringe on the fundamental right of parents to make childrearing decisions simply because a state judge believes a "better" decision could be made. Neither the Washington nonparental visitation statute generally—which places no limits on either the persons who may petition for visitation or the circumstances in which such a petition may be granted—nor the Superior Court in this specific case required anything more. Accordingly, we hold that § 26.10.160(3), as applied in this case, is unconstitutional.

Because we rest our decision on the sweeping breadth of § 26.10.160(3) and the application of that broad, unlimited power in this case, we do not consider the primary constitutional question passed on by the Washington Supreme Court—whether the Due Process Clause requires all nonparental visitation statutes to include a showing of harm or potential harm to the child as a condition precedent to granting visitation. We do not, and need not, define today the precise scope of the parental due process right in the visitation context. In this respect, we agree with Justice KENNEDY that the constitutionality of any standard for awarding visitation turns on the specific manner in which that standard is applied and that the constitutional protections in this area are best "elaborated with care." Because much state-court adjudication in this context occurs on a case-by-case basis, we would be hesitant to hold that specific nonparental visitation statutes violate the

Due Process Clause as a per se matter.* See, e.g., <u>Fairbanks v. McCarter, 330 Md. 39, 49–50, 622 A.2d 121, 126–127 (1993)</u> (interpreting best-interest standard in grandparent visitation statute normally to require court's consideration of certain factors); <u>Williams v. Williams, 256 Va. 19, 501 S.E.2d 417, 418 (1998)</u> (interpreting Virginia nonparental visitation statute to require finding of harm as condition precedent to awarding visitation).

* * *

There is thus no reason to remand the case for further proceedings in the Washington Supreme Court. As Justice KENNEDY recognizes, the burden of litigating a domestic relations proceeding can itself be "so disruptive of the parent-child relationship that the constitutional right of a custodial parent to make certain basic determinations for the child's welfare becomes implicated." In this case, the litigation costs incurred by Granville on her trip through the Washington court system and to this Court are without a doubt already substantial. As we have explained, it is apparent that the entry of the visitation order in this case violated the Constitution. We should say so now, without forcing the parties into additional litigation that would further burden Granville's parental right. We therefore hold that the application of § 26.10.160(3) to Granville and her family violated her due process right to make decisions concerning the care, custody, and control of her daughters.

Accordingly, the judgment of the Washington Supreme Court is affirmed.

It is so ordered.

---

* All 50 States have statutes that provide for grandparent visitation in some form. See <u>Ala.Code § 30–3–4.1 (1989)</u>; <u>Alaska Stat. Ann. § 25.20.065 (1998)</u>; <u>Ariz.Rev.Stat. Ann. § 25–409 (1994)</u>; <u>Ark. Code Ann. § 9–13–103 (1998)</u>; Cal. Fam.Code Ann. § 3104 (West 1994); <u>Colo.Rev.Stat. § 19–1–117 (1999)</u>; <u>Conn. Gen.Stat. § 46b–59 (1995)</u>; <u>Del.Code Ann., Tit. 10, § 1031(7) (1999)</u>; <u>Fla. Stat. § 752.01 (1997)</u>; <u>Ga.Code Ann. § 19–7–3 (1991)</u>; Haw.Rev.Stat. § 571–46.3 (1999); <u>Idaho Code § 32–719 (1999)</u>; <u>Ill. Comp. Stat., ch. 750, § 5/607 (1998)</u>; <u>Ind.Code § 31–17–5–1 (1999)</u>; <u>Iowa Code § 598.35 (1999)</u>; <u>Kan. Stat. Ann. § 38–129 (1993)</u>; <u>Ky.Rev.Stat. Ann. § 405.021 (Baldwin 1990)</u>; <u>La.Rev.Stat. Ann. § 9:344 (West Supp.2000)</u>; <u>La. Civ.Code Ann., Art. 136 (West Supp.2000)</u>; <u>Me.Rev. Stat. Ann., Tit. 19A, § 1803 (1998)</u>; <u>Md. Fam. Law Code Ann. § 9–102 (1999)</u>; Mass. Gen. Laws § 119:39D (1996); <u>Mich. Comp. Laws Ann. § 722.27b (Supp.1999)</u>; <u>Minn.Stat. § 257.022 (1998)</u>; <u>Miss.Code Ann. § 93–16–3 (1994)</u>; <u>Mo.Rev.Stat. § 452.402 (Supp.1999)</u>; <u>Mont.Code Ann. § 40–9–102 (1997)</u>; <u>Neb.Rev.Stat. § 43–1802 (1998)</u>; <u>Nev.Rev.Stat. § 125C.050 (Supp.1999)</u>; <u>N.H.Rev.Stat. Ann. § 458:17–d (1992)</u>; <u>N.J. Stat. Ann. § 9:2–7.1 (West Supp.1999–2000)</u>; <u>N.M. Stat. Ann. § 40–9–2 (1999)</u>; <u>N.Y. Dom. Rel. Law § 72 (McKinney 1999)</u>; <u>N.C. Gen.Stat. §§ 50–13.2, 50–13.2A (1999)</u>; N.D. Cent.Code § 14–09–05.1 (1997); <u>Ohio Rev.Code Ann. §§ 3109.051, 3109.11 (Supp.1999)</u>; <u>Okla. Stat., Tit. 10, § 5 (Supp.1999)</u>; <u>Ore.Rev.Stat. § 109.121 (1997)</u>; <u>23 Pa. Cons.Stat. §§ 5311–5313 (1991)</u>; <u>R.I. Gen. Laws §§ 15–5–24 to 15–5–24.3 (Supp.1999)</u>; <u>S.C.Code Ann. § 20–7–420(33) (Supp.1999)</u>; <u>S.D. Codified Laws § 25–4–52 (1999)</u>; <u>Tenn.Code Ann. §§ 36–6–306, 36–6–307 (Supp.1999)</u>; <u>Tex. Fam.Code Ann. § 153.433 (Supp.2000)</u>; Utah Code Ann. § 30–5–2 (1998); <u>Vt. Stat. Ann., Tit. 15, §§ 1011–1013 (1989)</u>; <u>Va.Code Ann. § 20–124.2 (1995)</u>; <u>W. Va.Code §§ 48–2B–1 to 48–2B–7 (1999)</u>; <u>Wis. Stat. §§ 767.245, 880.155 (1993–1994)</u>; <u>Wyo. Stat. Ann. § 20–7–101 (1999)</u>.

FYI

Troxel produced a total of six decisions from the Court. Justice Souter concurred in the judgment, concluding that the statute was facially unconstitutional. Justice Thomas concurred in the judgment, stating that he would apply strict scrutiny and noting that the state "lacks even a legitimate governmental interest. . .in second-guessing a fit parent's decision regarding visitation with fit parties."

Justice Scalia dissented in *Troxel* on the basis that substantive due process protection for parental rights should not be extended beyond what was recognized in the cases of *Meyer*, *Pierce*, and *Wisconsin v. Yoder*. Justice Stevens wrote a separate dissent, arguing that a parent's interests must be balanced against "the child's own complementary interest in preserving relationships that serve her welfare and protection" and concluding that "the Due Process Clause of the Fourteenth Amendment leaves room for states to consider the impact on a child of possibly arbitrary parental decisions that neither serve nor are motivated by the best interests of the child." Justice Kennedy also dissented, agreeing that parents have a fundamental constitutional right but concluding that it would be more appropriate to test the constitutionality of the "best interests" standard in the Washington statute based on factors such as whether the third party was a complete stranger, another parent, or a de facto parent. He was particularly concerned with cases in which a third party has acted in a caregiving role over a significant period of time.

For more on *Troxel*, see Ariela R. Dubler, *Constructing the Modern American Family: The Stories of* Troxel v. Granville, in Family Law Stories (Carol Sanger, ed., 2008).

Points for Discussion

a. *Troxel*

What governmental interests support the third party visitation laws enacted in all fifty states? Why does the plurality conclude that these interests are not sufficient to sustain the Washington statute? Justice O'Connor's plurality opinion in *Troxel* characterized the parental right as a "fundamental" one, a view shared by Justices Souter, Thomas, and Kennedy (and perhaps by Justice Stevens). Is Justice Thomas correct in concluding that any legislation infringing this right must therefore be subject to "strict scrutiny"?

David Meyer has noted that although the Supreme Court has routinely described family privacy rights as fundamental, it has taken a pragmatic and flexible approach to these cases rather than applying traditional strict scrutiny. David D. Meyer, *The Paradox of Family Privacy*, 53 Vand. L. Rev. 527 (2000); David D. Meyer, *Constitutional Pragmatism for a Changing American Family*, 32 Rutgers L.J. 711 (2001). How does the opinion in *Troxel* compare with other constitutional decisions you have read in the family law area?

b. Parental Presumptions

Courts deciding custody disputes between a legal parent and a non-parent do not apply the "best interests of the child" test usually used for disputes between parents. Rather, there is a longstanding presumption that a legal parent should be entitled to custody unless the parent is shown

Make the Connection

Custody and visitation rights for parents and third parties are discussed in Chapter 7.

to be unfit, or there is some other compelling reason to place the child in another person's custody. What constitutional arguments could be made for and against this presumption? What should a person other than a legal parent be required to establish in order to be awarded custodial rights and responsibilities?

c. Parental Rights in the Common Law

Make the Connection

The relationship of grandparents and grandchildren is discussed later in this chapter in *Moore v. City of East Cleveland, Ohio.*

Parental rights are deeply rooted in the common law tradition, which extended the father's power over his children until they reached the age of 21, even though children were treated as adults for some purposes at earlier ages. For example, children acquired the legal capacity to marry at age 12 for girls and 14 for boys, but could not marry without their fathers' consent before age 21. Children younger than seven were deemed to be incapable of committing crimes, children over fourteen were treated as having the same criminal responsibility as adults, and children between seven and fourteen could be held criminally responsible if the prosecution established they had sufficient intelligence to form a criminal intent. Children could be placed as apprentices by the age of seven, but their earnings belonged to their fathers until they turned 21. Under the common law, children could own property and enter into contracts, but had the power to disaffirm conveyances or contracts when they reach the age of majority. See generally Homer H. Clark, Jr., Domestic Relations §§ 8.1–8.2 (Student 2d ed. 1988).

Parents, Children and Torts

Although children are generally liable for their own torts, many jurisdictions have statutes making parents responsible as well. In some states, liability requires a showing that the parent was at fault, on grounds such as a failure to exercise reasonable control or supervision. See, e.g., <u>N.J. Stat. Ann. § 2A:53A-15 (2018)</u>; <u>Tenn. Code Ann. § 37–10–103 (2018)</u>. Some states impose vicarious liability on parents for a minor child's intentional torts, sometimes subject to a maximum recovery. See, e.g., <u>Cal. Civ. Code § 1714.1 (2018)</u>; <u>Distinctive Printing and Packaging Co. v. Cox, 443 N.W.2d 566 (Neb. 1989)</u>. <u>In the Interest of B.D., 720 So.2d 476 (Miss.1998)</u>, upheld a Mississippi statute authorizing orders against parents to make financial restitution for damage done by their children.

When a child suffers an injury, there are complex rules governing litigation or settlement of the child's claims in order to safeguard the child's interests. A parent does not ordinarily have the authority to settle the child's claim, unless the parent has been appointed as a guardian, and settlements are subject to the court's approval. See generally 1 Homer H. Clark, Jr., Domestic Relations § 9.2 (2d ed. 1987). Courts have sometimes declined to give effect to liability waivers signed by parents for children participating in activities such as skiing and horseback riding, concluding that a parent or guardian does not have authority to release a minor's future claim for negligence. See generally <u>BJ's Wholesale Club v. Rosen, 80 A.3d. 345 (Md. 2013)</u> (discussing cases).

Because a child's earnings were the property of his or her parent under the common law, a parent was entitled to recover in tort for the loss of a child's services or earnings if the child was negligently injured by a third person. See <u>Restatement (Second) of Torts § 703 (1977)</u>. Some courts have abolished this claim, however, on the basis that a child's services no longer have economic value. See, e.g., <u>Baxter v. Superior Court of Los Angeles County, 563 P.2d 871 (Cal. 1977)</u>. A few jurisdictions permit a parent to sue for loss of a child's consortium after a negligent injury, see, e.g., Gallimore v. Children's Hospital Medical Center, 617 N.E.2d 1052 (Ohio 1993), and Shockley v. Prier, 225 N.W.2d 495 (Wis. 1975), but others refuse to allow parents to bring this type of claim, see, e.g., Vitro v. Mihelcic, 806 N.E.2d 632 (Ill. 2004); Sizemore v. Smock, 422 N.W.2d 666 (Mich. 1988); Siciliano v. Capitol City Shows, Inc., 475 A.2d 19 (N.H. 1984); Roberts v. Williamson, 111 S.W.3d 113 (Tex. 2003); and Boucher v. Dixie Medical Center, a Div. of IHC Hospitals, Inc., 850 P.2d 1179 (Utah 1992). Courts have generally not been receptive to claims by children for the loss of parental consortium after tortious injury to their parents. See, e.g., Gaver v. Harrant, 557 A.2d 210 (Md. 1989); see also Restatement (Second) of Torts § 707A (1977); but see Villareal v. State Department of Transportation, 774 P.2d 213 (Ariz. 1989) and Campos v. Coleman, 123 A.3d 854 (Conn. 2015) (allowing action for loss of parental consortium).

When courts have been faced with tort actions against a parent on behalf of a child, many have refused to allow recovery based on a theory of parent-child immunity from suit. This area of the law has been in flux, however, with some states establishing an immunity rule and later abolishing it or creating exceptions for particular categories of cases, such as claims of sexual abuse. See, e.g., Newman v. Cole, 872 So.2d 138 (Ala. 2003) and Herzfeld v. Herzfeld, 781 So.2d 1070 (Fla. 2001); see also Restatement (Second) of Torts § 895G (1977) (rejecting parent-child tort immunity).

————————

Diamond v. Diamond

283 P.3d 260 (N.M. 2012)

OPINION

SERNA, JUSTICE.

{1} This appeal presents this Court with a matter of first impression: does the New Mexico Emancipation of Minors Act, NMSA 1978, §§ 32A–21–1 to –7 (1995) (the Act), which provides that a minor may be emancipated for "one or more purposes" set forth in the Act, *see* Section 32A–21–7(D), authorize a district court to declare a minor emancipated for some rather than all of those enumerated purposes? Based on the plain language and legislative purpose of the Act, we answer that question in the affirmative and accordingly reverse the Court of Appeals.

I. BACKGROUND

{2} Petitioner Jhette Diamond (Daughter), then sixteen years old, petitioned the district court in January 2007 for a declaration of emancipation pursuant to the Act. Daughter left the home of her mother Adrienne Diamond (Mother) at age thirteen and had been living with several different households since that time.

{3} The district court held a hearing on Daughter's petition in February 2007. Mother did not appear at the hearing or otherwise oppose the petition. Daughter, represented by counsel, told the district court that she had moved out of Mother's home due to domestic violence and substance abuse issues. Daughter had been working since the age of eleven, including for the past several years as a restaurant server and busser, while maintaining a high grade-point average as a sophomore at Española Valley High School. Counsel described Daughter as "focused on her future," and thriving with the support of the couple with whom she was living. Daughter had no intention of returning to live with Mother, who maintained a relationship with the man whose violent behavior and substance abuse had contributed to Daughter's decision to leave Mother's home in the first place.

{4} The district court concluded that by all accounts Daughter was capable of making appropriate choices for herself and covering her own expenses, describing Daughter's situation as "a classic case" for emancipation. Because Mother had not provided any financial support to Daughter before or after Daughter began living apart from Mother, Daughter asked if the emancipation order could be styled to reserve her right to pursue financial support from Mother. The court agreed provided that counsel could confirm that the Act authorized the court to do so.

{5} The district court issued a "Declaration of Emancipation of Minor" in March 2007, finding that Daughter had been living independently and managing her own financial affairs without support from Mother, determining that emancipation would be in Daughter's best interest, and declaring Daughter "an emancipated minor in all respects, except that she shall retain the right to support from [Mother]" pursuant to Section 32A–21–5(D) of the Act. Mother filed a pro se motion to set aside the declaration because she had not received adequate notice of the original emancipation hearing. Mother additionally argued that she had supported Daughter even after Daughter moved out by paying for Daughter's traffic tickets, medical and dental care, and school clothes, and "[was] always giving [Daughter] spending money." Mother also disputed that Daughter was managing her own financial affairs.

{6} The district court held a hearing on Mother's pro se motion in April 2007. Mother repeated her objections to Daughter's emancipation because, in her view, Daughter was not mature enough to act in her own best interest. The district court asked Mother for evidence or examples of Daughter's lack of maturity, and Mother could not think of any.

{7} Consistent with her prior representations to the court, Daughter testified that she had been working since age eleven. Daughter added that during the time she was still living with Mother, her earnings went to household expenses such as utility bills, and stated that "whenever my mom asked me for money, I gave it to her." Daughter also reiterated that she had left Mother's home due to violence that Mother's boyfriend perpetrated against both Mother and Daughter, as well as the boyfriend's chronic alcohol and drug abuse.

{8} The incident precipitating Daughter's decision to stop living with Mother, Daughter testified, took place in October 2003. One evening, in the course of an argument, Mother's boyfriend shook Mother and threw her against a bed. Mother began to have a panic attack, and her boyfriend departed. Although she was only thirteen years old at the time, Daughter drove Mother to the hospital. Some time after Mother and Daughter returned from the hospital, Mother's boyfriend reappeared at their home and demanded to see Mother. Daughter told him to leave. Mother's boyfriend pushed his way into the home, and when Daughter continued to block his access to Mother, the boyfriend picked Daughter up and threw her over a couch. Daughter kicked the boyfriend in the face and he again left the home.

{9} After this altercation, Daughter told Mother that she did not want Mother's boyfriend to come over to their home anymore. Instead of asking her boyfriend to stay away, Mother went to live with him at his home, leaving Daughter alone in their trailer with no water, gas, or electricity service due to unpaid bills. Daughter remained in the trailer until being evicted several months later in the middle of winter. During this period, Daughter continued to work and attend school full time. Because there was no food at Mother's home, Daughter frequently obtained food from a woman who employed her at a local restaurant.

{10} Daughter then lived for several months with neighbors, again while attending school full time and remaining employed. She later moved in with the brother of one of her neighbors, where she lived for several years, continuing to work at a local restaurant, paying for her own expenses and contributing to rent and other household expenses. Several months before filing her petition for emancipation, Daughter began living with members of the same extended family, a couple who allowed her to stay with them rent-free so that she could focus on school.

{11} Disputing Mother's assertions about having covered certain expenses, Daughter testified that it was actually a concerned teacher who paid for her traffic ticket, that Daughter herself paid for dental care, and that Medicaid covered the cost of medical care when Daughter broke her arm at school. Daughter acknowledged that on a single occasion Mother had purchased several items of clothing for her, but that she could not recall Mother ever providing her with spending money, contrary to Mother's claim that she "always" did so. Daughter testified that since living apart from Mother, she would visit Mother at her home approximately once a month but that she could remember only a handful of occasions when Mother visited her or otherwise attempted to contact her, including once when Mother turned up at Daughter's school to ask her for money.

{12} Daughter also explained why she was seeking emancipation. Although at that point in time she had already been living apart from her Mother for two to three years, paying her own expenses, attending school, and working, Daughter testified that she had difficulty obtaining medical insurance, accessing her school report cards, or applying for a driver's permit, all of which required parental consent. Emancipated status also would allow Daughter to open a bank account. Daughter stated that she would be uncomfortable if she were required to resume living with Mother, especially because Mother's abusive boyfriend remained a presence in Mother's home, and because she was doing well on her own.

{13} After hearing testimony from Mother and Daughter, the district court ruled from the bench that even assuming that all of Mother's contentions were true, emancipation remained in Daughter's best interest. The district court then re-declared Daughter to be emancipated and issued a formal order to that effect, which included the same provision as the court's prior order that Daughter was "an emancipated minor in all respects, except that she shall retain the right to support from [Mother]" pursuant to Section 32A–21–D(5) of the Act.

{14} As permitted by the district court's emancipation orders, in February 2008 Daughter filed a petition asking the district court to order Mother to pay retroactive and prospective child support to Daughter. Although Daughter's support petition was not expressly denominated as such, the parties and the district court treated it as an action to establish parentage and for support under the Uniform Parentage Act, NMSA 1978, §§ 40–11–1 to –23 (1986, as amended through 2004) (repealed and recodified at NMSA 1978, §§ 40–11A–101 to –903 (2009)).

{15} A hearing officer determined that Mother had not provided a home or financial support for Daughter since Daughter's emancipation. The hearing officer recommended that Mother be ordered to make support payments to Daughter in the amount of $390.00 per month from March 1, 2008 until Daughter reached the age of eighteen or graduated from high school, whichever event occurred later. The hearing officer reserved for later determination the issue of any child support obligation predating March 1, 2008 (including periods of time both predating and following Daughter's emancipation). The district court affirmed the hearing officer's report over Mother's written objections, and in January 2009 directed that a portion of Mother's retirement benefit, her sole source of income, be garnished and paid to Daughter.

{16} The parties filed several subsequent motions before the district court in summer and fall 2009, with Mother now represented by counsel. Mother principally argued that "New Mexico law does not allow child support for an emancipated minor." In these subsequent proceedings, Mother and Daughter repeated much of their prior testimony regarding disputed facts germane to the support issue. In addition, Daughter clarified that her separation from Mother took place in October 2004, rather than October 2003 as she had originally claimed. Daughter also testified that since petitioning for emancipation she had graduated from high school and was now a student at New Mexico State University. Mother, meanwhile, testified that she and Daughter were living together until December 2004 or January 2005. Mother also acknowledged that until March 2009, well past the time of Daughter's emancipation, she maintained an on-again, off-again relationship with the same boyfriend who had behaved violently toward Daughter.

{17} The district court reaffirmed its prior ruling that emancipation does not necessarily cut off a minor's right to child support. The court determined that Daughter began living apart from Mother permanently in January 2005, but that Mother's support obligation would begin in March 2005. The court concluded that Daughter was entitled to support from that time through May 2009, when Daughter graduated from high school at age eighteen, in an amount based on statutory guidelines and Mother's income. Accordingly, the court entered judgment in Daughter's favor in the amount of $15,278.00 (with $13,640.00 of that total owed as pre-emancipation support, and $1,638.00 owed as the remaining balance from the period post-dating Daughter's emancipation), and directed Mother to make specified monthly payments to fulfill her support obligation.

{18} Mother appealed the judgment entered against her in the support proceeding and a related order from the original emancipation proceeding. The Court of Appeals consolidated the two appeals. *Diamond v. Diamond*, 2011–NMCA–002, ¶ 1, 149 N.M. 133, 245 P.3d 578. Agreeing with Mother, the Court of Appeals held that "New Mexico law does not permit a minor emancipated pursuant to [the Act] to collect child support payments," and does not permit "an emancipating court to pick and choose the purposes for which a child is emancipated." The Court of Appeals reached this conclusion by determining that "a minor cannot be 'managing his own financial affairs,' " a prerequisite to emancipation under the Act, "if he is subject to his parent's control and is not allowed to retain the wages he has earned. Similarly, a minor cannot be 'managing his own financial affairs' if he is receiving financial and other support from his parents."

{19} Daughter subsequently petitioned this Court for writ of certiorari, presenting three closely interrelated questions, all of which require this Court to resolve whether the Act permits a district court to declare a minor emancipated for certain purposes while reserving that minor's right to seek support from her parent.

II. THE EMANCIPATION OF MINORS ACT

{20} The Legislature first adopted the Act in 1981, NMSA 1978, §§ 28–6–2 to –8 (1981, repealed and recodified at NMSA 1978, §§ 32A–21–1 to –7 (1995)), in response to a concern that "the law of this state is unclear as to the definition and consequences of emancipation of minors [and] that a legislative statement is required." Id. § 28–6–3. The Legislature therefore passed the Act to provide such a statement to "defin[e] emancipation and its consequences and to permit an emancipated minor to obtain a court declaration of his status." Id.; Section 32A–21–2.

{21} The Act defines an emancipated minor as any person sixteen years of age or older who "has entered into a valid marriage, whether or not the marriage was terminated by dissolution," who "is on active duty with any of the armed forces of the United States of America," or who has received a declaration of emancipation" pursuant to the Act. Section 32A–21–3. The Act sets forth three prerequisites to emancipation by judicial declaration. "Any person sixteen years of age or older may be declared an emancipated minor for one or more purposes enumerated in the [Act] if he is [1] willingly living separate and apart from his parents, guardian or custodian, [2] is managing his financial affairs and [3] the court finds it in the minor's best interest." Section 32A–21–4.

{22} In addition, the Act provides a procedural mechanism for a minor to obtain a declaration of emancipation. A minor seeking to be emancipated must file a verified petition with the children's court that "set[s] forth with specificity the facts" in support of such relief, Section 32A–21–7(A), and the court shall provide notice of the petition to the minor's parent, guardian or custodian, Section 32A–21–7(B). If the court determines the minor to be sixteen years of age or older and to fulfill the preconditions for emancipation, "the court may grant the petition unless, after having considered all of the evidence introduced at the hearing, it finds that granting the petition would be contrary to the best interests of the minor." Section 32A–21–7(C). Upon granting the petition, the court "shall immediately issue a declaration of emancipation containing specific findings of fact and one or more purposes of the emancipation, which shall be filed by the county clerk." Section 32A–21–7(D). Such a declaration "shall be conclusive evidence that the minor is emancipated." Section 32A–21–7(G).

{23} As for the legal effect of emancipation, under the Act

[a]n emancipated minor shall be considered as being over the age of majority for one or more of the following purposes:
A. consenting to medical, dental or psychiatric care without parental consent, knowledge or liability;
B. his capacity to enter into a binding contract;
C. his capacity to sue and be sued in his own name;
D. his right to support by his parents;
E. the rights of his parents to his earnings and to control him;
F. establishing his own residence;
G. buying or selling real property;
H. ending vicarious liability of the minor's parents. . .or
I. enrolling in any school or college.

Section 32A–21–5.

III. STANDARD OF REVIEW

{24} "The setting of child support is within the trial court's discretion and is reviewed on appeal only for an abuse of that discretion." *Styka v. Styka*, 1999–NMCA–002, ¶ 8, 126 N.M. 515, 972 P.2d 16. This appeal, however, does not implicate the district court's discretion in awarding support to Daughter so much as its determination that the Act allows an emancipated minor to pursue child support. "Statutory interpretation is a question of law, which we review de novo." *Hovet v. Allstate Ins. Co.*, 2004–NMSC–010, ¶ 10, 135 N.M. 397, 89 P.3d 69.

{25} In interpreting a statute, the Court's "primary goal is to ascertain and give effect to the intent of the legislature." *Jolley v. AEGIS*, 2010–NMSC–029, ¶ 8, 148 N.M. 436, 237 P.3d 738 (internal quotation marks and citation omitted). In assessing intent, "we look first to the plain language of the statute, giving the words their ordinary meaning, unless the Legislature indicates a different one was intended." *Oldham v. Oldham*, 2011–NMSC–007, ¶ 10, 149 N.M. 215, 247 P.3d 736 (internal quotation marks and citation omitted); *see also DeWitt v. Rent-A-Center, Inc.*, 2009–NMSC–032, ¶ 29, 146 N.M. 453, 212 P.3d 341 ("The first and most obvious guide to statutory interpretation is the wording of the statutes themselves."). When interpreting a statute, all sections of the statute "must be read together so that all parts are given effect." *High Ridge Hinkle Joint Venture v. City of Albuquerque*, 1998–NMSC–050, ¶ 5, 126 N.M. 413, 970 P.2d 599. Where the language of a statute is "clear and unambiguous, we must give effect to that language and refrain from further statutory interpretation." *Quynh Truong v. Allstate Ins. Co.*, 2010–NMSC–009, ¶ 37, 147 N.M. 583, 227 P.3d 73 (quoting *State v. Jonathan M.*, 109 N.M. 789, 790, 791 P.2d 64, 65 (1990)).

IV. DISCUSSION

A. Plain Language and Legislative History of the Act

1. "One or More. . .Purposes"

{26} Emancipation confers on eligible minors some or all of "the rights and status of adults." *Ortega v. Salt Lake Wet Wash Laundry, 156 P.2d 885, 890 (Utah 1945)*. In setting forth the nine possible legal effects of emancipation, the Act refers to "one or more of the [enumerated] purposes." Section 32A–21–5. Daughter interprets the Act to authorize a district court to "craft an order of emancipation to address only those purposes which meet the best interests of the child seeking emancipation," and asserts that there is nothing absurd about granting a minor many of the legal privileges of adulthood while in appropriate circumstances allowing that minor to pursue parental support. Mother in turn argues that where the Act refers to "one or more. . .purposes" of emancipation, the phrase should be interpreted to mean "all the purposes." According to Mother, allowing a district court to decide the individual purposes for which a minor is emancipated would lead to an "absurd scenario" where the minor could be freed from parental control but prevented from, for instance, establishing his or her own residence. In Mother's view, loss of any entitlement to parental support therefore is a necessary consequence of emancipation, because "[t]here's no such thing as a limited emancipation."

{27} The plain meaning of the phrase "one or more. . .purposes" is that a minor may be declared to be emancipated under the Act for a single enumerated purpose, for all nine enumerated purposes, or for any intermediate number of enumerated purposes. "As a rule of construction, the word 'or' should be given its normal disjunctive meaning unless the context of a statute demands otherwise," *Hale v. Basin Motor Co., 110 N.M. 314, 318, 795 P.2d 1006, 1010 (1990)*, or if "adherence to the literal use of the word leads to absurdity or contradiction," *State v. Block, 2011–NMCA–101, ¶ 21, 150 N.M. 598, 263 P.3d 940*. Our courts have employed this common-sense principle in a variety of statutory contexts. * * *

{28} The Act's reference to "one or more of the following purposes" for which emancipation may be granted cannot be viewed as haphazard or isolated. The Act employs this key phrase not only in enumerating the nine possible grounds for emancipation, Section 32A–21–5, but also in investing the district court with the authority to declare a minor to be emancipated, Section 32A–21–4 ("Any person sixteen years of age or older may be declared an emancipated minor for one or more of the purposes enumerated in the [Act]" if specified prerequisites are met.). The Act also directs a district court granting a minor's petition to "immediately issue a declaration of emancipation containing specific findings of fact and one or more purposes of the emancipation." Section 32A–21–7(D). This last reference to "one or more purposes" is especially significant, because there is no logical reason for requiring courts to identify the specific purposes for which emancipation is being granted if every emancipation automatically fulfills *all* of the enumerated purposes.

{29} "We must assume the legislature chose its words advisedly to express its meaning unless the contrary intent clearly appears." *State v. Maestas*, 2007–NMSC–001, ¶ 22, 140 N.M. 836, 149 P.3d 933 (quoting *Varoz v. N.M. Bd. of Podiatry*, 104 N.M. 454, 456, 722 P.2d 1176, 1178 (1986) (internal quotation marks and brackets omitted)). Not only does the Act fail to evidence any legislative intent contrary to the plain meaning of "one or more purposes," the history of its enactment provides persuasive indications of the Legislature's intent that district courts should tailor emancipation orders to the best interests of the minor in each particular case.

{30} As originally introduced, the legislation that ultimately became the Act included language consistent with Respondent's (and the Court of Appeals') interpretation, namely that "[a]n emancipated minor shall be considered as being over the age of majority *for the purpose of* " the nine specific grounds. The Legislature considered and rejected this phrasing, opting instead for the more flexible alternative of "one or more of the following purposes."

{31} Other revisions to the bill prior to enactment further illustrate the Legislature's preference that district courts retain the discretion to emancipate a minor in a manner consistent with that minor's individual circumstances and needs.
* * *

2. "Managing [One's] Own Financial Affairs"

{32} The Act requires that a minor must be living independently and "managing his own financial affairs" in order to be emancipated. Section 32A–21–4. Mother argues that "in the context of [the Act], 'managing his financial affairs' is synonymous with being financially independent, self-supporting, self-sufficient. . ., it is axiomatic that to be emancipated you must be self-supporting and if you are self-supporting you are not in need of or entitled to support." Daughter responds that managing one's financial affairs is not the equivalent of total financial self-sufficiency. We agree with Daughter.

{33} The Act does not define the phrase "managing [one's] financial affairs," but that term logically would include obtaining income and transacting for the necessities of life. Our caselaw usually employs the term in guardianship and conservatorship proceedings, where, for example, a court must find an adult "incapacitated and unable to manage an estate and financial affairs" in order to appoint a conservator for that person. *In re Conservatorship of Chisholm*, 1999–

NMCA–025, ¶ 12, 126 N.M. 584, 973 P.2d 261. Here, the district court determined that Daughter had been living independently and that Daughter had paid for all of her expenses out of her own earnings since March 2005, with no support from Mother. Daughter sought emancipation, in part, to obtain health insurance and open a bank account, further evidence of her intent and capacity to manage her own affairs but for certain legal impediments of minority.

{34} The Court of Appeals agreed with Mother and found the district court's interpretation of the Act "paradoxical," explaining that "a minor cannot be 'managing his own financial affairs' if he is receiving financial and other support from his parents." We do not see management of one's financial affairs and entitlement to support as inherently contradictory. Certainly, in other proceedings courts routinely award support without any finding or implication that the recipient is incapable of managing his or her affairs. *See generally Mitchell v. Mitchell, 104 N.M. 205, 214, 719 P.2d 432, 441 (Ct.App.1986)* (awarding spousal support based on circumstances of supporting spouse and recipient spouse).

{35} The Act itself contemplates that an emancipated minor may receive public assistance: An emancipated minor "shall not be denied benefits from any public entitlement program which he may have been entitled in his own right prior to the declaration of emancipation." Section 32A–21–6. A minor entitled to public assistance is necessarily not entirely self-supporting, at least not after he or she begins to receive the assistance payments. Under the Court of Appeals' interpretation of the Act, Daughter would be managing her own financial affairs if she were receiving financial support from the State, but not if she were receiving support from Mother. Mother does not offer any explanation for why the *source* of the support should be determinative of Daughter's ability to manage her affairs, and indeed such an approach would be inconsistent with our "strong public policy" favoring parental support where appropriate. *In re Estate of DeLara, 2002–NMCA–004, ¶ 10, 131 N.M. 430, 38 P.3d 198.* Finally, in the present case, the district court expressly did *not* emancipate Daughter with respect to her entitlement to support, so for that sole purpose she retained the status of minority. That determination explains why the district court set Daughter's eighteenth birthday or high school graduation, whichever occurred later, as the date terminating Mother's support obligation. Up until that moment, for support purposes only, Daughter remained a minor.

B. Partial and Complete Emancipation in Other States

{36} Although we find ample support for our interpretation of the Act in its plain language and legislative intent, a brief review of several other states' emancipation statutes, illustrative rather than exhaustive, indicates a diversity in approach to defining the legal effects of emancipation. Some states have determined that emancipation should always entail a fixed rather than a flexible set of legal consequences. For example, in contrast to the Act's provision that emancipation may be ordered for "one or more purposes," California's emancipation statute directs that an emancipated minor "shall be considered as being an adult for the following purposes," Cal. Fam.Code Ann. § 7050 (West 1992, operative Jan. 1, 1994), that is, for *all* of the seventeen purposes enumerated by the California statute, including "the minor's right to support by the minor's parents," *id.* § 7050(a), the parent's rights to "the minor's earnings and to control the minor," *id.* § 7050(b), and the minor's capacity to "establish [his or her] own residence," *id.* § 7050(e)(15). California courts have recognized the California legislature's deliberate choice to create a form of statutory emancipation with the same set of legal consequences for each affected minor.

{37} Consistent with California's approach and in contrast to ours, Vermont law provides that an emancipation order "shall recognize the minor as an adult for *all purposes* that result from reaching the age of majority, including. . .terminating parental support and control of the minor and [parental] rights to the minor's income." Vt. Stat. Ann. tit. 12, § 7156(a) (West 1995) (emphasis added), § 7156(a)(6). Pennsylvania state law does not set forth a specific statutory mechanism for a minor to obtain a declaration of emancipation, but nonetheless expressly provides that "[a] court shall not order either or both parents to pay for the support of a child if the child is emancipated." 23 Pa. Cons.Stat. Ann. § 4323(a) (West 1985).

* * *

{39} On the other hand, New Mexico is far from the only state where a minor's emancipation does not presumptively extinguish a parent's support obligation. Montana's emancipation statute probably resembles New Mexico's most closely. If a Montana court grants a petition for emancipation, it must issue an order that "specifically set[s] forth the rights and responsibilities that are being conferred upon the youth[, which] may include but are not limited to one or more" of a list of six purposes. Mont.Code Ann. § 41–1–503(2) (2009). Those purposes include the right to live in housing of the minor's choice, *id.* § 41–1–503(2)(b), the right to enter into contracts and incur debts, *id.* § 41–1–503(2)(d), the right to consent to medical care, *id.* § 41–1–503(2)(e), and the right to "directly receive and expend money to which the youth is entitled and to conduct the youth's own financial affairs," *id* . § 41–1–503(2)(c). The Montana statute, like ours, does not define emancipation to automatically end a parent's support obligation.

{40} At least one state goes further than New Mexico by not merely permitting but *mandating* parental support for emancipated minors. Under Michigan's emancipation statute, a court may declare a minor emancipated "for the purposes of, but not limited to, all of the following [fourteen purposes]," Mich. Comp.

Laws Ann. § 722.4e(1) (West 1968, as amended through 1988, effective Mar. 30, 1989), a list that does not include child support. Instead, Michigan law explicitly provides that "[t]he parents of a minor emancipated by court order are jointly and severally obligated to support the minor," except that the parents are not liable for debt incurred by the minor during the period of emancipation, id. § 722.4e(2).

{41} The point of the foregoing review is to illustrate the wide variety of approaches states employ to determine what legal consequences emancipation should have, particularly with respect to the provision of child support. Our Legislature could easily have decided that emancipation *ipso facto* extinguishes a parent's support obligation to a child, an alternative that it initially considered and that some other states have adopted. Instead, the Legislature ultimately chose to confer authority on the district courts to determine in each particular case whether an emancipated minor is entitled to support.

C. Emancipation at Common Law

{42} While our holding that the Act allows a district court to reserve a minor's right to financial support from a parent follows from the plain language of the Act, it is consistent with the treatment of emancipation under the common law. Historically, American courts recognized a "correlative" relationship between a parent's duty to support his or her minor child and the parent's entitlement to the child's services and earnings. 1 Homer H. Clark, Jr., *The Law of Domestic Relations in the United States* § 9.3, at 548–49 (2d ed.1987). Under this approach,

> the father [was] entitled to the services and earnings of his minor children, because he [was] bound to support and educate them. The right grows out of the obligation, and is correlative to it. When one ceases the other ceases also. The helplessness of the infant, demanding the tutelage and support of the father, in contemplation of law terminates in ordinary cases at twenty-one [then the age of majority], and the child becomes emancipated from parental control and entitled to his own earnings.

Campbell v. Cooper, 34 N.H. 49, at * 10 (1856). * * * More contemporary cases instead view the minor's reciprocal duty as submitting to the parent's control. *See, e.g., Howard Frank, M.D., P.C. v. Superior Court of Ariz.,* 722 P.2d 955, 958 (Ariz.1986) (noting that "emancipation frees parents and children from the reciprocal legal obligations of support and obedience").

{43} Emancipation developed largely to protect minors from claims against their wages asserted by their parents or by third parties. *See, e.g., Am. Prods. Co. v. Villwock,* 109 P.2d 570, 580 (Wash.1941) (noting that emancipation may be invoked "to protect the minor's earnings against the unfortunate parent's creditors." (quoting 1 James Schouler & Arthur W. Blakemore, *A Treatise on the Law of Marriage, Divorce, Separation and Domestic Relations,* § 807, at 897 (6th ed.1921));

Lackman v. Wood, 25 Cal. 147, 151 (1864) (Emancipation frees a minor "from parental control; he can claim his earnings thereafter as against his father."). A minor could only be emancipated through parental consent, although that consent could be implied as well as express. *Inhabitants of Lowell v. Inhabitants of Newport,* 66 Me. 78, 89 (1876). A parent's abandonment of a minor, or even oral expressions of an intent to abandon the minor, could constitute an implied consent to emancipation. *Kidd v. Joint Sch. Dist. No. 2, City of Richland Ctr. and Town of Richland,* 216 N.W. 499, 500 (Wis.1927); *see also Nightingale,* 15 Mass. at 274 ("But where the father has discharged himself of the obligation to support the child, or has obliged the child to support himself, there is no principle, but that of slavery, which will continue his right to receive the earnings of the child's labor. Thus, if the father should refuse to support a son. . .the law will imply an emancipation of the son. . . .").

{44} Courts have long recognized that common-law emancipation may be partial, that is, conferring some but not all of the aspects of adult status on the minor. * * *

{45} Prior to passage of the Act, New Mexico courts recognized emancipation under the common law. * * * As in other states, common-law emancipation in New Mexico could be express, where "the parent freely and voluntarily agrees" to allow a minor child to live independently and control his or her own earnings, or implied, where "the child is no longer subject to parental care and discipline,"

* * *

D. Public Policy Considerations

{47} The Legislature's decision to allow district courts to determine the extent of an emancipated minor's rights and responsibilities also comports with our state's public policy. "In New Mexico, there is a strong tradition of protecting a child's best interests in a variety of circumstances." *Sanders v. Rosenberg,* 122 N.M. 692, 694, 930 P.2d 1144, 1146 (1996) (internal quotation marks and citation omitted). Furthermore, "[i]t is well-settled law that when [a] case involves children, the trial court has broad authority to fashion its rulings in [the] best interests of the children." *Sanders,* 122 N.M. at 694, 930 P.2d at 1146 (internal quotation marks and citations omitted). In legal matters concerning minors, "the rule of 'best interests of the children' is essentially equitable." *State ex rel. Children, Youth & Families Dep't v. A.H.,* 1997–NMCA–118, ¶ 8, 124 N.M. 244, 947 P.2d 1064.

{48} More specifically, the district courts are properly "invested with broad discretion and flexibility in determining an award of child support." *DeTevis v. Aragon,* 104 N.M. 793, 800, 727 P.2d 558, 565 (Ct.App.1986) (citing *Henderson v. Lekvold,* 95 N.M. 288, 621 P.2d 505 (1980); *Spingola v. Spingola,* 91 N.M. 737,

580 P.2d 958 (1978)); *see also Fosmire v. Nicoleau,* 144 A.D .2d 8, 16 (N.Y.App. Div.1989) (In matters involving the protection of minor children, "the court must be allowed wide latitude and broad flexibility. . .because of the endless variety of human situations which can be presented in cases of this nature. There are no preordained answers and the result in any case will be totally dependent upon the unique facts involved therein.").

{49} Giving effect to the plain meaning of the Act is consistent with our state's public policy favoring judicial determination of the best interests of the minor. A district court could, for example, where appropriate declare a minor emancipated for a single purpose, such as "consenting to medical, dental or psychiatric care without parental consent, knowledge or liability," or attending college. Similarly, a district court has the discretion to declare a minor emancipated for a greater number of purposes, or all of the purposes, set forth in the Act. The critical inquiry remains the best interests of the minor, which the court determines on the basis of specific findings of fact. The mere possibility that a district court might abuse its discretion in declaring a minor emancipated for particular purposes does not provide a sufficient basis for reading words out of the Act.

V. CONCLUSION

{50} The Act provides that emancipation may be declared for "one or more purposes," including the minor's right to support by his or her parents. The district court based its decision to order post-emancipation support on a great deal of evidence regarding Daughter's and Mother's relationship, life choices, and financial circumstances. In rendering its judgment, the district court faithfully followed the procedural requirements of the Act and reached a result consistent with the Act's plain language. Because the Court of Appeals failed to give effect to that language, we reverse.

{51} IT IS SO ORDERED.

Points for Discussion

a. Parental Support Obligations

At common law, a father was primarily responsible for the support of his minor children, but the duty now extends equally to fathers and mothers. E.g. Rand v. Rand, 374 A.2d 900 (Md. 1977). Parental obligations are enforceable thorough a variety of civil and criminal remedies discussed in Chapter 7. See generally Homer H. Clark, Jr., Domestic Relations § 6.2 (Student 2d ed. 1988).

b. Age of Majority

Since the adoption of the Twenty-Sixth Amendment in 1971 giving 18-year-olds the right to vote, most states have reduced the age of majority to 18. Children attain full legal capacity at this age, but they are still subject to some restrictions, such as laws prohibiting purchase of liquor until age 21. In a few states, although the age of majority is 18, the parents' duty to support their children continues until age twenty-one. See, e.g., N.Y. Dom. Rel. L. § 240 1–b (2018). Depending on state laws, children are sometimes permitted to seek support after reaching the age of majority, either for educational expenses or when a child is disabled; see Chapter 7.

c. Emancipation

As discussed in *Diamond*, many states have statutes that authorize a minor to obtain a judicial declaration of emancipation, usually with the consent of the minor's parents or guardians. Such a decree allows the minor to live apart from his parents and to manage his or her own property and financial affairs. Typically, however, a parent's obligation of support ends once a child is emancipated. See generally Homer H. Clark, Jr., Domestic Relations § 8.3 (Student 2d ed. 1988).

Depending on the context, a child will be determined to be emancipated once the child marries, enlists in the military, or establishes his or her own residence and begins to earn his or her own living. For example, Parker v. Stage, 371 N.E.2d 513 (N.Y. 1977), held that a daughter who had left home to live with her boyfriend had emancipated herself and the parents could not be required to support her. Conversely, In re Marriage of Robinson, 629 P.2d 1069 (Colo.1981), found that when a child left home to take a summer job, earned money in that job, and then returned home, the child was not emancipated. See also State in Interest of R.R. v. C.R., 797 P.2d 459 (Utah Ct.App.1990).

Should a parent be permitted to emancipate a child in order to terminate the parent's duty of support? See, e.g., Dunson v. Dunson, 769 N.E.2d 1120 (Ind. 2002), which rejected a parent's petition, holding that the child must initiate an action to put himself or herself outside the parents' control and that the child must be self-supporting in fact. See generally Carol Sanger and Eleanor Willemsen, *Minor Changes: Emancipating Children in Modern Times*, 25 U. Mich. J.L. Reform 239 (1992).

d. Children in Need of Supervision

All or nearly all states have statutes authorizing juvenile proceedings against children under eighteen who run away from home or disobey their parents' reasonable instructions or are habitually truant from school. These are sometimes referred to as delinquency cases, and in such a proceeding, the court might order the child to return home and obey his or her parents' rules. If the child were placed away from his or her family, however, the parents would continue to be liable for the support of the child. See In re Sumey, 621 P.2d 108 (Wash. 1980); In Interest of S.E.S., 845 S.W.2d 140 (Mo.Ct.App.1993). On the overlap between delinquency jurisdiction and dependency proceedings, see In re R.T., 399 P.3d 1 (Cal. 2017). See generally Homer H. Clark, Jr., Domestic Relations § 9.5 (Student 2d ed. 1988).

When children refuse persistently to obey their parents, should the parents be able to terminate their duty of support? See, e.g., In re Thomas C., 691 A.2d 1140 (Conn. Super. Ct. 1996); Jennifer S. v. Marvin S., 568 N.Y.S.2d 515 (Fam. Ct. 1991). See generally Leslie J. Harris, et al., *Making and Breaking Connections Between Parents' Duty to Support and Right to Control Their Children*, 69 Or. L. Rev. 689 (1990).

e. Parental "Divorce"

Can a child bring an action to terminate the parental rights of his or her parents? Ryan v. Ryan, 677 N.W.2d 899 (Mich. Ct. App. 2004), held that the trial court had no subject matter jurisdiction to hear a teenager's claim for divorce from her parents. In one widely publicized case involving an 11-year-old boy, the court upheld the termination of his parents' rights and approved the boy's adoption by his foster parents. See Kingsley v. Kingsley, 623 So.2d 780 (Fla.Ct.App.1993). Although the child originally filed the petition, the court seemed to say that he could not sue, being a minor, but that an attorney could sue on his behalf as his "next friend."

In another high profile case, 12-year-old Walter Polovchak sought to obtain asylum and remain in Chicago with a cousin against the wishes of his parents after they decided to return to the Soviet Union. Although the parents' right to make this decision was eventually sustained, Walter turned 18 shortly after the final decision in the case and remained in the United States. See Polovchak v. Meese, 774 F.2d 731 (7th Cir. 1985). A similar attempt to seek asylum on behalf of the much younger Elian Gonzalez eventually resulted in the child's return to his father in Cuba. See Gonzalez v. Reno, 212 F.3d 1338 (11th Cir.2000).

Problem 4-4

Sara, a high school student, decided to leave home because of her father's insistence that she not have boys in her bedroom with the door closed. She moved in briefly with an aunt, and then to an apartment in a building owned by relatives. After three months living on her own, she brings a proceeding against her father for child support under the applicable statute. What obligations should her father have in this situation? (See <u>Chambers v. Chambers, 742 N.Y.S.2d 725 (App.Div.2002)</u>.)

Problem 4-5

After a major fight with his mother about whether he could have his ears pierced, a 12-year-old boy called the police and told them that his parents had marijuana in the house, describing exactly where it was hidden. The police went to the home, found eight pounds of marijuana, and arrested both parents, charging them with possession of marijuana for sale and distribution. What strategies might be employed to resolve the conflict within this family? (See Boulder Daily Camera, March 16, 1989, at 1; Melissa Healy, *Parents Ask Reunion with Tattling Teen*, L.A. Times, Sept. 9, 1999.)

Problem 4-6

Lori, age 15, has dated both boys and girls and is now in love with a 21-year-old woman named Ellen. When Lori's mother forbid her to continue her relationship with Ellen, Lori moved in with her mother's sister. Lori's mother has filed a petition to have Lori declared to be a "person in need of supervision" under a state law that applies to children who are "incorrigible, ungovernable or habitually disobedient and beyond the lawful control of a parent." What arguments could Lori make in response to her mother's petition? Should it matter whether Ellen's relationship with Lori could constitute a criminal offense because of the difference in their ages? (See <u>Matter of Lori M., 496 N.Y.S.2d 940 (Fam. Ct. 1985)</u>.)

Support Obligations for Adult Family Members

Support for elderly and disabled adults is provided today primarily by the government, in the form of Social Security, Medicare and Medicaid benefits. Family responsibilities including care for a parent fall within the scope of the Family and Medical Leave Act, <u>29 U.S.C. § 2612(a)(1) (2018)</u>, and an individual who provides sufficient financial support for a parent or other qualifying relative may be able to claim that person as a dependent for federal income tax purposes.

Many adults provide financial assistance to their parents, and about 30 states have laws that impose general duties of support for indigent persons on relatives. The right to enforce these duties is given either to the indigent person or to the state or to both. The primary purpose of these statutes is to shift some of the burden of supporting the poor from the state to family members. The relatives upon whom adult support obligations are imposed vary, with some states looking only to spouses and children, others including grandparents and grandchildren, and a few including brothers and sisters. See generally Seymour Moskowitz, *Filial Responsibility Statutes: Legal and Policy Considerations, 9 J. L. & Pol'y 709 (2001)*. See also Lee Anne Fennell, *Relative Burdens: Family Ties and the Safety Net, 45 Wm. & Mary L. Rev. 1453 (2004)*.

Courts generally conclude that family support statutes are constitutional; see Gregory G. Sarno, Annotation, *Constitutionality of Statutory Provision Requiring Reimbursement of Public by Child for Financial Assistance to Aged Parents, 75 A.L.R.3d 1159 (1977)*. But see Department of Mental Hygiene v. Kirchner, 388 P.2d 720 (Cal. 1964), remanded 380 U.S. 194 (1965), subsequent opinion 400 P.2d 321 (Cal. 1965), which held that a statute violated the state constitution when it was was applied to require a daughter's estate to reimburse the state for the expense of caring for the daughter's mother in a state mental hospital. Subsequent decisions suggest that the statutes are constitutional to the extent that they impose liability for support, but not if they make relatives liable for the costs of confinement, rehabilitation, treatment or supervision of indigent persons in state institutions. County of San Mateo v. Dell J., 762 P.2d 1202 (Cal. 1988). See also 1 Homer H. Clark, Jr., Domestic Relations § 7.7 (2d ed. 1987).

In re D.C.

115 Cal.Rptr.3d 837 (Ct. App. 2010), rev. denied (2011)

MARGULIES, J.

Appellant D.C., a minor, was continued as a ward of the court after police found stolen goods in his bedroom during a search of the apartment he shared with his mother and older brother. Police originally went to the apartment to conduct a probation search relating to the older brother, suspecting he might have been involved in local crimes. As they arrived, the officers obtained consent from appellant's mother to search the entire apartment. Appellant objected and attempted to block the officers' entry, but he relented when his mother told him to "get out of the way."

Appellant contends evidence of the stolen goods should have been suppressed because (1) his mother did not have the authority to consent to a search of his bedroom and (2) his objection to the officers' entry to the apartment precluded a consensual search under *Georgia v. Randolph* (2006) 547 U.S. 103, 126 S.Ct. 1515, 164 L.Ed.2d 208 (*Randolph*). While the arguments appellant raises might have prevailed were he an adult, we conclude his mother, as the parent of a minor child, had the authority to consent to a search of his bedroom and to override any objection he raised to the search of her apartment.

I. BACKGROUND

On November 25, 2009, the Alameda County District Attorney filed a wardship petition under Welfare and Institutions Code section 602, subdivision (a), alleging appellant, then age 15, had received stolen property (Pen.Code, § 496). The petition also alleged appellant had previously been found to have threatened a witness, in violation of Penal Code section 140.

Officer Morris, a police officer with the Oakland Housing Authority, testified that on October 26, 2009, he and other officers were called to an apartment building on a report of possible narcotics activity. After they arrived, an officer detained appellant's adult brother, suspecting he was involved in the reported activity. In the meantime, a building resident reported to a third officer that his apartment had been burglarized.

Running a check, the officers learned appellant's brother was on probation and the terms of his probation permitted warrantless searches. Officer Morris escorted the brother to the apartment where he lived with appellant and their mother, intending to conduct a probation search. On the way, they met appellant's mother and explained to her they wanted to search the apartment to confirm appellant's brother was not involved in the narcotics activity or the burglary. She consented to the search.

At the time, appellant was lingering nearby. As the officers approached the apartment door he barred their way, telling them, "You're not going to enter the apartment." When his mother told him to "get out of the way," appellant complied, stepping aside and remaining outside the apartment while the officers entered and began to search. During their search of appellant's bedroom, one of three in the apartment, the officers found some of the items reportedly taken in the burglary. By the time the officers completed their search of his bedroom, appellant was no longer outside the apartment.

The juvenile court denied appellant's motion to suppress the evidence taken from his room and found the allegations of the petition to be true. The court continued appellant as a ward of the court and continued him on probation in the custody of his mother.

II. DISCUSSION

Appellant contends the evidence found in his bedroom should have been suppressed because the warrantless search occurred without his consent and over his objection.

A. *Legal Background*

In reviewing a ruling on a motion to suppress, we defer to the trial court's factual findings when supported by substantial evidence, but we exercise our independent judgment in determining whether, on the facts so found, the search was lawful. A warrantless search is presumed to be unreasonable, and the prosecution bears the burden of demonstrating a legal justification for the search.

Consent has long been recognized as excusing the requirement of a search warrant. * * * The principles governing consent were established in *United States v. Matlock* (1974) 415 U.S. 164, 94 S.Ct. 988, 39 L.Ed.2d 242 (*Matlock*), in which the Supreme Court held that consent to a search given by a single resident of a residence occupied by several persons "is valid as against [an] absent, nonconsenting person" so long as the consenting resident "possesses common authority over [the] premises" with the absent resident. "Common authority" was defined in *Matlock* not as an issue of property law "but [as resting] rather on mutual use of the property by persons generally having joint access or control for most purposes, so that it is reasonable to recognize that any of the co-inhabitants has the right to permit the inspection in his own right and that the others have assumed the risk that one of their number might permit the common area to be searched."

In addition, officers may rely on the consent of a person whom they "reasonably and in good faith believe[ ]. . .ha[s] the authority to consent" to a particular search. (*People v. Ledesma* (2006) 39 Cal.4th 641, 703, 47 Cal.Rptr.3d 326, 140 P.3d 657.) Such apparent authority to consent exists if " 'the facts available to the officer at the moment. . ."warrant a man of reasonable caution in the belief" that the consenting party had authority over the premises.' " (*Illinois v. Rodriguez, supra,* 497 U.S. at p. 188, 110 S.Ct. 2793.)

B. *Appellant's Mother's Consent to the Search of His Bedroom*

Appellant argues that, if he were an adult, "there would be no question that his mother's consent would not have permitted" the search of his bedroom, since "[w]here bedrooms within a house have been appropriated for the exclusive use of one of the occupants," other residents cannot give valid consent to a search of the room. He contends the same rule should apply here, since there was no evidence regarding his mother's access to his bedroom.

As appellant argues, it has been held, outside the parent-child context, that adults sharing a residence but maintaining separate bedrooms do not have the apparent authority to consent to the search of one another's bedrooms, at least when officers have no other information about their living arrangements.

California courts, however, have come to a different conclusion when an adult child maintains a bedroom in the home of his or her parents. In *People v. Daniels* (1971) 16 Cal.App.3d 36, 93 Cal.Rptr. 628, the court held that the search of an adult child's bedroom in his parents' home made with the consent of a parent is reasonable "absent circumstances establishing the son has been given exclusive control over the bedroom." The court reasoned that "[p]arents with whom a son is living, on premises owned by them, do not ipso facto relinquish exclusive control over that portion thereof used by the son. To the contrary, the mere fact the son is permitted to use a particular bedroom, as such, does not confer upon him exclusive control thereof. [Citation.] His occupancy is subservient to the control of his parents. [Citations.] He may be excluded from the premises by them at any time." Similarly, in *People v. Oldham* (2000) 81 Cal.App.4th 1, 96 Cal.Rptr.2d 343, the court followed *Daniels* in finding valid a father's consent to the search of his adult son's bedroom. The son was a permanent resident in the home, and the father did not regularly enter his son's room, but the court held that the father's consent to the search was effective because "there was nothing to show [the son] had exclusive control over the bedroom he used or its contents. At most, the evidence showed there was joint control and Father possessed superior control because he had the right to exclude [the son] from the apartment."

When the child is a minor, there is an even stronger case for apparent authority in a parent to consent to the search of the child's bedroom. Unlike the parents of adult children, the parents of minor children have legal rights and obligations that both permit and, in essence, require them to exercise common authority over their child's bedroom. Parents have the "right to direct and control the activities of a minor child. . . . [Citations.] 'The liberty interest. . .of parents in the care, custody, and control of their children. . .is perhaps the oldest of the fundamental liberty interests. . . .' " (*Brekke v. Wills* (2005) 125 Cal.App.4th 1400, 1410, 23 Cal. Rptr.3d 609.) Conversely, parents have affirmative legal duties toward their minor children. Most fundamentally, parents have the "responsibility" to support their minor children (Fam.Code, § 3900) and must "exercise reasonable care, supervision, protection, and control" over their conduct (Pen.Code, § 272, subd. (a)(2); see *Williams v. Garcetti* (1993) 5 Cal.4th 561, 570–571, 20 Cal.Rptr.2d 341, 853 P.2d 507). "By imposing upon parents a duty to exercise reasonable care, supervision, protection, and control over their minor child, Penal Code section 272 is intended to 'safeguard children from those influences which would tend to cause them to become delinquent.' " (*Brekke v. Wills*, at p. 1411, 23 Cal.Rptr.3d 609.) Parents are also required to ensure their child's attendance at school (Ed.Code, §§ 48260.5, subds. (b)–(c), 48293) and may be held financially responsible for a minor child's misconduct.[2] "[O]ne purpose of the parental liability laws is to

---

[2]   See, e.g., Civil Code section 1714.1 (willful torts); Government Code section 38772, subdivision (b) (graffiti); Education Code section 48904, subdivision (a) (school injuries and property damage); Penal Code section 490.5, subdivision (b) (theft).

encourage responsibility in parents—that is, to encourage parents to exercise effective control over their children." (*Curry v. Superior Court* (1993) 20 Cal. App.4th 180, 187–188, 24 Cal.Rptr.2d 495.)

Think About It

How does the fact of parental responsibility for children support the ruling in this case?

Under *Matlock,* "common authority" over a residence is found if there is "mutual use of the property by persons generally having joint access or control for most purposes, so that it is reasonable to recognize that any of the co-inhabitants has the right to permit the inspection in his own right. . . ." Given the legal rights and obligations of parents toward their minor children, common authority over the child's bedroom is inherent in the parental role. Carrying out their duty of supervision and control requires a parent to have the ability to monitor their child's activities whenever the parent deems it appropriate, even when the child is in a bedroom nominally regarded as private. Proper exercise of parental duties therefore demands that the parent have "joint access or control" of a minor child's bedroom. This is true regardless of whether the parent finds it necessary to exercise that privilege frequently. Further, given the parental duty of control and supervision, it is reasonable "to recognize that [the parent] has the right to permit the inspection in his own right. . . ." (*Ibid.*) In the absence of evidence suggesting a parent has abdicated this role toward his or her child, police officers may reasonably conclude that a parent can validly consent to the search of a minor child's bedroom.

Although no California decision has addressed directly the apparent authority of a parent to consent to a search of the bedroom of a minor child, our case law has recognized that minor children are treated differently from adults under *Matlock.* * *

While there is very little evidence in the record regarding the relationship between appellant and his mother, what little information we have suggests his mother not only had apparent authority to consent to the search of his room, but actual authority as well. It is notable that when appellant's mother told him to let the officers pass, he moved aside, acknowledging his mother's superior authority. Thereafter, appellant did not attempt to intervene to prevent the search of his room, implicitly recognizing his mother's control over the entire premises.

* * *

Defendant also argues a parent cannot waive the Fourth Amendment rights of a child, citing *In re Scott K.* (1979) 24 Cal.3d 395, 155 Cal.Rptr. 671, 595 P.2d 105 (*Scott K.*), in which the Supreme Court ruled invalid a father's consent to the police search of his minor son's toolbox. The entire area of law governed by *Matlock,* however, concerns just this subject—the waiver by one occupant of the Fourth Amendment warrant requirement that would otherwise apply to a search of premises jointly occupied. There is no doubt that, under circumstances consistent with *Matlock,* a parent can waive the requirement of a warrant for the search of premises jointly occupied with a child, just as an unrelated cotenant can. *Scott K.* is not to the contrary. It announces no broad prohibition against parental waiver of children's Fourth Amendment rights. Rather, *Scott K.* holds only that the evidence presented was insufficient to demonstrate the father had the apparent authority over his minor son's toolbox necessary to consent to a search, reasoning "[j]uveniles are entitled 'to acquire and hold property' " and while "[p]arents may have a protectible interest in property belonging to children,. . .that fact may not be assumed." Concerning the issue relevant here, a parent's authority to consent to a search of a child's room, as opposed to a closed container within the room, *Scott K.* is consistent with our decision. The Supreme Court did not question the validity of the father's consent to the search of his son's room, but only the father's consent regarding the closed container belonging to his son. Because a person's authority to consent to the search of closed containers within a residence is evaluated separately from the authority to consent to a search of the residence itself, the ruling of *Scott K.* regarding the toolbox has no bearing on the issue here.

C. Appellant's Objection

Appellant also contends the police could not validly search his bedroom because he objected to their entry into the apartment.

The issue addressed in *Matlock* was the validity of the consent of one resident present at a home as against the rights of a second resident who, because of his or her absence from the home, had not given consent. A more complex situation is presented when two residents, both on the scene, disagree about police entry. Considering this situation in *Randolph, supra,* 547 U.S. 103, 126 S.Ct. 1515, the Supreme Court held that when a husband and wife disagree about police admittance to their home, a warrantless search cannot be justified on grounds of consent, notwithstanding the consent of one of the parties. Explaining its decision, the court began with the observation that in consent cases, "great significance [is] given to widely shared social expectations." Applying the principle, the court noted "it is fair to say that a caller standing at the door of shared premises would have no confidence that one occupant's invitation was a sufficiently good reason to enter when a fellow tenant stood there saying, 'stay out.' Without some very good reason, no sensible person would go inside under those conditions." The ordinary assumption, echoed in the law governing the relationship among cotenants of property, is that joint occupants have equal authority and grant access to their residence only upon mutual consent. Accordingly, the court concluded, "Since the co-tenant wishing to open the door to a third party has no recognized authority in law or social practice to prevail over a present and objecting co-tenant, his disputed invitation, without more, gives a police officer no better claim to reasonableness in entering than the officer would have in the absence of any consent at all."

If *Randolph* applies equally here, the juvenile court was required to grant the motion to suppress. When the officers sought consent to search from appellant's mother, appellant objected plainly and unmistakably, barring the door and prohibiting entry by police. On its facts, however, *Randolph* governs only a disagreement between joint *adult* occupants having apparently equal authority over a residence. Because of the unique nature of the rights and duties of parents with respect to their children, we conclude *Randolph* does not require the police to defer to an objecting minor child over a consent to search by his or her parent.

As discussed above, parents have a legal duty and a corresponding right to control and supervise the activities of their children. (*Brekke v. Wills, supra,* 125 Cal.App.4th at p. 1410, 23 Cal.Rptr.3d 609.) Unlike objecting cotenants, for whom there is "no recognized authority in law or social practice to prevail over" one another, a parent has legally recognized standing to prevail over the objections of a minor child, particularly concerning the control of premises owned or leased by the parent. That legal authority reflects common social expectation and practice regarding the relative power of children and parents.

Because of this difference in legal status and the traditional notions of parental authority underpinning it, the "widely shared social expectations" applicable to a disagreement between parent and minor child are different than those applicable to a disagreement between adult cotenants. A "caller standing at the door of shared premises", confronted with a parent inviting entry and a minor child objecting, would have little doubt that entry was authorized. *Randolph* recognized this difference, expressly noting that expectations, and therefore the reasonableness of an entry, might be different if "the people living together fall within some recognized hierarchy, like a household of parent and child or barracks housing military personnel of different grades," thereby permitting a "societal understanding of superior and inferior." Accordingly, under the analysis of *Randolph,* the police were not required to respect appellant's objection.

Appellant argues the officers' failure to honor his objection to their entry constituted a violation of his constitutional rights, noting minors are entitled to the protections of the Constitution and, in particular, the search and seizure provisions of the Fourth Amendment. (E.g., *New Jersey v. T.L.O.* (1985) 469 U.S. 325, 333, 105 S.Ct. 733, 83 L.Ed.2d 720 [minors protected by Fourth Amendment]; *In re William G.* (1985) 40 Cal.3d 550, 556–557, 221 Cal.Rptr. 118, 709 P.2d 1287 [same]; see also *In re Gault* (1967) 387 U.S. 1, 30–31, 87 S.Ct. 1428,

18 L.Ed.2d 527 [minors entitled to due process protections in delinquency proceedings].) While there is no question minors are entitled to the protection of the Fourth Amendment, adults and minors are not necessarily entitled to the same degree of constitutional protection. As noted in *Scott K., supra,* a search and seizure decision, "[b]y no means are the rights of juveniles coextensive with those of adults." "Minors' rights may be legitimately restricted to serve the state's interest in promoting the health and welfare of children. [Citation.] '[Even] where there is an invasion of protected freedoms "the power of the state to control the conduct of children reaches beyond the scope of its authority over adults." ' " To fulfill their duty of supervision, parents must be empowered to authorize police to search the family home, even over the objection of their minor children. While a minor child's Fourth Amendment rights may be narrower in these circumstances than those of an adult cohabiting with another, the difference is not great; police will still be required to obtain the consent of a person with common authority over the home—the parent—before the requirement of a search warrant is excused.

Appellant also argues that "[i]f a minor can give valid consent to search his residence, then he or she must also have the authority to deny consent." It is true some minor children have been found to have common authority over a family home and therefore to be capable of consenting to a search when their parents are not at home. The existence of such authority depends upon the child's age, maturity, and role in the family. (Compare *People v. Jacobs, supra,* 43 Cal.3d at pp. 481–482, 233 Cal.Rptr. 323, 729 P.2d 757 [11-year-old has no apparent authority to consent]; *United States v. Sanchez* (10th Cir.2010) 608 F.3d 685, 688–689 [15-year-old has common authority to consent]; see also *State v. Schwarz* (2006) 332 Mont. 243, 136 P.3d 989, 991–992 [as a matter of law under the Montana Constitution, a child under the age of 16 cannot give valid consent].)

The issue here, however, is not whether a minor child can deny consent to entry by the police into a family home *when parents are absent*. Rather, the issue here is whether a child's objection overrides simultaneous consent by a parent. Even those relatively rare cases finding authority in a minor child to consent to a search of the family home do not hold that a minor's consent is effective as against a parent's objection.

III. DISPOSITION

The judgment of the trial court is affirmed.

———————————

Points for Discussion

a. Children's Constitutional Rights

The Supreme Court has identified a variety of constitutional rights for children, including free speech rights, due process rights in the context of criminal prosecution, and the right to make decisions concerning contraceptive use and abortion. In many of these contexts, there is no conflict between children's constitutional rights and their parents' rights, and indeed in many cases it is the parents who act to vindicate their children's rights. In other circumstances, most notably in the cases concerning contraception and abortion, interests of parents and children may come into conflict. See generally Homer H. Clark, Jr., <u>Children and the Constitution, 1992 U. Ill. L. Rev. 1 (1992)</u>.

Many academic writers have addressed the questions of children's rights, some arguing for broader legal recognition of such rights. Among the early contributions to this debate, see Patricia M. Wald, *Making Sense Out of the Rights of Youth*, 4 Hum. Rts. Q. 13 (1974); and <u>Henry H. Foster, Jr. and Doris Jonas Freed, A Bill of Rights for Children, 6 Fam. L.Q. 343, (1972)</u>. For a more skeptical view, see Bruce C. Hafen, *Children's Liberation and the New Egalitarianism: Some Reservations About Abandoning Youth to Their "Rights,"* 1976 BYU L. Rev. 605. For a more recent discussion, articulating a developmental theory of children's rights, see Anne C. Dailey, <u>Children's Constitutional Rights, 95 Minn. L. Rev. 2099 (2011)</u>.

b. Children and Criminal Procedure

The opinion in *D.C.* cites <u>In re Gault, 387 U.S. 1 (1967)</u>, in which the Court held that a minor in a **juvenile delinquency** proceeding has rights under the Due Process Clause (a) to adequate notice of the charges, (b) to be advised of his right to counsel either of his own choosing or to be furnished by the state, (c) to confront the witnesses against him, to cross-examine them, and (d) to the privilege against self-incrimination.

In *Gault*, a 15-year-old boy had been picked up by the police after a complaint by a neighbor that he had made an obscene telephone call to her. He was held in a detention home for about four days, during which time a "hearing" was held before the juvenile judge in chambers, at which the boy's parents were present, but neither they nor the boy were represented by counsel. No one was sworn, the woman who complained of receiving the call did not appear, no record was made, but the boy was asked about his part in the obscene call and apparently admitted some participation. Another similar hearing was held later, still without counsel for the boy and without the presence of the complainant, as a result of which the boy was committed to the State Industrial School until he reached age 21, unless sooner discharged. The case came to the Court on a petition for habeas corpus, which was granted by the Supreme Court.

Justice Fortas reviewed the history of the juvenile court movement in the United States, and the theory that in juvenile delinquency proceedings the state acted as *parens patriae* for the child's benefit, rather than as the child's accuser. He found that the result of this approach was too often arbitrary action lacking in due process, and unfair to the child. He also found that the juvenile court approach had failed to reduce crime or rehabilitate juvenile offenders. The *Gault* case has generally been assumed to stand for the proposition that the fundamental guarantees of the Due Process Clause apply to children as well as to adults, and that they apply in proceedings that may result in a deprivation of liberty notwithstanding that the proceedings are labeled civil rather than criminal. See David S. Tanenhaus, The Constitutional Rights of Children: In re Gault and Juvenile Justice (2011).

Subsequent cases retreated from the broad principles announced in *Gault*. In re Winship, 397 U.S. 358 (1970), held that in the adjudicatory stage of a delinquency proceeding in which the child is charged with an offense which would be a crime if committed by an adult, the Due Process Clause requires that the standard of proof be the criminal standard of proof beyond a reasonable doubt. But McKeiver v. Pennsylvania, 403 U.S. 528 (1971), held that the Due Process Clause does not require preservation of the right to trial by jury in the adjudicatory phase of a juvenile delinquency proceeding. Beginning with the acknowledged proposition that the Court had refrained in past cases from holding that all the adult criminal's due process rights are applicable to juvenile delinquency proceedings, the Court refused to label such proceedings either "civil" or "criminal," and said that the standard is one of fundamental fairness. The Court concluded that a jury trial was not a necessary element of fundamental fairness.

c. Juvenile Justice and Delinquency Prevention

Congress began enacting juvenile crime legislation in the 1960s, and provides significant funding to states, local governments and organizations under the Juvenile Justice and Delinquency Prevention Act, codified at 34 U.S.C. § 11101 et seq. (2018). These programs are administered through the Office of Juvenile Justice and Delinquency Prevention in the U.S. Department of Justice. For an excellent introduction to the many complex policy issues in this area, see Elizabeth S. Scott and Laurence Steinberg, Rethinking Juvenile Justice (2010).

Juvenile Crime

State statutes often treat crimes committed by minors differently from the same crimes of adults, providing for specialized procedures and a different range of punishments. See generally Mark I. Soler et al., Representing the Child Client (2008 & Supp.).

d. Children and the Eighth Amendment

In a series of decisions, the Supreme Court has held that a death penalty sentence constitutes cruel and unusual punishment under the Eighth Amendment when it is imposed on a defendant for a crime committed before the individual reached age 18. See <u>Roper v. Simmons, 543 U.S. 551 (2005)</u>; see also <u>Thompson v. Oklahoma, 487 U.S. 815 (1988)</u> (finding that execution of a defendant for a crime committed before age 16 violated the Constitution). In addition, the Court held in <u>Graham v. Florida, 560 U.S. 48 (2010)</u> that the Eighth Amendment prohibits a mandatory sentence of life without parole for a juvenile convicted of a non-homicide offense, and extended this ruling to homicide offenses in <u>Miller v. Alabama, 567 U.S. 460 (2012)</u>. In <u>Montgomery v. Louisiana, 577 U.S. ____, 136 S.Ct. 2271 (2016)</u> the Court clarified that *Miller* stated a new substantive rule of constitutional law that must be applied retroactively by states on collateral review.

Global View: Children and International Human Rights Law

The United Nations <u>Convention on the Rights of the Child</u> (CRC), G.A. Res.44/25 (Annex), U.N. GAOR. 44th Sess., Supp. No. 49, at 166, U.N. Doc. A/44/49, 1577 U.N.T.S. 3 (Nov. 10, 1989), *reprinted at* 28 I.L.M. 1456 (1989), details a series of civil, political, economic, social and cultural rights of children, including rights to health care and education, to protection from abuse and neglect, to free expression of their views and participation in decision-making processes that concern them.

The CRC mandates that the best interest of the child "shall be a primary consideration" in all actions concerning children, whether taken by public or private social welfare institutions, courts of law, administrative authorities or other legislative bodies. It provides in Article 12 that a child "capable of forming his or her own views" has the right to express those views freely in any judicial or administrative proceeding concerning the child. The CRC protects familial rights, obligating governments to respect the "primary responsibility" of parents for the upbringing and development of the child in Articles 5 and 18, and including a requirement in Article 9 that a child shall not be separated from his or her parents against their will, unless competent authorities have determined (with appropriate procedural safeguards) that such a separation "is necessary for the best interests of the child."

Although the United States signed the CRC in 1995, it is the only nation in the world besides Somalia that has not ratified it. There are some potential conflicts between the CRC and United States laws, but opposition to the Convention has been primarily philosophical and political. See Susan Kilbourne, *Placing the Convention on the Rights of the Child in an American Context*, Human Rights, Spring 1999 at 7; Cynthia Price Cohen and Howard A. Davidson, eds., Children's Rights in America: U.N. Convention on the Rights of the Child Compared with United States Law (1990). The CRC's prohibition of capital punishment and life imprisonment without parole for juvenile offenders in Article 37(a), which was inconsistent with the laws in some states, no longer presents a conflict with U.S. law in light of the Supreme Court's decisions under the Eighth Amendment noted above.

The United States has ratified the Optional Protocol to the CRC on the Sale of Children, Child Prostitution, and Child Pornography, G.A. Res. 54–263 Annex, U.N. G.A.O.R., 54th Sess., U.N. Doc. A/RES/54/264 (May 25, 2000), and the Optional Protocol on the Involvement of Children in Armed Conflicts, G.A. Res. 54–263 Annex, U.N. G.A.O.R., 54th Sess., U.N. Doc. A/RES/54/264 (Mar. 16, 2001).

Care and Protection of Beth

587 N.E.2d 1377 (Mass 1992)

ABRAMS, JUSTICE.

A single justice has reserved and reported the correctness of a substituted judgment determination calling for a "no code"[1] order to be entered on the medical charts of an incompetent minor ward. A judge of the Holyoke Division of the

---

[1]   A "no code" order, also referred to as a "DNR" or do-not-resuscitate order, directs a hospital and staff not to employ extraordinary resuscitative measures in the event of cardiac or respiratory failure. "The terminology derives from the development in recent years, in acute care hospitals, of specialized 'teams' of doctors and nurses trained in the administration of cardiopulmonary resuscitative measures. If a patient goes into cardiac or respiratory arrest, the nurse in attendance causes a notice to be broadcast on the hospital's intercommunications system giving a code word and the room number. The members of the code team converge on the room immediately from other parts of the hospital." *Matter of Dinnerstein*, 6 Mass.App.Ct. 466, 469 n. 3, 380 N.E.2d 134 (1978).

District Court determined that an infant in a persistent vegetative coma would choose, were she competent, to have the "no code" order entered on her medical charts. For the reasons stated we affirm.

Facts. The child whose treatment is at issue was born on September 30, 1986. Her mother and putative father were both minors at the time. Less than one month after her birth, in response to a petition filed by the Department of Social Services (DSS), a District Court judge found the child to be in need of care and protection. By order of the District Court, DSS gained legal and physical custody of the child. On October 30, 1986, the child's mother was also found in need of care and protection and placed in DSS custody. In December of the same year, DSS returned physical custody of the child to her mother, while retaining legal custody.

Shortly thereafter, the mother and child were involved in an automobile accident. That accident, in which the straps on the child's car seat wrapped around her neck and cut off the supply of oxygen to her brain for a substantial period of time, left the child in an irreversible coma.

As a result of the accident, the child cannot see, hear, or engage in any purposeful movement. Her ability to breathe on her own is extremely limited. A breathing tube has been inserted directly into her lungs through an incision in her trachea, and her rate of breathing is controlled by a machine. She is fed through a feeding tube permanently inserted in her stomach. The child suffered cardiorespiratory arrests as a result of aspirating food regurgitated from her stomach. She was resuscitated on these occasions by extraordinary treatment, including the administration of medication to restart her heart. Although the child has undergone Nissen fundoplication surgery, which significantly decreases the likelihood that she will regurgitate food into her lungs, she nevertheless still runs the risk of such cardiorespiratory arrests.

On July 7, 1987, DSS and the child's mother jointly moved for appointment of a guardian ad litem for the child and entry of a substituted judgment decision as to what further medical care should be given to the child. Because both the child and her parents were minors, as well as under the legal custody of DSS, a guardian was appointed to represent the child.

The primary witness at the hearing for entry of substituted judgment was Dr. Stephen Lieberman, the director of the pediatric intensive care unit at Baystate Medical Center, where the child was hospitalized following the accident. Dr. Lieberman, who has extensive training and experience in treating children with neurological problems, was primarily responsible for the child from the time she was admitted to Baystate. After extensive testing, Dr. Lieberman determined that "there is nothing to indicate that she has any ability to function from her cerebral cortex. But she does function from a brain stem level where things are not under [her conscious] control."[4] He testified that the child is irreversibly in a state of coma from which "she will never regain [consciousness or] be able to function in any way." He testified that "there is really no potential for this condition to be reversed" except through the perfection of a complete brain transplant operation. Dr. Lieberman stated that, although there is medical controversy as to whether a person functioning at a brain stem level can feel pain, in his opinion, the child does not feel pain, or at least is not "able to localize it." He testified that entry of a "no code" order was completely consistent with medical ethics.

The District Court judge, substituting his judgment for the incompetent child, found that, if competent, the child would choose not to be resuscitated by extraordinary measures. He therefore ordered that "further ventilator treatment and resuscitative measures be withheld" in the event the child "suffers respiratory distress or cardiac arrest in the future." In addition, he ordered that the Nissen fundoplication surgery be performed in order to reduce the likelihood of the child's aspirating regurgitated food.

Pursuant to G.L. c. 211, § 3 (1990 ed.), the child's guardian ad litem sought relief from the District Court's DNR order before a single justice of this court. The single justice reserved and reported the matter after the parties[6] so requested and submitted a statement of agreed facts. The guardian argues that: (1) the judge's factual findings with respect to the effects of full code treatment clearly are erroneous; (2) the judge's determination that the child would choose to decline resuscitative medical treatment in the event of respiratory or cardiac arrest is without support in the record and the judge's findings; and (3) even if the judge's substituted judgment determination were correct, resuscitative treatment should nevertheless be administered because the State's interest in the preservation of

---

[4]   In other words, the child's lower brain, and not her upper brain, functions. The upper brain controls thinking and awareness. The lower brain controls only vegetative functions. Currently, only patients who have lost operation of both their upper and lower brain are classified as legally dead.

We note, however, that the definition of "death" is not static. It evolves with advances in medical technology and changes in social attitudes. Formerly, patients were declared dead when their heart and lungs ceased to function. See Black's Law Dictionary 488 (4th ed. 1968). Once the capacity to mechanically maintain cardiac and respiratory functions was developed, however, this definition was no longer adequate and was supplemented (either by statute or judicial decision) by the "total brain death" definition. See Black's Law Dictionary 360–361 (5th ed. 1979).

One commentator argues that our understanding of death should undergo another revision: when the upper brain ceases to function ("neocortical death"), the patient ought to be considered dead. According to this commentator, the values underlying the "total brain death" and "neocortical death" standard are compatible: the former, like the latter, rests on the view that consciousness is the sine qua non of human existence, since a person who is permanently unconscious will currently be declared dead even though her respiration could be mechanically maintained. K.G. Gervais, Redefining Death (Yale U. Press, 1986).

[6]   There are three parties to this matter: the guardian ad litem; DSS; and the judge of the District Court, whose motion to be designated a nominal party was allowed.

life outweighs the child's desire to have a "no code" order entered on her medical charts. The guardian requests that the order placing the child on "no code" status be vacated, and that we enter a judgment that the child would choose to have all extraordinary medical treatment continue in the event of further cardiac or respiratory arrests.

The "no code" determination. "Cardiac arrest occurs at some point in the dying process of every person, whatever the underlying cause of death. Hence the decision whether or not to attempt resuscitation is potentially relevant for all patients." Deciding to Forego Life-Sustaining Treatment: Ethical, Medical and Legal Issues in Treatment Decisions, President's Commission for the Study of Ethical Problems in Medicine and Biomedical and Behavioral Research, 235 (March, 1983). It is not surprising, then, that "no code" orders have become fairly routine.

Generally, "no code" orders do not require judicial oversight. Cf. *Brophy v. New England Sinai Hosp., Inc.*, 398 Mass. 417, 423, 497 N.E.2d 626 (1986) (unlike substituted judgment to discontinue artificial nutrition and hydration, DNR order entered on Brophy's chart at wife's request not reviewed by court). Courts should not be in the business of reviewing uncontroversial "no-code" cases simply because doctors and hospitals seek to shield themselves from liability. See Liacos, "Dilemmas of Dying," Legal and Ethical Aspects of Treating Critically and Terminally Ill Patients 149, 153 (Am.Soc'y of Law & Med., 1982) ("there is a difference between acting to preserve the interest of the patient and acting to preserve the interest of the profession"). "If hospitals ensure that decisionmaking practices are reasonable and that internal review and advice are readily available, decisions concerning resuscitation will seldom need to come before courts." Deciding to Forego Life-Sustaining Treatment, *supra at 252.*

In this case, however, the minor is incompetent by virtue of both her age and irreversible coma. Further, both parents still also minors, and the mother and child were in the legal custody of DSS. The guardian opposes the DNR order. Moreover, as in *Custody of a Minor (No. 1)*, 385 Mass. 697, 709, 434 N.E.2d 601 (1982), "the child already was within the jurisdiction of the court before the question whether a 'no code' order should be made * * * arose." In these circumstances, a judicial "no code" determination is appropriate. Cf. *id. at 709, 434 N.E.2d 601* (where, among other factors: (1) minor patient is ward of State in DSS custody; (2) child's mental faculties have not developed to point that he is competent to make decision; (3) parents have failed to exercise parental responsibilities toward child; and (4) child already was within the jurisdiction of the court, judicial determination of ["no code"] is appropriate); *Matter of Spring*, 380 Mass. 629, 636–637, 405 N.E.2d 115 (1980) ("[O]ur opinions should not be taken to establish any requirement of prior judicial approval that would not otherwise exist. * * * [A] variety of circumstances [are] to be taken into account in deciding whether there should be an application for a prior court order with respect to medical treatment of an incompetent patient." [Circumstances include whether the patient is in State custody, the patient's level of comprehension and mental ability, and whether the patient, spouse or guardian consent to the action]).

The right of incompetent individuals to refuse medical treatment is effectuated through the doctrine of substituted judgment. See, e.g., *Custody of a Minor* (No. 1), *supra*, 385 Mass. at 697, 434 N.E.2d 601; *Superintendent of Belchertown State School v. Saikewicz*, 373 Mass. 728, 738–739, 370 N.E.2d 417 (1977). In making a substituted judgment determination, the court "dons 'the mental mantle of the incompetent' and substitutes itself as nearly as possible for the individual in the decision-making process. * * * [T]he court does not decide what is necessarily the best decision but rather what decision would be made by the incompetent person if he or she were competent." *Matter of Moe*, 385 Mass. 555, 565, 432 N.E.2d 712 (1982), citing *Saikewicz, supra* 373 Mass. at 752, 370 N.E.2d 417, quoting *In re Carson*, 39 Misc.2d 544, 545, 241 N.Y.S.2d 288 (N.Y.Sup.Ct.1962). In determining what the incompetent person's choice would be, the judge should consider: (1) the patient's expressed preferences, if any; (2) the patient's religious convictions, if any; (3) the impact on the patient's family; (4) the probability of adverse side effects from the treatment; and (5) the prognosis with and without treatment. The judge must also "tak[e] into account the present and future incompetency of the individual as one of the factors which would necessarily enter into the decision-making process of the competent person." *Saikewicz, supra*, 373 Mass. at 752–753, 370 N.E.2d 417. The judge should also consider any countervailing State interests, which may include: (1) the preservation of life; (2) the protection of innocent third parties; (3) the prevention of suicide; and (4) the maintenance of the ethical integrity of the medical profession. The judge may consider any additional factors which appear to be relevant.

With respect to the foregoing factors, the judge found the following facts. Because of her infancy, the child had not expressed any wishes from which the judge could draw guidance. "[B]ecause of the absence of natural family involvement there is no information regarding the child's ethical, moral or religious values that the Court could examine." There would be little, if any, impact on the child's family because the family was never intact. "[T]he implications of a full-code effort would involve a substantial degree of bodily invasion." If the infant were to experience cardiac or respiratory arrest, in the absence of extraordinary measures, the child might die. Even with the full-code treatment, "the prognosis for the child * * * would remain terminal because of the untreatable 'brain-dead' condition." The child "has made no gains during her long hospitalization;" "at best [she] will live for an indefinite period in a vegetative coma without any real hope of improvement, and as to the brain damage itself the prognosis is hopeless." The judge's findings, excluding the one for which there is no support, * * * are sufficient to support the determination that the child would refuse resuscitative measures in the event of cardiac or respiratory arrest.

Arguing that the child has no dignity interest in being free of bodily invasions, the guardian states that the child "has no cognitive ability and therefore will suffer no 'indignity' that the medical care might be supposed to produce in a conscious person." "Cognitive ability" is not a prerequisite for enjoying basic liberties. In the law of this jurisdiction, incompetent people are entitled to the same respect, dignity and freedom of choice as competent people.

The guardian also argues that, in any event, "the necessity for the bodily invasions occasioned by the efforts to resuscitate have been greatly reduced by [the Nissen fundoplication] surgery." The fact that the invasions may be less frequent than before the surgery does not make any particular invasion less likely to offend the child's dignity.

The guardian claims that "treatment would not occasion any financial disruption of the ward's family, nor involve emotional disturbance which the ward would, if competent, find compelling." Although the guardian proposes that lack of financial disruption counsels in favor of continued treatment, we hardly think the guardian would accept the converse proposition. As we recently stated in <u>Doe, supra, 411 Mass. at 520 n. 15, 583 N.E.2d 1263</u>, "[t]he judge quite properly did not consider whether [the patient's] continued care would pose a burden of any kind on anyone. The cost of care in human or financial terms is irrelevant to the substituted judgment analysis." The guardian's second claim is controverted most strongly by the fact that both the child's mother and father have expressed their desire that extraordinary measures not be used to prolong the child's life. The mother testified: "I don't like to see her going through, suffering that she's going through. * * * I know what she was like before this accident. She was a very healthy baby, always smiling * * * and she's just laying there doing nothing, and it's not like my daughter." Moreover, the emotional disturbance which the ward herself, if competent, would experience as a result of her condition cannot be underestimated. Last, contrary to the guardian's assertions, there is no evidence that the decision to enter the "no code" order reflects the judge's own judgment about the quality of the child's life.

The guardian alternatively argues that, assuming that the judge was correct in deciding that the child would choose to refuse resuscitation, the State's interest in the preservation of life outweighs the child's wishes. As we have stated on previous occasions, the State's general interest in the preservation of life is not absolute. Here, as in <u>Saikewicz, supra, 373 Mass. at 742, 370 N.E.2d 417</u>, "[t]he interest of the State in prolonging a life must be reconciled with the interest of an individual to reject the traumatic cost of that prolongation. There is a substantial distinction in the State's insistence that human life be saved where the affliction is curable, as opposed to the State interest where, as here, the issue is not whether, but when, for how long, and at what cost to the individual that life may be briefly extended."

The substituted judgment decision and the entry of the "do not resuscitate" order are affirmed.

Nolan, Justice (dissenting).

A person is not obligated to take extraordinary means to prolong his life and, therefore, persons acting in behalf of others who are faced with such a decision, are not required to invoke extraordinary means.

However, the court again has approved application of the doctrine of substituted judgment when there is not a soupçon of evidence to support it. The trial judge did not have a smidgen of evidence on which to conclude that if this child who is now about five and one half years old were competent to decide, she would elect certain death to a life with no cognitive ability. The route by which the court arrives at its conclusion is a cruel charade which is being perpetuated whenever we are faced with a life and death decision of an incompetent person.

I dissent.

Points for Discussion

a. *Protection of Beth*

As the court says, if Beth's parents had been competent adults, it would not have been necessary to bring a legal proceeding to vindicate their desire for a "no code" order. What if Beth's parents had opposed the "no code" order? What should be the result if the parents were adults and disagreed concerning this type of major health care decision? See In re Jane Doe, 418 S.E.2d 3 (Ga. 1992); Curran v. Bosze, 566 N.E.2d 1319 (Ill. 1990).

Ordinarily, parents have the right to determine what medical care their children will receive, subject to the laws discussed in Chapter 5 that permit the state to intervene if withholding treatment would constitute child abuse or neglect. See generally Homer H. Clark, Jr., Domestic Relations § 9.3 (Student 2d ed. 1988).

b. Substituted Judgment

How can the doctrine of "substituted judgment" be used to determine whether to deny extraordinary treatment when the child involved is unconscious only about eight months old? If this doctrine is unrealistic in these circumstances, what other legal basis is there for deciding the case? See In re K.I., 735 A.2d 448 (D.C.1999), which applied a best interests test rather than a substituted judgment approach.

c. Infants with Severe Handicaps

Medical treatment decisions for infants with severe birth defects are governed by federal regulations, applicable to all hospitals receiving federal funds, designed to prevent instances of unlawful neglect, and implemented in response to cases such as United States v. University Hospital, State University of New York at Stony Brook, 729 F.2d 144, 146 (2d Cir.1984). See 45 C.F.R. § 84.55 (2018). The regulations encourage hospitals receiving federal funds to establish an Infant Care Review Committee (ICRC) to assist in developing standards and deciding on specific cases concerning medical treatment of infants, and require the posting of one of two forms of informational notice in the hospital, stating the hospital's policy, stating that nourishment and beneficial medical treatment should not be withheld from handicapped infants solely by reason of their mental or physical impairments. For discussion of the complex legal and ethical issues in these cases, see Carl E. Schneider, *Rights Discourse and Neonatal Euthanasia*, 76 Cal. L. Rev. 151 (1988); Martha A. Field, *Killing "The Handicapped"—Before and After Birth*, 16 Harv. Women's L. J. 79 (1993).

d. Mature Minors

Some states have a common law "mature minor" rule, which allows some mature minors to consent to treatment for non-serious illnesses or conditions. Some statutes may permit minors to consent to specific types of treatment, such as treatment for pregnancy, sexual assault, sexually transmitted diseases, alcohol and drug abuse, and in emergency situations. See, e.g., N.Y. Pub. Health L. § 2805–d (2018). Minors are in a special category with respect to abortion, as discussed in Chapter 2.

A mature minor may also have the right to refuse treatment, at least where the minor's parent concurs. Where the parent's opinion is adverse to the minor's and favors the treatment, the court said that would "weigh heavily" in the decision. See In re E.G., 549 N.E.2d 322 (Ill. 1989). See generally Rhonda Gay Hartman, *Coming of Age: Devising Legislation for Adolescent Medical Decision-Making*, 28 Am. J.L. & Med. 409 (2002); Walter Wadlington, *Minors and Health Care: The Age of Consent*, 11 Osgoode Hall L.J. 115 (1973).

There has been considerable debate over involuntary psychiatric treatment for minors. People v. Gainer, 566 P.2d 997 (Cal. 1977), held that the due process guarantees of both the U.S. and California Constitutions require a pre-commitment, trial-type

Make the Connection

Laws regarding medical decision-making for adult family members are discussed earlier in this chapter.

hearing for juveniles over fourteen being committed to state mental hospitals. The court expressly refrained from deciding what due process requires for children under fourteen. See also <u>P.F. v. Walsh, Jr., 648 P.2d 1067 (Colo.1982)</u> (holding a statute unconstitutional that authorized the admission of a minor to a state psychiatric hospital against his will, but with the approval of his parent or guardian.) In contrast, <u>Parham v. J.R., 442 U.S. 584 (1979)</u>, held that due process generally requires only a thorough psychiatric examination and an independent medical decision-making procedure, with periodic review of the child's status by hospital staff.

Problem 4-7

Karla was five months pregnant when she went into premature labor. Doctors informed her that her child had little chance of being born alive, and that if it was born alive, the baby would probably suffer from a variety of severe impairments including cerebral palsy, brain hemorrhaging, blindness, lung disease, pulmonary infections and mental retardation. Karla and her husband, Mark, informed the physicians and the hospital that they did not want heroic measures performed if the child was born prematurely, including resuscitation or life support machines, so that nature would take its course.

After meeting with the parents, the hospital administrators decided to have a neonatologist present at the birth and to wait until the child was born before deciding whether resuscitation was appropriate. The child was born alive the next day, and doctors placed her on ventilation to assist her breathing. Within a few days later, however, she suffered a brain hemorrhage causing severe physical and mental impairments. Karla and Mark have sued the hospital, alleging that the hospital was negligent in allowing emergency procedures to performed without their consent and that performing these procedures despite their instructions to the contrary constitutes a battery. Should the hospital be liable in these circumstances? (See <u>Miller v. HCA, 118 S.W.3d 758 (Tex. 2003)</u>.)

Guardianship

English law recognized many varieties of guardianship, created when a person was appointed to protect various interests of a child or a person under a disability, called the **ward**. A **guardian of the person** of a child is someone other than a parent who has custody of the child and is responsible for the child's care, education, and training. A **guardian of the estate** or property of the child is responsible for managing the child's property. The guardian of the estate is a fiduciary whose activities and obligations very closely resemble those of a trustee. Both a guardian of the person of the child and a guardian of the estate of a child must be appointed by a court. A **guardian ad litem** or GAL is appointed to represent and protect the interests of the child in particular litigation. See e.g. Fed. R. Civ. Proc. 17(c). The role of the GAL is discussed further in Chapter 7 and Chapter 8. For discussions of the various forms of guardianship, with references to statute and case law, see Homer H. Clark, Jr., Domestic Relations § 8.4 (Student 2d ed. 1988).

The expense and inconvenience of a financial guardianship may be avoided by the Uniform Transfer to Minors Act, enacted in many states, which establishes a simple and inexpensive way of making gifts of securities to children without either a guardianship or a trust. 8C U.L.A. 1 (2014). Gifts to minors under this statute are made by delivery of the security to a custodian for the minor. Such a gift conveys full legal title to the minor but enables the custodian to manage, invest and reinvest the property. If the child has a guardian, the guardian does not receive any rights with respect to the property given under the act. The act gives to the custodian broad powers of management, provides that the custodian is a fiduciary and provides convenient and inexpensive methods for the administration of the custodial property.

Statutes in many states authorize parents to appoint guardians of the child's person or estate by a will. See, e.g., Cal. Probate Code § 2108 (2018); Conn. Gen Stat. § 45a–596(a) (2018); N.Y. Dom. Rel. Laws § 81 (2018). Such an appointment must be confirmed by the appropriate court. See, e.g. In re Joshua S., 260 Conn. 182, 796 A.2d 1141 (2002); In re Slaughter, 738 A.2d 1013 (Pa.Super.Ct.1999). If only one parent of a child dies and the other is still alive, the surviving parent will ordinarily be granted custody of the child unless shown to be unfit. Cf. Guardianship of Stodden, 569 N.W.2d 621 (Iowa Ct. App.1997). Special statutes in some states allow a parent with a progressively chronic illness or irreversibly fatal illness to petition for appointment of a standby guardian, whose authority over the child becomes effective upon incapacity or death of the parent. See N.Y. Surr. Ct. Proc. Act § 1726 (2018); Guardianship of F.H., 632 N.Y.S.2d 777 (Surr.Ct.1995).

Problem 4-8

John moved in with Sherrie and her two children four years ago, and they were married two years later. The children have had no significant interaction with their father for the past seven years. Sherrie died unexpectedly a month ago, and John obtained an emergency order appointing him as temporary guardian of the children. Their father has now filed a petition for custody, asking that John's guardianship be terminated, invoking his rights as the children's natural and legal parent. How should the court evaluate this case? See Guardianship of B.H., 770 N.E.2d 283 (Ind. 2002).

D. Beyond the Nuclear Family

The marital and family privacy norms recognized in cases discussed earlier in this book, such as Griswold v. Connecticut, 381 U.S. 479 (1965) (Chapter 1), Michael H. v. Gerald D, 491 U.S. 110 (1989) (Chapter 2) and Troxel v. Granville, 530 U.S. 57 (2000) (Chapter 4), extend strong protection to nuclear family relationships, particularly family relationships based on marriage. See Anne C. Dailey, *Constitutional Privacy and the Just Family*, 67 Tul. L. Rev. 955 (1993); Richard F. Storrow, *The Policy of Family Privacy: Uncovering the Bias in Favor of Nuclear Families in American Constitutional Law and Policy Reform*, 66 Mo. L. Rev. 527 (2001). The Supreme Court has extended protection to nonmarital parent-child relationships in numerous decisions, including the lines of cases that began with Levy v. Louisiana, 391 U.S. 68 (1968) and Stanley v. Illinois, 405 U.S. 645 (1972), considered in Chapter 2. These two lines of cases are often ambivalent and contradictory, however, and ultimately reflect a strong preference for what Justice Scalia referred to as the "unitary family" in *Michael H.*

Contemporary demographic realities suggest that many adults and children do not live in nuclear families. The 2010 Census counted 116.7 million households in the United States, including 77.5 million "family households" containing at least one person related to the householder by birth, marriage, or adoption. Only 54.5 million of these households were husband-wife households, amounting to fewer than half of all households for the first time since these data have been kept. More than five million households consisted of three or more generations of family members, and large numbers of family households included stepchildren, adult children, siblings or other relatives of the householder. Of the 39.2 million nonfamily households, there were 31.2 million one-person households, and 8 million nonfamily households with two or more people. See U.S. Census Bureau, 2010 Census Briefs, Households and Families: 2010 (April 2012).

Moore v. City of East Cleveland, Ohio

431 U.S. 494 (1977)

Go Online

Listen to the <u>oral arguments</u> in *Moore* at the Oyez Project web site.

MR. JUSTICE POWELL announced the judgment of the Court, and delivered an opinion in which MR. JUSTICE BRENNAN, MR. JUSTICE MARSHALL, and MR. JUSTICE BLACKMUN joined.

East Cleveland's housing ordinance, like many throughout the country, limits occupancy of a dwelling unit to members of a single family. s 1351.02. But the ordinance contains an unusual and complicated definitional section that recognizes as a "family" only a few categories of related individuals, s 1341.08.[2] Because her family, living together in her home, fits none of those categories, appellant stands convicted of a criminal offense. The question in this case is whether the ordinance violates the Due Process Clause of the Fourteenth Amendment.

I

Appellant, Mrs. Inez Moore, lives in her East Cleveland home together with her son, Dale Moore Sr., and her two grandsons, Dale, Jr., and John Moore, Jr. The two boys are first cousins rather than brothers; we are told that John came to live with his grandmother and with the elder and younger Dale Moores after his mother's death.

In early 1973, Mrs. Moore received a notice of violation from the city, stating that John was an "illegal occupant" and directing her to comply with the ordinance. When she failed to remove him from her home, the city filed a criminal

---

[2]   Section 1341.08 (1966) provides:

" 'Family' means a number of individuals related to the nominal head of the household or to the spouse of the nominal head of the household living as a single housekeeping unit in a single dwelling unit, but limited to the following:

"(a) Husband or wife of the nominal head of the household.

"(b) Unmarried children of the nominal head of the household or of the spouse of the nominal head of the household, provided, however, that such unmarried children have no children residing with them.

"(c) Father or mother of the nominal head of the household or of the spouse of the nominal head of the household.

"(d) Notwithstanding the provisions of subsection (b) hereof, a family may include not more than one dependent married or unmarried child of the nominal head of the household or of the spouse of the nominal head of the household and the spouse and dependent children of such dependent child. For the purpose of this subsection, a dependent person is one who has more than fifty percent of his total support furnished for him by the nominal head of the household and the spouse of the nominal head of the household.

"(e) A family may consist of one individual."

charge. Mrs. Moore moved to dismiss, claiming that the ordinance was constitutionally invalid on its face. Her motion was overruled, and upon conviction she was sentenced to five days in jail and a $25 fine. The Ohio Court of Appeals affirmed after giving full consideration to her constitutional claims, and the Ohio Supreme Court denied review.

II

The city argues that our decision in Village of Belle Terre v. Boraas, 416 U.S. 1 (1974), requires us to sustain the ordinance attacked here. Belle Terre, like East Cleveland, imposed limits on the types of groups that could occupy a single dwelling unit. Applying the constitutional standard announced in this Court's leading land-use case, Villiage of Euclid, Ohio v. Ambler Realty Co., 272 U.S. 365 (1926), we sustained the Belle Terre ordinance on the ground that it bore a rational relationship to permissible state objectives.

But one overriding factor sets this case apart from Belle Terre. The ordinance there affected only unrelated individuals. It expressly allowed all who were related by "blood, adoption, or marriage" to live together, and in sustaining the ordinance we were careful to note that it promoted "family needs" and "family values." East Cleveland, in contrast, has chosen to regulate the occupancy of its housing by slicing deeply into the family itself. This is no mere incidental result of the ordinance. On its face it selects certain categories of relatives who may live together and declares that others may not. In particular, it makes a crime of a grandmother's choice to live with her grandson in circumstances like those presented here.

When a city undertakes such intrusive regulation of the family, neither Belle Terre nor Euclid governs; the usual judicial deference to the legislature is inappropriate. "This Court has long recognized that freedom of personal choice in matters of marriage and family life is one of the liberties protected by the Due Process Clause of the Fourteenth Amendment." Cleveland Board of Education v. LaFleur, 414 U.S. 632, 639–640 (1974). A host of cases, tracing their lineage to Meyer v. Nebraska, 262 U.S. 390, 399–401 (1923), and Pierce v. Society of the Sisters of the Holy Names of Jesus and Mary, 268 U.S. 510, 534–535 (1925), have consistently acknowledged a "private realm of family life which the state cannot enter." Prince v. Massachusetts, 321 U.S. 158, 166 (1944). See, e. g., Roe v. Wade, 410 U.S. 113, 152–153 (1973); Wisconsin v. Yoder, 406 U.S. 205, 231–233 (1972); Stanley v. Illinois, 405 U.S. 645, 651 (1972); Ginsberg v. New York, 390 U.S. 629, 639 (1968); Griswold v. Connecticut, 381 U.S. 479 (1965); id., at 495–496 (Goldberg, J., concurring); id., at 502–503 (White, J., concurring); Poe v. Ullman, 367 U.S. 497, 542–544 (1961) (Harlan, J., dissenting), cf. Loving v. Virginia, 388 U.S. 1, 12 (1967); May v. Anderson, 345 U.S. 528, 533 (1953); Skinner v. Oklahoma ex rel. Williamson, 316 U.S. 535, 541 (1942). Of course, the family is not beyond regulation. See Prince

v. Massachusetts, supra, 321 U.S. at 166. But when the government intrudes on choices concerning family living arrangements, this Court must examine carefully the importance of the governmental interests advanced and the extent to which they are served by the challenged regulation. See Poe v. Ullman, supra, 367 U.S., at 554 (Harlan, J., dissenting).

When thus examined, this ordinance cannot survive. The city seeks to justify it as a means of preventing overcrowding, minimizing traffic and parking congestion, and avoiding an undue financial burden on East Cleveland's school system. Although these are legitimate goals, the ordinance before us serves them marginally, at best. For example, the ordinance permits any family consisting only of husband, wife, and unmarried children to live together, even if the family contains a half dozen licensed drivers, each with his or her own car. At the same time it forbids an adult brother and sister to share a household, even if both faithfully use public transportation. The ordinance would permit a grandmother to live with a single dependent son and children, even if his school-age children number a dozen, yet it forces Mrs. Moore to find another dwelling for her grandson John, simply because of the presence of his uncle and cousin in the same household. We need not labor the point. Section 1341.08 has but a tenuous relation to alleviation of the conditions mentioned by the city.

III

The city would distinguish the cases based on *Meyer* and *Pierce*. It points out that none of them "gives grandmothers any fundamental rights with respect to grandsons," and suggests that any constitutional right to live together as a family extends only to the nuclear family essentially a couple and their dependent children.

To be sure, these cases did not expressly consider the family relationship presented here. They were immediately concerned with freedom of choice with respect to childbearing, e. g., *LaFleur*, Roe v. Wade, Griswold, supra, or with the rights of parents to the custody and companionship of their own children, Stanley v. Illinois, supra, or with traditional parental authority in matters of child rearing and education. *Yoder*, *Ginsberg*, *Pierce*, Meyer, supra. But unless we close our eyes to the basic reasons why certain rights associated with the family have been accorded shelter under the Fourteenth Amendment's Due Process Clause, we cannot avoid applying the force and rationale of these precedents to the family choice involved in this case.

* * *

Substantive due process has at times been a treacherous field for this Court. There are risks when the judicial branch gives enhanced protection to certain substantive liberties without the guidance of the more specific provisions of the

Bill of Rights. As the history of the *Lochner* era demonstrates, there is reason for concern lest the only limits to such judicial intervention become the predilections of those who happen at the time to be Members of this Court. That history counsels caution and restraint. But it does not counsel abandonment, nor does it require what the city urges here: cutting off any protection of family rights at the first convenient, if arbitrary boundary—the boundary of the nuclear family.

Appropriate limits on substantive due process come not from drawing arbitrary lines but rather from careful "respect for the teachings of history (and), solid recognition of the basic values that underlie our society". <u>Griswold v. Connecticut, 381 U.S., at 501</u> (Harlan, J., concurring). Our decisions establish that the Constitution protects the sanctity of the family precisely because the institution of the family is deeply rooted in this Nation's history and tradition. It is through the family that we inculcate and pass down many of our most cherished values, moral and cultural.

Ours is by no means a tradition limited to respect for the bonds uniting the members of the nuclear family. The tradition of uncles, aunts, cousins, and especially grandparents sharing a household along with parents and children has roots equally venerable and equally deserving of constitutional recognition. Over the years millions of our citizens have grown up in just such an environment, and most, surely, have profited from it. Even if conditions of modern society have brought about a decline in extended family households, they have not erased the accumulated wisdom of civilization, gained over the centuries and honored throughout our history, that supports a larger conception of the family. Out of choice, necessity, or a sense of family responsibility, it has been common for close relatives to draw together and participate in the duties and the satisfactions of a common home. Decisions concerning child rearing, which *Yoder, Meyer, Pierce* and other cases have recognized as entitled to constitutional protection, long have been shared with grandparents or other relatives who occupy the same household indeed who may take on major responsibility for the

> **FYI**
>
> Justices Brennan and Marshall wrote a concurring opinion emphasizing the "cultural myopia of the arbitrary boundary drawn by the East Cleveland ordinance," and the particular importance of the extended family form for black families. Justice Stevens concurred in the judgment, concluding that the ordinance was invalid as an unconstitutional taking of property without just compensation. Four justices dissented, in three separate opinions.
>
> For more of the story behind the *Moore* case, see Peggy Cooper Davis, Moore v. East Cleveland: *Constructing the Suburban Family*, in Family Law Stories 77 (Carol Sanger, ed. 2008)

rearing of the children.[15] Especially in times of adversity, such as the death of a spouse or economic need, the broader family has tended to come together for mutual sustenance and to maintain or rebuild a secure home life. This is apparently what happened here.[16]

Whether or not such a household is established because of personal tragedy, the choice of relatives in this degree of kinship to live together may not lightly be denied by the State. *Pierce* struck down an Oregon law requiring all children to attend the State's public schools, holding that the Constitution "excludes any general power of the State to standardize its children by forcing them to accept instruction from public teachers only." By the same token the Constitution prevents East Cleveland from standardizing its children and its adults by forcing all to live in certain narrowly defined family patterns.

Reversed.

Points for Discussion

a. Family vs. Non-Family Households

Three years before the *Moore* decision, the Court upheld a zoning ordinance in Village of Belle Terre v. Boraas, 416 U.S.1 (1974), that restricted the number of unrelated people who could live in the same household to two. Justice Marshall dissented on the basis that the ordinance violated the appellees' First Amendment freedom of association and their constitutional privacy rights. Why does the Court reach a different result in *Moore*?

b. Grandparents

The Supreme Court's opinion in *Troxel*, reprinted above, makes clear that grandparents' rights with respect to their grandchildren are generally subordinate to parental rights. Should the questions in *Troxel* be analyzed differently when grandparents have taken

Go Online

Information on Grandparents Raising Grandchildren is available from the Child Welfare Information Gateway.

on formal or informal responsibilities as caregivers? The question of kinship foster care is discussed in Chapter 5.

---

[15] Cf. Prince v. Massachusetts, 321 U.S. 158 (1944), which spoke broadly of family authority as against the State, in a case where the child was being reared by her aunt, not her natural parents.

[16] We are told that the mother of John Moore, Jr., died when he was less than one year old. He, like uncounted others who have suffered a similar tragedy, then came to live with the grandmother to provide the infant with a substitute for his mother's care and to establish a more normal home environment.

According to the U.S. Census Bureau, 2.7 million grandparents were raising their grandchildren in 2012. About 10% of all children lived in the same household with at least one grandparent, and two thirds of those households were maintained by the grandparent. Of the households maintained by grandparents, one in three had no parent present. About a third of the 7 million children who lived with a grandparent also had two parents present. See <u>Renee R. Ellis and Tavia Simmons, *Coresident Grandparents and Their Grandchildren: 2012* (2014)</u>.

Do grandparents have financial support obligations for their grandchildren? A Wisconsin statute provides that the parent of a dependent person under the age of eighteen must support a child of the dependent person, so far as the parent is able to do so, and to the extent that the dependent person is unable to do so. <u>Wis. Stat. Ann. §§ 49.90(1)(a)(2), 11 and 13(a) (2018)</u>. What is the likely purpose of this statute? See <u>In re Paternity of C.J.H., 439 N.W.2d 615 (Wis. Ct. App.1989)</u>. See also Patricia Donovan, *Will Grandparent Liability Help Curb Teenage Pregnancy?* 18 Fam. Plan. Persp. 264 (1986).

c. Functional Family Relationships

Before states began to recognize same-sex couple relationships through marriage, civil union or domestic partnership, a significant group of cases considered whether longstanding "functional" family relationships should be have legal consequences in various settings. E.g., <u>In re Guardianship of Kowalski, 382 N.W.2d 861, 865–67 (Minn. Ct. App.)</u>, cert. denied, <u>475 U.S. 1085 (1986)</u>, and <u>Braschi v. Stahl Associates, 543 N.E.2d 49 (N.Y. 1989)</u>. See generally Note, <u>*Looking for a Family Resemblance: The Limits of the Functional Approach to the Legal Definition of Family*, 104 Harv. L. Rev. 1640 (1991)</u>.

Similarly, case law and other developments have focused on broader recognition of children's relationships with adults who function as parents. See, e.g., Katherine T. Bartlett, <u>*Rethinking Parenthood as an Exclusive Status: The Need for Legal Alternatives When the Premise of the Nuclear Family Has Failed*, 70 Va. L. Rev. 879 (1984)</u>. De facto parent-child relationships are considered in Chapter 7.

d. Nannies, Teachers, and Scout Leaders

Should our notion of parental rights and responsibilities reflect the fact that a great deal of child care is carried out by various paid and unpaid care providers? See Melissa Murray, <u>*The Networked Family: Reframing the Legal Understanding of Caring and Caregivers*, 94 Va. L. Rev. 385 (2008)</u>; see also Tali Schaefer, <u>*Disposable Mothers: Paid In-Home Caretaking and the Regulation of Parenthood*, 19 Yale J. L. & Feminism 305 (2008)</u>. Laura Rosenbury argues that all sorts of other actors and institutions outside the family also play a significant role in children's socialization and development, and that parental prerogatives should give way to greater pluralism in this realm. See Laura A. Rosenbury, _Between Home and School_, 155 U. Pa. L. Rev. 833 (2007).

——————————

Stepparents

Millions of children share a household with a parent and another adult who is not their legal parent. Laws in many states encourage and facilitate stepparent adoptions, addressed in Chapter 3. What should be the legal effect of step-family relationships that are not formalized through adoption?

Stepparents typically lack authority to make medical or educational decisions for a child, although some states allow a stepparent or other person standing **in loco parentis** to act in particular circumstances. See, e.g., Ariz. Rev. Stat. § 44–133 (2018). Stepparents may be obligated to provide financial support for their stepchildren while living in the same household. See, e.g., Mo. Rev. Stat. § 453.400 (2018). After a divorce, or when the stepfamily no longer resides together, stepparents may be able to obtain custody or visitation rights under a **de facto parent** theory, considered further in Chapter 7. See generally Margaret M. Mahoney, _Stepparents as Third Parties in Relation to Their Stepchildren_, 40 Fam. L.Q. 81 (2006). See also Mary Ann Mason & David W. Simon, _The Ambiguous Stepparent: Federal Legislation in Search of a Model_, 29 Fam. L.Q. 445 (1995).

In some circumstances, stepparents have been required to support their stepchildren. For example, in Logan v. Logan, 120 N.H. 839, 424 A.2d 403 (1980), the New Hampshire Supreme Court concluded that the word "child" in the state's support statutes meant "either a natural child, an adopted child, or a stepchild." Other states have similar statutes, or have held that the duty to support a stepchild may be based on the common law. See, e.g., Del. Code Ann., tit. 13, §§ 501(b), 503 (2018); Kelley v. Iowa Department of Social Services, 197 N.W.2d 192 (Iowa 1972), appeal dismissed for want of a substantial federal question, 409 U.S. 813 (1972). The stepparent's duty of support is generally held to end when the marriage between the stepparent and the child's natural parent ends, however. Ruben v. Ruben, 461 A.2d 733 (N.H. 1983). The Washington statute imposing stepparent liability for support was held constitutional in Washington Statewide Organization of Stepparents v. Smith, 536 P.2d 1202 (Wash. 1975). Stepparent liability for support is discussed in Homer H. Clark, Jr., Domestic Relations 263–264 (Student 2d ed. 1988).

Problem 4-9

Joan and Terry, both divorced, purchased a seven-bedroom, four-bathroom house in a residential area and moved in with Joan's two children, age 16 and 19, and Terry's child, age 18. Local authorities have demanded that they vacate their home because the neighborhood is zoned for single-family dwellings, and the ordinance defines "family" as "One or more persons related by blood, marriage or adoption, occupying a dwelling unit as an individual housekeeping organization." What arguments can Joan and Terry make to challenge the ordinance? (See City of Ladue v. Horn, 720 S.W.2d 745 (Mo. App. E.D. 1986).)

Smith v. Organization of Foster Families for Equality & Reform

431 U.S. 816 (1977)

MR. JUSTICE BRENNAN delivered the opinion of the Court.

Appellees, individual foster parents and an organization of foster parents, brought this civil rights class action pursuant to 42 U.S.C.A. § 1983 in the United States District Court for the Southern District of New York, on their own behalf and on behalf of

Go Online

Listen to the oral arguments in *Smith* at the Oyez Project web site.

children for whom they have provided homes for a year or more. They sought declaratory and injunctive relief against New York State and New York City officials, alleging that the procedures governing the removal of foster children from foster homes provided in New York Social Services Law §§ 383(2) and 400, and in Title 18, New York Codes, Rules and Regulations § 450.14 violated the Due Process and Equal Protection Clauses of the Fourteenth Amendment. * * *

I

A detailed outline of the New York statutory system regulating foster care is a necessary preface to a discussion of the constitutional questions presented.

A

The expressed central policy of the New York system is that "it is generally desirable for the child to remain with or be returned to the natural parent because the child's need for a normal family life will usually best be met in the natural home and * * * parents are entitled to bring up their own children unless the best interests of the child would be thereby endangered," Soc.Serv.L. § 384–b(1) (a)(ii). But the State has opted for foster care as one response to those situations where the natural parents are unable to provide the "positive, nurturing family relationships" and "normal family life in a permanent home" that "offer the best opportunity for children to develop and thrive." § 384–b(1)(b), (1)(a)(i).

Foster care has been defined as "[a] child welfare service which provides substitute family care for a planned period for a child when his own family cannot care for him for a temporary or extended period and when adoption is neither desirable nor possible." Child Welfare League of America, Standards for Foster Family Care, 5 (1959). Thus, the distinctive features of foster care are first, "that it is care in a *family*, it is noninstitutional substitute care," and second, "that it is for a *planned* period—either temporary or extended. This is unlike adoptive placement, which implies a *permanent* substitution of one home for another." Kadushin, Child Welfare Services, 355 (1967).

Under the New York scheme children may be placed in foster care either by voluntary placement or by court order. Most foster care placements are voluntary. They occur when physical or mental illness, economic problems, or other family crises make it impossible for natural parents, particularly single parents, to provide a stable home life for their children for some limited period. Resort to such placements is almost compelled when it is not possible in such circumstance to place the child with a relative or friend, or to pay for the services of a homemaker or boarding school.

Voluntary placement requires the signing of a written agreement by the natural parent or guardian, transferring the care and custody of the child to an authorized child welfare agency. Soc.Serv.L. § 384–a(1). Although by statute the terms of such agreements are open to negotiation, Soc.Serv.L. § 384–a(2)(a), it is contended that agencies require execution of standardized forms.

* * * Foster parents, who are licensed by the State or an authorized foster care agency, Soc.Serv.L. §§ 376, 377, provide care under a contractual arrangement with the agency, and are compensated for their services. The typical contract expressly reserves the right of the agency to remove the child on request. Conversely, the foster parent may cancel the agreement at will.

The New York system divides parental functions among agency, foster parents and natural parents, and the definitions of the respective roles are often complex and often unclear. The law transfers "care and custody" to the agency, Soc.Serv.L. § 384–a; see also Soc.Serv.L. § 383(2), but day-to-day supervision of the child and his activities, and most of the functions ordinarily associated with legal custody, are the responsibility of the foster parent. Nevertheless, agency supervision of the performance of the foster parents takes forms indicating that the foster parent does not have the full authority of a legal custodian. Moreover, the natural parent's placement of the child with the agency does not surrender legal guardianship; the parent retains authority to act with respect to the child in certain circumstances. The natural parent has not only the right but the obligation to visit the foster child and plan for his future; failure of a parent with capacity to fulfill the obligation for more than a year can result in a court order terminating the parent's rights on the ground of neglect.

Children may also enter foster care by court order. * * * The consequences of foster care placement by court order do not differ substantially from those for children voluntarily placed, except that the parent is not entitled to return of the child on demand pursuant to Soc.Serv.L. § 384–a(2)(a); termination of foster care must then be consented to by the court. Soc.Serv.L. § 383(1).

B

The provisions of the scheme specifically at issue in this case come into play when the agency having legal custodianship determines to remove the foster child from the foster home, either because it has determined that it would be in the child's best interests to transfer him to some other foster home, or to return the child to his natural parents in accordance with the statute or placement agreement. Most children are removed in order to be transferred to another foster home. The procedures by which foster parents may challenge a removal made for that purpose differ somewhat from those where the removal is made to return the child to his natural parent.

Soc. Serv. L. § 383(2) provides that the "authorized agency placing out or boarding [a foster] child * * * may in its discretion remove such child from the home where placed or boarded." Administrative regulations implement this provision. The agency is required, except in emergencies, to notify the foster parents in writing 10 days in advance of any removal. The notice advises the foster parents that if they object to the child's removal they may request a "conference" with the social services department. The department schedules requested conferences within 10 days of the receipt of the request. The foster parent may appear with counsel at the conference, where he will "be advised of the reasons [for the removal of the child], and be afforded an opportunity to submit reasons why the child should not be removed." The official must render a decision in writing within five days after the close of the conference, and send notice of his decision to the foster parents and the agency. The proposed removal is stayed pending the outcome of the conference.

If the child is removed after the conference, the foster parent may appeal to the department of social services for a "fair hearing," that is, a full adversary administrative hearing, under Soc.Serv.L. § 400, the determination of which is subject to judicial review under N.Y.C.P.L.R. Art. 78; however, the removal is not automatically stayed pending the hearing and judicial review.

This statutory and regulatory scheme applies statewide. In addition, regulations promulgated by the New York City Human Resources Administration, Department of Social Services—Special Services for Children (SSC) provide even greater procedural safeguards there. Under SSC Procedure No. 5 (April 5, 1974), in place of or in addition to the conference provided by the state regulations, the foster parents may request a full trial-type hearing *before* the child is removed from their home. This procedure applies, however, only if the child is being transferred to another foster home, and not if the child is being returned to his natural parents.

One further preremoval procedural safeguard is available. Under Soc.Serv.L. § 392, the Family Court has jurisdiction to review, on petition of the foster parent or the agency, the status of any child who has been in foster care for 18 months or longer. The foster parents, the natural parents, and all interested agencies are made parties to the proceeding. Soc.Serv.L. § 392(4). After hearing, the court may order that foster care be continued, or that the child be returned to his natural parents, or that the agency take steps to free the child for adoption. Soc.Serv.L. § 392(7). Moreover, § 392(8) authorizes the court to issue an "order of protection" which "may set forth reasonable conditions of behavior to be observed for a specified time by a person or agency who is before the court." Thus, the court may order not only that foster care be continued, but additionally, "in assistance or as a condition of" that order that the agency leave the child with the present foster parent. In other words, § 392 provides a mechanism whereby a foster parent may obtain preremoval judicial review of an agency's decision to remove a child who has been in foster care for 18 months or more.

* * *

II

A

* * *

The appellees' basic contention is that when a child has lived in a foster home for a year or more, a psychological tie is created between the child and the foster parents which constitutes the foster family the true "psychological family" of the child. See Goldstein, Freud and Solnit, Beyond the Best Interests of the Child

(1973). That family, they argue, has a "liberty interest" in its survival as a family protected by the Fourteenth Amendment. Upon this premise they conclude that the foster child cannot be removed without a prior hearing satisfying due process. Appointed counsel for the children, however, disagrees, and has consistently argued that the foster parents have no such liberty interest independent of the interests of the foster children, and that the best interest of the children would not be served by procedural protections beyond those already provided by New York law. The intervening natural parents of children in foster care, also oppose the foster parents, arguing that recognition of the procedural right claimed would undercut both the substantive family law of New York, which favors the return of children to their natural parents as expeditiously as possible, and their constitutionally protected right of family privacy, by forcing them to submit to a hearing and defend their rights to their children before the children could be returned to them.

* * *

We therefore turn to appellees' assertion that they have a constitutionally protected liberty interest—in the words of the District Court, a "right to familial privacy," in the integrity of their family unit. This assertion clearly presents difficulties.

B

It is of course true that "freedom of personal choice in matters of * * * family life is one of the liberties protected by the Due Process Clause of the Fourteenth Amendment." There does exist a "private realm of family life which the state cannot enter," that has been afforded both substantive and procedural protection. * * *

First, the usual understanding of "family" implies biological relationships, and most decisions treating the relation between parent and child have stressed this element. *Stanley v. Illinois*, 405 U.S. 645, 651 (1972), for example, spoke of "[t]he rights to conceive and raise one's children" as essential rights, citing *Meyer v. Nebraska*, 262 U.S. 390 (1923), and *Skinner v. Oklahoma*, 316 U.S. 535 (1942).

A biological relationship is not present in the case of the usual foster family. But biological relationships are not exclusive determination of the existence of a family. The basic foundation of the family in our society, the marriage relationship, is of course not a matter of blood relation.

* * *

Thus the importance of the familial relationship, to the individuals involved and to the society, stems from the emotional attachments that derive from the intimacy of daily association, and from the role it plays in "promot[ing] a way of life" through the instruction of children, as well as from the fact of blood relationship. No one would seriously dispute that a deeply loving and interdependent relationship between an adult and a child in his or her care may exist even in the absence of blood relationship. At least where a child has been placed in foster care as an infant, has never known his natural parents, and has remained continuously for several years in the care of the same foster parents, it is natural that the foster family should hold the same place in the emotional life of the foster child, and fulfill the same socializing functions, as a natural family. For this reason, we cannot dismiss the foster family as a mere collection of unrelated individuals.

But there are also important distinctions between the foster family and the natural family. First, unlike the earlier cases recognizing a right to family privacy, the State here seeks to interfere not with a relationship having its origins entirely apart from the power of the State, but rather with a foster family which has its source in state law and contractual arrangements. The individual's freedom to marry and reproduce is "older than the Bill of Rights," <u>Griswold v. Connecticut, supra, 381 U.S., at 486</u>. Accordingly, unlike the property interests that are also protected by the Fourteenth Amendment, the liberty interest in family privacy has its source, and its contours are ordinarily to be sought, not in state law, but in intrinsic human rights, as they have been understood in "this Nation's history and tradition." * * * In this case, the limited recognition accorded to the foster family by the New York statutes and the contracts executed by the foster parents argue against any but the most limited constitutional "liberty" in the foster family.

A second consideration related to this is that ordinarily procedural protection may be afforded to a liberty interest of one person without derogating from the substantive liberty of another. Here, however, such a tension is virtually unavoidable. Under New York law, the natural parent of a foster child in voluntary placement has an absolute right to the return of his child in the absence of a court order obtainable only upon compliance with rigorous substantive and procedural standards, which reflect the constitutional protection accorded the natural family. Moreover, the natural parent initially gave up his child to the State only on the express understanding that the child would be returned in those circumstances. These rights are difficult to reconcile with the liberty interest in the foster family relationship claimed by appellees. * * * Whatever liberty interest might otherwise exist in the foster family as an institution, that interest must be substantially

> **FYI**
>
> Part III of the opinion analyzes the due process protections afforded to foster parents when an agency seeks to remove a child from their custody. These included an administrative hearing to review the agency's decision and the right to judicial review if the child had lived with the foster parents for 18 months. The Court found that these procedures were sufficient under the Constitution.

attenuated where the proposed removal from the foster family is to return the child to his natural parents.

* * * We are persuaded that, even on the assumption that appellees have a protected "liberty interest," the District Court erred in holding that the preremoval procedures presently employed by the State are constitutionally defective.

* * *

We deal here with issues of unusual delicacy, in an area where professional judgments regarding desirable procedures are constantly and rapidly changing. In such a context, restraint is appropriate on the part of courts called upon to adjudicate whether a particular procedural scheme is adequate under the Constitution. Since we hold that the procedures provided by New York State in § 392 and by New York City's SSC Procedure No. 5 are adequate to protect whatever liberty interest appellees may have, the judgment of the District Court is

> **FYI**
>
> Chief Justice Burger and Justices Stewart and Rehnquist concurred specially in this case, taking the position that "the interests asserted by the appellees are not of a kind that the Due Process Clause of the Fourteenth Amendment protects." In their view, New York's foster care program created no right in the foster family to remain intact, but rather was aimed at providing temporary care for the child until he or she can either be returned to his natural parents or placed in a permanent adoptive home.

Reversed.

Points for Discussion

a. Foster Parents and Due Process

Under the New York statutes described in *Smith v. OFFER*, foster parents have a number of procedural rights in the event children are removed from their care. Are these protections constitutionally necessary? If a state shifted children from one foster parent to another without providing notice or a hearing, would this violate the Due Process Clause? What if children were removed from foster parents and transferred to their natural parents without notice or a hearing? Several federal courts have concluded that foster parents have no constitutionally-protected liberty interests in this setting; see Drummond v. Fulton County Department of Family and Children's Services, 563 F.2d 1200 (5th Cir. 1977), cert. denied 437 U.S. 910 (1978); Procopio v. Johnson, 994 F.2d 325 (7th Cir. 1993).

b. Beyond the Best Interests of the Child

The Court cites Joseph Goldstein, Anna Freud, Albert J. Solnit, Beyond the Best Interests of the Child (1973). This book, written by experts in law and psychology, emphasized, for purposes of decisions on custody and adoption, that the child's interests should be paramount, that placements should provide the least detrimental available alternative for the child's development, and above all that placements should safeguard the child's need for continuity of relationships. The authors also stressed the idea that the child's psychological parent may be more important to the child than his or her legal or natural parent when the parent and child have been separated. The same authors wrote two additional books, elaborating on these ideas. The three books were later published in a single revised volume, Joseph Goldstein, Albert J. Solnit, Sonja Goldstein and Anna Freud, The Best Interests of the Child: The Least Detrimental Alternative (1996). Although very influential, this analysis has also been criticized. See Peggy Cooper Davis, "There is a book out . . .": *An Analysis of Judicial Absorption of Legislative Facts*, 100 Harv. L. Rev. 1539 (1987), and Michael Freeman, *The Best Interests of the Child? Is* The Best Interests of the Child *in the Best Interests of the Child?* 11 Int'l J. L. Pol'y & Fam. 360 (1997).

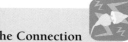

Make the Connection

Child welfare issues, including foster care and kinship foster care, are addressed in Chapter 5.

c. Family Placement Preferences

As noted in Chapter 3, state and federal laws state a preference for placing children with relatives for foster care or adoption. These preferences are not absolute, however, and courts must consider whether a familial placement is in the child's best interests. In some circumstances, the child's interests may be to remain with unrelated foster parents. See, e.g., Philip R. v. Eighth Judicial District Court, 416 P.3d 242 (Nev. 2018).

Sibling Relationships

Are siblings who live together in a household a family under the definitions considered in *Moore*? Siblings do not qualify for the legal benefits, or incur the legal obligations, that accompany spousal or parent-child relationships discussed in other parts of this chapter. Should they? See Jill Elaine Hasday, *Siblings in Law*, 65 Vand. L. Rev. 897 (2012).

Chapter 5

Child Maltreatment

Parents have a constitutionally-protected right to control their children's education and upbringing, recognized in cases such as <u>Meyer v. Nebraska, 262 U.S. 390 (1923)</u> and <u>Wisconsin v. Yoder, 406 U.S. 205 (1972)</u>, but the Supreme Court has also recognized that states have broad authority to enact legislation designed to protect children. See <u>Prince v. Massachusetts, 321 U.S. 158 (1944)</u>. When states act to remove children from their parents' care, or terminate parental rights, the courts must balance appropriate protection for fundamental parental rights with the compelling state interest in protecting children from harm.

In addition to this constitutional framework, the child welfare system in the United States is shaped by a cooperative federalism, in which the national government provides funding and defines the parameters for state laws under Title IV-B and IV-E of the Social Security Act. This chapter considers the complex interaction of state and federal law in this area, and explores the different ways in which state and local authorities respond to reports of neglect and abuse, work with families and children who come into the child welfare system, and proceed to termination of parental rights if the problems within the family cannot be remedied.

A. Responding to Child Abuse and Neglect

Child abuse and neglect have always been with us, often with the more or less tacit approval of public authorities. In the common law, the father was entitled to the custody of his children and had the right to exercise complete control over them. His right to discipline his children was subject to few limitations, and harsh punishments were not unusual. Poor, abandoned or orphaned children were placed in apprenticeships or institutions, where abuse and neglect were also common. Criminal law afforded some remedies to deter or punish cruelty to children, but they were not used often and were frequently ineffective because the crimes were hard to prove. For a review of this history, see <u>Mason P. Thomas, *Child Abuse and Neglect, Part I: Historical Overview, Legal Matrix and Social Perspectives,* 50 N.C. L. Rev. 293 (1972).</u>

In 1974, Congress passed the Child Abuse Prevention and Treatment Act (CAPTA), codified at 42 U.S.C. §§ 5101 et seq. (2018), which established a National Center on Child Abuse and Neglect in the U.S. Department of Health and Human Services, and provided grants for development of child abuse prevention and treatment programs. In 1980, the Adoption Assistance and Child Welfare Act (AACWA), codified at 42 U.S.C. §§ 621–628b, and 670–679b (2018), established new child protection requirements and set up a reimbursement program for state expenses incurred in the administration of adoption and foster care programs. These programs fall within Title IV-B of the Social Security Act for child welfare services, and under Title IV-E for foster care and adoption assistance. In 1997, the Adoption and Safe Families Act (ASFA) amended the IV-B and IV-E programs to reduce the time children spend in foster care and move them more quickly into adoptive or other permanent homes. For the history of this child welfare legislation, see Lela B. Costain, et al., The Politics of Child Abuse in America (1996), and Naomi R. Cahn, *Children's Interests in a Familial Context: Poverty, Foster Care and Adoption*, 60 Ohio St. L.J. 1189 (1999).

Go Online

Government sources in the United States estimate that 676,000 children were victims of abuse or neglect in 2016. About 75% of these children experienced neglect, 18% were physically abused, and 9% suffered sexual abuse, with some children experiencing multiple forms of abuse. Of this group, approximately 1750 children died as a result of abuse or neglect. Victimization rates were highest for children in their first year of life. See U.S. Department of Health and Human Services, Administration on Children, Youth and Families, Child Maltreatment 2016 (2018).

In the years after World War II many people in the medical profession became concerned about child abuse and began to classify and identify its symptoms. As physicians generally became more sensitive to the existence and indications of child abuse, the public became more aware of the problem, and legislators took steps to improve procedures for detecting and preventing child abuse. One important

Go Online

The Child Welfare Information Gateway has extensive information about federal and state child welfare systems including statistics, issue briefs, factsheets, and links to state statutes.

innovation came in the form of child abuse reporting laws, which require various individuals including physicians, teachers and child care providers to make a report when they suspect that a child has been abused or neglected. These laws were required by CAPTA; see 42 U.S.C. § 5106a(b)(2)(B) (2018).

In 2016, there were about 4.1 million reports of alleged child maltreatment, of which 65% came from mandated reporters such as health care workers, teachers, police officers, and social services staff. About 60% of these reports were "screened in," or accepted for investigation by child protective services. Of the nearly two million reports screened in, 90% received an investigation response, and about 25% of the reports investigated were found to be substantiated. See U.S. Department of Health and Human Services, Administration for Children and Families, Child Maltreatment 2016 (2018).

Go Online

Find state laws on reporting and responding to child abuse and neglect using the Child Welfare Information Gateway.

Once discovered, child maltreatment is usually addressed in a civil proceeding, typically divided into two stages. The adjudicatory stage is concerned with whether the child was abused or neglected within the meaning of the applicable state statute. This may be framed as an inquiry into whether the child is "dependent or neglected," sometimes referred to as a D&N proceeding, or whether this is a "child in need of assistance," also referred to as a CINA (or "China") proceeding.

If a court determines that the child has been abused or neglected, the second or dispositional stage considers what remedy best fits the circumstances. The court might release the child to the custody of his or her parents with or without a protective order or some form of supervision, or place the child in the custody of other persons, a foster home, the custody of a child care agency, or an institution. In a particularly serious case, the court might terminate parental rights completely. Beyond these civil remedies, child maltreatment may also be referred for prosecution under state criminal laws.

In Re Ethan H.

609 A.2d 1222 (N.H. 1992)

Johnson, Justice.

The defendant, Judith H., appeals from a Superior Court (*Groff,* J.) order finding that her son is an "abused child" under the Child Protection Act, RSA chapter 169–C. We reverse.

The defendant, a physician, is the mother of four children. On May 1, 1988, she observed her seven-year-old son, Ethan, throwing food at the dinner table. When she commanded Ethan to behave, he allegedly ignored her. In response, she took Ethan to a bedroom and struck his bare buttocks approximately six times with an imitation leather belt.

The next day, the local elementary school reported to the New Hampshire Division for Children and Youth Services (DCYS) that it had received an anonymous phone call that Ethan may have been struck by his mother. The DCYS immediately began to investigate the matter. On May 3, a social worker entered the defendant's home pursuant to a court order. She interviewed Ethan and observed several bruises on his lower back. Ethan admitted that his mother had struck him and that he had additional bruises on his buttocks.

Based on the social worker's observations, the District Court (*Gauthier,* J.) ordered on May 5 that Ethan be placed in protective supervision of the DCYS and "be immediately medically examined to document the physical injuries." Accordingly, the social worker took Ethan to the Nashua Memorial Hospital where he was examined by Dr. David Walker. According to Dr. Walker's affidavit, "Ethan * * * had bruises on his buttocks, lower back and a bruise and scrape on his right abdominal wall." Dr. Walker also recalls telling the social worker that, based on Ethan's condition, he "would have never thought that Ethan was abused." He later told the State's attorney that he "would *not* have suspected abuse nor filed a report as mandatory by law." (Emphasis added.)

The DCYS nonetheless proceeded with its investigation. On June 8, 1988, the District Court (*Howorth,* J.) conducted a hearing to determine whether Ethan was an "abused child" under the Child Protection Act. RSA 169–C:3, II defines an "abused child" as

"any child who has been:
(a) Sexually abused; or
(b) Intentionally physically injured; or
(c) Psychologically injured so that said child exhibits symptoms of emotional problems generally recognized to result from consistent mistreatment or neglect; or
(d) *Physically injured by other than accidental means.*"

(Emphasis added.) The district court found that "[Ethan] has incurred physical injury by other than accidental means within the meaning of RSA 169–C:3[,] II(d)."

The defendant appealed to the superior court for a *de novo* review pursuant to RSA 169–C:28. On December 20, 1988, the superior court conducted a hearing in which the DCYS called the defendant, the social worker, and Dr. Rantan Dandekar to testify.

On direct examination, the defendant admitted that Ethan's bruises were the result of corporal punishment. She also stated that she had previously "spanked" her children when she felt it was "judicious" and "proper." The remainder of the defendant's testimony regarded the facts surrounding the DCYS investigation. In questioning the defendant, the DCYS attorney made no attempt to establish whether Ethan was harmed or injured as a result of the blows. At the conclusion of the defendant's testimony, however, the trial court asked her whether Ethan cried upon being spanked, and she responded that he did cry.

Next, the DCYS called the social worker, who testified regarding her investigatory findings. The social worker recalled that "Ethan said that he received all [his bruises] from his mother hitting him with the belt." The social worker also recalled the defendant's statement that she "couldn't guarantee * * * that she wouldn't hit any of her children, including Ethan, with a belt [in the future]" and that "if Ethan had done something that she felt permitted using the belt, then she would use the belt." The DCYS attorney never asked the social worker whether in her opinion Ethan's bruises indicated harm or injury.

Finally, the DCYS called Dr. Dandekar to the witness stand. Dr. Dandekar testified that on May 6, the day after Dr. Walker examined Ethan on behalf of the DCYS, the defendant, apparently unaware of Dr. Walker's assessment of Ethan's bruises, had on her own initiative sent Ethan to Dr. Dandekar's office for an independent examination. Dr. Dandekar recalled that Ethan "had a bruise over his right thigh," "linear bruise[s] on * * * the right and left buttock," a "bruise which was just over the iliac crest," and a "healing abrasion" at "the point where the bottom and the stomach area meet." The DCYS never established whether this "healing abrasion" arose from the mother's punishment. Dr. Dandekar also testified that, based on the above observations, she would report the bruises to the DCYS because "by law [she was] supposed to report any non-accidental *bruises*." (Emphasis added.) The DCYS attorney did not ask Dr. Dandekar whether she observed any signs of harm or injury in treating Ethan; nor did the attorney ask Dr. Dandekar whether, in her professional opinion, the bruises themselves indicated harm or injury.

The DCYS presented no other testimony. Most notably, it did not call Dr. Walker, the physician who examined Ethan on behalf of the DCYS. As noted earlier, Dr. Walker signed an affidavit stating that he "would have never thought that Ethan was abused."

The defendant also presented three witnesses at the December 20 hearing. First, a lifelong friend testified that she had never observed any evidence of abuse in the defendant's relationship with her children. She also responded to the defendant's questions on redirect examination in the following manner:

"Q. What's been the standing joke about me and my kids with pretty well everybody as far as bruising goes?
A. Well, you just touch them and they're bruised.
Q. I used to yell at you when we lived together; isn't that right?
A. Uh-huh.
Q. Don't squeeze my arm, that will leave a huge bruise?
A. Uh-huh.
Q. Was that the standard thing among all our friends?
A. Very easily bruised, yes."

The DCYS attorney did not cross-examine the defendant's friend regarding the above testimony.

The defendant next called her sister, also a physician, who was sharing her home with the defendant's family at the time of the incident. The sister testified that the defendant "has a very strong attachment to her children" and is "a very, very concerned and loving mother." She also recalled that after Ethan was struck by his mother, he "was out * * * playing and running around and didn't appear to be injured in any way." She continued:

> "Ethan was as active as ever. Basketball. He was out running around and playing with his friends. There was absolutely no difference in his demeanor, saying he was sore when he sat down or that he hurt or anything like that. He was completely as normal as he always is."

On cross-examination, the DCYS attorney did not question the sister regarding her observations of Ethan. Instead, the attorney cross-examined her regarding Ethan's bruises (the presence of which had already been established by three other witnesses including the defendant). In response, the sister stated, "These children bruise very easily and they have numerous bruises on them at any given time from playing, going out in the woods, riding their bicycles, just roughhousing among themselves."

Finally, the defendant took the witness stand on her own behalf. She testified regarding, among other things, her philosophy on corporal punishment:

> "I believe corporal punishment, when done judiciously and appropriately for the situation and for the circumstances is a definite form of punishment. It's not the one people would ever use initially. I mean, you know, to strike out constantly at children and/or to use that as your only form of discipline would be ludicrous. But what I'm saying to you is that the circumstances warranted it. And you know your child and you know the situation. There are times when it can be appropriate."

The superior court upheld the district court's finding that Ethan was an "abused child." The defendant then appealed to this court. We remanded for reconsideration in light of our then recent decision in <u>Petition of Doe, 132 N.H. 270, 564 A.2d 433 (1989)</u>, and the superior court conducted a second hearing on October 5, 1990.

The DCYS presented no witnesses at the second hearing. The defendant, however, called three witnesses, including her father, a retired physician. His testimony concerned the relationship between pain, injury, and bruising. He opined that "[n]either bruising nor pain is a valid criteria [of determining injury]" and that "approximately 80 percent of the bruises that present at a doctor's office the patient has no idea how the bruises came [about]." He also explained that the buttocks is perhaps the safest area of the body upon which to administer corporal punishment. During an extremely short cross-examination covering only three pages in the trial transcript, the DCYS attorney did not significantly challenge the credibility of the father's testimony. Moreover, the attorney presented no evidence rebutting his testimony.

As noted earlier, <u>RSA 169–C</u>:3, II(d) defines an "abused child" as "any child who has been * * * [p]hysically injured by other than accidental means." In *Petition of Doe supra*, we addressed the proper scope of <u>RSA 169–C:3</u>, II(d). We noted that the provision, if interpreted literally, "is overly broad and could encompass well-being of the child." *Id.* at 277, <u>564 A.2d at 438</u>. We concluded that

> "a proper finding of child abuse under <u>RSA 169–C</u>:3, II(d) (Supp.1988) must include a determination of whether the alleged abusive act was committed under circumstances *indicating harm or threatened harm to the child's life, health, or welfare.* Such harm may be demonstrated by, for example, the severity of the intentionally inflicted injuries; *recurring or a threat of recurring injury;* or injury when a profile of the child's caretaker indicates a history of, or a propensity for, abuse. These examples are in no way intended to be limiting, as we recognize the myriad situations in which harm or threatened harm may exist."

Id. at 277–78, <u>564 A.2d at 438–39</u> (emphasis added).

In its decision of October 15, 1990, the superior court applied the above standards to the evidence presented at both the 1988 and 1990 hearings and found that Ethan was an "abused child" under RSA 169–C:3, II(d). The court first looked to the dictionary meaning of the term "bruise" and concluded that "[a] bruise is most certainly, by its plain meaning, an injury." The court then reasoned that

> "[t]he decision in *Petition of Jane Doe* acknowledges that conduct

Think About It

How did the decision in *Petition of Doe*, as described here, change the standard for proving child abuse under the New Hampshire statute?

causing minor injuries may constitute abuse if recurring injury or a threat of recurring injury is demonstrated. This is exactly the case here. [The defendant] intentionally struck her 6 year-old son with a belt across his bare buttocks about 6 times, causing linear bruises which were still visible after 5 days. Such 'strappings' had been occasioned to Ethan in the past as deemed required by his misbehavior. * * * [The defendant] also demonstrated her intent to continue to discipline her son in this manner in the future. On these facts, the Court finds that it has been established that the strapping of Ethan by [the defendant] was committed under circumstances indicating harm or threatened harm to the child's health and welfare. The Court finds that Ethan has been abused by the conduct of [the defendant]."

We will not reverse the superior court's findings "unless they are unsupported by the evidence or are erroneous as a matter of law." Upon reviewing the evidence presented at both the 1988 and 1990 hearings, we conclude that the superior court's finding that Ethan's bruises "indicat[ed] harm or threatened harm to [his] health and welfare" was unsupported by the evidence.

The defendant presented substantial evidence that Ethan, although bruised, was not harmed. First, her friend and sister both indicated that Ethan tended to bruise easily. Second, the sister indicated that Ethan was actively playing outside after the corporal punishment was administered. Third, the defendant's father testified regarding the tenuous relationship between bruising and harm. As noted earlier, the father's testimony went uncontroverted by any other professional witness. Indeed, the DCYS failed to present *any* testimony of its own indicating that Ethan was harmed or injured. This failure is stunning in light of the fact that the 1990 hearing occurred after this court remanded the matter for further consideration in light of *Petition of Doe*, the very case requiring "harm or threatened harm" for a finding of child abuse.

Additionally, the DCYS failed to present the testimony of Dr. Walker, *who examined Ethan on behalf of the DCYS*, at either hearing. In the absence of any showing to the contrary, we are left to presume that Dr. Walker was not called by the DCYS due to his opinion that he "would not have suspected abuse" based on Ethan's bruises.

Lastly, we note that neither in this case nor in *Petition of Doe* has this court been called upon to either condone or condemn the use of corporal punishment as a means of disciplining one's children. The legislature has already established as policy that *reasonable* corporal punishment is allowable. *See* RSA 627:6, I; *see also Petition of Doe, 132 N.H. at 277, 564 A.2d at 438*. This court's role is merely to determine if the acts alleged and found below, viewed in the light most favorable to the finder of fact, sustain a finding of "child abuse" within the meaning of RSA 169–C:3, II(d). Today, we hold only that the DCYS, by failing to establish that

Ethan's bruises were indicative of harm or injury, has not established child abuse under the standards set forth in *Petition of Doe*. We recognize that in future cases a child's bruises may be of such a nature as to establish *prima facie* evidence of "harm or threatened harm."

Because we conclude that no child abuse exists in this case, it is not necessary for us to address whether the defendant was justified in "strapping" Ethan under RSA 627:6, I, which provides that "[a] parent, guardian or other person responsible for the general care and welfare of a minor is justified in using force against such minor when and to the extent that he reasonably believes is necessary to prevent or punish such minor's misconduct." This statute merely codified the "well-recognized precept of Anglo-American jurisprudence that the parent of a minor child or one standing *in loco parentis* was justified in using a reasonable amount of force upon a child for the purpose of safeguarding or promoting the child's welfare." Bowers v. State, 126, 389 A.2d 341, 348 (Md. 1978).

Take Note

Note this discussion of New Hampshire's corporal punishment statute.

* * *

Points for Discussion

a. Corporal Punishment

What limits does the New Hampshire statute cited near the end of *Ethan H.* place on corporal punishment? Cf. State v. Leaf, 623 A.2d 1329 (N.H. 1993), affirming a second degree assault conviction of a father for beating his ten-year-old son with a belt. Would you favor the enactment of this type of statute? Other states also recognize a common law parental discipline defense. See, e.g., State v. Wade, 245 P.3d 1083 (Kan. Ct. App. 2010). For the arguments in favor of prohibiting corporal punishment, see Deanna Pollard, *Banning Child Corporal Punishment,* 77 Tul. L. Rev. 575 (2003).

How should the child's age affect the result in cases like this? In *Petition of Doe,* discussed in *Ethan H.,* the child was twenty-one months old when he misbehaved and his mother hit him with her hand, on two occasions. Should that conduct be treated as child abuse? Would it be excused under the New Hampshire corporal punishment statute, on the ground that the parent "reasonably believes [it] is necessary to prevent or punish" the child's misconduct? Would the parent's conduct in either *Petition of Doe* or *Ethan H.* amount to child abuse under the New

York statute, quoted below? If so, what would be an appropriate and effective disposition of the case?

b. Child Abuse Reporting Laws

As noted above, all states have child abuse reporting acts, and are required to have such acts as a condition on receiving federal funds. 42 U.S.C. § 5106a(b)(2) (B)(i) (2018). Under the federal law, state statutes must require child abuse reporting by classes of persons likely to come in contact with child abuse, such as doctors, nurses, other health care workers, school teachers or child care providers, and similar persons. The statutes also authorize reports by anyone who knows of or has reasonable cause to suspect child abuse. Reports are made to local child protective or law enforcement agencies. The statutes provide that any person reporting child abuse in good faith is immune from criminal or civil liability that might otherwise result from such a report, and good faith is usually presumed.

On reporting laws and the resulting immunity from liability, see Eli Newberger and Richard Bourne, *The Medicalization and Legalization of Child Abuse*, in Richard Bourne & Eli Newberger, Critical Perspectives on Child Abuse 139 (1979); Mark Hardin, Legal Barriers in Child Abuse Investigations: State Powers and Individual Rights, 63 Wash. L. Rev. 493 (1988); Douglas J. Besharov, *The Legal Aspects of Reporting Known and Suspected Child Abuse and Neglect*, 23 Vill. L. Rev. 458, 475 (1978).

State Reporting Requirements

Who is required to report suspected child abuse under the laws in your state? When, how, and to whom should these reports be submitted? A listing of state reporting statutes is available from the Child Welfare Information Gateway.

c. Child Abuse Registries

In *Petition of Doe* the court referred to the New Hampshire statute which requires that each instance of reported child abuse be entered in a central registry, whether or not probable cause is found. Reports for which probable cause is not found are kept in the registry for three years. If probable cause is found, the reports are kept in the registry for seven years. The court also cited Douglas J. Besharov, *Child Abuse Reporting and Investigation: Policy Guidelines for Decision Making*, 22 Fam. L.Q. 1, 12 (1988) which indicates that about 40% of all child abuse reports are unsubstantiated and dismissed. Most states have similar central registries of child abuse reports. For an example of a registry statute, see N.Y. Soc. Serv. L. § 422 (2018). Does the maintenance of these registries jeopardize the rights of persons whose names appear on them? See Valmonte v. Bane, 18 F.3d 992 (2d Cir.1994), holding the New York registry statute unconstitutional, and stating that 2,000,000 individuals were listed on the New York registry. See also Lee TT. v. Dowling, 664 N.E.2d 1243 (N.Y. 1996).

d. Parental Rights

Invoking the principle that they have a constitutionally-protected interest in the care, custody and management of their children, parents sometimes file suits under 42 U.S.C. § 1983 claiming that their constitutional parental rights have been infringed by the actions of child welfare officials responding to reports of abuse or neglect. Courts evaluating these cases hold that the state has a compelling interest in protecting children's welfare, and focus on whether the authorities had a reasonable suspicion that the child had been abused or was in danger of being abused. See, e.g., Croft v. Westmoreland County Children & Youth Services, 103 F.3d 1123 (3d Cir. 1997) (concluding that caseworker lacked "objectively reasonable grounds to believe the child had been sexually abused" based on an anonymous tip that young child had reported sleeping with her parents). Defendants in this type of case are typically accorded a qualified immunity from suit, which is available so long as they do not act in violation of rights that are clearly established in the law. E.g. Roska v. Peterson, 328 F.3d 1230 (10th Cir.2003).

e. Defining Abuse and Neglect

Another area of controversy has focused on the language of child abuse statutes. Broad and general statutes may give the trial courts too much discretion, permitting them to impose their own standards of family conduct on people from social and economic groups whose practices may be different, but who love their children and provide them with adequate care. To meet these criticisms, many child abuse statutes were made more specific, as with the New York statute reprinted below. Courts have generally upheld criminal child abuse statutes against constitutional vagueness challenges under the Due Process Clause. See, e.g. DuFresne v. State, 826 So.2d 272 (Fla. 2002), but see People v. Maness, 732 N.E.2d 545 (Ill. 2000) (finding statute regarding obligation to prevent sexual abuse unconstitutionally vague).

f. Parental Substance Use

Substance abuse may be the basis for a finding of neglect, but not all substance use by a parent rises to this level. For example, In re Drake M., 149 Cal. Rptr. 3d 875 (Ct. App. 2012), held that father's use of marijuana three times a week for chronic pain was not a basis for asserting dependency jurisdiction where there was no evidence to show that he was unable to adequately supervise or protect his son.

In the context of prenatal drug use, <u>New Jersey Division of Youth & Family Services v. A.L., 59 A.3d 576 (N.J. 2013)</u>, held that positive results of a screen for cocaine were not proof of actual harm or imminent danger to the child, as required by the state statute, where the baby's health was otherwise normal.

New York Family Court Act
§ 1012. Definitions

When used in this article and unless the specific context indicates otherwise:

* * *

(e) "Abused child" means a child less than eighteen years of age whose parent or other person legally responsible for his care

(i) inflicts or allows to be inflicted upon such child physical injury by other than accidental means which causes or creates a substantial risk of death, or serious or protracted disfigurement, or protracted impairment of physical or emotional health or protracted loss or impairment of the function of any bodily organ, or

(ii) creates or allows to be created a substantial risk of physical injury to such child by other than accidental means which would be likely to cause death or serious or protracted disfigurement, or protracted impairment of physical or emotional health or protracted loss or impairment of the function of any bodily organ, or

(iii) (A) commits, or allows to be committed, an offense against such child, defined in article one hundred thirty of the penal law; (B) allows, permits or encourages such child to engage in any act described in sections 230.25, 230.30 and 230.32 of the penal law; (C) commits any of the acts described in section 255.25 of the penal law; (D) allows such child to engage in acts or conduct described in article two hundred sixty-three of the penal law; or (E) permits or encourages such child to engage in any act or commits or allows to be committed against such child any offense that would render such child either a victim of sex trafficking or a victim of severe forms of trafficking in persons pursuant to 22 U.S.C. 7102 * * *; (F) provided, however, that (a) the corroboration requirements contained in the penal law and (b) the age requirement for the application of article two hundred sixty-three of such law shall not apply to proceedings under this article.

(f) "Neglected child" means a child less than eighteen years of age

   (i) whose physical, mental or emotional condition has been impaired or is in imminent danger of becoming impaired as a result of the failure of his parent or other person legally responsible for his care to exercise a minimum degree of care

      (A) in supplying the child with adequate food, clothing, shelter or education in accordance with the provisions of * * * the education law, or medical, dental, optometrical or surgical care, though financially able to do so or offered financial or other reasonable means to do so; or

      (B) in providing the child with proper supervision or guardianship, by unreasonably inflicting or allowing to be inflicted harm, or a substantial risk thereof, including the infliction of excessive corporal punishment; or by misusing a drug or drugs; or by misusing alcoholic beverages to the extent that he loses self-control of his actions; or by any other acts of a similarly serious nature requiring the aid of the court; provided, however, that where the respondent is voluntarily and regularly participating in a rehabilitative program, evidence that the respondent has repeatedly misused a drug or drugs or alcoholic beverages to the extent that he loses self-control of his actions shall not establish that the child is a neglected child in the absence of evidence establishing that the child's physical, mental or emotional condition has been impaired or is in imminent danger of becoming impaired as set forth in paragraph (i) of this subdivision; or

   (ii) who has been abandoned, in accordance with the definition and other criteria set forth in * * * the social services law, by his parents or other person legally responsible for his care.

(g) "Person legally responsible" includes the child's custodian, guardian,[1] any other person responsible for the child's care at the relevant time. Custodian may include any person continually or at regular intervals found in the same household as the child when the conduct of such person causes or contributes to the abuse or neglect of the child.

(h) "Impairment of emotional health" and "impairment of mental or emotional condition" includes a state of substantially diminished psychological or intellectual functioning in relation to, but not limited to, such factors as failure to thrive, control of aggressive or self-destructive impulses, ability to think and reason, or acting out or misbehavior, including incorrigibility, ungovernability or habitual truancy; provided, however, that such impairment must be clearly attributable to the unwillingness or inability of the respondent to exercise a minimum degree of care toward the child.

[NOTE: The references in subsection (e)(iii) of the statute relate to sex offenses; to various forms of promoting prostitution, to incest with an ancestor or descendant or with brother, sister, uncle, aunt, nephew or niece, and to sex performances by a child.]

N.Y. Fam. Ct. Act § 1012 (2018).

1   So in original. The word "or" should probably be inserted.

Problem 5-1

Do these scenarios constitute abuse or neglect within the New York statute, or under the equivalent statute in your jurisdiction?

(a) Scott and Karen are divorced, and Scott becomes concerned when their daughter, Jessica, tells Scott that Karen has been disciplining her with a wooden spoon. On one occasion, Karen caused a bruise on Jessica's buttocks about one inch in diameter. Scott reports his concern to the local social services agency, which investigates and learns that Karen uses the spoon rather than her hand because she believes it is wrong to hit with the hand, which represents love. She tells the investigator that she never hits Jessica in anger, that she spanks her only on the buttocks, over clothing, typically striking her about four times. Karen explains that her intent is not to harm but to cause a "sting" and to get the child's attention, and that she uses "the rod" because of what she has learned in parenting classes and teaching she receives at her church. After disciplining Jessica, Karen speaks to her about her behavior, they pray together, and Karen gives Jessica her forgiveness. When asked to stop using the rod, Karen refused. In all other respects, Jessica is well cared-for in her mother's home. (See In the Interest of J.P., 692 N.E.2d 338 (Ill. App. Ct. 1998).)

(b) Kimberly, age 17, is spending the weekend at her father's house when they get into an argument about whether she will attend her grandmother's birthday party. As punishment for refusing to go, Kimberly's father withdraws her driving privileges and takes the keys for the new car he recently purchased for her. Kimberly takes her father's keys, and demands that he exchange them for her keys. The father twists her arm behind her back and pries his keys out of her hand, Kimberly swears at him, and he slaps her in the face with an open hand. The fight continues for some time with pushing and the father's attempt at one point to spank Kimberly. Kimberly attempts to block the door when her father tries to leave and chases after him when he goes out another way. Kimberly calls her mother, who summons the police. (See State v. Hauenstein, 700 N.E.2d 378 (Ohio Ct.App.1997).)

(c) Tina lived with her two children, aged eight years and twenty-two months, and with two other adults. At about 9:30 p.m. Tina and other adults went to a Halloween party at a tavern several blocks away, leaving the eight-year-old watching television, and the baby asleep in a bedroom. The eight-year-old was able to use the telephone and Tina left with him the phone numbers of the tavern and a neighbor. At 11 p.m. two of Tina's adult friends checked on the children and found them all right, the older one still watching television. When Tina returned home at 2:00 a.m., she found the house full of smoke and both children dead of asphyxiation. The cause of the fire was not explained. Tina and the other adults were cigarette smokers and there were matches and candles in the house (See State v. Goff, 686 P.2d 1023 (Or. 1984). See also Matter of Sarah K., 536 N.Y.S.2d 958 (Fam.Ct.1989).)

(d) DT was a fourteen-year-old girl who one day took twenty-three adult migraine aspirin tablets, after which she called a doctor, who got her to the hospital, where she remained for a week. The doctor and a social worker at the hospital requested that DT's parents let her be tested at a local mental health center to evaluate her emotional stability, but the parents at first refused and consented only under threats of a juvenile court action. DT was evaluated as having "normal intelligence," but displaying "signs of depression, hostility, and impulsiveness." Placement in a foster home and individual therapy were recommended, but the parents refused to carry out the recommendations. (See In re Alyne E., 448 N.Y.S.2d 984 (Fam.Ct.1982). See also Bjerke v. D.T., 248 N.W.2d 808 (N.D.1976).)

(e) A fifth grade school teacher noticed that a girl in his class was often depressed, fatigued and unable to concentrate on her school work. The teacher talked with the child and learned that the child's parents regularly said that they did not love her, that she was a burden to them, that they wished she had never been born, that she was dumb and clumsy and that they wished they could get rid of her some way. At the same time they made her do most of the house cleaning and dish washing so that the child was too tired to do her homework or to pay attention in school. Should the teacher report this child as abused? (Cf. People v. D.A.K., 596 P.2d 747 (Colo. 1979). See also In the Matter of Shane T., 453 N.Y.S.2d 590 (Fam.Ct.1982).)

(f) When Sebastian M. was born, his urine tested positive for cocaine. His mother admitted that she had used cocaine once during the fifth month of her pregnancy and once again two days before his birth. She also admitted that she had smoked marijuana on a daily basis during her pregnancy. (See Matter of Stefanel Tyesha C., 556 N.Y.S.2d 280 (App. Div.), leave to appeal granted 559 N.Y.S.2d 813 (App. Div.) appeal discontinued and withdrawn 565 N.E.2d 520 (N.Y. 1990).)

(g) Nikolas is a four-year-old boy who is HIV positive, and his physician has recommended an experimental drug therapy for the child. Nikolas's mother, who also has HIV, decided to refuse the drug therapy in order to spare Nikolas the effects and risks of the treatment. She has told his doctor that if Nikolas's health begins to deteriorate significantly, she will reconsider her decision. (See In re Nikolas E., 720 A.2d 562 (Me. 1998).)

(h) In a criminal prosecution, can Terri be convicted for child abuse based on evidence that her husband Bert physically and sexually abused their seven-year-old son and eight-year-old daughter on numerous occasions? What additional evidence would the prosecution need to offer in a case such as this? (See State v. Williquette, 385 N.W.2d 145 (Wis. 1986).)

(i) A woman tells a counselor at a domestic violence shelter that her children have seen her husband beat her on several occasions, although she says that he has never beaten the children. His violence toward her has recently escalated in frequency and severity. The woman, after staying at the shelter for three nights, returns home with the children, and she refuses all offers of ongoing counseling or assistance. Based upon the woman's description of the recurrent violence in her relationship with her husband over a ten-year period, the counselor is convinced that the spousal abuse will continue. Does this constitute child abuse or neglect under the statute? Should the counselor report this to child protective services?

(j) At 14, R.T. began resisting her mother's efforts to control her behavior, running away from home for days at a time and falsely reporting that her mother had abused her. R.T. also ran away from her grandparents' home when her mother arranged for her to live there. By 17, she had given birth to two children, both of whom have been declared dependent, and lived on the street. May the court intervene on the basis that R.T. is a neglected child? (Cf. In re R.T., 399 P.3d 1 (Cal. 2017).)

——————————————

DeShaney v. Winnebago County Department of Social Services

489 U.S. 189 (1989)

CHIEF JUSTICE REHNQUIST delivered the opinion of the Court.

Go Online

Listen to the <u>oral arguments</u> in *De-Shaney* on the Oyez Project web site.

Petitioner is a boy who was beaten and permanently injured by his father, with whom he lived. The respondents are social workers and other local officials who received complaints that petitioner was being abused by his father and had reason to believe that this was the case, but nonetheless did not act to remove petitioner from his father's custody. Petitioner sued respondents claiming that their failure to act deprived him of his liberty in violation of the Due Process Clause of the Fourteenth Amendment to the United States Constitution. We hold that it did not.

I

The facts of this case are undeniably tragic. Petitioner Joshua DeShaney was born in 1979. In 1980, a Wyoming court granted his parents a divorce and awarded custody of Joshua to his father, Randy DeShaney. The father shortly thereafter moved to Neenah, a city located in Winnebago County, Wisconsin, taking the infant Joshua with him. There he entered into a second marriage, which also ended in divorce.

The Winnebago County authorities first learned that Joshua DeShaney might be a victim of child abuse in January 1982, when his father's second wife complained to the police, at the time of their divorce, that he had previously "hit the boy causing marks and [was] a prime case for child abuse." The Winnebago County Department of Social Services (DSS) interviewed the father, but he denied the accusations, and DSS did not pursue them further. In January 1983, Joshua was admitted to a local hospital with multiple bruises and abrasions. The examining physician suspected child abuse and notified DSS, which immediately obtained an order from a Wisconsin juvenile court placing Joshua in the temporary custody of the hospital. Three days later, the county convened an ad hoc "Child Protection Team"—consisting of a pediatrician, a psychologist, a police detective, the county's lawyer, several DSS caseworkers, and various hospital personnel—to consider Joshua's situation. At this meeting, the Team decided that there was insufficient evidence of child abuse to retain Joshua in the custody of the court. The Team did, however, decide to recommend several measures to protect Joshua, including enrolling him in a preschool program, providing his father with certain counselling services, and encouraging his father's girlfriend to move out of the home. Randy DeShaney entered into a voluntary agreement with DSS in which he promised to cooperate with them in accomplishing these goals.

Based on the recommendation of the Child Protection Team, the juvenile court dismissed the child protection case and returned Joshua to the custody of his father. A month later, emergency room personnel called the DSS caseworker handling Joshua's case to report that he had once again been treated for suspicious injuries. The caseworker concluded that there was no basis for action. For the next six months, the caseworker made monthly visits to the DeShaney home, during which she observed a number of suspicious injuries on Joshua's head; she also noticed that he had not been enrolled in school and that the girlfriend had not moved out. The caseworker dutifully recorded these incidents in her files, along with her continuing suspicions that someone in the DeShaney household was physically abusing Joshua, but she did nothing more. In November 1983, the emergency room notified DSS that Joshua had been treated once again for injuries that they believed to be caused by child abuse. On the caseworker's next two visits to the DeShaney home, she was told that Joshua was too ill to see her. Still DSS took no action.

In March 1984, Randy DeShaney beat four-year-old Joshua so severely that he fell into a life-threatening coma. Emergency brain surgery revealed a series of hemorrhages caused by traumatic injuries to the head inflicted over a long period of time. Joshua did not die, but he suffered brain damage so severe that he is expected to spend the rest of his life confined to an institution for the profoundly retarded. Randy DeShaney was subsequently tried and convicted of child abuse.

Joshua and his mother brought this action under 42 U.S.C. § 1983 in the United States District Court for the Eastern District of Wisconsin against respondents Winnebago County, its Department of Social Services, and various individual employees of the Department. The complaint alleged that respondents had deprived Joshua of his liberty without due process of law, in violation of his rights under the Fourteenth Amendment, by failing to intervene to protect him against a risk of violence at his father's hands of which they knew or should have known. The District Court granted summary judgment for respondents.

The Court of Appeals for the Seventh Circuit affirmed, 812 F.2d 298 (1987), holding that petitioners had not made out an actionable § 1983 claim for two alternative reasons.* * *

Because of the inconsistent approaches taken by the lower courts in determining when, if ever, the failure of a state or local governmental entity or its agents to provide an individual with adequate protective services constitutes a violation of the individual's due process rights, see *Archie v. City of Racine,* 847 F.2d 1211, 1220–1223, and n. 10 (C.A.7 1988) (en banc) (collecting cases), cert.

pending, No. 88–576, and the importance of the issue to the administration of state and local governments, we granted certiorari. We now affirm.

II

The Due Process Clause of the Fourteenth Amendment provides that "[n]o State shall * * * deprive any person of life, liberty, or property, without due process of law." Petitioners contend that the State deprived Joshua of his liberty interest in "free[dom] from * * * unjustified intrusions on personal security," by failing to provide him with adequate protection against his father's violence. The claim is one invoking the substantive rather than procedural component of the Due Process Clause; petitioners do not claim that the State denied Joshua protection without according him appropriate procedural safeguards, but that it was categorically obligated to protect him in these circumstances, see *Youngberg v. Romeo, 457 U.S. 307, 309 (1982)*.

But nothing in the language of the Due Process Clause itself requires the State to protect the life, liberty, and property of its citizens against invasion by private actors. The Clause is phrased as a limitation on the State's power to act, not as a guarantee of certain minimal levels of safety and security. It forbids the State itself to deprive individuals of life, liberty, or property without "due process of law," but its language cannot fairly be extended to impose an affirmative obligation on the State to ensure that those interests do not come to harm through other means. Nor does history support such an expansive reading of the constitutional text. Like its counterpart in the Fifth Amendment, the Due Process Clause of the Fourteenth Amendment was intended to prevent government "from abusing [its] power, or employing it as an instrument of oppression." Its purpose was to protect the people from the State, not to ensure that the State protected them from each other. The Framers were content to leave the extent of governmental obligation in the latter area to the democratic political processes.

Consistent with these principles, our cases have recognized that the Due Process Clauses generally confer no affirmative right to governmental aid, even where such aid may be necessary to secure life, liberty, or property interests of which the government itself may not deprive the individual. * * * If the Due Process Clause does not require the State to provide its citizens with particular protective services, it follows that the State cannot be held liable under the Clause for injuries that could have been averted had it chosen to provide them. As a general matter, then, we conclude that a State's failure to protect an individual against private violence simply does not constitute a violation of the Due Process Clause.

Petitioners contend, however, that even if the Due Process Clause imposes no affirmative obligation on the State to provide the general public with adequate protective services, such a duty may arise out of certain "special relationships" created or assumed by the State with respect to particular individuals. Petitioners argue that such a "special relationship" existed here because the State knew that Joshua faced a special danger of abuse at his father's hands, and specifically proclaimed, by word and by deed, its intention to protect him against that danger. Having actually undertaken to protect Joshua from this danger—which petitioners concede the State played no part in creating—the State acquired an affirmative "duty," enforceable through the Due Process Clause, to do so in a reasonably competent fashion. Its failure to discharge that duty, so the argument goes, was an abuse of governmental power that so "shocks the conscience" as to constitute a substantive due process violation.

We reject this argument. It is true that in certain limited circumstances the Constitution imposes upon the State affirmative duties of care and protection with respect to particular individuals. In *Estelle v. Gamble*, 429 U.S. 97 (1976), we recognized that the Eighth Amendment's prohibition against cruel and unusual punishment, made applicable to the States through the Fourteenth Amendment's Due Process Clause, *Robinson v. California*, 370 U.S. 660 (1962), requires the State to provide adequate medical care to incarcerated prisoners. 429 U.S., at 103–104. We reasoned that because the prisoner is unable " 'by reason of the deprivation of his liberty [to] care for himself,' " it is only " 'just' " that the State be required to care for him.

In *Youngberg v. Romeo*, 457 U.S. 307 (1982), we extended this analysis beyond the Eighth Amendment setting, holding that the substantive component of the Fourteenth Amendment's Due Process Clause requires the State to provide involuntarily committed mental patients with such services as are necessary to ensure their "reasonable safety" from themselves and others. As we explained, "[i]f it is cruel and unusual punishment to hold convicted criminals in unsafe conditions, it must be unconstitutional [under the Due Process Clause] to confine the involuntarily committed—who may not be punished at all—in unsafe conditions." *Id.*, see also *Revere v. Massachusetts General Hospital*, 463 U.S. 239, 244 (1983) (holding that the Due Process Clause requires the responsible government or governmental agency to provide medical care to suspects in police custody who have been injured while being apprehended by the police).

But these cases afford petitioners no help. Taken together, they stand only for the proposition that when the State takes a person into its custody and holds him there against his will, the Constitution imposes upon it a corresponding duty to assume some responsibility for his safety and general well-being. The rationale for this principle is simple enough: when the State by the affirmative exercise of its power so restrains an individual's liberty that it renders him unable to care for himself, and at the same time fails to provide for his basic human need—*e.g.*, food, clothing, shelter, medical care, and reasonable safety—it transgresses the substantive limits on state action set by the Eighth Amendment and the Due Process Clause. The affirmative duty to protect arises not from the State's knowledge of the individual's predicament or from its expressions of intent to help him, but from the limitation which it has imposed on his freedom to act on his own behalf. In the substantive due process analysis, it is the State's affirmative act of restraining the individual's freedom to act on his own behalf—through incarceration, institutionalization, or other similar restraint of personal liberty—which is the "deprivation of liberty" triggering the protections of the Due Process Clause, not its failure to act to protect his liberty interests against harms inflicted by other means.

The *Estelle-Youngberg* analysis simply has no applicability in the present case. Petitioners concede that the harms Joshua suffered did not occur while he was in the State's custody, but while he was in the custody of his natural father, who was in no sense a state actor.[9] While the State may have been aware of the dangers that Joshua faced in the free world, it played no part in their creation, nor did it do anything to render him any more vulnerable to them. That the State once took temporary custody of Joshua does not alter the analysis, for when it returned him to his father's custody, it placed him in no worse position than that in which he would have been had it not acted at all; the State does not become the permanent guarantor of an individual's safety by having once offered him shelter. Under these circumstances, the State had no constitutional duty to protect Joshua.

It may well be that, by voluntarily undertaking to protect Joshua against a danger it concededly played no part in creating, the State acquired a duty under state tort law to provide him with adequate protection against that danger. See Restatement (Second) of Torts § 323 (1965) (one who undertakes to render services to another may in some circumstances be held liable for doing so in a negligent fashion); see generally W. Keeton, D. Dobbs, R. Keeton, & D. Owen, Prosser and Keeton on the Law of Torts § 56 (5th ed. 1984) (discussing "special relationships" which may give rise to affirmative duties to act under the common law of tort). But the claim here is based on the Due Process Clause of the Fourteenth Amendment, which, as we have said many times, does not transform every tort

---

9   Complaint 16, App. 6 ("At relevant times to and until March 8, 1984 [the date of the final beating], Joshua DeShaney was in the custody and control of Defendant Randy DeShaney"). Had the State by the affirmative exercise of its power removed Joshua from free society and placed him in a foster home operated by its agents, we might have a situation sufficiently analogous to incarceration or institutionalization to give rise to an affirmative duty to protect. Indeed, several Courts of Appeals have held, by analogy to *Estelle* and *Youngberg,* that the State may be held liable under the Due Process Clause for failing to protect children in foster homes from mistreatment at the hands of their foster parents. See *Doe v. New York City Dept. of Social Services,* 649 F.2d 134, 141–142 (C.A.2 1981), after remand, 709 F.2d 782, cert. denied *sub nom. Catholic Home Bureau v. Doe,* 464 U.S. 864 (1983); *Taylor ex rel. Walker v. Ledbetter,* 818 F.2d 791, 794–797 (C.A.11 1987) (en banc), cert. pending *sub nom. Ledbetter v. Taylor,* No. 87–521. We express no view on the validity of this analogy, however, as it is not before us in the present case.

committed by a state actor into a constitutional violation. A State may, through its courts and legislatures, impose such affirmative duties of care and protection upon its agents as it wishes. But not "all common-law duties owed by government actors were * * * constitutionalized by the Fourteenth Amendment." *Daniels v. Williams, supra, 474 U.S., at 335*. Because, as explained above, the State had no constitutional duty to protect Joshua against his father's violence, its failure to do so—though calamitous in hindsight—simply does not constitute a violation of the Due Process Clause.

Judges and lawyers, like other humans, are moved by natural sympathy in a case like this to find a way for Joshua and his mother to receive adequate compensation for the grievous harm inflicted upon them. But before yielding to that impulse, it is well to remember once again that the harm was inflicted not by the State of Wisconsin, but by Joshua's father. The most that can be said of the state functionaries in this case is that they stood by and did nothing when suspicious circumstances dictated a more active role for them. In defense of them it must also be said that had they moved too soon to take custody of the son away from the father, they would likely have been met with charges of improperly intruding into the parent-child relationship, charges based on the same Due Process Clause that forms the basis for the present charge of failure to provide adequate protection.

The people of Wisconsin may well prefer a system of liability which would place upon the State and its officials the responsibility for failure to act in situations such as the present one. They may create such a system, if they do not have it already, by changing the tort law of the State in accordance with the regular law-making process. But they should not have it thrust upon them by this Court's expansion of the Due Process Clause of the Fourteenth Amendment.

Affirmed.

> **FYI**
>
> Justices Brennan, Marshall and Blackmun dissented in this case, stating: "Wisconsin's child-protection program thus effectively confined Joshua DeShaney within the walls of Randall DeShaney's violent home until such time as DSS took action to remove him. Conceivably, then, children like Joshua are made worse off by the existence of this program when the persons and entities charged with carrying it out fail to do their jobs." On this basis, they argued that this was not merely a case of refusal to provide affirmative services, but that the state had cut off private sources of aid to Joshua and therefore had a constitutional duty to protect him.
>
> For a behind-the-scenes look at the Supreme Court's decision to accept certiorari in *DeShaney*, see Linda Greenhouse's post, "A Second Chance for Joshua," on the New York Times "Opinionator" blog.

Points for Discussion

a. Injuries in Foster Care

Footnote 9 of the majority opinion in *DeShaney* raises, but does not decide, the question whether a state or its agencies might be liable under 42 U.S.C. § 1983 for placing a child in a foster home where the child is later injured. A number of cases have recognized liability when a state official acts with deliberate indifference to a substantial risk of serious harm to a child placed in foster care. See, e.g., Tamas v. Department of Social & Health Services, 630 F.3d 833 (9th Cir. 2010). State employees may have qualified immunity from suit under § 1983 if a reasonable official would not have understood that his or her conduct violated a constitutional right. See *Tamas*, supra; see also Norfleet v. Arkansas Dept. of Human Services, 989 F.2d 289 (8th Cir.1993).

> **Make the Connection**
>
> The principle invoked in *DeShaney*—that the state has no affirmative obligation to protect individuals from private violence—was also at the center of the Court's opinion in Town of Castle Rock v. Gonzales, 545 U.S. 748 (2005), reprinted in Chapter 4.

b. State Tort Claims

DeShaney suggests the possibility that state agencies might be liable under state tort law for children's injuries suffered at the hands of their parents or foster parents. Some courts have concluded that a state or state agency might be liable for negligence in either placing a child in a foster home where he was beaten, see Elton v. Orange County, 84 Cal.Rptr. 27 (Ct. App. 1970), or in failing to investigate and detect child abuse, see Department of Health and Rehabilitative Services v. Yamuni, 529 So.2d 258 (Fla.1988). Nichol v. Stass, 735 N.E.2d 582 (Ill. 2000) allowed a negligence action to proceed against foster parents following the death of a foster child. See also Miller v. Martin, 838 So.2d 761 (La. 2003) (state agency has vicarious liability for abuse inflicted by foster parents).

c. Failure to Report Abuse

Should a person required by statute to report child abuse be civilly or criminally liable for injuries to a child from the unreported child abuse? Most cases have refused to recognize a private right of action against a mandatory reporter who fails to report instances of child abuse when no report is made and a child is injured as a result. See, e.g., Cechman v. Travis, 414 S.E.2d 282 (Ga. Ct. App. 1991); but see Beggs v. State, Dept. of Social & Health Services, 247 P.3d 421 (Wash. 2011). Barber v. State, 592 So.2d 330 (Fla.Ct.App.1992), affirmed a conviction for failure to report sexual abuse in circumstances in which another person had already reported the particular incident.

Problem 5-2

Two female high school students were enrolled in a graphic arts class in a vocational technical school. They filed a complaint against the school, the school district, various individual teachers and administrators, and seven male students, under 42 U.S.C. § 1983. The complaint alleged that the plaintiffs were physically and sexually assaulted in the classroom, in an adjoining unisex bathroom and in a darkroom, two to four times a week from January to May. The plaintiffs alleged that a student teacher in charge of the class either heard of these activities or should have heard of them, and was or should have been in the classroom when these activities occurred. They also alleged that a school administrator was informed about the problem by one plaintiff and did nothing to correct the situation. Should defendants' motion to dismiss the complaint be granted under the authority of *DeShaney*? (See D.R. by L.R. v. Middle Bucks Area Vo-Tech. School, 972 F.2d 1364 (3d Cir.1992) (en banc).)

Nicholson v. Scoppetta

820 N.E.2d 840 (N.Y. 2004)

KAYE, CHIEF JUDGE.

In this federal class action, the United States Court of Appeals for the Second Circuit has certified three questions centered on New York's statutory scheme for child protective proceedings. The action is brought on behalf of mothers and their children who were separated because the mother had suffered domestic violence, to which the children were exposed, and the children were for that reason deemed neglected by her.

In April 2000, Sharwline Nicholson, on behalf of herself and her two children, brought an action pursuant to 42 USC § 1983, against the New York City Administration for Children's Services (ACS). The action was later consolidated with similar complaints by Sharlene Tillet and Ekaete Udoh—the three named plaintiff-mothers. Plaintiffs alleged that ACS, as a matter of policy, removed children from mothers who were victims of domestic violence because, as victims, they "engaged in domestic violence" and that defendants removed and detained children without probable cause and without due process of law. That policy, and its implementation—according to plaintiff-mothers—constituted, among other wrongs, an unlawful interference with their liberty interest in the care and custody of their children in violation of the United States Constitution.

In August 2001, the United States District Court for the Eastern District of New York certified two subclasses: battered custodial parents (Subclass A), and their children (Subclass B) (*Nicholson v. Williams*, 205 FRD 92, 95, 100 [ED N.Y.2001]). For each plaintiff, at least one ground for removal was that the custodial mother had been assaulted by an intimate partner and failed to protect the child or children from exposure to that domestic violence.

In January 2002, the District Court granted a preliminary injunction, concluding that the City "may not penalize a mother, not otherwise unfit, who is battered by her partner, by separating her from her children; nor may children be separated from the mother, in effect visiting upon them the sins of their mother's batterer" (*In re Nicholson*, 181 F.Supp.2d 182, 188 [ED N.Y. Jan. 20, 2002]; *see also Nicholson v. Williams*, 203 F.Supp.2d 153 [ED N.Y. Mar. 18, 2002] [108-page elaboration of grounds for injunction]).

The court found that ACS unnecessarily, routinely charged mothers with neglect and removed their children where the mothers—who had engaged in no violence themselves—had been the victims of domestic violence; that ACS did so without ensuring that the mother had access to the services she needed, without a court order, and without returning these children promptly after being ordered to do so by the court;[2] that ACS caseworkers and case managers lacked adequate training about domestic violence, and their practice was to separate mother and child when less harmful alternatives were available; that the agency's written policies offered contradictory guidance or no guidance at all on these issues; and that none of the reform plans submitted by ACS could reasonably have been expected to resolve the problems within the next year.

The District Court concluded that ACS's practices and policies violated both the substantive due process rights of mothers and children not to be separated by the government unless the parent is unfit to care for the child, and their procedural due process rights. The injunction, in relevant part, "prohibit[ed] ACS from carrying out *ex parte* removals 'solely because the mother is the victim of domestic violence,' or from filing an Article Ten petition seeking removal on that basis" (*Nicholson v. Scoppetta*, 344 F.3d 154, 164 [2d Cir.2003] [internal citations omitted]).

On appeal, the Second Circuit held that the District Court had not abused its discretion in concluding that ACS's practice of effecting removals based on a parent's failure to prevent his or her child from witnessing domestic violence against the parent amounted to a policy or custom of ACS, that in some circumstances

---

2   The District Court cited the testimony of a child protective manager that it was common practice in domestic violence cases for ACS to wait a few days before going to court after removing a child because "after a few days of the children being in foster care, the mother will usually agree to ACS's conditions for their return without the matter even going to court" (203 F.Supp.2d at 170).

the removals may raise serious questions of federal constitutional law, and that the alleged constitutional violations, if any, were at least plausibly attributable to the City. The Court hesitated, however, before reaching the constitutional questions, believing that resolution of uncertain issues of New York statutory law would avoid, or significantly modify, the substantial federal constitutional issues presented.

Given the strong preference for avoiding unnecessary constitutional adjudication, the importance of child protection to New York State and the integral part New York courts play in the removal process, the Second Circuit, by three certified questions, chose to put the open state statutory law issues to us for resolution. We accepted certification, and now proceed to answer those questions.

Certified Question No. 1: Neglect

"Does the definition of a 'neglected child' under <u>N.Y. Family Ct. Act § 1012(f), (h)</u> include instances in which the sole allegation of neglect is that the parent or other person legally responsible for the child's care allows the child to witness domestic abuse against the caretaker?"

We understand this question to ask whether a court reviewing an Article 10 petition may find a respondent parent responsible for neglect based on evidence of two facts only: that the parent has been the victim of domestic violence, and that the child has been exposed to that violence. That question must be answered in the negative. Plainly, more is required for a showing of neglect under New York law than the fact that a child was exposed to domestic abuse against the caretaker. Answering the question in the affirmative, moreover, would read an unacceptable presumption into the statute, contrary to its plain language.

<u>Family Court Act § 1012(f)</u> is explicit in identifying the elements that must be shown to support a finding of neglect. As relevant here, it defines a "neglected child" to mean:

> "a child less than eighteen years of age (i) whose physical, mental or emotional condition has been impaired or is in imminent danger of becoming impaired as a result of the failure of his parent or other person legally responsible for his care to exercise a minimum degree of care. . .
> "(B) in providing the child with proper supervision or guardianship, by unreasonably inflicting or allowing to be inflicted harm, or a substantial risk thereof, including the infliction of excessive corporal punishment; or by misusing a drug or drugs; or by misusing alcoholic beverages to the extent that he loses self-control of his actions; or by any other acts of a similarly serious nature requiring the aid of the court."

Thus, a party seeking to establish neglect must show, by a preponderance of the evidence (*see* Family Ct. Act § 1046[b][i]), first, that a child's physical, mental or emotional condition has been impaired or is in imminent danger of becoming impaired and second, that the actual or threatened harm to the child is a consequence of the failure of the parent or caretaker to exercise a minimum degree of care in providing the child with proper supervision or guardianship. The drafters of Article 10 were "deeply concerned" that an imprecise definition of child neglect might result in "unwarranted state intervention into private family life" (Besharov, Practice Commentaries, McKinney's Cons Laws of NY, Book 29A, Family Ct. Act § 1012 at 320, [1999 ed.]).

The first statutory element requires proof of actual (or imminent danger of) physical, emotional or mental impairment to the child. This prerequisite to a finding of neglect ensures that the Family Court, in deciding whether to authorize state intervention, will focus on serious harm or potential harm to the child, not just on what might be deemed undesirable parental behavior. "Imminent danger" reflects the Legislature's judgment that a finding of neglect may be appropriate even when a child has not actually been harmed; "imminent danger of impairment to a child is an independent and separate ground on which a neglect finding may be based" (*Dante M., 87 N.Y.2d at 79*). Imminent danger, however, must be near or impending, not merely possible.

In each case, additionally, there must be a link or causal connection between the basis for the neglect petition and the circumstances that allegedly produce the child's impairment or imminent danger of impairment. In *Dante M.,* for example, we held that the Family Court erred in concluding that a newborn's positive toxicology for a controlled substance alone was sufficient to support a finding of neglect because the report, in and of itself, did not prove that the child was impaired or in imminent danger of becoming impaired (87 N.Y.2d at 79). We reasoned, "[r]elying solely on a positive toxicology result for a neglect determination fails to make the necessary causative connection to all the surrounding circumstances that may or may not produce impairment or imminent risk of impairment in the newborn child." The positive toxicology report, in conjunction with other evidence—such as the mother's history of inability to care for her children because of her drug use, testimony of relatives that she was high on cocaine during her pregnancy and the mother's failure to testify at the neglect hearing—supported a finding of neglect and established a link between the report and physical impairment.

The cases at bar concern, in particular, alleged threats to the child's emotional, or mental, health. The statute specifically defines "impairment of emotional health" and "impairment of mental or emotional condition" to include

"a state of substantially diminished psychological or intellectual functioning in relation to, but not limited to, such factors as failure to thrive,

control of aggressive or self-destructive impulses, ability to think and
reason, or acting out or misbehavior, including incorrigibility, ungovernability or habitual truancy"

(Family Ct. Act § 1012[h]). Under New York law, "such impairment must be
clearly attributable to the unwillingness or inability of the respondent to exercise
a minimum degree of care toward the child." Here, the Legislature recognized that
the source of emotional or mental impairment—unlike physical injury—may be
murky, and that it is unjust to fault a parent too readily. The Legislature therefore
specified that such impairment be "clearly attributable" to the parent's failure to
exercise the requisite degree of care.

Assuming that actual or imminent danger to the child has been shown,
"neglect" also requires proof of the parent's failure to exercise a minimum degree
of care. * * *

"Minimum degree of care" is a "baseline of proper care for children that all
parents, regardless of lifestyle or social or economic position, must meet" (Besharov, at 326). Notably, the statutory test is "*minimum* degree of care"—not maximum, not best, not ideal—and the failure must be actual, not threatened.

Courts must evaluate parental behavior objectively: would a reasonable
and prudent parent have so acted, or failed to act, under the circumstances then
and there existing. The standard takes into account the special vulnerabilities of
the child, even where general physical health is not implicated. Thus, when the
inquiry is whether a mother—and domestic violence victim—failed to exercise a
minimum degree of care, the focus must be on whether she has met the standard
of the reasonable and prudent person in similar circumstances.

As the Subclass A members point out, for a battered mother—and ultimately
for a court—what course of action constitutes a parent's exercise of a "minimum
degree of care" may include such considerations as: risks attendant to leaving, if the
batterer has threatened to kill her if she does; risks attendant to staying and suffering
continued abuse; risks attendant to seeking assistance through government chan-
nels, potentially increasing the danger to herself and her children; risks attendant to
criminal prosecution against the abuser; and risks attendant to relocation. Whether
a particular mother in these circumstances has actually failed to exercise a minimum
degree of care is necessarily dependent on facts such as the severity and frequency
of the violence, and the resources and options available to her.

Only when a petitioner demonstrates, by a preponderance of evidence, that
both elements of section 1012(f) are satisfied may a child be deemed neglected
under the statute. When "the sole allegation" is that the mother has been abused
and the child has witnessed the abuse, such a showing has not been made. This

does not mean, however, that a child can never be "neglected" when living in a household plagued by domestic violence. Conceivably, neglect might be found where a record establishes that, for example, the mother acknowledged that the children knew of repeated domestic violence by her paramour and had reason to be afraid of him, yet nonetheless allowed him several times to return to her home, and lacked awareness of any impact of the violence on the children, as in *Matter of James MM., 294 A.D.2d at 632*; or where the children were exposed to regular and continuous extremely violent conduct between their parents, several times requiring official intervention, and where caseworkers testified to the fear and distress the children were experiencing as a result of their long exposure to the violence (*Matter of Theresa CC., 178 A.D.2d 687 [3d Dept 1991]*).

In such circumstances, the battered mother is charged with neglect not because she is a victim of domestic violence or because her children witnessed the abuse, but rather because a preponderance of the evidence establishes that the children were actually or imminently harmed by reason of her failure to exercise even minimal care in providing them with proper oversight.

Certified Question No. 2: Removals

Next, we are called upon to focus on removals by ACS, in answering the question:

"Can the injury or possible injury, if any, that results to a child who has witnessed domestic abuse against a parent or other caretaker constitute 'danger' or 'risk' to the child's 'life or health,' as those terms are defined in the N.Y. Family Ct. Act §§ 1022, 1024, 1026–1028?"

The cited Family Court Act sections relate to the removal of a child from home. Thus, in essence, we are asked to decide whether emotional injury from witnessing domestic violence can rise to a level that establishes an "imminent danger" or "risk" to a child's life or health, so that removal is appropriate either in an emergency or by court order.

While we do not reach the constitutional questions, it is helpful in framing the statutory issues to note the Second Circuit's outline of the federal constitutional questions relating to removals. Their questions emerge in large measure from the District Court's findings of an "agency-wide practice of removing children from their mother without evidence of a mother's neglect and without seeking prior judicial approval", and Family Court review of removals that "often fails to provide mothers and children with an effective avenue for timely relief from ACS mistakes."

Specifically, as to *ex parte* removals, the Circuit Court identified procedural due process and Fourth Amendment questions focused on whether danger to a child could encompass emotional trauma from witnessing domestic violence against a parent, warranting emergency removal. * * *

The Court also questioned whether "in the context of the seizure of a child by a state protective agency the Fourth Amendment might impose any additional restrictions above and beyond those that apply to ordinary arrests."

As to court-ordered removals, the Second Circuit recognized challenges based on substantive due process, procedural due process—the antecedent of Certified Question No. 3—and the Fourth Amendment. The substantive due process question concerned whether the City had offered a reasonable justification for the removals. The Second Circuit observed that "there is a substantial Fourth Amendment question presented if New York law does not authorize removals in the circumstances alleged."

> Finally, in certifying the questions to us, the Court explained that:
> "[t]here is. . .some ambiguity in the statutory language authorizing removals pending a final determination of status. Following an emergency removal, whether *ex parte* or by court order, the Family Court must return a removed child to the parent's custody absent 'an imminent risk' or 'imminent danger' to 'the child's life or health.' At the same time, the Family Court must consider the 'best interests of the child' in assessing whether continuing removal is necessary to prevent threats to the child's life or health. Additionally, in order to support removal, the Family Court must 'find[ ] that removal is necessary to avoid imminent risk. How these provisions should be harmonized seems to us to be the province of the Court of Appeals' "(344 F.3d at 169 [internal citations omitted]).

The Circuit Court summarized the policy challenged by plaintiffs and found by the District Court as "the alleged practice of removals based on a theory that allowing one's child to witness ongoing domestic violence is a form of neglect, either simply because such conduct is presumptively neglectful or because in individual circumstances it is shown to threaten the child's physical or emotional health" (*id.* at 166 n 5).

It is this policy, viewed in light of the District Court's factual findings, that informs our analysis of Certified Question No. 2. In so doing, we acknowledge the Legislature's expressed goal of "placing increased emphasis on preventive services designed to maintain family relationships rather than responding to children and families in trouble only by removing the child from the family" (*see Mark G. v. Sabol*, 93 N.Y.2d 710, 719 [1999] construing Child Welfare Reform Act of 1979 [L 1979, chs 610, 611]). We further acknowledge the legislative findings, made pursuant to the Family Protection and Domestic Violence Intervention Act of 1994, that

> "the corrosive effect of domestic violence is far reaching. The batterer's violence injures children both directly and indirectly. Abuse of a par-

ent is detrimental to children whether or not they are physically abused themselves. Children who witness domestic violence are more likely to experience delayed development, feelings of fear, depression and helplessness and are more likely to become batterers themselves" (L 1994, ch 222, § 1; *see also* People v. Wood, 95 N.Y.2d 509, 512 [2000] [though involving a batterer, not a victim]).

These legislative findings represent two fundamental—sometimes conflict in—principles. New York has long embraced a policy of keeping "biological families together" (Matter of Marino S., Jr., 100 N.Y.2d 361, 372 [2003]). Yet "when a child's best interests are endangered, such objectives must yield to the State's paramount concern for the health and safety of the child" (*id.* at 372).

As we concluded in response to Certified Question No. 1, exposing a child to domestic violence is *not* presumptively neglectful. Not every child exposed to domestic violence is at risk of impairment. *A fortiori,* exposure of a child to violence is not presumptively ground for removal, and in many instances removal may do more harm to the child than good. Part 2 of Article 10 of the Family Court Act sets forth four ways in which a child may be removed from the home in response to an allegation of neglect (or abuse) related to domestic violence: 1) temporary removal with consent; 2) preliminary orders after a petition is filed; 3) preliminary orders before a petition is filed; and 4) emergency removal without a court order. The issue before us is whether emotional harm suffered by a child exposed to domestic violence, where shown, can warrant the trauma of removal under any of these provisions.

* * *

Consent Removal

First, section 1021 provides that a child may be removed "from the place where he is residing with the written consent of his parent or other person legally responsible for his care, if the child is an abused or neglected child under this article" (Family Court Act § 1021). This section is significant because "many parents are willing and

Take Note

The rules that the court establishes here are different depending on how a child is removed from the home.

able to understand the need to place the child outside the home and because resort to unnecessary legal coercion can be detrimental to later treatment efforts" (Besharov, at 6).

Post-Petition Removal

If parental consent cannot be obtained, section 1027, at issue here, provides for preliminary orders after the filing of a neglect (or abuse) petition. Thus, according to the statutory continuum, where the circumstances are not so exigent, the agency should bring a petition and seek a hearing *prior to* removal of the child. In any case involving abuse—or in any case where the child has already been removed without a court order—the Family Court must hold a hearing as soon as practicable after the filing of a petition, to determine whether the child's interests require protection pending a final order of disposition (Family Ct Act § 1027[a]). As is relevant here, the section further provides that in any other circumstance (such as a neglect case), after the petition is filed any person originating the proceeding (or the Law Guardian) may apply for—or the court on its own may order—a hearing to determine whether the child's interests require protection, pending a final order of disposition.[8]

For example, in *Matter of Adam DD.* (112 A.D.2d 493 [3d Dept 1985]), after filing a child neglect petition, petitioner Washington County Department of Social Services sought an order under section 1027. At a hearing, evidence demonstrated that respondent-mother had told her son on several occasions that she intended to kill herself, and Family Court directed that custody be placed with petitioner on a temporary basis for two months. At the subsequent dispositional hearing, a psychiatrist testified that respondent was suffering from a type of paranoid schizophrenia that endangered the well-being of the child, and recommended the continued placement with petitioner. A second psychiatrist concurred. The Appellate Division concluded that the record afforded a basis for Family Court to find neglect because of possible impairment of the child's emotional health, and continued placement of the child with petitioner.

While not a domestic violence case, *Matter of Adam DD.* is instructive because it concerns steps taken in the circumstance where a child is emotionally harmed by parental behavior. The parent's repeated threats of suicide caused emotional harm that could be akin to the experience of a child who witnesses repeated episodes of domestic violence perpetrated against a parent. In this circumstance, the agency did not immediately remove the child, but proceeded with the filing of a petition and a hearing.

Upon such a hearing, if the court finds that removal is necessary to avoid imminent risk to the child's life or health, it is required to remove or continue

---

[8]   Under section 1028, a parent or person legally responsible for the care of a child may petition the court for return of the child after removal, if he or she was not present or given an adequate opportunity to be present at the section 1027 hearing. The factors to be considered when returning a child removed in an emergency mirror those considered in an initial determination under sections 1027 and 1022—best interests, imminent risk, and reasonable efforts to avoid removal.

the removal and remand the child to a place approved by the agency (Family Ct Act § 1027[b][i]). In undertaking this inquiry, the statute also requires the court to consider and determine whether continuation in the child's home would be contrary to the best interests of the child.

The Circuit Court has asked us to harmonize the "best interests" test with the calculus concerning "imminent risk" and "imminent danger" to "life or health" (344 F.3d at 169). In order to justify a finding of imminent risk to life or health, the agency need not prove that the child has suffered actual injury. Rather, the court engages in a fact-intensive inquiry to determine whether the child's emotional health is at risk. Section 1012(h), moreover, sets forth specific factors, evidence of which may demonstrate "substantially diminished psychological or intellectual functioning". As noted in our discussion of Certified Question No. 1, section 1012(h) contains the caveat that impairment of emotional health must be "clearly attributable to the unwillingness or inability of the respondent to exercise a minimum degree of care toward the child" (*see Matter of Theresa CC., 178 A.D.2d 687 [3d Dept 1991]*).

Importantly, in 1988, the Legislature added the "best interests" requirement to the statute, as well as the requirement that reasonable efforts be made "to prevent or eliminate the need for removal of the child from the home" (L 1988, ch 478, § 5). These changes were apparently necessary to comport with federal requirements under Title IV-E of the Social Security Act (42 USC § § 670–679a), which mandated that federal "foster care maintenance payments may be made on behalf of otherwise eligible children who were removed from the home of a specified relative pursuant to a voluntary placement agreement, or as the result of a 'judicial determination to the effect that continuation therein would be contrary to the welfare of the child and. . .that reasonable efforts [to prevent the need for removal] have been made' "The measures "ensure[d] that children involved in the early stages of child protective proceedings and their families receive appropriate services to prevent the children's removal from their homes whenever possible".

* * *

In this litigation, the City posits that the "best interests" determination is part of the Family Court's conclusion that there is imminent risk warranting removal, and concedes that whether a child will be harmed by the removal is a relevant consideration. The City thus recognizes that the questions facing a Family Court judge in the removal context are extraordinarily complex. As the Circuit Court observed, "it could be argued that the exigencies of the moment that threaten the welfare of a child justify removal. On the other hand, a blanket presumption in favor of removal may not fairly capture the nuances of each family situation" (344 F.3d at 174).

The plain language of the section and the legislative history supporting it establish that a blanket presumption favoring removal was never intended. The court *must do more* than identify the existence of a risk of serious harm. Rather, a court must weigh, in the factual setting before it, whether the imminent risk to the child can be mitigated by reasonable efforts to avoid removal. It must balance that risk against the harm removal might bring, and it must determine factually which course is in the child's best interests.

Additionally, the court must specifically consider whether imminent risk to the child might be eliminated by other means, such as issuing a temporary order of protection or providing services to the victim (Family Ct Act § 1027[b] [iv]). The Committee Bill Memorandum supporting this legislation explains the intent to address the situation "[w]here one parent is abusive but the child may safely reside at home with the other parent, the abuser should be removed. This will spare children the trauma of removal and placement in foster care" (Mem of Children and Families Standing Comm, Bill Jacket, L 1989, ch 727, at 7).

These legislative concerns were met, for example, in *Matter of Naomi R.* (296 A.D.2d 503 [2d Dept 2002]), where, following a hearing pursuant to section 1027, Family Court issued a temporary order of protection against a father, excluding him from the home, on the ground that he allegedly sexually abused one of his four children. Evidence established that the father's return to the home, even under the mother's supervision, would present an imminent risk to the health and safety of all of the children. Thus, pending a full fact-finding hearing, Family Court took the step of maintaining the integrity of the family unit and instead removed the abuser.

Ex Parte Removal by Court Order

If the agency believes that there is insufficient time to file a petition, the next step on the continuum should not be emergency removal, but *ex parte* removal by court order. Section 1022 of the Family Court Act provides that the court may enter an order directing the temporary removal of a child from home *before* the filing of a petition if three factors are met.

First, the parent must be absent or, if present, must have been asked and refused to consent to temporary removal of the child and must have been informed of an intent to apply for an order. Second, the child must appear to suffer from abuse or neglect of a parent or other person legally responsible for the child's care to the extent that immediate removal is necessary to avoid imminent danger to the child's life or health. Third, there must be insufficient time to file a petition and hold a preliminary hearing.

Just as in a <u>section 1027</u> inquiry, the court must consider whether continuation in the child's home would be contrary to the best interests of the child; whether reasonable efforts were made prior to prevent or eliminate the need for removal from the home; and whether imminent risk to the child would be eliminated by the issuance of a temporary order of protection directing the removal of the person from the child's residence.[11] Here, the court must engage in a fact-finding inquiry into whether the child is at risk and appears to suffer from neglect.

The Practice Commentaries suggest that <u>section 1022</u> may be unfamiliar, or seem unnecessary, to those in practice in New York City, "where it is common to take emergency protective action without prior court review" (Besharov, Practice Commentaries, McKinney's Cons Laws of NY, Book 29A, <u>Family Ct Act § 1022 at 10, [1999 ed]</u>). If, as the District Court's findings suggest, this was done in cases where a court order could be obtained, the practice contravenes the statute. <u>Section 1022</u> ensures that in most urgent situations, there will be judicial oversight in order to prevent well-meaning but misguided removals that may harm the child more than help. As the comment to the predecessor statute stated, "this section. . .[is] designed to avoid a premature removal of a child from his home by establishing a procedure for early judicial determination of urgent need" (Committee Comments, Family Ct Act repealed § 322 [1963]).

Whether analyzing a removal application under <u>section 1027</u> or <u>1022</u>, or an application for a child's return under <u>section 1028</u>, a court must engage in a balancing test of the imminent risk with the best interests of the child and, where appropriate, the reasonable efforts made to avoid removal or continuing removal. The term "safer course" should not be used to mask a dearth of evidence or as a watered-down, impermissible presumption.

Emergency Removal Without Court Order

Finally, <u>section 1024</u> provides for emergency removals without a court order. The section permits removal without a court order and without consent of the parent if there is reasonable cause to believe that the child is in such urgent circumstance or condition that continuing in the home or care of the parent presents an imminent danger to the child's life or health, and there is not enough time to apply for an order under <u>section 1022</u> (<u>Family Ct Act § 1024[a]</u>). Thus, emergency removal is appropriate where the danger is so immediate, so urgent that the child's life or safety will be at risk before an *ex parte* order can be obtained. The standard obviously is a stringent one.

<u>Section 1024</u> establishes an objective test, whether the child is in such circumstance or condition that remaining in the home presents imminent danger to life or

---

[11] The order must state the court's findings concerning the necessity of removal, whether respondent was present at the hearing and what notice was given.

health.[12] In construing "imminent danger" under section 1024, it has been held that whether a child is in "imminent danger" is necessarily a fact-intensive determination. "It is not required that the child be injured in the presence of a caseworker nor is it necessary for the alleged abuser to be present at the time the child is taken from the home. It is sufficient if the officials have persuasive evidence of serious ongoing abuse and, based upon the best investigation reasonably possible under the circumstances, have reason to fear imminent recurrence" (*Gottlieb v. County of Orange*, 871 F.Supp. 625, 628–629 [SD N.Y.1994], *citing Robison v. Via*, 821 F.2d 913, 922 [2d Cir1987]). The *Gottlieb* court added that, "[s]ince this evidence is the basis for removal of a child, it should be as reliable and thoroughly examined as possible to avoid unnecessary harm to the family unit" (871 F.Supp. at 629).

Section 1024 concerns, moreover, only the very grave circumstance of danger to life or health. While we cannot say, for all future time, that the possibility can *never* exist, in the case of emotional injury—or, even more remotely, the risk of emotional injury—caused by witnessing domestic violence, it must be a rare circumstance in which the time would be so fleeting and the danger so great that emergency removal would be warranted.

Certified Question No. 3: Process

Finally, the Second Circuit asks us:

"Does the fact that the child witnessed such abuse suffice to demonstrate that 'removal is necessary,' N.Y. Family Ct. Act §§ 1022, 1024, 1027, or that 'removal was in the child's best interests,' N.Y. Family Ct. Act §§ 1028, 1052(b)(i)(A), or must the child protective agency offer additional, particularized evidence to justify removal?"

The Circuit Court has before it the procedural due process question whether, if New York law permits a presumption that removal is appropriate based on the witnessing of domestic violence, that presumption would comport with *Stanley v. Illinois* (405 U.S. 645 [1972] [recognizing a father's procedural due process interest in an individualized determination of fitness]). All parties maintain, however, and we concur, that under the Family Court Act, there can be no "blanket presumption" favoring removal when a child witnesses domestic violence, and that each case is fact-specific. As demonstrated in our discussion of Certified Question No. 2, when a court orders removal, particularized evidence must exist to justify that determination, including, where appropriate, evidence of efforts made to prevent or eliminate the need for removal and the impact of removal on the child.

* * *

---

[12] Section 1022 also requires that the child be brought immediately to a social services department, that the agency make every reasonable effort to inform the parent where the child is and that the agency give written notice to the parent of the right to apply to family court for return of the child.

Accordingly, the certified questions should be answered in accordance with this Opinion.

* * *

Points for Discussion

a. Emergency Removal

The opinion in *Nicholson* describes four types of procedures that child protective workers may utilize to remove children from their parents: removal based on written consent from the parents (N.Y. Fam. Ct. Act § 1021), removal after the filing of a petition alleging abuse or neglect (N.Y. Fam. Ct. Act § 1027), removal based on an ex parte court order before the filing of an abuse or neglect petition (N.Y. Fam. Ct. Act § 1022), and emergency removal without a court order (N.Y. Fam. Ct. Act § 1024). When is each of these procedures appropriate? To what extent does this determination raise constitutional questions?

In Tenenbaum v. Williams, 193 F.3d 581 (2d Cir.1999), the court held that removal of a child from his or her parents without judicial process when there were no emergency circumstances violated the parents' procedural due process rights and was actionable under 42 U.S.C. § 1983. See also Hatch v. Department for Children, Youth and their Families, 274 F.3d 12 (1st Cir.2001). A Florida statute authorizing warrantless emergency removal of children from their homes was sustained in Doe v. Kearney, 329 F.3d 1286 (11th Cir.2003).

b. Domestic Violence and Child Abuse

There are strong correlations between child abuse and other domestic violence. Adults who batter a spouse or partner often abuse children in the household as well. Children are sometimes hurt in the course of adult domestic violence, either inadvertently or when they attempt to assist a battered parent. Parents who are victims of domestic violence may have difficulty protecting their children from abuse, or they may become violent toward their children.

Make the Connection

Family violence issues are discussed in Chapter 4.

See Howard A. Davidson, *Child Abuse and Domestic Violence: Legal Connections and Controversies*, 29 Fam. L.Q. 357 (1995).

One study concluded that of children who witness domestic violence in the home, 40% were physically abused and 28% of the girls reported sexual abuse.

Marie Roy, Children in the Crossfire: Violence in the Home—How Does It Affect Our Children? 103 (1988). Furthermore, "truancy, running away, drug and alcohol abuse, drug dealing, prostitution, assaultive behavior were common coping techniques" for these children; and "10% suffered from chronic enuresis and insomnia." Id. at 104.

The presence of adult domestic violence complicates the problem of a parent's liability for failure to prevent harm to a child. Statutes in some states provide an affirmative defense for a defendant who reasonably feared that action to stop the abuse would result in substantial bodily harm to the defendant or to the child. See, e.g., Iowa Code Ann. § 726.6.1e (2018); Minn. Stat. Ann. § 609.378 (2018). See also In the Matter of Glenn G., 587 N.Y.S.2d 464 (Fam. Ct. 1992) (finding battered mother had not abused children under the New York statute by failing to protect them from father's sexual abuse, but also concluding that she was guilty of neglect, which is a strict liability offense).

c. Secondary Abuse

Evidence suggests that whether or not they are physically abused, children who are exposed to domestic violence at home suffer a variety of long and short term consequences. Some cases have sustained findings of secondary abuse or neglect where a child is exposed to family violence, see, e.g., In re Heather A., 60 Cal.Rptr.2d 315 (Ct. App. 1996); In re Theresa "CC," 576 N.Y.S.2d 937 (App. Div.1991). Utah includes committing domestic violence in the presence of a child within the definition of child abuse. Utah Code Ann. § 76–5–109.1 (2018). In light of the opinion in *Nicholson*, how should child protection authorities approach these cases?

d. Collaborative Practice

In response to problems at the intersection of child protection and domestic violence, one important initiative has advocated greater collaboration between courts, the child welfare system, and the network of domestic violence service providers. A series of federally-funded demonstration projects have worked to implement and develop these recommendations. See Susan Schechter and Jeffrey L. Edelson, Effective Intervention in Family Violence and Child Maltreatment Cases: Guidelines for Policy and Practice (1999), published by the National Council of Juvenile and Family Court Judges and known as the "Greenbook."

Estelle v. McGuire

502 U.S. 62 (1991)

CHIEF JUSTICE REHNQUIST delivered the opinion of the Court.

Respondent Mark Owen McGuire was found guilty in a California state court of second-degree murder for the killing of his infant daughter. After unsuccessfully challenging his conviction on appeal in the state courts, McGuire sought federal habeas relief and the United States Court of Appeals for the Ninth Circuit set aside his conviction. 902 F.2d 749 (1990). We hold that in so doing the Court of Appeals exceeded the limited scope of federal habeas review of state convictions.

Go Online

Listen to the oral arguments in *Estelle* on the Oyez Project web site.

Make the Connection

These materials highlight particular problems in criminal law and procedure and the law of evidence that arise in the prosecution of crimes involving very young children.

McGuire and his wife brought their six-month-old daughter, Tori, to a hospital in Hayward, California. The baby was bluish in color and was not breathing. The attending physician noticed a large and relatively recent bruise on Tori's chest with multiple bruises around it, as well as black and blue marks around her ears. Efforts to revive the child were unsuccessful; Tori died 45 minutes after being brought to the hospital. An autopsy revealed 17 contusions on the baby's chest, 29 contusions in her abdominal area, a split liver, a split pancreas, a lacerated large intestine, and damage to her heart and one of her lungs. The autopsy also uncovered evidence of rectal tearing, which was at least six weeks old, and evidence of partially healed rib fractures, which were approximately seven weeks old.

The police questioned McGuire and his wife. McGuire stated his belief that Tori's injuries must have resulted from a fall off the family couch. He told the police that when his wife went out to make a telephone call, he went upstairs, leaving Tori lying on the couch; when he heard the baby cry, he came back downstairs to find her lying on the floor. After a police officer expressed skepticism at this explanation, McGuire replied that "[m]aybe some Mexicans came in" while he was upstairs. During separate questioning, McGuire's wife stated that she had not hit Tori, and that she was unsure whether her husband had done so.

McGuire was charged with second-degree murder. At trial, the prosecution introduced both the statements made by McGuire to police and the medical evidence, including the evidence of prior rectal tearing and fractured ribs. Two physicians testified that Tori was a battered child, relying in part on the prior rib and rectal injuries, as well as on the more recent injuries. McGuire's neighbor testified that she had seen McGuire carry Tori by one of her arms to the car and roughly pinch her cheeks together when she cried. The neighbor added that McGuire's wife had expressed fear in leaving Tori alone with McGuire, because he had been rough with the baby and "did bad things" to her.

In addition, the prosecution called a witness who had overheard a conversation between McGuire and his wife in the hospital emergency room the night of Tori's death. According to the witness, McGuire's wife several times insistently asked, "What really happened?" McGuire replied that he "didn't know," and that he "guessed" the baby fell off the couch. His wife continued to press for an answer, stating, "I am very patient. I can wait a long time. I want to know what really happened." Finally, she told McGuire that "the baby was alright when I left. You are responsible." McGuire's wife was called by the prosecution to testify at trial, after having been granted transactional immunity from future prosecution. In contrast to her prior statement to the police and her declarations at the hospital, she stated that she had beaten Tori on the day of her death before her husband arrived home. The jury convicted McGuire of second-degree murder.

The California Court of Appeal affirmed McGuire's conviction. The court observed that the evidence of prior rib and rectal injuries was introduced to prove "battered child syndrome." That syndrome exists when a child has sustained repeated and/or serious injuries by nonaccidental means. *People v. Bledsoe*, 36 Cal.3d 236, 249, 203 Cal.Rptr. 450, 458, 681 P.2d 291, 299 (1984). After reviewing California authority on the subject, the court concluded that "proof of Tori's 'prior injuries' tending to establish the 'battered child syndrome' was patently proper." The California Supreme Court denied review.

McGuire then filed a petition for habeas corpus relief in the United States District Court for the Northern District of California. That court denied relief. The Court of Appeals for the Ninth Circuit reversed and granted McGuire's habeas petition. The court ruled that the prior injury evidence was erroneously admitted to establish battered child syndrome, because no evidence linked McGuire to the prior injuries and no claim had been made at trial that the baby died accidentally. In addition, the court believed that the trial court's instruction on the use of prior act evidence allowed a finding of guilt based simply on a judgment that McGuire committed the prior bad acts.[1] The court concluded that the admission of the evidence, in conjunction with the prejudicial instruction, "rendered [McGuire's] trial arbitrary and fundamentally unfair" in violation of due process. We hold that none of the alleged errors rise to the level of a due process violation, and so reverse.

We first consider whether the admission of the prior injury evidence justified habeas relief. In ruling that McGuire's due process rights were violated by the admission of the evidence, the Court of Appeals relied in part on its conclusion that the evidence was "incorrectly admitted * * * pursuant to California law." Such an inquiry, however, is no part of a federal court's habeas review of a state conviction. We have stated many times that "federal habeas corpus relief does not lie for errors of state law." Today, we reemphasize that it is not the province of a federal habeas court to reexamine state court determinations on state law questions. In conducting habeas review, a federal court is limited to deciding whether a conviction violated the Constitution, laws, or treaties of the United States. 28 U.S.C. § 2241.

We thus turn to the question whether the admission of the evidence violated McGuire's federal constitutional rights. California law allows the prosecution to introduce expert testimony and evidence related to prior injuries in order to prove "battered child syndrome." *People v. Bledsoe, supra,* 36 Cal.3d, at 249, 203 Cal.Rptr., at 458, 681 P.2d at 299. The demonstration of battered child syndrome "simply indicates that a child found with [serious, repeated injuries] has not suffered those injuries by accidental means." Thus, evidence demonstrating battered child syndrome helps to prove that the child died at the hands of another and not by falling off a couch, for example; it also tends to establish that the "other," whoever it may be, inflicted

Think About It

What is the purpose of introducing "battered child syndrome" evidence? What risks does it present?

---

[1] The court instructed the jury:

"Evidence has been introduced for the purpose of showing that the Defendant committed acts similar to those constituting a crime other than that for which he is on trial. Such evidence, if believed, was not received, and may not be considered by you[,] to prove that he is a person of bad character or that he has a disposition to commit crimes. Such evidence was received and may be considered by you only for the limited purpose of determining if it tends to show three things:

"1. The impeachment of Daisy McGuire's testimony that she had no cause to be afraid of the Defendant.

"2. To establish the battered child syndrome, and

"3. Also a clear connection between the other two offense[s] and the one of which the Defendant is accused, so that it may be logically concluded that if the Defendant committed other offenses, he also committed the crime charged in this case.

"For the limited purpose for which you may consider such evidence, you must weigh it in the same manner as you do all other evidence in the case. You are not permitted to consider evidence for any other purpose."

the injuries intentionally. When offered to show that certain injuries are a product of child abuse, rather than accident, evidence of prior injuries is relevant even though it does not purport to prove the identity of the person who might have inflicted those injuries. Because the prosecution had charged McGuire with second-degree murder, it was required to prove that Tori's death was caused by the defendant's intentional act. Proof of Tori's battered child status helped to do just that; although not linked by any direct evidence to McGuire, the evidence demonstrated that Tori's death was the result of an intentional act by *someone,* and not an accident. The Court of Appeals, however, ignored the principle of battered child syndrome evidence in holding that this evidence was incorrectly admitted. For example, the court stated that "[e]vidence cannot have probative value unless a party connects it to the defendant in some meaningful way." We conclude that the evidence of prior injuries presented at McGuire's trial, whether it was directly linked to McGuire or not, was probative on the question of the intent with which the person who caused the injuries acted.

In holding the prior injury evidence inadmissible, the Court of Appeals also relied on the theory that, because no claim was made at trial that Tori died accidentally, the battered child syndrome evidence was irrelevant and violative of due process. This ruling ignores the fact that the prosecution must prove all the elements of a criminal offense beyond a reasonable doubt. In this second degree murder case, for example, the prosecution was required to demonstrate that the killing was intentional. Cal.Penal Code Ann. §§ 187, 189 (West 1988). By eliminating the possibility of accident, the evidence regarding battered child syndrome was clearly probative of that essential element, especially in light of the fact that McGuire had claimed prior to trial that Tori had injured herself by falling from the couch. The Court of Appeals, however, ruled that the evidence should have been excluded because McGuire did not raise the defense of accidental death at trial. But the prosecution's burden to prove every element of the crime is not relieved by a defendant's tactical decision not to contest an essential element of the offense. In the federal courts "[a] simple plea of not guilty * * * puts the prosecution to its proof as to all elements of the crime charged." <u>Mathews v. United States,</u> 485 U.S. 58, 64–65 (1988). Neither the Court of Appeals nor the parties have given us any reason to think that the rule is different in California. The evidence of battered child syndrome was relevant to show intent, and nothing in the Due Process Clause of the Fourteenth Amendment requires the State to refrain from introducing relevant evidence simply because the defense chooses not to contest the point.

Concluding, as we do, that the prior injury evidence was relevant to an issue in the case, we need not explore further the apparent assumption of the Court of Appeals that it is a violation of the due process guaranteed by the Fourteenth Amendment for evidence that is not relevant to be received in a criminal trial. We hold that McGuire's due process rights were not violated by the admission of the evidence.

II

The Court of Appeals, however, did not rely solely on a finding that the admission of the evidence was unconstitutional. It based its decision in part on a belief that the instruction given by the trial court, set forth in n. 1, *supra,* allowed the jury to consider the prior injury evidence for more than simply proof of the battered child syndrome, and thereby violated McGuire's due process rights. McGuire focuses on the portion of the instruction explaining to the jury that the prior injury evidence

> "was received and may be considered by you only for the limited purpose of determining if it tends to show * * * a clear connection between the other two offense[s] and the one of which the Defendant is accused, so that it may be logically concluded that if the Defendant committed other offenses, he also committed the crime charged in this case."

McGuire argues that, despite the absence of any direct evidence showing that he caused the rib and rectal injuries, the instruction told the jury to find that he had committed those prior offenses. Furthermore, he argues, the instruction left the jury with the mistaken impression that it could base its finding of guilt on the simple fact that he had previously harmed Tori. Under McGuire's reading, the instruction is transformed into a propensity instruction, allowing the jury to consider as evidence of his guilt the fact that his prior acts show a disposition to commit this type of crime. This, he contends, violates the Due Process Clause.

In arguing his point, McGuire makes much of the fact that, in giving its instruction, the trial court deviated in part from standard jury instruction 2.50 of the California Jury Instructions, Criminal (4th ed. 1979) (CALJIC).[3] As we have stated above, however, the fact that the instruction was allegedly incorrect under state law is not a basis for habeas relief. The only question for us is "whether the ailing instruction by itself so infected the entire trial that the resulting conviction violates due process." *Cupp v. Naughten,* 414 U.S. 141, 147 (1973); *Donnelly v. DeChristoforo,* 416 U.S. 637, 643 (1974) (" '[I]t must be established not merely

---

[3]   Meticulous compliance with CALJIC 2.50, as in effect at McGuire's trial, would have led the trial court to instruct the jury that the prior injury evidence

> "was received and may be considered by you only for the limited purpose of determining if it tends to show:
>
> "*A characteristic method, plan or scheme in the commission of criminal acts similar to the method, plan or scheme used in the commission of the offense in this case which would further tend to show* a clear connection between the other offense[s] and the one of which defendant is accused so that it may be logically concluded that if defendant committed the other offense[s] he also committed the crime charged in this case." (portion in italics was omitted from the actual jury instruction given at McGuire's trial).

that the instruction is undesirable, erroneous, or even 'universally condemned,' but that it violated some [constitutional right]' "). It is well established that the instruction "may not be judged in artificial isolation," but must be considered in the context of the instructions as a whole and the trial record. *Cupp v. Naughten, supra*, 414 U.S., at 147. In addition, in reviewing an ambiguous instruction such as the one at issue here, we inquire "whether there is a reasonable likelihood that the jury has applied the challenged instruction in a way" that violates the Constitution. *Boyde v. California*, 494 U.S. 370, 380 (1990). And we also bear in mind our previous admonition that we "have defined the category of infractions that violate 'fundamental fairness' very narrowly." *Dowling v. United States*, 493 U.S. 342, 352 (1990). "Beyond the specific guarantees enumerated in the Bill of Rights, the Due Process Clause has limited operation."

McGuire first claims that the instruction directed the jury to find that he had caused the prior injuries, thereby effectively taking that question from the jury. One might argue that the "two offense[s]" referred to in the instruction were McGuire's pinching of the child's cheeks and the lifting of the child by her arm. When read in context, however, we conclude that the most likely interpretation is that the reference was to the rectal tearing and fractured ribs. McGuire argues that, despite the lack of any direct evidence linking him to those injuries, the instruction directed the jury to find that he had committed them. This claim is clearly foreclosed, however, by the language of the instruction. The challenged portion of the instruction included the words "if the Defendant committed other offenses." By including this phrase, the trial court unquestionably left it to the jury to determine whether McGuire committed the prior acts; *only if* the jury believed he was the perpetrator could it use the evidence in deciding whether McGuire was guilty of the crime charged. Therefore, if the jury did not believe McGuire caused the prior injuries, he was not harmed by the challenged portion of the instruction. To the extent that the jury may have believed McGuire committed the prior acts and used that as a factor in its deliberation, we observe that there was sufficient evidence to sustain such a jury finding by a preponderance of the evidence. The proof of battered child syndrome itself narrowed the group of possible perpetrators to McGuire and his wife, because they were the only two people regularly caring for Tori during her short life. See *People v. Jackson*, 18 Cal.App.3d, at 507, 95 Cal.Rptr., at 921 ("Only someone regularly 'caring' for the child has the continuing opportunity to inflict these types of injuries; an isolated contact with a vicious stranger would not result in this pattern of successive injuries stretching through several months"). A neighbor testified that she had seen McGuire treat Tori roughly on two occasions, and that McGuire's wife was scared to leave Tori alone with McGuire because he "did bad things" to her; the neighbor further testified that she had never seen McGuire's wife abuse the child in any way. Furthermore, when being questioned by the police after Tori died, McGuire's wife stated that she observed bruises on the baby's body when bathing her. When asked by the police for an explanation, she replied, "I don't really know, you know, I am not the only one who is taking care of her." The evidence described, along with other evidence in the record, convinces us that there was sufficient proof for the jury to conclude, if it so desired, that McGuire caused the prior rib and rectal injuries.

McGuire also contends that, even if the determination of the perpetrator was left to the jury, the instruction constituted a "propensity" instruction, allowing the jury to base its determination of guilt in part upon the conclusion that McGuire had committed the prior acts and therefore had a propensity to commit this type of crime. While the instruction was not as clear as it might have been, we find that there is not a "reasonable likelihood" that the jury would have concluded that this instruction, read in the context of other instructions, authorized the use of propensity evidence pure and simple. It seems far more likely that the jury understood the instruction, to mean that *if* it found a "clear connection" between the prior injuries and the instant injuries, and *if* it found that McGuire had committed the prior injuries, then it could use that fact in determining that McGuire committed the crime charged. The use of the evidence of prior offenses permitted by this instruction was therefore parallel to the familiar use of evidence of prior acts for the purpose of showing intent, identity, motive, or plan. See, *e.g.*, Fed. Rule Evid. 404(b). Furthermore, the trial court guarded against possible misuse of the instruction by specifically advising the jury that the "[prior injury] evidence, if believed, was not received, and may not be considered by you[,] to prove that [McGuire] is a person of bad character or that he has a disposition to commit crimes." See n. 1, *supra*. Especially in light of this limiting provision, we reject McGuire's claim that the instruction should be viewed as a propensity instruction.

> **FYI**
>
> Justice O'Connor and Justice Stevens joined Part I of the Court's opinion but dissented from Part II, concluding that there was a reasonable likelihood that the jury had misapplied the prior acts instruction.

We therefore hold that neither the introduction of the challenged evidence, nor the jury instruction as to its use, "so infused the trial with unfairness as to deny due process of law." *Lisenba v. California*, 314 U.S. 219, 228 (1941). The judgment of the Court of Appeals is therefore

Reversed.

Points for Discussion

a. Prosecuting Child Abuse

Criminal prosecutions for child abuse present unusual problems for prosecutors, because the victims of these crimes may be too young to testify and there are often no other witnesses to the crimes that were committed. What evidence was available to the prosecutors in *Estelle*?

b. Syndrome Evidence

Precisely what sort of evidence falls within the definition of "battered child syndrome"? Does admitting this evidence as proof that the child was in fact abused run a substantial risk that innocent defendants will be convicted?

A more problematic example of medical syndrome evidence is "shaken baby syndrome." Children, particularly infants, can be seriously injured or even killed if they are badly shaken. While there may be no bruises or external signs of trauma, a medical examination can reveal injuries to the brain. Children with abusive head trauma may suffer long term disabling injuries, including blindness, seizures, and difficulty walking or talking. Cases include People v. Sargent, 970 P.2d 409 (Cal. 1999) (felony child abuse prosecution based on shaken baby syndrome evidence); Interest of Jac'Quez N., 669 N.W.2d 429 (Neb. 2003) (failure to seek treatment for infant's injuries caused by shaking is aggravated circumstance that justifies termination of parental rights without reasonable efforts to reunify family). The diagnosis is now medically controversial, however; see Commonwealth v. Millien, 50 N.E.3d 808 (Mass. 2016). See generally Deborah Tuerkheimer, *The Next Innocence Project: Shaken Baby Syndrome and the Criminal Courts*, 87 Wash. U. L. Rev. 1 (2009). See also Emily Bazelon, *Shaken-Baby Syndrome Faces New Questions in Court*, N.Y. Times, Feb. 2, 2011.

Prosecutors in child sexual abuse cases may attempt to offer expert testimony regarding Child Sexual Abuse Accommodation Syndrome, (CSAAS), in order to explain why a child victim might not complain to a parent or other authority figure about sexual abuse. Although the battered child syndrome turns on physical evidence, CSAAS rests on a psychological interpretation of the meaning of actions by a child. With some restrictions, expert testimony regarding CSAAS has been permitted. For example, United States v. Whitted, 11 F.3d 782 (8th Cir.1993), held that CSAAS testimony was admissible to inform the jury of the characteristics of sexually abused children, but that it could not be introduced to prove that sexual abuse had actually occurred. See also State v. J.Q., 617 A.2d 1196 (N.J. 1993) (holding that CSAAS was sufficiently reliable to allow an expert witness to describe traits found in victims, but that it could not be admitted for purposes beyond that limited scope).

c. Hearsay Evidence

In <u>Idaho v. Wright, 497 U.S. 805 (1990)</u>, the Supreme Court considered whether statements made by a two-and-a-half-year-old to the pediatrician who had examined her could be admitted under an exception to the hearsay rule. The Court noted that the Sixth Amendment Confrontation Clause requires that hearsay evidence be supported by "particularized guarantees of trustworthiness," and held that hearsay evidence used to convict a defendant must possess "indicia of reliability by virtue of its inherent trustworthiness, not by reference to other evidence at trial." The court pointed out that this evidence did not fall within one of the traditional exceptions to the hearsay rule, and concluded that "[c]orroboration of a child's allegations of sexual abuse. . .sheds no light on the reliability of the child's allegations regarding the identity of the abuser." Thus, admission of the hearsay evidence was reversible error, particularly in light of evidence that the doctor's interview with the child was conducted in a suggestive manner. Three Justices dissented, arguing that there was no constitutional bar to consideration of corroborating evidence in making the determination that hearsay evidence is trustworthy.

Many states have enacted statutes dealing with the introduction of hearsay statements by child victims in sexual abuse cases. See generally <u>Carol Schultz Vento, *Validity, Construction and Application of Child Hearsay Statutes*, 71 A.L.R.5th 637 (1999)</u>. These statutes must also comply with the Sixth Amendment, however, including the Supreme Court's more recent analysis of the Confrontation Clause in <u>Crawford v. Washington, 541 U.S. 1354 (2004)</u>. See, e.g., <u>People v. Moreno, 160 P.3d 242 (Colo. 2007)</u> (finding that state's child hearsay statute was unconstitutional). In <u>Ohio v. Clark, 576 U.S.   , 135 S.Ct. 2173 (2015)</u>, the Court held that testimony about a child's statements to his preschool teachers did not violate the Confrontation Clause under the test in *Crawford*.

With very young children, there is the further problem that the child may be unable to understand the duty to tell the truth and may not have the ability to distinguish between truth and falsity. Courts in a number of states have concluded, however, that testimonial incompetence is not a bar to admission of child hearsay statements concerning sexual abuse. See, e.g., <u>In re Cindy L., 947 P.2d 1340 (Cal. 1997)</u>; <u>Perez v. Florida, 536 So.2d 206 (Fla.1988)</u>; <u>Washington v. Doe, 719 P.2d 554 (Wash. 1986)</u>.

d. Special Courtroom Procedures

On the same day it decided Idaho v. Wright, the Court ruled in <u>Maryland v. Craig, 497 U.S. 836 (1990)</u>, that the Confrontation Clause did not categorically prohibit a procedure that allowed a child witness in a child abuse case to testify at trial, outside the defendant's physical presence, by one-way closed circuit television. The Court pointed out that the Maryland procedure preserved all elements of the confrontation right except the defendant's right to meet face-to-face with the witnesses at trial. Concluding that a state's interest in the physical and psychological well-being of child abuse victims was sufficiently important to outweigh the right to a face-to-face meeting, the Court noted that 37 states permitted use of videotaped testimony of sexually abused children, 24 states had authorized use of one-way closed circuit television testimony in child abuse cases, and eight states authorized use of a two-way closed circuit system.

In order to use the closed-circuit procedure, *Craig* requires the prosecution to make an adequate showing in the particular case that the procedure is necessary to protect the welfare of the child who will testify. The trial court must make a specific finding that the child would suffer emotional trauma from being required to testify in the courtroom in the presence of the defendant. Four Justices dissented in *Craig*, taking the view that the special reasons to suspend the guarantee of confrontation in these cases were matched by special reasons to insist on confrontation, particularly by the concern that child witnesses are more vulnerable to suggestion than adults and are often unable to separate fact from fantasy or suggestion in sexual abuse cases.

Medical Neglect

Parents have the right to determine what medical care their children will receive, but this right is constrained by state statutes that permit the state to intervene in circumstances in which withholding treatment constitutes abuse or neglect. In these cases, balancing the interest in maintaining family integrity and the interest in protecting children requires courts to make extremely difficult judgments, particularly when parents' objections to medical treatment are based on their religious beliefs.

Medical neglect cases may reach the courts when medical authorities seek authorization for blood transfusions or other medical procedures that parents oppose. State courts allow parents' wishes to be overruled when a child's life is in imminent danger, but they differ on whether intervention is appropriate when there is no immediate threat to the child's life. Compare <u>In re Green, 292 A.2d 387 (Pa. 1972)</u> (holding that state may not order surgery without showing of imminent danger) with <u>In re Sampson, 278 N.E.2d 918 (N.Y. 1972)</u> (affirming order for surgery and transfusion where child's life not in imminent danger).

Many states have enacted statutes providing that a parent's decision to treat his or her child by spiritual means through prayer is not sufficient to establish child maltreatment. These provisions do not limit the reporting obligations of mandatory reporters or the authority of state agencies to intervene, however. See, e.g., Colo. Rev. Stat. § 19–3–103 (2018); Conn. Gen. Stat. § 17a–104 (2018). If state officials do not have an opportunity to intervene, should parents be subjected to criminal prosecution for failure to obtain medical treatment that would have saved their child's life? The answer to this question has often turned on careful interpretation of spiritual treatment provisions in state statutes, which must inform parents clearly regarding how far the spiritual treatment defense may extend. Compare Walker v. Superior Court, 763 P.2d 852 (Cal. 1988) (allowing prosecution for involuntary manslaughter and felony child endangerment following death of child treated by spiritual means for acute meningitis); with Hermanson v. State, 604 So. 2d 775 (Fla. 1992) (quashing felony child abuse prosecution on basis that spiritual treatment statute failed to give notice of the point at which failure to get medical care becomes culpable negligence). See also State v. Neumann, 832 N.W.2d 560 (Wis. 2013) (affirming conviction of second degree reckless homicide against parents who failed to seek medical assistance for child who died from diabetic ketoacidosis). See generally James G. Dwyer, *Spiritual Treatment Exemptions to Child Medical Neglect Laws: What We Outsiders Should Think*, 76 Notre Dame L. Rev. 147 (2000).

B. Working with Families and Children

Although the details of child protection laws are different in different states, the process of working with families and children follows a generally consistent pattern. Proceedings typically begin with an investigation into allegations of abuse, neglect, or abandonment by the local social services or child welfare agency. The agency may seek an emergency order authorizing temporary placement of the child in protective care before the complaint against the parents is adjudicated.

At the adjudication stage, allegations of abuse or neglect are presented to a court, which must determine whether there is a sufficient factual and legal basis for state intervention in the family. If the court concludes that the child is **dependent** or **deprived**, within the meaning of the statutes, it must then determine an appropriate disposition for the case. At the disposition stage, the court typically orders a case plan or treatment plan, addressing such matters as what services will be provided to the family, and whether the child will remain with his or her family or be placed in foster care, a group home or with relatives. On the process of treatment planning, see <u>Marsha Garrison, *Child Welfare Decisionmaking: The Search for the Least Drastic Alternative*, 75 Geo. L.J. 1745, 1802–07 (1987)</u>.

Go Online

Find state <u>child welfare laws</u> through the Child Welfare Information Gateway web site.

If the case plan is successful, the child will be returned to the care of his or her parents. In 2016, just over half of all children who left foster care returned to their parent or principal caregiver. If the plan is not successful, state authorities may move to terminate parental rights and free the child for adoption or some other permanent solution. A court may terminate parental rights on the basis that a parent failed to make reasonable efforts to correct the conditions that were the basis for the adjudication. See, e.g., <u>In re D.F., 802 N.E.2d 800 (Ill. 2003)</u>; <u>Interest of Ty M., 655 N.W.2d 672 (Neb. 2003)</u>.

Reasonable Efforts and Family Preservation

The Adoption Assistance and Child Welfare Act (AACWA), <u>Pub. L. No. 96–272</u>, title I, 94 Stat. 501 (1980) required that states make reasonable efforts to preserve and reunify families prior to the placement of a child in foster care, to prevent or eliminate the need for removing a child from the child's home, and also to make it possible for a child to safely return to the child's home. <u>42 U.S.C. § 671(a)(15)(B) (2018)</u>. In making reasonable efforts, however, "the child's health and safety shall be the paramount concern." <u>42 U.S.C. § 671(a)(15)(A)</u>. A court may conclude that parental rights should not be terminated if the state has not provided appropriate services to the parents. See, e.g., <u>Matter of Star A., 435 N.E.2d 1080 (N.Y. 1982)</u>; <u>Parental Rights to B.P., 376 P.3d 350 (Wash. 2016)</u>.

Family preservation policies have been hampered by the chronic lack of resources available to state agencies for making reasonable efforts under AACWA. Litigation to enforce the reasonable efforts requirement reached the Supreme Court in <u>Suter v. Artist M., 503 U.S. 347 (1992)</u>. The Court held, however, that the act did not cre-

Go Online

Find state <u>laws addressing reasonable efforts</u> to preserve and reunify families through the Child Welfare Information Gateway.

ate enforceable rights within the meaning of <u>42 U.S.C.A. § 1983</u>, or an implied cause of action for private enforcement, concluding that the reasonable efforts language imposed "only a rather generalized duty on the State, to be enforced not by private individuals, but by the Secretary [of Health and Human Services]". In proceedings to terminate parental rights, courts determine whether reasonable efforts have been made on a case-by-case basis, and a court may consider the financial constraints within which state agencies operate in deciding whether reasonable efforts were made in a particular case. See <u>In re Shirley B., 18 A.3d 40 (Md. 2011)</u>.

Children are often placed in out-of-home care during the treatment phase of child welfare proceedings, most often in some type of foster care. The costs of this care to the states have been heavily subsidized by the federal government under Title IV-E of the Social Security Act. As foster care rates continued to climb through the 1980s and 1990s, the program grew increasingly expensive, and the family preservation policy was criticized for putting parents' rights ahead of children's interests. See, e.g., Richard Gelles, The Book of David: How Preserving Families Can Cost Children's Lives (1996); Elizabeth Bartholet, Nobody's Children (1999); but see Martin Guggenheim, <u>*Somebody's Children: Sustaining the Family's Place in Child Welfare Policy,* 113 Harv. L. Rev. 1716 (2000)</u>; Shawn Raymond, <u>*Where are the Reasonable Efforts to Enforce the Reasonable Efforts Requirement?: Monitoring State Compliance Under the Adoption Assistance and Child Welfare Act of 1980,* 77 Tex. L. Rev. 1235 (1999)</u>.

Congress responded to this controversy with the Adoption and Safe Families Act (ASFA), <u>Pub. L. No. 105–89</u>, 111 Stat. 2115 (1997), designed to move abused and neglected children more quickly into adoptive or other permanent homes. The new legislation substantially revised the Title IV-E system. Under ASFA, reasonable efforts are not required when a court determines that the parent has subjected the child to "aggravated circumstances," which may include abandonment, torture, chronic abuse or sexual abuse; or if a parent has committed murder, voluntary manslaughter, or a felony assault resulting in death or serious bodily harm to his or her child; or if the parent's rights to a sibling of the child have been involuntarily terminated. <u>42 U.S.C. § 671(a)(15)(D)</u>. When reasonable efforts are not required, ASFA law mandates "permanency hearings" within 30 days and requires states to move more quickly to terminate parental rights.

Go Online

The Children's Bureau in the U.S. Department of Health and Human Services provides a wide range of <u>statistical reports and other research</u> on adoption and foster care, child abuse and neglect, and child welfare.

One of the principal goals of ASFA was to reduce the problem known as foster care drift, and the legislation was designed to give state agencies one year to achieve family reunification or begin planning for termination of parental rights and adoption. The law requires that states have procedural safeguards to assure that each child in foster care has a permanency hearing no later than twelve months after the date the child entered foster care, and no less frequently than every twelve months after that time. 42 U.S.C. § 675(5)(C). State laws must require filing a petition for termination of parental rights for any child who has been in foster care for fifteen of the most recent 22 months, unless one of three exceptions is met. 42 U.S.C. § 675(5)(E). Under ASFA, the expectation is that termination of parental rights will occur even when there is no family waiting to adopt the child.

In Re H.G., A Minor

757 N.E.2d 864 (Ill. 2001)

JUSTICE McMORROW delivered the opinion of the court:

At issue in this appeal is the constitutionality of section 1(D)(m–1) of the Adoption Act (750 ILCS 50/1(D)(m–1) (West 1998)). Section 1(D)(m–1) provides, in part, that a parent may be found unfit if "[p]ursuant to the Juvenile Court Act of 1987, a child has been in foster care for 15 months out of any 22 month period." 750 ILCS 50/1(D)(m–1) (West 1998). The circuit court of Kane County, in cause No. 89115, * * * held section 1(D)(m–1) unconstitutional. Direct appeal was taken to this court and the cases were consolidated for review. For the reasons that follow, we affirm the judgment of the circuit court in cause No. 89115. * * *

Background

In 1980, Congress enacted the Adoption Assistance and Child Welfare Act (AACWA). See 42 U.S.C. §§ 620 through 628, 670 through 679a (1994). AACWA created a program which authorizes the federal government to reimburse the states for certain expenses incurred by the states in the administration of foster care and adoption services. To be eligible for federal funds under AACWA, the states must have in place a plan which provides, in pertinent part, that "reasonable efforts" will be made to prevent the removal of children from their homes into foster care and, after removal, that "reasonable efforts" will be made to reunify the children with their parents. See 42 U.S.C. § 671(a)(15) (1994); Suter v. Artist M., 503 U.S. 347 (1992). Through the establishment of the reimbursement program under AACWA, Congress sought to prevent the unnecessary placement of children in foster care. See generally C. Kim, Note, Putting Reason Back Into the Reasonable Efforts Requirement in Child Abuse and Neglect Cases, 1999 U. Ill. L.Rev. 287, 314.

Some time after the passage of AACWA, it became apparent to Congress that the courts and state agencies which were interpreting and implementing the "reasonable efforts" requirement of the Act were placing too great an emphasis on the goals of family preservation and reunification. As a result, a number of children were "languish[ing] in foster care" and "remain[ing] in limbo as to their permanency" while the states attempted to rehabilitate their parents. 1999 U. Ill. L.Rev. at 293. In response to this and other problems, Congress passed the Adoption and Safe Families Act of 1997. Pub.L. No. 105–89, 111 Stat. 2115 (codified as amended in various sections of 42 U.S.C.).

Among other issues, the Adoption and Safe Families Act of 1997 (ASFA) addressed the question of how long the states must pursue the goal of family reunification under the "reasonable efforts" standard. ASFA mandates that, to retain eligibility for federal funding, and unless certain exceptions apply, the states "shall file a petition to terminate the parental rights of [a] child's parents" when the child "has been in foster care under the responsibility of the State for 15 of the most recent 22 months." 42 U.S.C. § 675(5)(E) (Supp.1997). The exceptions to this rule requiring the filing of a petition to terminate parental rights are (1) the child is being cared for by a relative, (2) there is no compelling reason for filing such a petition, or (3) the state has not provided services necessary for the safe return of the child to the child's home. 42 U.S.C. § 675(5)(E) (Supp.1997).

In 1998, the General Assembly responded to Congress' enactment of the 15-month time frame for pursuing family reunification set forth in ASFA by adding section 1(D)(m–1) to the Adoption Act and section 2–13(4.5)(i) to the Juvenile Court Act of 1987 (705 ILCS 405/2–13(4.5)(i) (West 1998)). Section 2–13(4.5) of the Juvenile Court Act simply mirrors the language found in ASFA pertaining to the 15-month period for reunification. Section 2–13(4.5)(i) requires the Department of Children and Family Services to request the State to file a petition to terminate parental rights once a child has spent 15 months out of the most recent 22 months in foster care, unless one of the exceptions to filing such a petition listed in the federal legislation exists. See 705 ILCS 405/2–13(4.5)(i) (West 1998).

Section 1(D)(m–1) of the Adoption Act, however, goes a step further. Section 1(D)(m–1) creates a new ground of parental unfitness based upon the presumption that a parent is unfit if his or her child has been in foster care for 15 months out of a 22-month period. Section 1(D)(m–1) states that a parent may be unfit if:

> "Pursuant to the Juvenile Court Act of 1987, a child has been in foster care for 15 months out of any 22 month period * * * unless the child's parent can prove by a preponderance of the evidence that it is more likely than not that it will be in the best interests of the child to be returned to the parent within 6 months of the date on which a petition for termination of parental rights is filed under the Juvenile Court Act of 1987. The 15 month time limit is tolled during any period for which there is a court finding that the appointed custodian or guardian failed to make reasonable efforts to reunify the child with his or her family * * *." 750 ILCS 50/1(D)(m–1) (West 1998).

* * *

On March 12, 1996, the State filed a petition in the circuit court of Kane County in which it alleged that H.G. was a neglected minor. See 705 ILCS 405/2–3(1), 2–13 (West 1998). The allegations of neglect were contained in two counts, both of which asserted that H.G. was in an environment injurious to her welfare. See 705 ILCS 405/2–3(1)(b) (West 1998). Count I alleged that H.G.'s mother, E.W., had allowed H.G. to have contact with her father, in violation of an order of protection. Count II alleged that E.W. had "grabbed [H.G.'s] arm on two separate occasions causing a dislocation."

Following a temporary custody hearing (see 705 ILCS 405/2–10 (West 1998)), the circuit court determined that H.G. "did receive injuries" to her arm and, thus, that there was probable cause to believe that H.G. was neglected under count II of the State's petition. The court also found that it was "a matter of immediate and urgent necessity" (705 ILCS 405/2–10(2) (West 1998)) that H.G. be placed in the temporary custody of the Department of Children and Family Services (DCFS).

On October 10, 1996,[1] the circuit court entered an order adjudicating H.G. neglected based upon the allegations set forth in count II of the State's petition. See 705 ILCS 405/2–21 (West 1998).

On December 23, 1996,[2] the circuit court entered a dispositional order making H.G. a ward of the court. The court placed H.G. in the legal custody of DCFS and appointed the guardianship administrator of DCFS her legal guardian. See 705 ILCS 405/2–27(d) (West 1998). At the same time, the circuit court ordered E.W. to cooperate with DCFS and to follow a number of directives, including, inter alia, obtaining appropriate housing, participating in therapy, and completing parenting classes.

From December 1996 to August 1998, DCFS continued to monitor E.W.'s progress toward reaching the various goals and objectives that had been established for her. By the end of August 1998, DCFS concluded that E.W.'s progress was unsatisfactory and, therefore, that termination of her parental rights was warranted. On October 13, 1998, the State filed a petition for termination of parental rights. See 705 ILCS 405/2–13, 2–29 (West 1998). In that petition, the State alleged that E.W. was unfit under section 1(D)(m) of the Adoption Act (750 ILCS 50/1(D)(m) (West 1994)) because she had failed to make reasonable efforts to correct the conditions which were the basis for removal of H.G. or to make reasonable progress toward the return of the child within 12 months after adjudication. The matter was set for trial on March 11 and 12, 1999.

---

[1] E.W. waived the statutory, 90-day deadline for adjudication. See 705 ILCS 405/2114(b) (West 1998).

[2] The statutory, 30-day deadline for setting a dispositional hearing (see 705 ILCS 405/2–21(2) (West 1998)) was waived by agreement.

On March 8, 1999, E.W.'s attorney filed a motion for continuance because an indispensable witness was unavailable for trial. The circuit court granted the motion and continued the trial date until May 24 and 25. On May 17, the guardian ad litem for H.G. filed a motion seeking a continuance because he had an oral argument scheduled before the appellate court on May 25. The circuit court granted the motion and continued the case until October 8, 14 and 15. The circuit court chose dates some five months ahead because the court wished to avoid a piecemeal trial and because October 14 and 15 were the first consecutive, open dates on the court's calendar.

On October 4, 1999, the State filed an amended petition to terminate parental rights. In this petition, the State retained its allegation that E.W. was unfit under section 1(D)(m). In addition, for the first time, the State alleged that E.W. was unfit under section 1(D)(m–1) because H.G. had been in foster care for 15 out of the preceding 22 months.

On October 7, 1999, the circuit court vacated the October 8 trial date because a material witness for the State was on medical leave and was unable to appear in court. The court preserved the October 14 and 15 dates and instructed the State to determine whether the witness' testimony could be obtained by deposition. On October 13, 1999, the State filed a motion for continuance, which stated that the witness was physically unable to testify. On October 14, 1999, over E.W.'s objection, the motion for continuance was granted. The case was continued until January 27 and 28 and February 4, 2000. Also on October 14, on the circuit court's motion, the court struck the count in the State's amended petition which alleged that E.W. was unfit under section 1(D)(m–1) because that claim was not yet ripe.

On October 15, 1999, E.W. filed a petition to restore custody. See 705 ILCS 405/2–28(4) (West 1998). On October 26, 1999, the court ruled that this petition would be heard during the best interest portion of the termination hearing, if the case proceeded to that point.

On January 20, 2000, the State filed a second amended petition to terminate parental rights. This petition repeated the count under section 1(D)(m) that was still pending and added a second count, under section 1(D)(m–1), to replace the one the circuit court had struck in October.

On January 27, 2000, E.W. filed a motion to strike the second count of the State's petition. In this motion, E.W. asserted that section 1(D)(m–1) violates the federal and state constitutional guarantees of substantive due process and equal protection because it "is not narrowly tailored to achieve its manifest purpose, improperly shifts the burden of proof to a respondent parent, and improperly invites consideration of best interest issues at the fitness portion of a termination hearing."

On January 27, 2000, after hearing argument, the circuit court granted E.W.'s motion. In an oral ruling, the court determined that section 1(D)(m–1) implicated a fundamental interest, i.e., parental rights and, therefore, that the statute had to withstand strict scrutiny under the due process clause of the federal and state constitutions. The court held that section 1(D)(m–1) failed this test because it was not narrowly tailored. The court stated,

> "The problem is inherent in that this particular statute, unlike all of the other provisions for finding unfitness, relates not to conduct of a parent or an internal flaw of character or behavior or mental illness or physical infirmity, but rather the mere passage of time. I do agree that there is a due process problem."

The circuit court also held that section 1(D)(m–1) was "constitutionally infirm" because it shifted the burden of proof to the parent within the fitness proceeding and because it introduced the concept of best interests of the child into the determination of the unfitness of the parent.

At the conclusion of the circuit court's ruling from the bench, the State asked the court to stay any further proceedings on the termination petition. The court did so. Thus, count I of the State's petition, which alleges that E.W. is unfit under section 1(D)(m), is still pending, but is in abeyance. The State also sought leave to pursue an interlocutory appeal. The circuit court granted this request and, pursuant to Supreme Court Rule 308 (155 Ill.2d R. 308), stated that its holding that section 1(D)(m–1) is unconstitutional warranted interlocutory appeal. The circuit court also found, under Supreme Court Rule 304(a) (155 Ill.2d R. 304(a)), that there was no just reason for delaying appeal of the court's decision. Appeal was taken by the State directly to this court under Supreme Court Rule 302(a)(1) (134 Ill.2d R. 302(a)(1)). The State's appeal was docketed as case No. 89115.

In February 2000, the circuit court took evidence on E.W.'s petition to restore custody, which had been filed in October 1999. On March 7, the court determined that H.G. "can be cared for at home (of Mother) without endangering her health or safety." However, the court also concluded that return was not in H.G.'s best interests at that time. Accordingly, the court denied E.W.'s petition.

* * *

Analysis

* * *

Section 1(D)(m–1) creates a presumption of parental unfitness based upon a judicial finding that the parent's child has been in foster care for "15 months out of any 22 month period." 750 ILCS 50/1(D)(m–1) (West 1998). This statutory presumption is based solely upon the time the child has been in foster care; no inquiry is made into the parent's ability to provide the child with good care and treatment. The 15-month period may be tolled "during any period for which there is a court finding that the appointed custodian or guardian failed to make reasonable efforts to reunify the child with his or her family." Once a court finds that the child has been in foster care for 15 months, the parent may rebut the presumption of unfitness by showing it is more likely than not that it will be in the child's best interests to be returned to the parent within six months from the date the termination petition was filed.

On appeal, E.W. argues that section 1(D)(m–1) violates the guarantee of substantive due process provided by the United States and Illinois Constitutions. E.W. maintains that section 1(D)(m–1) impinges upon a fundamental liberty interest, the interest a parent has in raising his or her child. Thus, according to E.W., section 1(D)(m–1) must survive strict scrutiny, i.e., it must be narrowly tailored to serve a compelling governmental interest.

E.W. does not dispute that the State has a compelling interest in protecting the children of Illinois from harm and, hence, that the State has a compelling interest in identifying parents who pose a risk to the safety and well-being of their children and are therefore unfit. However, E.W. contends that section 1(D)(m–1) is not narrowly tailored to achieving this goal. E.W. focuses on section 1(D)(m–1)'s creation of a presumption of unfitness based upon a finding that a child has been in foster care for 15 months. E.W. argues that this statutory presumption does not narrowly identify unfit parents because it defines unfitness based solely on the passage of time rather than parental inability to care for children. Therefore, the statute may declare parents unfit even if they are, in fact, able to safely care for their children. Thus, according to E.W., section 1(D)(m–1) is unconstitutional.

The State, in response, concedes that section 1(D)(m–1) is subject to strict scrutiny. See In re R.C., 195 Ill.2d 291, 302–04, 253 Ill.Dec. 699, 745 N.E.2d 1233 (2001) (section of Adoption Act defining ground of unfitness is subject to strict scrutiny), citing Troxel v. Granville, 530 U.S. 57 (2000). The State maintains, however, that section 1(D)(m–1) survives this review. The State emphasizes that it has a compelling governmental interest in protecting the safety and welfare of the children of Illinois. The State asserts that "a fit parent does not allow his or her child to languish in foster care for 15 months" and argues that section 1(D)(m–1) narrowly identifies those parents who pose a danger to the health and safety of their children. We disagree.

To survive strict scrutiny, a statute must be narrowly tailored to serve a compelling interest. A statute is narrowly tailored if it uses "the least restrictive means consistent with the attainment of its goal." In re R.C., 195 Ill.2d at 303, 253 Ill.

Dec. 699, 745 N.E.2d 1233, citing Tully v. Edgar, 171 Ill.2d 297, 304–05, 215 Ill. Dec. 646, 664 N.E.2d 43 (1996). The presumption of unfitness set forth in section 1(D)(m–1) is not narrowly tailored to the compelling goal of identifying unfit parents because it fails to account for the fact that, in many cases, the length of a child's stay in foster care has nothing to do with the parent's ability or inability to safely care for the child but, instead, is due to circumstances beyond the parent's control. The record in the instant cause aptly illustrates this point.

On October 13, 1998, the State filed its initial motion to terminate the parental rights of E.W. This petition alleged only that E.W. was unfit under section 1(D)(m). No allegation was made that E.W. was unfit under section 1(D)(m–1), and no such allegation could have been made, as the 15-month time period for calculating H.G.'s stay in foster care could not begin to run until the enactment of section 1(D)(m–1), which had only recently occurred. Trial on the State's petition was originally set for March 11 and 12, 1999. On E.W.'s motion, the trial was continued until May 24 and 25 because an indispensable witness was unavailable. The case was continued again because the attorney and guardian ad litem for H.G. was required to appear in the appellate court for oral argument on May 25. The trial was then set for dates almost five months later, in October 1999. These dates were not chosen because of anything relating to E.W.'s ability to safely care for H.G. or because of any particular need of H.G. Instead, the October dates were chosen because they were the next available dates on which the circuit court would be able to conduct the trial without interruption.

The October 1999 date was also continued, on the State's motion, because a key witness was medically unable to testify. Only after this final continuance did the 15-month time frame of section 1(D)(m–1) become applicable to this case. On January 20, 2000, the State filed an amended petition to terminate parental rights in which it alleged that E.W. was unfit under section 1(D)(m–1). Nine of the 15 months covered by the State's allegation of unfitness under section 1(D)(m–1) were directly attributable to continuances which were necessary to bring the case to trial. Further, none of the nine-month period could be tolled under the portion of section 1(D)(m–1) which allows for tolling of the 15-month period because the continuances and court delays had nothing to do with whether "the appointed custodian or guardian failed to make reasonable efforts to reunify the child with his or her family." 750 ILCS 50/1(D)(m–1) (West 1998). Thus, in this cause, the passage of 15 months revealed nothing more than the fact that the judicial system's administrative needs may delay the resolution of certain cases. The fact that H.G. was in foster care for a 15-month period could not, by itself, warrant a presumption that E.W. is an unfit parent.

Other common situations illustrate the illogical reach of the presumption found in section 1(D)(m–1). For example, parents are frequently ordered to undergo drug treatment or other counseling as a condition to regaining custody of a child in foster care. Given the realities of limited funding, it is not uncommon for there to be waiting lists to receive such services. In such cases, DCFS might make every "reasonable effort[ ]" (750 ILCS 50/1(D)(m–1) (West 1998)) to get the parent the appropriate treatment yet be unable to do so in a prompt fashion simply because the program offering the counseling services is full. During the time DCFS attempts to enter the parent in the appropriate program, however, the 15-month period in section 1(D)(m–1) will continue to run. Thus, a delay which occurs through no fault of the parent or DCFS may trigger a finding of unfitness.

Many of the grounds of unfitness set forth in the Adoption Act, other than section 1(D)(m–1), employ time frames of one length or another. See, e.g., 750 ILCS 50/1(D)(c) (West 1998) (desertion for more than three months); 750 ILCS 50/1(D)(k) (West 1998) (habitual drunkenness or addiction to controlled substances for at least one year); 750 ILCS 50/1(D)(l) (West 1998) (failure to demonstrate a reasonable degree of interest in the child's welfare during the first 30 days following the child's birth). However, each of these grounds uses a time frame that measures some form of parental conduct, inaction or inability that relates to competence or the care given to a child. Section 1(D)(m–1), in contrast, improperly measures only the time that a child is in foster care. Cf. Stanley v. Illinois, 405 U.S. 645, 657 (1972) (under due process of the fourteenth amendment, statutory scheme to determine unfitness may not "foreclose[ ] the determinative issues of competence and care"). Because there will be many cases in which children remain in foster care for the statutory period even when their parents can properly care for them, we conclude that the presumption contained in section 1(D)(m–1) is not a narrowly tailored means of identifying parents who pose a danger to their children's health or safety.

The State emphasizes the importance of the rebuttal allowed by section 1(D)(m–1). The State maintains that, because section 1(D)(m–1) allows a parent to rebut the presumption of unfitness by showing that it will be in the best interests of the child to return home in six months, section 1(D)(m–1) strikes a proper balance between the interests of parents in the care and custody of their children and the interest of the State in protecting the safety of the children.

Citing Santosky v. Kramer, 455 U.S. 745 (1982), E.W. maintains, however, that it is inappropriate to introduce the concept of best interests during a fitness determination. E.W. further argues that, even if consideration of the best interests were appropriate during a fitness proceeding, that consideration does not sufficiently narrow the scope of the statute. As E.W. explains: "A parent contesting an allegation of unfitness under section [1(D)(m–1)] could present evidence of her ability to care for her child as part of the best interest phase of the unfitness hearing. The court could credit the parent's evidence as factually true and could rationally conclude that a parent is abundantly fit, i.e., perfectly capable of safely and adequately caring for the child, yet still conclude that the child's best interests will not be served by returning the child to the parent's home. Thus, in its natural operation, section [1(D)(m–1)] compels trial courts to make the Alice-in-Wonderland ruling that a fit parent is, by force of law, unfit."

We agree with the position advanced by E.W. The record in the instant cause illustrates the validity of her argument. While the State's motion to terminate parental rights was pending, E.W. filed a petition to restore custody. See 705 ILCS 405/2–28(4) (West 1998). The court deferred a hearing on that petition and stated that the petition would be considered after any findings of unfitness were made on the termination petition. After the circuit court held section 1(D)(m–1) unconstitutional and the State sought a stay of further proceedings on the termination petition, the court held a hearing on E.W.'s petition to restore custody. After hearing evidence, the court found "[t]hat the Minor can be cared for at home (of Mother) without endangering her health or safety." The court further found that it was not in the best interests of H.G. that the child be restored to the custody of E.W. Accordingly, the court denied the petition.

E.W. established to the circuit court's satisfaction that her child could be safely cared for in her home. However, as of the date of its ruling on the petition to restore custody, the court believed that reunification was not in the child's best interests. Consequently, had the fitness hearing under section 1(D)(m–1) gone forward, E.W. could have been declared unfit despite the court's finding that she was able to safely care for her child. Because this error is built into the statute's design, section 1(D)(m–1) cannot be considered narrowly tailored.

The State also argues that it has a compelling interest in ensuring that the time children spend in foster care is limited and in preventing foster care "drift." The State contends that section 1(D)(m–1) expresses the legislature's desire to obtain a permanent solution for children in foster care in an expeditious manner, regardless of whether that solution is returning the children to their parents or terminating the rights of the parents and making the children available for adoption. According to the State, the goal of achieving permanency is a compelling one that justifies the creation of section 1(D)(m–1). We disagree. The permanency achieved under section 1(D)(m–1) comes only after a finding that a parent is unfit. However, that determination of unfitness, as we have explained, is achieved in a way that is not narrowly tailored, as it must be to survive strict scrutiny. We decline to recognize that the State has a compelling interest in removing children from foster care in an expeditious fashion when that removal is achieved in an unconstitutional manner.

Section 1(D)(m–1) is not narrowly tailored to serve the compelling governmental interest of protecting the safety and well-being of the children of this state. We hold, therefore, that section 1(D)(m–1) violates the substantive due process guarantees of the federal and state constitutions. Accordingly, we affirm the judgment of the circuit court of Kane County.

* * *

Points for Discussion

a. Due Process

The court in *H.G.* considers the constitutional limits on state legislation that may infringe a parent's fundamental interest in raising his or her child. Because this interest is characterized as fundamental, the court applies strict scrutiny to the statute, asking whether it is narrowly tailored to serve a compelling governmental interest. There is no controversy about the state's compelling interest in protecting the safety and welfare of children, however. Cases like *H.G.* focus on the means the state has chosen to serve that purpose, asking whether the statute strikes the proper balance between the state's compelling interest and the parent's fundamental right. For an argument that this type of balancing can be better understood as a type of intermediate scrutiny, see David Meyer, *The Paradox of Family Privacy*, 53 Vand. L. Rev. 527 (2000).

b. Addressing Cultural, Class and Racial Bias

In Santosky v. Kramer, 455 U.S. 745 (1982), the Supreme Court held that the state must prove the grounds for termination of parental rights by clear and convincing evidence. The Court's opinion points out a number of factors that operate against parents in these cases, notes the "imprecise substantive standards that leave determinations unusually open to the subjective values of the judge," and states that because parents in these cases "are often poor, uneducated, or members of minority groups. . .such proceedings are often vulnerable to judgments based on cultural or class bias." 455 U.S. at 762–63.

Go Online

See *Addressing Racial Disproportionality in Child Welfare* (November 2016) on the Child Welfare Information Gateway web site.

In her book, Shattered Bonds: The Color of Child Welfare (2002), Dorothy Roberts described the enormous negative impact of the child welfare system on Black families. Roberts summarized government statistics that demonstrate a significant racial disparity in how children and families were treated.

Nationwide, 17% of all children were Black, while 42% of children in foster care were Black. Minority children were more likely to be taken from their homes and placed into foster care, while white children were more likely to remain at home and receive services there. Once removed from their families, Black children remained in foster care for much longer periods of time, and they were less likely to be returned home or adopted than other children. Part of this disparity can be explained by the disproportionate number of Black children who were living in poverty, but the statistics suggest that various institutionalized forms of racial bias are also a factor in these cases. What strategies could be adopted by courts or agencies to address these risks?

c. Indian Child Welfare Act

In addition to its provisions on adoption, discussed in Chapter 3, the Indian Child Welfare Act (ICWA) applies to the removal of Native American children from their homes and termination of parental rights. ICWA is intended to "promote the stability and security of Indian tribes and families by the establishment of minimum federal standards for the removal of Indian children from their families and the placement of such children in foster or adoptive homes." 25 U.S.C. § 1902 (2018). The higher standards established by ICWA preempt the applicable state law.

Under ICWA, any foster care placement or termination of parental rights to an Indian child must be based on proof that active efforts were made to provide services to prevent the breakup of the Indian family. 25 U.S.C. § 1912(d). The statute also requires clear and convincing evidence, including testimony of qualified expert witnesses, that continued custody by the parent or Indian custodian is likely to result in serious emotional or physical damage to the child. 25 U.S.C. § 1912(e). In addition, in a termination proceeding within ICWA there must be proof beyond a reasonable doubt. 25 U.S.C. § 1912(f). See, e.g., C.J. v. State, Dept. of Health and Social Services, 18 P.3d 1214 (Alaska 2001); L.G. v. State of Alaska, 14 P.3d 946 (Alaska 2000); In re Interest of D.S.P., 480 N.W.2d 234 (Wis. 1992).

State courts and officials do not always honor their obligations under ICWA, however. See Oglala Sioux Tribe v. Van Hunnik, 100 F. Supp. 3d 749 (D. S.D. 2015), which concluded that state courts and agencies in South Dakota violated the rights of Indian tribal members under ICWA and the Due Process Clause in the removal of children from their parents or custodians.

Go Online

See the Practical Guide to the Indian Child Welfare Act available online from the Native American Rights Fund.

If a trial court receives information to suggest that a child is a tribal member or might be eligible for membership in an Indian tribe, ICWA requires that the tribe be notified and permitted to intervene. See, e.g., In re Karla C., 6 Cal.Rptr.3d 205 (Ct. App. 2003). The tribe also has the right to seek to transfer jurisdiction over the proceeding to the tribal court. See, e.g., In re A.B., 663 N.W.2d 625 (N.D. 2003). On the possible conflict between ICWA and the federal Adoption and Safe Families Act, see In re D.B., 670 N.W.2d 67 (S.D. 2003).

As noted in Chapter 3, the Supreme Court narrowed the scope of ICWA with its ruling in Adoptive Couple v. Baby Girl, 570 U.S. 637 (2013), by limiting the application of § 1912(d) and § 1912(f). The Court held that these protections were not available to an unmarried biological father who had never had custody of the child, and who was not entitled to participate in the adoption proceeding under state law in South Carolina. The Court also ruled that the adoptive placement preferences in § 1915(a) were not applicable in this situation.

d. Representation for Children

Under CAPTA, states must provide children with a **guardian ad litem** (GAL) in any judicial proceedings concerning abuse and neglect. See 42 U.S.C. §5106a(b)(2)(B)(xiii) (2018). The GAL may be a lawyer or lay person who has received appropriate training and is appointed to represent the child and make recommendations to the court concerning the child's best interests. Traditionally, a GAL takes the child's wishes into account, but is not bound to by them. See, e.g., In Interest of Brandon S.S., 507 N.W.2d 94 (Wis. 1993). State laws reflect wide differences in defining the role of the GAL, however. See Jean Koh Peters, *How Children are Heard in Child Protective Proceedings, in the United States and Around the World, 2005: Survey Findings, Initial Observations, and Areas for Further Study*, 6 Nev. L.J. 922 (2006).

Go Online

Find state statutes on Representation of Children in Child Abuse and Neglect Proceedings on the Child Welfare Information Gateway.

Should children be entitled to representation by a lawyer rather than "best interests" representation by a GAL? This has been a subject of serious debate within the profession, and is discussed at greater length in Chapter 8. For an overview of the issues, see Barbara Ann Atwood, *The Uniform Representation of Children in Abuse, Neglect and Custody Proceedings Act: Bridging the Divide Between Pragmatism and Idealism*, 42 Fam. L.Q. 63 (2008).

e. Special Immigrant Juvenile Status

Undocumented minors present in the United States may be eligible for Special Immigrant Juvenile Status under 8 U.S.C. § 1101(a)(27)(J) (2018), which provides a pathway to becoming a lawful permanent resident. The statute requires that a family or juvenile court find that reunification with one or both of the child's parents "is not viable due to abuse, neglect, abandonment or a similar basis found under state law" and that it would not be in the child's best interest to be returned the child or parent's "previous country of nationality or country of last habitual residence." Procedures for obtaining this determination are different in each state. See, e.g., De Guardado v. Guardado Menjivar, 901 N.W.2d 243 (Minn. Ct. App. 2017); Fifo v. Fifo, 6 N.Y.S.3d 562 (App. Div. 2015).

Problem 5-3

Nadia was adjudicated to be a "child in need of protection" and placed in foster care before her first birthday. The dispositional order in the case required her mother to maintain a suitable home, abstain from alcohol and drugs, have counseling for substance abuse and undergo a psychological evaluation. Five years later, the state agency filed a notice that the mother had met the conditions of the order and that it intended to return Nadia to her care. Nadia's foster mother challenges the decision, arguing that it is in Nadia's best interests to remain in her foster home. How should the court decide this case? (See In Interest of Nadia S., 581 N.W.2d 182 (Wis. 1998).)

In Re Ashley S.

762 A.2d 941 (Maine 2000)

Saufley, J.

The father of Ashley S. appeals from the judgment of the District Court (Lewiston, Gorman, J.) finding Ashley to be in circumstances of jeopardy and awarding custody of Ashley to the Department of Human Services. 22 M.R.S.A. § § 4035, 4036 (1992 & Supp.2000). The father does not challenge the court's jeopardy finding but contends that the court erred when it found that "aggravated circumstances" existed pursuant to 22 M.R.S.A. § § 4002(1–B)(A)(1), 4036(1)(G–2) (Supp.2000) and that reunification efforts would be inconsistent with Ashley's permanency plan, 22 M.R.S.A. § 4041(2)(A1) (Supp.2000). We affirm the judgment.

I. BACKGROUND

On December 13, 1999, the Department of Human Services filed a petition for child protection order concerning two-year-old Ashley, alleging that Ashley was in circumstances of jeopardy based on her parents' severe neglect, domestic violence, and mental health problems. The Department also sought a preliminary protection order allowing Ashley's immediate removal from her parents' home. The court granted the preliminary protection order, and the Department removed Ashley from her parents' care on the same date.

The father waived his right to hearing on the preliminary protection order, and two months later, the court held hearings over the course of three days on the Department's petition for a protection order and its request for an order allowing the Department not to undertake reunification efforts. At trial, the father disputed only the Department's request to be relieved of its reunification obligations. The District Court found that Ashley was in circumstances of jeopardy, awarded custody of Ashley to the Department, and relieved the Department of its obligation to provide reunification services to the father.

The facts relevant to the father's appeal can be summarized as follows.[1] On December 13, 1999, at approximately 1:13 in the afternoon, the Lewiston Police Department received a phone call from Ashley's mother indicating that her two-month-old son, Eric Jr., had died in his sleep. Upon arriving at the apartment, the two responding detectives found the baby's corpse and Ashley in a shockingly unsanitary and dangerous apartment.

According to the investigating detectives, the apartment was in complete disarray, with dog excrement on the floor and garbage and trash piled everywhere. Although it was winter, the temperature inside the apartment was unusually warm, later reported to be above eighty degrees; and the odor of feces, urine, body odor, animals, and decaying food was overwhelming. Cockroaches were observed in the vicinity of Ashley's room and little bugs were flying around the trash and crawling on the walls. In the bathroom, there were gnats, and the tub was filled with trash bags full of clothing and other items. Dirty dishes and rotting foods filled the kitchen area. In sum, the two investigating detectives, who had almost twenty years of experience between them, described the apartment as one of the worst they had seen in their law enforcement careers.

The DHS caseworker who was called to the scene observed that the children's conditions reflected the shocking condition of the apartment and that Ashley

---

[1]   Because only the father appeals the court's judgment, the facts are recited to the extent that they are relevant to his appeal.

looked and smelled as if she had not been bathed in days, if not weeks, and was dressed in clothes that were covered with feces.

> I held her, and I immediately felt that her clothing was wet, so much that it had soaked through the arm that I was holding her by. . . . [W]hen we went to the police department, and upon takin[g] the clothes off of her, it was discovered that [the pants had] feces completely coating the inside, front and back. . . . It was very overwhelming. . . . [S]he had feces inside and outside of her stocking, shoes. It was all over—it was all over her body. In her hair.

According to Ashley's guardian ad litem, Ashley had to be "taken for medical treatment several times to try to determine why she was emitting a noticeable body odor even weeks after her removal from the [father's] home." Photographs and a video tape recording confirmed the testimony of the officers and the DHS caseworker.

Ashley's baby brother, Eric Jr., had been dead for approximately eight to twelve hours when the officers arrived. The previous evening, Eric Jr. had been put to bed, still in his car seat, in a bassinet inside the parents' bedroom. He was dressed in sweatpants and sweatshirt, and completely covered with a blanket. According to the father, it was routine for the parents to place the blanket over the baby's face to keep his pacifier from falling out.

Although it was typical for Eric Jr. to wake up one or more times during the night, he did not wake up that night. The next morning, when the mother left the apartment with Ashley's five-year-old stepsister, Katie, to run some errands, she did not feed or change the baby. From 7:30 A.M. until the mother's return just after 1:00 P.M., the father took no action to tend to Eric Jr. or Ashley's needs. Therefore, from approximately 11:00 P.M. until the next afternoon at 1:15 P.M., the two-month-old infant received no food, no care, and no attention whatsoever from his father. During those hours, Eric Jr. laid fully covered beneath a blanket in a sweltering apartment, right beside his father's bed, and died.[2] During the same period of time, Ashley was penned in a small room, covered in her own feces, unattended, and prevented from contact with her parents by a fence in the doorway of her room.

An evaluation of the father, completed after the baby's death, disclosed that the father "seems to feel no responsibility for his son's death, and did not seem to think it out of line to allow a small child like his youngest daughter to languish for hours in her room behind a locked gate." Ultimately, the court found that the father's "failure to even notice that [his] child was dead is clear and convincing evidence of deprivation of supervision."

---

[2]   The medical examiner testified that, although Sudden Infant Death Syndrome had been ruled out, the cause of death had not yet been established.

In a detailed and thoughtful opinion, the court concluded that the father had subjected Ashley to "chronic abuse or any other treatment that is heinous or abhorrent to society" and that reunification efforts would be inconsistent with her permanency plan. In light of the evidence that the father had the financial resources and the skills necessary to provide a clean and safe environment for his children,[3] the court concluded that the father willfully and grossly neglected the needs of his children. In so concluding, the court granted the Department's request not to commence reunification efforts. The father filed a timely appeal of the court's order.

II. DISCUSSION

The father contends that the court erred when it concluded that his treatment of Ashley met the statutory definition of "aggravated circumstances," as defined in 22 M.R.S.A. § 4002(1–B)(A)(1), and that providing reunification services would be inconsistent with Ashley's permanency plan. 22 M.R.S.A. § 4041(2)(A–1).[4] Specifically, the father argues that the court erred in interpreting the term "treatment that is heinous or abhorrent to society" as applied to the facts before it. 22 M.R.S.A. § 4002(1–B)(A)(1). We review de novo the court's interpretation of the statute for errors of law, and review the court's application of the statutory language to the facts at issue for abuse of discretion. See In re Heather C., 2000 ME 99, ¶ 26, 751 A.2d 448, 455; In re Christmas C., 1998 ME 258, ¶ 3, 721 A.2d 629, 630.

Ordinarily, when children are removed from their parents' custody, the Department is required to develop a rehabilitation and reunification plan designed to safely reunite the parents and children. 22 M.R.S.A. § 4041(1) (Supp.2000). Because families that enter the child protective system often suffer from a lack of resources, we have recognized the Department's role in this process as "important" in rehabilitating families for reunification. See In re Daniel C., 480 A.2d 766, 769 (Me.1984). Without the Department's efforts in this regard, families may not receive the help they need to correct the circumstances that brought their children into the State's custody in the first instance. See 22 M.R.S.A. § 4003(3) (Supp.2000). This aspect of the Department's responsibilities is even more crucial in light of the expedited timeframes recently enacted by the Legislature. 22 M.R.S.A. §§ 4038(1), 4052(2–A)(A) (Supp.2000).

---

[3]   The father received over $600 per month in Social Security benefits based on his temper disorder, and less than four months before Ashley was removed from his custody, he had received an additional $11,000 in retroactive benefits. The family supplemented his income with the mother's TANF benefits and income from her job. There also was testimony that the parents had previously been offered a full range of services in an unrelated matter with the DHS and had demonstrated that they had the skills to maintain a clean and safe environment for their children.

[4]   The court need only find one of these grounds for relieving the Department of its reunification responsibilities. In re Misty B., 2000 ME 67, ¶ 11, 749 A.2d 754, 757–58; 22 M.R.S.A. § 4041(2)(A–1) (Supp.2000).

The Legislature has recognized, however, that under certain circumstances, children cannot be returned home safely within a reasonably calculated time, even if reunification services are provided. See 22 M.R.S.A. §§ 4002(1–B), 4041(2)(A–1); In re Heather C., 2000 ME 99, ¶ 28, 751 A.2d at 456. Specifically, if the court finds the existence of an "aggravating factor," determines that continuation of reunification efforts is inconsistent with the permanency plan for the child, or if two placements of the child with the same parent have failed, the Department may be relieved of its reunification responsibilities. 22 M.R.S.A. § 4041(2)(A–1).

The Legislature adopted the "aggravating factors" language as part of an Act designed to facilitate "expeditious actions in child protection cases" in compliance with the federal Adoption and Safe Families Act. Adoption and Safe Families Act of 1997, Pub.L. No. 105–89, 111 Stat. 2115 (codified as amended at 42 U.S.C. 671(a)(15)(D) (2000)); L.D. 2246, Summary (118th Legis.1998); see also In re Heather C., 2000 ME 99, ¶ 27, 751 A.2d at 455–56. Section 4002 defines "aggravating factors," and provides, in relevant part:

> 1–B. Aggravating factor. "Aggravating factor" means any of the following circumstances with regard to the parent.
> A. The parent has subjected the child to aggravated circumstances including, but not limited to, the following:
> (1) Rape, gross sexual misconduct, gross sexual assault, sexual abuse, incest, aggravated assault, kidnapping, promotion of prostitution, abandonment, torture, chronic abuse or any other treatment that is heinous or abhorrent to society; or
> (2) Refusal for 6 months to comply with treatment required in a reunification plan.

22 M.R.S.A. § 4002(1–B)(A) (emphasis added).[6] If one of the "aggravating factors" is found, the court has the discretion to order the Department not to commence or to cease reunification efforts. In re Christmas C., 1998 ME 258, ¶ 7, 721 A.2d at 631; 22 M.R.S.A. § 4036(1)(G–2). Thus, the Act gives courts the discretion to identify the most egregious cases, from early stages of the child protective process, thereby allowing the Department to move towards achieving children's permanency without providing fruitless reunification services. 22 M.R.S.A. §§ 4002(1–B)(A), 4036(1)(G–2), 4041(2)(A–1).

The father contends that his actions cannot meet the statutory definition of "aggravated circumstances," because the statutory language encompasses only affirmative, criminal acts by a parent against a child. See 22 M.R.S.A. § 4002(1–B)

---

[6]   The Act also provides courts with the discretion to relieve the Department of its reunification efforts if the parent has been convicted of certain crimes and the victim was a child in the parent's household; the parental rights of the parent to the child's sibling have been terminated involuntarily; or the parent has abandoned the child. 22 M.R.S.A. § 4002(1–B) (Supp.2000). These provisions closely follow the language used in title 42, section 671 of the United States Code, which provides monetary assistance to states for expenditures related to "foster care and adoption assistance." * * *.

(A)(1). Because he only grossly neglected his daughter, and because he was not convicted of any crime, the father contends that his actions, as a matter of law, cannot meet the statutory definition of "treatment that is heinous or abhorrent to society."

Contrary to the father's assertions, the plain language of the statute does not limit the statute's reach to only affirmative or criminal acts. The statute provides courts with discretion to find an "aggravating factor" when "[t]he parent has subjected the child to. . .treatment that is heinous or abhorrent to society." 22 M.R.S.A. § 4002(1–B)(A) (emphasis added).[7] The word "subjected" has the plain meaning to "subdue," "expose," or "cause to undergo or experience." WEBSTER'S II NEW RIVERSIDE DICTIONARY 671 (Office Ed.1996). Parental treatment of a child that merely exposes the child to "heinous or abhorrent" circumstances may meet the statutory definition of an "aggravated circumstance." 22 M.R.S.A. § 4002(1–B)(A)(1). When a parent's treatment of a child exposes that child to heinous or abhorrent circumstances, the court may consider those circumstances, regardless of whether the parent placed the child in harm's way through action or inaction; it is not necessary that the parent be found to have somehow assaulted or otherwise affirmatively abused the child. It is necessary, however, that the parent's behavior fall far outside the norm of ordinary, fallible parental behavior.[8]

Neglect, that is, the failure to undertake the necessary and appropriate actions to keep children safe and well cared for, will rarely constitute the heinous or abhorrent treatment envisioned by the Legislature. There can be no question, however, that the severe neglect to which the father subjected Ashley and her infant brother was abhorrent. The children were ignored for hours, if not for days, in a shockingly unsanitary environment. They sat in their own excrement, unattended, unfed, and unwashed. They received no human contact for hours on end. Ashley was penned into a secluded room, where she could be ignored completely

---

[7] The laws of most states, pursuant to the Adoption and Safe Families Act of 1997, contain the "aggravated circumstances" language. Because Congress left it to the states to define what "aggravated circumstances" means, a wide variety of approaches has been found among the states. See, e.g., Conn. Gen. Stat. Ann. § 17a–111b(a) (West 2000); Iowa Code Ann. § 232.102(12) (West 2000); Neb. Rev. Stat. Ann. § 43–282.01(4) (Michie 2000); 42 Pa. Cons. Stat. § 6302 (2000); W. Va. Code Ann. § 49–6–5(a)(7)(A) (Michie 2000).

[8] Although the Legislature has not defined "heinous or abhorrent to society," our interpretation of that phrase is guided, in part, by the legislative history of this language. In 1985, the Legislature first added the phrase "heinous or abhorrent to society" to the Act and stated, in relevant part:

It is the intent of the Legislature that the court shall determine what circumstance constitutes a heinous or abhorrent parental act or failure to act. The Legislature intends the court to use its best judgment in making this determination according to generally accepted standards and mores of performance, behavior and responsibility in this culture; particularly in regard to the performance, behavior and responsibility of parents toward their children. . . .

P.L.1985, ch. 739, § 18.

by her father. Such gross disdain for the needs of the children falls so far outside the behavior expected of ordinary fallible parents as to be undeniably abhorrent.

Moreover, this was not the first time that Ashley had been subjected to such abject neglect. In 1998, when Ashley and Katie were living with the mother and father in another apartment in Lewiston, the Department responded to a referral indicating similar problems of serious neglect as well as a violent and abusive environment. The guardian ad litem reported that the case was eventually closed after Skill Builders praised the work that the parents had done. As noted in the guardian's report, however, the parents ceased making any efforts as soon as the Department stopped monitoring their care of the girls. A pattern emerged of parents who cleaned their home temporarily for the authorities, while in reality, they did nothing to improve the lives of their children. The record also confirms that whenever the parents moved, which they did frequently,[9] they quickly turned their new living quarters into shambles.

The court recognized the importance of placing the extraordinary neglect demonstrated on the day of the baby's death into context before determining whether to grant the Department's request that no further efforts at rehabilitation be made with the father. Specifically, the court found the following:

> As horrifying as the conditions in that apartment were, they must be seen in the context. If [these] were first time parents with no resources, and no training, the apartment would have been no less appalling but, perhaps, not the basis for a cease reunification order. However, these parties had a full range of opportunities offered to them during their previous involvement with DHS. In addition, although not wealthy by any stretch of imagination, [the parents] had many more resources available to them than many families in this area.

In sum, the evidence of unconscionable neglect by a parent who has access to his own resources, has had the benefit of rehabilitation resources, and has, nonetheless, chosen to wholly ignore his children's needs, is fully sufficient to support the court's findings that the father's treatment of Ashley was "heinous or abhorrent to society" and that the Department should be relieved of its reunification responsibilities.

We also reject the father's argument that the Legislature only intended criminal acts to be included as an "aggravated circumstance." See 22 M.R.S.A. § 4003 (1992 & Supp.2000). The plain language of the statute specifies that the list of enumerated acts is not an exclusive list. 22 M.R.S.A. § 4002(1–B)(A) (". . .including, but not limited to, the following. . ."). By using the "but not limited to" language, the Legislature intended courts to determine what constitutes "aggravated circumstances" depending on the circumstances. Id. Although the statute

---

[9]   The parents had moved approximately eighteen times by the time Katie was six years old.

references several criminal acts as illustrative of "aggravated circumstances," it also references other acts—abandonment, torture, and chronic abuse—which are not explicitly crimes. Id. Its inclusion of the final phrase, "other treatment that is heinous or abhorrent to society," evidences its inclusion of unprosecuted conduct. See id.[10] The statute plainly anticipates that certain acts, even when those acts do not result in a criminal prosecution, may meet the definition of "aggravated circumstances." See In re Heather C., 2000 ME 99, ¶¶ 25–26, 751 A.2d at 455. The extraordinary neglect to which Ashley and her infant brother were subjected falls within that definition.

Accordingly, applying the statutory definition to the facts at hand, we conclude that the District Court did not err in its interpretation of the statute nor exceed the bounds of its discretion when it found that the father's treatment of Ashley amounted to "treatment that is heinous or abhorrent to society." See id.[11] Moreover, contrary to the father's assertions, there was sufficient competent evidence in the record to support the District Court's factual findings.

The entry is: Judgment affirmed.

Points for Discussion

a. Aggravated Circumstances

As noted by the court in *Ashley S.*, the states have adopted statutes that define aggravated circumstances in which reunification efforts are not required, as directed by the federal Adoption and Safe Families Act. If this family had not been previously involved with the state social services agency, would the neglect described here be a sufficient basis for termination of parental rights without providing any reunification services to the family? If Ashley's younger brother had survived, would the unsanitary conditions of the apartment amount to "treatment that is heinous or abhorrent to society?"

Other cases applying the "aggravating factor" language of ASFA include Interest of Jac'Quez N., 669 N.W.2d 429 (Neb. 2003) (no services required when infant suffered serious injuries from shaking); Matter of Marino S., 795 N.E.2d 21 (N.Y. 2003) (efforts to reunite family not required after father's rape of older child and mother's failure to aid child afterward). See also In re Dashawn W., 992 N.E.2d 402 (N.Y. 2013) (affirming conclusion that reunification efforts would be

[10] It is also instructive that the "heinous or abhorrent" language was once part of a separate paragraph, unrelated to the list of crimes, but was consolidated with an abbreviated list of crimes when the Legislature enacted subsection 4002(1–B)(A) in 1997.
[11] For the same reasons, the court did not err when it found that reunification efforts would be inconsistent with Ashley's permanency plan. 22 M.R.S.A. § 4041(2)(A–1).

detrimental to child's best interests after the parent's repeated physical abuse of 5-month-old).

b. Abuse or Neglect of Siblings

A number of the categories of aggravated circumstances under ASFA involve the prior mistreatment of a different child, including a prior involuntary termination of a parent's rights with respect to another child, and crimes such as murder, manslaughter, or a serious assault on another child. See, e.g., Renee J. v. Superior Court, 28 P.3d 876 (Cal. 2001) (sustaining statute providing for termination without reunification services when parental rights over a sibling had previously been terminated and parent has not subsequently made a reasonable effort to treat the problems that led to removal of the sibling).

Foster Care

According to the federal definition, foster care is "24-hour substitute care for children outside their own homes." In September 2016 there were more than 437,000 children in some type of foster care in the United States, with about 32% placed in relative homes, 45% living with nonrelative foster families, 7% in institutions, 5% in group homes, 5% on trial home visits, 4% in preadoptive homes, and 1% living independently with supervision. One percent of children in foster care had run away. For 55% of children in foster care, the permanency goal was reunification with parents or principal caretakers, and for 26% of foster care children the permanency goal was adoption. More than 273,000 children entered foster care during the fiscal year, and about 250,000 children exited. Of the children who left foster care, about 20,000 were teenagers who "aged out" of the system. See U.S. Department of Health and Human Services, Administration on Children, Youth and Families, Foster Care Statistics 2016 (2018).

Despite federal financial assistance, many state foster care systems remain significantly underfunded. Foster care reform litigation in many cities and states has attempted to enforce the requirements of AACWA and ASFA and to raise constitutional due process and equal protection claims on behalf of children in foster care. See, e.g., Henry A. v. Willden, 678 F.3d 991 (9th Cir. 2012) (reversing dismissal of claims against Nevada under the 14th Amendment and the AACWA). These cases are usually filed as class action lawsuits in federal court. See, e.g., Brian A. ex rel. Brooks v. Sundquist, 149 F.Supp.2d 941 (M.D.Tenn.2000) (allowing class action to proceed). Many have resulted in settlement agreements and consent decrees. See, for example, Joel A. v. Giuliani, 218 F.3d 132 (2d Cir. 2000) (approving class action settlement with city and state child welfare officials).

In determining an out-of-home placement for a child, states must consider giving preference to a child's relatives, and must exercise due diligence to locate and notify grandparents and other adult relatives. See 42 U.S.C. § 671(a)(19) (2018). Parents and families may also arrange kinship care informally, without any intervention from the child welfare system. Research findings suggest that kinship care has significant benefits for children, but grandparents and other family care providers also face special challenges. See Margaret F. Brinig & Steven L. Nock, *How Much Does Legal Status Matter? Adoptions by Kin Caregivers*, 36 Fam. L.Q. 449 (2002). As national policy moved

Go Online

For an extensive listing of foster care reform cases see the Foster Care Reform Litigation Docket available from the National Center for Youth Law.

toward a greater emphasis on kinship care, the laws have changed to allow states to use federal foster care funding to create subsidized guardianship programs for kinship caregivers who become legal guardians. Some state statutes include strong preferences for placements with family members. See, e.g., In Interest of J.W., 226 P.3d 873 (Wyo. 2010) (reversing agency's placement of children with unrelated foster parents rather than uncle and aunt).

Although many states once discouraged or prohibited foster parents from adopting children placed in their care, federal law since 1980 has supported foster parents who wish to adopt by making adoption subsidies available from Title IV-E

Go Online

See "Working with Kinship Caregivers" on the Child Welfare Information Gateway.

foster care funds. Most children adopted today from foster care today are adopted by their foster parents, and various practices encourage this. For example, in "concurrent planning" cases, children are placed with foster parents who would consider adoption if reunification is not possible. The goal is to minimize the number of place-

ments that children experience, but it can be difficult for foster parents to work toward reunification and consider adoption at the same time. This conflict was at the heart of Smith v. Organization of Foster Families for Equality and Reform, 431 U.S. 816 (1977), reprinted in Chapter 4, in which the Supreme Court upheld procedures in New York that limited the rights of foster parents when the agency decided to remove a foster child from the foster home.

Any placement of a child in another state for foster care or adoption must comply with the Interstate Compact on the Placement of Children (ICPC), which every state has signed and enacted into law. The ICPC establishes a procedure for cross border placements, and requires that the appropriate public authorities in the receiving state must be notified in advance and must agree to receive a child before he or she is placed there, even if the placement will be with a relative. See, e.g., In re Yarisha F., 994 A.2d 296 (Conn. Ct. App. 2010) (reversing order that transferred guardianship to child's great-grandmother in another state without compliance with ICPC). The ICPC is designed to assure that the prospective placement is safe and suitable for the child, and provides for the placing entity to remain legally and financially responsible for the child.

The ICPC rules do not apply to a child who will be placed with a parent in another state, unless there is some concern that the parent may not be fit to care for the child, or if the child will continue to be a ward of the court or will remain in the custody of a public child welfare agency after going to live with the parent. The ICPC also does

Go Online

For more information on the ICPC, see the web site of the Association of Administrators of the Interstate Compact on the Placement of Children.

not apply to an informal placement by the child's parent or guardian with a close adult relative or non-agency guardian in another state. In addition, it does not apply to a placement of a child in a medical facility, psychiatric institution or boarding school in another state.

C. Terminating Parental Rights

State statutes establish grounds for involuntary termination of parental rights, which ends the parent-child relationship and frees the child for adoption. Statutory grounds typically include severe and chronic abuse and neglect of the child or other children in the same household, abandonment, failure to support or maintain contact with the child, or incapacity based on long-term mental illness or deficiency or alcohol or drug use. A child welfare case typically proceeds to termination of parental rights when the state's reasonable efforts to preserve or reunify the family have failed.

Go Online

Find state laws on involuntary termination of parental rights on the Child Welfare Information Gateway.

Recognizing that parents have a fundamental constitutional right to the care and custody of their minor children, the Supreme Court ruled in Santosky v. Kramer, 455 U.S. 745 (1982), that the state must prove the grounds for termination of parental rights by clear and convincing evidence. Under the same principles, parents have a right to notice and an opportunity for a hearing in proceedings involving their children. Note that each of a child's parents has an independent constitutional interest, and each parent's fitness must be adjudicated. See In re Sanders, 852 N.W.2d 524 (Mich. 2014) (holding that "one parent doctrine" was unconstitutional).

Before it decided *Santosky*, the Court rejected the claim that indigent parents have a constitutional right to court appointed counsel in termination proceedings. See Lassiter v. Department of Social Services of Durham County, 452 U.S. 18 (1981). Despite *Lassiter*, many states have statutes providing for court appointed counsel to indigent parents. E.g., Cal.Fam. Code § 7862 (2018); N.Y. (Judiciary) Family Court Act § 262 (2018); Matter of K.L.J., 813 P.2d 276 (Alaska 1991). In states that recognize a right to counsel, parents may challenge the outcome of termination proceedings on the basis of ineffective assistance of counsel. E.g. Matter of A.S., 87 P.3d 408 (Mont. 2004); Interest of E.R.W., 528 S.W.3d 251 (Tex. App. 2017).

In recognition of the basic constitutional importance of rights involving the family, the Supreme Court has held that an indigent parent must be permitted to appeal an order terminating parental rights without being obligated to prepay the costs of the appeal. M.L.B. v. S.L.J., 519 U.S. 102 (1996). In *M.L.B.*, the Court distinguished parental rights termination cases from other civil litigation, in which indigent persons have no constitutional right to proceed *in forma pauperis*.

Termination of the Parental Rights of John Doe

281 P.3d 95 (Idaho 2012)

EISMANN, JUSTICE.

This is an appeal from a judgment terminating the parental rights of a Mexican citizen and resident whose child was born in the United States to a citizen of this country on the ground that he had abandoned the child. We reverse the judgment of the magistrate court and remand this case with directions to order the Department of Health and Welfare to promptly deliver the child to her father in Mexico.

I. Factual Background.

John Doe (Father) is a citizen of Mexico who entered the United States illegally in 2003. In mid-2007, he married Jane Doe (Mother) in Payette, Idaho. Father spoke Spanish and Mother spoke English, and they needed an interpreter to converse with each other. After they were married, Father was arrested in Ontario, Oregon, when he attempted to open a bank account with a false social security number. He served three months in jail in Vale, Oregon, and was then transferred to a jail in Portland to be held for deportation. He agreed to voluntarily leave the United States and did so, returning to his parents' home in Salamanca, Guanajuato, Mexico. Mother also went to Mexico, but she returned to the United States after she became pregnant. Their child (Daughter) was born in the United States in November 2008. Mother also had a four-year-old son by another man. In March 2009, Father reentered the United States illegally in an attempt to be with his wife and Daughter, but he was caught in Arizona and returned to Mexico.

In March, 2009, Mother was living in Middleton, Idaho, with her boyfriend, who had a son who was about seven years old. On March 26, 2009, Mother and her boyfriend took his son to the hospital regarding severe bruising on his head. Because Mother and her boyfriend gave conflicting accounts of how the boy was injured, the medical personnel notified law enforcement. The investigation disclosed Mother's son had struck her boyfriend's son several times with a hairbrush. On March 27, 2009, Daughter and the boyfriend's son were taken into custody by law enforcement, and on the same day the county prosecuting attorney filed a petition under the Child Protective Act with respect to those children. The petition alleged that the name of Daughter's father was unknown and that he was in Mexico at an unknown address.

At the shelter care hearing held on March 31, 2009, Mother and her boyfriend stipulated that there was reasonable cause to believe that Daughter and boyfriend's son were abused and neglected and were therefore within the purview of the Child Protective Act. The children were then ordered to remain in the custody of the Department of Health and Welfare until the adjudicatory hearing.

On April 8, 2009, the prosecuting attorney filed an amended petition under the Child Protective Act. The amended petition added Mother's son as a child within the purview of the Child Protection Act. It alleged that Daughter and boyfriend's son were abused because Mother and her boyfriend should have known that Mother's son was physically and sexually abusing boyfriend's son and failed to protect him and that Mother's son was neglected because his parents were not providing him with necessary medical and behavioral treatment to prevent him from being a danger to others. There were no specific allegations that Daughter had been abused or neglected. The amended petition stated that the name and address of Daughter's father were unknown. On April 24, 2009, the prosecutor filed a second amended petition which added Father's name and his address in Mexico.

On May 27, 2009, Mother and her boyfriend appeared in court for an adjudicatory hearing. They stipulated that Daughter and boyfriend's son should remain in the protective custody of the Department. Pursuant to that stipulation, on June 3, 2009, the court entered a decree of protective supervision ordering that

Daughter would be in the custody of the Department of Health and Welfare for an indeterminate period not to exceed her eighteenth birthday.

On June 3, 2009, Father spoke by telephone from Mexico with the Department's caseworker assigned to this case. He told her that he would like to be involved in Daughter's life and to be reunited with Mother and her son. He also said he would like Mother to begin the process that would allow him to come into the United States lawfully. The caseworker asked if he would like to take part in the Department's upcoming meeting to make a plan regarding Daughter, and Father stated that he would be available by telephone. That meeting was held the following day, and Father participated by telephone. The Department's purpose for the meeting was to arrive at a plan to reunify Daughter with Mother, the parent from whom Daughter was taken. Because Daughter had not been taken from Father, there was at that point no consideration of having her live with him. During that meeting, Father stated that he wanted Daughter returned to Mother so they could all be a family.

Take Note!

As the husband of a U.S. citizen, the child's father could obtain a visa to enter and remain in the United States legally, but this is a process that must be initiated by the U.S. citizen spouse.

On June 16, 2009, Mother signed the case plan setting forth what she was required to do in order for Daughter to return to Mother's home. Although Idaho Code section 16–1621(3) states, "The plan shall state with specificity the role of the department toward *each* parent" (emphasis added), Father was not named as a participant in the plan, and the plan did not specify any role of the Department toward him. Father was not represented by counsel, nor had he even been made a party to the proceedings.

Father maintained monthly telephone contact with the caseworker to keep apprised of how Mother was progressing with the case plan. During the telephone conversation with the caseworker in July 2009, Father stated that Mother had not called him for about two weeks and that she may be upset because he learned that she was living with another man. He added that she had not been honest with him and wondered if she is still serious about their relationship. He also stated that he was very concerned about Daughter's welfare and would like to have some kind of contact with her. The caseworker responded that she would send him some pictures of daughter. The caseworker did so, but he did not receive them.

During the telephone conversation with the caseworker in August 2009, Father stated that he had talked with Mother over the telephone and she updated him on her progress. When he talked with the caseworker in September 2009, he stated that Mother had called him and was upset. He asked the caseworker if Mother was following the case plan and whether Daughter would be going home soon. The caseworker said there was no definite time period. During the November telephone conversation, the caseworker told Father that Daughter had been given a birthday party on her first birthday and was doing well. The caseworker also said that she would be working to allow Mother to have visitation with Daughter in Mother's home. In a report to the court filed on September 23, 2009, the caseworker wrote: "This worker has been able to speak with [Father] regarding his daughter. [He] would like to have [Daughter] sent to Mexico if [Mother] is not able to work the case plan and reunite with his daughter."

In February 2010, the caseworker informed Father that Mother was not doing what she was supposed to under her case plan, and the caseworker discussed placing Daughter with Father. He said he needed some help in order to keep his daughter, and the caseworker provided him with information to contact a person at the Mexican consulate in Boise. Father was to obtain a home study from the local office of Desarrollo Integral de la Familia (DIF), the Mexican equivalent to the Department. Father tried several times to contact the person, but was not able to talk with him until May 2010.

The next conversation between Father and the caseworker was in June 2010, because the caseworker had been on maternity leave. Father stated he had spoken to the person at the consulate, but that person stated he would have to talk with the caseworker. In July 2010, the DIF worker came to Father's home to conduct an investigation in order to prepare the home study.

On July 27, 2010, the prosecuting attorney filed a petition seeking to terminate Father's and Mother's parental rights in Daughter. Attached to the petition was a report to the court dated July 23, 2010. In that report, the caseworker stated the following regarding Father: "[Father] lives in Mexico he was deported from the United States before [Daughter] was born. This worker speaks with [Father] over the phone monthly regarding how [Daughter] is doing in the foster home. [Father] is interested in having [Daughter] live with him if [Mother] is unable to reunify with [Daughter]." Nevertheless, the caseworker recommended that Father's parental rights be terminated because he "has waited to contact the Mexican Consulate until the month of June 2010." The report also noted that the foster mother, who was a Department employee, and the foster father were willing to provide Daughter with a permanent home.

In August, the Department's caseworker told Father she would present the home study to the court if it was received in time. On September 15, 2010, the Mexican consulate emailed the report to the caseworker. The report stated that Father was financially, emotionally, physically, and mentally able to provide for

Daughter, that his home would be a suitable placement for Daughter, and that DIF would provide services to Father if Daughter were placed with him.

The termination hearing was held on September 29, 2010. At that hearing, the Department did not present the DIF report to the court. The caseworker testified that she disregarded the report because the Department had decided to terminate Father's parental rights. Thus, default was entered against Father, even though he had clearly not been properly served with process regarding the termination proceedings. On August 31, 2010, the prosecutor had obtained from the clerk of the court an order stating that Father's last known address was in Mexico and that he could be served by publication in a newspaper that had general circulation in Canyon County, Idaho. Obviously, service by publication in Canyon County was not intended to give Father any notice of the termination proceedings. On November 2, 2010, the court entered a judgment terminating Father's parental rights in Daughter. A judgment was also entered terminating Mother's parental rights.

Father ultimately obtained counsel and on February 24, 2011, his attorney filed a motion to set aside the default judgment. The prosecuting attorney resisted the motion, but after a hearing the magistrate court entered an order setting aside the judgment on the ground that there was no proper service. The matter was then tried on July 6 and 27, 2011. On December 7, 2011, the court entered a decree holding that Father had abandoned Daughter, that it would be in her best interests to remain in Idaho, and that Father's parental rights were terminated. Father then timely appealed.

II. Are the Court's Findings Supported by Substantial and Competent Evidence?

A court may grant a petition to terminate a parent-child relationship if the parent has abandoned the child and termination of the parental rights is in the child's best interests. I.C. § 16–2005(1)(a). " 'Abandoned' means the parent has willfully failed to maintain a normal parental relationship including, but not limited to, reasonable support or regular personal contact." Idaho Code section 16–2002(5). "Failure of the parent to maintain this relationship without just cause for a period of one (1) year shall constitute prima facie evidence of abandonment under this section. . . ." *Id.* "No universally applicable 'normal parental relationship' exists; whether such relationship exists depends on the circumstances of each case." *In re Adoption of Doe,* 143 Idaho 188, 191, 141 P.3d 1057, 1060 (2006).

"The petitioner holds and retains the burden of persuasion to show that abandonment has occurred. This includes a showing that the defendant parent is without just cause for not maintaining a normal relationship with the child." *Id.* at 192, 141 P.3d at 1061. Whether a matter has been proved by clear and convincing evidence is primarily a matter for the trial court. "On appeal, the appellate court does not reweigh the evidence to determine if it was clear and convincing." *Dep't.*

of Health and Welfare v. Doe, 149 Idaho 207, 210, 233 P.3d 138, 141 (2010). "Substantial and competent evidence is relevant evidence that a reasonable mind might accept to support a conclusion." *Anderson v. Harper's, Inc.*, 143 Idaho 193, 195, 141 P.3d 1062, 1064 (2006).

Abandonment. "[T]he willful failure to maintain a normal parental relationship can be based upon either the failure to pay reasonable support, or the failure to have regular personal contact, or some other failure." *Doe I v. Doe II*, 148 Idaho 713, 715, 228 P.3d 980, 982 (2010). The magistrate found that Father had abandoned Daughter because he had failed to pay support and had failed to have regular personal contact with Daughter.

The magistrate court found that Father "made no attempt to establish a relationship by the means that were available to him. [He] sent no letters, cards or gifts to [Daughter] through her custodian, IDHW [Idaho Department of Health and Welfare], despite the fact that he knew IDHW was capable of translating and delivering any such letter, card or gift to [Daughter]." This finding by the magistrate is clearly erroneous. In fact, it is absurd.

Mother left Mexico when she was pregnant. Father was a citizen of Mexico and the uncontradicted evidence was that he could not have come legally into the United States without Mother filing the appropriate documents to petition on his behalf. Mother did not do so. After Father was caught entering America illegally in 2009, he was barred from even petitioning to enter the country for ten years. 8 U.S.C. 1182(a)(9)(C)(i). When Daughter was ordered into the protective custody of the Department, she was seven months old. Having someone read letters to her from Father would not in any way create a parental relationship of any kind. Even by the time of trial, when she was two and one-half years old, reading letters from Father to her would not have helped develop a parental relationship. In fact, neither the Department nor the foster parents even told her who her Father was. By the time of the trial, Daughter was calling the foster father "Daddy." There is no way that Father could develop any relationship with Daughter without having personal contact with her, and that was not possible as long as Daughter was in the United States.

The magistrate judge also found that Father had abandoned Daughter because he "sent no support to Maria of any kind." The only evidence of Father's income was that he worked two to three days a week and that his salary was 800 to 900 pesos. Nine hundred pesos would be about $70.30. He lives in his parents' house with his sister, and they all work and contribute to provide support for those in the household. To determine a parent's ability to pay support for a child, the court must consider both the parent's income and the parent's living expenses. *In re Adoption of Doe*, 143 Idaho 188, 192, 141 P.3d 1057, 1061 (2006). The magistrate stated, "While the evidence shows that [Father] is a man of modest means, the record does show and this court finds that [Father] has been employed during the course of this case and that he has used those resources in the support of himself and his family in Mexico." That was the entire finding regarding Father's ability to have paid support for Daughter. There was no finding as to how much of Father's income was required for his share of the living expenses. Absent such evidence, the magistrate's finding that he could have provided some support to Daughter was clearly erroneous.

In order to prove that Father had abandoned the Daughter, the prosecutor had to prove by clear and convincing evidence that he had "*willfully* failed to maintain a normal parental relationship" with the children. I.C. § 16–2002(5) (emphasis added). "For one to willfully fail to do something, he or she must have the ability to do it." *Doe I v. Doe II,* 148 Idaho 713, 716, 228 P.3d 980, 983 (2010). There was no evidence that Father had the ability to establish any relationship with Daughter as long as she was in the custody of the Department and he was in Mexico, legally barred from entering the United States. Likewise, there is no evidence that he had the ability to pay support. Throughout the proceedings under the Child Protective Act and these proceedings, Father has consistently expressed the desire to have custody of Daughter, and he did all that he could do for that to happen.

In her report to the court, the caseworker stated that Father's parental rights should be terminated because he "has waited to contact the Mexican Consulate until the month of June 2010." He was told in February that the Department would consider placing Daughter with him and that he needed to contact a specific person at the Mexican consulate in Boise. He testified that he called the consulate several times, but was not able to make contact with that person until May. The caseworker herself testified that when she called the consulate and left a message asking that person to call her, it was a month before he did. The assertion that Father's parental rights should be terminated because it took him three months of trying before he was able to contact the person at the Mexican consulate certainly seems pretextual. It makes one wonder whether the real reason for seeking termination of Father's parental rights is the fact that a Department employee wanted to adopt Daughter.

Best interests of Daughter. The magistrate found that it was in Daughter's best interests to have Father's parental rights terminated so that she can be adopted by persons who can and will provide her with the guidance, care, and support that she has not had in Mother's custody. The court further found that it was contrary to her best interests "to be introduced at this late hour to the home of her father." The court stated that Daughter "has no relationship with [Father] or any other tie to Mexico whatsoever. The only home [Daughter] has ever known is Idaho and she is currently being well cared for and has bonded with her foster family in a pre-adoptive placement." This finding is clearly erroneous.

In making this finding, the magistrate court failed to recognize the significance of a parent's rights regarding his or her child. "A parent has a fundamental liberty interest in maintaining a relationship with his or her child." *In re Adoption of Doe*, 143 Idaho 188, 191, 141 P.3d 1057, 1060 (2006). In *Stockwell v. Stockwell*, 116 Idaho 297, 299, 775 P.2d 611, 613 (1989), we stated as follows:

> In custody disputes between a "non-parent" (i.e., an individual who is neither legal nor natural parent) and a natural parent, Idaho courts apply a presumption that a natural parent should have custody as opposed to other lineal or collateral relatives or interested parties. This presumption operates to preclude consideration of the best interests of the child unless the nonparent demonstrates either that the natural parent has abandoned the child, that the natural parent is unfit or that the child has been in the nonparent's custody for an appreciable period of time.

That same presumption applies here. There is no contention that Father abused or neglected Daughter, nor is there any contention that he is unfit to have her custody. Although the Department had custody of Daughter for slightly over two years by the trial date, that was not through any fault of Father. He could not lawfully enter the United States, and for almost two years of that time he was not even represented by counsel. He repeatedly expressed the desire to be with Daughter, and he did all that the Department told him to do in an attempt to obtain her custody. He was ultimately prevented from obtaining custody simply because the Department decided that Daughter should remain in the United States. Absent evidence that Father was unfit to have custody of Daughter, it was in Daughter's best interests to be placed with him once it was determined that Mother was unable to successfully complete her case plan.

Another Department employee testified: "I think it's in the best interest of [Daughter] obviously to remain in the United States because there's no comparison between being in Mexico and being in the United States, being a United States citizen. She has all the luxuries or all the things that we can offer." The fact that a child may enjoy a higher standard of living in the United States than in the country where the child's parent resides is not a reason to terminate the parental rights of a foreign national.

III. Conclusion.

We reverse the judgment of the magistrate court and remand this case with instructions for the court to order the Department to take all reasonable steps to promptly place Daughter with Father in Mexico.

───────────────

Points for Discussion

a. Jurisdiction

What is the basis for the court's jurisdiction in a termination of parental rights action? The <u>Uniform Child Custody Jurisdiction and Enforcement Act (UCCJEA)</u>, 9A U.L.A. (Part 1) 261 (1999), discussed in Chapter 7, provides for jurisdiction in a "child custody proceeding" in the child's "home state," generally defined as the state where the child has lived for six consecutive months immediately before to the commencement of the proceedings. See <u>UCCJEA § 102(7)</u> and <u>§ 201(a)</u>. Under the UCCJEA, the term "child custody proceeding" includes a wide range of matters, including proceedings for neglect, abuse, dependency, guardianship and termination of parental rights. <u>UCCJEA § 102(4).</u> If the child's home state is in another state or a foreign country, however, <u>UCCJEA § 204</u> allows a state court to exercise only temporary emergency jurisdiction. See, e.g., <u>In re Aiden L., 224 Cal. Rptr. 3d 400 (Ct. App. 2017)</u>.

The UCCJEA does not require that a court have personal jurisdiction to make a child custody determination, see <u>UCCJEA § 201(c)</u>, and most courts have concluded that it is not necessary in a proceeding to terminate parental rights based on what is known as the status exception to the personal jurisdiction rule. See, e.g., <u>In re Emma B., 169 A.3d 945 (Me. 2017)</u>; <u>In re R.W., 39 A.3d 682 (Vt. 2011)</u>. A state court may decline to exercise jurisdiction under <u>UCCJEA § 207</u> if it concludes that another forum is more appropriate. Cf. <u>Interest of John Doe, 926 P.2d 1290 (Haw. 1996)</u> (declining jurisdiction in TPR action concerning mother living in the Philippines whose only contact with state was allowing child's father to travel there with the child). Although personal jurisdiction may not be necessary, all parents have a constitutional right to notice and an opportunity for a hearing, and child welfare authorities have the obligation to make reasonable efforts to locate a child's parents and keep them informed about the proceedings. See, e.g., *In re R.W.*, supra.

b. Abandonment

Abandonment is a basis for involuntary termination of parental rights in many states, but statutes are often silent as to what constitutes abandonment, leaving it to the courts to elaborate this standard. For example, voluntary placement of a child in foster care was held not to constitute abandonment in <u>Matter of Guardianship of K.L.F., 608 A.2d 1327 (N.J. 1992)</u>. See also <u>Tennessee Baptist Children's Homes, Inc. v. Swanson, 2 S.W.3d 180 (Tenn.1999)</u>, which concluded that a state statute defining failure to provide financial support for four months as abandonment for purpose of terminating parental rights was unconstitutional. As discussed in the *John Doe* case, what is the test for abandonment in Idaho?

c. Incarceration

Should incarceration be a basis for terminating parental rights? Some states include imprisonment among the grounds justifying termination of parental rights. E.g., Cal. Fam. Code § 7825 (2018) (conviction of a felony where the crime shows unfitness); Or. Rev. Stat. § 109.322 (2018) (in prison not less than three years, where the child's welfare will be promoted by termination). But see State v. Stillman, 36 P.3d 490 (Or. 2001) (finding termination improper despite incarceration and history of drug abuse). Cases are collected in Gregory G. Sarno, Annotation, *Parent's Involuntary Confinement, or Failure to Care for Child as a Result Thereof, as Permitting Adoption Without Parental Consent*, 78 A.L.R.3d 712 (1977).

d. Safe Haven Laws

Many states have enacted "safe haven" laws since 1999 to allow the parent of an infant to relinquish custody and parental rights by bringing the child to designated locations such as hospitals or police stations. If there is no evidence of child abuse or neglect, the relinquishing parents are generally guaranteed anonymity and immunity from criminal prosecution for child abandonment. See, e.g., Matter of Doe, 3 A.3d 657 (N.J. Super. Ct. 2010); Matter of Doe, 883 N.Y.S.2d 430 (Fam. Ct. 2009).

e. Support Obligations

Statutes in a number of states continue to hold parents responsible for child support after their parental rights have been terminated, in some cases even after the child has been adopted. See, e.g., Illinois Department of Healthcare and Family Services v. Warner, 882 N.E.2d 557 (Ill. 2008); In re Adoption of Marlene, 822 N.E.2d 714 (Mass. 2005); and State v. Fritz, 801 A.2d 679 (R.I. 2002). What are the policy arguments for and against this approach? How long after termination of parental rights should support obligations continue?

Problem 5-4

When Richard was sentenced to a year in jail for drunk driving, his girlfriend Clarissa brought their two sons, an infant and a two-year-old, to visit him every week. Six months later, the boys were removed from Clarissa's care as a result of her neglect and substance abuse. They were placed with Richard's relatives, and for six months the state agency worked with both parents to develop a treatment plan. Shortly before his release date, however, Richard's sentence was extended by two years based on a prior conviction. At that point, the agency limited his contact with the children to cards or letters, and stopped communicating with him. The court stopped including Richard in case hearings, despite a state statute that allowed incarcerated parents to participate by telephone in these cases.

At the final hearing on termination, six months before Richard's release date, the court terminated Clarissa's parental rights. Richard offered proof that he had a job and housing lined up, that he had completed several courses and attended Alcoholics Anonymous meetings while in prison, and that he was on waiting lists for counseling and parenting classes. The state sought termination because he was still incarcerated, arguing that he had not demonstrated that he was willing and able to take responsibility for the children. How should the court decide this case? (See In re Mason, 782 N.W.2d 747 (Mich. 2010).)

Global View: Cross-Border Child Welfare Cases

International child welfare and parental rights cases pose special issues, which are often not well understood by local courts and agencies. Under Article 37(b) of the Vienna Convention on Consular Relations, child welfare authorities have an obligation to notify the appropriate foreign consulate whenever a guardian is appointed for a child (or other person lacking full legal capacity), if that child is a citizen of another country that has joined the VCCR or entered into a similar bilateral agreement with the United States. See, e.g., In Re R.W., 39 A.3d 682 (Vt. 2011); see generally Ann Laquer Estin, *Global Child Welfare: The Challenges for Family Law*, 63 Okla. L. Rev. 691 (2011). Detailed information on Consular Notification and Access is available on the U.S. State Department web site. Based on your reading of the *John Doe* case, what assistance might a foreign consulate be able to provide in a child welfare proceeding?

Cases involving undocumented immigrant parents and children are particularly challenging. Neither immigration status or the fact that a parent has been deported is a sufficient basis for termination of parental rights, see, e.g., Interest of M.M., 587 S.E.2d 825 (Ga. Ct. App. 2003); Interest of Angelica L., 767 N.W.2d 74 (Neb. 2009), and a court may not terminate parental rights based on the perceived advantages of living in the United States, see, e.g., Adoption of A.M.H., 215 S.W.3d 793 (Tenn. 2007). Caseworkers have the same obligation to make reasonable efforts at reunification of immigrant families, see In re B & J, 756 N.W.2d 234 (Mich. Ct. App. 2008), but these families may be ineligible for services such as food stamps and public assistance under federal law.

Children in the child welfare system may be able to petition for lawful permanent residence in the United States under the Special Immigrant Juvenile Status (SIJS) rules in 8 U.S.C. § 1101(a)(27)(J) (2018). For a child immigrant to be eligible, there must be a state court determination, before the child turns 21, that "reunification with 1 or both immigrant's parents is not viable due to abuse, neglect, abandonment or a similar basis found under State law." The court must also determine "that it would not be in the child's best interest to be returned to the [child's] or parent's previous country of residence."

In Interest of K.F.

437 N.W.2d 559 (Iowa 1989)

NEUMAN, JUSTICE.

This is an appeal from a juvenile court judgment severing a mother-child relationship. The controversy brings into sharp focus the painful choices thrust upon the State as *parens patriae* when a natural parent suffers from a chronic mental illness. We transferred the case to the court of appeals which, on a five to one vote, reversed the juvenile court. Having granted applications by the State and the child's guardian ad litem for further review, we now vacate the court of appeals decision and affirm the judgment of the juvenile court.

* * *

The grounds for termination of parental rights must be shown by clear and convincing proof. Iowa Code § 232.116(5)(c). Of particular significance here is the rule that mental disability, standing alone, is not a sufficient reason for the termination of the parent-child relationship. Nevertheless, we have said that it is a proper factor to consider and, when it contributes to a person's inability to parent, may be determinative on the issue of whether termination is required in the child's best interest.

With these principles in mind, we turn to the record before us and the arguments presented on appeal.

II.

The minor child, Kristi, was nine years old when the termination hearing was held. Her mother, appellant K.F. (Karen), suffers from schizophrenia, paranoid subtype. Since 1981, Karen has been subject to eleven involuntary commitments due to her mental illness. Thus Kristi has spent four and one-half years of her young life in out-of-home placements. The commitment which ultimately precipitated these proceedings occurred in December 1985. Kristi was placed in emergency foster care, followed by an adjudication that she was a child in need of assistance (CINA). *See* Iowa Code § 232.96. Pursuant to this adjudication, she has remained in foster care ever since.

As revealed by the testimony of Karen's psychiatrist, her illness is characterized by bizarre behavior brought on by delusions of persecution and paranoia. In general, the illness manifests itself through abnormalities in the thinking process (associational disturbances), inappropriate affect (disassociation in physical manifestation of emotion), autism (total self-absorption), and habit deterioration (for example, neglect of personal hygiene). Characteristically, the illness follows a predictable pattern: the patient denies the illness, loses touch with reality ("decompensates"), becomes delusional, and then exhibits bizarre behavior resulting in an involuntary commitment. After a period of hospitalization and drug therapy, the patient regains a hold on reality, is eventually discharged from commitment and then, because of denial of the illness, discontinues necessary medication and begins the cycle anew.

Karen's illness has followed this pattern for fifteen years, with the additional feature that she falls within the subgroup of schizophrenics who become acutely ill (psychotic) within one to two weeks of stopping medication. In the acute phase, Karen's delusions center on her belief that she is being persecuted by Mafia figures; a preoccupation with injustices she has suffered; and a belief that she has ties to the White House and famous persons who direct her activities. Her manner becomes irrational and aggressive, punctuated by excessive profanity and anger. She has in recent years caused numerous disturbances in shopping malls and in the offices of prospective employers, threatening neighbors with arson, voicing intentions to shoot the President, and threatening to kill a minister.

When in remission, Karen presents herself as polite and congenial, a doting and affectionate parent, and a tidy homemaker. She maintains her own apartment and satisfactorily manages her social security disability income. She has rarely missed a scheduled visit with Kristi and she has cooperated with case workers in planning suitable activities for them.

In spite of this outward ability to carry on a normal life, Karen's psychiatrist concedes that even with the help of medication, Karen's delusional system "never goes away 100 percent." The truth of his observation is exemplified by Karen's response to a question posed by the court in a CINA review hearing held in August 1987, approximately six months prior to the termination hearing:

Q: Have you tried—since last February or so, have you tried to maintain regular contact with Kristi through letters, if you weren't available for visits in the community?

A: Yes. And I'd like to explain, I was brain-washed down at Mt. Pleasant by pills that were brought in from Turkey, which you can communicate with each other in your mind, and this is already known fact in Japan and China. It's just that this—this country is not aware of it.

Six months later, discharged from any involuntary commitment status and defending her parental rights in these termination proceedings, Karen responded to a nearly identical inquiry as follows:

A: I once made a statement * * * in one of my hearings that I was given drugs to more or less mind read, read my mind, and thoughts were being put in my head at that time, that the Mafia was after me. Since I've been out of the hospital in June, I no longer have the drugs and no longer have the mind reading or mind interpretation, and I have no belief now that the Mafia is after me.

Q: Okay. You believe that was a result of the drugs that the doctors were giving you?

A: Not necessarily. I was receptive to this mind reading thing because I was on drugs. Whoever wanted to read my mind had to take the drug, which I was told is from Turkey.

Q: Okay. And since you're no longer taking that drug, you can't read those minds now; is that—

A: No, I couldn't mind read. They could mind read me.

Q: Okay.

A: And put thoughts in my mind, so that I would appear crazy if I said anything. Now, that may sound delusional to you now, but it's real. I have no—I've had no problems with that since June, though.

It is against this backdrop that we consider the State's petition to terminate Karen's parental rights, filed December 9, 1987. Brought in accordance with Iowa Code section 232.116(5), the burden rests upon the State to furnish clear and convincing proof that all of the following have occurred:

(1) The child has been adjudicated a child in need of assistance pursuant to section 232.96.

(2) The custody of the child has been transferred from the child's parents for placement pursuant to section 232.102 for at least twelve of the last eighteen months.

(3) There is clear and convincing evidence that the child cannot be returned to the custody of the child's parents as provided in section 232.102.

Iowa Code § 232.116(1)(e) (1987 Cum.Supp.).

Section 232.102 refers to potential harm to a child resulting from a variety of circumstances listed in section 232.2(6). In this case, the State's underlying CINA petition alleged that due to Karen's involuntary hospitalization, Kristi was without anyone to care for her.

Karen concedes that conditions (1) and (2) of section 232.116(1)(e) have been met. Kristi has been adjudicated in need of assistance and custody has been transferred for more than twelve months. We therefore address solely the sufficiency of the proof offered in support of the third necessary element. * * *

* * *

* * * The crucial question on this appeal is whether clear and convincing evidence exists in the record to support the termination. The court of appeals reversed the juvenile court on this ground. It focused on evidence of Karen's "steady improvement" as a result of bi-weekly intramuscular injections of Prolixin. It also characterized as inherently "unfair" the State's sudden movement toward termination now that the child has gained sufficient maturity to understand her mother's illness and, after four and one-half years of foster care, has patiently awaited reestablishment of their home. Moreover, the court concluded, the record did not provide the requisite proof that Karen would not in the future be capable of adequately ministering to her daughter's needs.

We would like to share the court of appeals' optimism about Karen and Kristi's future but our review of the record compels us to reach an opposite conclusion. The crucial question, as we see it, is not whether Karen's behavior while in remission convinces us that she is equal to the task of parenting Kristi. Were that the inquiry, our response—based on this record—would be cautiously optimistic. The decisive question, however, is whether Karen—if allowed to resume Kristi's care—would remain in remission and maintain a stable home for her, thus extinguishing the need for Kristi's continued CINA status. Our answer to that question, based on Karen's history and the prognosis offered by her own psychiatrist, is unequivocally negative.

Karen's psychiatrist, Dr. Chang, testified that there are those who suffer from schizophrenia who can successfully control the disease and its symptoms. Such individuals typically have insight into their illness and understand the necessity of maintaining contact with their physician and taking prescribed medication. When these individuals feel the symptoms of schizophrenia surfacing, they will actually seek out their physician and voluntarily commit themselves for in-patient treatment, if necessary. Regrettably, Karen has never displayed this insight. She denies that she suffers from any illness and resents what she interprets as interference by others in her life. She seeks autonomy and freedom from medication, believing that her medication is the source, rather than the cure, for her difficulties. When free of medication, however, normal life stress precipitates her acute psychotic symptoms. As noted by the trial court, this has been the recurring theme over the past eight years.

In spite of his strong belief that mentally ill persons like Karen have a right *not* to have the legal ties to their children severed under any circumstances, Dr. Chang expressed a grave concern that Karen's current cooperation in treatment was motivated solely by her desire to regain custody. He predicted that if she achieved that result she would remove herself and Kristi from the community, discontinue her medication and quickly become psychotic and incapable of providing for her child's most basic needs. Other witnesses who have worked closely with Karen echoed this same concern based on corroborating statements made by Karen.

Faced with the inevitability of requiring Kristi to endure repeated CINA proceedings and foster placements, here or elsewhere, for the remaining years of her childhood, we must ask whether such a way of life can possibly serve her best interest. To her credit, Kristi has survived the upsets in her life thus far with remarkable resilience. Nevertheless, the emotional strain of establishing relationships with multiple foster families, the unpredictability of her mother's behavior, and the obligation Kristi feels to provide Karen with emotional support, has already taken its toll. In the words of the clinical psychologist who evaluated Kristi in connection with these proceedings, Kristi is suffering from "considerable confusion, anxiety, and a lack of trust." Dr. Hutchison summarized his findings and recommendation as follows:

> Overall, Kristi's relationship with her mother is one of mixed feelings. There is love and caring along with fear and confusion. While she wants to retain a safe relationship with her mother, she also states that she would like to live with one family on a long term basis. She seems to be well aware that she cannot live with her mother and actually would not want to live with her.
> Based on this evaluation of Kristi, I would recommend that she be placed in a longterm, stable environment, either through longterm foster care or adoption. She needs the stability and security of knowing that she will not be moved from place to place so that she can allow herself to emotionally invest and receive from those around her.

As we consider the doctor's recommendation, we are confronted by a stern reality: termination of the parent-child relationship will not guarantee Kristi a permanent home. Nor can we overlook evidence that the termination itself will be stressful to Kristi. On balance, however, we concur in the juvenile court's judgment that termination "will provide the best opportunity for the security and permanence this child so desperately needs."

In summary, the State has proven by clear and convincing evidence that Kristi cannot be reunited with her mother now, or in the foreseeable future, without subjecting her to the same harm that would justify adjudicating her a child in need of assistance. No intervention up to this point has altered the repetition of the cycle. Given the fact that Kristi has already spent nearly half her life in foster care, we must view these tragic circumstances "with a sense of urgency." In re A.C., 415 N.W.2d at 614. We are convinced that termination is the only viable means by which Kristi can escape the cycle and relinquish her role as one of its victims.

* * * Finally, we briefly address Karen's contention that even if the evidence is deemed sufficient to support termination, we should not take that action because it would be "detrimental to the child * * * due to the closeness of the parent-child relationship." *See* Iowa Code § 232.116(3)(c). This statutory exception requires proof by clear and convincing evidence to justify its application. *See id.; see also* In re L.P., 370 N.W.2d 839, 842–43 (Iowa App.1985). Under this record, that standard cannot be met.

We note that all of the testimony and documentary evidence furnished by those persons who were acquainted with Karen and Kristi speak of an undeniable bond between them. The evidence also reveals, however, that the relationship is marked by as much ambivalence as affection. Because of Karen's unintentional but unrelenting preoccupation with persecutory delusions, and her tendency to "test out reality" on Kristi, an understandable distance has developed between them as Kristi attempts to physically and emotionally protect herself from Karen's often frightening behavior. As noted by Dr. Hutchison and others, Kristi's attitude toward her mother is a blend of love and fear, caring and confusion. In view of the paradoxical nature of the relationship, and the strength of the evidence otherwise supporting termination, we find no basis to set aside the juvenile court's judgment on this ground.

Points for Discussion

a. Placement Options

To what extent should the availability of a permanent adoptive placement for a child affect the court's decision whether to terminate parental rights? If evidence had been presented in *K.F.* that Kristi would be difficult to place in an adoptive home and that she wished to remain in contact with her mother, would these facts be relevant under the Iowa statutory scheme? See In Interest of S.J., 451 N.W.2d 827 (Iowa 1990), in which the court refused to terminate parental rights despite the fact that the parents could not care for their nine-year-old son, where his prospects for adoption were poor and his needs were being well met by an experienced foster parent.

b. Bonds Between Child and Parent

The Iowa statute governing parental rights termination provides that notwithstanding the existence of grounds for termination, the court need not terminate if "there is clear and convincing evidence that termination would be detrimental to the child due to closeness of the parent-child relationship". Iowa Code Ann. § 232.116(3)(c) (2018). What is the purpose of this statutory exception? The Court in *K.F.* found that the evidence was insufficient to support a finding under this provision that the termination would be detrimental. Although the court acknowledged an "undeniable bond" between the mother and daughter, it found that the relationship was "marked by as much ambivalence as affection." Since it is difficult to imagine a situation where there would be a sufficient basis to terminate parental rights and the child would not have ambivalent feelings, what type of evidence would a parent need to offer to satisfy this provision and avoid termination of parental rights?

c. Child's Wishes

Most custody statutes include the preference of the child as a factor to consider in deciding custody. E.g. Cal. Fam. Code § 3042 (2018); Conn. Gen. Stat. § 46b–56 (2018); Neb. Rev. Stat. § 42–364 (2018). In Georgia, a child of fourteen has the right to choose his custodian unless the parent chosen is unfit. Ga. Code § 19–9–3 (2018). Many statutes provide that the consent of a child to an adoption is required once the child has reached a specified age, generally twelve or fourteen years old. Colo. Rev. Stat. § 19–5–203(2) (2018); 750 Ill.Comp.Stat. § 50/12 (2018). Should a child's consent be required to terminate parental rights as well? See, e.g., Iowa Code Ann. § 232.116(3)(b) (2018) (providing that if a child over ten years old objects to the termination, the court need not grant the termination). See also In re Adoption No. T97036005, 746 A.2d 379 (Md. 2000) (holding that child has a due process right to be heard on whether father's rights are terminated).

d. Sibling Relationships

Should siblings have the opportunity to continue their relationship with each other after termination of parental rights? In re D.C., 4 A.3d 1004 (N.J. 2010), considered the application of the state's sibling visitation statute, concluding that the law created a presumption in favor of sibling visitation prior to adoption, and permitted orders for continued sibling visitation after an adoption. Many states take a different approach, however. See, e.g., Ken R. on behalf of C.R. v. Arthur Z., 682 A.2d 1267 (Pa. 1996) (holding that child has no standing to seek court-ordered visitation with siblings). See also In re Jamison, 4 N.E.3d 889 (Mass. 2014) (holding that juvenile court had jurisdiction to consider petition for visitation between a child in the custody of state social services agency and his three siblings under the guardianship of their aunt). See generally Randi Mandelbaum, *Delicate Balances: Assessing the Needs and Rights of Siblings in Foster Care to Maintain Their Relationships Post-Adoption*, 41 N. M. L. Rev. 1 (2011).

e. Parent with Disabilities

In *K.F.*, the mother's mental disability pre-existed the birth of her child, yet it took nine years for the State to seek to terminate her parental rights. What would justify such a long delay when the mother's condition appears to have followed a consistent pattern throughout the nine years? In cases of severe psychiatric illness, when there appears to be no possibility of improvement, courts have approved orders terminating parental rights immediately after the child's birth. See, e.g., Adoption of Christine, 542 N.E.2d 582 (Mass. 1989); In re the Interest of S.L.P., 432 N.W.2d 826 (Neb. 1988). Similarly, in the case of chronic drug or alcohol abuse, when numerous attempts at treatment have failed, child welfare authorities may remove a child from the parent's custody immediately after its birth. See In Interest of J.K., 495 N.W.2d 108 (Iowa 1993); In re Welfare of H.S., 973 P.2d 474 (Wash. Ct. App. 1999).

Some people may be successful parents despite significant disabilities. How should the authorities evaluate these cases? In re Adoption/Guardianship No. J9610436 and J9711031, 796 A.2d 778 (Md. 2002), held that the parental rights of a father with mental disability should not be terminated without clear and convincing evidence that he would not, even with proper assistance, be able to parent his children sufficiently in the reasonable future. See also In re D.A., 862 N.E.2d 829 (Ohio 2007), which reversed an order terminating parental rights based solely on the parents' mental retardation.

Note that the Americans with Disabilities Act (ADA) does not create a defense to an action for termination of parental rights. See, e.g., Adoption of Gregory, 747

N.E.2d 120 (Mass. 2001); Interest of Jane Doe, 60 P.3d 285 (Haw. 2002). However, a claim under the ADA against a state court, for failing to provide adequate accommodation for a hearing-impaired individual during a prolonged child custody dispute, was allowed to proceed in Popovich v. Cuyahoga County Ct. Com. Pl., 276 F.3d 808 (6th Cir. 2002).

CHAPTER 6

Family Dissolution

Dramatic changes in divorce laws, which began to occur around the world in the early 1970s, are often described as a revolution. In the United States, every state enacted non-fault divorce laws that have largely replaced the traditional fault grounds, and began to encourage couples to find means to resolve their differences outside the courtroom. Rules governing the financial aspects of divorce—property division and spousal support awards—also shifted to reflect the idea of marriage as a partnership, and to eliminate considerations of marital fault. Throughout this transformation, divorce has remained a subject of state law, with significant differences among the states and corresponding problems of jurisdiction and conflict of laws.

Couples who are not married when their relationships end confront many similar issues. Parties to a civil union or registered partnership must follow procedures for dissolving their union under state law that are often identical to the procedures for divorce. Cohabiting couples have no legal status to change or dissolve, and no legal framework to define their rights and responsibilities, but they often have property and financial disputes similar to those of married couples.

This chapter covers the major legal questions involved when couples divorce or dissolve their relationship, including the grounds and jurisdictional basis for court intervention, property and support remedies between members of the couple, the role of federal income tax and bankruptcy law, and the process of dispute resolution. Chapter 7 takes up those aspects of family dissolution that involve children.

A. Getting Divorced

Divorce laws today can only be understood against the background of rules that existed before the divorce revolution of the 1970s. Early divorce laws in the United States trace to English ecclesiastical law, which permitted couples to obtain a legal separation, called a **divorce a mensa et thoro**, based on adultery or other serious marital fault. Judicial divorce was not available in England until the Matrimonial Causes Act of 1857, but wealthy individuals were sometimes able to obtain a full divorce including the right to remarry by a special act of Parliament. In the English ecclesiastical law, a marriage annulment, called a ***divorce a vinculo matrimonii***, terminated the marriage retroactively and also freed the parties to marry again.

The English colonies that grew into the United States did not have ecclesiastical courts, but they brought the doctrines and practices of the ecclesiastical courts into their civil law. Those colonies settled by Lutherans and Calvinists generally permitted divorce, based on proof of serious marital fault such as adultery, cruelty or desertion, while those with a stronger Anglican tradition prohibited divorce. South Carolina had no general divorce statute until 1942, and New York allowed divorce only on the ground of adultery until 1966. The practice of legislative divorce was brought to the colonies and continued well into the nineteenth century. See, e.g., Maynard v. Hill, 125 U.S. 190 (1888).

From the early years of the United States, the variation among the divorce laws of different states prompted unhappily-married individuals to forum shop in order to obtain a divorce. See Nelson Manfred Blake, The Road to Reno: A History of Divorce in the United States (1962). The result of this was a highly complex set of jurisdictional and conflict of laws rules through which some states sought to restrain migratory divorce. Over time, these rules began to collapse under their own weight, until they were significantly rewritten in a series of Supreme Court decisions beginning in 1942 that helped clear a path for the revolution in state laws that followed. See Ann Laquer Estin, *Family Law Federalism: Divorce and the Constitution*, 16 Wm. & Mary Bill Rts. J. 381 (2007).

Although the divorce law on the books was quite strict until the no-fault revolution, the law in practice allowed much greater latitude for divorce. A couple who were in agreement about ending their marriage could often find a way to

Go Online

Divorce rates in the United States peaked between 1979 and 1981 at 5.3 divorces per 1000 population, and by 2009 had dropped to a rate of 3.4 divorces per 1000. Statistical Abstract of the United States 2012, Table 133 (2011).

Marriage and divorce statistics for the United States are collected from state authorities by the National Center for Health Statistics, based in the U.S. Centers for Disease Control and Prevention (CDC), and made available through the National Vital Statistics System.

Survey data on marriage and divorce are available from the U.S. Census Bureau. See Jamie M. Lewis and Rose M. Kreider, American Community Survey Reports, *Remarriage in the United States* (2015), and Diana B. Elliott and Tavia Simmons, American Community Survey Reports, *Marital Events of Americans: 2009* (2011).

obtain a divorce. In states that permitted divorce based on cruelty, courts routinely granted divorces in uncontested cases based on a fairly minimal showing of marital unkindness, despite the strict requirements reflected in case law. In New York, a husband might "confess" to adultery that had not occurred in order to obtain a divorce. Even before non-fault divorce appeared in the United States, a large majority of all divorces were not contested and divorce by consent was generally available. See Lawrence M. Friedman, *A Dead Language: Divorce Law and Practice Before No-Fault*, 86 Va.L. Rev. 1497 (2000). In states like New York, the difficulty in obtaining a divorce also led many people to seek annulment of their marriages.

Make the Connection

Grounds for annulment or declaration of invalidity are considered in Chapter 1.

Despite being widely avoided in practice, the traditional grounds for divorce could be significant in negotiations about alimony, property, and the custody and support of children. The existence or non-existence of statutory grounds gave important bargaining leverage to one party or the other. This often increased the hostility with which a couple entered the divorce process, which in turn increased the emotional and psychological harm that they and their children suffered. The idea that divorce was a legal remedy to be granted only to an innocent partner against one who was guilty of marital misconduct was criticized continuously for forty or fifty years before significant reforms were undertaken. Many people found the process of obtaining a divorce to be humiliating, and lawyers and judges worried that the fraud and perjury it involved brought the legal system into disrepute.

1. Divorce Grounds

Early experiments with non-fault divorce grounds in the 1930s included laws authorizing divorce based on incompatibility or a period of living separate and apart. See J. Herbie DeFonzo, Beneath the Fault Line: The Popular and Legal Culture of Divorce in Twentieth-Century America (1997). In 1970, the nation's first pure no-fault divorce law went into effect in California, and the Uniform Marriage and Divorce Act (UMDA) was approved by the National Conference of Commissioners on Uniform State Laws, now known as the Uniform Law Commission (ULC). Although not widely ratified, the UMDA served as a model for many state legislatures as they rewrote their laws, and the ULC later renamed it the Model Marriage and Divorce Act.

Uniform Marriage and Divorce Act

§ 302. Dissolution of Marriage; Legal Separation

(a) The [_____] court shall enter a decree of dissolution of marriage if:

* * *

(2) the court finds that the marriage is irretrievably broken, if the finding is supported by evidence that (i) the parties have lived separate and apart for a period of more than 180 days next preceding the commencement of the proceeding, or (ii) there is serious marital discord adversely affecting the attitude of one or both of the parties toward the marriage;

(3) the court finds that the conciliation provisions of Section 305 either do not apply or have been met;

* * *

(b) If a party requests a decree of legal separation rather than a decree of dissolution of marriage, the court shall grant the decree in that form unless the other party objects.

§ 305. Irretrievable Breakdown

(a) If both of the parties by petition or otherwise have stated under oath or affirmation that the marriage is irretrievably broken, or one of the parties has so stated and the other has not denied it, the court, after hearing, shall make a finding whether the marriage is irretrievably broken.

(b) If one of the parties has denied under oath or affirmation that the marriage is irretrievably broken, the court shall consider all relevant factors, including the circumstances that gave rise to filing the petition and the prospect of reconciliation, and shall:

(1) make a finding whether the marriage is irretrievably broken; or

(2) continue the matter for further hearing not fewer than 30 nor more than 60 days later, or as soon thereafter as the matter may be reached on the court's calendar, and may suggest to the parties that they seek counseling. The court, at the request of either party shall, or on its own motion may, order a conciliation conference. At the adjourned hearing the court shall make a finding whether the marriage is irretrievably broken.

(c) A finding of irretrievable breakdown is a determination that there is no reasonable prospect of reconciliation.

Uniform Marriage and Divorce Act (UMDA) §§ 302, 305, 9A U.L.A. (Part 1) 200–01, 242 (1998).

Desrochers v. Desrochers

347 A.2d 150 (N.H. 1975)

KENISON, CHIEF JUSTICE.

The parties married in September 1970. Their only child, a daughter, was born in January 1973. The parties separated in May of that year and the wife brought this libel for divorce the following September. A month later the parties agreed to and the court approved arrangements for custody, visitation and support. The defendant did not support his wife and child from the time of separation until the temporary decree. He made the payments called for by the decree from its entry until June 1975. In July 1974, the Hillsborough County Superior Court, Loughlin, J., held a hearing and made certain findings of fact. The critical portion of these findings is: "[T]he action was originally brought because the defendant did not work steadily and stated that he, when he learned that the plaintiff was pregnant, wanted a boy instead of a girl; if the plaintiff bore a girl he would like to put the child up for adoption. After the birth of the child [a daughter] the defendant became very attached to the child, has visited the child weekly except on two occasions, and has been faithfully making support payments under the temporary order of $25.00 a week. The defendant claims that he loves his wife, does not want a divorce. The wife claims that she no longer loves her husband, but since the filing of the divorce he has been an industrious worker and is very attached to the child." The superior court transferred without ruling the question "whether, on all the findings of fact, cause exists for granting a divorce under the provisions of RSA 458:7–a." This appeal was argued in September 1975. At the argument counsel informed the court that the defendant had stopped making support payments and had gone to Nevada in June 1975. At that time he had written to his attorney expressing his desire to remain married.

RSA 458:7–a (Supp.1973) provides: "A divorce from the bonds of matrimony shall be decreed, irrespective of the fault of either party, on the ground of irreconcilable differences which have caused the irremediable breakdown of the marriage. In any pleading or hearing of a libel for divorce under this section, allegations or evidence of specific acts of misconduct shall be improper and inadmissible, except where child custody is in issue and such evidence is relevant to establish that parental custody would be detrimental to the child or at a hearing where it is determined by the court to be necessary to establish the existence of irreconcilable differences. If, upon hearing of an action for divorce under this section, both parties are found to have committed an act or acts which justify a finding of irreconcilable differences, a divorce shall be decreed and the acts of one party shall not negate the acts of the other nor bar the divorce decree." This section must be applied in conjunction with RSA 458:7–b (Supp.1973) which precludes divorce when "there is a likelihood for rehabilitation of the marriage relationship" or when "there is a reasonable possibility of reconciliation."

RSA 458:7–a (Supp.1973) is the product of a national discussion regarding the proper grounds for divorce. It follows in important respects the California Family Law Act of 1969. That statute, and others following it, have been criticized for vagueness, but have been held to be sufficiently definite to afford due process of law. *Ryan v. Ryan*, 277 So.2d 266 (Fla.1973); *In re Marriage of Walton*, 28 Cal. App.3d 108, 104 Cal.Rptr. 472 (1972). A consensus has emerged that a period of separation due to marital difficulties is strong evidence of the irremediable breakdown of a marriage. * * * When asked to interpret a statute similar to RSA 458:7–a the Florida Court of Appeal stated: "The Legislature has not seen fit to promulgate guidelines as to what constitutes an 'irretrievably broken' marriage. It is suggested that this lack of definitive direction was deliberate and is desirable in an area as volatile as a proceeding for termination of the marital status. Consideration should be given to each case individually and predetermined policy should not be circumscribed by the appellate courts of this State.

"Thus, we are hesitant to set forth specific circumstances which trial courts could utilize as permissible indices of an irretrievable breakdown of the marital status. Were we to attempt to do so, we feel that the basic purpose of the new dissolution of marriage law would be frustrated. Such proceedings would either again become primarily adversary in nature or persons would again fit themselves into tailor-made categories or circumstances to fit judicially defined breakdown situations. It is our opinion that these two problems are the very ones which the Legislature intended to eliminate." *Riley v. Riley*, 271 So.2d 181, 183 (Fla.App.1972).

The existence of irreconcilable differences which have caused the irremediable breakdown of the marriage is determined by reference to the subjective state of mind of the parties. While the desire of one spouse to continue the marriage is evidence of "a reasonable possibility of reconciliation," it is not a bar to divorce. If one spouse resolutely refuses to continue and it is clear from the passage of time or other circumstances that there is no reasonable possibility of a change of heart, there is an irremediable breakdown of the marriage. H. Clark, Jr., Domestic Relations, § 12.5, at 351 (1968). Comment, *Irreconcilable Differences: California Courts Respond to No-fault Dissolutions*, 7 Loyola of L.A.L.Rev. 453, 459–60, 466, 485 *et seq.* (1974). The defendant may attempt to impeach the plaintiff's evidence of his or her state of mind regarding the relationship. If the trial court doubts plaintiff's evidence that the marriage has irremediably broken down, the court may continue the action to determine if reconciliation is possible. However, if the parties do not reconcile, dissolution should be granted.

Knowledge of the sources of marital discord is helpful in determining whether a breakdown is irremediable or whether there is a reasonable possibility of reconciliation. Yet the statutory test is the existing state of the marriage. The statute authorizes the trial court to receive evidence of specific acts of misconduct where it is determined by the court to be necessary to establish the existence of irreconcilable differences. This authority is an exception to the general rule of the statute excluding such evidence, and the intent of the statute to minimize the acrimony attending divorce proceedings.

The question whether a breakdown of a marriage is irremediable is a question to be determined by the trial court. RSA 458:7–a contemplates the introduction of factual testimony sufficient to permit a finding of irreconcilable differences which have caused the irremediable breakdown of the marriage. Nevertheless there are limits to the inquiry. "In the first place, there is the natural tendency to withhold information of a personal nature from anyone but a trusted and discreet adviser; secondly, any probing into personal matters against the wishes of the party examined would be objectionable * * *; and thirdly, the parties have come to court for a purpose. Their answers, which may be perfectly honest ones, will inevitably be slanted in the direction of their ultimate goal, which is divorce." *Bodenheimer, supra at 200* (1968). Within these limits the trial court must be adequately informed before acting in matters of such importance. But the statute does not contemplate a complete biopsy of the marriage relationship from the beginning to the end in every case. This is a difficult task, but judges face similar problems in other cases.

The separation of the parties for two and one-half years and the plaintiff's persistence in seeking a divorce during that period is evidence from which the trial court could find that this marriage has irremediably broken down.

Hagerty v. Hagerty

281 N.W.2d 386 (Minn. 1979)

STEPHEN L. MAXWELL, JUSTICE.

Appellant, the respondent below, in a marriage dissolution action appeals from a judgment granting the petition for dissolution and from the order denying her alternative motion for a new trial. We affirm.

Claire and William Hagerty were married in Chicago in 1947 and moved to Minnesota in 1965. They were parents of five children whose ages ranged from 17 to 28 years at the time of the 1978 dissolution proceedings. William had employment problems but was working at time of trial, and Claire, also employed, had started working about 1973. The three youngest children developed serious drug and behavior problems during the last few years of the marriage, and difficulties with communication and discipline precipitated the family's involvement with counseling and treatment programs by 1975, at which time William's alcoholism became apparent. All of those problems were sources of marital discord.

Claire, after unsuccessfully urging William to seek treatment for alcoholism, asked him in the summer of 1976 to leave the home. William moved out in August and filed for divorce in September. He made several unsuccessful attempts at reconciliation, but testified that no hope of reconciliation remained at the time of the proceedings. Claire claimed the marriage could be saved if William were treated for alcoholism, but she had not otherwise been willing to take him back.

Prior to the hearing on the dissolution petition, Claire had unsuccessfully sought a court order dismissing the petition unless her husband completed treatment for his alcoholism within 6 months and agreed to a one-year after-care program; if thereafter he wanted the dissolution she would not resist.

On April 6, 1978, the trial court dissolved the marriage after finding, among other things, that William suffered from alcoholism, a treatable disease; that it was a principal cause of marital discord which adversely affected his attitude towards the marriage; and that the marriage was irretrievably broken.

The pithy statement in appellant's brief that she "simply suggests that the alcoholism is the culprit and that Petitioner's assessment of the marriage is deluded," sets the scene. She then asks (1) how lucid are the perceptions of an alcoholic about the marriage; (2) whether the same perception would exist after recovery from alcoholism; and (3) whether the petitioner proved that the marriage was irretrievably broken.

The record amply supports the finding of serious marital discord, and Minn. St.1976, § 518.06, subd. 2, expressly permits a finding of irretrievable breakdown upon such evidence.[1]

Since the record also amply supports the findings of alcoholism as a principal cause of the discord and as a treatable disease, the issue is whether the petitioner's untreated alcoholism can or should defeat findings of discord and breakdown.

---

[1]   Minn.St.1976, § 518.06, applies to this action since the appeal was pending prior to the effective date of the 1978 amendment. It provided in pertinent part:

"Subdivision 1. A dissolution of a marriage may be granted by a court of competent jurisdiction upon a showing to the satisfaction of the court that there has been an irretrievable breakdown of the marriage relationship.

"Subd. 2. A court may make a finding that there has been an irretrievable breakdown of the marriage relationship if the finding is supported by evidence of any of the following:

* * *

"(6) Serious marital discord adversely affecting the attitude of one or both of the parties toward the marriage."

The statute was amended by L.1978, c. 722, §§ 22, 23, 63, effective March 1, 1979. Section 63 repealed subd. 2, and the repeal applies to actions pending prior to the effective date unless an appeal was pending or a new trial had been ordered. In that event the law in effect at the time of the order sustaining the appeal of the new trial governs. L.1978, c. 772, § 61(b)(d).

The "can" issue is one of statutory construction; the "should" issue is one of public policy.

1. *Statutory Construction:* Although irretrievable breakdown was the only ground for dissolution in the 1976 statute, several former grounds were retained in altered form in Minn.St.1976, § 518.06, subd. 2, as evidentiary guidelines for establishing that ground, and the guideline of serious marital discord was added. There was no requirement for reconciliation attempts or stay of dissolution for any specified, limited period. Without requirements indicating a legislative policy of affirmatively encouraging a possibility of reconciliation, the statute contemplates that the likelihood of reconciliation be considered in the determination of irretrievable breakdown along with the evidentiary guidelines.[2]

Commentators and cases in other jurisdictions which have interpreted the grounds in no-fault dissolution statutes generally agree that the underlying concern is whether a meaningful marriage exists or can be rehabilitated. With that concern as the central issue, irretrievable breakdown is a fact which can be shown where both parties acknowledge that a breakdown exists at the time of the proceedings and one sees no reconciliation possibility. See, *Flora v. Flora, 337 N.E.2d 846, 851 (Ind.App.1975)*; *Kretzschmar v. Kretzschmar, 48 Mich.App. 279, 210 N.W.2d 352 (1973)*. It can also be shown by evidence of only one party's belief that it is the existing state, particularly where the parties have been living apart. See, *In re Marriage of Franks, 542 P.2d 845, 852 (Colo.1975)*; Smith v. Smith, 322 So.2d 580 (Fla.App.1975); *Desrochers v. Desrochers, 115 N.H. 591, 594, 347 A.2d 150, 152 (1975)*.

Where one party urged that the marriage situation was remediable but the other refused to pursue counseling or reconciliation, the subjective factor proving irretrievable breakdown was established and dissolution was granted. See, *In re Marriage of Baier, 561 P.2d 20 (Colo.App.1977)*; *Kretzschmar v. Kretzschmar, 48 Mich.App. 279, 210 N.W.2d 352 (1973)*. In situations where statutes authorize counseling or continuance and the testimony of the party alleging breakdown might be impeachable or doubtful, a continuance is favored over a denial, with dissolution following in the event reconciliation is not accomplished. See, *Riley v. Riley, 271 So.2d 181, 184 (Fla.App.1972)*; *Desrochers v. Desrochers, supra*; Comment, 17 U.C.L.A.L.Rev. 1306, 1324–25 and note 135 (1970).

Because the courts look at the existing subjective attitude, evidence of cause is no more determinative than evidence of fault. * * * Similarly, the Supreme Court of Florida declared in Ryan v. Ryan, 277 So.2d 266, 271 (Fla.1973):

---

[2]   Compare Minn.St.1976, § 518.06, with N.H.Rev.Stat.Ann. §§ 458:7–a, 458:7–b (Supp.1977) where irremediable breakdown is based upon irreconcilable differences, but divorce is precluded when "there is a likelihood for rehabilitation" or "reasonable possibility of reconciliation."

" * * * The new statutory test for determining if a marriage is irretrievably broken is simply whether for whatever reason or cause (no matter whose 'fault') the marriage relationship is for all intents and purposes ended, no longer viable, a hollow sham beyond hope of reconciliation or repair."

Since, here, the issue of breakdown calls for a factual determination and since § 518.06 does not provide for a separate determination of the likelihood of reconciliation, the court could properly consider the impact of treatment upon both the husband's attitude and the existence of serious marital discord. If the evidence established, which it does not, that rehabilitation of this marriage was likely, the court would have been acting within its discretion in continuing the action.

Upon the evidence introduced, however, and under the prevailing view of the single ground for dissolution in no-fault statutes, the husband's untreated alcoholism cannot defeat findings of serious marital discord and irretrievable breakdown.

2. *Public Policy:* Appellant presents compelling arguments for requiring treatment before an alcoholic can obtain a marriage dissolution. The arguments are based upon social considerations regarding both divorce and alcoholism, two major public problems, and urge a significant "judicially carved" exception to the statute's liberal policy and broad language.

Both the Florida and New Hampshire courts were faced with similar requests to look beyond findings of irretrievable breakdown, and both espoused the view stated by the Florida court that "predetermined policy should not be circumscribed by the appellate courts * * *." *Riley v. Riley,* 271 So.2d 181, 183 (Fla. App.1972). * * *

This court recently expressed its rejection of judicial carving with regard to consideration of fault in property distribution decisions and said that the forum for excluding that factor was the legislature. See, *Elliott v. Elliott,* 274 N.W.2d 75, 77 (Minn.1978). Our position is consistent with the settled rule that extensions of statutory provisions are to be made by the legislature rather than the courts.

Based upon that judicial policy, we will not apply the requested alcoholism exception to the findings of discord and breakdown.

Affirmed.

———————————

Points for Discussion

a. Unilateral vs. Mutual Consent Divorce

Both *Desrochers* and *Hagerty* granted a divorce over the objection of one of the parties. Taking the same approach, In re Marriage of Morgan, 218 N.W.2d 552, 560 (Iowa 1974), contains this statement: "Marriage is a relationship between two people, and if one of those people has determined it shall not continue, this would seem to be plain evidence the relationship has broken down." Some states, however, have more restrictive statutes, in which a divorce may be denied where the parties disagree on whether their marriage is irretrievably broken. See, e.g., Gardner v. Gardner, 618 So.2d 108 (Miss.1993); Nieters v. Nieters, 815 S.W.2d 124 (Mo.Ct.App.1991).

As you review these materials, consider what would be the advantages and disadvantages of requiring mutual consent to terminate a marriage. In her book, *The Divorce Revolution* (1985), Lenore Weitzman points out that the old fault grounds for divorce gave bargaining leverage in financial negotiations to the spouse who did not wish to divorce. Marriage breakdown statutes have largely eliminated that leverage. Does this support an argument for a return to requiring fault grounds for divorce, or for requiring the consent of both parties? See Sweet v. Sweet, 462 A.2d 1031 (Conn. 1983).

b. Proof of Irretrievable Breakdown

Assume that in a divorce action by X against Y, the following was the only testimony:

Q. Have irreconcilable differences developed in your marriage?
A. (by X) Yes.
Q. Have those differences brought about a breakdown of your marriage?
A. Yes.
Q. Is there any possibility of reconciliation?
A. No.

Is this testimony a sufficient basis for granting a divorce under a marriage breakdown statute? See Note, 17 U.C.L.A. L. Rev. 1306, 1322 (1970). Is this testimony necessary in order for a court to grant a divorce? See Brunges v. Brunges. 837, 587 N.W.2d 554 (Neb. 1998) (trial court erred in relying on pleadings to find that marriage was irretrievably broken; statute requires hearing at which oral testimony or depositions are received into evidence).

Should the trial court in a pure no-fault state refuse to hear any evidence other than the testimony outlined above? Proof of marital misconduct is inadmissible in some jurisdictions. See Cal. Fam. Code § 2335 (2018) which excludes from evidence testimony concerning specific acts of marital misconduct, and Colo. Rev. Stat. § 13–20–206 (2018) which makes it illegal to file a pleading or cross-examine a witness so as to identify a third party alleged to be a "participant in misconduct of the adverse party."

c. No-Fault Divorce Grounds

More than forty states have enacted some version of marriage breakdown as a ground for divorce, which may be labeled "irretrievable breakdown," "irremediable breakdown," "irreconcilable differences," or "incompatibility." The New Hampshire and Minnesota statutes discussed in *Desrochers* and *Hagerty* are typical of the language used in these states. The remaining states allow divorce on the non-fault ground of living separate and apart, for periods ranging from six months to three years. This ground may be utilized less often because of the delay involved. Some states combine marriage breakdown or incompatibility with separation as a ground for divorce.

Go Online

Find a chart listing grounds for divorce and residency requirements for all states on the web page of the American Bar Association's Family Law Section.

About thirty-five states have retained their old fault grounds along with the new non-fault grounds, and a majority of states still allow courts to consider marital fault in deciding the financial aspects of a divorce. In these states, courts are sometimes required to decide whether to grant a divorce on fault or on non-fault grounds. For example, in Welsh v. Welsh, 761 A.2d 949 (Md. Ct. Spec. App. 2000), a court concluded that a divorce should be granted based on the parties' two year separation rather than on the ground of adultery, where the evidence established that the parties' relationship had deteriorated long before the husband left the marital home and that there was no adulterous relationship until after the parties separated. In Matter of Ross, 146 A.3d 1232 (N.H. 2016), when the spouses cross-petitioned for divorce on fault grounds, the court granted the divorce based on irreconcilable differences, concluding that husband's fault-based petition was barred on the basis of recrimination.

Until 2010, New York's only basis for non-fault divorce required mutual consent. A couple could divorce based on proof that they had lived apart pursuant to a separation agreement for at least a year. If spouses could not reach agreement, New York required proof of fault grounds. A significant portion of New York divorces were contested, with fault allegations and the threat of an expensive and unpleasant trial. Under the new ground added to the statute in 2010, divorce may be obtained based on an irretrievable breakdown of the marriage for a period of at least six months. No divorce can be granted, however, until the financial and other issues have been resolved by the parties or litigated by a court. See <u>N.Y. Dom. Rel. § 170 (7) (2018)</u>.

d. Counseling

In addition to the UMDA, a number of state statutes provide opportunities for counseling or conciliation. See, e.g., <u>Cal. Fam. Code §§ 1830 ff.</u>, <u>2334</u> (2018); <u>Iowa Code Ann. § 598.16 (2018)</u>. Should pre-divorce counseling be mandatory?

Client Counseling

How should a lawyer counsel a client who is contemplating filing for divorce? Should a lawyer ever discourage the client from proceeding? Should a lawyer refer a client for marital or individual psychological counseling or other professional assistance?

According to <u>Standard 2.1</u> of the <u>ABA Model Rules of Professional Conduct</u>, a lawyer advising a client "may refer not only to law but to other considerations such as moral, economic, social and political factors that may be relevant to the client's situation." What factors could a lawyer raise with his or her client in the context of a divorce? See also the <u>American Academy of Matrimonial Lawyers, Bounds of Advocacy</u>, which states in Standard 1.2 that "An attorney should advise the client of the emotional and economic impact of divorce and explore the feasibility of reconciliation." See generally Lynn D. Wardle, <u>*Counselors and Gatekeepers: The Professional Responsibilities of Family Lawyers in Divorce Cases*, 79 U.M.K.C. L. Rev. 417 (2010)</u>.

e. Divorce Rates

Allowing divorce without proof of fault was expected to lead to increased divorce rates. The American divorce rate increased markedly in the 1970's, but scholars have disagreed whether this was attributable to the enactment of divorce reform legislation. See Ira Mark Ellman and Sharon L. Lohr, <u>*Dissolving the Relationship Between Divorce Laws and Divorce Rates*, 18 Int'l Rev. L. & Econ. 341, 349–358 (1998)</u> (reviewing empirical literature and concluding that no-fault divorce did not cause an increase in divorce rates. See also H. Elizabeth Peters, *Marriage and Divorce: Informational Constraints and Private Contracting*, 76 Am. Econ. Rev. 437 (1986).

What public policies are appropriate to address high divorce rates? Some states have encouraged premarital counseling. For example, Florida reduces marriage license fees for couples who complete a marriage preparation course. See generally Matthew J. Astle, *An Ounce of Prevention: Marital Counseling Laws as an Anti-Divorce Measure*, 38 Fam. L.Q. 733 (2004).

f. Covenant Marriage

Louisiana enacted "covenant marriage" legislation in 1997, creating two kinds of marriage and divorce in the state. With the first type, divorce is allowed when the parties have lived separate and apart for six months, with other grounds based on fault. The second type, known as covenant marriage, is available at the parties' election; persons contracting a covenant marriage must undergo premarital counseling and may be divorced only on fault grounds or if they have lived separate and apart for two years (or for one year following a legal separation). La. Rev. Stat. § 9:272 (2018). Arizona and Arkansas have also enacted covenant marriage legislation. See Ariz. Rev. Stat. § 25–901 (2018); Ark. Code § 9–11–801 et seq. (2018). These laws are not likely to be given effect if the parties divorce in a jurisdiction that does not have covenant marriage. See Blackburn v. Blackburn, 180 So.3d 16 (Ala. Civ. App. 2015).

Go Online

See the information booklet available from the Louisiana Department of Justice, Office of the Attorney General, on Louisiana Laws on Community Property and Covenant Marriage.

Relatively small numbers of the marriages performed in these states have been covenant marriages. For a retrospective analysis by one of the drafters of the Louisiana legislation, see Katherine Shaw Spaht, *Covenant Marriage Seven Years Later: Its As Yet Unfulfilled Promise*, 65 La. L. Rev. 605 (2005).

Traditional Divorce Grounds and Defenses

Adultery. Adultery as a ground for divorce is defined as the voluntary sexual intercourse of a married person with a person other than the spouse. Homosexual contacts have been held to be adultery, and some statutes make this rule explicit. See, e.g., N.Y. Dom. Rel. § 170 (2018); S.B. v. S.J.B., 609 A.2d 124 (N.J. Super. Ct. Ch. Div. 1992); Bales v. Hack, 509 N.E.2d 95 (Ohio Ct. App. 1986); RGM v. DEM, 410 S.E.2d 564 (S.C. 1991); but see e.g. Matter of Blanchflower, 834 A.2d 1010 (N.H. 2003).

Adultery is also a criminal offense in some states, although more contemporary statutes have eliminated adultery from the list of sex crimes. See, e.g., Model Penal Code § 213.6, Note on Adultery and Fornication, Model Penal Code and Commentaries Part II, 430 (1980).

Desertion. Desertion as a ground for divorce is defined as (a) the voluntary separation by one spouse from the other, (b) with the intent not to resume marital cohabitation, (c) without the consent of the other spouse and (d) without justification. Most desertion statutes also impose a time requirement, most commonly a year, before desertion ripens into a ground for divorce. Conduct of one spouse that is so intolerable that the other is forced to leave the home is called constructive desertion, and may also be a ground for divorce.

Cruelty. Statutes making cruelty a ground for divorce require conduct that is "intolerable," "inhuman," "extreme," "grievous" or "barbarous." See, e.g., N.J. Stat. Ann. § 2A:34–2 (2018); N.Y. Dom. Rel. § 170(1) (2018). As noted above, however, courts applying these statutes in the years before no-fault divorce laws generally required very little by way of proof in uncontested divorce cases. According to the case law, however, a single act of cruelty is not sufficient to constitute grounds for divorce, unless the act is particularly outrageous or brutal. In addition, the plaintiff must prove that the cruelty had some effect upon his or her health before it will be held to be a ground for divorce. See, e.g., In re Marriage of Wade, 511 N.E.2d 156 (Ill. App. Ct. 1987).

Defenses to Divorce. Collusion, connivance, condonation and recrimination are the traditional affirmative defenses to a divorce action, inherited from the English ecclesiastical law. These may be established by statute or adopted by judicial decision, but they are mostly of historical interest, since they have no practical effect in a state with no-fault divorce grounds.

Collusion was defined as an agreement between the parties that one will not defend the suit or will appear to have committed a marital offense in order to obtain a divorce. Connivance occurred when the plaintiff consented to the defendant's commission of the marital offense. Condonation is defined as a resumption or continuance of marital cohabitation implying forgiveness on the part of the plaintiff spouse. Recrimination is the defense which occurred when the plaintiff was also shown to have engaged in conduct constituting a marital offense. In other words, if both parties engaged in marital misconduct, neither was permitted to obtain a divorce. See Surbey v. Surbey, 360 S.E.2d 873 (Va. Ct. App. 1987).

For further discussion of traditional and contemporary divorce grounds and defenses, and the evolution of no-fault divorce laws, see Homer H. Clark, Jr., Domestic Relations ch. 13 (Student 2d ed. 1988).

Problem 6-1

Your new client, Winona, tells you she wants a divorce from her husband, Hank. They have been married for five stormy years, during which Winona says that Hank has repeatedly humiliated her, publicly and privately, often when Hank was drunk. Hank became very angry at Winona several times, throwing glasses, smashing a hole in the wall, and hitting her hard enough to blacken one eye and cause painful bruises on four different occasions. Three times he forced her to have sexual relations in circumstances that would have constituted rape if they had not been married. Winona tells you that the effect upon her mental and physical health has been devastating, that she has lost weight, has trouble sleeping, and recently lost a good job because of her ill health.

Winona and Hank signed a prenuptial agreement in which each released all financial claims based on the marriage. In addition to a divorce, she would like to recover damages from Hank for all the harm he has caused her. Considering the laws in your state regarding divorces, marital torts, and premarital agreements, what advice would you give Winona? Would your advice differ depending whether or she could sue for divorce on the ground of cruelty? (See Hakkila v. Hakkila, 812 P.2d 1320 (N.M. Ct. App.1991); Twyman v. Twyman, 855 S.W.2d 619 (Tex.1993).)

Problem 6-2

Assume that you are a member of the Senate Judiciary Committee of your state legislature. As such a member, how would you react to the following proposed statute?

"(a) Any man and woman applying for a marriage license under the provisions of section ____, may file with their application a written contract, signed by both and duly acknowledged. Such contract may contain such provisions as the parties desire for the regulation of their marital rights and responsibilities, including, but not limited to, a provision establishing a limit on the duration of their marriage of not less than one year. Such contracts so filed shall be matters of public record and open to inspection.

"(b) On or after the date set by any contract filed under subsection (a) hereof for the termination of any marriage, the parties or either of them may file with the county clerk a written, signed and acknowledged statement that their marriage has terminated in accordance with the terms of the contract.

"(c) Either party to such contract may, at any time after such termination, bring suit in a court of competent jurisdiction to have adjudicated any financial, property, custody or other disputes arising out of the marriage or the marriage contract filed under subsection (a) hereof. Such disputes shall be decided by reference to the parties' contract filed under subsection (a) hereof if possible, but if not possible, in accordance with the applicable statutes and common law.

"(d) If no action under subsection (b) hereof is taken, contracts filed under subsection (a) hereof shall be deemed to be renewed for subsequent periods equal in length to the period of duration prescribed in the contract as originally filed. At any time the parties may file written, signed and acknowledged amendments to the contracts authorized by subsection (a)."

-----

2. Divorce Jurisdiction

In the era before no-fault divorce laws, when many individuals traveled to another state or country to obtain a divorce, jurisdiction and conflict of laws questions were at the core of domestic relations practice. Although migratory divorce is far less common today, the complex framework of divorce jurisdiction remains in place. Jurisdiction in divorce cases is unusual because the rules governing the courts' jurisdiction over termination of a marriage differ sharply from the rules governing jurisdiction over the financial aspects of divorce and the rules governing jurisdiction over child custody and support matters.

Make the Connection

For the jurisdictional requirements of cases involving child support and custody, see Chapter 7.

Von Schack v. Von Schack

893 A.2d 1004 (Maine 2006)

SAUFLEY, C.J.

[¶ 1] Mary Mulhearn Von Schack appeals from a divorce judgment entered in the District Court (West Bath, *Field, J.*). She raises a single question: When considering a complaint for divorce in which only the plaintiff is a Maine resident, does the Due Process Clause of the United States Constitution, U.S. CONST. amend. XIV, § 1, require a Maine court to have personal jurisdiction over the defendant in order to render a divorce judgment that dissolves the parties' marriage without determining the collateral issues of property division, parental rights, or support? We conclude that personal jurisdiction is not required in these limited circumstances, and we affirm the judgment of divorce.

I. BACKGROUND

[¶ 2] For purposes of this appeal, the parties do not dispute the following facts. Mary Mulhearn Von Schack and Wesley W. Von Schack were married in New York State in 1976 and have one daughter who was born on November 1, 1991. The parties lived in Pennsylvania and New York when they were a couple. Wesley moved to Maine in May 2004 to take a position as an executive in a corporation with offices in Maine. Mary has no contacts with Maine whatsoever. Wesley was unable to proceed with a divorce complaint in Pennsylvania or New York because he is not a resident and has failed to meet other statutory grounds.[1]

[¶ 3] Wesley filed a divorce complaint in the Maine District Court on November 5, 2004, after living in Maine for six months. In January 2005, Wesley had the complaint served on Mary personally in New York. Mary

New York revised its divorce law in 2010 to add a pure non-fault ground for divorce.

moved to dismiss the complaint on the grounds that Maine was not a convenient forum and the court lacked personal jurisdiction over her and lacked *in rem* jurisdiction over the parties' property.

[¶ 4] The court denied her motion to dismiss. In so doing, the court concluded first, that it could not grant any relief regarding parental rights and responsibilities because Maine was not the home state of the parties' child for purposes of the Uniform Child Custody Jurisdiction and Enforcement Act, 19–A M.R.S. §§ 1731–1742 (2005), and second, that because it lacked personal jurisdiction over Mary, it could not award support or divide property. It reasoned, however, that "the District Court has original jurisdiction over the dissolution of the parties' marriage and can enter an order regarding any real property in Maine." The court divorced the parties and left all property, spousal support, and parental issues to be litigated in a jurisdiction "that might have personal jurisdiction over both the parties and jurisdiction over the minor child." Mary timely appealed from the judgment.

II. DISCUSSION

[¶ 5] We begin our analysis with the District Court's conclusion, undisputed by the parties, that Mary "has no contacts with this state whatsoever," and that the court "lack[s]. . .personal jurisdiction over [Mary]." If the court erred in concluding that it lacks personal jurisdiction over Mary, it had the authority to enter a divorce judgment. If the court correctly concluded that it lacks personal jurisdic-

---

[1]   Specifically, New York is a state that does not allow no-fault divorces. See N.Y. DOM. REL. LAW § 170 (Consol. 1990 & Pamph. 2005)

tion, however, we must determine whether a court may grant a divorce when one party is not within the reach of the court's personal jurisdiction.

A. Personal Jurisdiction

[¶ 6] Although Maine's divorce statute permits a plaintiff to file a complaint for divorce if "[t]he plaintiff has resided in good faith in this State for 6 months prior to the commencement of the action," 19–A M.R.S. § 901(1)(A) (2005), it does not speak to jurisdiction. To determine whether Maine has personal jurisdiction over a defendant, we apply Maine's long arm statute, 14 M.R.S. § 704–A (2005):

> Any person, whether or not a citizen or resident of this State, who in person or through an agent does any of the acts hereinafter enumerated in this section, thereby submits such person, and, if an individual, his personal representative, to the jurisdiction of the courts of this State as to any cause of action arising from the doing of any of such acts:
>
> . . .
>
> **G.** Maintaining a domicile in this State while subject to a marital or family relationship out of which arises a claim for divorce, alimony, separate maintenance, property settlement, child support or child custody; or the commission in this State of any act giving rise to such a claim; or
>
> . . .
>
> **I.** Maintain any other relation to the State or to persons or property which affords a basis for the exercise of jurisdiction by the courts of this State consistent with the Constitution of the United States.

14 M.R.S. § 704–A(2).

[¶ 7] Pursuant to this long arm statute, the court could have obtained personal jurisdiction over Mary in three possible ways: (1) if she "[m]aintain[ed] a domicile in this State while subject to a marital or family relationship out of which arises a claim for divorce,"*id.* § 704–A(2)(G); (2) if she "commi[tted] in this State. . .any act giving rise to such a claim,"*id.*; or (3) if she "[m]aintain[ed] any other relation to the State or to persons or property which affords a basis for the exercise of jurisdiction by the courts of this State consistent with the Constitution of the United States,"*id.* § 704–A(2)(I). *See* Levy, *Maine Family Law* § 2.3 (5th ed. 2006).

[¶ 8] The parties agree that Mary never lived in Maine and never committed any acts in Maine related to the divorce. Accordingly, personal jurisdiction could not be asserted pursuant to section 704–A(2)(G). *See also Jackson v. Weaver,* 678 A.2d 1036, 1039 (Me.1996) (holding that satisfying section 704–A(2)(G) confers personal jurisdiction "to the extent that such personal jurisdiction comports with the requirements of due process").

[¶ 9] Similarly, section 704–A(2)(I) does not confer personal jurisdiction over Mary. Paragraph I permits the exercise of personal jurisdiction as long as a person has a relationship with the State of Maine, any Maine citizens, or Maine property that would afford a basis for jurisdiction consistent with the United States Constitution. 14 M.R.S. § 704–A(2)(I). Consistency with the Due Process Clause of the United States Constitution requires that: " '(1) Maine ha[s] a legitimate interest in the subject matter of this litigation; (2) the defendant, by his conduct, reasonably could have anticipated litigation in Maine; and (3) the exercise of jurisdiction by Maine's courts comports with traditional notions of fair play and substantial justice.' " *Jackson, 678 A.2d at 1039 (alteration in original)* (quoting *Murphy v. Keenan, 667 A.2d 591, 593 (Me.1995)*).

[¶ 10] We agree with the trial court that Mary lacks any relation to the State that would permit the court to exercise personal jurisdiction consistent with this test.   The unilateral decision of one spouse to move to Maine does not result in the other spouse "[m]aintain[ing] any other relation to. . .persons. . .which affords a basis for the exercise of jurisdiction by the courts of this State consistent with the Constitution of the United States." 14 M.R.S. § 704–A(2)(I). In such circumstances, the *nonresident* spouse did not engage in any conduct that would make it reasonable for her to have anticipated litigation in Maine.   Accordingly, section 704–A(2)(I) does not confer jurisdiction in the present case.

B. Jurisdiction Over Marital Status

[¶ 11] Because the court correctly concluded that it lacks personal jurisdiction over Mary, the question raised by Mary's appeal is whether the court could enter a valid judgment of divorce without obtaining personal jurisdiction over her. To answer this question, we begin by reviewing the evolution of United States Supreme Court jurisprudence regarding jurisdiction. In the late nineteenth century, the Court did not require personal jurisdiction for a state to determine the status of its citizen toward a nonresident. *Pennoyer v. Neff, 95 U.S. 714 (1877)*. In *Pennoyer,* the Court addressed a dispute over the ownership of land allegedly sold to satisfy a debt on a personal judgment. The Court held that a state's jurisdiction to render judgments *in personam* required personal service and that service by publication would not suffice. It took pains, however, to limit the scope of its holding and to clarify that the then current state of the law, allowing a state to determine the marital status of its own citizens, did not fall under this requirement. A state possessed the "absolute right to prescribe the conditions upon which the marriage relation between its own citizens shall be created, and the causes for which it may be dissolved."

[¶ 12] Following the reasoning of *Pennoyer,* the Court later stated, "each state, by virtue of its command over its domiciliaries and its large interest in the institution of marriage, can alter within its own borders the marriage status of the spouse domiciled there, even though the other spouse is absent." <u>Williams v. North Carolina, 317 U.S. 287, 298–99 (1942)</u>. Such a decree of marital status was entitled to full faith and credit in a sister state. <u>Id. at 303</u>. In its second opinion in the <u>Williams</u> case, the Court reiterated that "one State can grant a divorce of validity in other States. . .if the applicant has a *bona fide* domicil in the State of the court purporting to dissolve a prior legal marriage." <u>Williams v. North Carolina, 325 U.S. 226, 238 (1945)</u>.

[¶ 13] In 1945, the Supreme Court shifted its approach to jurisdictional determinations when it announced the now familiar standard for determining whether a court has jurisdiction over a person: the "minimum contacts" test. <u>Int'l Shoe Co. v. State of Washington, 326 U.S. 310, 316 (1945)</u>. The Court held,

> due process requires only that in order to subject a defendant to a judgment *in personam,* if he be not present within the territory of the forum, he have certain minimum contacts with it such that the maintenance of the suit does not offend "traditional notions of fair play and substantial justice."

<u>Id.</u> (quoting <u>Milliken v. Meyer, 311 U.S. 457, 463 (1940)</u>).

[¶ 14] It is important to recall that *International Shoe* was a commercial case, and did not involve marital relationships. Thus, even after the announcement of the minimum contacts test in *International Shoe,* the Court retained confidence in its holding in *Williams* allowing the exercise of jurisdiction by the state of residence of one, but not both, of the parties to a marriage. *See* <u>Estin v. Estin, 334 U.S. 541, 547 (1948)</u>. There, the Court observed the existence of public policy "considerations that have long permitted the State of the matrimonial domicile to change the marital status of the parties by an *ex parte* divorce proceeding, considerations which in the <u>Williams</u> cases we thought were equally applicable to any State in which one spouse had established a bona fide domicile."

What's That?

An ***ex parte divorce*** proceeding is one in which only one party appears in court.

[¶ 15] Nearly thirty years later, the Court considered whether the minimum contacts test should apply to *in rem* actions affecting property, as well as *in personam* actions. <u>Shaffer v. Heitner, 433 U.S. 186, 205–06 (1977)</u>. The Court concluded that "all assertions of state-court jurisdiction must be evaluated according to the standards set forth in *International Shoe* and its progeny," and that, "[t]o the extent that prior decisions are inconsistent with this standard, they are overruled." In reaching this holding, the Court reasoned that "[t]he fiction that an assertion of jurisdiction over property is anything but an assertion of jurisdiction over the owner of the property supports an ancient form without substantial modern justification." The Court again, however, seemed to signal a different approach to marriage and divorce. In a footnote, the Court noted, "[w]e do not suggest that jurisdictional doctrines other than those discussed in text, such as the particularized rules governing adjudications of status, are inconsistent with the standard of fairness."

[¶ 16] Since *Shaffer*, the Court has not considered whether a court enters a valid judgment of divorce when it determines only the marital status of the parties without obtaining personal jurisdiction over a defendant. The Court has held, however, that when child contact and support are at issue, personal jurisdiction is required. *Kulko v. Superior Court of California*, 436 U.S. 84 (1978). There the Court applied the minimum contacts analysis and determined that personal jurisdiction could not be exercised when the plaintiff sought to determine parental rights and support issues and the defendant had only the following contacts with the forum state: (1) he was married in the state, though it was neither party's domicile at that time; (2) he allowed the parties' children to live with their mother in the state for three months a year; and (3) he agreed to one child's decision to move to the forum state to live with her mother after the parties separated.

[¶ 17] In Maine, we have not yet considered whether a defendant must have minimum contacts with the State for a court to enter a divorce judgment when no property, parental rights, or support issues are determined. Since the United States Supreme Court's adoption of the minimum contacts analysis, we have observed that a court may not entertain a divorce action if a *plaintiff* fails to establish her domicile in Maine when the plaintiff's spouse is also not domiciled in Maine. *Belanger v. Belanger*, 240 A.2d 743, 746–47 (Me.1968); *see also* 19–A M.R.S. § 901(1)(A). We have also affirmed the dismissal of one count of a divorce complaint alleging a property interest in a trust for lack of personal jurisdiction. *Stanley v. Stanley*, 271 A.2d 636, 637–38 (Me.1970). We later held that "given sufficient contacts with the forum state, personal jurisdiction can be asserted over a non-resident who has received sufficient notice of a divorce action," such that a court can grant relief beyond a determination of marital status. *DeVlieg v. DeVlieg*, 492 A.2d 605, 607 (Me.1985).

[¶ 18] Thus, although we have inched toward it, we have not reached the question posed today: If a plaintiff establishes his or her domicile in Maine and the defendant has no contacts whatsoever with Maine, but has received adequate notice and an opportunity to be heard, do Maine courts have jurisdiction over the matter sufficient to decide only the issue of the parties' marital status?

[¶ 19] Presented with the same question, other state courts have consistently held that the forum court has jurisdiction to dissolve a domiciliary's marriage without distributing property or determining other rights that would require personal jurisdiction. *See, e.g., Abernathy v. Abernathy,* 267 Ga. 815, 482 S.E.2d 265, 267 (1997) (stating that personal jurisdiction is not required for a Georgia court to grant a divorce because the state only needs jurisdiction over the *res* of the marriage); *Jurado v. Brashear,* 782 So.2d 575, 577 n. 2 (La.2001) (acknowledging the right of a state to prescribe rules governing the marital status of a spouse domiciled in the state, even without personal jurisdiction over the defendant); *Dawson-Austin v. Austin,* 968 S.W.2d 319, 324–25 (Tex.1998), *cert. denied,* 525 U.S. 1067, 119 S.Ct. 795, 142 L.Ed.2d 657 (1999) (holding that jurisdiction to grant a divorce may exist without jurisdiction to adjudicate the parties' property rights); *Poston v. Poston,* 160 Vt. 1, 624 A.2d 853, 855(Vt.), *cert. denied,* 510 U.S. 816 (1993) (recognizing the "divisible divorce" doctrine which permits dissolution of a marriage although the court lacks personal jurisdiction over one party and cannot, therefore, resolve other issues raised in the divorce proceeding).

[¶ 20] As the California Supreme Court has observed, "[e]x parte divorces are a striking exception to the rule that a court must have personal jurisdiction over a party before it may adjudicate his substantial rights." *Whealton v. Whealton, 67 Cal.2d 656, 63 Cal.Rptr. 291, 432 P.2d 979, 982 (1967)*. A state's interest and that of the domiciliary spouse "justify subordinating the conflicting interests of the absent spouse and of any other interested jurisdiction."

Think About It

What are the implications of the **divisible divorce** doctrine mentioned here?

[¶ 21] New York itself affords full faith and credit to a sister state's divorce judgment, entered without personal jurisdiction over the defendant, as long as the judgment determines only the marital status of the parties. *Somma v. Somma,* 19 A.D.3d 477, 797 N.Y.S.2d 523, 524–25 (2005). To the extent that any property issues are addressed without personal jurisdiction over both parties, however, New York will not afford full faith and credit to those portions of the judgment.

[¶ 22] Although some courts have held that personal jurisdiction is unnecessary to dissolve a marriage because such a judgment amounts to an *in rem* judgment, *see, e.g., Schilz v. Superior Court,* 144 Ariz. 65, 695 P.2d 1103, 1106 (1985) (holding that a sister state's dissolution of a marriage was "an action *in rem* over the marriage status"), we decline to follow this line of reasoning. Based on our reading of *Shaffer,* we conclude that the United States Supreme Court has effectively abandoned this approach by concluding that both *in rem* and *in personam* "assertions of state-court jurisdiction must be evaluated according to the standards set forth in *International Shoe* and its progeny."

[¶ 23] We conclude that a judgment dissolving a marriage is not a property, or *in rem,* judgment, even if it has collateral effects on the parties' property rights. * * *

[¶ 24] Rather than being a property interest, marriage is a legal union resulting in a legally recognized status or relationship between the spouses. *See* 19–A M.R.S. § 650 (2005); *Belanger,* 240 A.2d at 746 (recognizing the state's interest in the marriage relation); BLACK'S LAW DICTIONARY 986 (7th ed. 1999). Marriage is a unique institution by which those who are married enter into a legally recognized personal relationship. *See* 19–A M.R.S. § 650; BLACK'S LAW DICTIONARY 986. The Legislature has recognized a number of grounds for dissolving a marriage through divorce. 19–A M.R.S. § 902 (2005). If the parties have "[i]rreconcilable marital differences," for instance, the law of Maine does not require the parties to remain in the marriage relationship. *Id.* § 902(1)(H).

[¶ 25] Because Maine has a unique interest in assuring that its citizens are not compelled to remain in such personal relationships against their wills and because no personal or real property interests would be determined in the proceeding, we conclude that Maine courts have jurisdiction to enter a divorce judgment without personal jurisdiction over the defendant upon compliance with 19–A M.R.S. § 901(1)(A) and all other procedural requirements. We do not, however, alter or re-evaluate the requirement of personal jurisdiction in any other type of litigation affecting the parties' children, financial responsibilities, or property.

[¶ 26] We also caution that when Maine lacks personal jurisdiction over a defendant in a divorce proceeding, Maine courts must exercise their limited jurisdiction with care. Courts must uphold the due process requirements of notice and an opportunity to be heard, *see DeVlieg,* 492 A.2d at 607 (acknowledging that the exercise of long-arm jurisdiction must comport with due process) and must consider a defendant's assertions of forum non conveniens if the exercise of jurisdiction would further a fraud or create an unwarranted burden or inconvenience for the defendant, *see Corning v. Corning,* 563 A.2d 379, 380 (Me.1989) (adopting the provision in the RESTATEMENT (SECOND) OF CONFLICT OF LAWS § 84 at 251 (1971) that allows a state to decline to exercise jurisdiction " 'if it is a seriously inconvenient forum for the trial of the action provided that a more appropriate forum is available to the plaintiff' "). By observing the necessity for basic due process rights of notice and an opportunity to be heard, and by carefully considering the convenience of Maine as a forum, the courts of Maine will continue to safeguard the rights of nonresident defendants while effectuating Maine's strong interest in protecting the rights of Maine residents to obtain judgments dissolving marriages in which they no longer wish to remain.

The entry is:

Judgment affirmed.

Points for Discussion

a. Divorce Jurisdiction

As illustrated by *Von Schack*, a court may have jurisdiction to terminate the marriage, but not to divide marital property, to order the payment of alimony or child support, or to determine parental responsibilities for children of the marriage. See also <u>Miller v. Miller, 861 N.E.2d 393 (Mass. 2007)</u>; <u>Crews v. Crews, 769 P.2d 433 (Alaska 1989)</u>; <u>Poston v. Poston, 624 A.2d 853 (Vt. 1993)</u>, cert. denied <u>510 U.S. 816 (1993)</u>.

b. Residence and Domicile

Statutes in all states define the connection that a petitioner must have with the state in order to obtain a divorce there, typically permitting a petitioner to file a divorce action if he or she has resided in the state for a specified time period. The period ranges from six weeks, see <u>Nev. Rev. Stat. Ann. § 125.020(2) (2018)</u>, to a year or more, see, e.g., <u>N.Y. Dom. Rel. L. § 230</u> (2018). In <u>Sosna v. Iowa 419 U.S. 393 (1975)</u>, the Supreme Court rejected the arguments that durational residence requirements for divorce petitioners violated the Due Process Clause and discriminated unfairly against recent arrivals to the state.

"Residence" and "domicile" are often used interchangeably in this context, but in some jurisdictions domicile is not sufficient if the petitioner resides somewhere else. See, e.g., <u>Midkiff v. Midkiff, 562 S.E.2d 177 (Ga. 2002)</u>; <u>Gutierrez v. Gutierrez, 921 A.2d 153 (Me. 2007)</u>, cf. <u>Caffyn v. Caffyn, 806 N.E.2d 415 (Mass. 2004)</u>.

Global View: International Divorce

The distinction between residence and domicile may be important for U.S. citizens living abroad, or for foreign citizens living in the United States. An expatriate American who decides to file for divorce in the United States may need to return and establish residence in a state. See, e.g., Conrad v. Conrad, 597 S.E.2d 369 (Ga. 2004). Conversely courts regularly allow divorce actions brought by foreign nationals to go forward, based on the strength of the petitioner's contacts with the forum state. Compare Sinha v. Sinha, 834 A.2d 600 (Pa.Super.Ct.2003) with Adoteye v. Adoteye, 527 S.E.2d 453 (Va. Ct. App. 2000).

When the respondent spouse lives in another country, there may be special requirements for service of process. See Ward v. Ludwig, 778 N.E.2d 650 (Ohio Ct. App. 2002), which applied the Hague Convention on the Service Abroad of Judicial and Extrajudicial Documents in Civil or Commercial Matters. See generally Ann Laquer Estin, International Family Law Desk Book 6–9 (2d ed. 2016).

c. Notice and an Opportunity for a Hearing

Even though personal jurisdiction is not required, *Von Schack* emphasizes that the respondent in a divorce action must be given notice and the opportunity to be heard as a matter of constitutional due process. Thus, state statutes and rules governing service of process apply in divorce actions as in other civil suits. Following the rule in Mullane v. Central Hanover Bank & Trust Co., 339 U.S. 306, 314 (1950), this notice must be "reasonably calculated, under all the circumstances, to apprise interested parties of the pendency of the action and afford them an opportunity to present their objections." Substituted service methods may be used if the respondent cannot be served within the state, including mail, or, service by publication or posting if the respondent's whereabouts are unknown. Note that courts have permitted substituted service by electronic means in some circumstances, including both email, see Safadjou v. Mohammadi, 964 N.Y.S.2d 801 (App. Div. 2013), and Facebook, see Baidoo v. Blood-Dzraku, 5 N.Y.S.3d 709 (Sup. Ct. 2015).

d. Same-Sex Marriage and Divorce

States that did not permit same-sex couples to marry reached different conclusions about whether they had jurisdiction to dissolve same-sex marriages entered into elsewhere. Compare O'Darling v. O'Darling, 188 P.3d 137 (Okla. 2008); Chambers v. Ormiston, 935 A.2d 956 (R.I. 2007); and Marriage of J.B. and H.B., 326 S.W.3d 654 (Tex. App. 2010) (concluding that courts did not have jurisdiction) with C.M. v. C.C., 867 N.Y.S.2d 884 (Sup. Ct. 2008); and Christiansen v. Christiansen, 253 P.3d 153 (Wyo. 2011) (assuming jurisdiction over divorce).

Courtney Joslin, in *Modernizing Divorce Jurisdiction: Same-Sex Couples and Minimum Contacts*, 91 Boston U. L. Rev. 1669 (2011), argues that the rule requiring domicile is anomalous and should be discarded in favor of some variation of the jurisdictional rules applied to other types of civil litigation. Would there be drawbacks to a regime that allowed personal jurisdiction over the parties as an alternative basis for divorce jurisdiction?

e. Dissolving Civil Unions and Domestic Partnerships

In those states that established civil union or registered partnership as an alternative to marriage, statutes define the requirements for divorce or dissolution of that status based on the requirements for dissolution of marriage. See, e.g., 750 Ill. Comp. Stat. 75/45 (2018). Couples who enter into a civil union or registered partnership in one state may encounter difficulty in obtaining a dissolution if their status is not recognized in the state where they reside. Courts in some states have concluded that they have subject matter jurisdiction to dissolve an out-of-state civil union based on general equity jurisdiction or comity principles. See, e.g., Hunter v. Rose, 975 N.E.2d 857 (Mass. 2012); Dickerson v. Thompson, 928 N.Y.S.2d 97 (App. Div. 2011); and Neyman v. Buckley, 153 A.3d 1010 (Pa. Super. Ct. 2016) (unpublished). Even when a court can dissolve the civil union or partnership, however, it may not may able to divide property or provide other financial relief. See O'Reilly Morshead v. O'Reilly-Morshead, 19 N.Y.S.3d 689 (Sup. Ct. 2015). To address this difficulty, some state statutes provide that by entering into a civil union or domestic partnership in the state, the partners consent to jurisdiction in that state for an action for dissolution, nullity or legal separation of the civil union or partnership. See generally Edward Stein, *The Topography of Legal Recognition of Same-Sex Relationships*, 50 Fam. Ct. Rev. 181 (2012).

f. Divisible Divorce

The rules applied in *Von Schack* emerged from a line of decisions in the U.S. Supreme Court considering when states are obligated under the Full Faith and Credit Clause of the U.S. Constitution to recognize divorce decrees issued in other states. These decisions established the bases for divorce jurisdiction, because most states did not wish to give divorces that would not be entitled to recognition in other states.

The modern doctrines start with Williams v. State of North Carolina, 317 U.S. 287 (1942) (*Williams I*), and Williams v. State of North Carolina, 325 U.S. 226 (1945) (*Williams II*), which began when two married residents of North Carolina, Mr. Williams and Mrs. Hendrix, went to Las Vegas for several months and obtained Nevada divorces from their respective spouses. Mr. Williams and Mrs. Hendrix married each other in Nevada as soon as the divorces were granted and returned to North Carolina, where local authorities prosecuted them for bigamous cohabitation.

In *Williams I*, the U.S. Supreme Court reversed their convictions, holding that a state court with jurisdiction based on the domicile of the plaintiff may enter a divorce decree entitled to recognition in other states. Based on the finding in the Nevada divorce decrees that Mr. Williams and Mrs. Hendrix were domiciled there, the Supreme Court concluded that Nevada had jurisdiction to grant the divorces and that North Carolina was required to extend full faith and credit to those decrees. This decision overruled Haddock v. Haddock, 201 U.S. 562 (1906), which had concluded that only the state of the "matrimonial domicile" could enter a divorce decree entitled to full faith and credit in other states.

The case was remanded to the North Carolina courts, and prosecutors argued in a second trial that the defendants had never acquired a bona fide domicile in Nevada and that therefore their divorces were invalid. The jury entered another verdict of guilty, which was upheld in *Williams II.* The Court concluded that a state in which a divorce is attacked could reexamine the finding of domicile made by the court that had entered the divorce, and refuse to recognize the divorce if it concluded that neither spouse had been domiciled in the divorcing state.

In two subsequent cases, however, the Supreme Court limited the circumstances in which an out-of-state divorce decree could be challenged. Sherrer v. Sherrer, 334 U.S. 343 (1948), involved a Florida divorce obtained by a wife whose husband participated in the Florida proceeding and did not dispute her assertion of a Florida domicile. When the husband attempted to attack Florida's jurisdiction in a subsequent proceeding in Massachusetts, the Court concluded that he was barred by doctrines of *res judicata* from attacking the Florida's court's finding of domicile because he had participated in the action in Florida. Johnson v. Muelberger, 340 U.S. 581 (1951), extended the doctrine of *Sherrer* to persons who were not parties to the divorce under attack. Based on *Sherrer* and *Johnson*, married couples who were in agreement to end their marriage could relatively easily go to a divorce haven like Nevada, stipulate to the court's jurisdiction, and obtain a decree entitled to recognition in every state.

Although the line of cases beginning with *Williams I* allowed for *ex parte* divorce, the Supreme Court did not take the same approach to actions concerning the financial incidents of divorce, such as alimony or property division. In Estin v. Estin, 334 U.S. 541 (1948), and Vanderbilt v. Vanderbilt, 354 U.S. 416 (1957), the Court refused to require states to give full faith and credit to out-of-state ex parte divorce decrees if that recognition would have financial consequences such as terminating the right to receive alimony. As noted by Justice Douglas's opinion in *Estin*, "The result in this situation is to make the divorce divisible—to give effect to the Nevada decree insofar as it affects marital status and to make it ineffective on the issue of alimony. It accommodates the interests of both Nevada and New York in this broken marriage by restricting each State to the matters of her dominant concern." For a discussion of the line of cases from *Williams I and II* through *Vanderbilt*, see Homer H. Clark, Jr., Domestic Relations § 12.2 (Student ed. 1988), and Ann Laquer Estin, *Family Law Federalism: Divorce and the Constitution*, 16 Wm. & Mary Bill Rts J. 381 (2007).

g. Is There a Right to Divorce?

The line of cases beginning with *Williams I and II* are based on the Full Faith and Credit Clause and focus primarily on the states' interests in regulating marriages and divorces of their citizens. These cases do not address the possibility that the Due Process Clause in the Fourteenth Amendment may

Think About It

In light of the fundamental right to marry identified in cases such as *Griswold* and *Loving*, would it be constitutional for a state to repeal its divorce laws entirely?

protect an individual right to divorce, although there is language in the opinions to suggest that some of the justices thought this was an important consideration. See Ann Laquer Estin, *Family Law Federalism: Divorce and the Constitution*, 16 Wm. & Mary Bill Rts J. 381 (2007).

Two subsequent cases considered more directly whether the Constitution protects the right to divorce. Boddie v. Connecticut, 401 U.S. 371 (1971), held that the states violated the Due Process Clause when they required indigent divorce plaintiffs to pay a filing fee of forty-five dollars, plus fifteen dollars for service of process by the sheriff, plus another forty or fifty dollars if service by publication was necessary. The Court's rationale was that "given the basic position of the marriage relationship in this society's hierarchy of values and the concomitant state monopolization of the means for legally dissolving this relationship, due process does prohibit a State from denying, solely because of inability to pay, access to its courts to individuals who seek judicial dissolution of their marriages." This ruling reflects the unique position of marriage and divorce in the legal system, the right to marry being viewed as a "fundamental right" under the Constitution, and other cases have upheld fee requirements for other types of civil litigation.

Sosna v. Iowa, 419 U.S. 393 (1975), considered a challenge to Iowa's one-year residence requirement for divorce petitioners, including the argument that it discriminated unfairly against recent arrivals to the state and violated the Due Process Clause under the principle in *Boddie*. The Supreme Court rejected this view, concluding that the residence requirement was constitutional.

Kulko v. Superior Court of California in and for the City and County of San Francisco

436 U.S. 84 (1978)

MR. JUSTICE MARSHALL delivered the opinion of the Court.

The issue before us is whether, in this action for child support, the California state courts may exercise *in personam* jurisdiction over a nonresident, nondomiciliary parent of minor children domiciled within the State. For reasons set forth below, we hold that the exercise of such jurisdiction would violate the Due Process Clause of the Fourteenth Amendment.

Go Online

Listen to the <u>oral arguments</u> in *Kulko* at the Oyez Project web site.

I

Appellant Ezra Kulko married appellee Sharon Kulko Horn in 1959, during appellant's three-day stopover in California en route from a military base in Texas to a tour of duty in Korea. At the time of this marriage, both parties were domiciled in and residents of New York State. Immediately following the marriage, Sharon Kulko returned to New York as did appellant after his tour of duty. Their first child, Darwin, was born to the Kulkos in New York in 1961, and a year later their second child, Ilsa, was born, also in New York. The Kulkos and their two children resided together as a family in New York City continuously until March 1972, when the Kulkos separated.

Following the separation, Sharon Kulko moved to San Francisco, California. A written separation agreement was drawn up in New York; in September 1972, Sharon Kulko flew to New York City in order to sign this agreement. The agreement provided, *inter alia,* that the children would remain with their father during the school year but would spend their Christmas, Easter and summer vacations with their mother. While Sharon Kulko waived any claim for her own support or maintenance, Ezra Kulko agreed to pay his wife $3,000 per year in child support for the periods when the children were in her care, custody and control. Immediately after execution of the separation agreement, Sharon Kulko flew to Haiti and procured a divorce there; the divorce decree incorporated the terms of the agreement. She then returned to California, where she remarried and took the name Horn.

The children resided with appellant during the school year and with their mother on vacations, as provided by the separation agreement, until December 1973. At this time, just before Ilsa was to leave New York to spend Christmas vacation with her mother, she told her father that she wanted to remain in California after her vacation. Appellant bought his daughter a one-way plane ticket, and Ilsa left, taking her clothing with her. Ilsa then commenced living in California with her mother during the school year and spending vacations with her father. In January 1976, appellant's other child, Darwin, called his mother from New York and advised her that he wanted to live with her in California. Unbeknownst to appellant, appellee Horn sent a plane ticket to her son, which he used to fly to California where he took up residence with his mother and sister.

Less than one month after Darwin's arrival in California, appellee Horn commenced this action against appellant in the California Superior Court. She sought to establish the Haitian divorce decree as a California judgment; to modify the judgment so as to award her full custody of the children; and to increase appellant's child support obligations. Appellant appeared specially and moved to quash service of the summons on the ground that he was not a resident of California and lacked sufficient "minimum contacts" with the State under *International Shoe Co. v. Washington,* 326 U.S. 310, 316 (1945), to warrant the State's assertion of personal jurisdiction over him.

The trial court summarily denied the motion to quash, and appellant sought review in the California Court of Appeal by petition for a writ of mandate. Appellant did not contest the court's jurisdiction for purposes of the custody determination, but, with respect to the claim for increased support, he renewed his argument that the California courts lacked personal jurisdiction over him. The appellate court affirmed the denial of appellant's motion to quash, reasoning that, by consenting to his children's living in California, appellant had "caused an effect in th[e] state" warranting the exercise of jurisdiction over him. 133 Cal.Rptr. 627, 628 (1976).

The California Supreme Court granted appellant's petition for review, and in a 4–2 decision sustained the rulings of the lower state courts. 19 Cal.3d 514, 138 Cal.Rptr. 586, 564 P.2d 353 (1977). It noted first that the California Code of Civil Procedure demonstrated an intent that the courts of California utilize all bases of *in personam* jurisdiction "not inconsistent with the Constitution." Agreeing with the court below, the Supreme Court stated that, where a nonresident defendant has caused an effect in the State by an act or omission outside the State, personal jurisdiction over the defendant in causes arising from that effect may be exercised whenever "reasonable." * * *

On Ezra Kulko's appeal to this Court, probable jurisdiction was postponed. We have concluded that jurisdiction by appeal does not lie, but, treating the papers as a petition for a writ of certiorari, we hereby grant the petition and reverse the judgment below.

II

The Due Process Clause of the Fourteenth Amendment operates as a limitation on the jurisdiction of state courts to enter judgments affecting rights or interests of nonresident defendants. See *Shaffer v. Heitner*, 433 U.S. 186, 198–200 (1977). It has long been the rule that a valid judgment imposing a personal obligation or duty in favor of the plaintiff may be entered only by a court having jurisdiction over the person of the defendant. *Pennoyer v. Neff*, 95 U.S. 714, 732–733 (1878); *International Shoe Co. v. Washington*, supra, 326 U.S., at 316. The existence of personal jurisdiction, in turn, depends upon the presence of reasonable notice to the defendant that an action has been brought. *Mullane v. Central Hanover Trust Co.*, 339 U.S. 306, 313–314 (1950), and a sufficient connection between the defendant and the forum State as to make it fair to require defense of the action in the forum. *Milliken v. Meyer*, 311 U.S. 457, 463–464 (1940). In this case, appellant does not dispute the adequacy of the notice that he received, but contends that his connection with the State of California is too attenuated, under the standards implicit in the Due Process Clause of the Constitution, to justify imposing upon him the burden and inconvenience of defense in California.

The parties are in agreement that the constitutional standard for determining whether the State may enter a binding judgment against appellant here is that set forth in this Court's opinion in *International Shoe Co. v. Washington*, supra: that a defendant "have certain minimum contacts with [the forum state] such that the maintenance of the suit does not offend 'traditional notions of fair play and substantial justice.'" 326 U.S., at 316, quoting *Milliken v. Meyer, supra, 311 U.S. at 463*. While the interests of the forum State and of the plaintiff in proceeding with the cause in the plaintiff's forum of choice are of course to be considered, see *McGee v. International Life Insurance Co., 355 U.S. 220, 223 (1957)*, an essential criterion in all cases is whether the "quality and nature" of the defendant's activity is such that it is "reasonable" and "fair" to require him to conduct his defense in that State. *International Shoe Co. v. Washington, supra, 326 U.S., at 316–317, 319*.

Like any standard that requires a determination of "reasonableness," the "minimum contacts" test of *International Shoe* is not susceptible of mechanical application; rather, the facts of each case must be weighed to determine whether the requisite "affiliating circumstances" are present. We recognize that this determination is one in which few answers will be written "in black and white. The greys are dominant and even among them the shades are innumerable." *Estin v. Estin,* 334 U.S. 541, 545 (1948). But we believe that the California Supreme Court's application of the minimum contacts test in this case represents an unwarranted extension of *International Shoe* and would, if sustained, sanction a result that is neither fair, just nor reasonable.

A

In reaching its result, the California Supreme Court did not rely on appellant's glancing presence in the State some 13 years before the events that led to this controversy, nor could it have. Appellant has been in California on only two occasions, once in 1959 for a three-day military stopover on his way to Korea, and again in 1960 for a 24-hour stopover on his return from Korean service. To hold such temporary visits to a State a basis for the assertion of *in personam* jurisdiction over unrelated actions arising in the future would make a mockery of the limitations on state jurisdiction imposed by the Fourteenth Amendment. Nor did the California court rely on the fact that appellant was actually married in California on one of his two brief visits. We agree that where two New York domiciliaries, for reasons of convenience, marry in the State of California and thereafter spend their entire married life in New York, the fact of their California marriage by itself cannot support a California court's exercise of jurisdiction over a spouse who remains a New York resident in an action relating to child support.

Finally, in holding that personal jurisdiction existed, the court below carefully disclaimed reliance on the fact that appellant had agreed at the time of separation to allow his children to live with their mother three months a year and that he had sent them to California each year pursuant to this agreement. As was noted below, to find personal jurisdiction in a State on this basis, merely because the mother was residing there, would discourage parents from entering into reasonable visitation agreements. Moreover, it could arbitrarily subject one parent to suit in any State of the Union where the other parent chose to spend time while having custody of their offspring pursuant to a separation agreement. As we have emphasized,

> "The unilateral activity of those who claim some relationship with a non-resident defendant cannot satisfy the requirement of contact with the forum State. * * * [I]t is essential in each case that there be some act by which the defendant purposefully avails [him]self of the privilege of conducting activities within the forum State * * *." *Hanson v. Denckla, supra,* 357 U.S., at 253.

The "purposeful act" that the California Supreme Court believed did warrant the exercise of personal jurisdiction over appellant in California was his "actively and fully consent[ing] to Ilsa living in California for the school year * * * and * * * sen[ding] her to California for that purpose." We cannot accept the proposition that appellant's acquiescence in Ilsa's desire to live with her mother conferred jurisdiction over appellant in the California courts in this action. A father who agrees, in the interests of family harmony and his children's preferences, to allow them to spend more time in California than was required under a separation agreement can hardly be said to have "purposefully availed himself" of the "benefits and protection" of California's laws. See *Shaffer v. Heitner*, supra, 433 U.S., at 216.[7]

Nor can we agree with the assertion of the court below that the exercise of *in personam* jurisdiction here was warranted by the financial benefit appellant derived from his daughter's presence in California for nine months of the year. This argument rests on the premise that, while appellant's liability for support payments remained unchanged, his yearly expenses for supporting the child in New York decreased. But this circumstance, even if true, does not support California's assertion of jurisdiction here. Any diminution in appellant's household costs resulted, not from the child's presence in California, but rather from her absence from appellant's home. Moreover, an action by appellee Horn to increase support payments could now be brought, and could have been brought when Ilsa first moved to California, in the State of New York; a New York court would clearly have personal jurisdiction over appellant and, if a judgment were entered by a New York court increasing appellant's child support obligations, it could properly be enforced against him in both New York and California.[9] Any ultimate financial advantage to appellant thus results not from the child's presence in California but from appellee's failure earlier to seek an increase in payments under the separation agreement. The argument below to the contrary, in our view, confuses the question of appellant's liability with that of the proper forum in which to determine that liability.

B

In light of our conclusion that appellant did not purposefully derive benefit from any activities relating to the State of California, it is apparent that the Califor-

---

[7] The court below stated that the presence in California of appellant's daughter gave appellant the benefit of California's "police and fire protection, its school system, its hospital services, its recreational facilities, its libraries and museums * * *." But, in the circumstances presented here, these services provided by the State were essentially benefits to the child, not the father, and in any event were not benefits that appellant purposefully sought for himself.

[9] A final judgment entered by a New York court having jurisdiction over the defendant's person and over the subject matter of the lawsuit would be entitled to Full Faith and Credit in any State. See New York ex rel. Halvey v. Halvey, 330 U.S. 610, 614 (1947). See also Sosna v. Iowa, 419 U.S. 393, 407 (1975).

nia Supreme Court's reliance on appellant's having caused an "effect" in California was misplaced. This "effects" test is derived from the American Law Institute's Restatement (Second) of Conflicts § 37 (1971), which provides:

> "A state has power to exercise judicial jurisdiction over an individual who causes effects in the state by an act done elsewhere with respect to any cause of action arising from these effects unless the nature of the effects and of the individual's relationship to the state make the exercise of such jurisdiction unreasonable."[11]

While this provision is not binding on this Court, it does not in any event support the decision below. As is apparent from the examples accompanying § 37 in the Restatement, this section was intended to reach wrongful activity outside of the State causing injury within the State, see, *e.g.*, Comment *a* (shooting bullet from one State into another), or commercial activity affecting state residents. Even in such situations, moreover, the Restatement recognizes that there might be circumstances that would render "unreasonable" the assertion of jurisdiction over the nonresident defendant.

The circumstances in this case clearly render "unreasonable" California's assertion of personal jurisdiction. There is no claim that appellant has visited physical injury on either property or persons within the State of California. C.f. *Hess v. Pawloski, 274 U.S. 352 (1927)*. The cause of action herein asserted arises, not from the defendant's commercial transactions in interstate commerce, but rather from his personal, domestic relations. It thus cannot be said that appellant has sought a commercial benefit from solicitation of business from a resident of California that could reasonably render him liable to suit in state court; appellant's activities cannot fairly be analogized to an insurer's sending an insurance contract and premium notices into the State to an insured resident of the State. C.f. *McGee v. International Life Ins. Co.* Furthermore, the controversy between the parties arises from a separation that occurred in the State of New York; appellee Horn seeks modification of a contract that was negotiated in New York and that she flew to New York to sign. As in *Hanson v. Denckla, 357 U.S., at 252*, the instant action involves an agreement that was entered into with virtually no connection with the forum State.

Finally, basic considerations of fairness point decisively in favor of appellant's State of domicile as the proper forum for adjudication of this case, whatever the merits of appellee's underlying claim. It is appellant who has remained in the State of the marital domicile, whereas it is appellee who has moved across the continent. Cf. *May v. Anderson, 345 U.S. 528, 534–535, n. 8 (1953)*. Appellant has at all times resided in New York State, and, until the separation and appellee's move to California, his entire family resided there as well. As noted above, appel-

---

[11] Section 37 of the Restatement has effectively been incorporated into California law. See Judicial Council Comment (9) to California Code Civ.Proc. § 410.10.

lant did no more than acquiesce in the stated preference of one of his children to live with her mother in California. This single act is surely not one that a reasonable parent would expect to result in the substantial financial burden and personal strain of litigating a child-support suit in a forum 3,000 miles away, and we therefore see no basis on which it can be said that appellant could reasonably have anticipated being "haled before a [California] court," *Shaffer v. Heitner*, 433 U.S., at 216. To make jurisdiction in a case such as this turn on whether appellant bought his daughter her ticket or instead unsuccessfully sought to prevent her departure would impose an unreasonable burden on family relations, and one wholly unjustified by the "quality and nature" of appellant's activities in or relating to the State of California. *International Shoe Co. v. Washington*, 326 U.S., at 319.

III

In seeking to justify the burden that would be imposed on appellant were the exercise of *in personam* jurisdiction in California sustained, appellee argues that California has substantial interests in protecting the welfare of its minor residents and in promoting to the fullest extent possible a healthy and supportive family environment in which the children of the State are to be raised. These interests are unquestionably important. But while the presence of the children and one parent in California arguably might favor application of California law in a lawsuit in New York, the fact that California may be the " 'center of gravity' " for choice of law purposes does not mean that California has personal jurisdiction over the defendant. And California has not attempted to assert any particularized interest in trying such cases in its courts by, *e.g.*, enacting a special jurisdictional statute.

California's legitimate interest in ensuring the support of children resident in California without unduly disrupting the children's lives, moreover, is already being served by the State's participation in the Uniform Reciprocal Enforcement of Support Act of 1968. This statute provides a mechanism for communication between court systems in different States, in order to facilitate the procurement and enforcement of child-support decrees where the dependent children reside in a State that cannot obtain personal jurisdiction over the defendant. California's version of the Act essentially permits a California resident claiming support from a nonresident to file a petition in California and have its merits adjudicated in the State of the alleged obligor's residence, without either party having to leave his or her own State. Cal.Code Civ.Proc. § 1650 et seq. New York State is a signatory to a similar act. Thus, not only may plaintiff-appellee here vindicate her claimed right to additional child support from her former husband in a New York court, but the uniform acts will facilitate both her prosecution of a claim for additional support and collection of any support payments found to be owed by appellant.[15]

It cannot be disputed that California has substantial interests in protecting resident children and in facilitating child-support actions on behalf of those children. But these interests simply do not make California a "fair forum," <u>Shaffer v. Heitner, supra, 433 U.S., at 215</u>, in which to require appellant, who derives no personal or commercial benefit from his child's presence in California and who lacks any other relevant contact with the State, either to defend a child-support suit or to suffer liability by default.

Take Note

The Uniform Reciprocal Enforcement of Support Act, cited here, has been replaced by the Uniform Interstate Family Support Act (UIFSA), discussed in Chapter 7.

IV

We therefore believe that the state courts in the instant case failed to heed our admonition that "the flexible standard of *International Shoe*" does not "herald[ ] the eventual demise of all restrictions on the personal jurisdiction of state courts." <u>Hanson v. Denckla, 357 U.S., at 251, 78 S.Ct., at 1238</u>. In <u>McGee v. International Life Insurance Co.</u>, we commented on the extension of *in personam* jurisdiction under evolving standards of due process, explaining that this trend was in large part "attributable to the * * * increasing nationalization of commerce * * * [accompanied by] modern transportation and communication [that] have made it much less burdensome for a party sued to defend himself in a State where he engages in economic activity." <u>355 U.S., at 222–223</u>. But the mere act of sending a child to California to live with her mother is not a commercial act and connotes no intent to obtain nor expectancy of receiving a corresponding benefit in the State that would make fair the assertion of that State's judicial jurisdiction.

Justices Brennan, White and Powell dissented in *Kulko* on the ground that the "appellant's connection with the State of California was not too attenuated under the standards of reasonableness and fairness implicit in the Due Process Clause, to require him to conduct his defense in the California courts."

---

[15]   Thus, it cannot here be concluded, as it was in <u>McGee v. International Life Insurance Co., 355 U.S., 220 at 223–224</u>, with respect to actions on insurance contracts, that resident plaintiffs would be at a "severe disadvantage" if in personam jurisdiction over out-of-state defendants were sometimes unavailable.

Accordingly, we conclude that the appellant's motion to quash service, on the ground of lack of personal jurisdiction, was erroneously denied by the California courts. The judgment of the California Supreme Court is, therefore,

Reversed.

Points for Discussion

a. Minimum Contacts

The Supreme Court in *Kulko*, quoting from earlier cases, says that in order to be subject to personal jurisdiction a defendant must "have certain minimum contacts with the [forum state] such that the maintenance of the suit does not offend 'traditional notions of fair play and substantial justice.' " What standards does the case offer for determining what fair play and substantial justice require in a child support proceeding? How do these standards compare to those applied in other types of cases? What does it mean to "conduct activities" in a particular state for purposes of a family law proceeding?

b. Personal Jurisdiction

As noted above, the three chief aspects of a divorce action rest on three different jurisdictional principles. Based on *Kulko*, courts agree that full personal jurisdiction is necessary to determine financial matters, including child support, alimony and equitable division of property. A judgment for alimony, child support or a division of property entered without personal jurisdiction may be attacked as a violation of the Due Process Clause, and will not be entitled to the protection of the Full Faith and Credit Clause. See, e.g., Baldwin v. Baldwin,170 P.2d 670 (Cal. 1946); Overby v. Overby, 457 S.W.2d 851 (Tenn. 1970). The Supreme Court seemed to require full personal jurisdiction in litigation over child custody in May v. Anderson, 345 U.S. 528 (1953), but this ruling has been largely disregarded, as discussed in Chapter 7.

c. Long-Arm Statutes

Some states have enacted long-arm statutes explicitly applicable to matrimonial suits. See, for example, 735 Ill. Comp. Stat. Ann. § 5/2–209 (2018), providing that in actions for divorce or legal separation a person submits to the courts' jurisdiction either by maintaining a matrimonial domicile in the state, or by committing any act within the state giving rise to the cause of action. Other states have long-arm statutes, like the California statute noted in *Kulko*, providing that the state may exercise personal jurisdiction over the defendant "upon any basis not inconsistent with the Constitution of this state or of the United States."

When a state's long-arm statute has no provision specifically addressed to divorce or support proceedings, courts have applied general long-arm provisions; see <u>Wright v. Wright, 276 A.2d 878 (N.J. Super. Ct. 1971)</u>; <u>Mizner v. Mizner, 439 P.2d 679 (Nev. 1968)</u>, cert. denied <u>393 U.S. 847 (1968)</u>. When there is no long-arm statute at all, jurisdiction was based solely minimum contacts and the Due Process Clause in <u>Stucky v. Stucky, 185 N.W.2d 656 (Neb. 1971)</u>.

Make the Connection

See Chapter 7 for coverage of UIFSA and jurisdictional issues in parentage and child support proceedings.

Kulko cites the Uniform Reciprocal Enforcement of Support Act (URESA), which has been replaced by the <u>Uniform Interstate Family Support Act (2008) (UIFSA)</u>, 9 U.L.A. (Part IB) 253 (Supp. 2018). UIFSA governs jurisdiction and enforcement of judgments in both spousal support and child support cases. All of the states have enacted UIFSA, including its long-arm provisions in <u>§ 201</u>. Under § 201(a)(4), a state court may exercise personal jurisdiction to determine parentage and establish a child support order over an individual who engaged in sexual intercourse in the state if the child may have been conceived by that act. Does this meet the constitutional requirements set out in *Kulko*? See also <u>Uniform Parentage Act (2017) § 604</u>, 9B U.L.A. (Supp. 2018).

d. Tag Jurisdiction

In <u>Burnham v. Superior Court of California, 495 U.S. 604 (1990)</u>, the Supreme Court held that minimum contacts are not necessary to support personal jurisdiction over a nonresident who is served with process while temporarily in the state, even in a suit unrelated to his activities in the state. *Burnham* arose from a divorce case similar to *Kulko*: Dennis and Francie Burnham lived with their children in New Jersey, and when they separated Francie moved to California with the children and filed for divorce. Francie had Dennis served when he came to California on a business trip and visited the children. Dennis Burnham challenged the assertion of jurisdiction in California, on the basis that his only contacts with the state were a few short visits to conduct business and see his children, but the Supreme Court reaffirmed the traditional view that service of process within the forum state was a constitutionally sufficient basis for assertion of jurisdiction over a nonresident. *Burnham* is criticized in Peter Hay, <u>*Transient Jurisdiction, Especially Over International Defendants: Critical Comments on* Burnham v. Superior Court of California, 1990 U. Ill. L. Rev. 593</u>.

e. In Rem and Quasi in Rem Jurisdiction

Since the Supreme Court's decision in <u>Shaffer v. Heitner, 433 U.S. 186 (1977)</u>, abolishing *quasi in rem* jurisdiction, the presence of the defendant's property in the state, without other contacts with the state, has not been treated as a sufficient basis to confer jurisdiction on the state's courts to enter a judgment against the owner of the property, even a judgment limited to the property. *Shaffer* does state that when claims to the property itself are the source of the lawsuit, it would be "unusual" for the state not to have jurisdiction. This suggests that the presence of marital property in a state might be sufficient to confer jurisdiction if the only claims involved that property.

Abernathy v. Abernathy, 482 S.E.2d 265 (Ga. 1997) wrestled with these issues in the case of a husband and wife who were married in Florida and lived together in Louisiana throughout their marriage. After the parties separated, the husband moved to Georgia and commenced a divorce proceeding, requesting that a divorce decree be granted and that all marital property located in Georgia be awarded to him. The court concluded it had jurisdiction over the marriage under cases such as Williams v. North Carolina, and concluded that it had *in rem* jurisdiction over all marital property located in Georgia. Two dissenting justices argued that this was more properly considered a *quasi in rem* proceeding, pointing out that the that the wife had no contacts at all with the state and the only marital property in Georgia was brought or acquired there by the husband after the separation.

Problem 6-3

(a) On the facts of *Kulko*, assume that the father failed to make the child support payments provided for in the original divorce decree covering periods when the children were with their mother in California. If a substantial arrearage accumulated, and the mother sued in California to collect the past due amount, would there be any basis for jurisdiction in California? (See Boyer v. Boyer, 383 N.E.2d 223 (Ill. 1978).)

(b) On the facts of *Kulko*, what should be the result if the father had visited the children in California once a year for three years, staying in the state about two weeks at each visit? If the mother brought suit in California, asking the court to increase child support, would the father's contacts with the state be sufficient to support jurisdiction? (See In Interest of S.A.V., 837 S.W.2d 80 (Tex.1992).)

(c) In a case such as *Burnham*, would it matter if the wife had asked the husband to come to California to see the children, and he had come solely for that purpose? Is this consistent with the policy arguments in *Kulko*? What if the husband had come to California solely to attend to business matters, having nothing to do with the children, and was served while in the state? What if he came to California to spend a week skiing at Lake Tahoe?

Problem 6-4

Lela and Roger were married in North Carolina and lived together in various countries during their marriage, including Egypt, Korea, the Philippines, India, Indonesia, Australia and Thailand. Each of these moves was determined by Roger's employment. During this time, they held North Carolina driver's licenses and maintained bank and investment accounts there. When they separated, Lela returned to North Carolina and filed for divorce. Roger was served in Bangkok, Thailand, and filed a motion to dismiss for lack of personal jurisdiction. Can the North Carolina court proceed with Lela's case? (See Sherlock v. Sherlock, 545 S.E.2d 757 (N.C. Ct. App. 2001).)

Client Counseling: Divorce Jurisdiction

A new client comes to you for representation in a divorce. She has recently separated from her husband and returned with her two children to live with her parents in this state. She tells you that she and her husband were married here ten years ago, but he has never lived here. She would like to get divorced, and needs financial support from her husband as well. What advice can you give her?

Federal Jurisdiction in Divorce and Family Law Disputes

Nothing in the text of the U.S. Constitution or federal jurisdictional statutes prevents parties who are citizens of different states from litigating divorce or other family law matters in federal courts pursuant to the courts' diversity jurisdiction under 28 U.S.C. § 1332 (2018). The federal courts, however, have developed a "domestic relations exception" to their diversity jurisdiction that was elaborated in early opinions, including Barber v. Barber, 62 U.S. (21 How.) 582 (1859); Simms v. Simms, 175 U.S. 162 (1899); and De La Rama v. De La Rama, 201 U.S. 303 (1906).

In Ankenbrandt v. Richards, 504 U.S. 689 (1992), the Supreme Court reaffirmed the domestic relations exception, but concluded that it did not apply in that case, which was a tort suit for damages brought by a mother against a father and his female companion for physical and sexual abuse of their daughters. The Court based the exception on words in the Judiciary Act of 1789 to the effect that the circuit courts had diversity jurisdiction over suits of a civil nature "at common law or in equity," pointing out that divorce and alimony proceedings fell historically within the jurisdiction of the English ecclesiastical courts and were neither suits in law nor equity. The Court bolstered its reading of the statute by noting that Congress had accepted this construction over many years. Under *Ankenbrandt,* the domestic relations exception is limited to suits for divorce, alimony decrees and child custody orders. Federal courts hear diversity actions for enforcement of spousal or child support decrees, so long as the claim is exclusively one for money damages. See also, e.g., Chevalier v. Barnhart, 803 F.3d 789 (6th Cir. 2015) (holding that domestic relations exception did not extend to claims for breach of contract and unjust enrichment).

The Supreme Court has also held that the federal habeas corpus statute may not be used to raise child custody disputes. See Lehman v. Lycoming County Children's Services Agency, 458 U.S. 502 (1982). When federal jurisdiction is asserted on the basis of a federal question, however, it is generally held that the domestic relations exception does not apply. Hooks v. Hooks, 771 F.2d 935 (6th Cir. 1985); Rubin v. Smith, 817 F.Supp. 987 (D.N.H. 1993).

———————

Dart v. Dart

597 N.W.2d 82 (Mich. 1999)

MARILYN J. KELLY, J.

We granted leave to determine whether the parties' English divorce judgment is entitled to full faith and credit under the principle of comity, and whether res judicata bars the action.

We hold that principles of comity and res judicata mandate that the Darts' foreign divorce judgment be enforced. The English court decided the property distribution issue on the merits, and no evidence was presented showing that plaintiff Katina Dart was denied due process. We affirm the decision of the Court of Appeals.

I. Facts

Plaintiff and defendant were married in 1980 and were residents of Okemos, Michigan until 1993, when they moved to England. The couple owned a large house in Okemos, situated on thirty-nine acres of land, valued at $1,500,000. The parties had two children. The defendant is the son of the founder of Dart Container Corporation, one of the largest family-controlled businesses in the United States. The defendant's earned income for the years 1992, 1993, and 1994, was

$313,009, $563,917, and $281,548, respectively. Between 1990 and 1993, the family's annual expenditures ranged from $300,000 to $600,000. The move to England made possible a September 1993 transfer of several hundred million dollars to the defendant from family trusts.

In 1974, before the marriage, the defendant's father established a trust for the benefit of defendant and his brother. For the transfer to occur, defendant had to renounce his United States citizenship and relocate outside the United States. The plaintiff refused to renounce her United States citizenship, and she also refused to renounce the citizenship of the children. She claims that, despite the relocation to London, England, she has always considered herself a resident and domiciliary of Okemos, Michigan.

In 1993, the parties jointly purchased a house near London for £2.75 million, and began renovations that took over a year to complete and cost another £3.5 million. They enrolled the children in the American School of London. Between 1993 and 1995, plaintiff asserts that she and the children made regular trips to Michigan for holidays, medical care, vacations, haircuts and other activities. Also, she maintained her Michigan driver's license and voted regularly in Michigan elections.

In September 1993, defendant received his distribution from the family trust which had a present, net value of £274 million (approximately $500,000,000). In the fall of 1994, plaintiff announced that she wanted a divorce. She revealed that what she had previously described to the defendant as a "one night stand" in 1989 had actually been a regular, adulterous affair with a man in Greece. The plaintiff asserted that she and defendant agreed to postpone the divorce action until she and the children returned to Michigan after the 1994–95 school year.

Despite the putative agreement, defendant filed for divorce in England on February 3, 1995. Plaintiff was served with process at the parties' home the following day. She contacted her American attorneys, and they filed a similar suit on her behalf in Michigan in the Ingham Circuit Court four days later. The parties remained in England until a consent order was entered in the English court on June 9, 1995, allowing plaintiff to return with the children to Michigan.

On March 21, 1995, in the Ingham Circuit Court, defendant moved for summary disposition pursuant to MCR 2.116(C)(4) and (6) on the bases of lack of jurisdiction and pendency of a prior proceeding. Following a hearing, the circuit court determined that jurisdiction was proper in Michigan and assumed jurisdiction over the children and the divorce proceeding. The court reserved for future decision the issue of jurisdiction over the parties' property.

Plaintiff also brought a jurisdictional challenge. The English court ruled on June 13, 1995, that jurisdiction was proper in England. Defendant then asked the Ingham Circuit Court to defer jurisdiction to the English court on the basis of *forum non conveniens.* After a hearing on August 7, 1995, the circuit court denied the motion and assumed jurisdiction over the parties' property.

Both suits proceeded. On October 27, 1995, a "decree absolute" of divorce was entered in the English court. This was followed by a seven-day trial in March 1996 in which plaintiff filed an answer claiming the "full range of financial ancillary relief available to a wife under the Matrimonial Causes Act [of] 1973."

Both sides presented expert witnesses who testified regarding the parties' assets and plaintiff's reasonable needs. On March 21, 1996, the English court issued a lengthy opinion in which it determined defendant's total net worth to be "about £400 million."

The court ruled that the reasonable needs or requirements of plaintiff, in light of her predivorce lifestyle and habits and the available assets, entitled her to £300,000 ($450,000) a year for life. However, the court held that, "In seeking to achieve justice [the court is] not limited to the reasonable annual expenditure of the wife. . .or to such other matters. . .described as constituting her 'reasonable requirements.' "

The court awarded the plaintiff a lump sum of £9 million ($13,500,000), the amount it felt necessary to achieve an equitable distribution. The plaintiff was also awarded the house in Okemos, Michigan, and its contents, that the parties agreed were worth approximately $1.5 million. She was awarded four paintings and her jewelry. The court also set child support in the amount of $95,400 a year for both children.

Defendant was awarded four automobiles and the balance of the marital estate. The English court expressly found that plaintiff was not entitled to a substantial share of defendant's family wealth. It was not a product of the marriage and had not been generated by the efforts of either party.

On March 29, 1996, defendant moved to stay or dismiss the Ingham Circuit Court proceedings, arguing that the English judgment was entitled to enforcement under the principle of comity and under the Uniform Foreign Money-Judgments Recognition Act, M.C.L. § 691.1151 *et seq.*; M.S.A. § 27.955(1) *et seq.* At the hearing on April 8, 1996, he urged, also, that the present action was barred by res judicata.

The circuit court judge denied the motion, finding that the English judgment was not entitled to recognition under the UFMJRA or the principle of comity. He reasoned that the English system of law was repugnant to the public policy of Michigan, and the English decision violated plaintiff's "right to have a fair and equitable distribution of property. . . ."

On appeal, in a per curium opinion, the Court of Appeals reversed, concluding that the "entire judgment, including the property division as well as the child support and lump-sum awards," should be enforced under the UFMJRA. 224 Mich.App. 146, 150, 568 N.W.2d 353 (1997).

* * *

The Court of Appeals also concluded that comity mandated that the English judgment be respected. Plaintiff had a fair hearing on the merits at which she was present, represented by counsel, and actively participated. Thus, she was accorded due process.

Finally, the Court of Appeals reasoned that res judicata barred the case from being relitigated because the English court had considered the property, alimony, and child support claims and issued a final order. The English court did not consider child custody or visitation. These issues were within the purview of the Ingham Circuit Court under the Uniform Child Custody Jurisdiction Act, M.C.L. § 600.653; M.S.A. § 27A.653.

When plaintiff appealed, we granted leave on October 12, 1998.

II. Analysis

The Court of Appeals correctly held that comity dictated that the judgment should be enforced because the plaintiff was accorded due process. Since the English judgment adjudicated the property issue, the plaintiff is barred from relitigating that issue under res judicata.

> Comity is defined as the recognition which one nation allows within its territory to the legislative, executive, or judicial acts of another nation, having due regard both to international duty and convenience and to the rights of its own citizens or of other persons who are under the protection of its laws. [*Bang v. Park,* 116 Mich.App. 34, 39, 321 N.W.2d 831 (1982), *citing* 16 Am.Jur.2d, Conflict of Laws, § 10, pp. 27–29 (currently § 15, pp. 25–26).]

Comity mandates that this foreign judgment be given force and effect. The seminal United States Supreme Court case of *Hilton v. Guyot,*[2] set forth the factors that

---

2   159 U.S. 113, 202–203, 16 S.Ct. 139, 40 L.Ed. 95 (1895).

the federal courts use in recognizing and giving full effect to the judgment of foreign countries under comity:

> Where there has been opportunity for a full and fair trial abroad before a court of competent jurisdiction, conducting the trial upon regular proceedings, after due citation or voluntary appearance of the defendant, and under a system of jurisprudence likely to secure an impartial administration of justice between the citizens of its own country and those of other countries, and there is nothing to show either prejudice in the court or in the system of laws under which it was sitting, or fraud in procuring the judgment, or any other special reason why the comity of this nation should not allow it full effect, the merits of the case should not, in an action brought in this country upon the judgment, be tried afresh, as on a new trial or an appeal, upon the mere assertion of the party that the judgment was erroneous in law or in fact.

Michigan courts have used the *Hilton* criteria. In *Growe v. Growe*,[3] the appellee began a domestic relations action in Ontario. A judgment for alimony and custody of the parties' minor children was rendered by the Supreme Court of Ontario. Later, the defendant left Canada, obtained a Nevada divorce, and began living in Wayne County, Michigan. The appellee commenced suit in Wayne Circuit Court seeking support arrearages. The trial court dismissed the appellee's action, and the Court of Appeals, in reviewing the appellee's request for relief, noted:

> Faced as we are here with a judgment from a court of competent jurisdiction which lies but the breadth of a river from the instant court, closer, indeed, than most of the remaining 49 States, and a court which draws its concepts of law from the same roots as ours, comity supplies a rational and well-founded reason for affording relief to this plaintiff. Any appellate court faced with the compelling elements this Court finds before it would be derelict if it did not examine minutely this burgeoning concept of jurisprudence.

In upholding the Ontario judgment under the principle of comity, the Court of Appeals held:

> A review of the judgment will indicate whether or not the basic rudiments of due process were followed, whether the parties were present in court, whether a hearing on the merits was had.

Here, both parties participated and were represented by counsel in the English court proceedings. Plaintiff initially challenged jurisdiction in the English court. She asserted that defendant had not been "habitually" a resident of England for twelve months. Justice Johnson of the Family Division of the High Court of Justice ruled in defendant's favor, concluding that England was his main home and that he intended to stay there.

---

3   2 Mich.App. 25, 138 N.W.2d 537 (1965).

* * *

The English court heard evidence pertaining to the value of the Dart Container Corporation, as well as defendant's salary and other real and personal property. It heard evidence regarding plaintiff's nonmonetary contributions to the marriage as well. It considered the home in Michigan, paintings, jewelry, and cars.

The parties agree that the factors that the English courts examine when dividing property are substantially the same as those used in Michigan. In *Sparks v. Sparks, supra,* this Court set forth the appropriate factors to consider in the division of marital property:

> (1) duration of the marriage, (2) contributions of the parties to the marital estate, (3) age of the parties, (4) health of the parties, (5) life status of the parties, (6) necessities and circumstances of the parties, (7) earning abilities of the parties, (8) past relations and conduct of the parties, and (9) general principles of equity. [*Id.* at 159–160, 485 N.W.2d 893.]

Section 25 of the Matrimonial Causes Act[4] requires that an English court consider nearly identical factors in dividing marital property.

Plaintiff argues that English courts apply a different rationale in cases involving large assets. In her brief, she asserts that the English court principally examined her financial needs to determine the appropriate award, not the marital assets.

In *Preston v. Preston,*[5] the English court announced a formula to be applied in cases in which the available resources are large. *Preston* established that there is a maximum sum to be awarded. This so-called "*Preston* ceiling" limits the award to an amount that satisfies the court's estimation of a wife's needs for support. Lord Justice Ormrod wrote in *Preston:*

> I think that on the true construction of § 25 there does come a point, in cases where the available resources are very large,. . .when the amount required to fulfill its terms "levels off," and redistribution of capital as such, in some unspecified ratio begins, which is outside the section.

Had the English court actually used this formulation to divide the parties' marital assets, we might agree with plaintiff that she was denied due process. However, the English court did not use the *Preston* ceiling. Instead, it determined that the defendant's holdings and trust income were not marital property. Justice Johnson explained:

> [I]f you had a case where the husband and wife together built up a vast property empire, I see no reason why the wife's contribution should not entitle her to 50%. There is said to be a distinction between the wife

---
[4]   English Matrimonial Causes Act, 1973, § 25.

[5]   1981 2 FLR 331.

whose contribution was child care and the wife who actually worked in the business, doing the books or whatever, it was. If Mr. and Mrs. Dart had started with nothing and in a back street somewhere in Detroit they had started making plastic objects and over the period of 20 or 30 years they had [ended] up with an empire worth £1,000 million, I would see every reason for Mrs. Dart having half of it. Personally, I do not have any difficulty with that. Whether the English law permits it or not is another matter, but that is not this case.

Normally, property received by a married party as an inheritance, but kept separate from marital property, is deemed to be separate property not subject to distribution. *Lee v. Lee*, 191 Mich.App. 73, 477 N.W.2d 429 (1991). The trust income from the Dart Container Corporation was never marital property. Although the defendant worked for Dart Container Corporation during the marriage, his compensation was the salary and bonuses that he earned. His cumulative salary and bonuses over the course of the marriage were far less than the $14.5 million property award that plaintiff received.

The Dart fortune and defendant's interest in it exist independently of defendant's workplace activities or the marriage partnership.[6]

* * *

Thus, the English court's treatment of defendant's interests in the Dart family trusts and assets as separate property, rather than marital assets, did not violate plaintiff's right to due process.

Moreover, plaintiff's assertion that the English court failed to consider marital property is flawed. The English judgment awarded her the $1.5 million house in Okemos, some paintings, and a car. It also awarded child support in the amount of more than $90,000 a year. Certainly, the English court could not have divided these marital assets had there been no discovery. We find that the plaintiff was accorded due process in the English proceeding.

Consequently, res judicata bars the plaintiff from relitigating the property distribution issue. The English court decided this issue on the merits. Res judicata bars a subsequent action between the same parties when the evidence or essential facts are identical. *Eaton Co. Bd. of Co. Rd. Comm'rs v. Schultz*, 205 Mich.App. 371, 375, 521 N.W.2d 847 (1994). A second action is barred when (1) the first action was decided on the merits, (2) the matter contested in the second action was or could have been resolved in the first, and (3) both actions involve the same parties or their privies.

---

[6]   We recognize that, in certain situations, a spouse's separate assets, or the appreciation in their value during the marriage, may be included in the marital estate.

Michigan courts have broadly applied the doctrine of res judicata. They have barred, not only claims already litigated, but every claim arising from the same transaction that the parties, exercising reasonable diligence, could have raised but did not. *Gose v. Monroe Auto Equipment Co.*, 409 Mich. 147, 160–163, 294 N.W.2d 165 (1980); *Sprague v. Buhagiar*, 213 Mich.App. 310, 313, 539 N.W.2d 587 (1995).

Here, the Michigan divorce action involves the same parties with the same assets and the same children as the English action. We have already determined under our comity analysis that the English judgment is valid. The fact that it does not address custody or visitation is not fatal to its preclusive effect with respect to property distribution. The Ingham Circuit Court has jurisdiction over the questions of custody and visitation, pursuant to the Uniform Child Custody Jurisdiction Act, *supra*. See *Braden v. Braden*, 217 Mich.App. 331, 338–339, 551 N.W.2d 467 (1996). Accordingly, res judicata bars relitigation of the present action.

III. Conclusion

We affirm the Court of Appeals decision to give deference to the English divorce judgment under the principle of comity. It was evident from the judgment rendered in England that plaintiff had a fair hearing on the merits, that she was present, represented by counsel, and actively participated. Thus, the present action is barred by res judicata.

WEAVER, C.J., and TAYLOR, CORRIGAN, and YOUNG, JJ., concur with MARILYN J. KELLY, J.

MICHAEL F. CAVANAGH, J. (*dissenting*).

I must part company with the majority on the deference shown to the English Court's judgment. While I agree with Justice Kelly that the English Court did not apply the *Preston*[1] "ceiling" rule in this case, but rather steered away from such a ruling to find the bulk of defendant's assets to be nonmarital property, I am unpersuaded that such a finding removes the English decision from the looming shadow of *Preston*.

As even the majority tacitly admits, the application of the *Preston* rule in a case such as this (or in any case for that matter) would likely raise serious due process concerns. The mere existence of such a rule, and the apparent statutory basis for the rule cited by Lord Justice Ormrod in adopting it,[2] suggests that, at least in cases in which substantial assets are involved, the goals of the English judicial system in marital dissolution cases differ substantially from the framework of

---

[1]   *Preston v. Preston*, 1981 2 FLR 331.

[2]   See *Preston* at 339.

our state, as reviewed by us in *Sparks*.[3] Where plaintiff was in the exact position necessary for her to suffer the ill effects not only of the *Preston* rule, but also the underlying statutory and judicial rationales for it, I cannot say, particularly in view of the asset division undertaken by the English Court, that she escaped unscathed by the effects of the adverse predispositions demonstrated.

In reaching this conclusion, it is necessary to consider, given the majority's reliance on the determination of the trust assets as nonmarital in nature, what sort of effect would have occurred had Justice Johnson of the English Court found the entire amount of disputed property (including the trust assets) to consist of marital assets. While the justice postulated he personally would not have had difficulty awarding plaintiff half the assets in such a case, he also noted that whether that would be permitted under law was another matter. Indeed, the *Preston* rule would appear to dictate that, regardless of his decision, plaintiff, from the beginning of the English case, was predestined to receive only a fraction of the disputed assets, regardless of the determinations of the Court on whatever substantive issues there might have been (including the marital property issue). It is difficult to give due process credence to a system in which the result would remain adverse to the plaintiff whether or not she prevailed on the point the majority determines the case should be decided upon.

Accordingly, while not, in large part, disputing the authorities cited by the majority as a general matter, I am nonetheless convinced that the operation of the English system of marital asset division in cases involving substantial assets reflects considerations very different from our own, and that such considerations cast a shadow on the decision sufficient to preclude Michigan courts, with our well-established criteria for property distribution in divorce cases, from recognizing a decision that is not only from another land, but truly foreign to the concepts underlying Michigan law. Accordingly, I respectfully dissent from the Court's decision.

BRICKLEY, J., concurs with MICHAEL F. CAVANAGH, J.

Think About It

The dissenters argue that application of the English "*Preston* rule" to a property division raises serious due process concerns. Does this argument seem correct? If so, would all differences in substantive law raise due process concerns? What makes these differences a matter of due process?

---

3   *Sparks v. Sparks*, 440 Mich. 141, 485 N.W.2d 893 (1992).

Points for Discussion

a. Comity

The statement quoted by the court in *Dart* from the case of Hilton v. Guyot, 159 U.S. 113 (1895), lists the factors courts typically apply in determining whether to extend comity to a foreign court decree. These focus on questions such as jurisdiction and notice and opportunity for a hearing, as well as whether the matter was heard "under a system of jurisprudence likely to secure an impartial administration of justice between citizens of its own country and those of other countries." Courts in the United States regularly extend comity to family law judgments entered by foreign courts in circumstances that satisfy these requirements. See, e.g., Kalia v. Kalia, 783 N.E.2d 623 (Ohio Ct. App. 2002) (child support order); Bliss v. Bliss, 733 A.2d 954 (D.C.1999) (custody order) cf. Luxembourg ex rel. Ribeiro v. Canderas, 768 A.2d 283 (N.J. Super. Ct. Ch. Div.2000) (denying enforcement of support order entered without personal jurisdiction over obligor). See also Restatement (Third) Foreign Relations Law §§ 484–486 (1987); Restatement (Second) Conflict of Laws § 98 (1971).

b. Jurisdictional Grounds

What jurisdictional basis is required for an American court to extend comity to a foreign court judgment? Many of the cases addressing this question consider migratory divorce decrees from Mexico or the Dominican Republic during the period before no-fault divorce reforms. In general, courts in the United States have required that one party be domiciled in the forum when a foreign court takes jurisdiction over a divorce. See, e.g., Atassi v. Atassi, 451 S.E.2d 371 (N.C. Ct. App. 1995) (denying recognition to divorce obtained in Syria by husband who was a U.S. citizen domiciled in North Carolina). When both parties appear in a foreign divorce proceeding, however, the jurisdictional basis may not be open to a later dispute. See, e.g., Rosenstiel v. Rosenstiel, 209 N.E.2d 709 (N.Y. 1965). Statutes enacted in several states purport to limit state court consideration of "foreign law" in family law cases, by restricting the use of common law comity and inconvenient forum doctrines, and by limiting the scope of contractual choice of law and forum selection agreements. See, e.g., Kan. Stat. § 60–5101 et seq. (2018); Okla. Stat. tit. 12, § 20 (2018).

Courts in many other countries base jurisdiction to resolve matters of personal status such as divorce on the parties' nationality. See generally Lennart Palsson, Marriage and Divorce, in III International Encyclopedia of Comparative Law (Private International Law) ch. 16 (1978). Should this distinction make a difference to an American court in deciding whether to extend comity to a foreign divorce decree?

Problem 6-5

Tony and Fabienne were French citizens who had been married for 20 years when Tony was transferred to New York by his employer. They purchased a home and moved to New York with their children, spending school vacation periods largely in France. After living in New York for almost fifteen years, Fabienne filed for divorce in New York. A week later, Tony filed for divorce in France, and asked the New York court to dismiss his wife's action on jurisdictional grounds. Should the court dismiss the suit? Should it make a difference if Tony had already obtained a divorce from the French courts when he asked the New York court to dismiss her action? (See Bourbon v. Bourbon, 687 N.Y.S.2d 426 (App. Div. 1999) and 751 N.Y.S.2d 302 (App. Div. 2002).)

Global View: Religious Divorce

American courts may recognize foreign-country divorce decrees entered by religious authorities in countries such as Israel or Egypt where those decrees are given effect for civil purposes, provided that there was an appropriate jurisdictional basis and that both spouses had notice and an opportunity to be heard. See, e.g., Chaudry v. Chaudry, 388 A.2d 1000 (N.J. Super. Ct. App. Div. 1978); Shapiro v. Shapiro, 442 N.Y.S.2d 928 (Sup. Ct. 1981).

A divorce or annulment obtained from religious authorities within the United States has no secular legal effect, but may be important to the parties for religious reasons. New York has legislation designed to address the interaction of civil and religious divorce proceedings in traditional Jewish communities, where a woman must have a document known as a *get* in order to remarry. See N.Y. Dom. Rel. Law § 253(3) (2018). See generally Ann Laquer Estin, *Toward a Multicultural Family Law*, 38 Fam. L.Q. 501 (2004) and Ann Laquer Estin, *Unofficial Family Law*, 94 Iowa L. Rev. 449 (2009).

Couples may choose to resolve their differences through mediation or arbitration, which is sometimes conducted within a particular cultural or religious framework. Agreements to arbitrate are governed by state law, and an arbitrated resolution of a divorce dispute may be enforceable in state courts. These issues are considered later in this chapter.

B. Financial Remedies

Marriage has significant financial consequences for individuals and families. Some of these are governed by property law, including inheritance and community property law. Couples may also use marital contracts, discussed in Chapter 1, to shape their obligations to each other. Marriage is also an important consideration for purposes of income tax, bankruptcy, Social Security and other areas of public law.

Make the Connection

Couples who live together without marriage may also make financial claims at the end of their relationship, based on property, contract and restitution theories. See *Marvin v. Marvin* and *Morone v. Morone* in Chapter 1, and the *Hofstad* case in this chapter.

Divorce also has significant financial consequences. Marriage is understood to be an economic partnership, and contemporary divorce laws emphasize that both parties' contributions to the partnership should be recognized and compensated when the partnership ends. All states provide for division of property and spousal support awards at the time of divorce. Although long-term spousal support orders are rare, transitional support orders are more common, with the goal of assisting a financially dependent partner in becoming economically self-sufficient.

1. Property Division

Property division is often the most complex aspect of divorce litigation. As a first step, the parties (and their lawyers) identify and locate all of the property owned by either spouse, as well as their liabilities. In many states, they must also classify these assets either as separate property or as marital or community property, depending on the jurisdiction. The assets must also be valued, and while this is a simple process for a bank account or vehicle, parties may need to retain experts to value assets such as a pension or a business. Finally, in their settlement negotiations or in a litigated proceeding, the parties or the court will decide on an appropriate division of assets and liabilities between the spouses.

Go Online

Find a chart listing and categorizing property division statutes of all states on the web page of the American Bar Association's Family Law Section.

deCastro v. deCastro

616 N.E.2d 52 (Mass. 1993)

ABRAMS, JUSTICE.

Edson deCastro, the husband, appeals from the judge's division of the marital property, specifically the division of stock in Data General Corporation (Data General). Jean deCastro, the wife, argues that she has been damaged by the husband's stay of that portion of the judgment nisi of divorce which awarded her fifty percent of the Data General stock. She also requests damages and attorney's fees on the theory that the husband's appeal is frivolous. We allowed the wife's petition for direct appellate review.

The judge entered findings of fact, a rationale and an order. We recite those facts pertinent to the appeal. The parties were married in Norwich, Connecticut, on November 16, 1963. The wife was a schoolteacher and the husband worked at Digital Equipment Corporation. They lived in Newton. For the first part of the marriage, the parties pooled their savings. In 1967, a daughter was born, and the wife discontinued her work. In 1968, the husband, with four others, formed a new company called Data General Corporation. The husband contributed $15,000 from the joint savings account to the start of Data General. The parties purchased a home in Southborough, in order to be close to Data General's headquarters.

Two other children were born, one in 1970 and the other in 1972. The wife remained at home, caring for the children and her husband. Data General was a successful venture, and the parties' life-style reflected that. The judge found that they owned the Southborough property, eight automobiles, an airplane, and a boat. The parties skied, generally spent one week each winter in a warm climate, and belonged to the Westboro Tennis Club.

In 1980, the husband became involved with another woman and left the marital home. The judge found that the husband did not want the wife to divorce him, and that the husband continued to visit, and occasionally spent the night. The judge also found that, during the years 1980 to 1986, the husband and wife had sexual intercourse on various occasions.

After the husband moved out of the marital home, the wife began to work as a librarian for the school department of Thompson, Connecticut. The husband continued to pay the expenses of the households. He also paid family and education expenses. Since returning to employment in 1980, the wife has contributed all of her salary to the maintenance of herself and the children. In 1981 and 1982, the husband purchased land on Lake Winnepesaukee, Wolfeboro, New Hampshire, on which to build a vacation home for the wife. Since 1982, the wife and the children have spent most summers in Wolfeboro.

The husband, in his name, owns a significant number of shares in Data General. The judge included the following findings:

April 16, 1968: Mr. deCastro acquired 315,220 shares when Data General Corporation was formed

January 4, 1974: Mr. deCastro purchased 100 shares when Data General went on the New York Stock Exchange

February 15, 1980: Date of parties' separation, Mr. deCastro owned 315,320 shares

November 8, 1983: Data General Common Stock split 2 for 1—As of November 8, 1983, Mr. deCastro owned 630,640 shares

February 28, 1984: Mr. deCastro exercised stock options and purchased 207,666 shares

November, 1984: Mr. deCastro sold 50,000 shares of Data General to pay taxes, repay part of his loan to Data General and to have funds to exercise the June 19, 1985, option

June 19, 1985: Mr. deCastro exercised stock option and purchased 59,000 shares of Data General

April 2, 1986: Mr. deCastro was granted the option to purchase 50,000 shares of Data General, which to date remains unexercised

June 28, 1991: Mr. deCastro owns 847,306 shares of Data General and an option to purchase an additional 50,000 shares at below market value.

The judge also considered the wife's contribution. He found that the wife assumed ninety percent of the responsibility for the physical and mental needs of the children. She was responsible for all cooking and care of the interior of the house, and for the maintenance of her car and those of the children. The wife was responsible for entertaining both her family and the husband's, and for purchasing gifts. The wife transported the children to school, athletic events, dancing school, music lessons and other events, arranging car pools when necessary. She also acted as the disciplinarian, setting and enforcing the rules. The wife was responsible for purchasing the children's clothing, the food, and any household necessities, and managed the money for these and other expenses. She attended ninety percent of the athletic events, parent-teacher conferences and other events, accompanied the children on college tours and spent all summers with them. In addition, she took them on several trips. The wife also was responsible for the religious and moral upbringing of the children. The judge concluded that: "Throughout the period of separation, the wife maintained a stable home atmosphere for the children by continuing good relationships with relatives, friends and neighbors. Because of such stability, the children are well-balanced, bright and athletic and never in trouble." The judge also noted that the husband was attentive to the children when his schedule permitted.

1. *The division of the Data General stock.* The husband challenges the judge's division of the Data General stock. He claims that the judge failed to consider all [of] the factors G.L. c. 208, § 34 (1990 ed.),[2] and also to make appropriate findings. The husband also argues that the judge did not make the rationale for his decision regarding the division of assets implicit or explicit. We do not agree.

General Laws, c. 208, § 34, gives the judge the discretion to "make a fair and just assignment of the spouses' property." *Bianco v. Bianco,* 371 Mass. 420, 422, 358 N.E.2d 243 (1976), quoting Inker, Walsh & Perocchi, Alimony and Assignment of Property: The New Statutory Scheme in Massachusetts, 10 Suff.U.L.R. 1, 4 (1975). This discretion is not unlimited. In *Bowring v. Reid,* 399 Mass. 265, 503 N.E.2d 966 (1987), we outlined a procedure probate judges should follow in assigning property under G.L. c. 208, § 34. "[A] judge must make findings indicating that he has considered all factors relevant under § 34, and has not considered any irrelevant factors." In reviewing a judge's decision under G.L. c. 208, § 34, we use a two-step analysis. We first determine whether the judge considered all the § 34 factors, and no others. We then evaluate whether the conclusions follow from the findings and rulings. Any conclusions the judge makes will be reversed only if "plainly wrong and excessive," but the judge's findings and rulings must make clear the reasons for these conclusions.

The husband claims that the probate judge issued findings of fact that were "woefully inadequate" with regard to the factor of contribution to the acquisition, preservation, and appreciation of marital assets. The husband contends that the Data Gen-

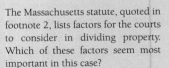

Think About It

The Massachusetts statute, quoted in footnote 2, lists factors for the courts to consider in dividing property. Which of these factors seem most important in this case?

---

[2]   General Laws c. 208, § 34 (1990 ed.), as amended St.1990, c. 467, effective March 29, 1991, provides in pertinent part: "Upon divorce or upon a complaint in an action brought at any time after a divorce, whether such a divorce has been adjudged in this commonwealth or another jurisdiction, the court of the commonwealth, provided there is personal jurisdiction over both parties, may make a judgment for either of the parties to pay alimony to the other. In addition to or in lieu of a judgment to pay alimony, the court may assign to either husband or wife all or any part of the estate of the other, including but not limited to, all vested and nonvested benefits, rights and funds accrued during the marriage and which shall include, but not be limited to, retirement benefits, military retirement benefits if qualified under and to the extent provided by federal law, pension, profit-sharing, annuity, deferred compensation and insurance. In determining the amount of alimony, if any, to be paid, or in fixing the nature and value of the property, if any, to be so assigned, the court, after hearing the witnesses, if any, of each party, shall consider the length of the marriage, the conduct of the parties during the marriage, the age, health, station, occupation, amount and sources of income, vocational skills, employability, estate, liabilities and needs of each of the parties and the opportunity of each for future acquisition of capital assets and income. In fixing the nature and value of the property to be so assigned, the court shall also consider the present and future needs of the dependent children of the marriage. The court may also consider the contribution of each of the parties in the acquisition, preservation or appreciation in value of their respective estates and the contribution of each of the parties as a homemaker to the family unit."

eral stock was the greatest single asset of the marital estate and that the judge failed to make findings, based on the evidence, as to the husband's revolutionary designs, the founding and developing of Data General, and the husband's unique role in the computer industry.

* * * The judge considered the contributions of both the husband and the wife to the marriage. He found that "during the first three (3) years of the parties' marriage, the husband provided the majority of the financial contribution to the marital estate and that since 1967, the husband provided virtually all of the financial contribution to the marital estate but that the wife contributed almost all of the homemaking responsibilities and that since 1980 when she returned to work all of her salary has gone to family expenses." He also found that, after the separation, the wife maintained the stability of the family, and that, as a result of this, the children were balanced and successful.

The findings the judge made support the conclusion that he considered all of the factors required under § 34. The judge was not compelled to consider the husband's contributions to the computer industry in distributing the marital property. We conclude that the judge's findings with regard to contribution to the marital estate were more than adequate.[3]

We next determine whether the judge's rationale makes clear, either expressly or implicitly, the reasons for his distribution of the Data General stock. The husband argues that the rationale does not follow logically from the findings of fact or the underlying evidence heard at trial. He also claims that the judge did not apply existing case law properly to the facts of the case.

In his rationale, the judge noted that, in the first years of their marriage, both parties worked and managed to save $15,000, which the husband then invested in Data General. The judge acknowledged that, after 1967, the husband made all of the financial contribution to the family until 1980, when the wife reentered the work force and contributed her earnings to the maintenance of herself, the children, and their stations in life. The judge also explained: "From the beginning this [marriage] was a partnership in which both parties contributed to the raising of the children and to the accumulation of marital assets. Over the years their efforts became focused—hers on the home and the children—his on his work at the Corporation." The judge noted: "When the assets of this type of marriage are

---

[3]   The husband "acknowledges that the trial court * * * nominally considered and made findings on all the statutory factors. * * * "He asserts, however, that "under the heading of 'Contribution to the Acquisition, Preservation and Appreciation of the marital assets * * * the findings are hopelessly flawed when contrasted with the evidence. * * * ' " We do not agree. That argument is based solely on the fact that, in the husband's view, the evidence of the husband's "genius" was not accorded sufficient weight by the judge. Because we reject the husband's claim that "genius" is a factor under § 34, we reject the husband's argument that the judge did not weigh the evidence correctly. We add that our reading of the record amply supports the judge's findings and rulings.

divided by a Probate Court, justice and equality require that both the financial contributions in the accumulation of these assets and the non-financial contribution in the raising of the children and taking care of the home must be taken into account."

The husband claims that the judge's ruling with regard to the division of the Data General stock was plainly wrong and excessive and should be set aside. The husband asserts that the judge abused his discretion because his division of property did not reflect the "super-contribution" of the husband. The husband claims that the judge erred because he failed to make a finding about the husband's "genius." He suggests that his "genius" alone engendered the considerable estate.[4] The judge's rationale for the division of the marital property follows from the findings that both parties contributed to the marriage, one focusing on work outside the home and the other focusing on work within the home and with the children. The judge recognized that the contributions to the acquisition, preservation, and appreciation in value of the stock made by the wife were not quantifiable. He also recognized that the marriage had been a partnership, and that she had focused on the children and the home. The judge concluded that the wife made an equal contribution to the marriage. Therefore, the judge divided the Data General stock equally. The judge's rationale follows from his findings, which were based on ample evidence.

The husband's argument otherwise is simply a resurrection of the discarded idea that the wage earner is entitled to most if not all of the benefits of the paid work. Section 34 does not require the judge to limit his order to consideration of which party made the greater financial contribution to the acquisition of the assets. That narrow focus and analysis is precisely what the Legislature tried to avoid in § 34. The marriage-as-partnership concept, embodied in G.L. c. 208, § 34, recognizes that one party often concentrates on the financial side of the family while the other concentrates on homemaking and child care. Both parties contributed to developing a substantial marital estate, the husband by working at Data General and the wife by raising bright, happy, stable children and caring for the home. "The concept of property assignment or equitable division under [§ 34] must be read to apply in a broad sense to the value of *all* contributions of the respective spouses towards the marital enterprise; it contemplates something *more* than determining which spouse's money purchased a particular asset" (emphasis added). *Pare v. Pare, supra*, 409 Mass. at 297, 565 N.E.2d 1195; ("Property division * * * is based on the joint contribution of the spouses to the marital enterprise," quoting Inker et al., 10 Suff.U.L.R. 11).

---

[4]   The husband's argument could be made by any person whose ideas, skills, and judgment made that person highly financially successful in that person's business, industry or profession.

In sum, the judge correctly analyzed the marital estate under G.L. c. 208, § 34. He considered all the factors and did not consider any irrelevant factors. The husband's suggestion that his contributions to the computer industry should have been considered in dividing the marital property is unsupported by statute or case law. There was no error.

* * *

FYI

The court also held that the stay granted by the Court of Appeals forbidding the transfer of shares awarded to the wife was too broad.

Conclusion. We affirm the judge's division of the Data General stock. We rule that the stay was too broad and that it is dissolved as of the date this opinion is issued. We remand the case to the Probate Court for a determination of damages, if any, based on the difference between the value on the date the stay issued and the value on the date of this opinion of the Data General shares the transfer of which was erroneously stayed.

Points for Discussion

a. Marital and Community Property

State property laws follow one of three distinct patterns. Most states are "marital property" states, which require the divorce court to classify the property owned by the spouses at the time of divorce as either marital or separate, and then authorize the court to divide all marital property. Marital property is typically defined as all property acquired during the marriage except property acquired by gift, devise or descent; property acquired in exchange for property acquired by gift, devise or descent; or property excluded by agreement of the parties. This was the approach of the original Uniform Marriage and Divorce Act (UMDA), 9A U.L.A. (Part 1) 288–89 (1998), enacted with some modifications in Colorado, Kentucky, Missouri, Minnesota and Illinois. In a few of the marital property states, the statutes permit a division of separate property as well as marital property where the division of marital property alone would be unfair.

About fourteen states have statutes that authorize the courts to divide all of the property owned by both spouses at the time of the divorce, regardless of when, how or by whom the property was acquired or how the title is held. This is sometimes referred to as a "hotchpot" approach; see, e.g., UMDA § 307, Alternative A, 9A U.L.A. (Part 1) 288 (1998). Both marital property and hotchpot states come from the common law property tradition, in which each spouse has full authority to manage and control of any property titled in his or her name during the course of the marriage. How would you characterize the Massachusetts statute, which is quoted in footnote 2 of *DeCastro*?

A third group of states, including Arizona, California, Idaho, Louisiana, Nevada, New Mexico, Texas, and Washington, have community property laws, which govern management and use of property both during a marriage and when the marriage ends by death or divorce. During marriage, each spouse has an interest in any community property held by the other, and each spouse has fiduciary obligations to the other. See, for example, *Schlueter v. Schlueter*, reprinted in Chapter 4. See also See, e.g., Uniform Marriage and Divorce Act § 307, Alternative B, 9A U.L.A. (Part 1) 288–89 (1998). Because marital property laws were largely inspired by the community property tradition, the definition and treatment of marital and community property are very similar for purposes of divorce.

Although Wisconsin is a marital property state for purposes of divorce, it has enacted the Uniform Marital Property Act, 9A U.L.A. (Part 1) 103 (1998), which provides that each spouse has an undivided one-half interest in any marital property during the marriage. Wis. Stat. Ann. § 767.255 (2018).

Uniform Marriage and Divorce Act

Section 307. Disposition of Property

* * *

(b) For purposes of this Act only, "marital property" means all property acquired by either spouse subsequent to the marriage except:

(1) property acquired by gift, bequest, devise or descent;

(2) property acquired in exchange for property acquired prior to the marriage or in exchange for property acquired by gift, bequest, devise or descent;

(3) property acquired by a spouse after a decree of legal separation;

(4) property excluded by valid agreement of the parties; and

(5) the increase in value of property acquired prior to the marriage.

Uniform Marriage and Divorce Act § 307(b), 9A U.L.A. (Part 1) 289 (1998) (original 1970 version).

---

b. Equitable Distribution

In many states, statutes call for an "equitable distribution" of the parties' property. See UMDA § 307(a), 9A U.L.A. (Part 1) 288 (1998). In some states, however, statutes create a rebuttable presumption favoring an equal division of marital property. See, e.g., Wis. Stat. § 767.61(3) (2018). What are the arguments for and against the use of presumptions in these cases? Does the Massachusetts statute quoted in *deCastro* address this question? Does *deCastro* suggest that an award of half the marital estate to a homemaker should be required?

The shift toward equitable distribution and more generous property division awards for homemakers was an important aspect of the divorce reform legislation of the 1970s. The drafters of the Uniform Marriage and Divorce Act intended more substantial property division to prevent the need for ongoing alimony or maintenance payments after divorce. This may be possible in a case like *deCastro*, but most divorcing couples do not have enough property to provide either party with substantial financial protection. See Marsha Garrison, *Good Intentions Gone Awry: The Impact of New York's Equitable Distribution Law on Divorce Outcomes*, 57 Brook. L. Rev. 621, 728 (1991). In most cases, the family's financial welfare after the divorce will be dependent primarily upon the spouses' earnings.

In most states, there is no equivalent to equitable distribution for unmarried couples. Thus, rather than dividing all of the property accumulated during a cohabitation relationship, courts address specific assets that are jointly titled or to which both members of the couple have contributed in some fashion. This process is considered later in this chapter.

c. Marital Fault

To what extent should marital fault, such as adultery, desertion or cruelty, be considered in determining the amount of the property awarded to either spouse? Many state statutes provide explicitly that courts may not consider marital misconduct. E.g., Cal. Fam. Code § 2335 (2018); Colo. Rev. Stat. § 14–10–113(1) (2018); Wis. Stat. § 767.61 (2018). In contrast to these laws, the Massachusetts statute applied in *deCastro* authorizes the court to take into account "the conduct of the parties during the marriage." Did the court take into account the husband's involvement with another woman? Should the court have done this?

A few states have special rules for extreme or egregious misconduct, such as a serious violent felony, see, e.g., Brancoveanu v. Brancoveanu, 535 N.Y.S.2d 86 (App.Div.1988) (attempted murder) or a pattern of physical and emotional abuse, see, e.g., Havell v. Islam, 718 N.Y.S.2d 807 (Sup.Ct.2000). Cf. Mosbarger v. Mosbarger, 547 So.2d 188 (Fla.Ct.App.1989) (equal property division despite wife shooting at husband). Other states have permitted consideration of medical and financial needs that resulted from serious spousal abuse as one factor in determining a marital property division. See Petition of Fenzau, 54 P.3d 43 (Mont. 2002). See generally Ira Ellman, *The Place of Fault in a Modern Divorce Law*, 28 Ariz. St. L.J. 773 (1996).

d. Economic Misconduct

Courts dividing marital property also consider financial misconduct such as waste or dissipation of assets, with or without explicit statutory authority. Herron v. Johnson, 714 A.2d 783 (D.C.1998), defined dissipation as the disposition of marital property by a spouse in a manner designed to circumvent equitable distribution. See, e.g., Sands v. Sands, 497 N.W.2d 493 (Mich. 1993) (allocating to wife property that husband had attempted to conceal); G.M. v. M.M., 23 N.Y.S.3d 859 (Sup. Ct. 2015) (affirming unequal division after husband diverted income from marital estate to support second family). In community property jurisdictions, fraud or waste of community assets may be taken into consideration in the division of property at the time of divorce, as discussed in Schlueter v. Schlueter, 975 S.W.2d 584 (Tex.1998), reprinted in Chapter 4. See, e.g., Marriage of Kamgar, 226 Cal. Rptr. 3d 234 (Ct. App. 2017) (husband breached fiduciary duties by undisclosed and reckless investment decisions).

How should a court consider behavior such as gambling or illegal activities that affect the parties' financial circumstances at the time of divorce? In Kittredge v. Kittredge, 803 N.E.2d 306 (Mass. 2004), the court held that gambling losses are not always a dissipation of marital assets, and ruled that courts should inquire into the circumstances including the parties' overall contributions to the marital estate. Linda G. v. James G., 64 N.Y.S.3d 17 (App. Div. 2017), upheld an unequal distribution in favor of the wife in light of financial difficulties caused by husband's insider trading and subsequent trial, conviction, and incarceration). See generally Lewis Becker, *Conduct of a Spouse That Dissipates Property Available for Equitable Distribution: A Suggested Analysis*, 52 Ohio St. L.J. 95 (1991). See also G.M. v. M.M., 23 N.Y.S.3d 859 (Sup. Ct. 2015), which affirmed an unequal property division in favor of a wife based on evidence that the husband had been diverting income from the marital estate for a substantial period of time to support a second family.

e. Marital Debts

In addition to dividing marital property, courts in a divorce case may allocate responsibility for payment of the parties' debts. Like assets, debts may also be classified as marital or separate; see, e.g., Dodson v. Dodson, 955 P.2d 902 (Alaska 1998); In re the Marriage of Speirs, 956 P.2d 622 (Colo.Ct.App.1997); Jonas v. Jonas, 660 N.Y.S.2d 487 (App. Div. 1997); Alford v. Alford, 120 S.W.3d 810 (Tenn.2003). See also Marriage of Curda-Derickson, 668 N.W.2d 736 (Wis. Ct. App.2003) (criminal restitution order not classified as marital debt).

Note, however, that allocation of a joint debt by the court or the parties at the time of a divorce does not affect the relationship between the creditor and the spouses. See, e.g., Harriman v. Harriman, 710 A.2d 923 (Me.1998). This has important implications in the event that the spouse to whom a joint debt is allocated files for bankruptcy or otherwise fails to pay. Bankruptcy issues are discussed later in this chapter.

f. Tax Liabilities

Potential tax liabilities should be carefully evaluated in the settlement of divorce cases. These may be taken into account by a court as a factor in achieving an equitable distribution, e.g. Marriage of Maurer, 623 N.W.2d 604 (Minn.2001), particularly when the spouses anticipate tax consequences as an immediate result of the property division, as is the case when assets will be sold to facilitate the distribution. See Solomon v. Solomon, 857 A.2d 1109 (Md. 2004). Courts are typically unwilling to adjust the valuation of marital assets based upon hypothetical future tax liabilities, such as those involved in the sale of a business. E.g. Schuman v. Schuman, 658 N.W.2d 30 (Neb. 2003). Divorce tax issues are discussed later in this chapter.

g. Pets as Property

Pets and other animals are generally treated as personal property under the law. For example, Zelenka v. Pratte, 912 N.W.2d 723 (Neb. 2018), ordered replevin of a French bulldog that the petitioner had received as a gift from his former partner during their relationship.

Courts have resisted using child custody principles in disputes concerning pets, see, e.g., Marriage of Enders, 48 N.E.3d 1277 (Ill. App. Ct. 2015) (rejecting claim for pet visitation rights). In Travis v. Murray, 977 N.Y.S.2d 621 (Sup. Ct. 2013), however, the court allowed the parties to present evidence on what award of a shared animal would be "best for all concerned," explaining: "[E]ach side will have the opportunity to prove not only why she will benefit from having Joey in her life but why Joey has a better chance of living, prospering, loving and being loved in the care of one spouse as opposed to the other." In several states, statutes now direct courts to allocate sole or joint ownership of a pet in divorce cases, taking the animal's well-being into account. See, e.g., 750 Ill. Comp. Stat. 5/503(n) (2018).

Problem 6-6

Ethel and Ross were married for 30 years and had two grown children at the time of their divorce. The applicable statute requires a court to consider the parties' respective contributions during the marriage. Ross's earnings totaled $248,000 during the marriage, while Ethel's were $51,000. In addition, Ethel offered expert testimony to prove that her services as a homemaker had a monetary value of $217,000. Should Ethel receive a larger share of the marital property on this basis? (See Raley v. Raley, 437 S.E.2d 770 (W. Va. 1993).)

Problem 6-7

After Christina married Esteban, a professional athlete earning several million dollars a year, he made frequent large gifts to various friends and relatives, including Rolex watches, new cars, and travel expenses. A year later, Christina discovered that there were also many gifts going to a woman named Ashley, who was pregnant with his child. In the divorce proceedings that followed, Christina presented evidence of more than $500,000 in community property spent on Ashley (as well as her baby and her mother), approximately $100,000 in gifts and loans to members of Esteban's family, and another $100,000 in checks and cash advances for which Esteban had no explanation. How should these amounts be treated in division of the community estate? (See Loaiza v. Loaiza, 130 S.W.3d 894 (Tex. App. 2004).)

Problem 6-8

Ava and Dan purchased a condominium unit to live in during their marriage, which dropped in value by more than $75,000 and was "underwater"—worth less than the amount of their mortgage—when they separated. Dan thinks they should abandon the condo and let the property go into foreclosure; Ava wants to live in the property and have the full balance of the unpaid debt treated as a marital liability. How should the court decide this dispute? (See Byrne v. Byrne, 128 So.3d 2 (Fla. Ct. App. 2012).)

Middendorf v. Middendorf

696 N.E.2d 575 (Ohio 1998)

LUNDBERG STRATTON, JUSTICE.

In this case, we examine the legal standards for determining when appreciation in separate property becomes marital property for purposes of the division of property in a domestic relations case under R.C. 3105.171. Max asserts that in order for a court to determine that an increase in separate property is marital property, the court must find that both spouses have expended significant marital funds or labor directly contributing to the increase or that the non-owning spouse must contribute substantial work to improvement and maintenance of the separate property. We disagree.

In <u>Worthington v. Worthington (1986), 21 Ohio St.3d 73, 21 OBR 371, 488 N.E.2d 150</u>, this court affirmed a trial court's decision that held that the increase in value of separate property is marital property where the increase in value is the result of the couples' expenditure of a substantial sum of marital funds and labor. The court in <u>Worthington</u> held:

"A trial court, in determining the division of property pursuant to the factors contained in R.C. 3105.18 and all other relevant factors, does not abuse its discretion by apportioning the appreciation in value of non-marital property as a marital asset, where significant marital *funds and labor* are expended to improve and maintain such property." (Emphasis added.)

However, the General Assembly codified a new definition of "marital" and "separate property" in <u>R.C. 3105.171</u>, which became effective on January 1, 1991. 143 Ohio Laws, Part III, 5226, 5452. <u>R.C. 3105.171(A)(3)(a)</u>, as amended, states:

" 'Marital property' means, subject to division (A)(3)(b) of this section, all of the following:
" * * *

"(iii) * * * all income and appreciation on separate property, due to the labor, monetary, or in-kind contribution of *either or both of the spouses* that occurred during the marriage." (Emphasis added.) 144 Ohio Laws, Part I, 1754–1755.

<u>R.C. 3105.171(A)(6)(a)</u> states:

" 'Separate property' means all real and personal property and any interest in real or personal property that is found by the court to be any of the following:
" * * *

"(iii) Passive income and appreciation acquired from separate property by one spouse during the marriage."

Finally, <u>R.C. 3105.171(A)(4)</u> states:

" 'Passive income' means income acquired other than as a result of the labor, monetary, or in-kind contribution of either spouse."

It is within the province of a court to construe laws enacted by the legislature. The primary purpose of interpretation is to ascertain the intent of the legislature. In interpreting legislative intent, the court must first look to the language of the statute. If the language of the statute is unambiguous, then the statute must be applied pursuant to its plain meaning.

The plain language of R.C. 3105.17(A)(3)(a)(iii) unambiguously mandates that when *either* spouse makes a labor, money, or in-kind contribution that *causes* an increase in the value of separate property, that increase in value is deemed marital property.

The definition in R.C. 3105.171(A)(3)(a)(iii) differs from the "joint efforts" test in *Worthington* in that *Worthington* required an effort by *both* spouses before any increase in the value of separate property due to such efforts would be classified as marital

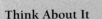

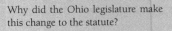

Think About It

Why did the Ohio legislature make this change to the statute?

property. R.C. 3105.171(A)(3)(a)(iii) requires only an expenditure or effort by *either* spouse. Thus, R.C. 3105.171(A)(3)(a)(iii) in effect supersedes *Worthington* for purposes of defining when appreciation of separate property is marital property. Accordingly, the appellate court did not err in affirming the trial court's interpretation of R.C. 3105.171, that an increase in the value of separate property due to *either* spouse's efforts is marital property.

We must now determine if there was sufficient evidence to support the trial court's determination that there was an increase in the value of the stockyard during Max and Pat's marriage and that the increase was *due to* the labor, money, or in-kind contributions made by Max. R.C. 3105.171(A)(3)(a)(iii). If the evidence indicates that the appreciation of the separate property is *not due* to the input of Max's (or Pat's) labor, money, or in-kind contributions, the increase in the value of the stockyard is passive appreciation and remains separate property. R.C. 3105.171(A)(6)(a)(iii); 3105.171(A)(4).

A trial court has broad discretion in making divisions of property in domestic cases. A trial court's decision will be upheld absent an abuse of discretion. "Abuse of discretion" is more than an error of law or judgment; it implies that the court acted in an unreasonable, arbitrary, or unconscionable fashion. If there is some competent, credible evidence to support the trial court's decision, there is no abuse of discretion. Therefore, if there is some competent, credible evidence that there was an increase in the value of the stockyard during the marriage and that the increase in the valuation was due to labor, money, or in-kind contributions of either Max or Pat, or both, the increase in valuation is classified as marital property and subject to division.

On remand from the court of appeals, the magistrate hired Philip Brandt as an independent expert to value the stockyard. Brandt testified that the value of the stockyard when the Middendorfs were married was $201,389 and the value in December 1992, the stipulated date for purposes of determining value, was

$309,930. Thus, the increase was $108,541. Both the magistrate and the court rejected the defense expert's testimony and found the court-appointed expert more credible. This testimony provided credible evidence of an increase in the value of the stockyard during the Middendorfs' marriage.

The second issue upon which we must determine if credible evidence has been submitted is whether this increase in value of the stockyard was *due to* labor, monetary, or in-kind contribution by Max.

The stockyard business primarily involves buying hogs from farmers and then reselling them to the slaughterhouse. As a sideline, the stockyard would contract with farmers to feed the hogs until the hogs reached a marketable size, whereupon they would be sold to a meatpacking company. This arrangement has a reciprocal benefit: the farmer is relieved of the risks associated with owning the hog (disease, market fluctuation) and the stockyard is relieved of having to care for the hogs.

Max argues that there is no evidence that the increase in the stockyard's value was due to his funds or labor. Max asserts that the increase was due solely to passive appreciation from "market changes." However, Max's position fails to take into account all of the other factors contributing to the increase.

Passive forces such as market conditions may influence the profitability of a business. However, it is the employees and their labor input that make a company productive. In today's business environment, executives and managers figure heavily in the success or failure of a company, and in the attendant risks (*e.g.*, termination, demotion) and rewards (*e.g.*, bonuses, stock options) that go with the respective position. These individuals are the persons responsible for making pivotal decisions that result in the success or failure of the company. There is no reason that these factors should not likewise be relevant in determining a spouse's input into the success of a business.

It is true that the stockyard business has inherent, uncontrollable risks, such as market fluctuation and death of the livestock due to disease, which affect profitability. However, monitoring market prices in order to make timely purchases and sales, deciding the numbers of hogs purchased, and deciding whether to contract with farmers to care for hogs are a few of the calculated decisions made by the stockyard management that also affect profitability. Thus, no matter how high hog prices went, the business would not operate, let alone increase in value, without the necessary ingredients of labor and leadership from the owners and management. Making these calculated decisions was part of Max's responsibilities as a livestock buyer and co-owner of the stockyard. Max testified that he spent long hours working there, which included buying and selling hogs.

Both the trial court and the court of appeals found that these efforts directly contributed to the appreciation of the company assets. The trial court found that "the increase in value of Middendorf Stockyard Company was the direct result of the pivotal role which [Max] played in the management of the company during the course of the marriage." The appeals court found that the Max "played a vital role in the management of the Stockyards. * * * [He] clearly dedicated himself to his work, spending significant amounts of time working to keep his business profitable in an increasingly risky market." Absent an abuse of discretion, we will not disturb these findings of fact.

Although we note that Pat contributed substantial efforts to the family relationship that freed Max of the responsibilities of the home and children and enabled him to devote more time to the business, we need not reach the issue of the value of her contributions. Because Max's efforts contributed to the appreciation of the Middendorf Stockyards, the requirements of R.C. 3105.171(A)(3)(a)(iii) are met, as the statute requires the contribution of only one spouse. Thus, we find some competent, credible evidence that Max's interest in the stockyard increased in value by $108,541, during Max and Pat's marriage, due to Max's labor. Therefore, the trial court did not abuse its discretion in finding that the $108,541 appreciation of the stockyard was a marital asset to be divided between Max and Pat. Accordingly, we affirm the judgment of the court of appeals.

Judgment affirmed.

Points for Discussion

a. Marital and Separate Property

As noted above, divorce courts in most states must differentiate separate property from marital or community property before making an equitable distribution. Many states apply a presumption that all property acquired by either spouse subsequent to the marriage and prior to a decree of divorce or legal separation is marital property. This presumption may be overcome by a showing that the property was acquired by one of the methods listed in the definition of separate property. E.g., Colo. Rev. Stat. § 14–10–113(3) (2018); Minn. Stat. Ann. § 518.54(5) (2018); Mo. Ann. Stat. § 452.330(3) (2018); see also UMDA § 307(c) [Alternative B], 9A U.L.A. (Part 1) 289 (1998). See In re Marriage of Fields, 779 P.2d 1371 (Colo.Ct.App.1989), cert. dismissed 781 P.2d 1040 (Colo.1989).

b. Length of Marriage

If a couple lived together prior to their marriage, the question sometimes arises whether property acquired while they were cohabitating should be treated as marital or community property. A number of states permit consideration of property acquired during the cohabitation period, see, e.g., <u>Northrop v. Northrop, 622 N.W.2d 219 (N.D. 2001)</u>; <u>Marriage of Burton, 758 P.2d 394 (Or. Ct. App. 1988)</u>; <u>Marriage of Meyer, 620 N.W.2d 382 (Wis. 2000)</u>; but other states do not, see, e.g., <u>Loughlin v. Loughlin, 910 A.2d 936 (Conn. 2006)</u>. See also <u>Matter of Munson, 146 A.3d 153 (N.H. 2016)</u> (holding that court may consider premarital cohabitation as a factor in making equitable distribution).

Similarly, courts must sometimes decide when a marriage has ended for community and marital property purposes. In some states the marital community ends on the date of separation, see, e.g., <u>Cal. Fam. Code § 771 (2012)</u>, although the courts may apply a high standard for what constitutes a sufficient separation. See, e.g., <u>Marriage of Hardin, 45 Cal.Rptr.2d 308 (Ct. App. 1995)</u>; <u>Marriage of Norviel, 126 Cal.Rptr.2d 148 (Ct. App. 2002)</u>. In other states, the marriage does not end until a decree is entered, see, e.g., <u>Alston v. Alston, 629 A.2d 70 (Md. 1993)</u>; <u>Giha v. Giha, 609 A.2d 945 (R.I.1992)</u>. Both *Alston* and *Giha* involved spouses who won lottery prizes after the parties' separation but prior to their divorce; in both cases the lottery winnings were divided by the divorce court as marital property. See also <u>Seizer v. Sessions, 940 P.2d 261 (Wash. 1997)</u>.

c. Appreciation and Income from Separate Property

State laws vary considerably on the problem addressed in *Middendorf*: how to characterize appreciation in the value of separate property that occurs during the marriage. Community property states generally treat active increases in the value of separate property—those that result from the spouses' efforts—as belonging to the community, while passive increases remain part of the separate estate. Statutes in many of the marital property states, including the Ohio statute discussed in *Middendorf*, make a similar distinction. There are also states in which all increases in value of separate property are treated as marital property, see, e.g., <u>Colo. Rev. Stat. Ann. § 14–10–113(4) (2018)</u> and <u>Pa. Cons. Stat. tit. 23 § 3501 (2018)</u>, and states in which all increases in the value of separate property remain separate, see, e.g., <u>750 Ill. Comp. Stat. Ann. § 5/503 (2018)</u>. What if an increase in value is partly active and partly passive? In <u>Macdonald v. Macdonald, 532 A.2d 1046 (Me.1987)</u>, the court ruled that an auto dealership was separate property, but that the marital estate was entitled to the portion of the increase in the value of the business that was attributable to marital effort. See also <u>Kaaa v. Kaaa, 58 So.3d 867 (Fla. 2010)</u>.

Marital Agreements

Spouses may enter agreements regarding their property rights, including terms such as when their property will be characterized as marital or separate, or which state's marital property law will apply. For the rules governing marital agreements, see Chapter 1.

Different states also treat income received from separate property during the marriage under different rules, treating it either as separate property, or as marital or community property, or as separate property unless it was produced by spousal efforts. See e.g. Marriage of Gottsacker v. Gottsacker, 664 N.W.2d 848 (Minn.2003); Cal. Fam. Code § 770(3) (2018); 750 Ill. Comp. Stat. Ann. § 5/503(c)(2) (2018).

As was the case with the stockyard involved in *Middendorf*, these rules mean that some assets may have a mixed character, with their part of their value separate and part marital. Property may also have mixed character if it was acquired using both separate and marital or community assets. For example, one spouse might use separate resources for the down payment on a house, and marital funds to pay off the mortgage debt. See, e.g., Fields v. Fields, 931 N.E.2d 1039 (N.Y. 2010).

d. Transmutation and Commingling

Two important doctrines provide a basis on which separate property may become marital or community property.

Commingling results when separate and marital properties are inextricably combined, so that the respective contributions of the two estates cannot be traced. Based on a presumption that property acquired during marriage is marital or community property, this mingling results in the combined asset being characterized as marital property. For example, in Van Ness v. Van Ness, 482 N.E.2d 1049 (Ill. App. Ct. 1985), marital and separate property were combined to improve a house, which was then sold and the proceeds used to buy another house, which was ultimately treated as marital property.

Transmutation occurs when a spouse transfers property during the marriage in circumstances suggesting that the spouse intended to change its beneficial ownership from separate to marital property. The most common example occurs when property that was purchased with separate funds is titled either in a joint tenancy or tenancy by the entireties. This typically raises a rebuttable presumption that the owner intended to make a gift to the marital estate, and the property becomes marital unless the owner is able to rebut the presumption. See J. Thomas Oldham, *Tracing, Commingling, and Transmutation*, 23 Fam. L.Q. 219 (1989).

In some states, transmutation can occur when a couple deals with their property as if it were marital. For example, Miller v. Miller, 105 P.3d 1136 (Alaska 2005) considered whether the parties had demonstrated an intent that the family home be marital property after thirteen years of living there together, cleaning and maintaining it, and paying taxes and insurance from marital funds. California regulates transmutation by statute, authorizing couples to accomplish transmutation by agreement, but requiring that in some cases it be done in a writing consented to by the person adversely affected by the transmutation. See Cal. Fam. Code §§ 850–853 (2018), applied in Marriage of Benson, 116 P.3d 1152 (Cal. 2005).

e. Source of Funds Rule

How should a court treat passive increases and decreases in the value of an asset that is partly marital and partly separate? In many states, this is accomplished using the source of funds rule, which determines the ratio of marital and separate investments in the property, and applies those percentages to the property value at the time of a divorce. See, e.g. In re Marriage of Moore, 618 P.2d 208 (Cal. 1980); In re Marriage of Looney, 286 S.W.3d 832 (Mo. Ct. App. 2009).

f. Trusts

Family estate planning may introduce significant complications into the process of marital property division; see, e.g. Marriage of Robert v. Zygmunt, 652 N.W.2d 537 (Minn.Ct.App.2002). Some cases conclude that a spouse's beneficial interest in a trust is neither marital nor separate property, particularly when the interest is contingent or the trust is revocable. See Marriage of Rosenblum, 602 P.2d 892 (Colo. Ct. App. 1979); Williams v. Massa, 728 N.E.2d 932 (Mass. 2000); but see Bentson v. Bentson, 656 P.2d 395 (Or. Ct. App. 1983). Other cases treat beneficial interests in trusts as separate property, leading to the further problem of classifying trust income and any appreciation in the value of trust assets during the marriage. See In re Balanson, 25 P.3d 28 (Colo.2001). Even if a trust is neither separate nor marital property, a court may consider the trust as part of the parties' economic circumstances in making an equitable division of marital property. See generally Michael Diehl, *The Trust in Marital Law: Divisibility of a Beneficiary Spouse's Interests on Divorce*, 64 Tex. L. Rev. 1301 (1986).

g. Choice of Law

The diversity among the states' treatment of the division of property in divorce creates obvious choice of law problems when a divorce occurs between spouses who have lived and acquired property in a number of places during their marriage. The traditional rule in the United States has been that the legal rights of the spouses in real estate they own at the time of divorce are governed by the law of the situs of the property, while their rights in movable property are governed by the law of the place where they were domiciled at the time it was acquired. See Peter Hay et al., Conflict of Laws §§ 14.6, 14.9, 14.10 (6th ed. 2018); Restatement (Second) Conflict of Laws §§ 234, 258(2) (1971).

There are important exceptions to these doctrines. If the parties have entered into a valid premarital or marital agreement, that agreement will generally control choice of law and property distribution questions. Divorce courts routinely apply the law of the forum to property division questions, unless there is an objection from one of the spouses. In some community property states, statutes have created the institution of **quasi-community property**, which is defined as real or personal property, wherever located, which was acquired by the spouses while domiciled outside the community property state and which would have been community property if the spouses had been domiciled in the community property state at the time the property was acquired. In effect, this amounts to a choice of law

Think About It

In view of the many practical difficulties inherent in the traditional choice of law rule, would it be preferable for all states to apply the law of the forum to property division questions, assuming that the forum had personal jurisdiction over both parties and that they had not entered into a different agreement?

rule that allows the court to apply its own community property law to all of the couple's property. See, e.g., Ariz.Rev.Stat.Ann. § 25–318 (2018); Cal.Fam.Code § 125 (2018); see Friedrich K. Juenger, *Marital Property and the Conflict of Laws: A Tale of Two Countries*, 81 Colum. L. Rev. 1061 (1981).

Problem 6-9

A wife buys a house before her marriage for a price of $100,000, paying $20,000 in cash and executing a note and mortgage for the balance. During the marriage the note is paid off out of marital funds. On divorce the house is appraised at $150,000. In the various states discussed above, how much of the property is marital and how much separate on divorce? (See Thomas v. Thomas, 377 S.E.2d 666 (Ga. 1989); Noyes v. Noyes, 617 A.2d 1036 (Me.1992).)

Problem 6-10

At the time Arthur and Ruth were married, Arthur owned a certificate of deposit worth $7500 and a mutual fund account worth $12,500. Several years later, Arthur purchased a beach house for $230,000, taking title in his name alone. For the down payment on the property, Arthur cashed in his CD, which had value of $10,000, and the mutual fund, which was worth $20,000. Five years later, when Arthur and Ruth divorced, the beach house was valued at $330,000, with a mortgage balance of $190,000. Under the different approaches discussed here, what portion of the value of the beach house would be considered marital property? (See Clum v. Graves, 729 A.2d 900 (Me. 1999); but see Warner v. Warner, 807 A.2d 607 (Me. 2002).)

Problem 6-11

After Janice and Ralph were married, Ralph's parents made gifts to him of one third of the shares in a corporation that owned their family farm. Throughout the twenty years that Janice and Ralph were married, Ralph and his brother worked the farm, growing and selling the crops, paying the expenses and banking the profits. During the same period, Janice acted as a farm wife, keeping house, getting the meals, caring for a kitchen garden and raising five children. At the time of the parties' divorce, Ralph's share of the farm had increased substantially in value. Should the increase be treated as marital property? (See <u>Meservey v. Meservey, 841 S.W.2d 240 (Mo.Ct.App.1992)</u>; cf. <u>Nardini v. Nardini, 414 N.W.2d 184 (Minn.1987)</u>; <u>Marschner v. Marschner, 621 N.W.2d 339 (N.D.2001)</u>.)

Problem 6-12

After he married Linda, Buddy was ordained as a minister and established Union Oaks, a religious organization with tax-exempt status under Internal Revenue Code. Buddy and Linda transferred their property to Union Oaks in exchange for promissory notes totaling $200,000. Union Oaks provided Buddy and Linda with a parsonage, and paid for their vehicles, travel, and various other personal expenses. In addition, Union Oaks paid Buddy a small salary. When Linda and Buddy separated twenty years later, they did not own any significant property beyond the promissory notes from Union Oaks, which have never been paid. Union Oaks has assets of more than $1.3 million, however, generated primarily through a series of real estate transactions. There is very little evidence that Union Oaks has ever conducted any community or religious activities. Can Linda collect a portion of the Union Oaks assets as marital property? (See <u>Medlock v. Medlock, 642 N.W.2d 113 (Neb. 2002)</u>; see also <u>Neibaur v. Neibaur, 125 P.3d 1072 (Idaho 2005)</u>.)

Hofstad v. Christie

240 P.3d 816 (Wyo. 2010)

HILL, JUSTICE.

[¶ 1] Appellant Jerald Korwin Hofstad challenges the district court's judgment equally partitioning a home owned by him and Appellee Cathryn Anne Christie as tenants in common. We affirm.

Think About It

As you study the materials in this chapter, consider the different approaches that state laws take to the assets and earnings of married or cohabiting couples at the end of their relationship.

ISSUES

[¶ 2] Mr. Hofstad lists four issues:

1. Did the district court below commit reversible error when it applied Alaska and Montana law and treated an unmarried couple as family members for purposes of dividing real property owned jointly as tenants in common?

2. Did the district court below commit reversible error when it found unequal contributions toward the purchase price of the property, there was no specific evidence of a gift, and yet the district court presumed that a gift of the excess contribution was intended?

3. Did the district court below improperly assign the burden of proof to the donor to prove the negative—that no gift was made?

4. Where there was no family relationship, and no specific evidence of any intended gift, should the property be divided according to the proven unequal contributions of the parties?

FACTS

[¶ 3] From February of 1996 to July of 2007, Mr. Hofstad and Ms. Christie were involved in a relationship and lived together for extended periods of time, but never married. However, their relationship produced twin boys born in 1996. The couple and their children, including five children from Mr. Hofstad's prior relationship, lived together in Casper from 1998 to 2005. Their home, located on Monument Road, was owned alone by Mr. Hofstad.

[¶ 4] In 2005, Hofstad decided to purchase a new home in Casper located at 1120 Donegal Street. At the time he entered into the contract on the Donegal home, he and Ms. Christie were separated. However, in April of 2005, the parties reconciled, and the warranty deed of the Donegal home conveyed the property to "Jerald K. Hofstad and Cathryn Anne Christie, grantee(s)." Mr. Hofstad paid the down payment, the closing costs, and entered into the loan obligation for the Donegal home. He used $124,053.15 from the sale of the Monument Road home, which was sold in May of 2005, to pay down the mortgage on the Donegal home.

[¶ 5] From May of 2005 until July of 2007, the parties and their children lived in the Donegal home. Mr. Hofstad paid all mortgage payments and utilities. Christie contributed to various improvements and was the homemaker of the home. In July of 2007, Christie moved out of the Donegal home.

[¶ 6] In December of 2007, Christie filed suit seeking partition of the Donegal home. After a bench trial, the court ruled that the home should be partitioned equally. The court reasoned that although Mr. Hofstad and Christie contributed unequal monetary amounts to the Donegal home, with Mr. Hofstad contributing substantially more money than Ms. Christie, Mr. Hofstad nevertheless failed to prove that there was not a family relationship or donative intent. Ms. Christie was awarded $70,767.40, one-half of the home's equity. Mr. Hofstad appealed that decision.

* * *

DISCUSSION

[¶ 8] It is widely accepted that, "if the instrument does not specify the shares of each co-tenant, it will be presumed that they take equal, undivided interests." *Bixler v. Oro Management,* 2004 WY 29, ¶ 19, 86 P.3d 843, 850 (Wyo.2004); see also 20 Am.Jur.2d *Cotenancy and Joint Ownership* § 121 (1995). However, this presumption may be rebutted by parol evidence, such as proof that the co-tenants contributed unequal amounts toward the purchase price of the property, and there is neither a family relationship among the co-tenants nor any evidence of donative intent on the part of those who contributed more than their pro rata amounts toward the purchase price. *Bixler,* ¶ 19, 86 P.3d at 850 (citations omitted); see also *D.M. v. D.A.,* 885 P.2d 94, 96 (Alaska 1994). See *Lawrence v. Harvey,* 186 Mont. 314, 607 P.2d 551, 556–57 (1980).

[¶ 9] In the instant case, both parties agree that the Donegal property is held by them as tenants in common, inasmuch as the warranty deed did not specify a joint tenancy. Also, both parties agree with the district court's assessment that Mr. Hofstad contributed a substantially greater financial amount. Having established that the parties are tenants in common, but that Mr. Hofstad contributed substantially more money than Ms. Christie towards the property, we are faced with considering whether there is either evidence of a family relationship or evidence of donative intent on the part of Mr. Hofstad, or lack thereof.

[¶ 10] First, we consider the more difficult of the two questions: whether there is evidence of the existence of a family relationship. Mr. Hofstad argues that the district court improperly applied a family presumption to himself and Ms. Christie as an "unmarried couple." Mr. Hofstad insists that there is absolutely no family relationship between himself and Ms. Christie because they are not related and they are unmarried. This is a matter of first impression in Wyoming, so we therefore look to other jurisdictions for guidance. A Missouri court stated as follows:

The record is clear that for several years prior to his death Phillips and Margaret conducted their joint household in the same manner as if they were married. Such a relationship, even in the absence of sexual relations, gave rise to a "family relation" between Margaret and Phillips. *Wells v. Goff,* [361 Mo. 1188] 239 S.W.2d 301 (Mo.1951); *Manning v. Driscoll's Estate,* 174 S.W.2d 921 (Mo.App.1943). In each of those cases a woman filed a claim against the estate of a male decedent for general housework performed for him during his lifetime. In each case, a "family relation" was found to exist.

Johnston v. Estate of Phillips, 706 S.W.2d 554, 556 (Mo.Ct.App.1986). Similarly, an Oregon court stated:

[T]he legislature expressly defined "members of the same family" to mean "persons who are members of a family as parents, stepparents, grandparents, spouses, sons-in-law, daughters-in-law, brothers, sisters, children, stepchildren, adopted children or grandchildren." The definition expressly requires a family *relationship* between "persons." In particular, those persons must be members of a family "as" parents, stepparents, and so on. As the department correctly observes, a person cannot be a parent to himself, a spouse to himself, his own child, his own in-law, or have any of the other relationships specified in the statute. In keeping with that understanding of the legislature's intended meaning, the statute consistently uses plural rather than singular references (*e.g.,* corporate "officers," corporate "directors," and family "members"). *See Schuette v. Dept. of Revenue,* 326 Or. 213, 217–18, 951 P.2d 690 (1997) (the repeated use of a singular or plural noun form provides some indication of the legislature's intent). [Emphasis in original.]

Finally, as the department correctly argues, even apart from the definition provided by the legislature, the term "family" is a "quintessential example" of a collective noun—*i.e.,* a noun that most naturally refers to a collection of things or persons as a unit. *See Webster's Third New Int'l Dictionary* 444 (unabridged ed. 2002) (defining "collective": "1 a *of a word or term:* indicating a number of persons or things considered as constituting one group or aggregate *family* and *flock* are *collective* words> b *of a noun or pronoun:* singular in form but sometimes or always plural in construction *family* in 'the family were proud' is a *collective* word>"). Various dictionary definitions of the word "family" similarly denote a group of individuals with a common affiliation or ancestry.

Empl. Dep't v. Stock Secrets, Inc., 210 Or.App. 426, 150 P.3d 1090, 1092 (2007).

[¶ 11] Our own statute defines "family members" as follows:

(x) "Member of the minor's family" means the minor's parent, stepparent, spouse, grandparent, brother, sister, uncle or aunt, whether of whole or half blood or by adoption[.]

Wyo. Stat. Ann. § 34–13–114(a)(x) (LexisNexis 2009).

[¶ 12] Even the United States Supreme Court recognizes that "family is a much broader term" than just parents and their children. *Moore v. City of East Cleveland*, 431 U.S. 494, 543, 97 S.Ct. 1932, 52 L.Ed.2d 531 (1977). The district court in this case echoed that sentiment when it stated in its conclusions of law that:

> Mr. Hofstad and Ms. Christie cohabited and shared an intimate relationship which resulted in the birth of two children of that relationship, and they resided together with their children at the 1120 Donegal residence, and accordingly, there was a family relationship[.]

[¶ 13] Although the term "family relationship" is by no means absolute, we agree with the district court and Ms. Christie that in this case, the parties do share a family relationship, largely by way of their sharing two children. Even if Mr. Hofstad and Ms. Christie are not married, nor related by blood, that they lived together on and off for approximately ten years, all the while sharing an intimate relationship which resulted in the birth of their twins is evidence that a family relationship exists. Mr. Hofstad and Ms. Christie may never consider themselves "family," having never been married; however, their twin sons bind the four of them inextricably and forever, resulting in a family *relationship*. We disagree with Mr. Hofstad's argument that he does not share a family relationship with Ms. Christie.

[¶ 14] Next we turn to whether or not there was any evidence of donative intent on the part of Mr. Hofstad, who argues that not only did he not gift Ms. Christie one-half of the value of the Donegal home, but also that she should have been required to actually prove that a gift of one-half of the value of the home was given to her.

[¶ 15] Again, because this is an issue of first impression in Wyoming, we look to other states for direction. Other states have applied the "equal share presumption rule" to tenancies in common. In *D.M.*, the plaintiffs rebutted the general presumption of equal shares between tenants in common by demonstrating unequal contribution to equity in real property. There, the court found that this evidence created a presumption that they intended to share property in proportion to their respective contributions, and that was enough to rebut the general presumption of equal shares. *D.M.*, 885 P.2d at 97–98. The court held that if the parties intend to hold a tenancy in common in a particular proportion or if intent to determine proportion by a particular method can be discovered, this intent controls over the equal share presumption rule of cotenancy. Nonetheless, the court recognized that the common law presumptions concerning the respective interests of tenants in common where one contributes unequally to the purchase price are not applicable where the relationship between the parties indicates that one might have intended to make a gift to the other. *Id., at 97*, n. 7 (citing *People v. Varel*, 351 Ill. 96, 184 N.E. 209, 211 (1932); *Wood v. Collins*, 812 P.2d 951, 956 (Alaska 1991)).

In *Wood*, the court held that where the parties cohabitate and share an intimate relationship, it is more likely than otherwise that one party may contribute more of the acquisition or upkeep costs and still expect an equal share of the property. The court in *Wood* went on to explain that the court must still find, however, that it was in fact the intent of the party making the excess contribution to confer it on the other party as a gift.

[¶ 16] Using the rules of cotenancy, when the conveyance is taken in both names, the parties would be presumed to share equally or to share based upon the amount contributed, if the contributions were traceable (rebuttable by donative intent or a family relationship). *West v. Knowles*, 50 Wash.2d 311, 311 P.2d 689 (1957); A.C. Freeman on Cotenancy and Partition, 172 § 105 *Presumption of Relative Interests* (2nd ed. 1886). See, e.g., *Mayo v. Jones*, 8 Wash.App. 140, 505 P.2d 157 (Wash.App.1972); *Huls v. Huls*, 98 Ohio App. 509, 130 N.E.2d 412 (1954); *Williams v. Monzingo*, 235 Iowa 434, 16 N.W.2d 619 (Iowa 1944). Such rules of cotenancy could also result in requiring a showing of who paid various items, such as taxes, mortgage payments, or repairs. 2 Tiffany, Law of Real Property 282, § 461 (1939 and 2001 Cum.Supp.). The difficulty with the application of the rules of cotenancy is that their mechanical operation does not consider the nature of the relationship of the parties. While this may be appropriate for commercial investments, a mechanistic application of these rules will not often accurately reflect the expectations of the parties.

[¶ 17] In *Beal v. Beal*, 282 Or. 115, 577 P.2d 507 (1978), the Supreme Court of Oregon found that property accumulated during cohabitation should be divided by determining the express or implied intent of the parties. There, Barbara and Raymond Beal, recently divorced, purchased property together, listing themselves as husband and wife. Both contributed to the down payment, Barbara paying $500.00 more than Raymond. Barbara made the first monthly payment; Raymond made all subsequent payments. The parties lived together in the house and both contributed to the household. After two years, Barbara moved out. Raymond remained and made all monthly payments on the house. The court decided the property dispute should be resolved by looking at the parties' intent. Before Barbara moved out, the trial court found that the parties intended to pool their resources for their common benefit. Therefore, both parties were held to have an undivided interest in the property. The court rejected the regular rules of cotenancy, which would have required the parties to share expenses based upon their ownership share, because these rules failed to account for the relationship between the parties. Instead, the court stated,

> We believe a division of property accumulated during a period of cohabitation must be begun by inquiring into the intent of the parties, and if an intent can be found, it should control that property distribution. While this is obviously true when the parties have executed a written agree-

ment, it is just as true if there is no written agreement. The difference is often only the sophistication of the parties. Thus, absent an express agreement, courts should closely examine the facts in evidence to determine what the parties implicitly agreed upon. . . .

. . . .

. . .we hold that courts, when dealing with the property disputes of a man and a woman who have been living together in a nonmarital domestic relationship, should distribute the property based upon the express or implied intent of those parties.

Beal, 577 P.2d at 510. We agree with *Beal* that property accumulated before separation should be divided by determining the express or implied intent of the parties. Here, the district court stated that

Mr. Hofstad's representation and promise that Ms. Christie would be a "co-owner" or "equal owner" of the 1120 Donegal residence, and that if they would get back together again he would put title to the property in both names, is evidence of donative intent on his part with respect to the equal undivided one-half interest in the property vested in Ms. Christie.

After reviewing the record, we agree with the district court. Among the evidence that leads us to this conclusion is that in 2005, after the parties were briefly separated, they became engaged, and Mr. Hofstad represented to Ms. Christie that he would "change," they would be married within three months, that he would undergo counseling, and that Ms. Christie would be a co-owner or equal owner in the Donegal home. Furthermore, as conclusive evidence of Mr. Hofstad's intent, he put Ms. Christie's name on the Donegal deed after they rekindled their relationship. He initiated the purchase of the Donegal property of his own volition, but switched course after rekindling his relationship with Ms. Christie. We find this to be persuasive evidence of Mr. Hofstad's donative intent.

CONCLUSION

[¶ 18] The district court's judgment partitioning equally a home the parties owned as tenants in common is affirmed. Given the parties' children and living situation over the course of the past ten years, a family relationship existed. Furthermore, given the circumstances surrounding the purchase of 1120 Donegal and the parties' reconciliation, evidence of donative intent existed. We affirm the district court.

Points for Discussion

a. Cohabitant Claims

Because couples who are not married under state law do not have access to equitable distribution and other remedies under state divorce laws, their property rights are governed by property and contract law and restitution principles. How would this case be resolved if the couple had been married to each other?

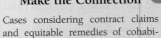

Make the Connection

Cases considering contract claims and equitable remedies of cohabitants are included in Chapter 1.

b. Property Law Remedies

All states have statutes governing the rights of co-tenants to partition jointly-owned real property, and many states also allow actions for partition of personal property. Partition actions are typically equitable proceedings, in which courts apply a range of equitable defenses. See generally Leonard A. Girard, *Equitable and Contractual Defenses to Partition*, 18 Stan. L. Rev. 1428 (1966). For cohabiting couples in many states, a partition action serves as the functional equivalent of equitable division for jointly-owned property. See, e.g., Brooks v. Allen, 137 A.3d 404 (N.H. 2016), which approved an equitable partition of real estate owned by an unmarried couple during their 20-year relationship, over one partner's objection that this was an improper "divorce-like" remedy.

Why does the court in *Hofstad* ask whether there was a "family relationship" between Mr. Hofstad and Ms. Christie? On what basis does the court conclude that equal partition of the property is appropriate? Would the case have been decided differently if he had not put her name on the title?

c. Contract Remedies

As noted in Chapter 1, courts in most jurisdictions enforce express agreements between cohabitants. Courts in a number of jurisdictions also allow cohabitants to bring claims based on an implied contract theory at the end of their cohabitation. For example, the *Beal* case, cited in *Hofstad*, concluded that "courts, when dealing with the property disputes of a man and woman who have been living together in a nonmarital domestic relationship, should distribute the property based upon the express or implied intent of the parties." See also Ireland v. Flanagan, 627 P.2d 496 (Or. Ct. App. 1981); Watts v. Watts, 405 N.W.2d 303 (Wis. 1987); Goode v. Goode, 396 S.E.2d 430 (W. Va. 1990); Reed v. Parrish, 286 P.3d 1054 (Alaska 2012). Other states have rejected the implied contract approach, however. See, e.g., Morone v. Morone, 413 N.E.2d 1154 (N.Y. 1980). See generally George L.

Blum, Annotation, <u>*Property Rights Arising from Relationship of Couple Cohabiting Without Marriage,* 69 A.L.R.5th 219 (1999 & Supp.)</u>

If Mr. Hofstad had not put Ms. Christie's name on the deed to the property, could she have claimed a share of the equity on an implied contract theory? How would a case like *Hofstad* be handled in a jurisdiction that does not recognize equitable or implied contract claims between unmarried cohabitants?

d. Equitable Remedies

Should states permit cohabitants to bring equitable actions for property division without requiring proof of an express or implied contract? In Washington, courts divide property of couples in "committed intimate relationships." See, e.g., <u>Olver v. Fowler, 168 P.3d 348 (Wash. 2007)</u>. Other states utilize restitution principles to compensate one partner's investment of money or services in a property or business owned by the other partner, but do not order compensation for less tangible contributions. See generally Ann Laquer Estin, <u>*Ordinary Cohabitation,* 76 Notre Dame L. Rev. 1381 (2001)</u>.

Restatement (Third) of Restitution and Unjust Enrichment § 28 (2011)

(1) If two persons have formerly lived together in a relationship resembling marriage, and if one of them owns a specific asset to which the other has made substantial, uncompensated contributions in the form of property or services, the person making such contributions has a claim in restitution against the owner as necessary to prevent unjust enrichment upon the dissolution of the relationship.

(2) The rule of subsection (1) may be displaced, modified, or supplemented by local domestic relations law.

Brebaugh v. Deane

118 P.3d 43 (Ariz. Ct. App. 2005) rev. den. (2006)

PORTLEY, J.

¶ 1 We examine whether stock options that had not vested before the petition for dissolution was served can be divided as community property. Because we find that the trial court needs to determine whether the unvested stock options were compensation for past performance, incentives for future performance or some combination of both, we reverse that portion of the decree of dissolution and remand the matter to the trial court.

FACTUAL AND PROCEDURAL BACKGROUND

¶ 2 William J. Brebaugh ("Husband") and Nancy L. Deane ("Wife") were divorced after thirty years of marriage. Husband is the vice president of enrollment at Apollo Group, Inc./University of Phoenix ("Apollo"). Wife teaches art in the Scottsdale School District. The parties were unable to resolve whether Husband's unvested stock options were community property. After their trial, the court determined the unvested stock options were community property and awarded Wife one-half of those options. Husband appealed and we have jurisdiction pursuant to Arizona Revised Statutes ("A.R.S.") section 12–2101(B) (2003).

DISCUSSION

¶ 3 Husband received blocks of stock options from his employer during the marriage. The parties agreed that stock options that had vested prior to the date the petition was served were community property. They also agreed that stock options he received after service were his separate property. They could not agree, however, whether the options he received during the marriage but could not be exercised until after service of the petition were community or separate property.

¶ 4 The trial court, after consideration of testimony, memoranda and proposed findings of fact and conclusions of law, noted that the issue was how any community interest in the unvested options should be determined. After noting that Arizona has not examined the issue, the trial court examined the "time rule" outlined in *In re Marriage of Hug*, 154 Cal.App.3d 780, 201 Cal.Rptr. 676 (1984), and rejected Husband's claim that the unvested options were intended as incentive for his future employment. It determined that Husband had failed to demonstrate by clear and convincing evidence that the options that had not vested before service of process were his sole and separate property.

¶ 5 On appeal, Husband contends that we should allocate the community and separate property interests in unvested stock options using a formula that favors the future efforts of the employee-spouse. *See generally* In re Marriage of Nelson, 177 Cal.App.3d 150, 222 Cal.Rptr. 790 (1986). Wife contends that there was insufficient evidence to suggest that the options were granted for Husband's future efforts. She argues that the options were compensation for work during the marriage and, therefore, are entirely community property. In the alternative, she contends that a time rule that emphasizes the employee's past efforts is the appropriate formula in this case. *See generally* Hug, 154 Cal.App.3d 780, 201 Cal.Rptr. 676. * * *

¶ 6 Stock options are a form of compensation. *See* In re Marriage of Robinson and Thiel, 201 Ariz. 328, 332, ¶ 9, 35 P.3d 89, 93 (App.2001). "Property acquired by either spouse during marriage is presumed to be community property, and the spouse seeking to overcome the presumption has the burden of establishing a separate character of the property by clear and convincing evidence." Thomas v. Thomas, 142 Ariz. 386, 392, 690 P.2d 105, 111 (App.1984). Property acquired after service of a petition for dissolution is considered separate property if the parties get divorced. *See* A.R.S. § 25–211 (2000).

¶ 7 In Arizona, the community has an interest in the property earned during the marriage. *See* Van Loan v. Van Loan, 116 Ariz. 272, 274, 569 P.2d 214, 216 (1977) (holding that to the extent a spouse acquires unvested pension benefits from community efforts, that property right is divisible upon dissolution). However, compensation for a spouse's post-dissolution efforts is sole and separate property. *See* A.R.S. § 25–213(B) (Supp.2004); In re Marriage of Kosko, 125 Ariz. 517, 518, 611 P.2d 104, 105 ("any portion of a recovery which represents compensation for post-dissolution earnings of the. . .spouse is the separate property of that spouse"). As such, we hold that unvested stock options are analogous to pension plans.

¶ 8 Arizona courts have held that "pension rights, whether vested or nonvested, are community property insofar as the rights were acquired during marriage." Johnson v. Johnson, 131 Ariz. 38, 41, 638 P.2d 705, 708 (1981) (footnotes omitted); *accord* Van Loan, 116 Ariz. at 274, 569 P.2d at 216. Other jurisdictions also consider unvested stock options analogous to unvested pension benefits in determining the community interest. Thus, if the stock options are intended as compensation for Husband's efforts during marriage, they are community property. If, however, the options are, in part, intended to induce future employment, then, to that extent, they are Husband's separate property.

¶ 9 Most jurisdictions have applied a time rule for determining the community's interest in unvested stock options. *See, e.g.,* Baccanti v. Morton, 434 Mass.

787, 752 N.E.2d 718, 727–28 (2001) (citing cases). In determining whether the community has an interest in the unvested stock options granted during the marriage, the court must determine the extent to which the stock options were compensation for a spouse's effort during the marriage. In making that determination, the court must consider the employer's purpose for awarding the stock options.

¶ 10 As the trial court recognized, the purpose of stock options varies widely. A company may award stock options as compensation for past services or performance, as incentive to remain with the company, or to garner favorable tax consequences. Therefore, we agree that "[t]rial courts should be vested with broad discretion to fashion approaches which will achieve the most equitable results under the facts of each case." Hug, 201 Cal.Rptr. at 685.

¶ 11 Here, the trial court concluded that Husband's stock options compensated him for work performed during the marriage and rejected his claim that the options were solely intended to encourage him to remain with Apollo. It concluded, based on the date the options were granted, that all options granted during the marriage, whether vested or not at the time of service, were community property. The stock option agreements do not, however, appear to support that conclusion.

¶ 12 The stock option agreements provide that the options were intended to encourage key employees to remain and to enhance Apollo's ability to attract new employees "by providing an opportunity to have a proprietary interest in the success of [Apollo,]" and as an incentive to "focus on [its] long-term growth." The agreements provided that the options could vest on an accelerated basis if Apollo reached certain profit goals and the stock price reached a designated amount. Alternatively, and regardless of Apollo's performance, twenty-five percent of the options would vest annually beginning the year after the options were awarded.

¶ 13 Apollo's chief financial officer, Kenda Gonzalez, moreover, testified that stock options generally are granted as an incentive for employees to remain with a company, to think like stockholders and thereby consider the company's long-term benefits. She also testified that Apollo grants options based on the employee's level of responsibility within the company, not for past performance. Husband's expert accountant testified that Apollo's stock options were an inducement to keep him with the company and not to reward him for past performance.

¶ 14 Wife's expert accountant testified that Husband's stock options were compensation for past efforts. She opined that because Apollo's enrollment had increased significantly during Husband's tenure as vice president of enrollment, which increased the gross income for the corporation, his salary and bonuses alone were inadequate compensation. Husband admitted that he would not stay with the company if he only received his salary and bonuses. Husband received regular merit raises and bonuses during his employment, but did not receive stock options on a regular basis.

¶ 15 If the stock options were intended solely as compensation for work performed or deferred compensation, the trial court's characterization would be correct. It does not appear, however, that the court considered the fact that the agreements specifically stated that the options were intended to encourage key employees to remain with Apollo and enhance Apollo's ability to attract new employees. The language of the agreements sufficiently rebuts the presumption that the options granted during the marriage are entirely community property.

¶ 16 We have found only two jurisdictions that have held that unvested stock options were entirely community property. In *Bodin v. Bodin,* a Texas appellate court affirmed the trial court's ruling that unvested stock options, like military retirement benefits, were a community asset because they constituted a contingent interest in property earned during the marriage. 955 S.W.2d 380, 381 (Tex. Ct.App.1997). The *Bodin* court, however, did not analyze whether the unvested stock options were for past performance or incentive for future performance, or whether that purpose might limit the community's interest in the stock options to the extent the unvested options were intended as compensation for post-divorce services. * * *

¶ 18 In Wisconsin, the court of appeals presumed that unvested stock options were community property. *See Chen v. Chen,* 142 Wis.2d 7, 416 N.W.2d 661, 665 (Ct.App.1987). *Chen* held that the employee spouse failed to rebut the presumption because the stock option agreement stated that the options were intended to reward past contributions to the employer and to induce continued employment. The court stated that "it would be mere conjecture to attempt to separate the portion of the net profits attributable to [the employee spouse's] post-divorce efforts" because the increase in value was due, in part, "to market forces and innumerable other variables."

¶ 19 Here, if the trial court concludes, after reviewing the agreements, that the unvested stock options were, even in part, incentives for future performance, it should analyze the issue under *Hug* and *Nelson,* and use a time rule to determine the community and separate property interests in the unvested stock options. Our conclusion is supported by the fact that a similar fractional formula is used to determine the community's interest in unvested pension or retirement plans. When properly applied, the time rules equitably allocate the portion of the stock options attributable to future services.

¶ 20 A majority of courts that have examined whether unvested stock options that vest after separation or service of the petition have accepted two primary time-rule formulas for allocating unvested stock options. The first is the *Hug* formula which is most appropriate for stock options that are granted for past services but cannot be exercised until after the separation or service of process because the formula gives more weight to the employee's entire tenure with the employer during marriage. Under the *Hug* formula,

> the number of options determined to be community [is] the product of a fraction in which the numerator [is] the period in months from the commencement of the spouse's tenure with his employer to the date of the couple's separation, and the denominator [is] the period in months between commencement of employment and the date when each group of options first bec[o]me[s] exercisable. This fraction [is] then multiplied by the number of shares of stock which c[an] be purchased with each block of options, yielding the community figure.

Nelson, 222 Cal.Rptr. at 793 (*citing Hug, 201 Cal.Rptr. at 678*).

¶ 21 Conversely, the *Nelson* formula is more appropriate for stock options which are intended to compensate an employee for future efforts. The *Nelson* formula assumes that the period of employment prior to the granting of the option did not contribute to the employee earning the stock options and should not be included in the time used to calculate the community's interest in the options. In Nelson, the numerator of the fraction is "the number of months from the date of grant of each block of options to the date of the couple's separation, while the denominator [is] the period from the time of each grant to its date of exercisability." This fraction is also multiplied by the number of shares to be purchased to determine the community figure.

* * *

¶ 23 "The valuation of assets is a factual determination that must be based on the facts and circumstances of each case." Kelsey v. Kelsey, 186 Ariz. 49, 51, 918 P.2d 1067, 1069 (App.1996). As noted in *Hug,* "since the purposes underlying stock options differ, reference to the facts of each particular case must be made to reveal the features and implications of a particular employee stock option." Because the nature of stock options differ and trial courts will have to resolve options on an ad hoc basis, we decline to adopt a single formula for valuing stock options upon dissolution.

¶ 24 Although Husband contends that his options were incentive for future performance and Wife contends they were for past performance, we will leave it to the trial court to determine whether the disputed options were incentives for the future, compensation for past performance, or some combination of both. Once it makes that determination, it can decide which time-rule formula is most appropriate.

¶ 25 The primary factor the trial court should consider is the employer's intent in awarding the options. In determining the employer's intent, the court should consider whether there is any expressly stated purpose in the employment agreement or stock option agreement, and the adequacy of other compensation or the compensation scheme as a whole, *see Hug, 154 Cal.App.3d at 790, 201 Cal.Rptr. 676* (stock options may be in lieu of higher current compensation or as bonus). If the employer's intent in granting the unvested options was to compensate the employee for past or current service, the options are community property and the *Hug* formula is applicable. If, however, the intent was to provide an incentive for the employee's future performance, the *Nelson* formula should be used to allocate the unvested options.

¶ 26 Accordingly, we reverse the portion of the decree dividing the unvested stock options and remand for further findings consistent with this opinion.

* * *

Points for Discussion

a. Vested and Unvested Stock Options

In *Brebaugh*, the parties agreed that vested stock options received during the marriage were community property, but disagreed about the characterization of unvested stock options. Davidson v. Davidson, 578 N.W.2d 848 (Neb. 1998), offered this explanation of these terms:

> An employee stock option is an employee's contractual right to purchase an employer's stock during a specified period at a predetermined price. An employee stock option may be vested and matured, vested and unmatured, or unvested. If the employee has an absolute right to exercise the option immediately, the option is vested and matured. If the employee cannot exercise the option until some future date, but the employee has an absolute right to exercise the option on that date, the option is vested and unmatured. If the option cannot be exercised until some future date and the option is subject to divestment, the option is unvested.

Davidson, 578 N.W.2d at 853.

Many court decisions have concluded that unvested stock options received during a marriage can properly be classified as marital property, but a small minority of jurisdictions hold that unvested stock options may not treated as marital property. See generally Tracy A. Thomas, *The New Marital Property of Employee Stock Options*, 35 Fam. L.Q. 497 (2001). What are the arguments for and against treating unvested stock options as marital property?

**Further Reading:
Stock Options**

Lester Barenbaum, et al., The Family Lawyer's Guide to Stock Options (2007).

If a court determines that unvested stock options are marital property, how can they be divided? If options can only be exercised at some time in the future, how can the court determine their value? If the options are unvested, how should the court take the risk that they will not vest into account? See *Davidson, 578 N.W.2d at 858–59*; Diana Richmond, *The Challenges of Stock Options*, 35 Fam. L.Q. 251 (2001).

b. Time Rules

In allocating unvested options between the marital and separate estates, most courts apply some version of the "time rule" described in *Brebaugh*. Time rules are also used to divide other assets that are acquired over a period of time, such as an employment bonus or pension. In general, these rules begin by determining the period of months or years over which the asset was earned or acquired, and then determine what portion of that time period was during the marriage.

If the court determines on remand that the options involved in *Brebaugh* were granted for past services, how should they be divided? What if the court determines that they were intended as compensation for future services? See generally David S. Rosettenstein, *Exploring the Use of the Time Rule in the Distribution of Stock Options on Divorce*, 35 Fam. L.Q. 263 (2001).

c. Pension Plans

Brebaugh points out that Arizona treats both vested and unvested pension rights acquired during a marriage as community property. All or nearly all states agree that vested pension rights may be marital property, following a trend started in the mid-1970s. See In re Marriage of Brown, 544 P.2d 561 (Cal. 1976), which emphasized the fact that pension benefits are a form of deferred compensation for services performed by an employee.

An employee has a vested pension right if the employee has completed the period of employment necessary to give the employee an indefeasible right to a pension that will be payable in the future, when the employee reaches retirement age. An employee may enforce the right to a vested pension even if he or she has left or been discharged by that employer, although a vested pension may be subject to defeasance if the holder dies before the date on which the pension matures. See In re Marriage of Grubb, 745 P.2d 661 (Colo.1987). In most states, unvested pensions are also divisible as marital property. See Broadhead v. Broadhead, 737 P.2d 731 (Wyo.1987) (citing cases).

Although there is a substantial consensus that pensions should be characterized as marital property, there is a wider range of views on the appropriate methods for determining how much of a pension is marital property and how the marital portion should be distributed. The case law is collected in Elizabeth Barker Brandt, *Valuation, Allocation, and Distribution of Retirement Plans at Divorce: Where are We?* 35 Fam. L.Q. 469 (2001). Pension plans may be divided using a "Qualified Domestic Relations Order" or QDRO, under the federal Employee Retirement Income Security Act of 1974 (ERISA), described below.

Logistics of dividing an **employee benefit plan** also depend on whether the plan involved is a ***defined-contribution plan***, in which the employer maintains an individual account for each employee with a readily determined value, or a ***defined-benefit plan***, under which the employer pays a benefit at retirement according to a formula, based on variables such as the employee's length of service and highest monthly salary. See In re the Marriage of Lehman, 955 P.2d 451 (Cal. 1998); In re the Marriage of Kelm, 912 P.2d 545 (Colo. 1996). Defined-contribution plans are much easier to value and divide in divorce cases.

d. Deferred Compensation

In addition to stock options and pension plans, courts treat many other forms of deferred compensation as marital or community property subject to equitable distribution. For example, courts have divided:

* accumulated paid vacation and sick leave days, see Schober v. Schober, 692 P.2d 267 (Alaska 1984), but see Marriage of Abrell, 923 N.E.2d 791 (Ill. 2010);

* a year-end or other bonus payment, see In re Marriage of Griswold, 48 P.3d 1018 (Wash. Ct. App. 2002), King v. Howard, 158 A.3d 878 (Del. 2017);

* contingent fee payments and commissions paid for work done during the marriage, see, McDermott v. McDermott, 986 S.W.2d 843 (Ark. 1999) (attorney's contingent fee contracts); Niroo v. Niroo, 545 A.2d 35 (Md. 1988) (insurance renewal commissions); but see Green v. Green, 806 S.E.2d 45 (N.C. Ct. App. 2017) (contingent fees are not deferred compensation):

- payments under professional sports contracts for games played during the marriage, see, e.g., <u>In re Marriage of Sewell, 817 P.2d 594 (Colo.Ct.App.1991)</u>; <u>Gastineau v. Gastineau, 573 N.Y.S.2d 819 (N.Y.Sup.Ct.1991)</u>, <u>Chambers v. Chambers, 840 P.2d 841 (Utah Ct.App.1992)</u>; and

- proceeds from a Nobel Prize award received by a spouse for scientific work done during the marriage, see <u>Ketterle v. Ketterle, 814 N.E.2d 385 (Mass. App. Ct. 2004)</u>.

Some courts have classified intellectual property rights acquired during the marriage as marital property, and treat the income that flows from these rights as a form of deferred compensation. See, e.g., <u>In re Marriage of Zaentz, 267 Cal. Rptr. 31 (Ct. App. 1990)</u>; <u>Teller v. Teller, 53 P.3d 240 (Haw. 2002)</u>; <u>Marriage of Heinze, 631 N.E.2d 728 (Ill. App. Ct. 1994)</u>; <u>In re Marriage of Monslow, 912 P.2d 735 (Kan. 1996)</u>; <u>Dunn v. Dunn, 802 P.2d 1314 (Utah Ct.App.1990)</u>. See also <u>Rodrigue v. Rodrigue, 218 F.3d 432 (5th Cir.2000)</u> (holding that the federal Copyright Act does not preempt state community property laws). See also <u>Canisius v. Morgenstern, 35 N.E.3d 385 (Mass. App. Ct. 2015)</u>, which considered the problem of allocating royalties from wife's best-selling novel written during the marriage, when she also carried out significant publicity and promotional work for the the book after the couple separated.

e. Disability, Workers' Compensation, and Personal Injury Awards

Under the majority rule, referred to as the "analytic approach," the portion of disability pensions, workers' compensation awards, and personal injury damages that is intended to reimburse expenses incurred or earnings lost during the marriage is marital property and subject to equitable distribution. See, e.g. <u>Weisfeld v. Weisfeld, 545 So.2d 1341 (Fla.1989)</u> (workers' compensation award); <u>Hardin v. Hardin, 801 S.E.2d 774 (Ga. 2017)</u> (disability insurance); <u>Marshall v. Marshall, 902 N.W.2d 223 (Neb. 2017)</u> (personal injury settlement). In some states, however, courts read the statutory presumption that property received during a marriage is marital to require that the entire amount of any claim accrued or award received during the marriage must be treated as marital property. E.g. <u>In re Marriage of DeRossett, 671 N.E.2d 654 (Ill. 1996)</u>; <u>Drake v. Drake, 725 A.2d 717 (Pa. 1999)</u>. Note that the characterization of this property as marital does not determine how it will be distributed between the parties. In *DeRossett*, for example, the court found the husband's workers' compensation settlement to be marital property, and awarded 30% of it to the wife.

f. Dividing Deferred Compensation Interests

After a court determines that some type of compensation, which will be received in the future, constitutes marital or community property, it can employ one of three broad approaches to dividing the marital share. For vested benefits, with a net present value that can be readily ascertained, the court may award the interest to one spouse and offset that value against other property in the marital estate. Alternatively, if it is possible to calculate the marital portion of the asset that will or may be received in the future, the court may enter an order dividing the interest based on that formula but deferring the actual distribution of the asset until it is received. A third approach is for the court to reserve jurisdiction over the issue, so that the parties can come back to court when the asset is actually received. See Marriage of Kelm, 912 P.2d 545 (Colo. 1996).

The "immediate offset" approach has some advantages, particularly when the interest can be readily valued and when it is a relatively minor part of the marital estate. Courts often strongly favor this approach, because it winds up the conflict between the parties. E.g. Ruggles v. Ruggles, 860 P.2d 182 (N.M. 1993); cf. Blanchard v. Blanchard, 731 So.2d 175 (La.1999). What are the advantages of the deferred distribution and reserved jurisdiction approaches?

Federal Pension and Retirement Laws

ERISA. The Employee Retirement Income Security Act of 1974 (ERISA), 29 U.S.C.A. § 1003(a)(1) (2018), regulates most employee benefit plans in the United States. Initially, ERISA contained a provision forbidding assignment or alienation of pension benefits, and some courts held that this prevented divorce courts from dividing pensions in divorce. Congress amended ERISA in 1984 to allow state courts to order deferred distribution of pension benefits by making a "qualified domestic relations order" (QDRO) for alimony, child support or marital property. The interactions between ERISA and divorce laws are complex, and must be carefully navigated by divorce lawyers.

Go Online

Basic information about QDROs is available from the Employee Benefits Security Administration in the U.S. Department of Labor.

The Supreme Court has considered the interaction between ERISA and state laws in several cases, including Boggs v. Boggs, 520 U.S. 833 (1997), which concluded that the surviving spouse provisions of ERISA preempt aspects of Louisiana community property law, and Egelhoff v. Egelhoff, 532 U.S. 141 (2001), which concluded that ERISA preempts a state statute providing that designations of a spouse as beneficiary of a life insurance or pension plan are automatically revoked in the event of a divorce. Kennedy v. Plan Administrator for DuPont Savings and Investment Plan, 555 U.S.

285 (2009), concluded that a savings and investment plan administrator had a duty under ERISA and the plan documents to follow the beneficiary designation on file for a divorced plan participant in favor of his ex-wife, where he failed to execute a new beneficiary designation. The Court concluded that the participant's former wife's waiver of her interest, in a divorce decree that did not amount to a QDRO, was not effective where it was inconsistent with the plan documents.

Social Security Benefits. Under the federal Social Security Act, an individual who was married for ten years or more may claim benefits at retirement based upon his or her former spouse's earnings record, see 42 U.S.C. § 402(b) and (c); § 416(d) (2018). See generally Grace Ganz Blumberg, *Adult Derivative Benefits in Social Security*, 32 Stan. L. Rev. 233 (1980). Social security benefits are not marital property, however, and may not be divided on divorce. See, e.g., Jackson v. Sollie, 141 A.3d 1122 (Md. 2016); Neville v. Neville, 791 N.E.2d 434 (Ohio 2003). This rule applies even if the parties have agreed by contract to divide future Social Security benefits. See, e.g., In re Marriage of Anderson, 252 P.3d 490 (Colo. Ct. App. 2010). Courts may take the benefits into account as part of their consideration of the parties' economic circumstances, however. See Matter of Marriage of Brane, 908 P.2d 625 (Kan. Ct. App. 1995); Pongonis v. Pongonis, 606 A.2d 1055 (Me.1992); but see In re Marriage of Crook, 813 N.E.2d 198 (Ill. 2004).

Railroad Retirement Act. Hisquierdo v. Hisquierdo, 439 U.S. 572 (1979) held that the Railroad Retirement Act preempted California community property law, so that the California divorce court did not have authority to divide the railroad retirement pension of the employee husband. Congress subsequently amended the Railroad Retirement Act to permit the division of a part of the pension benefits, the so-called Tier II payments. See 45 U.S.C. § 231m(b)(2) (2018). An award to the non-employee spouse may not, under *Hisquierdo,* be made indirectly by including the pension in marital property and giving the non-employee spouse other property equal to her share in the pension. Belt v. Belt, 398 N.W.2d 737 (N.D.1987).

Military Retirement Pay. Following *Hisquierdo*, the Supreme Court considered military retirement pay in McCarty v. McCarty, 453 U.S. 210 (1981), and decided that it was not community property subject to division on divorce. Following the decision in *McCarty*, Congress passed the Uniformed Services Former Spouses' Protection Act, (USFSPA), codified at 10 U.S.C. § 1408 (2018). USFSPA overruled *McCarty,* providing that disposable retired or retainer pay may be treated by a state court as the property of the member of the armed forces and that individual's spouse, and may be ordered by that court to be paid directly to the spouse or former spouse if he or she was married to the member of the armed forces during ten years of military service. The manner and amounts of the division are generally left to the state divorce courts, but the statute is quite complex.

Since USFSPA, state courts have generally treated military pensions as marital or community property, to the extent earned during marriage, and thus available for distribution on divorce.

Military disability benefits are not subject to division under USFSPA. See <u>Mansell v. Mansell, 490 U.S. 581 (1989)</u>; see generally Mark E. Sullivan, The Military Divorce Handbook (2d ed. 2011). This causes difficulties when a veteran decides, at some point after a divorce that involved a division of military pay, to waive a portion of his or her retirement pay in order to receive military disability benefits. This waiver has the effect of reducing the spouse's share as well. Although a number of state courts held that an individual making this election could be required to indemnify his or her former spouse, the Supreme Court concluded that the statute does not permit this. See <u>Howell v. Howell, 581 U.S. ___, 137 S.Ct. 1400 (2017)</u>. The Court made clear, however, that state courts are free to consider this possibility in making the initial division of assets, or as part of the circumstances in setting or modifying spousal support orders.

Further Reading: Deferred Compensation

- David Clayton Carrad, The Complete QDRO Handbook: Dividing ERISA, Military, and Civil Service Pensions and Collecting Child Support from Employee Benefit Plans (3d ed. 2009).

- Gary A. Shulman & David I. Kelley, Dividing Pensions in Divorce: Negotiating and Drafting Safe Settlements with QDROs and Present Values (3d ed. 2010).

- Kristi Anderson Wells and Jon Eric Stuebner, The Executive Compensation Handbook: Stock Option Awards, Restricted Stock Grants, Cash Bonuses, Incentives and Other Non-Qualified Deferred Compensation in Divorce (2018).

Problem 6-13

When Eloise and Nelson divorced after twenty-five years of marriage, Nelson had worked for his current employer for twenty years and was vested in the employer's "defined benefit" pension plan. Nelson planned to work another ten years, until the earliest date when he would be eligible to retire with full benefits under the plan. The actual amount that he will receive under the defined benefit formula will be determined at the time of his retirement, based on his number of years of employment with the company and his salary on the date he retires. How should the court divide the pension? (See In re the Marriage of Kelm, 912 P.2d 545 (Colo. 1996).)

Problem 6-14

At the time of his divorce from Jennifer, Louis was 55 years old and a senior partner at a large accounting firm. Under the partnership agreement, Louis was required to retire at age 62. Because Louis had ten years of service as a partner, he was eligible for a supplemental benefit designed as an incentive for early retirement. The supplemental benefit is worth two times the partner's annual salary if he or she retires at age 56, with the amount decreasing each month until it reaches zero at age 62. Jennifer and Louis have been married more than twenty years. If Louis takes the early retirement incentive, should the payment be treated as community property? (See In re the Marriage of Drapeau, 114 Cal.Rptr.2d 6 (Ct. App. 2001).)

———————

Bowen v. Bowen

473 A.2d 73 (N.J. 1984)

O'Hern, J.

This case concerns the valuation and equitable distribution of a spouse's minority stock interest in a closely held corporation. The specific question is whether a court, in effecting distribution of the assets, and faced with difficulty in fixing value, should permit the stockholder husband to retain ownership of all of the stock and award the wife an equitable one-half interest in the stock. We hold that a court should not and reverse the judgment below.

The parties were married in 1955 and had four children. At the time of trial, three children were emancipated and an 18-year-old son was beginning college. During the early years of the marriage, the plaintiff worked and helped to put defendant through engineering school. After graduation, defendant worked for Union Carbide until 1971, when he left to take a position with a small manufacturing corporation. In 1973, he and two other employees of that company formed the Polycel Corporation, of which he is now a 22% shareholder. He became a full-time employee of Polycel in 1976. Polycel is engaged in plastics manufacturing and is located in a rented factory in Bound Brook. In 1979, its gross sales were over $3,000,000 and its net income was $144,235.

The parties separated in March 1979. The plaintiff continued to live in the family home. At the time of trial she was employed as a secretary. The major assets of the parties were the family home in Hillsborough and the 22% interest in Polycel.

In view of the length of the marriage and the contributions of both, the court directed that the marital assets be divided equally between husband and wife. The family home was to be sold as soon as possible, and after payment of the expenses of sale, previously incurred college debts, and certain other debts, the net proceeds were to be divided equally.

Concerning the equitable distribution of the defendant's 22% interest in Polycel Corporation, the court, confronted with testimony valuing the stock anywhere from a minimum value of $70,854 to a maximum of $338,279, concluded that determining the fair market value of the stock solely from the valuations made by the accountants would be nothing more than conjecture. It ordered what it recognized to be "an entirely new and more practical scheme of distribution." It directed that the defendant retain all of the stock, but that the plaintiff be awarded an "equitable one-half interest in said stock." Defendant was to retain all indicia of ownership, including the right to vote at shareholders' meetings, but he was to share with the plaintiff all dividends and proceeds from the sale or transfer of any stock.

To prevent avoidance of dividends by payment of excessive salaries, bonuses, or fringe benefits, the court fixed the then current amount of these items, $48,000 per year, as base compensation to the defendant and ordered that all future income in excess thereof be deemed stock dividends to be divided between the parties. The court ordered that one-half of the gross amount of such dividends was to be paid by the husband to the plaintiff with each to pay his or her own taxes. The judgment also required defendant to report annually to plaintiff the total of all benefits and expenses received by him and paid for by Polycel that might be used for both business and personal reasons. These were presumed to be 40% attributable to business with the balance regarded as a dividend. The other officers and directors were to be informed of the judgment and notified that they would be personally responsible to the plaintiff for any losses she might sustain as a result of a sham agreement between the parties disposing of the husband's interest.

The judgment also provided rehabilitative alimony in the amount of $300 per month for three years, $700 per month permanent alimony, and $200 per month child support.

The dispute here is not over the general principles applicable to such cases. The trial court recognized the controlling principles of *Borodinsky v. Borodinsky, 162 N.J.Super. 437, 393 A.2d 583 (App.Div.1978)*, which bear restating here:

It seems almost doctrinal that the elimination of the source of strife and friction is to be sought by the judge in devising the scheme of distribution, and the financial affairs of the parties should be separated as far as possible. If the parties cannot get along as husband and wife, it is not likely they will get along as business partners. [*Id.* at 443, 393 A.2d 583.]

* * *

The difference between *Borodinsky* and this case is that here the husband retained the same role in the close corporation as he had before. There would be no occasion for deadlock or forced liquidation or dissolution.[1] He would continue to be a successful wage earner. The result proposed by the court is not without its interesting aspects. Nonetheless, in our view, the disadvantages of the continuing relationship between the parties outweigh the problems of proof that confront a court in such a situation.

The restrictions may inhibit the corporation's ability to conduct its affairs without judicial supervision. In reality the husband would become an 11% owner. Although there would be no occasion for deadlock, the court has created a new interest in the corporation, something the other shareholders did not want, as evidenced by their buy-sell agreement. Limiting the husband's future earnings makes earning potential a separate element of the equitable distribution, a concept we disapproved in *Mahoney v. Mahoney*, 91 N.J. 488, 453 A.2d 527 (1982). Treating certain business expenses as a dividend poses additional income tax problems for the parties. Furthermore, the other two owners may be placed in an unfair situation since defendant's compensation and expenses will have to be monitored and they may be personally liable if they seek to disentangle themselves from him.

Each of these problems poses a potential "source of strife and friction" that should be eliminated. We hold that a court faced with what it considers inadequate proofs of value must nonetheless eliminate the sources of continuing disquiet between the parties. It must therefore resolve the question of value in the divorce proceedings. If need be, it can marshall additional proofs to enable it to fix a value for the disputed asset.

We have recently had occasion to review again the principles that shall guide courts in fixing the value of business enterprises. *Dugan v. Dugan*, 92 N.J. 423, 457 A.2d 1 (1983). In that case, the issue was the calculation of goodwill attributable to a professional legal corporation. We recognized that

[t]here are probably few assets whose valuation imposes as difficult, intricate and sophisticated a task as interests in close corporations. They cannot be realistically evaluated by a simplistic approach which is based solely on book value,

---

[1] We note that it is not inappropriate to distribute stock in kind when there are no issues of corporate control. That solution will rarely, if ever, be applicable in a close corporation situation.

which fails to deal with the realities of the good will concept, which does not consider investment value of a business in terms of actual profit, and which does not deal with the question of discounting the value of a minority interest.

In this case each of these issues was present. Generally speaking, we have held there is no essential difference so far as equitable distribution principles are concerned between an interest in an individual business and one held in corporate name: "The form should not control."

There is no single formula that will apply to each enterprise: "Each case presents a unique factual question, the solution to which is not within the ambit of any exact science. The reasonableness of any valuation depends upon the judgment and experience of the appraiser and the completeness of the information upon which his conclusions are based." *Lavene v. Lavene,* 162 N.J.Super. 187, 193, 392 A.2d 621 (Ch.Div.1978) (on remand from 148 N.J.Super. 267, 372 A.2d 629).

In arriving at a federal estate or gift tax value for close corporation stock, "[n]o general formula may be given that is applicable to the many different valuation situations." Rev.Rul. 59–60, 1959–1 C.B. 237. Nevertheless, most experts and courts have used the IRS's Revenue Ruling 59–60 as the guide in valuing the close corporation. The goal is to arrive at a fair market value for a stock for which there is no market. To do this, the IRS recommends that "all available financial data, as well as all relevant factors affecting the fair market value, should be considered." *Id.* at § 4.01.

Among the factors listed in the Ruling as "fundamental and requir[ing] careful analysis" are the history of the firm, the nature of the company, the outlook for the industry, the book value of the stock, the size of the block to be valued, the earning and dividend-paying capacities of the company, and the existence of goodwill or other intangible assets. Generally, greater weight will be given to earnings factors for those companies that sell products or services, and to asset values for investment or holding companies. *Id.* at § 5. In addition, earnings factors must be capitalized. Choosing the appropriate capitalization rate is "one of the most difficult problems in valuation." *Id.* at § 6. Among the considerations that go into a capitalization rate are the nature of the business, the risk involved, and the stability of earnings.

The Ruling warns against an inflexible approach to valuing. Methods such as taking an average of several factors are disapproved. *Id.* at § 7. However, restrictive arrangements, such as buy-sell agreements, may be used, along with other factors, to arrive at the value of the stock. *Id.* at § 8. Since the three Polycel shareholders have made their interest subject to a buy-sell agreement, we first consider its application to this case.[2]

(a) Buy-Sell Agreement

Ordinarily the value that people put on an asset is the most productive place to start such an inquiry: * * *

Stern v. Stern, 66 N.J. 340, 345, 331 A.2d 257 (1975), recognized that placing "a precise or even an approximately accurate value upon an interest in a professional partnership, when the partner whose interest is in question intends to continue as a member of the firm is no easy matter." In that case, the Court considered the most accurate and certainly the most useful method for purposes of equitable distribution to be the formula for the calculation and payment of a partner's interest to his personal representative upon death. But the circumstances were different from those presented to the court here. The evidence in *Stern* was that the formula was revised quarterly, was obviously intended to reflect the elements of the enterprise's worth, other than the individual's capital account, and that the payments occasioned by death were to be funded with the proceeds of life insurance on the lives of the several partners. The *Stern* Court held that a trial court would be justified in adding to this sum the value of defendant's capital account, treating the total as the presumptive value of the defendant's partnership interest in the firm. Once it is established that the books of the firm are well kept and that the value of the partners' interests are in fact periodically and carefully reviewed, then the presumption would be subject to attack only upon the submission of clear and convincing proofs.

Those elements were not present here. The buy-sell agreement among the three stockholders prohibited a transfer of the stock unless offered to the other stockholders or the corporation at a price computed in the agreement. The agreement provided that each partner's share would be determined on the basis of book value, provided that the minimum value of defendant's interest was $25,000. It provided that book value was to be established by the corporation's accountant. In the event of disagreement with a shareholder's accountant, "then a Certified Public Accountant shall be appointed by the presiding judge of the Somerset County Court * * * [who] shall determine the book value of the shares of corporate stock in accordance with this formula and the determination by said Accountant shall be binding upon all parties to this Agreement." The formula established by the

---

[2]   We have discussed Revenue Ruling 59–60 because it is commonly employed, and its principles were used in the trial below. We recognize, however, that there are other acceptable methods of valuation, *see, e.g.,* Righter v. United States, 439 F.2d 1204, 194 Ct.Cl. 400 (1971) (comparative appraisal technique), and we make no judgment as to what method the court should use on remand. *See* Note, *The Effect of Corporate Control on Valuation of Closely Held Corporate Stock for Federal Estate and Gift Tax Purposes,* 1982 *U.Ill.L.Rev.* 775; Schreier and Joy, *Judicial Valuation of "Close" Corporation Stock:* Alice in Wonderland *Revisited,* 31 *Okla.L.Rev.* 853 (1978).

agreement specifically excluded goodwill or other intangible assets but otherwise specified how accounts receivable, inventory, machinery, fixtures, taxes, and life insurance policies were to be valued. In addition, the agreement provided for installment payments over a period of years with stated interest. The agreement also provided that the parties would periodically fix a value in a Certificate of Agreed Value. No Certificate existed here.

We agree with the trial court's conclusion that this buy-sell should not control because it did not contemplate the circumstances when the stockholder's status with the corporation and his fellow stockholders was to remain the same. Under these circumstances, Polycel's assets of goodwill and other intangibles (including considerable technical expertise) should have been included to reflect fair value. We note that the procedure endorsed in *Stern*—adding to the base value set by the partnership agreement the value of the capital account that was outside the agreement, 66 *N.J.* at 346, 331 *A.*2d 257—might be used when a corporate buy-sell is similarly trustworthy but incomplete. The addition of goodwill calculated in accordance with the guidelines of *Dugan v. Dugan, 92 N.J. 423, 457 A.2d 1 (1983),* would yield presumptive evidence of value. Determination of an appropriate capitalization rate would be based upon rates of return in comparable publicly traded securities, or on sales of comparable businesses.

Here, neither party sought to rely upon the buy-sell agreement, although the defendant's expert testified that he had recently calculated the value on that basis at $92,473. The effect of a buy-sell agreement in a matrimonial settlement cannot be regarded as facially dispositive, but must be considered in light of all of the circumstances and its provisions. A central inquiry is whether it represents an arm's-length agreement to fix real value for the triggering event that has occurred. *Rogers v. Rogers, 296 N.W.2d 849 (Minn.1980)* (buy-sell agreement given two-step effect for purposes of marital distribution).

Finally, the defendant argues that the court should not value his interest above its buy-sell value, since if he must sell his shares, the price he would receive would be limited by the buy-sell restriction. But there should be no reason to sell the shares since the court can fashion the distribution so that a sale need not occur. Furthermore, to give the buy-sell agreement conclusive effect would not recognize the realities of the present situation: The shareholder will not sell the stock and, one hopes, will not die. In other words, he will continue to experience the benefits of being a 22% shareholder and an employee.

Under the conditions stated in *Stern,* an up-to-date buy-sell agreement will provide presumptive evidence of value of a minority share in a firm. All those conditions were not present here and so the court below was obliged to consider the other proofs. It may choose to give evidentiary weight to the agreement insofar as it is reliable although incomplete.

(b) Gross Operating Profit Capitalization

As previously noted, the range of proofs was extreme indeed, going from $70,000 to $338,000. Yet, each of the experts was soft at the margins of his opinion. The husband's expert agreed that he would not recommend that his client sell his share for the figure of $70,000 since the client was gainfully employed in the business and it had an intrinsically higher value for him. Conversely, the wife's expert conceded that there was a wide range of values and in his redirect examination suggested that his "bottom line" figure was $180,000. There was also evidence that in a recent financial statement the husband himself had fixed the value of his interest in Polycel at $132,000 and the husband's accountant had fixed the buy-sell value at $92,000.

Expert opinion testimony of an accountant is not significantly different from any other form of expert testimony: Reliability can be established by showing general acceptance in the scientific community through proofs of expert testimony, scientific and legal writings, or judicial opinions. Those principles applicable to scientific testimony can be helpful here in evaluating expert opinion testimony as to value.

Plaintiff's accountant based his high figure of $338,000 upon the application of an earnings capitalization rate of five to the net profit of the company. While earnings capitalization is one factor in valuation, *compare* Rev.Rul. 59–60, at § 4.01(d), § 4.02(d), and § 6, plaintiff's accountant could offer no basis in generally accepted accounting principles for his capitalization rate of five as applied to the net profit from sales figures. It was simply his opinion, "from experience", "[j]ust historical in other businesses that I have dealt with." The range of rates was anywhere from five to twelve, according to plaintiff's accountant. He chose the low end of the range to reflect defendant's minority interest in Polycel, but offered no external proof to justify his choice.

We hold that a court should not base an opinion on theories of value that lack support in the record, demonstrated market reliability, or general acceptance.

* * *

The sources of an expert's testimony must be relevant as well as reliable. The parties must present evidence that has demonstrated market reliability (*e.g.,* data of comparable corporations that are publicly traded) or is otherwise generally accepted as reliable by experts or by courts (*e.g.,* relevant appraisal manuals, authoritative industry guides, or factual foundations in the record before the court).

(c) Formula Approach

The other method of valuation used below was a formula approach based on <u>Revenue Ruling 59–60</u>, devised by the IRS for valuing property for federal tax purposes. As we described it in *Dugan,* a formula approach "requires a determination of income from the tangible assets, and subtraction of that income from the total income. The residual is capitalized and the balance is designated goodwill." <u>92 N.J. at 436, 457 A.2d 1</u>.[5]

The experts differed in their application of the formula in several respects. Plaintiff's accountant believed a return of 10% on fixed assets was appropriate, while defendant's held out for 12 1/2%. Both employed a capitalization rate of 20% (5 times return on intangibles) but disagreed over whether a 30% discount for defendant's minority interest should be applied. Plaintiff's expert said he "built in a discount" by not using a higher capitalization factor of 7 or 8. The parties also disagreed over whether the sale of one piece of machinery was to be considered an extraordinary income item and whether the earnings should be capitalized before or after taxes.[6]

In resolving these issues, the court could consider the appointment of an independent expert to assist it. We have emphasized the important role that court-appointed experts may play in resolving issues of technical complexity before a court. We also recognize that it may be overbroad in cases of this magnitude to employ three expert witnesses, each of whom must be compensated, to arrive at fair value. But the Case Information Statement and other discovery methods can

---

[5]   Although both accountants described their appraisals as based on <u>Revenue Ruling 59–60</u>, both incorporated the provisions of <u>Rev.Rul. 68–609, 1968–2 C.B. 327</u>, which supplemented <u>Rev.Rul. 59–60</u>. It provides:

The "formula" approach may be stated as follows:

A percentage return on the average annual value of the tangible assets used in a business is determined, using a period of years (preferably not less than five) immediately prior to the valuation date. The amount of the percentage return on tangible assets, thus determined, is deducted from the average earnings of the business for such period and the remainder, if any, is considered to be the amount of the average annual earnings from the intangible assets of the business for the period. This amount (considered as the average annual earnings from intangibles), capitalized at a percentage of say, 15 to 20 percent, is the value of the intangible assets of the business determined under the "formula" approach.

The percentage of return on the average annual value of the tangible assets used should be the percentage prevailing in the industry involved at the date of valuation, or (when the industry percentage is not available) a percentage of 8 to 10 percent may be used.

The 8 percent rate of return and the 15 percent rate of capitalization are applied to tangibles and intangibles, respectively, of businesses with a small risk factor and stable and regular earnings; the 10 percent rate of return and 20 percent rate of capitalization are applied to businesses in which the hazards of business are relatively high.

[6]   The parties disagreed over whether to use three or four years' earnings in applying <u>Rev.Rul. 59–60</u>. That Ruling recommends the use of five or more years. *Id.* at § 4.02(d). In *Dugan,* we expressed a preference for the use of five years' earnings, <u>92 N.J. at 441, 457 A.2d 1</u>, but since Polycel Corporation is relatively young, the parties' ultimate choice of a lesser number may be acceptable.

be used to narrow the issues so that a court will employ an independent expert to assist it only in evaluating the points of difference. We believe that method could be used here to fix the value after reliance upon an independent expert to resolve the differences expressed in employing Revenue Ruling 59–60.

Naturally, the ultimate responsibility for disposition of the assets would remain with the Family Part. A fair and workable system of distribution still must be made. One of the problems below was that there was no liquid value for the husband's stock, and if it were ordered sold, the price would be fixed by the buy-sell agreement. Hence, defendant argued, there was no way to distribute the stock fairly. Perhaps, part of the defendant's share of the proceeds of the sale of the house could be used to make a down payment on the plaintiff's share of the corporate property with the balance being paid out over an extended period of time on terms the court may determine. The issue of alimony may have to be reviewed in light of the revised equitable distribution plan.

In sum, we hold: (1) courts must arrive at a value for closely held corporate stock to effect equitable distribution of the asset to one spouse; (2) a comprehensive buy-sell agreement will provide presumptive evidence of such value; (3) opinions of value not based upon evidence in the record or of proven acceptance in the field should be given little weight; and (4) courts should employ independent experts under Rule 5:3–3 when necessary to resolve specific disagreements between the parties' experts. The judgment of the Appellate Division is reversed and the cause remanded to the trial court for further proceedings in accordance with this opinion.

Points for Discussion

a. Business Valuation

As *Bowen* indicates, many courts begin their treatment of the business valuation question with a reference to Revenue Ruling 59–60, 1959–1 C.B. 237, in particular to the list of factors included there. See also Nardini v. Nardini, 414 N.W.2d 184 (Minn.1987). Unfortunately the general guidelines in that ruling do not go very far toward determining values in specific cases, as *Bowen* makes clear. For this reason, expert testimony is central to most business valuation disputes. See generally Arnold H. Rutkin, *Valuation of a Closely Held Corporation, Small Business or Professional Practice*, in 2 Valuation and Distribution of Marital Property (2004).

Bowen also holds that opinions offered by valuation experts must be based on "evidence in the record or of proven acceptance in the field." Plaintiff's expert used an earnings capitalization approach, but did not have a persuasive explanation of the capitalization rate he selected. What guidance does the court provide regarding the evidence that could be offered to support an expert's valuation opinion?

b. Shareholder Agreements

Is the court in *Bowen* correct in saying that the shareholder agreement should not control the value in this case? Courts in divorce cases have frequently considered whether to value the stock in a closely-held corporation in accordance with a restrictive shareholder agreement. Other examples include In re Marriage of Nichols, 33 Cal.Rptr.2d 13 (Ct. App. 1994); Lyon v. Lyon, 439 N.W.2d 18 (Minn.1989); In re Marriage of DeCosse, 936 P.2d 821 (Mont. 1997); Brozek v. Brozek, 874 N.W.2d 17 (Neb. 2017); Hertz v. Hertz, 657 P.2d 1169 (N.M. 1983); Kaye v. Kaye, 478 N.Y.S.2d 324 (App.Div.1984).

There are many different varieties of shareholder agreements. The agreement in *Bowen* provided that a shareholder wishing to sell his shares had to offer them first to the other shareholders at book value. This was not a **buy-sell agreement**, in which one party, usually the corporation, agrees to buy the stock of a stockholder who wishes to withdraw from the corporation based on a formula for determining the value of the shares. **Book value** is the value of the corporation's assets as shown on the books of the corporation, less the present liabilities. The total book value divided by the number of outstanding shares gives the book value of each share. Since the book value is based on a valuation of assets in accordance with accounting principles, which normally require the use of historical cost, book value may not be a very close indication of the current value of the company's assets. It also completely ignores the profit-making potential of the business.

c. Capitalization of Earnings

The court in *Bowen* describes valuation testimony based on a capitalization of earnings. This approach requires first computing the earnings of the asset based on its past history, usually over a number of years. The assumption is made that these earnings will continue into the future. In order to generate a valuation based upon projected earnings, the expert must determine what rate of return should be expected for an asset of this type in similar economic conditions. Once an appropriate rate of return is established, it is applied to the earnings to determine the capital value of the business. Many divorce cases rely on this methodology. See, e.g., Wright v. Wright, 904 P.2d 403 (Alaska 1995); Olsen v. Olsen, 873 P.2d 857 (Idaho 1994); and Neuman v. Neuman, 842 P.2d 575 (Wyo.1992). See also Alan S. Zipp, *Divorce Valuation of Business Interests: A Capitalization of Earnings Approach*, 23 Fam. L.Q. 89 (1989).

For example, an asset generating earnings of $40,000 per year that is expected to produce a return on investment of 20% per year would be worth $200,000; while an asset with the same earnings that is expected to produce a return of 10%

per year would be worth $400,000, an asset expected to produce a return of 8% per year would be worth $500,000, and an asset expected to generate a return of only 5% per year would be worth $800,000. Notice that different rates of return applied to the same earnings generate very large differences in valuation.

Business valuations often refer to an earnings multiple. The multiple is the reciprocal of the rate of return. For a 20% rate of return, the earnings multiple is 5, for a 10% rate of return it is 10, for an 8% rate of return it is 12.5, and for a 5% rate of return it is 20.

Capitalization of Earnings			
Asset Value	Annual Earnings	Rate of Return	Earnings Multiple
$ 200,000	$40,000 per year	20% per year	5 times earnings
$ 400,000	$40,000 per year	10% per year	10 times earnings
$ 500,000	$40,000 per year	8% per year	12.5 times earnings
$ 800,000	$40,000 per year	5% per year	20 times earnings

Using Business Principles

Business valuation is an important topic in other subjects, including corporate law and estate and gift tax, and an understanding of basic business principles is important for divorce lawyers. For more on these questions, see these sources:

- Robert W. Hamilton and Richard A. Booth, Business Basics for Law Students: Essential Concepts and Applications (4th ed. 2006).

- William A. Klein et al., Business Organization and Finance: Legal and Economic Principles (11th ed. 2010).

- Shannon Pratt and Alina V. Niculita, The Lawyer's Business Valuation Handbook (2010).

In re the Marriage of McReath

800 N.W.2d 399 (Wis. 2011)

PATIENCE DRAKE ROGGENSACK, J.

¶ 1 We review a published opinion of the court of appeals affirming the circuit court's order that Timothy McReath (Tim) pay Tracy McReath (Tracy) $796,720 to equalize the property division upon the couple's divorce, as well as $16,000 per month for 20 years in maintenance. The questions presented are: (1) whether the entire value of the salable professional goodwill of Tim's interest in Orthodontic Specialists, S.C. can be counted as divisible property in a marital estate, and (2) if the answer to the first question is yes, did the circuit court double count the value of the professional goodwill in Orthodontic Specialists when it based Tracy's maintenance award on Tim's expected future earnings from Orthodontic Specialists.

¶ 2 We conclude the entire value of the salable professional goodwill was properly counted as divisible property in the marital estate. Moreover, we conclude that the circuit court did not double count the professional goodwill from Orthodontic Specialists in the maintenance award. Accordingly, we affirm the decision of the court of appeals.

I. BACKGROUND

A. Facts

¶ 3 This case requires us to review the circuit court's order dividing marital property and awarding maintenance in a divorce proceeding. Tracy and Tim were married on August 27, 1988. Three children, all of whom were minors at the time the divorce proceedings were initiated, were born of their marriage.

¶ 4 In 1991, Tim received his dental degree, and in 1993, he received a master's degree in orthodontia. Accordingly, most of Tim's dental education was pursued during the marriage. Tim took out student loans to fund his education, all of which were repaid with marital funds.

¶ 5 Upon receiving his masters in orthodontia, Tim worked as an associate at Orthodontic Specialists for two years. Tim then purchased the Baraboo and Portage locations of Orthodontic Specialists from Dr. Grady.

¶ 6 Tim paid approximately $930,000 for the two locations of Orthodontic Specialists. A portion of this purchase price was attributed to a noncompete agreement that Dr. Grady signed and to transitional services that Dr. Grady provided Tim. Specifically, Tim testified that $100,000 was for the physical assets, corporate name, and corporate goodwill. The remaining $830,000 was for, as Tim described, "Dr. Grady's name, the noncompete clause, and the employment agreement that Dr. Grady would stay on to introduce me to his existing patients, [and] to counsel me through the process of learning how to do business."

¶ 7 With regard to the noncompete agreement, Tim testified that he would not have purchased Orthodontic Specialists for as high of a price as he did without a noncompete agreement because, "[Dr. Grady] could have just opened up a business just down the street and I'm assuming that he would have taken not only the majority of patients with him but the majority of the future patients in the area." Tim also testified that he was not aware of any transaction in the field of orthodontics, for any substantial value, that took place without a noncompete agreement. According to Tim, "the name of the practitioner is always weighted very heavily as opposed to the goodwill or the value of the name of the practice or corporation."

¶ 8 Tim has worked as the sole owner of Orthodontic Specialists since he purchased it from Dr. Grady. Tim has historically averaged a 60-hour work week. This is significantly more than the average orthodontist who works only 35 hours per week. Recently, Tim has reduced the number of hours he works to approximately 45 hours per week. Tim has no plans to sell or dispose of his practice.

¶ 9 Tim has been very successful in operating Orthodontic Specialists. His annual gross business revenues in the five years leading up to the divorce ranged from $1.6 million to in excess of $1.8 million. In the same five years, Tim received an average yearly net cash flow from Orthodontic Specialists of $697,522. Notably, Orthodontic Specialists maintains the only orthodontic offices in Baraboo and Portage.

¶ 10 The success of Orthodontic Specialists has resulted in a relatively high standard of living for the McReath family. They have significant assets and little, if any, personal debt.

¶ 11 Unlike Tim, Tracy does not have a professional degree. She is a high school graduate with some college credits, but no college degree. Tracy worked outside the home while Tim was attending dental school. Throughout much of their marriage, however, Tracy worked as a homemaker and the primary caretaker for the couple's children. Specifically, she was completely out of the workforce from 1993 to 2000. From 2000 to 2008, she performed some financial and clerical duties for Orthodontic Specialists. In this position, she was paid $15,000 to $16,000 per year. The circuit court found Tracy has a current earning capacity of $14.50 per hour, or $30,160 annually.

B. Procedural History

¶ 12 On May 16, 2007, Tracy filed a petition for divorce in Sauk County Circuit Court. Upon entering the order of divorce, the circuit court, among other things, divided the marital property and awarded maintenance to Tracy.

¶ 13 Regarding the marital property division, with the exception of the value of Orthodontic Specialists, the parties stipulated to the value of their marital assets. They also stipulated to a division of assets with a balancing payment. Hearings were held on the appropriate fair market valuation of Orthodontic Specialists, and resulted in a valuation of $1,058,000. This was the value given by Tracy's expert, Craig Billings (Billings). The court rejected the $415,000 valuation of Tim's expert, Dennis Ksicinski (Ksicinski).[8]

¶ 14 Having valued Orthodontic Specialists at $1,058,000, the court turned to dividing the assets. The court found that there was no reason to deviate from the presumption of equal property division in Wis. Stat. § 767. 61(3) (2009–10). It then combined the $1,058,000 valuation of Orthodontic Specialists with the other, stipulated-to, assets in the marital estate. Because, among other assets, Tim was the stipulated owner of Orthodontic Specialists, Tim's total assets exceeded Tracy's by $1,593,440. As such, to equalize the property division, the court awarded Tracy $796,720, to be paid at the rate of no less than $80,000 per year plus accrued interest.

¶ 15 Next, to set maintenance, the court used Tim's average annual earnings from Orthodontic Specialists over the preceding five years, i.e., $697,522. However, because the $697,522 salary was based on Tim working 50–70 hours per week, the court adjusted the figure to reflect a 40-hour work week. Consequently, the court set Tim's expected annual income from Orthodontic Specialists at $465,000 (rounded). Next, the court took its finding that Tracy had a current earning capacity of $14.50 per hour, or $30,160 annually. The court then added these income calculations to the other sources of income available to the parties, specifically rental and investment income, and found that Tim's total annual

---

[8] In accepting Billings' valuation, the court highlighted that Billings had "provided a comprehensive and thorough evaluation" of the business and "[h]is conclusions were supported by direct work with the practice including a site visit or visits, conversations with [Tim, a] review of the financial records" and "external information sources unique to the profession such as surveys and professional journal data."

The court found Ksicinski's valuation problematic because, among other things, Ksicinski relied significantly on information provided by Tim and did little independent or critical analysis; Ksicinski used only financial data from 2007 (one of Orthodontic Specialists' worst financial years in terms of net income) in making his valuations; Ksicinski did not look to outside sources and industry norms to support his conclusions; and Ksicinski's valuation was not supported by the record given the fact that Tim had bought the practice in the 1990s for over $900,000 and the business grossed in excess of $1.6 million per year.

income was $535,806 (or $44,650/month) and Tracy's total annual income was $75,944 (or $6,328/month).

¶ 16 With these figures in hand, the court considered the statutory factors set forth in Wis. Stat. § 767.56 in deciding whether to award maintenance. In considering these factors, the court found that it was unlikely that Tracy would ever have Tim's earning capacity or an income that would allow for a standard of living comparable to that enjoyed during the marriage. The court also underscored that Tracy had contributed to the dental education and increased earning capacity of Tim. Based on these findings, the court awarded Tracy maintenance in the amount of $16,000 per month for a period of 20 years.

¶ 17 Tim appealed and the court of appeals affirmed. *McReath v. McReath,* 2010 WI App 101, 329 Wis.2d 155, 789 N.W.2d 89. * * *

¶ 20 We granted review and now affirm the court of appeals.

II. DISCUSSION

A. Standard of Review

¶ 21 The division of marital property and the calculation of maintenance are matters typically left to the sound discretion of the circuit court. We do not disturb a circuit court's discretionary determinations about property division and the calculation of maintenance unless the court erroneously exercised its discretion. A circuit court erroneously exercises its discretion if it makes an error of law. The issues presented here concern whether the circuit court applied incorrect legal standards in dividing marital property and calculating maintenance.

¶ 22 When an issue of law arises while we are reviewing a circuit court's exercise of discretion, we review that issue independently, but benefiting from the analyses of the court of appeals and circuit court. Moreover, in deciding legal issues, we uphold the circuit court's findings of fact unless they are clearly erroneous. "[T]he valuation of marital assets is a finding of fact." *Liddle v. Liddle,* 140 Wis.2d 132, 136, 410 N.W.2d 196 (Ct.App.1987).

B. Marital Estate and Goodwill

¶ 23 Chapter 767 of the Wisconsin Statutes, "Actions Affecting the Family," sets forth how a presiding court should divide the marital estate upon divorce. Wisconsin Stat. § 767.61(1) requires the court to divide the property of the parties upon divorce. Section 767.61(2) identifies property that is subject to division by describing the limited types of property that generally are not subject to division on divorce. The property subject to division is considered the marital estate for purposes of property division upon divorce. *Steinke v. Steinke*, 126 Wis.2d 372, 380, 376 N.W.2d 839 (1985).

¶ 24 When engaged in dividing the marital estate, a circuit court is to proceed under the presumption of equal division. Wis. Stat. § 767.61(3). Dividing the estate equally "effectuates the policy that each spouse makes a valuable contribution to the marriage and that each spouse should be compensated for his or her respective contributions." *Steinke*, 126 Wis.2d at 380–81, 376 N.W.2d 839. We have explained the rationale behind equal division when one spouse leaves the work force to care for the couple's domestic needs:

> Part of the rationale in creating the presumption of equal property division is that the homemaking partner has contributed services which have enabled the financially supporting partner to achieve his or her station in life, and in so doing the homemaking partner has lost ground in the job market.

Id. (internal quotation marks and citation omitted). Despite the presumption of equal division, the court has the discretion to alter the distribution after considering numerous factors.

¶ 25 Property valued for the purpose of dividing the marital estate should be valued at its fair market value. "Fair market value is the price that property will bring when offered for sale by one who desires but is not obligated to sell and bought by one who is willing but not obligated to buy."

¶ 26 In this case, the issue is whether the entire value of the salable professional goodwill in Orthodontic Specialists is included in the marital estate subject to division under Wis. Stat. § 767.61. Subsection 767.61(2) does not explicitly exclude professional goodwill from the divisible marital estate. Consequently, we turn to the applicable case law and policy considerations to decide whether the entire value of the salable professional goodwill is subject to property division.

Think About It

Property valuation in divorce is usually based on fair market value. How does this principle influence the definition of martial property interests in professional goodwill or an academic degree?

¶ 27 Defining professional goodwill is a necessary starting point. In 1967, we recognized a business's goodwill as a divisible marital asset. *Spheeris v. Spheeris*, 37 Wis.2d 497, 155 N.W.2d 130 (1967). In doing so, we underscored the difficulty in defining the concept, but set forth the following definition:

> In its broadest sense the intangible asset called good will may be said to be reputation; however, a better description would probably be that

element of value which inheres in the fixed and favorable consideration of customers arising from an established and well-conducted business.

Id. at 504, 155 N.W.2d 130 (footnote and internal quotation marks omitted). Similarly, the court of appeals has advanced the following definition:

The advantage or benefit which is acquired by an establishment beyond the mere value of the capital stock, funds, or property employed therein, in consequence of the general public patronage and encouragement which it receives from constant or habitual customers on account of its local position, or common celebrity, or reputation for skill or affluence, or punctuality, or from other accidental circumstances or necessities, or even from ancient partiality or prejudices.

Holbrook v. Holbrook, 103 Wis.2d 327, 345, 309 N.W.2d 343 (Ct.App.1981) (citing 38 Am.Jur.2d., Goodwill § 1 (1968)). Stated another way, goodwill is "[a] business's reputation, patronage, and other intangible assets that are considered when appraising the business, [especially] for purchase; the ability to earn income in excess of the income that would be expected from the business viewed as a mere collection of assets." *Black's Law Dictionary* 763 (9th ed.2009). Simply stated, goodwill is "an asset of recognized value beyond the tangible assets of [a business]." *Taylor v. Taylor,* 222 Neb. 721, 386 N.W.2d 851, 857 (1986).

¶ 28 Originally, it was posited that goodwill did not inhere in professional businesses because professional businesses depend on the skill and reputation of the professional. *Holbrook,* 103 Wis.2d at 346, 309 N.W.2d 343. However, courts and scholars now recognize goodwill in professional businesses. *See, e.g., id.* at 347–49, 309 N.W.2d 343; *Peerenboom v. Peerenboom,* 147 Wis.2d 547, 550–52, 433 N.W.2d 282 (Ct.App.1988); *Golden v. Golden,* 270 Cal.App.2d 401, 75 Cal. Rptr. 735, 737–38 (1969); Christopher A. Tiso, *Present Positions on Professional Goodwill: More Focus or Simply More Hocus Pocus?,* 20 J. Am. Acad. Matrimonial L. 51, 52 (2006). When goodwill inheres in a professional business, it is most properly classified as "professional goodwill."

* * *

¶ 31 While *Spheeris* involved a commercial business, subsequent Wisconsin cases have recognized goodwill in professional practices. In *Holbrook,* Mr. Holbrook was a partner in a large law firm. The court of appeals considered whether the circuit court had erroneously determined that the goodwill in Mr. Holbrook's partnership interest in the law firm was a divisible marital asset. In concluding that the circuit court did err, the court began its discussion with a blanket statement that, standing alone, would imply the court was prohibiting any inclusion of professional goodwill in the divisible marital estate. The court stated, "[w]e are not persuaded that the concept of professional goodwill as a divisible marital asset should be adopted in Wisconsin."

¶ 32 However, the court's subsequent discussion focused on its assumption that professional goodwill cannot be sold, and "accrues to the benefit of the owners only through increased salary." For instance, the court compared the professional goodwill in Mr. Holbrook's partnership interest to a professional degree. It opined that "[l]ike an educational degree, a partner's theoretical share of a law firm's goodwill *cannot be exchanged on an open market: it cannot be assigned, sold, transferred, conveyed or pledged.* . . . In both cases, the 'asset' involved *is not salable* and has computable value to the individual only to the extent that it promises increased future earnings." Moreover, the court underscored that, apart from receiving the value of his capital account, Mr. Holbrook was "[e]thically and contractually. . .prevented from otherwise disposing of his interest" in the firm.

¶ 33 Accordingly, Wisconsin courts considering the valuation of professional goodwill subsequent to *Holbrook* have limited *Holbrook's* assertion that professional goodwill is not part of the divisible marital estate to situations where the professional goodwill is nonsalable. For example, in *Peerenboom,* the court of appeals concluded that the goodwill in a divorcing spouse's dental practice could be a divisible marital asset. The court distinguished *Holbrook:*

> *Holbrook.* . .involved the division of an individual lawyer's interest in a large law firm. The court explained that due to ethical and contractual considerations, his interest in the law firm's goodwill could not be exchanged or sold on the open market. The court concluded therefore that it would be inequitable to compel "a professional practitioner to pay a spouse a share of intangible assets at a judicially determined value that could not be realized by a sale or another method of liquidating value."
>
> . . .
>
> In contrast, in this case the record shows no ethical or contractual barrier to [Dr. Peerenboom's] disposing of his interest in his dental practice. Accordingly, to the extent that the evidence shows that the goodwill exists, is marketable, and that its value is something over and above the value of the practice's assets and the professional's skills and services, it may be included as an asset in the marital estate and be subject to division.

Id. at 551–52, 433 N.W.2d 282 (quoting *Holbrook,* 103 Wis.2d at 351, 309 N.W.2d 343).

¶ 34 Similarly, in *Sommerfield v. Sommerfield,* 154 Wis.2d 840, 454 N.W.2d 55 (Ct.App.1990), the court of appeals held that the circuit court erred when, for the purpose of setting the value of Mr. Sommerfield's accounting practice, it disregarded the expert witness's valuation of the practice's goodwill. Starting with the premise that goodwill can be a marketable asset, the court underscored the expert's opinion that a noncompete agreement covering two years would be the normal condition under which a practice like Mr. Sommerfield's would be sold. Concluding that there was no evidence that such a noncompete agreement would be unenforceable, the court held that the circuit court erroneously found that there was not separate, marketable goodwill in Mr. Sommerfield's practice that could be included in the divisible marital estate.

¶ 35 In accordance with previous Wisconsin case law, we conclude today that when valuing a business interest that is part of the marital estate for purposes of divorce, a circuit court shall include the value of the salable professional goodwill attendant to the business interest. In addition to the above discussed case law, this conclusion is supported by Wis. Stat. § 767.61 and the policy considerations behind § 767.61.

¶ 36 First, while Wis. Stat. § 767.61(2) excludes specific property from the marital estate, professional goodwill is not listed therein. Moreover, under § 767.61(3), we presume that the marital estate should be divided equally. As aforementioned, the presumption of equal division recognizes the contributions of each spouse to the marriage, including a homemaker spouse's lost earning capacity from being out of the job market. Where the salable professional good-will is developed during the marriage, it defies the presumption of equality to exclude it from the divisible marital estate. As one court has explained:

> [T]he wife, by virtue of her position of wife, made to that [goodwill] value the same contribution as does a wife to any of the husband's earn-ings and accumulations during the marriage. She is as much entitled to be recompensed for that contribution as if it were represented by the increased value of stock in a family business.

Golden, 75 Cal.Rptr. at 738.[15]

¶ 37 In sum, pursuant to Wis. Stat. § 767.61, Wisconsin case law and the policy supporting the presumption of equality in the division of the marital estate, we hold that a circuit court shall include salable professional goodwill in the divis-ible marital estate when the business interest to which the goodwill is attendant is an asset subject to § 767.61.

¶ 38 Tim urges us to require circuit courts to divide professional goodwill into two subgroups, "personal" goodwill and "enterprise" goodwill, and to create a presumption that personal goodwill is excluded from the marital estate. This is an approach taken by some courts and scholars.

¶ 39 When professional goodwill is so divided, enterprise goodwill is char-acterized as "[g]oodwill in a professional practice. . .attributable to the business enterprise itself by virtue of its existing arrangements with suppliers, customers or

---

[15]   In *Golden v. Golden,* 270 Cal.App.2d 401, 75 Cal.Rptr. 735 (1969), the non-professional spouse was the wife. We recognize that the roles could easily be reversed, with the non-professional spouse being the husband.

others, and its anticipated future customer base due to factors attributable to the business." *Id.* (quoting <u>Yoon v. Yoon, 711 N.E.2d 1265, 1268 (Ind.1999)</u>); *see also* <u>May v. May, 214 W.Va. 394, 589 S.E.2d 536, 541–42 (2003)</u>. Personal goodwill, on the other hand, is characterized as the goodwill that is "attributable to the individual owner's personal skill, training or reputation," i.e., it is "the goodwill that depends on the continued presence of a particular individual." <u>Id.</u> (quoting <u>Yoon, 711 N.E.2d at 1268–69</u>); *see also* <u>May, 589 S.E.2d at 542</u>.

¶ 40 Some courts that divide professional goodwill into enterprise and personal goodwill have concluded that enterprise goodwill is included in the divisible marital estate, and personal goodwill is not. This conclusion is based in large part on the belief that enterprise goodwill is salable, while personal goodwill is not. For instance, in <u>Yoon</u>, the Supreme Court of Indiana included enterprise goodwill in the divisible estate, explaining that while "[i]t is not necessarily marketable in the sense that there is a ready and easily priced market for it, [ ] it is in general transferable to others and has a value to others." With respect to personal goodwill, however, the *Yoon* court explained that because personal goodwill depends on the continued presence of the particular professional, it "represents nothing more than the future earning capacity of the individual." Consequently, based on its belief that personal goodwill is not salable, the *Yoon* court excluded personal goodwill from the marital estate.

¶ 41 After reviewing cases that distinguish between personal and enterprise goodwill, we choose not to require circuit courts to draw a distinction between personal and enterprise goodwill when dividing a marital estate that includes professional goodwill. This is so because the premise on which the distinction is grounded—that enterprise goodwill is salable and personal goodwill is not—is mistaken. As evidenced by the facts of the case at hand, Tim testified that when he bought Orthodontic Specialists for $930,000, nearly 90 percent of the sale price was for the professional goodwill. Tim described this goodwill as including elements of "personal" goodwill: "Dr. Grady's name, the noncompete clause, and the employment agreement that Dr. Grady would stay on to introduce me to his existing patients." Therefore, as this case demonstrates, in some situations, personal goodwill is salable.

C. Maintenance and Double Counting

¶ 42 Having concluded that a circuit court shall consider salable professional goodwill, including what some courts term "personal" goodwill, as a divisible marital asset, we now set forth the law applicable to the second issue presented. The second issue presented is whether the circuit court double counted the value of Tim's professional goodwill by basing Tracy's maintenance award on Tim's expected future earnings when the future earnings will arise from Orthodontic

Specialists. Under Tim's line of reasoning, the circuit court counted the goodwill once when it treated the goodwill as a divisible marital asset. Tim contends that the court then counted professional goodwill a second time when it awarded maintenance based on his past earnings from Orthodontic Specialists, given that professional goodwill increased those past earnings.

¶ 43 We begin with an overview of maintenance in Wisconsin. Maintenance awards upon a divorce are governed by Wis. Stat. § 767.56. Pursuant to § 767.56, a circuit court "may grant an order requiring maintenance payments to either party for a limited or indefinite length of time" after considering a list of enumerated factors.[17] As aforementioned, it is within the circuit court's discretion to determine the amount and duration of maintenance. However, the factors enumerated in § 767.56 should be the "touchstone of analysis" when a court sets maintenance. *LaRocque v. LaRocque*, 139 Wis.2d 23, 32, 406 N.W.2d 736 (1987).

¶ 44 There are two objectives that an award of maintenance seeks to meet. The first objective is support of the payee spouse. This objective may not be met by merely maintaining the payee spouse at a subsistence level. Rather, maintenance should support the payee spouse at the pre-divorce standard. This standard should be measured by "the lifestyle that the parties enjoyed in the years immediately before

Think About It

How would you assess Tracy's maintenance claim in light of the different factors listed in the Wisconsin statute in footnote 17?

---

17   Those factors are:

(1) The length of the marriage.

(2) The age and physical and emotional health of the parties.

(3) The division of property made under s. 767.61.

(4) The educational level of each party at the time of marriage and at the time the action is commenced.

(5) The earning capacity of the party seeking maintenance, including educational background, training, employment skills, work experience, length of absence from the job market, custodial responsibilities for children and the time and expense necessary to acquire sufficient education or training to enable the party to find appropriate employment.

(6) The feasibility that the party seeking maintenance can become self-supporting at a standard of living reasonably comparable to that enjoyed during the marriage, and, if so, the length of time necessary to achieve this goal.

(7) The tax consequences to each party.

(8) Any mutual agreement made by the parties before or during the marriage, according to the terms of which one party has made financial or service contributions to the other with the expectation of reciprocation or other compensation in the future, if the repayment has not been made, or any mutual agreement made by the parties before or during the marriage concerning any arrangement for the financial support of the parties.

(9) The contribution by one party to the education, training or increased earning power of the other.

(10) Such other factors as the court may in each individual case determine to be relevant.

the divorce and could anticipate enjoying if they were to stay married." The second objective is fairness, which aims to "compensate the recipient spouse for contributions made to the marriage, give effect to the parties' financial arrangements, or prevent unjust enrichment of either party."

¶ 45 When determining the appropriate maintenance award, we have instructed courts to start with "the proposition that the dependent partner may be entitled to 50 percent of the total earnings of both parties" and then make any needed adjustments after considering the Wis. Stat. § 767.56 factors. Notwithstanding the proscribed starting point, "[t]he payment of maintenance is not to be viewed as a permanent annuity." *Vander Perren v. Vander Perren,* 105 Wis.2d 219, 230, 313 N.W.2d 813 (1982). Rather, maintenance is "designed to maintain a party at an appropriate standard of living, under the facts and circumstances of the individual case, until the party exercising reasonable diligence has reached a level of income where maintenance is no longer necessary."

¶ 46 As is the case here, concerns about double counting sometimes arise when awarding maintenance. We first pronounced the rule against double counting in *Kronforst v. Kronforst,* 21 Wis.2d 54, 123 N.W.2d 528 (1963). At issue in *Kronforst* was the counting of Mr. Kronforst's interest in his employment profit-sharing trust. The trust was set up so that, upon termination of his employment, Mr. Kronforst could either withdraw his interest from the trust or have his interest disbursed to him in monthly installments over ten years. When dividing the marital estate upon the couple's divorce, the circuit court included, as a divisible asset, Mr. Kronforst's interest in the trust and awarded the interest to him.

¶ 47 On review, we concluded that the circuit court properly included Mr. Kronforst's interest in the trust in the divisible estate. We held, however, that the circuit court erred when it also considered the payments from the trust as Mr. Kronforst's income when calculating maintenance. We underscored that at the time of trial, Mr. Kronforst was on extended medical leave, and therefore, "all probabilities" were that he would not return to work, meaning that his interest in the trust would not grow. As such, we opined:

> We view the matter no differently than if the $9,749 had constituted cash in a bank deposit standing in defendant's name. Such an asset cannot be included as a principal asset in making division of the estate and then also as an income item to be considered in awarding alimony.

Id. at 64, 123 N.W.2d 528.

¶ 48 Our case law since *Kronforst* has refined the rule against double counting. In *Hommel v. Hommel,* 162 Wis.2d 782, 471 N.W.2d 1 (1991), we held that, generally, it did not violate the rule against double counting to include "investment income from assets awarded to a spouse as part of an equal division of property pursuant to a divorce settlement [when] calculating that spouse's income for purposes of revising a maintenance award to the payee spouse." In so holding, we relied in part on the court of appeal's rationale and holding in *Pelot v. Pelot,* 116 Wis.2d 339, 342 N.W.2d 64 (Ct.App.1983).

* * *

¶ 52 * * * As in *Pelot,* in the typical property division case involving a pension, the trial court may determine the present value of the pension. When the present value of a pension plan is calculated, that present value is based, in part, on projected future benefit payments. *See generally Pelot,* 116 Wis.2d at 341–43, 342 N.W.2d 64; *see also Bloomer v. Bloomer,* 84 Wis.2d 124, 130–32, 267 N.W.2d 235 (1978) (explaining how numerous courts have calculated the present value of pension funds for property division purposes). Therefore, assuming the employee spouse is awarded the present value of the asset, he or she does not receive the value of the asset at the time of the property division. Rather, the spouse receives that value via future payments. Accordingly, * * * it would be double counting to count the present value of the pension as a divisible asset and also count the future payments as income, since the income, up to the valuation placed on the pension at the time of the division, are one and the same.

¶ 53 Contrarily, when an income earning asset is assigned to one spouse, as in *Hommel,* that spouse, generally, receives the full fair market value of that asset at the time of the property division. Stated otherwise, if the spouse was awarded income property, that spouse could turn around and sell the income property the next day and, thereby, attain the value of the property. The spouse could also elect to keep the property and earn income from it. As the spouse earns income, he or she does not lose the value of the property because he or she always has the option to sell the property for fair market value. Therefore, unlike pension benefit payments (up to the present value placed on the pension at the time of the division), the value of investment property is separate from the income it generates. Consequently, as *Hommel* held, counting income from income earning assets will typically not implicate double counting.

> **Think About It**
>
> What is the basis for the distinction the court draws here between pension benefits and investment property?

* * *

D. Application

a. Goodwill

¶ 55 We now apply the legal principles set forth above to the facts and circumstances of this case. Starting with the value of professional goodwill in Orthodontic Specialists, Tim contends that the entire value of the salable professional goodwill in Orthodontic Specialists should not be included in the divisible marital estate. Specifically, Tim would like what he classifies as personal goodwill to be excluded. Notably, Tim does not argue that, if, as a matter of law, the entire value of Orthodontic Specialists' salable goodwill is includable in the marital estate, the circuit court's finding that Orthodontic Specialists' value is $1,058,000 was clearly erroneous. Nor does he challenge that the property should be divided equally.

¶ 56 Pursuant to our conclusion above, the entire amount of *salable* professional goodwill was appropriately included in the marital estate. Here, Tim has not shown that the $1,058,000 value placed on Orthodontic Specialists includes nonsalable goodwill. Rather, the facts indicate the contrary. In particular, Tim bought the practice, over a decade ago, for $930,000. Approximately 90 percent of this purchase price was paid for goodwill. Moreover, Tim testified that this goodwill included "Dr. Grady's name, the noncompete clause, and the employment agreement that Dr. Grady would stay on to introduce me to his existing patients, [and] to counsel me through the process of learning how to do business," much of which is included in what Tim classifies as personal goodwill.

¶ 57 As the sale from Dr. Grady to Tim shows, personal goodwill in an orthodontic practice is salable. It is appropriate to include the salable goodwill from Orthodontic Specialists in the divisible marital estate.

¶ 58 Moreover, the record is replete with evidence that Tracy contributed to the development and success of Orthodontic Specialists. There is no question that she helped to create the business's goodwill. Consequently, under the statutory presumption of an equal division of the marital estate and the contributions of both parties to the creation of the marital estate herein, the circuit court did not erroneously exercise its discretion when it included the goodwill associated with Orthodontic Specialists in the marital estate and divided it on a 50:50 basis. Stated otherwise, the circuit court did not erroneously exercise its discretion when it included the entire $1,058,000 value of Orthodontic Specialists' goodwill in the marital estate.

b. Double counting

¶ 59 Tim argues that the circuit court double counted the value of his professional goodwill when it included the goodwill in the divisible marital estate, and then based Tracy's maintenance award on Tim's expected future earnings. According to Tim, the expected future earnings also included the value of the goodwill because it was calculated using Tim's average income over the preceding five years which was increased by the goodwill. We disagree.

¶ 60 We start by underscoring our directive in *Cook* that the rule against double counting is advisory and not absolute. *Cook, 208 Wis.2d at 180, 560 N.W.2d 246*. As set forth above, the double counting rule does not prohibit the inclusion of investment income from assets awarded to a spouse as part of property division when calculating maintenance. *Hommel, 162 Wis.2d at 792, 471 N.W.2d 1*. This is so because the value of the investment asset is separate from the income it produces. Contrarily, pension benefit payouts (until they reach the amount of the valuation given the pension as an asset at the time of the property division) do not create value separate from the pension as an asset at the time of the property division. *Olski, 197 Wis.2d at 243–51, 540 N.W.2d 412*; *Pelot, 116 Wis.2d at 343, 342 N.W.2d 64*. Applying these principles to the case at hand, we conclude that the salable professional goodwill in Orthodontic Specialists is similar to an asset that produces income.

¶ 61 As with an income producing asset, the value of Orthodontic Specialists at the time of the property division had a set value, namely, $1,058,000. If Tim so chose, at the time of the property division, he could have sold Orthodontic Specialists and realized this value. Or, he could retain Orthodontic Specialists, earn income from it and sell it at a later time. Consequently, Tim has the option of continuing to generate substantial income from Orthodontic Specialists without diminishing its value. Specifically, the circuit court found that if Tim works 40 hours per week, Tim's income will be $465,000 annually. As with income from an income earning asset, this income is separate from the value of Orthodontic Specialists as it existed at the time of the property division. Consequently, the circuit court did not double count Orthodontic Specialists' professional goodwill and, therefore, did not erroneously exercise its discretion when it awarded Tracy $16,000 per month, for 20 years, in maintenance.

III. CONCLUSION

¶ 62 We conclude the entire value of salable professional goodwill was properly counted as divisible property in the marital estate. Moreover, we conclude that the circuit court did not double count the professional goodwill from Orthodontic Specialists in the maintenance award. Accordingly, we affirm the decision of the court of appeals.

The decision of the court of appeals is affirmed.

————————

Points for Discussion

a. Professional Goodwill

Courts have wrestled with the question of when it is appropriate to value and divide professional goodwill in a divorce case. Many jurisdictions take the approach urged by Dr. McReath in this case, attempting to distinguish between enterprise goodwill, which may be marital property, and personal goodwill, which belongs to the professional spouse. See, e.g., Yoon v. Yoon, 711 N.E.2d 1265 (Ind. 1999); In re Marriage of Zells, 572 N.E.2d 944 (Ill. 1991). Other courts have ordered division of goodwill in a professional practice without making the distinction between enterprise and personal goodwill. See, e.g., In re Marriage of Huff, 834 P.2d 244 (Colo.1992). There are also decisions holding that the goodwill of a professional practice is not property for purposes of equitable distribution on divorce. See, e.g., Powell v. Powell, 648 P.2d 218 (Kan. 1982). See generally Allen Parkman, *The Treatment of Professional Goodwill in Divorce Proceedings*, 18 Fam. L.Q. 213 (1984).

In *McReath*, the court focuses on what it describes as saleable goodwill, making a distinction between professional practices that can be bought and sold, such as orthodontia or accounting practices, and those that cannot, specifically law practices. Another opinion that takes a similar approach to this problem is Hanson v. Hanson, 738 S.W.2d 429 (Mo.1987), in which the court wrote:

> Proof of the existence of goodwill is particularly troublesome in a professional context. This difficulty is a product of the fact that the reputation of the individual practitioner and the goodwill of his enterprise are often inextricably interwoven. Because of the difficulties inherent in separating the reputation of the professional from that of his enterprise, evidence that other professionals are willing to pay for goodwill when acquiring a practice is, in our view, the only acceptable evidence of the existence of goodwill. Thus, as a matter of proof, the existence of goodwill is shown only when there is evidence of a recent actual sale of a similarly situated professional practice, an offer to purchase such a practice, or expert testimony and testimony of members of the subject profession as to the existence of goodwill in a similar practice in the relevant geographic and professional market. Absent such evidence, one can only speculate as to the existence of goodwill.

738 S.W.2d at 434, 435. Is *McReath* correct that the focus on saleable goodwill avoids the problem of dividing personal goodwill?

Although the majority of goodwill cases consider professional practices, similar questions can arise with other types of business ventures. See. e.g., Moore v. Moore, 779 S.E.2d 533 (S.C. 2015) (concluding that 20 % of the goodwill value of lighting company was personal to wife).

b. Noncompetition Agreements

When Dr. McReath purchased his orthodontics practice from Dr. Grady, most of the sales price was attributable to an employment and noncompetition agreement signed by Dr. Grady. This is common in the purchase and sale of many types of professional practices and other businesses. If Dr. McReath decided to sell the practice, he would likely have to sign a similar agreement. How should this affect the determination of whether or not the goodwill in the practice should be treated as marital property? See In the Matter of the Marriage of Slater and Slater, 245 P.3d 676 (Or.Ct. App. 2010) (holding that valuation of chiropractic business could not be based on assumption that husband would execute noncompetition agreement).

If Dr. McReath were to divorce while receiving payments under a noncompetition agreement for a practice he had purchased or established during his marriage, should those payments be characterized as marital property? Courts have concluded that if such an agreement substantially restricts an individual's future earning opportunities, it may not be included in the marital estate. E.g. Lowe v. Lowe, 372 N.W.2d 65 (Minn.Ct.App.1985). If such an agreement does not restrict income and employment opportunities, however, it may be treated as compensation for goodwill and other assets transferred to the buyer, and included in the marital estate; e.g. In re the Marriage of Gilbert-Sweere, 534 N.W.2d 294 (Minn. Ct.App.1995); In re Marriage of Gillespie, 948 P.2d 1338 (Wash. Ct. App. 1997).

Buying and Selling a Law Practice

Traditional ethics principles held that law practices cannot be sold, primarily because the lawyer's clients must be left free to consult other lawyers and may not be urged to continue with the purchaser of a practice. Under Rule 1.17 of the ABA Model Rules of Professional Conduct, however, lawyers may sell or purchase a law practice as long as certain conditions are met. See also Cal. Prof. Conduct Rule 2–300 (2018).

c. Goodwill in Law Practices

Despite the traditional ethical prohibition on sales of law practices, some courts have found the goodwill of law practices to be marital or community property subject to equitable division on divorce. See, e.g., In re Marriage of Nichols, 33 Cal.Rptr.2d 13 (Ct. App. 1994); In re Marriage of Huff, 834 P.2d 244 (Colo.1992). Other courts have concluded that the goodwill of a solo practitioner's law practice cannot be divided on divorce as marital or community property. See <u>Prahinski v. Prahinski, 582 A.2d 784 (Md. 1990)</u>.

d. Double Counting

The court in *McReath* also considers the double counting problem that arises with some marital assets. One reason that courts give for excluding "personal goodwill" from the valuation of a professional practice is a concern that the same earnings should not be divided twice, once in a marital property division and again in a spousal support award. See, e.g., <u>Grunfeld v. Grunfeld, 731 N.E.2d 142 (N.Y. 2000)</u>; <u>Marriage of Schneider, 824 N.E.2d 177 (Ill. 2005)</u>. Does the court in *McReath* address this issue satisfactorily?

Think About It

What arguments would support treating the value of a non-saleable professional practice as marital property in the context of a divorce?

McReath notes that the same concern is raised in cases dividing pension benefits. Courts in many states have held that once pension benefits are divided, it is improper to consider pension income for purposes of awarding spousal support, but states are sharply divided over the correct treatment of this question.

Problem 6-15

Vincent is a retired police officer who has operated a landscaping business for 15 years. His company has six employees, but Vincent is the only one who speaks English and the only one who deals directly with clients. The business has tangible assets worth $320,000. In their divorce, Vincent's wife Joan retains an expert who concludes that the value of the landscaping business is $460,000, including the tangible assets and $140,000 in goodwill. What arguments or evidence could Vincent offer to try to rebut the expert's business valuation? (See <u>Moretti v. Moretti, 766 A.2d 925 (R.I. 2001)</u>.)

In Re Marriage of Olar

<u>747 P.2d 676 (Colo. 1987) (en banc)</u>

VOLLACK, JUSTICE.

The issue presented in this case is whether an educational degree constitutes marital property subject to division upon dissolution of marriage, overruling

<u>*Graham v. Graham,* 194 Colo. 429, 574 P.2d 75 (1978)</u>, or in the alternative, if an educational degree is not marital property, whether the wife was entitled to maintenance under the facts of this case, including the contributions made by the wife towards her husband's education. The court of appeals held that the trial court did not abuse its discretion by not awarding the wife maintenance, because she failed to meet the threshold requirements of need set forth in <u>section 14–10–114(1)(a) and (b), 6B C.R.S. (1987)</u>. *In re Marriage of Olar,* No. 84CA0329 (Colo.App. Oct. 17, 1985) (not selected for publication). We affirm in part, reverse in part and remand the case for further proceedings.

I.

The petitioner, Sally K. Olar (wife), and the respondent, Terry T. Olar (husband), were married on September 5, 1970, and separated on June 26, 1982. When the couple separated, the wife was unaware that she was pregnant with the couple's only child. By the time that the decree of dissolution was entered on December 23, 1983, the child born of the marriage was eleven months old, and the wife was an unemployed, full-time student living with her parents in Munster, Indiana. The husband was living in Copeland, Texas, earning a gross salary of $35,000 per year as a laboratory manager.

At the time of their marriage, the wife had graduated from high school and the husband was in his first year of undergraduate studies. During the twelve-year marriage, with the exception of one year in which he worked full-time, the husband was a full-time student, acquiring undergraduate and graduate degrees. For the seven years prior to their separation in June of 1982, the Olars resided in Fort Collins, Colorado, where the husband attended Colorado State University (C.S.U.). At the time of the permanent orders hearing on December 15, 1983, the husband had completed his doctoral dissertation and was only required to present his work before a dissertation committee to obtain the doctoral degree in physiology and biophysics. Throughout the marriage, the wife worked full-time, and at the time of separation she was a bookkeeper with a gross income of $1,200 per month. The wife continued her employment until June 15, 1983, with the exception of nine weeks maternity leave, until she moved to Indiana to commence her full-time studies. She moved in with her parents who provided her and the child room and board with an agreed upon value of $400 per month, which the parents advanced her as a loan to be paid back when possible.

The husband's actual educational costs were financed by a combination of veteran's benefits for his past military service, tuition waivers, student loans, fellowships, and graduate student stipends. In the late 1970's, the husband also received in excess of $8,000 as an inheritance from his father and this sum was co-mingled with the assets of the parties, some of it going for a down-payment on a mobile home in which the couple lived until their separation. Throughout their marriage, the parties acquired little in the way of marital assets. According to the wife, during the years 1979 to 1982 her income totaled $47,398 and the husband's income totaled $26,628. The marital property consisted of two motor vehicles, furniture and miscellaneous property, a mobile home worth approximately $10,000, and at the time of dissolution, a savings account containing $1,100. Both parties had debts from credit cards and the husband had student loan debts of approximately $5,400.

The wife filed for dissolution of the marriage in January of 1983 in Larimer County District Court. At the dissolution hearing, the wife claimed that she was entitled to maintenance which would represent compensation for her working full-time throughout the marriage to assist in providing almost a complete doctoral education for her husband. The wife claimed that she had an agreement with her husband whereby he would support her during her efforts to achieve a college education for herself after his education was completed. She had an expert testify as to the value of a college education for her, comparing what she could expect to earn as a high school graduate and a college graduate. The wife did not specifically argue that the husband's graduate degrees were marital property and did not offer testimony on the potential worth of his degrees if discounted to present value, or the amount that she contributed to his education.

The husband claimed that there was no formal agreement between the parties that he would finance her education. He argued that his education was not marital property under Colorado law, and that the wife was not entitled to maintenance because she was capable of supporting herself. The custody of the minor child was not at issue and was awarded to the wife subject to reasonable and liberal visitation rights for the husband.

The trial court held that the wife was not eligible for maintenance because she failed to establish the threshold of need necessary to justify such an award under <u>section 14–10–114, 6B C.R.S. (1987)</u>. The court found that the wife was capable of supporting herself and although she had a young minor child to care for, nothing suggested that the child required her mother's full-time presence at home. The trial court ordered the husband to pay to the wife $350 per month as child support. As to the marital property, the court ordered that the proceeds of the sale of the mobile home, totalling $4,914.60, and the savings account of $1,100 should be combined, and the wife should receive the sum of $5,000, with the balance going to the husband. The court noted that this was not an equal distribution, but stated that this award was in keeping with dictum contained in <u>Graham v. Graham, 194 Colo. 429, 574 P.2d 75 (1978)</u>,[1] and would go towards

---

[1]   In *Graham,* we stated that the contribution of a spouse to the education of the other spouse could be taken into consideration by the court when dividing marital property. <u>194 Colo. at 433, 574 P.2d at 78</u>.

assisting the wife in continuing her education while working part-time. The court specifically held that the education of the husband was not marital property, and for this reason, found that the student loans of the husband, likewise, were not marital obligations, and ordered that the husband assume those debts without contribution from the wife.

The wife appealed the judgment to the court of appeals, claiming that the trial court erred in denying her maintenance because she failed to satisfy a threshold requirement of need. The court of appeals affirmed the trial court, stating that "[a] trial court may use an award of maintenance as a tool to balance equities and compensate a spouse whose work has enabled the other spouse to obtain an education, so long as the spouse seeking maintenance meets the statutory threshold requirements of need set forth in § 14–10–114(1)(a) and (b), C.R.S." The court of appeals held the trial court did not abuse its discretion in finding that the wife failed to establish the requisite need.

II.

We granted certiorari to reconsider our decision in _Graham v. Graham, 194 Colo. 429, 574 P.2d 75 (1978)_, which held that an educational degree is not marital property. This reconsideration is based upon the recognition of the harsh and often unfair outcome in a dissolution proceeding where one spouse has postponed his or her own career and educational goals to support and contribute to the career and educational goals of the other spouse. The pursuit of advanced educational degrees and professional training often results in a deferral of earning capacity by the spouse who receives that educational degree or advanced training at the expense of the current standard of living of the couple. When a couple collectively works towards the attainment of an advanced educational degree or career goal, there is an expectation of a higher standard of living in the future. If a dissolution of the marriage occurs just as the graduate degree is attained, or the career goal achieved, or just subsequent to the attainment of the goal, the spouse that contributed to and supported the other spouse has his or her expectations of the higher standard of living frustrated, and as a result of the collective sacrifice and deferment of acquiring other possessions, is left in a position where there is little marital property to divide. The contributions to the other spouse's education or career goals are often made at the expense of the supporting spouse's own education or career goal. The supporting spouse is left without the resources to recover from the years of deferring the acquisition of property and security. It is with the recognition of this potential for injustice that we examine the status of an educational degree in the context of the dissolution of a marriage.

In considering the status of an educational degree in the dissolution of a marriage, we do not work on a clean slate. In _Graham v. Graham, 194 Colo. 429,_

574 P.2d 75 (1978), we held that an educational degree is not marital property within the meaning of section 14–10–113(2), 6B C.R.S. (1987), which states that "[f]or purposes of this article only, 'marital property' means all property acquired by either spouse subsequent to the marriage except:"

(a) Property acquired by gift, bequest, devise, or descent;
(b) Property acquired in exchange for property acquired prior to the marriage or in exchange for property acquired by gift, bequest, devise, or descent;
(c) Property acquired by a spouse after a decree of legal separation; and
(d) Property excluded by valid agreement of the parties.

In applying this definition to an educational degree, we have stated:

An advanced degree is a cumulative product of many years of previous education, combined with diligence and hard work. It may not be acquired by the mere expenditure of money. It is simply an intellectual achievement that may potentially assist in the future acquisition of property. In our view, it has none of the attributes of property in the usual sense of that term.

Graham, 194 Colo. at 432, 574 P.2d at 77.

Our position in *Graham* is followed by the majority of jurisdictions to address this issue. *E.g., Nelson v. Nelson, 736 P.2d 1145 (Alaska 1987); Wisner v. Wisner, 129 Ariz. 333, 631 P.2d 115 (App.1981); In re Marriage of Sullivan, 134 Cal. App.3d 634, 184 Cal.Rptr. 796 (1982); vacated, 37 Cal.3d 762, 209 Cal.Rptr. 354, 691 P.2d 1020 (1984)* (statute amended to provide for the community to be reimbursed for community contributions to education of a party); *Hughes v. Hughes, 438 So.2d 146 (Fla.App.1983); In re Marriage of Weinstein, 128 Ill.App.3d 234, 83 Ill.Dec. 425, 470 N.E.2d 551 (1984); Archer v. Archer, 303 Md. 347, 493 A.2d 1074 (1985); Drapek v. Drapek, 399 Mass. 240, 503 N.E.2d 946 (1987); Ruben v. Ruben, 123 N.H. 358, 461 A.2d 733 (1983); Mahoney v. Mahoney, 91 N.J. 488, 453 A.2d 527 (1982); Hodge v. Hodge, 513 Pa. 264, 520 A.2d 15 (1986); Wehrkamp v. Wehrkamp, 357 N.W.2d 264 (S.D.1984); Petersen v. Petersen, 737 P.2d 237 (Utah App.1987). Contra, O'Brien v. O'Brien, 66 N.Y.2d 576, 498 N.Y.S.2d 743, 489 N.E.2d 712 (1985).*[2]

---

[2] The *O'Brien* decision is based on portions of the New York Equitable Distribution Law which provides that a court consider the efforts one spouse has made to the other spouse's career. *See* N.Y.Dom.Rel.Law § 236(B)(5) (McKinney 19__). The analysis in *O'Brien* is illustrative of the equitable concerns of the working spouse who contributes to the other spouse's career, however, it has a limited application beyond New York.

One commentator also argues that a spouse's professional degree and license should be considered a career asset to be divided, and provides a clear picture of the surprising injustice which resulted from the institution of the no-fault divorce law in the United States. L. Weitzman, *The Divorce Revolution* 124–29 (1985).

The doctrine of stare decisis imposes upon us a duty to exercise extreme care in overruling settled law. On the other hand, "[a] rule directed to the disposition of property in a dissolution proceeding can only be as sound as the economic reality which it attempts to service." *In re Marriage of Grubb*, 745 P.2d 661, 664 (Colo.1987). In *Grubb*, we reconsidered the status of pension plans as marital property and found that our prior case law, which rejected the concept of pension plans as marital property, did not adequately account for the true nature of retirement plans. We recognized that retirement benefits were a form of deferred compensation for consideration for past services performed by an employee and constituted part of the compensation earned by the employee. Educational degrees are very different in nature from pension plans. While a pension plan is difficult to place a value upon, it is possible. We find that the value of an educational degree is too dependent upon the attributes and future choices of its possessor to be fairly valued.

Other courts have noted the difference between professional licenses or degrees and vested but unmatured pension plans. The Maryland Court of Appeals noted that while pension rights constitute a current asset which the individual has a contractual right to receive, the future enhanced income resulting from a professional degree is a "mere expectancy." *Archer v. Archer*, 493 A.2d at 1079, citing *Deering v. Deering*, 292 Md. 115, 437 A.2d 883 (1981) (case holding a vested but unmatured pension right is marital property). The New Jersey Supreme Court stated that "[a] professional license or degree represents the opportunity to obtain an amount of money only upon the occurrence of highly uncertain future events. By contrast, the vested but unmatured pension at issue in *Kikkert [v. Kikkert*, 88 N.J. 4, 438 A.2d 317 (N.J.1981)], entitled the owner to a definite amount of money at a certain future date." *Mahoney*, 453 A.2d at 531. The *Mahoney* court further stated that "[v]aluing a professional degree in the hands of any particular individual at the start of his or her career would involve a gamut of calculations that reduces to little more than guesswork." We agree with this analysis, and therefore reaffirm our holding in *Graham*, holding that an educational degree is not marital property.

In *Graham* we stated, "[a] spouse who provides financial support while the other spouse acquires an education is not without a remedy." Here, it is the adequacy of the remedy with which we are concerned. The contribution of one spouse to the education of the other spouse may be taken into consideration when marital property is divided. This remedy is effective only if sufficient marital property has been accumulated by the parties during their marriage. In *Graham*, and the case at bar, the parties were divorced shortly after the husband acquired his degree. The situation in which the dissolution of marriage occurs before the benefits of the advanced degree can be realized, and where no marital property is accumulated, requires us to look to another remedy for the inequity that results for the working spouse. Another option mentioned in *Graham* was an award of maintenance as a need is demonstrated. The trial court could make an award of maintenance based on all relevant factors including the contribution of one spouse to the education of the other spouse. For this remedy, we look to section 14–10–114, 6B C.R.S. (1987), which sets forth the standards for awarding maintenance.

III.

Under Colorado's maintenance statute, maintenance is available only if property is insufficient to provide for the financial needs of the spouse. In this case, the accumulated marital property was insufficient to fairly compensate the wife for her contributions and expectations in the husband's educational degree. However, the trial court determined that the wife was not entitled to maintenance because she was capable of supporting herself, and therefore failed to establish "the threshold necessary to justify an award of maintenance." In our view, the trial court's holding does not adequately address the unfairness which results when one spouse sacrifices his or her own educational goals to support his or her spouse. Such an interpretation is not required by section 14–10–114, 6B C.R.S. (1987). Subsection (1) provides that a court may grant maintenance to either spouse if it finds that the spouse seeking maintenance:

(a) Lacks sufficient property, including marital property apportioned to him, to provide for his reasonable needs; and
(b) Is unable to support himself through appropriate employment or is the custodian of a child whose condition or circumstances make it appropriate that the custodian not be required to seek employment outside the home.

Take Note!

The statute construed here, based on UMDA § 308(a), requires that a spouse seeking support after a divorce make a threshold showing of need.

Once the court deems it just to award a spouse maintenance, the court considers all relevant factors including: the financial resources of the party seeking maintenance; the time necessary to acquire sufficient education or training to enable the party seeking maintenance to find appropriate employment and that party's future earning capacity; the standard of living established during the marriage; the duration of the marriage; the age and condition of the spouse seeking maintenance; and the ability of the spouse paying maintenance to meet his or her needs. § 14–10–114(2), 6B C.R.S. (1987). In consideration of whether to award maintenance, the trial court applies a two-part test evidenced by the statute. First, the trial court must determine whether a spouse is entitled to maintenance under section 14–10–114(1). Second, the trial court determines the amount of maintenance to be awarded once entitlement has been established. In setting the amount of maintenance, the trial court considers various factors including the standard of living established during the marriage.

As interpreted by the trial court, the threshold of need required by section 14–10–114(1), evidenced by the requirement that the spouse seeking maintenance have insufficient property to provide for his "reasonable needs" and be "unable to support himself through appropriate employment," is a high threshold requiring a spouse to establish that he or she lacks the minimum resources to sustain human life. The phrases "reasonable needs" and "appropriate employment" need not be viewed so narrowly.

In *Graham,* we stated that one of the remedies available to the working spouse, where no marital property was accumulated, is an award of maintenance if "a need is demonstrated." In *In re the Marriage of McVey,* 641 P.2d 300, 301 (Colo.App.1981), the court of appeals stated that "a trial court may use an award of maintenance *as a tool to balance equities and compensate a spouse whose work has enabled the other spouse to obtain an education;* however, this tool is available for use only where the spouse seeking maintenance meets the statutory threshold requirements of need." (Emphasis added). This "threshold of need" was not defined in *McVey,* but appears to have incorporated the concept of the minimum requirements to sustain life. This interpretation does not give sufficient weight to the word "reasonable" contained in the phrase "reasonable needs."[3] The determination of what a spouse's "reasonable needs" are, is dependent upon the particular facts and circumstances of the parties' marriage. *See Moss v. Moss,* 190 Colo. 491, 549 P.2d 404 (1976) (in the award of alimony, each case depends on its own particular facts and circumstances and an award of alimony in gross is not unacceptable per se).

The second factor to be considered in deciding whether a spouse is entitled to maintenance is whether the spouse is able to find "appropriate employment" for his or her support. § 14–10–114(1)(b). In the interest of fairness, the determination of what constitutes "appropriate employment" under subsection (b) requires that the party's economic circumstances and reasonable expectations established during the marriage be considered. In *In re Marriage of Angerman,* 44 Colo.App. 298, 612 P.2d 1166 (1980), the court of appeals affirmed the award of maintenance to the

---

[3]   The Utah Court of Appeals noted the rigidity of the interpretation of the "reasonable needs" requirement of section 14–10–114, noting that in cases such as *Graham,* "where divorce occurs shortly after the degree is obtained, traditional alimony analysis would often work hardship because, while both spouses have modest incomes at the time of divorce, the one is on the threshold of a significant increase in earnings. Moreover, the spouse who sacrificed so the other could attain a degree is precluded from enjoying the anticipated dividends the degree will ordinarily provide. * * * In such cases, alimony analysis must become more creative to achieve fairness, and an award of 'rehabilitative' or 'reimbursement' alimony, not terminable upon remarriage, may be appropriate." *Petersen v. Petersen,* 737 P.2d at 242 n. 4.

wife in the sum of $200 per month while the wife was matriculating in a master's degree program for music. The trial court found that the parties had intended that "appropriate employment" for the wife meant a career in opera or in the teaching of music, and that the wife's employment as a keypunch operator was only a temporary position "dictated by the financial needs of the husband's education."

The word "appropriate" is defined as "specially suitable" or "proper." Webster's Third New International Dictionary 106 (1969). The word "appropriate" limits the otherwise harsh results of denying a spouse maintenance if any kind of employment is attainable. The employment must be suited to the individual, including that individual's expectations and intentions as expressed during the marriage. The consideration of the parties' reasonable expectations and intentions gives full meaning to the phrase "appropriate employment." Any statement or intimation to the contrary in our prior decision in *Graham* and contained in the court of appeals' decision of *McVey* is hereby expressly disapproved. We think it appropriate for the trial court to reconsider the award of maintenance.[24]

Accordingly, we affirm the court of appeals' holding that an educational degree was not marital property, but reverse the judgment and remand the case to the court of appeals with directions to return the case to the district court for further proceedings as to the issue of maintenance.

> **FYI**
>
> On remand, the trial court awarded Sally Olar $600 a month in maintenance for four years, to continue regardless of her remarriage, but to be terminable upon her death. The trial court found that a bookkeeper's job paying $1200 a month would not enable the petitioner to support herself in accordance with "the parties' expectations had the parties remained together or had petitioner obtained her bachelor's degree." In re Marriage of Olar, District Court, County of Larimer, State of Colorado, Civil Action No. 83–DR–15, August 12, 1988.

---

[24] Other courts have considered the problem of how to fairly compensate a working spouse who has supported the other spouse while he or she obtains a professional degree. One jurisdiction has created what is known as "reimbursement alimony" which awards maintenance to the supporting spouse in an amount to equal the money spent by the supporting spouse towards the education. *Mahoney v. Mahoney,* 91 N.J. 488, 453 A.2d 527 (1982). Another court held that the supporting spouse was entitled to restitution of the money spent towards the attainment of the other spouse's degree in order to prevent unjust enrichment of the student-spouse. *See Hubbard v. Hubbard,* 603 P.2d 747 (Okla.1979). We recognize that our approach to compensating a spouse for his or her support of the other spouse in the attainment of an educational degree is to a certain extent limited by the statutory framework contained in the Uniform Dissolution of a Marriage Act. Other courts, interpreting their own statutory provisions regarding maintenance, have held that a demonstrated capacity of self-support on the part of the supporting spouse is but one factor to be considered in the awarding of maintenance, recognizing that a spouse who is capable of supporting someone through school will in most cases be capable of supporting him or herself after the marriage is dissolved. *See Washburn v. Washburn,* 101 Wash.2d 168, 677 P.2d 152 (1984).

Points for Discussion

a. Academic Degrees as Property

A large majority of the states do not treat educational degrees as marital property subject to equitable distribution. See <u>Simmons v. Simmons, 708 A.2d 949, 955 fn. 7 (Conn. 1998)</u> (citing decisions). In New York, however, degrees and professional licenses may be treated as property under <u>O'Brien v. O'Brien, 489 N.E.2d 712 (N.Y. 1985)</u>.

New York's equitable distribution law requires that courts consider any direct or indirect contributions made to the acquisition of marital property, including the expenditures, contributions or services of one spouse to the career of the other party. <u>N.Y. Dom. Rel. L. § 236[B][5][d](7) (2018)</u>. *O'Brien* read this language to permit courts to award not merely the amount of the supporting spouse's direct financial contributions to the acquisition of a degree or license, but to value the enhanced earning capacity that resulted from the degree and then award an equitable share of that value. A spouse seeking to share in the value of a degree must show that he or she made a substantial contribution to its acquisition. See, e.g., <u>Higgins v. Higgins, 857 N.Y.S.2d 171 (App. Div. 2008)</u>.

How can a spouse's enhanced earning capacity be measured? Is this analogous to professional goodwill?

For additional background on *O'Brien*, see Ira Mark Ellman, O'Brien v. O'Brien: *A Failed Reform, Unlikely Reformers, in* Family Law Stories 269 (Carol Sanger, ed. 2008).

b. Celebrity Goodwill

Under the New York approach, other types of career enhancement development may also treated as marital property. In <u>Elkus v. Elkus, 572 N.Y.S.2d 901 (App. Div. 1991)</u>, motion for leave to appeal dismissed <u>588 N.E.2d 99 (N.Y. 1992)</u> the wife became an internationally acclaimed opera star during the marriage, in part due to the assistance and coaching of her husband. The court held that to the extent that her career appreciation was due to the husband's efforts and contributions, the appreciation was marital property to be divided on divorce. See also <u>Golub v. Golub, 527 N.Y.S.2d 946 (N.Y.Sup.1988)</u>; <u>Piscopo v. Piscopo, 557 A.2d 1040 (N.J. Super. Ct. App.Div.1989)</u>. How would this type of marital property be valued and divided?

c. Reimbursement Alimony

Courts that have concluded that academic degrees are not marital property face the further question of whether and how to compensate the supporting spouse for his or her contributions to the other spouse's education, a problem sometimes described as the "diploma dilemma." There are a number of approaches described in footnote 24 of the *Olar* decision, including an award of what is sometimes called "reimbursement" alimony. See Mahoney v. Mahoney, 453 A.2d 527, 533 (N.J. 1982). On what basis could an award of reimbursement maintenance be calculated? See Lambert v. Lambert, 376 S.E.2d 331 (W. Va. 1988); Hoak v. Hoak, 370 S.E.2d 473 (W. Va. 1988).

In addition to academic degrees, what other contributions might be compensated in this manner? Would a spousal support award be preferable to property division in cases of professional or celebrity goodwill accumulated during a marriage? Would reimbursement alimony be appropriate to compensate one spouse for payment of the other's separate debts? See Zullo v. Zullo, 613 A.2d 544 (Pa. 1992).

Problem 6-16

Tom and Diana began living together while they were in college, and Tom proposed to Diana on the day he was accepted to medical school. After six years and two children, Tom filed for a divorce. Tom is a resident in internal medicine, and Diana runs an in-home day care business she used to support the family while Tom was in medical school. Tom earns about $60,000 a year, and Diana earns about $12,000 a year. Diana has hired a valuation expert who has computed that Tom's increased earnings over his working life as a result of his medical degree will be more than $ 800,000. How should Diana be compensated for her contributions to Tom's medical degree? Would you answer be different if Tom and Diana were not married? (See In re Marriage of Francis, 442 N.W.2d 59 (Iowa 1989).)

Problem 6-17

Anthony and Claire began living together without marrying, holding themselves out as husband and wife, working together in Anthony's machine shop business. They took equal salaries, but when they incorporated the business, all of the shares were placed in Anthony's name. Claire came up with the idea to make a bright-colored purse-sized flashlight, and the business became extremely successful. When their relationship ended after 25 years, the business was worth hundreds of millions of dollars. Does Claire have a legal basis to seek compensation for her contributions for Anthony's success? How would her rights be different if they had actually married at the outset of their relationship? (See <u>Maglica v. Maglica, 78 Cal.Rptr.2d 101 (Ct. App. 1998)</u>.)

---

2. Spousal Support

All states authorize awards of spousal support, also known as alimony or maintenance, after a divorce. In the English ecclesiastical law, alimony orders were a continuation of the husband's duty of support for his wife, entered as part of a ***divorce a mensa et thoro***, roughly equivalent to a legal separation. A wife who was at fault was not entitled to alimony. American law adopted the practice of granting alimony as an incident to absolute divorce. With the elimination of fault grounds for divorce, however, the purposes of spousal support have shifted.

Today, if any spousal support is ordered at all, it is usually for a relatively short time period, with the purpose of assisting a financially dependent spouse in making a transition to economic self-sufficiency. This is often characterized as rehabilitative or transitional support. Support orders may be entered on a permanent or indefinite basis in some situations, generally those in which he parties have dramatically different earnings and one spouse's prospects for financial independence are limited. In a few states, spousal support may be awarded to compensate one spouse for contributions to the marriage that cannot adequately be covered with property division orders; this is sometimes referred to as reimbursement or restitutionary alimony.

Property division and spousal support orders have significantly different characteristics and legal consequences. For example, spousal support orders are typically modifiable on proof that relevant circumstances have changed since the divorce decree was entered, while a decree dividing the spouses' property is generally not modifiable, except on proof of grounds which warrant reopening the judgment. In addition, spousal support usually terminates on the remarriage of the recipient or the death of either party, while these events do not affect the obligation to make property distribution payments.

Go Online

Find a chart listing the <u>spousal support statutes</u> for all states on the web page of the American Bar Association's <u>Family Law Section</u>.

Tax and Bankruptcy Considerations

As discussed later in this chapter, spousal support and property division awards are treated differently under federal tax and bankruptcy laws. Alimony payments ordered or agreed to prior to 2019 may be deductible from the payor's income and included in the recipient's income for purposes of federal income taxes. Division of property is not a taxable event and property distribution payments are not deductible. Property obligations have historically been dischargeable in bankruptcy, while alimony obligations have not.

Because these distinctions have significant practical and economic consequences for the parties, they must be carefully considered in negotiating and settling divorce cases. To a certain extent, parties to a settlement may use the differences to structure an agreement to their advantage. Courts do not always accept the parties' characterization of a payment, however, particularly for purposes of federal income tax or bankruptcy laws.

In re the Marriage of Hutchings

250 P.3d 324 (Okla. 2011)

REIF, J.:

[1] ¶ 1 The issues presented on certiorari review are whether the trial court considered the relevant factors under Oklahoma law for determining an appropriate amount of support alimony, and whether the trial court's award of support alimony is supported by the evidence. We hold that the court's award of support alimony was insufficient and an abuse of discretion.

¶ 2 Elizabeth Hutchings (wife) and Dean Hutchings (husband) were married on March 12, 1983. At the time of the marriage, both parties had a high school diploma. The wife was twenty years old, pregnant, and working as a nurse's aide. The husband was twenty-one and working for a manufacturing company. The parties did not own any real property.

¶ 3 The couple's first child was born in August 1983, and three more children were born of the marriage in August 1985, July 1987, and January 1989. The wife quit her job as a nurse's aide when she began having health problems with the first child. By a joint decision of the parties, the wife continued to stay home and to take care of the children until they were older. The wife was the primary caretaker of the children for approximately sixteen years of the twenty-two year marriage.

¶ 4 In July 1998, the wife began working part-time as a birth certificate clerk at St. John Medical Center, and continued to care for the parties' children. By the time of trial, she had held that job full time for four years, earning $22,927.93 in 2007. She is at the top amount she can earn for that position, with no opportunity for advancement.

¶ 5 At trial, the wife testified that she did not earn enough to support herself. Even with the husband's $900 contribution, at the time of trial she had a shortfall of around $1,200 per month. She used money from her savings, from what she had left from the sale of the rental house, to cover her expenses. When she has to add expenses such as health insurance, she estimated that the shortfall would be around $1,825 per month. She testified that she wanted to become self-supportive by obtaining a master's degree in social work in which she would earn $35,000 to $39,000 per year. She started part-time classes at junior college in January 2008, and estimated that her college expenses would be a total of $23,850 over five years.

¶ 6 After seven years at the manufacturing company, the husband began working for American Airlines. He started out painting planes and worked his way up to crew chief, earning over $70,000 per year at the time of trial. The husband also earned extra income, generally in cash, through independent painting and construction jobs. The husband testified that in 2007 he received cash in the amount of $4,500 for three painting jobs, and a W-2 showed he earned $1,200 from U.S. Medical. The husband also acquired a pension and a 401(k) plan at American Airlines, and flying benefits.

¶ 7 After the birth of their first child in 1983, the parties purchased an unfinished house and five acres. It took fourteen to fifteen years to complete the house, with the wife helping with some of the physical labor to finish it. The house was sold shortly after its completion, and the parties then built a second home where they lived for about five years. The parties then moved into a lakefront home, where they lived until separation. The house was 2,100 square feet, with a private boat dock and access to a swimming pool and tennis court. At the time of separation, the parties also owned a rental house and a vacant lot, and each party had a vehicle.

¶ 8 The parties separated on July 17, 2005, after twenty-two years of marriage. The husband moved out of the marital residence and began living with another woman. Two minor children, and one child who had aged out, continued to live with the wife. Following the separation, the wife moved into a one-bedroom apartment, and she plans to purchase a home about half the size of the prior marital residence with her half of the proceeds from the sale of the marital home. She believes she can only afford a house in the range of $75,000 to $85,000.

¶ 9 The husband purchased a newly built, 1,600 square foot home after the separation, with a purchase price of $159,000. He paid $34,000 in cash as a down payment from his $40,000 sales proceeds from the sale of the marital residence. He travels monthly, often accompanied by his girlfriend, both domestically as well as to Jamaica, Switzerland, and Australia.

¶ 10 On September 13, 2005, the wife filed for divorce. The parties entered into a partial temporary order in October 2005, whereby the wife was granted temporary custody of the minor children and the husband was ordered to pay $931.26 per month in child support. Later that month, the parties entered into an agreed temporary order whereby the wife retained custody of the minor children, and the husband was ordered to pay the wife $2,000 per month as a combination of temporary child support and temporary payment of jointly acquired indebtedness. After the sale of the rental property, the husband began paying the wife $1,800 per month as the combined payment of child support and jointly acquired debt. Then, following the aging out of the youngest child in June 2007, the husband paid the wife $900 per month without a court order until trial.

¶ 11 The divorce was granted in March 2008. The parties had resolved all issues by the time of trial except for support alimony and payment of the joint 2006 taxes. The wife had requested $2,200 per month support alimony for five years, for a total of $132,000, in order to pursue the social work degrees. The wife requested that the husband be ordered to pay the parties' 2006 joint taxes of $2,678, which were incurred based on the sale of the rental house and the husband's sale of American Airlines stock. The husband argued that he should not have to pay the wife any support alimony and that she should pay her share of the taxable gain on the rental property. He also requested credit for monies he had paid to the wife under the agreed temporary order.

¶ 12 The trial court awarded her $250 per month for three years, for a total of $9,000 in support alimony. The Court of Civil Appeals affirmed, stating that "[w]hile the facts of this case might have supported a higher amount of support alimony, we cannot say the award was *against all reason*." (Emphasis added.) The appellate court noted that there will be a significant earning disparity between the husband and wife. The appellate court also stated that "Wife agreed that she was asking for $23,800 for reimbursement of tuition for undergraduate and graduate degrees, but if she chose to change her profession to nursing, that would have been free through a program at St. John's, except for owing St. John's two-years of employment at $18 per hour. Wife was adamant about not wanting to be a nurse." (Footnote omitted.)

¶ 13 The wife sought certiorari on the grounds that the court not only failed to apply the relevant factors to this case, but wrongfully read the record to conclude that if the wife chose to change her profession to nursing, it would have been free through a program at St. John Hospital. The wife states that the record does not support that she would receive a free education, but only minimal tuition assistance in a field she did not wish to pursue. She avers that when parties divorce, there is no precedent to force an occupation chosen by the husband on the wife.

¶ 14 In divorce actions, the trial court is vested with wide discretion in awarding alimony. On appeal, the court will not disturb the trial court's judgment regarding alimony absent an abuse of discretion or a finding that the decision is clearly contrary to the weight of the evidence.[2]

¶ 15 Alimony is an allowance for the maintenance of a party. In awarding alimony, although each case depends on its own facts and circumstances, the amount must be reasonable. Oklahoma defines support alimony as a need-based concept, with a purpose of cushioning the economic impact of the post-marriage transition and readjustment to gainful employment. Demonstrated need is shown by the totality of proof of the spouse's financial condition.

¶ 16 Support alimony is based on a consideration of relevant factors including: demonstrated need during the post-divorce economic readjustment period; the parties' station in life; the length of the marriage and the ages of the spouses; the earning capacity of the parties as well as their physical condition and financial means; the accustomed style of living of the parties; evidence of a spouse's own income-producing capacity and the time needed to make the post-divorce transition for self-support.

¶ 17 In *Durland v. Durland, 1976 OK 102, 552 P.2d 1148*, the court increased an alimony award from $36,000 to $48,000 where the parties had been married nineteen years, the wife earned a minimal income and was not trained for any particular employment, and one of the children required special care. Also, in *Peyravy v. Peyravy, 2003 OK 92, 84 P.3d 720*, the court determined that a trial court's award of support alimony in the amount of $24,000, was insufficient where the parties had been married for twenty-two years, the husband had supported the family, the husband's average monthly income paid by the family's corporations was $9,100, and the wife's health inhibited her ability to work full time outside the home. The *Peyravy* court noted that in *Mocnik v. Mocnik, 1992 OK 99, 838 P.2d 500*, the court increased an alimony award from $60,000 to $120,000 where the parties had been married for eighteen years, the husband earned $215,000 a year,

---

[2] The appellate court's finding that "we cannot say the award was against all reason" was not a proper statement of the standard of review.

and the wife had an earning capacity of $20,000. Moreover, in <u>Aronson v. Aronson, 1970 OK 74, 468 P.2d 493</u>, the court increased an alimony award of $60,500 to $90,750 where the parties had been married for fifteen years, the husband was a doctor earning $60,000 a year, and the wife worked as a substitute elementary school teacher, earning only $500 per month. The *Peyravy* court further noted that in other cases with similar circumstances, the court refused to reduce awards of support alimony which were significantly more than $24,000.

¶ 18 Here, the parties had been married for over twenty-two years when they became separated, and the husband's income was more than three times that of his wife. The evidence indicates that the wife's current income potential is insufficient to meet her meager living expenses. She has no opportunity for advancement without additional education and training, and her educational and training goals are reasonable under the circumstances,[10] allowing her to increase her income potential. The parties' earning capacities are significantly disparate. The trial court's award of $250 per month leaves the wife with a substantial shortfall every month, even with her living in a one-bedroom apartment. The husband, by contrast, enjoyed a lavish lifestyle during the separation. The wife has a clearly-demonstrated need for more income during the post-matrimonial economic readjustment period.

¶ 19 The amount awarded by the trial court does not provide the wife with the necessary opportunity for post-marital economic readjustment. The trial court failed to properly consider the appropriate factors under Oklahoma law for setting support alimony. Based on the length of the marriage, the ability of the husband to pay, the needs of the wife for living expenses and education, and her current income potential, the trial court's support alimony award of $9,000 to wife was insufficient and an abuse of discretion. Divorce cases are of equitable cognizance, and this Court ordinarily orders the disposition the trial court should have made. We therefore re-calculate the support alimony to award the wife $1,500 per month for 36 months, for a total of $54,000. The trial court's support alimony award is reversed and the matter is remanded with instructions to enter a support alimony award of $54,000, payable at $1,500 per month for 36 months.

* * *

¶ 20 ALL JUSTICES CONCUR.

---

[10]   The wife's choice of an educational endeavor should not be limited to the pursuit of a nursing degree, as chosen by the husband, where her unequivocal testimony was that she did not want to be a nurse.

Points for Discussion

a. Eligibility for Spousal Support

Case law and the literature on spousal support describe at least three primary purposes for spousal support awards: support, compensation, and rehabilitation. See, e.g., In re Marriage of LaRocque, 406 N.W.2d 736 (Wis. 1987). What was the purpose of the award in *Hutchings*?

State statutes vary greatly in when they permit spousal support orders. Statutes based on the Uniform Marriage and Divorce Act § 308(a), 9A U.L.A. (Part 1) 446 (1998), discussed in the *Olar* case above, require the court to make an initial finding that the applicant lacks property to provide for her reasonable needs and is unable to support herself by appropriate employment or is a child's custodian making it appropriate that she not seek employment. E.g. Mo. Ann. Stat. § 452.335 (2018). What does this suggest about the appropriate purposes of a spousal support order?

Other states, such as Illinois or Pennsylvania, authorize courts to award alimony when the judge finds it "necessary" on the basis of a long list of relevant factors. 750 Ill. Comp. Stat. § 5/504 (2018); 23 Pa. Cons. Stat. § 3701 (2018). Texas, which had no law authorizing spousal awards until 1995, permits alimony only in extremely limited circumstances. Tex. Fam. Code Ann. §§ 8.001–8.011 (2018). Arizona authorizes courts to consider whether the marriage was of long duration so that the applicant is of an age which may preclude the possibility of adequate employment. Ariz. Rev. Stat. Ann. § 25–319 (2018). Massachusetts amended its alimony statutes in 2011 to provide more specific limits on the amount and duration of support awards. See Mass. Gen. Laws ch. 208 §§ 48–55 (2018).

As with the trial court ruling in *Hutchings*, the case law often reflects strong reluctance by judges to award more than minimal spousal support. As some courts put it, alimony is "disfavored." The percentage of divorce decrees that include alimony orders is small, with most studies indicating figures under 20%. Moreover, many of these cases involve short term, rehabilitative awards. See Lenore J. Weitzman, The Divorce Revolution: The Unexpected Social and Economic Consequences for Women and Children in America 143–183 (1985).

b. Factors in Determining Support Awards

Once a spouse establishes that he or she meets the statutory criteria for spousal support, the court must determine the amount and duration of any award. Statutes commonly include a list of factors to be considered by the court and the admonition to enter an order that is "just" or "reasonable." E.g. Uniform Marriage and Divorce Act § 308(b), 9A U.L.A. (Part 1) 446 (1998). According to an empirical study in New York state, the factors that courts weigh most heavily in deciding alimony cases are the length of the parties' marriage and the relative earning power of the spouses. Marsha Garrison, <u>*How Do Judges Decide Divorce Cases? An Empirical Analysis of Discretionary Decision Making*, 74 N.C. L. Rev. 410, 521 (1996)</u>. Which factors were important to the court in *Hutchings*? As a counterpoint to *Hutchings*, see <u>Jandreau v. LaChance, 116 A.3d 1273 (Me. 2015)</u>, finding that denial of spousal support was an abuse of discretion given the substantial income disparity between the parties. In Jandreau, the wife's only income was $14,212 per year in disability benefits, and husband earned $87,896 per year working as a machinist.

c. Fault

States are almost evenly divided between jurisdictions in which courts are permitted to consider marital misconduct in deciding whether to order spousal support and in what amounts, see, e.g., <u>Mass. Gen. Laws ch. 208, § 34 (2018)</u>; <u>23 Pa. Cons. Stat. § 3701 (2018)</u>; and jurisdictions in which courts are prohibited from considering misconduct in determining support awards, see, e.g., <u>Uniform Marriage and Divorce Act § 308(b)</u>. Compare <u>Rodriguez v. Rodriguez, 13 P.3d 415 (Nev. 2000)</u> (court abused discretion in denying alimony on basis of extramarital affair) with <u>Griffith v. Griffith, 506 S.E.2d 526 (S.C. Ct.App.1998)</u> (adultery a criminal offense in South Carolina and an absolute bar to alimony). Even in states that permit consideration of fault, other factors may weigh in favor of a support award. See, e.g., <u>Mani v. Mani, 869 A.2d 904 (N.J. 2005)</u>; <u>Congdon v. Congdon, 578 S.E.2d 833 (Va. Ct. App. 2003)</u>. Which of these approaches reflects the better policy? If marital fault has been made irrelevant to the grant or denial of divorce, what is the argument for considering fault in setting support?

d. Rehabilitation

As with the order in *Hutchings*, limited term spousal support orders are frequently intended to enable a dependent spouse to get the education or training necessary to be financially self-sufficient. The general policies favoring time-limited rehabilitative alimony rather than indefinite awards have seemed unfair and inappropriate in cases involving older wives in long-term marriages, who had no employment skills and no realistic possibility of becoming economically independent. In many states, appellate courts have refused to sustain short-term support awards in these cases unless there was evidence in the record to support the conclusion that the dependent spouse would be able to meet his or her financial needs at the end of the transitional support period. See, e.g., <u>In re Marriage of Morrison, 573 P.2d 41 (Cal. 1978)</u>; <u>Sinn v. Sinn, 696 P.2d 333 (Colo.1985)</u>. See Joan M. Krauskopf, <u>*Rehabilitative Alimony: Uses and Abuses of Limited Duration Alimony*, 21 Fam. L.Q. 573 (1988)</u>. What kind of evidence would meet this requirement?

e. Alimony for Caregivers

Many state statutes, including those based on the UMDA, suggest that a spousal support order may be appropriate when one spouse will have primary responsibility for child care following a divorce. In practice, alimony is rarely awarded on this basis alone. See Ann Laquer Estin, *Maintenance, Alimony, and the Rehabilitation of Family Care*, 71 N.C. L. Rev. 721 (1993), for an argument that spousal support orders should be used to support post-divorce caregiving for children. Should reimbursement alimony be awarded to spouses who have made financial or career sacrifices for the benefit of children during a marriage?

f. Spousal Support for Husbands

Courts decide cases involving spousal support orders for husbands, but they are not as numerous as cases involving wives. See, e.g., Stone v. Stone, 488 S.E.2d 15 (W. Va. 1997) (14-year marriage; rehabilitative alimony for paramedic husband seeking additional education); but see Metz v. Keener, 573 N.W.2d 865 (Wis. Ct.App.1997) (no maintenance for husband after short term marriage; husband received 40% of marital estate with value in excess of $1 million comprised entirely of wife's assets).

Orr v. Orr, 440 U.S. 268 (1979) held that an Alabama statute that only authorized courts to order husbands, but not wives, to pay alimony was a violation of the Equal Protection Clause of the Fourteenth Amendment to the Constitution. The Court rejected Alabama's justifications for the statute, including the state's preference for allocating to wives a dependent role in the family; the goal of protecting a wife as a "needy spouse"; and the compensation of women for past gender discrimination in marriage. The Court said that the "old notion" that the man has the primary responsibility for providing a home and its essentials could no longer justify gender-based discrimination, and that the existing process already considered the parties' relative financial circumstances. On remand the Alabama court decided to make alimony available to husbands rather than abolishing it entirely. Orr v. Orr, 374 So.2d 895 (Ala.Ct.App.1979).

g. Income Equalization

The court in In re Marriage of LaRocque, 406 N.W.2d 736 (Wis. 1987), held that after long term marriages, a reasonable starting point for determining maintenance is an equal division of the parties' total post-divorce income. What would this rule have meant in the *Hutchings* case? Courts in other states have divided on the question of whether equalization of income is an appropriate basis for a spousal support award. Cases rejecting this approach include Reichert v. Reichert, 516 N.W.2d 600 (Neb. 1994) and Stone v. Stone, 488 S.E.2d 15 (W. Va. 1997). Cases which have allowed this approach include Gardner v. Gardner, 748 P.2d

1076 (Utah 1988); and Guiel v. Guiel, 682 A.2d 957 (Vt. 1996). See also Jana B. Singer, *Divorce Reform and Gender Justice*, 67 N.C. L. Rev. 1103, 1117–1121 (1989), suggesting a formula for equal post-divorce sharing of income amounting to one year of income sharing for each two years of marriage.

h. Spousal Support Guidelines

In a few states, support guidelines established by court rules set presumptive levels of spousal support. Pennsylvania's spousal support guidelines, which apply to temporary alimony situations, begin with the difference between the two spouses' incomes, and require the higher earning spouse to pay a percentage of that difference to the lower earning spouse. For couples with dependent children, the presumptive spousal support payment is 30% of the difference in earnings. For couples with no dependent children, the figure is 40 %. See Mascaro v. Mascaro, 803 A.2d 1186 (Pa. 2002) (construing guidelines in high income case). 23 Pa. Cons. Stat. § 4322 (2012) and Pa. R.Civ.P. 1910.16–4, Part IV (2004). In Colorado, the statute applied in *Olar* has been replaced with one that incorporates a guideline, and requires court to compute and consider the guideline amount in most spousal support cases. See Colo. Rev. Stat. §14–10–114 (2018). See generally Twila B. Larkin, *Guidelines for Alimony: The New Mexico Experiment*, 38 Fam. L.Q. 29 (2004) (describing guidelines used in ten different states).

The American Academy of Matrimonial Lawyers (AAML) has developed a spousal support formula, which takes into account both parties' income, the length of the marriage, and a series of factors that would justify deviation from the formula amount. See Mary Kay Kisthardt, *Re-thinking Alimony: The AAML's Considerations for Calculating Alimony, Spousal Support or Maintenance*, 21 J. Am. Acad. Matrim. Lawyers 61 (2008). Boemio v. Boemio, 994 A.2d 911 (Md. 2010), held that it was within the trial court's discretion to consult the AAML guidelines in setting an alimony award.

i. Temporary Support

State statutes generally authorize the courts to grant alimony or spousal support during the pendency of the divorce suit, often called temporary alimony or alimony *pendente lite*. See, e.g. Cal.Fam.Code § 3600 (2018); Colo.Rev.Stat.Ann. § 14–10–108 (2018); Fla. Stat. Ann. § 61.071 (2018); Mass.Ann.L. ch. 208, § 17 (2018); N.J.Stat.Ann. § 2A:34–23 (2018); N.Y.Dom.Rel.L. § 236[B][6][a] (2018); 23 Pa. Cons. Stat. § 3702 (2018). Since the purpose of these payments is to maintain the applicant's standard of living as far as possible during the litigation, the amount awarded has no necessary relation to what might be awarded after the divorce. Burlini v. Burlini, 191 Cal.Rptr. 541 (Ct. App. 1983).

j. Support Claims by Cohabitants

Although courts in most jurisdictions utilize property and restitution principles to address the financial rights of cohabitants at the end of their relationships, very few jurisdictions allow claims for ongoing support in this situation. In most states, a cohabitant can obtain support after the relationship ends only by proving an express promise to pay support. See, e.g., Posik v. Layton, 695 So.2d 759 (Fla. Dist. Ct. App. 1997).

Since the decision in Marvin v. Marvin, 557 P.2d 106 (Cal. 1976), reprinted in Chapter 1, "palimony" has been available in California on an implied contract theory. Cases are collected in William H. Danne, Jr., *Annotation, "Palimony" Actions for Support Following Termination of Nonmarital Relationships,* 21 A.L.R.6th 351 (2007 & Supp.) New Jersey courts also allowed support claims by cohabitants based on implied contract, until a 2009 statute mandated that such contracts must be in writing and must be made with independent advice of counsel for both sides. See N.J. Stat. Ann. § 25:1–5(h) (2018).

k. Attorney's Fees

Statutes also authorize courts to require one spouse to pay part or all of the other spouse's reasonable attorney fees in a divorce action. Attorney fees are awarded on substantially the same reasoning as temporary spousal support: if the applicant requires legal advice to present a claim or defense, does not have the money to pay a lawyer, and the other spouse is able to bear that expense, the other spouse will be ordered to do so. In determining what fees are reasonable, the trial court may consider factors such as the nature of the case, its difficulty, the amount of money or property involved, the degree of skill or experience required and employed in the case, the degree of success attained, and the number of hours spent. See generally Jane Massey Draper, Annotation, *Excessiveness or Adequacy of Attorneys' Fees in Domestic Relations Cases,* 17 A.L.R.5th 366 (1994).

> **Make the Connection**
>
> Attorneys' fees in divorce actions raise special issues for federal income tax and bankruptcy purposes, and a range of ethical issues discussed in Chapter 8.

Problem 6-18

Harold and Wendy had been married for fifteen years when they divorced. Wendy was age 37 and Harold was 40, and their three children were 14, 10 and 6 years old. The parties separated when Harold left home, telling Wendy that he had fallen in love with one of her friends. During the marriage, Wendy did not work outside the home, but assumed full responsibility for homemaking and care of the children. Harold worked as a stockbroker and his annual income was $300,000. Harold retained an expert witness, who testified that Wendy had a college degree, was in good health, and could earn $60,000 per year. The parties have agreed on an equal division of the marital estate, which has a net value of $400,000, and they agree that Wendy will receive custody of the children and child support. Wendy is requesting alimony in the amount of one third of Harold's earned income until her death or remarriage. What arguments would you make for and against Wendy's claim?

Problem 6-19

When Harry and Winnie were married, Harry was 48 and Winnie was 45 years old. Harry received an annual salary of $200,000 from a construction firm that he owned and operated and had a net worth in excess of $5 million. Although it was highly profitable, the firm paid low dividends for tax reasons and had retained net earnings of ten million dollars. Before the marriage, Winnie had been a sociology professor at a state university with an annual salary of $48,000. She stopped working when she married Harry because he insisted that she should not work. Harry always gave Winnie plenty of money, and they lived on a scale corresponding to his wealth.

Although Harry seemed kind and affectionate before the marriage, after about two years he began to spend most of his evenings playing poker or drinking in his favorite bar with friends or business associates. On two occasions he hit Winnie hard enough to leave bruises on her face and arms. Winnie could not persuade Harry to see a marriage counselor with her, and after four years of marriage, she sued for divorce. Her old job was no longer available to her and she has not been able to find a new teaching position. Winnie is now working as a saleswoman in a department store, earning about $1,000 per month. Should she receive spousal support in these circumstances? On what basis?

Legal Separation and Separate Maintenance

A married couple who no longer wish to live together, but do not want to dissolve their marriage, may enter into a separation agreement. In some states, they may obtain a court decree that defines their financial rights and obligations, often known as a separate maintenance decree, which may provide for spousal support payments. Signing an agreement or obtaining a court order may be important for tax reasons, so that any support paid will qualify as alimony under the rules described later in this chapter.

As with divorce, the grounds for legal separation vary from state to state, ranging from traditional fault grounds such as desertion or cruelty, to no-fault grounds such as living separate and apart or irretrievable breakdown. See, e.g. Tenn. Code § 36–4–102 (2018), Wis. Stat § 767.35(1) (2018). See also Theisen v. Theisen, 716 S.E.2d 271 (S.C. 2011), construing the state statute providing for separate maintenance to require that the parties must be living separately. In many states, there is a simplified procedure for converting a legal separation into a divorce. See, e.g., Wis. Stat § 767.35(5) (2018).

In the Matter of Raybeck

44 A.3d 551 (N.H. 2012)

Lynn, J.

The respondent, Bruce Raybeck, appeals an order of the Laconia Family Division (*Sadler,* J.), recommended by the Marital Master (*Garner,* M.), ruling that the respondent was required to continue paying alimony to the petitioner, Judith Raybeck. We vacate and remand.

I

The relevant facts are as follows. The parties were divorced in Texas in August 2005 after a forty-two-year marriage. The respondent was awarded property in North Carolina and Texas, and the petitioner was awarded property in Laconia, New Hampshire. The divorce decree, based upon the parties' agreement, obligated the respondent to pay the petitioner alimony of $25,000 per year for ten years, in yearly installments. That obligation would cease, however, if the petitioner "cohabitates with an unrelated adult male."

Approximately three months before the January 2010 alimony payment was due, the petitioner moved out of her Laconia house and rented it to reduce her expenses. She moved into the upper level of a single family home in Plymouth owned by Paul Sansoucie, a man she had met through an online dating service. Sansoucie lived on the lower level and did not charge the petitioner for rent. She did, however, pay about $300 per month for food and often cooked for him. They also shared living space on the middle level of the house. When the respondent learned that the petitioner lived with another man, he stopped paying alimony. In response, the petitioner asked the family division to enforce the alimony agreement and require the respondent to resume his support payments.

After a hearing, the marital master recommended a finding that the petitioner was not cohabiting with Sansoucie under the terms of the divorce decree, and the family division approved the recommendation ordering the respondent to continue his alimony payments. This appeal followed.

II

In his brief, the respondent argues that the court erred as a matter of law in concluding that the petitioner was not cohabiting with Sansoucie under the terms of the divorce decree. The respondent abandoned that argument at oral argument, however, arguing instead that "the trial court below was not able to establish a workable definition of what constitutes cohabitation," and asking this court to adopt a standard of cohabitation enacted recently by legislative initiative in Massachusetts. *See An Act Reforming Alimony in the Commonwealth,* 2011 Mass. Acts ___ (H.B. 3617, ch. 124 § 49(d)).* The petitioner argues that the trial court acted within its discretion in concluding that she was not cohabiting with another man as that term was intended in the divorce decree.

---

* That Act provides, in section 49(d), that:

(d) General term alimony shall be suspended, reduced or terminated upon the cohabitation of the recipient spouse when the payor shows that the recipient has maintained a common household, as defined below, with another person for a continuous period of at least 3 months.

(1) Persons are deemed to maintain a common household when they share a primary residence together with or without others. In determining whether the recipient is maintaining a common household, the court may consider any of the following factors:

(i) oral or written statements or representations made to third parties regarding the relationship of the cohabitants;

(ii) the economic interdependence of the couple or economic dependence of 1 party on the other;

(iii) the common household couple engaging in conduct and collaborative roles in furtherance of their life together;

(iv) the benefit in the life of either or both of the common household parties from their relationship;

(v) the community reputation of the parties as a couple; or

(vi) other relevant and material factors.

In reviewing the trial court's ruling, we accept its factual findings unless they lack support in the record or are clearly erroneous. *State v. Michelson,* 160 N.H. 270, 272, 999 A.2d 372 (2010). The application of the appropriate legal standard to those facts, however, is a question of law, which we review *de novo.*

Neither the legislature nor this court has had occasion to define "cohabitation" as that term is often used in a divorce decree. Because the divorce decree here reflects the parties' agreement, we will interpret the cohabitation clause according to its common meaning. *See Kessler v. Gleich,* 161 N.H. 104, 108, 13 A.3d 109 (2010). The trial court applied the following standard:

> [E]vidence of a sexual relationship is admissible, but not necessarily required, for a finding of cohabitation. . . . [T]here must be more to the relationship than just occupying the same living area or sharing some or all of the expenses incurred by both parties. The evidence should reflect a common and mutual purpose to manage expenses and make decisions together about common and personal goals, and a common purpose to make mutual financial and personal progress toward those goals.

Applying this definition, the court concluded that the petitioner and Sansoucie did not cohabit. In support of that decision, the court found, among other facts, that the petitioner was forced to relocate when the respondent first announced that he would discontinue the alimony payments; that she and Sansoucie sleep on different floors of the house although they do share a common living area; that she does not pay rent but pays for food; and that their financial relationship is limited to her paying for food in exchange for shelter. The court also found, however, evidence indicating that there was a personal component to their relationship. They had, for example, shared rooms during their travels together. In a letter to her children, the petitioner stated that she and Sansoucie had discussed marriage but did not marry for "personal and financial reasons." Specifically, the petitioner wrote that "neither of us is sure if we want to remarry. Financial matters become so complicated at our age. . . ." The record also reflected that the petitioner's son-in-law referred to Sansoucie as the petitioner's boyfriend in a Christmas letter. Notwithstanding the evidence of a personal connection, the trial court ruled that the petitioner and Sansoucie did not cohabit in light of their financial situation.

Our common law lacks a definition of cohabitation as that term is used in divorce decrees and separation agreements. Dictionary definitions confirm the trial court's conclusion that to qualify a living arrangement as one of cohabitation there must be a personal connection beyond that of roommates or casual bedfellows. *Black's Law Dictionary,* for example, defines **cohabitation** as "[t]he fact or state of living together, esp[ecially] as partners in life, usu[ally] with the suggestion of sexual relations." *Black's Law Dictionary* 296 (9th ed.2009). *The Oxford English Dictionary* defines it as "liv[ing] together as husband and wife, esp[ecially] without legal marriage." 1 *Oxford English Dictionary* 447 (6th ed.2007). *Ballentine's*

Law Dictionary defines it as "a dwelling together of a man and a woman in the same place in the manner of husband and wife." *Ballentine's Law Dictionary* 214 (3d ed.1967); see also *The New Oxford American Dictionary* 330 (2d ed.2005) ("live together and have a sexual relationship without being married"); *Webster's Third New International Dictionary* 440 (unabridged ed.2002) ("[T]o live together as or as if as husband and wife. The mutual assumption of those marital rights, duties and obligations which are usually manifested by married people, including but not necessarily dependent on sexual relations.").

Common law standards from other jurisdictions contain similar articulations. *See, e.g., State v. Arroyo*, 181 Conn. 426, 435 A.2d 967, 970 (1980) ("[Cohabitation] is the mutual assumption of those marital rights, duties and obligations which are usually manifested by married people, including but not necessarily dependent on sexual relations."); *Cook v. Cook*, 798 S.W.2d 955, 957 (Ky.1990) (cohabitation is "mutually assum[ing] the duties and obligations normally assumed by married persons"); *Fisher v. Fisher*, 75 Md.App. 193, 540 A.2d 1165, 1169 (1988) (cohabitation "envisions at least the normally accepted attributes of a marriage"); *Frey v. Frey*, 14 Va.App. 270, 416 S.E.2d 40, 43 (1992) (cohabitation "has been consistently interpreted by courts as encompassing both a permanency or continuity element and an assumption of marital duties"); *see also Gordon v. Gordon*, 342 Md. 294, 675 A.2d 540, 546 n. 8 (1996) (rejecting proposition that cohabitation is synonymous with common residence). Similarly, *Corpus Juris Secundum* states: "Generally, where alimony is sought to be modified on the basis of cohabitation with another by the recipient spouse, cohabitation is an arrangement in which the couple reside together on a continuing conjugal basis or hold themselves out as man and wife." 27B C.J.S. *Divorce* § 656, at 334 (2005). The notes of that treatise elaborate: "Where the term 'cohabitation' is used in a divorce decree. . ., court must look to whether the parties have assumed obligations, including support, equivalent to those arising from a ceremonial marriage."

After carefully reviewing these authorities, we follow them in defining cohabitation as a relationship between persons resembling that of a marriage. As such, cohabitation encompasses both an element of continuity or permanency as well as an assumption of marital obligations. *Cf. Frey*, 416 S.E.2d at 43. As the trial court recognized, whether two people are cohabiting will depend on the facts and circumstances of each particular case. Beyond living together on a continual basis, many factors are relevant to the inquiry. Primary among them are the financial arrangements between the two people, such as shared expenses, whether and to what extent one person is supporting the other, the existence and use of joint bank accounts or shared investment or retirement plans, a life insurance policy carried by one or both parties benefiting the other, and similar financial entanglements.

We observe, however, that, in considering the financial arrangements, the age of the putative couple may be an important consideration. Where, as here, the individuals are senior citizens, support of one by the other may have less significance than with younger people not only because older individuals may be more financially secure than their younger counterparts, but also because older individuals may have estate plans in place to benefit children of prior relationships.

Also important is the extent of the personal relationship, including evidence of an intimate connection, how the people hold themselves out to others, the presence of common friends or acquaintances, vacations spent together, and similar signs of an ongoing personal commitment. Evidence of a sexual relationship should also be considered, but is not dispositive. Here too, the age of the couple may be relevant in weighing this factor; for older people, a sexual component to intimacy may not be as significant as it would be for younger couples.

In addition, the shared use and enjoyment of personal property is an indication of cohabitation, such as common use of household rooms, appliances, furniture, vehicles, and whether one person maintains personal items, such as toiletries or clothing, at the residence of the other. So, too, are indications that family members and friends view the relationship as one involving an intimate personal commitment. Taken together, these factors will support a finding of cohabitation if they indicate that two people are so closely involved that their relationship resembles that of marriage.

Because the trial court did not have the benefit of the standard we articulate here for determining whether the relationship between the petitioner and Sansoucie amounted to cohabitation, we vacate and remand the case for the master to reconsider the matter in light of the standard we have established.

Vacated and remanded.

Points for Discussion

a. Modification of Spousal Support

Spousal support orders are generally modifiable, either pursuant to express statutory provision or the state's common law. The usual basis for a modification is that there has been a change in the economic circumstances of the parties. For example, UMDA § 316(a) provides that alimony awards may only be modified "upon a showing of changed circumstances so substantial and continuing as to make the terms unconscionable." Most states authorize modification only prospectively, with respect to installments coming due after the date on which the motion to modify was filed. See, e.g., UMDA § 316(a).

The question sometimes arises whether a divorce decree that does not provide for spousal support can be modified to provide for payments based on a later change of circumstances. Courts are divided on this point; In re Marriage of Carlson, 338 N.W.2d 136, 139 (Iowa 1983), suggests that if a divorce decree is silent upon the question of alimony or states that no alimony will be ordered, the decree cannot be modified later to allow alimony, even if there is a change in the parties' circumstances. In order to protect one spouse's opportunity to receive support payments in the future, a separation agreement or divorce decree sometimes provides for alimony of $1 per year.

b. Changes in Income

Support payments may be terminated or reduced when the recipient obtains a job that provides more substantial income than what was anticipated at the time the support obligation was determined. E.g., Marriage of Rohde-Giovanni, 676 N.W.2d 452 (Wis. 2004). Support payments are not generally increased when the payer's income increases, see, e.g., Marriage of Weber, 91 P.3d 706 (Or. 2004), although an increase may be ordered if the original award was inadequate in light of the parties' standard of living during the marriage, e.g. Marriage of Peterka, 675 N.W.2d 353 (Minn.Ct.App.2004); Crews v. Crews, 751 A.2d 524 (N.J. 2000); Wharton v. Wharton, 424 S.E.2d 744 (W. Va. 1992). See also Dan v. Dan, 105 A.3d 118 (Conn. 2014) (holding that increase in former husband's income was not a sufficient justification to increase alimony award).

If the payer's income decreases, courts may terminate or reduce the spousal support obligation, depending on the circumstances. Courts are more sympathetic to payers who seek modification when their income decreases as a result of a health problem or job loss or retirement at a normal retirement age, see, e.g., Smith v. Smith, 419 A.2d 1035 (Me.1980) (payer aged and in bad health); and less sympathetic to early retirement, see, e.g., Pimm v. Pimm, 601 So.2d 534 (Fla.1992). The relative circumstances of both parties are also an important consideration. See, e.g., Miller v. Miller, 734 A.2d 752 (N.J. 1999) (income imputed to husband's assets).

Although spousal support obligations are not dischargeable in bankruptcy, property division obligations may be discharged. Courts treat discharge of property division obligations in bankruptcy proceedings as a change in circumstances that may result in a modification of spousal support. See, e.g., In re Marriage of Lynn, 123 Cal.Rptr.2d 611 (Ct. App. 2002); Low v. Low, 777 S.W.2d 936 (Ky.1989); Siragusa v. Siragusa, 843 P.2d 807 (Nev. 1992); Richardson v. Richardson, 868 P.2d 259 (Wyo.1994). Bankruptcy issues are addressed later in this chapter.

c. Termination of Spousal Support

In many states, spousal support terminates automatically on the remarriage of the recipient. E.g. N.J.Stat.Ann. § 2A:34–25 (2018); see also Cal.Fam.Code "§ 4337 (2018); Colo.Rev.Stat.Ann. § 14–10–122(2) (2018); UMDA § 316(b). These statutes permit the parties to agree otherwise, and sometimes permit a court to order support that will not terminate on remarriage. Where there is no such statute, courts sometimes treat the remarriage only as a change in circumstances which may justify termination of alimony. Compare O'Brien v. O'Brien, 623 N.E.2d 485 (Mass. 1993) with Matter of Marriage of Grage, 819 P.2d 322 (Or. Ct. App. 1991), and Johnson v. Johnson, 580 A.2d 503 (Vt. 1990). Courts have divided on the question whether a support obligation that terminated with recipient's remarriage can be reinstated if the marriage ends in divorce or annulment. See, e.g., Watts v. Watts, 547 N.W.2d 466 (Neb. 1996) (reversing termination of alimony where recipient's second marriage was void.)

Spousal support obligations also generally terminate on the death of either party. Some statutes provide that a support obligation may survive the payer's death if the decree or the separation agreement provide expressly for this result. E.g. Uniform Marriage and Divorce Act § 316(b); see also Oedekoven v. Oedekoven, 920 P.2d 649 (Wyo.1996). Alternatively, the court might order, or the parties might agree, that the paying spouse will maintain insurance on his or her life for the benefit of the receiving spouse.

In Massachusetts, legislation enacted in 2011 (and quoted in *Raybeck*) provides for termination of alimony in the event of the recipient's remarriage, cohabitation or death, or when the obligor reaches the age for retirement with full Social Security benefits, except on a showing of good cause by clear and convincing evidence. See Mass. Gen. Laws ch. 208, § 49 (2018). The statute includes a schedule that defines the permissible duration of alimony awards. For marriages that last five years or less, alimony can generally last only for half the number of years of the marriage. This percentage increases with the length of the marriage. Alimony can be awarded for an indefinite period if the marriage continued for twenty years or more, and a court may deviate from these time limits if it is "required in the interests of justice." See generally Young v. Young, 81 N.E.3d 1165 (Mass. 2017) (reversing and remanding award based on a percentage of spouse's income); and Zaleski v. Zaleski, 13 N.E.3d 967 (Mass. 2014) (affirming award of rehabilitative rather than general term alimony).

d. Cohabitation

The court in *Raybeck* defines cohabitation as "a relationship between persons resembling that of marriage." This is consistent with the law in many other jurisdictions. See, for example, Cal. Fam. Code § 4323 (2018), construed in In re Marriage of Bower, 117 Cal.Rptr.2d 520 (Ct. App. 2002); and <u>Conn. Gen Stat. § 46b–86(b) (2018)</u>, construed in <u>DeMaria v. DeMaria, 724 A.2d 1088 (Conn. 1999)</u>. Some states define cohabitation as a basis for terminating support to require not only living with a new partner but also holding oneself out as that person's spouse; e.g. <u>N.Y. Dom. Rel. Law § 248 (2012)</u>. In New Jersey, an amendment to the statutes reversed a body of case law on this point, allowing for termination of alimony if the recipient cohabits with another person, defined in this way: "cohabitation involves a mutually supportive, intimate personal relationship in which a couple has undertaken duties and privileges that are commonly associated with marriage or civil union but does not necessarily maintain a single common household." <u>N.J. Stat. Ann. § 2A:34:23(n) (2018)</u>.

Before the changes to the New Jersey statute, <u>Konzelman v. Konzelman, 729 A.2d 7 (N.J. 1999)</u>, considered whether the parties should be permitted to agree to a stricter cohabitation rule when they settle the issues in their divorce by agreement. Other cases involving agreements to terminate support on cohabitation include <u>Perri v. Perri, 608 N.E.2d 790 (Ohio Ct. App. 1992)</u>; and <u>Kripp v. Kripp, 849 A.2d 1159 (Pa. 2004)</u>.

e. Nonmodifiable Spousal Support

In negotiating the terms of their divorce, parties may agree to terms that would have been beyond the authority of the divorce court. One important example is a stipulation that support payments will not be modifiable in the event of a change in circumstances. See <u>UMDA § 306(f)</u>, An offer to agree to "non-modifiable" support for a limited term may be an important bargaining concession, particularly if the spouse who will be paying support wants to be assured that the recipient will not be able to have the payment term extended. See, e.g., <u>In re Marriage of Thompson, 640 P.2d 279 (Colo.Ct.App.1982)</u>; <u>In re Marriage of Nichols, 469 N.W.2d 619 (Wis. 1991)</u>. The rules on how to create a non-modifiable obligation are different in each state, and counsel should be certain that both parties to the divorce have considered the full range of scenarios in which they might want an opportunity to request modification before they waive the right to do so. For an illustration of the risks in this area, see <u>Bradley v. Bradley, 76 A.3d 395 (Md. Ct. Spec. App. 2013)</u> (dismissing motion to modify maintenance filed by payor who was bankrupt, permanently disabled, and living on Social Security payments that were less than his monthly maintenance obligation).

Problem 6-20

If a trial court orders spousal support payments for three years, to enable a spouse to obtain a nursing degree, and that spouse remarries after one year, should the support payments terminate? (See <u>Self v. Self, 861 S.W.2d 360 (Tenn.1993)</u>.)

Problem 6-21

(a) On the facts of *Raybeck*, what if Judith and Paul had signed a contract providing that each would contribute equally to all of the expenses of their joint lives, including food, rent, clothing, furniture, utilities, transportation, recreation, and medical care? Could Judith continue to receive spousal support? (See In re Marriage of Dwyer, 825 P.2d 1018 (Colo.Ct.App.1991).)

(b) What if the evidence in a case showed that, five years after a divorce, an ex-wife who was receiving spousal support had purchased a home in joint tenancy with another woman where they lived together, dividing all household expenses equally and maintaining a joint credit union account where they both deposit their paychecks and the spousal support payments? Although they have taken vacations together, and send out a joint Christmas letter, the two women occupy separate bedrooms, and state that there is no sexual contact or physical attraction between them. Both see themselves as heterosexual, and date men occasionally. Should the court grant a motion to terminate spousal support? (See In re Marriage of Weisbruch, 710 N.E.2d 439 (Ill. App. Ct. 1999).)

––––––––––––

Enforcement of Property and Support Orders

Once a property division order is final, it is not subject to modification and can be enforced like any other judgment. This includes enforcement in other states, which must give the judgment full faith and credit. Because support orders are modifiable, they are not entitled to full faith and credit in other jurisdictions until a specific claim for arrearages has been reduced to judgment in the state where the support order was entered. See Sistare v. Sistare, 218 U.S. 1 (1910). State courts may enforce out-of-state spousal support orders based on comity, however, and consider claims for modification in those enforcement proceedings. See, e.g., Worthley v. Worthley, 283 P.2d 19 (Cal. 1955), and Lowery v. Lowery, 591 A.2d 81 (Vt. 1991).

Today, spousal support orders can be enforced under the Uniform Interstate Family Support Act (UIFSA), which is discussed in more detail in Chapter 7. Although UIFSA applies both to obligations for child support and obligations for spousal support, its provisions are somewhat different in each context. The principal difference is that the issuing tribunal retains "continuing exclusive jurisdiction" under UIFSA § 211 over a spousal support order throughout the entire existence of the support obligation. See In re Marriage of Rassier, 118 Cal.Rptr.2d 113 (Ct. App. 2002); Hornblower v. Hornblower, 94 A.3d 1218 (Conn. App. Ct. 2014).

A spousal support obligor who has the ability to pay and fails to do so may be subject to contempt proceedings, which may be either civil or criminal. See generally <u>Hicks on Behalf of Feiock v. Feiock, 485 U.S. 624 (1988)</u>.

Civil contempt proceedings are intended to coerce the defendant into complying with the court's decree. The act must be within his or her power to perform, and the contempt order must state how the contempt may be purged. A defendant may be imprisoned following a citation for civil contempt for an indefinite term, until he or she complies with the court's decree. See, e.g., <u>McDaniel v. McDaniel, 262 A.2d 52 (Md. 1970)</u>.

Criminal contempt proceedings have the purpose of punishing repeated or aggravated disobedience of court orders. In a criminal contempt proceeding, all of the safeguards of criminal law and procedure apply, and commitment is for a definite term. A sentence for criminal contempt, based on a failure to pay child support, was entered in the case of <u>Moss v. Superior Court, 950 P.2d 59 (Cal. 1998)</u>. State laws vary on whether there must be proof beyond a reasonable doubt that the debtor had the ability to pay in a criminal contempt proceeding, or whether the inability to pay may be treated as an affirmative defense, on which the defendant bears the burden of proof. See, e.g., <u>Moss, supra.</u>

Global View: Spousal Support and Property Issues in International Cases

Courts in the United States enforce foreign country judgments on the basis of comity rather than full faith and credit. See, e.g., <u>Dart v. Dart, 568 N.W.2d 353 (Mich. Ct. App. 1997)</u>, reprinted earlier in this chapter. See also <u>Wolff v. Wolff, 389 A.2d 413 (Md. Ct. Spec App.1978)</u>, aff'd <u>401 A.2d 479 (Md. 1979)</u>; <u>Downs v. Yuen, 748 N.Y.S.2d 131 (App. Div. 2002)</u> (enforcing $10 million judgment rendered by a Hong Kong court in a divorce action). Foreign country spousal support orders are generally entitled to recognition and enforcement under UIFSA. Obtaining enforcement abroad for financial orders from courts in the United States is often a more complicated process. See generally Ann Laquer Estin, <u>*International Divorce: Litigating Marital Property and Support Rights*, 45 Fam. L.Q. 293 (2011)</u>.

C. Federal Tax and Bankruptcy Law

Family law is primarily state law, but federal laws play a substantial role in regulating the financial aspects of divorce. One example of this is the law regarding pension and retirement benefits addressed earlier in this chapter, and another example is the law regulating child support enforcement discussed in Chapter 7. For divorce practitioners, it is also essential to understand the impact that federal income tax and bankruptcy laws may have on their clients' financial circumstances after a divorce. These laws may be an important consideration in deciding whether to structure payments after a divorce as property division or spousal support.

1. Income Tax

Divorce tax has long been a complicated subject. Alimony payments ordered or agreed to prior to 2019 could be deducted from the income of the payer and included in the taxable income of the receiving spouse under the Internal Revenue Code. See 26 U.S.C. § 71(a), § 215 (2018). This was not true of payments made to carry out a property division between husband and wife, or payments made for child support. This difference gave a divorcing couple an opportunity to structure their settlement to reduce their overall tax obligation, particularly in situations where the two individuals' incomes place them in significantly different tax brackets. In order to have payments treated as alimony for tax purposes, the parties' separation or divorce agreement or decree had to conform to various requirements set out in the Internal Revenue Code at 26 U.S.C. § 71. See Jim Tankersley, *'Hurry Up and Get a Divorce'? For the Rich, There's an Incentive*, N.Y. Times, July 2, 2018. Although the rules have been changed for alimony payments ordered or agreed to after 2018, many individuals will remain subject to the traditional rules.

Go Online

Tax information for Divorced or Separated Individuals is available from the U.S. Internal Revenue Service online and in Publication 504.

Transfers of property between spouses at the time of a divorce are not taxable. Under 26 U.S.C. § 1041(a) (2018), no gain or loss is recognized on transfers of property between spouses, or between former spouses, if the transfer is incident to a divorce. In order to be incident to the divorce, the transfer must occur within a year of the termination of the marriage or be related to the cessation of the marriage. Where the transfer is within § 1041(a), the spouse who receives the property takes the transferor's adjusted basis in the property. See § 1041(b)(2). When the spouse who receives the property later sells or transfers it, that spouse will owe taxes on any gain associated with the property, measured by the difference between the sale price and the basis at which the spouse received the property. Thus, a division of property may have significant income tax consequences for one of the parties at some time in the future. State laws vary on the question of whether a court may consider potential taxes in dividing marital property, but parties must carefully consider this issue in evaluating a proposed settlement.

Special rules govern the tax treatment of gains on the sale of a marital residence. Under 26 U.S.C. § 121(a) (2018), a taxpayer may exclude from income up to $250,000 of gain from the sale of a home that was used as a principal residence for at least two of the five years before the sale. In the context of divorce or separation, it is somewhat easier to meet the principal residence requirement where the property was transferred under § 1041(a) or where the spouse or former spouse was granted use of the property under a divorce or separation agreement. See 26 U.S.C. § 121(d)(3). There are also complex tax problems when a married couple agree that one party's shares in a closely held corporation will be redeemed by the corporation at the time of divorce. In some circumstances, this transfer may qualify for nonrecognition treatment under § 1041. See Craven v. United States, 215 F.3d 1201 (11th Cir. 2000)

Unmarried couples couples are not eligible to transfer property under § 1041 when they break up. For example, Reynolds v. Commissioner, 77 T.C.M. (CCH) 1479 (1999) held that settlement of property interests at the end of long term cohabitation relationship would be characterized as sale of the taxpayer's interest in joint assets. In *Reynolds*, the transaction was a taxable event, but no gain was recognized because the payment the taxpayer received was less than her basis in the items she relinquished.

Bock v. Dalbey

815 N.W.2d 530 (Neb. 2012)

CONNOLLY, J.

SUMMARY

The district court dissolved the marriage of Jennifer Lynn Dalbey, the appellant, and Matthew John Bock. We granted Dalbey's petition for further review on one question: Does a trial court in a marital dissolution action have the discretion to order the parties to file a joint income tax return? We conclude it does not. The Nebraska Court of Appeals affirmed the trial court's order requiring the parties to file a joint tax return. It cited cases showing that courts have conflicting views and agreed with those courts holding that trial courts do have this discretion. Because a trial court can equitably adjust its division of the marital estate to account for a spouse's unreasonable refusal to file a joint return, we reverse, and remand the cause to the Court of Appeals with directions for further disposition.

BACKGROUND

The parties married in 2006. The district court entered its dissolution decree in August 2010. Many of the facts of this case deal with the district court's division of the marital assets. But the issue here is the court's order requiring that the parties file a joint tax return for 2008 and 2009. The parties filed a joint return for the 2007 tax year. But they had not filed any tax return for 2008 or 2009. The district court, without citing authority, ordered the parties to file a joint return. It allocated the unspecified refunds or assessments to be shared by the parties in a ratio that equaled each party's contribution of adjusted gross income to their total adjusted gross income. The record does not show what their individual income contributions were for the 2008 and 2009 tax years, but it does show that Bock earned substantially more income than Dalbey.

In affirming, the Court of Appeals framed the issue as whether the Supremacy Clause of the U.S. Constitution barred the district court from ordering the parties to file a joint return. The federal tax code allows married individuals to elect whether to file joint or separate returns. But the Court of Appeals determined that this election did not conflict with a state court's order to file jointly. It stated that domestic relations law is generally a state law matter outside of federal jurisdiction.

ASSIGNMENT OF ERROR

In her petition for further review, Dalbey assigns that the Court of Appeals erred in affirming the district court's order that the parties file a joint income tax return.

STANDARD OF REVIEW

We independently review questions of law decided by a lower court.

ANALYSIS

Ordinarily, a trial court in Nebraska should not consider the speculative tax consequences of its distribution orders unless it has ordered the immediate liquidation or sale of an asset or a party must sell an asset to satisfy a monetary judgment. But the questions here are (1) whether a district court can consider the tax consequences of one party's refusal to file a joint return in dividing the marital estate and (2) whether it has discretion to order the parties to file a joint return to preserve assets for the marital estate or to equalize its division of the estate.

Married individuals can elect whether to file a joint or separate return.[4] For joint returns, the federal government taxes the income of a married couple in the aggregate.[5] Filing jointly generally, but not always, produces substantial tax savings.[6] But a "[h]usband and wife filing a joint return are jointly and severally liable for all tax for the taxable year (not merely the amount shown on the return), including interest, additions for negligence, and fraud penalties if applicable."[7] The right of election under the federal tax code and the possible exposure to liability have prompted several courts to hold that a trial court cannot order a party to file a joint return.

Few courts, however, have decided this question. This may partially be because marital tax experts advise divorcing couples to privately negotiate an agreement to file a joint return. Generally, if the parties have agreed to file a joint return, the trial court can incorporate or rely on the agreement in equitably dividing the marital estate and enforce the agreement if necessary. But other appellate courts have disagreed on whether a trial court, outside of a party's agreement, can compel a party to a divorce proceeding to file a joint return.

Of the courts that have held that a trial court cannot compel a party to file a joint return, *Leftwich v. Leftwich*[10] is the most cited case. There, unless the wife agreed to file joint tax returns for 2 years of the marriage, the husband would owe about $40,000 in additional taxes. So the trial court conditioned the wife's receipt of her share of marital property upon her filing the joint returns, with the understanding that the husband would pay any additional taxes. The District of Columbia appellate court, concerned with the wife's liability exposure, reversed:

> The propriety of considering tax matters in divorce proceedings, however, does not serve as a license for the trial court to compel a party to execute a joint return. The trial court is not at liberty to alter basic precepts of federal or of state tax law. . . .

> . . . A married individual possesses complete discretion to file a separate return, or, with the concurrence of his or her spouse, a joint return. . . .

> To sanction the trial court's effectively ordering a spouse to cooperate in filing a joint return would nullify the right of election conferred upon married taxpayers by the Internal Revenue Code. Such a right is not inconsequential; its exercise affects potential criminal and/or civil liabilities of taxpayers. . . . Married individuals filing a joint return expose themselves to joint and several liability for any fraudulent or erroneous aspect of the return.

The wife's exposure to liability was the critical factor in the court's holding:

---

4   I.R.C. § 6013 (2006).
5   See I.R.C. § 6013(d)(3).
6   See Leon Gabinet, Tax Aspects of Marital Dissolution § 3:3 (rev.2d ed.2005).
10   Leftwich v. Leftwich, 442 A.2d 139 (D.C.1982).

Given the wife's substantial interest in the choice of a filing status, with its concomitant consequences, we find that it was error for the trial court to impose a coercive construction of [I.R.C.] § 6013 [the federal statute permitting a husband and wife to elect to file jointly or separately] on appellant.

Furthermore, the *Leftwich* court reasoned that even if the trial court could override the wife's election to file a separate return, under equity principles, it should not have resorted to a coercive remedy when a less intrusive one existed: "[T]he trial court well could have remedied any perceived tax disadvantage to the husband by altering the disposition of the marital property." Other courts that hold a trial court cannot compel the filing of a joint return have also held the trial court may nonetheless consider the tax disadvantages of filing separate returns in its equitable division of the marital estate.

But other appellate courts have held that a trial court can compel a party to file a joint tax return.[15] Of these cases, *Bursztyn v. Bursztyn* is a recent, prominent decision on which the Nebraska Court of Appeals relied. The *Bursztyn* court conceded that good arguments exist on both sides of the issue. It noted, however, that in New Jersey, a trial court is statutorily required to consider the tax consequences of its alimony and equitable distribution rulings. The *Bursztyn* court considered an abridgment of an individual's choice whether to file joint or separate tax returns to be a minor intrusion of the parties' individual rights. Finally, the court concluded that because a trial court has discretion to allocate federal tax exemptions for dependent children, it could, when appropriate, compel the parties to file joint tax returns to preserve the marital estate.

Yet the *Bursztyn* court was nonetheless persuaded by the *Leftwich* court's reasoning that altering the equitable distribution of marital property was a less intrusive option to remedy a tax disadvantage that a spouse incurs because of the other spouse's election to file a separate return. So the *Bursztyn* court tempered its decision that a trial court has discretion to order joint tax returns as follows: "In general, we believe trial courts should avoid compelling parties to execute joint tax returns because of the potential liability to which the parties would be exposed, and because there generally exists a means by which to compensate the parties for the adverse tax consequences of filing separately." In short, the *Bursztyn* court required a trial court to consider the equitable adjustment remedy before resorting to a coercive order to file a joint return.

But in other appellate decisions—including the Nebraska Court of Appeals' decision in this appeal—courts holding that trial courts have discretion to com-

---

[15] See, *In re Marriage of Zummo*, 167 Ill.App.3d 566, 521 N.E.2d 621, 118 Ill.Dec. 339 (1988); *Theroux v. Boehmler*, 410 N.W.2d 354 (Minn.App.1987); *Bursztyn v. Bursztyn*, 379 N.J.Super. 385, 879 A.2d 129 (2005); *Fraase v. Fraase*, 315 N.W.2d 271 (N.D.1982); *Ahmad, supra* note 9. See, also, *In re Marriage of LaFaye*, 89 P.3d 455 (Colo.App.2003).

pel the parties to file joint tax returns have not required a coercive order to be the remedy of last resort. That is, they have not considered whether adjusting the equitable distribution of marital property is a less intrusive way to remedy a spouse's unprincipled refusal to file a joint tax return. But we believe that it is the preferable remedy for four reasons.

First, the U.S. Tax Court is not bound by orders compelling the parties to sign a joint return. It will look to the husband and wife's intent, and if one of them signed only because a state court ordered him or her to do so, the return may or may not be treated as a joint return.[18] This means that a trial court cannot know with certainty whether its equitable division of the marital estate based on consideration of a joint tax return will be given effect by federal authorities or courts.

Second, an order compelling the parties to file joint tax returns is a mandatory injunction. A mandatory injunction is an equitable remedy that commands the subject of the order to perform an affirmative act to undo a wrongful act or injury. It is considered an extreme or harsh remedy that should be exercised sparingly and cautiously. Further, an injunction, in general, is an extraordinary remedy that a court should ordinarily not grant except in a clear case where there is actual and substantial injury. And a court should not grant an injunction unless the right is clear, the damage is irreparable, and the remedy at law is inadequate to prevent a failure of justice. Finally, when a statute provides an adequate remedy at law, equity will not entertain jurisdiction, and a party must exhaust the statutory remedy before it may resort to equity.

Here, the statutory remedy is found in Neb.Rev.Stat. § 42–365 (Reissue 2008). This statute authorizes a trial court to equitably distribute the marital estate according to what is fair and reasonable under the circumstances. Because § 42–365 is broad in its scope, we agree with the decisions of courts that hold a trial court may adjust its equitable division of the marital estate to account for the tax consequences of filing separate returns.

Therefore, under § 42–365, we hold that if a party seeking an equitable adjustment presents the court with the tax disadvantages of filing separate returns, a trial court may consider a party's unreasonable refusal to file a joint return. Evidence of a tax disadvantage would normally include the parties' calculated joint and separate returns for comparison. But because we conclude that § 42–365 permits a court to adjust its division of the marital estate to fit the equities of the case, we agree with the *Leftwich* court that equity principles weigh against permitting a trial court to resort to the coercive remedy of compelling a party to file a joint tax return.

---

[18] Compare *Price v. Commissioner,* 86 T.C.M. (CCH) 203 (2003), with *Anderson v. Commissioner,* 47 T.C.M. (CCH) 1123 (1984).

Third, a resisting spouse's exposure to liability under the federal tax code is too difficult to predict if compelled to file a joint return. We agree with the Court of Appeals that trial courts in marital dissolution proceedings can order the parties to take actions with tax consequences, such as allocating the dependency exemptions. But allocating dependency exemptions is not analogous to compelling a spouse to file a joint tax return because of the potential liability. And we doubt that a trial court could be certain that the spouse resisting a joint return would not be exposed to joint and several liability for the tax consequences of the return.

In its decision, the Court of Appeals noted that the tax code provides relief from joint and several liability for an "innocent spouse."[26] Obtaining relief under the innocent spouse statute, however, is far from certain. The regulations are complicated,[27] and predicting liability would frequently require considerable tax expertise.

A divorcing spouse compelled to sign a joint return faces potential liability on two fronts. First of all, I.R.C. § 6015(b) and (c) can provide relief from an under*statement* of tax or a divorced spouse's portion of an assessed deficiency, but these provisions do not provide relief from an under*payment* of reported tax. Because subsections (b) and (c) do not apply to underpayments of tax, a claimant can seek equitable relief from an underpayment of tax only under § 6015(f). Among the multiple factors that federal tax regulators will consider are whether the claimant had reason to know that the tax would not be paid and whether the claimant significantly benefited from the unpaid liability. Summed up, for a divorcing spouse with little or no taxable income for the tax year, signing a joint tax return may pose considerable liability risk with no appreciable benefit.

Next, to seek relief from understatements of tax or assessed deficiencies under I.R.C. § 6015(b) and (c), an innocent spouse must *not* have had knowledge of the other spouse's "item" on the joint tax return that resulted in the understatement or deficiency assessment.[30] "A spouse knowing of the facts giving rise to a deficiency has actual knowledge, even if he or she does not understand the tax consequences of the facts or the error in the return's treatment of the item."[31] The knowledge component applies to both omissions of income and erroneous deductions, although the test can differ depending on whether omitted income or an erroneous deduction is at issue. In general, however, federal courts review these issues for whether a reasonably prudent person, under the circumstances, would have known that the return contained a substantial understatement of tax or that further investigation was required. If so, and the claimant did not take reasonable steps to investigate, relief will be denied.

---

26   See I.R.C. § 6015(b) and (c) (2006).
27   See Bittker & Lokken, *supra* note 7, §§ 111.3A.2 and 111.3A .3.
30   See I.R.C. § 6015(b)(1)(B) and (c)(3)(C).
31   See Bittker & Lokken, *supra* note 7, § 111.3A.3 at 4 (citing regulations and case examples).

These rules show that a coerced filing of a joint tax return can be fraught with unanticipated liability. Because the risks frequently outweigh the benefits, in private negotiations a spouse will often not agree to a joint return without the other spouse's agreement to share in the tax savings and to promise indemnity. We believe that these decisions are best left to the parties to negotiate after considering the risks and benefits of a joint return. If a spouse unreasonably refuses to file a joint return, the other spouse can take the matter up with the court.

Fourth, the rules related to filing deadlines under the federal tax code create practical hurdles to allowing a trial court to compel the parties to file joint returns. Under § 6013(b) of the tax code, a husband and wife can only elect to file a joint return for up to 3 years after they filed separate returns. But the opposite is not true. If the husband and wife filed a joint return, they cannot revoke that decision after the filing time limits for the taxable year have expired.[36]

So if a trial court orders a party to file a joint return, he or she will usually have to comply quickly or risk being held in contempt. Yet even if the party appeals the order, the party cannot revoke the joint return. The party's only avenue for relief from federal tax liability is the tax code's innocent spouse statute. As discussed, that option is a precarious road at best. Thus, the tax code's time limitations also weigh against permitting trial courts to order the parties to file a joint return.

For all of these reasons, we hold that a trial court does not have discretion to compel parties seeking marital dissolution to file a joint income tax return.

CONCLUSION

We conclude that the Court of Appeals erred in holding that a district court has discretion to compel the parties to a marital dissolution proceeding to file a joint income tax return. Because a trial court can equitably adjust its division of the marital estate to account for a spouse's unreasonable refusal to file a joint return, resort to a coercive remedy that carries potential liability is unnecessary. We therefore reverse that portion of the Court of Appeals' decision affirming the district court's order requiring the parties to file a joint tax return. We remand the cause to the Court of Appeals with directions to remand the cause to the district court with directions to vacate that portion of its order that we have reversed.

REVERSED AND REMANDED WITH DIRECTIONS.

---

[36] See I.R.C. § 6013(f)(4); 26 C.F.R. § 1.6013–1(a)(1) (2011).

Points for Discussion

a. Joint Income Tax Filing

As *Bock* suggests, it will be financially advantageous for some divorcing couples to continue filing joint tax returns during the pendency of their divorce. For this reason, tax issues should be considered early in divorce proceedings. Taxpayers will be treated as married for a given tax year if, as of the last day of the year, they have not received a final divorce or separation decree. If one spouse files separately, however, both must file separately.

If the parties file separate returns, temporary support payments made by one spouse to the other may be treated as alimony under the rules discussed above, which means that the spouse receiving the payments must include them in his or her income and pay taxes on the amount received. Similarly, temporary support paid in the months prior to the divorce in the year in which the divorce becomes final may be taxable to the recipient as alimony.

b. Innocent Spouse Protections

A married couple who file joint income tax returns during their marriage remain jointly and severally liable for any underpayment of taxes for those years, including interest and penalties that may be assessed. As *Bock* considers, this may present a substantial risk to a spouse who has not had knowledge or control of the parties' financial affairs. The "innocent spouse" provisions in 26 U.S.C. § 6015 (2018) provide some relief in this situation, with particular protections for divorced or separated

Go Online

Tax Information for Innocent Spouses is available from the U.S. Internal Revenue Service online and in Publication 971.

individuals in § 6015(c) and (f). See, e.g., Aranda v. Commissioner, 432 F.3d 1140 (10th Cir. 2005), and Baranowicz v. Commissioner, 432 F.3d 972 (9th Cir. 2005).

c. Children as Dependents

Bock also refers to court decisions allocating the dependency exemption for federal income tax purposes between a child's parents. Generally, under 26 U.S.C. § 152 (2018), if a child's parents are divorced, the parent having custody of the child during the greater portion of the calendar year is entitled to claim the child as a dependent. This allows the parent to parent to claim child tax credits, which increased in value and became refundable under the 2017 tax legislation. The other parent may claim the child as a dependent if the parent with primary custody signs a written declaration that he or she will not claim the child as a dependent. Many state court cases have held that courts have jurisdiction to order the custodial parent to execute such a declaration as part of the financial provisions of a divorce decree. See, e.g., <u>Young v. Young, 453 N.W.2d 282 (Mich. Ct. App. 1990)</u>; <u>Babka v. Babka, 452 N.W.2d 286 (Neb. 1990)</u>. The same test is applied to parents who have never married. <u>King v. Commissioner, 121 T.C. 245 (2003)</u>.

d. Taxes and Unmarried Couples

Unmarried couples cannot file joint tax returns, but one member of the couple may be able to claim head of household status or treat the other partner as a dependent under <u>26 U.S.C. § 152(a)(2)</u> and § 152(d)(2)(h). In addition, these couples face significantly different treatment for purposes of federal estate and gift taxes and taxation of employment benefits. See <u>Frank S. Berall, *Tax Consequences of Unmarried Cohabitation*, 23 QLR 395 (2004)</u>.

Further Reading: Divorce Taxation

- Melvyn B. Frumkes and Brian C. Vertz, Frumkes and Vertz on Divorce Taxation (16th ed. 2017).

- Jack Zuckerman, The 1040 Handbook: A Guide to Income and Asset Discovery (7th ed. 2018).

2. Bankruptcy

The goal of federal bankruptcy laws is to give insolvent debtors a fresh start by discharging their debts, a process that releases the debtor from personal liability and prohibits his or her creditors from taking action against the debtor to try to collect those debts. Since 2005, eligibility for a liquidation discharge under Chapter 7 of the Bankruptcy Code has been subject to a means test, and most individual debtors with regular income are now required to proceed under Chapter 13. Although Chapter 13 allows for discharge of a wider range of debts, the debtor must first enter into a plan and repay his or her creditors as far as possible over three to five years. An individual who operates a business as a sole proprietor may file for bankruptcy protection under Chapter 11, and a "family farmer" or fisherman may file under Chapter 12.

Bankruptcy is a common companion to divorce, and lawyers practicing family law need to be alert to several sets of issues. A filing for bankruptcy relief by either husband or wife prior to or during the litigation of a divorce will trigger the automatic stay provisions of the federal bankruptcy laws. See <u>11 U.S.C. § 362(a) (2018)</u>. The automatic stay provision applies to any proceeding that "seeks to determine the division of property that is property of the estate," but it does not apply to proceedings to establish or modify a domestic support obligation or to proceedings to collect a domestic support obligation from property that is not part of the bankruptcy estate. See <u>11 U.S.C. § 362(b)(2)</u>. It also has no effect on the court's jurisdiction to enter a divorce decree or orders concerning nonfinancial aspects of the divorce case, such as child custody and visitation. See, e.g., <u>Klass v. Klass, 831 A.2d 1067 (Md. 2003)</u>. In order to proceed with the property aspects of

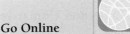

Go Online

Detailed information on U.S. bankruptcy laws and procedures is available from the web page of the <u>U.S. Bankruptcy Courts</u>.

The U.S. Trustee's office in the Department of Justice publishes a basic <u>Bankruptcy Information Sheet</u> in many different languages

a divorce case, the non-debtor spouse must have the automatic stay lifted by the bankruptcy court. See, e.g., <u>In re White, 851 F.2d 170 (6th Cir.1988)</u>. In some cases, the federal bankruptcy court may decide equitable distribution issues under state law in an adversary proceeding. See, e.g., <u>In re Simeone, 214 B.R. 537 (Bankr. E.D. Pa.1997)</u>, <u>In re Secrest, 453 B.R. 623 (Bankr. E.D. Va. 2011)</u>.

Bankruptcy laws are also an important consideration in any divorce case in which the parties have financial obligations to each other that will continue after the court enters the divorce decree. In this situation, the spouses may be debtors, creditors, or both. For many years, bankruptcy laws permitted debtors to discharge property division obligations arising from a separation or divorce, but not obligations for alimony or child support. Congress amended these rules in 1994 and 2005, and dischargeability now depends on two factors: whether the debt falls within the definition of a "domestic support obligation" under <u>11 U.S.C. §101(14A) (2018)</u>, and whether the bankruptcy proceeding has been filed as a liquidation proceeding under Chapter 7, or a reorganization proceeding under Chapter 11, Chapter 12, or Chapter 13.

11 U.S.C. § 101(14A) (2018):
Domestic Support Obligation

The term "domestic support obligation" means a debt that accrues before, on, or after the date of the order for relief in a case under this title, including interest that accrues on that debt as provided under applicable nonbankruptcy law notwithstanding any other provision of this title, that is—

(A) owed to or recoverable by—

    (i) a spouse, former spouse, or child of the debtor or such child's parent, legal guardian, or responsible relative; or

    (ii) a governmental unit;

(B) in the nature of alimony, maintenance, or support (including assistance provided by a governmental unit) of such spouse, former spouse, or child of the debtor or such child's parent, without regard to whether such debt is expressly so designated;

(C) established or subject to establishment before, on, or after the date of the order for relief in a case under this title, by reason of applicable provisions of—

    (i) a separation agreement, divorce decree, or property settlement agreement;

    (ii) an order of a court of record; or

    (iii) a determination made in accordance with applicable nonbankruptcy law by a governmental unit; and

(D) not assigned to a nongovernmental entity, unless that obligation is assigned voluntarily by the spouse, former spouse, child of the debtor, or such child's parent, legal guardian, or responsible relative for the purpose of collecting the debt.

In re Phegley

443 B.R. 154 (B.A.P. 8th Cir. 2011)

SALADINO, BANKRUPTCY JUDGE.

John Phegley appeals the bankruptcy court's memorandum and order dated August 3, 2010, and the judgment pursuant thereto dated August 9, 2010, which determined that Mr. Phegley's debts for monthly maintenance payments and attorney's fees pursuant to a state court marriage dissolution proceeding are excepted from discharge pursuant to 11 U.S.C. § 523(a)(5). For the reasons stated below, we affirm.

BACKGROUND

John J. Phegley ("John") and Sheri L. Phegley ("Sheri") were married on May 9, 1998, and lived in Missouri. On June 3, 2009, the Circuit Court of Jackson County Missouri entered a Judgment and Decree of Dissolution of Marriage ("Decree") that dissolved the marriage of John and Sheri. The Decree provided, *inter alia,* that the parties were awarded joint physical and legal custody of the two minor children of the marriage. John was ordered to pay child support to Sheri in the amount of $325.00 per month.

The Decree further provided that John shall pay to Sheri:

[T]he sum of one thousand two hundred fifty and 00/100 dollars ($1,250.00) per month as and for contractual maintenance for a period of forty-eight (48) months beginning on the 1st day of July, 2009 and continuing on the 1st day of each month until the final payment is due at which time [John's] maintenance obligation shall terminate; provided, however, that such maintenance may earlier terminate upon [Sheri's] re-marriage or the death of either party.

In addition, John and Sheri were each awarded certain specified items of marital property and John was ordered to pay Sheri $32,371.98 as equalization of property. Finally, the Decree provided that John "shall pay a portion of [Sheri's] attorney's fees in the amount of nine thousand one hundred seventy-eight and 69/100 dollars ($9,178.69). . . ."

On September 2, 2009, John filed a Chapter 13 bankruptcy petition. Subsequently, Sheri filed a complaint to determine dischargeability of indebtedness pursuant to 11 U.S.C. § 523. In the complaint, Sheri contended that the attorney's fees of $9,178.69 and the monthly maintenance payments of $1,250.00 are non-dischargeable as domestic support obligations pursuant to U.S.C. § 523(a)(5).[2] John asserts that the debts are not domestic support obligations, but instead are a division of marital property and should not be excepted from discharge.

The bankruptcy court found that the maintenance payments and attorney's fees awarded in the Decree are nondischargeable as domestic support obligations pursuant to § 523(a)(5). John appeals.

---

[2] Sheri also asserted that the debts were nondischargeable pursuant to § 523(a)(15), but the bankruptcy court previously ruled that since this was a Chapter 13 case, the § 523(a)(15) issue was not ripe for consideration. Thus, the trial dealt only with § 523(a)(5).

STANDARD OF REVIEW

The determination of whether an award arising out of marital dissolution proceedings was intended to serve as an award for alimony, maintenance, or support, or whether it was intended to serve as a property settlement is a question of fact to be decided by the bankruptcy court. We review the bankruptcy court's findings of fact for clear error and its conclusions of law de novo.

DISCUSSION

In its opinion, the bankruptcy court correctly identified the general legal principles applicable to this matter as follows:

Pursuant to 11 U.S.C. § 101(14A), the term "domestic support obligation" means:

[A] debt that accrues before, on, or after the date of the order for relief in a case under this title, including interest that accrues on that debt as provided under applicable nonbankruptcy law notwithstanding any other provision of this title, that is—

(A) owed to or recoverable by—

(i) a spouse, former spouse, or child of the debtor or such child's parent, legal guardian, or responsible relative; or

. . .

(B) in the nature of alimony, maintenance, or support (including assistance provided by a governmental unit) of such spouse, former spouse, or child of the debtor or such child's parent, without regard to whether such debt is expressly so designated;

(C) established or subject to establishment before, on, or after the date of the order for relief in a case under this title, by reason of applicable provisions of—

(i) a separation agreement, divorce decree, or property settlement agreement;

. . .

(D) not assigned to a nongovernmental entity, unless that obligation is assigned voluntarily by the spouse, former spouse, child of the debtor, or such child's parent, legal guardian, or responsible relative for the purpose of collecting the debt.

This definition was enacted by the Bankruptcy Abuse Prevention and Consumer Protection Act of 2005 ("BAPCPA") and has an impact throughout the Bankruptcy Code on issues of discharge, the automatic stay, priorities, exemptions, the means test, and the calculation of disposable income in a Chapter 13 case. For purposes of the case at hand, discharge is at issue. Domestic support obligations are not discharged in Chapter 13 cases. *See* 11 U.S.C. § 1328(a) and 11 U.S.C. § 523(a)(5). Further, domestic support obligations are priority claims pursuant to 11 U.S.C. § 507(a)(1)(A). If, on the other hand, the obligation is not a domestic support obligation, it would fall under 11 U.S.C. § 523(a)(15), which obligations are not excepted from discharge in Chapter 13 cases, nor are they entitled to priority status. In this case, the requirements of § 101(14A)(A) and (C) are satisfied and not at issue; but whether the debt is in the nature of alimony, maintenance, or support as required under § 101(14A)(B) is the issue of this adversary proceeding.

The BAPCPA amendments that added § 101(14A) and altered §§ 523(a)(5) and (15) did not change the standard for whether an obligation is in the nature of support. When deciding whether a debt should be characterized as one for support or property settlement, the crucial question is the function the award was intended to serve. *Adams v. Zentz,* 963 F.2d 197, 200 (8th Cir.1992); *Boyle v. Donovan,* 724 F.2d 681, 683 (8th Cir.1984) (citing *Williams v. Williams (In re Williams),* 703 F.2d 1055, 1057 (8th Cir.1983)); *see Kruger v. Ellis (In re Ellis),* 149 B.R. 925, 927 (Bankr.E.D.Mo.1993) (finding that in order to determine whether an award represents a property settlement or a maintenance obligation, a court must look to the function an award was intended to serve).

Whether a particular debt is a support obligation or part of a property settlement is a question of federal bankruptcy law, not state law. A divorce decree's characterization of an award as maintenance or alimony does not bind a bankruptcy court but is however a starting point for the determination of the award's intended function. The burden of proof under § 523(a)(5) is on the party asserting that the debt is nondischargeable.

Take Note

The determination of whether a debt is a "domestic support obligation" is controlled by federal and not state law.

Factors considered by the courts in making this determination include: the language and substance of the agreement in the context of surrounding circumstances, using extrinsic evidence if necessary; the relative financial conditions of the parties at the time of the divorce; the respective employment histories and prospects for financial support; the fact that one party or another receives the marital property; the periodic nature of the payments; and whether it would be difficult for the former spouse and children to subsist without the payments.

Exceptions from discharge for spousal and child support deserve a liberal construction, and the policy underlying § 523 favors the enforcement of familial obligations over a fresh start for the debtor, even if the support obligation is owed directly to a third party. *See Holliday v. Kline (In re Kline),* 65 F.3d 749 (8th Cir.1995); *Williams v. Kemp (In re Kemp),* 242 B.R. 178, 181 (8th Cir. BAP 1999), *aff'd* 232 F.3d 652 (8th Cir.2000).

After correctly describing the above legal standards, the bankruptcy court then proceeded to apply those standards to the facts of this case. First, in determining that the monthly maintenance payments awarded by the Decree did constitute domestic support obligations excepted from discharge pursuant to § 523(a)(5), the bankruptcy court noted that the Decree specifically held that the monthly maintenance payments were necessary so that Sheri could continue her education and pursue her teaching certificate and that she could not presently earn sufficient income to support herself. In addition, the Decree provided that the monthly maintenance payments would terminate upon death or remarriage. Those factors are indicative of domestic support obligations. As the bankruptcy court found, the state court "clearly took into account the parties' income and expenses, their employment at the time of dissolution and ability to obtain a job, [Sheri's] continuing schooling and whether [Sheri] could support herself without monthly maintenance payments during the time period that she was continuing her education." Those findings are clearly supported by the record and are not clearly erroneous.

John's primary argument on appeal is that the Decree granted the "maintenance" payments to Sheri only because John was awarded the marital asset referred to as "renewal premiums." As a former insurance agent, John was entitled to receive additional income if and when any insurance policies he had previously sold are renewed by the insured and the premiums are paid. Thus, the renewal premium income is contingent upon the policies being renewed, and John was awarded all of the rights to that potential income. His theory appears to be that the state court judge only awarded the "maintenance" payments as a way of dividing the contingent renewal premium income. However, as discussed in the preceding paragraph, that position simply is not supported by the record.

At oral argument, John's attorney took the position that the Eighth Circuit Court of Appeals was wrong in *Williams* and its progeny when it said that the court should look to the function the award was intended to serve when assessing whether an award was intended as support. Instead, he argues that the better approach is to look at the "source of the funding" for the award, rather than at the intent or function of the award. Even if we could entertain such an argument, we disagree that such an approach is the better way to proceed. In any event, this court simply cannot ignore the long-standing precedent from the Eighth Circuit Court of Appeals in *Williams*.

The bankruptcy court's determination that the function and purpose of the maintenance payments were to provide support to Sheri is amply supported by the record and will not be overturned.

The bankruptcy court also found that the attorney fee award was in the nature of support. The disparities in the parties' education, training, employment history, and earning capacity all led the bankruptcy court to find that the attorney fee award was made to balance those disparities and was, therefore, intended as support. The record supports the bankruptcy court's finding.

Accordingly, we affirm the decision of the bankruptcy court.

Points for Discussion

a. *Phegley*

What are the different amounts John was required to pay Sheri in their divorce decree? Which of these does the court consider in this case? How would you characterize each of these items for bankruptcy purposes? What is the consequence of the court's characterization of these payments?

What was the court's rationale in concluding that the amount awarded for attorney's fees constituted a DSO? Should the result have been different if the debtor had been ordered to pay this amount directly to his ex-wife's lawyers? See generally In re Kassicieh, 425 B.R. 467 (Bankr. N.D. Ohio 2010).

b. Domestic Support Obligations

As previously noted, a debtor cannot discharge a Domestic Support Obligation (DSO) in liquidation proceedings under Chapter 7 or reorganization proceedings under Chapters 11, 12, or 13. See 11 U.S.C. §523(a)(5) and § 1328(a) (2018). The Code extends other important protections to DSOs as well. Under § 507(a)(1), a DSO has the highest priority among all unsecured claims. For a debtor in Chapter 7, this preserves whatever resources are available for these family support needs. Because DSOs are not dischargeable, both the debtor and the creditor have a significant interest in making sure that any DSO is addressed in a bankruptcy proceeding. Another way in which the Bankruptcy Code protects DSOs is by exempting claims to establish or modify support obligations from the automatic stay under § 362(b)(2).

c. Other Divorce or Separation Obligations

The court in *Phegley* did not address the property equalization payment, on the basis that the issue was not ripe for consideration. If John had been proceeding under Chapter 7, his property equalization debt would not have been dischargeable, even if it did not qualify as a DSO, since it was a debt "to a spouse, former spouse, or child of the debtor. . .incurred by the debtor in the course of a divorce or separation or in connection with a separation agreement, divorce decree or other order of a court of record. . . ." See 11 U.S.C. § 523 (a)(15) (2018). In a contempt proceeding brought after a former husband obtained a Chapter 7 bankruptcy discharge of joint debts owed to third parties, the court in Collins v. Collins, 136 A.3d 708 (Me. 2016), applied 11 U.S.C. § 523(a)(15) and concluded that the husband's obligations to his ex-wife with respect to those debts, as well as the obligations owed directly to her, had survived the discharge.

In Chapter 13 proceedings, however, a property equalization debt from a divorce or separation may be discharged. See 11 U.S.C. § 1328(a) (2018) (listing debts that are not dischargeable under Chapter 13). See, e.g., In re Boller, 393 B.R. 569 (Bankr. E.D. Tenn. 2008). See also Beth Holliday, Construction and Application of Bankruptcy Abuse and Consumer Protection Act's Provision Defining Domestic Support Obligations, 56 A.L.R. Fed. 2d 439 (2011).

d. Third Party Debts in Divorce

One spouse's obligation to pay a joint debt owed to a third-party creditor also typically falls outside the Bankruptcy Code's definition of domestic support obligations. While a divorce court may order one party to pay certain marital debts, or the couple may agree that one party will pay debts for which the couple are jointly liable, creditors will not be bound by the court's orders or the parties' settlement agreement. If the spouse who was made responsible for a joint debt defaults, the creditor will be free to collect it from the other spouse. This result is almost guaranteed if the spouse who is responsible for paying obtains a bankruptcy discharge. When this occurs, a former husband or wife who is then obligated to pay the debt can seek indemnification from the spouse to whom the debt was assigned in the divorce.

This raises a further question as to how the obligation to indemnify should be treated in a bankruptcy proceeding. In Chapter 7 proceedings, courts have concluded that an obligation to indemnify a former spouse falls within the scope of §523(a)(15), quoted above, and that it was therefore nondischargeable. See, e.g., In re Wodark, 425 B.R. 834 (B.A.P. 10th Cir. 2010); Quinn v. Quinn, 528 B.R. 203 (D. Mass. 2015); Howard v. Howard, 336 S.W.3d 433 (Ky. 2011).

Debts and Divorce

Couples who are separating or divorcing should usually pay off as much of their shared debt as possible. When there are significant obligations between the couple or to third parties that will survive a divorce, lawyers should be certain to counsel clients about the risk of bankruptcy and to consider whether those debts can be secured.

e. Judicial Liens

Because of the risk that obligations running from one spouse to the other under a divorce decree will later be discharged in bankruptcy, parties often seek to secure those obligations as far as possible at the time of the decree. The court may impose a judicial lien against property owned by the debtor-spouse, such as a residence, in order to secure the debt. Under 11 U.S.C. § 522(f), a debtor may not avoid the fixing of a judicial lien securing a domestic support obligation. See 11 U.S.C. § 522(f)(1)(A)(2012). See generally Sheryl Scheible Wolf, *Divorce, Bankruptcy and Metaphysics: Avoidance of Marital Liens Under § 522(f) of the Bankruptcy Code*, 31 Fam. L.Q. 513 (1997).

f. Joint Bankruptcy

Married couples are eligible to petition jointly for bankruptcy protection under 11 U.S.C. § 302(a) (2018). This is another area where same-sex couples faced significant difficulty before federal laws extended recognition to same-sex marriage. In re Simmons, 584 B.R. 295 (Bankr. N.D. Ill. 2018) held that a same-sex couple who had obtained a civil union in Illinois, where that status was "substantively identical" to marriage, were eligible to file a joint petition under Chapter 13. The court in In re Villaverde, 540 B.R. 431 (Bankr. C.D. Cal. 2015), reached the opposite result with respect to a couple who had registered as domestic partners under California law.

Problem 6-22

Jane was divorced from Tom three years ago and was awarded custody of their two children. Tom is a brilliant but eccentric engineer who had a small but profitable consulting business, from which he earned about $200,000 a year. When Jane and Tom were divorced, he received his consulting business, with a value of $600,000, and Jane received the marital residence, with equity of $200,000. Tom was ordered to pay Jane $200,000 in five equal yearly installments with interest. The decree also ordered him to make payments on the home mortgage of $1500 each month and pay Jane $500 per month as alimony and $1000 per month as child support.

Tom began drinking heavily after the divorce, and his business deteriorated. He made some of the monthly payments the court ordered, but within a year he filed a petition in bankruptcy, seeking to discharge his obligation to pay the home mortgage and his business debts as well as obligations to Jane under the divorce decree. What arguments would you make for Jane in this situation? What arguments would you make for Tom? If Tom is able to have his $200,000 debt to Jane discharged, does she have any other remedies she can pursue in the divorce action? What if Tom is able to pull his life back together, and resume his consulting business? (Cf. <u>Birt v. Birt, 96 P.3d 544 (Ariz. Ct. App.2004)</u>; <u>Jeffords v. Scott, 624 N.W.2d 384 (Wis. Ct. App.2000)</u>.)

Further Reading: Bankruptcy Law

- <u>Janet Leach Richards, *A Guide to Spousal Support and Property Division Claims Under the Bankruptcy Abuse Prevention and Consumer Protection Act of 2005*, 41 Fam. L.Q. 227 (2007)</u>.

- Lynne F. Riley and Maria C. Furlong, *Intersection of Divorce and Bankruptcy: BAPCPA and Other Developments*, 16 Norton Ann. Surv. Bankr. L. 15(2010).

- Shayna M. Steinfeld and Bruce R. Steinfeld, The Family Lawyer's Guide to Bankruptcy (4th ed. 2018).

D. Settlements, Decrees and Dispute Resolution

Most divorce cases are settled through a process of negotiation between the parties or their lawyers. Lawyers face a particularly difficult task in this setting, where the parties may be angry or emotional, the issues at stake are complex and important, and the settlement will have long term consequences for the couple and their children. Mediation, arbitration and collaborative law present important alternatives to traditional litigation of divorce disputes, and help lawyers and divorcing parties work toward better resolution of these cases.

Divorce negotiations are shaped by a larger framework of divorce law and by the procedural safeguards that the law imposes on "private ordering" in divorce disputes. See <u>Robert H. Mnookin and Lewis Kornhauser, *Bargaining in the Shadow of the Law: The Case of Divorce*, 88 Yale L.J. 950 (1979)</u>, and Robert H. Mnookin, *Divorce Bargaining: The Limits on Private Ordering*, 18 U. Mich. J. L. Reform 1015 (1985). There is a useful literature on the process of negotiation, including Roger Fisher, William L. Ury and Brue Patton, Getting to Yes: Negotiating Agreement Without Giving In (rev. ed. 2011).

One advantage of private ordering in divorce is that the parties may be able to include terms in their settlement agreement that a court would not otherwise have authority to order. For example, in many states couples may enter enforceable agreements on payment of college expenses or other post-majority support for their children. See, e.g., Zetterman v. Zetterman, 512 N.W.2d 622 (Neb. 1994). Another example is an agreement for nonmodifiable spousal support, discussed above.

Negotiation of the issues in a divorce case may be carried on by the parties alone, by the parties' lawyers, or by the parties with the assistance of a mediator. Mediation, sometimes referred to as "facilitated negotiation," may be conducted by a lawyer or a non-lawyer mediator, whose function is to assist the parties in reaching agreement. Ideally, mediation produces better outcomes for the parties, saves the time and expense of litigation, and reduces the hostility that is often created or exacerbated by adversary proceedings.

Some states require couples to attempt mediation in cases with disputed custody or visitation issues. See, e.g. Cal.Fam.Code § 3170 (2018); N.C.Gen.Stat. § 50–13.1(b) (2018); and Wis.Stat.Ann. § 767.405 (2018). In others, courts have discretion to order mediation. E.g. Colo.Rev.Stat.Ann. § 14–10–129.5 (2018); Minn.Stat.Ann. § 518.619 (2018).

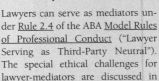

Lawyer-Mediators

Lawyers can serve as mediators under Rule 2.4 of the ABA Model Rules of Professional Conduct ("Lawyer Serving as Third-Party Neutral"). The special ethical challenges for lawyer-mediators are discussed in Chapter 8.

Critics have pointed to particular risks of mediation in certain types of cases, and argued that mediation in divorce cases should be voluntary rather than mandatory. See Trina Grillo, *The Mediation Alternative: Process Dangers for Women*, 100 Yale L.J. 1545 (1991). The concerns are particularly strong where there is a history of domestic violence between the parties; see Penelope E. Bryan, *Killing Us Softly: Divorce Mediation and the Politics of Power*, 40 Buff. L. Rev. 441 (1992), and Penelope Eileen Bryan, *Reclaiming Professionalism: The Lawyer's Role in Divorce Mediation*, 28 Fam. L.Q. 177 (1994). Many state statutes now reflect this concern with provisions to prevent courts from requiring mediation in cases where there has been a history of domestic violence. See, e.g., Fla.Stat. § 44.102(2)(c) (2018);

see also <u>Cal. Fam. Code § 3181 (2018)</u> (requiring mediator to meet with parties separately in cases with domestic violence issues).

Collaborative Law

Divorce lawyers in many states now offer an alternative dispute resolution process, known as "collaborative law." This is a voluntary process, in which couples and their lawyers agree at the outset to resolve the case by negotiation rather than litigation, with the understanding that both lawyers will withdraw from representing their clients if negotiations are ultimately not successful. Numerous state bar ethics committees have approved the use of this process, and several states have adopted collaborative law rules or statutes. See, e.g., <u>Cal. Fam. Code § 2013 (2018)</u>, <u>Tex. Fam Code § 15.001</u> et seq. (2018). Some of these are based on the <u>Uniform Collaborative Law Act (2010), 7 U.L.A. (Part IB) (Supp. 2018)</u>. See generally <u>*Special Issue on Collaborative Law*, 38 Hofstra L. Rev. 411 (2010)</u>. Resources on collaborative law include Pauline H. Tesler, Collaborative Law: Achieving Effective Resolution in Divorce without Litigation (3d ed. 2016).

Winegeart v. Winegeart

910 N.W.2d 906 (S.D. 2018)

GILBERTSON, CHIEF JUSTICE

[¶ 1.] Eryn Marie Winegeart appeals the circuit court's order to sell real estate she jointly owned with Weston Lee Winegeart, her former spouse. The order permits the payment of realtor fees, but Eryn asserts the parties orally agreed in mediation to sell the property without paying realtor fees. We affirm.

Facts and Procedural History

[¶ 2.] Weston and Eryn Winegeart first married in 2005, divorced, then married for a second time in 2012. The parties owned a home in Pierre, where they resided with their three children: B.C., K.L., and J.C. On October 4, 2016, Weston filed for divorce. Eryn subsequently obtained a protection order against Weston, and both parties vacated the home. Weston moved to Texas.

[¶ 3.] On January 9, 2017, the circuit court ordered the parties to undergo mediation. The parties attended one mediation session on March 9. After the session, Weston signed an agreement with a real-estate agent to list the jointly owned real estate. The listing agreement included a commission for the realtor. On March 10, a third party signed an agreement to purchase the property for $330,000. Eryn refused to sign the purchase agreement, asserting that during mediation, Weston had orally agreed to sell the property without paying for a realtor.

[¶ 4.] On March 22, 2017, Weston filed a motion asking the court to order Eryn to sign the purchase agreement. The parties deposed the mediator on March 30. Over the objection of Weston's attorney, the mediator testified that it was his "understanding. . .that there were no Realtor commissions to be paid, that this was going to be a private sale." The court held a hearing to consider the motion on March 31. The court found that the parties had not entered into an enforceable oral agreement in regard to realtor fees. The court granted Weston's request and ordered Eryn to sign the purchase agreement.

[¶ 5.] On April 15, 2017, after the circuit court issued its order requiring Eryn to sign the purchase agreement, the parties entered into a property-settlement agreement. On April 18, the circuit court granted a divorce on the grounds of irreconcilable differences. The court determined custody, set child support, and incorporated the parties' April 15 property-settlement agreement.

[¶ 6.] Eryn appeals the circuit court's March 31, 2017 order requiring her to sign the purchase agreement. She asks this Court to enter an order requiring Weston to pay her "the realtor fees incurred as a result of his violation of the oral mediated agreement." Thus, Eryn raises the following issue: Whether the court erred by ordering her to sign the purchase agreement.

Standard of Review

[¶ 7.] This appeal involves interpreting South Dakota's Uniform Mediation Act, SDCL chapter 19–13A. Statutory interpretation is a question of law reviewed de novo. _Pitt-Hart v. Sanford USD Med. Ctr., 2016 S.D. 33, ¶ 7, 878 N.W.2d 406, 409_. The circuit court's factual findings are reviewed under the clearly erroneous standard. _Aguilar v. Aguilar, 2016 S.D. 20, ¶ 9, 877 N.W.2d 333, 336_.

Analysis and Decision

[¶ 8.] Eryn argues the circuit court erred by entering its March 31, 2017 order requiring her to sign the purchase agreement. Eryn asserts that the parties entered into an enforceable oral agreement during mediation on March 9, 2017, and that the court "abused its discretion in refusing to enforce" that agreement.

Weston raises a number of reasons to reject Eryn's argument. First, as a matter of first impression in South Dakota, he argues that communications occurring in the course of mediation are confidential and cannot be used to prove the existence of an agreement. Second, he argues that even if such communications could be used as evidence of an oral agreement, Eryn signed a confidentiality agreement that prevents relying on those communications. Third, he argues that even if the parties' mediation communications could be used as evidence to establish an oral agreement in this case, the circuit court's factual finding that he did not agree to sell the home without paying realtor fees is not clearly erroneous. And finally, he argues that even if Eryn is correct that the parties entered into such an agreement on March 9, 2017, that agreement was superseded by the parties' April 15, 2017 agreement.

1   [¶ 9.] The question whether an oral agreement arising out of mediation is enforceable is a question of first impression in this jurisdiction. South Dakota adopted the Uniform Mediation Act (UMA) in 2008. SDCL chapter 19–13A. Under the UMA, a mediation communication "means a statement, whether oral or in a record or verbal or nonverbal, that occurs during a mediation or is made for purposes of considering, conducting, participating in, initiating, continuing, or reconvening a mediation or retaining a mediator." SDCL 19–13A–2(2). As a general rule, "a mediation communication is privileged. . .and is not subject to discovery or admissible in evidence in a proceeding[.]" SDCL 19–13A–4(a); *see also* SDCL 19–19–515 ("All verbal or written information relating to the subject matter of a mediation which is transmitted between any party to a dispute and a mediator or any agent, employee, or representative of a party or a mediator is confidential."). Thus, "[i]n a proceeding,. . .[a] mediation party may refuse to disclose, and may prevent any other person from disclosing, a mediation communication." SDCL 19–13A–4(b)(1).

[¶ 10.] The exceptions to the mediation-communication privilege enumerated in SDCL 19–13A–6 seem to support the conclusion that an oral agreement occurring in the course of mediation is unenforceable. The UMA specifically excepts mediation communications "in an *agreement evidenced by a record* signed by all parties to the agreement[.]" SDCL 19–13A–6(a)(1) (emphasis added). The specific inclusion of *written* agreements in SDCL 19–13A–6 implies that *nonwritten* agreements are not excepted from the mediation-communication privilege. *See In re Estate of Flaws*, 2012 S.D. 3, ¶ 20, 811 N.W.2d 749, 754 (applying the canon of construction *expressio unius est exclusio alterius*). Indeed, as the Utah Supreme Court has noted, the Uniform Law Commission (ULC) "explained in a comment to the Uniform Mediation Act that oral agreements were intentionally *not* included in the list of exceptions to mediation privilege." *Reese v. Tingey Constr.*, 177 P.3d 605, 609–10 (Utah 2008) (emphasis added). As the ULC explained, the exception for written agreements is noteworthy only for what is not included: oral agreements. The disadvantage of exempting oral settlements is that nearly everything said during a mediation session could bear on either whether the parties came to an agreement or the content of the agreement. In other words, an exception for oral agreements has the potential to swallow the rule of privilege. As a result, mediation participants might be less candid, not knowing whether a controversy later would erupt over an oral agreement.

Unif. Mediation Act § 6 cmt. 2 (Unif. Law Comm'n, amended 2003).

[¶ 11.] Judicial opinions from other jurisdictions agree that only written agreements are enforceable under the UMA. Aside from South Dakota, the UMA has been adopted by the District of Columbia and by the States of Hawaii, Idaho, Illinois, Iowa, Nebraska, New Jersey, Ohio, Utah, Vermont, and Washington. Of these eleven other jurisdictions, it appears that five have had occasion to address this question, and all five suggest that an oral agreement is unenforceable. *Billhartz v. Billhartz*, No. 5–13–0580, 2015 WL 2058961, at *8 (Ill. App. Ct. May 4, 2015) ("The Uniform Mediation Act. . .contemplates that a signed, written agreement is admissible and enforceable following mediation and that oral communications generally are not."); *Shriner v. Friedman Law Offices, P.C., L.L.O.*, 23 Neb.App. 869, 877 N.W.2d 272, 290 (2016) ("The Uniform Mediation Act. . .establishes a privilege for mediation communications, which generally are not subject to discovery or admissible in evidence in a proceeding."); *Willingboro Mall, Ltd. v. 240/242 Franklin Ave., L.L.C.*, 215 N.J. 242, 71 A.3d 888, 890 (2013) ("[P]arties that intend to enforce a settlement reached at mediation must execute a signed written agreement."); *Akron v. Carter*, 190 Ohio App.3d 420, 942 N.E.2d 409, 415–16 (2010) (holding mediation communications "privileged and. . .neither discoverable nor admissible" where party sought to introduce those communications "in an effort to prove that an oral contract of settlement arose out of the mediation"); *Reese*, 177 P.3d at 610 (rejecting an oral-agreement exception to the mediation-communication privilege and concluding that "a court can enforce only a mediation agreement that has been reduced to writing"). While these decisions are not per se binding on this Court, the Legislature has instructed that "[i]n applying and construing this chapter, consideration should be given to the need to promote uniformity of the law with respect to its subject matter among States that enact it." SDCL 19–13A–13; *see also* SDCL 2–14–13 ("Whenever a statute appears in the code of laws enacted by § 2–16–13 which, from its title, text, or source note, appears to be a uniform law, it shall be so interpreted and construed as to effectuate its general purpose to make uniform the law of those states which enact it.").

[¶ 12.] Even so, additional analysis is required to apply the foregoing opinions in this case. These opinions are premised on the evidentiary reality that if mediation communications are not subject to discovery or admissible in evidence, then generally the only way to prove the terms of an agreement is to reduce it to a signed writing. *See, e.g.,* <u>Reese, 177 P.3d at 609–10</u>. But South Dakota's version of the UMA potentially provides another avenue for establishing the terms of a settlement reached during mediation that has not been reduced to writing. Under § 7(b)(1) of the UMA, "[a] mediator may disclose. . .whether a settlement was reached[.]" But unlike every other jurisdiction that has adopted the UMA, the South Dakota Legislature modified the language of our corresponding statute; thus, in South Dakota, a mediator may disclose "whether a settlement was reached *and if so the terms thereof*[.]" SDCL 19–13A–7(b)(1) (emphasis added).[3]

[¶ 13.] The foregoing invites the question whether a mediator may disclose the terms of an *oral* settlement reached during mediation. On one hand, an oral settlement is a settlement, and <u>SDCL 19–13A–7(b)(1)</u> permits a mediator to disclose the terms of a settlement. But on the other hand, "[e]xcept as otherwise provided in <u>§ 19–13A–6</u>, a mediation communication is privileged as provided in subsection (b) and is not subject to discovery or admissible in evidence in a proceeding unless waived or precluded as provided by § 19–13A–5." <u>SDCL 19–13A–4(a)</u>. Thus, <u>SDCL 19–13A–4(a)</u> omits <u>SDCL 19–13A–7(b)(1)</u> from the list of circumstances under which the mediation-communication privilege does not apply. So the choice must be made whether to add <u>SDCL 19–13A–7(b)(1)</u> to <u>SDCL 19–13A–4(a)</u>'s list of circumstances under which the privilege does not apply, or to read the word *settlement* in <u>SDCL 19–13A–7(b)(1)</u> to permit the disclosure of the terms of only a settlement that has been reduced to writing.

[¶ 14.] <u>SDCL 19–13A–7(b)(1)</u> should not be read to permit a mediator to disclose the terms of a purported oral settlement reached during mediation. As noted above, the purpose of the mediation-communication privilege is to encourage participants to be candid by shielding their negotiations from later disclosure. *Unif. Mediation Act* § 6 cmt. 2. But if a mediator may disclose mediation communications under <u>SDCL 19–13A–7(b)(1)</u>, then the purpose of the mediation-communication privilege can be easily subverted: while one party to a negotiation cannot disclose settlement negotiations occurring during mediation, the same evidence could be admitted by simply subpoenaing the mediator to testify. And as the ULC pointed out in the model act, "nearly everything said during a mediation session could bear on either whether the parties came to an agreement or the content of the agreement." *Unif. Mediation Act* § 6 cmt. 2. Thus, permitting a mediator to disclose the terms of a purported oral settlement also "has the potential to swallow the rule of privilege." Id. But perhaps most important of all, this narrow reading harmonizes <u>SDCL 19–13A–7(b)(1)</u> with its counterparts in other jurisdictions that have enacted the UMA, thereby carrying out the Legislature's

---

3   While the mediation acts of the District of Columbia and the States of Hawaii, Idaho, Illinois, Iowa, Nebraska, New Jersey, Ohio, Utah, Vermont, and Washington also permit a mediator to disclose "whether a settlement was reached," none of them permit a mediator to disclose the terms of such settlement. * * *

directive to consider chapter 19–13A in light of other jurisdictions' treatment of the UMA. *See* SDCL 19–13A–13.

2   [¶ 15.] Even if SDCL 19–13A–7(b)(1) permitted a mediator to disclose mediation communications relating to a purported oral agreement, Eryn was still precluded under chapter 19–13A from introducing the mediator's testimony in this case. "[M]ediation communications are confidential to the extent agreed by the parties or provided by other law or rule of this State." SDCL 19–13A–8. In this case, the parties entered into a confidentiality agreement prior to engaging in mediation. Under that agreement, the parties agreed to the following provision:

> 5. Confidentiality: The parties and the mediator will abide by the follow-ing confidentiality provisions:
>
> > a. All discussions, representations and statements made during the mediation will be privileged as settlement negotiations. *The parties will not attempt to discover or use as evidence in any legal proceeding anything related to the mediation, including any communications or the thoughts, im-pressions or notes of the mediator.* No document produced in mediation which is not otherwise discoverable will be admissible by the parties in any legal proceedings for any purpose, including impeachment.
> > b. The parties will not subpoena the mediator, any members of his staff or any legal records or documents of the mediator in any proceedings of any kind.
> > c. The mediator will not discuss the mediation process or disclose any communications made during the process to any person except his staff as necessary.

(Emphasis added.) So regardless of whether the mediator's testimony regarding the terms of the purported oral settlement would normally be admissible under SDCL 19–13A–7(b)(1), that testimony is not admissible in this case by agreement of the parties.

[¶ 16.] Even if the mediator's testimony were admissible, Eryn still has the burden of proving the elements of a contract. The "[e]lements essential to exis-tence of a contract are: (1) [p]arties capable of contracting; (2) [t]heir consent; (3) [a] lawful object; and (4) [s]ufficient cause or consideration." SDCL 53–1–2. " 'There must be mutual assent or a meeting of the minds on all essential elements or terms in order to form a binding contract.' Whether there is mutual assent is a fact question determined by the words and actions of the parties." *Vander Heide v. Boke Ranch, Inc.*, 2007 S.D. 69, ¶ 20, 736 N.W.2d 824, 832 (quoting *Read v. McKennan Hosp.*, 2000 S.D. 66, ¶ 23, 610 N.W.2d 782, 786). As noted above, a circuit court's "factual findings will not be disturbed unless they are clearly errone-ous." *Aguilar*, 2016 S.D. 20, ¶ 9, 877 N.W.2d at 336.

[¶ 17.] The circuit court found that Eryn did not meet her burden of proving the parties had a meeting of the minds. During the hearing on Weston's motion to require Eryn to sign the purchase agreement, the court said: "I don't see a mediated agreement. I see a draft." Indeed, during that hearing, Eryn's attorney admitted that the first draft agreement he submitted following the mediation did not include a provision forbidding the payment of realtor fees. If anything, that draft supports Weston's claim that the parties did not reach an agreement regarding realtor fees during the March 9, 2017 mediation. Eryn's attorney also admitted at the hearing that the parties then revised the first draft several times, making numerous additions. Only then did Eryn's attorney produce a draft that included a provision forbidding the payment of realtor fees. And perhaps most telling, the April 15, 2017 agreement that Eryn signed explicitly states: "[P]arties *disagree* as to the employment of a real estate broker[.]" (Emphasis added.) In light of the foregoing, the court's factual finding that there was not a meeting of the minds is not clearly erroneous; even considering the mediator's testimony, "a complete review of the evidence" does not create "a definite and firm conviction that a mistake has been made." *Id.*

[¶ 18.] Finally, even if the mediator's testimony were admissible and the circuit court's factual finding on mutual assent were clearly erroneous, Eryn would still not be entitled to relief. As noted above, the parties both signed an agreement dated April 15, 2017—after the purported oral agreement of March 9, 2017. "The execution of a contract in writing. . .supersedes all the oral negotiations or stipulations concerning its matter which preceded or accompanied the execution of the instrument." SDCL 53–8–5. The April 15 agreement includes the following provision:

> 1. COMPLETE AGREEMENT: Each of the parties is fully and completely informed of the financial and personal status of the other and each has given full thought to the making of this Agreement, and all obligations herein contained and *each of the parties understands the agreements and obligations assumed by the other* with the express understanding and agreement they *are in full satisfaction of all obligations for which each of the parties now has or might hereafter otherwise have toward the other.*

(Emphasis added.) Not only does the April 15 agreement not forbid the payment of realtor fees, it expressly acknowledges that the parties disagreed on that term:

> [T]he parties hereto agree that the Plaintiff shall market the family residence as expeditiously and in the most cost effective manner as possible; parties disagree as to the employment of a real estate broker; the minimum price the parties agree to will be the sum of $325,000. The parties agree that in the event the house is sold, all of the outstanding expenses, including advance taxes, closing costs, mortgage, and any other personal services owed shall be paid out of said sale proceeds. Any deficiency from the sale is Plaintiff's responsibility; and any profits shall be split equally between the parties.

Eryn cannot now modify the April 15 agreement by extrinsic evidence of an earlier purported agreement. *Roseth v. Roseth,* 2013 S.D. 27, ¶ 15, 829 N.W.2d 136, 142. Thus, the question whether the parties entered into an oral agreement on March 9, 2017, that forbade the payment of realtor fees is immaterial.

Conclusion

[¶ 19.] Eryn is not entitled to relief. South Dakota's Uniform Mediation Act does not permit a mediator to disclose the terms of a settlement produced in mediation unless that settlement has been reduced to writing. Even if the mediator's testimony were normally admissible, Eryn signed a confidentiality agreement that precluded the introduction of such evidence. Additionally, if the mediator's testimony were considered, the circuit court's finding that the parties did not mutually assent to selling their home without paying realtor fees still would not be clearly erroneous. And in any event, Eryn cannot rely on the purported oral agreement of March 9, 2017, to modify the written agreement of April 15, 2017.

[¶ 20.] We affirm. Weston's request for appellate attorney's fees is granted in the amount of $10,400.

Points for Discussion

a. Confidentiality

Winegeart cites the Uniform Mediation Act, 7A U.L.A. (Part III) 447 (2017), drafted in collaboration with the ABA Section on Dispute Resolution, which establishes a privilege of confidentiality for mediators and participants. What public policies support this privilege? Are these different from the polices reflected in evidence rules, such as the Indiana rule cited here (based on Federal Rule of Evidence 408)? Under the various authorities cited in *Horner,* when would testimony regarding mediation communications be prohibited?

b. Defenses to Mediated Agreements

Numerous cases have applied contract defenses to mediated settlement agreements. For example, Vitakis-Valchine v. Valchine, 793 So.2d 1094 (Fla. Ct.App.2001), held that a mediated settlement agreement may be set aside based on improper coercion during the mediation process. Under a Texas statute that makes a mediated agreement binding and irrevocable after certain formalities, see Tex. Fam. Code § 6.602(b) (2012), the courts concluded that a dispute regarding an ambiguous term had to be referred back to the mediator to determine what the parties had intended. See Milner v. Milner, 361 S.W.3d 615 (Tex. 2012).

What about an agreement that has not been reduced to writing? Issues sometimes arise when one party repudiates or refuses to sign a written agreement after mediation. State statutes may require certain formalities for a mediated agreement to be binding. See, e.g., 19–A Me. Rev. Stat. § 251 (2018), applied in Dewhurst v. Dewhurst, 5 A.3d 23 (Me. 2010). Herrera v. Herrera, 974 P.2d 675 (N.M. Ct.App.1999), rejected a husband's statute of frauds defense where he acknowledged that he had agreed to the terms of a mediated settlement.

c. Role of Counsel in Mediation

Lawyers for the parties in divorce cases may participate in mediation, or may be involved only in preparing their clients for mediation sessions and reviewing whatever agreements the parties reach. When mediation is mandatory, lawyers should advise clients regarding whether it is appropriate, and consider whether there is some basis, such as a history of domestic violence, for asking that the court not require mediation. Lawyers can help prepare clients for mediation by providing information about the process, about the client's alternatives to a mediated settlement, and about legal considerations. This information can help a client to establish goals for the mediation that may shape an appropriate settlement. For a discussion of the lawyer's role in mediation, see Craig A. McEwen et al., *Bring in the Lawyers: Challenging the Dominant Approaches to Ensuring Fairness in Divorce Mediation*, 79 Minn. L. Rev. 1317 (1995).

Further Reading: Mediation

- Jay Folberg, et al., Divorce and Family Mediation: Models, Techniques, and Applications (2004).

- Jane C. Murphy and Robert Robinson, Family Mediation: Theory and Practice (2d ed. 2015).

Separation and Settlement Agreements

An agreement reached in mediation or other settlement negotiations is usually reduced to writing in the form of a separation agreement, stipulation, or consent judgment. Drafting skills come to the forefront at this stage, as separation agreements are subject to the same interpretation problems as other types of contracts. See, e.g., <u>Matter of Marriage of Wessling, 747 P.2d 187 (Kan. Ct. App. 1987)</u> (interpreting cohabitation clause), and <u>Pacifico v. Pacifico, 920 A.2d 73 (N.J. 2007)</u> (rejecting doctrine of *contra proferentum* when both parties had lawyers who participated in drafting and revising the agreement).

Like other contracts, marital separation agreements can be set aside on the basis of fraud, duress, or undue influence. See <u>Sally Burnett Sharp, *Fairness Standards and Separation Agreements: A Word of Caution on Contractual Freedom*, 132 U. Pa. L. Rev. 1399 (1984)</u>. State statutes and court rules typically require disclosure of the parties' assets and other important financial information before their agreement is approved by the court. See, e.g., <u>Cal. Fam. Code § 2105 (2018)</u>, discussed in <u>Elden v. Superior Court, 62 Cal.Rptr.2d 322 (Ct. App. 1997)</u>.

Divorcing couples present their agreement to the court for its approval. Courts usually accept these agreements, particularly when both parties are represented by counsel, and statutes in some jurisdictions limit the scope of the court's review. For example, <u>UMDA § 306</u> provides that parties may enter into a written separation agreement, and states that the terms of the agreement, except those providing for child support, custody or visitation, are binding on the court unless the court finds, "after considering the economic circumstances of the parties and any other relevant evidence produced by the parties. . .that the separation agreement is unconscionable." See, e.g., <u>In re Marriage of Manzo, 659 P.2d 669 (Colo. 1983)</u>; see also <u>Pouech v. Pouech, 904 A.2d 70 (Vt. 2006)</u>.

Self-Represented Divorce Litigants

In many divorce cases, neither of the parties has a lawyer, and in a large majority of divorce cases at least one of the parties appears without counsel. This presents challenges for everyone involved, though an individual appearing **pro se** is generally required to adhere to the usual rules and procedures. See, e.g., <u>Ezell v. Lawless, 955 A.2d 202 (Me. 2008)</u>. A lawyer representing an individual whose spouse is appearing pro se has particular ethical obligations under <u>Rule 4.3</u> of the ABA <u>Model Rules of Professional Conduct</u>. Many state court systems or bar associations have developed handbooks or web sites with information to assist pro se litigants. See generally <u>Carolyn D. Schwartz, Note, *Pro Se Divorce Litigants: Frustrating the Traditional Role of the Trial Court Judge and Court Personnel*, 42 Fam. Ct. Rev. 655 (2004)</u>.

If one of the parties to a separation agreement subsequently challenges it as unfair, the challenge will be more difficult if that person was represented by counsel. See, e.g., Levine v. Levine, 436 N.E.2d 476 (N.Y. 1982). Courts do not set aside agreements on the basis that one of the parties did not have legal representation, see, e.g., Casto v. Casto, 508 So.2d 330, 334 (Fla.1987), but they may question an agreement if the attorney who drafted it for one spouse led the other to believe that the lawyer was representing both parties. In Hale v. Hale, 539 A.2d 247, 254 (Md. Ct. Spec. App. 1988), the court wrote: "We feel that when a husband and wife are contemplating a separation agreement, it should be obvious to an attorney that he *cannot* adequately represent the interests of both parties", while *Levine*, 436 N.E.2d at 478, took a different approach: "While the absence of independent representation is a significant factor to be taken into consideration when determining whether a separation agreement was freely entered into, the fact that each party retained the same attorney does not, in and of itself, provide a basis for rescission." In Marriage of Egedi, 105 Cal.Rptr.2d 518 (Ct. App. 2001), the court allowed enforcement of a marital settlement agreement prepared by a single attorney who acted "only as a scrivener" and obtained informed written waivers of the potential conflict of interests from both parties.

Can a Lawyer Be "Just a Scrivener"?

How should a lawyer proceed if asked to prepare a separation agreement for a divorcing couple? Can the lawyer undertake this type of limited representation, or does it present a conflict of interest under Rule 1.7 of the ABA Model Rules of Professional Conduct? According to the American Academy of Matrimonial Lawyers' Bounds of Advocacy Standard 3.1, "An attorney should not represent both husband and wife even if they do not wish to obtain independent representation." Is it possible to say that the lawyer acting as a scrivener is not "representing" either party?

A separation or settlement agreement may be merged or incorporated into the final divorce decree, which has the effect of substituting the rights and duties under the decree in place of those created by the agreement. Whether or not a merger has occurred may have significant consequences for the parties after their divorce, particularly regarding the remedies available if one of the parties does not fulfill his or her obligations and the question whether the court can order a modification. Depending on the law of the state where the divorce takes place, the parties may be able to determine whether or not to have their agreement merge into the decree. E.g. <u>UMDA § 306</u>. This is a complex question, and may have significant consequences if not handled carefully. See, e.g., <u>McMahon v. Shea, 688 A.2d 1179 (Pa. 1997)</u> (ruling that husband could pursue malpractice claim against attorneys who failed to merge alimony agreement into final decree).

Problem 6-23

Steven and Laura, both lawyers, were married for thirty years when they separated and divorced. They agreed to an approximately equal division of their assets, including an account with Madoff Investment Services which they believed to be worth $5.4 million. Steven kept the account, and agreed to pay Laura $2.7 million as her share. Two years later, Steven learned that Madoff had committed extensive securities fraud and the account was actually worthless. Is there a basis on which he can have the agreement set aside? Does it matter whether the agreement was incorporated or merged into the divorce decree? (See <u>Simkin v. Blank, 968 N.E.2d 459 (N.Y. 2012)</u>.)

Problem 6-24

After thirteen years of marriage, Jim asked Donna to sign a separation agreement that gave her assets worth $225,000 from property Jim owned worth almost $10 million. Donna consulted a lawyer and showed him a general listing of Jim's property, and the lawyer advised her not to sign the agreement. Jim told Donna he would "blow up" her house and throw bleach over her clothes if she refused to sign. Although Donna signed the agreement, she asked the court to invalidate it when Jim presented it to the court for approval in the divorce proceedings. How should the court evaluate her request? (See <u>Casto v. Casto, 508 So.2d 330, 334 (Fla.1987)</u>.)

Problem 6-25

When Albert and Constance divorced, their separation agreement provided that Albert would "cause to be allocated" to Constance one-half of his military pension rights. After Albert retired, he and Constance began receiving payments pursuant to this agreement. Three years later, Albert applied for military disability benefits, which were offset against his retirement pay. As a result, his payments more than doubled, while hers fell by more than eighty percent. What kinds of contract claims arguments might Constance raise against Albert? (See <u>Krapf v. Krapf, 786 N.E.2d 318 (Mass. 2003)</u>.)

Faherty v. Faherty

477 A.2d 1257 (N.J. 1984)

GARIBALDI, J.

The question posed in this appeal is whether an arbitration provision in a separation agreement, entered into by the parties prior to their divorce and incorporated in their divorce judgment, is enforceable. The Chancery Division and the Appellate Division enforced the arbitration provision. We granted certification, and now modify and affirm, as modified, the Appellate Division's judgment.

I

Susan Faherty (Susan) and J. Roger Faherty (Roger) were divorced in 1977 after seventeen years of marriage. At that time, they had four dependent children. Prior to their divorce, the parties, both of whom were represented by counsel, negotiated and executed a Property Settlement Agreement (Agreement). The trial court incorporated the Agreement in the final judgment of divorce, which expressly recited that the court had made no "findings as to the reasonableness thereof."

The Agreement is detailed and governs equitable distribution, spousal support, child custody, and child support. Paragraph 25 of the Agreement provides that any financial dispute arising out of the Agreement must be arbitrated as a condition precedent to court action; the arbitration must be conducted under the rules of the American Arbitration Association (AAA); and the arbitrator's decision is binding on the parties. Paragraph 20 permits modification of payments due to changed circumstances but, in the event of a dispute over the necessity for such modification, requires arbitration as a condition precedent to judicial relief.

The Agreement also contains several paragraphs dealing with the equitable distribution of the parties' assets. Under the terms of the Agreement, Roger transferred the marital home in Summit, New Jersey to Susan, who also retained all the tangible personal property in the home and a Jeep. Paragraph 7 required Roger, over a ten-year period, to pay Susan ten promissory notes totalling $165,000 as "an adjustment of accounts as part of the division in lieu of statutory equitable distribution of marital assets."[1] In the event of Roger's death, the notes were to

---

[1]   Paragraph 7 provides in part:

The parties shall make an adjustment of accounts as part of the division in lieu of statutory equitable distribution of marital assets by the payment by the husband to the wife of $165,000., payable as follows: by a series of ten non-interest bearing notes, due annually commencing on October 1, 1978, with privileges of prepaying without credit or penalty, which notes shall be considered to be in default 30 days after due date and thereafter bear 8% interest plus reasonable collection charges, *said notes to be treated as commercial obligations binding on the husband's estate as debts; neither his death nor any act* of the wife other than her death, shall limit or modify this obligation * * *. [Emphasis added.]

be treated as a debt of his estate. As security for the payment of the notes, Roger was required to furnish stock to be held in an escrow account and to secure a $100,000 term life insurance policy.

Paragraph 29 provides for adjustment of support under certain circumstances. Roger was a successful investment banker employed by his closely-held family corporation. The parties recognized that Roger's ability to meet his spousal-support obligations under the Agreement was contingent on his company's earnings. To avoid the possibly unjust consequences of requiring Roger to pay the full support required in the Agreement in years when his company did not make a profit, the parties in paragraph 29 provided:

> 29. (a) The parties to this Agreement recognize that the husband's obligation provided for in paragraph 2 may, under the circumstances that his employer, Faherty & Swartwood, Inc., may not have substantial pre-tax earnings, be difficult for him to perform.
> (b) Any arrearages which may develop in payment of the obligations provided for in paragraph 2 shall be *weighed* in connection with the amount of his fixed annual salary and the fiscal year-end pre-tax earnings of the said employer, since a distribution of said earnings or a loan on the basis of such earnings is expected to be the sole way in which the husband could meet the said obligations, or make up any arrearages which may accumulate thereunder.
> (c) Nothing in this paragraph shall be deemed to apply to, modify or limit any portion of this Agreement with the exception of the said paragraph 2. [Emphasis added.]

Further, the Agreement included the following clauses: a release by each party of all equitable division of marital assets and all community property interests except for those provided in the Agreement; an integration clause stating that the Agreement represented the parties' entire understanding and that "there are no representations, promises, warranties, covenants or undertakings other than those expressly set forth herein"; a default clause, whereby Roger agreed that if he should default in performing any obligation under the Agreement, he would pay to Susan counsel fees she reasonably incurred to enforce her rights under the Agreement; and a provision that the Agreement shall be governed by the laws of New Jersey.

The present case arose when Susan moved in the Chancery Division for an order fixing past-due alimony and child support and compelling discovery of defendant's business records. Susan claimed that Roger was in arrears of $25,400 in support payments and had defaulted on one of the equitable-distribution promissory notes of $25,000. Roger cross-moved, seeking to compel arbitration of the arrearages pursuant to paragraphs 20 and 25 and seeking arbitration as to the amounts of future payments because he claimed significantly changed circumstances. The Chancery Division issued an order compelling arbitration of arrearages of alimony and child support as well as the issue of modification of future payments of alimony and child support in accordance with the Agreement.

Subsequently, the parties selected an arbitrator according to the rules of the AAA. The issues submitted to arbitration were Susan's claims for arrearages in alimony and child support, for future alimony and child support, as well as Roger's claim that both the arrearages in alimony and child support and future payments thereof should be reduced due to his changed circumstances.

The arbitration took several months. It included several lengthy days of examination, cross-examinations, exchange of post-hearing and reply briefs, and, finally, the entry of the arbitrator's award on January 18, 1981. The arbitrator made no written findings of fact and neither of the parties requested a written transcript.

The arbitrator's award fixed the alimony arrearages of $37,648 and child support arrearages of $12,284. The award also denied Roger's requests for reduction in future alimony, if any, and future child support. Thereafter, Susan moved in the Chancery Division to confirm the arbitration award. Roger cross-moved to vacate the arbitrator's award and to obtain court hearings for modification of his prior and future payments due to his changed circumstances and for modification of his payments in lieu of equitable distribution.

The Chancery Division confirmed the arbitration award and denied Roger's motion. Although Roger had originally petitioned the court to compel arbitration, in his appeal to the Appellate Division, for the first time, he challenged the validity of the arbitration clause and also sought to overturn the Chancery Division's confirmation of the arbitration award. The Appellate Division, in a brief *per curiam* opinion, found that all issues of law raised by Roger were clearly without merit.

Roger makes two basic claims. The first is that arbitration of domestic disputes between former spouses regarding alimony and child support should not, as a matter of public policy, be permitted to be settled outside the courts, and therefore the arbitration clause in the Agreement should not be enforced. The second is that the arbitration award in this case was erroneous and should be overturned.

II

Although it is clear that marital separation agreements are enforceable in this state insofar as "they are just and equitable," *Schlemm v. Schlemm, 31 N.J. 557, 158 A.2d 508 (1960)*, this Court has never before addressed the question of the enforceability of an arbitration clause in a separation agreement.

In this state, as in most American jurisdictions, arbitration is a favored remedy. It permits parties to agree to resolve disputes outside of the court system. A court generally will enforce an arbitration agreement unless it violates public policy.

In recent years arbitration has been used more frequently as a viable means of resolving domestic disputes that arise under separation agreements. *See* Comment, "The Enforceability of Arbitration Clauses in North Carolina Separation Agreements," 15 *Wake Forest L. Rev.* 487 (1979). In other jurisdictions around the country courts have consistently enforced arbitration clauses to settle matrimonial disputes. * * *

This issue has been addressed in only one case in this state. *See* <u>Wertlake v. Wertlake, 127 N.J.Super. 595, 318 A.2d 446 (Ch.Div.1974)</u>, rev'd, <u>137 N.J.Super. 476, 349 A.2d 552 (App.Div.1975)</u>. Although the Chancery Division in *Wertlake* cited cases from several jurisdictions upholding arbitration of disputes over alimony and child support and cited no contrary precedent, it held that child support was a nonarbitrable issue because of the state's exclusive *parens patriae* relationship to children. The Appellate Division reversed, holding that the validity of the arbitration clause was not in controversy since the parties had submitted their dispute to the court and had not sought arbitration. Thus, the lower court's statement on arbitration was mere dicta. <u>Wertlake v. Wertlake, supra, 137 N.J.Super. at 490–91, 349 A.2d 552</u>. Therefore, today's decision is written on a clean slate.

III

Our arbitration statute, <u>N.J.S.A. 2A:24–1 to–11</u>, recognizes the validity of arbitration as a means of resolving contractual disputes between parties.[2] As discussed earlier in this opinion, New Jersey has long recognized the validity and enforceability of separation agreements between divorcing spouses. *See* <u>Schlemm, supra, 31 N.J. 557, 158 A.2d 508</u>. Enforcement of arbitration clauses pertaining to alimony as within such agreements is a logical extension of the view, expressed in *Schlemm,* that parties should be granted as much autonomy as possible in the ordering of their personal lives. Since parties may settle spousal support rights and obligations by contract, <u>Schlemm, supra, 31 N.J. at 581, 158 A.2d 508</u>, there is no policy reason to prohibit their submitting disputes arising out of such contracts to binding arbitration. It is fair and reasonable that parties who have agreed to be bound by arbitration in a formal, written separation agreement should be

---

[2] 2A:24–1. Arbitration provisions; validity and effect.

A provision in a written contract to settle by arbitration a controversy that may arise therefrom or a refusal to perform the whole or a part thereof or a written agreement to submit, pursuant to section 2A:24–2 of this title, any existing controversy to arbitration, whether the controversy arise out of contract or otherwise, shall be valid, enforceable and irrevocable, except upon such grounds as exist at law or in equity for the revocation of a contract.

so bound. Rather than frowning on arbitration of alimony disputes, public policy supports it. We recognize that in many cases arbitration of matrimonial disputes may offer an effective alternative method of dispute resolution. As commentators have noted, the advantages of arbitration of domestic disputes include reduced court congestion, the opportunity for resolution of sensitive matters in a private and informal forum, reduction of the trauma and anxiety of marital litigation, minimization of the intense polarization of parties that often occurs, and the ability to choose the arbitrator. In this sensitive and intensely private area of domestic disputes, arbitration expressly contracted for by the spouses is highly desirable. We accordingly hold today that under the laws of New Jersey, parties may bind themselves in separation agreements to arbitrate disputes over alimony. As is the case with other arbitration awards, an award determining spousal support would be subject to the review provided in <u>N.J.S.A. 2A:24–8</u>.

IV

Our inclination to embrace arbitration in all phases of matrimonial disputes is tempered, however, by our knowledge that in such cases competing public policy considerations abound. Accordingly, the principle issue involved here is whether public policy prohibits arbitration from resolving child support and custody disputes.

Although it is generally accepted that spouses may enter enforceable agreements to arbitrate alimony disputes, some commentators have suggested that arbitration is unsatisfactory to resolve disputes concerning child support or custody because of the court's traditional role as *parens patriae*. Traditionally, courts under the doctrine of *parens patriae* have been entrusted to protect the best interests of children. Children's maintenance, custody-visitation, and overall best interests have always been subject to the close scrutiny and supervision of the courts despite any agreements to the contrary. Some commentators see arbitration as a dangerous encroachment on this jurisdiction. *See* Holman & Noland, "Agreement and Arbitration: Relief to over-litigation in domestic relations disputes in Washington," 12 *Willamette L.J.* 527, 537 (1976). Since parents cannot by agreement deprive the courts of their duty to promote the best interests of their children, it is argued that they cannot do so by arbitration.

Detractors notwithstanding, there has been a growing tendency to recognize arbitration in child support clauses. We do not agree with those who fear that by allowing parents to agree to arbitrate child support, we are interfering with the judicial protection of the best interests of the child. We see no valid reason why the arbitration process should not be available in the area of child support; the advantages of arbitration in domestic disputes outweigh any disadvantages.

Nevertheless, we recognize that the courts have a nondelegable, special supervisory function in the area of child support that may be exercised upon review of an arbitrator's award. We therefore hold that whenever the validity of an arbitration award affecting child support is questioned on the grounds that it does not provide adequate protection for the child, the trial court should conduct a special review of the award. This review should consist of a two step analysis. First, as with all arbitration awards, the courts should review child support awards as provided by N.J.S.A. 2A:24–8.[3] Second, the courts should conduct a *de novo* review unless it is clear on the face of the award that the award could not adversely affect the substantial best interests of the child.

An arbitrator's award that grants all the requested child support would generally satisfy this second test because it is always in the child's best interest to have as much support as possible. Clearly such an award does not adversely affect the best interest of the child. In such cases, the spouse challenging the award would be limited to the statutory grounds for vacation or modification provided in N.J.S.A. 2A:24–8 because the state's interest in protecting the child has already been established. Thus, only an arbitrator's award that either reduced child support or refused a request for increased support could be subject to court review beyond the review provided by statute, because only such an award could adversely affect the interests of the child. However, even awards reducing support would be subject to court review only if they adversely affected the *substantial* best interests of the child. The substantial best interests of the child are not affected when the reduction in support or the denial of additional support is petty or frivolous, but only when it actually and materially affects the child's standard of living.

While several states have enforced agreements to arbitrate child support disputes, arbitration of custody and visitation issues has been deemed to be an unacceptable infringement of the court's *parens patriae* role. We do not reach the question of whether arbitration of child custody and visitation rights is enforceable since that issue is not before us. However, we note that the development of a fair and workable mediation or arbitration process to resolve these issues may be more beneficial to the children of this state than the present system of courtroom confrontation. *See* Schepard, Philbrick & Rabino, "Ground Rules for

---

[3] 2A:24–8. Vacation of award; rehearing.

The court shall vacate the award in any of the following cases:

a. Where the award was procured by corruption, fraud or undue means;

b. Where there was either evident partiality or corruption in the arbitrators, or any thereof;

c. Where the arbitrators were guilty of misconduct in refusing to postpone the hearing, upon sufficient cause being shown therefor, or in refusing to hear evidence, pertinent and material to the controversy, or of any other misbehaviors prejudicial to the rights of any party;

d. Where the arbitrators exceeded or so imperfectly executed their powers that a mutual, final and definite award upon the subject matter submitted was not made.

When an award is vacated and the time within which the agreement required the award to be made has not expired, the court may, in its discretion, direct a rehearing by the arbitrators.

Custody Mediation and Modification," 48 *Alb.L.Rev.* 616 (1984). Accordingly, the policy reasons for our holding today with respect to child support may be equally applicable to child custody and visitation cases.

As we gain experience in the arbitration of child support and custody disputes, it may become evident that a child's best interests are as well protected by an arbitrator as by a judge. If so, there would be no necessity for our *de novo* review. However, because of the Court's *parens patriae* tradition, at this time we prefer to err in favor of the child's best interest.

V

Finally, we must decide whether the arbitrator's award should be confirmed in the present case. *N.J.S.A.* 2A:24–1 to–11 grants arbitrators "extremely broad powers and extends judicial support to the arbitration process subject only to limited review." *Barcon Assocs., Inc. v. Tri-County Asphalt Corp., supra*, 86 *N.J.* at 187, 430 A.2d 214.

Before turning to the facts of the present case, we note that the arbitrator made no written findings of fact. The AAA rules do not require such findings, but because alimony and child support are always subject to modification for changed circumstances, we suggest, but do not mandate, that the arbitrator in all future domestic dispute arbitrations make reasonably detailed findings of fact upon which she or he bases the arbitration award. Such findings will aid not only the court's review of the award but also will aid later arbitrators in determining requests for modification. Certainly, such findings of fact should be prepared if requested by either of the parties.

With these admonitions in mind, we find that in this case, the arbitrator's award is not subject to heightened scrutiny to protect the interests of the children because the award enforced their rights and protected their interests against Roger's claim of changed circumstances. In this case the state's interest in the welfare of the children has been protected and there is no public policy reason to subject the award to *de novo* review.

Of the statutory grounds for vacation of an arbitration award, Roger relies on *N.J.S.A.* 2A:24–8d, which provides that an arbitration award may be vacated:

> d. Where the arbitrators exceeded or so imperfectly executed their powers that a mutual, final and definite award upon the subject matter submitted was not made.

Roger bases his claim on the contention that the arbitrator failed to weigh the evidence presented to him. Roger first claims that if the arbitrator had weighed the evidence of his income and his closely-held corporations' earnings, as required by paragraph 29(b) of the Agreement, he could not have made the award that he made. We have no record in this case and Roger has failed to provide any support for this contention. Next, Roger claims that the promissory notes, which, under the terms of the Agreement, were equitable distribution, were actually disguised alimony and as such should be subject to modification for changed circumstances. In the absence of any evidence to the contrary and in view of the language of the clause in issue, we hold that Roger failed to show that the arbitrator violated N.J.S.A. 2A:24–8d. Accordingly, there is no reason to vacate or modify the award on these grounds.

We are empowered to modify or correct arbitration awards in certain cases. N.J.S.A. 2A:24–9 allows us to correct errors when there was an evident miscalculation of figures or an evident mistake. Paragraph 29(d) of the Agreement provided that if Roger paid the November 1, 1977 real estate taxes on the family home in Summit, New Jersey, he would get a credit for that payment when any accumulated arrears were subsequently adjusted. It is undisputed that Roger paid $1,313.75 in real estate taxes and that the arbitrator failed to give him credit for that payment.

> **FYI**
>
> *Faherty* left open the question whether arbitration was permissible in child custody and visitation disputes, and the court later decided in Fawzy v. Fawzy, 973 A.2d 347 (N.J. 2009), that the right to family privacy and parental autonomy "subsumes the right to submit issues of child custody and parenting time to an arbitrator for disposition," with arbitral awards to be enforced by the courts unless there is a showing of adverse impact or harm to the child.

Further, under N.J.S.A. 2A:24–8(d), an award shall be vacated when the arbitrator exceeded his power. Since the parties agreed that the arbitrator would decide legal issues in accordance with the law of New Jersey, the award should not have granted Susan alimony in the future since she had remarried. Accordingly, that part of the award is vacated.

With the exception of correcting these two minor errors, we approve the arbitrator's award as having satisfied all of the statutory and public policy requirements for confirmation.

The judgment of the Appellate Division is modified and as modified affirmed.

———————

Points for Discussion

a. Arbitration Statutes

Almost every state has enacted either the 1956 Uniform Arbitration Act or the 2000 revised version. Uniform Arbitration Act (UAA), 7 U.L.A. (Part 1A) 1

(2009). Under either version of the UAA, the process requires first that the parties enter into an agreement to arbitrate. A court may decide matters such as whether an agreement to arbitrate exits, whether a particular controversy is subject to an agreement to arbitrate, and whether a contract containing an agreement to arbitrate is enforceable. Once the arbitrator makes an award, one of the parties may seek judicial confirmation. The court must confirm the arbitration award unless grounds are established to vacate, modify, or correct it, for example, if there is proof of fraud or corruption, if the arbitrators exceeded their powers or refused to hear material evidence; or if there was no arbitration agreement. Once a court order is entered confirming an award, it may be enforced in the same manner as any other judgment or decree.

A number of states have statutes or court rules that provide specifically for family law arbitration. See, e.g., Ind. Code § 34–57–5–1 et seq. (2018); Mich. Comp. L. § 600.5071 (2018); N.C. Gen Stat. § 50–41 et seq. (2018); and N.J. Sup. Ct. R. 5:1–5 (2018). The Uniform Family Law Arbitration Act, 9 U.L.A. (Part 1B) (Supp. 2018), approved in 2016, was designed to work in tandem with the UAA. It has been enacted in Arizona and Hawaii.

b. Arbitration Agreements and Court-Ordered Arbitration

The parties in *Faherty* agreed at the time of their divorce settlement to arbitrate any future financial disputes. A number of cases have upheld arbitration provisions included in premarital agreements. See, e.g., LaFrance v. Lodmell, 144 A.3d 373 (Conn. 2016); Kelm v. Kelm, 623 N.E.2d 39 (Ohio 1993). Should the judge in a divorce case be permitted to order binding arbitration when the parties fail to reach an agreement on some issue in a divorce case? See Gustin v. Gustin, 652 N.E.2d 610 (Mass. 1995), which allowed a judge to require the parties to submit a property division dispute to a court-appointed intermediary, who would then make a recommendation to the judge, but held that the judge could not delegate the duty to make an equitable division of property. See also Biel v. Biel, 336 N.W.2d 404 (Wis. Ct.App.1983), which struck a court's order directing mediation-arbitration of custody and visitation issues. Why would a court order parties to arbitrate a family law dispute?

c. Child Support and Custody Arbitration

As discussed in *Faherty*, courts traditionally have maintained jurisdiction over child support and custody issues in order to protect the best interests of children. How does the court balance the policies that favor arbitration with the courts' role as **parens patriae**? See also Masters v. Masters, 513 A.2d 104 (Conn. 1986) (enforcing agreement to submit child support disputes to arbitration).

Fawzy v. Fawzy, 973 A.2d 347 (N.J. 2009), approved arbitration of these issues, holding that a child custody arbitration award was subject to review only for the possibility of an adverse impact or harm to the child. Other courts have concluded that custody issues are not appropriate subjects for arbitration, see, e.g., <u>Kelm v. Kelm, 749 N.E.2d 299 (Ohio 2001)</u>, or hold that the courts retain more extensive authority to review custody arbitration awards, see, e.g., <u>Miller v. Miller, 620 A.2d 1161 (Pa. Super. Ct.1993)</u>.

Statutes in many states allow for arbitration of custody or child support, but extend courts greater responsibilities in reviewing these awards. E.g. <u>Mich. Comp. L. § 600.5080 (2018)</u>; <u>Wis. Stat. Ann. § 802.12(3) (2018)</u>. The Uniform Family Law Arbitration Act was drafted to include child-related disputes, with additional safeguards, but includes an opt-out provision for states that do not take this approach. See also Elizabeth A. Jenkins, <u>*Validity and Construction of Provisions for Arbitration of Disputes as to Alimony or Support Payments or Child Visitation or Custody Matters*, 38 A.L.R.5th 69 (1996)</u>.

Global View: Religious Arbitration in Family Law Disputes

Arbitration presents one distinct advantage for members of some cultural or religious groups: the opportunity to present their family disputes to a decision-maker who is familiar with their cultural or religious practices. For example, couples in Jewish communities may enter into arbitration agreements conferring authority on a rabbinic tribunal known as a *bet din,* and the tribunal's awards will usually be enforceable in the civil courts within the parameters of state arbitration laws. See, e.g., <u>Lang v. Levi, 16 A.3d 980 (Md. Ct. Spec. App. 2011)</u>.

Muslim tribunals may also enter arbitration awards in divorce disputes that are then presented to the secular courts for enforcement. Although this takes place routinely in a number of countries, including Great Britain, the prospect of "Sharia arbitration" became highly controversial in Ontario in 2003, and the Ontario legislature eventually amended its Arbitration Act to require that all arbitration must be based on the law of Ontario or another Canadian jurisdiction. See Natasha Bakht, *Religious Arbitration in Canada: Protecting Women by Protecting Them from Religion*, 19 Canadian J. Women & L. 119 (2007).

Divorce Procedures and Consequences

Divorce actions developed from a mixture of equity, statutory law, and some remnants of ecclesiastical law, and are generally governed by the same procedural rules as other civil actions. Normally the spouses are the only parties to the divorce action. Although children of a marriage are generally not parties to the divorce action, many states authorize the appointment of an attorney or other representative for the child. These issues are considered in Chapter 7 and Chapter 8. As ordinary civil proceedings, divorce actions are subject to the usual civil discovery rules, which allow each spouse an opportunity to determine whether there is property to be divided, what that property is, what its value may be, and whether it is marital or separate.

To preserve the status quo during divorce litigation, the courts frequently enter preliminary injunctions forbidding transfers of property and restraining the parties from harassing each other or removing any children from the jurisdiction without the consent of the other parent. In some states, these orders take effect automatically upon the filing of a petition for divorce or legal separation followed by personal service on the respondent. E.g., Colo. Rev. Stat. § 14–10–107(4)(b) (2018). Either spouse may apply to the court for temporary orders addressing matters such as parenting time, child support, spousal support, or rights to use or have access to property such as the marital home while divorce proceedings are pending.

Even when the parties have reached a settlement agreement, most states require that they make a court appearance to finalize their divorce. States may allow divorce by affidavit or summary judgment without a personal appearance in some circumstances. See, e.g., Colo. Rev. Stat. § 14–10–120.3 (2018); Minn. Stat. Ann. § 518.195(1) (2018); Mont. Code Ann. § 40–4–130 (2018). If the parties have not agreed to a settlement, the issues are usually tried to the court, although some states provide for jury trials in divorce actions. See generally Jeffrey F. Ghent, *Right to Jury Trial in State Court Divorce Proceedings*, 56 A.L.R.4th 955 (1987).

After a court makes permanent orders or accepts the parties' settlement agreement and issues a divorce decree, it becomes a final judgment that may be enforced with all of the remedies available for enforcement of civil judgments. A divorce decree is not subject to modification, except for particular issues such as child support and parenting time that remain subject to modification based on changes in circumstances (by statute or according to the parties' agreement).

A final divorce decree terminates the marriage of the parties, and may have other consequences, such as terminating wills or insurance policies in which one spouse names the other as a beneficiary, or terminating spousal joint tenancies in land. State statutes have taken different approaches to this question. See generally

Uniform Probate Code § 2–804, 8 U.L.A. (Part III) 330 (2013). In 2018, the Supreme Court upheld Minnesota's retroactive application of a statute that automatically revoked the designation of the insured's former spouse as beneficiary of his life insurance policy. Sveen v. Melin, 584 U.S. ___, 138 S.Ct. 1815 (2018).

As noted earlier in this chapter, the rules are especially complex with respect to beneficiary designations in pension plans governed by the federal Employee Retirement Income Security Act (ERISA). The Supreme Court has held several times that ERISA preempts inconsistent provisions of state law; see also Hillman v. Maretta, 569 U.S. 483 (2013) (holding that state law is preempted by Federal Employees' Group Life Insurance Act).

These are typically default rules, and parties may reach a different agreement if they wish to continue insurance coverage or leave a bequest to a former spouse. There are many traps for the unwary, however, and couples should consider their situation carefully. Note that in some states, courts are required to ask or notify parties at the time of their divorce about the need to update beneficiary designations. See, e.g., Utah Code § 30–3–5(e) (2018).

Sahin v. Sahin

758 N.E.2d 132 (Mass. 2001)

SPINA, J.

Selcuk T. Sahin (wife) filed a complaint against Kenan E. Sahin (husband) seeking relief from a prior divorce judgment by means of an independent equity action and pursuant to Mass. R. Civ. P. 60(b)(6), 365 Mass. 828 (1974). She alleged that fraud perpetrated by the husband had resulted in a divorce judgment that was manifestly unconscionable. A Probate and Family Court judge granted the husband's motion for summary judgment and dismissed the wife's complaint. We granted the wife's application for direct appellate review and now affirm the judgment of the Probate and Family Court.

1. *Background.* In the underlying action, the wife filed for divorce from the husband on June 30, 1994, following twenty-eight years of marriage. The central issue at trial was the value of the husband's business, Kenan Systems Corporation (KSC), a computer company founded in 1982 that developed billing software used primarily by telecommunications companies. Expert testimony was presented by each party, including a balance sheet showing actual revenue for the period January 1, 1995–June 30, 1995, and projected revenue for the period July

1, 1995–December 31, 1995 (1995 spreadsheet).[1] Based on all of the information that was presented, the judge concluded that the fair market value of the husband's interest in KSC was $4,912,717. Because the wife sought a specific cash payment, rather than a percentage of stock ownership in KSC, the judge awarded the husband 100% of the outstanding shares in KSC but ordered him to pay the wife 30% of KSC's established value, or $1,473,815, in annual instalments [sic] over five years. A judgment for divorce nisi was issued on February 22, 1996. The judgment became absolute on May 23, 1996.

In January, 1999, nearly three years after issuance of the divorce judgment, Lucent Technologies, Inc. (Lucent), announced that it was acquiring KSC in exchange for 12.88 million shares of Lucent, then valued at $1.48 billion. The sale was completed by March 1, 1999, and KSC became a wholly owned subsidiary of Lucent.

In light of the explosion in value of KSC and, consequently, in the husband's wealth, the wife filed with the Probate and Family Court a complaint seeking relief from the prior divorce judgment by means of an independent equity action and pursuant to rule 60(b)(6). She asserted that there were compelling and exceptional circumstances necessitating review of the division of property between the parties, particularly the huge disparity between the $4.9 million valuation of KSC in 1996 and its $1.48 billion sale price in 1999. The wife alleged that the gross discrepancy between the estimated fair market value of KSC in 1996 and its established fair market value in 1999 could not be explained by any market condition, by the economy, or by any internal changes in the company, including its product line or marketing strategy. Rather, it was the wife's contention that this discrepancy was directly attributable to the husband's misrepresentations and omissions during the divorce proceedings of material facts pertaining to KSC's financial outlook, which constituted fraud and denied the wife her day in court.[5]

---

[1]   A Probate and Family Court judge had ordered that all discovery be completed by July 27, 1995. Both the wife's expert and the husband's expert valued Kenan Systems Corporation (KSC) as of June 30, 1995.

[5]   The wife alleged the following misrepresentations and omissions by the husband: (1) in July, 1993, the husband had reported at a meeting that KSC's business plan predicted 1996 revenues of $65–90 million and 1999 revenues of $130–245 million; (2) as early as 1994, the husband had received offers from Dunn & Bradstreet, Sema Group, and IBM to purchase KSC (or its products) for amounts in excess of $4.2 million; (3) in contrast to the husband's testimony at the divorce trial that KSC's future was risky and pessimistic, he testified in later unrelated litigation that, even as early as 1994, KSC was well positioned for success; (4) the financial projections in the 1995 spreadsheet had been prepared on a worst case scenario basis, the spreadsheet did not include any information about contracts signed after June 30, 1995, and it did not include any revenue from the United States Postal Service from October, 1995, through December, 1995; (5) the 1995 spreadsheet understated revenues from several known contracts signed before June 30, 1995, by $2.7 million; (6) the 1995 spreadsheet did not disclose three software licensing agreements signed by the husband between August, 1995, and October, 1995, for total fees in excess of $9.3 million; and (7) KSC signed several new licensing agreements in early 1996, including one with France Telecom that had a value of $10.5 million.

Following the completion of discovery, the husband filed a motion for summary judgment on the grounds that there were no genuine issues of material fact, that the wife's bases for asserting fraud were insufficient as a matter of law, and that her claims were time barred. The judge first concluded that, viewing all of the evidence in the light most favorable to the wife, there was no evidence that she had been defrauded by the husband. Furthermore, even if she had been able to present evidence of fraud by the husband, there was no exception in rule 60(b) that would allow the judge to grant the wife relief more than one year after entry of the divorce judgment. Accordingly, the Probate and Family Court entered a judgment of dismissal on June 6, 2000.

The wife now argues that the judge erred in concluding that there was no avenue by which she was entitled to relief from the prior divorce judgment more than one year after the entry of such judgment. She contends that she should have been afforded relief pursuant to (1) an independent equity action under rule 60(b); (2) an action to set aside the judgment for "fraud [on] the court"; and (3) a claim under rule 60(b)(6). The wife asserts that her evidence demonstrated that the fair market value of KSC at the time of the divorce was corrupted by the husband's fraudulent scheme to misrepresent and omit significant facts that impeded her ability to obtain an accurate valuation of the company. As such, the husband's motion for summary judgment should have been denied.

2. *Independent equity action.* Rule 60 sets forth a comprehensive framework for obtaining relief from a final judgment or order, balancing the competing needs for finality and flexibility to be certain that justice is done in light of all the facts. Rule 60(b) provides, in pertinent part, as follows:

> "On motion and upon such terms as are just, the court may relieve a party or his legal representative from a final judgment, order, or proceeding for the following reasons: (1) mistake, inadvertence, surprise, or excusable neglect; (2) newly discovered evidence which by due diligence could not have been discovered in time to move for a new trial under Rule 59(b); (3) fraud (whether heretofore denominated intrinsic or extrinsic), misrepresentation, or other misconduct of an adverse party. . .or (6) any other reason justifying relief from the operation of the judgment. The motion shall be made within a reasonable time, and for reasons (1), (2), and (3) not more than one year after the judgment, order or proceeding was entered or taken. . . . This rule does not limit the power of a court to entertain an independent action to relieve a party from a judgment, order, or proceeding, or to set aside a judgment for fraud upon the court."

The wife would not have been able to prevail on a motion for relief from judgment pursuant to rule 60(b)(2) or (3) because her complaint was filed more than one year after the final judgment in the divorce proceeding was entered. Unlike actions brought pursuant to subsections (b)(1), (2), and (3), which are subject to the one-year time limitation, there is no specified time limitation for bringing an independent action for relief from judgment. Mass. R. Civ. P. 60(b). That said, however, "a party should not be able to avoid the one-year or 'reasonable time' limits of Rule 60(b) simply by commencing an independent action seeking the same relief." J.W. Smith & H.B. Zobel, Rules Practice § 60.16, at 488 (1977 & Supp.2001). See United States v. Beggerly, 524 U.S. 38, 46, 118 S.Ct. 1862, 141 L.Ed.2d 32 (1998) ("If relief may be obtained through an independent action in a case such as this, where the most that may be charged. . .is a failure to furnish relevant information that would at best form the basis for a [r]ule 60 [b] [3] motion, the strict 1-year time limit on such motions would be set at naught"). To the extent that the claims raised by a party's independent action appear to fall within those provisions of rule 60(b) that mandate a specific time limitation, but that materialized too late to file in a motion to the court which rendered the judgment, the party must raise some additional ground or reason justifying relief after the expiration of the time limitation.

Rule 60(b) does not identify the bases for an independent action. This substantive determination is made by recourse to "judicial principles governing untimely requests for equitable relief from fraudulent judgments" that existed prior to the adoption of rule 60(b). Historically, relief from a valid and final judgment required more than a showing of common-law fraud.

Cases addressing the scope of fraud necessary to support an independent action under the current version of rule 60(b) have continued to follow this principle. See United States v. Beggerly, supra at 46–47, 118 S.Ct. 1862 (independent actions reserved for those cases where relief from final judgment necessary to prevent a grave miscarriage of justice).

The wife has not presented any evidence to demonstrate that equity mandates granting her relief from the divorce judgment. The 1993 business plan setting forth projected revenues for 1996 and 1999 was not a statement of facts but merely of financial estimates. See Rodowicz v. Massachusetts Mut. Life Ins. Co., 192 F.3d 162, 175–176 (1st Cir.1999) (statements of opinion or belief as to business operations, made without certainty, do not rise to level of statements of fact and do not constitute fraudulent misrepresentations). Moreover, during the divorce proceedings, the wife never deposed the KSC employee who prepared the business plan. The wife also never deposed the two KSC employees on whose testimony she now relies to support her allegation that the husband received offers to invest in or purchase KSC as early as 1994. As to the purported "offer" by Dunn & Bradstreet, the wife was on notice of it pursuant to documents she received from State Street Bank during discovery. The husband's statements in 1995 as to KSC's financial future, whether optimistic or pessimistic, were also opinions, not facts.

To the extent that the 1995 spreadsheet understated or omitted potential streams of revenue, it was clear that the financial information for the time period from July 1, 1995, through December 31, 1995, constituted projected estimates. The wife admits that, during the divorce proceedings, she never deposed the former KSC controller, who prepared the 1995 spreadsheet, to ascertain how it was assembled and what potential revenues were not included. Moreover, the wife's expert prepared his own analysis of the fair market value of KSC and did not indicate that he relied on the 1995 spreadsheet as a source of information for his report.

With respect to the wife's claim that the husband failed to disclose the existence of three licensing agreements entered into during the fall of 1995, as described in her request for production of documents, we note that the husband objected to the request on the basis of confidentiality. The husband asserted that he was prohibited from disclosing this information absent a court order or the permission of the customers. There is no evidence that the wife sought either a court order or permission from the customers, notwithstanding the fact that the husband made KSC's customer lists available to the wife.

The husband admits that he did not disclose to the wife the existence of several new licensing agreements that were signed during 1996 on the ground that he had no duty to produce such documents after the divorce trial was over. He also contends that he was never asked to speculate about any potential future contracts. "A division of marital assets anticipates a final and equitable distribution of the property owned by the parties at the time of the divorce, and it is from those assets only that a judge can make her division. . . . Thus, in making a division of assets the judge [is] limited, for better or worse, to the property owned by the parties at the time of the divorce." Heins v. Ledis, 422 Mass. 477, 483–484, 664 N.E.2d 10 (1996). See Baccanti v. Morton, 434 Mass. 787, 794–796, 752 N.E.2d 718 (2001) (spouse's existing stock options, although uncertain in value and not yet vested, considered assets that may be included when dividing marital estate). The new licensing agreements at issue herein were not entered into until 1996, and there was no indication that negotiations had been manipulated to postpone the execution of such agreements until after the divorce trial was over. The licensing agreements did not become existing assets of KSC for valuation purposes until 1996. Therefore, they would not be included in the determination of the appropriate division of property.[10]

Based on our review of the record, we conclude that the husband's alleged fraud in misrepresenting and failing to disclose significant financial information about KSC during the divorce proceedings, and the wife's "newly discovered" evidence of such fraud, do not justify granting the wife equitable relief from the divorce judgment under rule 60(b). She has failed to present any evidence demonstrating that enforcement of the judgment would be manifestly unconscionable. Much of the evidence that the wife contends was imperative to an accurate valuation of KSC was, in fact, available to her during the earlier proceedings. While the wife's experts in the present equity action were prepared to testify that the husband's financial misrepresentations and omissions had a significant and material impact on the valuation of KSC, those experts have not suggested that they could have predicted that KSC would explode in value and be worth $1.48 billion by 1999, particularly in light of the major fluctuations in the fortunes of computer companies. The husband did not conceal a marital asset from the wife—KSC was known, valued (albeit imperfectly), and divided. As such, the wife was afforded her day in court. We recognize that there may be instances when allowing a particular judgment to stand would be so contrary to principles of equity as to tip what would otherwise be ordinary fraud into the special category that can invoke a court's inherent power to breach finality. The wife has not presented evidence that this is such a case.

3. *Fraud on the court*. The wife's claim that she is entitled to relief from the divorce judgment because the husband's alleged misrepresentations and omissions constituted "fraud upon the court" under rule 60(b) is equally unavailing. Even if the wife's allegations were true, the husband's conduct did not amount to fraud on the court.

There is no time limitation that would bar a judge from setting aside a judgment for fraud upon the court. See Mass. R. Civ. P. 60(b). "A 'fraud on the court' occurs where 'it can be demonstrated, clearly and convincingly, that a party has sentiently set in motion some unconscionable scheme calculated to interfere with the judicial system's ability impartially to adjudicate a matter by improperly influencing the trier or unfairly hampering the presentation of the opposing

---

[10] In reliance on G.L. c. 208, § 34, the wife asserts that the division of property between former spouses can be examined at any time after the divorce for fairness and reasonableness. Her argument is without merit. "Property settlements are designed largely to effectuate a final and complete settlement of obligations between the divorcing spouses. While alimony is modifiable on the showing of a material change in circumstances. . .property settlements are not." *Heins v. Ledis*, 422 Mass. 477, 483, 664 N.E.2d 10 (1996). See *Drapek v. Drapek*, 399 Mass. 240, 244, 503 N.E.2d 946 (1987). Contrast *Brash v. Brash*, 407 Mass. 101, 102–105, 551 N.E.2d 523 (1990) (complaint for division of marital assets could be heard ten years after entry of judgment of divorce nisi where such judgment did not include division of marital assets).

party's claim or defense.' " <u>Paternity of Cheryl, 434 Mass. 23, 35, 746 N.E.2d 488 (2001)</u>, quoting <u>Rockdale Mgt. Co. v. Shawmut Bank, N.A., 418 Mass. 596, 598, 638 N.E.2d 29 (1994)</u>. The doctrine embraces "only that species of fraud which does, or attempts to, defile the court itself, or is a fraud perpetrated by officers of the court so that the judicial machinery can not perform in the usual manner its impartial task of adjudging cases that are presented for adjudication." <u>Pina v. McGill Dev. Corp., 388 Mass. 159, 165, 445 N.E.2d 1059 (1983)</u>, quoting <u>Lockwood v. Bowles, 46 F.R.D. 625, 631 (D.D.C.1969)</u>. "A party seeking to demonstrate fraud on the court must prove 'the most egregious conduct involving a corruption of the judicial process itself. Examples are bribery of judges, employment of counsel to 'influence' the court, bribery of the jury, and the involvement of an attorney (an officer of the court) in the perpetration of fraud.'"[11] Conduct such as nondisclosure to the adverse party or the court of facts pertinent to the matter before it, without more, does not constitute fraud on the court for purposes of setting aside a judgment under rule 60(b).

4. *Relief under <u>Mass. R. Civ. P. 60(b)(6)</u>*. We next consider the wife's argument that she was entitled to relief from the divorce judgment pursuant to <u>Mass. R. Civ. P. 60(b)(6)</u>, the catchall provision of that rule. "In essence, rule 60(b)(6) vests 'power in courts adequate to enable them to vacate judgments whenever such action is appropriate to accomplish justice.' " <u>Parrell v. Keenan, 389 Mass. 809, 815, 452 N.E.2d 506 (1983)</u>, quoting <u>Klapprott v. United States, 335 U.S. 601, 615, 69 S.Ct. 384, 93 L.Ed. 1099 (1949)</u>. In the interest of finality of judgments, relief under rule 60(b)(6) is only to be granted in extraordinary circumstances. Moreover, relief under rule 60(b)(6) is only appropriate when justified by some reason other than those set forth in rule 60(b)(1)–(5). "In other words, to prevail under rule 60(b)(6), a party must show that there is a reason to justify the relief, and also that the reason is not within the grounds set forth in rule 60(b)(1)–(5)." Parrell v. Keenan, supra at 814–815, <u>452 N.E.2d 506</u>. The wife's proffered reasons for relief—the husband's alleged fraud in misrepresenting and failing to disclose significant financial information about KSC and her "newly discovered" evidence of such fraud—clearly fall within subsections (2) and (3) of rule 60(b). Because the wife's arguments are not requests for relief independent of subsections (b)(1)–(5), she may not seek relief under rule 60(b)(6).

Judgment affirmed.

———————

---

[11]   The wife has not presented any evidence that the husband's attorneys were involved in the perpetration of any alleged fraud on the court.

Points for Discussion

a. Reopening Divorce Judgments

Most jurisdictions have rules, often based on Rule 60(b) of the Federal Rules of Civil Procedure, providing for relief from a judgment or order on grounds including mistake, inadvertence, surprise or excusable neglect; fraud, and other misconduct of an adverse party. As noted in *Sahin*, a motion for 60(b) relief on these grounds must be made within a reasonable time after the judgment is entered and often within a specific time limit, such as six months or one year. For an example of a successful challenge, see <u>Weinstein v. Weinstein, 882 A.2d 53 (Conn. 2005)</u> in which the courts reopened a divorce judgment based on allegations that the husband had failed to disclose an offer to purchase his share of a company, which husband had valued at $40,000, for $2.5 million. California has enacted a statute extending the time limits and expanding the grounds for setting aside divorce judgments. See, e.g., <u>Cal. Fam. Code § 2120</u> et seq. (2018), applied in <u>Marriage of Brewer, 113 Cal.Rptr.2d 849 (Ct. App. 2001)</u> (setting aside agreement and judgment based on mutual mistake as to value of community property assets).

The remedy invoked in *Sahin* was an independent suit in equity to obtain relief from the judgment. By its terms, Rule 60(b) does not limit the court's power to entertain this type of action. As the court notes, however, this type of action requires proof of relatively more serious defects with the process. Traditionally, courts have held that this relief is available only in cases of extrinsic fraud, in which the plaintiff was deprived of the opportunity to present his or her case fully in a fair adversary hearing. E.g. <u>Jorgensen v. Jorgensen, 193 P.2d 728 (Cal. 1948)</u>. Although the distinction between extrinsic and intrinsic fraud has been criticized, it is still sometimes applied in the case law. See, e.g., <u>Marriage of Gance, 36 P.3d 114 (Colo.Ct.App.2001)</u>.

b. Tort Claims

Courts have sometimes allowed plaintiffs to proceed with tort actions for damages rather than a suit to set aside the decree. See, e.g. <u>Worton v. Worton, 286 Cal.Rptr. 410 (Ct. App. 1991)</u>; <u>Hess v. Hess, 580 A.2d 357 (Pa. Super. Ct. 1990)</u>. In <u>d'Elia v. d'Elia, 68 Cal.Rptr.2d 324 (Ct. App. 1997)</u>, the California Court of Appeal affirmed a $3.9 million damages award against an ex-husband on common law claims of intentional and negligent misrepresentation and breach of fiduciary duty in connection with a divorce settlement agreement, but reversed a judgment for even larger damages premised on violations of state securities laws, concluding that securities laws do not apply to the division of community property in a divorce case.

Courts have also considered whether claims regarding fraud committed during divorce proceedings fall within the federal Racketeer Influenced and Corrupt Organizations Act (RICO), 18 U.S.C. § 1961 et seq. (2018). See, e.g., Grimmett v. Brown, 75 F.3d 506 (9th Cir.1996); DeMauro v. DeMauro, 115 F.3d 94 (1st Cir.1997).

This is an area in which lawyers for all parties in a divorce proceeding should be extremely careful. In Rucker v. Schmidt, 794 N.W.2d 114 (Minn. 2011), after an ex-wife recovered more than $4 million in damages from her former husband for fraudulent misrepresentation concerning the value of his business interests, she was permitted to bring another action against his lawyer for fraud and aiding and abetting under a statute that allows claims for treble damages against lawyers who engage in deceit or collusion. The court declined to treat the lawyer and client as having sufficient privity of interest to trigger res judicata. Not all jurisdictions take this approach to the privity question, however. See, e.g., Chaara v. Lander, 45 P.3d 895 (N.M. Ct. App. 2002).

c. Discovery and Due Diligence

The opinion in *Sahin* points out that the wife (and her lawyer) never took a number of steps in discovery, such as depositions of certain key witnesses, that might have allowed her to obtain a more accurate valuation of the company. How did that affect the outcome of her action to set aside the divorce decree? Does she have any other avenues of relief available after the courts reject her attempt to reopen the judgment?

In cases of an attorney's mistake, inadvertence, or neglect in representing a client, the client's usual remedy is a malpractice claim. Depending on the circumstances and the timing, the client may be able to have the judgment reopened under Rule 60(b)(1) or 60(b)(6) based on the attorney's misconduct. See, e.g., Marriage of Orcutt, 253 P.3d 884 (Mont. 2011). The client must also act with due diligence, however. In Marriage of Goldsmith, 962 N.E.2d 517 (Ill. App. Ct. 2011), the court emphasized that when a spouse waives the right to conduct formal discovery and accepts a representation that the other party has made a full disclosure, the spouse "does so at his or her peril." A divorce judgment was reopened in Marriage of Hunt, 353 P.3d 911 (Colo. Ct. App. 2015), where the husband violated rules imposing affirmative disclosure obligations on parties in domestic relations cases.

Problem 6-26

When Debra and Paul divorced after three years of marriage, they signed a separation agreement in which Paul received all of the stock in his business, known as AFI, and the marital residence. Debra received $350,000 and a Nissan Pathfinder. Paul told Debra during their negotiations that AFI was worth $6 million, approximately the same amount as its value when they were married. Four months after the divorce, Debra read in the newspaper that Paul had sold AFI for $30 million. Evidently, Paul had been negotiating the sale for most of the past year. The same law firm represented Paul in the divorce and the sale of his company. What advice would you give her in these circumstances?

Problem 6-27

Denise found out that a group of coworkers had won the lottery, and intended to give her twenty percent of the $6 million jackpot. She filed for divorce before claiming her share, and arranged for the checks and paperwork to be sent to her at her mother's address. Denise did not tell her husband, Thomas, about the winnings, and did not list them either as community or separate property on her financial disclosure forms. Denise and Thomas entered into a settlement agreement that was approved by the court. Two years later, when Thomas learned of the lottery prize, he filed a motion to set aside the divorce decree. Does he have a claim against Denise? (See <u>Marriage of Rossi, 108 Cal.Rptr.2d 270 (Ct. App. 2001)</u>.)

Problem 6-28

When Rebecca and Wesley divorced, they signed an agreement providing that Wesley would keep his tool and die company, worth $6 million, and that he would pay Rebecca $230,000 a year in spousal support which they labeled as "non-modifiable and not subject to judicial review." The court entered a divorce decree based on their agreement. After the divorce, Wesley ceded day-to-day operation of the company to his son from a prior marriage, who committed serious financial improprieties and bankrupted the company within two years. Can Wesley have the judgment reopened or the agreement set aside? (See <u>Rose v. Rose, 795 N.W.2d 611 (Mich. Ct. App. 2010)</u>.)

CHAPTER 7

Parental Responsibilities

Whether married or unmarried, all parents share significant moral and legal responsibility for their children. Once parentage is established, this includes the obligation to provide financial support, and these duties are now enforced thorough a complex administrative and judicial process involving both the state and federal governments. Although parents have a broad right to determine their children's upbringing, this principle does not provide a basis for resolving disputes between parents over major decisions concerning their child's welfare. When parents disagree, courts may be called upon to assign rights and responsibilities between parents based on the best interests of the child. In some cases, third parties with no legal status as parents may also seek a share of this responsibility. This chapter explores the law's approach to both domains of parental responsibility: child support, and the allocation of authority to make decisions and provide residential care for children.

A. Child Support

Go Online

For detailed information on state child support laws and policies, see the web sites of the <u>National Conference of State Legislators</u> and the <u>Office of Child Support Enforcement</u> in the in the U.S. Department of Health and Human Services.

Child support law in the United States has become a cooperative project of the state and federal government, structured and funded under Title IV-D of the Social Security Act. Working within this program, every state has adopted the <u>Uniform Interstate Family Support Act (UIFSA)</u>, designed to facilitate the process of collecting support across state boundaries. Every state has adopted child support guidelines that use a numeric formula to establish a presumptive support award, and all states have implemented a variety of child support enforcement techniques, including such measures as suspending professional and driver's licenses of delinquent support obligors.

1. Establishing Jurisdiction

With our highly mobile population and more than fifty different jurisdictions, each one with distinct child support laws, the first problem in a child support case is often determining where the action should begin. As a matter of constitutional due process, courts must have personal jurisdiction over a potential obligor to enter a support order. See Kulko v. Superior Court, 436 U.S. 84 (1978), reprinted in Chapter 6. This requirement generates significant complications in the many cases in which the child in need of support does not reside in the same state where the obligor is located.

Parker v. Alaska Department of Revenue

960 P.2d 586 (Alaska 1998)

PER CURIAM.

Steve Parker, a resident of California, challenges the superior court's jurisdiction in an action seeking a judgment of paternity and child support. Parker was stationed in Ketchikan in 1978 while a member of the United States Coast Guard. During this time, he engaged in sexual intercourse with an Alaska resident. This contact resulted in the conception of a child, also an Alaska resident, for whom the State seeks the decree in this case. We hold that the trial court properly exercised personal jurisdiction over Parker.

Under the catch-all provision of our "long-arm" statute, AS 09.05.015(c), personal jurisdiction may be exercised to the extent permitted by the due process clause of the Fourteenth Amendment to the United States Constitution. *See Alaska Telecom, Inc. v. Schafer*, 888 P.2d 1296, 1299 (Alaska 1995). For the exercise of personal jurisdiction over a nonresident defendant to be constitutional, the defendant must have sufficient "minimum contacts" with the forum state so that maintaining a suit in the forum state "does not offend 'traditional notions of fair play and substantial justice.' " *International Shoe Co. v. Washington*, 326 U.S. 310, 316, 66 S.Ct. 154, 90 L.Ed. 95 (1945) (quoting *Milliken v. Meyer*, 311 U.S. 457, 463, 61 S.Ct. 339, 85 L.Ed. 278 (1940)).

Jurisdiction is permissible over a nonresident defendant where his contacts with the forum are such that he could reasonably anticipate being haled into court in the forum state. See *Burger King Corp. v. Rudzewicz*, 471 U.S. 462, 474, 105 S.Ct. 2174, 85 L.Ed.2d 528 (1985).

"The unilateral activity of those who claim some relationship with a non-resident defendant cannot satisfy the requirement of contact with the forum State. . . . [I]t is essential in each case that there be some act by which the defendant purposefully avails [him]self of the privilege of conducting activities within the forum State. . . ."

Puhlman v. Turner, 874 P.2d 291, 293 (Alaska 1994) (quoting *Hanson v. Denckla*, 357 U.S. 235, 253, 78 S.Ct. 1228, 2 L.Ed.2d 1283 (1958)). A nonresident defendant must have fair warning that his activities may foreseeably subject him to jurisdiction in Alaska.

If the defendant's activities in the forum state are "continuous and systematic," the forum may assert "general jurisdiction" over the defendant, and the cause of action need not arise out of the contacts with the forum state. However, where the cause of action arises out of the contacts with the forum state, the court may have "specific jurisdiction," even where the defendant has only one contact with the forum state.

This case involves specific jurisdiction; the paternity action arises directly out of Parker's conduct in the state. In cases involving specific jurisdiction, "if the defendant has 'purposefully directed' his activities at residents of the forum, and the litigation results from alleged injuries 'that arise out of or relate to' those activities," he should reasonably anticipate being haled into court in that forum. Specific jurisdiction "is justified on the basis of the relationship among the defendant, the forum, and the litigation." *Glover v. Western Air Lines, Inc.*, 745 P.2d 1365, 1367 (Alaska 1987) (citing *Helicopteros Nacionales de Colombia v. Hall*, 466 U.S. 408, 414 & n. 8, 104 S.Ct. 1868, 80 L.Ed.2d 404 (1984)).

Parker purposefully directed his activities at the mother of his child, resulting in the child's birth. A person engaging in sexual intercourse with a resident of Alaska while in Alaska should foresee the possibility that a child might be born and that a paternity and support action might be brought. A number of authorities support this view. *See, e.g., Bell v. Arnold*, 248 Ga. 9, 279 S.E.2d 449, 450 (1981); *People ex rel. Black v. Neby*, 265 Ill.App.3d 203, 202 Ill.Dec. 630, 638 N.E.2d 276, 277 (1994); *Larsen v. Scholl*, 296 N.W.2d 785, 790 (Iowa 1980); *Jones v. Chandler*, 592 So.2d 966, 972 (Miss.1991); *State, Dep't of Soc. Servs. v. Cummings*, 2 Neb. App. 820, 515 N.W.2d 680, 684 (1994). We therefore conclude that Parker had sufficient minimum contacts with Alaska.

Once minimum contacts are established, we must then decide whether the exercise of personal jurisdiction comports with traditional notions of fair play and substantial justice. Because Parker purposefully directed his activities at an Alaskan resident, he must demonstrate "compelling circumstances which render Alaska's exercise of jurisdiction. . .so unreasonable as to constitute a denial of due process." However, Parker failed to demonstrate or argue any compelling interest against the exercise of personal jurisdiction both in the trial court and on appeal.[3]

We reject all of Parker's other arguments because they are dependent on his incorrect assertion that insufficient minimum contacts exist in this case. The judgment is AFFIRMED.

Points for Discussion

a. Personal Jurisdiction

The U.S. Supreme Court established constitutional parameters for personal jurisdiction over nonresident defendants in child support cases in Kulko v. Superior Court of California In and For City and County of San Francisco, 436 U.S. 84 (1978), reproduced in Chapter 6, and Burnham v. Superior Court, 495 U.S. 604 (1990). As the court notes in *Parker*, other state courts have also concluded that sexual intercourse within the state is a sufficient basis for specific jurisdiction over parentage and support claims concerning a child who may have been born as a result. State courts applying the minimum contacts test in *Kulko* have concluded that other relatively minor connections between a parent and a state are not a sufficient basis for jurisdiction, however. See, e.g., Beale v. Haire, 812 So.2d 356 (Ala.Ct.Civ.App.2001); In re the Marriage of Crew, 549 N.W.2d 527 (Iowa 1996); Katz v. Katz, 707 A.2d 1353 (N.J. Super. Ct. 1998). In many cases, therefore, the courts in the state where a child lives will not be able to assert jurisdiction over child support claims against the child's non-resident parent.

b. Uniform Interstate Family Support Act (UIFSA)

Jurisdiction in child support cases is governed by the Uniform Interstate Family Support Act (UIFSA), 9 U.L.A. (Part 1B) (Supp. 2018) (as amended in 2008), which has been adopted in every state. Important provisions of UIFSA are reprinted in the Appendix. In addition to interstate cases, UIFSA applies to cross-border child support proceedings involving Indian tribes, the District of Columbia, Puerto Rico, and the Virgin Islands. See UIFSA § 102(26). On the jurisdiction of Indian tribes, see State v. Central Council of Tlingit and Haida

---

[3]   In his reply brief Parker raises for the first time the argument that Alaska would be an inconvenient forum. We reject this assertion because Parker fails to show that defense of the suit would be burdensome or that any witnesses or evidence are located in California. *Cf. Volkswagenwerk, A.G.,* 611 P.2d at 502 (holding that although "[i]nconvenience to at least some parties" would occur because "legal doctrine, documents, exhibits, witnesses, and counsel" from Germany and Alaska would be involved, exercise of personal jurisdiction would not violate due process). Further, the State has a fundamental interest as a matter of social policy in requiring parents to support their children. The child was conceived in Alaska and resides in Alaska. As the child's home state, Alaska has an interest in protecting the child.

Indian Tribes of Alaska, 371 P.3d 255 (Alaska 2016). International application of UIFSA is considered later in this chapter.

UIFSA § 201 enumerates a number of bases for personal jurisdiction over non-residents, including several that may go beyond the limits articulated in *Kulko*. For example, § 201(a)(5) provides that a state's courts will have jurisdiction over an individual for purposes of litigating support if the child lives in the state as a result of that person's "acts or directives." See, e.g., Franklin v. Virginia Department of Social Services, 497 S.E.2d 881 (Va. Ct. App. 1998) (upholding long arm jurisdiction); McNabb v. McNabb, 65 P.3d 1068 (Kan. Ct. App. 2003) (concluding there was no jurisdiction); and Windsor v. Windsor, 700 N.E.2d 838 (Mass. App. Ct. 1998) (same). Is this provision consistent with *Kulko*?

UIFSA provides for a two-state process, discussed in the next case, which is available when it is not possible to obtain personal jurisdiction over a potential obligor. Using this procedure, a support proceeding may be commenced in one state and transmitted to the support enforcement agency of another state where it is possible to obtain personal jurisdiction over the respondent.

c. Inconvenient Forum

Under the doctrine of ***forum non conveniens*** a court with personal and subject matter jurisdiction may decline to exercise jurisdiction if there is a more convenient forum in which to resolve the dispute. As indicated in footnote 3, the defendant in *Parker* raised this defense on appeal. Why did the court reject this argument? No provision in UIFSA provides for an inconvenient forum defense, and courts have not agreed on whether to read it into the statute. Compare Perdomo v. Fuller, 974 P.2d 185 (Okla.Ct.App.1998) (allowing transfer on basis of inconvenient forum), with Ervin v. Ervin, 265 P.3d 1272 (Mont. 2011) (holding that an inconvenient forum defense is inapplicable under UIFSA).

UIFSA was designed to facilitate interstate litigation, with procedures designed to allow discovery in another state, see UIFSA § 318, and special rules of evidence and procedure allowing for the admission of testimony and other evidence taken in another state, see UIFSA § 316. Do these procedures resolve the problems that an inconvenient forum provision would address?

Problem 7-1

While visiting France from her home in Virginia, Jane had a short romance with Edward, an American filmmaker living in Paris, and became pregnant. After their daughter was born in Virginia, Edward spent an afternoon visiting with her there and then returned to his home in Paris. While Edward was in Virginia, Jane took photographs of him playing with the baby. She also has letters he wrote to her after the visit, referring to the child as "our daughter." Can Jane bring an action in Virginia to establish paternity and a child support order? (See <u>Bergaust v. Flaherty, 703 S.E.2d 248 (Va. Ct. App. 2011)</u>.)

Problem 7-2

During their marriage, Reginald subjected Susan to serious physical and mental abuse. When Susan learned she was pregnant, she left Reginald and moved into a shelter. After Reginald's threats escalated, she moved to her father's home in another state, where the baby was born a few months later. Susan has filed for child support orders in her new state. Reginald has no other connections to the state. Can the court take jurisdiction under <u>UIFSA § 201</u>? (See <u>In re Marriage of Malwitz, 99 P.3d 56 (Colo.2004)</u>; <u>Powers v. District Court of Tulsa County, 227 P.3d 1060 (Okla. 2009)</u>.)

Department of Human Services v. Leifester

<u>721 A.2d 189 (Maine 1998)</u>

WATHEN, C.J.

Defendant Gregory Leifester appeals from the judgment of the Superior Court (Androscoggin County, *Marden*, J.) awarding plaintiff Julie A. Young $21,346 as reimbursement for past child support pursuant to the Uniform Interstate Family Support Act (UIFSA). Because the court did not err in accepting an unverified amendment to Young's Uniform Support Petition and in ordering Leifester to pay retroactive child support, we affirm the judgment.

The facts may be summarized as follows: Julie Young gave birth to her son Travis in 1982. Young never requested child support from Leifester nor did she initiate a court action to obtain support. In 1996 the Maine Department of Human Services (DHS), at the request of the State Attorney's Office of Maryland, filed a Uniform Support Petition on behalf of Young pursuant to the Uniform Interstate Family Support Act (UIFSA). UIFSA authorizes the state responding to a Uniform Support Petition, in this case Maine, to commence a child support proceeding at the request of a petitioner or an enforcement agency

Think About It

How did the Maine Department of Human Serivces come to initiate this proceeding?

in another state. *See* <u>19 M.R.S.A. § 423</u> (Pamph.1996) (current version at <u>19–A M.R.S.A. § 3001 (1998)</u>).

Young's petition alleged that Leifester was the father of Travis and requested a determination of paternity as well as an award of child support and medical coverage as required by Maine statutes. The petition, which was verified as required by UIFSA, did not specifically request collection of arrears or retroactive child support. In March of 1997, DHS filed an amendment, sent by the Maryland State Attorney's Office at Young's request, that altered the petition only by including a request for the collection of arrears or retroactive child support.

After testing demonstrated a strong likelihood that he was the father of Travis, Leifester stipulated to paternity at the hearing and agreed to the amount of his ongoing weekly child support obligation. The court determined paternity, established ongoing child support, and ordered Leifester to reimburse Young $21,346 for past child support. On appeal, Leifester challenges only the order for past child support.

Leifester first argues that the court erred as a matter of law in accepting the amendment to Young's petition, adding the request for retroactive child support. It is well settled that the decision to grant leave to amend a pleading is within the sound discretion of the trial court.

* * *

Leifester next argues that UIFSA does not authorize the court to order him to pay past child support. Because this is an issue of law, we review the decision of the Superior Court de novo. UIFSA includes within the powers of the responding tribunal the authority to "[i]ssue or enforce a support order, modify a child support order or render a judgment to determine parentage," as well as to "[d]etermine the amount of any arrearages and specify a method of payment." <u>19 M.R.S.A. § 423–D(2)(A), (D)</u> (Pamph.1996) (current version at <u>19–A M.R.S.A. § 3005(2)(A), (D) (1998)</u>). Moreover, UIFSA broadly defines the term "support order":

> The court concludes that the trial court did not exceed the bounds of its discretion in allowing the amendment.

> "Support order" means a judgment, decree or order, whether temporary, final or subject to modification, for the benefit of a child, a spouse or a former spouse, which provides for monetary support, health care, arrearages or reimbursement, and may include related costs and fees, interest, income withholding, attorney's fees and other relief.

19 M.R.S.A. § 421(21) (Pamph.1996) (current version at 19–A M.R.S.A. § 2802(22) (1998)).

Maine's substantive law regarding paternity and child support is the Uniform Act on Paternity, which the court applied pursuant to that provision of UIFSA requiring the application of state substantive law. The Uniform Act on Paternity allows the court to order past child support:

> If paternity has been determined or has been acknowledged according to the laws of this State, the liabilities of the father may be enforced in the same or other proceedings by the mother, the child or the public authority that has furnished or may furnish the reasonable expenses of pregnancy, confinement, education, support or funeral expenses. Chapter 7, subchapter I–A applies to an award of past support, which is calculated by applying the current child support guidelines to the period for which past support is owed.

19 M.R.S.A. § 272 (Pamph.1996) (current version at 19–A M.R.S.A. § 1553 (1998)); *see also Mushero v. Ives*, 949 F.2d 513, 518 (1st Cir.1991) (stating that "the right to collect retroactive support is conclusively established in Maine's paternity statutes"). Thus, the court properly applied the substantive law of Maine and ordered Leifester to pay for the past support of Travis.

Finally, Leifester assigns error to the court's method of computing his obligation for past child support. Leifester argues that the award must be based on reimbursement for actual and reasonable expenditures, citing *White v. Allen*, 667 A.2d 112 (Me.1995). *White v. Allen*, however, lost any value as precedent by virtue of amendments to 19 M.R.S.A. § 272. Section 272 was amended to require that liability for past support be calculated by applying the child support guidelines to the period for which past support is owed. *See* 19 M.R.S.A. § 272. In turn, the child support guidelines mandate the use of the child support tables in computing an award of past support. See 19 M.R.S.A. § 316(1), (1–A) (Pamph.1996) (current version at 19–A M.R.S.A. § 2006(1), (2) (1998)). In this case, the court relied upon a child support worksheet prepared by DHS, applying the child support guidelines to the period for which prior support was owed, in correctly computing that Leifester was responsible for $21,346 in past child support.

The entry is:

Judgment affirmed.

————————

Points for Discussion

a. Two-State Proceedings

Under UIFSA, several types of proceedings may involve more than one state. Cases such as *Leifester* arise when there is no existing support order and it is not possible to obtain jurisdiction over the respondent in the state where the child and the party seeking support reside. As in *Leifester*, establishment of a support order may require a determination of paternity as the first step. In other cases, when there is already a support order in place, a two-state proceeding may be utilized to enforce the support order, either directly or following registration of the order in the responding state. Finally, a two-state proceeding may be required if either party seeks modification of an existing support order. Enforcement and modification proceedings are considered in more detail below.

Take Note!

In an action brought to determine parentage and establish child support orders under UIFSA, the court may not litigate custody and visitation issues unless it has an independent jurisdictional basis to hear these claims. See UIFSA § 104(b)(2).

In a two-state proceeding under UIFSA, the case begins with a court in the jurisdiction where support is sought, referred to as the initiating tribunal. The matter is sent to a responding tribunal, which applies its own procedural and substantive law, including rules on choice of law, to its determination of parentage or establishment of a support order. See UIFSA § 303. If the responding tribunal is enforcing an order entered in another state, however, the law of the issuing state governs the nature, extent, amount and duration of current support payments and the computation and payment of arrearages. See UIFSA § 604(a).

b. Retroactive Child Support

Under the Maine statutes cited in *Leifester*, child support orders may date back to the child's birth. Cf. Rydberg v. Johnson, 583 N.W.2d 631 (N.D.1998) (concluding that court had authority, but upholding trial court's decision not to award past support), and O'Meara v. Doherty, 761 N.E.2d 965 (Mass. App. Ct. 2002) (allowing recovery but significantly reducing amount). Some states do not permit retroactive support awards; see, e.g., Santa Clara County v. Perry, 956 P.2d 1191 (Cal. 1998); In re Paternity of P.J.W., 441 N.W.2d 289 (Wis. Ct. App.1989).

Courts have considered whether claims for retroactive support may be barred based on equitable defenses such as **laches**. E.g. In re State ex rel. Reitenour, 807 A.2d 1259 (N.H. 2002) (allowing recovery despite delay); In the Matter of Norton, 93 P.3d 804 (Or. Ct. App. 2004) (denying recovery). In Carnes v. Kemp, 821

N.E.2d 180 (Ohio 2004), the court allowed an emancipated adult child to pursue a paternity determination and retroactive support from birth through emancipation from her biological father. See also Santagate v. Tower, 833 N.E.2d 171 (Mass. Ct. App. 2005) (granting restitutionary recovery to mother more than 27 years after father deserted family). See generally Jeffrey W. Santema, Annotation, *Liability of Father for Retroactive Child Support on Judicial Determination of Paternity*, 87 A.L.R.5th 361 (2001).

Problem 7-3

Mother and Father live together with their child in Arizona. When Mother and Father separate, Father moves with the child to California. What would be needed for Father to obtain a child support order in California under UIFSA? If Father cannot get an order in California, how should he proceed? In each scenario, what state's law would govern Mother's support obligations? How would jurisdiction be determined if Mother had moved to California, and Father had remained in Arizona with the child?

Problem 7-4

Melissa, who was married and living in Wisconsin, had an affair with Felipe while she was visiting in Oklahoma. Nine months after her visit, Melissa gave birth to a daughter at her home in Wisconsin. When the child was almost two years old, Felipe filed a petition in Oklahoma seeking a determination of paternity as well as visitation and an order that the child's surname be changed to his. Does the court have jurisdiction over his claims? Must Melissa litigate in Oklahoma? (See Perdomo v. Fuller, 974 P.2d 185 (Okla.Ct.App.1998).)

Problem 7-5

Gary and Carol lived together in Nebraska with their son Brad. When Brad was two years old, Carol moved with him to Washington to help care for an elderly relative. After several months, Carol decided to remain in Washington, and filed for a divorce. The court granted the divorce, but refused to enter a child support order because it had no jurisdiction over Gary. Twelve years later, after Carol was seriously injured in an accident, she decided to seek child support from Gary. Should Carol be permitted to collect retroactive support? How could she go about doing this? What state's law would govern this question? (See Willers ex rel. Powell v. Willers, 587 N.W.2d 390 (Neb. 1998).)

——————

2. Determining Support

One of the central innovations of the federal child support enforcement program under Title IV-D of the Social Security Act was the requirement enacted in 1984 that every state must develop a formula or guideline to determine presumptive child support orders. See 42 U.S.C. § 667 (2018). Guidelines were mandated to bring child support awards up to a level more nearly equal to the actual cost of raising children, to reduce the inconsistencies and variations existing between awards, and to enable the courts to arrive at awards more quickly and easily. These guidelines apply both to marital and nonmarital children, see Shuba v. Division of Child Support Enforcement ex rel. Reese, 564 A.2d 1084 (Del.1989); Holtz v. State ex rel. Houston, 847 P.2d 972 (Wyo.1993), and also apply to support for children in the custody of the state or someone other than a parent. See In re Joshua W., 617 A.2d 1154 (Md. Ct. Spec. App. 1993) (child in state foster care).

There are several types of child support guidelines. The simplest provides that a stated percentage of the non-custodial parent's income must be paid to the custodial parent. This percentage varies with the number of children being supported. Illinois used this form of guideline for many years, applying percentages ranging from twenty to fifty percent of the obligor's net income. 750 Ill.Comp. Stat.Ann. § 5/505 (2018).

A majority of the states base their guidelines on the "income shares model," which was initially developed using economic studies about the cost of raising children at various levels of family income. See, e.g., Thomas Espenshade, Investing in Children: New Estimates of Parental Expenditures (1984). See also Robert Williams, *Guidelines for Setting Levels of Child Support Orders*, 21 Fam. L.Q. 281, 286–289 (1987). The model assumes that parents with higher incomes will spend more on their children than parents with lower incomes, and that parents with more children will spend less per child than parents with fewer children.

Go Online

Find a chart listing Child Support Guidelines for all states on the web page of the American Bar Association's Family Law Section.

Income shares guidelines are based on estimates of the marginal expenditures made for children in different types of households. This type of formula assumes that there is a base amount of income available to meet the needs of the adults in each household, and asks how much more would be needed to maintain the same standard of living if children were added into the household. For a critique of this model, see Ira Mark Ellman, *Fudging Failure: The Economic Analysis Used to Construct Child Support Guidelines*, 2004 U. Chi. Legal F. 167. Guidelines used in Massachusetts and the District of Columbia take a different approach, considering the comparative economic circumstances of both the child's parents, and attempt to provide a more equal living standard in the child's two homes. For a useful discussion of the "equal living standards" approach, see Marsha Garrison, *The Goals and Limits of Child Support Policy*, in Child Support: The Next Frontier 16 (J. Thomas Oldham & Marygold S. Melli, eds. 2000).

P.O.P.S. v. Gardner

998 F.2d 764 (9th Cir. 1993)

FARRIS, J., CIRCUIT JUDGE:

Parents Opposed to Punitive Support challenged the constitutionality of the Washington State Child Support Schedule. The district court granted the State's motion for summary judgment. The court ruled that the Schedule did not violate the Equal Protection or the Due Process Clauses of the Fourteenth Amendment.

We affirm.

Facts

Congress has mandated that each state develop presumptive child support guidelines. *See* 42 U.S.C. § 667(b) (1988). Governor Booth Gardner created an Executive Task Force in June 1985 to investigate Washington state's child support program. The Task Force issued a final report in September 1986 recommending that the State adopt a presumptive child support schedule. After numerous public hearings and meetings, the Child Support Schedule Commission presented a schedule to the Legislature which it passed into law.

The Schedule is used to determine the amount of child support parents must pay upon divorce. The economic table, one of five parts of the Schedule, sets forth the basic child support obligation based on the combined family net income and number of children. The table operates similarly to a tax table, mandating different support levels at different income levels. The basic support obligation is allocated between the parents based on each parent's share of the family's net income.

The Schedule permits deviations from the presumptive support obligation, but requires written findings of fact to explain any such deviation. Wash.Rev. Code § 26.19.035(2). Several bases for deviation are enumerated: wealth, income of other adults in the household, liens or extraordinary debt, child support or maintenance received or paid, children from other relationships, and nonrecurring income. *Id.* at § 26.19.075. The court may also deviate if the child spends a significant amount of time with the obligated parent. *Id.* at § 26.19.075(1)(d). The Washington Supreme Court has held that the enumerated reasons for deviation are not exclusive. *In re Marriage of Booth,* 114 Wash.2d 772, 791 P.2d 519, 521 (1990).

P.O.P.S. challenges the constitutionality of the Schedule, claiming that it violates the Due Process and Equal Protection Clauses of the Fourteenth Amendment. P.O.P.S. also claims that the Schedule's economic table creates an irrebuttable presumption that violates the plaintiffs' right to procedural due process.

Discussion

I. *REBUTTABILITY OF THE CHILD SUPPORT SCHEDULE*

P.O.P.S. argues that parents cannot rebut the basic support obligation, because the State has not revealed the assumptions underlying the economic table. By "assumptions", P.O.P.S. means the individual cost components of the table. P.O.P.S. contends that because the cost components of the economic table are incapable of being discovered, parents cannot demonstrate that the table under- or overstates their basic support obligation. P.O.P.S. argues, for example, that noncustodial parents cannot demonstrate that the economic table overestimates housing costs for their child, because they cannot determine what percentage of their basic support obligation is assumed to be housing costs.

The district court held that the Schedule, including the economic table, is rebuttable and that only equity constrained the judge's authority to deviate. The State presented two surveys that purport to show that one out of five support orders deviate from the presumptive support level. P.O.P.S. recognizes that the courts can deviate from the Schedule, but argues that parents cannot obtain a deviation by arguing that the economic table does not accurately reflect their child rearing expenses. P.O.P.S. maintains that the surveys do not show that any litigants have obtained a deviation by attacking the assumptions underlying the economic table.

P.O.P.S. introduced declarations from economists, practitioners and judges, stating that in practice the economic table is irrebuttable. They testify that courts simply will not consider the argument that individualized child care costs differ from those assumed by the economic table, because they do not know the underlying assumptions of the table. On summary judgment, we must construe the evidence in favor of the nonmoving party. Although there is strong evidence to the contrary, we assume *arguendo* that the economic table is irrebuttable.

"Procedural due process imposes constraints on governmental decisions which deprive individuals of 'liberty' or 'property' interests within the meaning of the Due Process Clause of the Fifth or Fourteenth Amendment." *Mathews v. Eldridge*, 424 U.S. 319, 332 (1976). P.O.P.S. does not deny that the State has the authority to require divorced parents to provide for their children, rather, P.O.P.S. maintains that the requirements of procedural due process prevent the State from ordering its members to pay child support without affording them an opportunity to demonstrate that the award does not reflect the "actual" cost of rearing their particular child. P.O.P.S. opines broadly that the Supreme Court has long disfavored irrebuttable presumptions. But not all so-called irrebuttable presumptions are unconstitutional. *See, e.g.,* *Michael H. v. Gerald D.*, 491 U.S. 110, 119 (1989); *Weinberger v. Salfi*, 422 U.S. 749, 772 (1975).

In *Michael H.*, the Supreme Court upheld a California law that conclusively presumed that a child born to a married woman living with her husband is the child of the husband. Based solely on the legal presumption, the State declared that the husband of the child's mother was the child's father, despite blood tests that showed a ninety-eight percent probability that another man was the child's natural father. The natural father claimed that the presumption violated his right to procedural due process, because it terminated his liberty interest in his relationship with his child without affording him an opportunity to demonstrate his paternity in an evidentiary hearing. The Court rejected his procedural due process claim, finding that the presumption was a substantive rule of law which must be reviewed for fundamental fairness.

Make the Connection

Michael H. is reprinted in Chapter 2.

Similarly, the economic table is the implementation of a substantive rule of law. P.O.P.S.'s contention that parents cannot demonstrate that the economic table overstates their actual child-rearing costs misses the point. The table does not purport to provide merely for the child's subsistence, rather it is designed to sustain the child at a standard of living concomitant with her divorcing parents' income. The measure of that standard is subjective. Washington state declares it to be irrelevant whether the noncustodial parent actually spent less than the amount indicated in the economic table to support her children before divorce; the table tells parents what they ought to spend. To the extent that the presumption is conclusive, it is a substantive rule of law based upon a determination by the Legislature as a matter of social policy, that divorcing parents will be required to sustain their children at a certain standard of living determined by the parents' income. We reject P.O.P.S.'s procedural due process challenge and proceed to its substantive claim.

II. *SUBSTANTIVE DUE PROCESS*

The rights to marry, have children, and maintain a relationship with one's children are fundamental rights protected by the Fourteenth Amendment's Due Process Clause. *See* <u>Stanley v. Illinois, 405 U.S. 645, 651 (1972)</u> (children); <u>Loving v. Virginia, 388 U.S. 1, 12 (1967)</u> (marriage). Statutes that directly and substantially impair those rights require strict scrutiny. *See* <u>Zablocki, 434 U.S. at 387</u>. According to P.O.P.S., the financial pressures created by the Schedule alienate noncustodial parents from their children, cause divorces between noncustodial parents and their new spouses, deter new marriages, and prevent noncustodial parents from having more children with their new spouses. P.O.P.S. argues that because the Schedule impacts family relationships, we should apply strict scrutiny to the Schedule. We reject the argument.

> **Make the Connection**
>
> <u>Stanley v. Illinois</u> is reprinted in Chapter 2; <u>Loving v. Virginia</u> is reprinted in Chapter 1.

In <u>Zablocki v. Redhail, 434 U.S. 374, 375 (1978)</u>, the Supreme Court applied strict scrutiny to a state statute that forbade noncustodial parents who had child support obligations from marrying without obtaining court permission. Any marriage entered into without compliance with the statute was void and the persons acquiring illegal marriage licenses were subject to criminal penalties. P.O.P.S.'s reliance on *Zablocki* is misplaced. Unlike the statute in <u>Zablocki</u>, the Schedule does not directly interfere with family relationships. The Schedule does not bar noncustodial parents from entering or maintaining family relationships. In fact, the Statute employs the method for enforcing child support orders that the Court approved in *Zablocki*—adjusting award criteria. Some noncustodial parents may feel discouraged from getting married because of obligations to their own children but nothing in the Statute limits or restricts remarriage:

> By reaffirming the fundamental character of the right to marry, we do not mean to suggest that every state regulation which relates in any way to the incidents of or prerequisites for marriage must be subjected to rigorous scrutiny. To the contrary, reasonable regulations that do not significantly interfere with decisions to enter into the marital relationship may legitimately be imposed.

P.O.P.S. argues that the Schedule results in child support orders that are so high that they effectively bar some noncustodial parents from getting remarried. P.O.P.S. cites anecdotal evidence from several noncustodial parents who claim to have had marital difficulties because of their child support obligation, but all of those parents did remarry despite alleged financial pressures. The Schedule does not directly and substantially interfere with marriage. Moreover, if a noncustodial parent could show that he was so burdened by his child support obligation that he could not get married, the court would have the authority to deviate from the presumptive award on that basis. *See* Wash.Rev.Code §§ 26.19.075(1)(c), (e) and (4). Such a claim would not require the parent to rebut the assumptions underlying the economic table, and therefore, P.O.P.S.'s challenge to the economic table is irrelevant to whether the Schedule is constitutional. The Schedule provides that neither parent's total child support obligation may exceed forty-five percent of net income, further diminishing the likelihood that excessive awards will prevent marriage. *Id.* at § 26.19.065(1).

P.O.P.S. also asserts that noncustodial parents are so frustrated by the operation of the Schedule that they do not spend as much time with their children. The fact that some parents take their financial frustrations out on their children does not afford them extra protection under the Due Process Clause. The Schedule does not discourage parents from spending time with their children. It explicitly permits courts to deviate from the presumptive support level if the noncustodial parent spends a "significant amount of time" with his children. *Id.* at § 26.19.075(d).

The burden of child support awards may very well discourage some people from having additional children and may discourage some from entering new marriages. But all financial obligations impact family decisions. Providing financial and emotional support is the responsibility one assumes by choosing to have children. Every obligation imposed by the State cannot be subject to strict scrutiny. Such a holding would turn the doctrine of strict scrutiny "into a virtual engine of destruction for countless legislative judgments which have heretofore been thought wholly consistent with the Fifth and Fourteenth Amendments to the Constitution." *Weinberger*, 422 U.S. at 772.

The judgment of the legislature must stand if there is a rational relationship between the operation of the Schedule and the policy that the Schedule serves. The Legislature intended to accomplish three goals by creating a statewide child support schedule:

> (1) Increasing the adequacy of child support orders through the use of economic data as the basis for establishing the child support schedule;
> (2) Increasing the equity of child support orders by providing for comparable orders in cases with similar circumstances; and
> (3) Reducing the adversarial nature of the proceedings by increasing voluntary settlements as a result of the greater predictability achieved by a uniform statewide child support schedule.

Wash.Rev.Code § 26.19.001. P.O.P.S. recognizes that these are legitimate state interests, but argues that the Schedule is not a rational means of achieving the goals. We cannot agree. Requiring judges to follow the table unless they articulate a good reason to deviate decreases the likelihood that individual judges will erroneously award insufficient support. Because the most important factors for setting support are income and number of children, similarly situated people will pay similar amounts for child support. The presumptive nature of the table promotes voluntary settlements as the parties have fewer issues about which they can argue. Thus, adopting a presumptive support schedule is a rational means of achieving the State's legitimate goals.

P.O.P.S. contends that the State's methodology for developing the economic table inflated the presumptive child support level above the actual costs of rearing children in Washington. P.O.P.S. discusses at length several perceived flaws in the table. The discussion serves only to prove that the appropriate level of child support is a debatable issue dependent on policy and value judgments. On issues of social policy, the state has the power to make such judgments as long as they are not made arbitrarily. The table was developed based on economic studies and hard data. The presumptive support levels are not arbitrary.

III. *EQUAL PROTECTION*

P.O.P.S. argues that the Schedule violates the equal protection rights of the children of noncustodial households. The Statute provides that the child support schedule shall be applied to determine the presumptive support. Children from other relationships are not to be counted to determine the basic support obligation. However, the court may deviate from the basic support obligation if either parent has children from other relationships to whom she owes a duty of support. *Id.* at § 26.19.075(1)(e). The Schedule explicitly permits the court to consider children from the noncustodial household. P.O.P.S. contends that the Equal Protection Clause dictates stricter guidelines for the consideration of noncustodial children. The Fourteenth Amendment does not mandate the rigid social policy prescriptions urged by P.O.P.S.

In *Lipscomb v. Simmons, 962 F.2d 1374 (9th Cir. 1992)* (*en banc*), we upheld an Oregon statute that provided aid to foster parents who were not related to their foster children, but denied state aid to foster parents who were related to their foster children. We held that because the law did not affect a suspect class or directly interfere with a fundamental right, it need only have a rational basis. We held further that we "need not ascertain the actual reason for the classification but may consider any facts from which the state reasonably could have concluded that the challenged classification would promote a legitimate state purpose."

Children of noncustodial parents do not constitute a suspect class. The schedule does not directly and substantially interfere with fundamental rights. *See Califano, 434 U.S. at 54*; *see also Lipscomb, 962 F.2d at 1379* (holding that the government has no affirmative obligation to facilitate the exercise of constitutional rights). We review the Schedule under the rational basis test.

P.O.P.S. maintains that the state does not have even a rational basis for "discriminating" against children of noncustodial households. The Schedule does not discriminate. Courts may deviate from the basic support obligation when either parent has other children. Thus the court can insure that children from noncustodial families are not unduly burdened by the child support award. The State presented evidence that the most frequent reason for deviating is the existence of other children. P.O.P.S. complains that the Schedule does not give the court any guidance for deviating from the presumptive amount based on other children. The State need not create a perfect Schedule; it need only have a rational basis for the statute:

> In the area of economics and social welfare, a State does not violate the Equal Protection Clause merely because the classifications made by its laws are imperfect. If the classification has some "reasonable basis," it does not offend the Constitution simply because the classification "is not made with mathematical nicety or because in practice it results in some inequality."

Dandridge v. Williams, 397 U.S. 471, 485 (1970) (citations omitted).

The divorcing parents are jointly responsible for the presumptive support amount, and therefore, it is rational for the presumptive support calculation to include only the children for whom both divorcing parents have responsibility.

We have carefully examined all of P.O.P.S.'s constitutional challenges. They find no support in the Constitution.

Affirmed.

Points for Discussion

a. *P.O.P.S.*

Was the court in *P.O.P.S.* correct in rejecting the argument that the guidelines should be rebuttable, as a matter of Due Process, if the table fails to reflect the actual child rearing expenses in a particular household? What about the plaintiff's other arguments? See also Coghill v. Coghill, 836 P.2d 921 (Alaska 1992), Georgia Department of Human Resources v. Sweat, 580 S.E.2d 206 (Ga. 2003), and Gallaher v. Elam, 104 S.W.3d 455 (Tenn.2003).

b. Rules vs. Standards

Before the enactment of support guidelines, child support awards were left to the discretion of the trial judge. The judge was authorized to take account of such factors as the financial resources of the child and the parents, the standard of living which the child would have enjoyed if the marriage had continued, the child's physical, emotional and educational needs, and the needs of the non-custodial parent. See <u>Uniform Marriage and Divorce Act § 309</u>, 9A U.L.A. (Part I) 573 (1998). Statutes like this remain in force in many states, but for most purposes the guidelines now control the determination of child support.

The transformation in the legal treatment of child support, from open-ended discretionary decision-making to "bright-line" decision-making, has been dramatic. Do the guidelines in general accomplish the purposes for which they were originally designed? See Charles Brackney, *Battling Inconsistency and Inadequacy: Child Support Guidelines in the States*, 11 Harv. Women's L.J. 197 (1988).

c. Deviations from the Guidelines

As noted in *P.O.P.S.*, support orders may deviate from the presumptive guideline amount, but only if the court makes explicit findings concerning the basis for deviation. See See <u>42 U.S.C. § 667(b)(2) (2018)</u>; see, e.g., <u>Lembo v. Lembo, 624 A.2d 1089 (R.I.1993)</u>; <u>Matter of Marriage of Booth, 791 P.2d 519 (Wash. 1990)</u>. This has led to substantial litigation on permissible grounds for deviation. Over time, many states' guidelines have been revised to address some of these issues. For example, the Colorado child support guidelines include an adjustment to income to reflect support obligations for other children, <u>Colo.Rev.Stat. § 14–10–115(7) (d) and (d.5) (2018)</u>; formulas for allocating child care costs, <u>§ 14–10–115(11)</u>, and educational and transportation expenses, <u>§ 14–10–115(13)</u>; and an adjustment in cases of shared and split residential care, <u>§§ 14–10–115(14)(b) and (c)</u>.

d. High Income Cases

Another recurring problem, which has led to changes in the guidelines over time, is how to handle cases in which one parent's income exceeds the highest figure listed in the guidelines. Some courts have concluded that the guidelines are not applicable, and return to the discretionary standards for determining support. <u>Anonymous v. Anonymous, 631 So.2d 1030 (Ala.Civ.App. 1993)</u>. Others states use the top guideline figure as a presumptive minimum award, and give the court discretion to order a larger amount, based on the child's reasonable needs and the other factors courts considered before the enactment of child support guidelines. See, e.g., <u>In re Marriage of Van Inwegen, 757 P.2d 1118 (Colo.Ct.App. 1988)</u>; <u>McCarty v. Faried, 499 S.W.3d 266 (Ky. 2016)</u>; <u>Voishan v. Palma, 609 A.2d 319 (Md. 1992)</u>; <u>Rodriguez v. Rodriguez, 860 S.W.2d 414 (Tex.1993)</u>; <u>Harris v. Harris, 714 A.2d 626 (Vt. 1998)</u>.

In other states, courts have extrapolated from the highest income figures on the table, see, e.g., <u>Black v. Black, 812 S.W.2d 480 (Ark. 1991)</u>, or applied a flat percentage to income that exceeds the level in the table, see <u>Finley v. Scott, 707 So.2d 1112 (Fla.1998)</u>. In these states, or in those with guidelines based on a straight percentage of income formula, there is the potential for extremely large child support awards. Should this be a basis for deviation from the guidelines? See also <u>Marriage of McCausland, 152 P.3d 1013 (Wash. 2007)</u>, which held that it was error for a trial court to extrapolate mechanically when parents' income exceeded the amounts included in the guidelines, concluding that an award exceeding the guidelines must be supported by written findings of fact. See also <u>Hanrahan v. Bakker, 186 A.3d 958 (Pa. 2018)</u> (court must consider reasonable needs of children in high income cases).

e. Agreements to Deviate

How should a court evaluate a settlement agreement that deviates significantly from the child support guidelines? In some states, courts must make express findings explaining any deviation from the guidelines. See, e.g., <u>In re Paternity of Perry, 632 N.E.2d 286 (Ill. App. Ct. 1994)</u>; <u>Cox v. Cox, 776 P.2d 1045 (Alaska 1989)</u>; <u>Zarrett v. Zarrett, 574 N.W.2d 855 (N.D.1998)</u>. Should the court approve an agreement to waive support in exchange for custody or a surrender of visitation rights? See <u>Blisset v. Blisset, 526 N.E.2d 125 (Ill. 1988)</u> (agreement to waive support in exchange for surrender of visitation rights unenforceable); <u>Kelley v. Kelley, 449 S.E.2d 55 (Va. 1994)</u> (waiver of child support in divorce decree vacated as void); but see <u>McNattin v. McNattin, 450 N.W.2d 169 (Minn.Ct.App.1990)</u> (wife who agreed not to seek child support in exchange for custody must establish change in circumstances in order to secure award.) Conversely, what about an agreement to pay significantly greater support than the guidelines would require? Cf. <u>Laughlin v. Laughlin, 229 P.3d 1002 (Alaska 2010)</u>, which refused to approve a couple's agreement to establish a special fund for their children in lieu of child support.

f. Nonparents and Child Support

Courts generally refuse to impose child support obligations on stepparents; see, e.g., <u>In re Glaude and Fogg, 855 A.2d 494 (N.H. 2004)</u> (stepfather not obligated to pay child support). In <u>T.F. v. B.L., 813 N.E.2d 1244 (Mass. 2004)</u>, the court refused to enforce an agreement between the child's mother and the mother's domestic partner that the partner would pay support for a child born during their relationship. The ALI Principles of the Law of Family Dissolution (ALI Principles) propose in § 3.03 that a partner may be held responsible to pay support in these circumstances under estoppel principles. See also <u>Marriage of Snow, 862 N.E.2d 664 (Ind. 2007)</u> (in loco parentis status not sufficient basis for imposing child support obligation); <u>Poncho v. Bowdoin, 126 P.3d 1221 (N.M. Ct. App. 2005)</u> (equitable adoption is not a basis for imposing child support obligation).

The law is more complex with respect to grandparents. While grandparents generally are not held responsible for child support, statutes may impose liability in cases involving minor children who become parents. See, e.g., <u>N. C. Gen. Stat. § 50–13.4 (2018)</u>, applied in <u>Whitman v. Kiger, 533 S.E.2d 807 (N.C. Ct. App. 2000)</u>, providing that parents of an unemancipated minor child, who is also a custodial or noncustodial parent of a child, share the liability for their grandchild's support. See also <u>A.N. v. S.M., 756 A.2d 625 (N.J. Super. Ct. App. Div.2000)</u>, which held that a court should impute income to a 15-year-old father of a child who had no income other than his allowance and who was not permitted to work by his own father, and held that a judge could direct child's grandfather to pay difference between the imputed amount and what the father could afford to pay. When a child has minor parents, and the child's custodial parent is receiving TANF assistance, the state may hold the parents of the child's noncustodial parent jointly and severally liable for any child support. See 42 U.S.C. § 666(a) (18) (2018).

Make the Connection

Chapter 4 addresses legal obligations to support parents and other family members.

Problem 7-6

After their divorce, Susan is earning $2,000 a month and Ed is earning $4,000 a month. Susan has primary custody of their son, Charles. Under the guidelines in their state, this translates to a presumptive child support order of $1,000 a month.

(a) Should the court adjust this amount downward if Ed proves that Susan has remarried, and her new husband earns more than $12,000 a month? (See In re Marriage of Gehl, 486 N.W.2d 284 (Iowa 1992).) *NO bc child not his responsibity*

(b) Should the court adjust this amount downward if Ed proves that he is paying $1,000 a month to help support his elderly mother? (See Butler v. Gill, 61 Cal. Rptr.2d 781 (Ct. App. 1997).) *NO*

(c) Should the court increase this amount to help cover tuition for Charles at a private secondary school? Should it matter why Susan wants to enroll Charles in private school? (See In re Barrett, 841 A.2d 74 (N.H. 2004).) *yes, will matter why she wants to enroll him*

(d) Should the court decrease this amount if Ed proves that he has remarried and has two new children to support? (See Salazar v. Attorney General of Texas, 827 S.W.2d 41 (Tex. App. 1992).) *NO*

Problem 7-7

Slavomir had been a resident of the United States for several years when he filed for divorce from his wife Eva, who lives in the Slovak Republic. After the divorce, Eva filed a petition with a state court in the United States seeking child support for their daughter. Under the applicable guidelines, Slavomir would be obligated to pay $500 a month, but he argues that the court should deviate from this figure because the cost of living is much lower in the Slovak Republic, asserting that his daughter's reasonable needs can be met on half of this amount. Should the court grant the deviation? (See Gladis v. Gladisova, 856 A.2d 703 (Md. 2004); People ex rel. A.K., 72 P.3d 402 (Colo.Ct.App.2003).)

Problem 7-8

When Mary and Robert divorced, the court entered a shared custody order that placed their children with Robert for 75% of the year and with Mary for 25% of the year. Mary has a monthly net income of $4,000 a month and Robert's net monthly income is $16,000. Based on the applicable child support guidelines, the combined support obligation of both parents is $6,000 a month. How should child support be allocated between Robert and Mary in this situation? (See Colonna v. Colonna, 855 A.2d 648 (Pa. 2004); see also Marriage of Turk, 12 N.E.3d 40 (Ill. 2014).)

Problem 7-9

A year after moving in together, Jamie and Keon had a child. Six months later, they broke up, and Jamie brought an action to secure child support. She presented evidence that her monthly expenses were $4,200, and her net monthly earnings from part-time employment were about $700. Keon, a professional athlete, had net monthly earnings of $50,000. The applicable child support guidelines require a noncustodial parent with one child to pay twenty percent of his or her net earnings as child support. Should the court order Keon to pay $10,000 a month in child support? If Keon's earnings increase substantially, should the support order be increased? (See In re Keon C., 800 N.E.2d 1257 (Ill. App. Ct. 2003); see also Johnson v. Superior Court, 77 Cal.Rptr.2d 624 (Ct. App. 1998); In re Paternity of Tukker M.O., 544 N.W.2d 417 (Wis. 1996).)

Problem 7-10

Emilio and Carey lived together for several years without marrying, and had two children together. Carey filed a petition for child support after they separated, and her attorney has served discovery requests seeking information about Emilio's finances. Emilio has offered to stipulate that his income exceeds $1.2 million per year, and that he could pay any reasonable amount of child support. Carey believes that Emilio earns more than $300,000 per month, which would result in a presumptive award under the guidelines of $30,000 per month. Emilio has requested a protective order on the grounds that the discovery request was unduly burdensome and not reasonably calculated to lead to the discovery of admissible evidence. Should the court grant his motion? How should his child support obligation be determined? (See Estevez v. Superior Court, 27 Cal.Rptr.2d 470 (Ct. App. 1994); In re Marriage of Hubner, 114 Cal.Rptr.2d 646 (Ct. App. 2001).)

Lauderman v. Wyoming Department of Family Services

232 P.3d 604 (Wyo. 2010)

GOLDEN, JUSTICE.

[¶ 1] Lisa Lauderman, (Mother) and Russell Nomura (Father) have one child. The Department of Family Services (DFS) filed a motion to modify child support. After a hearing, the district court reduced Father's child support obligation. Mother appeals. We affirm.

ISSUES

[¶ 2] Mother presents multiple issues, but they can be reduced into two main issues. First, Mother argues the district court abused its discretion in calculating the parties' respective incomes. Second, Mother argues the district court abused its discretion in admitting certain letters into evidence.

FACTS

[¶ 3] Mother and Father never married but they had one child together in 1999. Mother has always had custody of the child. In 2004, Father's child support obligation was set at $263.00 per week. In early 2007, Father fell $3,419.00 in arrears. He paid the arrears in full. In November 2007, DFS filed a Petition for Modification of Child Support.

[¶ 4] The district court held an evidentiary hearing on the Petition. After the hearing, the district court made the following findings:

3. At the time of the trial in this matter, the Respondent, Lauderman, was the mother of two (2) minor children, the child at issue who is nine (9) years of age, and an infant daughter born in June, 2009. She was employed at L & H Industrial, Inc., as a welder from May, 2007 until her termination in November, 2007, as a result of her pregnancy.

4. At the time of the trial in this matter, the Respondent, Nomura, was a self-employed dry waller operating his own business referred to as RNR Drywall, Inc. Mr. Nomura is the sole officer and shareholder of the business.

5. Respondent Lauderman should be imputed a net income as she is voluntarily unemployed. The Court should impute her income from prior years and based on her 2007 W-2. The fact that she is a stay-at-home mother should have no bearing on the imputed income.

6. Respondent Lauderman is capable of earning $16.00 per hour and her income is based on the following calculations:

$ 33,280.00	Gross income ($16.00 x 2080 hours per year)
-$ 0.00	Federal income (tax credits are higher than taxes owed)
-$ 2,053.00	Social Security
-$ 483.00	Medicare
$ 30,744.00	annual net income (does not include tax credits)

Divided by 12 months = $2,562.00 net monthly income

7. Respondent Nomura's net monthly income is based upon his 2008 actual earnings and his earning capability in the future, rather than what he earned during more prosperous economic times.

8. To use Respondent Nomura's prior years' income would result in imputing a net income that would result in an impossibly high child support obligation and would set this party up for failure. Therefore, 2008 is the only year that should be used to determine the Respondent Nomura's net monthly income.

9. Respondent Nomura's net monthly income is derived from using this net revenues from RNR Drywall in the amount of $21,518.05. This is the amount of actual money that was available to Nomura from the business during 2008. This amount is derived by adding the operating income of $5,076.78, plus the income from the sale of an asset (truck) in the amount of $16,441.27.

10. The health insurance of $2,256.38 should be added back in and counted towards the Respondent Nomura's net income as his net revenues from the business were reduced by this line item and is not for the benefit of the child.

11. Depreciation of $107.20 should further be added back to Mr. Nomura's net revenues since Wyoming law does not allow depreciation to reduce someone's net income.

12. Officer salary of $17,840.48 should count towards Mr. Nomura's net income.

13. Unemployment benefits of $3,490.00 should count towards Mr. Nomura's net income.

14. The Section 179, Depreciation of $36,032.95, should not be included in the net monthly income of Mr. Nomura. The Court finds that this is not a paper deduction, but rather, is an actual expenditure (for a truck) and should be entirely deducted.

15. The 2008 draws of $54,940.34 should not be used for determining the Respondent Nomura's income in 2008. To count the 2008 draws from the business as income for the Respondent Nomura in 2008 would be unfairly inflating his income because it comes from money that was earned in prior years.

16. The net income of the Respondent Nomura is determined as follows:

$ 21,518.08	2008 net revenues from RNR Drywall
$ 3,490.00	Unemployment
$ 2,256.38	Health Insurance
$ 107.20	Depreciation
$ 17,840.48	Officer Salary (no calculation avail. for personal taxes)
$ 45,212.14	annual net income

Divided by 12 months = $3,767.68 net monthly income

17. Child support is therefore calculated at $650.00 according to the child support guidelines in effect at the time of entry of this Order based upon mother's imputed net monthly income of $2,562.00; and father's net monthly income of $3,767.68.

In sum, Father's child support obligation was reduced from $263.00 per week to $650.00 per month.

DISCUSSION

Standard of Review

[¶ 5] We review a district court's order on a petition to modify child support to determine if the district court has abused its discretion. Our review entails evaluation of the sufficiency of the evidence to support the district court's decision. In evaluating the evidence, we afford to the prevailing party every favorable inference while omitting any consideration of evidence presented by the unsuccessful party. Findings of fact not supported by the evidence, contrary to the evidence, or against the great weight of the evidence cannot be sustained. Similarly, an abuse of discretion is present " 'when a material factor deserving significant weight is ignored.' "

Analysis

[¶ 6] We begin by noting that Mother's appellate argument is premised on the belief that the district court deviated from the presumptive child support amount calculated pursuant to Wyo. Stat. Ann. § 20–2–307. Mother's argument is misplaced. The district court did not deviate from the presumptive child support amount. What Mother actually takes issue with, and what we will discuss, is the district court's computation of income for the respective parties.

[¶ 7] Determination of child support amounts is governed by statute. The first step in calculating child support is determining the parents' respective monthly net incomes. "Income" and "net income" are defined in <u>Wyo. Stat. Ann. § 20–2–303(a)</u> as:

> (ii) "Income" means any form of payment or return in money or in kind to an individual, regardless of source. Income includes, but is not limited to wages, earnings, salary, commission, compensation as an independent contractor, temporary total disability, permanent partial disability and permanent total disability worker's compensation payments, unemployment compensation, disability, annuity and retirement benefits, and any other payments made by any payor, but shall not include any earnings derived from overtime work unless the court, after considering all overtime earnings derived in the preceding twenty-four (24) month period, determines the overtime earnings can reasonably be expected to continue on a consistent basis. In determining income, all reasonable unreimbursed legitimate business expenses shall be deducted. Means tested sources of income such as Pell grants, aid under the personal opportunities with employment responsibilities (POWER) program, food stamps and supplemental security income (SSI) shall not be considered as income. Gross income also means potential income of parents who are voluntarily unemployed or underemployed;
>
> (iii) "Net income" means income as defined in paragraph (ii) of this subsection less personal income taxes, social security deductions, cost of dependent health care coverage for all dependent children, actual payments being made under preexisting support orders for current support of other children, other court-ordered support obligations currently being paid and mandatory pension deductions. Payments towards child support arrearage shall not be deducted to arrive at net income[.]

<u>Wyo. Stat. Ann. § 20–2–303(a)(ii) and (iii) (LexisNexis 2009)</u>.

Mother's Income

[¶ 8] Mother first objects to the district court's finding that she was voluntarily unemployed. The evidence supports this finding. Mother had worked as a welder in 2007. After she was let go from that job, she decided to be a stay-at-home mother. Mother testified that there were welding jobs currently available in her town, which she was physically capable of performing. She wasn't applying for them because she didn't want to be away from her children. Given this testimony, it was well within the district court's discretion to find Mother voluntarily unemployed. *See, e.g.,* <u>*In re Paternity of IC*, 971 P.2d 603, 607 (Wyo.1999)</u> (voluntarily leaving job to return to school constitutes voluntary unemployment).

[¶ 9] Mother next objects to the amount of income imputed to her. In 2007, when she was working as a welder, she was earning $16.00 per hour. Mother testified that jobs were available at the time of the hearing and were paying $16.00

per hour. Mother's own evidence supports the <u>district court's</u> decision to impute to her a salary of $16.00 per hour.

[¶ 10] Mother's objection continues that the district court abused its discretion when it did not subtract any amount for federal income tax. The district court's calculations show that it considered federal income tax. It determined the tax credits available to Mother exceeded the amount of federal income tax owed based on the imputed salary. In making this determination, the district court adopted figures provided by the DFS indicating the amount of earned income credit and child tax credit would be more than the federal income tax due. The district court's reliance on the DFS calculation is reasonable under the circumstances.

Father's Income

[¶ 11] Turning to Father's income, Mother contends Father should be found to be voluntarily underemployed. The evidence shows that Father worked as a drywaller for 18 years. He owned and operated a drywall business in the Jackson area. When business declined in the Jackson area Father relocated to Worland. Despite his attempts to keep the business going, Father testified there was simply no work available: "I've hit every job there is. I've stopped on every job site there is. I've spoke [sic] with every contractor there is in Jackson, Worland, Thermop [sic], surrounding areas. I have contacts nationwide, and everybody's out of work right now." Father even looked for jobs in the oil field sector but was unable to find anything. Given the evidence, we find no credence in Mother's contentions that Father isn't looking hard enough or in a wide enough geographic scope.

[¶ 12] Mother next takes issue with the district court's computation of Father's income. First, she argues the district court should have included in-kind benefits Father received from his business as income. Mother does not, however, identify any in-kind benefits received by Father. We therefore need not consider this argument further.

[¶ 13] Mother also argues the district court erred in not including certain draws Father took from his business in 2008 as income. Father's accountant, however, explained that draws are unrelated to business income. Draws come from money already in the business that could have been earned at any time during the business's existence. At the time of the hearing, the business had only approximately $9,000.00. Father's future income, therefore, would be limited to amounts earned during the current year. Under the circumstances, the district court did not abuse its discretion in not factoring the draws into Father's income for child support purposes.

[¶ 14] Finally, Mother argues the district court abused its discretion in using Father's 2008 income instead of his 2007 income. The district court explained its decision in its order. It did not use Father's 2007 income because it did not accurately reflect current economic conditions. The district court determined Father was not likely to be able to earn the same amount in the future. Given the well-documented collapse of the construction industry, as well as Father's testimony as to how the economic downturn is affecting him personally, we find the district court was within its discretion in relying on Father's 2008 actual income as more appropriately indicative of Father's future earning capacity.

[¶ 15] In *Woodward v. Woodward, 428 P.2d 389 (Wyo.1967)*, a case wherein a father's earning capacity had deteriorated, this Court stated

> the trial court has found that, due to no fault or choice of his own, the father of the children does not now have an earning capacity or income sufficient to enable him to pay more than the amount required by the court's decree.
>
> * * * *
>
> . . .[S]hould the future earning capacity and ability of the father be bettered, either by improvement in his health or through his securing of more remunerative employment or additional estate, the door remains open to show such changed condition, and modification of the court decree may be had.
> The law never intends to require the impossible, and an award without ability to pay would have been a fruitless gesture which could not inure to the benefit of the minor children whose welfare is of primary concern to courts.

The same comments apply here.

Introduction of Letters

[¶ 16] During the hearing, to support his testimony that he had been actively looking for work, Father offered multiple letters from contractors stating they had no work available for him. The district court admitted the letters into evidence over Mother's several objections including a hearsay objection. The decision of whether or not to admit evidence lies within the discretion of the trial court. We will not disturb the trial court's ruling absent abuse of that discretion. As always, even if this Court determines that the trial court erred in ruling on the admissibility of evidence, we disregard errors which are harmless.

[¶ 17] We need not discuss whether the admission of the letters constituted error because, even if it did, Mother was not prejudiced by such introduction. The district court listened to Mother's objections and admitted the letters over the objections stating "[t]he Court can give them the weight that it determines, so I don't think that it's going to be prejudicial." There is no further indication that the district court relied on the letters, nor was it necessary for the district court to do so. Father testified extensively as to his continuing job search. The letters do nothing more than corroborate that testimony. *See* Rudy v. Bossard, 997 P.2d 480, 484 (Wyo.2000) (no prejudice in admission of letter when letter did nothing more than corroborate testimony).

CONCLUSION

[¶ 18] We find no abuse of discretion in the district court's calculation of the parties' respective incomes for child support purposes. The decision is reasonable under the circumstances. We also find no harm in the introduction of letters corroborating Father's extensive testimony on his attempts to find work. Affirmed.

HILL, JUSTICE, dissenting.

[¶ 19] I respectfully dissent because my review of this case convinces me that the proceedings that are included in the record on appeal are insufficient to disturb the status quo. In 2004, a New Jersey court set Father's child support obligation at $263.00 per week. That judgment was registered in Wyoming in 2005 and under its terms, Father has been required to pay that much in child support to Mother since that time (although he has not always done so). The child at issue in this appeal is nearing 11 years of age as we address the difficulties that this case poses.

[¶ 20] In Wyoming it is traditional to set child support as a monthly figure and so I would calculate that figure like this: $263.00 x 52 weeks = $13,676.00 per year ÷ 12 months = $1,139.6666 rounded to $1,139.67 per month. In her brief, Mother contends/concedes that Father should pay $1,109.88, if the "facts and figures" that can be gleaned from the record on appeal are deemed to be accurate enough to provide the basis for a reliable decision in that regard. Mother concedes she can do some work and earn approximately $1,269.73 per month.

[¶ 21] During the months May through November in 2007, just before the birth of her youngest child, Mother earned $16.00 an hour as a welder, although she only worked for seven months during that year (she was discharged late in her pregnancy). So, in addition to the child she shares with Father, Mother now has the care of an infant child born of a recent relationship. Mother's contention is that, while she is capable of doing some work, she cannot go back to welding full-time. This is so because she cannot arrange adequate child care for her infant child because the work shifts for welders are 12-hour shifts. In addition, she must, of course, provide parenting for the older child who is the beneficiary of Father's child support.

[¶ 22] The district court determined that Mother was capable of working 40 hours a week, 52 weeks a year, at a pay rate of $16.00 an hour ($33,280.00 annually). Although Father has historically earned significantly more than he did in 2008, the district court determined that Father's income for 2008 was $3,767.68 per month. The year 2008 was chosen because that was the year "hard-times" hit in the construction industry (Father owns a dry-wall company). Based on that calculation, Father was to pay Mother $650.00 per month in child support. The district court's equation is just not an acceptable means of calculating child support. The evidence suggested that Father was capable of earning significantly more than the amount attributed to him (and very likely was earning more). The testimony suggested that Father used his construction company to pay many of his living expenses, including transportation and housing. Although the Internal Revenue Service allows such "deductions" and "adjustments" for income tax purposes, this Court should not permit adequate child support to hinge upon how talented a parent's accountant (and the taxpayer himself) is at the art of income tax avoidance. See *Durham v. Durham*, 2003 WY 95, ¶¶ 8–12, 74 P.3d 1230, 1233–34 (Wyo.2003); *Bailey v. Bailey*, 954 P.2d 962, 967 (Wyo.1998); 3 Anteau, et al., *Family Law Litigation Guide with Forms: Discovery, Evidence, Trial of Child Support Issues* § 34.04 [b] (Imputed Income) (2008).

[¶ 23] We have held that the district court's discretion with respect to child support is limited by Wyoming's statutes that govern that subject. Wyo. Stat. Ann. §§ 20–2–301 through 20–2–315 (LexisNexis 2009); *Steele v. Steele*, 2005 WY 33, ¶ 12, 108 P.3d 844, 849 (Wyo.2005).

> Judicial discretion is a composite of many things, among which are conclusions drawn from objective criteria; it means a sound judgment exercised with regard to what is right under the circumstances and without doing so arbitrarily or capriciously.

Vaughn v. State, 962 P.2d 149, 151 (Wyo.1998). Under the facts and circumstances presented here, the district court decision is not "right." It applies two widely divergent formulas in calculating the parties' incomes and produces a result that is an affront to both the letter and the spirit of the statutes governing child support.

[¶ 24] For these reasons I would remand this matter to the district court with directions that the "Order on Petition for Modification of Support" state a conclusion that Father's obligation to pay child support must remain unchanged.

———————

Points for Discussion

a. *Lauderman*

In *Lauderman*, the custodial parent was unemployed at the time of the support hearing. How does the court determine whether to impute income to her, and how much to impute, for purposes of applying the child support guidelines? Why does the court reject the mother's argument that income should also be imputed to the father? Does the dissent have the better argument here?

b. Defining Income

Most child support guidelines include broad definitions of income, like the Wyoming statute quoted in *Lauderman*, and courts construe these statutes broadly when deciding whether certain payments should be treated as income for guidelines purposes. See, e.g., Dunn v. Dunn, 952 P.2d 268 (Alaska 1998) (IRA dividends); In re the Marriage of Long, 921 P.2d 67 (Colo.Ct.App.1996) (military Basic Allowance for Quarters); In re Jerome, 843 A.2d 325 (N.H. 2004) (annuity payments from personal injury settlement); Marriage of Cheriton, 111 Cal.Rptr.2d 755 (Ct. App. 2001) (proceeds from exercise of stock options). Monetary gifts that a parent receives from family members on a regular basis are sometimes treated as income, see, e.g., Marriage of Rogers, 820 N.E.2d 386 (Ill. 2004); but see Styka v. Styka, 972 P.2d 16 (N.M. Ct.App.1998). See also Harshman v. Harshman, 158 A.3d 506 (Me. 2017) (ongoing distributions from trust fund included in income); Guilford County ex rel. Easter v. Easter, 473 S.E.2d 6 (N.C. Ct. App. 1996) (gifts from third parties may be considered as a basis for deviation from guidelines).

c. Business Income

As demonstrated in *Lauderman*, the problem of determining income for a parent who is self-employed or who operates a business raises many difficulties. Numerous courts have addressed questions such as whether acquisition of a capital asset constitutes an ordinary and necessary business expense, see, e.g., Kamm v. Kamm, 616 N.E.2d 900 (Ohio 1993); the proper treatment of depreciation expenses, see, e.g., Labar v. Labar, 731 A.2d 1252 (Pa. 1999); and how to characterize retained earnings in a closely-held Subchapter S corporation, see, e.g., Zold v. Zold, 911 So.2d 1222 (Fla. 2005). This process may require significant factual investigation; see, e.g., Pyle v. Pyle, 162 A.3d 814 (Me. 2017) (comparing information from tax returns and bank deposits).

d. Irregular Income

For support obligors with income that fluctuates significantly from year to year, a court may average several years' income and use that figure to determine an appropriate support award. See, e.g., In re Marriage of Nelson, 698 N.E.2d 1084 (Ill. App. Ct. 1998); In re Knickerbocker, 601 N.W.2d 48 (Iowa 1999); but see <u>Schaeffer v. Schaeffer, 717 N.E.2d 915 (Ind.Ct.App.1999)</u> (five-year income average not appropriate where obligor's income had increased steadily).

State courts and legislatures take different approaches to the treatment of inheritances, trust distributions, and non-recurring items of income such as a lump sum personal injury settlement or capital gains on the sale of an asset. Compare <u>In re A.M.D., 78 P.3d 741 (Colo. 2003)</u> (gifts and inheritances are income for child support purposes under state statute) with <u>Humphreys v. DeRoss, 790 A.2d 281 (Pa. 2002)</u> (gifts and inheritances are not income under state child support statute); see also <u>Lasche v. Levin, 977 A.2d 361 (D.C. 2009)</u>. Even if the corpus of such a payment is not included in income, interest or other income the funds generate may be treated as income. See also Genna Rosten, Annotation, <u>*Consideration of Obligor's Personal-Injury Recovery or Settlement in Fixing Alimony or Child Support,* 59 A.L.R.5th 489 (1998)</u>.

Problem 7-11

David obtains a divorce from Patricia and the court awards him custody of their child. David proves that during their marriage, Patricia received $250,000 a year from a discretionary trust set up by her father. The trust principal consists of securities worth five million dollars, and it produces an income of five hundred thousand dollars a year. The trust instrument makes a local bank the trustee, and provides that the trustee shall have uncontrolled discretion to distribute the income and principal from the trust to Patricia or her descendants for expenses the trustee determines to be necessary for the beneficiaries' health, welfare, comfort, support, maintenance or education, or, if the trustee finds it advisable, no such payments may be made and the income not paid may be added back in to the corpus of the trust. The corpus of the trust is to go to her descendants on her death. Should Patricia's income from the trust be taken into account in arriving at a child support order under the guidelines? (See <u>In re Marriage of Jones, 812 P.2d 1152 (Colo.1991)</u>.)

───────

In Re the Marriage of Little

<u>975 P.2d 108 (Ariz 1999)</u> (en banc)

McGregor, Justice.

In this opinion, we consider the standard courts should apply in determining whether a non-custodial parent's voluntary decision to leave his or her employment to become a full-time student constitutes a sufficient change in circumstances to warrant a downward modification of the parent's child support obligation.

I.

The parties divorced in November 1995. The court ordered appellant Billy L. Little, Jr., an Air Force lieutenant, to pay $1,186 per month for the support of his two young children. In August 1996, appellant resigned his commission in the Air Force, a position that paid $48,000 in yearly salary plus benefits, and chose to enroll as a full-time student at Arizona State University College of Law rather than to seek employment.

Upon leaving the Air Force, appellant petitioned the court to reduce his child support obligation to $239 per month. The trial court concluded that appellant had failed to prove a substantial and continuing change of circumstances in accordance with Arizona Revised Statutes (A.R.S.) §§ 25–327.A and 25–503.F, and denied his request for modification. The trial court specifically found that appellant voluntarily left his employment to further his own ambition; that he failed to consider the needs of his children when he made that decision; and that to reduce his child support obligation would be to his children's immediate detriment and their previously established needs. The trial court did reduce appellant's child support obligation to $972 per month on the ground that appellee Lisa L. Little had acquired a higher paying job.[1]

The court of appeals, applying a good faith test to determine whether appellant acted reasonably in voluntarily leaving his employment, held that the trial court abused its discretion in finding that appellant's decision to terminate his employment and pursue a law degree was unreasonable. Because we hold that a court, rather than rely upon a good faith test, must balance a number of factors to determine whether to modify a child support order to reflect a substantial and continuing change of circumstances, we vacate the opinion of the court of appeals and affirm the decision of the trial court.

II.

A.

The decision to modify an award of child support rests within the sound discretion of the trial court and, absent an abuse of that discretion, will not be disturbed on appeal. See *Fought v. Fought*, 94 Ariz. 187, 188, 382 P.2d 667, 668 (1963). An abuse of discretion exists when the record, viewed in the light most favorable to upholding the trial court's decision, is "devoid of competent evidence to support" the decision.

---

[1]   Throughout law school, appellant has financed his education and child support obligation through student loans and, according to his own assertions, has paid child support at the average rate of $800 per month.

B.

Arizona's law governing modification of child support orders, codified at A.R.S. §§ 25–327.A and 25–503.F, states that a court should modify a child support order only if a parent shows a substantial, continuing change of circumstances. Guidelines adopted by this court provide procedural guidance in applying the substantive law. See A.R.S. § 25–501.C; Appendix to <u>A.R.S. § 25–320</u>, Child Support Guidelines (Guidelines); *see also* <u>In re Marriage of Pacific, 168 Ariz. 460, 815 P.2d 7 (App.1991)</u> (holding that the Guidelines are not substantive law, but function rather as a source of guidance to trial courts in applying the substantive statutory and case law). According to the Guidelines, when a parent is unemployed or working below his or her full earning potential, a trial court calculating the appropriate child support payment may impute income to that parent, up to full earning capacity, if the parent's earnings are reduced voluntarily and not for reasonable cause. *See* Guidelines 4.e. The Guidelines also state that the trial court may elect not to impute income to a parent if he or she is enrolled in reasonable occupational training that will establish basic skills or is reasonably calculated to enhance earning capacity. *See* Guidelines 4.e.2. Significantly, both the governing statute and the Guidelines recognize that a parent's child support obligation is paramount to all other financial obligations, and that a parent has a legal duty to support his or her biological and adopted children. *See* A.R.S. § 25–501.C; *see also* Guidelines 2.b, d.

C.

Arizona's appellate courts have considered whether a court should modify a child support order to reflect a change in an obligor parent's employment in the contexts of incarceration, sale of a business, retirement, layoff, and strike. We have not, however, considered the issue of what effect a parent's voluntary decision to forego employment and become a full-time student has upon that parent's obligation to pay child support.

A number of other jurisdictions have considered the issue that confronts us. Courts in sister jurisdictions have applied one of three tests to determine whether to modify a child support order when a parent voluntarily terminates his or her employment. See Lewis Becker, <u>Spousal and Child Support and the "Voluntary Reduction of Income" Doctrine, 29 Conn. L. Rev. 647, 658 (1997)</u>. The first of these tests, the good faith test, "considers the actual earnings of a party rather than his earning capacity, so long as" he or she acted in good faith and not "primarily for the purpose of avoiding a support obligation" when he or she terminated employment. The second test, designated the strict rule test, "disregards any income reduction produced by voluntary conduct and. . .looks at the earning capacity of a party in fashioning a support obligation." The third test, referred to as the intermediate test, balances various factors to determine "whether to use actual income or earning capacity in making a support determination." Each of the tests evidences its own strengths and weaknesses, and each reflects the public policy of its adopting jurisdiction.

Other jurisdictions have detected three fundamental flaws in the good faith test, which assigns the highest value to the obligor parent's individual freedom of choice. First, the test erroneously "assumes that a divorced or separated party to a support proceeding will continue to make decisions in the best overall interest of the family unit," when often, in fact, the party will not. Second, the test fails to attach sufficient importance to a parent's existing obligation to support his or her children. As one court explained, the good faith test allows a parent to be "free to retire, take a vow of poverty, write poetry, or hawk roses in an airport, if he or she sees fit," provided only that his or her motivation for acting is not to shirk a child support obligation. *Deegan v. Deegan*, 254 N.J.Super. 350, 603 A.2d 542, 546 (1992). Third, once the party seeking a downward modification provides a seemingly good faith reason for leaving employment, the burden of proof often shifts to the party opposing the reduction to then show that the reason given is merely a sham. Even if the burden of proof does not shift, the trial court is still left with the difficult task of evaluating a party's subjective motivation. While all those factors influence our decision to reject the good faith test, we regard the primary shortcoming of the good faith test as being its focus upon the parent's motivation for leaving employment rather than upon the parent's responsibility to his or her children and the effect of the parent's decision on the best interests of the children.

The strict rule test also contains a fatal flaw. This test is too inflexible because it considers only one factor, the parent's earning capacity, in determining whether to modify a child support order when a parent voluntarily leaves employment. We decline to adopt the strict rule test because it allows no consideration of the parent's individual freedom or of the economic benefits that can result to both parent and children from additional training or education.

We reject both these extreme approaches and instead adopt an intermediate balancing test that considers a number of factors, consistent with A.R.S. §§ 25–327.A, 25–503.F, 25–501.C, and the Guidelines.

D.

Arizona law prescribes that "[t]he obligation to pay child support is primary and other financial obligations are secondary." A.R.S. § 25–501.C. Thus, the paramount factor a trial court must consider in determining whether a voluntary change in employment constitutes a substantial and continuing change in circumstances sufficient to justify a child support modification is the financial impact of the parent's decision on the child or children the support order protects. If a reduction in child support due to a non-custodial parent's voluntary decision to change his or her employment status places a child in financial peril, then the court generally should not permit a downward modification.

In many instances, the impact on the children will not be so severe as to place the children in peril. In those circumstances, courts must consider the overall reasonableness of a parent's voluntary decision to terminate employment and return to school. The answers to several questions will provide relevant information. The court should ask whether the parent's current educational level and physical capacity provide him or her with the ability to find suitable work in the marketplace. If so, the decision to leave employment is less reasonable. See *Patterson v. Patterson*, 102 Ariz. 410, 415, 432 P.2d 143, 148 (1967) (refusing to reduce a father's child support award on the grounds that "no showing was made that he lacked the ability or capacity to work" and because a father's obligation to his children "cannot be diminished because he preferred to be idle rather than industrious or [that]. . .his own improprieties. . .caused a diminution in his medical practice income"). In contrast, answers to other questions make the parent's decision to leave employment more reasonable. If the additional training is likely to increase the parent's earning potential, the decision is more likely to be found reasonable. *See* Guidelines 4.e.2; *see also* *Rubenstein v. Rubenstein*, 655 So.2d 1050, 1052 (Ala.Civ.App.1995) (holding that the trial court did not abuse its discretion in failing to impute additional income to a father who, while completing a residency program that would increase his future income potential, continued to fulfill his current support obligation). The court should also consider the length of the parent's proposed educational program, because it matters whether the children are young enough to benefit from the parent's increased future income. *See* *Overbey v. Overbey*, 698 So.2d 811, 815 (Fla.1997) (considering as a factor in its refusal to reduce a father's child support obligation the fact that "the older child will reach majority before the father finishes school" and the younger child will do so "only a few years thereafter"). The court also should inquire whether the parent is able to finance his or her child support obligation while in school through other resources such as student loans or part-time employment. *See* *Baker v. Grathwohl*, 97 Ohio App.3d 116, 646 N.E.2d 253, 255 (1994) (discussing the fact that the trial court was not convinced that the obligor father would not be able to obtain part-time employment during law school). Finally, the court should consider whether the parent's decision is made in good faith, as a decision to forego employment and return to school usually will not be reasonable or made in good faith if the parent acts to avoid a child support obligation.

We do not intend to suggest that the factors listed above are exhaustive of the relevant areas of inquiry. The primary task for a trial court is to decide each case based upon " 'the best interests of the child, not the convenience or personal preference of a parent.' " <u>*Department of Soc. Servs. v. Ewing*, 22 Va.App. 466, 470</u> <u>S.E.2d 608, 611 (1996)</u> (quoting <u>*Brody v. Brody*, 16 Va.App. 647, 432 S.E.2d 20,</u> <u>22 (1993)</u>). Trial courts therefore retain discretion to " 'consider the nature of the changes and the reasons for the changes, and. . .determine whether, under all the circumstances, a modification is warranted.' " <u>*In re Marriage of Clyatt*, 267 Mont.</u> <u>119, 882 P.2d 503, 505 (1994)</u> (quoting <u>*In re Marriage of Rome*, 190 Mont. 495,</u> <u>621 P.2d 1090, 1092 (1981)</u>).

We believe the balancing test described above comports not only with Arizona's public policy, but also with a national policy trend that favors strictly enforcing child support obligations. Several states, including Alabama, Florida, Maine, Montana, New Mexico, Ohio, and Virginia, recently have held that a parent's voluntary return to school does not justify a downward modification of his or her child support obligation. *See* <u>*Overbey*, 698 So.2d at 811</u>; <u>*Ewing*, 470 S.E.2d at</u> <u>608</u>; <u>*Harvey v. Robinson*, 665 A.2d 215 (Me.1995)</u>; <u>*Clyatt*, 882 P.2d at 503</u>; <u>*Baker*,</u> <u>646 N.E.2d at 253</u>; <u>*Johnson v. Johnson*, 597 So.2d 699 (Ala.Civ.App.1992)</u>; <u>*Wolcott*</u> <u>*v. Wolcott*, 105 N.M. 608, 735 P.2d 326 (N.M.App.1987)</u>. Moreover, the federal government has passed laws recognizing that the duty to support one's children is paramount. For instance, federal bankruptcy law excepts debts "to a. . .child of the debtor, for. . .support of such. . .child, in connection with a separation agreement, divorce or other order of a court of record" from discharge in bankruptcy proceedings. <u>11 U.S.C.A. § 523(a)(5) (West Supp.1998)</u>. Recently-enacted federal criminal legislation provides that a parent who "wilfully fails to pay a support obligation with respect to a child who resides in another State shall be punished" by fine and/or up to six months imprisonment for the first offense, and by fine and/or up to two years imprisonment for subsequent offenses. <u>18 U.S.C.A. § 228 (West</u> <u>Supp.1998)</u>. In addition, Congress authorized the Bureau of Justice Assistance to provide grants to states "to develop, implement, and enforce criminal interstate child support legislation and coordinate criminal interstate child support efforts." <u>42 U.S.C.A. § 3796cc (West 1994)</u>.

* * *

Applying the balancing test to the facts involved here, we conclude that the trial court did not abuse its discretion when it refused appellant's request for a downward modification of his child support obligation. First, the negative impact of the requested reduction on appellant's children, had the trial court granted it, would have been substantial. The trial court found that such a reduction "would be to the children's immediate detriment and their previously established needs." The record also reveals that appellee earns only $1,040 per month in salary. This income places the Little family well below the 1998 federal poverty level.[3] Without their father's support, appellant's children would face significant economic hardship. Second, appellant holds Bachelor of Arts and Master of Business Administration degrees. Appellant, by asking the trial court to assume he will earn more money when he completes law school than he could have earned in the private business sector, invited the court to engage in speculation. Therefore, while appellant's children are young enough to benefit from any increased income their father earns, the speculative nature of the increase justified giving this factor minimal weight. Third, the record does not reflect that appellant, upon leaving the Air Force, even attempted to obtain suitable employment in the Phoenix metropolitan area that would have allowed him to be close to his children and fulfill his financial obligations to them. Fourth, appellant has been able to finance his law school education and most of his child support obligation through student loans. Nothing in the record suggests that appellant is unable to obtain part-time employment to fulfill the remainder of his child support obligation. Finally, the trial court specifically found that appellant failed to act in good faith and instead endeavored to further his own ambition when he chose to forego employment and become a full-time student. Thus, the trial court did not abuse its discretion when it determined that appellant failed to act in his children's best interests when he voluntarily left full-time employment to enroll in law school.

E.

We realize that the "responsibilities of begetting a family many times raise havoc with dreams. Nevertheless, the duty [to support one's children] persists, with full authority in the State to enforce it." _Romano v. Romano, 133 Vt. 314, 340 A.2d 63, 64 (1975)_. We therefore vacate the opinion of the court of appeals and affirm the decision of the trial court.

Points for Discussion

a. Imputed Income

As suggested by *Lauderman* and *Little*, courts may impute income to a parent who is unemployed or underemployed in an initial support determination or a support modification. *Little* describes different tests courts have applied to this problem; the issue is addressed by statute or court rules in some jurisdictions. As illustrated by the *Lauderman* case, courts in states with income shares guidelines

---

[3]   The 1998 Department of Health and Human Services Poverty Guidelines list the poverty level for a family of three as $13,650 annually. *See* 63 Fed.Reg. 9235–38 (1998). Mrs. Little's annual salary is $12,480.

may also impute income to an unemployed custodial parent. Tetreault v. Coon, 708 A.2d 571 (Vt. 1998).

Many cases have considered incarcerated child support obligors. Some courts have taken the view that this is involuntary unemployment and an appropriate basis for modification, e.g. Wills v. Jones, 667 A.2d 331 (Md. 1995). Other courts have refused to reduce support obligations in this situation, e.g. In re Marriage of Thurmond, 962 P.2d 1064 (Kan. 1998); Yerkes v. Yerkes, 824 A.2d 1169 (Pa. 2003). Under a new policy, in effect since January 2017, the federal regulations that govern child support enforcement prohibit states from treating incarceration as voluntary unemployment in establishing or modifying child support orders. See 45 CFR 302.56(c)(3) (2018). See also the discussion of Child Support and Incarceration on the web page of the National Conference of State Legislators.

Child Support and Criminal Law

Lawyers with a criminal defense practice may encounter child support issues in two ways: when a client faces state or federal criminal charges for failure to pay child support, or when a client's arrest or conviction on other charges means that he or she will no longer be able to pay court-ordered child support. Federal regulations require states to have procedures for review and adjustment of child support orders when a noncustodial parent will be incarcerated for more than 180 days. See 45 CFR § 303.8 (2018). How (and when) should defense lawyers counsel their clients about child support obligations and other parental responsibilities?

b. Modification of Support

As *Little* demonstrates, child support orders may be modified upon proof of a substantial change in circumstances, and states must have procedures for periodic review and adjustment of support orders. Some support guidelines include a formula providing for modification when there is a certain percentage difference between a prior award and the amount due under the guidelines in the new circumstances. See, e.g., Colo. Rev. Stat. Ann. § 14–10–122(b) (2018) (less than a 10% difference between an award and the guidelines is deemed not a substantial and continuing change of circumstances). To facilitate this kind of reevaluation, parents may agree or be ordered to exchange their tax returns on a regular basis. See, e.g., <u>Decker v. Decker, 48 N.Y.S.3d 827 (App. Div. 2017)</u>. Because child support orders are issued by the court, they cannot be modified by private agreement without court approval. See, e.g., <u>Court v. Kiesman, 850 A.2d 330 (Me.2004)</u> (holding that parent's agreement to give used truck as payment for three years of child support was unenforceable).

Each installment due under a child support order becomes vested as a final judgment when it accrues and is unpaid, and for this reason only future installments of child support may be modified. This rule facilitates enforcement of child support orders, and is required by federal law. See <u>42 U.S.C.A. § 666(a)(9)(C) (2018)</u>. Under some state statutes, retroactive modification to increase support is permitted if one of the parties has misrepresented or failed to disclose income or other relevant information. See, e.g., <u>23 Pa. Cons. Stat. Ann. § 4352(e) (2018)</u>, applied in <u>Albert v. Albert, 707 A.2d 234 (Pa.Super.Ct.1998)</u>.

The motion to modify is treated as a continuation of the original proceeding, and <u>UIFSA § 205</u> confers continuing exclusive jurisdiction on a tribunal that has entered a support order if the obligor, the obligee, or the child is residing in the forum state. UIFSA's jurisdictional requirements for support modification proceedings are discussed in more detail below.

Informal Modification

Lawyers should always advise clients paying family support support that an informal agreement to modify support will not bind the other party unless it has been approved by a court. Many cases have ordered parents to pay large amounts of arrearages in this situation. See, e.g., <u>In re Laura, 13 A.3d 330 (N.H. 2010)</u>. See also <u>Culver v. Culver, 17 A.3d 1048 (Conn. App. Ct. 2011)</u>, which held that an oral agreement to modify support was not enforceable and that the defendant owed $225,000 in past due child support.

c. Termination of Support

A parent's legal obligation to support his or her child usually ends when the child reaches the age of majority or is otherwise emancipated. Emancipation, discussed in Chapter 4, generally occurs when a child marries, enlists in the military, or leaves home and becomes self-supporting. Although the age of majority was 21 under the common law, most states have reduced the age of majority by statute to 18. Some states extend the parental obligation to pay support beyond the legal age of majority, typically until the child finishes high school. In New York, children have a right of support until age 21. See N.Y. Fam. Ct. Act § 413(1)(a) (2018). States may allow support to continue beyond the age of majority for educational purposes or in cases of disability; these issues are discussed in the next case and the notes that follow. In most states, parties may stipulate in a separation agreement or consent judgment that child support will continue beyond the usual age of majority. The separate question of whether courts have authority to order post-majority support for educational or other expenses is taken up in the following case and notes.

State laws may provide that a parent's obligation to pay support terminates when the parent dies, see, e.g., Benson ex rel. Patterson v. Patterson, 830 A.2d 966 (Pa. 2003), or that the obligation to pay support does not end on the death of the obligor, but becomes a claim against the parent's estate, see, e.g., L.W.K. v. E.R.C., 735 N.E.2d 359 (Mass. 2000). See also Uniform Marriage and Divorce Act § 316(c), 9A U.L.A. (Part 2) 102 (1998). The cases are collected in Susan L. Thomas, Annotation, *Death of Obligor as Affecting Decree for Child Support*, 14 A.L.R.5th 557 (1993).

In most states, a parent's obligation to pay support terminates automatically when his or her parental rights are terminated. See McCabe v. McCabe, 78 P.3d 956 (Okla. 2003) (listing cases). In a few jurisdictions, child support obligations may continue after termination, see, e.g., State v. Fritz, 801 A.2d 679 (R.I. 2002). Child support obligations also end when paternity is disestablished; see, e.g., Walter v. Gunter, 788 A.2d 609 (Md. 2002).

Go Online

Links to state laws regarding termination of child support are available on the web site of the National Conference of State Legislatures.

Problem 7-12

Two years after his divorce from Cheryl, David was laid off from his job as assistant plant manager at a local woolen mill. David had worked at the mill more than twenty years, and was earning $60,000 when it closed. He will be able to draw unemployment benefits for a year, but he does not anticipate being able to find new employment that will pay more than $20,000 a year. When he files a motion to modify child support, Cheryl argues that he could earn $50,000 in a position similar to his old job if he relocated from Maine to Minnesota, North Carolina, or Mexico. Cheryl earns $15,000 a year cleaning offices and working as a cook on weekends. What income should the court impute to David? (See Wrenn v. Lewis, 818 A.2d 1005 (Me. 2003); see also Quintana v. Eddins, 38 P.3d 203 (N.M. Ct. App. 2001).)

Problem 7-13

While Richard and Barbara were married, Richard worked as a stagehand, earning the union wage of $20 per hour for theater work and $15 per hour for television work. He phoned the union hall each day for jobs, and because of his seniority could usually have his choice of the work available. Before the separation, Richard worked two or three theater jobs each day, often including nights and weekends and sometimes as many as sixteen hours in a day. His average earnings were $5000 to $6000 a month. After the parties separated, Richard began taking only television work, and is now earning approximately $3000 a month. Barbara argues that the court should impute income to Richard based on his demonstrated ability to earn greater amounts of money; Richard argues that he shifted to television work so that he could work regular eight hour days and spend more time with their seven year old daughter. Should the court impute additional income to Richard? (See In re Marriage of Simpson, 841 P.2d 931 (Cal. 1992).)

Problem 7-14

When Jerry and Judith divorced, Jerry had primary residential custody of their two children, and Judith, who was unemployed, was ordered to pay child support of $25 per month. Two years later, the state child support enforcement agency filed a motion to modify support. The evidence showed that Judith had remarried and was self-employed as a beautician, working only 24 hours a week because of the expense of daycare for her new daughter. A state statute provides that "absent substantial justification, it should be assumed that a parent is able to earn at least the federal minimum wage and to work 40 hours per week." How should the court compute Judith's income? (See Marriage of Milano, 936 P.2d 302 (Kan. Ct. App. 1997).)

———————

Style v. Shaub

955 A.2d 403 (Pa. Super. Ct. 2008)

OPINION BY DONOHUE, J.:

¶ 1 Appellant Sharon L. Style ("Style") appeals the order of the Court of Common Pleas of Lancaster County, Pennsylvania dismissing a petition for child support filed on behalf of her adult son, Dustin Charles Shaub ("Dustin"). After careful review, we affirm.

¶ 2 Style and Ronald C. Shaub ("Shaub") married on August 31, 1984 and their son, Dustin, was born on January 3, 1987. In November 1999, they separated and Style filed a petition requesting child support for Dustin, which was granted. The couple divorced on July 5, 2002.

¶ 3 On January 3, 2005, Dustin turned 18 years old and in July 2005 he completed high school. Pursuant to Pa.R.C.P.1910.19(e), the Lancaster County Domestic Relations Office ("Domestic Relations Office"), sent Style notice that the child support order for Dustin would be terminated unless she notified them within thirty (30) days of any basis for continuing support. Neither Style nor Dustin responded to the Domestic Relations Office's Rule 1910.19(e) notice.[1] On June 6, 2005, the trial court ordered Shaub to cure arrearages owed to Style for past support, but determined that further child support for Dustin would be terminated. On July 14, 2005, after finding that Shaub had paid all arrears and fees, the trial court entered an order terminating child support for Dustin.

¶ 4 On October 25, 2006, Style filed a new complaint for child support on Dustin's behalf. In the new complaint, Style alleged that Dustin, now 19, had psychiatric and medical limitations that precluded him from maintaining gainful employment to support himself. On January 31, 2007, the trial court dismissed Style's complaint. On February 7, 2007, Style filed a *pro se* request for an evidentiary hearing, which was granted. The trial court conducted the evidentiary hearing on June 1, 2007.

¶ 5 At the hearing, testimony revealed that Dustin has had a long history of psychiatric and medical disabilities, including diagnoses for Attention Deficit Hyperactivity Disorder ("ADHD"), Oppositional Defiant Disorder ("ODD"), dysthymia (also referred to as chronic depression), and Atypical Autism. Dustin testified that he had been taking various medications for these conditions for most of his life.

---

[1]   At the evidentiary hearing, Style testified that she "did not have any money to do anything" and that she "didn't have the funds to hire a lawyer to do it." She further testified that she sent "the paper back stating that Dustin was disabled and has disabilities, and they sent my paper back stating that I needed to file some other kind of paper."

¶ 6 A review of Dustin's employment history showed that he had attempted three jobs, with mixed success. For example, he had been able to perform as a dishwasher at Pizza Hut, but could not handle a job at Dollar Store because he lost concentration and would just wander about the store. In September 2006, Dustin began attending the Hiram G. Andrews Center (the "Andrews Center"), a residential institution in Johnstown, Pennsylvania which provides vocational training to disabled individuals.[2] Lewis Hogarth ("Hogarth"), his vocational evaluator at the Andrews Center, opined that Dustin could handle a job as a kitchen worker or custodian staff, and that while he worked slowly he could handle a variety of tasks and was courteous and cooperative. Hogarth's report indicated that Dustin reads at an 8th grade level, can do mathematics at a 9th grade level, and has a full scale IQ of 78.

¶ 7 The trial court dismissed Style's complaint for two reasons. First, the trial court found that because Style and Dustin failed to respond to the Rule 1910.19(e) notice from the Domestic Relations Office, they were estopped from demanding a new support order directing Shaub to pay child support for Dustin as an adult. Second, the trial court determined that Style and Dustin had presented insufficient evidence to rebut the presumption that Dustin, having reached the age of majority and completed high school, was unable to engage in profitable employment at a supporting wage. On appeal, Style challenges both of these rulings.

¶ 8 This Court's standard and scope of review regarding a child support order is well-settled:

> In reviewing an order entered in a support proceeding, an appellate court has a limited scope of review. The trial court possesses wide discretion as to the proper amount of child support and a reviewing court will not interfere with the determination of the court below unless there has been a clear abuse of discretion. The function of the appellate court is to determine whether there is sufficient evidence to sustain the order of the hearing judge. An abuse of discretion is not merely an error of judgment; rather, it occurs when the law is overridden or misapplied, or the judgment exercised is manifestly unreasonable or the result of partiality, bias or ill-will.

Kotzbauer v. Kotzbauer, 937 A. 2d 487, 489 (Pa.Super. 2007) (internal citations omitted).

¶ 9 Our Court has not previously addressed the issue of whether it is permissible to assert a post-majority claim for support after a previous support order was terminated pursuant to Rule 1910.19(e). Our decisions in this area have all addressed the uninterrupted continuation of support after age 18, *see, e.g., Com.*

---

[2]   Style testified that she filed the new support complaint because she had lost her job and tuition at the Andrews Center had become a financial burden to her.

ex. rel. Cann v. Cann, 274 Pa.Super. 274, 418 A.2d 403, 405 (1980), or a first request for support of a mentally or physically disabled adult child. *See Kotzbauer; see also Hanson v. Hanson,* 425 Pa.Super. 508, 625 A.2d 1212, 1214 (1993).

* * *

¶ 13 Although the pre-majority child support order was properly terminated pursuant to Rule 1910.19(e), we do not agree with the trial court that Style was estopped from filing a new request for support. Without determining the applicability of the doctrine of equitable estoppel generally to issues of child support like the one presented here, it is clear that under the law of Pennsylvania, a finding of estoppel must be based upon a demonstration of detrimental reliance by the party asserting the doctrine. Here Shaub offered no evidence to show any detrimental reliance on his part to the termination of the original (pre-majority) child support order.

¶ 14 In Pennsylvania, the duty to support a child generally ceases when the child reaches the age of majority, which is defined as either eighteen years of age or when the child graduates from high school, whichever comes later. *Blue v. Blue,* 532 Pa. 521, 616 A.2d 628 (1992). 23 Pa.C.S.A. § 4321(3), however, provides that "[p]arents may be liable for the support of their children who are 18 years of age or older." In applying section 4321(3), this Court has found that there is a presumption that the duty to support a child ends when the child reaches majority:

> Ordinarily a parent is not required to support his adult child but there is a well recognized exception supported by abundant authority that where such child is too feeble physically or mentally to support itself the duty on the parent continues after the child has attained its majority.

Commonwealth ex. rel. O'Malley v. O'Malley, 105 Pa.Super. 232, 161 A. 883, 884 (1932); *see also Verna v. Verna,* 288 Pa.Super. 511, 432 A.2d 630, 632 (1981); *Colantoni v. Colantoni,* 220 Pa.Super. 46, 281 A.2d 662, 664 (1971).

¶ 15 This presumption is not rebuttable if the child becomes disabled only *after* reaching the age of majority. *See Overseers of Mount Pleasant v. Wilcox,* 12 Pa.C.C. 447, 2 Pa. Dist. 628, 1893 WL 3104 (Pa.Quar.Sess.1893) (holding that where a child attained majority and became self-supporting, father's common law liability ceased and could not be restored by a subsequent change in the child's condition); *see also O'Malley,* 161 A. at 884. The public policy behind such rationale is apparent, as there must be a logical end point to a parent's obligation to support his or her child. Otherwise, an adult child could theoretically sue their elderly parents for support after sustaining a debilitating injury well after reaching the age of majority.

¶ 16 When the disability resulting in the child's inability to be self-sufficient already exists at the time the child reaches the age of majority, however, the presumption is rebuttable by the adult child upon proof that there are "conditions that make it impossible for her or him to be employed." In *Hanson*, John and Nancy Hanson divorced in 1987 by entering into a divorce settlement that acknowledged that their youngest daughter, Mary, "had certain handicaps which impair[ed] her employment capabilities." In the divorce settlement, the Hansons agreed that they would both keep Mary on their medical and dental insurance plans provided by their employers, but did not otherwise provide any support payments for Mary's care. Several years later, after Mary had reached the age of majority, Nancy filed a petition against John seeking child support for Mary, who lived with Nancy and had held several part-time minimum wage jobs. In rejecting John's contention that he had no legal duty to pay for the support of his adult daughter, this Court ruled that "[t]here is a duty on parents to support a child that has a physical or mental condition, *which exists at the time the child reaches its majority,* that prevents the child from being self-supporting."

¶ 17 Applying the rule in *Hanson* to this case, when Dustin turned eighteen and completed high school, a presumption arose that Shaub's legal obligation to pay child support had ended. Because Dustin's psychiatric and medical disabilities existed before he reached the age of majority, however, this presumption was rebuttable upon proof from Dustin that his disabilities prevented him from being self-supporting. Accordingly, the new complaint for child support filed by Style on Dustin's behalf should not have been dismissed as a matter of law.

Think About It

Why does the court draw this distinction between disabilities that arise before a child reaches the age of majority and those that begin later? See also In re Jacobson, 842 A.2d 77 (N.H. 2004).

¶ 18 Despite this determination, we nevertheless affirm the trial court's order denying the request for child support because we agree with the trial court that Dustin failed to present sufficient evidence to rebut the presumption in this case. To rebut the presumption that a parent has no obligation to support an adult child, "the test is whether the child is physically and mentally able to engage in profitable employment and whether employment is available to that child at a supporting wage." *Hanson, 625 A.2d at 1214*, *citing Com. ex. rel. Groff v. Groff, 173 Pa.Super. 535, 98 A.2d 449 (1953)*; and *Commonwealth v. Gilmore, 97 Pa.Super. 303 (1929)*. The adult child has the burden of proof on these issues. *See, e.g., Verna, 432 A.2d at 632*. Our scope of review is limited to a determination of whether the trial court committed an abuse of discretion or an error of law when making a determination in this regard.

¶ 19 With regard to the first part of the test, namely whether the child is physically and mentally able to engage in profitable employment, the trial court found that "the testimony presented on Dustin's behalf [was] neither convincing [n]or complete enough to meet the standard of proof [in this case]." In addition to their own testimony, Style and Dustin offered the expert testimony of Mr. Hogarth, Dustin's vocational evaluator at the Andrews Center. Mr. Hogarth testified that he had evaluated Dustin's performance of a variety of work tasks over a three-week period and found that Dustin demonstrated adequate oral communication skills, but lacked initiative, motivation and was easily distracted. Mr. Hogarth testified that distractions might be alleviated by medication for ADHD. Mr. Hogarth also noted that he observed improvement in Dustin by the third week of evaluation. Dustin was able to perform a variety of physical tasks, worked slowly but consistently, was punctual, performed a satisfactory amount and quality of work with some supervision, and was courteous and cooperative. In sum, although Mr. Hogarth described Dustin "as a person in need of rehabilitative services," he opined that he "gave him a guarded diagnosis for successful entry in the workforce at the present time."

¶ 20 Style's testimony regarding Dustin's abilities was considerably more negative.[4] She testified that Dustin had an unsuccessful work history, that he always "needs a structured environment," and that he requires constant supervision. She further testified that in her view Dustin is not capable of living on his own and that he is not employable.

¶ 21 Based upon the testimony presented, the trial court found that Style and Dustin had not proven that Dustin is not able to engage in profitable employment. The trial court summarized its findings as follows:

> In short, this Court is not certain that Dustin's work history reflects his lack of ability, but rather a bad choice in employment opportunities. The Court further believes that Dustin is capable of doing a job with a minimally distracting environment and simple repetitive tasks, rather than jobs which required him to be in a varied environment and change quickly from one task to another, particularly on his own initiative.

> * * *

> Dustin appears to be able to work, albeit at a job which involves consistent behavior and a minimum of distractibility. We all have our limits on the type of job we can perform. Dustin has those limitations, also, but that doesn't mean he cannot work within his limitations.

> * * *

---

[4]   The trial court offered the following observation regarding Dustin's testimony at the evidentiary hearing: "He sat comfortably on the witness stand and answered questions with a demeanor that gave no indication of the problems ascribed to him by his Mother."

Although the Court does not believe it was purposeful, Dustin and his mother have been choosing jobs randomly from the newspaper or internet, rather than trying to find one compatible with Dustin's limitations and needs.

Based upon our review of the record, we conclude that the trial court's findings are adequately supported by the evidence presented at the evidentiary hearing, and that the trial court did not abuse its discretion or commit an error of law when making its determination.

¶ 22 With regard to the second part of the test for rebutting the presumption, namely whether employment is available to the child at a supporting wage, the trial court found that Style and Dustin presented little or no evidence in this regard:

> [T]he Court lacks the information about Dustin's needs and what he could reasonably make at a job suited to him to enable the Court to calculate whether Dustin can make a supporting wage. Dustin made $6.25 [per hour] at the Pizza Hut and $7.00 [per hour] at the Dollar Store. The Court can assume that Dustin could now make at least minimum wage, which would provide him with a supporting wage, but this would be an assumption only, not a provable fact.
> Dustin has the burden of proof in this matter. It is not up to the Court to fill in the blanks in his testimony and supply those elements missing from his case. If expert testimony had been available to describe Dustin's disabilities and their ramifications, there might have been an appropriate conclusion to be drawn. But even Mr. Hogarth, the vocational expert, failed to discuss in detail the types of jobs that might be available.

¶ 23 Based upon our review of the record, we agree with the trial court that Style and Dustin did not prove what types of jobs Dustin is capable of performing, how much compensation Dustin could reasonably expect to receive from such employment, whether or not such jobs were available in the local marketplace, or whether Dustin could support himself on this level of compensation. As the trial court notes, although Mr. Hogarth gave Dustin "a guarded diagnosis for successful entry in the workforce," he offered no testimony describing the types of jobs Dustin could successfully perform or whether such jobs were then available in the Lancaster County area. Without evidence, we are constrained by our standard of review to affirm the trial court's order denying child support.

¶ 24 Order affirmed.

———————————

Points for Discussion

a. Support for Disabled Adult Children

Courts in many states have authority to order post-majority support for a child who is unable to be self-supporting as a result of a physical or mental disability at the time of his or her parents' divorce. In addition to *Style*, see Koltay v. Koltay, 667 P.2d 1374 (Colo.1983). Statutes in some states limit this authority, however; see, e.g., Pierce v. Pierce, 770 A.2d 867 (R.I.2001). Is there a statutory basis for the post-majority support requested in *Style*? What additional evidence might have helped Dustin to prevail in this case?

Style notes that the court would not have authority to order parents to support a child who becomes disabled after reaching the age of majority. What if the parents of a disabled child divorce after their child has reached adulthood? See Geygan v. Geygan, 973 N.E.2d 276 (Ohio. Ct. App. 2012), which held that the court had no jurisdiction to enter support and custody orders for a child who was 38 years old at the time of his parents' divorce. That court pointed out that there are different state statutes that provide a structure for care and management of adults with disabilities. Some states impose more extensive family support obligations. See, e.g., In re Guardianship of M.A.S., 266 P.3d 1267 (Mont. 2011), which applied a state statute providing that "it is the duty of the father, the mother, and the children of any poor person who is unable to provide self-maintenance by work to maintain that person to the best of their ability." See Mont. Code Ann. § 40–6–214 (2018). Legal responsibilities for adult family members are also considered in Chapter 4.

b. Post-Minority Educational Expenses

Should courts have authority to order parents to contribute to the educational expenses of children who have reached the age of majority? In states that allow child support to continue to age 21, expenses such as college tuition may be included in a child support order.

Some state statutes grant very explicit authority to the courts to order educational support beyond the normal age of majority. See, e.g., Iowa Code § 598.21F (2018) (allowing "postsecondary education subsidy"); Or. Rev. Stat. § 107.108(4) (2018) (support may be ordered for a child between age 18 and 21 attending a school, college or university). In other states, courts have ordered this type of support even without clear statutory authorization. See, e.g., Newburgh v. Arrigo, 443 A.2d 1031 (N.J. 1982). Other courts have concluded there is no basis under state law to award post-majority educational support. See, e.g., Ex parte Christopher, 145 So.3d 60 (Ala. 2013); In re Marriage of Plummer, 735 P.2d 165 (Colo.1987); Grapin v. Grapin, 450 So.2d 853 (Fla.1984); Wood v. Wood, 361

S.E.2d 819 (Ga. 1987); Adam v. Adam, 624 A.2d 1093 (R.I.1993). State statutes may prohibit awards of educational expenses beyond high school. See, e.g., N.H. Rev. Stat. § 461–A:14 V (2018). Courts that do not have authority to order parents to provide post-majority support often have authority to enforce agreements between the parents for such support. See, e.g., Minn. Stat. § 518.551 subd. 5d (2018); Zetterman v. Zetterman, 512 N.W.2d 622 (Neb. 1994).

If a court has authority to order postmajority educational support, how should it set the amount and duration? See, e.g., Newburgh v. Arrigo, 443 A.2d 1031 (N.J. 1982), listing factors for courts to consider in evaluating the claim for contribution to higher education. See generally Madeline Marzano-Lesnevich and Scott Adam Laterra, *Child Support and College: What is the Correct Result?*, 22 J. Am. Acad. Matrim. Law. 335 (2009). In Allen v. Allen, 54 N.E.3d 344 (Ind. 2016), the court concluded that authorization to order "post-secondary" educational support did not include graduate or professional school expenses.

Does a statute granting courts authority to order divorced parents to pay post-majority educational support raise constitutional concerns? Curtis v. Kline, 666 A.2d 265 (Pa. 1995), concluded that there was no rational basis for treating children with married parents differently than children with divorced parents, but other cases have concluded that such statutes are constitutional. See, e.g., In re Marriage of Crocker, 22 P.3d 759 (Or. 2001); Childers v. Childers, 575 P.2d 201 (Wash. 1978).

Problem 7-15

Charles and Helen lived together for five years, and had two young children when they separated. Charles, a professional athlete, earned a gross income of $60,000 per month, and a net income of approximately $40,000. Helen seeks child support under the state guidelines, which set the support amount for two children at 32% of the obligor's net income, or $12,800 per month. Helen asks the court to order support of $2,000 per month, and that an additional $10,800 per month to be paid into a trust fund that would fund child support if Charles' income decreases in the future, and which would also be available to the children for college tuition and other post-majority expenses. Charles has objected to this, arguing that an award of $2000 per month exceeds the children's current needs, and pointing out that courts in the jurisdiction have no authority to enter orders for post-majority support. Can the court create the trust fund? (See Nash v. Mulle, 846 S.W.2d 803 (Tenn.1993).)

Further Reading: Child Support

- Andrea H. Beller and John W. Graham, Small Change: The Economics of Child Support (1996).

- J. Thomas Oldham and Marygold S. Melli, eds., Child Support: The Next Frontier (2000).

3. Enforcing Support

Public efforts to enforce family support obligations have a long history, going back at least to the English Poor Laws enacted at the end of the sixteenth century. See Jacobus tenBroek, *California's Dual System of Family Law: Its Origin, Development and Present Status: Part I*, 16 Stan. L. Rev. 257, 283–86 (1964). Several dozen states enacted the 1910 Uniform Desertion and Nonsupport Act, and all states eventually adopted the 1950 Uniform Reciprocal Enforcement of Support Act, designed to provide a civil remedy when the support obligor and the child in need of support lived in different states. See generally William J. Brockelbank, Interstate Enforcement of Family Support;The Runaway Pappy Act (2d ed. 1971).

As noted above, child support laws are enacted and enforced primarily at the state level, within a structure established by federal law. Congress initially required states to establish child support enforcement programs in order to receive funding for the Aid to Families with Dependent Children (AFDC) program in 1950, and then enacted more comprehensive legislation in 1975, with substantial amendments in 1984, 1988, 1992, and 1996. Since 1996, the AFDC program has been replaced by block grants for Temporary Assistance for Needy Families (TANF), but states are still required to comply with the IV-D requirements to receive full funding for TANF. On the federalism questions raised by Congress's extensive role in setting child support policy, see Ann Laquer Estin, *Sharing Governance: Family Law in Congress and the States*, 18 Cornell J. L. & Pub. Pol'y 267 (2009).

In order to get the full allocation of TANF funds, every state must have a state plan for child and spousal support pursuant to 42 U.S.C. § 654, and provide services for establishment of paternity, and establishment, modification or enforcement of child support. States must implement various support enforcement procedures outlined in 42 U.S.C. § 666 (2018). Despite its tie to TANF, child support services under Title IV-D are available to all families, even those who are not eligible for TANF payments. The parent of a child who is receiving public assistance payments must assign his or her child support claim to the state, however, and the state may enforce that claim against the obligor parent and recoup its TANF expenditures from the amounts it collects. See 42 U.S.C.A. § 608(a)(3). TANF recipients are also required to cooperate in establishing a child's paternity; see generally S.D. v. Dep't of Human Services, 781 A.2d 1105 (N.J. Super. Ct. App. Div. 2001).

Make the Connection

Federal laws addressing establishment of parentage are discussed in Chapter 2.

Efforts to improve interstate child support enforcement have been one important focus of the IV-D program. Congress created the U.S. Commission on Interstate Child Support in 1988, and subsequently enacted many of its recommendations into law. See generally Margaret Campbell Haynes, *Supporting Our Children: A Blueprint for Reform*, 27 Fam. L.Q. 7 (1993). These include the Full Faith and Credit for Child Support Orders Act (FFCCSOA), 28 U.S.C. § 1738B (2018) which requires that states recognize and enforce support orders from other states. To facilitate interstate enforcement, Congress also required the states to enact the Uniform Interstate Family Support Act (UIFSA). See 42 U.S.C. § 666(f) (2018).

Go Online

Data on custodial parents and child support is available from the U.S. Census Bureau. See Timothy Grall, Current Population Reports, Custodial Mothers and Fathers and Their Child Support: 2015 (2018).

Welsher v. Rager

491 S.E.2d 661 (N.C. Ct. App. 1997)

TIMMONS-GOODSON, JUDGE.

This action arises out of plaintiff Rosemarie Welsher's attempt to enforce a New York child support order. Plaintiff and defendant Paul Rager were divorced in 1980. In 1985, plaintiff petitioned for a court order recognizing an agreement for support executed by plaintiff and defendant on 17 January 1985. The order entered on 11 February 1985 in Monroe County, New York District Court provided, in pertinent part, that defendant was to be "legally responsible for the support" of the couple's two sons, Jeremy (born 26 May 1974) and Michael (born

26 November 1976). The order obligated defendant to make payments of $45.00 per week. Defendant signed the order voluntarily, waiving his right, both to be represented by an attorney and to object to the matter in family court.

Plaintiff still resides in New York. However, defendant has moved to Winston-Salem, North Carolina; and has refused to make any of the $45.00 payments since 6 July 1995. At that time, Jeremy and Michael were twenty-one and eighteen, respectively, and Michael had just graduated from high school.

Plaintiff initiated the present action by filing a petition requesting registration and enforcement of the 1985 New York child support order in Forsyth County, North Carolina. At the time that this petition was filed, Jeremy and Michael were aged twenty-two and nineteen, respectively. The petition claimed arrearage of $1,789.64 as of 11 April 1996, and included both a copy of the original order for support and a copy of New York's Uniform Support of Dependent's Law section 31–3, which establishes the age of emancipation in the State of New York at twenty-one years.

Defendant responded by filing an "Answer for Civil Suit," which alleged, in pertinent part, that the couple's original 1980 divorce decree only obligated him to support the children until they were eighteen and out of high school; that he did not knowingly agree to pay support until the children reached twenty-one; and that he felt that making support payments to an "adult" over the age of eighteen was unjustifiable. Accordingly, defendant asked that the court relieve him of any obligation under the 1985 order for support. The answer was made in an unverified written statement and included no documentation pertaining to the divorce decree. We note that at no time did defendant seek to modify his obligation based on Jeremy's emancipation.

The matter was heard by Judge Roland H. Hayes during the 30 July 1996 civil session of Forsyth County District Court. After hearing the arguments of both parties and examining plaintiff's evidence, the trial court granted defendant's motion to dismiss, and denied plaintiff's request for continued support. Plaintiff appeals.

* * * We, therefore, proceed immediately to plaintiff's third assignment of error by which she argues that the trial court erred in failing to apply New York law in deciding whether to enforce the 1985 New York support order. Plaintiff contends that the Uniform Interstate Family Support Act (UIFSA), recently enacted by the North Carolina General Assembly, requires that a support order be interpreted according to the law of the state in which it is issued. We agree.

The Uniform Reciprocal Enforcement of Support Act (URESA) was repealed by the North Carolina General Assembly effective 1 January 1996. In its place, the legislature adopted UIFSA in Chapter 52C of our General Statutes. Both URESA and

UIFSA were promulgated and intended to be used as procedural mechanisms for the establishment, modification, and enforcement of child and spousal support obligations. See N.C. Gen.Stat. § 52C–3–301 (1995), official comment. Under URESA, a state had jurisdiction to establish, vacate, or modify an obligor's support obligation even when that obligation had been created in another jurisdiction. The result was often multiple, inconsistent obligations existing for the same obligor and injustice in that obligors could avoid their responsibility by moving to another jurisdiction and having their support obligations modified or even vacated.

UIFSA was designed to correct this problem. See Patricia Wick Hatamyar, _Critical Applications and Proposals for Improvement of the Uniform Interstate Family Support Act and The Full Faith and Credit for Child Support Orders Act_, 71 St. John's L.Rev. 1 (1997); David H. Levy & Cecilia A. Hynes, _Highlights of the Uniform Interstate Family Support Act_, 83 Ill. B.J. 647 (1997). UIFSA establishes a one order system whereby all states adopting UIFSA are required to recognize and enforce the same obligation consistently. A priority scheme is established for the recognition and enforcement of multiple existing support obligations. *See* N.C. Gen.Stat. § 52C–2–207(a)(1995). In instances where only one tribunal has issued a support order, that order becomes the one order to be recognized and enforced by states adopting UIFSA. *See* N.C.G.S. § 52C–2–207(a)(1). For example, the official comment to section 52C–6–603 of the North Carolina General Statutes notes,

> [a]lthough RURESA specifically subjects a registered order to "proceedings for reopening, vacating, or staying as a support order of this State," these remedies are not authorized under UIFSA. While a foreign support order is to be enforced and satisfied in the same manner as if it had been issued by a tribunal of the registering state, the order to be enforced remains an order of the issuing state. Conceptually, the responding state is enforcing the order of another state, not its own order.

N.C. Gen.Stat. § 52C–6–603 (1995), official comment. The one order system is applicable even where the state initiating the order has not adopted UIFSA.

Once the validity of the one order is determined, enforcement by the registering tribunal is obligatory, with two exceptions. The registering tribunal may vacate or modify the order if (1) both parties consent to the modification, or (2) the child, the obligor and the individual obligee have all permanently left the issuing state and the registering state can claim personal jurisdiction over all of them. *See* N.C. Gen.Stat. § 52C–2–205 (1995), official comment.

A non-registering party may also avoid enforcement of an order by successfully contesting its registration. Upon filing, a support order becomes registered in North Carolina and, unless successfully contested, must be recognized and enforced. N.C.G.S § 52C–6–603. The procedure for contesting a registered order is set out in Part Two of Article 6 of UIFSA, entitled "Contest of Validity of Enforcement." Under section 52C–6–607 of the General Statutes, a party seeking to vacate an order's registration has the burden of proving at least one of seven narrowly-defined defenses. The possible defenses are as follows: (1) the issuing tribunal lacked jurisdiction; (2) the order was fraudulently obtained; (3) the order has been vacated, suspended or modified; (4) the issuing tribunal has been stayed pending appeal; (5) the remedy sought is not available in this state; (6) payment has been made in full or in part; and (7) enforcement is precluded by the statute of limitations. N.C. Gen.Stat. § 52C–6–607(a)(1995). If the defending party either fails to contest the registration or does not establish a defense under 52C–6–607(a), the registering tribunal is required by law to confirm the order. N.C.G.S. § 52C–6–607(c).

In terms of choice of law, URESA generally required that the law applied in interpreting and/or enforcing the support order be that of the state in which enforcement was sought. *See* Pieper v. Pieper, 90 N.C.App. 405, 368 S.E.2d 422 (holding that URESA could not be used to enforce a foreign support order requiring support until

Take Note

The grounds listed here are the only defenses available to an individual opposing registration and enforcement.

age 22 since such an order could not have been issued under North Carolina law), *aff'd*, 323 N.C. 617, 374 S.E.2d 275 (1988). However, UIFSA provides, "The law of the issuing state governs the nature, extent, amount, and duration of current payments and other obligations of support and the payment of arrears under the order." N.C. Gen.Stat. § 52C–6–604(a)(1995). The official comment to section 52C–6–604 notes that this means "an order for the support of a child until age 21 must be recognized and enforced in that manner in a state in which the duty of support of a child ends at age 18." N.C.G.S. § 52C–6–604, official comment.

* * *

Plaintiff's support order became registered in North Carolina upon filing. Applying the appropriate law, UIFSA, the record is devoid of a defense under section 52C–6–607 of the General Statutes, which would justify vacating a properly registered support order. Under UIFSA, unless the court finds that the defendant has met his burden of proving one of the specified defenses, enforcement is compulsory. The trial court's single finding of fact in the present case was that the children had reached eighteen. Under URESA, such a finding may have been sufficient to deny enforcement since North Carolina law would have governed interpretation of the order, and provided for emancipation at eighteen. *See* Pieper, 90 N.C.App. 405, 368 S.E.2d 422. However, as URESA has been repealed, New York law, which provides that the age of emancipation is twenty-one, must be applied in enforcing the 11 February 1985 foreign order.

Moreover, the record is devoid of any evidence that either (1) both parties consented to a modification, or (2) the issuing state had lost continuing, exclusive jurisdiction over the order. Hence, no court of this jurisdiction may properly vacate or modify this order. *See* N.C.G.S. § 52C–2–205. If defendant wishes to have the order modified or vacated, he must pursue the matter in New York, which maintains continuing, exclusive jurisdiction over the order.

* * *

In her final assignment of error, plaintiff contends that the trial court erred in failing to use New York law in interpreting the order, as required by the Federal Full Faith and Credit for Child Support Orders Act (FFCCSOA), 28 U.S.C. § 1738B. Again, we agree.

* * *

We note that the trial court, applying New York law could properly find that defendant was not liable for any arrearage as to Jeremy, because Jeremy had reached the age of 21 prior to the 6 July 1995 date on which defendant ceased to make court-ordered support payment. However, the trial court is still without authority to modify the $45.00 a week payment, as such modification is not allowed under UIFSA and FFCCSOA. The New York order does not provide a per child break-down regarding defendant's support obligation, but merely provides that $45.00 per week is to be paid for both children. Absent further knowledge as to whether an adjustment would be permitted under New York law for Jeremy's emancipation, and in what proportion, enforcement of the order in any amount less than $45.00 per week would be an impermissible modification of the New York order. Defendant's only recourse, in this case, then, is to seek modification of his child support obligation in New York, based upon Jeremy's emancipation. *See State, Dept. of Rev. v. Skladanuk,* 683 So.2d 624 (Fla.Dist.Ct.App.1996) (holding that FFCCSOA prevented Florida court from modifying the terms of a New York order as written regardless of the defendant's inability to pay and that the defendant was required to seek modification of his child support obligation in New York).

In sum, because the trial court failed to apply New York law in accordance with UIFSA and FFCCSOA, its order is vacated, and this matter is remanded to the trial court for hearing and the entry of an order not inconsistent with this opinion.

Reversed and remanded.

———————————

Points for Discussion

a. Continuing Exclusive Jurisdiction

Welsher illustrates one of the key aspects of UIFSA: Once a court or administrative tribunal in a state has issued a support order, that tribunal has continuing exclusive jurisdiction (CEJ) under UIFSA § 205(a) if the state remains the residence of the obligor, the individual obligee, or the child, or if the parties consent to a continuation of jurisdiction by that tribunal. In addition to the *Welsher* case, see Cohen v. Cohen, 25 N.E.3d 840 (Mass. 2015); State ex rel. Harnes v. Lawrence, 538 S.E.2d 223 (N.C. Ct. App. 2000); Scanlon v. Witrak, 42 P.3d 447 (Wash. Ct. App. 2002). See also Teseniar v. Spicer, 74 P.3d 910 (Alaska 2003) (finding continuing exclusive jurisdiction in Alaska where mother and child remained in the state). How does UIFSA's continuing jurisdiction language apply to a situation in which the custodial parent and children had left the original forum state and then resumed residency there? See Klingel v. Reill, 841 N.E.2d 1256 (Mass. 2006).

Once a tribunal loses its continuing exclusive jurisdiction, it may no longer modify the child support order, which may be registered for modification purposes in another state. UIFSA § 205(b) allows a tribunal in another state to assume jurisdiction if several conditions are satisfied. Each individual party must file a consent with the original court agreeing to the assumption of jurisdiction by the new tribunal, and the new tribunal must have jurisdiction over at least one of the individual parties or be located in the state of residence of the child. See Knabe v. Brister, 65 Cal.Rptr.3d 493 (Ct. App. 2007); Peace v. Peace, 737 A.2d 1164 (N.J. Super. Ct. Ch. Div. 1999).

b. UIFSA Registration and Enforcement

Welsher also illustrates the registration and enforcement aspects of UIFSA in a multistate context. Once a support order is registered in a state under UIFSA § 603, it is enforceable in the same manner as an order issued by a court in that state. The court can apply the same procedures to a registered out-of-state order that it applies in enforcing its own orders, but the court is not permitted to modify the order unless certain other conditions are present, as discussed in the notes below.

UIFSA § 604(a) provides that the law of the issuing state governs "the nature, extent, amount and duration of current payments" and "the computation and payment of arrearages" under the order. Section 604(b) directs that, in proceedings to collect arrearages, the court must apply whichever state's statute of limitations is longer. See, e.g., Clemmons v. Office of Child Support Enforcement, 47 S.W.3d 227 (Ark. 2001), Marriage of Morris, 32 P.3d 625 (Colo. Ct. App. 2001); North Carolina v. Bray, 503 S.E.2d 686 (N.C. Ct. App. 1998); Attorney General v. Litten, 999 S.W.2d 74 (Tex. App. 1999). Under § 604(c), the responding tribunal applies the enforcement procedures and remedies of its own state to enforce current support and collect arrears and interest.

In an enforcement proceeding under UIFSA, the only defenses available to a support obligor are the ones listed in UIFSA § 607(a), quoted by the court in *Welsher* and listed in the chart below. What other defenses might a support obligor want to assert in an enforcement action?

Defenses to Registration or Enforcement of Support Orders under UIFSA
• The issuing tribunal lacked personal jurisdiction over the contesting party - § 607(a)(1)
• The order was obtained by fraud - § 607(a)(2)
• The order has been vacated, suspended or modified by a later order - § 607(a)(3)
• The issuing tribunal has stayed the order pending appeal - § 607(a)(4)
• There is a defense under the law of the enforcing state to the remedy sought - § 607(a)(5)
• Full or partial payment has been made - § 607(a)(6)
• The statute of limitations under § 604 precludes enforcement of some or all of the alleged arrearages - § 607(a)(7)
• The alleged controlling order is not the controlling order under § 207 - § 607(a)(8)

c. Modification Jurisdiction

UIFSA provides for registration of a child support order that was issued in another state for modification, or modification and enforcement, if the requirements of § 611(a) or § 613 are met. Section 611(a)(1) requires that the child, the support obligor and the party entitled to receive support do not reside in the issuing state, that the party seeking modification is not a resident of the new state, and that the respondent is subject to personal jurisdiction in the new state. The drafters of UIFSA have described this by saying that the party seeking a modification must "play an away game" by going to the state where the other party lives. Alternatively, § 611(a)(2) allows a tribunal in the new state to assume jurisdiction if the child is a resident of the state, any individual party is subject to personal jurisdiction in the state, and all of the individual parties file consents. Under § 613, a tribunal may assume jurisdiction to modify an order from another state if all of the individual parties reside in the new state and the child does not still reside in the issuing state. Once a court or administrative tribunal in a new state modifies a child support order, it becomes the tribunal with continuing exclusive jurisdiction. Cases applying UIFSA § 611(a), and concluding that the court has no jurisdiction to modify support orders, include Porro v. Porro, 675 N.W.2d 82 (Minn. Ct. App. 2004); Casiano v. Casiano, 815 A.2d 638 (Pa. Super. Ct. 2002); and LeTellier v. LeTellier, 40 S.W.3d 490 (Tenn.2001).

UIFSA § 611(b) provides that modification of a registered child support order from another state is "subject to the same requirements, procedures, and defenses" that apply to other support modification proceedings in the state, and that the modified order may be enforced and satisfied in the same manner. This means that the new state's law, including its support guidelines, will apply. See, e.g., Alaska Child Support Enforcement Division v. Bromley, 987 P.2d 183 (Alaska 1999); Marriage of Crosby and Grooms, 10 Cal.Rptr.3d 146 (Ct. App. 2004); Groseth v. Groseth, 600 N.W.2d 159 (Neb. 1999); Matter of Marriage of Cooney, 946 P.2d 305 (Or. Ct. App. 1997). There is an important exception, however, incorporated in § 611(c) and (d).

Under UIFSA § 611(c), the tribunal in the new state "may not modify any aspect of a child support order that may not be modified under the law of the issuing state, including the duration of the obligation of support." According to the comments to this section, this means that if child support was ordered through age 21 in the issuing state, the new forum state may not automatically terminate support at age 18. Conversely, if the law governing the original support order terminates support at 18, the new tribunal cannot continue it to a later age. See, e.g., Kerr v. Kerr, 100 S.W.3d 912 (Mo. Ct. App. 2003); Matter of Marriage of Cooney, 946 P.2d 305 (Or. Ct. App. 1997); Badeaux v. Davis, 522 S.E.2d 835, (S.C. Ct. App. 1999).

The limits on modification under § 611(c) have also been applied to modification proceedings under § 613; see, e.g., Riggle v. Riggle, 52 P.3d 360 (Kan. Ct. App. 2002) (duration of support obligation not modifiable in Kansas despite fact that all parties and the children are now residents of the state); Freddo v. Freddo, 983 N.E.2d 1216 (Mass. App. Ct. 2013) (Florida support order terminating at age 18 may not be extended in Massachusetts).

Note that a party may not avoid the limitations on modification in UIFSA § 611 by commencing an original action for child support in a new state in which jurisdiction can be obtained over the support obligor. See UIFSA § 201(b), applied in Vailas v. Vailas, 939 N.E.2d 565 (Ill. App. Ct. 2010) and In re Marriage of Cepukenas v. Cepukenas, 584 N.W.2d 227 (Wis. 1998). Spencer v. Spencer, 882 N.E.2d 886 (N.Y. 2008), ruled that a petition for de novo determination of child support in New York, where support may continue until a child reaches age 21, was not permitted in light of UIFSA and a prior Connecticut child support order that had terminated when the child turned 18. See also <u>Hennepin County v. Hill, 777 N.W.2d 252 (Minn. Ct. App. 2010)</u>.

In light of the limitations on modification in <u>UIFSA § 611</u>, can a court with jurisdiction to modify child support order an obligor to contribute toward a child's post-majority college expenses when the original order was entered in a state that does not allow this type of order? See <u>Marshak v. Weser, 915 A.2d 613 (N.J. Super. Ct. App. Div. 2007)</u>; <u>In re Schneider, 268 P.3d 215 (Wash. 2011)</u> (refusing to order support for college expenses that would extend duration of order). Conversely, if the court with jurisdiction to modify is in a state that does not allow post-majority educational support, and the original order was entered in a state that does, can the new court enforce or enter an order to require a parent to assist with educational expenses? See <u>In re Scott, 999 A.2d 229 (N.H. 2010)</u> (holding that college support order was modifiable under UIFSA § 611, and rejecting claim for educational support.)

d. FFCCSOA

The court in *Welsher* cites the federal Full Faith and Credit for Child Support Orders Act (FFCCSOA), <u>28 U.S.C. § 1738B (2018)</u>, which requires states to recognize and enforce child support orders from other states. Although UIFSA and FFCCSOA were intended to be consistent, the rules governing modification jurisdiction in <u>UIFSA § 611(a)</u> are more restrictive than the comparable provision in FFCCSOA. Courts have reached different conclusions as to whether FFCCSOA can be interpreted to include the requirements of UIFSA, or whether it must be treated as preempting any inconsistent provisions of UIFSA. Compare <u>Draper v. Burke, 881 N.E.2d 122 (Mass. 2008)</u> with <u>Roberts v. Bedard, 357 S.W.3d 554 (Ky. Ct. App. 2011)</u>. See also <u>Marriage of Basileh, 912 N.E.2d 814 (Ind. 2009)</u>.

Global View: International Child Support

UIFSA and the federal IV-D system are also available to establish and enforce child support orders at the international level. The United States has designated a series of <u>"foreign reciprocating countries"</u> for child support purposes under <u>42 U.S.C. § 659a (2018)</u>, and every state has also entered into similar state-level reciprocal agreements with one or more foreign jurisdictions.

The United States has ratified the 2007 <u>Hague Convention on the International Recovery of Child Support and Other Forms of Family Maintenance</u> (Child Support Convention), which was implemented through federal legislation tied to the IV-D child support enforcement program and the amendments to UIFSA. See Battle Rankin Robinson, *Integrating an International Convention into State Law: The UIFSA Experience*, 43 Fam. L.Q. 61 (2009). The Office of Child Support Enforcement in the U.S. Department of Health and Human Services serves as the Central Authority for the United States under the Convention.

Under UIFSA 2008, a foreign child or spousal support order is eligible for registration and enforcement if it was entered by a tribunal in a "foreign country" as that term is defined in UIFSA § 102(5). This definition includes four groups of countries: countries that have been declared to be "foreign reciprocating countries" under U.S. law, countries with a state-level reciprocal child support agreement, countries that have enacted laws or procedures that are "substantially similar" to UIFSA, and countries in which the Child Support Convention is in effect. An order from another country that does not meet the definition of "foreign country" under UIFSA § 102(5) can be enforced on the basis of comity. See UIFSA § 104(a). UIFSA § 615 provides a basis for state courts to modify foreign country child support orders if the court in the foreign country has no jurisdiction to do so. UIFSA 2008 includes specialized rules and procedures in Article 7 for cases under the Child Support Convention. See UIFSA § 702.

e. Equitable Defenses

Prior to UIFSA, courts sometimes excused payments of support arrearages based on equitable defenses, such as waiver, estoppel or laches. One common situation arose when parents agreed informally to reduce or terminate child support, without seeking court approval of their new agreement. Parties cannot contractually modify the terms of a child support decree, see, e.g., In re Marriage of Monicken, 593 N.W.2d 509 (Wis. Ct. App. 1999), but courts have sometimes applied waiver or estoppel doctrines to prevent a custodial parent from pursuing a claim for arrears in this situation. In some states, a custodial parent who has concealed the whereabouts of a child from the support obligor may be estopped from collecting support arrearages for the period of concealment. See, e.g., In re Marriage of Damico, 872 P.2d 126 (Cal. 1994).

In interstate cases, however, the requirements of UIFSA § 607 effectively prevent support obligors from asserting equitable defenses. See Child Support

Enforcement Division of Alaska v. Brenckle, 675 N.E.2d 390 (Mass. 1997) (obligor's laches defense not cognizable under UIFSA).

Statutes and case law in some jurisdictions also bar support obligors from asserting particular equitable defenses. See, e.g., Cal. Fam. Code § 291(d) (2018) (barring laches defense except with respect to judgment owed to the state), discussed in In re Marriage of Fellows, 138 P.3d 200 (Cal. 2004). See also Wynn v. Craven, 799 S.E.2d 172 (Ga. 2017) (laches does not apply to claims for uncollected child support); Aguero v. Aguero, 976 P.2d 1088 (Okla. Ct. App. 1999) (equitable defenses not available in child support enforcement actions); Paternity of John R.B., 690 N.W.2d 849 (Wis. 2005) (applying statute limiting equitable defenses to support enforcement).

Child Support and Bankruptcy

Child support orders are "domestic support obligations" under the Bankruptcy Code, see 11 U.S.C. § 101(14A) (2018), and are not dischargeable in a bankruptcy proceeding. See Chapter 6.

f. Visitation Interference

Many cases and statutes provide that the obligations to pay support and make the child available for parenting time or visitation are independent. Thus, a support obligor may not unilaterally withhold payments when the custodial parent does not comply with visitation orders, and a custodial parent may not deny parenting time when the support obligor fails to make child support payments. See UIFSA § 305(d) (responding tribunal may not condition payment of a support order on compliance with visitation provisions); Hermosillo v. Hermosillo, 962 P.2d 891 (Alaska 1998) (financial sanctions for interference with visitation may not be offset against support arrearages). For similar reasons, the court concluded in Perkinson v. Perkinson, 989 N.E.2d 758 (Ind. 2013), that a parent's agreement to give up parenting time in exchange for relief from paying child support was unenforceable.

In extreme cases, courts may attempt to use child support payments as leverage to obtain a parent's cooperation with visitation. See, e.g., N.Y. Dom.Rel.L. § 241 (2018), which provides that interference with visitation is not a defense to enforcement of child support or grounds for an order cancelling arrears, but may be the basis for a prospective order suspending payments in response to such interference. See also Welch v. Welch, 519 N.W.2d 262 (Neb. 1994). In a case in which one parent moved to abate his support obligation after the other parent took the children to Uruguay and refused to return them, the court ordered that child support continue but that the payments be deposited into a trust account. Marriage of Popa and Garcia, 995 N.E.2d 521 (Ill. App. Ct. 2013). Note, however, that courts enforcing support orders under UIFSA do not acquire jurisdiction to make rulings in collateral custody or visitation disputes between the parties. See UIFSA § 314. See generally Ira Mark Ellman, *Should Visitation Denial Affect the Obligation to Pay Support?* 36 Ariz. St. L.J. 661 (2004).

Client Counseling: Support Obligor

If you represented a noncustodial parent subject to a child support order whose children have been concealed by the other parent, what advice would you give your client?

g. Nonparentage

Under UIFSA § 607 how would a court address the argument that a support obligor is not the parent of a child? An order disestablishing paternity has the effect of terminating any future obligation for child support, but in most states it does not cancel

Make the Connection

Paternity disestablishment laws are considered in Chapter 2.

the obligation to pay arrearages that have accumulated. See, e.g., McBride v. Jones, 803 So.2d 1168 (Miss.2002). In Maryland, an individual cannot be held liable for child support arrearages after a paternity declaration is vacated, see Walter v. Gunter, 788 A.2d 609 (Md. 2002), but this rule does not apply in cases under UIFSA. See UIFSA § 315, which states: "A party whose parentage of a child has been previously determined. . .may not plead nonparentage as a defense to a proceeding under this [act]." See also Department of Human Resources v. Mitchell, 12 A.3d 179 (Md. Ct. Spec. App. 2011).

Problem 7-16

Deborah and Edward divorced in Texas when their son was five years old, and Edward was ordered to pay child support. Thirty years after the divorce, Deborah seeks to register her divorce decree in Oklahoma and collect more than $72,000 in support arrearages from Edward. If Oklahoma has no statute of limitations on enforcement of child support orders, but Texas law provides that a judgment becomes dormant if there is no attempt to execute it within twelve years, does

Edward have a good defense to registration and enforcement in Oklahoma? (See Thornton v. Thornton, 247 P.3d 1180 (Okla. 2011).)

Problem 7-17

Husband, Wife, and Children live together in Florida. Wife files an action for divorce in Florida, and obtains a child support and custody order there.

(a) Assume that Husband later moves alone to Georgia, and stops paying support. Can Wife have the Florida support order enforced in Georgia? How would such a proceeding be handled under UIFSA?

(b) Assume that Husband moves alone to Georgia, and takes a great new job. Where should Wife file to get the child support order increased?

(c) Assume that Husband moves alone to Georgia and then loses his job. Where should Husband file to get the child support order decreased?

(d) Would your answers be any different if Wife and Children had also moved to Georgia after the Florida order was entered?

Problem 7-18

Mom, Dad, and their kids live together in New York. When Mom and Dad split up, Dad and the kids move to Pennsylvania and Mom moves to Michigan.

(a) Assume there was no proceeding commenced in New York before the parties left the state. What can Dad do to secure a child support order against Mom?

(b) Assume instead that Dad obtained an initial support order in New York before the parties relocated, and that Mom's income has increased. Where should Dad file to get the child support order increased? (Cf. Kasdan v. Berney, 587 N.W.2d 319 (Minn. Ct. App. 1999).)

(c) Assume that Dad had obtained a support order in New York, and that Mom has lost her job in Michigan. Where should she file to get the child support order decreased?

(d) Assume that Mom loses her job in Michigan and moves to Pennsylvania. Can a tribunal in Pennsylvania modify the New York child support order?

(e) Assuming that Pennsylvania can modify the New York child support order on the facts of (c) or (d), can the court change the duration of support payments (i.e. terminate before the child reaches age 21)?

Problem 7-19

Several years after Valerie and Keith were divorced in Arizona, Valerie moved to Texas and Keith moved to Kansas. Valerie eventually assigned her child support rights under the Arizona divorce decree to the state of Texas, which registered the order for enforcement in Kansas, seeking accumulated arrears of $17,000 as well as a wage assignment for $640 per month in current support. Keith filed a response, arguing that the amount of arrearages was not computed correctly, and requesting that the court enter a new order establishing support payments consistent with the Kansas guidelines. What should the Kansas tribunal do with this case? (See <u>Gentzel v. Williams, 965 P.2d 855 (Kan. Ct. App. 1998)</u>.)

Problem 7-20

David and Linda had a brief sexual encounter one October, and Linda gave birth to a daughter the following July. Although they all lived in the same town for several years, Linda never told David, during her pregnancy or afterward, that he was the girl's father. When the child was 14, she wanted to meet her father, and Linda requested assistance in locating David from the local Child Support Enforcement agency. She then filed claims for prospective and retroactive child support. A blood test confirmed David's paternity, and he comes to you for advice. Retroactive support under the guidelines would amount to more than $20,000. What arguments might he make? (See <u>Matter of Loomis, 587 N.W.2d 427 (S.D.1998)</u>.)

Problem 7-21

Mark and Theresa had a longstanding friendship and occasionally had sex. They lost contact for a while, and when Mark saw Theresa again, he learned that she had given birth to a child. Theresa implied that Mark was the father, and he began to give her money and to visit the child. Because Theresa was receiving public support payments, the local District Attorney's office brought suit against Mark to establish paternity and a support order. Mark had himself and the child tested by a DNA laboratory, and learned that he was not the child's father. When he complained to Theresa about the lawsuit, she said she would ask the DA's office not to proceed with the litigation. Neither Theresa nor Mark did anything to follow up, however, and the court entered a default judgment declaring Mark to be the child's father and imposing a monthly support obligation. Two years later, the state begins an enforcement action against Mark, seeking wage withholding and a drivers' license suspension. Does Mark have a defense to this action? (See <u>County of Los Angeles v. Warmoth, 72 Cal.Rptr.2d 902 (Ct.App.1998)</u>.)

Child Support Enforcement Mechanisms

The IV-D child support program requires states to enact a range of procedures to increase the effectiveness of support enforcement. See 42 U.S.C. § 666(a) (2018). This includes making particular enforcement mechanisms available under state law, including:

- automatic wage withholding orders under § 666(a)(1), see People ex rel. Sheppard v. Money, 529 N.E.2d 542 (Ill.1988);

- procedures to apply state income tax refunds to past due child support obligations under § 666(a)(3);

- automatic real and personal property liens to collect support arrearages without prior judicial or administrative hearings under § 666(a)(4); and

- authority to withhold, suspend or restrict the use of driver's licenses, business and professional licenses, and recreational and sporting licenses of individuals owing overdue support under § 666(a)(16), see Alaska Department of Revenue v. Beans, 965 P.2d 725 (Alaska 1998).

Additional support enforcement mechanisms are authorized by federal law, including:

- offset of federal income tax refunds for delinquent support under 42 U.S.C. § 652(b) (2018);

- restrictions or denial of passports to obligors with arrearages of more than $2,500 under 42 U.S.C. § 652(k) (2018), see Eunique v. Powell, 302 F.3d 971 (9th Cir. 2002);

- garnishment of Social Security payments under 42 U.S.C. § 659 (2018), see, e.g., Lang v. Social Security Administration, 612 F.3d 960 (8th Cir. 2010);

- use of a Qualified Domestic Relations Order (QDRO) to access the obligor's retirement benefits under 29 U.S.C. § 1056(d)(3) (2018), see Nkopchieu v. Minlend, 718 S.E.2d 470 (Va. Ct. App. 2011).

Turner v. Rogers

564 U.S. 431 (2011)

JUSTICE BREYER delivered the opinion of the Court.

South Carolina's Family Court enforces its child support orders by threatening with incarceration for civil contempt those who are (1) subject to a child support order, (2) able to comply with that order, but (3) fail to do so. We must decide whether the Fourteenth Amendment's Due Process

Go Online

Listen to the oral arguments in *Turner* on the Oyez Project website.

Clause requires the State to provide counsel (at a civil contempt hearing) to an *indigent* person potentially faced with such incarceration. We conclude that where as here the custodial parent (entitled to receive the support) is unrepresented by counsel, the State need not provide counsel to the noncustodial parent (required to provide the support). But we attach an important caveat, namely, that the State must nonetheless have in place alternative procedures that assure a fundamentally fair determination of the critical incarceration-related question, whether the supporting parent is able to comply with the support order.

I

A

South Carolina family courts enforce their child support orders in part through civil contempt proceedings. Each month the family court clerk reviews outstanding child support orders, identifies those in which the supporting parent has fallen more than five days behind, and sends that parent an order to "show cause" why he should not be held in contempt. S.C. Rule Family Ct. 24 (2011). The "show cause" order and attached affidavit refer to the relevant child support order, identify the amount of the arrearage, and set a date for a court hearing. At the hearing that parent may demonstrate that he is not in contempt, say, by showing that he is not able to make the required payments. See *Moseley v. Mosier,* 279 S.C. 348, 351, 306 S.E.2d 624, 626 (1983) ("When the parent is *unable* to make the required payments, he is not in contempt"). If he fails to make the required showing, the court may hold him in civil contempt. And it may require that he be imprisoned unless and until he purges himself of contempt by making the required child support payments (but not for more than one year regardless). See S.C.Code Ann. § 63–3–620 (Supp.2010) (imprisonment for up to one year of "adult who wilfully violates" a court order); *Price v. Turner,* 387 S.C. 142, 145, 691

<u>S.E.2d 470, 472 (2010)</u> (civil contempt order must permit purging of contempt through compliance).

B

In June 2003 a South Carolina family court entered an order, which (as amended) required petitioner, Michael Turner, to pay $51.73 per week to respondent, Rebecca Rogers, to help support their child. (Rogers' father, Larry Price, currently has custody of the child and is also a respondent before this Court.) Over the next three years, Turner repeatedly failed to pay the amount due and was held in contempt on five occasions. The first four times he was sentenced to 90 days' imprisonment, but he ultimately paid the amount due (twice without being jailed, twice after spending two or three days in custody). The fifth time he did not pay but completed a 6-month sentence.

After his release in 2006 Turner remained in arrears. On March 27, 2006, the clerk issued a new "show cause" order. And after an initial postponement due to Turner's failure to appear, Turner's civil contempt hearing took place on January 3, 2008. Turner and Rogers were present, each without representation by counsel.

The hearing was brief. The court clerk said that Turner was $5,728.76 behind in his payments. The judge asked Turner if there was "anything you want to say." Turner replied,

> "Well, when I first got out, I got back on dope. I done meth, smoked pot and everything else, and I paid a little bit here and there. And, when I finally did get to working, I broke my back, back in September. I filed for disability and SSI. And, I didn't get straightened out off the dope until I broke my back and laid up for two months. And, now I'm off the dope and everything. I just hope that you give me a chance. I don't know what else to say. I mean, I know I done wrong, and I should have been paying and helping her, and I'm sorry. I mean, dope had a hold to me."

The judge then said, "[o]kay," and asked Rogers if she had anything to say. After a brief discussion of federal benefits, the judge stated,

> "If there's nothing else, this will be the Order of the Court. I find the Defendant in willful contempt. I'm [going to] sentence him to twelve months in the Oconee County Detention Center. He may purge himself of the contempt and avoid the sentence by having a zero balance on or before his release. I've also placed a lien on any SSI or other benefits."

The judge added that Turner would not receive good-time or work credits, but "[i]f you've got a job, I'll make you eligible for work release." When Turner asked why he could not receive good-time or work credits, the judge said, "[b]ecause that's my ruling."

The court made no express finding concerning Turner's ability to pay his arrearage (though Turner's wife had voluntarily submitted a copy of Turner's application for disability benefits. Nor did the judge ask any followup questions or otherwise address the ability-to-pay issue. After the hearing, the judge filled out a prewritten form titled "Order for Contempt of Court," which included the statement:

> "Defendant (was) (was not) gainfully employed and/or (had) (did not have) the ability to make these support payments when due

But the judge left this statement as is without indicating whether Turner was able to make support payments.

C

While serving his 12-month sentence, Turner, with the help of *pro bono* counsel, appealed. He claimed that the Federal Constitution entitled him to counsel at his contempt hearing. The South Carolina Supreme Court decided Turner's appeal after he had completed his sentence. And it rejected his "right to counsel" claim. The court pointed out that civil contempt differs significantly from criminal contempt. The former does not require all the "constitutional safeguards" applicable in criminal proceedings. 387 S.C., at 145, 691 S.E.2d, at 472. And the right to government-paid counsel, the Supreme Court held, was one of the "safeguards" not required.

Turner sought certiorari. In light of differences among state courts (and some federal courts) on the applicability of a "right to counsel" in civil contempt proceedings enforcing child support orders, we granted the writ. Compare, *e.g.,* *Pasqua v. Council,* 186 N.J. 127, 141–146, 892 A.2d 663, 671–674 (2006); *Black v. Division of Child Support Enforcement,* 686 A.2d 164, 167–168 (Del.1996); *Mead v. Batchlor,* 435 Mich. 480, 488–505, 460 N.W.2d 493, 496–504 (1990); *Ridgway v. Baker,* 720 F.2d 1409, 1413–1415 (C.A.5 1983) (all finding a federal constitutional right to counsel for indigents facing imprisonment in a child support civil contempt proceeding), with *Rodriguez v. Eighth Judicial Dist. Ct., County of Clark,* 120 Nev. 798, 808–813, 102 P.3d 41, 48–51 (2004) (no right to counsel in civil contempt hearing for nonsupport, except in "rarest of cases"); *Andrews v. Walton,* 428 So.2d 663, 666 (Fla.1983) ("no circumstances in which a parent is entitled to court-appointed counsel in a civil contempt proceeding for failure to pay child support"). Compare also *In re Grand Jury Proceedings,* 468 F.2d 1368, 1369 (C.A.9

Think About It

Consider the ways in which this distinction between civil and criminal contempt proceedings is important to the analysis in this case.

1972) *(per curiam)* (general right to counsel <u>in civil contempt proceedings</u>), with <u>Duval v. Duval, 114 N.H. 422, 425–427, 322 A.2d 1, 3–4 (1974)</u> (no general right, but counsel may be required on case-by-case basis).

* * *

III

A

We must decide whether the Due Process Clause grants an indigent defendant, such as Turner, a right to state-appointed counsel at a civil contempt proceeding, which may lead to his incarceration. This Court's precedents provide no definitive answer to that question. This Court has long held that the Sixth Amendment grants an indigent defendant the right to state-appointed counsel in a *criminal* case. <u>Gideon v. Wainwright, 372 U.S. 335 (1963)</u>. And we have held that this same rule applies to *criminal contempt* proceedings (other than summary proceedings). <u>United States v. Dixon, 509 U.S. 688, 696 (1993)</u>; <u>Cooke v. United States, 267 U.S. 517, 537 (1925)</u>.

> **FYI**
>
> In Part II of the opinion, the Court concludes that the case is not moot despite the fact that Turner completed his 12-month prison sentence in 2009, because the controversy "falls within a special category of disputes that are 'capable of repetition' while 'evading review.'"

But the Sixth Amendment does not govern civil cases. Civil contempt differs from criminal contempt in that it seeks only to "coerc[e] the defendant to do" what a court had previously ordered him to do. <u>Gompers v. Bucks Stove & Range Co., 221 U.S. 418, 442 (1911)</u>. A court may not impose punishment "in a civil contempt proceeding when it is clearly established that the alleged contemnor is unable to comply with the terms of the order." <u>Hicks v. Feiock, 485 U.S. 624, 638</u>, n. 9. And once a civil contemnor complies with the underlying order, he is purged of the contempt and is free. <u>Id., at 633</u> (he "carr[ies] the keys of [his] prison in [his] own pockets" (internal quotation marks omitted)).

Consequently, the Court has made clear (in a case not involving the right to counsel) that, where civil contempt is at issue, the Fourteenth Amendment's Due Process Clause allows a State to provide fewer procedural protections than in a criminal case. <u>Id., at 637–641</u> (State may place the burden of proving inability to pay on the defendant).

This Court has decided only a handful of cases that more directly concern a right to counsel in civil matters. And the application of those decisions to the present case is not clear. On the one hand, the Court has held that the Fourteenth Amendment requires the State to pay for representation by counsel in a *civil* "juvenile delinquency" proceeding (which could lead to incarceration). *In re Gault,* 387 U.S. 1, 35–42 (1967). Moreover, in *Vitek v. Jones,* 445 U.S. 480, 496–497 (1980), a plurality of four Members of this Court would have held that the Fourteenth Amendment requires representation by counsel in a proceeding to transfer a prison inmate to a state hospital for the mentally ill. Further, in *Lassiter v. Department of Social Servs. of Durham Cty.,* 452 U.S. 18 (1981), a case that focused upon civil proceedings leading to loss of parental rights, the Court wrote that the

> "pre-eminent generalization that emerges from this Court's precedents on an indigent's right to appointed counsel is that such a right has been recognized to exist only where the litigant may lose his physical liberty if he loses the litigation."

And the Court then drew from these precedents "the presumption that an indigent litigant has a right to appointed counsel only when, if he loses, he may be deprived of his physical liberty."

On the other hand, the Court has held that a criminal offender facing revocation of probation and imprisonment does *not* ordinarily have a right to counsel at a probation revocation hearing. *Gagnon v. Scarpelli,* 411 U.S. 778 (1973); see also *Middendorf v. Henry,* 425 U.S. 25 (1976) (no due process right to counsel in summary court-martial proceedings). And, at the same time, *Gault, Vitek*, and *Lassiter* are readily distinguishable. The civil juvenile delinquency proceeding at issue in *Gault* was "little different" from, and "comparable in seriousness" to, a criminal prosecution. In *Vitek*, the controlling opinion found *no* right to counsel. 445 U.S., at 499–500 (Powell, J., concurring in part) (assistance of mental health professionals sufficient). And the Court's statements in *Lassiter* constitute part of its rationale for *denying* a right to counsel in that case. We believe those statements are best read as pointing out that the Court previously had found a right to counsel *"only "* in cases involving incarceration, not that a right to counsel exists in *all* such cases (a position that would have been difficult to reconcile with *Gagnon*).

B

Civil contempt proceedings in child support cases constitute one part of a highly complex system designed to assure a noncustodial parent's regular payment of funds typically necessary for the support of his children. Often the family receives welfare support from a state-administered federal program, and the State then seeks reimbursement from the noncustodial parent. See 42 U.S.C. §§ 608(a)(3) (2006 ed., Supp. III), 656(a)(1) (2006 ed.); S.C.Code Ann. §§ 43–5–65(a)(1), (2) (2010 Cum.Supp.). Other times the custodial parent (often the mother, but sometimes the father, a grandparent, or another person with custody) does not receive government benefits and is entitled to receive the support payments herself.

The Federal Government has created an elaborate procedural mechanism designed to help both the government and custodial parents to secure the payments to which they are entitled. See generally *Blessing v. Freestone,* 520 U.S. 329, 333 (1997) (describing the "interlocking set of cooperative federal-state welfare programs" as they relate to child support enforcement); 45 CFR pt. 303 (2010) (prescribing standards for state child support agencies). These systems often rely upon wage withholding, expedited procedures for modifying and enforcing child support orders, and automated data processing. 42 U.S.C. §§ 666(a), (b), 654(24). But sometimes States will use contempt orders to ensure that the custodial parent receives support payments or the government receives reimbursement. Although some experts have criticized this last-mentioned procedure, and the Federal Government believes that "the routine use of contempt for non-payment of child support is likely to be an ineffective strategy," the Government also tells us that "coercive enforcement remedies, such as contempt, have a role to play." Brief for United States as *Amicus Curiae* 21–22, and n. 8 (citing Dept. of Health and Human Services, National Child Support Enforcement, Strategic Plan: FY 2005–2009, pp. 2, 10). South Carolina, which relies heavily on contempt proceedings, agrees that they are an important tool.

We here consider an indigent's right to paid counsel at such a contempt proceeding. It is a civil proceeding. And we consequently determine the "specific dictates of due process" by examining the "distinct factors" that this Court has previously found useful in deciding what specific safeguards the Constitution's Due Process Clause requires in order to make a civil proceeding fundamentally fair. *Mathews v. Eldridge,* 424 U.S. 319, 335 (1976) (considering fairness of an administrative proceeding). As relevant here those factors include (1) the nature of "the private interest that will be affected," (2) the comparative "risk" of an "erroneous deprivation" of that interest with and without "additional or substitute procedural safeguards," and (3) the nature and magnitude of any countervailing interest in not providing "additional or substitute procedural requirement [s]."

The "private interest that will be affected" argues strongly for the right to counsel that Turner advocates. That interest consists of an indigent defendant's loss of personal liberty through imprisonment. The interest in securing that freedom, the freedom "from bodily restraint," lies "at the core of the liberty protected by the Due Process Clause." *Foucha v. Louisiana,* 504 U.S. 71, 80 (1992). And we have made clear that its threatened loss through legal proceedings demands "due process protection." *Addington v. Texas,* 441 U.S. 418, 425 (1979).

Given the importance of the interest at stake, it is obviously important to assure accurate decisionmaking in respect to the key "ability to pay" question. Moreover, the fact that ability to comply marks a dividing line between civil and criminal contempt, *Hicks,* 485 U.S., at 635, n. 7, reinforces the need for accuracy. That is because an incorrect decision (wrongly classifying the contempt proceeding as civil) can increase the risk of wrongful incarceration by depriving the defendant of the procedural protections (including counsel) that the Constitution would demand in a criminal proceeding. See, *e.g.,* <u>*Dixon,* 509 U.S., at 696</u> (proof beyond a reasonable doubt, protection from double jeopardy); <u>*Codispoti v. Pennsylvania,* 418 U.S. 506, 512–513, 517 (1974)</u> (jury trial where the result is more than six months' imprisonment). And since 70% of child support arrears nationwide are owed by parents with either no reported income or income of $10,000 per year or less, the issue of ability to pay may arise fairly often. See E. Sorensen, L. Sousa, & S. Schaner, Assessing Child Support Arrears in Nine Large States and the Nation 22 (2007) (prepared by The Urban Institute), online at <u>http://aspe.hhs.gov/hsp/07/assessing-CS-debt/report.pdf</u> (as visited June 16, 2011, and available in Clerk of Court's case file); *id.,* at 23 ("research suggests that many obligors who do not have reported quarterly wages have relatively limited resources"); Patterson, <u>Civil Contempt and the Indigent Child Support Obligor: The Silent Return of Debtor's Prison, 18 Cornell J. L. & Pub. Pol'y 95, 117 (2008)</u>. See also, *e.g.,* <u>*McBride v. McBride,* 334 N.C. 124, 131</u>, n. 4, <u>431 S.E.2d 14, 19</u>, n. 4 (1993) (surveying North Carolina contempt orders and finding that the "failure of trial courts to make a determination of a contemnor's ability to comply is not altogether infrequent").

On the other hand, the Due Process Clause does not always require the provision of counsel in civil proceedings where incarceration is threatened. See <u>*Gagnon,* 411 U.S. 778</u>. And in determining whether the Clause requires a right to counsel here, we must take account of opposing interests, as well as consider the probable value of "additional or substitute procedural safeguards."

Think About It

What are the policy implications of the fact that most obligors who owe support arrears have no reported income or an income of $10,000 per year or less?

Doing so, we find three related considerations that, when taken together, argue strongly against the Due Process Clause requiring the State to provide indigents with counsel in every proceeding of the kind before us.

First, the critical question likely at issue in these cases concerns, as we have said, the defendant's ability to pay. That question is often closely related to the question of the defendant's indigence. But when the right procedures are in place, indigence can be a question that in many—but not all—cases is sufficiently straightforward to warrant determination *prior* to providing a defendant with counsel, even in a criminal case. Federal law, for example, requires a criminal defendant to provide information showing that he is indigent, and therefore entitled to state-funded counsel, *before* he can receive that assistance. See 18 U.S.C. § 3006A(b).

Second, sometimes, as here, the person opposing the defendant at the hearing is not the government represented by counsel but the custodial parent *un*represented by counsel. See Dept. of Health and Human Services, Office of Child Support Enforcement, Understanding Child Support Debt: A Guide to Exploring Child Support Debt in Your State 5, 6 (2004) (51% of nationwide arrears, and 58% in South Carolina, are not owed to the government). The custodial parent, perhaps a woman with custody of one or more children, may be relatively poor, unemployed, and unable to afford counsel. Yet she may have encouraged the court to enforce its order through contempt. Cf. Tr. Contempt Proceedings (Sept. 14, 2005), App. 44a–45a (Rogers asks court, in light of pattern of nonpayment, to confine Turner). She may be able to provide the court with significant information. Cf. *id.,* at 41a–43a (Rogers describes where Turner lived and worked). And the proceeding is ultimately for her benefit.

A requirement that the State provide counsel to the noncustodial parent in these cases could create an asymmetry of representation that would "alter significantly the nature of the proceeding." *Gagnon, supra,* at 787. Doing so could mean a degree of formality or delay that would unduly slow payment to those immediately in need. And, perhaps more important for present purposes, doing so could make the proceedings *less* fair overall, increasing the risk of a decision that would erroneously deprive a family of the support it is entitled to receive. The needs of such families play an important role in our analysis.

Third, as the Solicitor General points out, there is available a set of "substitute procedural safeguards," which, if employed together, can significantly reduce the risk of an erroneous deprivation of liberty. They can do so, moreover, without incurring some of the drawbacks inherent in recognizing an automatic right to counsel. Those safeguards include (1) notice to the defendant that his "ability to pay" is a critical issue in the contempt proceeding; (2) the use of a form (or the equivalent) to elicit relevant financial information; (3) an opportunity at the hearing for the defendant to respond to statements and questions about his financial status, (*e.g.,* those triggered by his responses on the form); and (4) an express finding by the court that the defendant has the ability to pay. See Tr. of Oral

Arg. 26–27; Brief for United States as *Amicus Curiae* 23–25. In presenting these alternatives, the Government draws upon considerable experience in helping to manage statutorily mandated federal-state efforts to enforce child support orders. It does not claim that they are the only possible alternatives, and this Court's cases suggest, for example, that sometimes assistance other than purely legal assistance (here, say, that of a neutral social worker) can prove constitutionally sufficient. Cf. *Vitek,* 445 U.S., at 499–500 (Powell, J., concurring in part) (provision of mental health professional). But the Government does claim that these alternatives can assure the "fundamental fairness" of the proceeding even where the State does not pay for counsel for an indigent defendant.

While recognizing the strength of Turner's arguments, we ultimately believe that the three considerations we have just discussed must carry the day. In our view, a categorical right to counsel in proceedings of the kind before us would carry with it disadvantages (in the form of unfairness and delay) that, in terms of ultimate fairness, would deprive it of significant superiority over the alternatives that we have mentioned. We consequently hold that the Due Process Clause does not *automatically* require the provision of counsel at civil contempt proceedings to an indigent individual who is subject to a child support order, even if that individual faces incarceration (for up to a year). In particular, that Clause does not require the provision of counsel where the opposing parent or other custodian (to whom support funds are owed) is not represented by counsel and the State provides alternative procedural safeguards equivalent to those we have mentioned (adequate notice of the importance of ability to pay, fair opportunity to present, and to dispute, relevant information, and court findings).

We do not address civil contempt proceedings where the underlying child support payment is owed to the State, for example, for reimbursement of welfare funds paid to the parent with custody. Those proceedings more closely resemble debt-collection proceedings. The government is likely to have counsel or some other competent representative. Cf. *Johnson v. Zerbst,* 304 U.S. 458, 462–463 (1938) ("[T]he average defendant does not have the professional legal skill to protect himself when brought before a tribunal with power to take his life or liberty, *wherein the prosecution is presented by experienced and learned counsel* " (emphasis added)). And this kind of proceeding is not before us. Neither do we address what due process requires in an unusually complex case where a defendant "can fairly be represented only by a trained advocate." *Gagnon,* 411 U.S., at 788; see also Reply Brief for Petitioner 18–20 (not claiming that Turner's case is especially complex).

IV

The record indicates that Turner received neither counsel nor the benefit of alternative procedures like those we have described. He did not receive clear notice that his ability to pay would constitute the critical question in his civil contempt proceeding. No one provided him with a form (or the equivalent) designed to elicit information about his financial circumstances. The court did not find that Turner was able to pay his arrearage, but instead left the relevant "finding" section of the contempt order blank. The court

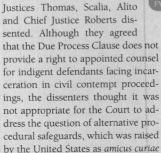

Justices Thomas, Scalia, Alito and Chief Justice Roberts dissented. Although they agreed that the Due Process Clause does not provide a right to appointed counsel for indigent defendants facing incarceration in civil contempt proceedings, the dissenters thought it was not appropriate for the Court to address the question of alternative procedural safeguards, which was raised by the United States as *amicus curiae* and not by the parties.

nonetheless found Turner in contempt and ordered him incarcerated. Under these circumstances Turner's incarceration violated the Due Process Clause.

We vacate the judgment of the South Carolina Supreme Court and remand the case for further proceedings not inconsistent with this opinion.

It is so ordered.

Points for Discussion

a. Reforms After *Turner*

Following the decision in *Turner*, the federal Office of Child Support Enforcement issued new rules requiring states to establish guidelines for use of contempt actions. Before filing a civil contempt action, the state child support agency must screen the case for information regarding the noncustodial parent's ability to pay, and give notice to the defendant that his or her ability to pay constitutes the critical question in the civil contempt action. See 45 CFR 303.6(c)(4) (2018).

b. Civil and Criminal Contempt

As in *Turner*, contempt proceedings for the enforcement of child support are usually civil or remedial in nature. See In re Marriage of Nussbeck, 974 P.2d 493 (Colo.1999) (discussing punitive and remedial contempt); Jones v. Maryland, 351 Md. 264, 718 A.2d 222 (1998). Should a support obligor who refuses to find employment be subject to civil contempt sanctions? See Maryland Rule 15–207, discussed in <u>Ott v. Frederick County Department of Social Services, 694 A.2d 101</u> <u>(Md. 1997)</u> (providing for constructive civil contempt).

The distinction between civil and criminal contempt was also important in another child support case decided by the Supreme Court. <u>Hicks v. Feiock, 485</u> <u>U.S. 624 (1988)</u>, considered the burden of proof on the question of whether a delinquent child support obligor has the ability to make the payments that have been ordered. *Hicks* concluded that a state may place the burden of proof on the support obligor in a civil contempt proceeding, so that he or she would be required to prove an inability to pay as an affirmative defense. If applied to a criminal contempt proceeding, however, the Court held that California's statutory presumption that the support obligor remained able to make the required payments would violate the due process clause.

c. Criminal Nonsupport Laws

In addition to civil laws providing for child support enforcement and the possibility of contempt sanctions, states may prosecute parents under criminal law for failure to support their children. Depending on the state statute, this is either a misdemeanor or felony offense. In a study conducted in the 1970s, David Chambers concluded that the rate of violation of support orders was significantly reduced when public agencies initiated prosecutions quickly and courts were willing to impose jail sentences as a sanction. David Chambers, Making Fathers Pay (1979). See generally Homer H. Clark, Jr., Domestic Relations § 6.5 (Student 2d ed. 1988).

In interstate cases the Deadbeat Parents Punishment Act, <u>18 U.S.C. § 228</u> <u>(2012),</u> establishes a federal crime based on willful failure to pay child support ordered for a child who resides in another state. The crime in <u>§ 228</u> may be charged as a felony, punishable by fines and imprisonment for up to two years as well as mandatory restitution of all unpaid support. In <u>United States v. Ballek, 170</u> <u>F.3d 871 (9th Cir.1999)</u>, the court held that the finding of willfulness required by the Act could be premised on defendant's failure to seek available employment that would have earned him enough money to meet his child support obligations. The court also rejected defendant's argument that this construction of the statute violated the Thirteenth Amendment. See also <u>United States v. Fuller, 751 F.3d</u> <u>1150 (10th Cir. 2014)</u>, which upheld a defendant's conviction based on evidence that he was willfully underemployed as a part-time musician. Defendants may be convicted even after demonstrating that they could not pay the full amount ordered, provided they failed to pay the portion of the obligation they could afford; see <u>United States v. Mattice, 186 F.3d 219 (2d Cir.1999)</u>; <u>United States</u> <u>v. Mathes, 151 F.3d 251 (5th Cir.1998)</u>. Defendants may defend against a prosecution under the CSRA by showing that the underlying support obligation was imposed by a court without personal jurisdiction over the defendant. See, e.g.,

United States v. Kramer, 225 F.3d 847 (7th Cir.2000); United States v. Bigford, 365 F.3d 859 (10th Cir.2004).

Problem 7-22

David was prosecuted for his failure to support nine children he fathered with four different women, with accumulated arrearages of more than $25,000. After David entered a plea, the judge imposed a sentence of three years in prison and five years of probation, subject to this condition: while on probation, David cannot have any more children unless he demonstrates that he has the ability to support them and that he is supporting the children he already has. Can David challenge this sentence? On what basis? (See State v. Oakley, 629 N.W.2d 200 (Wis. 2001), motion for reconsideration denied 635 N.W.2d 760 (Wis. 2001).)

──────────

B. Parenting Time

Child custody and visitation disputes between parents are governed almost exclusively by state law. Litigation of parenting disputes is significantly complicated by the fact that families are often highly mobile, and may be spread across different parts of the country or the world. In addition, children's circumstances may change over time, and courts may remain involved in these cases until children reach the age of majority. Although all courts and legislatures agree with the principle that these disputes must be decided on the basis of the best interests of the child, they may approach this question differently.

1. Jurisdiction: Working with the UCCJEA

Traditionally, adjudication of child custody and parental rights was treated as a status determination, and jurisdiction was based on the child's domicile in the state. Restatement, Conflict of Laws § 117 (1934). This approach was gradually replaced by the view that any state with a substantial interest in the child's welfare might take jurisdiction of a custody case, a view clearly articulated in Sampsell v. Superior Court, 197 P.2d 739 (Cal. 1948), and eventually adopted in every state through the Uniform Child Custody Jurisdiction Act (UCCJA), 9 U.L.A. (Part 1A) 261 (1999).

By providing for concurrent jurisdiction in more than one state, however, the UCCJA created the possibility of competing litigation and contradictory decrees entered by courts in different states. A party who was disappointed by one court's ruling could "seize and run," moving with the child and seeking a new order, in a different state, modifying the initial decree. Because of the rule that child custody decrees always remain subject to modification to protect the child's best interests, they were not generally seen as subject to the constraints of the Full Faith and Credit Clause. See, e.g., Kovacs v. Brewer, 356 U.S. 604 (1958). In 1980, Congress enacted the Parental Kidnapping Prevention Act (PKPA), codified at 28 U.S.C. § 1738A (2012), to address the problem of interstate recognition and enforcement of custody decrees. Differences between the requirements of the UCCJA and the PKPA created enormous complexity and confusion, however. In the words of Professor Homer Clark, custody cases under these statutes could "be analyzed in terms technical enough to delight a medieval property lawyer." Homer H. Clark, Jr., Domestic Relations 494 (Student 2d ed. 1988).

The 1997 Uniform Child Custody Jurisdiction and Enforcement Act (UCCJEA), 9 U.L.A. (Part IA) 649 (1999), eliminated some of the difficulties that had arisen under the UCCJA, and works more effectively with the PKPA and the federal Violence Against Women Act. Every state in the United States except Massachusetts has adopted the UCCJEA. See generally Patricia M. Hoff, *The ABC's of the UCCJEA: Interstate Child Custody Practice Under the New Act*, 32 Fam. L.Q. 267 (1998). Case law is collected in David Carl Minneman, *Construction and Operation of the Uniform Child Custody Jurisdiction and Enforcement Act*, 100 A.L.R.5th 1 (2002). The UCCJEA is reprinted with additional commentary in Robert G. Spector, *Uniform Child Custody Jurisdiction and Enforcement Act with Prefatory Note and Comments*, 32 Fam. L.Q. 303 (1998). Important provisions of the UCCJEA are reprinted in the Appendix.

In the Interest of Brilliant

86 S.W.3d 680 (Tex App. 2002)

ANN CRAWFORD McCLURE, JUSTICE.

This appeal centers on the recently adopted Uniform Child Custody Jurisdiction and Enforcement Act. Mother, father, and child are former residents of Massachusetts, all of whom relocated to Texas. When the mother expressed her intent to return to Massachusetts, the father filed suit and obtained a temporary restraining order prohibit-

Go Online

The full text of the UCCJEA and information on its adoption in different states is available from the Uniform Laws Commission.

ing the removal of the child from the jurisdiction of the court. Although she was duly served, the mother left Texas with the child and returned to Massachusetts, later claiming that her relocation to Texas was merely a temporary absence. The trial court denied the mother's plea to the jurisdiction and subsequently entered a default judgment naming the father as sole managing conservator. We conclude that Texas has jurisdiction under the UCCJEA, but we reverse the default judgment and remand for a trial on the merits.

Factual Summary

Kaylee Lynn-Marie Brilliant was born in Massachusetts on June 15, 1999. She was conceived when her mother, Kristen Lynn Fox (Kristen), was a seventeen-year-old high school student. Reginald Brilliant (Regi) is Kaylee's father but he and Kristen have never married. Kristen moved in with Regi in March 1999 and they continued living together until April 16, 2000, when Regi moved to Texas. Regi grew up in El Paso and his family continued to live here. The record reveals that the couple had planned to relocate to El Paso and Regi, an employee of Home Depot, requested a job transfer. When the transfer came through, Regi loaded a U-Haul truck with all of his new family's belongings, except for the clothing Kristen needed to finish the last two months of high school. During their brief separation, Kristen lived with her mother and wrote letters in which she told Regi she was anxious "to start my new life down there with you." As planned, Kristen and Kaylee arrived in El Paso on June 12.

On June 15, 2000, Kristen completed and signed a rental application adding her name to the lease on their apartment. She filled out job applications with Blockbuster and Payless Shoe Source, although neither of these is signed nor dated. Kaylee's immunization records were transferred to an El Paso clinic and Regi discovered that the child's shots had not been kept current. While the record does not indicate when the parties applied for a social security card in Kaylee's name, the Social Security Administration mailed Kaylee's card—postmarked April 1, 2000—to Regi's father's home in El Paso.

Kristen soon expressed displeasure with Texas. She wrote Regi a letter on July 10, telling him "that it just wasn't working out, she was leaving, she and the baby were going back to Massachusetts." Regi filed suit on July 19 and on July 21, he obtained a temporary restraining order preventing Kristen from removing Kaylee from El Paso County. Kristen was served with the restraining order on July 22 but she did not move out of the couple's apartment until July 24, when her mother arrived in town. Kristen and Kaylee stayed in the motel with Kristen's mother until July 27, when all three of them left El Paso for Massachusetts in violation of the restraining order. Kristen and Kaylee spent a total of forty-five days in Texas.

Kristen filed a paternity suit in Massachusetts on August 3. She did not file an answer in the Texas suit but instead filed a plea to the jurisdiction on August 7. On August 16, she filed an amended plea to the jurisdiction to which she attached her own affidavit and a certified copy of a letter from the Massachusetts court to the associate judge of the El Paso court. A hearing on the plea proceeded before the associate judge on August 9 and Kristen appealed the adverse ruling to the referring court. The *de novo* hearing before the Honorable Alfredo Chavez took place on August 18. Kristen did not appear for the hearing. Judge Chavez ultimately denied the plea. On October 26, Kristen, represented by new counsel, urged a motion for new trial and, in the alternative, a motion for reconsideration. Again, Kristen did not appear. In denying the relief requested, the trial court stated:

> It's this Court's opinion that Texas had jurisdiction over the case at that time. To grant the new trial and to decline jurisdiction, even on an inconvenient forum basis would be to condone the blatant disregard for court orders by the respondent, which highly disturbs this Court. And I'm not going to do that.

The following day, Regi and his attorney appeared before Judge Chavez. They advised the court that the two attorneys who had represented Kristen had been employed solely for the purpose of pursuing the plea to the jurisdiction and Kristen, having failed to file an answer, was in default. Regi's counsel also represented that she had advised Kristen's attorney following the hearing on the motion for new trial that she intended to pursue a default judgment the next day. Neither counsel nor Kristen appeared. The court found that it had jurisdiction of the cause and of the parties, that all persons entitled to citation were properly cited, that a jury was waived, and that a record was taken. He appointed Regi as sole managing conservator of Kaylee, appointed Kristen as possessory conservator and entered a standard possession order. Child support was fixed at $150 per month. From this order, Kristen brings two issues for review: (1) Texas lacked subject matter jurisdiction to make an initial child custody determination under the Uniform Child Custody Jurisdiction and Enforcement Act (UCCJEA); and (2) the default judgment was improper because Kristen did not receive forty-five days' notice of the trial setting.

* * *

Uniform Child Custody Jurisdiction and Enforcement Act

In her first issue for review, Kristen contends that the trial court lacked subject matter jurisdiction to make an initial child custody determination. Generally, there are three jurisdictional elements: (1) jurisdiction over the subject matter; (2) jurisdiction over the person or res; and (3) power to render the particular relief awarded. Subject matter jurisdiction is essential to the authority of a court to decide a case; it is never presumed and cannot be waived.

Jurisdiction here is predicated upon the UCCJEA which Texas adopted effective September 1, 1999. The Act was designed to address the "inconsistency of interpretation of the [former] UCCJA and the technicalities of applying the PKPA."[1] McGuire v. McGuire, 18 S.W.3d 801, 806 (Tex.App.-El Paso 2000, no pet.), *citing* Sampson & Tindall, TEXAS FAMILY CODE ANNOTATED § 152.001, Introductory Comment, p. 410 (1999). The new act prioritizes home state jurisdiction. Sampson & Tindall, TEXAS FAMILY CODE ANNOTATED § 152.001, Commissioners' Official Prefatory Note to UCCJEA p. 464 (2001). The clear purpose of the UCCJEA, like that of the former UCCJA, is to discourage and eliminate child snatching, to avoid jurisdictional competition, to avoid continued relitigation of custody decisions, and to promote cooperation between the states to ensure that a custody decision is rendered in the state that can better determine the best interest of the child.

Home State

"Home state" is defined in the Act:

(7) 'Home state' means the state in which a child lived with a parent or a person acting as a parent for at least six consecutive months immediately before the commencement of a child custody proceeding. In the case of a child less than six months of age, the term means the state in which the child lived from birth with a parent or a person acting as a parent. A period of temporary absence of a parent or a person acting as a parent is part of the period.

TEX.FAM.CODE ANN. § 152.102(7) (Vernon Supp.2002). In turn, "commencement" as used in the definition "means the filing of the first pleading in a proceeding." TEX.FAM.CODE ANN. § 152.102(5). Commentary suggests that although the definition of "home state" has been reworded slightly, no substantive change from the UCCJA was intended. Sampson & Tindall, TEXAS FAMILY CODE ANNOTATED § 152.102, *Commissioners' Comment* p. 470 (2001).

Section 152.201 provides the hierarchy for determining whether a state has jurisdiction to make an initial child custody determination:

§ 152.201. Initial Child Custody Jurisdiction
(a) Except as otherwise provided in Section 152.204, a court of this state has jurisdiction to make an initial child custody determination only if:
(1) this state is the home state of the child on the date of the com-

---

[1]   "PKPA" is the acronym for the Parental Kidnaping Prevention Act of 1980, 28 U.S.C.A.§ 1738A (West 2002). Although the PKPA prioritized "home state" jurisdiction, the former UCCJA as adopted by the National Conference of Commissioners on Uniform State Law authorized four independent jurisdictional bases without prioritization. The Texas version of the former Act prioritized home state jurisdiction. *See* former TEX.FAM.CODE ANN.§ 152.003 (Vernon 1996).

mencement of the proceeding[2] or was the home state of the child within six months before the commencement of the proceeding and the child is absent from this state but a parent or person acting as a parent continues to live in this state;

(2) a court of another state does not have jurisdiction under Subdivision (1), or a court of the home state of the child has declined to exercise jurisdiction on the ground that this state is the more appropriate forum under Section 152.207 or 152.208, and:

   (A) the child and the child's parents, or the child and at least one parent or a person acting as a parent, have a significant connection with this state other than mere physical presence; and

   (B) substantial evidence is available in this state concerning the child's care, protection, training, and personal relationships;

(3) all courts having jurisdiction under Subdivision (1) or (2) have declined to exercise jurisdiction on the ground that a court of this state is the more appropriate forum to determine the custody of the child under Section 152.207 or 152.208; or

(4) no court of any other state would have jurisdiction under the criteria specified in Subdivision (1), (2), or (3).

TEX.FAM.CODE ANN. § 152.201. For our purposes, the commentary is again insightful:

> The six-month extended home state provision of Subsection (a)(1) has been modified slightly from the UCCJA. The UCCJA provided that home state jurisdiction continued for six months when the child had been removed by a person seeking the child's custody or for other reasons and a parent or a person acting as a parent continues to reside in the home state. Under this Act, it is no longer necessary to determine why the child has been removed. The only inquiry relates to the status of the person left behind. This change provides a slightly more refined home state standard than the UCCJA or the PKPA, which also requires a determination that the child has been removed 'by a contestant or for other reasons.'

Sampson & Tindall, TEXAS FAMILY CODE ANNOTATED § 152.201, *Commissioners' Comment* p. 478 (2001).

Framing the Issue

Both parties agree that Texas was not Kaylee's home state as she had not resided here for the requisite six month period. Kristen contends that Massachusetts has home state status because her 45-day residence in Texas was merely a "temporary absence" as that term is used in Section 152.102(7). Regi contends

---

[2]   One court has concluded that the "date of commencement of the proceeding" means the date of commencement of a proceeding in a Texas court. *In re McCoy*, 52 S.W.3d 297, 306 (Tex.App.-Corpus Christi 2001, orig. proceeding).

that Kristen "moved" from Massachusetts to Texas so that no parent continued to live in Massachusetts; consequently, neither Texas nor Massachusetts has home state jurisdiction and Texas may assert "significant connections" jurisdiction under Section 152.201(a)(2)(A). We must first consider the meaning of "temporary absence."

Temporary Absence

Kristen claims that she is not and never was a resident of the State of Texas, nor was their daughter. She contends that a temporary absence from the home state does not constitute new residency when the stay is less than six months. * * *

Think About It

Why does it matter whether Massachusetts has home state status under the UCCJEA?

* * *

We are faced here with a situation in which Kristen moved from Massachusetts to Texas. Had she returned to Massachusetts before suit was filed, we might be more inclined to find her absence temporary. But at the time suit was filed in Texas, no one lived in Massachusetts—Kristen, Regi, and Kaylee were all living in Texas. Although Kristen and Kaylee returned to Massachusetts, Kristen was restrained from removing the child from El Paso County. She did so anyway.[6] The UCCJEA was designed to prevent the gamesmanship and forum shopping that has occurred here. Kristen chose to relocate to Texas and although, regrettably, she did not wish to remain, she cannot bootstrap her relocation to a "temporary absence" from Massachusetts by skipping town with the child in direct violation of a court order. Consequently, neither Texas nor Massachusetts had home state jurisdiction.

Kristen argues that Massachusetts has already determined it has home state status and has expressed its intent to exercise jurisdiction. By letter dated August 15, 2000, a judge of the Probate and Family Court Department, Norfolk Division, advised the associate judge below as follows:

> Given the facts set forth in Ms. Fox's Affidavit, which in pertinent part are essentially undisputed, it would appear that Massachusetts and not Texas is the child's home state under the UCCJA. Massachusetts was the child's home state within six months of the date(s) upon which the ac-

---

[6]   In effect, this case presents the reverse of the scenario envisioned by Section 152.208 which, generally speaking, requires a court to decline jurisdiction when the court has acquired jurisdiction under the UCCJEA because a person seeking to invoke its jurisdiction has engaged in unjustifiable conduct. *See* TEX. FAM. CODE ANN. § 152.208(a). Here, Kristen attempted to avoid jurisdiction in Texas by fleeing the state after being served with a restraining order.

tions were filed in each court. It would, therefore, appear that the fact that the mother and child resided briefly in Texas (June July 2000) would not confer subject matter jurisdiction in Texas. Moreover, the child was born in Massachusetts, and mother and the child currently reside in, and have significant lifelong connections to, Massachusetts.

After reviewing the enclosed, and your, [sic] file, I respectfully submit that for the reasons set forth above, you decline to take further action and dismiss the action pending before you in order that any question of subject matter jurisdiction can be put to rest.

Think About It

Note the communication between the judges in Massachusetts and Texas that occurred in this case. Why did the Massachusetts court conclude that Massachusetts was the child's home state? Why did the Texas court reject this conclusion?

Without question, the Texas proceeding was filed first, and it was filed at a time when all parties resided in Texas. Thus, the provisions of Section 152.206(a) are inapplicable. TEX.FAM. CODE ANN. § 152.206(a) (a court of this state may not exercise its jurisdiction under the UCCJEA if, at the time of the commencement of the proceeding, a proceeding concerning the custody of the child has been commenced in a court of another state). Nor can we conclude that Section 152.206(b) applies (if a Texas court determines that a child custody proceeding has been commenced in another state having jurisdiction substantially in accordance with the Act, the Texas court shall stay its proceeding and communicate with the court of the other state; if the court of the state having jurisdiction substantially in accordance with this chapter does not determine that the Texas court is a more appropriate forum, the Texas court shall dismiss the proceeding). As we have detailed, Massachusetts was not Kaylee's home state.

We must next consider whether it was appropriate for Texas to exercise jurisdiction on the basis of significant connections. This necessitates a showing by Regi that (1) the child has no home state or the home state has declined to exercise jurisdiction; (2) it is in the best interest of the child because the child and at least one of its parents have a significant connection with Texas beyond mere physical presence; and (3) there is available in Texas substantial evidence concerning the child's present or future care, protection, training, and personal relationships. TEX. FAM.CODE ANN. § 152.201(a)(2).

Significant Connections

At the hearing, Regi and his father testified concerning Kaylee's connections to Texas. Bruce Brilliant testified that he has lived in El Paso since 1975 and is employed with United States Customs. He has seven other children besides Regi, five of whom still live at home. These four girls and one boy range from two to eleven years of age. The extended family saw Kaylee on a frequent basis and the children would play together. His home featured "a great big play room and there's nothing but toys." Kaylee had a place in their family and "[s]he loved it there." He also explained Regi's and Kristen's plans to raise their family in Texas:

[T]hey were going to go ahead and go get a house. As a matter of fact, I had the ticket to bring her down here. And after that, she was going to get a job. And my wife even said I'll go over, pick up the baby, take you to work, bring the baby to the house and the baby can play with the kids all day long.

Q: Was that acceptable to Kristen?
A: Yes.

As the father of eight children, he had helped Kristen with child care, teaching her that she could not mix the formula with plain tap water, that she needed to sterilize the bottles, boil the water and the nipples. He had warned her that if she preferred to use the microwave, she should not put the nipples in it.

Regi testified that Kaylee's medical records were transferred to Texas and that the child was behind in her immunizations. He brought her current "except for the TB. She had an appointment for the 14th, but she wasn't here." The Social Security Administration was advised that Kaylee's residence was in Texas.

As we have noted, Kristen did not appear at the hearing so the record contains only the affidavit attached to her plea to the jurisdiction. In it, she claimed that Regi obtained the temporary restraining order by making fraudulent representations to the court. She also alleged that he had made misrepresentations to her concerning "life in his home state of Texas." The affidavit does not specify what those misrepresentations were, nor did Kristen offer evidence to establish any. With regard to significant connections, she made the following statements without elaboration:

- I have lived in Quincy, Massachusetts all of my life and was living in Quincy when I met Reginald Brilliant.

* * *

- I was 17 years old when I became pregnant and was living at home with my mother in Quincy, Massachusetts.
- When I was six months pregnant, Reginald Brilliant and I moved in together.
- We lived together at 81 Island Street, Marshfield, Massachusetts for approximately one year and four months.

* * *

- I always had reservations about making such a drastic move with my young baby as I had always been extremely close to my mother;

and my ties in Massachusetts, where I had lived all of my life, were very strong.

* * *

- I intend to stay in the Commonwealth of Massachusetts permanently.
- I have been the sole caretaker of my daughter, Kaylee, since her birth.
- Kaylee has become extremely attached to my mother, Lynn Fox, with whom we both live.

Kaylee lived with both of her parents from the time of her birth until April 15, 2000 and again from June 12, 2000 until July 24, 2000. She lived with her mother and her maternal grandmother from mid-April until June 12, 2000.[7] Lynn Fox did not testify in person or by affidavit. There was no evidence presented concerning the environment in Massachusetts, other than that Kaylee's medical care had been neglected. Certainly, evidence of Kaylee's connections to Massachusetts could have been presented but Kristen, electing not to appear, offered nothing more than conclusory comments about her attachments to Massachusetts and her mother, and Kaylee's attachment to her grandmother. We are disinclined to accord much weight to attachments Kaylee may have developed in the months following her return to Massachusetts in July 2000 when the move was in complete and utter disregard of a court order. Moreover, jurisdiction is determined based upon the existing circumstances at the time suit is filed in Texas. We thus conclude that it was in Kaylee's best interest for Texas to assume jurisdiction because she and her father had a significant connection to Texas other than mere physical presence, and, based on the record before us, Texas was a repository of substantial evidence concerning her present or future care, training, and personal relationships. Consequently, Texas was authorized to exercise its jurisdiction based on significant connections. Kristen's first issue for review is overruled.

Default Judgment

On the day after the trial court denied the motion for new trial, Regi and his attorney appeared and obtained a default judgment which appointed Regi as the sole managing conservator of Kaylee. Kristen contends that she had entered an "appearance" such that she was entitled to notice of the hearing. Regi urges us to construe the trial court's order as a judgment **nihil dicit**.

The Supreme Court has discussed three types of default judgments that contrast to "a judgment upon trial." The first is the traditional no-answer default. Second is the judgment *nihil dicit*, which occurs when a defendant has (1) entered some plea, usually of a dilatory nature, but one which does not place the merits of

---

[7]   Although she was again living with her mother and maternal grandmother from July 24 forward, we determine jurisdiction based upon the circumstances as they existed on the date suit was filed.

the plaintiff's case in issue; or (2) withdrawn his answer. A no-answer default and a judgment *nihil dicit* are so similar that the same rules apply to each with respect to the effect and validity of the judgment.

A judgment *nihil dicit* is proper when a party appears but has filed no answer on the merits. It is stronger than a no-answer default in that a judgment *nihil dicit* acts as a confession of judgment. These two types of judgments contrast with a post-answer default judgment, in which an answer is on file but the defendant fails to appear at trial. The difference is that a post-answer default constitutes neither an abandonment of the answer nor an implied confession of any issues joined by the answer. A judgment cannot be entered on the pleadings; the plaintiff must offer evidence and prove his case as in a judgment upon a trial.

At oral argument, Regi conceded that none of the cases involving judgments *nihil dicit* to which he has directed our attention involved a suit affecting the parent-child relationship in which the trial court was charged with determining a child's best interest. Moreover, none of the cases which he cites addresses whether a judgment *nihil dicit* may be taken without notice. Even the Texas Quarries case, which Regi suggests is factually similar, reveals that a notice of the trial setting was provided. See Texas Quarries v. Pierce, 244 S.W.2d 571, 572 (Tex.Civ.App.-San Antonio 1951, no writ).

An original answer may consist of motions to transfer venue, pleas to the jurisdiction, pleas in abatement, or any other dilatory pleas. Tex.R.Civ.P. 85. If a timely answer has been filed, or the respondent has otherwise made an appearance in a contested case, she is entitled to notice of the trial setting as a matter of due process. Even a pro se answer in the form of a signed letter that identifies the parties, the case, and the defendant's current address, constitutes a sufficient appearance to require notice to that party of any subsequent proceedings.

Kristen's plea to the jurisdiction constituted an appearance. When a party has appeared, she is entitled to notice of trial pursuant to Rule 245. The rule provides that the "[c]ourt may set contested cases on written request of any party. . .with reasonable notice of not less than forty-five days to the parties of a first setting for trial. . . ." Tex.R.Civ.P. 245. A trial court's failure to comply with the rules of notice in a contested case deprives a party of the constitutional right to be present at the hearing, to voice her objections in an appropriate manner, and results in a violation of fundamental due process. Thus, if the respondent does not have notice of the trial setting as required by Rule 245, the default judgment should be set aside because it is ineffectual. We sustain the second issue for review. The judgment is reversed and remanded for trial on the merits.

———————

Points for Discussion

a. *Brilliant*

What alternative approaches to the jurisdictional question under the UCCJEA were available to the court in *Brilliant*? Consider the purposes of the UCCJEA, as described by the court, and evaluate whether the opinion vindicates or frustrates these purposes.

b. Scope of the UCCJEA

The UCCJEA applies to any "child-custody proceeding," broadly defined in § 102(4) as "a proceeding in which legal custody, physical custody, or visitation with respect to a child is at issue." The definition includes proceedings for divorce, separation, neglect, abuse, dependency, guardianship, paternity, termination of parental rights, and protection from domestic violence, but it does not include juvenile delinquency or contractual emancipation proceedings.

Jurisdiction for purposes of adoption presents somewhat distinct issues, and the drafters of the UCCJEA did not include adoption within the scope of the statute, largely in deference to the Uniform Adoption Act, which includes its own jurisdictional rules. The UAA has only been adopted in Vermont, however, and courts in a number of states now apply the UCCJEA in adoption cases.

Make the Connection

Jurisdiction over adoption proceedings is discussed in Chapter 3, and jurisdiction in parental rights termination cases is addressed in Chapter 5.

In applying the UCCJEA, the term "State" is defined in § 102(15) to include any state in the United States as well as the District of Columbia, Puerto Rico, the U.S. Virgin Islands, and any "territory or insular possession subject to the jurisdiction of the United States" (such as Guam or American Samoa). As drafted, the UCCJEA also provides that states will treat Indian tribes as states in making jurisdictional determinations, and will recognize and enforce child-custody determinations made by tribes "under factual circumstances in substantial conformity with the jurisdictional standards" of the UCCJEA. See UCCJEA § 104. See, e.g., Garcia v. Gutierrez, 217 P.3d 591 (N.M. 2009); Kelly v. Kelly, 806 N.W.2d 133 (N.D. 2011). As discussed below, UCCJEA § 105 extends similar treatment to foreign countries.

c. Home State Jurisdiction

UCCJEA § 201(a)(1) gives jurisdictional priority to the courts of a state that "is the home State of the child on the date of commencement of the proceeding, or was the home State of the child within six months before the commencement of the proceeding and the child is absent from this State but a parent or person acting as a parent continues to live in this state." As defined in § 102(7), "Home State means the State in which a child lived with a parent or person acting as a parent for at least six consecutive months immediately before the commencement of a child-custody proceeding." The definition provides that the home state of a child less than six months of age is "the state in which the child lived from birth" with a parent or a person acting as a parent. As noted by the court in *Brilliant*, the definition of "home state" also provides that a period of temporary absence may be part of the six-month period. This temporary absence issue can be central to the determination of jurisdiction. See, e.g. Sarpel v. Eflanli, 65 So.3d 1080 (Fla. Dist. Ct. App. 2011).

The combined effect of § 201(a)(1) and § 102(7) is to allow a state to continue exercising "home state" jurisdiction for six months after the child has left the state, as long as a parent or person acting as a parent continues to live in the state. See, e.g., Welch-Doden v. Roberts, 42 P.3d 1166 (Ariz. Ct.App. 2002). This provides an important protection against the type of "seize and run" tactics that complicated custody litigation and often harmed children under the prior statutes.

d. Significant Connection Jurisdiction

When no state can exercise jurisdiction under the home state provision of the UCCJEA, or when a court with home state jurisdiction declines to exercise it, § 201(a)(2) allows a state court to take jurisdiction if two requirements are met. The child and at least one parent or person acting as a parent must have "a significant connection with this state other than mere physical presence," and there must be "substantial evidence" available in the state "concerning the child's care, protection, training and personal relationships." How did the Texas court in *Brilliant* apply this test? Could the court in Massachusetts have asserted jurisdiction on this basis? What happens under § 201 if no state can assert home state jurisdiction, and there is also no state where the child has a significant connection?

e. Simultaneous Proceedings

Under UCCJEA § 206, a court may not exercise jurisdiction if, at the time a proceeding is commenced, there is a pending custody proceeding concerning the same child in another state, and the other court is exercising jurisdiction substantially in conformity with the UCCJEA. See, e.g., Pierce v. State, 172 A.3d 190 (Vt. 2017). Note that this rule does not apply to a court exercising temporary emergency jurisdiction under § 204, or situations in which the first court has declined to exercise jurisdiction.

f. Judicial Communication

Jurisdictional conflicts and other questions that arise between courts in custody litigation may be addressed by direct judicial communication, authorized by UCCJEA § 110. See, e.g., Fitzpatrick v. McCrary, 182 A.3d 737 (Me. 2018). Parties must either be permitted to participate in the communication or, given an opportunity to present facts and legal arguments before a decision on jurisdiction is made. Except for communications regarding matters such as calendars and court records, a record must be made of any judicial communication and the parties must be promptly informed and granted access to the record.

g. Emergency Jurisdiction

In urgent situations, when a child is present within a state and the child has been abandoned or "it is necessary in an emergency to protect the child because the child, or a sibling or parent of the child, is subjected to or threatened with mistreatment or abuse," UCCJEA § 204 allows a state court to assume emergency jurisdiction. Court decisions have stressed that this jurisdiction is temporary, continuing only as long as necessary to protect the child's safety. See, e.g., In re C.T., 121 Cal.Rptr.2d 897 (Ct. App. 2002) (approving emergency order entered in sexual abuse case). Various provisions in § 204 address the limited duration of emergency orders and procedures for judicial communication with the court that would otherwise have jurisdiction. See, e.g., Beauregard v. White, 972 A.2d 619 (R.I. 2009) (finding that although several orders fell within court's emergency jurisdiction, circumstances did not justify continuing exercise of jurisdiction on this basis).

h. Declining Jurisdiction

A court with jurisdiction under the UCCJEA may decline to exercise it on two different grounds. A court may decline to exercise jurisdiction based on the inconvenient forum provisions in § 207, if it determines that a court of another state is a more appropriate forum. Section 207 lists factors the state court should consider in making this determination, including whether domestic violence has occurred and is likely to continue in the future and which state could best protect the parties and the child, the length of time the child has resided outside the state, the distance between the courts in the two states, the relative financial circumstances of the parties, any agreement between the parties as to which state should assume jurisdiction, the nature and location of necessary evidence, each court's ability to decide the matter expeditiously, and the familiarity of the court in each state with the facts and issues in the case. Under § 207, the court must hold a hearing or allow the parties to submit information on these factors. See, e.g., Rice v. McDonald, 390 P.3d 1133 (Alaska 2018); In re the Marriage of Fontenot, 77 P.3d 206 (Mont. 2003).

Another basis for declining to exercise jurisdiction is in UCCJEA § 208, which requires that a court decline to exercise its jurisdiction if that jurisdiction came about "because a person invoking the jurisdiction has engaged in unjustifiable conduct," unless certain exceptions apply. See, e.g., In re Lewin, 149 S.W.3d 727 (Tex. App.2004) (declining to exercise jurisdiction after a child was wrongfully retained in the state in a case within the Hague Convention on the Civil Aspects of International Child Abduction).

i. Choice of Law

What state's law should a court apply in deciding parental responsibility questions? In an action for termination of parental rights as part of a stepparent adoption proceeding, within the scope of UCCJEA, Crouch v. Smick, 24 N.E.3d 300 (Ill. App. Ct. 2014), concluded that "if an Illinois court is determined to be the home state for jurisdiction, it is necessarily the state with the most significant relationship for choice-of-law purposes and Illinois law applies." See also State ex rel. S.O., 122 P.3d 686 (Utah Ct. App. 2005).

Global View: International Custody Disputes

Courts must treat foreign countries as if they were states of the United States for purposes of applying the jurisdictional provisions of the UCCJEA, see § 105(a), and must recognize and enforce child custody determinations made in foreign countries "under factual circumstances in substantial conformity with the jurisdictional standards" of the UCCJEA, see § 105(b). Many cases have applied these rules. See, e.g., Atchison v. Atchison, 664 N.W.2d 249 (Mich. Ct. App. 2003) (holding that court in Canada had continuing exclusive jurisdiction under the UCCJEA); In re Marriage of Medill, 40 P.3d 1087 (Or. Ct. App. 2002) (concluding that Germany was the child's home state under the UCCJEA). See generally Robert G. Spector, *International Child Custody Jurisdiction and the Uniform Child Custody Jurisdiction and Enforcement Act*, 33 N.Y.U. J. Int'l L. & Pol. 251 (2000).

Recognition of a foreign decree is not required if the foreign proceeding did not afford both parties with the "fundamental indicia of due process—notice and the opportunity to be heard," Maqsudi v. Maqsudi, 830 A.2d 929 (N.J. Super. Ct. Ch.Div.2002). UCCJEA § 105(c) provides that a court "need not apply the provisions of [the UCCJEA] when the child custody law of the other country violates fundamental principles of human rights."

In 2010, the United States signed the 1996 Hague Convention on Jurisdiction Applicable Law, Recognition, Enforcement and Co-operation in Respect of Parental Responsibility and Measures for the Protection of Children (Child Protection Convention). Implementation of the Child Protection Convention would be accomplished through a combination of federal legislation and amendments to the UCCJEA.

Problem 7-23

Mother and Father live together with their children for three years in Arizona. When Mother and Father separate, Mother moves with the children to Colorado.

(a) Can Mother bring a child custody proceeding in Colorado under the UCCJEA? *depends how long has lived there*

(b) Can Father bring a child custody proceeding in Arizona under the UCCJEA?

(c) Would your answers be different if Mother did not tell Father where she had gone with the children until she had been there for a year?

(d) How would your answers be different if Father had also moved away from Arizona?

(e) How would your answers be different if the family had lived together initially in Mexico rather than Arizona? *— we treat foreign country as state*

(f) What should happen if the Mother had abandoned the children in Colorado several weeks after moving there?

(g) Assume that Mother lived with the children in Colorado for three months, and then moved them to Washington for two months, and then to Hawaii for three months. Can she bring a child custody proceeding in Hawaii? On what basis? How might Father challenge the jurisdiction of the court in Hawaii? *→ NO unless emergency* *∟ Father should argue inconvenient forum*

Problem 7-24

Jeffrey and Alesha lived together in Illinois when they separated. Alesha moved to her family's home in Texas, and Jeffrey filed a petition for dissolution of their marriage in Illinois. A month later, when Jeffrey learned that Alesha was pregnant, he amended his petition to request custody of the unborn child. He also asked the court to grant an injunction ordering Alesha to move back to Illinois until the child was born and to "provide him with all relevant information regarding the pregnancy." Does the court in Illinois have jurisdiction over Jeffrey's claims? Would your answer be different if Jeffrey and Alesha were not married, and he filed a petition in Illinois for determination of the child's parentage? (See Marriage of Skelton, 815 N.E.2d 1176 (Ill. App. Ct. 2004); see also Sara Ashton McK v. Samuel Bode M., 974 N.Y.S.2d 434 (App. Div. 2013).)

Client Counseling: Custody Jurisdiction

Your client tells you that he and his wife have a two-year-old daughter and their marriage is not in good shape. His wife left town about three months ago with the child, without telling him she was leaving. Your client learned only yesterday that she returned to her hometown in another state, a small town where her father is a leading citizen. Your client would like to retrieve his daughter and bring a claim for custody. What advice can you give him? How would your advice change if they had been gone for six months? (Cf. Stokes v. Stokes, 751 P.2d 1363 (Alaska 1988); In re Marriage of Verbin, 595 P.2d 905 (Wash. 1979).)

Billhime v. Billhime

952 A.2d 1174 (Pa. Super. Ct. 2008)

¶ 1 Lisa Billhime Nistri ("Mother") appeals from the order of the Court of Common Pleas of Montour County denying her motion to relinquish jurisdiction in this custody action to the state of Florida. After careful review, we reverse and remand.

¶ 2 Mother and Darin Billhime ("Father") are the parents of twin boys born in Orlando, Florida on December 3, 1996. The family remained in Florida until 2001, when they relocated to Montour County, Pennsylvania. Mother and Father separated in early 2004, at which time a custody action was filed in the Court of Common Pleas of Montour County. The trial court subsequently awarded primary physical custody of the children to the Mother and partial physical custody to the Father. In March 2005, Mother and the children moved back to Orlando, Florida,[1] where they continue to live at this time. Following the relocation to Florida, the trial court modified the custodial arrangement, with Mother retaining primary physical custody but permitting Father to enjoy custody during the boys' spring, Thanksgiving and Christmas vacations, as well as nearly all of their summer vacation.

---

[1]   In July 2004, Mother filed a Petition to Relocate to Florida with the children. The trial court denied the Petition, but in March 2005 this Court reversed that decision, permitting the relocation of Mother and children to Florida.

¶ 3 Unfortunately, the transition to this custodial schedule proved difficult and multiple petitions for contempt were filed and adjudicated in the trial court in Montour County. On June 8, 2006, Father filed a petition with the trial court seeking primary custody of the children. On February 28, 2007, Mother responded by filing a motion requesting that the trial court relinquish jurisdiction over this child custody action to the Circuit Court for the 9th Judicial Circuit in and for Orange County, Florida. Following an evidentiary hearing, the trial court denied Mother's motion to relinquish jurisdiction, ruling that "[c]ontinuing jurisdiction over the custody case above captioned shall remain with the courts of the Commonwealth of Pennsylvania." Order, 6/15/07. In its written opinion dated June 19, 2007, the trial court explained that it denied Mother's motion because "there exists evidence that the children and one of the parents continues to have a significant connection with this Commonwealth."

¶ 4 This timely appeal followed. In accordance with our standard of review, this Court will not disturb a decision to exercise or decline jurisdiction absent an abuse of discretion by the trial court. *Wagner v. Wagner*, 887 A.2d 282, 285 (Pa. Super.2005). An abuse of discretion occurs when the court has overridden or misapplied the law, when its judgment is manifestly unreasonable, or when there is insufficient evidence of record to support the court's findings. Based on our careful review of the record, we conclude that the trial court abused its discretion and that its decision to deny Mother's motion to relinquish jurisdiction must be reversed.

¶ 5 In its written opinion, the trial court found that it retained exclusive continuing jurisdiction to modify custody orders in this case pursuant to section 5422(a) of the Uniform Child Custody Jurisdiction and Enforcement Act ("UCCJEA"), 23 Pa.C.S.A. § 5401 *et seq.* Section 5422(a) provides as follows:

> **§ 5422. Exclusive, continuing jurisdiction**
>
> **(a) General rule.**—Except as otherwise provided in section 5424 (relating to temporary emergency jurisdiction), a court of this Commonwealth which has made a child custody determination consistent with section 5421 (relating to initial child custody jurisdiction) or 5423 (relating to jurisdiction to modify determination) has exclusive, continuing jurisdiction over the determination until:
>
> > (1) a court of this Commonwealth determines that neither the child, nor the child and one parent, nor the child and a person acting as a parent have a significant connection with this Commonwealth and that substantial evidence is no longer available in this Commonwealth concerning the child's care, protection, training and personal relationships;
> >
> > (2) a court of this Commonwealth or a court of another state determines that the child, the child's parents and any person acting as a parent do not presently reside in this Commonwealth.

¶ 6 <u>Subsection 5422(a)(1)</u> thus provides that the courts of this Commonwealth will exercise exclusive continuing jurisdiction to modify child custody orders originally entered here unless the child, or a child and at least one parent (or a person acting as a parent), no longer have a "significant connection" with Pennsylvania. For the child, the lack of a continuing "significant connection" with the Commonwealth is established if the court finds that substantial evidence concerning the child's "care, protection, training and personal relationships" is no longer available here.

¶ 7 In denying mother's motion to relinquish jurisdiction, the trial court relied almost exclusively on Father's continuing "significant connection" with Pennsylvania. The trial court found that Father is the fifth-generation owner of a farm in Montour County, retains a Pennsylvania driver's license, has an active equitable distribution action pending in the local court, and enjoys the majority of visitation time with his children in the state.

¶ 8 In contrast, however, the trial court's opinion does not focus in any detail on whether the *children* continue to maintain a "significant connection" to Pennsylvania, noting only that the boys visit here on three occasions per year and spend time with their father, friends and paternal grandfather. A review of the record of the evidentiary hearing reveals that little evidence was introduced regarding the continuing availability in Pennsylvania of "substantial evidence concerning the child's care, protection, training and personal relationships," as is expressly required by section 5422(a)(1) of the UCCJEA.

¶ 9 In fact, essentially all of the evidence presented at the evidentiary hearing demonstrates that information relating to the children's welfare is now located in the state of Florida. For example, the children's medical care is provided in Florida, including by their pediatrician, dentist and orthodontist. They attend a private school in Florida, performing well, earning high grades and regularly being named to the honor roll and the headmaster's list. Through their school, they are involved in basketball, football, soccer, baseball, golf, safety patrols and extracurricular art classes. The boys also participate in Cub Scouts in Florida and are actively involved in their Orlando-based church. They have good friends and significant family in the Orlando area, including a grandmother, aunts and uncles, and cousins.

¶ 10 Based upon the above evidence, the record in this case does not support a finding that the children retain a "significant connection" with Pennsylvania, as required by subsection 5422(a)(1) of the UCCJEA. As a result, the Court of Common Pleas of Montour County no longer has exclusive continuing jurisdiction to modify its previously entered child custody orders.

¶ 11 In the absence of exclusive continuing jurisdiction, a Pennsylvania court may nevertheless modify a child custody order it previously issued if it has jurisdiction to make an initial determination under section 5421 of the UCCJEA. 23 Pa.C.S.A. § 5422(b); *Wagner v. Wagner,* 887 A.2d 282, 287 (Pa.Super.2005). Because the trial court did not address the applicability of section 5421 in connection with its initial consideration of Mother's motion to relinquish jurisdiction, we remand for consideration and decision on this issue. In the event the trial court determines that it lacks jurisdiction to make an initial custody determination pursuant to section 5421, it should grant Mother's motion and relinquish jurisdiction of custody matters relating to these two children to the courts of the state of Florida.

¶ 12 Order reversed. Case remanded. Jurisdiction relinquished.

Points for Discussion

a. Child Custody Determination

UCCJEA § 102(11) defines a "modification" as "a child-custody determination that changes, replaces, supersedes, or is otherwise made after a previous determination concerning the same child." This provision is expanded by the broad statutory definition of "child-custody determination" under § 102(3) as: "a judgment, decree, or other order of a court providing for the legal custody, physical custody, or visitation with respect to a child. The term includes a permanent, temporary, initial, and modification order. The term does not include an order relating to child support or other monetary obligation of an individual." See, e.g., Snow v. Snow, 74 P.3d 1137 (Or. Ct. App. 2003).

b. Exclusive Continuing Jurisdiction

UCCJEA § 202 and § 203 provide that a state that makes an initial child custody determination retains exclusive continuing jurisdiction over the case unless one of two conditions are met. Under § 202(a)(1), a court in the state with exclusive continuing jurisdiction may conclude "that neither the child, nor the child and one parent, nor the child and a person acting as a parent have a significant connection with this State and that substantial evidence is no longer available in this State concerning the child's care, protection, training, and personal relationships." Under § 202 (a)(2), a court in any state may determine "that the child, the child's parents, and any person acting as a parent do not presently reside in" the state. Why did the UCCJEA drafters limit the inquiry under § 202(a)(1) to the court in the state with continuing jurisdiction?

California courts have held as a matter of law that a "significant connection" exists to support continuing exclusive jurisdiction so long as a parent who exercises visitation rights continues to live in the state. See Grahm v. Superior Court,

34 Cal.Rptr.3d 270 (Cal. Ct. App. 2005). See also White v. Harrison White, 760 N.W.2d 691 (Mich. Ct. App. 2008) (reviewing cases); Watson v. Watson, 724 N.W.2d 24 (Neb. 2006). How is this different from the court's approach in *Bill-hime*? Which approach seems preferable to you, and why?

Several cases decided under § 202(a)(2) have pointed out that the statutory language focuses on whether the child and the parents "presently reside in" the original jurisdiction, citing the Commissioners' Notes for the statute which indicate that this term "is not used in the sense of a technical domicile." See, e.g., Parenting of A.B.A.M., 96 P.3d 1139 (Mont. 2004); In re Lewin, 149 S.W.3d 727 (Tex. App.2004). But see Brandt v. Brandt, 268 P.3d 406 (Colo. 2012) (holding that initial decree state did not lose jurisdiction during mother's military service outside the state). Because the determination whether any of the parties "presently reside in" the state is made at the time the action to modify is filed, it does not matter whether they may have resided somewhere else for a period of time and then returned. See In re Parenting of A.B.A.M., 96 P.3d 1139 (Mont. 2004).

c. PKPA

The federal Parental Kidnapping Prevention Act, 28 U.S.C. § 1738A (2018), limits the circumstances in which one court may modify a custody determination made by a court in another state. Under § 1738(f), a state court may modify a custody determination from another state if it has jurisdiction to make a custody determination and the court of the other state "no longer has jurisdiction, or it has declined to exercise such jurisdiction to modify. . . ." In states that have not enacted the UCCJEA, or states that have a non-uniform version of the Act, the PKPA may operate to prevent modification that would otherwise be permitted under state law. See, e.g., Scott v. Somers, 903 A.2d 663 (Conn. Ct. App. 2006) (concluding that Connecticut could not modify a Florida custody order under the PKPA).

The PKPA applies to adoption proceedings. See, e.g., In re Adoption of Baby E.Z., 266 P.3d 702 (Utah 2011). State courts have disagreed as to whether it applies to proceedings for termination of parental rights brought by public child welfare authorities in one state following private custody litigation in a different state. See generally In re Higera N., 2 A.3d 265 (Maine 2010).

Finally, note that the PKPA does not provide a means for resolving an impasse in the event that courts in two different states reach different conclusions as to which state has jurisdiction and what the PKPA requires in a particular case. See Thompson v. Thompson, 484 U.S. 174 (1988) (holding that Congress did not intend to create a cause of action in federal court to enforce the PKPA). Should Congress amend the statute to allow federal jurisdiction in these cases?

d. Forum Selection Agreements

As a rule, parties may not confer subject matter jurisdiction on a court by consent or waiver. Thus, courts have been unwilling to enforce stipulations that a particular court will exercise or retain jurisdiction in a custody case. E.g. <u>MacDougall v. Acres, 693 N.E.2d 663 (Mass. (1998)</u>; <u>Friedman v. Nevada Eighth Judicial District Court, 264 P.3d 1161 (Nev. 2011)</u>. When the parties stipulate to jurisdiction in a forum that has subject matter jurisdiction, courts are more willing to enforce an agreement. See, e.g., <u>In re Marriage of Hilliard, 533 N.E.2d 543 (Ill. App. Ct. 1989)</u>. Courts may also rely on such a stipulation as a basis to decline jurisdiction under UCCJEA § 207.

e. Registration and Enforcement of Custody Determinations

UCCJEA Article 3 creates a procedure for registration and enforcement of a child-custody determination, if it was made by a court in another state or country based on factual circumstances that satisfy the jurisdictional standards of the UCCJEA. See, e.g., in <u>In re Sophia G.L., 890 N.E.2d 470 (Ill. 2008)</u>. A petitioner who seeks enforcement of a child-custody determination may also obtain a warrant to take physical custody of the child if the child is "likely to suffer serious imminent physical harm or removal from this State." <u>UCCJEA § 311(a)</u>.

Military Families

When a parent is in military service, there are additional procedural and substantive rules in custody and visitation cases, beginning with the Servicemembers Civil Relief Act, <u>50 U.S.C. App. § 501 et seq. (2018)</u>, which is expressly applicable to custody proceedings. See, e.g., <u>Marriage of Harris, 922 N.E.2d 626 (Ind. Ct. App. 2010)</u>; cf. <u>Griffin v. Griffin, 916 N.W.2d 292 (Mich. Ct. App. 2018)</u>. See generally Sara Estrin, *The Servicemembers Civil Relief Act: Why and How this Act Applies to Child Custody Proceedings*, 27 Law & Ineq. 211 (2009).

Many states have enacted legislation to address the custody and visitation rights of a parent called to active duty in the armed forces. In 2012, the Uniform Law Commission approved the <u>Uniform Deployed Parents Custody and Visitation Act (DPCVA)</u>, 9 U.L.A. (Part IB) (Supp. 2018), which integrates with the UCCJEA, and provides expedited procedures for temporary custody orders during deployment. The DPCVA encourages parents to agree to a custody arrangement during deployment, and includes safeguards designed to balance the interests of the service member and the other parent, and protect the best interests of the children involved.

Problem 7-25

Husband, Wife, and Children live together in Florida. Husband files an action for divorce in Florida, and obtains a child custody order there. Three years later, Husband moves to Georgia with the children.

(a) Can Husband have the Florida custody order modified in Georgia after he and the children have lived there for a year? After ten years?

(b) Can Wife have the visitation provisions of the Florida order enforced in Georgia? How should such a proceeding be handled under the UCCJEA?

(c) Would your answers be any different if Wife had also moved to another state after the Florida order was entered?

(d) Would your answers be any different if the parties had been living in France, and the original custody order was entered by a court in France?

Problem 7-26

A year after Ann and Robert were divorced, the court in Texas modified their divorce decree and permitted Robert to move with their children to another state. Over the next five years, Robert and the children moved three more times. Ann flew several times a year to visit the children, and they returned each summer to visit Ann in Texas, staying up to a month. When Ann learned that Robert was planning to relocate outside the country with the children, she petitioned the court in Texas for a modification of custody. What arguments can Robert make to challenge the jurisdiction of the Texas court? How should the court decide this question? (See In re Forlenza, 140 S.W.3d 373 (Tex.2004).)

Problem 7-27

Hector and Josefina were divorced in the Dominican Republic, and she agreed that their sons could live with him. Josefina remarried and moved to New York. After she was granted lawful permanent resident status, she brought the boys to live with her. Three months later, Hector was arrested in New York for threatening Josefina. The court issued protective orders and released Hector without bail, based on his representation that he lived in New York. When Josefina filed a petition in New York for a change of custody, alleging an extensive history of domestic violence, an investigation by social services indicated that the boys were frightened of their father and had been doing well in New York with their mother. Can the New York court decide this case? Would your analysis differ if Hector had returned to the Dominican Republic before Josefina filed her petition? (See Hector G. v. Josefina P., 2 Misc.3d 801, 771 N.Y.S.2d 316 (Sup.Ct.2003).)

Problem 7-28

Tanya and Joe moved to Colorado in August, and separated five months later. Joe relocated to Nebraska, and Tanya and Joe signed an agreement stating that custody matters would be decided under Colorado law, that their daughter would live with Tanya in Colorado, and that Joe would have parenting time with the child every summer for the month of August. Joe brought the child to Nebraska that summer, but then refused to return her and filed an action for divorce and custody in Nebraska. When Tanya is notified of the proceeding, how should she respond? If the court in Nebraska enters a custody order, is it enforceable in Colorado? (Cf. In re the Parental Responsibilities of L.S., 257 P.3d 201 (Colo. 2011).)

Problem 7-29

When Maria and her husband were divorced in Mexico, she was granted primary legal and physical custody of their children, with visitation rights for her husband. After she relocated with the children to California six months later, her husband began making threats to kill her and take the children. Maria has filed a request in California for a civil protection order restraining him from any contact with her or the children. Does the state court have jurisdiction under the UCCJEA to enter this order? (See In re Marriage of Fernandez-Abin, 120 Cal.Rptr.3d 227 (Ct. App. 2011).)

Personal Jurisdiction in Custody Cases

One of the long-standing puzzles of child custody jurisdiction law concerns the role of personal jurisdiction in these cases. Because custody proceedings were traditionally treated as an adjudication of status, personal jurisdiction was not required. In May v. Anderson, 345 U.S. 528 (1953), however, the Supreme Court concluded that a child custody order entered without personal jurisdiction over the respondent was not entitled to full faith and credit in another state. Although some courts have relied on *May* in refusing to give full faith and credit to custody decrees of other states, see e.g. Dean v. Dean, 447 So.2d 733 (Ala.1984), the PKPA requires that states enforce and refuse to modify child custody determinations of other states without regard to whether the court that made the determination had personal jurisdiction over the parties. Moreover, UCCJEA § 201(c) provides that "[p]hysical presence of, or personal jurisdiction over, a party or a child is neither necessary nor sufficient to make a child-custody determination." State courts routinely conclude that even cases involving complete termination of parental rights fall within the status exception to the personal jurisdiction requirement. See, e.g., In re R.W., 39 A.3d 682 (Vt. 2011).

The Supreme Court has not revisited the question of personal jurisdiction in custody cases since its decision in *May*. The Court cited *May* when it ruled in Kulko v. Superior Court, 436 U.S. 84 (1978), that personal jurisdiction is required in child support cases, but a footnote in Shaffer v. Heitner, 433 U.S. 186 (1977), suggests that status questions remain an exception to the usual rules governing personal jurisdiction. See also Stanley v. Illinois, 405 U.S. 645, 657 n. 9 (1972) (suggesting that an unwed father's parental rights may be terminated based on service by mail or notice by publication). Some scholars have concluded that these cases have overruled a strict reading of *May*, see Brigitte Bodenheimer & Neeley-Kvarme, *Jurisdiction Over Child Custody After* Shaffer *and* Kulko, 12 U.C. D. L. Rev. 229, 251 (1979). For the argument that personal jurisdiction is necessary in custody cases, see Rhonda Wasserman, *Parents, Partners and Personal Jurisdiction*, 1995 U. Ill. L. Rev. 813 (1995).

2. Assigning Parental Responsibilities

In the United States and around the world, the primary consideration in allocating parental responsibilities is the best interests of the child. This has not always been the case: at common law, a father had the primary right to custody of his children. During the nineteenth century, courts began to award custody to mothers, and eventually began to presume that children of "tender years" should be placed with their mothers. See Mary Ann Mason, From Father's Property to Children's Rights: The History of Child Custody in the United States (1994). When one parent has sole or primary custody, the other has traditionally been entitled to visitation rights.

During the 1970s and 1980s, states began to authorize joint custody awards, in which both parents shared responsibilities for legal decision-making and physical care of children. Many state statutes now stress the goal of keeping both parents involved in the child's life. States have adopted new terminology designed to reinforce this goal and reduce the stigma associated with older terms like "visitation" or "non-custodial parent." Decision-making authority may be referred to as exercising parental responsibilities or functions (rather than as legal custody), and time spent caring for the child may be described as parental contact, parenting time, or residential time (rather than as physical custody or visitation.) In some states, the idea of custody has been discarded entirely in favor of "parenting plans," in which the parties or the court allocate decision-making responsibilities and physical care for the child and agree on a method of dispute resolution in the event of disagreements between the parents.

Go Online

Find a chart listing statutes and Custody Criteria for all states on the web page of the American Bar Association's Family Law Section.

The same principles govern allocation of parental responsibility for children born to unmarried couples. See, e.g., Ysla v. López, 684 A.2d 775 (D.C. 1996) (awarding joint legal custody to unmarried parents despite the mother's objections). Note, however, that state laws may assign custody of a nonmarital child to the child's birth mother as an initial matter, particularly if the other parent's parentage has not been established. See, e.g. In re Vernor, 94 S.W.3d 201 (Tex. App. 2002).

In Re Marriage of Kovacs

854 P.2d 629 (Wash. 1993) (en banc)

ANDERSEN, CHIEF JUSTICE.

Facts of Case

The father in this marriage dissolution action seeks review of a Court of Appeals decision which reversed the trial court's order awarding primary residential care of the parties' three minor children to the father rather than to the mother. The father argues that the Court of Appeals applied the wrong legal standard when it held that the parent who has been the primary caregiver of the children during marriage must be designated as the primary residential parent in a dissolution action, unless that parent's personality, conduct or parenting style is found to have had an adverse impact on the children. We agree with the father and reverse the Court of Appeals.

John and Marcia Kovacs were married in August 1982. At the time of the marriage John owned a small janitorial business in Alaska and Marcia was working in a restaurant.

The Kovacs have three children, Johnny, who is now 10 years old; Courtney, who is 9 years old; and Billy, who is 6 years old. During the marriage Marcia generally stayed at home to care for the children and the family home while John worked outside the home to financially care for the family. Marcia worked outside the home for only a short time prior to the separation.

In 1984, John was forced to sell his janitorial business to meet an IRS obligation. He worked for the new owner of the business for a time, but problems developed in the employment relationship and John was fired in the spring of 1988.

After John lost his job, the couple decided to move to California where job opportunities appeared to be better than those in Alaska. The couple agreed that Marcia would stay with the children in Spokane, where Marcia's parents lived, until John was able to find a job and housing in California. Marcia and the children moved to Spokane in late April 1989. They lived with Marcia's parents until the Kovacs' furniture arrived and Marcia was able to move into a duplex owned by her parents. John joined the family 3 or 4 weeks later, on May 22, 1989. Then, in mid-June, John went to California to look for work.

He found a job in California on August 18, 1989, and later moved into a three-bedroom townhouse in a planned residential community in Irvine, California. Marcia traveled to Irvine in October 1989 to see the new home but did not tell John at that time that she intended to file for dissolution of their marriage. It was not until John arrived in Spokane in November 1989 to move his family to California that Marcia told him the marriage was over. John returned to California and Marcia remained in Spokane with the three children.

She apparently filed a petition for dissolution of marriage in Spokane County Superior Court on December 20, 1989. A *temporary* parenting plan, awarding Marcia primary residential placement of the children pending final resolution of the action, was apparently entered in March 1990.

Testimony before the trial court indicated that Marcia was the primary caregiver and was generally responsible for the day-to-day care of the children's needs during the marriage and during the period of separation.

The record reflects the problems that existed within the family and with each parent.

During the approximately 18 months the couple was living apart, Marcia became romantically involved with another man, she left the children with various relatives during times when she was traveling to and from the man's home in Olympia, and was cited for two alcohol-related driving offenses. She was arrested for driving while under the influence of alcohol in October 1989 after she was involved in an automobile accident. The children, who were in the automobile at the time, were temporarily removed from Marcia's care and placed in a foster home for 2 days.

At trial both parents sought primary residential placement of the children.

Both parents had apparently agreed to be evaluated by the father's expert witness, a clinical psychologist. The psychologist interviewed each parent alone, administered personality tests to each parent, observed the children alone and observed each parent with the children. With the information gained through the testing, the interviews and observation the psychologist concluded that Marcia has a personality disorder. The psychologist testified that although an individual with a personality disorder could "get by as a parent", the personality disorder would inevitably affect parenting.

The psychologist testified that although the children were "adequately adjusted", they appeared to respond better to the father's directions than the mother's. He stated that the oldest child was the most difficult of the three to manage and that child needed the firm limit setting that the father was able to provide. While stating the question was "relatively close", the psychologist recommended that the father be awarded primary residential placement of the children because the father "is a more stable individual who will provide a more structured stable environment for the children."

The mother's expert was a counselor who met the mother for the first time just a few days before trial. She observed the mother and children together the day before trial began. The counselor did not administer any tests and did not meet the father. The counselor recommended the children be placed with the mother. The counselor said she found the children to be "in pretty good shape, so whatever either parent has done, they must have done a pretty good job." She also said the children told her that they wanted to live with their mother. The counselor, noting that the mother was the primary caregiver of the children, stated, "Children can get along without a lot of things, but they don't get along well without nurturing from a mother."

The trial court followed the recommendation of the father's expert and awarded primary residential placement of the children to the father. The children moved to their father's home in California in January 1991, just a few days after the conclusion of the trial, and have continued to reside there during this appeal. A stay of the trial court's order was denied by the Court of Appeals on January 18, 1991.

On appeal the Court of Appeals reversed the trial court's order, and remanded for a new trial, holding that placement with the parent who had acted as the primary caregiver was *required* unless the child had been harmed by the conduct of the primary caregiver. *In re Marriage of Kovacs,* 67 Wash.App. 727, 730–31, 840 P.2d 214 (1992). We granted the father's petition for review.

One issue is presented.

Issue

Does the Parenting Act of 1987 create a presumption that placement of a child with the parent who has been the primary caregiver is always in the child's best interests absent proof that the primary caregiver's personality, conduct or parenting style has harmed the child's physical, mental or emotional well being?

Decision

CONCLUSION. The Parenting Act of 1987 does not create a presumption in favor of placement with the primary caregiver. Instead, the Act requires consideration of seven factors and provides that the child's relationship with each parent be the factor given the greatest weight in determining the permanent residential placement.

We have not yet construed the residential provisions of the Parenting Act of 1987 (hereinafter Parenting Act or the Act), Laws of 1987, ch. 460.

Washington's Parenting Act represents a unique legislative attempt to reduce the conflict between parents who are in the throes of a marriage dissolution by focusing on continued "parenting" responsibilities, rather than on winning custody/visitation battles. The Act replaced the terms "custody" and "visitation" with the concepts of "parenting plans" and "parental functions". Ordinarily parents involved in a marriage dissolution action are required to develop a parenting plan that: (1) provides for a method of resolving future disputes about the children; (2) allocates decisionmaking between the parents; and (3) makes residential provisions for each child. It is only the *residential placement* of the parties' children that is at issue in the present case.

In ordering a parenting plan, the trial court is required to provide for the residential schedule or placement of the child. The residential placement is to be in the best interests of the child and is to be made only after certain factors have been considered by the court. The Parenting Act revised the factors previously considered by the trial court under former law, but continues to give the trial court broad discretion when making the determination.

A trial court's ruling dealing with the placement of children is reviewed for abuse of discretion. A trial court abuses its discretion when its decision is manifestly unreasonable or based on untenable grounds.

In the present case the Court of Appeals held that the trial court abused its discretion because it failed to find circumstances supporting a "change" of placement from the primary caregiver (the mother) to the father. In ruling as it did, the Court of Appeals relied on a 1975 case, <u>Wildermuth v. Wildermuth, 14 Wash.App. 442, 542 P.2d 463 (1975)</u>. Although *Wildermuth* was a *modification of custody* case, the Court of Appeals found the language of the former modification statute and the language of the policy section of the Parenting Act of 1987 to be similar.[13]

The Court of Appeals interpreted the Parenting Act to *require* placement with the parent who has provided the primary daily care of the child, unless the trial court finds that the personality or parenting style of the primary caregiver has resulted in harm to the child.

The language from the Act which the Court of Appeals believed compelled this conclusion is the following:

> Parents have the responsibility to make decisions and perform other parental functions necessary for the care and growth of their minor children. *In any proceeding between parents under this chapter, the best interests of the child shall be the standard by which the court determines and allocates the parties' parental responsibilities.* The state recognizes the fundamental importance of the parent-child relationship to the welfare of the child, and that the relationship between the child and each parent should be fostered unless inconsistent with the child's best interests. *The best interests of the child are served by a parenting arrangement that best maintains a child's emotional growth, health and stability, and physical care. Further, the best interest of the child is ordinarily served when the existing pattern of interaction between a parent and child is altered only to the extent necessitated by the changed relationship of the parents or as required to protect the child from physical, mental, or emotional harm.*

(Italics ours.) <u>RCW 26.09.002</u>.

That policy section, however, must be read in conjunction with the following placement provisions:

> (1) OBJECTIVES. The objectives of the permanent parenting plan are to:
> (a) Provide for the child's physical care;
> (b) Maintain the child's emotional stability;
> (c) Provide for the child's changing needs as the child grows and matures, in a way that minimizes the need for future modifications to the permanent parenting plan;
> (d) Set forth the authority and responsibilities of each parent with respect to the child, consistent with the criteria in <u>RCW 26.09.187</u> and <u>26.09.191</u>;
> (e) Minimize the child's exposure to harmful parental conflict;

---

[13] *Kovacs,* <u>67 Wash.App. at 731, 840 P.2d 214</u>. The case presently before the court involves the *initial* permanent placement decision *not* a modification of placement, which would be governed by <u>RCW 26.09.260</u>.

(f) Encourage the parents, where appropriate under RCW 26.09.187 and 26.09.191, to meet their responsibilities to their minor children through agreements in the permanent parenting plan, rather than by relying on judicial intervention; and

(g) To otherwise protect the best interests of the child consistent with RCW 26.09.002.

RCW 26.09.184(1).

(3) RESIDENTIAL PROVISIONS.

(a) The court shall make residential provisions for each child which encourage each parent to maintain a loving, stable, and nurturing relationship with the child, consistent with the child's developmental level and the family's social and economic circumstances. The child's residential schedule shall be consistent with RCW 26.09.191. Where the limitations of RCW 26.09.191 are not dispositive of the child's residential schedule, the court shall consider the following factors:

(i) The relative strength, nature, and stability of the child's relationship with each parent, including whether a parent has taken greater responsibility for performing parenting functions relating to the daily needs of the child;

(ii) The agreements of the parties, provided they were entered into knowingly and voluntarily;

(iii) Each parent's past and potential for future performance of parenting functions;

(iv) The emotional needs and developmental level of the child;

(v) The child's relationship with siblings and with other significant adults, as well as the child's involvement with his or her physical surroundings, school, or other significant activities;

(vi) The wishes of the parents and the wishes of a child who is sufficiently mature to express reasoned and independent preferences as to his or her residential schedule; and

(vii) Each parent's employment schedule, and shall make accommodations consistent with those schedules.

Factor (i) shall be given the greatest weight.

RCW 26.09.187(3)(a).

In interpreting the above statutory language certain principles of statutory construction apply. These are as follows: (1) a statute which is clear on its face is not subject to judicial interpretation; (2) an ambiguity will be deemed to exist if the statute is subject to more than one reasonable interpretation; (3) if a statute is subject to interpretation, it will be construed in the manner that best fulfills the legislative purpose and intent; and (4) in determining the legislative purpose and intent the court may look beyond the language of the Act to legislative history.

On its face, the language of the Parenting Act may be interpreted as requiring placement with the primary caregiving parent, absent a showing of harm to the child, or it may be interpreted as allowing a trial court to weigh all factors and then place the child with the parent the trial court believes will best meet the needs of the child, whether or not that parent has been the primary caregiver. Because it is subject to more than one reasonable interpretation, the Parenting Act is subject to judicial construction.

The Act's history actually began several years before it was proposed to the Legislature. During the early 1980's the Legislature considered several bills that would have amended the custody provisions of the marriage dissolution act. Many of these bills were "joint custody" bills which would have created a presumption for shared or split parenting of children after dissolution of marriage. Following the 1983 legislative session, an ad hoc committee, which included lawyers, state legislators, family law professors, child psychiatrists and psychologists, began working on a compromise draft that eventually became the Parenting Act of 1987. The ad hoc committee included advocates of a shared parenting (joint custody) presumption as well as advocates of a primary caregiver presumption.

The ad hoc committee's first proposed draft was introduced in bill form to the Legislature in 1986. The policy section of the proposed bill differed from that eventually enacted in 1987 in that it stated:

> *It is presumed* that the best interest of the child is served when the existing pattern of interaction between a parent and child is altered only to the extent necessitated by the changed relationship of the parents or as required to protect the child from physical, mental, or emotional harm.

(Italics ours.) House Bill 1618, § 1, 49th Legislature (1986) (part).

The bill further included a presumption to be applied by a trial court when designating primary residential placement of a child. The bill stated that the trial court was to first determine whether there was a primary caregiver for the child. If so, then "[i]t is presumed that the child's best interests are served by awarding the child's residence to the primary caregiver". House Bill 1618, § 8(4)(a), 49th Legislature (1986) (part). The proposed presumption section was weakened somewhat during the 1986 legislative session. However, the bill did not pass at that session.

* * *

While the statements of individual lawmakers and others before the Senate Judiciary Committee cannot be used to conclusively establish the intent of the Legislature as a whole, they can be instructive in showing the reasons for the changes in the legislation. This is particularly true where, as here, the legislative record does not reflect any contrary intent. * * *

The law as enacted also changed the policy section proposed by the drafters by replacing the language creating a presumption to a statement that the best interests of a child are "*ordinarily* served when the existing pattern of interaction between a parent and child is altered only to the extent necessitated by the changed relationship of the parents or as required to protect the child from physical, mental, or emotional harm." (Italics ours.) RCW 26.09.002 (part).

Marcia Kovacs, the mother in the case before the court, argues that this language "allows alteration of the existing parental relationship only as required to protect the children from physical, mental, or emotional harm." However, where physical, mental or emotional harm to the child are at issue, the limitations provided for in RCW 26.09.191(2) or (3) would apply. The mother essentially argues that the law presumes that placement with the primary caregiver is in the child's best interests and that the presumption can only be overcome by a showing of harm to the child. This argued interpretation of the law is clearly contrary to the Legislature's intent.

> The opinion describes revisions made to the legislation in the following session, and quotes statements from the legislative record indicating that the sponsors had abandoned the "tie-breaker presumption" in favor of the primary caretaker in order to secure passage of the legislation.

Further evidence of the Legislature's intent is demonstrated by its concern that the parent who had been awarded temporary residential placement of the child *not* be given unfair advantage when the permanent parenting plan was entered. RCW 26.09.197 requires a trial court awarding temporary residential placement to "give particular consideration" to (1) which parent has taken greater responsibility during the last 12 months for performing parenting functions relating to the daily needs of the child and (2) which parenting arrangements will cause the least disruption to the child's emotional stability while the action is pending, as well as to the seven factors listed in RCW 26.09.187(3)(a). In enacting these temporary parenting plan provisions, the Legislature recognized "the importance to the child's emotional stability of maintaining established patterns of care during what is generally a highly chaotic and emotionally stressful time." 1987 Proposed Parenting Act Commentary and Text, at 18 (available at Wash.State Archives). These same two considerations are not among the factors to be considered when developing the residential provisions of a *permanent* parenting plan.

The Act further states:

> In entering a permanent parenting plan, the court shall not draw any presumptions from the provisions of the temporary parenting plan.

RCW 26.09.191(4).

The *Family Law Deskbook* explains:

The temporary parenting plan is to be based upon a look at the *preceding 12 months* to determine the relationship of the children with each parent subject, of course, to the other limitations. In the permanent parenting plan, the court is to evaluate the ability of each parent to perform the parenting functions for each child *prospectively*. Drawing any presumption from the temporary plan is inappropriate.

(Italics ours.) Washington State Bar Ass'n, *Family Law Deskbook* 45–25 (1989).

It is thus clear to us from the legislative history that the Legislature not only did not intend to create any presumption in favor of the primary caregiver but, to the contrary, intended to reject any such presumption.

In establishing the seven statutory factors set forth in RCW 26.09.187(3)(a), the Legislature has provided the trial court guidance, along with the flexibility it needs, to make these difficult decisions.

On appeal, the mother in this case initially also challenged the trial court's findings of fact relating to the stability of each parent and the trial court's conclusion that the evidence supported placement of the children with the father. An appellate court may not substitute its findings for those of the trial court where there is ample evidence in the record to support the trial court's determination. While the evidence in this case is contradictory, there is ample evidence to support the trial judge's findings of fact.

The record reflects that the decision of the trial court in this case was based on a consideration of the statutory factors set forth in RCW 26.09.187(3)(a), and on the evidence presented, including testimony of expert witnesses. On the record presented, we cannot conclude that the trial court's decision was based on untenable grounds or that it was manifestly unreasonable. We hold, therefore, that the trial court did not abuse its discretion in awarding residential placement of the children to the father.

> **FYI**
>
> For more of the facts of *Kovacs*, see In re Marriage of Kovacs, 840 P.2d 214 (Wash Ct. App. 1992). See also Jane W. Ellis, *The Washington State Parenting Act in the Courts: Reconciling Discretion and Justice in Parenting Plan Disputes*, 69 Wash. L. Rev. 679 (1994).

The Court of Appeals is reversed and the parenting plan ordered by the trial court is affirmed.

Points for Discussion

a. Parenting Plans

Under many state statutes, including the Washington law addressed in *Kovacs*, either the parties or the court must come up with a parenting plan to allocate parental rights and responsibilities. See also Colo. Rev. Stat. § 14–10–124(7) (2018); 750 Ill. Comp. Stat. 5/602.1(b) (2018); Mont. Code Ann. § 40–4–234 (2018). The requirements for these plans vary from state to state, but typically they include provisions designating a residential schedule and allocating responsibility for educational, medical, and other important decisions. The use of parenting plans reflects the more complex custodial arrangements that are now common, and the requirement to develop such a plan may facilitate the process of settling custody disputes. Some states only require parenting plans in joint custody cases. See generally Daniel J. Hyman, Parenting Plans: Meeting the Challenges with Facts and Analysis (2018).

Section 2.03(2) of the ALI Principles of the Law of Family Dissolution (2000) (ALI Principles) defines a parenting plan as "a set of provisions for allocation of custodial responsibility and decisionmaking responsibility on behalf of a child and for resolution of future disputes between the parents." See generally Katharine T. Bartlett, *U.S. Custody Law and Trends in the Context of the ALI Principles of the Law of Family Dissolution*, 10 Va. J. Soc. Pol'y & L. 5 (2002).

b. Child's Best Interests

In *Kovacs*, as in all parenting disputes, the court's ultimate goal is to determine what result will be in the best interests of the children. It is much easier to state this standard than to implement it. On the facts of *Kovacs*, what were the primary arguments on behalf of the mother, and the primary arguments for the father? How did the court resolve these competing claims?

Custody determinations are generally left to the broad discretion of the trial court judge, but state legislatures seek to shape this discretion with statutes that enumerate factors the court should consider. Was the statute that applied in *Kovacs* helpful in resolving the case? How do the factors in this statute compare with the factors listed in Uniform Marriage and Divorce Act (UMDA) § 402, reprinted below?

On the challenges of applying the best interests test, see Jon Elster, *Solomonic Judgments: Against the Best Interest of the Child*, 54 U. Chi. L. Rev. 1 (1987); Robert Mnookin, *Child Custody Adjudications: Judicial Functions in the Face of Indeterminacy*, 39 L. & Contemp. Probs. 226 (1975); Carl E. Schneider, *Discretion, Rules and Law: Child Custody and the UMDA's Best-Interest Standard*, 89 Mich. L. Rev. 2215 (1991).

UMDA § 402. Best Interest of Child

The court shall determine custody in accordance with the best interest of the child. The court shall consider all relevant factors including:

(1) the wishes of the child's parent or parents as to his custody;

(2) the wishes of the child as to his custodian;

(3) the interaction and interrelationship of the child with his parent or parents, his siblings, and any other person who may significantly affect the child's best interest;

(4) the child's adjustment to his home, school, and community; and

(5) the mental and physical health of all individuals involved.

The court shall not consider conduct of a proposed custodian that does not affect his relationship to the child.

9A U.L.A. (Part 2) 282 (1998).

c. Primary Caretaker

The primary caretaker presumption discussed in *Kovacs* has been debated as a means of channeling the wide discretion given to trial judges in custody cases. Many scholars have endorsed some form of the primary caretaker rule, particularly with respect to the custody of young children. See, e.g., David Chambers, *Rethinking the Substantive Rules for Custody Disputes in Divorce*, 83 Mich. L. Rev. 477 (1984); Martha Fineman, *Dominant Discourse, Professional Language, and the Legal Change in Child Custody Decisionmaking*, 101 Harv. L. Rev. 727 (1988). Although state courts and legislatures treat the role of the primary caretaker as an important consideration in determining custody, most states have not been willing to establish a presumption.

Section 2.08(1) of the ALI Principles recommended that custodial responsibilities should be allocated "so that the proportion of custodial time the child spends with each parent approximates the proportion of time each parent spent performing caretaking functions for the child" prior to the separation or the filing of the action. See Custody of Kali, 792 N.E.2d 635 (Mass. 2003). This "approximation" standard was initially proposed in Elisabeth S. Scott, *Pluralism, Parental Preference, and Child Custody*, 80 Cal. L. Rev. 615 (1992). Until 2018, West Virginia followed this approach, with a statute that replaced the primary caretaker presumption previously adopted in <u>Garska v. McCoy, 278 S.E.2d 357 (W. Va. 1981)</u>. But see <u>W. Va. Code § 48–9–206(a) (2018)</u> (no presumptions in allocation of parental responsibilities).

d. Children's Wishes

Both <u>UMDA § 402</u> and the Washington statute quoted in *Kovacs* include the children's wishes among the factors that courts must consider in allocating parental responsibilities. How should a court determine the children's wishes? Note that <u>UMDA § 404</u> permits the court to interview children in chambers rather than having them testify as witnesses in the court proceeding. When a judge interviews a child in chambers, without the presence of the parties or their lawyers, many jurisdictions require that the interview be recorded in some fashion, with a record available to the parties in the event of an appeal. See, e.g., <u>N.D. McN v. R.J.H, 979 A.2d 1195 (D.C. 2009)</u>; <u>Uherek v. Sathe, 917 A.2d 306 (N.J. Super. Ct. App. Div. 2007)</u>; <u>Ynclan v. Woodward, 237 P.3d 145 (Okla. 2010)</u>.

Courts and commentators emphasize the importance of hearing a child's views without pressuring the child to take sides in the parents' dispute. E.g., <u>Marriage of Doty, 629 N.E.2d 679 (Ill. App. Ct. 1994)</u>; see generally <u>Joan B. Kelly, *Psychological and Legal Interventions for Parents and Children in Custody and Access Disputes: Current Research and Practice,* 10 Va. J.Soc. Pol'y & L. 129 (2002)</u>; Frederica K. Lombard, *Judicial Interviewing of Children in Custody Cases: An Empirical and Analytical Study*, 17 U.C. Davis L. Rev. 807 (1984). When a guardian ad litem or a custody investigator has been appointed, the child's wishes may be communicated indirectly through that individual. The question whether children should have the right to participate as parties in custody litigation is discussed later in this chapter.

Some custody statues go further than simply directing a court to consider children's wishes in allocating parental responsibilities. Under <u>W. Va. Code § 48–9–206 (2018)</u> courts are directed to "accommodate, if the court determines it is in the best interests of the child, the firm and reasonable preferences of a child who is fourteen years of age or older, and with regard to a child under 14 years of age, but sufficiently matured that he or she can intelligently express a voluntary preference for one parent, to give that preference the weight warranted by the circumstances." California gives a child who is 14 or older a right to address the court concerning custody or visitation unless the court determines that would not be in the child's best interests. See <u>Cal. Fam. Code § 3042 (2018)</u>.

e. Parental Misconduct

Statutes based on <u>UMDA § 402</u> state that a court may not consider "conduct of a proposed custodian that does not affect his relationship to the child." The court's statement of the facts in *Kovacs* suggests that the trial court considered the mother's romantic involvement with another man and her alcohol-related driving offenses in reaching its custody determination. Could this type of evidence be considered under the UMDA rule?

Substance abuse may be a significant factor in some parental responsibilities cases. To what extent should this question be framed in terms of whether the uses are legal or illegal? Courts have begun to consider custody issues in states that allow for medical or recreational marijuana use. The Maine statutes provide specifically for this problem; see Daggett v. Sternick, 109 A.3d 1137 (Me. 2015) (applying 22 Me. Rev. Stat. § 2423–E (3), and concluding that the father's use of medical marijuana impaired his ability to parent his child).

f. Domestic Violence

Clearly, a history of child abuse by one parent would weigh significantly in any court's assessment of the child's best interests, but courts in the past were much less willing to recognize that a history of spousal abuse within a family was relevant to custody determination. See Naomi R. Cahn, *Civil Images of Battered Women: The Impact of Domestic Violence on Child Custody Decisions*, 44 Vand. L. Rev. 1041 (1991). Most state statutes now require that courts consider evidence of domestic violence in assigning parental responsibilities. Many also provide presumptions against joint custody in cases where there has been domestic violence. E.g. Mass. Gen. L. 208 § 31A (2018). See also Caven v. Caven, 966 P.2d 1247 (Wash. 1998) (reversing joint decision-making order in case involving domestic violence); Marriage of Hynick, 727 N.W.2d 575 (Iowa 2007) (affirming denial of joint physical care in case involving domestic violence.)

g. Custody Experts

The evidence in *Kovacs* included testimony from a psychologist retained as an expert witness by the father, and a counselor who met briefly with the mother and children. What kind of information did these experts provide to the court? How helpful or influential was their testimony in this case? Should the courts permit custody experts to give their opinions on the ultimate issue of which parent should be given primary custody?

Studies suggest that custody evaluation reports exert considerable influence on the judges who are ultimately responsible for making custody determinations. Experience also suggests, however, that the quality of these reports varies widely. See, e.g., In re Marriage of Rebouche, 587 N.W.2d 795 (Iowa Ct.App.1998) (reversing trial court custody decision based on biased custody report). A full custody evaluation is also an expensive undertaking, although some jurisdictions provide for a custody investigation to be performed at a lower cost by an agency such as the welfare department, social services agency, or probation office.

Expert Witness Testimony

Experts including psychiatrists, psychologists, and social workers may be retained by the parties or appointed by the court in custody cases to evaluate the parents and the children and to make recommendations concerning the children's best interests. In some states, statutes regulate this practice. See, e.g., Colo. Rev. Stat. § 14–10–127 (2018). Evaluators commonly use clinical interviews and psychological testing in formulating their opinions, but often these methods have not been subjected to the type of testing and scrutiny usually required for admission of expert witness testimony under state rules of evidence based on Fed. R. Evid. 702. See generally Mary Johanna McCurley, et al., *Protecting Children from Incompetent Forensic Evaluations and Expert Testimony*, 19 J. Amer. Acad. Matrim. Lawyers 277 (2005). On efforts to improve the quality and reliability of these evaluations, see James N. Bow and Francella A. Quinnell, *A Critical Review of Child Custody Evaluation Reports*, 40 Fam. Ct. Rev. 164 (2002). See generally Marc J. Ackerman and Andrew W. Kane, Psychological Experts in Divorce Actions (4th ed. 2005).

Problem 7-30

Odette and Douglas are in the process of a divorce, and attempting to negotiate terms for a parenting agreement for their twelve year old daughter and eight year old son. Odette was the children's primary caregiver, and though she is a devoted mother she also suffers from a psychiatric illness characterized as acute or latent schizophrenia. Douglas wants to have the children live with him, but his business requires extensive travel from time to time. Odette strongly objects to losing custody. The children have indicated a desire to live with their father, but they have also said that they love their mother. What kind of parenting plan might be devised in this case? (Cf. Odette R. v. Douglas R., 399 N.Y.S.2d 93 (Fam. Ct.1977).)

Problem 7-31

When David and Jane divorce, both of them seek custody of their teenaged daughter, Andrea. The evidence at trial indicates that although David has a long history of battering Jane, he has never directly harmed Andrea. Andrea is closely bonded with her father, who is attentive and loving and significantly involved in her schoolwork and extracurricular activities. By contrast, Andrea does not relate well with her mother. In interviews with a social worker, Andrea denies ever witnessing her father's violent behavior, and expresses a strong preference to live with him. How should the court approach this case? (See Wissink v. Wissink, 749 N.Y.S.2d 550 (App. Div. 2002).)

Problem 7-32

During a contested hearing on custody and visitation, the trial judge becomes aware that the child's mother and her partner smoke cigarettes at home around her eight-year-old daughter. On its own motion, the court enters a restraining order prohibiting either one from smoking in the child's presence. On appeal, the mother argues that the court has exceeded its authority and violated her fundamental constitutional rights. Should the court's order be reversed? (See In re Julie Anne, 780 N.E.2d 635 (Ohio Ct. Com.Pl.2002).)

Palmore v. Sidoti

466 U.S. 429 (1984)

Go Online

Listen to the oral arguments in *Palmore* on the Oyez Project web site.

CHIEF JUSTICE BURGER delivered the opinion of the Court.

We granted certiorari to review a judgment of a state court divesting a natural mother of the custody of her infant child because of her remarriage to a person of a different race.

I

When petitioner Linda Sidoti Palmore and respondent Anthony J. Sidoti, both Caucasians, were divorced in May 1980 in Florida, the mother was awarded custody of their 3-year-old daughter.

In September 1981 the father sought custody of the child by filing a petition to modify the prior judgment because of changed conditions. The change was that the child's mother was then cohabiting with a Negro, Clarence Palmore, Jr., whom she married two months later. Additionally, the father made several allegations of instances in which the mother had not properly cared for the child.

After hearing testimony from both parties and considering a court counselor's investigative report, the court noted that the father had made allegations about the child's care, but the court made no findings with respect to these allegations. On the contrary, the court made a finding that "there is no issue as to either party's devotion to the child, adequacy of housing facilities, or respectability of the new spouse of either parent."

The court then addressed the recommendations of the court counselor, who had made an earlier report "in [another] case coming out of this circuit also involving the social consequences of an interracial marriage. _Niles v. Niles, 299 So.2d 162._" From this vague reference to that earlier case, the court turned to the present case and noted the counselor's recommendation for a change in custody because "[t]he wife [petitioner] has chosen for herself and for her child, a life-style unacceptable to the father *and to society.* . . . The child. . .is, or at school age will be, subject to environmental pressures not of choice." (emphasis added).

The court then concluded that the best interests of the child would be served by awarding custody to the father. The court's rationale is contained in the following:

> "The father's evident resentment of the mother's choice of a black partner is not sufficient to wrest custody from the mother. It is of some significance, however, that the mother did see fit to bring a man into her home and carry on a sexual relationship with him without being married to him. Such action tended to place gratification of her own desires ahead of her concern for the child's future welfare. *This Court feels that despite the strides that have been made in bettering relations between the races in this country, it is inevitable that Melanie will, if allowed to remain in her present situation and attains school age and thus more vulnerable to peer pressures, suffer from the social stigmatization that is sure to come.*" (emphasis added).

The Second District Court of Appeal affirmed without opinion, 426 So.2d 34 (1982), thus denying the Florida Supreme Court jurisdiction to review the case. See Fla. Const., Art. V, § 3(b)(3); _Jenkins v. State, 385 So.2d 1356 (Fla.1980)_. We granted certiorari, and we reverse.

II

The judgment of a state court determining or reviewing a child custody decision is not ordinarily a likely candidate for review by this Court. However, the court's opinion, after stating that the "father's evident resentment of the mother's choice of a black partner is not sufficient" to deprive her of custody, then turns to what it regarded as the damaging impact on the child from remaining in a racially mixed household. This raises important federal concerns arising from the Constitution's commitment to eradicating discrimination based on race.

The Florida court did not focus directly on the parental qualifications of the natural mother or her present husband, or indeed on the father's qualifications to have custody of the child. The court found that "there is no issue as to either party's devotion to the child, adequacy of housing facilities, or respectability of the new spouse of either parent." This, taken with the absence of any negative finding as to the quality of the care provided by the mother, constitutes a rejection of any claim of petitioner's unfitness to continue the custody of her child.

The court correctly stated that the child's welfare was the controlling factor. But that court was entirely candid and made no effort to place its holding on any ground other than race. Taking the court's findings and rationale at face value, it is clear that the outcome would have been different had petitioner married a Caucasian male of similar respectability.

A core purpose of the Fourteenth Amendment was to do away with all governmentally imposed[1] discrimination based on race. See *Strauder v. West Virginia*, 100 U.S. 303, 307–308, 310 (1880). Classifying persons according to their race is more likely to reflect racial prejudice than legitimate public concerns; the race, not the person, dictates the category. See *Personnel Administrator of Mass. v. Feeney*, 442 U.S. 256, 272 (1979). Such classifications are subject to the most exacting scrutiny; to pass constitutional muster, they must be justified by a compelling governmental interest and must be "necessary. . .to the accomplishment" of their legitimate purpose, *McLaughlin v. Florida*, 379 U.S. 184, 196 (1964). See *Loving v. Virginia*, 388 U.S. 1, 11 (1967).

The State, of course, has a duty of the highest order to protect the interests of minor children, particularly those of tender years. In common with most states, Florida law mandates that custody determinations be made in the best interests of the children involved. Fla.Stat. § 61.13(2)(b)(1) (1983). The goal of granting custody based on the best interests of the child is indisputably a substantial governmental interest for purposes of the Equal Protection Clause.

It would ignore reality to suggest that racial and ethnic prejudices do not exist or that all manifestations of those prejudices have been eliminated. There is a risk that a child living with a stepparent of a different race may be subject to a variety of pressures and stresses not present if the child were living with parents of the same racial or ethnic origin.

The question, however, is whether the reality of private biases and the possible injury they might inflict are permissible considerations for removal of an infant child from the custody of its natural mother. We have little difficulty con-

---

[1] The actions of state courts and judicial officers in their official capacity have long been held to be state action governed by the Fourteenth Amendment. Shelley v. Kraemer, 334 U.S. 1 (1948); Ex parte Virginia, 100 U.S. 339, 346–347 (1880).

cluding that they are not.[2] The Constitution cannot control such prejudices but neither can it tolerate them. Private biases may be outside the reach of the law, but the law cannot, directly or indirectly, give them effect. "Public officials sworn to uphold the Constitution may not avoid a constitutional duty by bowing to the hypothetical effects of private racial prejudice that they assume to be both widely and deeply held." *Palmer v. Thompson,* 403 U.S. 217, 260–261 (1971) (White, J., dissenting).

This is by no means the first time that acknowledged racial prejudice has been invoked to justify racial classifications. In *Buchanan v. Warley,* 245 U.S. 60 (1917), for example, this Court invalidated a Kentucky law forbidding Negroes to buy homes in white neighborhoods.

> "It is urged that this proposed segregation will promote the public peace by preventing race conflicts. Desirable as this is, and important as is the preservation of the public peace, this aim cannot be accomplished by laws or ordinances which deny rights created or protected by the Federal Constitution."

Whatever problems racially mixed households may pose for children in 1984 can no more support a denial of constitutional rights than could the stresses that residential integration was thought to entail in 1917. The effects of racial prejudice, however real, cannot justify a racial classification removing an infant child from the custody of its natural mother found to be an appropriate person to have such custody.[3]

The judgment of the District Court of Appeal is reversed.

──────────

Points for Discussion

a. Equal Protection and Child Custody

Describe the Court's equal protection analysis in *Palmore.* Under this analysis, can a family court ever consider race as a factor in making custody decisions? In

---

[2]   In light of our holding based on the Equal Protection Clause, we need not reach or resolve petitioner's claim based on the Fourteenth Amendment's Due Process Clause.

[3]   This conclusion finds support in other cases as well. For instance, in Watson v. Memphis, 373 U.S. 526 (1963), city officials claimed that desegregation of city parks had to proceed slowly to "prevent interracial disturbances, violence, riots, and community confusion and turmoil." The Court found such predictions no more than "personal speculations or vague disquietudes," and held that "constitutional rights may not be denied simply because of hostility to their assertion or exercise." In Wright v. Georgia, 373 U.S. 284 (1963), the Court reversed a Negro defendant's breach-of-peace conviction, holding that "the possibility of disorder by others cannot justify exclusion of persons from a place if they otherwise have a constitutional right (founded upon the Equal Protection Clause) to be present."

Matter of Davis v. Davis, 658 N.Y.S.2d 548 (App.Div.1997), the court considered the custody dispute of an interracial couple concerning their two-year-old son. The father, who was African-American, argued that his biracial household would provide more support for the child than the mother's all-white household. Under *Palmore*, is this an appropriate consideration? See also Marriage of Gambla and Woodson, 853 N.E.2d 847 (Ill. Ct. App. 2006); Ebirim v. Ebirim, 620 N.W.2d 117 (Neb. Ct. App. 2000).

Do equal protection principles bar decision-making in custody disputes based on the ethnicity, sex, religion, or sexual orientation of a parent or child? What about immigration status? See Rico v. Rodriguez, 120 P.3d 812 (Nev. 2005), which concluded that a trial court's consideration of the parents' immigration status in granting custody of nonmarital children to their father, who was a legal permanent resident, did not violate the due process and equal protection rights of their mother, who had immigrated illegally with the children from Mexico.

Make the Connection

Race-matching policies in foster care and adoption are discussed in Chapter 3.

b. Religion and Child Custody

Courts have generally concluded that parents' religious affiliations or practices are not a permissible basis for making an initial custody determination. See, e.g., Osteraas v. Osteraas, 859 P.2d 948 (Idaho 1993); Zummo v. Zummo, 574 A.2d 1130 (Pa. Super. Ct. 1990); Hudema v. Carpenter, 989 P.2d 491 (Utah Ct.App.1999). When a child has an established religious identity, however, courts are more likely to weigh this factor in making a decision. See, e.g., Bonjour v. Bonjour, 592 P.2d 1233 (Alaska 1979); Burrows v. Brady, 605 A.2d 1312 (R.I.1992).

Courts sometimes consider ways in which religiously-motivated conduct could affect the child's best interests. See, e.g., Harrison v. Tauheed, 256 P.3d 851 (Kan. 2011). In rare cases, courts deciding custody disputes conclude that one parent's religious views present a serious risk of harm to the child. See, e.g., Burnham v. Burnham, 304 N.W.2d 58 (Neb. 1981); Leppert v. Leppert, 519 N.W.2d 287 (N.D.1994); cf. Quiner v. Quiner, 59 Cal.Rptr. 503 (Ct.App.1967). See generally James G. Dwyer, *Parents' Religion and Children's Welfare: Debunking the Doctrine of Parents' Rights*, 82 Cal. L. Rev. 1371 (1994).

c. Lesbian, Gay and Transsexual Parents

Many courts have considered whether sexual orientation or sexual activity by a gay or lesbian parent can be a basis for denying custody or imposing limits on a parent's time with the child. In more recent cases, courts require proof that the parent's behavior has a direct and harmful effect on the child before imposing such limits, but these rulings differ significantly in what they consider sufficient proof of harm to justify restrictions. Compare <u>Damron v. Damron, 670 N.W.2d 871 (N.D.2003)</u> (ruling that "a custodial parent's homosexual household is not grounds for modifying custody. . .in the absence of evidence that environment endangers or potentially endangers the children's physical or emotional health or impairs their emotional development"); with <u>Ex parte H.H., 830 So.2d 21 (Ala.2002)</u> (reaffirming rule that a trial court has discretion to deny custody on the basis of parent's homosexual conduct or relationship) and <u>Pulliam v. Smith, 501 S.E.2d 898</u> (N.C. 1998) (modifying custody after father's same-sex partner moved into his home). In <u>McGriff v. McGriff, 99 P.3d 111 (Idaho 2004)</u>, the court concluded that sexual orientation cannot be a factor in awarding or modifying custody or visitation following the Supreme Court's ruling in *Lawrence v. Texas.* See also <u>Marriage of Black, 392 P.3d 1041, 1048 (Wash. 2017)</u> ("We are not confident that the trial court here approached the parenting plan with an attitude of neutrality regarding sexual orientation that fairness demands.") See generally Patricia M. Logue, *The Rights of Lesbian and Gay Parents and Their Children*, 18 J. Amer. Acad. Matrimonial Lawyers 95 (2002).

Further Reading

Courtney G. Joslin et al., Lesbian, Gay Bisexual and Transgender Family Law (2017–18 ed.).

In <u>J.L.S. v. D.K.S., 943 S.W.2d 766 (Mo.Ct.App.1997)</u>, the court concluded that visitation between two young children and their father was not appropriate after his sex reassignment surgery, citing the children's need for more time to prepare mentally and emotionally to resume their relationship. But see <u>Christian v. Randall, 516 P.2d 132 (Colo. Ct. App. 1973)</u> (reversing change of custody ordered on basis of custodial parent's transsexual change). See also <u>Michael P. Sullivan, Annotation, *Parent's Transsexuality as Factor in Award of Custody of Children, visitation Rights, or Termination of Parental Rights*, 59 A.L.R.4th 1170 (1988)</u>.

Problem 7-33

Two Alaska Native parents dispute the custody of their eight-year-old son. The child's mother has a job in Juneau, and lives with a non-Native person she intends to marry. The father works on commercial fishing boats during the fishing season, and otherwise leads "the traditional subsistence existence of village Alaska, hunting, trapping, fishing and picking berries." If the father obtains custody, he plans to have the boy live with him in his village and stay with his aunt during the fishing season. Can the court evaluate the parents' different ways of life in determining how to allocate parental responsibility? (See <u>Carle v. Carle, 503 P.2d</u>

1050 (Alaska 1972); see also <u>Red Elk v. McBride, 344 P.3d 818 (Alaska 2015)</u>; <u>Jones v. Jones, 542 N.W.2d 119 (S.D.1996)</u>.)

Problem 7-34

When Ruth was 16, she married Rodney in a religious ceremony and began living in a polygamous household with Rodney, his two other wives, and their children. Ruth had two children with Rodney, and left his household several years later with her children. Rodney admits his paternity and has sued for custody of the children. Ruth's lawyer points out that Rodney is breaking the law, and argues that his 20 children are often supervised by a single adult while the other adults are at work. Can the court consider these factors in deciding whether to allow Rodney to share custody of the children? (Cf. <u>Sanderson v. Tryon, 739 P.2d 623 (Utah 1987)</u>.)

Rodrigue v. Brewer

<u>667 A.2d 605 (Maine 1995)</u>

Dana, Justice.

Suzanne Brewer appeals from the judgment entered in the Superior Court (Waldo County, *MacInnes, A.R.J.*) affirming a judgment of the District Court (Belfast, *Staples*, J.) providing for shared parental rights and responsibilities of their two and a half year old son, Kenai, with primary physical residence alternating every four weeks, parental rights and responsibilities over his religious upbringing being allocated to the mother, and parental rights and responsibilities over his education being allocated to the father. We affirm the judgment.

Suzanne Brewer and Barry Rodrigue were married in December 1989 after a brief courtship. They separated in February 1990, sometime after their child's conception. Although the couple reconciled briefly, they permanently separated in May 1992. The District Court determined that shared parental rights and responsibilities were called for but found that despite the willingness of Brewer and Rodrigue to share in parenting on an equal basis, their inability to separate themselves from their marital conflicts compelled the court to establish a detailed plan of parental contact with Kenai and to allocate certain functions between the parents. The Superior Court reviewed the findings of the District Court and held that the findings were neither clearly erroneous nor an abuse of discretion. This appeal followed.

When the Superior Court acts as an intermediate appellate court, we will directly review the decision of the District Court. The paramount consideration for the trial court when allocating parental rights and responsibilities is the best interests of the child. 19 M.R.S.A. § 752(5) (Supp.1994); *Lane v. Lane,* 446 A.2d 418, 419–20 (Me.1982). In doing so, the trial court "must seek not merely to preserve the child from harm, but to discern, 'as a wise, affectionate and careful parent,' what custody arrangement will further the child's best interests." *Cyr v. Cyr,* 432 A.2d 793, 796 (Me.1981) (citing *Sheldon v. Sheldon,* 423 A.2d 943, 946 (Me.1980)). The trial court's decision is entitled to substantial deference, and we will let the trial court's findings stand unless clearly erroneous. We have stated in a custody case that the "essential impact of the 'clearly erroneous rule' is that the trial judge's findings stand unless they clearly cannot be correct because there is no competent evidence to support them." *Harmon v. Emerson,* 425 A.2d 978, 982 (Me.1981) (emphasis in original).

Brewer complains that the court's allocation of sole responsibility for Kenai's education to Rodrigue on the basis of his relative educational qualifications was an abuse of discretion. The record indicates that at the time of the hearing Rodrigue, then age 44, was pursuing two Ph.D. degrees: one at the University of Maine in History and the other at Laval University in Quebec City in Geography, and working as a research assistant at the University of Maine. In contrast, Brewer was a high school graduate, a full-time mother, and had worked as a teacher's aide and was currently doing some part-time bookkeeping. The court relied on the testimony of three experts and the parties. Dr. Hamrick testified that compared to the father she would have more concern about the mother's ability to make appropriate choices for Kenai's education and growth. Dr. Gaffney described the father as "an intelligent, sophisticated, sensitive man, a hard-working, dedicated academician and father." Gaffney also stated that the mother frequently deals with problems by withdrawing entirely from communication, and Hamrick testified that "as the development tasks of the child become that of separation from the parent. . .the kinds of difficulties [the mother] has with resolving conflict are going to become very significant." There is no suggestion that the court based its decision exclusively on an analysis of the parties' relative educational credentials. The challenged factual findings are not clearly erroneous. Nor was the allocation of responsibility to Barry an abuse of discretion.

Further, given Kenai's young age and the uncertainty of the parents' future living situations, Brewer questions the timing of the court's allocation of specific tasks to either parent. Generally, the allocation of parental rights and responsibilities can be modified if circumstances between the parties change. *See* 19 M.R.S.A. § 752(12); *Rowland v. Kingman,* 629 A.2d 613 (Me.1993), *cert. denied,* 510 U.S. 1074, 114 S.Ct. 884, 127 L.Ed.2d 78 (1994) (party filed motion to modify parental rights and responsibilities when party with primary residence intended to relocate out of state). If there is a change in circumstances that substantially affects the best interests of the child, either parent may petition the court to have the plan modified. *Villa v. Smith, 534 A.2d 1310, 1312 (Me.1987)*.

Brewer complains that it is not in Kenai's best interest given his need for stability for the primary residence to alternate monthly between Belfast and Quebec City. Because Rodrigue proposed to reside in Quebec City for perhaps eighteen months, the court's allocation of a shared primary residence required Kenai to readjust to a new home environment every four weeks.

The trial court had before it testimony that although both Rodrigue and Brewer are caring, loving, and capable people who desire to parent Kenai, the intense conflict between them substantially impairs their ability to cooperate in that parenting. At the time of the hearing Kenai was rotating between his parents' homes every two or three days. Dr. Gaffney testified that transitions were stressful and longer visits would diminish that stress. He recommended that the court's order concerning parental responsibilities be postponed for one year while the parents engage in co-parenting counseling. Dr. Gaffney testified that if the decision could not be postponed until the parents were offered the opportunity to develop better skills for conflict resolution, he would recommend the allocation of sole parental responsibility to Brewer. Dr. Hamrick testified that because of the importance of maintaining Kenai's bond with each parent, joint parental responsibility is the favored arrangement. She also favored alternating the child's residence every three or four weeks until he reached school age.

Although the record indicates that both parents are equally willing and capable of parenting and both requested the 50:50 arrangement to continue even when Rodrigue was in Quebec, Brewer finds fault with the trial court's order because it did not adopt the expert's suggestion that in the short run the ultimate parenting power reside not with either parent but with a "guardianship of some sort or some third party." Even assuming that the court had the authority to suspend parental rights, *see* 19 M.R.S.A. § 752(6), neither parent was economically able to afford the services of a "third" parent. Moreover, the court did urge the parties to undergo co-parenting counseling after Rodrigue returns from Quebec. The court's decision to provide for joint parental responsibility and alternating primary custody for four week periods was not an abuse of discretion.

The entry is:

Judgment affirmed.

RUDMAN, Justice, dissenting.

I respectfully dissent.

I have no quarrel with the District Court's findings of fact in this case. On the basis of those undisputed findings, however, the court must act within the bounds of its discretion in assigning parental rights and responsibilities. We review the court's assignment of parental rights for an abuse of the court's discretion in determining the consequences of its factual findings. Discretion is not an absolute standard. The discretion accorded a trial court varies according to the principles identified as controlling a particular discretionary determination. When we say we review the court's determination for abuse of discretion we mean we have the responsibility to determine whether the court acted within the principles identified as bounding that discretionary determination. If the court acts within its principled bounds, its determination is entitled to deference. If, however, as here, the court's determination strays from these principles, that determination constitutes an abuse of the court's discretion.

The Source of Discretion in Assigning Parental Rights is Equity

The source of the principles that limit the court's discretion in parental rights determinations is venerable. The court's power derives from its general equity jurisdiction. *Roussel v. State*, 274 A.2d 909, 917–22 (Me.1971).

> The King, as pater patriae, has the direction of infants, which charge is administered in his Court of Chancery.

Id. at 918 (quoting *DeManneville v. DeManneville*, 10 Vesey Jr's 52 (1804)).

> That was not a jurisdiction to determine rights as between a parent and a stranger, or as between a parent and a child. It was a paternal jurisdiction, a judicially administrative jurisdiction, in virtue of which the Chancery Court was to act on behalf of the Crown, as being the guardian of all infants, in place of a parent, and as if it were the parent of the child, thus superseding the natural guardianship of the parent.

Roussel v. State, 274 A.2d at 918 (quoting *The Queen v. Gyngall*, 2 Q.B. 232 (1893)).

The guardianship jurisdiction of Chancery, with all its old authority and bounded by its old principles, survives in the courts of Maine. In determining parental responsibility incident to its statutory divorce jurisdiction, a Maine trial court applies these principles of equity under its full equitable jurisdiction.

> We find that the Legislature intended for courts in determining issues of custody in divorce proceedings to apply the equitably-based principles which are applied to custody determinations made under the full equitable jurisdiction, (deriving from the English Court of Chancery) which was originally granted by the Legislature to the Supreme Judicial Court in 1874.

Harmon v. Emerson, 425 A.2d at 984.

Principles Limiting Discretion in Assigning Parental Rights

When properly exercised, a trial court's historic equitable discretion to assign parental rights and responsibilities is entitled to substantial deference. <u>Ziehm v. Ziehm, 433 A.2d 725, 730 (Me.1981)</u> (citing <u>Cooley v. St. Andre's Child Placing Agency, 415 A.2d 1084, 1086 (Me.1980)</u>). The court, however, may not do as it pleases. In discharging its responsibility to exercise its original equity jurisdiction over the custody of infants, the trial court must apply the substantive principles of equity.

A judge in discharging his sobering responsibility of deciding the care and custody of a minor child acts not at all as a mere arbiter between two adult adversaries, simply reacting to the evidence they may see fit to adduce in support of their respective positions. Rather, his function is that described in the oft-quoted words used by Judge Cardozo in <u>Finlay v. Finlay, 240 N.Y. 429, 148 N.E. 624, 626 (1925)</u>:

> He acts as *parens patriae* to do what is best for the interest of the child. He is to put himself in the position of a "wise, affectionate and careful parent" and make provision for the child accordingly. . . . He is not adjudicating a controversy between adversary parties, to compose their private differences. He is not determining rights "as between a parent and a child" or between one parent and another. He "interferes for the protection of infants, *qua infants*, by virtue of the prerogative which belongs to the [state] as *parens patriae*."

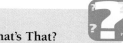

What's That?

The doctrine of ***parens patriae*** gives the state standing to bring suit to protect citizens who are not otherwise able to protect themselves.

<u>Ziehm v. Ziehm, 433 A.2d at 728</u>.

In *Ziehm* we not only identified the best interest of the child as the fundamental principle limiting the court's discretion in assigning parental rights, we adopted Justice Cardozo's explication of that principle. The trial court's guiding equitable principle in determining parental rights and responsibilities is not to effect an even-handed division between the parents. Its guiding principle is to act in the best interest of the child. Our legislature has mandated that historic equitable principle, to act in the best interest of the child, as the standard for custody determinations at divorce. <u>19 M.R.S.A. § 752 (1981 & Supp.1994)</u>.

Although we have said repeatedly that the "delicate balancing" of the factors set forth in <u>19 M.R.S.A. § 752</u> is left to the sound discretion of that judge who has the single opportunity to observe the individuals involved and therefore is in the best position to act on behalf of the State as a wise, affectionate, and careful parent, as the reviewing court here we must measure the trial court's balancing against a principled standard decreed not only by the historic traditions of equity but by our statute. We have said that as long as there is rational support for the trial court's determination of parental rights we will not overturn it. *Sheldon v. Sheldon*, 423 A.2d 943, 946 (Me.1980). But that "rational support," the reason for the court's determination, must fall within the principle established by equity, articulated by Cardozo, and adopted by this Court. Just any reason will not do. Mere evidence on the record will not do. Discretionary justification is not a question of clear error of fact. A court is not free to disregard professional witnesses' advice without articulating a principled rationale, grounded in the best interest of the child, for having done so. A court is not free to seek to assign parental rights and responsibilities by balancing them "equally" between one parent and another. It is not enough for the court to simply declare its determination to be in the best interest of the child. The record in the instant case provides no rational support for the court's determination that it is in the best interest of this child to be divided equally between two warring parents.

The Best Interest of the Child

The trial court here dealt with the custody of a child less than three years of age. The court's decision provided for shared parental rights and shared primary residence, the child to live with each parent for alternating periods of four weeks duration. The court's decree contemplated the father would reside temporarily in Quebec and perhaps then permanently in Alaska and the mother would reside in Belfast, Maine. The decree further ordered the father was to have sole control over the child's education and the mother to have sole control over the child's religious training.

The trial court heard testimony from the parties and from three expert witnesses: two psychologists and a bilingual primary educator. The testimony of the three expert witnesses, called to address the best interest of the child, does not support the court's order assigning shared responsibility.

The linguist refused to give an opinion on anything other than the general virtue of bilingual education and the availability of bilingual education in Quebec. He specifically, clearly, and properly refused to address the psychological and social issues associated with moving a child back and forth every four weeks between Quebec and Belfast but limited his testimony to addressing factors of the linguistic challenge facing a child in such an arrangement. His positive evaluation of bilingual education provides nothing to guide the court in assessing the difficult psychological questions involved here.

Evidence addressing the psychological best interest of the child came in the form of testimony by the psychologists. *Both* expressed their explicit and unequivocating belief that these parents would be incapable of sustaining a joint parenting arrangement.

One of the psychologists, a university counselor who did initial couple therapy for the parties but later provided individual counseling for the father alone, advised that joint responsibility should not be assigned unless a third-party mediator were appointed to negotiate the inevitable conflicts between the parents. She characterized continuing mediation as an "essential ingredient" in any assignment of shared responsibilities. Unfortunately she did not address what should happen if mediation were unavailable. Her testimony therefore provided only an insoluble conundrum for a court financially locked out of the disposition she advised. There must be no shared responsibility, she said, but neither should either parent be given "most" authority. Her advice recommended against both of the only two avenues open to the court and provided no rational basis for choosing either.

The other psychologist, a clinical and school practitioner, also advised against shared responsibility. He recommended that joint responsibility could not work unless the parties could be given time first for counseling to develop an ability to resolve their deep seated conflicts. This psychologist, however, did testify expressly as to a recommended disposition should such help be unavailable. He advised that if a decision had to be made as things stood, the mother should be given sole parental responsibility.

The trial court found that "even though the parties are intelligent and reasonably mature, they are unable to divorce themselves from the stress and rancor that characterized their short term marriage." The court then, recognizing the incapability of the parents to work together, having before it no helpful psychological information from the linguist and an impossible recommendation from the counselor, chose to ignore the clinical psychologist's direct advice. Although there is *no evidence of any kind* in the record that shared parenting responsibility here is in the best interest of the child, the trial court assigned shared responsibility.

I am sympathetic to the financial and time strictures that bar the trial court from structuring what could be an optimal solution to this difficult dispute. That limited resources make recommended alternatives impossible, however, does not mean that the court by default must assign the very joint parenting responsibility both psychologists recommended against. There is no rational support in the record for the court's assigning to these parents, in light of the unavailability of mediation or further counseling, shared parental rights and responsibilities.

The court parceled out parental rights with obvious attention to balancing the parents' interests. Four weeks with father. Four weeks with mother. Educational responsibility to father. Religious responsibility (that the mother did not seek and had not asked for) to mother. The court's strain to effect a kind of legal equipoise is palpable. Such balancing, however, does not satisfy equity's principled command that the court must make its determination in the best interest of the child.

The court's assignment of joint parental rights and responsibilities, split as to time and split as to function, impels the parties, who universally have been determined to be incapable of resolving their conflicts, into certain conflict. In ignoring the expert advice before it and failing to articulate any evidentiary rationale for doing so, and in structuring an artificially balanced division of rights, the court acted as "mere arbiter between the adult adversaries." The trial court did what Justice Cardozo warned against and determined parental rights as between one parent and another. A determination of parental rights that acts to balance parental interests without evidence that such balancing is in the best interest of the child constitutes an abuse of the court's discretion.

Internal Consistency of a Discretionary Order

A second principle, beyond the equitable and statutory requirement that the court must act in the best interest of the child, also bounds a trial court's discretion. A court order must be internally consistent. As the trial court must follow applicable principles of equity, so must it follow principles of logic. It must avoid issuing an inherently contradictory order. The District Court order allocating parental rights and responsibilities between Barry Rodrigue and Suzanne Brewer fails to adhere to this fundamental principle of discretion. The order is internally inconsistent.

The order assigns to Rodrigue and Brewer the ultimate in shared parental rights and obligations: to provide their son a primary home. This shared responsibility for guiding and guarding their child's growth and development, just provided by the trial court, is immediately shattered by the trial court's assigning to the father sole decision-making power over the boy's education. The court has given the father the power to place the child in any school he decides, even if such placement destroys shared residency.

Such an inherently contradictory allocation of parental rights and responsibilities cannot be justified as a response to the parents' inability to resolve their conflicts. Although shared parental rights and responsibilities generally may be appropriate, such co-parenting is not always in the best interest of the child and is especially inappropriate when the parties are found to be "unable to divorce themselves from the stress and rancor that characterized their short-term marriage."

I would vacate the judgment of the District Court.

———————————

Points for Discussion

a. Joint Custody

What are the potential benefits and risks of joint parental responsibility? The court in *Rodrigue* approved an award of shared decision-making and primary residence to the parents of a three-year-old who would be living in different cities and who had a history of "intense conflict." Why does the majority conclude this is appropriate? Is the dissenting opinion more persuasive in this case? If the dissenting opinion had prevailed, and the case had been remanded, how should the lower court have resolved the dispute?

Some states have statutory presumptions in favor of some form of joint custody. See, e.g., Fla. Stat. Ann. § 61.13(2)(c)(2) (2018); Iowa Code Ann. § 598.41(2) (2018). Other state statutes disfavor joint custody, unless both parents have agreed to it. See, e.g., Vt. Stat. Ann. tit. 15, § 665(a)(2018). California has eliminated its former presumption favoring joint custody. See Cal. Fam. Code § 3040(c) (2018). Note that state statutes may treat shared legal decision-making authority differently from shared physical custody or residence orders. See Marriage of Hansen, 733 N.W.2d 683 (Iowa 2007) (holding that the custody statute established a presumption of joint legal custody, but no presumption of joint physical care). In deciding whether joint custody is appropriate, courts consider the parents' ability to communicate and cooperate, but as *Rodrigue* suggests, this is not always determinative. See Santo v. Santo, 141 A.3d 74 (Md. 2016), which approved joint custody with tie-breaking provisions for two parents who had been unable to cooperate or communicate effectively.

b. Child Development and Custody Guidelines

What assistance can child development research provide to parents, lawyers, and judges seeking to minimize the negative impact of family separation on children? Many experts recommend that very young children should not be alternating between two residences, in order to protect the child's primary attachments during early childhood. The conventional wisdom on this point was strongly influenced by Joseph Goldstein, Anna Freud, and Albert J. Solnit, Beyond the Best Interests of the Child (3d ed. 1984), which insisted on the importance of continuity and stability in the life of the child, and urged courts to focus on the child's psychological and emotional relationships with his or her parents. For a more recent analysis, see Joan B. Kelly and Michael E. Lamb, *Using Child Development Research to Make Appropriate Custody and Access Decisions for Young Children*, 38 Fam. & Concil. Cts. Rev. 297 (2005).

Applying these ideas, many courts refuse to approve alternating residential custody for young children, particularly where parents live at a great distance. See, e.g. West v. Lawson, 951 P.2d 1200 (Alaska 1998) (vacating order that provided for six-month alternating custody schedule between Alaska and Nevada); Bainbridge v. Pratt, 68 So.3d 310 (Fla. Dist. Ct. App. 2011) (reversing annually rotating custody plan for school-age child); In re Marriage of Swanson, 656 N.E.2d 215 (Ill. App. Ct. 1995); Wiseman v. Wall, 718 A.2d 844 (Pa.Super.Ct.1998) (alternating week shared custody of one-year-old nonmarital child).

c. Parental Contact Orders

Contemporary statutes emphasize the importance for children of frequent and continuing contact with both parents after a divorce. See, e.g., Cal. Fam. Code § 3020 (2018). For this reason, when one parent is awarded sole or primary physical care of a child, the other parent is entitled to visitation, which is also known as parenting time, parental contact, or residential time. These terms are intended to signal that both parents maintain an important role as parents in their children's lives.

Some jurisdictions have developed standard visitation guidelines. See, e.g., Utah Code Ann. §§ 30–3–35, 30–3–35.5 (2018); Indiana Parenting Time Guidelines (2017) (applied in Malicoat v. Wolf, 792 N.E.2d 89 (Ind.Ct.App.2003).) These guidelines typically establish a standard minimum visitation schedule, and make some attempt to reflect the different needs of children at different stages of development. Guidelines may establish a presumption, so that a court is required to explain any deviations from the guidelines. But see Drury v. Drury, 32 S.W.3d 521 (Ky.Ct.App.2000) (holding that court may not apply standard visitation schedule adopted by local rule without making findings of fact as to the child's best interests).

Parenting time or visitation rights may be denied, terminated, or restricted if visitation would be seriously detrimental to the child. See, e.g., UMDA § 407(a) (visitation may be denied if court finds it would endanger seriously the child's physical, mental, moral, or emotional health). Some statutes list particular circumstances in which visitation may be limited. See, e.g., Colo. Rev. Stat. § 14–10–129(3) (2018) (listing crimes which may disqualify a parent from visitation).

Rather than denying all contact between a parent and child, a court may order supervised visitation. See, e.g., Monette v. Hoff, 958 P.2d 434 (Alaska 1998) (mother posed a risk of abduction and flight); Bodine v. Bodine, 528 N.E.2d 973 (Ohio Ct. App. 1988) (denial of request for visitation supervision was abuse of discretion when father had history of violent outbursts); Mary D. v. Watt, 438 S.E.2d 521 (W. Va. 1992) (court entering supervised visitation order must determine that child will be safe from emotional and psychological trauma).

d. Custody Mediation and Arbitration

Some states require mediation of custody and visitation issues prior to a contested hearing, see, e.g. Cal. Fam. Code §§ 3170–3177 (2018), and other states allow courts to order the parties to attempt to mediate these disputes, see, e.g. Colo. Rev. Stat. § 14–10–129.5 (2018). Mediation is usually not required where there is a history of domestic violence. See, e.g. Iowa Code § 598.7 (2018). After mediation, the parties' parenting plan or custody agreement is presented to the court for its approval and incorporation into a court order.

Make the Connection

Mediation and arbitration in family disputes is addressed in Chapter 6.

In some states, parents may agree to arbitrate custody disputes, within the general parameters of state arbitration laws. See Fawzy v. Fawzy, 973 A.2d 347 (N.J. 2009). Other states do not allow this, see, e.g., Kelm v. Kelm, 749 N.E.2d 299 (Ohio Ct. App. 2001), or require that courts must review a custody arbitration award to determine whether it is in the child's best interests, see Harvey v. Harvey, 680 N.W.2d 835 (Mich. 2004). Courts cannot require parties to submit custody disputes to binding arbitration, see, e.g., Gates v. Gates, 716 A.2d 794 (Vt. 1998). Parents often agree in their separation agreement or parenting plan that any future disputes will be submitted to mediation. See, e.g., Gould v. Gould, 523 S.E.2d 106 (Ga. Ct. App. 1999).

Further Reading: Joint Custody

- John N. Hartson, et al, Creating Effective Parenting Plans: A Developmental Approach for Lawyers and Divorce Professionals (2006).

- Joan H. McWilliams, Parenting Plans for Families After Divorce (2011).

- Isolini Ricci, Mom's House/Dad's House (2d ed. 1997).

Problem 7-35

Arthur and Susan have two adopted daughters, ages seven and five. Although the children have lived with their mother for the past two years, Arthur has filed for divorce and requested shared legal and physical custody of the girls. A psychiatrist retained by Susan as an expert has given the opinion, after interviewing the children and Susan, that adopted children have a special need for security which would be impaired by joint physical custody and the parents' different approaches to child care. He also gave his opinion that Susan should have sole legal custody, based on Susan's belief that she and Arthur will not be able to cooperate. Arthur has retained two expert witnesses, who are both of the opinion that it is important for the girls to maintain their relationship with their father, and that the parents should have joint physical custody. The children wish to live with their mother. Should the court order joint custody over Susan's objections? (See Beck v. Beck, 432 A.2d 63 (N.J. 1981).)

Miller v. Smith

989 A.2d 537 (Vt. 2009)

¶ 1. Mother appeals from the family court's order regarding parent-child contact. This is the third time the parties have been before this Court arguing over the details of their parent-child contact schedule. In this appeal, mother argues that the family court erred by refusing to order father to take the parties' six-year-old child to a gymnastics class during father's scheduled visitation period. We affirm the family court's order.

¶ 2. The parties divorced after a short marriage. Their daughter, B.S., is now six years old. Mother has sole legal and physical rights and responsibilities in the minor child. In November 2008, father filed a motion to enforce a provision, effective on the child's sixth birthday, providing him with an additional overnight visit. Father interpreted the term "overnight" to mean a 24-hour period, and he thus sought to have the child from five p.m. on a certain day until five p.m. the following day. Mother objected, asserting that father's visitation ended at the beginning of the school day or 9 a.m. on nonschool days. Mother maintained that father's plan would be disruptive to the child and not in her best interests. Following a hearing, the court issued an order setting forth the contact schedule. Father's additional overnight was provided on Tuesdays, once per month. The court explained that as a matter of judicial finality and economy, it could not continue to tinker with the parties' visitation schedule. It stated that the schedule was now clear—the additional overnight was in place. It was now time for the family to turn their attention to something else and stick by the schedule they had developed. The court thus granted father's motion to enforce and denied the parties' remaining requests.

¶ 3. Mother then filed a motion, asking the court to clarify that father must bring the child to her scheduled activities on his visitation days. Father responded and also asked the court to correct an inadvertent error in its decision. The court then issued another entry order responding to these requests. It explained that the family court could not referee the details of how the child spent her time with father. Father was an adult and during his time with B.S. he would have to make decisions about the child's activities. The court expected that father would respect the child's wishes, but in the end, it was a private matter that the court would not supervise. The court noted that any other approach was unthinkable. The court had no ability or any role in deciding if gymnastics on Tuesdays were better for the child than an afternoon spent at father's house. If the court issued an order requiring father to take the child to after-school activities, the parties would then be back with an endless stream of disputes over the value and reasonableness of various activities. The court could provide blocks of time to each parent. Within reason, how each parent spent that time was left to the individual parent who was caring for the child at the time. Mother appealed from this decision.

¶ 4. Mother argues that the court's order interferes with her right under 15 V.S.A. §§ 664–665 to choose the child's activities. In a related vein, mother asserts that the court seemed to agree at the hearing that father should take the child to activities chosen by mother and, thus, it should have entered an order to this effect.

¶ 5. These arguments are without merit. While mother suggests that the court agreed with her position at the hearing, the record plainly shows that the court rejected mother's approach. The family court acted well within its discretion in refusing to police the child's recreational activities during her visitation with father. Our decision in *Gazo v. Gazo,* 166 Vt. 434, 697 A.2d 342 (1997), is instructive. In that case, we recognized that the parent who does not have physical responsibility for a child "has a right to some measure of parent-child contact unless the best interests of the child[ ] require otherwise." The court may impose conditions on visitation if clearly required by the child's best interests, which is not to suggest that the custodial parent can impose restrictions unilaterally. "If the custodial parent desires that restrictions be imposed, she must ask the court to impose them." As we observed in *Gazo,* "[w]ithout mutual tolerance and understanding, these rights of visitation can become a nightmare for both parents and a disaster for the child or children involved." (alteration in original) (quotation omitted).

¶ 6. In *Gazo,* the court prohibited the mother, who had been awarded legal and physical rights and responsibilities for the parties' two children, from imposing "any limitations on who the children see or what the children do when they are having parent-child contact with the [father]." We found that while the court's finding was supported by the evidence, its order was overly broad "to the extent that it interferes with the award of parental rights and responsibilities to [the mother]." We went on, however, to strike that portion of the court's order as "unnecessary," now that a specific schedule of visitation was in place "leaving nothing to [mother]'s discretion." We further held that if the mother wanted to impose restrictions on the father's actions during visitation, she would have to seek further court intervention for that purpose.

¶ 7. In this case, the court specifically rejected mother's proposed restrictions, and we find no abuse of the family court's discretion in ruling on this motion to clarify. Mother essentially argues that she has the right to control the child's activities during father's visitation. This is the "nightmare" situation we foretold in *Gazo*. If the custodial parent were allowed to establish routines and restrictions within a noncustodial parent's time at her whim, the contact with father would be little more than a babysitting function with mother having filled the time with instructions and conditions. There are certainly times when the parent awarded parental rights and responsibilities will want to establish conditions, such as where the child has a strict vegetarian diet but the noncustodial parent gives the child hamburger each night of a visit, the mother could ask the court to consider making adherence to a vegetarian diet mandatory. However, to allow the custodial parent to schedule the child for time that is supposed to be spent with the noncustodial parent ignores the legislative mandate that children should continue "to have the opportunity for maximum continuing physical and emotional contact with both parents." It would also, as the trial court aptly noted, bring the parties back before the court "with an endless string of disputes over the reasonableness and value of sports, music lessons, gymnastics classes and friends' birthday parties." As the family court explained, it "can provide blocks of time to each parent. Within reason, how each spends it has to be left to the individual decision of the parent who is caring for [the child] at the time."

Affirmed.

Points for Discussion

a. Major Decisions

Orders allocating custody or parental responsibility assign the legal right to make major decisions concerning the child's life, and an award of sole legal custody ordinarily allows the custodial parent to make these decisions unilaterally. Still, courts are regularly called upon to decide parenting disputes, whether or not the parents share legal decision-making authority. Some of the more commonly litigated issues include:

- whether a child will attend public or parochial school, see, e.g., Griffin v. Griffin, 699 P.2d 407 (Colo.1985), Von Tersch v. Von Tersch, 455 N.W.2d 130 (Neb. 1990), whether home schooling is appropriate, see, e.g., In re Kurowski, 20 A.3d 306 (N.H. 2011), or whether a child should be enrolled in a program for gifted and talented children, see, e.g., Lombardo v. Lombardo, 507 N.W.2d 788 (Mich. Ct. App. 1993);

- major health care decisions concerning the child, such as consent for elective surgery, see, e.g., <u>Brzozowski v. Brzozowski, 625 A.2d 597 (N.J.Super. Ct. Ch. Div. 1993)</u>, whether a child will be immunized, see, e.g., <u>Winters v. Brown, 51 So.3d 656 (Fla. Dist. Ct. App. 2011)</u>, whether the child will see a particular therapist, see, e.g., <u>Avren v. Garten, 710 S.E.2d 130 (Ga. 2011)</u>, or the entry of a "do not resuscitate" order for comatose child, see, e.g. <u>In re Doe, 418 S.E.2d 3 (Ga. 1992)</u>;

- the child's religious observance, see, e.g., <u>Kendall v. Kendall, 687 N.E.2d 1228 (Mass. 1997)</u>, <u>Sagar v. Sagar, 781 N.E.2d 54 (Mass. App. Ct. 2003)</u>;

- the child's extracurricular activities, see e.g. <u>Mord v. Peters, 571 So.2d 981 (Miss.1990)</u> (flying lessons), <u>Pogue v. Pogue, 370 A.2d 539 (N.J. Super. Ct. Ch. Div. 1977)</u> (debating whether 15-year-old should be enjoined from playing basketball until his grades improved); and

- the child's name, see, e.g. <u>Gubernat v. Deremer, 657 A.2d 856 (N.J. 1995)</u>, <u>Doherty v. Wizner, 150 P.3d 456 (Or. Ct. App. 2006)</u>.

See also <u>Kirkpatrick v. Eighth Judicial District, 64 P.3d 1056 (Nev. 2003)</u>, which held that a divorced father was not constitutionally entitled to notice and an opportunity for a hearing before his teenaged daughter received court permission to marry. Are there decisions that should require consent of both parents, even if one parent has sole custody?

Even when parents have joint legal custody, courts are reluctant to step into and resolve these types of conflicts, sometimes allocating the final say on disputed matters to the primary residential parent. (This was true in the *Griffin* and *Brzozowski* cases, supra, but not in *Lombardo* and *Doe*.)

A number of cases have addressed the standing of noncustodial parents to make constitutional or civil rights claims on behalf of their children. In <u>Elk Grove Unified School District v. Newdow, 542 U.S. 1 (2004)</u>, the Supreme Court concluded that a noncustodial father had no standing to bring his own constitutional challenge to the state law that required daily recitation of the Pledge of Allegiance in his daughter's school. See also <u>Crowley v. McKinney, 400 F.3d 965 (7th Cir. 2005)</u> (upholding dismissal of father's civil rights suit against school district and principal); and <u>Fuentes v. Board of Education, 907 N.E.2d 696 (N.Y. 2009)</u> (ruling that noncustodial parent has no right to control child's education absent express permission in custody order). The ruling in *Elk Grove* was abrogated ten years later, however, when the Court abandoned the prudential standing doctrine in <u>Lexmark International, Inc. v. Static Control Components, Inc., 572 U.S. 118 (2014)</u>.

b. Dispute Resolution

Consider the shared parenting order in the *Rodrigue* case. Did that order provide an appropriate dispute resolution mechanism? The wide range of potential parenting disputes suggested by cases such as *Rodrigue* and *Miller* illustrates the value of establishing a process for dispute resolution in all shared parenting cases, whether or not the arrangement is labeled as joint custody. For example, parents may agree to submit any future parenting disputes to mediation. See, e.g., Gould v. Gould, 523 S.E.2d 106 (Ga. Ct. App. 1999) (dismissing custody modification action for failure to comply with mediation provision).

Another system, which was developed for working with high-conflict families, involves the appointment of a special master or parenting coordinator who assists parties in resolving their disagreements, and who may also be given authority to decide some parenting disputes, subject to general supervision of the trial court. See, e.g., the Oklahoma Parenting Coordinator Act, 43 Okl. Stat. § 120.1 (2018), applied in Fultz v. Smith, 97 P.3d 651 (Okla.Civ.App.2004). See also Jordan v. Jordan, 14 A.3d 1136 (D.C. 2011); Harrison v. Harrison, 376 P.3d 173 (Nev. 2018); see generally *Guidelines for Parenting Coordination*, 44 Fam. Ct. Rev. 164 (2006).

c. Parent Education

Along with custody mediation requirements, states have developed parent education programs to reduce the adversarial nature of the divorce process and help focus parents' attention on the needs of their children. States may require that divorcing couples with minor children attend an approved seminar or counseling concerning the effects of divorce on children, see, e.g., Iowa Code § 598.15 (2018); N.H. Rev. Stat. Ann. § 458–D:1 (2018), or give the courts authority to order parents to attend counseling or classes. Kagin v. Kopowski, 10 F.Supp.2d 756 (E.D.Ky.1998) upheld an order to attend a parent education course against a First Amendment challenge where the class was sponsored by a local church. See also Nelson v. Nelson, 954 P.2d 1219 (Okla.1998). Connecticut's parent education requirement was sustained in Dutkiewicz v. Dutkiewicz, 957 A.2d 821 (Conn. 2008).

Problem 7-36

Although Mother and Father have joint legal custody of their daughter, age 16, Mother has sole physical custody. Father learns that the daughter is twenty weeks pregnant and planning to have an abortion. He immediately files a motion asking the court to enjoin Mother from allowing the abortion to proceed without his consent. The state statute provides that a physician may not perform an abortion on a minor "without first having obtained the written consent of one of the parents or the legal guardian of the minor pregnant woman." Is Father's consent required in this situation? (See S.H. v. D.H., 796 N.E.2d 1243 (Ind.Ct.App.2003).)

Problem 7-37

Paul and Anne agree to share physical custody of their three-year-old daughter after their divorce. Paul, who has been blind since birth, plans to hire a nanny to help him, but he objects to Anne's demand that he have the nanny move into his home and be present at all times when the child is in his care. Paul is a very successful businessman who has lived and traveled independently for many years; he has cared for the child alone in the past and does not feel the need to have the nanny in his home overnight. How should the court evaluate Anne's request? (See Clark v. Madden, 725 N.E.2d 100 (Ind.Ct.App.2000).)

Renaud v. Renaud

721 A.2d 463 (Vt. 1998)

JOHNSON, J.

Daniel Renaud (father) appeals from a divorce judgment of the Franklin Family Court. He contends the court: (1) abused its discretion in awarding Gail Renaud (mother) sole legal and physical parental rights and responsibilities notwithstanding the court's finding that mother had interfered with the relationship between the child and father; and (2) erroneously divided the marital estate. We affirm.

The parties were married in October 1989. They had one child, a son, born in January 1994. In May 1996, the parties separated following father's disclosure that he was having an affair with a co-worker and wanted a divorce. At the time of trial in April and May of 1997, mother was living with the three-year-old child in the marital home, and father was living with the co-worker and her children.

Both parties worked full time in supervisory positions for the federal government. Before the separation, both shared in attending to the minor's childcare needs. Mother arranged her work schedule to have Fridays off to spend with the child. Father took the child to daycare in the morning, visited him there during the day, and brought him home at night. Mother generally took time off from work when the child was sick, purchased his clothes, and did his laundry. The court found that both parents provided the child with love, discipline, structure, and guidance, and that either would be fit to serve as the custodial parent.

Following the separation, father voluntarily moved out, and mother and child continued to reside in the family home. Almost immediately, mother began to impede father's contact with the child, forcing father to file a number of motions to establish an emergency visitation schedule. Following a hearing in July 1996, the court established a temporary visitation schedule. Thereafter, mother filed a succession of relief-from-abuse petitions, alleging that father had physically and sexually abused the minor. The allegations ranged from evidence of diaper rash, to sunburn, cuts and bruises, and inappropriate touching. These petitions further disrupted father's contact with the child, resulting in periods of noncontact and supervised visitation.

None of the abuse allegations was substantiated, and all of the petitions were ultimately dismissed. Indeed, the court found that father had never abused the minor, that the factual support for the "excessive number of motions and petitions" was "weak at best," and that mother had, in fact, "imagined abuse where there was no abuse." The court further found that mother's actions were the result of a heightened distrust of father because of his marital unfaithfulness, and that her "baseless suspicions ha[d] adversely affected [the minor] in that he is no longer as loving towards [father] as he once was." A team of psychiatric experts appointed by the court observed that the child interacted well with each parent, but noted that mother's repeated accusations had damaged the child's relationship with father, and warned that if such accusations continued they could seriously compromise the father-child relationship.

The court awarded sole parental rights and responsibilities to mother, albeit "with some hesitation." The court found that the child had an extremely close emotional relationship with mother and that "upsetting that relationship [was] likely to be detrimental to [the child]." The court further observed that mother had sought counseling to overcome her emotional problems resulting from the divorce, and concluded that she would be able "in a reasonable period of time. . . [to] help repair the damage she caused to the relationship between [father] and [the child]," and could "actively encourage frequent and open contact" between them. To further ensure that this occurred, the court specifically ordered mother to encourage the child to develop a warm and loving relationship with father, forbade either parent from making disparaging remarks about the other in the minor's presence, and ordered extensive visitation with father totaling about fifty percent of the minor's time. This appeal followed.

I.

In light of the court's express findings that mother had undermined the child's relationship with father by filing excessive and baseless abuse allegations, father contends that the court's decision to award mother sole parental rights and responsibilities was a patent abuse of discretion. Like the trial court here, we are reluctant to condone any conduct by a parent that tends to diminish the child's relationship with the other parent. Indeed, in awarding parental rights and responsibilities, the court is statutorily required to consider "the ability and disposition of each parent to foster a positive relationship and frequent and continuing contact with the other parent, including physical contact, except where contact will result in harm to the child or to a parent." 15 V.S.A. § 665(b)(5). Across the country, the great weight of authority holds that conduct by one parent that tends to alienate the child's affections from the other is so inimical to the child's welfare as to be grounds for a denial of custody to, or a change of custody from, the parent guilty of such conduct. See generally Annotation, *Alienation of Child's Affections as Affecting Custody Award,* 32 A.L.R.2d 1005 (1953) (collecting cases).

The paramount consideration in any custody decision, however, is the best interests of the child. See *Bissonette v. Gambrel,* 152 Vt. 67, 70, 564 A.2d 600, 602 (1989); *Lafko v. Lafko,* 127 Vt. 609, 618, 256 A.2d 166, 172 (1969). Children are not responsible for the misconduct of their parents toward each other, and will not be uprooted from their home merely to punish a wayward parent. See *Nickerson v. Nickerson,* 158 Vt. 85, 90, 605 A.2d 1331, 1334 (1992) (attention should be directed to needs of the children rather than actions of parents). Nevertheless, a child's best interests are plainly furthered by nurturing the child's relationship with both parents, and a sustained course of conduct by one parent designed to interfere in the child's relationship with the other casts serious doubt upon the fitness of the offending party to be the custodial parent. See *Young v. Young,* 212 A.D.2d 114, 628 N.Y.S.2d 957, 958 (1995) (interference with relationship between child and noncustodial parent raises " 'a strong probability that the offending party is unfit to act as a custodial parent' ") (quoting *Maloney v. Maloney,* 208 A.D.2d 603, 617 N.Y.S.2d 190, 191 (1994)); see also *McAdams v. McAdams,* 530 N.W.2d 647, 650 (N.D.1995) ("[A] parent who willfully alienates a child from the other parent may not be awarded custody based on that alienation.").

This is not to say that evidence of alienation of affection automatically precludes the offending parent from obtaining custody. See *Slinkard v. Slinkard,* 589 S.W.2d 635, 636 (Mo.Ct.App.1979) ("[A]lthough alienation of a child's affections from his natural parent and interference with visitations rights may be grounds for change of. . .custody, they do not compel such a result."). The best interests of the child remains the paramount consideration. Courts should be wary, however, of over-reliance on such otherwise significant considerations as the child's emotional attachment to, or expressed preference for, the offending parent, or on such factors as stability and continuity. For as one court has observed, "The desires of young children, capable of distortive manipulation by a bitter, or perhaps even well-meaning, parent, do not always reflect the long-term best interest of the children." *Nehra v. Uhlar,* 43 N.Y.2d 242, 401 N.Y.S.2d 168, 372 N.E.2d 4, 7 (N.Y.1977). And although stability is undoubtedly important, the short-term disruption occasioned by a change of custody may be more than compensated by the long-term benefits of a healthy relationship with both parents.

Thus, where the evidence discloses a continual and unmitigated course of conduct by a parent designed to poison a child's relationship with the other parent, a change of custody from the offending parent may well be in the child's long-term best interests. See _Begins v. Begins_, 168 Vt. 3, 721 A.2d 469, 473 (1998) (court abused its discretion in awarding custody to father where single most significant factor contributing to sons' estrangement from mother was constant poisoning of relationship by father); see also _Lewin v. Lewin_, 186 Cal.App.3d 1482, 231 Cal.Rptr. 433, 437 n. 4 (1986) (change of custody compelled where mother engaged in ongoing conduct intended and designed to interfere with development of healthy father-daughter relationship); _Thurman v. Thurman_, 73 Idaho 122, 245 P.2d 810, 815 (1952) (trial court abused discretion in refusing to award custody to mother where father had "by design and planning" interfered with mother's visitation rights); _In re Leyda_, 355 N.W.2d 862, 866 (Iowa 1984) (trial court abused discretion in awarding custody to mother where evidence disclosed that she had "sought to obscenely denigrate and deny the emotional relationship between [the child] and her father").

A more subtle, but no less invidious, form of interference in parent-child relations may take the form of persistent allegations of physical or sexual abuse. In _Young_, for example, the court reversed an award of custody to the mother where the trial court had inexplicably ignored uncontradicted evidence that the mother had filed numerous false accusations of sexual abuse by the father. As the court observed, "[t]hese repeated uncorroborated and unfounded allegations of sexual abuse brought by the mother against the father cast serious doubt upon her fitness to be the custodial parent." 628 N.Y.S.2d at 962. Other decisions are to similar effect. See, e.g., _Lewin_, 231 Cal.Rptr. at 437 n. 4 (change of custody compelled where mother had "made numerous bizarre, outrageous and totally unfounded accusations" of child abuse against father); _In re Wedemeyer_, 475 N.W.2d 657, 659 (Iowa Ct.App.1991) (upholding change of custody where mother's "flagrant and continuing destructive conduct," including persistent allegations that father was "an insane sex addict who masturbates and performs sexual acts with animals," had interfered with children's association with father); _Ellis v. Ellis_, 747 S.W.2d 711, 715 (Mo.Ct.App.1988) (change of custody justified where mother had "used the device of making a false accusation of sexual abuse against [father] as a weapon to cut off his access to [the child]").

The situation is more difficult where the allegations of abuse, although ultimately found to be baseless, may initially be in doubt. Society has a strong interest in encouraging parents to take action if they suspect that their child is being abused. Accordingly, courts should infer an ulterior motive in the filing of such charges only where a parent knew, or reasonably should have known, that they were groundless. Here, the court found that the factual support for mother's relief-from-abuse petitions was "weak at best," and that mother "imagined abuse where there was no abuse" because of her emotional distress and distrust of husband. The record amply supports these findings, but the findings do not indicate whether mother knew or reasonably should have known that the petitions were groundless.

The record mitigates in favor of mother in this regard. The evidence showed that she did not act precipitously in filing the petitions, but consulted with the child's pediatrician and therapist, as well as her own therapist, about her suspicions. The child's pediatrician recalled at the first relief-from-abuse hearing that mother had expressed grave concern that father was neglecting the child's physical well-being, and did not appear to be acting out of malice or spite. Moreover, while he informed her that the child's physical condition did not necessarily suggest abuse or neglect, he also told her that if the child's sunburns continued he would "be quite alarmed," and would feel that the "caregiver [father] is not able to protect [the child] from an obvious source of harm." Although the court ultimately dismissed the petition, finding no evidence of abuse, it did express concern about the sunburn and bruises, and urged father to "re-double [his] efforts to be vigilant."

Mother also expressed her concerns to the child's therapist. She was particularly anxious about statements by the child suggesting that father had manipulated the child's penis. The therapist recalled at the second relief-from-abuse hearing that mother "chiefly wanted guidance." Although he ultimately concluded that it was unlikely the child had been abused, he was sufficiently concerned to contact Social and Rehabilitation Services. Later, when mother informed him that she had filed a relief-from-abuse petition, the therapist reassured her that he would have done the same under the circumstances. Although the court again found the allegations of abuse to be groundless, it stressed that it was "not at all suggesting that the mother's reaction wasn't appropriate. She was obviously concerned. She was obviously worried. But we don't find anything devious about what she did here. . .basically as a concerned mother under the circumstances."

Mother's therapist also contacted SRS on mother's behalf after hearing her concerns. Like the pediatrician and the child's therapist, he believed that mother was primarily seeking expert guidance and reassurance that the child was being well cared for.

Thus, the record evidence does not support a finding that mother's purpose was to alienate the child from his father, or that her concerns were wholly unreasonable. It is particularly significant in this regard that mother repeatedly sought expert guidance before acting and received ambiguous messages, suggesting on the one hand that the physical evidence of abuse was weak, but on the other hand that her concerns were not entirely unfounded and certainly warranted investigation.

The trial court also focused on the relatively transient nature of mother's emotional distress, finding it "likely that, in a reasonable period of time, [mother] will be less distrustful of [father] and will help repair the damage she caused to the relationship between [father and child]." Although there was conflicting evidence on this point, substantial credible expert evidence supported the conclusion that mother's actions were a transient reaction to a highly volatile emotional situation, and that she had progressed to the point where she could within a reasonable period of time cooperate with father and foster a healthy relationship with the child. We note that the child's tender years may facilitate the healing process envisioned by the court, whereas an older child might not be so amenable to change.

Indeed, the evidence and the findings here contrast sharply with those in another case decided today, _Begins, 168 Vt. at 303, 721 A.2d at 473_. There, the family court awarded the father parental rights and responsibilities for two teenage boys, notwithstanding its express finding that the father had willfully poisoned the mother's relationship with the boys and had demonstrated no inclination to act otherwise. The court had also found that the mother had been the children's primary care provider before the separation, and was the custodian of choice in all other significant respects. We thus concluded that an award to the father in these circumstances would seriously impede the mother's opportunity to reestablish a healthy relationship with her sons in the future, and that reversal of the judgment was compelled. Here, in contrast, the court expressly found that mother's actions were transitory, unlikely to be repeated, and subject to cure.

Finally, we note that the court awarded father extremely liberal visitation, resulting in a nearly equal sharing of time with the child. This fact, coupled with the court's finding that a change of custody would be highly detrimental to the minor, and that mother would be able to foster a healthy relationship with father within a reasonable period of time, leads us to conclude that the court did not abuse its discretion in awarding parental rights and responsibilities to mother. We hasten to remind the parties, however, that the court's ruling is subject to future modification, and underscore the court's specific admonishment to mother to encourage a warm and loving relationship between father and child.

Points for Discussion

a. High-Conflict Divorce

Custody statutes often include a "friendly parent" provision, like the one quoted in _Renaud_, requiring the court to consider whether a proposed custodian will encourage the child's relationship with his or her other parent. As the court notes in _Renaud_, it relied on this provision in a companion case, _Begins v. Begins, 721 A.2d 469 (Vt. 1998)_, to reverse a custody award made to a father who had alienated his sons from their mother. What is the distinction the court draws between these two cases? See also _Cloutier v. Lear, 691 A.2d 660 (Me.1997)_; _Mar-_

riage of Lemcke, 623 N.W.2d 916 (Minn.Ct.App.2001); McAdams v. McAdams, 530 N.W.2d 647 (N.D.1995); and Knutsen v. Cegalis, 172 A.3d 180 (Vt. 2017).

Ongoing parental conflict after divorce causes serious harm to children, and many courts have experimented with new procedures to work with parents in high conflict cases, such as the use of parenting coordinators, described above. See generally Mitchell A. Baris et al., Working With High-Conflict Families of Divorce: A Guide for Professionals (2001); Joan B. Kelly, *Psychological and Legal Interventions for Parents and Children in Custody and Access Disputes: Current Research and Practice*, 10 Va. J. Soc. Pol'y & L. 129 (2002); Janet R. Johnston, et al., *Ongoing Postdivorce Conflict: Effects on Children of Joint Custody and Frequent Access*, 59 Am. J. Orthopsychiatry 576 (1989).

b. Parental Alienation

Children may resist spending time with a parent after separation for a wide variety of reasons, which may or may not be the result of the other parent's indoctrinating behavior. Although the idea of a "parental alienation syndrome" has circulated widely in case law and literature, it has not been supported by clinical research, and has not been accepted as a psychiatric diagnosis. See Joan B. Kelly and Janet R. Johnston, *The Alienated Child: A Reformulation of Parental Alienation Syndrome*, 39 Fam. Ct. Rev. 249 (2001). Kelly and Johnston argue that there is a broad continuum of behavior here, and a child may have a realistic estrangement from a parent based on the child's experiences with that parent. At the extreme end of the continuum, however, children caught in high-conflict divorce disputes may have significantly distorted and exaggerated reactions to a parent. Finding appropriate and helpful legal and therapeutic interventions for these cases is extremely challenging. See generally Barbara Jo Fidler, et al., Children Who Resist Post-Separation Parental Contact: A Differential Approach for Legal and Mental Health Professionals (2012).

c. Child Abuse Allegations

A history of child abuse is clearly an appropriate basis for denying or limiting parental contact, reflected in many state statutes. See, e.g., Colo. Rev. Stat. § 14–10–129 (3)(a) (2018); Md. Code Ann. Fam. Law § 9–101(b)(2018), Tex. Fam. Code § 153.004(b) (2018); Depending on the circumstances, however, courts may permit visitation with restrictions or supervision. See, e.g. Nelson v. Jones, 944 P.2d 476 (Alaska 1997); Mary Ann P. v. William R.P., 475 S.E.2d 1 (W. Va. 1996).

Although the court in *Renaud* concluded that the mother's allegations were unfounded, the court also concluded that she had acted appropriately by seeking expert guidance. This is an extremely difficult and controversial aspect of custody litigation, which must be very carefully handled by lawyers and the courts. One useful resource is Ann M. Haralambie, Child Sexual Abuse in Civil Cases: A Guide to Custody and Tort Actions (2003). As suggested in *Renaud*, repeated, unsubstantiated allegations of abuse by a custodial parent are sometimes the basis for orders changing custody. See, e.g., Watson v. Poole, 495 S.E.2d 236 (S.C. Ct.App.1997); Young v. Young, 628 N.Y.S.2d 957 (App.Div.1995).

Visitation Enforcement

The obligations to make children available for parenting time and to pay child support are independent of each other, and a parent who resorts to a "self-help" remedy by refusing to pay child support to try to pressure the other parent to cooperate may be held in contempt of court. Because of the importance of both child support and parenting time to children's well-being, courts are generally unwilling to condition child support payments on the other parent's cooperation with visitation. A few cases have approved this technique in extreme circumstances. See, e.g., Welch v. Welch, 519 N.W.2d 262 (Neb. 1994); see also Copeland v. Copeland, 235 So.3d 91 (Miss. 2017) (concluding that children had forfeited their right to support based on their "clear and extreme" conduct toward father); Appert v. Appert, 341 S.E.2d 342 (N.C. Ct. App. 1986) (citing cases).

Conduct by one parent that obstructs or denies the other parent's court-ordered parenting time may be subject to sanctions for civil contempt, see, e.g., Wells v. Wells, 549 A.2d 1039 (Vt. 1988); In re Marriage of Farr and Martin, 940 P.2d 679 (Wash. Ct. App. 1997); or criminal contempt, see Carlson v. Carlson, 748 S.E.2d 304 (Ga. Ct. App. 2013). Some states allow for an award of damages in this situation. See, e.g., Alaska Stat. § 25.20.140 (2018); Colo. Rev. Stat. § 14–10–129.5 (2018).

In extreme cases, a court may modify the custody orders as a remedy for interference in the child's relationship with the other parent. See, e.g., Ashlock v. District Court, 717 P.2d 483 (Colo.1986); Doe v. Doe, 239 P.3d 774 (Idaho 2010); Clark v. Clark, 422 N.W.2d 793 (Neb. 1988); Russell v. Russell, 948 P.2d 1351 (Wyo.1997). Contra Everett v. Everett, 433 So.2d 705 (La.1983) (interference not a sufficient basis for modification); Campbell v. Campbell, 604 A.2d 33 (Me.1992). See generally Margaret M. Mahoney, *The Enforcement of Child Custody Orders by Contempt Remedies*, 68 U. Pitt. L. Rev. 835 (2007).

Every state provides for suspending drivers' licenses of obligors who fail to pay child support, as noted earlier in this chapter. A number of states have extended the same remedy to cases of parents who have been found to be in contempt of court for visitation abuse. See, e.g., 625 Ill. Cons. Stat. 5/7–701 et seq. (2018). Under the Illinois statutes, visitation or parenting time interference is also a misdemeanor offense. See 720 Ill. Cons. Stat. 5/10–5.5 (2018).

Problem 7-38

Several years after their divorce, Chris notified his ex-wife, Sara, of the dates he planned to take their two children for his allotted four weeks of summer parenting time. When he came to pick up the children, however, they were not at home. Chris eventually got a court order specifying the dates for his visitation, but his daughter Caroline, age 13, refused to go with him. Because this had happened numerous times, Chris's attorney advised him to seek contempt sanctions against Sara for her failure to comply with the court's orders. Sara claims that she could not comply with the court's order because Caroline refuses to cooperate. What are Sara's obligations in this situation? (See Marriage of Rideout, 54 P.3d 1212 (Wash. 2002).)

Problem 7-39

Elena's ex-husband, Kevin, was awarded substantial parenting time with their two children, but he has been inconsistent and unpredictable about spending time with them. Elena files a motion asking the court to require Kevin to exercise his visitation with the children or, in the alternative, that he be required to pay for child care when he does not appear. Can the court grant Elena's motion? (See Marriage of Mitchell, 745 N.E.2d 167 (Ill. App. Ct. 2001).)

Matter of Stapleford

931 A.2d 1199 (N.H. 2007)

HICKS, J.

The parties' minor children, currently thirteen and fifteen years old, appeal a recommended order of a Marital Master (*Cross,* M.) approved by the Derry Family Division (*Sadler,* J.) denying their motion to intervene in their parents' divorce proceedings. We affirm.

The record supports the following. Cheryl Stapleford (mother) and Richard Stapleford (father) were married on October 17, 1992. On December 10, 2004, the parties filed for divorce. On July 27, 2005, the court appointed a guardian ad litem (GAL) to represent the interests of the parties' two children. On April 14, 2005, the Derry Family Division entered a temporary order awarding the mother primary physical custody of the children.

On May 17, 2006, the GAL submitted a preliminary report recommending, against their preference, that the children live primarily in Milford with their mother. Subsequently, upon his attorney's recommendation, the father retained

Attorney Kevin Buchholz to represent the children. On August 9, 2006, Buchholz filed a motion, on behalf of the children, to modify the court's temporary orders. The court denied the motion because the children were not parties to the case. Buchholz then filed a motion to intervene on behalf of the children.

At a hearing held on the motion to intervene, Buchholz asserted a due process and statutory right of the children to be heard. He argued that the court cannot give substantial weight to the children's preferences consistent with RSA 461–A:6, II (Supp.2006) if they are not allowed to intervene when a GAL makes a recommendation contrary to their preferences.

The mother argued that intervention was unnecessary because the GAL had already represented the children's preferences in his reports. The GAL explained that the children wanted to live in Chester with their father because "they lived in Chester their entire life, their grandparents are ill. . .and they want to be there for their grandparents." He also noted that their preference, in his opinion, had more to do with their familiarity with Chester than with whom they wanted to live. The GAL opposed intervention, asserting that it would unduly empower the children, encourage them to violate rules, make parenting harder, and otherwise confuse them.

The master denied the motion to intervene, finding that the GAL had represented the children's best interests and had adequately reported their preferences. He further noted in his order:

> The children's attorney offers more specific examples than the GAL of why the children feel as they do, but not only has the Court already heard some of those specifics from the parties themselves, but the examples are also not qualitatively different as to cause concern about the appropriateness of the Court's Temporary Order dated June 14, 2006.

On appeal, the children argue that: (1) they have a statutory right to intervene as parties to their parents' divorce; (2) the trial court committed an unsustainable exercise of discretion in failing to apply the proper intervention test and denying their motion to intervene; (3) they have a due process right to intervene; and (4) they were denied due process at the hearing on the motion to intervene. We address these issues in order.

The children argue that RSA 461–A:6, II creates a statutory right to intervene for mature minors. We review questions of statutory interpretation *de novo*. The statute states, in pertinent part, that "[i]f the court finds by clear and convincing evidence that a minor child is of sufficient maturity to make a sound judgment, the court may give substantial weight to the preference of the mature minor child as to the determination of parental rights and responsibilities." When construing a statute, we examine its language, ascribing the plain and ordinary meaning to the words used by the legislature. We can neither ignore the plain language of the legislation nor add words which the lawmakers did not see fit to include. Here, RSA 461–A:6, II does not address intervention at all, and we will not add those words to the statute. Accordingly, the statute does not create a right for mature minors to intervene in their parents' divorce proceedings.

We next address the children's claim that the court committed an unsustainable exercise of discretion in failing to apply our customary intervention test and denying intervention. The children point to the traditional intervention test, which provides: "A person who seeks to intervene in a case must have a right involved in the trial and his interest must be direct and apparent; such as would suffer if not indeed be sacrificed were the court to deny the privilege." *Snyder v. N.H. Savings Bank,* 134 N.H. 32, 35, 592 A.2d 506 (1991) (quotations, brackets and emphasis omitted).

In New Hampshire, this standard has never been applied to children seeking to intervene in their parents' divorce. The children arguably have a right and interest involved in the outcome of the divorce, most notably regarding the issue of custody. However, the children are minors, maturity notwithstanding, and minors do not have the same legal rights as do adults in the legal system. *See Miller v. Miller,* 677 A.2d 64, 66 (Me.1996) ("[A]t common law. . .children do not possess the requisite legal capacity to participate in litigation in their own names."). This is why the law provides for representation of a minor's interests through a GAL. *See* RSA 461–A:16 (Supp.2006); *see also* 43 C.J.S. *Infants* § 329 (2004). The traditional intervention test, therefore, cannot be applied to the minors in this case to allow them to intervene in their parents' divorce. Accordingly, we cannot say that the trial court committed an unsustainable exercise of discretion in failing to apply the traditional intervention test.

The children next argue that their due process rights under the Fourteenth Amendment of the United States Constitution and Part I, Article 2 of the New Hampshire Constitution were violated at the hearing below and by the trial court's denial of their motion to intervene.

We first note that although the children's brief refers to "substantive due process," the brief addresses purely procedural due process concerns. Merely using the word "substantive" is insufficient to articulate a substantive due process argument. Accordingly, we will conduct only a procedural due process analysis.

We address the children's argument under the State Constitution, citing federal opinions for guidance only. This court is the final arbiter of the due process requirements of the State Constitution.

We first address the children's argument that they have a due process right to intervene in their parents' divorce. The first step of a due process analysis is to determine whether a legally protected interest has been implicated. We will assume in this case, without deciding, that the "children have a [protected] liberty interest in the outcome of their parents' divorce." *Miller*, 677 A.2d at 68.

Next, we determine whether due process requires that the children be permitted to intervene in their parents' divorce by employing a three-prong balancing test, considering: (1) the private interest affected by the official action; (2) the risk of an erroneous deprivation of such interest through the procedures used and the probable value, if any, of additional or substitute procedural safeguards; and (3) the government's interest, including the function involved and the fiscal and administrative burdens that additional or substitute procedural requirements would entail. *In re Father 2006–360*, 155 N.H. 93, 94–96, 921 A.2d 409, 411 (2007); *Mathews v. Eldridge*, 424 U.S. 319, 335, 96 S.Ct. 893, 47 L.Ed.2d 18 (1976).

We first address the children's interest. The minors' "most immediate interest. . .is in the custodial outcome." *Miller*, 677 A.2d at 68. More specifically, the children's interest is in achieving the best possible outcome, whether that is in line with their preferences at the time or not. RSA 461–A:6 (Supp.2006) includes many factors for the court's consideration, all of which aim to protect the children's interests by achieving the best outcome for them, in satisfaction of the first prong.

We next address the risk of an erroneous outcome for the children without their intervention. We find that the children's interests are well protected by the existing process. "The [GAL] is already an advocate for the best interest of the children in all of its complex dimensions." RSA 461–A:16 ensures that the GAL conducts a detailed investigation and advocates for the children's best interests. The court need not accept the GAL's recommendation, and the court may agree or disagree with a minor's wishes. Poorly performing GALs are subject to fines and disciplinary action under RSA 461–A:16, VI(c), (d). Further, the adversarial nature of a divorce proceeding provides an effective check and balance system. A parent who opposes the GAL's recommendation will likely expose any mistakes made by the GAL, through cross-examination or otherwise.

Finally, we examine the State's interest, including the function involved and the fiscal and administrative burdens that intervention by the children would entail. In divorce proceedings, the State's primary interest is "the best interests of the child." RSA 461–A:6, I. As discussed above, we find that the best interests of the children are well-protected by the current system. Additionally, we agree with *Miller* that "[d]ivorce litigation would be complicated exponentially by the involvement of children as parties." If children were allowed to intervene, they could participate in discovery, depose and cross-examine witnesses, and appeal the court's ruling. Should siblings disagree among themselves, they could each hire their own attorney to advocate for their individual preferences. We need not further detail the chaos that would ensue if we were to hold that every mature minor has a due process right to intervene in their parents' divorce litigation.

Accordingly, after weighing the above factors, we hold that the children have no due process right to intervene in their parents' divorce. Because the State Constitution is at least as protective of individual liberties in these circumstances as the Federal Constitution, *see In re Samantha L.*, 145 N.H. 408, 414, 761 A.2d 1093 (2000); *Mathews*, 424 U.S. at 335, 96 S.Ct. 893, we reach the same result under the Federal Constitution.

Given that we hold, as a matter of law, that the children have no right to intervene in their parents' divorce, we need not address their argument that they were denied due process at the hearing on the motion to intervene.

Affirmed.

——————————

Global View: The Child's Right to be Heard

Article 12 of the United Nations Convention on the Rights of the Child (CRC) states that a child "who is capable of forming his or her own views" has the right "to express those views freely in all matters affecting the child, the views of the child being given due weight in accordance with the age and maturity of the child." More specifically, under the CRC the child should "be provided the opportunity to be heard in any judicial and administrative proceedings affecting the child, either directly, or through a representative or an appropriate body, in a manner consistent with the procedural rules of national law." The United States has signed the CRC, but has not ratified it. Is representation by a GAL, as described in *Stapleford*, consistent with Article 12?

Points for Discussion

a. Children's Participation?

Other courts have also reached the conclusion that children do not have a constitutional right to participate in divorce or custody proceedings. See Miller v.

<u>Miller, 677 A.2d 64 (Me. 1996)</u>; <u>In re Marriage of Hartley, 886 P.2d 665 (Colo. 1994)</u>; and <u>Ihinger v. Ihinger, 824 A.2d 601 (Vt. 2003)</u>. See also <u>Marriage of Osborn, 135 P.3d 199 (Kan. Ct. App. 2006)</u>, which held that an 11-year-old child had no standing to file a motion to modify parenting time in her parents' divorce case.

As noted above, custody statues frequently direct the courts to consider children's wishes in allocating parental responsibilities. Under these statutes, it may be an abuse of discretion for the court to refuse to hear from a child. See, e.g., <u>Holiday v. Holiday, 247 P.3d 29 (Wyo. 2011)</u>. How can children's voices be heard if children are not joined as parties to the litigation?

> **Make the Connection**
>
> As discussed in Chapter 5, federal law requires that states provide some form of representation for children in abuse and neglect proceedings. How are these cases different from parenting disputes?

b. Types of Representation for Children

Statutes in many states, as well as <u>UMDA § 310</u>, permit but do not usually require the court to appoint an attorney to represent the child in a contested custody case. Traditionally, such an attorney serves as a **guardian ad litem**, charged with representing the child's best interests rather than the child's wishes. In some cases, the GAL is not an attorney, and may serve primarily as an advisor for the child or an investigator assisting the court. This may be similar to the role performed by CASA volunteers (Court Appointed Special Advocates) in child welfare cases.

In contrast to best-interests representation based on the GAL model, courts in some jurisdictions may appoint an attorney to serve as the child's legal advocate, representing the child's position in the proceedings. On the distinction between a GAL and a lawyer for the child, see <u>Betz v. Betz, 575 N.W.2d 406 (Neb. 1998)</u> and <u>Clark v. Alexander, 953 P.2d 145 (Wyo. 1998)</u>. See generally Melissa A. Kucinski, A Practical Handbook for the Child's Attorney: Effectively Representing Children in Custody Cases (2018). The American Bar Association approved a set of Standards of Practice for Lawyers Representing Children in Custody Cases, reprinted at <u>37 Fam. L.Q. 131 (2003)</u>. The Standards defines two distinct roles: the Child's Attorney, who provides independent legal counsel to a child; and the Best Interests Attorney, who provides legal services for the purpose of protecting a child's best interests.

> **Make the Connection**
>
> The distinct responsibilities of lawyers representing a child's best interests and lawyers acting as counsel for a child are considered in Chapter 8.

Problem 7-40

In their custody dispute, Mother alleges that she should have sole custody because Father has sexually abused their daughter. Various mental health professionals have treated the daughter, who is 17, over several years, and the parents have agreed that her treatment records should be provided to the psychologist who has been appointed to serve as a custody evaluator. The daughter's guardian ad litem opposes production of her records, and has asserted a statutory therapist-patient privilege on her behalf. Should the parents be permitted to waive the daughter's privilege? (See Attorney ad Litem for D.K. v. Parents of D.K., 780 So.2d 301 (Fla.Ct.App.2001); Abrams v. Jones, 35 S.W.3d 620 (Tex.2000). See also Harder v. Anderson, Arnold, Dickey, Jensen, Gullickson and Sanger, L.L.P., 764 N.W.2d 534 (Iowa 2009) (noncustodial parent not entitled to obtain children's mental health records unless release would be in the children's best interest); Rinehart v. Svensson, 169 A.3d 198 (Vt. 2017) (same).)

Parents, Grandparents and De Facto Parents

Sometimes adults who do not have a legal parent-child relationship with a particular child seek to be awarded custody or visitation rights. This type of parenting dispute raises two distinct legal questions: who has standing to bring this type of action, and what substantive standard should

Make the Connection

Troxel v. Granville is reprinted in Chapter 4.

be applied in disputes between a parent and someone without that status. The answer to both of these questions is influenced by the Supreme Court's decision in Troxel v. Granville, 530 U.S. 57 (2000).

Troxel concluded that a court order granting visitation to grandparents, under a Washington statute that allowed "any person at any time" to bring an action for visitation rights, violated the mother's fundamental constitutional right to make decisions concerning the care, custody and control of her minor children. In *Troxel*, there were no allegations that the mother was an unfit parent, and no evidence that it would be harmful to the children to have only the amount of visitation with their grandparents that the mother had allowed. The Court held that the Washington statute was unconstitutional as applied to the facts of that case, suggesting that other circumstances might not present the same constitutional problem.

State statutes take different approaches to the threshold question of who has standing bring a claim for custody or visitation with a child. Very open-ended statutes, like the one considered in *Troxel*, may create constitutional problems, because the burden of litigation may be a significant intrusion into the parent-child relationship. Other state statutes restrict standing much more narrowly, however, excluding some individuals who have a strong and important parent-like relationships with a child. Statutes based on UMDA § 401(d)(2) permit a person other than a parent to commence a child custody proceeding only if the child is not in the physical custody of one of the child's parents.

Once the question of standing is determined, non-parents seeking court-ordered custody or visitation rights also face a different burden of proof than the best interests test applied to disputes between parents. Historically, state statutes and court decisions reflected a strong presumption in favor of the legal or natural parent in these cases, and a non-parent typically had to prove that the parent was unfit or that it would be harmful to the child for the court to deny the non-parent's claim for custody or visitation. See, e.g., Calif. Fam. Code § 3041 (2018); see generally Watkins v. Nelson, 748 A.2d 558 (N.J. 2000). The natural parent presumption has been weakened in many states, but some version of it appears to be required by the *Troxel* ruling. See, e.g., In re Marriage of O'Donnell-Lamont, 91 P.3d 721 (Or. 2004).

Both the third-party standing rules and the natural parent presumption are applied in a wide variety of contexts, including claims made by stepparents, grandparents, and other relatives, or foster parents and prospective adoptive parents. Often in these cases, the child has spent time in the physical custody of the adult who is seeking to continue their relationship. See, e.g., In re Custody of C.C.R.S., 892 P.2d 246 (Colo.1995); Guinta v. Doxtator, 794 N.Y.S.2d 516 (App. Div. 2005); Bowie v. Arder, 490 N.W.2d 568 (Mich. 1992). Should children be seen as having a right to maintain relationships with important adults in their lives? See Gilbert Holmes, *The Tie That Binds: The Constitutional Right of Children to Maintain Relationships With Parent-Like Individuals*, 53 Md. L. Rev. 358 (1994). See also Katharine T. Bartlett, *Rethinking Parenthood as an Exclusive Status: The Need for Legal Alternatives When the Premise of the Nuclear Family has Failed*, 70 Va. L. Rev. 879 (1984); John DeWitt Gregory, *Blood Ties: A Rationale for Child Visitation by Legal Strangers*, 55 Wash. & Lee L. Rev. 351 (1998).

Go Online

Find a chart listing statutes and criteria for Third-Party Visitation for all states on the web page of the American Bar Association's Family Law Section.

Thorndike v. Lisio

154 A.3d 624 (Me. 2017)

SAUFLEY, C.J.

[¶ 1] Jessica Ann Lisio appeals from a judgment of the District Court (Rockland, *Raimondi, J.*) finding that Tammy J. Thorndike is a de facto parent of two of Lisio's biological children. We discern no error in the court's determinations that Thorndike "has undertaken a permanent, unequivocal, committed, and responsible parental role in [each] child's life," and that "there are exceptional circumstances sufficient to allow the court to interfere with" the biological parents' parental rights. *Pitts v. Moore*, 2014 ME 59, ¶ 27, 90 A.3d 1169 (quotation marks omitted). Accordingly, we affirm the judgment.

I. BACKGROUND

[¶ 2] The facts are drawn from the procedural record of the case and the court's supported findings of fact. *See Kilborn v. Carey*, 2016 ME 78, ¶ 3, 140 A.3d 461. Lisio and Thorndike, who lives as a man, met in 2005 when Lisio's son, Caden, was one year old. They began living together in Bath in August 2007. Thorndike was not working at the time because he had suffered a back injury. Lisio was working as a newspaper carrier. Thorndike cared for Caden while Lisio was working. He got the child ready in the morning, delivered him to and from preschool, bathed him, read to him, played with him, took him to medical appointments, and acted in all ways as a loving father to Caden.

[¶ 3] Thorndike and Lisio decided to have a child together in 2007 or 2008. Lisio arranged to be artificially inseminated, and she became pregnant with Arianna. She and Thorndike registered as domestic partners in early 2009, during the pregnancy. Arianna was born on May 11, 2009.

[¶ 4] Lisio returned to work about one week after Arianna was born. She began working as a certified nursing assistant and also maintained her paper route. Thorndike was a stay-at-home parent who did all the things a parent does—changing diapers, making bottles, being up at night with the baby, and continuing to take care of Caden. Thorndike also took care of housekeeping chores and attended Arianna's doctor appointments with Lisio. At those appointments, Thorndike presented himself as Arianna's father. Lisio, Thorndike, and the two children did things together and functioned as a loving family.

[¶ 5] When Arianna was eight or nine months old, Thorndike and Lisio began having problems in their relationship. Lisio had a brief affair with another person, though the parties remained together and maintained the same parental roles. The couple decided to move to Wiscasset and make a fresh start. Thorndike began to work at a Rockland restaurant during the day, and Lisio, who had stopped delivering newspapers, worked as a CNA at night. Each of them cared for the children while the other was at work. The relationship continued to deteriorate, however, and Thorndike began a relationship with someone else and moved out in 2012.

[¶ 6] After moving out, Thorndike continued to call the children every day before bedtime, and the children visited him, though the parties disagree about how frequently. By the end of 2012, Lisio had a new boyfriend, Joshua Cote. Cote was working for a carnival and traveled seasonally in New England. Lisio would bring the children and stay with him during weekends. After Cote found out that Thorndike was transgender, Cote demanded that Thorndike pay child support if he wanted to see the children. Thorndike made some payments but did not pay regular child support.

[¶ 7] During the last week of June 2014, while the children were visiting Thorndike for the weekend, Caden revealed to Thorndike that Cote had been hitting him, and Caden had bruises. Caden said that Lisio had said not to tell.

[¶ 8] Thorndike called his sister and organized a meeting with his parents and Lisio's parents. At the end of the weekend, the children went to stay with Lisio's parents, consistent with Caden's wishes, and a report was made to the Department of Health and Human Services. The Department substantiated the report and opened an investigation. The children remained with Lisio's parents until the end of 2014.

[¶ 9] Lisio was very angry with Thorndike for his role in reporting the abuse instead of talking to her about it. Lisio refused to allow any contact, even by phone, between Thorndike and the children after June 2014, taking the position that Thorndike had no rights. Thorndike was able to get some clothes to the children through Lisio's mother, but that was the full extent of his contact with the children until the court entered a judgment requiring contact in 2016.

[¶ 10] On September 17, 2014, Thorndike filed a complaint for a determination of paternity and parental rights and responsibilities. Lisio opposed the complaint, arguing that Thorndike had no parental rights. The court (*Mathews, M.*) entered a case management order in November 2014 directing that a de facto parentage action complying with the requirements of <u>Pitts, 2014 ME 59, ¶ 35, 90 A.3d 1169</u>, must be filed and the complaint served on Caden's biological father. In January 2015, Thorndike moved to amend his complaint to allege de facto parenthood and submitted an affidavit. See id.

[¶ 11] The next month, the court (*Sparaco, J.*) entered an order finding that Caden's biological father had not yet been served and directing the biological parents to submit affidavits within twenty days after the biological father's service. Due to issues of service on Caden's biological father, the court proceeded to address Thorndike's standing in October 2015 without service having been completed. *See id.* The court found that Thorndike had made a prima facie showing of de facto parenthood and therefore had standing. *See id.*

[¶ 12] Mediation was scheduled, and Caden's biological father was served in Arkansas, where he is incarcerated. Caden's biological father filed a letter with the court in January 2016 opposing Thorndike's claim of de facto parenthood.

[¶ 13] After mediation, issues of de facto parenthood and the parties' parental rights and responsibilities remained in dispute. The court (*Raimondi, J.*) held an evidentiary hearing on March 10, 2016. The court heard testimony from Thorndike and his sister, and from Lisio and Cote. The court found, by clear and convincing evidence, that Thorndike was a de facto parent. *See id.* ¶ 36. The court entered a parental rights and responsibilities order that provided for the children's primary residence to be with Lisio, for the parties to share parental rights and responsibilities, for each party to refrain from doing anything to estrange the children from the other party, and for the children to have contact with Thorndike on a gradually increasing schedule that would ultimately place the children in his care every other weekend and one evening every other week. *See id.* ¶ 37.

[¶ 14] On April 20, 2016, Thorndike filed a motion to correct the findings of fact with respect to the court's reference to a witness as Lisio's sister when she is actually Thorndike's sister. <u>M.R. Civ. P. 52(b), 60(a)</u>. On the same day, Lisio filed her timely notice of appeal.

[¶ 15] After briefs had been filed in this appeal, we directed the court to act on Thorndike's motion to correct. The court granted the motion and corrected the judgment to properly identify the testifying witness as Thorndike's sister. Although the parties were afforded the opportunity to request additional briefing after the ruling on the motion to correct, neither party made such a request. The judgment remained otherwise unchanged, and we now consider Lisio's appeal.

II. DISCUSSION

[¶ 16] The process employed in this case was consistent with the procedures that we outlined in *Pitts*, and neither party argues that there was any procedural defect. Lisio argues only that the court erred in its factual findings and that there is insufficient credible evidence to support the court's determination of Thorndike's de facto parenthood. To review the court's decision, we (A) summarize the law of de facto parenthood and (B) review the court's findings in this case.

A. Law of De Facto Parenthood

[¶ 17] The Maine Parentage Act did not take effect until July 1, 2016, after the court had already held a hearing and entered its judgment in this matter. *See* P.L. 2015, ch. 296, §§ A–1, D–1 (effective July 1, 2016) (codified at 19–A M.R.S. §§ 1831–1939 (2016)). Thus, the trial court relied on the case law in effect at the time of the hearing and decision, which required a person seeking to establish de facto parenthood to show, by clear and convincing evidence, that "(1) 'he or she has undertaken a permanent, unequivocal, committed, and responsible parental role in the child's life,' and (2) 'there are exceptional circumstances sufficient to allow the court to interfere with the legal or adoptive parent's rights.' " *C.L. v. L.L.*, 2015 ME 131, ¶ 20, 125 A.3d 350 (quoting *Pitts*, 2014 ME 59, ¶ 27, 90 A.3d 1169). "We review the court's findings of fact for clear error and its conclusions of law de novo." *Kilborn*, 2016 ME 78, ¶ 16, 140 A.3d 461.

[¶ 18] To satisfy the first element for establishing de facto parenthood, a person must have "participated in the child's life as a member of the child's family. . .reside[d] with the child and, with the consent and encouragement of the legal parent, perform[ed] a share of caretaking functions." *Pitts*, 2014 ME 59, ¶ 28, 90 A.3d 1169 (quotation marks omitted). "Only by establishing that he or she provided some actual caretaking functions can a petitioner be successful." *Id.* The evidence must show "the intent of the legal parent and the putative de facto parent to co-parent, as measured before the dissolution of their relationship, or the intent of the legal parent that the non-parent act as parent in place of the legal parent." *Id.*

[¶ 19] To satisfy the second element, exceptional circumstances must be established by showing that " 'the child's life would be substantially and negatively affected if the person who has undertaken a permanent, unequivocal, committed, and responsible parental role in that child's life is removed from that role.' " *Kilborn*, 2016 ME 78, ¶ 22, 140 A.3d 461 (quoting *Pitts*, 2014 ME 59, ¶ 29, 90 A.3d 1169 (plurality opinion)).

B. Review of Court Findings

[¶ 20] Although there were a few minor errors in the court's extensive factual findings, the errors are not of the kind that could affect the outcome and are harmless. *See* M.R. Civ. P. 61. The court's error in finding that the parties' relationship began earlier than the parties testified that it did may seem significant, but the court found that Thorndike's *parental* role did not begin until August 2007 when Thorndike began to live with Lisio and Caden, and that date is not in dispute.

[¶ 21] The other findings that Lisio disputes were not clearly erroneous. Specifically, there is no evidence in the record that Caden's biological father, as Lisio now states, resided with Lisio and Caden until Caden was two years old; there is evidence that Thorndike did not move out of the home until mid-2012; the evidence shows only Lisio's engagement to Cote, not any legal commitment; and even if Lisio is correct that the children have been doing well with Lisio and Cote since the Department's involvement, the court did not err in finding that Lisio failed to acknowledge the harm done to the children by denying Thorndike contact after he acted to keep Caden safe from abuse.

[¶ 22] The court's findings of fact support its ultimate determinations that (1) Thorndike undertook "a permanent, unequivocal, committed, and responsible parental role" in the children's lives, _Pitts_, 2014 ME 59, ¶ 27, 90 A.3d 1169 (quotation marks omitted), and (2) especially given that Thorndike worked with extended family to prevent child abuse, the children's lives "would be substantially and negatively affected" if Thorndike were removed from his "permanent, unequivocal, committed, and responsible parental role," _Kilborn_, 2016 ME 78, ¶ 22, 140 A.3d 461 (quotation marks omitted).

[¶ 23] As the court found, Thorndike and Lisio raised Caden together from age three, became domestic partners, and had Arianna together as a couple. Thorndike, with Lisio's consent and encouragement, undertook "a permanent, unequivocal, committed, and responsible parental role" in the children's lives, attending to their daily needs and caring for them as a loving parent. _Pitts_, 2014 ME 59, ¶ 27, 90 A.3d 1169 (quotation marks omitted). He resided with them until 2012 and after that cared for them at visits and demonstrated a willingness to act decisively when necessary to protect the children from harm. See id. The court did not err in finding that the children's lives "would be substantially and negatively affected" if Thorndike were removed from his parental role. _Kilborn_, 2016 ME 78, ¶ 22, 140 A.3d 461 (quotation marks omitted).

[¶ 24] The court did not err in finding that both elements set forth in _Pitts_ were established by clear and convincing evidence. *See id.*; _Pitts_, 2014 ME 59, ¶¶ 27–29, 90 A.3d 1169. Accordingly, we affirm the court's finding that Thorndike is the de facto parent of Caden and Arianna.

The entry is:

Judgment affirmed.

Points for Discussion

a. De Facto Parenthood

Courts in many states extend standing in parental responsibility cases to a parent's spouse or cohabiting partner based on a finding that the partner stands in loco parentis or is a de facto or equitable parent. See, e.g., V.C. v. M.J.B., 748 A.2d 539 (N.J. 2000); Custody of B.M.H., 315 P.3d 470 (Wash. 2013); In re H.S.H.-K., 533 N.W.2d 419 (Wis. 1995). In in some states, statutes define the basis for this type of third-party standing. See, e.g., Ariz. Rev. Stat. § 25–409 (2018); Haw. Rev. Stat. § 571–46(a)(2) (2018).

In other states, courts have rejected these approaches. See, e.g., Parentage of Scarlett Z-D., 28 N.E.3d 776 (Ill. 2015); Petition of Ash, 507 N.W.2d 400 (Iowa 1993); Jones v. Barlow, 154 P.3d 808 (Utah 2007); Titchenal v. Dexter, 693 A.2d 682 (Vt. 1997). What are the policy arguments against allowing a person who is not a legal parent to seek decision-making rights or parenting time?

Several states that formerly rejected the de facto parent approach have reconsidered the question and begun to embrace it, recognizing that it is particularly important for same-sex couples, who may have agreed to share parenting before they were legally permitted to marry. See, e.g., Conover v. Conover, 146 A.3d 433 (Md. 2016); Brooke S.B. v. Elizabeth A.C.C., 61 N.E.3d 89 (N.Y. 2016). See generally Courtney G. Joslin et al., *Lesbian, Gay, Bisexual and Transgender Family Law* ch. 7 (2017–18 ed.)

Make the Connection

As discussed in Chapter 2, a parent's spouse or cohabitant may be a presumed parent of a child born during their relationship.

As noted in the opinion in *Thorndike*, Maine codified the de facto parent rule in its 2016 Parentage Act. See Me. Rev. Stat. tit. 19, § 1891 (2018); see also Del Code Ann., tit. 13, §8–201(c) (2018); and Uniform Parentage Act (2017) § 609. Under the UPA and the Maine and Delaware statutes, an individual who is adjudicated to be a de facto parent becomes the child's legal legal parent for all purposes.

The ALI Principles recognize both a "parent by estoppel" and a "de facto parent," and extend a right to notice and an opportunity to participate to individuals in these two categories. Section 2.18 gives preference to legal parents over de facto parents in the allocation of custodial responsibility, however, and precludes an allocation of responsibility to other adults over the parent's objections except in limited circumstances. See A.H. v. M.P., 857 N.E.2d 1061 (Mass. 2006) (discussing the ALI approach).

b. What About *Troxel*?

Can the de facto parent doctrine be reconciled with the constitutional protection for parental rights protected by Troxel v. Granville, 530 U.S. 57 (2000)? How does the test described in *Thorndike* at ¶ 17, adopted by the Maine Supreme Court in Pitts v. Moore, 90 A.3d 1169 (2014), satisfy the requirements of *Troxel*? See generally Conover v. Conover, 146 A.3d 433, 443–446 (Md. 2016).

Cases extending rights to de facto parents emphasize that this status can only be created with the consent of a legal parent, who allowed or encouraged the child to form a parent-like relationship with the third party. See, e.g., *Conover*, 146 A.3d at 447. Taking the consent principle a step further, some state courts have concluded that express agreements in which a parent extends custody rights to a third party may be enforced, if consistent with the child's best interests. See, e.g., Frazer v. Goudschaal, 295 P.3d 542 (Kan. 2013), and In re Bonfield, 780 N.E.2d 241 (Ohio 2002).

c. More than Two Parents?

What about the biological father of the older child in the *Thorndike* case? Can a child with two legal parents also have a de facto parent? See In re Parentage of M.F., 228 P.3d 1270 (Wash. 2010), which held that a stepfather could not seek de facto parent status when the child's mother and father were both exercising parental responsibility.

Note, however, that the UPA allows a court to adjudicate a child to have more than two legal parents, "if the court finds that failure to recognize more than two parents would be detrimental to the child." UPA (2017) § 613(c) (Alternative B). See also Me. Rev. Stat. tit. 19–a, § 1853(2) (2018).

d. Stepparent Custody Orders

Courts have also relied on the in loco parentis approach in disputes between a parent and a person who took on a parental role while married to the child's other parent. See, e.g., Paquette v. Paquette, 499 A.2d 23 (Vt. 1985), which held that:

> "if a stepparent stands in loco parentis to a child of the marital household, custody of that child may be awarded to the stepparent if it is shown by clear and convincing evidence that the natural parent is unfit or that extraordinary circumstances exist to warrant such a custodial order, and that it is in the best interests of the child for custody to be awarded to the stepparent."

See also Young v. Young, 845 A.2d 1144 (Me.2004); Edwards v. Edwards, 777 N.W.2d 606 (N.D. 2010). See generally Margaret M Mahoney, Stepfamilies and the Law (1994); Susan L. Pollet, *Still a Patchwork Quilt: A Nationwide Survey of State Laws Regarding Stepparent Rights and Obligations*, 48 Fam. Ct. Rev. 528 (2010).

As a substantive matter, despite the traditional presumption in favor of the legal or biological parent, courts in some cases have applied a best interests standard in deciding custody disputes between a child's legal parent and stepparent, particularly after the death of the child's custodial parent. See, e.g., Charles v. Stehlik, 744 A.2d 1255 (Pa. 2000); cf. Tailor v. Becker, 708 A.2d 626 (Del.1998) (applying Delaware statute giving stepparents the right to seek custody of a child on the death of the custodial natural parent). Ordinarily, on the death of a child's custodial parent, the right to custody reverts to the child's surviving noncustodial parent, and a stepparent or another relative who sought custody would have to show that the legal parent was unfit or had abandoned the child. See, e.g. Custody of N.A.K., 649 N.W.2d 166 (Minn.2002); Carr v. Prader, 725 A.2d 291 (R.I.1999); Florio v. Clark, 674 S.E.2d 845 (Va. 2009). See also Sacha M. Coupet, *"Ain't I a Parent?": The Exclusion of Kinship Caregivers from the Debate Over Expansions of Parenthood*, 34 N.Y.U. Rev. L. & Soc. Change 595 (2010).

e. Support Obligations of De Facto, Equitable and Stepparents

Should nonparents who seek custody or visitation have a responsibility to assist with the child's financial support? For de facto parents, the obligation should be clear. See, e.g., Pitts v. Moore, 90 A.3d 1169, 1183 (Me. 2014) ("We cannot emphasize enough that parenthood is forever, whether the relationship is biological, adoptive, or de facto. The role of a de facto parent is no less permanent than that of any other parent. . . . The obligation of a de facto parent to pay child support, too, remains in force until modified by the court, or the child turns eighteen or graduates from secondary school, or marries, or joins the armed services.") See also L.S.K. v. H.A.N., 813 A.2d 872 (Pa. Super. Ct. 2002) (partner who sought in loco parentis status estopped from claiming that she had no duty of support). Cf. T.F. v. B.L., 813 N.E.2d 1244 (Mass. 2004) (declining to enforce promise to pay child support in co-parenting agreement).

For a third party without legal parental status, support obligations are not typical. State statutes and common law rules may impose a support duty on stepparents with respect to children living in the same household, but this obligation typically ends when they no longer live together. See, e.g., Harmon v. Department of Social and Health Services, 951 P.2d 770 (Wash. 1998); see generally David B. *Sweet, Annotation: Stepparent's Postdivorce Duty to Support Stepchild*, 44 A.L.R. 4th 520 (1986).

f. Grandparent Visitation and Custody

When a grandparent (or other relative or friend) provides substantial parental care for a child, this may be sufficient to meet the test of de facto parenthood, but numerous cases have set a fairly high threshold in this context. See, e.g., Chapman

v. Hopkins, 404 P.3d 638 (Ariz. Ct. App. 2017); Davis v. McGuire, 186 A.3d 837 (Me. 2018); Suarez v. Williams, 44 N.E.3d 915 (N.Y. 2015). The test for standing under grandparent visitation statutes is typically somewhat easier to establish. As the Supreme Court noted in *Troxel,* every state has some form of grandparent visitation statute. Courts considered the validity of these statutes after *Troxel,* with a variety of results. Some state courts concluded that their grandparent visitation statutes sufficiently addressed the constitutional concerns outlined in *Troxel.* See, e.g., Marriage of Harris, 96 P.3d 141 (Cal. 2004); Rideout v. Riendeau, 761 A.2d 291 (Me.2000). Other courts interpreted or reinterpreted their statutes to cure potential constitutional defects. See Blixt v. Blixt, 774 N.E.2d 1052 (Mass. 2002); Matter of E.S., 863 N.E.2d 100 (N.Y. 2007); Hiller v. Fausey, 904 A.2d 875 (Pa. 2006) (reviewing cases, and concluding that requirements of statute "combined with the presumption that parents act in a child's best interest" were sufficient protection for parents' constitutional rights). Other courts have concluded that their statutes were invalid either facially, see, e.g., Wickham v. Byrne, 769 N.E.2d 1 (Ill. 2002); DeRose v. DeRose, 666 N.W.2d 636 (Mich. 2003); or as applied, see, e.g., Brice v. Brice, 754 A.2d 1132 (Md. Ct.Spec.App.2000).

In light of the *Troxel* opinion, reprinted in Chapter 4, what elements must be included in a statute of this type to satisfy the constitutional concerns articulated by the Supreme Court?

g. Conflict of Laws

Variations between the laws of different states regarding de facto parent status or grandparent visitation rights give rise to conflict of laws questions. These cases fall generally within the scope of the Uniform Child Custody Jurisdiction and Enforcement Act (UCCJEA) and the Parental Kidnapping Prevention Act (PKPA), discussed earlier in this chapter, as well as the Full Faith and Credit Clause of the U.S. Constitution. For example, in S.D. v. K.H., 98 N.E.3d 375 (Ohio Ct. App. 2018), an Ohio court with exclusive, continuing jurisdiction under the UCCJEA declined to recognize a California order that established a third person as another parent of the child. See also LeDoux-Nottingham v. Downs, 210 So.3d 1217 (Fla. 2017), in which a Florida court recognized and enforced a Colorado order awarding grandparent visitation, despite the fact that the same order could not have been entered in Florida.

Problem 7-41

Dawn and her husband Michael had been trying unsuccessfully to conceive a child for several years when her friend Audria moved into their home. The three of them considered themselves a family, and began to engage in intimate relations together. After Audria became pregnant, Dawn went with Audria to her medical appointments, and used her medical insurance to cover Audria's pregnancy and delivery. Dawn shared caretaking duties for the child, who is almost two years old.

When her relationship with Michael deteriorated several months ago, Dawn and Audria moved out with the child. Dawn plans to file for divorce, and would like to have the court approve a "tricustody" arrangement, in which she shares parental responsibilities with Audria and Michael. What advice would you give her? (See Dawn M. v. Michael M., 47 N.Y.S.3d 898 (Sup. Ct. 2017).)

Problem 7-42

Bob and Betty have two young children, who have spent a great deal of time with Bob's parents. Bob and Betty have a difficult relationship with Bob's parents, who frequently criticize Betty and have urged Bob, in front of the children, to divorce her. They disagree often about how the children are disciplined and their activities and bedtime schedules. After Bob's father fired Bob from his job in the family business, Bob and Betty cut off all contact with his parents, and no longer allow them to speak with or give gifts to the children. Under *Troxel* and the third-party standing rules in your state, can Bob's parents file an action seeking visitation with the children two weekends every month? If so, should the court grant the visitation that Bob's parents request? (See Hawk v. Hawk, 855 S.W.2d 573 (Tenn.1993).)

---

3. Modification, Relocation and Child Abduction

Parental responsibility orders are modifiable, either pursuant to statute or at common law. If a party seeks modification in the state that entered the initial decree, the proceeding is considered a continuation of the original case. As discussed earlier in this chapter, jurisdiction to modify a custody determination is controlled initially by UCCJEA § 202, which provides for exclusive continuing jurisdiction in the original forum state as long as the child has a significant connection to the state and substantial evidence is available there concerning the child's care, protection, training and personal relationships. If modification is sought in a different state, the jurisdictional requirements of UCCJEA § 203 must be satisfied.

A party seeking modification of custody or visitation has the burden of proof, and typically will be required to show that circumstances have changed or additional facts have come to light. See, e.g., Shoff v. Shoff, 534 N.E.2d 462 (Ill. App. Ct. 1989); Betterton v. Betterton, 752 S.W.2d 417 (Mo. Ct. App.1988). Some statutes impose a higher threshold; under UMDA§ 409, a motion to modify a custody decree cannot be made within two years unless there is reason to believe the child's present environment may seriously endanger the child, and the court must find both a change in circumstances and also either that the child's custodian has agreed to the change, or that the child has already been integrated into the petitioner's family, or that the present environment seriously endangers the child's "physical, mental, moral or emotional health."

When one parent has sole or primary physical custody or placement of a child, courts modify parenting time orders to increase the other parent's time with the child whenever it serves the child's best interests. See, e.g., Turley v. Turley, 5 S.W.3d 162, (Mo.1999); Braatz v. Braatz, 706 N.E.2d 1218 (Ohio 1999). Under UMDA § 407(b), a court may not restrict visitation "unless it finds that the visitation would endanger seriously the child's physical, mental, moral or emotional health." A number of states make it easier to modify shared parenting orders, particularly when ongoing parental conflict has made shared responsibility unworkable. See, e.g., In re Marriage of Dullard, 531 N.E.2d 854 (Ill. App. Ct. 1988); McCauley v. Schenkel, 977 S.W.2d 45 (Mo.Ct.App.1998); Moody v. Moody, 715 P.2d 507 (Utah 1985). Courts in many states have held that custody orders that shift custody automatically at some point in the future are improper. See Knutsen v. Cegalis, 989 A.2d 1010 (Vt. 2009) (collecting cases)

Numerous recent decisions have addressed custody modification issues in the context of parents deployed in military service. See, e.g., Marriage of Grantham, 698 N.W.2d 140 (Iowa 2005); Fischer v. Fischer, 157 P.3d 682 (Mont. 2007); Faucett v. Vasquez, 984 A.2d 460 (N.J. Super. Ct. App. Div. 2009). The Uniform Deployed Parents Custody and Visitation Act 9 U.L.A. (Part IB) (Supp. 2018),, approved by the Uniform Law Commission in 2012, is intended to promote a fair balance of the interests of a parent who is deployed in the armed services and the other parent and the best interests of the children involved.

Some of the most challenging modification questions arise when one parent seeks to move away with the couple's children. Geographic distance can make shared parenting difficult or impossible. Depending on the age of the children, the distances involved, and the resources available to the parents, relocation presents a risk that the child's relationship with the left-behind parent may be seriously diminished. Courts and legislatures have struggled to develop standards that balance the different interests in these cases, experimenting with presumptions, shifting burdens of proof, and long lists of factors for courts to consider.

Arthur v. Arthur

54 So.3d 454 (Fla. 2010)

QUINCE, C.J.

Shawn M. Arthur seeks review of the decision of the Second District Court of Appeal in *Arthur v. Arthur*, 987 So.2d 212 (Fla. 2d DCA 2008), on the ground that it expressly and directly conflicts with three decisions of the First District Court of Appeal, *Sylvester v. Sylvester*, 992 So.2d 296 (Fla. 1st DCA 2008); *Janousek v. Janousek*, 616 So.2d 131 (Fla. 1st DCA 1993); and *Martinez v. Martinez*, 573 So.2d 37 (Fla. 1st DCA 1990). We have jurisdiction. Based on our reasoning below, we quash the Second District's decision in *Arthur* to the extent it is inconsistent with this opinion, and approve the First District's decisions in *Sylvester, Janousek*, and *Martinez* to the extent that they are consistent with our analysis and holding.

FACTS AND PROCEDURAL BACKGROUND

In a dissolution of marriage action, the trial court granted shared parental responsibility, designating Josette A. Arthur (the Wife) as the primary residential parent. Shawn M. Arthur (the Husband) was granted reasonable visitation of the child. *See Arthur v. Arthur*, 987 So.2d 212, 213 (Fla. 2d DCA 2008). Moreover, and most pertinent to our decision in this case, the trial court authorized the Wife to permanently relocate with the parties' minor child to the state of Michigan after the child reached the age of three. At the time of trial, the minor child was sixteen months old. In granting the Wife's relocation request, the trial court reasoned that the relocation was proper because the Wife proposed to move to the area where she grew up and had family, and the area was close to the Husband's extended family. Regarding its reasons for delaying the relocation until the child reached the age of three, the trial court explained:

> [T]he Court is cognizant that children between infancy and approximately 3 years of age need more frequent contact with both parents in order to properly bond with the parents. But for the Court's concern for the Husband's ability to bond with his son, the Wife's relocation would have been granted without further delay.

On appeal, the Husband argued that the trial court erred by determining that the Wife could relocate with the child approximately twenty months after the final hearing. More specifically, the Husband asserted that the trial court's ruling was a prospective determination of the child's best interest and that the court lacked authority to make such a determination. * * * The Second District Court of Appeal disagreed and held that the trial court did not exceed its authority in granting the relocation request upon the child reaching the age of three. The district court rejected the Husband's claim that the trial court found relocation not to be in the best interest of the child as of the day of the trial. Instead, the Second

District concluded that the trial court's detailed findings in the final judgment supported the Wife's relocation request. * * *

The Husband petitioned this Court for discretionary review of the Second District's decision in *Arthur.* His petition was based on express and direct conflict with the First District's decisions in *Sylvester, Janousek,* and *Martinez.* We granted review to resolve this conflict.

ANALYSIS

Section 61.13001, Florida Statutes (2006), titled "Parental relocation with a child," establishes the procedures involved in the relocation of a child, whether relocation is sought after agreement between the parties or alternatively contested by one party. In the case of a contested relocation, the Legislature has stated that "[n]o presumption shall arise in favor of or against a request to relocate with the child when a primary residential parent seeks to move the child and the move will materially affect the current schedule of contact, access, and time-sharing with the nonrelocating parent or other person." § 61.13001(7), Fla. Stat. (2006). Instead, section 61.13001(8) states:

> The parent or other person wishing to relocate has the burden of proof if an objection is filed and must then initiate a proceeding seeking court permission for relocation. The initial burden is on the parent or person wishing to relocate to prove by a preponderance of the evidence that relocation is in the best interest of the child. If that burden of proof is met, the burden shifts to the nonrelocating parent or other person to show by a preponderance of the evidence that the proposed relocation is not in the best interest of the child.

In addition to the burden that the parties must meet, the statute outlines several factors a trial court must consider before reaching a decision on a parent's request for permanent relocation. Section 61.13001(7) provides that the court shall evaluate:

> (a) The nature, quality, extent of involvement, and duration of the child's relationship with the parent proposing to relocate with the child and with the nonrelocating parent, other persons, siblings, half-siblings, and other significant persons in the child's life.
>
> (b) The age and developmental stage of the child, the needs of the child, and the likely impact the relocation will have on the child's physical, educational, and emotional development, taking into consideration any special needs of the child.
>
> (c) The feasibility of preserving the relationship between the nonrelocating parent or other person and the child through substitute arrangements that take into consideration the logistics of contact, access, visitation, and time-sharing, as well as the financial circumstances of the parties; whether those factors are sufficient to foster a continuing mean-

ingful relationship between the child and the nonrelocating parent or other person; and the likelihood of compliance with the substitute arrangements by the relocating parent once he or she is out of the jurisdiction of the court.

(d) The child's preference, taking into consideration the age and maturity of the child.

(e) Whether the relocation will enhance the general quality of life for both the parent seeking the relocation and the child, including, but not limited to, financial or emotional benefits or educational opportunities.

(f) The reasons of each parent or other person for seeking or opposing the relocation.

(g) The current employment and economic circumstances of each parent or other person and whether or not the proposed relocation is necessary to improve the economic circumstances of the parent or other person seeking relocation of the child.

(h) That the relocation is sought in good faith and the extent to which the objecting parent has fulfilled his or her financial obligations to the parent or other person seeking relocation, including child support, spousal support, and marital property and marital debt obligations.

(i) The career and other opportunities available to the objecting parent or objecting other person if the relocation occurs.

(j) A history of substance abuse or domestic violence as defined in s. 741.28 or which meets the criteria of s. 39.806(1)(d) by either parent, including a consideration of the severity of such conduct and the failure or success of any attempts at rehabilitation.

(k) Any other factor affecting the best interest of the child or as set forth in s. 61.13.

* * *

More recently, the First District decided *Sylvester,* a case with facts similar to those presented in the instant case. In *Sylvester,* the trial court granted the wife's relocation request but delayed relocation until the child reached five years of age and/or started kindergarten, finding that it was not in the best interest of the child to be immediately separated from the husband. At the time of the hearing the child was three years old. The trial court determined that current relocation was not in the best interest of the child because it believed that the child needed more time to acclimate to the marital dissolution. Rather, the court found that the child would be emotionally and psychologically capable of handling a deferred relocation. On appeal, the First District reversed the trial court's order, holding that the trial court erred in permitting relocation two years from the date of the hearing. Noting its decision in *Janousek,* the district court found that "the proper cause of action is to determine whether relocation is presently appropriate and consider future relocation based on the circumstances existing at that time." The district court recognized its disagreement with the Second District's decision in *Arthur,* to the extent that *Arthur* allowed a trial court "to look into its crystal ball and determine whether relocation would be in the best interest in the future." The court further noted that "[i]t is difficult enough to determine the present emotional and psychological needs of a child; it is impossible to speculate what those needs will be in two years."

Relying on the above case law, the Husband alleges two errors with the trial court's judgment. First, he argues that because there was no evidence presented to the trial court as to the child's best interests twenty months after the final hearing, the trial court acted beyond its authority in making a prospective finding of the minor child's best interests. In support of this argument, he claims that the trial court should have determined the child's best interests as of the time of the final hearing, not the child's best interests twenty months later. He alleges that the trial court's conclusion was inconsistent with its determination that such relocation could not occur until twenty months after the final hearing and its findings concerning the impact of relocation on the child's ability to bond with the Husband. Second, the Husband asserts that the trial court's grant of relocation based upon a prospective finding of best interests impermissibly shifts the burden of proof to him in any attempt to readdress the best interest issue before the prospective date of relocation.

Upon review of the Husband's arguments and the well-reasoned analyses in the First District's opinions in *Martinez, Janousek*, and *Sylvester,* we conclude that a best interests determination in petitions for relocation must be made at the time of the final hearing and must be supported by competent, substantial evidence. In this case, the trial court authorized the relocation based in part on its conclusion that relocation would be in the best interests of the child twenty months from the date of the hearing. Such a "prospective-based" analysis is unsound. Indeed, a trial court is not equipped with a "crystal ball" that enables it to prophetically determine whether future relocation is in the best interests of a child. Any one of the various factors outlined in section 61.13001(7) that the trial court is required to consider, such as the financial stability of a parent or the suitability of the new location for the child, could change within the extended time period given by the court before relocation. Because trial courts are unable to predict whether a change in any of the statutory factors will occur, the proper review of a petition for relocation entails a best interests determination *at the time of the final hearing,* i.e. a "present-based" analysis.

Although the trial court in this case did not utilize this "present-based" analysis, we conclude that if it had done so, the court would have denied the relocation request. Our reading of the order indicates that the court did not agree that a relocation at the time of the hearing was in the best interests of the child. We find the most telling phrase of the order to be the court's statement that "[b]ut for the Court's concern for the Husband's ability to bond with his son, the Wife's relocation would have been granted without further delay." In its consideration of subsection (b) of section 61.13001(7), the court found that "[r]equiring the Wife to wait until the child turns three (3) years old allows the Husband and child the time necessary to form a lasting bond with each other." Thus, although the court may have favored relocation once the child reached three years of age, it is clear that the court found that relocation was not in the best interests of the child at the time of the hearing. Therefore, the petition for relocation should have been denied.

Based on our determination that the trial court's prospective best interest determination was erroneous, we conclude that it is unnecessary to address the Husband's claim of trial court error. Thus, we make no decision as to whether trial court's grant of relocation in this case improperly shifted the burden of proof to the Husband in a future attempt to prevent relocation.

CONCLUSION

Based on the above analysis, we quash the Second District's decision in *Arthur* to the extent it is inconsistent with this opinion, and approve the decisions of the First District in *Martinez, Janousek,* and *Sylvester* to the extent they are consistent with the foregoing opinion. We vacate the provision in the final judgment of dissolution permitting the Wife to relocate after twenty months and remand this case to the Second District with directions to remand to the trial court to deny the Wife's request for relocation.

* * *

It is so ordered.

Points for Discussion

a. Presumptions and Burdens of Proof

The Florida statute construed in *Arthur* expressly rejects presumptions for or against relocation, and imposes an initial burden of proof on the party seeking to relocate to show that the move is in the best interests of the child. What kinds of evidence might a parent like Josette Arthur present to meet this burden? After this showing is made, the Florida statute shifts the burden to the party opposing relocation, to show that a move would not be in the best interest of the child. What evidence would you expect a parent in Shawn Arthur's situation to present?

Historically, some courts have strongly disfavored removal, placing a heavy burden of proof on the custodial parent seeking to relocate with the child. Courts in both New York and California moved in the mid-1990s to make it easier for a parent with primary custody to relocate. See Tropea v. Tropea, 665 N.E.2d 145 (N.Y. 1996); and In re Marriage of Burgess, 913 P.2d 473 (Cal. 1996). Washington has a rebuttable presumption allowing a primary custodial parent to relocate with the child. See <u>Wash. Rev. Code § 26.09.520 (2018)</u>, applied in <u>Marriage of Horner, 93 P.3d 124 (Wash. 2004)</u>. After the Colorado Supreme Court established a presumption in favor of relocation, however, the state legislature responded with a statute eliminating the presumption. See <u>Colo. Rev. Stat. § 14–10–129 (2018)</u>, construed in <u>Marriage of Ciesluk, 113 P.3d 135 (Colo. 2005)</u>. The Alabama statute includes a presumption that relocation is not in the best interest of a child. See <u>Ala. Code §§ 30–3–160 to 30–3–169.10. (2018)</u> ("Alabama Parent-Child Relationship Protection Act.")

The <u>Proposed Model Relocation Act (1997)</u>, drafted by the American Academy of Matrimonial Lawyers (AAML), includes three alternative approaches to assigning the burden of proof in these cases, reflecting the inability of the drafters to reach a consensus and leaving this issue to state legislatures to decide. What are the policy arguments for a presumption in favor of granting relocation requests? What are the policy arguments for a presumption against relocation? Is the burden shifting approach, as illustrated by the Florida statute, a better approach? Should the court's approach be any different if the question arises at the time of an initial custody determination, as in *Arthur*, or if it comes up on a motion to modify sometime after the initial orders are entered?

Relocation Restrictions

In some jurisdictions, a child's custodial parent has the right to determine the child's place of residence. To protect against the risk that the parent will simply move away with the child, separation agreements and court orders may expressly prohibit the primary parent from relocating outside the state (or beyond a certain distance within the state) without consent of the other parent or a court order.

b. Notice

The Florida relocation statute applied in *Arthur* gives a parent seeking to relocate with a child two alternatives. Unless the parent has entered into a signed agreement with "every other person entitled to access or time-sharing with the child," he or she must file a petition to relocate, have it served, and obtain the court's permission to relocate. See <u>Fla. Stat. § 61.13001 (2), (3) (2018)</u>. Similarly, Pennsylvania's relocation statute requires notice of a proposed relocation, and prohibits relocation unless "every individual who has custody rights" consents to relocation or does not object after notice, or the court approves the proposed relocation after a hearing. See <u>23 Pa. Cons. Stat. Ann. § 5337 (2018)</u>.

c. Relocation Factors

Consider the different factors included in the Florida statute cited in *Arthur*. Which of these factors seem to favor relocation on the facts of the case? Which factors suggest that relocation would not be in the child's best interests? How would these factors be different in a case involving a child who was three years old rather than sixteen months? For a more extensive list of factors drawn from the case law in this area, see W. Dennis Duggan, *Rock-Paper-Scissors: Playing the Odds With the Law of Child Relocation*, 45 Fam. Ct. Rev. 193, 209–10 (2007). See generally Linda D. Elrod, *National and International Momentum Builds for More Child Focus in Relocation Disputes*, 44 Fam. L.Q. 341 (2010).

d. Relocation Research

The academic literature on relocation is sharply polarized between writers who emphasize the importance of protecting the child's relationship with a primary caretaker, and writers who stress the importance of frequent and continuing contact with both parents. For an attempt to evaluate these studies and the growing body of empirical research on the effects of relocation on children, see Nicola Taylor & Marilyn Freeman, *International Research Evidence on Relocation: Past, Present, and Future*, 44 Fam. L.Q. 317 (2010). Taylor and Freeman suggest that relocation research needs to take better account of other factors that are often present in the divorce context, such as ongoing interparental conflict and the financial and other burdens of significant travel between the parents' homes. See also Patrick Parkinson, Judy Cashmore & Judi Single, *The Need for Reality Testing in Relocation Cases*, 44 Fam. L.Q. 1 (2010).

Global View: International Relocation

International moves raise the same types of problems as other relocation cases, and courts generally apply the same legal standards to requests for international relocation. See, e.g., In re Marriage of Condon, 73 Cal.Rptr.2d 33 (Ct. App. 1998) (Australia); Hayes v. Gallacher, 972 P.2d 1138 (Nev. 1999) (Japan); Lenz v. Lenz, 79 S.W.3d 10 (Tex. 2002) (Germany). However, the burden and expense of travel between the parents' homes is often much greater in these cases, cultural and language barriers may limit the child's ability to remain closely connected with parents in two different worlds, and jurisdiction and conflict of laws questions may encourage forum shopping tactics that do not serve the child's best interests.

> If a parent relocates to or from another country with a child, without court permission or the other parent's consent, there may be further issues under the Hague Child Abduction Convention, discussed below. At a meeting in 2010, an international group of judges and other experts agreed to a set of guidelines to address relocation disputes known as the Washington Declaration on International Family Relocation.

e. Parent's Right to Travel?

If the father in *Arthur* had decided to relocate away from the child, could the court have ordered him to remain in the area for several years until he had bonded with the child? If not, why not? See Allbright v. Allbright, 215 P.3d 472 (Idaho 2009) (finding an abuse of discretion when the trial court ordered parent to remain in the state). Cf. Carlton v. Carlton, 873 S.W.2d 801 (Ark. 1994). See also D'Onofrio v. D'Onofrio, 365 A.2d 27 (N.J. Super. Ct. Ch.Div.) aff'd 365 A.2d 716 (N.J. Super. Ct. App.Div.1976), which noted that the noncustodial parent is free to move away from the children in order to seek out a better or different life-style, and suggested that the custodial parent should have the same opportunity.

If the mother had sought permission to relocate in order to take a new job, or to follow a new spouse, could the court have ordered her not to move away? Numerous cases have held that courts cannot order the parents to live in a particular location, especially when a parent is already living in a different place. See, e.g., Spahmer v. Gullette, 113 P.3d 158 (Colo. 2005); Smith v. McDonald, 941 N.E.2d 1 (Mass. 2010); Custody of D.M.G., 951 P.2d 1377 (Mont. 1998); Lane v. Schenck, 614 A.2d 786 (Vt. 1992).

Problem 7-43

When Kimberly and Roger divorced, the court awarded them joint legal custody, and awarded Kimberly primary physical custody, provided that she continue to live in one of two counties near Roger's residence. The order stated that if she elected to move away, primary physical care of the children would shift automatically to Roger. Kimberly would like to have the freedom to relocate, and is considering an appeal. What arguments could she make to have the order set aside? (See Marriage of Seitzinger, 775 N.E.2d 282 (Ill. App. Ct. 2002); see also Rego v. Rego, 259 P.3d 447 (Alaska 2011).)

Problem 7-44

Christopher and Deborah were married in Australia and their two children were born there. The family moved to Los Angeles, but their marriage deteriorated after several years. Deborah took the children and flew to Australia, without informing Christopher first, and then refused to tell him where the children were living. Christopher filed a divorce action in California and a proceeding under the Hague Child Abduction Convention in Australia, and the Australian Family Court ordered the children returned to the United States.

In California, Deborah has requested sole legal custody and permission to return to Australia with the children, who are 5 and 7. She argues that the children's primary emotional attachment is to her, that that she does not have a settled base in California and would be better able to support herself financially in Australia, and that all her extended family lives there. Deborah proposes that the children would spend four school vacation periods, totaling about 13 weeks a year, with their father in California. Christopher opposes the move. How should the court approach this case? (See In re Marriage of Condon, 73 Cal.Rptr.2d 33 (Ct. App. 1998).)

State v. Vakilzaden

742 A.2d 767 (Conn. 1999)

BERDON, J.

On December 11, 1997, the defendant, Anthony Vakilzaden, was charged with one count of custodial interference in the first degree in violation of General Statutes § 53a–97 (a)(2) and one count of conspiracy to commit custodial interference in the first degree in violation of General Statutes §§ 53a–48 and 53a–97 (a)(2). The charges arose from a criminal complaint that the defendant aided and abetted his nephew, Orang Fabriz, in interfering with the custodial rights of Lila Mirjavadi, the wife of Fabriz, with respect to their child, Saba Fabriz. The defendant moved to dismiss the charges filed against him based on the theory that Fabriz, as the child's father, was a joint custodian of Saba. The trial court granted the defendant's motion to dismiss, relying on this court's decision in Marshak v. Marshak, 226 Conn. 652, 628 A.2d 964 (1993). The trial court concluded that the state had not demonstrated that Mirjavadi was the sole custodian of the child at the time of the alleged interference.

* * * The pivotal issue in this appeal is whether this court should reconsider *Marshak.*

In *Marshak*, the plaintiff wife brought a civil action seeking damages against several defendants for conspiracy to interfere with her custodial rights to her children arising from the defendants' actions in helping her husband remove the children from her custody. Her husband subsequently fled the country with the children. On the basis of authority from other jurisdictions and § 700 of the Restatement (Second) of Torts, the trial court found three of the four defendants liable to the plaintiff for having conspired with her husband and for having aided and abetted him to commit the tort of child abduction, and awarded monetary damages to the plaintiff. On appeal, we reversed the trial court's judgment, concluding that the defendant was not liable to the plaintiff because the plaintiff's husband had joint legal custody of the children at the time of the alleged acts in question. Joint custody was based wholly on the fact that the parties were still married at the time of the abduction,[5] and that neither party had filed for dissolution of the marriage, nor had they sought any type of court intervention affecting custody. In *Marshak*, we stated that "a factual predicate for any tort related to child abduction. . .is the unlawful custody of a child." Thus, having determined that where joint custody was inferred from their marital status, we reversed the judgment in favor of the plaintiff as there could be no unlawful custody at the time of the defendant's actions.

Marshak may be distinguishable from the present case on the ground that a court order permitting only limited, supervised visitation between a father and a child satisfies the sole custody requirement of *Marshak*. If a parent has sole custody, a person in the position of the defendant, who allegedly assisted the father in the abduction of the child, properly may be charged with the crime of custodial interference.

Although we could reinstate the information against the defendant on that basis, we do not stop there. We conclude that *Marshak* should be overruled, and that the dismissal of the criminal information in the present case was improper on that ground. We therefore reverse the trial court's judgment dismissing the information and remand the case for further proceedings according to law.

* * *

Mirjavadi and Fabriz, both Iranian citizens, were married in their homeland in 1990. They have one daughter, Saba. In September, 1995, when Saba was one and one-half years old, the family traveled together to the United States on a tem-

---

[5] General Statutes § 45a–606 provides in relevant part: "The father and mother of every minor child are joint guardians of the person of the minor, and the powers, rights and duties of the father and the mother in regard to the minor shall be equal. . . ."

porary visa. Mirjavadi and Fabriz separated approximately one month after their arrival in the United States. Mirjavadi retained physical custody of their daughter and moved into her brother's home in Stamford. Fabriz moved in with his uncle, the defendant, who, at the time in question, was a resident of New Jersey.

Mirjavadi applied for political asylum and, in January, 1996, brought an action for the dissolution of her marriage to Fabriz in the Superior Court for the judicial district of Stamford. On February 5, 1996, a hearing was held on Fabriz's motion seeking visitation rights with Saba. Fabriz notified the court that he was not seeking any form of custody, but, rather, an order of visitation. After making it clear that (1) physical custody of Saba would remain with Mirjavadi and (2) visitation with Fabriz would be supervised based on his risk of flight with Saba and his past abusive behavior, the trial court, Harrigan, J., ordered the parties to consult with the family relations division of the Superior Court and to report back to the court if and when the details of a visitation agreement between the parties had been reached.

That same day, Fabriz and Mirjavadi informed the trial court that they had come to an agreement as to the terms of supervised visitation. The court entered the order for visitation pursuant to their agreement, which allowed Fabriz three hours of supervised visitation per week in the presence of appointed monitors.

On September 30, 1996, Fabriz, while accompanied by the defendant, purchased two one-way tickets to Istanbul, Turkey, for a flight departing from John F. Kennedy Airport in New York on October 5, 1996. The names listed on the tickets were Orang and Saba Fabriz.

On October 5, 1996, at 2 p.m., Mirjavadi drove Saba to the Stamford Mall to turn Saba over to Fabriz for a regularly scheduled visit supervised by attorney Maria Varone, the appointed monitor. The defendant also was present.

Varone indicated to police that during the visit, Fabriz went into one of the mall stores with Saba while she remained outside the store talking with the defendant. Varone further stated that although she was not sure about the time as she was not wearing a watch, she estimated that between 4:15 and 4:30 p.m., she became concerned as to Fabriz' whereabouts. Fabriz never emerged from the store. Varone and the defendant searched for Fabriz and Saba to no avail. Mirjavadi returned to the mall at the scheduled time of 5 p.m. to retrieve Saba, at which time Varone informed Mirjavadi that Fabriz had disappeared with Saba. Mirjavadi has had no contact with Saba since October 5, 1996.

In *Marshak*, we indicated that recognition of "the tort of child abduction or custodial interference, as applied to either a parent or third party, might well play an important role in encouraging the speedy return of abducted children to the custodial parent. . . ." Marshak v. Marshak, supra, 226 Conn. at 665, 628 A.2d 964. Under the facts and circumstances of that case this issue was put off for another day. Today is that day.

The state argues that we should overrule *Marshak* and allow joint custodians to be held criminally liable if, in abducting their own child, their intent is to deprive the other joint custodian of his or her equal parental rights permanently or for a protracted period of time in accordance with General Statutes § 53a–98. We agree that *Marshak* should be overruled and that a joint custodian is not inherently immune from criminal prosecution based solely on his or her status as joint custodian if the state can prove all elements of the custodial interference statute, including both knowledge and intent, beyond a reasonable doubt.[8]

* * *

In *Marshak* we held that, "[t]he absence of a specific finding by the trial court that the defendant had conspired with or aided the children's father at a time after the father had been stripped of any legal entitlement to custody of the children is fatal to the plaintiff's claim." Marshak v. Marshak, supra, 226 Conn. at 667–68, 628 A.2d 964. "The trial court did not find that the defendant had knowingly conspired with the plaintiff's husband. . .or had aided and abetted his actions at a time other than when [the husband] had joint legal custody of the children." Quite simply, the legal premise underlying our holding in *Marshak* was faulty. We were wrong to conclude that a joint custodian could never, under any scenario, be liable for custodial interference.

---

8   Although we are concerned with the domestic violence hypothetical posed by the amicus curiae Connecticut Women's Education and Legal Fund (CWEALF), we do not agree with its legal conclusions. "CWEALF believes that adoption of the State's proposed rule places women who want to leave the family home with their children—because of an abusive husband or an abusive father—in. . .[a] peculiar position. . . . CWEALF believes that the state's construction of the custodial interference statute will, in many cases, eliminate from consideration the mens rea element of the statute." We disagree. The state is still required to prove, beyond a reasonable doubt, that the accused (1) intended to hold the child permanently or for a protracted period of time (2) knowing that he had no legal right to do so. See General Statutes §§ 53a–97 and 53a–98. Although we are sensitive to the concerns and needs specific to abuse situations, as the amicus points out, "[parents owe] common-law and statutory duties to their children. . . ." (Common-law duty to protect and safeguard minor children from harm; see also Uniform Child Custody Jurisdiction Act, General Statutes § 46b–90 et seq., which allows emergency custody orders when "it is necessary in an emergency to protect the child because he has been subjected to or threatened with mistreatment or abuse. . . ." General Statutes § 46b–93 [a][3] [B]). Thus, a parent who temporarily "abducts" a child in an effort to safeguard that child from an abusive situation, but seeks appropriate legal redress under § 46b–93 (a)(3)(B) as soon as is feasible under the circumstances, could not meet the necessary mens rea for custodial interference because he or she would have the legal right to take the child to protect him or her. We are confident that our law enforcement authorities and our courts will be sensitive to this reality.

General Statutes § 45a–606 provides in relevant part that "[t]he father and mother of every minor child are joint guardians of the person of the minor, and the powers, rights and duties of the father and the mother in regard to the minor shall be equal. . . ." When one parent purposefully deprives the other joint custodian of their joint lawful custody of the minor child, a de facto sole custody situation is effectively created. Such extrajudicial measures taken by an abducting parent cannot be lawful, and we were wrong to conclude otherwise in *Marshak*.

> **FYI**
>
> There were two concurring opinions in *Vakilzaden*, agreeing with the majority that a joint custodian could be subject to criminal liability under the statutes. Three justices wrote to emphasize their view that the state must prove, as an "essential element" of the charge, that the joint custodian had knowledge that he or she had no legal right to take the child. The opinion states: "By ignoring the element of knowledge, the state proposes a rule that would allow criminal liability to be imposed upon a joint custodian who infringes upon the other parent's custodial rights but who is merely acting to protect the child. The risk that criminal liability will be imposed upon a parent who takes her child to avoid further abuse to herself or her child is decidedly contrary to the public policy of this state. . . ." The second concurring opinion, while agreeing with this view, notes that the issue is addressed in footnote 8 of the majority opinion.
>
> Does the court's discussion in footnote 8 adequately address this issue?

In reaching this conclusion, we are persuaded by the interpretation of similar statutes in other jurisdictions. In construing its analogous statute, the Maine Supreme Court, in State v. Butt, 656 A.2d 1225, 1227 (Me.1995), noted: "In the absence of a court order awarding custody of children, both parents are jointly entitled to their care, custody, and control. . . . Although as a parent, [the defendant husband] had rights of custody in regard to his children, so too did his wife. . .the mother of those children. [The defendant] can point to no convincing reason or any authority why, absent a court order, [the statute] does not prohibit one parent from depriving the other parent of their legal right to joint custody. [The defendant], after all, deprived [his wife] of any and all contact with the children. . . . Accordingly, the jury was entitled to find that [the defendant] knew that he had no legal right to take. . .his children, and to keep them from their mother." (Citation omitted.)

Similarly, in construing Alaska's custodial interference statutes, that state's Appellate Court posed this question: "Did the Alaska Legislature intend [the statutes] to reach the conduct of a parent whose right to physical custody of the child remains undiminished but whose conduct deprives the other parent of his or her right to custody?" Strother v. State, 891 P.2d 214, 219 (Alaska App.1995). That court answered in the affirmative, as do we. "The crime of custodial interference was designed to protect any custodian from deprivation of his or her custody rights—even if that deprivation results from the actions of a person who also has a right to. . .custody of the child. The crime does not focus on the legal status of the defendant, but rather focuses on the defendant's actions, the effect of the defendant's actions, and the intent with which those actions were performed."

In this case, the state asserts that it will be able to prove that the defendant was present during the family court hearings, he was often present with Fabriz for the supervised visits with Saba, he assisted Fabriz with the purchase of plane tickets to Turkey, he facilitated Fabriz's getaway from the mall the day he took Saba, and he interfered with the police investigation, ensuring that Fabriz was not detained by the police. In short, the state has proffered sufficient evidence with which a jury could find beyond a reasonable doubt that the defendant conspired with Fabriz to deprive Mirjavadi of her lawful joint custody in Saba. Accordingly, in the interest of justice, this court's decision in Marshak v. Marshak, supra, 226 Conn. 652, 628 A.2d 964, is overruled.

The judgment is reversed and the case is remanded for further proceedings according to law.

Points for Discussion

a. Custodial Interference

Many states have recognized a cause of action for child abduction or custodial interference based on Restatement (Second) of Torts § 700 (1977). See Anonymous v. Anonymous, 672 So.2d 787 (Ala.1995); Stone v. Wall, 734 So.2d 1038 (Fla.1999); Kessel v. Leavitt, 511 S.E.2d 720 (W. Va. 1998). But see Larson v. Dunn, 460 N.W.2d 39 (Minn.1990), which declined to recognize the tort, suggesting that contempt sanctions and criminal prosecution were better remedies. See generally William B. Johnson, *Annotation, Liability of Legal or Natural Parent, or One Who Aids and Abets, for Damages Resulting from Abduction of Own Child*, 49 A.L.R. 4th 7 (1986). Wolf v. Wolf, 690 N.W.2d 887 (Iowa 2005), upheld an award of actual and punitive damages against mother for tortious interference with father's custody right).

b. Criminal Statutes

The federal kidnapping statute, 18 U.S.C. § 1201 (2018), does not apply to abduction "of a minor by the parent thereof," even if the abducting parent had no legal right to take the child. See, e.g., United States v. Sheek, 990 F.2d 150 (4th Cir. 1993).

Most states have enacted statutes that impose criminal penalties on parents who take children either without a privilege to do so or in violation of a custody decree. In some states, a parent may be convicted of child abduction even when he or she shares joint custody of the child. E.g. People v. Harrison, 402 N.E.2d 822 (Ill. App. Ct. 1980); State v. Butt, 656 A.2d 1225 (Me.1995). In the words of one court: "when a child is entrusted to joint custodians, neither custodian may take exclusive physical custody of the child in a manner that defeats the rights of the other joint custodian." Strother v. Alaska, 891 P.2d 214, 223 (Alaska Ct. App.1995) (citing other cases). See generally Homer H. Clark, Jr., Domestic Relations § 11.2 (Student 2d ed. 1988).

Go Online

Resources on preventing and responding to parental child abductions are available from the National Center for Missing and Exploited Children and the US. State Department.

c. Preventing Child Abduction

A number of states have adopted the 2006 Uniform Child Abduction Prevention Act, 9 U.L.A. (Part 1A) (Supp. 2018), which provides guidelines for courts to follow to help identify families at risk for child abduction and measures that can help to prevent this. See generally Patricia M. Hoff, *"UU" UCAPA: Understanding and Using UCAPA to Prevent Child Abduction*, 41 Fam. L.Q. 1 (2007).

Global View: International Kidnapping

The International Parental Kidnapping Crime Act (IPKCA), 18 U.S.C. § 1204 (2018), provides for fines and imprisonment for up to three years for "whoever removes a child from the United States or retains a child (who has been in the United States) outside the United States with intent to obstruct the lawful exercise of parental rights." The term "parental rights" is defined in the statute to mean joint or sole physical custody, including visiting rights. See, e.g., United States v. Fazal-Ur-Raheman-Fazal, 355 F.3d 40 (1st Cir.2004).

In addition, when a child is removed from the child's country of "habitual residence," it may be possible to secure an order to return the child under the provisions of the Hague Convention on the Civil Aspects of International Child Abduction, 9 I.L.M. 1501 (1980). The Child Abduction Convention was implemented in the United States by the International Child Abduction Remedies Act (ICARA), 22 U.S.C. § 9001 et seq. (2018). On the interaction between the IPKCA and the Hague Child Abduction Convention, see United States v. Ventre, 338 F.3d 1047 (9th Cir.2003).

Abbott v. Abbott

560 U.S. 1 (2010)

JUSTICE KENNEDY delivered the opinion of the Court.

This case presents, as it has from its inception in the United States District Court, a question of interpretation under the Hague Convention on the Civil Aspects of International Child Abduction (Convention), Oct. 24, 1980, T. I. A. S. No. 11670, S. Treaty Doc. No. 99–11. The United States is a

Go Online

Listen to the oral arguments in *Abbott* on the Oyez Project website.

contracting state to the Convention; and Congress has implemented its provisions through the International Child Abduction Remedies Act (ICARA), 102 Stat. 437, 42 U. S. C. §11601 *et seq.* The Convention provides that a child abducted in violation of "rights of custody" must be returned to the child's country of habitual residence, unless certain exceptions apply. Art. 1,. The question is whether a parent has a "righ[t] of custody" by reason of that parent's *ne exeat* right: the authority to consent before the other parent may take the child to another country.

I

Timothy Abbott and Jacquelyn Vaye Abbott married in England in 1992. He is a British citizen, and she is a citizen of the United States. Mr. Abbott's astronomy profession took the couple to Hawaii, where their son A. J. A. was born in 1995. The Abbotts moved to La Serena, Chile, in 2002. There was marital discord, and the parents separated in March 2003. The Chilean courts granted the mother daily care and control of the child, while awarding the father "direct and regular" visitation rights, including visitation every other weekend and for the whole month of February each year.

Chilean law conferred upon Mr. Abbott what is commonly known as a ***ne exeat*** right: a right to consent before Ms. Abbott could take A. J. A. out of Chile. See Minors Law 16,618, art. 49 (Chile), App. to Pet. for Cert. 61a (granting a *ne exeat* right to any parent with visitation rights). In effect a *ne exeat* right imposes a duty on one parent that is a right in the other. After Mr. Abbott obtained a British passport for A. J. A., Ms. Abbott grew concerned that Mr. Abbott would take the boy to Britain. She sought and obtained a "*ne exeat* of the minor" order from the Chilean family court, prohibiting the boy from being taken out of Chile.

In August 2005, while proceedings before the Chilean court were pending, the mother removed the boy from Chile without permission from either the father or the court. A private investigator located the mother and the child in Texas. In February 2006, the mother filed for divorce in Texas state court. Part of the relief she sought was a modification of the father's rights, including full power in her to determine the boy's place of residence and an order limiting the father to supervised visitation in Texas. This litigation remains pending.

Mr. Abbott brought an action in Texas state court, asking for visitation rights and an order requiring Ms. Abbott to show cause why the court should not allow Mr. Abbott to return to Chile with A. J. A. In February 2006, the court denied Mr. Abbott's requested relief but granted him "liberal periods of possession" of A. J. A. throughout February 2006, provided Mr. Abbott remained in Texas.

In May 2006, Mr. Abbott filed the instant action in the United States District Court for the Western District of Texas. He sought an order requiring his son's return to Chile pursuant to the Convention and enforcement provisions of the ICARA. In July 2007, after holding a bench trial during which only Mr. Abbott testified, the District Court denied relief. The court held that the father's *ne exeat* right did not constitute a right of custody under the Convention and, as a result, that the return remedy was not authorized. 495 F. Supp. 2d 635, 640.

The United States Court of Appeals for the Fifth Circuit affirmed on the same rationale. The court held the father possessed no rights of custody under the Convention because his *ne exeat* right was only "a veto right over his son's departure from Chile." 542 F. 3d 1081, 1087 (2008). The court expressed substantial agreement with the Court of Appeals for the Second Circuit in *Croll v. Croll*, 229 F. 3d 133 (2000). Relying on American dictionary definitions of "custody" and noting that *ne exeat* rights cannot be " 'actually exercised' " within the meaning of the Convention, *Croll* held that *ne exeat* rights are not rights of custody. *Id.*, at 138–141 (quoting Art. 3(*b*), Treaty Doc., at 7). A dissenting opinion in *Croll* was filed by then-Judge Sotomayor. The dissent maintained that a *ne exeat* right is a right of custody because it "provides a parent with decisionmaking authority regarding a child's international relocation."

The Courts of Appeals for the Fourth and Ninth Circuits adopted the conclusion of the *Croll* majority. See *Fawcett v. McRoberts*, 326 F. 3d 491, 500 (CA4 2003); *Gonzalez v. Gutierrez*, 311 F. 3d 942, 949 (CA9 2002). The Court of Appeals for the Eleventh Circuit has followed the reasoning of the *Croll* dissent. *Furnes v. Reeves*, 362 F. 3d 702, 720, n. 15 (2004). Certiorari was granted to resolve the conflict.

II

The Convention was adopted in 1980 in response to the problem of international child abductions during domestic disputes. The Convention seeks "to secure the prompt return of children wrongfully removed to or retained in any

Contracting State," and "to ensure that rights of custody and of access under the law of one Contracting State are effectively respected in the other Contracting States." Art. 1, Treaty Doc., at 7.

The provisions of the Convention of most relevance at the outset of this discussion are as follows:

"Article 3: The removal or the retention of the child is to be considered wrongful where—
"*a* it is in breach of rights of custody attributed to a person, an institution or any other body, either jointly or alone, under the law of the State in which the child was habitually resident immediately before the removal or retention; and
"*b* at the time of removal or retention those rights were actually exercised, either jointly or alone, or would have been so exercised but for the removal or retention.

. . . . .

"Article 5: For the purposes of this Convention—
"*a* 'rights of custody' shall include rights relating to the care of the person of the child and, in particular, the right to determine the child's place of residence;
"*b* 'rights of access' shall include the right to take a child for a limited period of time to a place other than the child's habitual residence.

. . . . .

"Article 12: Where a child has been wrongfully removed or retained in terms of Article 3. . .the authority concerned shall order the return of the child forthwith."

The Convention's central operating feature is the return remedy. When a child under the age of 16 has been wrongfully removed or retained, the country to which the child has been brought must "order the return of the child forthwith," unless certain exceptions apply. See, *e.g.,* Arts. 4, 12. A removal is "wrongful" where the child was removed in violation of "rights of custody." The Convention defines "rights of custody" to "include rights relating to the care of the person of the child and, in particular, the right to determine the child's place of residence." Art. 5(*a*). A return remedy does not alter the pre—abduction allocation of custody rights but leaves custodial decisions to the courts of the country of habitual residence. Art. 19. The Convention also recognizes "rights of access," but offers no return remedy for a breach of those rights. Arts. 5(*b*), 21.

The United States has implemented the Convention through the ICARA. The statute authorizes a person who seeks a child's return to file a petition in state or federal court and instructs that the court "shall decide the case in accordance with the Convention." 42 U. S. C. §§ 11603(a), (b), (d). If the child in question has been "wrongfully removed or retained within the meaning of the Convention," the child shall be "promptly returned," unless an exception is applicable. § 11601(a)(4).

III

As the parties agree, the Convention applies to this dispute. A. J. A. is under 16 years old; he was a habitual resident of Chile; and both Chile and the United States are contracting states. The question is whether A. J. A. was "wrongfully removed" from Chile, in other words, whether he was removed in violation of a right of custody. This Court's inquiry is shaped by the text of the Convention; the views of the United States Department of State; decisions addressing the meaning of "rights of custody" in courts of other contracting states; and the purposes of the Convention. After considering these sources, the Court determines that Mr. Abbott's *ne exeat* right is a right of custody under the Convention.

A

"The interpretation of a treaty, like the interpretation of a statute, begins with its text." *Medellín v. Texas*, 552 U. S. 491, 506 (2008). This Court consults Chilean law to determine the content of Mr. Abbott's right, while following the Convention's text and structure to decide whether the right at issue is a "righ[t] of custody."

Chilean law granted Mr. Abbott a joint right to decide his child's country of residence, otherwise known as a *ne exeat* right. Minors Law 16,618, art. 49 (Chile), provides that "[o]nce the court has decreed" that one of the parents has visitation rights, that parent's "authorization. . .shall also be required" before the child may be taken out of the country, subject to court override only where authorization "cannot be granted or is denied without good reason." Mr. Abbott has "direct and regular" visitation rights and it follows from Chilean law, that he has a shared right to determine his son's country of residence under this provision. To support the conclusion that Mr. Abbott's right under Chilean law gives him a joint right to decide his son's country of residence, it is notable that a Chilean agency has explained that Minors Law 16,618 is a "right to authorize the minors' exit" from Chile and that this provision means that neither parent can "unilaterally" "establish the [child's] place of residence." Letter from Paula Strap Camus, Director General, Corporation of Judicial Assistance of the Region Metropolitana, to National Center for Missing and Exploited Children (Jan. 17, 2006).

The Convention recognizes that custody rights can be decreed jointly or alone, see Art. 3(*a*); and Mr. Abbott's joint right to determine his son's country of residence is best classified as a joint right of custody, as the Convention defines that term. The Convention defines "rights of custody" to "include rights relating to the care of the person of the child and, in particular, the right to determine the child's place of residence." Art. 5(*a*). Mr. Abbott's *ne exeat* right gives him both the joint "right to determine the child's place of residence" and joint "rights relating to the care of the person of the child."

Mr. Abbott's joint right to decide A. J. A.'s country of residence allows him to "determine the child's place of residence." The phrase "place of residence" encompasses the child's country of residence, especially in light of the Convention's explicit purpose to prevent wrongful removal across international borders. And even if "place of residence" refers only to the child's street address within a country, a *ne exeat* right still entitles Mr. Abbott to "determine" that place. "[D]etermine" can mean "[t]o fix conclusively or authoritatively," Webster's New International Dictionary 711 (2d ed. 1954) (2d definition), but it can also mean "[t]o set bounds or limits to," *ibid.* (1st definition), which is what Mr. Abbott's *ne exeat* right allows by ensuring that A. J. A. cannot live at any street addresses outside of Chile. It follows that the Convention's protection of a parent's custodial "right to determine the child's place of residence" includes a *ne exeat* right.

Mr. Abbott's joint right to determine A. J. A.'s country of residence also gives him "rights relating to the care of the person of the child." Art. 5(*a*). Few decisions are as significant as the language the child speaks, the identity he finds, or the culture and traditions she will come to absorb. These factors, so essential to self-definition, are linked in an inextricable way to the child's country of residence. One need only consider the different childhoods an adolescent will experience if he or she grows up in the United States, Chile, Germany, or North Korea, to understand how choosing a child's country of residence is a right "relating to the care of the person of the child." The Court of Appeals described Mr. Abbott's right to take part in making this decision as a mere "veto," but even by that truncated description, the father has an essential role in deciding the boy's country of residence. For example, Mr. Abbott could condition his consent to a change in country on A. J. A.'s moving to a city outside Chile where Mr. Abbott could obtain an astronomy position, thus allowing the father to have continued contact with the boy.

That a *ne exeat* right does not fit within traditional notions of physical custody is beside the point. The Convention defines "rights of custody," and it is that definition that a court must consult. This uniform, text-based approach ensures international consistency in interpreting the Convention. It forecloses courts from relying on definitions of custody confined by local law usage, definitions that may undermine recognition of custodial arrangements in other countries or in different legal traditions, including the civil-law tradition. And, in any case, our own legal system has adopted conceptions of custody that accord with the Convention's broad definition. Joint legal custody, in which one parent cares for the child while the other has joint decisionmaking authority concerning the child's welfare, has become increasingly common. See Singer, Dispute Resolution and the Postdivorce Family: Implications of a Paradigm Shift, 47 Family Ct. Rev. 363, 366

(2009) ("[A] recent study of child custody outcomes in North Carolina indicated that almost 70% of all custody resolutions included joint legal custody, as did over 90% of all mediated custody agreements"); E. Maccoby & R. Mnookin, Dividing the Child: Social and Legal Dilemmas of Custody 107 (1992) ("[F]or 79% of our entire sample, the [California] divorce decree provided for joint legal custody"); see generally Elrod, Reforming the System to Protect Children in High Conflict Custody Cases, 28 Wm. Mitchell L. Rev. 495, 505–508 (2001).

Ms. Abbott gets the analysis backwards in claiming that a *ne exeat* right is not a right of custody because the Convention requires that any right of custody must be capable of exercise. The Convention protects rights of custody when "at the time of removal or retention those rights were actually exercised, either jointly or alone, or would have been so exercised but for the removal or retention." Art. 3(b). In cases like this one, a *ne exeat* right is by its nature inchoate and so has no operative force except when the other parent seeks to remove the child from the country. If that occurs, the parent can exercise the *ne exeat* right by declining consent to the exit or placing conditions to ensure the move will be in the child's best interests. When one parent removes the child without seeking the *ne exeat* holder's consent, it is an instance where the right would have been "exercised but for the removal or retention."

The Court of Appeals' conclusion that a breach of a *ne exeat* right does not give rise to a return remedy would render the Convention meaningless in many cases where it is most needed. The Convention provides a return remedy when a parent takes a child across international borders in violation of a right of custody. The Convention provides no return remedy when a parent removes a child in violation of a right of access but requires contracting states "to promote the peaceful enjoyment of access rights." Art. 21. For example, a court may force the custodial parent to pay the travel costs of visitation, see, *e.g.*, Viragh v. Foldes, 415 Mass. 96, 109–111, 612 N. E. 2d 241, 249–250 (1993), or make other provisions for the noncustodial parent to visit his or her child, see §11603(b) (authorizing petitions to "secur[e] the effective exercise of rights of access to a child"). But unlike rights of access, *ne exeat* rights can only be honored with a return remedy because these rights depend on the child's location being the country of habitual residence.

Any suggestion that a *ne exeat* right is a "righ[t] of access" is illogical and atextual. The Convention defines "rights of access" as "includ[ing] the right to take a child for a limited period of time to a place other than the child's habitual residence," Art. 5(b), and ICARA defines that same term as "visitation rights," §11602(7). The joint right to decide a child's country of residence is not even arguably a "right to take a child for a limited period of time" or a "visitation righ[t]." Reaching the commonsense conclusion that a *ne exeat* right does not fit these definitions of "rights of access" honors the Convention's distinction between rights of access and rights of custody.

Ms. Abbott argues that the *ne exeat* order in this case cannot create a right of custody because it merely protects a court's jurisdiction over the child. Even if this argument were correct, it would not be dispositive. Ms. Abbott contends the Chilean court's *ne exeat* order contains no parental consent provision and so awards the father no rights, custodial or otherwise. Even a *ne exeat* order issued to protect a court's jurisdiction pending issuance of further decrees is consistent with allowing a parent to object to the child's removal from the country. This Court need not decide the status of *ne exeat* orders lacking parental consent provisions, however; for here the father relies on his rights under Minors Law 16,618. Mr. Abbott's rights derive not from the order but from Minors Law 16,618. That law requires the father's consent before the mother can remove the boy from Chile, subject only to the equitable power family courts retain to override any joint custodial arrangements in times of disagreement. Minors Law 16,618; see 1 J. Atkinson, Modern Child Custody Practice §6–11 (2d ed. 2009) ("[T]he court remains the final arbiter and may resolve the [dispute between joint custodians] itself or designate one parent as having final authority on certain issues affecting the child"); *Lombardo v. Lombardo*, 202 Mich. App. 151, 159, 507 N. W. 2d 788, 792 (1993) ("[W]here the parents as joint custodians cannot agree on important matters such as education, it is the court's duty to determine the issue in the best interests of the child"). The consent provision in Minors Law 16,618 confers upon the father the joint right to determine his child's country of residence. This is a right of custody under the Convention.

B

This Court's conclusion that Mr. Abbott possesses a right of custody under the Convention is supported and informed by the State Department's view on the issue. The United States has endorsed the view that *ne exeat* rights are rights of custody. In its brief before this Court the United States advises that "the Department of State, whose Office of Children's Issues serves as the Central Authority for the United States under the Convention, has long understood the Convention as including *ne exeat* rights among the protected 'rights of custody.' " Brief for United States as *Amicus Curiae* 21; see *Sumitomo Shoji America, Inc. v. Avagliano*, 457 U. S. 176, 184–185, n. 10 (1982) (deferring to the Executive's interpretation of a treaty as memorialized in a brief before this Court). It is well settled that the Executive Branch's interpretation of a treaty "is entitled to great weight." There is no reason to doubt that this well-established canon of deference is appropriate here. The Executive is well informed concerning the diplomatic consequences resulting from this Court's interpretation of "rights of custody," including the likely reaction of other contracting states and the impact on the State Department's ability to reclaim children abducted from this country.

C

This Court's conclusion that *ne exeat* rights are rights of custody is further informed by the views of other contracting states. In interpreting any treaty, "[t]he 'opinions of our sister signatories'. . .are 'entitled to considerable weight.' " *El Al Israel Airlines, Ltd. v. Tsui Yuan Tseng, 525 U. S. 155, 176 (1999)* (quoting *Air France v. Saks, 470 U. S. 392, 404 (1985)*). The principle applies with special force here, for Congress has directed that "uniform international interpretation of the Convention" is part of the Convention's framework. See §11601(b)(3)(B).

A review of the international case law confirms broad acceptance of the rule that *ne exeat* rights are rights of custody. In an early decision, the English High Court of Justice explained that a father's "right to ensure that the child remain[ed] in Australia or live[d] anywhere outside Australia only with his approval" is a right of custody requiring return of the child to Australia. *C. v. C.*, [1989] 1 W. L. R. 654, 658 (C. A.). Lords of the House of Lords have agreed, noting that *C. v. C.*'s conclusion is "settled, so far as the United Kingdom is concerned" and "appears to be the majority [view] of the common law world." See *In re D (A Child)*, [2007] 1 A. C. 619, 628, 633, 635 (2006).

The Supreme Court of Israel follows the same rule, concluding that "the term 'custody' should be interpreted in an expansive way, so that it will apply [i]n every case in which there is a need for the consent of one of the parents to remove the children from one country to another." CA 5271/92 *Foxman v. Foxman*, [1992], §§3(D), 4 (K. Chagall transl.). The High Courts of Austria, South Africa, and Germany are in accord. See Oberster Gerichtshof [O. G. H.] [Supreme Court] Feb. 5, 1992, 2 Ob 596/91 (Austria) ("Since the English Custody Court had ordered that the children must not be removed from England and Wales without the father's written consent, both parents had, in effect, been granted joint custody concerning the children's place of residence"); *Sonderup v. Tondelli*, 2001(1) SA 1171, 1183 (Constitutional Ct. of South Africa 2000) ("[The mother's] failure to return to British Columbia with the child. . .was a breach of the conditions upon which she was entitled to exercise her rights of custody and. . .therefore constituted a wrongful retention. . .as contemplated by [Article 3] of the Convention"); Bundesverfassungsgericht [BVerfG] [Federal Constitutional Court of Germany] July 18, 1997, 2 BvR 1126/97, ¶15 (the Convention requires a return remedy for a violation of the "right to have a say in the child's place of residence"). Appellate courts in Australia and Scotland agree. See *In the Marriage of Resina* [1991] FamCA 33 (Austl., May 22, 1991), ¶¶ 18–27; *A. J. v. F. J.*, [2005] CSIH 36, 2005 1 S. C. 428, 435–436.

It is true that some courts have stated a contrary view, or at least a more restrictive one. The Canadian Supreme Court has said *ne exeat* orders are "usually intended" to protect access rights. *Thomson v. Thomson*, [1994] 3 S. C. R. 551, 589–590, 119 D. L. R. (4th) 253, 281; see *D. S. v. V. W.*, [1996] 2 S. C. R. 108,

134 D. L. R. (4th) 481. But the Canadian cases are not precisely on point here. *Thomson* ordered a return remedy based on an interim *ne exeat* order, and only noted in dicta that it may not order such a remedy pursuant to a permanent *ne exeat* order. See [1994] 3 S. C. R., at 589–590, 119 D. L. R. (4th), at 281. *D. S.* involved a parent's claim based on an implicit *ne exeat* right and, in any event, the court ordered a return remedy on a different basis. See [1996] 2 S. C. R., at 140–141, 142, 134 D. L. R. (4th), at 503–504, 505.

French courts are divided. A French Court of Appeals held that "the right to accept or refuse the removal of the children's residence" outside of a region was "a joint exercise of rights of custody." *Public Ministry* v. *M. B.*, [CA] Aix-en-Provence, 6e ch., Mar. 23, 1989, Rev. crit. dr. internat. Privé 79(3), July–Sept. 1990, 529, 533–535. A trial court in a different region of France rejected this view, relying on the mother's "fundamental liberty" to establish her domicil. See *Attorney for the Republic at Périgueux* v. *Mrs. S.*, [T. G. I.] Périgueux, Mar. 17, 1992, Rev. cr. dr. internat. Privé 82(4) Oct.– Dec. 1993, 650, 651–653, note Bertrand Ancel, D. 1992, note G. C.

Scholars agree that there is an emerging international consensus that *ne exeat* rights are rights of custody, even if that view was not generally formulated when the Convention was drafted in 1980. At that time, joint custodial arrangements were unknown in many of the contracting states, and the status of *ne exeat* rights was not yet well understood. See 1980 Conférence de La Haye de droit international privé, Enlèvement d'enfants, morning meeting of Wed., Oct. 8, 1980 (discussion by Messrs. Leal & van Boeschoten), in 3 Actes et Documents de la Quatorzième session, pp. 263–266 (1982) (Canadian and Dutch delegates disagreeing whether the Convention protected *ne exeat* rights, while agreeing that it should protect such rights). Since 1980, however, joint custodial arrangements have become more common. And, within this framework, most contracting states and scholars now recognize that *ne exeat* rights are rights of custody. * * *

A history of the Convention, known as the Pérez-Vera Report, has been cited both by the parties and by Courts of Appeals that have considered this issue. See 1980 Conférence de La Haye de droit international privé, Enlèvement d'enfants, E. Pérez-Vera, Explanatory Report (Pérez-Vera Report or Report), in 3 Actes et Documents de la Quatorzième session, pp. 425–473 (1982). We need not decide whether this Report should be given greater weight than a scholarly commentary. * * * It suffices to note that the Report supports the conclusion that *ne exeat* rights are rights of custody. The Report explains that rather than defining custody in precise terms or referring to the laws of different nations pertaining to parental rights, the Convention uses the unadorned term "rights of custody" to recognize "*all* the ways in which custody of children can be exercised" through "a flexible interpretation of the terms used, which allows the greatest possible number of cases to be brought into consideration." Thus the Report rejects the notion that because *ne exeat* rights do not encompass the right to make medical or some other important decisions about a child's life they cannot be rights of custody. Indeed, the Report is fully consistent with the conclusion that *ne exeat* rights are just one of the many "ways in which custody of children can be exercised."

D

Adopting the view that the Convention provides a return remedy for violations of *ne exeat* rights accords with its objects and purposes. The Convention is based on the principle that the best interests of the child are well served when decisions regarding custody rights are made in the country of habitual residence. See Convention Preamble. Ordering a return remedy does not alter the existing allocation of custody rights, Art. 19, but does allow the courts of the home country to decide what is in the child's best interests. It is the Convention's premise that courts in contracting states will make this determination in a responsible manner.

Custody decisions are often difficult. Judges must strive always to avoid a common tendency to prefer their own society and culture, a tendency that ought not interfere with objective consideration of all the factors that should be weighed in determining the best interests of the child. This judicial neutrality is presumed from the mandate of the Convention, which affirms that the contracting states are "[f]irmly convinced that the interests of children are of paramount importance in matters relating to their custody." Convention Preamble. International law serves a high purpose when it underwrites the determination by nations to rely upon their domestic courts to enforce just laws by legitimate and fair proceedings.

To interpret the Convention to permit an abducting parent to avoid a return remedy, even when the other parent holds a *ne exeat* right, would run counter to the Convention's purpose of deterring child abductions by parents who attempt to find a friendlier forum for deciding custodial disputes. Ms. Abbott removed A. J. A. from Chile while Mr. Abbott's request to enhance his relationship with his son was still pending before Chilean courts. After she landed in Texas, the mother asked the state court to diminish or eliminate the father's custodial and visitation rights. The Convention should not be interpreted to permit a parent to select which country will adjudicate these questions by bringing the child to a different country, in violation of a *ne exeat* right. Denying a return remedy for the violation of such rights would "legitimize the very action—removal of the child—that the home country, through its custody order [or other provision of law], sought to prevent" and would allow "parents to undermine the very purpose of the Convention." *Croll, 229 F. 3d, at 147* (Sotomayor, J., dissenting). This Court should be most reluctant to adopt an interpretation that gives an abducting parent an advantage by coming here to avoid a return remedy that is granted, for instance, in the United Kingdom, Israel, Germany, and South Africa.

Requiring a return remedy in cases like this one helps deter child abductions and respects the Convention's purpose to prevent harms resulting from abductions. An abduction can have devastating consequences for a child. "Some child psychologists believe that the trauma children suffer from these abductions is one of the worst forms of child abuse." H. R. Rep. No. 103–390, p. 2 (1993). A child abducted by one parent is separated from the second parent and the child's support system. Studies have shown that separation by abduction can cause psychological problems ranging from depression and acute stress disorder to posttraumatic stress disorder and identity-formation issues. See N. Faulkner, Parental Child Abduction is Child Abuse (1999), (as visited May 13, 2010, and available in Clerk of Court's case file). A child abducted at an early age can experience loss of community and stability, leading to loneliness, anger, and fear of abandonment. See Huntington, Parental Kidnapping: A New Form of Child Abuse (1982), in American Prosecutors Research Institute's National Center for Prosecution of Child Abuse, Parental Abduction Project, Investigation and Prosecution of Parental Abduction (1995) (App. A). Abductions may prevent the child from forming a relationship with the left-behind parent, impairing the child's ability to mature. See Faulkner, *supra*, at 5.

IV

While a parent possessing a *ne exeat* right has a right of custody and may seek a return remedy, a return order is not automatic. Return is not required if the abducting parent can establish that a Convention exception applies. One exception states return of the child is not required when "there is a grave risk that his or her return would expose the child to physical or psychological harm or otherwise place the child in an intolerable situation." Art. 13(b), Treaty Doc., at 10. If, for example, Ms. Abbott could demonstrate that returning to Chile would put her own safety at grave risk, the court could consider whether this is sufficient to show that the child too would suffer "psychological harm" or be placed "in an intolerable situation." See, *e.g.*, <u>Baran v. Beaty, 526 F. 3d 1340, 1352–1353 (CA11 2008)</u>; <u>Walsh v. Walsh, 221 F. 3d 204, 220–221 (CA1</u>

Justice Stevens dissented in *Abbott*, joined by Justice Thomas and Justice Breyer, and argued that use of the return remedy in the circumstances of *Abbott* was contrary to the Convention's text and purpose. The dissenters emphasized that "[t]he drafters' primary concern at the time the Convention was drafted was to remedy abuses by noncustodial parents who attempt to circumvent adverse custody decrees. . .by seeking a more favorable judgment in a second nation's family court system." Based on the treaty language, they rejected the conclusion that Mr. Abbott's veto power was a right "relating to the care of the child" or a right to determine the child's place of residence, arguing that the court's broad reading of this language "eviscerates the distinction the Convention draws between rights of custody and rights of access."

2000). The Convention also allows courts to decline to order removal if the child objects, if the child has reached a sufficient "age and degree of maturity at which it is appropriate to take account of its views." Art. 13(*b*), Treaty Doc., at 10. The proper interpretation and application of these and other exceptions are not before this Court. These matters may be addressed on remand.

* * *

The judgment of the Court of Appeals is reversed, and the case is remanded for further proceedings consistent with this opinion.

It is so ordered.

_____

Points for Discussion

a. Hague Abduction Countries

As noted in *Abbott*, the United States implemented the Child Abduction Convention with the International Child Abduction Remedies Act (ICARA), currently codified at <u>22 U.S.C. § 9001 et seq. (2018)</u>. More than 90 other countries have ratified or acceded to the Child Abduction Convention, but the United States has not yet accepted all of these accessions. The threshold question in any case brought under the Convention is whether the treaty was in effect between the United States and the country where the child is claimed to have been habitually resident at the time of the wrongful removal or retention. Cases in which the Child Abduction Convention is not available as a remedy present a much more difficult problem for a left-behind parent. See, e.g., <u>Taveras v. Taveraz, 477 F.3d 767 (6th Cir. 2007)</u>. See generally Patricia E. Apy, *Managing Child Custody Cases Involving Non-Hague Contracting States*, 14 J. Am. Acad. Matrim. L. 77 (1997).

Go Online

Extensive information the Child Abduction Convention is available from the U.S. State Department's <u>web page</u> and the <u>Hague Conference on Private International Law</u>.

b. Wrongful Removal or Retention

The test of wrongful removal or retention in Article 3 of the Child Abduction Convention requires proof that the plaintiff had custodial rights under the law of the child's habitual residence, and that at the time of the removal or retention the plaintiff was actually exercising those rights (or would have been, but for the child's removal to or retention in another country). Friedrich v. Friedrich, 78 F.3d 1060 (6th Cir.1996) (*Friedrich II*) considered whether a plaintiff was actually exercising custodial rights under German law at the time the child was removed to the United States, and concluded that a court should find exercise whenever "a parent with de jure custody rights keeps, or seeks to keep, any sort of regular contact with his or her child." Id. at 1064.

c. Habitual Residence

A number of different Hague conventions rely on the concept of "habitual residence," which is treated as a question of fact, avoiding the legal technicalities embodied in terms such as domicile or nationality. The term is not defined in the Child Abduction Convention, but it is crucial to its application. See Friedrich v. Friedrich, 983 F.2d 1396 (6th Cir. 1993) (*Friedrich I*) ("We agree that habitual residence must not be confused with domicile. To determine the habitual residence, the court must focus on the child, not the parents, and examine past experience, not future intentions."), and Feder v. Evans-Feder, 63 F.3d 217 (3d Cir. 1995) ("[W]e believe that a child's habitual residence is the place where he or she has been physically present for an amount of time sufficient for acclimatization and which has a 'degree of settled purpose' from the child's perspective.")

Determination of habitual residence is problematic in cases in which the child has been moved from one country to another, particularly when the child's parents have different intentions with respect to the child's residence. The Ninth Circuit Court of Appeals suggested in Mozes v. Mozes, 239 F.3d 1067 (9th Cir.2001), that courts should consider whether there is evidence of a shared parental intent regarding the child's residence. Although this approach has been followed in several federal circuits, see, e.g., Gitter v. Gitter, 396 F.3d 124 (2d Cir. 2005), Koch v. Koch, 450 F.3d 703 (7th Cir. 2006), and Ruiz v. Tenorio, 392 F.3d 1247 (11th Cir. 2004), it has been criticized in others, see, e.g., Robert v. Tesson, 507 F.3d 981 (6th Cir. 2007), Stern v. Stern, 639 F.3d 449, 451 (8th Cir. 2011).

d. Rights of Custody and Access

Abbott illustrates one type of problem that arises in the determination of whether a plaintiff had "rights of custody" as defined by Article 5 under the law of the habitual residence. See also Furnes v. Reeves, 362 F.3d 702 (11th Cir.2004) (considering "joint parental responsibility" under Norwegian law); and Gil v. Rodriguez, 184 F.Supp.2d 1221 (M.D.Fla.2002) (father's custodial rights under Venezuelan law for child under age 7). As noted in *Abbott*, Article 21 of the Convention suggests that the Central Authorities of participating countries may assist with applications to secure access or visitation rights, but the return remedy of the Convention is not available to a parent who has only rights of access. See Cantor v. Cohen, 442 F.3d 196 (4th Cir. 2006). In the United States, ICARA allows judicial proceedings to secure access rights, see 22 U.S.C. § 9003(b) (2018), but the courts do not agree on whether there is jurisdiction for this purpose in federal court. Compare Cantor v. Cohen, 442 F.3d 196 (4th Cir. 2006), with Ozaltin v. Ozaltin, 708 F.3d 355 (2d Cir. 2013).

e. Exceptions to the Return Obligation

At the end of its opinion in *Abbott*, the Supreme Court points out that the obligation to return a child under the Child Abduction Convention is subject to exceptions. These are set out in Articles 12, 13 and 20 of the Convention. In the United States, ICARA provides that two of these exceptions, based on a grave risk of harm under Article 13(b) or a human rights concern under Article 20, must be proven by clear and convincing evidence. See 22 U.S.C. § 9003(e) (2018).

One Year/Child Well Settled. Article 12 of the Child Abduction Convention provides that return of a child "shall be ordered forthwith" when the child was wrongfully removed or retained in the year prior to the commencement of the return proceedings. Even when proceedings are commenced after more than a year, however, the Convention provides that the child shall be returned "unless it is demonstrated that the child is now settled in its new environment." See, e.g., In re Robinson, 983 F.Supp. 1339 (D.Colo.1997) (concluding that child should not be returned because the petition was not filed within a year and the child was well settled in the new environment). In Lozano v. Alvarez, 572 U.S. 1 (2014), the Supreme Court resolved a split among the federal circuits, ruling unanimously that equitable tolling principles did not apply to the one-year rule in Article 12. The Court concluded that background rules of U.S. law should not be grafted onto the Abduction Convention, even if those rules might help to deter abductions.

Consent/Acquiesence. Under Article 13(a), the authorities need not order return of a child if there is proof that the party seeking return consented to or subsequently acquiesced in the removal or retention in another country. Numerous cases therefore consider whether the parents of a child have agreed to the child's residence in another country for a period of time, see, e.g., Toren v. Toren, 191 F.3d 23 (1st Cir.1999).

Grave Risk of Harm. Under Article 13(b), a court may deny a return order when a defendant shows a "grave risk" that the child's return "would expose the child to physical or psychological harm or otherwise place the child in an intolerable situation." Most of the litigation over exceptions to return have fallen in this category, and many cases have quoted the opinion in Friedrich v. Friedrich, 78 F.3d 1060 (6th Cir.1996), which suggested that only two situations would meet this test: when returning the child means sending the child to "a zone or war, famine, or disease" or when there is "serious abuse or neglect, or extraordinary emotional dependence" and the country of habitual residence cannot give the child adequate protection for some reason.

Child's Objections. Under Article 13, authorities may refuse to return a child based on a finding "that the child objects to being returned and has attained an age and degree of maturity at which it is appropriate to take account of its views." There is no age at which these views are automatically given effect, see, e.g. England v. England, 234 F.3d 268 (5th Cir.2000) (views of 13-year-old not considered without proof of child's maturity). Under Article 4, however, the Convention no longer applies once a child reaches age 16. Concerning the defense based on a child's objections to return, see de Silva v. Pitts, 481 F.3d 1279 (10th Cir. 2007) and Karkkainen v. Kovalchuk, 445 F.3d 280 (3d Cir. 2006).

Human Rights. Article 20 allows the authorities to refuse return of a child "if this would not be permitted by the fundamental principles of the requested State relating to the protection of human rights and fundamental freedoms." As noted above, this defense requires proof by clear and convincing evidence in the United States, and it has almost never been used either in the United States or in other Hague countries. See, e.g., Hazbun Escaf v. Rodriguez, 200 F.Supp.2d 603 (E.D.Va.2002). What principles of human rights might be implicated by a return order in a child abduction case? For an argument in favor of expanding the use of this defense, see Merle H. Weiner, *Strengthening Article 20*, 38 U.S.F. L. Rev. 701 (2004).

f. Domestic Violence Issues

Many cases brought under the Child Abduction Convention involve a fact pattern in which a custodial mother who has been a victim of domestic violence takes her children and moves to another country. This was not a situation that the drafters considered when the Convention was adopted, and the case law reflects considerable difficulty that courts have had in applying the Convention in this context. When children are the victims of physical or sexual abuse, the grave risk of harm exception under Article 13(b) provides a basis for refusing return, although even in this situation courts inquire whether it is possible to devise a means of returning the child safely to the habitual residence. E.g. Danaipour v. McLarey, 286 F.3d 1 (1st Cir.2002). If violence directed at the custodial parent is sufficiently serious, a court may conclude that it presents a grave risk to the child as well. E.g. Walsh v. Walsh, 221 F.3d 204 (1st Cir.2000). A number of writers have considered the dilemma presented by these cases; see, e.g., Merle H. Weiner, *International Child Abduction and the Escape from Domestic Violence*, 69 Fordham L. Rev. 593 (2000). See also Van de Sande v. Van de Sande, 431 F.3d 567 (7th Cir. 2005) (evidence of serious family violence sufficient to establish grave risk of harm).

g. Return and Appeals

In <u>Chafin v. Chafin, 568 U.S. 165 (2013)</u>, the Court ruled unanimously that a return order under the Convention, and the child's subsequent return from the United States to her mother in Scotland, did not moot the case for purposes of the father's appeal. Acknowledging that it was not clear whether the father could obtain a "re-return" of the child from Scotland if he prevailed on appeal, the Court held that this uncertainty did not deprive the appellate court of jurisdiction. The Court also noted that if the father were to prevail on appeal, he might obtain relief from the lower court's judgment for more than $94,000 in fees and expenses in connection with the child's return.

Chafin reflects an obvious policy problem: should trial courts routinely grant stays of Hague return orders, in order to allow the losing party an opportunity to appeal? The Supreme Court's answer to this was no, noting that the Convention mandates a prompt return. The Court encouraged lower courts to "take steps to decide these cases as expeditiously as possible, for the sake of the children who find themselves in such an unfortunate situation."

Further Reading: Child Abduction Convention

- Ann Laquer Estin, International Family Law Desk Book (2d ed. 2016).

- Jeremy D. Morley, The Hague Abduction Convention: Practical Issues and Procedures for the Family Lawyer (2017).

- Rhona Schuz, The Hague Child Abduction Convention: A Critical Analysis (2013).

Problem 7-45

After a romance developed between Wim, who lived in Belgium, and Christina, who lived in New York, Christina learned that she was pregnant with Wim's child. Because there was free medical care available in Belgium, Wim persuaded her to have the baby there. Christina traveled to Belgium on a tourist visa, bringing only two suitcases, and lived there for six months until the child was born. By then, the parties' relationship had deteriorated, and Christina obtained a U.S. passport for the infant and returned with him to New York. Wim made several trips to New York over the next three months, but the parties' attempts to reconcile were not successful. Wim has filed a petition to return the baby to Belgium under the Child Abduction Convention. What issues must the court resolve? (See Delvoye v. Lee, 329 F.3d 330 (3d Cir. 2003).)

Problem 7-46

After planning their move for several years, Robert and Julie sold their house and moved from Minnesota to Israel in July with their two sons, who were 6 and 9 years old. The children enrolled in school, made friends, and began to learn Hebrew, but Julie was unhappy and wanted to return to the U.S. with the children. To prevent this, Robert procured an ex parte restraining order from a rabbinical court in Israel with jurisdiction over child custody matters. After Robert agreed that Julie could take the children back to Minnesota for a visit the next summer, Julie consulted a lawyer, who told her that she would probably lose custody of her children in the Israeli rabbinical court. At the end of their school year, Julie flew to Minnesota with the boys and filed an action for a legal separation and custody in the state courts. She refused to return to Israel with the children, and four months later Robert filed a petition under the Hague Convention in federal district court. What arguments might Julie make in response to Robert's petition? (Cf. Silverman v. Silverman, 338 F.3d 886 (8th Cir. 2003).)

CHAPTER 8

The Lawyer's Role in Family Disputes

Lawyers practicing in family law face unique challenges. Clients in these cases are often unhappy and under significant personal and financial stress. Family disputes can be emotionally charged, with the potential for serious and long-lasting effects for the parties and those who are closest and most important to them. Because the law in this area tends to be open-ended or subject to significant judicial discretion—as when courts determine a "fair and equitable" division of property, or the "best interests of the child"—the process may seem arbitrary or unfair. The familiar paradigm of the zealous advocate seems problematic in this setting, but lawyers are not always skilled at or prepared for the challenges of problem-solving, promoting settlement and helping clients to balance different and conflicting goals.

Bounds of Advocacy

The American Academy of Matrimonial Lawyers (AAML) has developed standards of conduct known as the Bounds of Advocacy to provide guidance for lawyers in family disputes.

The special challenges of family law practice have consequences for lawyers: bar authorities report that a significant portion of the grievances filed against attorneys stem from representation in divorce and family law disputes. This chapter considers how the familiar professional responsibility principles apply in this setting, and explores two unusual roles performed by attorneys in family law cases: serving as a mediator or "third party neutral," and working with children as clients.

Wood v. McGrath, North, Mullin & Kratz, P.C.

589 N.W.2d 103 (Neb. 1999)

CONNOLLY, J.

We granted the appellant, Beverly J. Wood's petition for further review of the Nebraska Court of Appeals' decision. The Court of Appeals concluded that as a matter of law, Timothy J. Pugh, an attorney with the appellee, the law firm of McGrath, North, Mullin & Kratz, P.C. (McGrath), did not breach the standard of care or commit legal malpractice by failing to inform Wood that the law relating to two issues relevant to a divorce settlement was unsettled and that the settlement resolved those issues against her. We reverse the Court of Appeals' decision and conclude that the doctrine of judgmental immunity does not apply to an attorney's failure to inform a client of unsettled legal issues relevant to a settlement agreement.

BACKGROUND

We set out the facts focusing on the issues raised in Wood's petition for further review. For a more detailed recitation of the facts, see *Wood v. McGrath, North,* 7 Neb.App. 262, 581 N.W.2d 107 (1998).

Wood brought a legal malpractice action against McGrath, alleging that Pugh had negligently represented her in a dissolution action. The underlying dissolution action was concluded by settlement and decree. In her petition against McGrath, Wood alleged that Pugh allowed her to accept less than her share of the marital estate and was negligent by, inter alia, failing to inform her that (1) the settlement reflected a distribution which excluded all rights to then unvested stock options which her husband held through his employment at Werner Enterprises, Inc.; (2) the state of the law indicated that a trial court could likely include all such stock options within the marital estate; (3) the settlement reflected a distribution which excluded approximately $210,489 from the marital estate to account for potential capital gains tax on the stock that the couple owned; and (4) the state of the law indicated that a trial court could likely value the Werner stock without deducting any potential capital gains tax.

At trial, Wood testified that Pugh told her the settlement awarded her 40 percent of the marital estate and that when she asked if that was appropriate, she said Pugh told her a judge would award her anywhere from 35 to 50 percent— that she could do better or worse than the settlement by going to trial. However, Wood testified that Pugh never discussed the different terms of the settlement, never mentioned any alternatives to settling, never provided any reasons to reject the settlement, and never discussed the potential outcome of a trial. She stated that she would not have signed the agreement if Pugh had told her that a trial court might include the unvested stock options as part of the marital estate and that a trial court might prohibit the deduction of potential capital gains tax when valuing the stock, contrary to what the settlement proposed.

Two attorneys testified as expert witnesses for Wood. David Domina stated that when a property settlement raises the issue of unvested stock options, the decision is the client's whether to pursue the issue to trial or to nonetheless settle the issue and that a lawyer breaches the applicable standard of care by failing to inform the client of the existence of the issue and the related law. Domina testified that when a settlement agreement deducts potential capital gains taxes from the value of a marital estate, a lawyer breaches the applicable standard of care by failing to inform a client of the effect of the deduction and the related law. Paul Galter testified that given the terms of the settlement agreement presented to Wood, Pugh breached the standard of care because Pugh did not give Wood sufficient information on the unvested stock options and capital gains tax issues. Galter stated that Pugh had a duty to tell Wood that the agreement raised the issues; to explain their effects to Wood; and to explain what the relevant law on the issues was, including what courts in other jurisdictions had held, before permitting her to sign the agreement.

At the close of Wood's evidence, McGrath moved for a directed verdict, which the court sustained on the issues of the stock valuation and the exclusion of unvested stock options.

On appeal, Wood asserted, inter alia, that the trial court erred in granting McGrath's directed verdict, arguing that Pugh breached the standard of care by failing to properly advise her in regard to the settlement agreement.

The Court of Appeals noted that the law on both the inclusion of unvested stock options in the marital estate and the consideration of potential capital gains taxes in valuing the estate were unsettled in Nebraska at the time the parties entered into the agreement. _Wood v. McGrath, North_, 7 Neb.App. 262, 581 N.W.2d 107 (1998). Accordingly, the court held that the judgmental immunity rule applied and concluded that Pugh's acts and omissions relating to the issues were not negligent as a matter of law. The court then stated that "Pugh, upon exercise of informed judgment, was not obligated to give additional advice regarding the unsettled nature of relevant legal principles."

* * *

ANALYSIS

Wood argues that the doctrine of judgmental immunity does not apply to Pugh's failure to inform her of the law relating to the unvested stock options and capital gains tax deduction issues; that the settlement resolved those issues against her; and that given the body of law on the issues at the time, a trial judge might have resolved those issues in her favor. McGrath notes that the law regarding those issues was unsettled in Nebraska when Pugh represented Wood and argues that the doctrine of judgmental immunity applies to an attorney's decision regarding unsettled law, citing _Baker v. Fabian, Thielen & Thielen_, 254 Neb. 697, 578 N.W.2d 446 (1998). McGrath thus contends that when presenting a client with a settlement, an attorney has no duty to inform a client of possible options when the law relating to a relevant issue is unsettled.

In *Baker, supra*, this court held that an attorney is not liable for an error in judgment on a point of law which has not been settled by this court and on which reasonable doubt may be entertained by well-informed lawyers. Thus, an attorney's judgment or recommendation on an unsettled point of law is immune from suit, and the attorney has no duty to accurately predict the future course of unsettled law. This immunity rule encourages practicing attorneys in this state to predict, in a professional manner, the outcome of legal issues relevant to their clients' cases. See Canon 7, EC 7–3 and 7–5, of the Code of Professional Responsibility. However, Pugh's recommendations (or lack thereof) on the unvested stock options and capital gains tax issues are not before us. Rather, the issue is whether the doctrine of judgmental immunity applies to Pugh's failure to inform Wood that the law relating to unvested stock options and potential capital gains tax issues, while unsettled in Nebraska, were settled in other jurisdictions in a manner which would have been favorable to Wood. The question of whether an attorney owes a duty to inform a client of the unsettled nature of relevant law was not addressed in *Baker*. Thus, we must determine whether to extend the *Baker* judgmental immunity rule to an attorney's failure to inform a client of unsettled legal issues relevant to a settlement agreement.

"[W]e insist that lawyers. . .advise clients with respect to settlements with the same skill, knowledge, and diligence with which they pursue all other legal tasks." *Bruning v. Law Offices of Ronald J. Palagi*, 250 Neb. 677, 689, 551 N.W.2d 266, 272 (1996) (citing *Grayson v. Wofsey, Rosen, Kweskin & Kuriansky*, 231 Conn. 168, 646 A.2d 195 (1994)). See, also, *McWhirt v. Heavey*, 250 Neb. 536, 550 N.W.2d 327 (1996). We declined in *McWhirt v. Heavey*, 250 Neb. at 547, 550 N.W.2d at 335, " 'to adopt a rule that insulates attorneys from exposure to malpractice claims arising from their negligence in settled cases if the attorney's conduct has damaged the client.' " We decline to adopt such a rule now.

The decision to settle a controversy is the client's. See Canon 7, EC 7–7. If a client is to meaningfully make that decision, he or she needs to have the information necessary to assess the risks and benefits of either settling or proceeding to trial. "A lawyer should exert his or her best efforts to ensure that decisions of a client are made only after the client has been informed of relevant considerations." Canon 7, EC 7–8. The desire is that a client's decision to settle is an informed one.

The attorney's research efforts may not resolve doubts or may lead to the conclusion that only hindsight or future judicial decisions will provide accurate answers. The attorney's responsibilities to the client may not be satisfied concerning a material issue simply by determining that a proposition is doubtful or by unilaterally deciding the issue. Where there are reasonable alternatives, the attorney should inform the client that the issue is uncertain, unsettled or debatable and allow the client to make the decision. 2 Ronald E. Mallen & Jeffrey M. Smith, Legal Malpractice § 17.15 at 531–32 (4th ed.1996).

Additionally, an allegation that an attorney is negligent by failing to inform a client of an unsettled legal issue relevant to a settlement does not demand that an attorney accurately predict the future course of unsettled law. Thus, an allegation that an attorney did not properly inform a client of relevant unsettled legal issues does not provide the same need for immunity from suit as does an attorney's judgment or recommendation in an area of unsettled law.

* * *

Ultimately, we cannot support what would be the clear result of extending the judgmental immunity rule in the instant case. If we conclude that the judgmental immunity rule applies to an attorney's failure to inform a client of unsettled legal issues relevant to a settlement, an attorney could forgo conducting research or providing a client with information on a relevant legal issue once he or she determined that the legal issue at hand was unsettled in this state. We fail to see how this result promotes the settlement of disputes in a client's best interests.

We conclude that the doctrine of judgmental immunity does not apply to an attorney's failure to inform a client of unsettled legal issues relevant to a settlement. Our conclusion makes no judgment as to whether Pugh was negligent. It imposes no additional duty as a matter of law to research or inform a client on unsettled legal matters. Rather, it simply directs that consistent with *Bruning v. Law Offices of Ronald J. Palagi*, 250 Neb. 677, 551 N.W.2d 266 (1996); *McWhirt v. Heavey*, 250 Neb. 536, 550 N.W.2d 327 (1996); and *McVaney v. Baird, Holm, McEachen*, 237 Neb. 451, 466 N.W.2d 499 (1991), whether an attorney is negligent for such a failure is determined by whether the attorney exercised the same skill, knowledge, and diligence as attorneys of ordinary skill and capacity commonly possess and exercise in the performance of all other legal tasks. At the same time, an attorney's ultimate recommendation in an area of unsettled law is immune from suit. *Baker v. Fabian, Thielen & Thielen, supra.* Such a result gives the client the benefit of both professional advice and the information necessary to make an informed decision whether to settle a dispute.

CONCLUSION

The Court of Appeals erred in concluding that Pugh was not negligent as a matter of law in failing to inform Wood of the unsettled nature of the law regarding whether unvested stock options were part of the marital estate and whether the marital estate's unvested stock options should have been valued without deducting potential capital gains tax. Accordingly, we reverse the Court of Appeals' decision and remand the cause to the Court of Appeals with directions to remand the cause to the district court for a new trial.

REVERSED AND REMANDED FOR A NEW TRIAL.

Points for Discussion

a. Client Autonomy

The *Wood* case applies the American Bar Association's Model Code of Professional Responsibility, which has been replaced by the ABA's <u>Model Rules of Professional Conduct</u> (Model Rules). All states use some version of the Model Rules. <u>Model Rule 1.2(a)</u> requires a lawyer to abide by a client's decision in important matters such as the decision to settle a case. Lawyers must also keep their clients reasonably informed about the status of a matter, and give the client whatever information is reasonably necessary so that the client can make informed decisions. <u>Model Rule 1.4</u>.

Go Online

Information about and the text of the ABA Model Rules, and links to state ethics rules, are available from the <u>ABA Center for Professional Responsibility</u>. The <u>California Rules of Professional Conduct</u>, are available from the State Bar of California.

b. Competence and Diligence

The Model Rules require that a lawyer provide competent representation to clients, reflecting a sufficient level of legal knowledge, skill, thoroughness and preparation, see <u>Model Rule 1.1</u>; and also require that a lawyer act with reasonable diligence and promptness in representing a client, see <u>Model Rule 1.3</u>. A lawyer who fails to exercise an appropriate level of diligence and competence may be subject to a malpractice action brought by the client, or an attorney discipline proceeding under the applicable ethics rules. See, e.g., <u>People v. Aron, 962 P.2d 261 (Colo.1998)</u> (attorney suspended for failure to research custody issues and failure to advise client of criminal consequences for violating custody order.)

Neglect. An obvious example of the attorney's failure to act competently or diligently occurs when the lawyer neglects a client's case. This occurs all too often, as the disciplinary cases demonstrate. See, e.g., <u>Van Sloten v. State Bar of California, 771 P.2d 1323 (Cal. 1989)</u>; <u>People v. Felker, 770 P.2d 402 (Colo.1989)</u> (preparation of the case on the way to the courthouse is a ground for discipline); <u>In re Smith, 659 N.E.2d 896 (Ill. 1995)</u>. See <u>James L. Rigelhaupt, Jr., *Annotation, Attorney's Liability for Negligence In Cases Involving Domestic Relations*, 78 A.L.R.3d 255 (1977)</u>.

Advice to Settle. Courts have found lawyers answerable in malpractice for negligently advising a client to settle a case. Frequently, the claim is based on the lawyer's failure to discover important financial information. See <u>Grayson v. Wof-</u>

sey, Rosen, Kweskin and Kuriansky, 646 A.2d 195 (Conn. 1994); Meyer v. Wagner, 709 N.E.2d 784 (Mass. 1999), Ziegelheim v. Apollo, 607 A.2d 1298 (N.J. 1992). See generally Andrew S. Grossman, *Avoiding Legal Malpractice in Family Law Cases: The Dangers of Not Engaging in Financial Discovery*, 33 Fam. L.Q. 361 (1999); Lewis Becker, *Ethical Concerns in Negotiating Family Law Agreements*, 30 Fam. L.Q. 587 (1996). See also McMahon v. Shea, 688 A.2d 1179 (Pa. 1997) (failure to advise client regarding controlling law): Gamez v. State Bar of Texas, 765 S.W.2d 827 (Tex. App. 1988) (failure to discuss question of income tax exemptions for children).

Make the Connection

Should the ex-wife in Sahin v. Sahin, 758 N.E.2d 132 (Mass. 2001), reprinted in Chapter 6, have a malpractice claim against her lawyers? What about the unmarried father in Heidbreder v. Carton, 645 N.W.2d 355 (Minn. 2002), reprinted in Chapter 3?

c. Confidentiality

A lawyer is obligated to maintain client confidences, with very limited authority to reveal information relating to the representation. Model Rule 1.6 permits a lawyer to reveal confidential information if the lawyer reasonably believes it is necessary to prevent "reasonably certain death or substantial bodily harm," to prevent the client from committing a crime or fraud that is "reasonably certain to result in substantial injury to the financial interests or property of another and in furtherance of which the client has used or is using the lawyer's services," or to prevent, mitigate or rectify substantial injury to the financial interests or property of another resulting from a crime or fraud by the client "in furtherance of which the client has used the lawyer's services."

Applying these rules, how should a lawyer proceed when his or her client has abducted a child? If the lawyer knows the location of the client and the child, but has been instructed not to reveal it, what response can the lawyer give if the court asks where the client is? See People v. Chappell, 927 P.2d 829 (Colo.1996) (disbarring attorney for assisting client in child abduction); In re Marriage of Decker, 606 N.E.2d 1094 (Ill. 1992) (sentencing attorney for contempt for refusing to disclose information regarding client's whereabouts); but see Brennan v. Brennan, 422 A.2d 510 (Pa. Super. Ct. 1980) (information covered by attorney-client privilege).

In some states, lawyers are exempt from the child abuse reporting obligations discussed in Chapter 5, in order to protect confidential client information. Even when lawyers are not exempt by statute, some authorities suggest that they are bound by the requirements of Rule 1.6, and may not report child abuse or neglect unless necessary to prevent reasonably certain death or substantial bodily harm. See, e.g., Indiana State Bar Association, Ethics Opinion No. 2 of 2015, but cf.

Utah State Bar, Ethics Advisory Committee Opinion No. 97–12 (1998). The AAML Bounds of Advocacy takes the position in Standard 2.26 that: "An attorney should disclose evidence of a substantial risk of physical or sexual abuse of a child by the attorney's client." See generally Lisa Hansen, *Comment, Attorneys' Duty to Report Child Abuse*, 19 J. Amer. Acad. Matrim. L. 59 (2004).

Make the Connection

Confidentiality is also protected by the attorney-client privilege under the law of evidence, but the scope of the ethical obligation is much broader than the scope of the evidentiary privilege.

What are a lawyer's alternatives if the lawyer discovers that a client has been concealing assets from his or her spouse? An ethics opinion in New York concluded that a lawyer with knowledge that a client had fraudulently omitted assets from a financial statement, signed by the lawyer and filed with the court, had a duty either to persuade the client to undo the fraud or withdraw the document. N.Y. Ethics Op. 781 (2004). What if the lawyer does not learn about a failure to disclose property until after a separation agreement has been signed and a divorce decree is entered? Should a divorce lawyer be held liable in tort for misrepresenting a client's financial circumstances? See Simms v. Seaman, 69 A.3d 880 (Conn. 2013) (ruling that lawyer was shielded by "litigation privilege," but noting other jurisdictions that have abrogated privilege by statute for claims of fraud).

d. Conflicts of Interest

Can a lawyer represent both spouses in an uncontested divorce? Model Rule 1.7 permits a lawyer to undertake simultaneous representation in some circumstances, but not if the representation involves "the assertion of a claim by one client against another client represented in the same litigation or other proceeding before a tribunal." This rule prohibits joint representation in a divorce, custody, or child support matter. The AAML Bounds of Advocacy state that "[a]n attorney should not represent both husband and wife even if they do not wish to obtain independent representation," see Standard 3.1; and also that "[a]n attorney should not simultaneously represent both a client and a person with whom the client is sexually involved," see Standard 3.3.

Other ethics rules have permitted joint representation in divorce cases if the lawyer reasonably believed he or she would be able to provide competent and diligent representation and both clients consented after full disclosure of the risks of common representation. See, e.g., Levine v. Levine, 436 N.E.2d 476 (N.Y. 1982). This is still the rule in California; see In re Marriage of Egedi, 105 Cal.Rptr.2d 518 (Ct. App. 2001) (applying Cal. R. Prof. Conduct 3–310). Joint representation is fraught with peril for an attorney, however, and the case law includes both malpractice and discipline cases where lawyers improperly handled conflicting representation. E.g. <u>Ishmael v. Millington, 50 Cal.Rptr. 592 (Ct. App. 1966)</u>.

Lawyers face a different conflict of interest problem when they have represented one or both of the parties in another matter prior to their separation and divorce. All of the usual conflict of interest rules apply in this situation, particularly <u>Model Rules 1.7</u> and <u>1.9</u>. See, e.g., <u>People ex rel. Cortez v. Calvert, 617 P.2d 797 (Colo.1980)</u>; <u>Buntrock v. Buntrock, 419 So.2d 402 (Fla.App.1982)</u>; <u>Matter of Sexson, 613 N.E.2d 841 (Ind.1993)</u>; <u>Shih Ping Li v. Tzu Lee, 85 A.3d 144 (Md. 2014)</u>; <u>Grover v. Virdi, 516 N.Y.S.2d 27 (App. Div. 2d Dep't 1987)</u>. The same rule may apply to subsequent representation of one member of a cohabiting couple. See <u>In re Wilder, 764 N.E.2d 617 (Ind. 2002)</u> (lawyer who represented cohabiting couple in various business matters could not represent one of them in separating their affairs at the end of their relationship).

Joint representation of natural and adoptive parents is also problematic. An attorney was disbarred in <u>Stark County Bar Association v. Hare, 791 N.E.2d 966 (Ohio 2003)</u>, for misconduct including conflicts of interest, charging excessive fees, and misrepre-

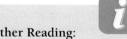

Further Reading:

Barbara Glesner-Fines, Ethical Issues in Family Representation (2010).

senting fees paid to the birth mother. In a termination of parental rights case, the court in <u>Baker v. Marion County Office of Family and Children, 810 N.E.2d 1035 (Ind. 2004)</u> refused to set aside the termination on the basis that joint representation of the parents did not result in a conflict of interest. When would joint misrepresentation of both parents be improper in a termination proceeding? See <u>In re Priscilla D., 5 A.3d 677 (Me. 2010)</u>.

e. Zealous Representation

How should a lawyer proceed when a client wants to take an extremely aggressive position, or is overly passive, or seeks an outcome that does not seem to be in the best interests of the children? What if a client is uncertain whether to proceed with a divorce? The professional conduct rules direct a lawyer to exercise independent judgment and render candid advice, which may be based on "moral, economic, social and political" considerations in addition to the law. See <u>Model Rule 2.1</u>. According to <u>AAML Standard 1.2</u>, a lawyer should advise the client of the emotional and economic impacts of divorce, and the feasibility of reconciliation. <u>Standard 6.1</u> provides that: "An attorney representing a parent should consider the welfare of, and seek to minimize the adverse impact of the divorce on, the minor children," and <u>Standard 6.2</u> states that: "An attorney should not permit a client to contest child custody, contact or access for either financial leverage or vindictiveness."

Lawyers may not bring frivolous claims or seek to delay litigation for strategic purposes; see Model Rules 3.1 and 3.2. Courts may impose sanctions on lawyers in these circumstances; e.g. Heal v. Heal, 762 A.2d 463 (R.I.2000). A lawyer's representation of a client does not constitute an endorsement of the client's views and activities, see Model Rule 1.2(b), and a lawyer may seek to withdraw if a client insists on pursuing objectives that the lawyer considers repugnant or with which the lawyer has a fundamental disagreement, see Model Rule 1.16(b)(4). In re Rose Lee Ann L., 718 N.E.2d 623 (Ill. 1999), held that a lawyer should be permitted to withdraw as attorney for parents in an abuse and neglect proceeding if the lawyer believes the clients may present a serious risk of bodily harm to the child. See also Office of Disciplinary Counsel v. Lombardi, 770 N.E.2d 1013 (Ohio 2002), in which a lawyer was suspended for financially assisting a client who defied a court's custody order and went into hiding in another state with the child.

f. Self-Represented Litigants

More often than not, one or both parties in a family law matter are not represented by lawyers. **Pro se** representation is particularly common in uncontested cases and cases in which the couple do not have children. See Robert B. Yegge, *Divorce Litigants Without Lawyers*, 28 Fam. L.Q. 407 (1994). This raises issues both of a lawyer's responsibility in dealing with an unrepresented party, see Model Rule 4.3, and the broader question of lawyers' responsibilities in making legal services available to persons of limited means. See also AAML Bounds of Advocacy Standard 3.2.

Unbundled Legal Services

One response to the high rate of pro se representation in family law has been a move toward "unbundling" legal services, by allowing lawyers to offer some but not all of the services usually encompassed by representation of a client. This may include legal counseling for pro se litigants, or serving as a "consulting attorney" for parties in mediation. See generally Forrest S. Mosten and Elizabeth Potter Scully, Unbundled Legal Services: A Family Lawyer's Guide (2017).

Model Rule 1.2(c) states that "A lawyer may limit the scope of the representation if the limitation is reasonable under the circumstances and the client gives informed consent." See, e.g., Lerner v. Laufer, 819 A.2d 471 (N.J. Super. Ct. App. Div. 2003), which allowed a lawyer to limit the scope of his representation to reviewing a mediated divorce settlement agreement. A number of jurisdictions have rules governing limited scope representation in family law. See, e.g., Cal. R. Ct. 5.425; Fla. Fam. L. R. Civ. P. 12.040.

g. Attorney's Fees

Legal fees must be reasonable, see <u>Model Rule 1.5(a)</u>. Courts sometimes conclude that very substantial fees are reasonable under the circumstances of particular cases. See, e.g., <u>Paul, Weiss, Rifkind, Wharton & Garrison v. Koons, 780 N.Y.S.2d 710 (Sup.Ct.2004)</u> (fees amounted to more than $3.9 million in international custody dispute in which wealthy client directed firm to "leave no stones unturned" and work "full-speed-ahead" on every front that could be pursued). Courts have disapproved of "nonrefundable" retainer fees in divorce matters. E.g. <u>Dayton Bar Association v. Schram, 787 N.E.2d 1184 (Ohio 2003)</u>. AAML <u>Standard 4.1</u> states that fee agreements should be in writing.

A lawyer may not charge "any fee in a domestic relations matter, the payment or amount of which is contingent upon the securing of a divorce or upon the amount of alimony or support, or property settlement in lieu thereof." <u>Model Rule 1.5(d)(1)</u>. The AAML Bounds of Advocacy go further, providing also that an attorney should not charge a fee contingent on the custody or visitation provisions obtained. See <u>Standard 4.5</u>. For a case in which a lawyer was sanctioned and held liable in malpractice for charging an illegal contingent fee in a large asset divorce case, based on a jury's finding that the $4.8 million fee was not paid by the client as a gift or bonus, see <u>Goldstein v. Commission for Lawyer Discipline, 109 S.W.3d 810 (Tex.Ct.App.2003)</u>.

Sex with Clients?

Movies and television programs often portray divorce lawyers having sexual relationships with their clients, and the original version of the ABA Model Rules did not expressly prohibit this. <u>Model Rule 1.8(j)</u> now states: "A lawyer shall not have sexual relations with a client unless a consensual sexual relationship existed between them when the client-lawyer relationship commenced." AAML <u>Standard 3.4</u> provides that an attorney should never have a sexual relationship with a client, opposing counsel or a judicial officer in the case during the time of the representation. See <u>Attorney Grievance Com'n of Maryland v. Culver, 849 A.2d 423 (Md. 2004)</u>. See also <u>California Formal Ethics Opinion 1987–92</u>. Note that sexting may constitute a sexual relationship within the scope of Rule 1.8(j). See, e.g., <u>Disciplinary Matter Involving Stanton, 376 P.3d 693 (Alaska 2016)</u>; <u>Disciplinary Counsel v. Bartels, 87 N.E.3d 155 (Ohio 2016)</u>. Sexual relations between a lawyer and a client may be but are not necessarily grounds for a malpractice claim, see <u>Vallinoto v. DiSandro, 688 A.2d 830 (R.I.1997)</u>.

Further Reading: Divorce Lawyers

- Lynn Mather, Craig McEwen, & Richard J. Maiman, Divorce Lawyers at Work: Varieties of Professionalism in Practice (2001).

- Austin Sarat & William L.F. Felstiner, Divorce Lawyers and Their Clients: Power and Meaning in the Legal Practice (1995).

Problem 8-1

Assume that you are a lawyer in private practice and you meet with a new client in a divorce action who appears to be in a state of extreme emotional and psychological distress.

(a) Do you have a duty to refer the client to appropriate professionals for consultation and psychotherapy? Would failure to do so constitute malpractice? Could your law firm have a counselor on staff to provide this type of assistance to the firm's family law clients?

(b) How should you proceed if your client is generally uncooperative, appears to be seriously depressed, and is asked to sign a separation agreement that would waive spousal support and relinquish primary custody of the couple's children? See Model Rule 1.14. (Cf. Talbot v. Schroeder, 475 P.2d 520 (Ariz. Ct. App. 1970).)

Lawyer Serving as a Third-Party Neutral

Family law matters may be subject to mediation or arbitration, as discussed in Chapters 6 and 7, and lawyers may serve as mediators or arbitrators. ABA Model Rule 2.4 governs the professional obligations of a lawyer serving as a third-party neutral. In this role, the lawyer assists "two or more persons who are not clients of the lawyer" to reach resolution of a dispute. The lawyer must inform unrepresented parties that the lawyer is not representing them, and must generally explain to them the difference between representing a client and serving as a third-party neutral. Under Model Rule 1.12, a lawyer who serves as a third-party neutral faces some limitations on future representation of any of the parties to the proceeding. Cf. Matluck v. Matluck, 825 So.2d 1071 (Fla.Ct.App. 2002) (former divorce mediator's law firm disqualified from representing husband in in post-dissolution proceedings); In re W.R., 966 N.E.2d 1139 (Ill. App. Ct. 2012) (former custody mediator disqualified from representing father in neglect action). See also Isaacson v. Isaacson, 792 A.2d 525 (N.J. Super. Ct. App. Div. 2002), which held that an attorney appointed as a mediator could not also serve as guardian ad litem representing the interests of the children.

Go Online

Lawyers serving in a third party neutral role may be subject to specialized ethical rules such as the American Bar Association's Model Standards of Practice for Family and Divorce Mediation (2001).

May a lawyer-mediator also draft documents for mediation clients, such as divorce petitions and settlement agreements for filing with the court? Authorities in Ohio have approved this practice, see Ohio Board of Commissioners on Grievances and Discipline, Op. No. 2009–4, 2009 WL 1764110 (2009), while other ethics authorities have concluded that this role is improper; see Texas Prof. Ethics Comm., Op. No. 583, 2008 WL 4897790 (2008); Utah State Bar Ethics Advisory Op. Comm., Op. 05–03, 2005 WL 3779039 (2005).

Ethics authorities have also weighed in on the practice of collaborative law, discussed in Chapter 6, a process in which clients retain lawyers for the limited purpose of settling the dispute without litigation. According to the ABA, this does not violate the Model Rules of Professional Conduct. See "Ethical Considerations in Collaborative Law Practice," ABA Formal Ethics Op. No. 07–447 (2007); see also the Uniform Collaborative Law Act (2010). Numerous state ethics committees have approved collaborate law practice. See, e.g., N.J. Sup. Ct. Advisory Comm. on Prof. Ethics, Op. 699, 2005 WL 3890576 (2005), but see Colo. Ethics Op. 115, Ethical Considerations in the Collaborative and Cooperative Law Contexts (2007).

Representing Children

Lawyers representing children face an extremely complex set of challenges. First, the lawyer must determine whether he or she has been appointed to serve as a guardian *ad litem* (GAL), charged with representing the child's best interests, or as an advocate, serving as counsel to the child. In addition, the lawyer's role may differ depending upon whether the lawyer is representing the child in a juvenile court prosecution, an abuse and neglect proceeding, an adoption or parentage case, or a custody dispute. Legal representation for children in juvenile court cases was mandated by the Supreme Court in In re Gault, 387 U.S. 1 (1967), and representation for children in child protection cases is required under the federal Child Abuse Prevention and Treatment Act, 42 U.S.C. § 5106(a)(2)(B)(ii) (2018).

Important consequences flow from the distinction between guardian and advocate, including such matters as whether the attorney may file motions and examine witnesses, whether the attorney may file a report with the court, and

On children's right to partici- pate in a divorce or custody proceeding, see <u>Matter of Sta- pleford, 931 A.2d 1199 (N.H. 2007)</u>, reprinted in Chapter 7.

whether the attorney may testify. Although non-lawyers cannot serve as counsel to the child, they may be appointed as a GAL or "special advo- cate." Courts have struggled to clarify these roles, and define how children's representatives may participate in dif- ferent types of proceedings.

Georgia State Bar Formal Advisory Opinion No. 10-2

<u>Approved, 720 S.E.2d 647 (Ga. 2012)</u>

QUESTION PRESENTED:

May an attorney who has been appointed to serve both as legal counsel and as guardian ad litem for a child in a termination of parental rights case advocate termination over the child's objection?

SUMMARY ANSWER:

When it becomes clear that there is an irreconcilable conflict between the child's wishes and the attorney's considered opinion of the child's best interests, the attorney must withdraw from his or her role as the child's guardian ad litem.

OPINION:

Relevant Rules

This question squarely implicates several of Georgia's Rules of Professional Conduct, particularly, Rule 1.14. Rule 1.14, dealing with an attorney's ethical duties towards a child or other client with a disability, provides that "the lawyer shall, as far as reasonably possible, maintain a normal client-lawyer relationship with the client." Comment 1 to Rule 1.14 goes on to note that "children as young as five or six years of age, and certainly those of ten or twelve, are regarded as having opinions that are entitled to weight in legal proceedings concerning their custody."

This question also involves Rule 1.2, Scope of Representation, and Rule 1.7, governing conflicts of interest. Comment 4 to Rule 1.7 indicates that "[l]oyalty to a client is also impaired when a lawyer cannot consider, recommend or carry out an appropriate course of action for the client because of the lawyer's other competing responsibilities or interests. The conflict in effect forecloses alternatives that would otherwise be available to the client."

Finally, this situation implicates Rule 3.7, the lawyer as a witness, to the extent that the guardian ad litem must testify and may need to advise the court of the conflict between the child's expressed wishes and what he deems the best interests of the child. Similarly, Rule 1.6, Confidentiality of Information, may also be violated if the attorney presents the disagreement to the Court.

Statutory Background

Georgia law requires the appointment of an attorney for a child as the child's counsel in a termination of parental rights proceeding.[4] The statute also provides that the court may additionally appoint a guardian ad litem for the child, and that the child's counsel is eligible to serve as the guardian ad litem. In addition to the child's statutory right to counsel, a child in a termination of parental rights proceedings also has a federal constitutional right to counsel.

In Georgia, a guardian ad litem's role is "to protect the interests of the child and to investigate and present evidence to the court on the child's behalf." The best interests of the child standard is paramount in considering changes or termination of parental custody. *See, e.g.,* Scott v. Scott, 276 Ga. 372, 377 (2003) ("[t]he paramount concern in any change of custody must be the best interests and welfare of the minor child"). The Georgia Court of Appeals held in In re A.P. [291 Ga. App. 690, 691 (2008)] based on the facts of that case that the attorney-guardian ad litem dual representation provided for under O.C.G.A. § 15–11–98(a) does not result in an inherent conflict of interest, given that "the fundamental duty of both a guardian ad litem and an attorney is to act in the best interests of the [child]."

This advisory opinion is necessarily limited to the ethical obligations of an attorney once a conflict of interest in the representation has *already arisen*. Therefore, we need not address whether or not the dual representation provided for under O.C.G.A. § 15–11–98(a) results in an inherent conflict of interest.[9]

---

[4]   O.C.G.A. § 15–11–98(a) ("In any proceeding for terminating parental rights or any rehearing or appeal thereon, the court *shall* appoint an attorney to represent the child as the child's counsel and *may* appoint a separate guardian ad litem or a guardian ad litem who may be the same person as the child's counsel") (emphasis added).

[9]   See, e.g., Wis. Ethics Op. E–89–13 (finding no inherent conflict of interest with the dual representation of an attorney and guardian but concluding that if a conflict does arise based on specific facts, the attorney's ethical responsibility is to resign as the guardian).

Discussion

The child's attorney's first responsibility is to his or her client. Rule 1.2 makes clear that an attorney in a normal attorney-client relationship is bound to defer to a client's wishes regarding the ultimate objectives of the representation. Rule 1.14 requires the attorney to maintain, "as far as reasonably possible. . .a normal client-lawyer relationship with the [child]." An attorney who "reasonably believes that the client cannot adequately act in the client's own interest" may seek the appointment of a guardian or take other protective action. Importantly, the Rule does not simply direct the attorney to act in the client's best interests, as determined solely by the attorney. At the point that the attorney concludes that the child's wishes and best interests are in conflict, the attorney should petition the court for removal as the child's guardian ad litem, disclosing only that there is a conflict which requires such removal.

The attorney should not reveal the basis of the request for the appointment of a guardian ad litem to preserve confidentiality and so as not to compromise the child's position.[14] An exception to the duty of confidentiality may arise "[w]here honoring the duty of confidentiality would result in the children's exposure to a high risk of probable harm."[15]

The attorney should not reveal further information received during the representation, nor should the attorney otherwise use the information received from the child in confidence to advocate a position not desired by the child. This contrasts with the attorney's ability to disclose such information to the court in service of the child's wishes.

The attorney is under an affirmative ethical obligation to seek to have a new guardian ad litem appointed following his withdrawal as guardian, as Comment 3 to Rule 1.14 explains that "the lawyer should see to [the appointment of a legal representative] where it would serve the client's best interests." If the conflict between the attorney's view of the child's best interests and the child's view of his or her own interests is severe, the attorney may seek to withdraw entirely following Rule 1.16 or seek to have a separate guardian appointed.

The attorney may not withdraw as the child's counsel and then seek appointment as the child's guardian ad litem, as the child would then be a former client to whom the former attorney/guardian ad litem would be adverse.

---

[14]   See In re Georgette, 785 N.E.2d 356, 367 (Mass. 2003).
[15]   In re Christina W., 639 S.E.2d 770, 778 (W. Va. 2006).

This conclusion is in accord with many other states.[20] For instance, Ohio permits an attorney to be appointed both as a child's counsel and as the child's guardian ad litem.[21] Ohio ethics rules prohibit continued service in the dual roles when there is a conflict between the attorney's determination of best interests and the child's express wishes. Court rules and applicable statutes require the court to appoint another person as guardian ad litem for the child. An attorney who perceives a conflict between his role as counsel and as guardian ad litem is expressly instructed to notify the court of the conflict and seek withdrawal as guardian ad litem.[24] This solution (withdrawal from the guardian ad litem role once it conflicts with the role as counsel) is in accord with an attorney's duty to the client.

Connecticut's Bar Association provided similar advice to its attorneys, and Connecticut's legislature subsequently codified that position into law.[26] Similarly, in Massachusetts, an attorney representing a child must represent the child's expressed preferences, assuming that the child is reasonably able to make "an adequately considered decision. . .even if the attorney believes the child's position to be unwise or not in the child's best interest."[27] Even if a child is unable to make an adequately considered decision, the attorney still has the duty to represent the child's expressed preferences unless doing so would "place the child at risk of substantial harm." In New Jersey, a court-appointed attorney needs to be "a zealous advocate for the wishes of the client. . .unless the decisions are patently absurd or pose an undue risk of harm."[29] New Jersey's Supreme Court was skeptical that an attorney's duty of advocacy could be successfully reconciled with concern for the client's best interests.[30]

In contrast, other states have developed a "hybrid" model for attorneys in child custody cases serving simultaneously as counsel for the child and as their

---

[20] See, e.g., Wis. Ethics Op. E–89–13, Conflicts of Interests; Guardians (1989) (providing that dual representation as counsel and guardian ad litem is permitted until conflict between the roles occurs, and then the attorney must petition the court for a new guardian ad litem); Ariz. Ethics Op. 86–13, Juvenile Proceedings; Guardians (1986) (providing that a "lawyer may serve as counsel and guardian ad litem for a minor child in a dependency proceeding so long as there is no conflict between the child's wishes and the best interests of the child").

[21] Ohio Board of Comm'rs. on Griev. and Discipline, Op. 2006–5, 2006 WL 2000108, at *1 (2006).

[24] Id., quoting In re Baby Girl Baxter, 17 Ohio St. 3d 229, 479 N.E.2d 257 (1985) (superseded by statute on other grounds).

[26] See Conn. Bar Ass'n Comm. on Prof. Ethics, CT Eth. Op. 94–29, 1994 WL 780846, at *3 (1994); In re Tayquon, 821 A.2d 796, 803–04 (Conn. App. 2003) (discussing revisions to Conn. Gen. Stat. § 46b–129a).

[27] See Mass Comm. For Public Counsel Servs., Performance Standards, Standard 1.6(b), at 8–10; See also In re Georgette, 785 N.E.2d 356, 368 (Mass. 2003).

[29] In re Mason, 701 A.2d 979, 982 (N.J. Super. Ct. Ch. Div. 1997) (internal citations omitted).

[30] See In re M.R., 638 A.2d 1274, 1285 (N.J. 1994).

guardian ad litem.[31] This "hybrid" approach "necessitates a modified application of the Rules of Professional Conduct." That is, the states following the hybrid model, acknowledge the "'hybrid' nature of the role of attorney/guardian ad litem which necessitates a modified application of the Rules of Professional Conduct," excusing strict adherence to those rules. The attorney under this approach is bound by the client's best interests, not the client's expressed interests. The attorney must present the child's wishes and the reasons the attorney disagrees to the court.

Although acknowledging that this approach has practical benefits, we conclude that strict adherence to the Rules of Professional Conduct is the sounder approach.

Conclusion

At the point that the attorney concludes that the child's wishes and best interests are in conflict, the attorney should petition the court for removal as the child's guardian ad litem, disclosing only that there is a conflict which requires such removal. The attorney should not reveal the basis of the request for the appointment of a guardian ad litem to preserve confidentiality and so as not to compromise the child's position. The attorney should not reveal further information received during the representation, nor should the attorney otherwise use the information received from the child in confidence to advocate a position not desired by the child. The attorney is under an affirmative ethical obligation to seek to have a new guardian ad litem appointed following his withdrawal as guardian. If the conflict between the attorney's view of the child's best interests and the child's view of his or her own interests is severe, the attorney may seek to withdraw entirely following Rule 1.16 or seek to have a separate guardian appointed.

---

[31]   See Clark v. Alexander, 953 P.2d 145, 153–54 (Wyo. 1998); In re Marriage of Rolfe, 216 Mont. 39, 51–53, 699 P.2d 79, 86–87 (Mont. 1985); In re Christina W., 639 S.E.2d at 777 (requiring the guardian to give the child's opinions consideration "where the child has demonstrated an adequate level of competency [but] there is no requirement that the child's wishes govern."); see also Veazey v. Veazey, 560 P.2d 382, 390 (Alaska 1977) ("[I]t is equally plain that the guardian is not required to advocate whatever placement might seem preferable to a client of tender years.") (superseded by statute on other grounds); Alaska Bar Assn Ethics Committee Op. 85–4 (November 8, 1985)(concluding that duty of confidentiality is modified in order to effectuate the child's best interests); Utah State Bar Ethics Advisory Opinion Committee Op. No. 07–02 (June 7, 2007) (noting that Utah statute requires a guardian ad litem to notify the Court if the minor's wishes differ from the attorney's determination of best interests).

Points for Discussion:

a. GAL or Advocate?

How is the GAL role distinct from that of counsel for the child? Clark v. Alexander, 953 P.2d 145 (Wyo.1998), which approved a hybrid model of representation, held that a lawyer serving as GAL for three children in the same family was not bound by their wishes regarding custody, and did not need to withdraw when they expressed conflicting preferences, although he was obligated to inform the court of the children's preferences and explain the basis for his disagreement. As a GAL, the lawyer was expected to conduct an investigation, and could disclose information to the court that would otherwise be confidential, although the court noted that it was always best to seek the child's consent first. As an attorney, the GAL could file motions, present evidence, examine and cross-examine witnesses, and make argument to the court, but he could not also be a fact witness at the hearing.

Many writers endorse the advocate model, particularly for children who are old enough to reason and communicate effectively. See, e.g., Katharine Hunt Federle, *The Ethics of Empowerment: Rethinking the Role of Lawyers in Interviewing and Counseling the Child Client*, 64 Fordham L. Rev. 1655 (1996); Martin Guggenheim, *The Right to Be Represented but Not Heard: Reflections on Legal Representation for Children*, 59 N.Y.U. L. Rev. 76 (1984). For a caution on this point, see Emily Buss, *Confronting Developmental Barriers to the Empowerment of Child Clients*, 84 Cornell L. Rev. 895 (1999). For an account of the experience of representing children, see Emily Buss, *"You're My What?" The Problem of Children's Misperceptions of Their Lawyers' Roles*, 64 Fordham L. Rev. 1699 (1996).

b. Professional Responsibilities of a GAL

The attorney-client privilege may operate differently when a lawyer is appointed as guardian ad litem for a child. See In re Christina W., 639 S.E.2d 770 (W. Va. 2006) (holding that GAL may have obligation to disclose information to safeguard child's best interests); People v. Gabriesheski, 262 P.3d 653 (Colo. 2011) (child's statements to GAL in child welfare proceeding not privileged in stepfather's subsequent criminal prosecution when child recanted accusations).

Note that a lawyer serving as a GAL may be subject to professional discipline for actions taken while in that role. See In re Disciplinary Proceeding Against Whitney, 120 P.3d 550 (Wash. 2005) (lawyer disbarred for lying to court and obstructing disciplinary inquiry). In most jurisdictions, however, a GAL has an absolute quasi-judicial

Go Online

Resources and information for lawyers representing children are available from the National Association of Counsel for Children.

immunity from lawsuits for negligence. See, e.g., <u>Kimbrell v. Kimbrell, 331 P.3d 915 (N.M. 2014)</u>; <u>Paige K.B. v. Molepske, 580 N.W.2d 289 (Wis.1998)</u>; see also <u>Kirtley v. Rainey, 326 F.3d 1088 (9th Cir.2003)</u> (court-appointed GAL is not a state actor for purposes of § 1983). Lawyers appointed as counsel for children rather than as guardians ad litem may not enjoy the immunity from tort liability that generally applies to a GAL. See <u>Fox v. Wills, 890 A.2d 726 (Md. 2006)</u>.

c. Standards of Practice

The American Bar Association has developed practice standards for lawyers representing children as either attorney for the child or a "best interests attorney." <u>Standards of Practice for Lawyers Representing Children in Custody Cases</u> (2003), reprinted at <u>37 Fam. L.Q. 131 (2003)</u>, and discussed in <u>Linda D. Elrod, *Raising the Bar for Lawyers Who Represent Children: ABA Standards of Practice for Custody Cases*, 37 Fam. L.Q. 105 (2003)</u>. See also the ABA <u>Standards of Practice for Lawyers Who Represent Children in Abuse and Neglect Cases</u> (1996).

The 2007 <u>Uniform Representation of Children in Abuse, Neglect, and Custody Proceedings Act (URCANCPA)</u>, reprinted at <u>42 Fam. L.Q. 1 (2008)</u>, integrates these two sets of ABA standards, and also addresses the role of the non-lawyer representative for a child, such as Court Appointed Special Advocate (CASA), referred to as a "best interests advocate." Under all of these standards, a child's attorney has a traditional attorney-client relationship with the child, including duties to maintain the child's confidences and abide by the child's decisions about the objectives of representation.

Problem 8-2

When C.C. was three years old his father, Ronald, fatally shot C.C.'s mother. C.C. was found to be dependent, and a petition was filed for termination of Ronald's parental rights. C.C.'s court-appointed lawyer has argued in support of termination, but C.C. has told both his therapist and his lawyer that he wants to live with Ronald. Ronald has asked the judge to remove C.C.'s counsel and appoint a new lawyer. C.C.'s lawyer has asked to be reappointed as GAL. C.C. is now age five. How should the court proceed? (Cf. <u>Castro v. Houchuli, 343 P.3d 457 (Ariz. Ct. App. 2015)</u>.)

Further Reading: Representing Children

- Melissa A. Kucinski, A Practical Handbook for the Child's Attorney: Effectively Representing Children in Custody Cases (2018).

- Jennifer L. Renne, <u>Legal Ethics in Child Welfare Cases</u> (2004).

Appendix
SELECTED STATUTORY PROVISIONS

Uniform Parentage Act (2017)

9B U.L.A. (Supp. 2018)

ARTICLE 1 GENERAL PROVISIONS

* * *

§ 102. Definitions.

In this [act]:

(1) "Acknowledged parent" means an individual who has established a parent-child relationship under [Article] 3.

Go Online

The full text and information on state adoptions for different versions of the Uniform Parentage Act is available from the Uniform Law Commission.

(2) "Adjudicated parent" means an individual who has been adjudicated to be a parent of a child by a court with jurisdiction.

(3) "Alleged genetic parent" means an individual who is alleged to be, or alleges that the individual is, a genetic parent or possible genetic parent of a child whose parentage has not been adjudicated. The term includes an alleged genetic father and alleged genetic mother. The term does not include:

(A) a presumed parent;

(B) an individual whose parental rights have been terminated or declared not to exist; or

(C) a donor.

(4) "Assisted reproduction" means a method of causing pregnancy other than sexual intercourse. The term includes:

(A) intrauterine or intracervical insemination;

(B) donation of gametes;

(C) donation of embryos;

(D) in-vitro fertilization and transfer of embryos; and

(E) intracytoplasmic sperm injection.

(5) "Birth" includes stillbirth.

(6) "Child" means an individual of any age whose parentage may be determined under this [act].

(7) "Child-support agency" means a government entity, public official, or private agency, authorized to provide parentage-establishment services under Title IV-D of the Social Security Act, 42 U.S.C. sections 651 through 669.-

(8) "Determination of parentage" means establishment of a parent-child relationship by a judicial or administrative proceeding or signing of a valid acknowledgment of parentage under [Article] 3.

(9) "Donor" means an individual who provides gametes intended for use in assisted reproduction, whether or not for consideration. The term does not include:

(A) a woman who gives birth to a child conceived by assisted reproduction[, except as otherwise provided in [Article] 8]; or

(B) a parent under [Article] 7[or an intended parent under [Article] 8].

(10) "Gamete" means sperm, egg, or any part of a sperm or egg.

(11) "Genetic testing" means an analysis of genetic markers to identify or exclude a genetic relationship.

(12) "Individual" means a natural person of any age.

(13) "Intended parent" means an individual, married or unmarried, who manifests an intent to be legally bound as a parent of a child conceived by assisted reproduction.

(14) "Man" means a male individual of any age.

(15) "Parent" means an individual who has established a parent-child relationship under § 201.

(16) "Parentage" or "parent-child relationship" means the legal relationship between a child and a parent of the child.

(17) "Presumed parent" means an individual who under § 204 is presumed to be a parent of a child, unless the presumption is overcome in a judicial proceeding, a valid denial of parentage is made under [Article] 3, or a court adjudicates the individual to be a parent.

(18) "Record" means information that is inscribed on a tangible medium or that is stored in an electronic or other medium and is retrievable in perceivable form.

(19) "Sign" means, with present intent to authenticate or adopt a record:

(A) to execute or adopt a tangible symbol; or

(B) to attach to or logically associate with the record an electronic symbol, sound, or process.

(20) "Signatory" means an individual who signs a record.

(21) "State" means a state of the United States, the District of Columbia, Puerto Rico, the United States Virgin Islands, or any territory or insular possession under the jurisdiction of the United States. The term includes a federally recognized Indian tribe.

(22) "Transfer" means a procedure for assisted reproduction by which an embryo or sperm is placed in the body of the woman who will give birth to the child.

(23) "Witnessed" means that at least one individual who is authorized to sign has signed a record to verify that the individual personally observed a signatory sign the record.

(24) "Woman" means a female individual of any age.

§ 103. Scope.

(a) This [act] applies to an adjudication or determination of parentage.

(b) This [act] does not create, affect, enlarge, or diminish parental rights or duties under law of this state other than this [act].

[(c) This [act] does not authorize or prohibit an agreement between one or more intended parents and a woman who is not an intended parent in which the woman agrees to become pregnant through assisted reproduction and which provides that each intended parent is a parent of a child conceived through assisted reproduction. If a birth results under the agreement and the agreement is unenforceable under [cite to law of this state regarding surrogacy agreements], the parent-child relationship is established as provided in [Articles] 1 through 6.]

Legislative Note: A state should enact subsection (c) if the state does not enact Article 8 or otherwise does not permit surrogacy agreements.

* * *

§ 105. Applicable Law.

The court shall apply the law of this state to adjudicate parentage. The applicable law does not depend on:

(1) the place of birth of the child; or

(2) the past or present residence of the child.

* * *

§ 107. Establishment of Maternity and Paternity.

To the extent practicable, a provision of this [act] applicable to a father-child relationship applies to a mother-child relationship and a provision of this [act] applicable to a mother-child relationship applies to a father-child relationship.

ARTICLE 2 PARENT-CHILD RELATIONSHIP

§ 201. Establishment of Parent-Child Relationship.

A parent-child relationship is established between an individual and a child if:

(1) the individual gives birth to the child[, except as otherwise provided in [Article] 8];

(2) there is a presumption under § 204 of the individual's parentage of the child, unless the presumption is overcome in a judicial proceeding or a valid denial of parentage is made under [Article] 3;

(3) the individual is adjudicated a parent of the child under [Article] 6;

(4) the individual adopts the child;

(5) the individual acknowledges parentage of the child under [Article] 3, unless the acknowledgment is rescinded under § 308 or successfully challenged under [Article] 3 or 6;[or]

(6) the individual's parentage of the child is established under [Article] 7[; or

(7) the individual's parentage of the child is established under [Article] 8].

Legislative Note: A state should include paragraph (7) if the state includes Article 8 in this act. If the state does not enact Article 8 but otherwise permits and recognizes surrogacy agreements by statute, the state should include a reference to the statute in paragraph (7).

§ 202. No Discrimination Based on Marital Status of Parent.

A parent-child relationship extends equally to every child and parent, regardless of the marital status of the parent.

§ 203. Consequences of Establishing Parentage.

Unless parental rights are terminated, a parent-child relationship established under this [act] applies for all purposes, except as otherwise provided by law of this state other than this [act].

§ 204. Presumption of Parentage.

(a) An individual is presumed to be a parent of a child if:

(1) except as otherwise provided under[[Article] 8 or] law of this state other than this [act]:

(A) the individual and the woman who gave birth to the child are married to each other and the child is born during the marriage, whether the marriage is or could be declared invalid;

(B) the individual and the woman who gave birth to the child were married to each other and the child is born not later than 300 days after the marriage is terminated by death, [divorce, dissolution, annulment, or declaration of invalidity, or after a decree of separation or separate maintenance], whether the marriage is or could be declared invalid; or

(C) the individual and the woman who gave birth to the child married each other after the birth of the child, whether the marriage is or could be declared invalid, the individual at any time asserted parentage of the child, and:

(i) the assertion is in a record filed with the [state agency maintaining birth records]; or

(ii) the individual agreed to be and is named as a parent of the child on the birth certificate of the child; or

(2) the individual resided in the same household with the child for the first two years of the life of the child, including any period of temporary absence, and openly held out the child as the individual's child.

(b) A presumption of parentage under this § may be overcome, and competing claims to parentage may be resolved, only by an adjudication under [Article] 6 or a valid denial of parentage under [Article] 3.

ARTICLE 3 VOLUNTARY ACKNOWLEDGMENT OF PARENTAGE

§ 301. Acknowledgment of Parentage.

A woman who gave birth to a child and an alleged genetic father of the child, intended parent under [Article] 7, or presumed parent may sign an acknowledgment of parentage to establish the parentage of the child.

§ 302. Execution of Acknowledgment of Parentage.

(a) An acknowledgment of parentage under § 301 must:

(1) be in a record signed by the woman who gave birth to the child and by the individual seeking to establish a parent-child relationship, and the signatures must be attested by a notarial officer or witnessed;

(2) state that the child whose parentage is being acknowledged:

(A) does not have a presumed parent other than the individual seeking to establish the parent-child relationship or has a presumed parent whose full name is stated; and

(B) does not have another acknowledged parent, adjudicated parent, or individual who is a parent of the child under [Article] 7[or 8] other than the woman who gave birth to the child; and

(3) state that the signatories understand that the acknowledgment is the equivalent of an adjudication of parentage of the child and that a challenge to the acknowledgment is permitted only under limited circumstances and is barred two years after the effective date of the acknowledgment.

(b) An acknowledgment of parentage is void if, at the time of signing:

(1) an individual other than the individual seeking to establish parentage is a presumed parent, unless a denial of parentage by the presumed parent in a signed record is filed with the [state agency maintaining birth records]; or

(2) an individual, other than the woman who gave birth to the child or the individual seeking to establish parentage, is an acknowledged or adjudicated parent or a parent under [Article] 7[or 8].

§ 303. Denial of Parentage.

A presumed parent or alleged genetic parent may sign a denial of parentage in a record. The denial of parentage is valid only if:

(1) an acknowledgment of parentage by another individual is filed under § 305;

(2) the signature of the presumed parent or alleged genetic parent is attested by a notarial officer or witnessed; and

(3) the presumed parent or alleged genetic parent has not previously:

(A) completed a valid acknowledgment of parentage, unless the previous acknowledgment was rescinded under § 308 or challenged successfully under § 309; or

* * *

§ 305. Effect of Acknowledgment or Denial of Parentage.

(a) Except as otherwise provided in sections 308 and 309, an acknowledgment of parentage that complies with this [article] and is filed with the [state agency maintaining birth records] is equivalent to an adjudication of parentage of the child and confers on the acknowledged parent all rights and duties of a parent.

(b) Except as otherwise provided in sections 308 and 309, a denial of parentage by a presumed parent or alleged genetic parent which complies with this [article] and is filed with the [state agency maintaining birth records] with an acknowledgment of parentage that complies with this [article] is equivalent to an adjudication of the nonparentage of the presumed parent or alleged genetic parent and discharges the presumed parent or alleged genetic parent from all rights and duties of a parent.

* * *

§ 308. Procedure for Rescission.

(a) A signatory may rescind an acknowledgment of parentage or denial of parentage by filing with the [relevant state agency] a rescission in a signed record which is attested by a notarial officer or witnessed, before the earlier of:

(1) 60 days after the effective date under § 304 of the acknowledgment or denial; or

(2) the date of the first hearing before a court in a proceeding, to which the signatory is a party, to adjudicate an issue relating to the child, including a proceeding that establishes support.

(b) If an acknowledgment of parentage is rescinded under subsection (a), an associated denial of parentage is invalid, and the [state agency maintaining birth records] shall notify the woman who gave birth to the child and the individual who signed a denial of parentage of the child that the acknowledgment has been rescinded. Failure to give the notice required by this subsection does not affect the validity of the rescission.

§ 309. Challenge after Expiration of Period for Rescission.

(a) After the period for rescission under § 308 expires, but not later than two years after the effective date under § 304 of an acknowledgment of parentage or denial of parentage, a signatory of the acknowledgment or denial may commence a proceeding to challenge the acknowledgment or denial, including a challenge brought under § 614, only on the basis of fraud, duress, or material mistake of fact.

(b) A challenge to an acknowledgment of parentage or denial of parentage by an individual who was not a signatory to the acknowledgment or denial is governed by § 610.

* * *

§ 311. Full Faith and Credit.

The court shall give full faith and credit to an acknowledgment of parentage or denial of parentage effective in another state if the acknowledgment or denial was in a signed record and otherwise complies with law of the other state.

* * *

ARTICLE 4 REGISTRY OF PATERNITY

PART 1—GENERAL PROVISIONS

§ 401. Establishment of Registry.

A registry of paternity is established in the [state agency maintaining the registry].

§ 402. Registration for Notification.

(a) Except as otherwise provided in subsection (b) or § 405, a man who desires to be notified of a proceeding for adoption of, or termination of parental rights regarding, his genetic child must register in the registry of paternity established by § 401 before the birth of the child or not later than 30 days after the birth.

(b) A man is not required to register under subsection (a) if[:

(1)] a parent-child relationship between the man and the child has been established under this [act] or law of this state other than this [act][; or

(2) the man commences a proceeding to adjudicate his parentage before a court has terminated his parental rights].

(c) A man who registers under subsection (a) shall notify the registry promptly in a record of any change in the information registered. The [state agency maintaining the registry] shall incorporate new information received into its records but need not seek to obtain current information for incorporation in the registry.

§ 403. Notice of Proceeding.

An individual who seeks to adopt a child or terminate parental rights to the child shall give notice of the proceeding to a man who has registered timely under § 402(a) regarding the child. Notice must be given in a manner prescribed for service of process in a civil proceeding in this state.

§ 404. Termination of Parental Rights: Child Under One Year of Age.

An individual who seeks to terminate parental rights to or adopt a child is not required to give notice of the proceeding to a man who may be the genetic father of the child if:

(1) the child is under one year of age at the time of the termination of parental rights;

(2) the man did not register timely under § 402(a); and

(3) the man is not exempt from registration under § 402(b).

§ 405. Termination of Parental Rights: Child at Least One Year of Age.

If a child is at least one year of age, an individual seeking to adopt or terminate parental rights to the child shall give notice of the proceeding to each alleged genetic father of the child, whether or not he has registered under § 402(a) unless his parental rights have already been terminated. Notice must be given in a manner prescribed for service of process in a civil proceeding in this state.

* * *

ARTICLE 5 GENETIC TESTING

§ 501. Definitions.

In this [article]:

(1) "Combined relationship index" means the product of all tested relationship indices.

(2) "Ethnic or racial group" means, for the purpose of genetic testing, a recognized group that an individual identifies as the individual's ancestry or part of the ancestry or that is identified by other information.

(3) "Hypothesized genetic relationship" means an asserted genetic relationship between an individual and a child.

(4) "Probability of parentage" means, for the ethnic or racial group to which an individual alleged to be a parent belongs, the probability that a hypothesized genetic relationship is supported, compared to the probability that a genetic relationship is supported between the child and a random individual of the ethnic or racial group used in the hypothesized genetic relationship, expressed as a percentage incorporating the combined relationship index and a prior probability.

(5) "Relationship index" means a likelihood ratio that compares the probability of a genetic marker given a hypothesized genetic relationship and the probability of the genetic marker given a genetic relationship between the child and a random individual of the ethnic or racial group used in the hypothesized genetic relationship.

§ 502. Scope of [Article]; Limitation on Use of Genetic Testing.

(a) This [article] governs genetic testing of an individual in a proceeding to adjudicate parentage, whether the individual:

(1) voluntarily submits to testing; or

(2) is tested under an order of the court or a child-support agency.

(b) Genetic testing may not be used:

(1) to challenge the parentage of an individual who is a parent under [Article] 7[or 8]; or

(2) to establish the parentage of an individual who is a donor.

Legislative Note: *A state should include the bracketed reference to Article 8 if the state includes Article 8 in this act.*

§ 503. Authority to Order or Deny Genetic Testing.

(a) Except as otherwise provided in this [article] or [Article] 6, in a proceeding under this [act] to determine parentage, the court shall order the child and any other individual to submit to genetic testing if a request for testing is supported by the sworn statement of a party:

(1) alleging a reasonable possibility that the individual is the child's genetic parent; or

(2) denying genetic parentage of the child and stating facts establishing a reasonable possibility that the individual is not a genetic parent.

(b) A child-support agency may order genetic testing only if there is no presumed, acknowledged, or adjudicated parent of a child other than the woman who gave birth to the child.

(c) The court or child-support agency may not order in utero genetic testing.

(d) If two or more individuals are subject to court-ordered genetic testing, the court may order that testing be completed concurrently or sequentially.

(e) Genetic testing of a woman who gave birth to a child is not a condition precedent to testing of the child and an individual whose genetic parentage of the child is being determined. If the woman is unavailable or declines to submit to genetic testing, the court may order genetic testing of the child and each individual whose genetic parentage of the child is being adjudicated.

(f) In a proceeding to adjudicate the parentage of a child having a presumed parent or an individual who claims to be a parent under § 609, or to challenge an acknowledgment of parentage, the court may deny a motion for genetic testing of the child and any other individual after considering the factors in § 613(a) and (b).

(g) If an individual requesting genetic testing is barred under [Article] 6 from establishing the individual's parentage, the court shall deny the request for genetic testing.

(h) An order under this section for genetic testing is enforceable by contempt.

* * *

§ 506. Genetic Testing Results; Challenge to Results.

(a) Subject to a challenge under subsection (b), an individual is identified under this [act] as a genetic parent of a child if genetic testing complies with this [article] and the results of the testing disclose:

(1) the individual has at least a 99 percent probability of parentage, using a prior probability of 0.50, as calculated by using the combined relationship index obtained in the testing; and

(2) a combined relationship index of at least 100 to 1.

(b) An individual identified under subsection (a) as a genetic parent of the child may challenge the genetic testing results only by other genetic testing satisfying the requirements of this [article] which:

(1) excludes the individual as a genetic parent of the child; or

(2) identifies another individual as a possible genetic parent of the child other than:

(A) the woman who gave birth to the child; or

(B) the individual identified under subsection (a).

(c) Except as otherwise provided in § 511, if more than one individual other than the woman who gave birth is identified by genetic testing as a possible genetic parent of the child, the court shall order each individual to submit to further genetic testing to identify a genetic parent.

* * *

ARTICLE 6 PROCEEDING TO ADJUDICATE PARENTAGE

PART 1—NATURE OF PROCEEDING

* * *

§ 602. Standing to Maintain Proceeding.

Except as otherwise provided in [Article] 3 and sections 608 through 611, a proceeding to adjudicate parentage may be maintained by:

(1) the child;

(2) the woman who gave birth to the child, unless a court has adjudicated that she is not a parent;

(3) an individual who is a parent under this [act];

(4) an individual whose parentage of the child is to be adjudicated;

(5) a child-support agency[or other governmental agency authorized by law of this state other than this [act]];

(6) an adoption agency authorized by law of this state other than this [act] or licensed child-placement agency; or

(7) a representative authorized by law of this state other than this [act] to act for an individual who otherwise would be entitled to maintain a proceeding but is deceased, incapacitated, or a minor.

§ 603. Notice of Proceeding.

(a) The [petitioner] shall give notice of a proceeding to adjudicate parentage to the following individuals:

(1) the woman who gave birth to the child, unless a court has adjudicated that she is not a parent;

(2) an individual who is a parent of the child under this [act];

(3) a presumed, acknowledged, or adjudicated parent of the child; and

(4) an individual whose parentage of the child is to be adjudicated.

(b) An individual entitled to notice under subsection (a) has a right to intervene in the proceeding.

(c) Lack of notice required by subsection (a) does not render a judgment void. Lack of notice does not preclude an individual entitled to notice under subsection (a) from bringing a proceeding under § 611(b).

§ 604. Personal Jurisdiction.

(a) The court may adjudicate an individual's parentage of a child only if the court has personal jurisdiction over the individual.

(b) A court of this state with jurisdiction to adjudicate parentage may exercise personal jurisdiction over a nonresident individual, or the [guardian or conservator] of the individual, if the conditions prescribed in [cite to this state's § 201 of the Uniform Interstate Family Support Act] are satisfied.

(c) Lack of jurisdiction over one individual does not preclude the court from making an adjudication of parentage binding on another individual.

* * *

PART 2—SPECIAL RULES FOR PROCEEDING TO ADJUDICATE PARENTAGE

§ 606. Admissibility of Results of Genetic Testing.

(a) Except as otherwise provided in § 502(b), the court shall admit a report of genetic testing ordered by the court under § 503 as evidence of the truth of the facts asserted in the report.

(b) A party may object to the admission of a report described in subsection (a), not later than [14] days after the party receives the report. The party shall cite specific grounds for exclusion.

(c) A party that objects to the results of genetic testing may call a genetic-testing expert to testify in person or by another method approved by the court. Unless the court orders otherwise, the party offering the testimony bears the expense for the expert testifying.

(d) Admissibility of a report of genetic testing is not affected by whether the testing was performed:

> (1) voluntarily or under an order of the court or a child-support agency; or

> (2) before, on, or after commencement of the proceeding.

§ 607. Adjudicating Parentage of Child with Alleged Genetic Parent.

(a) A proceeding to determine whether an alleged genetic parent who is not a presumed parent is a parent of a child may be commenced:

> (1) before the child becomes an adult; or

> (2) after the child becomes an adult, but only if the child initiates the proceeding.

(b) Except as otherwise provided in § 614, this subsection applies in a proceeding described in subsection (a) if the woman who gave birth to the child is the only other individual with a claim to parentage of the child. The court shall adjudicate an alleged genetic parent to be a parent of the child if the alleged genetic parent:

> (1) is identified under § 506 as a genetic parent of the child and the identification is not successfully challenged under § 506;

> (2) admits parentage in a pleading, when making an appearance, or during a hearing, the court accepts the admission, and the court determines the alleged genetic parent to be a parent of the child;

> (3) declines to submit to genetic testing ordered by the court or a child-support agency, in which case the court may adjudicate the alleged genetic parent to be a parent of the child even if the alleged genetic parent denies a genetic relationship with the child;

> (4) is in default after service of process and the court determines the alleged genetic parent to be a parent of the child; or

(5) is neither identified nor excluded as a genetic parent by genetic testing and, based on other evidence, the court determines the alleged genetic parent to be a parent of the child.

(c) Except as otherwise provided in § 614 and subject to other limitations in this [part], if in a proceeding involving an alleged genetic parent, at least one other individual in addition to the woman who gave birth to the child has a claim to parentage of the child, the court shall adjudicate parentage under § 613.

§ 608. Adjudicating Parentage of Child with Presumed Parent.

(a) A proceeding to determine whether a presumed parent is a parent of a child may be commenced:

(1) before the child becomes an adult; or

(2) after the child becomes an adult, but only if the child initiates the proceeding.

(b) A presumption of parentage under § 204 cannot be overcome after the child attains two years of age unless the court determines:

(1) the presumed parent is not a genetic parent, never resided with the child, and never held out the child as the presumed parent's child; or

(2) the child has more than one presumed parent.

(c) Except as otherwise provided in § 614, the following rules apply in a proceeding to adjudicate a presumed parent's parentage of a child if the woman who gave birth to the child is the only other individual with a claim to parentage of the child:

(1) If no party to the proceeding challenges the presumed parent's parentage of the child, the court shall adjudicate the presumed parent to be a parent of the child.

(2) If the presumed parent is identified under § 506 as a genetic parent of the child and that identification is not successfully challenged under § 506, the court shall adjudicate the presumed parent to be a parent of the child.

(3) If the presumed parent is not identified under § 506 as a genetic parent of the child and the presumed parent or the woman who gave birth to the child challenges the presumed parent's parentage of the child, the court shall adjudicate the parentage of the child in the best interest of the child based on the factors under § 613(a) and (b).

(d) Except as otherwise provided in § 614 and subject to other limitations in this [part], if in a proceeding to adjudicate a presumed parent's parentage of a child, another individual in addition to the woman who gave birth to the child asserts a claim to parentage of the child, the court shall adjudicate parentage under § 613.

§ 609. Adjudicating Claim of De Facto Parentage of Child.

(a) A proceeding to establish parentage of a child under this § may be commenced only by an individual who:

(1) is alive when the proceeding is commenced; and

(2) claims to be a de facto parent of the child.

(b) An individual who claims to be a de facto parent of a child must commence a proceeding to establish parentage of a child under this section:

(1) before the child attains 18 years of age; and

(2) while the child is alive.

(c) The following rules govern standing of an individual who claims to be a de facto parent of a child to maintain a proceeding under this section:

(1) The individual must file an initial verified pleading alleging specific facts that support the claim to parentage of the child asserted under this section. The verified pleading must be served on all parents and legal guardians of the child and any other party to the proceeding.

(2) An adverse party, parent, or legal guardian may file a pleading in response to the pleading filed under paragraph (1). A responsive pleading must be verified and must be served on parties to the proceeding.

(3) Unless the court finds a hearing is necessary to determine disputed facts material to the issue of standing, the court shall determine, based on the pleadings under paragraphs (1) and (2), whether the individual has alleged facts sufficient to satisfy by a preponderance of the evidence the requirements of paragraphs (1) through (7) of subsection (d). If the court holds a hearing under this subsection, the hearing must be held on an expedited basis.

(d) In a proceeding to adjudicate parentage of an individual who claims to be a de facto parent of the child, if there is only one other individual who is a parent or has a claim to parentage of the child, the court shall adjudicate the individual who claims to be a de facto parent to be a parent of the child if the individual demonstrates by clear-and-convincing evidence that:

(1) the individual resided with the child as a regular member of the child's household for a significant period;

(2) the individual engaged in consistent caretaking of the child;

(3) the individual undertook full and permanent responsibilities of a parent of the child without expectation of financial compensation;

(4) the individual held out the child as the individual's child;

(5) the individual established a bonded and dependent relationship with the child which is parental in nature;

(6) another parent of the child fostered or supported the bonded and dependent relationship required under paragraph (5); and

(7) continuing the relationship between the individual and the child is in the best interest of the child.

(e) Subject to other limitations in this [part], if in a proceeding to adjudicate parentage of an individual who claims to be a de facto parent of the child, there is more than one other individual who is a parent or has a claim to parentage of the child and the court determines that the requirements of subsection (d) are satisfied, the court shall adjudicate parentage under § 613.

§ 610. Adjudicating Parentage of Child with Acknowledged Parent.

(a) If a child has an acknowledged parent, a proceeding to challenge the acknowledgment of parentage or a denial of parentage, brought by a signatory to the acknowledgment or denial, is governed by sections 309 and 310.

(b) If a child has an acknowledged parent, the following rules apply in a proceeding to challenge the acknowledgment of parentage or a denial of parentage brought by an individual, other than the child, who has standing under § 602 and was not a signatory to the acknowledgment or denial:

(1) The individual must commence the proceeding not later than two years after the effective date of the acknowledgment.

(2) The court may permit the proceeding only if the court finds permitting the proceeding is in the best interest of the child.

(3) If the court permits the proceeding, the court shall adjudicate parentage under § 613.

§ 611. Adjudicating Parentage of Child with Adjudicated Parent.

(a) If a child has an adjudicated parent, a proceeding to challenge the adjudication, brought by an individual who was a party to the adjudication or received notice under § 603, is governed by the rules governing a collateral attack on a judgment.

(b) If a child has an adjudicated parent, the following rules apply to a proceeding to challenge the adjudication of parentage brought by an individual, other than the child, who has standing under § 602 and was not a party to the adjudication and did not receive notice under § 603:

> (1) The individual must commence the proceeding not later than two years after the effective date of the adjudication.

> (2) The court may permit the proceeding only if the court finds permitting the proceeding is in the best interest of the child.

> (3) If the court permits the proceeding, the court shall adjudicate parentage under § 613.

§ 612. Adjudicating Parentage of Child of Assisted Reproduction.

(a) An individual who is a parent under [Article] 7 or the woman who gave birth to the child may bring a proceeding to adjudicate parentage. If the court determines the individual is a parent under [Article] 7, the court shall adjudicate the individual to be a parent of the child.

(b) In a proceeding to adjudicate an individual's parentage of a child, if another individual other than the woman who gave birth to the child is a parent under [Article] 7, the court shall adjudicate the individual's parentage of the child under § 613.

§ 613. Adjudicating Competing Claims of Parentage.

(a) Except as otherwise provided in § 614, in a proceeding to adjudicate competing claims of, or challenges under § 608(c), 610, or 611 to, parentage of a child by two or more individuals, the court shall adjudicate parentage in the best interest of the child, based on:

> (1) the age of the child;

> (2) the length of time during which each individual assumed the role of parent of the child;

> (3) the nature of the relationship between the child and each individual;

> (4) the harm to the child if the relationship between the child and each individual is not recognized;

(5) the basis for each individual's claim to parentage of the child; and

(6) other equitable factors arising from the disruption of the relationship between the child and each individual or the likelihood of other harm to the child.

(b) If an individual challenges parentage based on the results of genetic testing, in addition to the factors listed in subsection (a), the court shall consider:

(1) the facts surrounding the discovery the individual might not be a genetic parent of the child; and

(2) the length of time between the time that the individual was placed on notice that the individual might not be a genetic parent and the commencement of the proceeding.

Alternative A

(c) The court may not adjudicate a child to have more than two parents under this [act].

Alternative B

(c) The court may adjudicate a child to have more than two parents under this [act] if the court finds that failure to recognize more than two parents would be detrimental to the child. A finding of detriment to the child does not require a finding of unfitness of any parent or individual seeking an adjudication of parentage. In determining detriment to the child, the court shall consider all relevant factors, including the harm if the child is removed from a stable placement with an individual who has fulfilled the child's physical needs and psychological needs for care and affection and has assumed the role for a

§ 614. Precluding Establishment of Parentage by Perpetrator of Sexual Assault.

(a) In this section, "sexual assault" means [cite to this state's criminal rape statutes].

(b) In a proceeding in which a woman alleges that a man committed a sexual assault that resulted in the woman giving birth to a child, the woman may seek to preclude the man from establishing that he is a parent of the child.

(c) This section does not apply if:

(1) the man described in subsection (b) has previously been adjudicated to be a parent of the child; or

(2) after the birth of the child, the man established a bonded and dependent relationship with the child which is parental in nature.

(d) Unless § 309 or 607 applies, a woman must file a pleading making an allegation under subsection (b) not later than two years after the birth of the child. The woman may file the pleading only in a proceeding to establish parentage under this [act].

(e) An allegation under subsection (b) may be proved by:

(1) evidence that the man was convicted of a sexual assault, or a comparable crime in another jurisdiction, against the woman and the child was born not later than 300 days after the sexual assault; or

(2) clear-and-convincing evidence that the man committed sexual assault against the woman and the child was born not later than 300 days after the sexual assault.

(f) Subject to subsections (a) through (d), if the court determines that an allegation has been proved under subsection (e), the court shall:

(1) adjudicate that the man described in subsection (b) is not a parent of the child;

(2) require the [state agency maintaining birth records] to amend the birth certificate if requested by the woman and the court determines that the amendment is in the best interest of the child; and

(3) require the man pay to child support, birth-related costs, or both, unless the woman requests otherwise and the court determines that granting the request is in the best interest of the child.

PART 3—HEARING AND ADJUDICATION

* * *

§ 617. Proceeding Before Birth.

[Except as otherwise provided in [Article] 8, a][A] proceeding to adjudicate parentage may be commenced before the birth of the child and an order or judgment may be entered before birth, but enforcement of the order or judgment must be stayed until the birth of the child.

Legislative Note: *A state should include the bracketed phrase on Article 8 if the state wishes to recognize in statute surrogacy agreements and includes Article 8 in this act.*

§ 618. Child as Party; Representation.

(a) A minor child is a permissive party but not a necessary party to a proceeding under this [article].

(b) The court shall appoint [an attorney, guardian ad litem, or similar person] to represent a child in a proceeding under this [article], if the court finds that the interests of the child are not adequately represented.

§ 619. Court to Adjudicate Parentage.

The court shall adjudicate parentage of a child without a jury.

* * *

§ 623. Binding Effect of Determination of Parentage.

(a) Except as otherwise provided in subsection (b):

(1) a signatory to an acknowledgment of parentage or denial of parentage is bound by the acknowledgment and denial as provided in [Article] 3; and

(2) a party to an adjudication of parentage by a court acting under circumstances that satisfy the jurisdiction requirements of [cite to this state's § 201 of the Uniform Interstate Family Support Act] and any individual who received notice of the proceeding are bound by the adjudication.

(b) A child is not bound by a determination of parentage under this [act] unless:

(1) the determination was based on an unrescinded acknowledgment of parentage and the acknowledgment is consistent with the results of genetic testing;

(2) the determination was based on a finding consistent with the results of genetic testing, and the consistency is declared in the determination or otherwise shown;

(3) the determination of parentage was made under [Article] 7[or 8]; or

(4) the child was a party or was represented by [an attorney, guardian ad litem, or similar person] in the proceeding.

(c) In a proceeding for [divorce, dissolution, annulment, declaration of invalidity, legal separation, or separate maintenance], the court is deemed to have made an adjudication of parentage of a child if the court acts under circumstances that satisfy the jurisdiction requirements of [cite to this state's § 201 of the Uniform Interstate Family Support Act] and the final order:

(1) expressly identifies the child as a "child of the marriage" or "issue of the marriage" or includes similar words indicating that both spouses are parents of the child; or

(2) provides for support of the child by a spouse unless that spouse's parentage is disclaimed specifically in the order.

(d) Except as otherwise provided in subsection (b) or § 611, a determination of parentage may be asserted as a defense in a subsequent proceeding seeking to adjudicate parentage of an individual who was not a party to the earlier proceeding.

(e) A party to an adjudication of parentage may challenge the adjudication only under law of this state other than this [act] relating to appeal, vacation of judgment, or other judicial review.

Legislative Note: A state should include the bracketed reference to Article 8 if the state wishes to recognize in statute surrogacy agreements and includes Article 8 in this act.

ARTICLE 7 ASSISTED REPRODUCTION

§ 701. Scope of [Article].

This [article] does not apply to the birth of a child conceived by sexual intercourse[or assisted reproduction under a surrogacy agreement under [Article] 8].

Legislative Note: A state should include the bracketed phrase concerning a surrogacy agreement if the state wishes to recognize in statute surrogacy agreements and includes Article 8 in this act.

§ 702. Parental Status of Donor.

A donor is not a parent of a child conceived by assisted reproduction.

§ 703. Parentage of Child of Assisted Reproduction.

An individual who consents under § 704 to assisted reproduction by a woman with the intent to be a parent of a child conceived by the assisted reproduction is a parent of the child.

§ 704. Consent to Assisted Reproduction.

(a) Except as otherwise provided in subsection (b), the consent described in § 703 must be in a record signed by a woman giving birth to a child conceived by assisted reproduction and an individual who intends to be a parent of the child.

(b) Failure to consent in a record as required by subsection (a), before, on, or after birth of the child, does not preclude the court from finding consent to parentage if:

(1) the woman or the individual proves by clear-and-convincing evidence the existence of an express agreement entered into before conception that the individual and the woman intended they both would be parents of the child; or

(2) the woman and the individual for the first two years of the child's life, including any period of temporary absence, resided together in the same household with the child and both openly held out the child as the individual's child, unless the individual dies or becomes incapacitated before the child attains two years of age or the child dies before the child attains two years of age, in which case the court may find consent under this subsection to parentage if a party proves by clear-and-convincing evidence that the woman and the individual intended to reside together in the same household with the child and both intended the individual would openly hold out the child as the individual's child, but the individual was prevented from carrying out that intent by death or incapacity.

§ 705. Limitation of Spouse's Dispute of Parentage.

(a) Except as otherwise provided in subsection (b), an individual who, at the time of a child's birth, is the spouse of the woman who gave birth to the child by assisted reproduction may not challenge the individual's parentage of the child unless:

(1) not later than two years after the birth of the child, the individual commences a proceeding to adjudicate the individual's parentage of the child; and

(2) the court finds the individual did not consent to the assisted reproduction, before, on, or after birth of the child, or withdrew consent under § 707.

(b) A proceeding to adjudicate a spouse's parentage of a child born by assisted reproduction may be commenced at any time if the court determines:

(1) the spouse neither provided a gamete for, nor consented to, the assisted reproduction;

(2) the spouse and the woman who gave birth to the child have not cohabited since the probable time of assisted reproduction; and

(3) the spouse never openly held out the child as the spouse's child.

(c) This § applies to a spouse's dispute of parentage even if the spouse's marriage is declared invalid after assisted reproduction occurs.

§ 706. Effect of Certain Legal Proceedings Regarding Marriage.

If a marriage of a woman who gives birth to a child conceived by assisted reproduction is [terminated through divorce or dissolution, subject to legal separation or separate maintenance, declared invalid, or annulled] before transfer of gametes or embryos to the woman, a former spouse of the woman is not a parent of the child unless the former spouse consented in a record that the former spouse would be a parent of the child if assisted reproduction were to occur after a [divorce, dissolution, annulment, declaration of invalidity, legal separation, or separate maintenance], and the former spouse did not withdraw consent under § 707.

§ 707. Withdrawal of Consent.

(a) An individual who consents under § 704 to assisted reproduction may withdraw consent any time before a transfer that results in a pregnancy, by giving notice in a record of the withdrawal of consent to the woman who agreed to give birth to a child conceived by assisted reproduction and to any clinic or health-care provider facilitating the assisted reproduction. Failure to give notice to the clinic or health-care provider does not affect a determination of parentage under this [act].

(b) An individual who withdraws consent under subsection (a) is not a parent of the child under this [article].

§ 708. Parental Status of Deceased Individual.

(a) If an individual who intends to be a parent of a child conceived by assisted reproduction dies during the period between the transfer of a gamete or embryo and the birth of the child, the individual's death does not preclude the establishment of the individual's parentage of the child if the individual otherwise would be a parent of the child under this [act].

(b) If an individual who consented in a record to assisted reproduction by a woman who agreed to give birth to a child dies before a transfer of gametes or embryos, the deceased individual is a parent of a child conceived by the assisted reproduction only if:

(1) either:

(A) the individual consented in a record that if assisted reproduction were to occur after the death of the individual, the individual would be a parent of the child; or

(B) the individual's intent to be a parent of a child conceived by assisted reproduction after the individual's death is established by clear-and-convincing evidence; and

(2) either:

(A) the embryo is in utero not later than [36] months after the individual's death; or

(B) the child is born not later than [45] months after the individual's death.

ARTICLE 8 SURROGACY AGREEMENT

Legislative Note: A state should include Article 8 if the state wishes to recognize in statute surrogacy agreements.

PART 1—GENERAL REQUIREMENTS

§ 801. Definitions.

In this [article]:

(1) "Genetic surrogate" means a woman who is not an intended parent and who agrees to become pregnant through assisted reproduction using her own gamete, under a genetic surrogacy agreement as provided in this [article].

(2) "Gestational surrogate" means a woman who is not an intended parent and who agrees to become pregnant through assisted reproduction using gametes that are not her own, under a gestational surrogacy agreement as provided in this [article].

(3) "Surrogacy agreement" means an agreement between one or more intended parents and a woman who is not an intended parent in which the woman agrees to become pregnant through assisted reproduction and which provides that each intended parent is a parent of a child conceived under the agreement. Unless otherwise specified, the term refers to both a gestational surrogacy agreement and a genetic surrogacy agreement.

§ 802. Eligibility to Enter Gestational or Genetic Surrogacy Agreement.

(a) To execute an agreement to act as a gestational or genetic surrogate, a woman must:

(1) have attained 21 years of age;

(2) previously have given birth to at least one child;

(3) complete a medical evaluation related to the surrogacy arrangement by a licensed medical doctor;

(4) complete a mental-health consultation by a licensed mental-health professional; and

(5) have independent legal representation of her choice throughout the surrogacy arrangement regarding the terms of the surrogacy agreement and the potential legal consequences of the agreement.

(b) To execute a surrogacy agreement, each intended parent, whether or not genetically related to the child, must:

(1) have attained 21 years of age;

(2) complete a medical evaluation related to the surrogacy arrangement by a licensed medical doctor;

(3) complete a mental-health consultation by a licensed mental health professional; and

(4) have independent legal representation of the intended parent's choice throughout the surrogacy arrangement regarding the terms of the surrogacy agreement and the potential legal consequences of the agreement.

§ 803. Requirements of Gestational or Genetic Surrogacy Agreement: Process.

A surrogacy agreement must be executed in compliance with the following rules:

(1) At least one party must be a resident of this state or, if no party is a resident of this state, at least one medical evaluation or procedure or mental-health consultation under the agreement must occur in this state.

(2) A surrogate and each intended parent must meet the requirements of § 802.

(3) Each intended parent, the surrogate, and the surrogate's spouse, if any, must be parties to the agreement.

(4) The agreement must be in a record signed by each party listed in paragraph (3).

(5) The surrogate and each intended parent must acknowledge in a record receipt of a copy of the agreement.

(6) The signature of each party to the agreement must be attested by a notarial officer or witnessed.

(7) The surrogate and the intended parent or parents must have independent legal representation throughout the surrogacy arrangement regarding the terms of the surrogacy agreement and the potential legal consequences of the agreement, and each counsel must be identified in the surrogacy agreement.

(8) The intended parent or parents must pay for independent legal representation for the surrogate.

(9) The agreement must be executed before a medical procedure occurs related to the surrogacy agreement, other than the medical evaluation and mental health consultation required by § 802.

§ 804. Requirements of Gestational or Genetic Surrogacy Agreement: Content.

(a) A surrogacy agreement must comply with the following requirements:

(1) A surrogate agrees to attempt to become pregnant by means of assisted reproduction.

(2) Except as otherwise provided in sections 811, 814, and 815, the surrogate and the surrogate's spouse or former spouse, if any, have no claim to parentage of a child conceived by assisted reproduction under the agreement.

(3) The surrogate's spouse, if any, must acknowledge and agree to comply with the obligations imposed on the surrogate by the agreement.

(4) Except as otherwise provided in sections 811, 814, and 815, the intended parent or, if there are two intended parents, each one jointly and severally, immediately on birth will be the exclusive parent or parents of the child, regardless of number of children born or gender or mental or physical condition of each child.

(5) Except as otherwise provided in sections 811, 814, and 815, the intended parent or, if there are two intended parents, each parent jointly and severally, immediately on birth will assume responsibility for the financial support of the child, regardless of number of children born or gender or mental or physical condition of each child.

(6) The agreement must include information disclosing how each intended parent will cover the surrogacy-related expenses of the surrogate and the medical expenses of the child. If health-care coverage is used to cover the medical expenses, the disclosure must include a summary of the health-care policy provisions related to coverage for surrogate pregnancy, including any possible liability of the surrogate, third-party-liability liens, other insurance coverage, and any notice requirement that could affect coverage or liability of the surrogate. Unless the agreement expressly provides otherwise, the review and disclosure do not constitute legal advice. If the extent of coverage is uncertain, a statement of that fact is sufficient to comply with this paragraph.

(7) The agreement must permit the surrogate to make all health and welfare decisions regarding herself and her pregnancy. This [act] does not enlarge or diminish the surrogate's right to terminate her pregnancy.

(8) The agreement must include information about each party's right under this [article] to terminate the surrogacy agreement.

(b) A surrogacy agreement may provide for:

(1) payment of consideration and reasonable expenses; and

(2) reimbursement of specific expenses if the agreement is terminated under this [article].

(c) A right created under a surrogacy agreement is not assignable and there is no third-

* * *

ARTICLE 9 INFORMATION ABOUT DONOR

§ 901. Definitions.

In this [article]:

(1) "Identifying information" means:

(A) the full name of a donor;

(B) the date of birth of the donor; and

(C) the permanent and, if different, current address of the donor at the time of the donation.

(2) "Medical history" means information regarding any:

(A) present illness of a donor;

(B) past illness of the donor; and

(C) social, genetic, and family history pertaining to the health of the donor.

§ 902. Applicability.

This [article] applies only to gametes collected on or after [the effective date of this [act]].

§ 903. Collection of Information.

A gamete bank or fertility clinic licensed in this state shall collect from a donor the donor's identifying information and medical history at the time of the donation. If the gamete bank or fertility clinic sends the gametes of a donor to another gamete bank or fertility clinic, the sending gamete bank or fertility clinic shall forward any identifying information and medical history of the donor, including the donor's signed declaration under § 904 regarding identity disclosure, to the receiving gamete bank or fertility clinic. A receiving gamete bank or fertility clinic licensed in this state shall collect and retain the information about the donor and each sending gamete bank or fertility clinic.

§ 904. Declaration Regarding Identity Disclosure.

(a) A gamete bank or fertility clinic licensed in this state which collects gametes from a donor shall:

(1) provide the donor with information in a record about the donor's choice regarding identity disclosure; and

(2) obtain a declaration from the donor regarding identity disclosure.

(b) A gamete bank or fertility clinic licensed in this state shall give a donor the choice to sign a declaration, attested by a notarial officer or witnessed, that either:

(1) states that the donor agrees to disclose the donor's identity to a child conceived by assisted reproduction with the donor's gametes on request once the child attains 18 years of age; or

(2) states that the donor does not agree presently to disclose the donor's identity to the child.

(c) A gamete bank or fertility clinic licensed in this state shall permit a donor who has signed a declaration under subsection (b)(2) to withdraw the declaration at any time by signing a declaration under subsection (b)(1).

§ 905. Disclosure of Identifying Information and Medical History.

(a) On request of a child conceived by assisted reproduction who attains 18 years of age, a gamete bank or fertility clinic licensed in this state which collected, stored, or released for use the gametes used in the assisted reproduction shall make a good-faith effort to provide the child with identifying information of the donor who provided the gametes, unless the donor signed and did not withdraw a declaration under § 904(b)(2). If the donor signed and did not withdraw the declaration, the gamete bank or fertility clinic shall make a good-faith effort to notify the donor, who may elect under § 904(c) to withdraw the donor's declaration.

(b) Regardless whether a donor signed a declaration under § 904(b)(2), on request by a child conceived by assisted reproduction who attains 18 years of age, or, if the child is a minor, by a parent or guardian of the child, a gamete bank or fertility clinic licensed in this state shall make a good-faith effort to provide the child or, if the child is a minor, the parent or guardian of the child, access to nonidentifying medical history of the donor.

§ 906. Recordkeeping.

A gamete bank or fertility clinic licensed in this state which collects, stores, or releases gametes for use in assisted reproduction shall collect and maintain identifying information and medical history about each gamete donor. The gamete bank or fertility clinic shall collect and maintain records of gamete screening and testing and comply with reporting requirements, in accordance with federal law and applicable law of this state other than this [act].

* * *

Uniform Interstate Family Support Act (UIFSA) (2008)

9 U.L.A. (Part 1B) (Supp. 2018)

ARTICLE 1. GENERAL PROVISIONS

* * *

§ 102. Definitions.

In this [act]:

* * *

(3) "Convention" means the Convention on the International Recovery of Child Support and Other Forms of Family Maintenance, concluded at The Hague on November 23, 2007.

Go Online

The full text and information on state adoptions of the Uniform Interstate Family Support Act is available from the Uniform Law Commission.

(4) "Duty of support" means
an obligation imposed or imposable by law to provide support for a child, spouse, or former spouse, including an unsatisfied obligation to provide support.

(5) "Foreign country" means a country, including a political subdivision thereof, other than the United States, that authorizes the issuance of support orders and:

(A) which has been declared under the law of the United States to be a foreign reciprocating country;

(B) which has established a reciprocal arrangement for child support with this state as provided in Section 308;

(C) which has enacted a law or established procedures for the issuance and enforcement of support orders which are substantially similar to the procedures under this [act]; or

(D) in which the Convention is in force with respect to the United States.

* * *

(8) "Home state" means the state or foreign country in which a child lived with a parent or a person acting as a parent for at least six consecutive months

immediately preceding the time of filing of a [petition] or comparable pleading for support and, if a child is less than six months old, the state or foreign country in which the child lived from birth with any of them. A period of temporary absence of any of them is counted as part of the six-month or other period.

* * *

(26) "State" means a state of the United States, the District of Columbia, Puerto Rico, the United States Virgin Islands, or any territory or insular possession under the jurisdiction of the United States. The term includes an Indian nation or tribe.

* * *

(28) "Support order" means a judgment, decree, order, decision, or directive, whether temporary, final, or subject to modification, issued in a state or foreign country for the benefit of a child, a spouse, or a former spouse, which provides for monetary support, health care, arrearages, retroactive support, or reimbursement for financial assistance provided to an individual oblige in place of child support. The term may include related costs and fees, interest, income withholding, automatic adjustment, reasonable attorney's fees, and other relief.

(29) "Tribunal" means a court, administrative agency, or quasi-judicial entity authorized to establish, enforce, or modify support orders or to determine parentage of a child.

* * *

§ 104. Remedies Cumulative.

(a) Remedies provided by this [act] are cumulative and do not affect the availability of remedies under other law or the recognition of a foreign support order on the basis of comity.

(b) This [act] does not:

(1) provide the exclusive method of establishing or enforcing a support order under the law of this state; or

(2) grant a tribunal of this state jurisdiction to render judgment or issue an order relating to [child custody or visitation] in a proceeding under this [act].

§ 105. Application of [Act] to Resident of Foreign Country and Foreign Support Proceeding.

(a) A tribunal of this state shall apply [Articles] 1 through 6 and, as applicable, [Article] 7, to a support proceeding involving:

(1) a foreign support order;

(2) a foreign tribunal; or

(3) an obligee, obligor, or child residing in a foreign country.

(b) A tribunal of this state that is requested to recognize and enforce a support order on the basis of comity may apply the procedural and substantive provisions of [Articles] 1 through 6.

(c) [Article] 7 applies only to a support proceeding under the Convention. In such a proceeding, if a provision of [Article] 7 is inconsistent with [Articles] 1 through 6, [Article] 7 controls.

ARTICLE 2. JURISDICTION

§ 201. Bases for Jurisdiction over Nonresident.

(a) In a proceeding to establish or enforce a support order or to determine parentage of a child, a tribunal of this state may exercise personal jurisdiction over a nonresident individual [or the individual's guardian or conservator] if:

(1) the individual is personally served with [citation, summons, notice] within this state;

(2) the individual submits to the jurisdiction of this state by consent, by entering a general appearance, or by filing a responsive document having the effect of waiving any contest to personal jurisdiction;

(3) the individual resided with the child in this state;

(4) the individual resided in this state and provided prenatal expenses or support for the child;

(5) the child resides in this state as a result of the acts or directives of the individual;

(6) the individual engaged in sexual intercourse in this state and the child may have been conceived by that act of intercourse;

(7) the individual asserted parentage of a child in the [putative father registry] maintained in this state by the [appropriate agency]; or

(8) there is any other basis consistent with the constitutions of this state and the United States for the exercise of personal jurisdiction.

(b) The bases of personal jurisdiction set forth in subsection (a) or in any other law of this state may not be used to acquire personal jurisdiction for a tribunal of this state to modify a child support order of another state unless the requirements of Section 611 are met, or, in the case of a foreign support order, unless the requirements of Section 615 are met.

§ 202. Duration of Personal Jurisdiction.

Personal jurisdiction acquired by a tribunal of this state in a proceeding under this [act] or other law of this state relating to a support order continues as long as a tribunal of this state has continuing, exclusive jurisdiction to modify its order or continuing jurisdiction to enforce its order as provided by Sections 205, 206, and 211.

§ 203. Initiating and Responding Tribunal of State.

Under this [Act], a tribunal of this state may serve as an initiating tribunal to forward proceedings to a tribunal of another state and as a responding tribunal for proceedings initiated in another state or a foreign country.

§ 204. Simultaneous Proceedings

(a) A tribunal of this state may exercise jurisdiction to establish a support order if the [petition] or comparable pleading is filed after a pleading is filed in another state or a foreign country only if:

(1) the [petition] or comparable pleading in this state is filed before the expiration of the time allowed in the other state or foreign country for filing a responsive pleading challenging the exercise of jurisdiction by the other state or foreign country;

(2) the contesting party timely challenges the exercise of jurisdiction in the other state or foreign country; and

(3) if relevant, this state is the home state of the child.

(b) A tribunal of this state may not exercise jurisdiction to establish a support order if the [petition] or comparable pleading is filed before a [petition] or comparable pleading is filed in another state or foreign country if:

(1) the [petition] or comparable pleading in the other state or foreign country is filed before the expiration of time allowed in this state for filing a responsive pleading challenging the exercise of jurisdiction by this state;

(2) the contesting party timely challenges the exercise of jurisdiction in this state; and

(3) if relevant, the other state or foreign country is the home state of the child.

§ 205. Continuing, Exclusive Jurisdiction to Modify Child-Support Order.

(a) A tribunal of this state that has issued a child-support order consistent with the law of this state has and shall exercise continuing, exclusive jurisdiction to modify its child-support order if the order is the controlling order and:

(1) at the time of the filing of a request for modification this state is the residence of the obligor, the individual obligee, or the child for whose benefit the support order is issued; or

(2) even if this state is not the residence of the obligor, the individual obligee, or the child for whose benefit the support order is issued, the parties consent in a record or in open court that the tribunal of this state may continue to exercise jurisdiction to modify its order.

(b) A tribunal of this state that has issued a child-support order consistent with the law of this state may not exercise continuing, exclusive jurisdiction to modify the order if:

(1) all of the parties who are individuals file consent in a record with the tribunal of this state that a tribunal of another state that has jurisdiction over at least one of the parties who is an individual or that is located in the state of residence of the child may modify the order and assume continuing, exclusive jurisdiction; or

(2) its order is not the controlling order.

(c) If a tribunal of another state has issued a child-support order pursuant to [the Uniform Interstate Family Support Act] or a law substantially similar to that Act which modifies a child-support order of a tribunal of this state, tribunals of this state shall recognize the continuing, exclusive jurisdiction of the tribunal of the other state.

(d) A tribunal of this state that lacks continuing, exclusive jurisdiction to modify a child-support order may serve as an initiating tribunal to request a tribunal of another state to modify a support order issued in that state.

(e) A temporary support order issued ex parte or pending resolution of a jurisdictional conflict does not create continuing, exclusive jurisdiction in the issuing tribunal.

* * *

§ 210. Application of [Act] to Nonresident Subject to Personal Jurisdiction.

A tribunal of this state exercising personal jurisdiction over a nonresident in a proceeding under this [act], under other law of this state relating to a support order, or recognizing a foreign support order may receive evidence from outside this state pursuant to Section 316, communicate with a tribunal of outside this state pursuant to Section 317, and obtain discovery through a tribunal outside this state pursuant to Section 318. In all other respects, Articles 3 through 6 do not apply and the tribunal shall apply the procedural and substantive law of this state.

§ 211. Continuing, Exclusive Jurisdiction to Modify Spousal-Support Order.

(a) A tribunal of this state issuing a spousal-support order consistent with the law of this state has continuing, exclusive jurisdiction to modify the spousal-support order throughout the existence of the support obligation.

(b) A tribunal of this state may not modify a spousal-support order issued by a tribunal of another state or a foreign country having continuing, exclusive jurisdiction over that order under the law of that state or foreign country.

(c) A tribunal of this state that has continuing, exclusive jurisdiction over a spousal-support order may serve as:

(1) an initiating tribunal to request a tribunal of another state to enforce the spousal-support order issued in this state; or

(2) a responding tribunal to enforce or modify its own spousal-support order.

ARTICLE 3: CIVIL PROVISIONS OF GENERAL APPLICATION

§ 301. Proceedings under [Act]

(a) Except as otherwise provided in this [act], this [article] applies to all proceedings under this [act].

(b) An individual [petitioner] or a support enforcement agency may initiate a proceeding authorized under this [Act] [act] by filing a [petition] in an initiating tribunal for forwarding to a responding tribunal or by filing a [petition] or a comparable pleading directly in a tribunal of another state or a foreign country which has or can obtain personal jurisdiction over the [respondent].

* * *

§ 303. Application of Law of this State.

Except as otherwise provided in this [act], a responding tribunal of this state shall:

(1) apply the procedural and substantive law generally applicable to similar proceedings originating in this state and may exercise all powers and provide all remedies available in those proceedings; and

(2) determine the duty of support and the amount payable in accordance with the law and support guidelines of this state.

§ 304. Duties of Initiating Tribunal.

(a) Upon the filing of a [petition] authorized by this [Act], an initiating tribunal of this state shall forward the [petition] and its accompanying documents:

(1) to the responding tribunal or appropriate support enforcement agency in the responding state; or

(2) if the identity of the responding tribunal is unknown, to the state information agency of the responding state with a request that they be forwarded to the appropriate tribunal and that receipt be acknowledged.

(b) If requested by the responding tribunal, a tribunal of this state shall issue a certificate or other document and make findings required by the law of the responding state. If the responding tribunal is in a foreign country, upon request the tribunal of this state shall specify the amount of support sought, convert that amount into the equivalent amount in the foreign currency under applicable official or market exchange rate as publicly reported, and provide any other documents necessary to satisfy the requirements of the responding foreign tribunal.

§ 305. Duties and Powers of Responding Tribunal

(a) When a responding tribunal of this state receives a [petition] or comparable pleading from an initiating tribunal or directly pursuant to Section 301(b), it shall cause the [petition] or pleading to be filed and notify the [petitioner] where and when it was filed.

(b) A responding tribunal of this state, to the extent not prohibited by other law, may do one or more of the following:

(1) establish or enforce a support order, modify a child-support order, determine the controlling child-support order, or determine parentage of a child;

(2) order an obligor to comply with a support order, specifying the amount and the manner of the compliance;

(3) order income withholding;

(4) determine the amount of any arrearages, and specify a method of payment;

(5) enforce orders by civil or criminal contempt, or both;

(6) set aside property for satisfaction of the support order;

(7) place liens and order execution on the obligor's property;

(8) order an obligor to keep the tribunal informed of the obligor's current residential address, electronic-mail address, telephone number, employer, address of employment, and telephone number at the place of employment;

(9) issue a [bench warrant; capias] for an obligor who has failed after proper notice to appear at a hearing ordered by the tribunal and enter the [bench warrant; capias] in any local and state computer systems for criminal warrants;

(10) order the obligor to seek appropriate employment by specified methods;

(11) award reasonable attorney's fees and other fees and costs; and

(12) grant any other available remedy.

(c) A responding tribunal of this state shall include in a support order issued under this [act], or in the documents accompanying the order, the calculations on which the support order is based.

(d) A responding tribunal of this state may not condition the payment of a support order issued under this [act] upon compliance by a party with provisions for visitation.

(e) If a responding tribunal of this state issues an order under this [act], the tribunal shall send a copy of the order to the [petitioner] and the [respondent] and to the initiating tribunal, if any.

(f) If requested to enforce a support order, arrears, or judgment or modify a support order stated in a foreign currency, a responding tribunal of this state shall convert the amount stated in the foreign currency to the equivalent amount in dollars under the applicable official or market exchange rate as publicly reported.

* * *

§ 314. Limited Immunity of [Petitioner].

(a) Participation by a [petitioner] in a proceeding under this [act] before a responding tribunal, whether in person, by private attorney, or through services provided by the support enforcement agency, does not confer personal jurisdiction over the [petitioner] in another proceeding.

(b) A [petitioner] is not amenable to service of civil process while physically present in this state to participate in a proceeding under this [act].

(c) The immunity granted by this section does not extend to civil litigation based on acts unrelated to a proceeding under this [act] committed by a party while present in this state to participate in the proceeding.

§ 315. Nonparentage as Defense.

A party whose parentage of a child has been previously determined by or pursuant to law may not plead nonparentage as a defense to a proceeding under this [act].

§ 316. Special Rules of Evidence and Procedure.

(a) The physical presence of a nonresident party who is an individual in a tribunal of this state is not required for the establishment, enforcement, or modification of a support order or the rendition of a judgment determining parentage of a child.

* * *

(f) In a proceeding under this [act], a tribunal of this state shall permit a party or witness residing outside this state to be deposed or to testify under penalty of perjury by telephone, audiovisual means, or other electronic means at a designated tribunal or other location. A tribunal of this state shall cooperate with other tribunals in designating an appropriate location for the deposition or testimony.

* * *

§ 317. Communications Between Tribunals.

A tribunal of this state may communicate with a tribunal outside this state in a record, or by telephone, electronic-mail, or other means, to obtain information concerning the laws, the legal effect of a judgment, decree, or order of that tribunal, and the status of a proceeding in the other state or foreign country. A tribunal of this state may furnish similar information by similar means to a tribunal outside this state.

§ 318. Assistance With Discovery.

A tribunal of this state may:

(1) request a tribunal outside this state to assist in obtaining discovery; and

(2) upon request, compel a person over which it has jurisdiction to respond to a discovery order issued by a tribunal outside this state.

* * *

ARTICLE 4. ESTABLISHMENT OF SUPPORT ORDER OR DETERMINATION OF PARENTAGE

§ 401. Establishment of Support Order

(a) If a support order entitled to recognition under this [act] has not been issued, a responding tribunal of this state with personal jurisdiction over the parties may issue a support order if:

(1) the individual seeking the order resides outside this state; or

(2) the support enforcement agency seeking the order is located outside this state.

(b) The tribunal may issue a temporary support order if the tribunal determines that such an order is appropriate and the individual ordered to pay is:

(1) a presumed father of the child;

(2) petitioning to have his paternity adjudicated;

(3) identified as the father of the child through genetic testing;

(4) an alleged father who has declined to submit to genetic testing;

(5) shown by clear and convincing evidence to be the father of the child;

(6) an acknowledged father as provided by [applicable state law];

(7) the mother of the child; or

(8) an individual who has been ordered to pay child support in a previous proceeding and the order has not been reversed or vacated.

(c) Upon finding, after notice and opportunity to be heard, that an obligor owes a duty of support, the tribunal shall issue a support order directed to the obligor and may issue other orders pursuant to Section 305.

§ 402. Proceeding to Determine Parentage.

A tribunal of this state authorized to determine parentage of a child may serve as a responding tribunal in a proceeding to determine parentage of a child brought under this [act] or a law or procedure substantially similar to this [act].

* * *

ARTICLE 6. REGISTRATION, ENFORCEMENT, AND MODIFICATION OF SUPPORT ORDER

PART 1. REGISTRATION AND ENFORCEMENT OF SUPPORT ORDER

§ 601. Registration of Order for Enforcement.

A support order or income-withholding order issued in another state or a foreign support order may be registered in this State for enforcement.

* * *

§ 603. Effect of Registration for Enforcement.

(a) A support order or income-withholding order issued in another state or a foreign support order is registered when the order is filed in the registering tribunal of this state.

(b) A registered support order issued in another state or a foreign country is enforceable in the same manner and is subject to the same procedures as an order issued by a tribunal of this state.

(c) Except as otherwise provided in this [act], a tribunal of this state shall recognize and enforce, but may not modify, a registered support order if the issuing tribunal had jurisdiction.

§ 604. Choice of Law.

(a) Except as otherwise provided in subsection (d), the law of the issuing state or foreign country governs:

(1) the nature, extent, amount, and duration of current payments under a registered support order;

(2) the computation and payment of arrearages and accrual of interest on the arrearages under the support order; and

(3) the existence and satisfaction of other obligations under the support order.

(b) In a proceeding for arrears under a registered support order, the statute of limitation of this state, or of the issuing state or foreign country, whichever is longer, applies.

(c) A responding tribunal of this state shall apply the procedures and remedies of this state to enforce current support and collect arrears and interest due on a support order of another state or a foreign country registered in this state.

(d) After a tribunal of this or another state determines which is the controlling order and issues an order consolidating arrears, if any, a tribunal of this state shall prospectively apply the law of the state or foreign country issuing the controlling order, including its law on interest on arrears, on current and future support, and on consolidated arrears.

PART 2. CONTEST OF VALIDITY OR ENFORCEMENT.

§ 605. Notice of Registration of Order.

(a) When a support order or income-withholding order issued in another state or a foreign support order is registered, the registering tribunal of this state shall notify the nonregistering party. The notice must be accompanied by a copy of the registered order and the documents and relevant information accompanying the order.

(b) A notice must inform the nonregistering party:

(1) that a registered order is enforceable as of the date of registration in the same manner as an order issued by a tribunal of this state;

(2) that a hearing to contest the validity or enforcement of the registered order must be requested within [20] days after notice, unless the registered order is under Section 707;

(3) that failure to contest the validity or enforcement of the registered order in a timely manner will result in confirmation of the order and enforcement of the order and the alleged arrearages and precludes further contest of that order with respect to any matter that could have been asserted; and

(4) of the amount of any alleged arrearages.

* * *

(d) Upon registration of an income-withholding order for enforcement, the support enforcement agency or registering tribunal shall notify the obligor's employer pursuant to [the income-withholding law of this State].

* * *

§ 607. Contest of Registration or Enforcement.

(a) A party contesting the validity or enforcement of a registered support order or seeking to vacate the registration has the burden of proving one or more of the following defenses:

(1) the issuing tribunal lacked personal jurisdiction over the contesting party;

(2) the order was obtained by fraud;

(3) the order has been vacated, suspended, or modified by a later order;

(4) the issuing tribunal has stayed the order pending appeal;

(5) there is a defense under the law of this state to the remedy sought;

(6) full or partial payment has been made;

(7) the statute of limitation under Section 604 Section 604 precludes enforcement of some or all of the alleged arrearages; or

(8) the alleged controlling order is not the controlling order.

(b) If a party presents evidence establishing a full or partial defense under subsection (a), a tribunal may stay enforcement of a registered support order, continue the proceeding to permit production of additional relevant evidence, and issue other appropriate orders. An uncontested portion of the registered support order may be enforced by all remedies available under the law of this state.

(c) If the contesting party does not establish a defense under subsection (a) to the validity or enforcement of a registered support order, the registering tribunal shall issue an order confirming the order.

§ 608. Confirmed Order.

Confirmation of a registered support order, whether by operation of law or after notice and hearing, precludes further contest of the order with respect to any matter that could have been asserted at the time of registration.

PART 3. REGISTRATION AND MODIFICATION OF CHILD-SUPPORT ORDER
OF ANOTHER STATE

§ 609. Procedure to Register Child Support Order of Another State for Modification.

A party or support enforcement agency seeking to modify, or to modify and enforce, a child support order issued in another state shall register that order in this state in the same manner provided in Sections 601 through 608 if the order has not been registered. A [petition] for modification may be filed at the same time as a request for registration, or later. The pleading must specify the grounds for modification.

§ 610. Effect of Registration for Modification.

A tribunal of this state may enforce a child support order of another state registered for purposes of modification, in the same manner as if the order had been issued by a tribunal of this state, but the registered support order may be modified only if the requirements of Section 611 or 613 have been met.

§ 611. Modification of Child Support Order of Another State.

(a) If Section 613 does not apply, upon [petition] a tribunal of this state may modify a child-support order issued in another state which is registered in this state if, after notice and hearing, the tribunal finds that:

(1) the following requirements are met:

(A) neither the child, nor the obligee who is an individual, nor the obligor resides in the issuing state;

(B) a [petitioner] who is a nonresident of this state seeks modification; and

(C) the [respondent] is subject to the personal jurisdiction of the tribunal of this state; or

(2) this state is the residence of the child, or a party who is an individual is subject to the personal jurisdiction of the tribunal of this state, and all of the parties who are individuals have filed consents in a record in the issuing tribunal for a tribunal of this state to modify the support order and assume continuing, exclusive jurisdiction.

(b) Modification of a registered child-support order is subject to the same requirements, procedures, and defenses that apply to the modification of an order issued by a tribunal of this state and the order may be enforced and satisfied in the same manner.

(c) A tribunal of this state may not modify any aspect of a child-support order that may not be modified under the law of the issuing state, including the duration of the obligation of support. If two or more tribunals have issued child-support orders for the same obligor and same child, the order that controls and must be so recognized under Section 207 establishes the aspects of the support order which are nonmodifiable.

(d) In a proceeding to modify a child-support order, the law of the state that is determined to have issued the initial controlling order governs the duration of the obligation of support. The obligor's fulfillment of the duty of support established by that order precludes imposition of a further obligation of support by a tribunal of this state.

(e) On the issuance of an order by a tribunal of this state modifying a child-support order issued in another State, the tribunal of this state becomes the tribunal having continuing, exclusive jurisdiction.

(f) Notwithstanding subsections (a) through (e) and Section 201(b), a tribunal of this state retains jurisdiction to modify an order issued by a tribunal of this state if:

(1) one party resides in another state; and

(2) the other party resides outside the United States.

* * *

§ 613. Jurisdiction to Modify Child-Support Order of Another State When Individual Parties Reside in This State.

(a) If all the parties who are individuals reside in this state and the child does not reside in the issuing state, a tribunal of this state has jurisdiction to enforce and modify the issuing state's child-support order in a proceeding to register that order.

(b) A tribunal of this state exercising jurisdiction under this section shall apply the provisions of [Articles] 1 and 2, this [article], and the procedural and substantive law of this state to the proceeding for enforcement or modification. [Articles] 3, 4, 5, 7, and 8 do not apply.

§ 614. Notice to Issuing Tribunal of Modification.

Within [30] days after issuance of a modified child-support order, the party obtaining the modification shall file a certified copy of the order with the issuing tribunal that had continuing, exclusive jurisdiction over the earlier order, and in each tribunal in which the party knows the earlier order has been registered. A party who obtains the order and fails to file a certified copy is subject to appropriate sanctions by a tribunal in which the issue of failure to file arises. The failure to file does not affect the validity or enforceability of the modified order of the new tribunal having continuing, exclusive jurisdiction.

PART 4. REGISTRATION AND MODIFICATION OF FOREIGN CHILD-SUPPORT ORDER

§ 615. Jurisdiction to Modify Child-Support Order of Foreign Country.

(a) Except as otherwise provided in Section 711, if a foreign country lacks or refuses to exercise jurisdiction to modify its child-support order pursuant to its laws, a tribunal of this state may assume jurisdiction to modify the child-support order and bind all individuals subject to the personal jurisdiction of the tribunal whether the consent to modification of a child-support order otherwise required of the individual pursuant to Section 611 has been given or whether the individual seeking modification is a resident of this state or of the foreign country.

(b) An order issued by a tribunal of this state modifying a foreign child-support order pursuant to this section is the controlling order.

* * *

Uniform Child-Custody Jurisdiction and Enforcement Act (UCCJEA)

9 U.L.A. (Part 1A) 649 (1999)

[ARTICLE] 1 GENERAL PROVISIONS

* * *

§ 102. Definitions.

In this [Act]:

(1) "Abandoned" means left without provision for reasonable and necessary care or supervision.

(2) "Child" means an individual who has not attained 18 years of age.

Go Online

The full text and information on state adoptions of the Uniform Child Custody Jurisdiction and Enforcement Act is available from the Uniform Law Commission.

(3) "Child-custody determination" means a judgment, decree, or other order of a court providing for the legal custody, physical custody, or visitation with respect to a child. The term includes a permanent, temporary, initial, and modification order. The term does not include an order relating to child support or other monetary obligation of an individual.

(4) "Child-custody proceeding" means a proceeding in which legal custody, physical custody, or visitation with respect to a child is an issue. The term includes a proceeding for divorce, separation, neglect, abuse, dependency, guardianship, paternity, termination of parental rights, and protection from domestic violence, in which the issue may appear. The term does not include a proceeding involving juvenile delinquency, contractual emancipation, or enforcement under [Article] 3.

(5) "Commencement" means the filing of the first pleading in a proceeding.

(6) "Court" means an entity authorized under the law of a State to establish, enforce, or modify a child-custody determination.

(7) "Home State" means the State in which a child lived with a parent or a person acting as a parent for at least six consecutive months immediately before the commencement of a child-custody proceeding. In the case of a child less than six months of age, the term means the State in which the

child lived from birth with any of the persons mentioned. A period of temporary absence of any of the mentioned persons is part of the period.

(8) "Initial determination" means the first child-custody determination concerning a particular child.

(9) "Issuing court" means the court that makes a child-custody determination for which enforcement is sought under this [Act].

(10) "Issuing State" means the State in which a child-custody determination is made.

(11) "Modification" means a child-custody determination that changes, replaces, supersedes, or is otherwise made after a previous determination concerning the same child, whether or not it is made by the court that made the previous determination.

(12) "Person" includes government, governmental subdivision, agency, or instrumentality, or any other legal or commercial entity.

(13) "Person acting as a parent" means a person, other than a parent, who:

(A) has physical custody of the child or has had physical custody for a period of six consecutive months, including any temporary absence, within one year immediately before the commencement of a child-custody proceeding; and

(B) has been awarded legal custody by a court or claims a right to legal custody under the law of this State.

(14) "Physical custody" means the physical care and supervision of a child.

(15) "State" means a State of the United States, the District of Columbia, Puerto Rico, the United States Virgin Islands, or any territory or insular possession subject to the jurisdiction of the United States.

[(16) "Tribe" means an Indian tribe, or band, or Alaskan Native village which is recognized by federal law or formally acknowledged by a State.]

(17) "Warrant" means an order issued by a court authorizing law enforcement officers to take physical custody of a child.

§ 103. Proceedings Governed by Other Law.

This [Act] does not govern an adoption proceeding or a proceeding pertaining to the authorization of emergency medical care for a child.

§ 104. Application to Indian Tribes.

(a) A child-custody proceeding that pertains to an Indian child as defined in the Indian Child Welfare Act, 25 U.S.C. 1901 et seq., is not subject to this [Act] to the extent that it is governed by the Indian Child Welfare Act.

[(b) A court of this State shall treat a tribe as a State of the United States for purposes of [Articles] 1 and 2.]

[(c) A child-custody determination made by a tribe under factual circumstances in substantial conformity with the jurisdictional standards of this [Act] must be recognized and enforced under the provisions of [Article] 3.]

§ 105. International Application of [Act].

(a) A court of this State shall treat a foreign country as a State of the United States for purposes of applying [Articles] 1 and 2.

(b) A child-custody determination made in a foreign country under factual circumstances in substantial conformity with the jurisdictional standards of this [Act] must be recognized and enforced under [Article] 3 of this [Act].

(c) The court need not apply the provisions of this [Act] when the child custody law of the other country violates fundamental principles of human rights.

§ 106. Effect of Child-Custody Determination.

A child-custody determination made by a court of this State that had jurisdiction under this [Act] binds all persons who have been served in accordance with the laws of this State or notified in accordance with Section 108 or who have submitted to the jurisdiction of the court, and who have been given an opportunity to be heard. As to those persons, the determination is conclusive as to all decided issues of law and fact except to the extent the determination is modified.

* * *

§ 108. Notice to Persons Outside State.

(a) Notice required for the exercise of jurisdiction when a person is outside this State may be given in a manner prescribed by the law of this State for service of process or by the law of the State in which the service is made. Notice must be given in a manner reasonably calculated to give actual notice but may be by publication if other means are not effective.

(b) Proof of service may be made in the manner prescribed by the law of this State or by the law of the State in which the service is made.

(c) Notice is not required for the exercise of jurisdiction with respect to a person who submits to the jurisdiction of the court.

§ 109. Appearance and Limited Immunity.

(a) A party to a child-custody proceeding, including a modification proceeding, or a petitioner or respondent in a proceeding to enforce or register a child-custody determination, is not subject to personal jurisdiction in this State for another proceeding or purpose solely by reason of having participated, or of having been physically present for the purpose of participating, in the proceeding.

(b) A person who is subject to personal jurisdiction in this State on a basis other than physical presence is not immune from service of process in this State. A party present in this State who is subject to the jurisdiction of another State is not immune from service of process allowable under the laws of that State.

(c) The immunity granted by subsection (a) does not extend to civil litigation based on acts unrelated to the participation in a proceeding under this [Act] committed by an individual while present in this State.

§ 110. Communication Between Courts.

(a) A court of this State may communicate with a court in another State concerning a proceeding arising under this [Act].

(b) The court may allow the parties to participate in the communication. If the parties are not able to participate in the communication, the parties shall be given the opportunity to present facts and legal arguments before a decision on jurisdiction is made.

* * *

[ARTICLE] 2: JURISDICTION

§ 201. Initial Child-Custody Jurisdiction.

(a) Except as otherwise provided in Section 204, a court of this State has jurisdiction to make an initial child-custody determination only if:

(1) this State is the home State of the child on the date of the commencement of the proceeding, or was the home State of the child within six months before the commencement of the proceeding and the child is absent from this State but a parent or person acting as a parent continues to live in this State;

(2) a court of another State does not have jurisdiction under paragraph (1), or a court of the home State of the child has declined to exercise jurisdiction on the ground that this State is the more appropriate forum under Section 207 or 208, and:

(A) the child and the child's parents, or the child and at least one parent or a person acting as a parent have a significant connection with this State other than mere physical presence; and

(B) substantial evidence is available in this State concerning the child's care, protection, training, and personal relationships;

(3) all courts having jurisdiction under paragraph (1) or (2) have declined to exercise jurisdiction on the ground that a court of this State is the more appropriate forum to determine the custody of the child under Section 207 or 208; or

(4) no State would have jurisdiction under paragraph (1), (2), or (3).

(b) Subsection (a) is the exclusive jurisdictional basis for making a child-custody determination by a court of this State.

(c) Physical presence of, or personal jurisdiction over, a party or a child is neither necessary nor sufficient to make a child-custody determination.

§ 202. Exclusive, Continuing Jurisdiction.

(a) Except as otherwise provided in Section 204, a court of this State that has made a child-custody determination consistent with Section 201 or 203 has exclusive, continuing jurisdiction over the determination until:

(1) a court of this State determines that neither the child, nor the child and one parent, nor the child and a person acting as a parent have a significant connection with this State and that substantial evidence is no longer available in this State concerning the child's care, protection, training, and personal relationships; or

(2) a court of this State or a court of another State determines that the child, the child's parents, and any person acting as a parent do not presently reside in this State.

(b) A court of this State which has made a child-custody determination and does not have exclusive, continuing jurisdiction under this section may modify that determination only if it has jurisdiction to make an initial determination under Section 201.

§ 203. Jurisdiction to Modify Determination.

Except as otherwise provided in Section 204, a court of this State may not modify a child-custody determination made by a court of another State unless a court of this State has jurisdiction to make an initial determination under Section 201(a)(1) or (2) and:

> (1) the court of the other State determines it no longer has exclusive, continuing jurisdiction under Section 202 or that a court of this State would be a more convenient forum under Section 207; or

> (2) a court of this State or a court of the other State determines that the child, the child's parents, and any person acting as a parent do not presently reside in the other State.

§ 204. Temporary Emergency Jurisdiction.

(a) A court of this State has temporary emergency jurisdiction if the child is present in this State and the child has been abandoned or it is necessary in an emergency to protect the child because the child, or a sibling or parent of the child, is subjected to or threatened with mistreatment or abuse.

(b) If there is no previous child-custody determination that is entitled to be enforced under this [Act] and a child-custody proceeding has not been commenced in a court of a State having jurisdiction under Sections 201 through 203, a child-custody determination made under this section remains in effect until an order is obtained from a court of a State having jurisdiction under Sections 201 through 203. If a child-custody proceeding has not been or is not commenced in a court of a State having jurisdiction under Sections 201 through 203, a child-custody determination made under this section becomes a final determination, if it so provides and this State becomes the home State of the child.

(c) If there is a previous child-custody determination that is entitled to be enforced under this [Act], or a child-custody proceeding has been commenced in a court of a State having jurisdiction under Sections 201 through 203, any order issued by a court of this State under this section must specify in the order a period that the court considers adequate to allow the person seeking an order to obtain an order from the State having jurisdiction under Sections 201 through 203. The order issued in this State remains in effect until an order is obtained from the other State within the period specified or the period expires.

(d) A court of this State which has been asked to make a child-custody determination under this section, upon being informed that a child-custody proceeding has been commenced in, or a child-custody determination has been made by, a court of a State having jurisdiction under Sections 201 through 203, shall immediately communicate with the other court. A court of this State which is exercising jurisdiction pursuant to Sections 201 through 203, upon being informed that a child-custody proceeding has been commenced in, or a child-custody determination has been made by, a court of another State under a statute similar to this section shall immediately communicate with the court of that State to resolve the emergency, protect the safety of the parties and the child, and determine a period for the duration of the temporary order.

§ 205. Notice; Opportunity to Be Heard; Joinder.

(a) Before a child-custody determination is made under this [Act], notice and an opportunity to be heard in accordance with the standards of Section 108 must be given to all persons entitled to notice under the law of this State as in child-custody proceedings between residents of this State, any parent whose parental rights have not been previously terminated, and any person having physical custody of the child.

(b) This [Act] does not govern the enforceability of a child-custody determination made without notice or an opportunity to be heard.

(c) The obligation to join a party and the right to intervene as a party in a child-custody proceeding under this [Act] are governed by the law of this State as in child-custody proceedings between residents of this State.

§ 206. Simultaneous Proceedings.

(a) Except as otherwise provided in Section 204, a court of this State may not exercise its jurisdiction under this [article] if at the time of the commencement of the proceeding, a proceeding concerning the custody of the child has been commenced in a court of another State having jurisdiction substantially in conformity with this [Act], unless the proceeding has been terminated or is stayed by the court of the other State because a court of this State is a more convenient forum under Section 207.

(b) Except as otherwise provided in Section 204, a court of this State, before hearing a child-custody proceeding, shall examine the court documents and other information supplied by the parties pursuant to Section 209. If the court determines that a child-custody proceeding has been commenced in a court in another State having jurisdiction substantially in accordance with this [Act], the court of this State shall stay its proceeding and communicate with the court of the other State. If the court of the State having jurisdiction substantially in accordance with this [Act] does not determine that the court of this State is a more appropriate forum, the court of this State shall dismiss the proceeding.

(c) In a proceeding to modify a child-custody determination, a court of this State shall determine whether a proceeding to enforce the determination has been commenced in another State. If a proceeding to enforce a child-custody determination has been commenced in another State, the court may:

(1) stay the proceeding for modification pending the entry of an order of a court of the other State enforcing, staying, denying, or dismissing the proceeding for enforcement;

(2) enjoin the parties from continuing with the proceeding for enforcement; or

(3) proceed with the modification under conditions it considers appropriate.

§ 207. Inconvenient Forum.

(a) A court of this State which has jurisdiction under this [Act] to make a child-custody determination may decline to exercise its jurisdiction at any time if it determines that it is an inconvenient forum under the circumstances and that a court of another State is a more appropriate forum. The issue of inconvenient forum may be raised upon motion of a party, the court's own motion, or request of another court.

(b) Before determining whether it is an inconvenient forum, a court of this State shall consider whether it is appropriate for a court of another State to exercise jurisdiction. For this purpose, the court shall allow the parties to submit information and shall consider all relevant factors, including:

(1) whether domestic violence has occurred and is likely to continue in the future and which State could best protect the parties and the child;

(2) the length of time the child has resided outside this State;

(3) the distance between the court in this State and the court in the State that would assume jurisdiction;

(4) the relative financial circumstances of the parties;

(5) any agreement of the parties as to which State should assume jurisdiction;

(6) the nature and location of the evidence required to resolve the pending litigation, including the testimony of the child;

(7) the ability of the court of each State to decide the issue expeditiously and the procedures necessary to present the evidence; and

(8) the familiarity of the court of each State with the facts and issues of the pending litigation.

(c) If a court of this State determines that it is an inconvenient forum and that a court of another State is a more appropriate forum, it shall stay the proceedings upon condition that a child-custody proceeding be promptly commenced in another designated State and may impose any other condition the court considers just and proper.

(d) A court of this State may decline to exercise its jurisdiction under this [Act] if a child-custody determination is incidental to an action for divorce or another proceeding while still retaining jurisdiction over the divorce or other proceeding.

§ 208. Jurisdiction Declined by Reason of Conduct.

(a) Except as otherwise provided in Section 204 [or by other law of this State], if a court of this State has jurisdiction under this [Act] because a person seeking to invoke its jurisdiction has engaged in unjustifiable conduct, the court shall decline to exercise its jurisdiction unless:

(1) the parents and all persons acting as parents have acquiesced in the exercise of jurisdiction;

(2) a court of the State otherwise having jurisdiction under Sections 201 through 203 determines that this State is a more appropriate forum under Section 207; or

(3) no court of any other State would have jurisdiction under the criteria specified in Sections 201 through 203.

(b) If a court of this State declines to exercise its jurisdiction pursuant to subsection (a), it may fashion an appropriate remedy to ensure the safety of the child and prevent a repetition of the unjustifiable conduct, including staying the proceeding until a child-custody proceeding is commenced in a court having jurisdiction under Sections 201 through 203.

(c) If a court dismisses a petition or stays a proceeding because it declines to exercise its jurisdiction pursuant to subsection (a), it shall assess against the party seeking to invoke its jurisdiction necessary and reasonable expenses including costs, communication expenses, attorney's fees, investigative fees, expenses for witnesses, travel expenses, and child care during the course of the proceedings, unless the party from whom fees are sought establishes that the assessment would be clearly inappropriate. The court may not assess fees, costs, or expenses against this State unless authorized by law other than this [Act].

* * *

[ARTICLE] 3: ENFORCEMENT

§ 301. Definitions.

In this [article]:

(1) "Petitioner" means a person who seeks enforcement of an order for return of a child under the Hague Convention on the Civil Aspects of International Child Abduction or enforcement of a child-custody determination.

(2) "Respondent" means a person against whom a proceeding has been commenced for enforcement of an order for return of a child under the Hague Convention on the Civil Aspects of International Child Abduction or enforcement of a child-custody determination.

§ 302. Enforcement Under Hague Convention.

Under this [article] a court of this State may enforce an order for the return of the child made under the Hague Convention on the Civil Aspects of International Child Abduction as if it were a child-custody determination.

§ 303. Duty to Enforce.

(a) A court of this State shall recognize and enforce a child-custody determination of a court of another State if the latter court exercised jurisdiction in substantial conformity with this [Act] or the determination was made under factual circumstances meeting the jurisdictional standards of this [Act] and the determination has not been modified in accordance with this [Act].

(b) A court of this State may utilize any remedy available under other law of this State to enforce a child-custody determination made by a court of another State. The remedies provided in this [article] are cumulative and do not affect the availability of other remedies to enforce a child-custody determination.

* * *

§ 305. Registration of Child-Custody Determination.

(a) A child-custody determination issued by a court of another State may be registered in this State, with or without a simultaneous request for enforcement, by sending to [the appropriate court] in this State:

(1) a letter or other document requesting registration;

(2) two copies, including one certified copy, of the determination sought to be registered, and a statement under penalty of perjury that to the best

of the knowledge and belief of the person seeking registration the order has not been modified; and

(3) except as otherwise provided in Section 209, the name and address of the person seeking registration and any parent or person acting as a parent who has been awarded custody or visitation in the child-custody determination sought to be registered.

* * *

§ 306. Enforcement of Registered Determination.

(a) A court of this State may grant any relief normally available under the law of this State to enforce a registered child-custody determination made by a court of another State.

(b) A court of this State shall recognize and enforce, but may not modify, except in accordance with [Article] 2, a registered child-custody determination of a court of another State.

* * *

§ 311. Warrant to Take Physical Custody of Child.

(a) Upon the filing of a petition seeking enforcement of a child-custody determination, the petitioner may file a verified application for the issuance of a warrant to take physical custody of the child if the child is immediately likely to suffer serious physical harm or be removed from this State.

(b) If the court, upon the testimony of the petitioner or other witness, finds that the child is imminently likely to suffer serious physical harm or be removed from this State, it may issue a warrant to take physical custody of the child. The petition must be heard on the next judicial day after the warrant is executed unless that date is impossible. In that event, the court shall hold the hearing on the first judicial day possible. The application for the warrant must include the statements required by Section 308(b).

(c) A warrant to take physical custody of a child must:

(1) recite the facts upon which a conclusion of imminent serious physical harm or removal from the jurisdiction is based;

(2) direct law enforcement officers to take physical custody of the child immediately; and

(3) provide for the placement of the child pending final relief.

(d) The respondent must be served with the petition, warrant, and order immediately after the child is taken into physical custody.

(e) A warrant to take physical custody of a child is enforceable throughout this State. If the court finds on the basis of the testimony of the petitioner or other witness that a less intrusive remedy is not effective, it may authorize law enforcement officers to enter private property to take physical custody of the child. If required by exigent circumstances of the case, the court may authorize law enforcement officers to make a forcible entry at any hour.

(f) The court may impose conditions upon placement of a child to ensure the appearance of the child and the child's custodian.

* * *

§ 315. Role of [Prosecutor or Public Official].

(a) In a case arising under this [Act] or involving the Hague Convention on the Civil Aspects of International Child Abduction, the [prosecutor or other appropriate public official] may take any lawful action, including resort to a proceeding under this [article] or any other available civil proceeding to locate a child, obtain the return of a child, or enforce a child-custody determination if there is:

(1) an existing child-custody determination;

(2) a request to do so from a court in a pending child-custody proceeding;

(3) a reasonable belief that a criminal statute has been violated; or

(4) a reasonable belief that the child has been wrongfully removed or retained in violation of the Hague Convention on the Civil Aspects of International Child Abduction.

(b) A [prosecutor or appropriate public official] acts on behalf of the court and may not represent any party.

* * *

Index

References are to pages